THE GOSPEL
ACCORDING TO
ST. JOHN

THE GOSPEL
ACCORDING TO
ST. JOHN

AN INTRODUCTION
WITH COMMENTARY AND NOTES
ON THE GREEK TEXT

C. K. BARRETT

Second Edition

THE WESTMINSTER PRESS
Philadelphia

First published in 1955
Second impression (corrected) 1956
Eleventh impression 1976
Second edition 1978

Second edition © C. K. Barrett 1978

Published by The Westminster Press ®
Philadelphia, Pennsylvania

PRINTED IN THE UNITED STATES OF AMERICA
9 8 7 6 5 4 3 2

Library of Congress Cataloging in Publication Data

Barrett, Charles Kingsley.
  The Gospel according to St. John.

  Includes bibliographical references and indexes.
  1. Bible. N.T. John — Commentaries. I. Title.
BS2615.3.B3 1978   226′.5′077   78-2587
ISBN 0-664-21364-2

CONTENTS

PREFACE

I T is now a little more than a quarter of a century since I completed
the first edition of this Commentary. It was not published till 1955
because it had been written for a series and was rejected by the
publisher; it was too long and detailed. It is no small part of my debt
to SPCK, and in particular to the late Dr F. N. Davey, that the un-
wanted commentary, which I refused to shorten, on the ground that it
was at that time impossible to write a commentary on the Fourth
Gospel that was both short and worth reading, came after some inevitable delay to the birth. I can see it now as a juvenile work, and if
today I were to set about a commentary on John it would be a different
book. But life is short, and I have had to be content to revise the old
one, much of which remains, though scarcely a page remains untouched
and parts have been pretty radically rewritten. There is also a good
deal of new material.

The last twenty five years have witnessed a fast-flowing stream of
commentaries, monographs, and articles on the Fourth Gospel; many
of them are of the highest quality. I have read by no means all; even if
in the period my attention had not been directed rather to Paul than to
John I should not have been able to do so. I have made it clear to the
publishers that I did not understand the production of a new edition of
my Commentary to involve a full bibliographical guide to the Johannine
literature of the period since the first was issued. I am not competent to
produce such a guide, and those who seek one should look elsewhere—
to E. Malatesta's Bibliography, to surveys by E. Haenchen and E.
Käsemann, to the splendid and still unfinished review by H. Thyen
(*Theologische Rundschau* 39 (1974–5), 1–69, 222–52, 289–330; 42 (1977),
211–70), and to the great commentaries by R. Schnackenburg and
R. E. Brown. From what I have read, however, I have learnt much, and
what I have learnt is reflected in this new book. Not infrequently I have
learnt by disagreeing, and I am scarcely less grateful to those on whom I
have sharpened my wits in controversy than to those with whose ideas
I have found myself in enthusiastic agreement. This does not mean that
I have ceased to be grateful to earlier guides, of whom now none sur-
vives: Hoskyns, and his editor—to me, much more than editor—Noel
Davey; C. H. Dodd; and Rudolf Bultmann, who died about a week
after the manuscript of the new edition left my hands.

Though I have tried to read some at least of the latest books and to learn from them, this Commentary, even in its new state, will seem to many to be old-fashioned. To some of the most popular modern opinions I do not subscribe. I do not believe that Qumran holds the key to John; I do not believe that it is a Palestinian work, aimed at Diaspora Judaism; I do not believe that it is possible to isolate sources, unless perhaps we should describe Mark as a source; I do not believe that John intended to supply us with historically verifiable information regarding the life and teaching of Jesus, and that historical traditions of great worth can be disentangled from his interpretative comments. I believe that John does more to interpret the Nag Hammadi texts than they do to interpret John. Before my readers dismiss all this as out of date I should like for their reflection to recall one of the Durham characters of a past generation. P. J. Heawood was a professor of mathematics who was also a diligent reader of the Old Testament in Hebrew and the New Testament in Greek. He died in 1955 at the age of 93. One of his foibles was to correct his watch on January 1 each year, and at no other time. 'Professor Heawood,' a friend might say to him, 'your watch is five hours slow.' 'No,' he would reply, 'it is not slow; it is seven hours fast.'

It remains to offer my thanks: to SPCK, for kindness in the past and patience and help in the present; to Dr J. McHugh, for the loan of books not otherwise easily available; to scholars in many lands who have sent me innumerable books and off-prints dealing with the Fourth Gospel. I wish I could have referred at appropriate points to all of these, but a writer on John has the best of precedents for omitting all but the most essential matters.

Durham University   C. K. BARRETT.
August 1976–*January* 1978.

LIST OF ABBREVIATIONS

I N this book 'John' signifies both the Fourth Gospel, and the Fourth Evangelist. No assumption is implied regarding the identity of the latter. For the shortened titles used for some ancient books (including papyri and inscriptions) see the Index of References. In addition to the conventional contractions the following abbreviations are used in the references:

GRAMMARS AND DICTIONARIES

Bauer, *Wörterbuch*	*Griechisch-Deutsches Wörterbuch zu den Schriften des Neuen Testaments and der übrigen urchristlichen Literatur*, by W. Bauer, 1958. E.T., *Greek-English Lexicon of the New Testament and Other Early Christian Literature*, ed. William F. Arndt and F. W. Gingrich, 1957.
B.D.	*Grammatik des neutestamentlichen Griechisch*, by F. Blass, revised by A. Debrunner, 1949; Anhang, 1950. E.T., *A Greek Grammar of the New Testament and other Early Christian Literature*, ed. Robert W. Funk, 1961.
B.D.B.	*A Hebrew and English Lexicon of the Old Testament*, by F. Brown, S. R. Driver, and S. A. Briggs, 1906.
E. Bib.	*Encyclopaedia Biblica*, edited by T. K. Cheyne and J. S. Black, 1914.
G.K.	*Gesenius' Hebrew Grammar* as edited and enlarged by E. Kautzsch, translated by G. W. Collins and A. E. Cowley, 1898.
Jastrow	*A Dictionary of the Targumin, the Talmud Babli and Yerushalmi, and the Midrashic Literature*, compiled by M. Jastrow, 1926.
K.B.	*Lexicon in Veteris Testamenti Libros*, by L. Koehler and W. Baumgartner, 1948–53.
Lewis and Short	*A Latin Dictionary*, by C. T. Lewis and C. Short, 1907.
L.S.	*A Greek-English Lexicon*, by H. G. Liddell and R. Scott: new edition by H. Stuart Jones and R. McKenzie, 1925–40.
M. i	*A Grammar of New Testament Greek*, Volume i, *Prolegomena*, by J. H. Moulton, 1908.
M. ii	*A Grammar of New Testament Greek*, Volume ii, by J. H. Moulton and W. F. Howard, 1929.

M. III   *A Grammar of New Testament Greek*, Volume III, by N. Turner, 1963.

M.M.   *The Vocabulary of the Greek Testament, illustrated from the papyri and other non-literary sources*, by J. H. Moulton and G. Milligan, 1914–29.

Moule, *Idiom Book*   *An Idiom Book of New Testament Greek*, by C. F. D. Moule, 1953.

Palmer   *A Grammar of the Post-Ptolemaic Papyri*, Volume 1, Part 1 (Publications of the Philological Society, XIII), by L. R. Palmer, 1946.

Radermacher   *Neutestamentliche Grammatik* (Handbuch zum Neuen Testament, 1.1), by L. Radermacher, 1911.

Robertson   *A Grammar of the Greek New Testament in the Light of Historical Research*, by A. T. Robertson, 1919.

Rutherford   *The New Phrynichus, being a revised text of the Ecloga of the Grammarian Phrynichus*, with introduction and commentary, by W. G. Rutherford, 1881.

T.W.N.T.   *Theologisches Wörterbuch zum Neuen Testament*, edited by G. Kittel, subsequently by G. Friedrich, 1932—(in progress). E.T., *Theological Dictionary of the New Testament*, 1964—

Turner, *Insights*   *Grammatical Insights into the New Testament*, by N. Turner, 1965.

W.M.   *A Treatise on the Grammar of New Testament Greek*, by G. B. Winer, translated with large additions by W. F. Moulton, 1882.

COMMENTARIES ON (OR INCLUDING) JOHN

Bauer   *Das Johannes-Evangelium* (Handbuch zum Neuen Testament 6), by W. Bauer, 1933.

Bernard   *A Critical and Exegetical Commentary on the Gospel according to St John*, by J. H. Bernard, 1928.

Brown   *The Gospel according to John*, Anchor Bible 29, 29A, by R. E. Brown, Vol. 1, 1966; Vol. 2, 1970.

Bultmann   *Das Evangelium des Johannes* (Kritisch-exegetischer Kommentar über das Neue Testament), by R. Bultmann, 1950; Ergänzungshefte, 1950, 1957. E.T., *The Gospel of John*, 1971.

Fenton   *The Gospel according to John*, New Clarendon Bible, by J. C. Fenton, 1970.

Field   *Notes on the Translation of the New Testament*, by F. Field, 1899.

Hoskyns   *The Fourth Gospel*, by E. C. Hoskyns, edited by F. N. Davey, 1940.

Lagrange   *Évangile selon Saint Jean*, by M.-J. Lagrange, 1948.

Lightfoot	*St John's Gospel: a Commentary*, by R. H. Lightfoot, 1956.
Lindars	*The Gospel of John*, New Century Bible, by B. Lindars, 1972.
Loisy	*Le quatrième Évangile* (deuxième édition refondue), by A. Loisy, 1921.
Morris	*The Gospel according to John*, by L. Morris, 1974.
Odeberg	*The Fourth Gospel interpreted in its relation to Contemporaneous Religious Currents in Palestine and the Hellenistic-Oriental World*, by H. Odeberg, 1929.
Pallis	*Notes on St John and the Apocalypse*, by Alex. Pallis, n.d.
S.B.	*Kommentar zum Neuen Testament aus Talmud und Midrasch*, by H. L. Strack and P. Billerbeck, 1922–8.
Sanders	*A Commentary on the Gospel according to St John*, Black's New Testament Commentaries, by J. N. Sanders, edited and completed by B. A. Mastin, 1968.
Schlatter	*Der Evangelist Johannes*, by A. Schlatter, 1958.
Schnackenburg I, II, III	*Das Johannesevangelium*, Herders Theologischer Kommentar zum Neuen Testament, by R. Schnackenburg. Vol. 1, 1965; Vol. 2, 1971, Vol. 3, 1976. E.T. of Vol. 1, *The Gospel according to St John*, 1968.
Strachan	*The Fourth Gospel, its Significance and Environment*, by R. H. Strachan, 1941.
Westcott	*The Gospel according to St John*, by B. F. Westcott, 1903.

OTHER BOOKS AND STUDIES ON JOHN

Bacon	*The Fourth Gospel in Research and Debate*, by B. W. Bacon, 1910.
Becker, *Reden*	*Die Reden des Johannesevangeliums und der Stil der gnostischen Offenbarungsrede*, by H. Becker, ed. by R. Bultmann. *F.R.L.A.N.T.* 68 (N.F. 50), 1956.
Borgen	*Bread from Heaven*, by P. Borgen. *Supplements to Nov. T.*, 10, 1965.
Burney	*The Aramaic Origin of the Fourth Gospel*, by C. F. Burney, 1922.
Cullmann, *Circle*	*The Johannine Circle*, by O. Cullmann, E.T., 1976.
'Dialectical Theology'	'The Dialectical Theology of St John', by C. K. Barrett, in *Essays*, 49–69.
Dodd, *Interpretation*	*The Interpretation of the Fourth Gospel*, by C. H. Dodd, 1953.
Dodd, *Tradition*	*Historical Tradition in the Fourth Gospel*, by C. H. Dodd, 1963.
Goguel	*Le Quatrième Évangile* (*Introduction au Nouveau Testament*, II), by M. Goguel, 1924.
Guilding	*The Fourth Gospel and Jewish Worship*, by A. Guilding, 1960.

Howard — *The Fourth Gospel in Recent Criticism and Interpretation*, by W. F. Howard, new edition, revised by C. K. Barrett, 1955.

J. & Q. — *John and Qumran*, edited by J. H. Charlesworth, 1972.

Judaism — *The Gospel of John and Judaism*, by C. K. Barrett, E.T., 1975.

Käsemann, *Testament* — *The Testament of Jesus*, by E. Käsemann. E.T., 1968.

Martyn — *History and Theology in the Fourth Gospel*, by J. L. Martyn, 1968.

Meeks — *The Prophet-King: Moses Traditions and the Johannine Christology*, by W. A. Meeks. *Supplements to Nov. T.*, 14, 1967.

'Menschensohn' — 'Das Fleisch des Menschensohnes (Joh 6, 53)', by C. K. Barrett, in *Jesus und der Menschensohn, für Anton Vögtle*, edited by R. Pesch and R. Schnackenburg, 1975.

Prologue — *The Prologue of St John's Gospel*, by C. K. Barrett, 1971. Reprinted in *Essays*, 27–48.

Sanders, *Early Church* — *The Fourth Gospel in the Early Church*, by J. N. Sanders, 1943.

Schweizer — *Ego Eimi . . .*, by E. Schweizer, 1939.

Sidebottom — *The Christ of the Fourth Gospel*, by E. M. Sidebottom, 1961.

'The Father is greater than I' — ' "The Father is greater than I" (Jo 14, 28): Subordinationist Christology in the New Testament', by C. K. Barrett, in *Neues Testament und Kirche, für R. Schnackenburg*, edited by J. Gnilka, 144–59, 1974.

'Theocentric' — 'Christocentric or Theocentric? Observations on the Theological Method of the Fourth Gospel', by C. K. Barrett, in *La Notion biblique de Dieu, Bibliotheca Ephemeridum Theologicarum Lovaniensium*, 41, edited by J. Coppens, 361–76, 1976.

'Theological Vocabulary' — 'The Theological Vocabulary of the Fourth Gospel and of the Gospel of Truth', by C. K. Barrett, in *Current Issues in New Testament Interpretation, Essays in honor of O. A. Piper*, edited by W. Klassen and G. F. Snyder, 210–23, 297f., 1962.

OTHER BOOKS ON THE NEW TESTAMENT
AND RELATED SUBJECTS

Abrahams, *Studies* I and II — *Studies in Pharisaism and the Gospels*, First and Second Series, by I. Abrahams, 1917 and 1924.

Beginnings — *The Beginnings of Christianity, Part I: The Acts of the Apostles*, edited by F. J. Foakes Jackson and K. Lake, 1920–33.

Benoit I, II, III — *Exégèse et Théologie*, Vol. I, 1961; Vol. II, 1961; Vol. III, 1968.

Betz — *Lukian von Samosata; religionsgeschichtliche und paränetische Parallelen. Texte und Untersuchungen*, 76, 1961.

Black — *An Aramaic Approach to the Gospels and Acts*, by M. Black. Third Edition, 1967.

Bonsirven — *Le Judaïsme Palestinien au temps de Jésus-Christ*, by J. Bonsirven, 1934.

Bornkamm I, II, III, IV — G. Bornkamm, *Das Ende des Gesetzes* (= *Gesammelte Aufsätze* I, 1966); *Studien zu Antike und Urchristentum* (= *Ges. Aufs.* II, 1970); *Geschichte und Glaube I* (= *Ges. Aufs.* III, 1968); *Geschichte und Glaube II* (= *Ges. Aufs.* IV, 1971).

Bousset-Gressmann — *Die Religion des Judentums im späthellenistischen Zeitalter*, by W. Bousset. Third edition, edited by H. Gressmann. Handbuch zum Neuen Testament, 21, 1926.

Braun — *Qumran und das Neue Testament*, by H. Braun, in *Th. R.* 28 (1962), 192–234; the whole republished in two volumes, 1966.

Bultmann, *P.C.* — *Primitive Christianity in its Contemporary Setting*, by R. Bultmann, E. T., 1956.

Bultmann, *Theology* — *Theology of the New Testament*, by R. Bultmann, E.T., Vol. 1, 1952; Vol. 2, 1955.

C.A.H. — *The Cambridge Ancient History*, edited by J. B. Bury, S. A. Cook, F. E. Adcock, and M. P. Charlesworth, 1923–39.

Conzelmann, *Theology* — *An Outline of the Theology of the New Testament*, by H. Conzelmann, E.T., 1969.

Creed — *The Gospel according to St Luke*, by J. M. Creed, 1930.

Cullmann, *Christology* — *Christology of the New Testament*, by O. Cullmann, E.T., 1959.

Cullmann, *Salvation* — *Salvation in History*, by O. Cullmann, E.T., 1967.

Cullmann, *V. & A.* — *Vorträge und Aufsätze* 1925–1962, by O. Cullmann. Ed. by K. Fröhlich, 1966.

Danby — *The Mishnah*, translated from the Hebrew with Introduction and brief Explanatory Notes by H. Danby, 1933.

Daube, *N.T.R.J.* — *The New Testament and Rabbinic Judaism*, by D. Daube, 1956.

Davies, *Land* — *The Gospel and the Land*, by W. D. Davies, 1974.

Deissmann — *Light from the Ancient East*, by A. Deissmann; English translation, 1911.

Delitzsch — ספרי הברית החדשה (The New Testament in Hebrew), translated by F. Delitzsch, 1904.

Derrett, *Law* — *Law in the New Testament*, by J. D. M. Derrett, 1970.

Dinkler, *Signum* — *Signum Crucis*, by E. Dinkler, 1967.

Dodd, *A.S.* — *According to the Scriptures*, by C. H. Dodd, 1952.

Essays	*New Testament Essays*, by C. K. Barrett, 1972.
Fitzmyer, *Essays*	*Essays on the Semitic Background of the New Testament*, by J. A. Fitzmyer, 1971.
Haenchen, *Weg*	*Der Weg Jesu*, by E. Haenchen, 1966.
Hahn, *Titel*	*Christologische Hoheitstitel*, by F. Hahn, Second edition, 1964.
Hahn, *Titles*	*The Titles of Jesus in Christology*, by F. Hahn (abridged E.T. of the foregoing), 1969.
Hennecke-Schneemelcher	*Neutestamentliche Apokryphen in deutscher Übersetzung*, by E. Hennecke. Third edition, by W. Schneemelcher. Vol. 1, 1959; Vol. 2, 1964.
Higgins, *Son of Man*	*Jesus and the Son of Man*, by A. J. B. Higgins, 1964.
Hort	*The Christian Ecclesia*, by F. J. A. Hort, 1914.
H.S.G.T.	*The Holy Spirit and the Gospel Tradition*, by C. K. Barrett, 1947.
Jeremias, *Abba*	*Abba*, by J. Jeremias, 1966.
Jeremias, *Eucharistic Words*	*The Eucharistic Words of Jesus*, by J. Jeremias, E.T. Second edition, 1966.
Jeremias, *Jerusalem*	*Jerusalem in the Time of Jesus*, by J. Jeremias, E.T., 1969.
Jeremias, *Theology* 1	*New Testament Theology*, by J. Jeremias, Vol. 1, 1971.
Klausner	*Jesus of Nazareth, his Life, Times and Teaching*, by J. Klausner, E.T., 1925.
Lipsius-Bonnet	*Acta Apostolorum Apocrypha*, edited by R. A. Lipsius and M. Bonnet. Three volumes, 1959.
McNamara, *T. & T.*	*Targum and Testament*, by M. McNamara, 1972.
Richardson, *Theology*	*An Introduction to the Theology of the New Testament*, by A. Richardson, 1958.
Schürer	*A History of the Jewish People in the Time of Jesus Christ*, by E. Schürer; English translation, 1885–96.
Schweitzer	*The Mysticism of Paul the Apostle*, by A. Schweitzer; English translation, 1931.
Schweizer, *Beiträge*	*Beiträge zur Theologie des Neuen Testaments*, by E. Schweizer, 1970.
Schweizer, *Jesus*	*Jesus*, by E. Schweizer, E.T., 1971.
Singer	*The Authorised Daily Prayer Book of the United Hebrew Congregations of the British Empire*, with a new translation by S. Singer, 1912.
Stendahl, *Scrolls*	*The Scrolls and the New Testament*, edited by K. Stendahl, 1958.
Stenning	*The Targum of Isaiah*, edited with a translation by J. F. Stenning, 1949 (1953).
Torrey	*Our Translated Gospels*, by C. C. Torrey, n.d.

PERIODICALS

C.B.Q.	Catholic Biblical Quarterly.
E.T.	The Expository Times.
H.T.R.	Harvard Theological Review.
H.U.C.A.	Hebrew Union College Annual.
J.B.L.	Journal of Biblical Literature.
J.Q.R.	The Jewish Quarterly Review.
J.R.B.	The Bulletin of the John Rylands Library.
J.T.S.	The Journal of Theological Studies.
N.T.S.	New Testament Studies.
Nov. T.	Novum Testamentum.
R.B.	Revue Biblique.
S.J.T.	Scottish Journal of Theology.
St. Th.	Studia Theologica.
Th. L. Z.	Theologische Literaturzeitung.
Th. Z.	Theologische Zeitschrift.
Z.N.T.W.	Zeitschrift für die neutestamentliche Wissenschaft.

ACKNOWLEDGEMENT

I am indebted to the Delegates of the Clarendon Press, who have permitted me to draw upon articles I have contributed to the *Journal of Theological Studies* (old series 48 (1947), 155–69; new series 1 (1950), 1–15), and to reproduce passages from M. R. James's translation of the Acts of Pilate, the Acts of Thomas, and the Gospel of Peter from his *The Apocryphal New Testament*, and from H. Danby's translation of *The Mishnah*. My thanks for permission to quote from copyright translations are also due to the Loeb Classical Library (the edition of Josephus by H. St J. Thackeray and R. Marcus), to the Executors of the late Dr C. G. Montefiore (*A Rabbinic Anthology*, by C. G. Montefiore and H. Loewe), and to Messrs Parker and Son, Ltd. (A. C. McGiffert's edition of Eusebius's *Ecclesiastical History* in the series of Post-Nicene Christian Fathers). Particular thanks are due to Basil Blackwell, Publisher, for permission to quote from *The Gospel of John* by Rudolf Bultmann.   C.K.B.

INTRODUCTION

1

THE GOSPEL, ITS CHARACTERISTICS
AND PURPOSE

1. THE PROBLEM OF THE FOURTH GOSPEL

THE purpose of an introduction to any ancient book is that its environment may shed light upon the work under consideration, and that in turn the book may be used to illuminate its environment. This is inevitably a complicated process, for no book is completely detachable from its surroundings, but it is particularly difficult in the investigation of the Fourth Gospel, and at the same time particularly important, for this book holds a key-place in the movement of early Christian thought. The difficulty arises out of the fact that the evidence on the basis of which the gospel may be related to its environment, and the usual critical questions of date, authorship, and the like, answered, is at once complex and considerable in bulk, yet also inconclusive.

For example, if for the moment we set aside the Christian affiliations of the gospel, against what background of thought must it be viewed and interpreted? For many years the prevailing critical opinion was that John was 'the gospel of the Hellenists'[1]; it was written by a Greek thinker for Greeks; it marks a decisive point in the hellenization of the Christian faith. Undoubtedly, as will appear, there is much evidence to support this view. More recently, however, there has been a strong tendency to emphasize the significance for John of the Old Testament and of Judaism; thus, for example, 'The gospel is through and through Palestinian. The notion that it is in any sense Hellenistic is contrary to its whole tenour.'[2] Again, it cannot be doubted that there is in the gospel thoroughly Jewish material. The coexistence of these two strains of thought recalls their earlier combination in Hellenistic Judaism[3]; but whatever precedents may be invoked, it cannot be maintained that the background of the gospel (and a fortiori its relation to its background) is simple. The publication (for the most part since the first edition of this Commentary was written) of the Qumran texts cannot be said to have made it less complex.

The question of the authorship of the book is tantalizing. Both in regard to patristic references to persons named John, and in regard to

---

[1] The title of a book by B. W. Bacon (edited by C. H. Kraeling, 1933).
[2] W. Temple, *Readings in St John's Gospel* (1945), xix. See also *Judaism*, especially 8–15.
[3] See C. H. Dodd, *J.R.B.* 19 (1935), 329–43; also his *Interpretation*.

3

patristic allusions to and quotations of the gospel, there was already a Johannine problem in the second century. Viewed from one angle the evidence that the gospel was written, as tradition affirms, by John the son of Zebedee, seems overwhelming; from another, it is very unsatisfactory. Within the gospel itself there are passages which read like the recollections of an eye-witness; there are others of which it seems impossible to vindicate the historical credibility, both because of their inherent improbability, and because they bear the marks of long reflection and meditation upon earlier tradition. How can these divergent impressions be harmonized? The evidence is not sufficient to permit a simple answer. The complexity of the internal evidence is bound up with the question whether we now have the gospel in the form in which its author left it, or, as it may perhaps be better put, with the question what we mean by the author of the gospel. Its composition is now widely held to have been a sequence of successive redactions, and it is disputed whether the main process of editing (to which the name 'John' may for convenience be attached) marked the beginning or the end of this, or perhaps some intermediate point.

A third and even more difficult and important question has now been hinted at. Whoever the author may have been, what was his intention in writing the gospel? Why did he write as he did? Was his intention to record historical events in a plain accurate style, and even to correct earlier reports? Or did he write as a mystic, concerned not with historical but with transcendental truth and interested in narrative only for the allegorical significance it conveyed? The passages referred to above as supporting the view that the gospel was written by an eye-witness suggest the former alternative, but this is not the whole of the evidence, and there is undoubtedly some that points in the opposite direction. John does use his narratives as sources of teaching, and in some respects at least they are used as allegories, whether they ever were more than allegories (from the historical point of view) or not.

The state of affairs which results from this complicated and inconclusive body of evidence is not merely one of historical and critical uncertainty. We are confronted also with the problem of interpretation. Is the gospel to be taken as the report of an apostolic eye-witness, the priceless legacy bequeathed to the church by the beloved disciple himself? Or is it the anonymous (or pseudonymous) product of an unknown author in the second century? Is it to be taken as a supremely reliable historical record of the words and deeds of Jesus? Or is it a set of mystical variations upon a theological theme? Is it a free, individualistic, rewriting of earlier material, unhampered by the fetters of tradition? Or should we see in it a rigid ecclesiastical correction of such speculation? If it was not written by an apostle, and if it is something more than, and other than, a straightforward historical record, what right has it to a place in the church's canon of Scripture, and, granted its place, how is it to be read and interpreted? What is its authority, and what is its importance in Christian theology?

These questions, and many more, are raised, and are now widely recognized as raised, by the gospel before us. It is not claimed that they receive final or satisfactory answers in this book, but they have been kept constantly in mind. Some, particularly those regarding authorship, date, and composition, cannot now be answered with certainty, though much can be learnt by studying them. The peculiar character of the Fourth Gospel is due, it appears, to a twofold conviction, shared by its author, whom I shall consider to be the man (or group) who would accept responsibility for the book as we read it in the ancient MSS., with other New Testament writers but expressed by him with unusual intensity and in a unique form. The conviction is, first, that the actual history of Jesus of Nazareth is of paramount significance because in it the eternal God confronted men, enabling faith and offering to faith the gift of eternal life; and, secondly, that the mere historical data of the life of Jesus are trivial, apart from the faith, God-given, that he is the Word become flesh. Accordingly, 'these are written that you may believe' (20.31); not that you may have a reliable account of what Jesus really did and taught, but that, whatever the details of his ministry may have been, you may believe. It is of fundamental importance to John that Jesus did in fact live and die and rise from the dead; but he uses the material in his gospel so that men may recognize their relation to God in Jesus, rather than to convey interesting information about him. He means to write both history and theology—theological history. The historical and theological grounds and consequences of this observation will be noted in the course of the present commentary.

2. LITERARY CHARACTERISTICS AND STRUCTURE

The Greek style of the Fourth Gospel is highly individual. It closely resembles that of 1, 2, and 3 John (on the precise relation between the gospel and the epistles see below, pp. 59ff.); otherwise it stands alone in the New Testament. It is not easy to characterize. It is neither bad Greek nor (according to classical standards) good Greek. Solecisms are avoided; and so are all the fine and characteristic subtleties of the Greek language. In spite of the absence of these niceties the style remains not only clear but very impressive, charged with a repetitive emphasis and solemn dignity which are felt even in translation. John's vocabulary is very small, but even so many of his most frequently used words occur comparatively rarely in the Synoptic Gospels. For example:

	Matthew	Mark	Luke	John
ἀγαπᾶν, ἀγάπη	9	6 (5)	14	44
ἀλήθεια, ἀληθής, ἀληθινός	2	4	4	46
γινώσκειν	20	13 (12)	28	57 (56)
γραφή (sing.)	0	1	1	11

εἰμι (1 sing. pres.)	14	4	16	54
ἐργάζεσθαι, ἔργον	10 (9)	3	3	35
ζωή	7	4	5	35 (34)
Ἰουδαῖοι	5	6	5	67 (66)
κόσμος	8	2	3	78
κρίνειν	6	0	6	19
μαρτυρεῖν				
μαρτυρία, μαρτύριον	4	6	5	47
μένειν	3	2	7	40 (39)
παροιμία	0	0	0	4
πατήρ (of God)	45 (44)	4	17 (16)	118
πέμπειν	4	1	10	32
τηρεῖν	6	1 (0)	0	18
τιθέναι ψυχήν	0	0	0	8
φανεροῦν	0	1	0	9
φιλεῖν	5	1	2	13
φῶς	7	1	7 (6)	23

Conversely some common synoptic expressions are rare in John, or absent altogether:

	Matthew	Mark	Luke	John
ἄρχεσθαι	13	26 (25)	31	2 (1)
βάπτισμα	2	4	4	0
βασιλεία	57 (55)	20	46	5
δαιμόνιον	11 (9)	11	23	6 (all in the accusation that Jesus was possessed by a demon)
δίκαιος (of men)	17 (15)	2	10 (9)	0
δύναμις	13 (12)	10	15	0
ἐλεεῖν, ἔλεος, σπλαγχνίζεσθαι	16	7 (6)	13	0
εὐαγγελίζεσθαι, εὐαγγέλιον	5	7	10	0
καθαρίζειν	7	4	7	0
καλεῖν	26	4	43	2
κηρύσσειν	9	12	9	0
λαός	14	3 (2)	37 (36)	3 (2)
μετανοεῖν, μετάνοια	7 (6)	3	14	0
παραβολή	17	13	18	0
προσεύχεσθαι, προσευχή	19 (17)	13 (12)	22 (21)	0
τελώνης	8	3	10	0.[1]

[1] These lists are based on those in Goguel, 244f. The most significant words have been selected and the numbers verified.

John can hardly be said to create a new vocabulary, yet his choice of words is undoubtedly distinctive. His Greek moves slowly and within narrow limits, which clearly distinguish it from the other gospels; but it must be acknowledged to be an adequate instrument for the author's purpose. In spite of the small vocabulary the reader never receives the impression of an ill-equipped writer at a loss for the right word; rather that of a teacher who is confident that his message can be summed up in a few fundamental propositions which he has learnt to express with studied economy of diction.

John's style may be more particularly studied by the examination of a number of characteristic expressions and usages.[1] These may be briefly set out as follows.

(i) *Parataxis*. This is perhaps the most striking feature of John's style. Greek in general is characteristically hypotactic; that is, the sentences are joined together by connecting particles, or by the use of a subordinating participle. John, however, very frequently links short complete sentences simply by the use of καί. The usage is far too common for enumeration, but as an example John 9.6f. may be observed: . . . ἔπτυσεν . . . καὶ ἐποίησεν . . . καὶ ἐπέθηκεν . . . καὶ εἶπεν . . . καὶ ἐνίψατο καὶ ἦλθεν. For an analysis of the different forms of parataxis see M. II, 420–3. There may be noted here also the adversative use of καί. See M. II, 469, where 1.5 and 17.11 are mentioned as the best examples, and 21 other passages are referred to.

(ii) *Asyndeton*. Sometimes John's sentences are not even linked by means of καί, but are simply laid side by side. When sentences beginning with a verb of speaking are excluded (such sentences are found in asyndeton in good Greek), 39 instances may be quoted (1.40,42,45, 47; 2.17; 4.6,7,30; 5.12,15; (6.23); 7.32,41; 8.27; 9.9(*ter*),13,16,35,40; 10.21,22; 11.35,44; 12.22(*bis*),29; 13.22,23; 16.19; 19.29; 20.18,26; 21.3,11,12,13,17), while the numbers in the Synoptic Gospels are much smaller (Schweizer, 91f.).

(iii) οὖν. Not only does John use this particle very frequently (*c.* 190 times; rest of the New Testament, *c.* 303), he uses it in a very unusual way. It loses its argumentative force and becomes simply a narrative link (110 times; rest of the New Testament 4; Schweizer, 89f.). This is an unmistakable feature of John's style.

(iv) ἐκεῖνος. This pronoun is used substantivally (in singular) by John 44 times; in the rest of the New Testament (apart from 1 John) it is so used only 21 times. Allowing for the length of the books, this means that the usage is 19 times more frequent in the gospel than elsewhere in the New Testament (Schweizer, 90f.).

(v) ἐμός. In New Testament Greek generally we meet the genitive of the personal pronoun (μου). John has ἐμός 39 times, that is, more

---

[1] See especially Schweizer, 87–99; also Goguel, 242–61, Howard, 276–81, and E. Ruckstuhl, *Die literarische Einheit des Johannesevangeliums* (1951).

frequently than in all the other New Testament books put together. Moreover, he uses the possessive pronoun with repetition of the article (e.g. ὁ λόγος ὁ ἐμός) 29 times, with only one other such use in the rest of the New Testament, and that in 1 John (1.3) (Schweizer, 88f.).

(vi) ἀφ' ἑαυτοῦ, ἀπ' ἐμαυτοῦ. This expression occurs 13 times in John, 3 times (but all plural, ἀφ' ἑαυτῶν) in the rest of the New Testament (Schweizer, 93).

(vii) ἐκ with the genitive in place of the partitive genitive, occurs at least 42 times in John (Schweizer, 92).

(viii) *Epexegetic* ἵνα, ὅτι. The frequency of ἵνα-clauses in John is particularly striking, and many of them express no sense of purpose (e.g. 6.29, τοῦτό ἐστιν τὸ ἔργον τοῦ θεοῦ ἵνα πιστεύητε . . .; cf. 3.19, αὕτη δέ ἐστιν ἡ κρίσις ὅτι τὸ φῶς ἐλήλυθεν . . .). These epexegetical clauses, especially with ἵνα, are very rare in the rest of the New Testament. See below, p. 9.

(ix) οὐ (μή) . . . ἀλλά. This construction occurs *c.* 75 times. Cf. 7.49; 8.55; 12.27; 15.25; 16.20. With a following ἵνα (elliptically) it is found in the New Testament only at John 1.8; 9.3; 11.52 and 1 John 2.19 (Schweizer, 91).

Some of these stylistic features are really significant; for example, the Johannine ἀφ' ἑαυτοῦ, ἀπ' ἐμαυτοῦ points to a fundamental element in John's Christology (see especially on 5.19); others have importance chiefly in the fact that, since they occur uniformly throughout the gospel, they serve as evidence for its integrity. Dr E. Schweizer, whose work on these Johannine '*characteristica*' is perhaps the most illuminating of all, thinks that, while the integrity of the gospel as a whole is demonstrated, the following two deductions may be drawn: (*a*) The *pericopae* 2.1–10,13–19; 4.46–53; 12.1–8,12–15 seem to stand out from the rest of the gospel, though they have certainly been worked over by the author of the whole (100). On these passages see below, pp. 17f. (*b*) 'There results a certain division between Discourses and Narratives' (Schweizer, 106). On this point it will be well to be cautious. Narrative and discourse call for different characteristics of style, and when the whole is admittedly so uniform it seems better not to posit two distinct sources for these parts of the gospel.

One very important question remains regarding the distinctive Johannine style. May it be regarded as a native Greek product, or is it due to the influence of Aramaic? Most students of the gospel are disposed to allow some Semitic influence upon the Greek of the gospel, but the degree of influence postulated varies from critic to critic. C. F. Burney[1] and C. C. Torrey[2] have argued that our present Greek gospel was translated from an earlier Aramaic document, now no longer extant; less radical views are maintained by J. H. Moulton and

---

[1] See under 'Abbreviations'.
[2] See under 'Abbreviations'; also *The Four Gospels* (n.d.); 'The Aramaic Origin of the Gospel of John', *H.T.R.* 16 (1923), 305–44.

W. F. Howard.[1] E. C. Colwell[2] argued that no Aramaic influence could be traced in the gospel. There is a good introduction to and discussion of the question in M. Black's *Aramaic Approach*, and it is dealt with in most recent commentaries. See also the survey article, 'From Burney to Black. The Fourth Gospel and the Aramaic Question', *C.B.Q.* 26 (1964), 323–39, by Schuyler Brown. Here it will be possible to present only a small selection of the evidence, and to discuss it very briefly.

First may be taken several points of style that have already been noted.

(i) *Parataxis* is as characteristic of Aramaic as it is rare in good Greek. The adversative use of 'and' is also Semitic.

(ii) *Asyndeton* also is common in Aramaic (not Hebrew).

(iii) See (viii) above, p. 8, on the use of ἵνα and ὅτι. Some of the unusual constructions of these words have been accounted for as mistranslations of the Aramaic ד (*d*[e] or *di*), which is used not only as a conjunction (=ἵνα or ὅτι) but also as a mark of the genitive relation, and as a relative particle. It is claimed that these uses have sometimes been confounded by the writer of the Greek gospel. Thus Burney (69–78) claimed that ἵνα wrongly renders ד (= the relative) at 1.8; 5.7; 6.30,50; 9.36; 14.16, ὅτι at (?1.16); 8.45; 9.17. See M. II, 436f., Black, 70–83, and the notes on the passages.

The following points may now be added.

(iv) A number of Aramaic words appear in transliteration, with translations or equivalents: 1.38 ('Ραββί, ὃ λέγεται μεθερμηνευόμενον διδάσκαλε); 1.41,42; 4.25; 9.7; 11.16; 19.13,17; 20.16; 21.2; cf. 12.13.

(v) Some of John's words are held to be drawn from or based upon Aramaic. The lake of Galilee is called θάλασσα (sea), not by the natural word λίμνη (lake). This is a Semitic usage. αὐξάνειν ('to increase') is used at 3.30 in the sense 'to become great'. The Aramaic רבי (*r*[e]*bhi*) has both these meanings. πιστικός (12.3) is a well-known crux. It is perhaps a transliteration of פיסתקא (*pistaqa*) (Black, 223ff.). Finally must.be noted the often remarked ambiguity of John's use of ὑψοῦν (see on 3.14), by which he means both 'to exalt' and 'to lift up on the cross'. This verbal play is stronger and clearer in Syriac and in Palestinian Aramaic, since in those languages אזדקף ('*ezd*[e]*qeph*) means not only 'to be lifted up' but also 'to be crucified' (which the Greek ὑψωθῆναι does not normally mean). See Black, 141. The different suggestion made by McNamara (quoted on 3.14) points equally to Aramaic usage.

(vi) *Constructions.* See (iii) above. Other alleged examples of Aramaic constructions are: (*a*) *Relative resumed by pronoun in agreement*: 1.27 (οὗ οὐκ εἰμὶ ἐγὼ ἄξιος ἵνα λύσω αὐτοῦ τὸν ἱμάντα); (1.33); 13.26; (18.9); cf. 9.36. See M. II, 434f.; Black, 100f. (*b*) *The Aramaic relative* particle ד *is indeclinable*; this may account for the curious Greek of

[1] See M. I, *passim*, and especially M. II, 411–85 (by W. F. Howard).
[2] *The Greek of the Fourth Gospel* (1931).

the following passages: 6.37,39; 10.29; 17.2,11,12,24 (Burney, 101–3). See M. II, 437; Black, 79ff. (c) *Ethic Dative with a verb of motion.* There is a possible case at 20.10. Black, 102f. (d) *Positive adjective used for comparative*: perhaps 1.15,30. Black, 117. (e) *Cardinal numerals for ordinals*: 20.1,19. M. II, 439; Black, 124. (f) *Auxiliary use of* ὑπάγειν (אזל, *'ªzal*): perhaps 12.11; 15.16. (g) *Impersonal plural*: 15.6; 20.2. M. II, 447f.; Black, 126ff. (h) *Greek aorist for Semitic static perfect* (where a Greek present would have been more suitable): perhaps 11.14. Black, 129. (i) *Historic present, and periphrastic present and imperfect.* These tenses are common in John and may, but do not necessarily, indicate Aramaic influence. M. I, 120–2, 225–7; II, 451f., 456f.; Black, 130ff. (j) *Casus pendens* is frequent in John (Burney, 63–5, counts 27 examples) as in Aramaic. See M. II, 424; Black, 51f. (k) *The construction* πιστεύειν εἰς occurs 33 times in John (Burney, 34). It might represent the Hebrew האמין ב (*he'ᵉmin bᵉ*). or Aramaic הימין ב (*hemin bᵉ*). M. I, 67f.; II, 463. (l) *The Hebrew infinitive absolute* (this is not a regular Aramaic construction) may be represented by the dative χαρᾷ in 3.29. M. II, 443f.

(vii) *Mistranslations.* It has been alleged that in many places the present text of John reveals mistranslation of an underlying Aramaic text. The mistranslation can be detected by retranslating the faulty Greek text into Aramaic. Many of these alleged errors are ruled out by the application of the two canons laid down by Dr Black (8): 'The mistranslation must at least be credible; and the conjectured Aramaic must be possible.' Application of this principle, as Dr Black himself shows, has the effect of thinning down considerably the number of alleged Aramaisms. See however 11.33, 38.

(viii) *Traces of poetic structure*, such as parallelism, alliteration, and the like. It has often been claimed that the Prologue (1.1–18) is poetic in structure; on this question see below, pp. 150f. Some sayings attributed to the Baptist show parallel form, and are held by Dr Black (145–9) to show the structure of Aramaic verse (John 1.15,30; 3.27–36).

A brief sketch of the evidence for the Aramaic quality of John's Greek has now been given. It is extremely difficult to estimate the weight of such evidence, and it is not likely that any two students would entirely agree in their judgement. It is indisputable that the older any piece of traditional material is the closer it must stand to the Aramaic spoken by Jesus and his contemporaries. This fact may account for the parallelism in the sayings attributed by John to the Baptist. But what of the miscellaneous Aramaisms that remain as possible or probable in the Greek of the gospel? They are certainly too few (if we leave out parataxis and asyndeton) to prove that the Greek was translated from an Aramaic gospel, and probably too few to prove that the Aramaic tradition lies anywhere close to the surface. Thus for example it is quite probable that Aramaic usage is the reason why the evangelists (except Luke) refer to the θάλασσα rather than the λίμνη of Galilee; but John did not take the word from Aramaic but from Greek traditional sources, probably including Mark. πιστικός may be rightly explained from the Aramaic פיסתקא, but John did not take the word directly from an Aramaic source but from Mark, or some similar Greek source. John knew, from the Old Testament as well as Christian tradition, that Jesus ὑψώθη; starting from this he may have simply reflected that when Jesus mounted on the cross he ascended at the same time to the Father. When the evidence is sifted in this way only a very few points remain in addition to the general impression produced by the paratactic and asyndetic style of the gospel as a whole. What does this amount to? Here, especially, personal judgement will be heard, and certainty cannot be attained. It does however seem probable that John, though not translating Aramaic documents, was accustomed to think and speak in Aramaic as well as in Greek. It is true that Deissmann (127–32) has shown that parataxis occurs in uneducated Greek texts where Semitic influence cannot be suspected; but John, though he may not have had a formal Greek education, was not an uncultivated writer. On the other hand, there are certain particulars in which John's style resembles that of Greek mystical writings, and if Semitic paronomasia can occasionally be conjecturally recovered, similar phenomena in Greek can be detected with certainty (e.g. 15.1–3; note also the double meaning found in ἄνωθεν, 3.3,7, which can hardly be paralleled in Aramaic, and the play on τὰ ἴδια, οἱ ἴδιοι, in 1.11, of which the same is true). Perhaps it is safest to say that in language as in thought John treads, perhaps not unconsciously, the boundary between the Hellenic and the Semitic; he avoids the worst kind of Semitism, but retains precisely that slow and impressive feature of Aramaic which was calculated to produce the effect of solemn, religious Greek, and may perhaps have influenced already the liturgical language of the church.

The structure of the gospel is simple in outline, complicated in detail. The book falls into four clear parts, with an appendix, as follows:

(a) 1.1–18, Prologue;
(b) 1.19—12.50, Narratives, Conversations, and Discourses;
(c) 13.1—17.26, Jesus alone with his Disciples;
(d) 18.1—20.31, the Passion and Resurrection;
(e) 21.1–25, an Appendix (see below, pp. 576f.).

Most students of the gospel accept some such analysis, though with differences in detail. Thus Miss Guilding (46) differs only slightly:

Prologue	1.1–18
(1) The manifestation of the Messiah to the world	1.19—4.54
(2) The manifestation of the Messiah to the Jews	6,5,7—12
(3) The manifestation of the Messiah to the Church	13—20
Epilogue	21

C. H. Dodd (*Interpretation*, 289) is even closer to what is proposed here with

A. The Proem	1
B. The Book of Signs	2—12
C. The Book of the Passion	13—20
	(or 21)

It is certainly correct to note a break between chs. 12 and 13, but doubtful whether the whole of ch. 1 should be taken as introductory, doubtful whether John distinguishes so sharply between the world and the Jews (and cf. 12.20), and perhaps undesirable to combine the last discourses, the passion narrative, and the resurrection narrative under one heading.

On (*a*) nothing need be said here. It is held by some to have been originally composed in metrical form and to have suffered interpolation; for a discussion of these questions see below, pp. 150f.; it seems that to each a negative answer should be given. (*d*) and (*e*) likewise call for no detailed discussion here. Both are given in the form of a straightforward narrative, though in each detailed study will reveal how John has reworked the traditional material he received so as to bring out its theological significance. This theological operation does not, however, radically affect the structure (though it does affect the chronology—see pp. 15–18, 21, 24) of the story. The bulk of the gospel falls into sections (*b*) and (*c*).

(*b*) contains a great variety of material. There are simple narratives containing little or no teaching (e.g. 4.46–54; 6.16–21); conversations, simple (e.g. 1.45–51) or, more commonly, controversial (e.g. 8.21–59); and, often merging into the conversations, prolonged discourses pronounced by Jesus (e.g. 5.19–47). This disparate material is not left in juxtaposed fragments, but narrative, discourse, and debate are woven together into units, which in turn stand in recognizable relationship to each other. To take the clearest of examples: the discourse on the bread of life (6.26–59) clearly arises out of the miracle in which Jesus supplies a multitude with bread (6.5–13). In the 'sign' (σημεῖον) the truth of the discourse is implicit; the two are complementary. Again it will be remarked at once that the 'bread of life' chapter forms a complement to the 'water of life' discourse (4.10–26). The discourse does not always follow the action to which it corresponds; for example, it is at 8.12 that Jesus announces that he is the light of the world; the corresponding miracle (the gift of sight to a man born blind) is found in ch. 9. There are moreover abundant cross-references; for example, 'light' appears also at 3.19–21; 12.35f.,46 (cf. 11.9f.), as well as in the Prologue. The total number of distinct themes is small: Life (including water of life and bread of life), Light, the relation of Jesus to the Father, the Shepherd, Sabbath controversy: these cover nearly all the material in chs. 1—12. This section of the gospel has been described (see above) as a 'book of signs', but it may be questioned whether the gospel itself justifies this use of the word *sign*; see below, pp. 75–8.

The movement of thought in this long section of the gospel may now be roughly sketched. A few verses which are connecting links and little more are omitted.

(i) 1.19—2.11. The paragraph opens with the negative witness of the Baptist to himself, and his positive witness to Jesus as the Lamb and Son (or Elect One) of God. It is because of his testimony that the first disciples attach themselves to Jesus and go with him to the marriage feast at Cana. This incident is closely linked with the foregoing by chronological notes (1.29,35,43; 2.1) and leads up to the faith of the disciples (2.11) which is prompted by the sign. Jesus has now appeared as the Envoy of God, accompanied by believing disciples.

(ii) 2.13—4.54. To set himself up in this way at the head of a group of believers was to detach himself from the main body of Judaism. This is brought out in 2.13–22, where the main point (for John) is not the purification of the Temple but the prediction that the killed and risen body of Jesus would take the place of the Temple. This theme had already been foreshadowed in the wedding miracle. It is now expounded in two discourses. In 3.3,5 it is pointed out to Nicodemus that even Israel cannot expect simply to pass into the kingdom of God through the mere lapse of time; only rebirth gives access to the kingdom. In ch. 4 (after a return to John and his witness to validate the claims made by Jesus) Jesus reaches a wider audience and offers to Samaritans also the living water which is that of which the water of Jacob's well was but a shadow, and thereby makes possible worship in Spirit and in truth. The Samaritans declare that he is the Saviour of the world, and the truth of their pronouncement is emphasized in the next narrative, in which Jesus gives life to the household of one who is probably to be thought of as a Gentile. This miracle (4.46–54) like that of 2.1–11 takes place at Cana—a fact that helps to bind the material together.

(iii) In 5.2–9 a miracle story is very simply narrated. The event however took place on the Sabbath, and this fact sets in motion a long discourse. Jesus grounds his sabbath work on his unity with the Father, who is always active, and thus a Christological point of the utmost importance is brought forward, and throughout the chapter the dependence of the Son upon, and his unity with, the Father are discussed. This unity, and the humble obedience in which it is expressed, provide the basis upon which the claims made in the following sections must be understood.

(iv) 6.1–71. After the Christological material of (iii) an advance is made upon (ii), where Jesus claimed to be able to give the water of life. He now claims that he himself is the bread of life. This declaration is made on the basis of a sign (the feeding of the multitude) drawn from the earlier tradition, to which was attached another, the walking on the lake. The claims of Jesus provoke a twofold reaction: many of his followers leave him, but Peter avows faith in him as the Holy One of God (cf. Mark 8.29 and parallels).

(v) 7.1–52; 8.12–59 (on 7.53—8.11 see below, pp. 589ff.). In this paragraph narrative is reduced to a minimum, and the teaching material is highly argumentative. The two main themes used hitherto—the claim of Jesus to give life to the world and the controversy regarding his person—are both brought to the clearest and most forceful expression (7.39; 8.25). In 8.12 the statement is made which leads naturally to the next paragraph. Again we see how John binds his material together.

(vi) 9.1—10.42. In ch. 9 the theme of Jesus as the light of the world is worked out with a liberal use of dramatic irony, and perhaps with thinly veiled reference to the circumstances in which John was writing; see pp. 137f. The Jews examine the healed man and, through him, Jesus himself, unaware that the light in their midst is convincing them of the blindness that boasts of sight and refuses to see. The miraculous cure is alluded to in ch. 10, but the main theme is the description of Jesus as the good shepherd. This theme is however closely related to that of the light of the world, since there are those who come to the light, as there are sheep who know and obey their shepherd, and since there are those who claim to be shepherds and are not, as there are those who claim that they see but do not.

(vii) 11.1–44. Jesus is the resurrection and the life. This, no new theme in the gospel, is brought out with supreme vividness and power by the narrative, told at length, of the raising of Lazarus; 11.45–57 is a connecting link which is equally the conclusion of (vii) and the introduction to (viii).

(viii) 12.1–36. This paragraph deals with the meaning of the passion. The anointing (12.1–8) points forward to the death of Jesus, the entry (12.12–19) to his glory. In 12.20–36, the sayings prompted by the arrival of the Greeks, both these aspects of the passion are brought out: the hour of death is the hour of glory (12.23).

12.37–50 forms a theological conclusion and summary of the ministry as a whole. This paragraph corresponds to the Prologue and is of scarcely less theological significance. It would not be wrong to give it the status of an Epilogue to the public ministry. See the notes.

Finally, after this analysis of the main body of the gospel, we may turn to the incidents and discourses of the last night of the life of Jesus, contained in chs. 13—17 (on which see further below, pp. 454ff.). This body of material is on a larger scale, but follows a pattern similar to that of the earlier units. It opens with a symbolic action, the washing of the disciples' feet, and then proceeds through dialogue to what is, in chs. 15f., almost pure discourse, uninterrupted by question and answer. The conversation and discourse serve to bring out the meaning of the relationship established by the feet-washing and of the approaching passion of Jesus, which is itself prefigured in the humble love embodied in the act of service which he performs for his friends. After this exposition the crucifixion is recounted (as has been noted) in plain terms with little theological comment. The closest parallel to this in the body of the gospel is the account of the raising of Lazarus (11.1–44). Here also the theological discussion precedes the event itself, which is narrated quite simply; and in this narrative also the climax of Jesus' speech is found in a prayer (11.41f.; cf. ch. 17). In the passion narrative the conversation between Jesus and Pilate, in addition to a number of incidents, provides a setting for theological comment.

If this analysis of the gospel be received, two consequences must also be accepted. (a) Since the material is disposed in accordance with a theological and literary scheme, it is idle to seek in John a chronology of the ministry of Jesus. This is not to deny the existence of valuable historical material in John; but the material has been digested and expressed organically in an organism which is primarily theological. (b) Theories of dislocation (see below, pp. 21–6) are not proved when it is shown that, by manipulation, the components of the gospel can be reshuffled into a neater narrative. The question is whether these components, as they stand, take their proper place in the theological structure of the book.

3. SOURCES

Articles by D. M. Smith (*N.T.S.* 10 (1964), 336–51) and R. Kysar (*Nov. T.* 15 (1973), 134–52) speak of an emerging consensus with regard to the source-criticism of John. Dr Smith's conclusions are summed up (and approved) by Dr Kysar as the basis for his further advance as follows (p. 134):

First, John did not use the synoptic gospels, even though he may have drawn some of his material from a tradition having some points of contact with the synoptic oral tradition; second, some interest in the genre of johannine *Reden* seemed to be arising; and third, the fundamentally semitic background of the johannine tradition seemed agreed upon, thanks in part to the discoveries at Qumran.

I have to acknowledge (and the fact is courteously recognized by Dr Kysar on p. 152, note 1) that I do not share in this consensus. I have no doubt at all that John used sources (see below), and I believe it to be profitable to consider from point to point what sources may have been at his disposal and how he may have edited them; but the unity not only of style (see above, pp. 5–11) but also of theological purpose which is so characteristic of the gospel means that the only sources we can with any probability isolate are those which have a known independent existence.

(i) *The Synoptic Gospels.* It will be shown to be probable (see below, pp. 42–6) that John was familiar with Mark, and probable also, though in a smaller degree, that he knew Luke. Where Mark and John agree closely together, as occasionally they do, there is no simpler or

15

better hypothesis than that John drew his material from Mark, not in slavish imitation, but with the frequent recollections which a well-known and authoritative source would inspire. If however the hypothesis is accepted it is necessary to ask in what ways John used this, his only identifiable documentary source. The answer to this question is briefly as follows (on the historical and theological relation between John and the synoptic tradition see below, pp. 46–54). John used freely what Marcan material suited his purpose. He omitted a great deal of Mark, and included much not contained in Mark. When he was simply narrating an incident contained in Mark, he naturally recalled and repeated a number of Marcan words and phrases; but the Marcan material remained subject to his own main purpose and plan. Mark certainly did not dictate the shape of the Fourth Gospel. For example, John took over the Marcan narrative of the feeding of the multitude; he tells the story as simply as Mark, and uses some of Mark's language. But, for him, the narrative finds its significance as the text of a long and very characteristically Johannine discourse to which there is no formal parallel in Mark. An even better example is to be found in the Marcan baptism story. It is almost certain that John knew the story (see on 1.32–4), and he makes a vital theological use of it: it was the descent of the dove upon Jesus which supplied the evidence that he was the Son (or Elect One) of God, who should baptize with the Holy Spirit. Yet the narrative as such John completely omits.

Similar remarks may be made with regard to the synoptic sayings. The teaching of John is for the most part cast in a different mould from that of the synoptics. In place of short pithy sayings and parables we have long discourses which, though they do not in general pursue single direct lines of thought, cover a good deal of ground in a circuitous way. Closer examination however reveals that the Johannine discourses are often built upon, and contain, embedded within them, sayings identical with or similar to those of the synoptics.[1] The long discourse, already referred to, in John 6 seems to rest upon the synoptic saying, 'This [that is, This Bread, or This loaf] is my body' (Mark 14.22). This saying is never actually quoted, but in places (e.g. 6.51) it lies very close to the surface. In the last discourses especially certain important synoptic *logia* are used in a most significant way. The scene (chs. 13—17) opens with the washing of the disciples' feet by Jesus, a deed representative of his love for them and symbolical of the act of humility shortly to be performed in the crucifixion. This recalls Luke 22.27 (I am among you as ὁ διακονῶν), and the more theological parallel in Mark 10.45. A like love is required of the disciples (13.14,34; 14.15; 15.12,17); this 'new commandment' recalls the commandment to love the neighbour as oneself (Mark 12.31 and parallels; cf. 10.35–44 and parallels). The disciples who are thus united in the love of Christ

---

[1] See Howard, 216f., 306f.; Dodd, *Tradition*, 335–65.

must expect to be hated by the world (15.18–21); with this may be compared the last Beatitude, Matt. 5.11f.; Luke 6.22f. Just as Jesus is sent into the world and thus incurs its hatred, so he sends his disciples. This fundamental thought (13.16,20; 15.20; 17.3,8,18,23,25; cf. 20.21) also recalls the Synoptic Gospels, e.g. Matt. 10.24; Luke 6.40. It will be observed that, though notable synoptic sayings reappear in various forms in John (only a few examples have been given here), they are almost invariably recast. This may mean that John used collections of sayings similar to but not identical with those which have been preserved in the synoptics. This is probably true and is confirmed by the existence of aphorisms in John which have no parallel in the Synoptic Gospels.[1] But it is probably true also, and is suggested by comparison with John's treatment of the synoptic incidents, that he deliberately worked over the synoptic sayings, illustrating them by symbolic narratives, expanding them into discourses, and condensing them into new aphorisms.

John's treatment of the synoptic material, though by no means irresponsible, is certainly free, and there follows from it an important observation, the significance of which must be fully weighed. If we did not possess Mark it would be quite impossible to separate the apparently Marcan sections from the rest of John and recognize their origin in a distinct source. In themselves they are not distinctive, because they have been made part of John's general scheme. This means, on the one hand, that (with the possible exceptions of a few Lucan elements) no other sources can be distinguished in John.[2] Those, it should be noted, who reject John's knowledge of Mark are in even deeper darkness. On the other hand, it must be regarded as probable that such sources, whether written or oral, existed, since there is no reason to suppose that whatever John did not draw from Mark he made up out of his own head. It should be recognised that beyond this point all source-criticism of John is guess-work. All that can be done with any show of objectivity is to classify the material in the gospel and consider what kind of source might lie behind it.

(ii) *Material akin to the synoptic tradition.* Several Johannine narratives have the form of synoptic incidents but do not occur in Matthew, Mark, or Luke. The following may be reckoned here:

2.1–11, the Marriage Feast at Cana;
4.46–54, the Nobleman's Son;
5.1–9, the Cure of the Lame Man;
9.1–7, the Cure of the Man born Blind.

In view of Dr Schweizer's observation (see above, p. 8) it may be necessary to add:

2.13–19, the Cleansing of the Temple;

[1] See Howard, 306.
[2] On the relation between John and *P. Eg.* 2 see below, p. 110; H. I. Bell and T. C. Skeat, *Fragments of an Unknown Gospel* (1935); C. H. Dodd, *New Testament Studies* (1953), 12–52; G. Mayeda, *Das Leben-Jesu-Fragment Papyrus Egerton 2* (1946).

12.1–8, the Anointing;

12.12–15, the Entry into Jerusalem.

These incidents might all have been drawn from Mark; but there are differences between the Johannine and Marcan accounts, and the possibility must be allowed that John used another source. See the notes on each passage; the most probable view is that in each Mark was at least one contributing source even if other traditions (including possibly Luke) were combined with it.

If we did not possess Mark all these stories might have been reckoned together, and with (for example), the feeding of the multitude (6.5–13) and the walking on the lake (6.16–21). The treatment of them is comparable with that given to the Marcan episodes; 5.1–9 and 9.1–7 in particular are used as the basis of theological exposition in the same way as the feeding of the multitude. It is possible that 4.46–54 is a variation or adaptation of the Q miracle of the cure of the centurion's servant (Matt. 8.5–13; Luke 7.2–10), but apart from this possibility it is useless to speculate on the source whence the incidents were drawn, or even to say whether one source or several is involved, and whether the source (or sources) was written or oral.

Even less conclusive results are obtained if the teaching material is considered. A list of aphorisms, recalling, in form, those of the Synoptic Gospels, is given by W. F. Howard (267), but it is impossible to trace them to a source.

(iii) *A Signs Source.* One of the two main sources isolated by Bultmann was called by him the σημεῖα-Quelle. The hypothesis has been taken up by other students of the gospel, notably R. T. Fortna, in *The Gospel of Signs* (1970).[1] For a full critical account of Bultmann's hypothesis see D. M. Smith, *The Composition and Order of the Fourth Gospel* (1965).[2] It is clear (see above, pp. 12ff.) that the first twelve chapters of the gospel contain as a major element a sequence of miraculous events: the turning of the water into wine at Cana, the cure of the officer's son, the healing of the lame man at the pool, the feeding of the five thousand, the walking on the lake, the cure of the blind man, and the raising of Lazarus. Some of these events are described by the word σημεῖον. Bultmann's suggestion is that these, together with some other material,[3] were drawn from a single source, which was marked by a somewhat superstitious belief in the miraculous (*Wunderglaube*) and represented Jesus as a θεῖος ἀνήρ—one of a not uncommon class of semi-supernatural, thaumaturgic teachers of antiquity.[4] The independent existence of such

[1] I may refer to my review in *J.T.S.* 22 (1971), 571–4.

[2] I may refer to my review in *J.T.S.* 17 (1966), 438–41.

[3] Dr Smith reconstructs the source, with references to the appropriate passages in Bultmann's commentary, as follows: 1.35–49; 2.1–12; 4.4–9, 16–19, 25–30, 40, 46, 47, 50–54; 6.1–3, 5, 7–13, 16–22, 25; 7.2–10; 5.2–15; 7.19–23; 9.1–3, 6–21, 24–28, 34–38; 10.40–42; 11.2, 3, 5–7, 11–19, 33, 34, 38–44; 12.37, 38; 20.30, 31. I have ignored a few small omissions.

[4] See below, p. 74.

a source cannot, Bultmann agrees, be demonstrated on linguistic grounds (though it may be confirmed by them), but it is possible to see from time to time indications of the evangelist's editing. Not for him the source's crude faith in the wonder-worker; rather, he understands the signs as a symbolic representation of the revelation made by Jesus, which like the discourses, challenged men to a decision about himself. Will they or will they not accept him as the Revealer? There are a few places where the use of the word σημεῖον suggests that it has been drawn from a source; thus the first miracle at Cana is described as an ἀρχὴ τῶν σημείων (2.11), and the second as δεύτερον σημεῖον (4.54). There is however no further enumeration of signs, and general references such as 6.26 can prove no more than that there was a tradition that Jesus worked a good many miracles (cf. 20.30). The use of the word σημεῖον is discussed below (see pp. 75–8); here it must be noted that not all the miracles in the supposed Signs Source are described by this term (it is not applied to the cure of the lame man at the pool, the walking on the lake, and only incidentally to the cure of the blind man, 9.16, and the raising of Lazarus, 11.47), and that the word ἔργον is also used significantly by John (see below, p. 75).

Further discussion at this point would occupy space that cannot be spared. It must be plainly said that there is nothing at all incredible in the suggestion that there was available to John a source containing a sequence of miracle stories described as signs and intended to evoke faith in Jesus as a wonder-worker, though in 6.5–13; 6.16–21; and possibly in 4.46–54; 5.1–9 the Synoptic Gospels too may have contributed to John's narrative. It may have been so; but I see no evidence that proves, or indeed could prove, that it was so, or even that the hypothesis has such a weight of probability as to make it a valuable exegetical tool. To say this is not to deny the value of the observations made by Bultmann, Dr Fortna, and others, which suggest (among other things) that there were different views of the significance of the miracles of Jesus. Such different views did exist, and to examine and compare them is an important part of the historical and theological study of the gospel. But to say that they existed is not necessarily to say that one of them was to be found in a source and the other in the editorial work of the user of the source. It may well be that both existed in the mind of John himself.

(iv) *The Discourses.* One of the most striking features of John is the great bulk of discourse material, which is far more extensive than the narratives which have so far been mentioned, and unlike them, is given in a form peculiar to this gospel. May it be said that the discourses were drawn by the final editor of the gospel from a special source different from those which provided him with the miracle and other stories? This opinion has been maintained, but it seems to rest on inadequate grounds and to be in conflict with some of the facts. (a) As with the narrative material, it must be recognized that there are no compelling and objective literary phenomena on which the hypothesis can rest. The characteristics of Johannine style (see above, pp. 7ff.) are found in the discourses, the narratives, and the editorial framework. (b) The discourses are in general thematically attached to miracles —the Bread of Life to the feeding miracle, the Light of the World to the cure of the blind man—and it is surely somewhat improbable that a narrative source and a discourse source happened fortuitously to fit together as happily as the combination of event and interpretation that we find in the gospel. Moreover, it sometimes happens (e.g. in chs. 4, 9, and 11) that narrative and discourse are woven together. (c) The combination of event and interpretation seems to have been characteristic of the earlier gospel forms.[1] It would be quite wrong to argue that there cannot have been a collection of discourse material earlier than John (especially of the kind that Bultmann has in mind—see below), but on the whole the balance of probability is against it.

One of Bultmann's major sources was called by him *Offenbarungsreden*, Revelation Discourses.[2] These discourses were not Christian in origin (and therefore do not fall under objection (c) above) but based on an oriental gnosis adopted by disciples of John the Baptist. When the evangelist, who originally was such a disciple, became a Christian he adapted the gnostic discourses as utterances of Jesus. This involved the Christianizing and historicizing of the gnostic myth, which when placed on the lips of the historical Jesus necessarily took on a new meaning. Bultmann thinks that one of the gnostic discourses is the source underlying the Prologue, which thus becomes a crucial example for the study of his theory. See in this Commentary pp. 149ff.; also *Essays*, 27–48. The considerations noted above, and others that apply to particular examples, make Bultmann's hypothesis unconvincing; but this judgement on a literary question in no way diminishes the importance of Bultmann's views on the relation between John and the gnostic myth. See below, pp. 38–41.

John's use of a Discourse Source is as unprovable as his use of a Signs Source; and the existence of the former is perhaps less probable

---

[1] The *Gospel of Thomas* contains a series of sayings of Jesus with virtually no narrative. The most probable view however is that this work was excerpted from earlier sources (including probably one or more of the canonical gospels) for use in gnostic circles. Among earlier sources even the document 'Q' as reconstructed by B. H. Streeter (*The Four Gospels* (1936), 291) contains a little narrative matter. But it is doubtful whether this 'Q' ever existed (*E.T.* 54 (1943), 320–3).

[2] For this too see D. M. Smith, op. cit. The source as Dr Smith reconstructs it runs as follows: 1.1–5, 9–12, 14, 16; 3.6, 8, 11–13, 18, 20, 21, 31–36; 7.37, 38; 4.13, 14, 23, 24; 6.27, 35, 33, 48, 47, 44, 45, 37; 5.17, 19–21, 24–26; 11.25, 26; 5.30–32, 37, 39, 40; 7.16–18; 5.41–44; 8.14, 16, 19; 7.6, 7, 28, 29, 33, 34; 8.50, 54, 55, 43, 42, 44, 47, 45, 46, 51; 8.12; 12.44, 45; 9.39; 12.47–49; 8.50, 23, 28, 29; 9.5, 4; 11.9, 10; 12.35, 36; 10.11, 12, 1–4, 8, 10, 14, 15, 27–30, 9; 12.27–29, 31, 32; 8.31, 32, 34, 35, 38; 17.1, 4–6, 9–14, 16, 17, 20–23; 13.31, 32; 15.1–2, 4–6, 9, 10, 14, 16, 18–20, 22, 24, 26; 16.8, 12–14, 16, 20–24, 28; 14.1–4, 6, 7, 9, 10, 12, 14, 16–19, 26, 27; 18.37. I have not taken account of fragments of verses, or of a few small doubts about Bultmann's meaning.

than the existence of the latter. To say this however is not to deny either that synoptic and other *logia* (see above) underlie the discourses, or that the discourses (together with the corresponding signs) may have had an independent existence before the publication of the gospel. The hypothesis that they were in the first place sermons delivered by the evangelist and subsequently (perhaps even after his death) arranged in the gospel has much to commend it (see below, pp. 26, 133f.); but this is very different from the hypothesis that the discourse material was derived by John from an earlier source.

(v) *A Judaean Source.* Comparison with the Synoptic Gospels reveals at once that much of the material peculiar to John is set not in Galilee but in the south, in Judaea or in the city of Jerusalem itself. Only in chs. 2, 4, 6, 7 does Jesus appear outside the southern area. From this fact has been drawn the inference that John possessed a special 'Judaean' or 'Jerusalem Source', from which he derived his information. This is a possible inference, but quite beyond the limits of proof. It is equally possible that John drew his Judaean material from current tradition; possible also that, for reasons of his own, he attached to Jerusalem material which, when it reached him, had no location or even a different location. Certainly John has a great interest in the Jewish feasts, which required, or accounted for, the presence of Jesus in Jerusalem; and his placing of material in the capital city of Judaism corresponds to his frequent use of the general phrase 'the Jews' instead of the particular designations—Pharisees, Sadducees, Herodians—found in the Synoptic Gospels. It is easy to overvalue the importance of topographical features of the gospel, or at least to value them in the wrong way. See W. D. Davies, *Land*, 298–335.

(vi) *The Passion Narrative.* The question may be raised whether John's passion narrative is or is not dependent upon the Marcan (or some similar) story. If John's passion narrative is independent it is a very important source of his gospel (or, perhaps, a very important part of the Judaean source). The view taken in this commentary, however, is that the Johannine passion story is an edited version of the Marcan, into which John has introduced some fresh material. He has retold the story from his own point of view, giving full place to his own special interests, and, it may be, including some additional historical information, though this probably amounts to little, but he does not offer a complete independent passion narrative. This position can be maintained (or attacked) only on the basis of detailed examination of the text, for which reference must be made to the notes on chs. 18, 19, 20.

4. THEORIES OF DISPLACEMENT AND REDACTION

The gospel defies precise analysis into sources. This is not to say that sources were not employed in its construction, but only that continuous sources (with the exception of Mark) cannot be traced. It is moreover true that when the gospel is read through, in spite of a general impression of unity, certain indications of disunity and dislocation are found. The narrative does not always proceed straightforwardly; some of the connections are bad, and sometimes there are no connections at all. Occasionally a piece seems to be out of its proper setting. It is on the basis of these observations that theories of accidental displacement of parts of the gospel, and of editorial redaction, have been founded. Those who have proposed such theories often disagree sharply among themselves—a fact which tends to diminish confidence in their results—and the number[1] of different proposals for restoring the original text of the gospel is very large. In this paragraph only a few examples will be given. Further discussion will be found at various points in the commentary, but this book is likely still to fall under the condemnation cf Dr D. M. Smith, who writes (op. cit., xv), 'Unfortunately, he [Barrett] does not argue the case against displacements with the same consistency and cogency with which Bultmann argued for them, but such a comparable argumentation is precisely what is demanded.' From one point of view this complaint is entirely justified. Every one of Bultmann's suggestions is worthy of detailed consideration, and he argues his case with unsurpassed learning and skill. The following comments however may be made. (1) If every proposal were examined in full this book would be a great deal longer than I intend it to be. (2) A question of general principle is involved which does not need to be repeated every time: I take it that if the gospel makes sense as it stands it can generally be assumed that this is the sense it was intended to make. That it may seem to me to make better sense when rearranged I do not regard as adequate reason for abandoning an order which undoubtedly runs back into the second century—the order, indeed, in which the book was *published*. This consideration leads to (3), the question what we mean by John, whether as person or book. Questions of authority and canon are raised here, but I defer them to a later point, and refer back to my definition of the author as 'the man (or group) who would accept responsibility for the book as we read it in the ancient MSS.' *Someone* published it substantially as it now stands; and I continue to make the assumption that he knew his business, and that it is the first duty of a commentator to bring out this person's meaning.[2] This meaning will be brought out

---

[1] Several theories of partition and redaction are summarized in Howard, 297–302. By far the most elaborate of recent theories is that of R. Bultmann, for which see the invaluable account and discussion of D. M. Smith, op. cit. Bultmann (see his commentary, vii–xii) reads the gospel in the following order (I omit a few minor points): 1.1–3.21; 3.31–6, 22–30, 4.1–54; 6.1–59; 5.1–47; 7.15–24; 8.13–20; 7.1–14, 25–9; 8.48–50, 54, 55; 7.30, 37–44, 31–6, 45–52; 8.41–7, 51–3, 56–9; 9.1–41; 8.12; 12.44–50; 8.21–9; 12.34–6; 10.19–21, 22–6, 11–13, 1–10, 14–18, 27–42; 11.1–12.33; 8.30–40; 6.60–71; 12.37–43; 13.1–30; 17.1–26; 13.31–5; 15.1–16.33; 13.36–14.31; 18.1–21.25. For the work of his ecclesiastical redactor see pp. 3of.

[2] '*It goes without saying that the exegesis must expound the complete text*, and the critical analysis is the servant of this exposition. The case is only otherwise where glosses of a secondary redaction occur' (Bultmann, 17; his italics).

all the better if it is possible to detect editorial processes by which pieces of material are switched from one place to another, one connection to another. If such manipulation can be demonstrated it must be gratefully accepted as a valuable guide to interpretation. But this brings us back to the question whether the alleged displacements are in fact convincing—not whether they are possible, but whether they are convincing; not whether the several passages concerned could once have stood in a different order, but whether only the hypothesis that they did so stand makes sense of the work before us. This is a condition extremely difficult to fulfil.

A few suggested displacements will be mentioned, most of them going back to the time before Bultmann's consistent carrying through of the inquiry but taken up and elaborated by him.

(i) 3.22–30, which seems to interrupt the Nicodemus discourse (3.31 follows upon 3.21), should be removed and placed between 2.12 and 2.13. This change also improves the itinerary, since Jesus, in Galilee in 2.1–12, is next brought εἰς τὴν ᾿Ιουδαίαν γῆν (3.22) before going up to Jerusalem at 2.13.

(ii) Ch. 6 should stand between chs. 4 and 5. Again the itinerary is improved. As the gospel stands, Jesus is in Galilee (4.54); goes up to Jerusalem (5.1); crosses the sea of Galilee (6.1—there being no indication that he has left Jerusalem); walks in Galilee, being unable to walk in Judaea (7.1—because the Jews were seeking to kill him, though he had not been in Jerusalem since 5.47). If the suggested emendation is made the course of events is as follows: Jesus is in Galilee (4.54), crosses the sea (6.1), goes up to Jerusalem (5.1), and returns, for security, to Galilee (7.1).

(iii) 7.15–24 should be read after 5.47. It continues the argument of ch. 5, and interrupts the connection between 7.14 and 7.25.

(iv) 10.19–29 should be read after 9.41. The σχίσμα of 10.19 follows naturally upon the miracle of ch. 9, and so does the remark of 10.21 (μὴ δαιμόνιον δύναται τυφλῶν ὀφθαλμοὺς ἀνοῖξαι;). Further, 10.18 is admirably taken up by 10.30.

(v) Chs. 15 and 16 should be taken at some point before 14:31, which closes the upper-room discourses. The order adopted by Bernard (xx–xxiii; xxxii) is 13.1–31a; 15.1–27; 16.1–33; 13.31b–8; 14.1–31.

(vi) 18.13–24 is out of order. (a) It is difficult to understand the movements of Jesus in relation to Annas and Caiaphas; (b) the story of Peter's denial is given in two parts. Some such arrangement as that of the Sinaitic Syriac (which gives the order of verses 13, 24 ,14, 15, 19–23, 16–18) should be adopted.

Some theories of dislocation are supported by the observation that many of the displaced passages are of the same length, or are multiples of the same length; the mechanical process of dislocation then becomes easier to understand, since sheets, originally loose or detached from a papyrus roll, or leaves of a codex, could conceivably be placed in the wrong order.

In addition to the questions of principle mentioned above the following general observations may be made.

(i) There is no textual evidence in support of any of the proposed alterations (except that of the Sinaitic Syriac in 18.13–24). This is by no means a fatal objection but it means that the hypotheses in question can be held only in the form of the belief that the autograph copy of the gospel was itself damaged. This must almost certainly carry back the damage to the lifetime of the evangelist, who, one would think, would probably have had the opportunity of remedying the mishap.

(ii) 'This evangelist is not interested in itineraries' (Strachan, 81). The movement of the gospel is dictated by theological rather than by chronological and topographical considerations. A particularly striking example is to be found in ch. 5 (see above, p. 13).

(iii) Further, even his theological thought does not habitually move in straight lines. It is rather his custom to regard a question from one point of view, and then adopt another, sometimes taking up a somewhat different subject between the two treatments.

(iv) While the proposed alterations generally improve some connections, they often worsen others.

Theories of redaction differ from theories of dislocation in that they account for the present unsatisfactory state of the gospel by the hypothesis of an editor whose work was responsible for the perversion of an original text, or the faulty combination of documents. They resemble theories of dislocation, however, in that they are so numerous and various that a detailed account of them cannot be given in this book. As a comparatively simple, and persuasive, example may be given the theory of B. W. Bacon,[1] who assigns to a redactor the following passages: 1.6–8, 15; 2.1–12, 13–25; 3.31–6; 4.43–5, (46b), (54); 5.28f.; 6.29b,40b, 44b,(54b); 7.1,14,37–9; 10.7,8b,9,22f.; 12.29f.,33,42f.,44–50; 13.16,20, 36–8; 18.9,14–18,24–7; 19.34,35,37; 20.24–9; 21; (7.53—8.11); (12.8); (21.25).

This list has not a little in common with the passages Bultmann describes as redactional. For an account of these see D. M. Smith, op. cit., 213–26; an assessment of the validity and significance of the redaction theory follows, 227–38. Dr Smith correctly observes that 'the novelty of Bultmann's redactional theory consists in the way in which he related it to the problem of the order of the gospel, maintaining that the same redactor(s) who found the gospel in fragments and assembled it in its present order also made certain additions that would make this original and dubiously orthodox document acceptable to the developing orthodoxy of the church of the early second century' (213). It is the historical and theological interests, rather than literary phenomena,

---

[1] Collected in Howard, 299. See Bacon, 472–527.

that mark out the redactor's work and distinguish it from the evangelist's own; these interests Dr Smith subdivides as sacramentalism, apocalyptic eschatology, conformity to the synoptics, the beloved disciple and the attestation of the gospel. A few miscellaneous redactions are not covered by these headings.

Some redaction theories founder on the linguistic unity of the gospel (see above, pp. 5ff.), but not Bultmann's; his stands or falls by exegetical and theological considerations, and it is impossible to apply these in brief compass in this Introduction. They have however been applied at a number of points in the Commentary, and raise questions of the highest importance. What *was* John's attitude to sacraments? to eschatology? to history? I have argued in this book, and elsewhere,[1] that John was not an anti-sacramentalist, whose work was interpolated by an orthodox sacramentalist, but a profound theologian, capable of acceptance, but of highly critical acceptance, of the sacraments; that he had not abandoned futurist eschatology in the interests of a purely present Christian experience, but was a profound theologian, capable of holding present and future together in unity. And so on. If I am right in these views, the case for redaction[2] falls to the ground. But the question is one that can only be argued out 'on the ground', in the bayonet-fighting of detailed exegesis.

This discussion may, though it should not, have given the reader the impression that I believe that John, in writing the gospel, was a mere inanimate plectrum in the hands of the Spirit. This is not so; the book (whatever doctrine of inspiration one may hold) was produced by normal literary processes, and it is very probable that these were complex rather than simple. The gospel may have passed through as many as five stages of composition,[3] though if this is so it seems to me no longer possible to distinguish them. I hint below at a suggestion, to be developed later in the Introduction (pp. 133f.), that seems to me plausible; it should be described by no stronger word, and students of this gospel should be ready to admit that there is a great deal that they do not know. It may be said of the whole gospel and not merely of the last discourses, 'These rearrangements only gain consistency at the cost of creating fresh problems ... But the chief difficulty is that the material is treated as if John had planned the whole complex as a unity, whereas in fact the contents are loosely strung together with very little progression of thought. . . . If it can be accepted that John picks up one theme after another for further development, without giving much attention to the overall unity, there is no reason to abandon the order which has come down to us (Lindars, 461).[4]

---

[1] *Essays*, 58–69; *Judaism*, 69–76; 'The Father is greater than I'.
[2] Except in a few places such as perhaps 4.9; 5.3f.; 7.53–8.11; 19.35; 21.24; perhaps the whole of ch. 21.
[3] Brown, XXXIV–XXXIX.
[4] Dr Lindars himself believes that what we have is a second edition of the gospel. The main features of the second edition are (*a*) the Prologue (1.1–18) replaces the

Neither displacement theories nor redaction theories are needed to explain the present state of the gospel, in which certain roughnesses undoubtedly remain, together with an undoubted impression of a vigorous unity of theme. It was not for nothing that the image of the 'seamless robe' was applied by Strauss to the gospel itself. It shows a genuine unity of language and style, which is no more than the outward expression of an inward unity of thought and purpose; but this unity was imposed upon material drawn in the first place from a variety of sources, and composed, it may be, over a fairly considerable period. Much of the discourse material in the gospel can be readily understood as having been originally delivered in sermons. An incident from the life of Jesus was narrated, and the evangelist-preacher expounded its significance for the life and thought of the church. As this process was repeated and prolonged a body of material would grow under his hands until it was capable of formulation in the shape of a gospel. The formulation, however, would be no easy task. Not only would the original sources be disparate; the several sections, or homilies, would not necessarily dovetail into one another. The evangelist was, however, aided in his work by two principles which tended strongly towards unification. In the first place, he possessed an extraordinary grasp of the theological significance of the earlier gospel tradition as a whole. He was able to see its total significance in its parts; to present, not a miscellaneous collection of the deeds and words of Jesus, but a unified conception of his person, which shone out in various ways in the several traditions about him (see further below, pp. 51–4). In the second place, he was impelled by a purpose which gave unity to his work. In an age when the first formulations of the Christian faith were seen by some to be unsatisfactory, when gnosticism in its various forms was perverting the Gospel and adopting it for its own uses, he attempted and achieved the essential task of setting forth the faith once delivered to the saints in the new idiom, for the winning of new converts to the church, for the strengthening of those who were unsettled by the new winds of doctrine, and for the more adequate exposition of the faith itself.

---

original opening; (*b*) ch. 6 was inserted to demonstrate that Moses 'wrote of me' (5.46); (*c*) the Lazarus material (11.1–46; 12.9–11) was added, causing considerable rearrangement; (*d*) chs. 15, 16, and probably 17, were added, breaking the connection between 14.31 and 18.1.

2

THE NON-CHRISTIAN BACKGROUND OF
THE GOSPEL

EVEN a short sketch of the world of thought in which John was composed would extend beyond the limits of this Introduction.[1] The background of the gospel is unusually complicated. It is difficult to draw sharp lines. Men and ideas travelled fast and far in the first and second centuries after Christ, and cults and philosophies mingled together and influenced one another. It was an age of syncretism. The older religions of the Mediterranean world had for many been dissolved in the acids of scepticism; but newer faiths were moving in from the east and in varying degrees establishing themselves upon the basis of late Greek philosophy, which itself became more and more religious; while it must be remembered that the first century witnessed also the revival (fostered by Augustus) of the ancient Roman religion, as well as the beginnings of Emperor worship. Even Judaism, as will appear, did not stand wholly outside this process of cross-fertilization, and rabbinic as well as Hellenistic Judaism shows its effects. Important, however, as this mingling of Greek and Hebraic is (see below, pp. 39ff.), it remains true that in the first century it is possible to pick out, as the two main strands of developing thought, the Old Testament tradition, preserved in the Jewish church, and the general trend of Greek religious philosophy. They were capable of mixing (and the syncretistic phenomenon of gnosticism is of great importance in the study of John), but in themselves they differed widely.

1. THE OLD TESTAMENT[2]

John is certainly dependent on the Old Testament, but his use of it differs from that of other New Testament writers, and is far from simple. His direct quotations are fewer, and he comparatively rarely uses the 'proof-texts' by which the earliest Christians often sought to show that Jesus was the Messiah whose coming was prophesied in the Old Testament.

[1] Further material can be found in my *The New Testament Background: Selected Documents* (1956), a book which came into being as a byproduct of my preparation for the first edition of this Commentary.

[2] See C. H. Dodd, *According to the Scriptures* (1952); B. Noack, *Zur johanneischen Tradition* (1954), 71–89; B. Lindars, *New Testament Apologetic* (1961); E. D. Freed, *Old Testament Quotations in the Gospel of John* (1965).

It seems that John regularly used the LXX in making his Old Testament quotations, but that he was capable of going direct to the Hebrew, and on occasion did so. He may have used other traditional versions and interpretations. The evidence for these statements is set out in the following analysis of his quotations.

(i) In the following five passages the LXX Greek agrees exactly with the Hebrew of the passage quoted, and John agrees with both.

John	10.16	Ezek. 34.23; 37.24
	10.34	Ps. 81(82).6
	12.38	Isa. 53.1 (LXX and John prefix κύριε)
	16.22	Isa. 66.14
	19.24	Ps. 21(22).19

No conclusion can be drawn regarding the source whence these quotations were drawn.

(ii) The following passages are not exact quotations but adaptations which might be based on either the Hebrew or the Greek text. On each see the commentary.

John	1.51	Gen. 28.12
	6.31	Exod. 16.14f.; Ps. 77(78).24f.
	6.45	Isa. 54.13
	7.42	Ps. 88(89).4f.; Mic. 5.1(2); and perhaps other passages
	12.13	Ps.117(118).25f.
	12.27	Ps. 6.3; 41(42).7
	15.25	Ps. 34(35).19; 68(69).5
	19.28f.	Ps. 68(69).22
	19.36	Exod. 12.10,46; Num. 9.12; Ps. 33(34).21

(iii) In one place John sides with the Hebrew against the Greek (see the note).

John 19.37   Zech. 12.10

(iv) In one place there is a superficial but probably illusory agreement of John with LXX against the Hebrew.

John 2.17: ὁ ζῆλος τοῦ οἴκου σου καταφάγεταί με.

Ps. 68.10 (LXX): ὁ ζῆλος τοῦ οἴκου σου καταφάγεταί με (so B; but Bᵇ, א, R have κατέφαγέ(ν) με).

Ps. 69.10 (Heb.): קנאת ביתך אכלתני.

John (with the MS. B of the LXX) has the future καταφάγεται while the Hebrew has the perfect אכלתני ('ᵃkalathni). But the LXX reading is far from certain; and the future is a possible rendering of the Hebrew perfect.

(v) The remaining passages merit individual consideration.

John 1.23; Isa. 40.3. John agrees verbally with the LXX except that in place of ἑτοιμάσατε (also used at Mark 1.3) he has εὐθύνατε (Aquila and Theodotion have ἀποσκευάσατε, Symmachus, εὐτρεπίσατε).

John's is a possible rendering of the Hebrew (פנו, *pannu*), but it may have been suggested by other LXX passages (see the notes).

John 12.15; Zech. 9.9. John's form of the prophecy has striking differences from both Hebrew and Greek; see the notes.

John 12.40; Isa. 6.10. John, the Hebrew, and the LXX are all different, but John is perhaps a little nearer the Hebrew than the LXX; see the notes.

John 13.18; Ps. 40(41).10. In having the singular ἄρτον John agrees with the Massoretic Hebrew (לחמי, *lahmi*) against the LXX (ἄρτους); but the Hebrew text represented by the LXX differs only in pointing, and it would be unwise to argue on the basis of this passage that John used the Hebrew text, though it is quite possible that he did so (see further in the commentary).

This brief analysis suggests, as has been said, that John regularly used the LXX, but that he was able to use, and on occasion did use, the Hebrew.[1] It is impossible to conclude that he always used the Hebrew and neglected the Greek; he quotes too often in agreement with the LXX for this to be likely. It is possible that he also knew other versions of the Old Testament. The quotation of 12.41 is introduced as spoken by Isaiah because 'he saw his [that is, Christ's] glory'. This may have been suggested by some such version as that of the Targum of Isa. 6.5 which declares that Isaiah saw 'the glory of the *shekhinah* of the King of the ages' (יקר שכינת מלך עלמיא). This one small piece of evidence, however, must not be unduly pressed.

The comparative rarity of 'proof-texts' in John has already been mentioned. Several of those which are used occur in the passion narrative, and give it a distinctly primitive appearance. To draw, however, from the small number of explicit quotations the conclusion that John had less interest in and a smaller knowledge of the Old Testament than the other evangelists would be a serious mistake. Closer examination of the gospel shows that the Old Testament themes, often crudely set forth in the earlier gospels, have thoroughly permeated John's thought, and appear, often without reference to particular passages of the Old Testament, again and again.[2] Two examples may be given. At Mark 7.6f., Isa. 29.13 is quoted as predicting the hypocrisy of the Pharisees, who pay lip-service to God, yet by their deeds reject what is shown to be his true will. John does not quote the verse from Isaiah, but brings out its substance with a vivid and dramatic sense of the irony involved; for example, in the story of Nicodemus (3.1–21); in the discussion of the witness of the Old Testament and John the Baptist (5.31–47); in 7.19–24, where the Jews who practise

---

[1] An alternative hypothesis, which must not be dismissed, is that the use of Hebrew lies further back, in John's sources; e.g. it may be that at 19.37 John did not himself use the Old Testament but an earlier Christian translation of the verse in question.

[2] See *J. T.S.* old series 48 (1947), 155–69. The argument of the following paragraphs, and some quotations, have been taken from this article.

circumcision on the Sabbath complain of Jesus' healing work on that day; in 8.39–44, where the professed sons of Abraham seek to murder an innocent man; and, most dramatically, at 18.28, where the Jews who are about to compass the crucifixion of Jesus refuse to enter the Praetorium in order that they may not be defiled. In all these passages John emphasizes the same theme as Mark, with, however, one very significant difference. In Mark the proof-text 'is applied to a particular piece of hypocrisy. Men invent or adjust a law so as to excuse themselves from the moral obligation of caring for their parents. . . . In John, on the other hand, the good thing neglected, which is contrasted with lip-service, is not an ethical practice but a proper response to Jesus. This is an alteration very characteristic of John.'

As a second example, the conversation in Mark 12.29–33 may be considered. There are references here to Deut. 4.35; 6.4f.; Lev. 19.18; 1 Sam. 15.22. 'There is no verbal parallel in John, but it is perhaps not too much to say that no Old Testament themes have more deeply influenced the evangelist than these—the theme of the divine unity, and the command of love.' So central indeed are these themes in John that illustration of them is needless. Of course, they are reinterpreted: the unity of God now means the unity of the Father and the Son, and the command to love the neighbour (the fellow-Israelite) becomes the requirement of mutual love within the church; but this reinterpretation signifies only that John is a Christian user of the Old Testament. The Old Testament themes, never formally buttressed by the quotation of texts, are Christologically worked out.

John, then, develops the synoptic use of the Old Testament in a characteristically subtle way. At its most characteristic this differs most widely from the *pesher* interpretation of the Qumran sect. When John declares (12.39f.), This is why they could not believe, because Isaiah said, He has blinded their eyes and hardened their heart, he is not far from the simple commentary which cites the text and continues, Its *pesher* is . . . But, though the writers of the Scrolls, especially perhaps of the *Hodayoth*, have undoubtedly absorbed the language and spirit of the Old Testament (it is this that accounts for most of the resemblances between the Scrolls and the New Testament), John's profound thematic usage, founded as it is upon the figure of Jesus, is hard to parallel. John also uses Old Testament material extensively in the symbolical language which abounds in his gospel. This is seen most clearly in the extended allegories of the Shepherd (10.1–16) and the Vine (15.1–6). Neither of these looks back to a single Old Testament passage, but each is full of Old Testament imagery. For details, see the notes.

The Old Testament, therefore, so well known and understood that John could use it not piecemeal but as a whole, may be taken as an essential element in the background of the gospel. We now proceed to examine his relation to the channels in which the Old Testament tradition was propagated in the first century.

2. JUDAISM[1]

The Old Testament tradition, preserved in written documents, was also handed down in the living stream of Judaism. This ran in the first century (as it had always run) in numerous channels; in particular it now flowed in the stream of apocalyptic and in the stream of rabbinic thought. It may be said that apocalyptic was the successor of the prophetic, rabbinical thought the successor of the legal, part of the Old Testament; but this is only very approximately true. The apocalyptic and rabbinic literatures can no more be separated than the Law and the Prophets,[2] and neither can be separated from non-Jewish influences; yet a distinction between them is convenient for analysis.

It might seem at a first glance that John bears no relation at all to the apocalyptic literature; this, however, is not so. It must in the first place be recognized that apocalyptic is not exclusively concerned with the future. Apocalypse means the unveiling of secrets; very frequently the secrets disclose future events, but sometimes they make known present facts, especially facts regarding the life of heaven, divine and angelic beings, and the like. The two kinds of secret pass over into one another, since an unveiling of what is eternally present in heaven may well indicate what may be expected to happen in the future on earth. New Testament apocalyptic is in general concerned with the future, though the Johannine apocalypse, for example, describes vividly the worship of heaven as it is; but the gospel may equally be looked upon as apocalyptic in the sense that it unveils present reality. Jesus can declare heavenly things (ἐπουράνια) because he is the Son of man, who is in heaven (3.12f.). There is no question here of declaring the future, only the imparting of heavenly truth. Certainly, in this place and in others like it John is not simply writing in the Old Testament tradition; Greek and other non-Jewish influences have helped to mould his thought. But these influences were also at work upon Jewish apocalyptic, and the parallelism between John and apocalyptic writers is not invalidated by such facts.

A consideration of John's terminology points to his familiarity with apocalyptic. He can speak of Jesus not only as Messiah (not necessarily an apocalyptic term) and as King, but also as Son of man (a title hardly found except in the apocalyptic writings). Jesus speaks both of the kingdom of God, and of his own kingdom, and it is quite clear that each is an other-worldly kingdom (3.3,5; 18.36). For men there lies ahead a resurrection (a literal coming out of their tombs, 5.28; cf. 11.43f.), and, after that, judgement (5.29). The fact that John is able to speak also of a present resurrection and a present judgement in no way alters the facts that he speaks of a future resurrection and judgement

[1] See *Judaism*.
[2] The Qumran literature (see below, pp. 33f.) contains both apocalyptic and legal elements.

and that his thought is formed upon an apocalyptic frame; it means that his eschatology is Christian eschatology (see below, pp. 67–70). The judgement will be carried out by Jesus as Son of man (5.27); accordingly it is made clear that after his departure to the Father he will 'come' (14.3,18; 21.22). The blessing conferred on men by God through Christ is eternal life (3ωή αἰώνιος), the life of the age (αἰών) to come, a fundamental notion of apocalyptic. In addition to this basic apocalyptic terminology the use of such metaphors as the germinating seed (12.24) and the ripening harvest (4.35–8) may be noted.

There can be no doubt that John, distinctive though the pattern of his thought is, was by no means out of touch with the world of Jewish apocalyptic, though his knowledge may well have reached him through Christian channels. That he carried through a drastic reorientation of apocalyptic eschatology is equally clear; on this see below, pp. 67–70.

Rabbinic Judaism grew out of the movement for the re-establishment of a reformed Judaism in the time of Ezra, and is worthily reckoned the heir of Old Testament religion; yet there is excellent evidence that it was not free from non-Jewish influence—for example, the large number of Greek and Latin loan-words taken into the Hebrew and Aramaic of the Talmud and Midrash. The rabbinic literature covers a vast field of human activity and thought. It deals with matters of criminal and civil, as well as religious, law. From law it passes over to ethical instruction and exhortation. It contains a good deal of theology, mostly in homiletic form, and it is messianic and eschatological though not as a rule apocalyptic. It contains history, mingled with folk-tales and legends which incidentally describe, often in detail, the customs of those who narrated them; it gives many liturgical details and much biblical exegesis, and it lays bare the bases of a varied religion, sometimes practical and sometimes mystical. John reveals numerous contacts with rabbinic Judaism over much of this wide area. The following examples may be given.[1]

Certain elementary processes of criminal law are assumed; an accused person must be allowed the right to speak before the judges (7.51), and the consentient testimony of at least two witnesses is necessary for the establishing of any fact (8.17). Religious law naturally occupies a larger place than criminal, and here John knows that the commandment that a child should be circumcised on the eighth day took precedence of the sabbath law; if the eighth day fell on a Sabbath it was nevertheless legitimate to make all necessary preparations for, and to perform, the operation (7.22f.). On the other hand, to carry a mattress on the Sabbath was illegal (5.10). It is probable, though not certain, that 7.37ff. shows John's awareness of a ritual practice carried out in Jerusalem at the feast of Tabernacles before the destruction of

---

[1] On all the Johannine references in the following paragraph see the notes, where the most important rabbinic parallels are cited. Fuller information will usually be found in S.B.

the Temple, and described in the Mishnah (and elsewhere). Knowledge of rabbinic exegesis appears at 1.51 and 8.56, for John evidently thinks of the angels ascending and descending on Jesus (as they had been said to do on Jacob), and knows that Abraham went into all the days of history and therefore saw in advance the day of the Messiah. Rabbinic theology and mysticism also appear in John, for the description of the Logos and his relation to God in the Prologue corresponds exactly to much that was said by the Rabbis about the Torah; and the language used to describe the unity of the Father and the Son calls to mind sayings about the unity existing between God and Israel.

In the passages which have been referred to, and in all similar passages, great caution is necessary. No part of the rabbinic literature was written down until a date later than the composition of John. Direct literary relationship is out of the question, and some apparent parallels may be merely fortuitous. But when all such allowances have been made it remains very probable that John himself (or perhaps the authors of some of his sources) was familiar with the oral teaching which at a later date was crystallized in the Mishnah, the Talmud, and the Midrashim.

Apocalyptic and Rabbinic Judaism remain important elements in the background of the Fourth Gospel, and it would be misleading if they were overlooked; but they were by no means the whole of Judaism. On Hellenistic Judaism see below, pp. 39ff.; in Alexandria and no doubt elsewhere in the Diaspora Greek thought affected Jewish to an even greater extent than in Palestine (above p. 27). Even in Palestine the various schools of Pharisaism cannot now be regarded as constituting a single and uniform normative Judaism. This has always been known; the accounts in Philo (*Prob.* 75–91; *Hypothetica* 11, 1–18) and Josephus (*Bel.* 11, 119–61; *Ant.* XIII, 171f.) of the Essenes showed that there were groups of Jews whose Jewishness was emotionally intense but in content affected by non-Jewish ideas. To this evidence must now be added that of the so-called Dead Sea Scrolls,[1] discovered at or near Qumran near the Dead Sea. Whether those who composed and copied the Scrolls are rightly described as Essenes is a question that need not be discussed here; the label that they should bear is far less important than the fact that they existed and were the sort of people that they were. They were in many ways very different from John the Baptist and Jesus; perhaps even more different from John the Evangelist. They separated themselves from the Temple not because they believed in worship in spirit and truth, unrestricted to any locality (John 4.21–4), but because they disapproved of the officiating priests, their calendar and their conduct. They maintained the Law, as they understood and interpreted it, with

---

[1] The best introduction is in the two books by Millar Burrows: *The Dead Sea Scrolls* (1956), and *More Light on the Dead Sea Scrolls* (1958). For the texts see E. Lohse, *Die Texte aus Qumran* (1964); for translation, G. Vermes, *The Dead Sea Scrolls in English* (1962). See also J. H. Charlesworth, ed., *John and Qumran* (1972).

the greatest rigour. They did not mix with but withdrew from the common life of their people to live in isolation, though also in community. Yet in this, and in some other ways, they manifest parallels with primitive Christianity. The Christians did not withdraw to the desert but they did form a clearly marked community, which developed its own organization and institutions. That John and Qumran both teach a 'modified dualism' is broadly true, but not very significant, since this modified dualism is to be found also in the Old Testament, which is well aware of the way in which good and evil, happiness and pain, life and death, light and darkness, stand over against each other, yet is committed to belief in one supreme God, responsible for the whole of creation and accessible to all, even though some may decide against him, choosing darkness rather than light. More significant than this kind of dualism are (a) the piety of the *Hodayoth* (though here the canonical Psalter is a major source, available also to John), and (b) the Qumran community's sense that it is itself the scene and the instrument of the realization of eschatology. It is this conviction that leads to parallels between the use of Scripture by John and at Qumran (though here too there are differences—see p. 30).

The greatest importance of the Qumran discoveries (and it is very great indeed) is their enrichment of our knowledge of first-century Palestine, the first home of the early church. The student of primitive Christianity (including of course Johannine Christianity) should make himself as familiar with the Scrolls as he can (just as he should with the rabbinic literature, the apocalypses, Philo, and Josephus). But when the passages in John (and I have done my best to point these out in the commentary) which are really illuminated, and whose exegesis is in any degree determined, by the Scrolls are counted up the result is extremely meagre. Now that the excitement of the first discoveries is past it is possible to see that Qumran has not revolutionized the study of the New Testament—certainly it has not revolutionized the study of John.

3. GREEK PHILOSOPHY

Over against the Old Testament, though in part allied with its descendants, stood the Greek tradition; but it must be understood that when John wrote the 'Greek tradition' meant something different from the classical philosophy of the golden age of Greece. The purely Hellenic had given place to the Hellenistic. The superb self-confidence of the fifth century B.C. had collapsed; rational thought had compromised with mysticism; eclecticism, both in philosophy and religion, was the order of the day. Mere antiquity was almost superstitiously reverenced, though, it may be added, reverenced rather than understood. Homer was allegorized so that his improper stories might become vehicles of religion. Sacraments, asceticism, and debauch ere p̂ actised according to taste and opportunity in the search for union with the divine, the immortality of the divine spark enclosed within its earthy prison.

Philosophic schools, of course, still existed, though most philosophic instruction consisted in the teaching of rhetoric. The Academy, for example, looked back to Plato, whose thought it developed in a sceptical direction which the Master would hardly have approved. Plato, however, in the first century after Christ was both more and less than a great personal teacher of a philosophical system; he was an atmosphere, absorbed though not understood by many who had never read his works. He had given definite expression to the notion of a real world, invisible and eternal, of which this world of appearance and time-sequence was but a transient and imperfect copy. Out of this contrast came the conception of mind, far superior to the flesh, and the ideal of a life of abstraction and contemplation, in which the mind, freed from matter and fixed upon the truly real, became one with God, the Idea of the Good. There is not a little of this popular Platonism in John. Jesus declares that he is not of this world but ἐκ τῶν ἄνω, while his opponents are of this world, ἐκ τῶν κάτω (8.23; cf. 18.36). This contrast of an upper and a lower world complements the perhaps more characteristically Jewish contrast between the present world and the world to come, and may be said to look back to Plato. Again, when Jesus speaks of himself as the 'true' (ἀληθινός) vine (15.1; cf. 1.9, the true light, 6.32, the true bread), included among other notions is that of an archetypal, ideal vine, of which others are mere copies.

In addition to the Platonic only one philosophical 'school' need be noted, the Stoic; though it is very doubtful whether John shows any direct relationship with real Stoicism. It is true that a superficial contact appears at once in the use of the term Logos (see below, pp. 73f.; 152-5), for Logos plays a vital part in the Stoic view of the world. All things in the universe were pervaded (it was believed) by Logos, itself a fine, impalpable material substance. The word Logos had two meanings: it could mean the immanent reason, the inward rational property (λόγος ἐνδιάθετος), and equally, speech, the outward expression of the inward thought (λόγος προφορικός). Logos was divine, and Logos expressed itself in material objects, animate and inanimate. Logos was God and Logos was the universe: Stoic physics was hardly separable from pantheism. Germs of the divine Logos (λόγοι σπερματικοί) might however be especially looked for in the mind of man, itself a fragment of the universal mind, and there therefore existed a natural kinship between the soul of man and the rational soul of the universe. It followed that what a man had to do in order to achieve the ideal life was to live in accordance with the Logos which was both within and around him—he had to live κατὰ λόγον, and if he did so he became a child of God. More, if he could but bring his material nature into subjection to his rational nature he was no less than God, since then the governing part of his life was Logos, a fraction or spark of the universal Logos, than which the Stoic had no other God. When we turn to John we find not only the word Logos, but also the statement that the Logos is the light which illuminates every man (1.9), as the Stoics believed that every man shared, however slightly, in the universal reason. We learn that the incarnate Logos came to 'his own' (1.11); that his own sheep heard his voice (10.3f.), that all who were 'of the truth' heard his voice (18.37), that he came to gather together into one the scattered children of God (11.52), and that those to whom the λόγος τοῦ θεοῦ came were called θεοί (10.35). On all these passages the commentary must be consulted; but it may here be generally stated that John, in spite of these similarities, is, both in his Logos doctrine and in his anthropology, far removed from Stoicism. The Logos came indeed to his own (εἰς τὰ ἴδια); but—a penetrating comment on the gospel story—his own (οἱ ἴδιοι) did not receive him (1.11), and there are no men naturally, in virtue of an inward logos, children of God. Men must receive from Christ power to become children of God (1.12).

John is no Stoic; yet it is important to set out very briefly the Stoic belief, not for its own sake but on account of the synthesis of Platonism and Stoicism which first became popular in the first century B.C., chiefly, it seems, under the influence of Posidonius (*fl. c.* 100 B.C.), and helped to make possible the religious developments which will shortly be mentioned. Methods (by no means always consistent) were found for reconciling Stoic pantheism with the Platonic idea of a transcendent God. The divine (and strictly immaterial) pattern of the universe, on the basis of which (according to the Platonic cosmogony) the visible universe was made, was amalgamated with the divine (and material) Logos which (according to the Stoics) was immanent in the universe. This amalgamation is, however, implied rather than expressed in the fragments of Posidonius which have been preserved, and in the writings of other philosophers, such as Philo, who were probably dependent on him. The fact is that Hellenistic religious philosophers drew upon Platonic cosmogony and Stoic physics (and upon Pythagoreanism), upon the ethics of all schools, and upon non-Greek contributions, in their attempts to meet the need for a philosophy which should supply a scientific basis for religion and a satisfying guide for life. John reflects this situation, but never allows the attentive reader to forget that he is a theologian, and in some sense a historian, rather than a philosopher. That is, he finds his 'guide for life'—the way, the truth, and the life—not in a system but in a historical person.

4. RELIGIONS OF SALVATION

Along with the more or less rational concepts of Hellenistic philosophy went a growing belief in destiny, and in astrology. Man, living under the circle of the stars, was directed by them and enslaved to the divinities or demons who inhabited them, or were represented by them. If he was to escape from the circle of fate he must find some means by which, leaving behind his bodily nature, he might mount to the heavenly sphere beyond the stars and live immortal in communion with God. Clearly this process could be complete only at death; but already in life he must seek and find, if he could, both assurance regarding his ultimate fate and some foretaste of it. Merely rational knowledge was not sufficient to gain such an end. Man without a saviour or revealer was lost. Saviours and revealers, religions and philosophies, there were in considerable number in the Hellenistic world, and John, setting forth, in that world, and with the intention of being understood by it, the true Saviour and the true revelation, seems to have made use of the ideas which were in circulation in it.

Broadly speaking, salvation might be sought by one of two means. The first is that represented by the mystery religions.[1] While these differed widely from one another in detail, and drew their beliefs and practices from diverse sources, they all are alike in certain particulars. Each rested on a myth, a tale of the Saviour God, which generally included his death and resurrection; each offered a means of initiation by which the neophyte was numbered among the servants of his Lord, a sacrament or sacraments by which the participant was infused with the divine life, and so assured that after his death he would successfully pass through the astral powers and win immortality in union with God. In terminology at least, John is not without contact with these religions. John contains the story of the wonders, and especially of the death and resurrection of the Saviour, told as the record of his own movement from earthly humility to divine exaltation.[2] In the story of the Saviour's violent death we read that there proceeded from his corpse water and blood, which could be taken to represent the two sacraments of the church. These sacraments (see further below, pp. 82–5) are also alluded to in specific statements.[3] Access to the kingdom of God is granted only to those who have received divine generation by the divinely appointed means (1.12; 3.3,5); Jesus promised a 'bread of life' which is his own sacrificed flesh; only those who eat this flesh, and drink his blood, have the divine life sought by all religious men (6.51,53). So far, at least, a parallelism exists, but it is much less pronounced than the differences between John and the mystery religions, and indeed can be made plausible only by placing disproportionate emphasis on a small number

[1] See (among other works) R. Reitzenstein, *Die hellenistischen Mysterienreligionen* (1927); S. Angus, *The Mystery-Religions and Christianity* (1925); A. D. Nock, 'Early Gentile Christianity and its Hellenistic Background', in *Essays on the Trinity and the Incarnation*, edited by A. E. J. Rawlinson (1928), now separately reprinted (1964), with a valuable bibliography; A. D. Nock, *Conversion* (1933); R. Bultmann, *Primitive Christianity in its Contemporary Setting* (1956), 156–61; A. Loisy, *Les Mystères païens et le Mystère chrétien* (1930).

[2] Note here also the Hellenistic figure of the θεῖος ἀνήρ; see below, p. 74.

[3] For the possibility that these may be redactional interpolations see p. 83, and the notes on the verses in question.

of passages. Jesus, unlike the divine heroes of the mystery myths, had lived, and very recently, a real human life; the myth was not only myth but history. The sacraments, moreover, bear distinct traces of having grown out of the earlier eschatological sacraments of primitive Christianity, and John's presentation of them is accompanied by a radical criticism (see below, pp. 84f.). John's picture, however, of the divine Saviour who passed through death to life in order to make that same life available to his followers by sacramental means belongs to the world in which the mystery cults were winning an increasing popularity.

Salvation was for some a matter of sacraments, *opera operata* in which the participant, though often encouraged to good behaviour, received in the rite itself the divine gift of salvation and the assurance of immortality. A second medium of salvation may be summed up in the word 'gnosis'.[1] The goal sought was the same; but 'this alone brings salvation for man—the knowledge (γνῶσις) of God' (*C.H.* x, 15). Man's way of escape was to know God and thus to know himself. Gnosis involved knowledge of cosmogony, generally in the form of a cosmological myth which accounted for the strange mixture of matter and divine reason of which man was composed; and, corresponding to the cosmology, a soteriology which was often quite independent of cultus and consisted of knowledge of the way by which one might in the goodness of God pass safely through the planetary spheres. Personal union with God and apotheosis were the final goal, and it was anticipated in the earthly experience of those who by abstraction and the mortification of the flesh caused themselves to be born again by the divine will. This kind of religion is found (with many variations) in the gnostic systems (Christian and other), but, as far as the New Testament is concerned, most significantly in the *Corpus Hermeticum*, a body of literature dating from the second, third, and fourth centuries but incorporating matter almost certainly early enough to be contemporary with John. No direct literary relationship can be traced, but it seems clear that John was working with similar presuppositions and along similar lines to those of the Hermetic authors. He never uses the word γνῶσις (perhaps intentionally), but knowledge is a vital theme of the gospel; to know God and his Envoy is eternal life (17.3). In both John and the *Hermetica* God is light and life, and light and life are the blessings enjoyed by those who are united with God. The notion of divine

[1] It is useful tō retain the term gnosticism for the Christian heresy of the second and later centuries, gnosis for the related pre-Christian phenomenon, though there are limits to the extent to which this distinction can be carried through. The literature on the whole field is immense. The following, among other works, will be found useful: Bultmann (as in n. 1, p. 37), 162–71; R. McL. Wilson, *The Gnostic Problem* (1958), and *Gnosis and the New Testament* (1968); Dodd, *Interpretation*, 10–53, 97–130; H. Jonas, *Gnosis und spätantiker Geist* (1954 (1934)), and *The Gnostic Religion* (1958); R. Reitzenstein, *Poimandres* (1904); U. Bianchi, ed., *Le Origini dello Gnosticismo* (1967). Particularly important are the two volumes of selected texts, edited in the first instance by W. Foerster, and in E.T. by R. McL. Wilson: *Gnosis I* (1972), and *Gnosis II* (1974).

begetting, or rebirth, occupies an important place in the *Hermetica*, though the means of regeneration is not, as in the mysteries, sacramental; the mediation between God and man is here effected by a mediating Logos, or Heavenly Man. All this indicates clearly the background of thought from which John emerged, and when this background is recognized it is no longer surprising that (so far as we know) the first users of the gospel were gnostics (see pp. 65f., 112ff.). Once more, there are differences as well as resemblances, and they arise primarily out of the fact that John was concerned with a Logos who had become flesh. Mere abstraction from the physical universe and absorption in mystical speculation were not the means to receive such a Logos.

Now that some (but not all; see below) of the evidence has been briefly set out it is possible to review the position occupied by the Fourth Gospel in the world in which it was written. It was pointed out above that some scholars claim that the gospel is exclusively Palestinian and in no way related to the Hellenistic world (they seem to forget that Palestine was part of the Hellenistic world), while others treat it as an example of purely Hellenistic religious philosophy. Neither of these extreme positions can be maintained. The fact, and it seems indisputable, is that both Jewish and Hellenistic elements are to be found in the gospel, and not lying side by side in a manner that could easily be disposed of by a source hypothesis, but fused into a unitary presentation of the universal significance of Jesus. John, for ends that doubtless seemed to him good, sets forth a synthesis of Jewish and Greek thought. He was not the first to do so. The pressure of Greek influence affected both the form and content of Palestinian Judaism, and Jewish propagandists had long used the language and thought-forms of Hellenism in order to express their own religious experience and to commend their faith to men of other races. It might be expected that this Hellenistic Judaism would form a close parallel to John's own achievement; and this is in fact true.

The fusion of Greek and Hebrew thought had been effected in two ways, which correspond to the two expressions of Hellenistic thought that have already been noted; and naturally enough, since both the mystery religions and the gnostic systems were the product of oriental faiths and speculation which sought to express themselves in a Hellenistic milieu. It seems, though the evidence is not quite conclusive, that attempts had been made to express Judaism as a mystery cult. As early as 139 B.C. Jews in Rome, practising a cult which had spread from Phrygia, were worshipping a God called Sabazius, in whose name we may see a mingling of the Hebrew Sabaoth (יהוה צבאות, the Lord of Hosts) with a Phrygian title of Dionysus.[1] It has been held[2] that Philo

---

Valerius Maximus I, iii, 2. See Schürer, II, ii. 233f.
[2] Notably by E. R. Goodenough, *By Light, Light* (1935).

also bears witness to an attempt to express Judaism as the supreme mystery (cf. e.g. *Cher.* 49; ἐγὼ παρὰ Μωυσεῖ τῷ θεοφιλεῖ μυηθεὶς τὰ μεγάλα μυστήρια). But in view of the extreme disgust with which Philo regards the cults of his day (e.g. *Spec.* 1, 319: Moses rejects τὰ περὶ τελετὰς καὶ μυστήρια καὶ πᾶσαν τὴν τοιαύτην τερθρείαν καὶ βωμολοχίαν) it seems certain that he did no more than occasionally apply in metaphor terminology that was sufficiently well known to himself and his readers. Philo is rather the outstanding representative of the second, non-cultic, kind of assimilation of Judaism to Hellenistic thought and practice. Like the authors of the *Hermetica*, and at an earlier date, he is concerned with the knowledge of God, and he believes this knowledge to be attainable, without the use of material media, on the basis of a given revelation, by means of abstraction and meditation. The revelation is both a cosmology and a soteriology, and of course is to be found in the Old Testament, though it is surprising how much of current Hellenistic philosophy Philo is able to draw from the books of Moses. By dint of allegory the narratives of the Pentateuch are harnessed and made to serve the homiletic and missionary purposes Philo cherished.

This assimilation of Judaism and its fundamental documents to Hellenism had begun, long before the time of Philo, in the Wisdom literature. The figure of Wisdom (חכמה, σοφία) herself furnished an intermediate divine being capable of adaptation on both philosophical and religious lines, and was succeeded in Philo by the Logos, who, with other powers (δυνάμεις), performs the will of God and acts as the means by which God creates the world. To this thought there are parallels in John (see especially the commentary on the Prologue); but it is here less important to adduce detailed parallels between John and Philo (no literary relationship can, it seems, be proved) than to observe that the two authors were confronted by similar tasks. Both had minds well stocked with the fundamental ideas of Hellenistic religion, and both with this equipment did their best to set out in the most attractive way possible an originally Semitic faith. Both were in this process brought into relation with the gnostic movement whose entry into Europe corresponded roughly with the period spanned by the work of Philo and John. Important as the *Hermetica* are (see above, pp. 38f.), Philo is an even more important witness to the pre-Christian gnosis which is part of the background of John. There is little doubt or dispute that this gnosis plays some part in the make-up of Johannine thought. Was this part positive or negative? That is, Was John concerned to controvert the ideas of gnosis, even though he used some of its language? Or did he adopt both the language and the thought, or some of the thought, of gnosis as a means of expounding and commending, perhaps incidentally of modifying, the Christian faith? A related question may be put in literary form: At what stage did gnostic material enter the substance of the gospel? Did John take over and Christianize fundamentally gnostic material (see above, pp. 19ff., on the Revelation Discourses), or did he introduce gnostic language into the non-gnostic primitive Christian tradition?[1] This chapter, which is primarily, and briefly, descriptive, is not the place at which to attempt to answer these questions (see especially pp. 140–4); but it is important to show that they are raised by serious study of the background of the gospel.

[1] The question may be illustrated by reference to the Odes of Solomon and the Mandaean literature, which are referred to again below, pp. 65f, 112f. The Odes are gnostic, but are they the kind of early gnostic material that was a source for John, or do they represent a gnosticizing kind of Christianity and owe their origin to the influence of John (or similar Christian literature)? The Mandaean literature as it stands is much later than John, but may bear witness to much earlier beliefs in some respects akin to Johannine thought; should the pre-Mandaean material be thought of as a source for John, or should John be thought of as one of the sources for Mandaean gnosticism?

3

THE CHRISTIAN BACKGROUND OF THE GOSPEL

1. THE SYNOPTIC TRADITION

(i) *Literary*. In the earlier period of the critical study of the New Testament a view commonly held was that John knew Mark, and possibly Luke and even Matthew too. A good example is provided by B. H. Streeter (*The Four Gospels*, first edn. 1924),[1] who concludes that John knew Mark well, that he knew, and assumed that his readers knew, Luke, and that he is likely to have known Matthew since there is evidence that Matthew was current in Asia. John made little use of Matthew because he did not like its apocalyptic and Judaistic tendencies. Both literary and theological relations suggest that 'the Gospels of Mark, Luke and John form . . . a series, Luke being dependent on Mark, and John on both the others' (pp. 424f.).

This position was attacked by P. Gardner-Smith (*St John and the Synoptic Gospels*, 1938). The logic of his argument is clear: the question he has in mind is 'whether it is easier to account for the similarities between St John and the Synoptists without a theory of literary dependence, or to explain the discrepancies if such a theory has been accepted' (p. x). Before proceeding with this question he makes two preliminary points. (1) The evangelist must have been a member of a local church, and would be dependent primarily not upon written documents but on the oral tradition current in that church. (2) It is wrong to concentrate on the few resemblances between John and the other gospels; the differences are far more extensive and should be given proportionate weight. After surveying the material as a whole Gardner-Smith reaches the conclusion that the resemblances, such as they are, can be adequately, and indeed best, explained on the basis of oral tradition. There is thus no ground for the view that John knew any of the Synoptic Gospels as written works, for even the framework of the gospel was provided not so much by literary models as by the common Christian preaching.

John's independence of the Synoptic Gospels has now been very widely accepted, though often with some modification. Thus P. Borgen[2] thinks

---

[1] I may refer here to an article in which I have reviewed this question in *E.T.* 85 (May 1974), 228–33. I am indebted to the former Editor, Dr C. L. Mitton, for permission to make use of material contained in this article.

[2] *N.T.S.* 5 (1959), 246–59.

that 'units of synoptic material have been added to the Johannine tradition' (259), and P. Parker[1] that 'the Fourth Evangelist must somewhere, sometime, have been associated with Luke in the Christian missionary enterprise' (336). I do not share what is now the popular opinion, for reasons given partly in this chapter and partly in the notes on relevant passages; I may refer also to the article already cited (where the views of a number of scholars are considered).

The facts which have convinced most students of the synoptic problem that Mark (or a document closely resembling it) was used by Matthew and Luke are the occurrence in Matthew and Luke of Marcan episodes in the Marcan order, and the use by Matthew and Luke of Marcan language. Analogous facts may, to a smaller extent, be observed in regard to John. The following is a list, which is certainly not complete, of corresponding passages which occur *in the same order* in both Mark and John.

		Mark	John
(a)	The work and witness of the Baptist	1.4–8	1.19–36
(b)	Departure to Galilee	1.14f.	4.3
(c)	Feeding of the Multitude	6.34–44	6.1–13
(d)	Walking on the Lake	6.45–52	6.16–21
(e)	Peter's Confession	8.29	6.68f.
(f)	Departure to Jerusalem	9.30f. 10.1,32,46	7.10–14
(g)	The Entry {transposed in John[2] The Anointing	11.1–10 14.3–9	12.12–15 12.1–8
(h)	The Last Supper, with predictions of betrayal and denial	14.17–26	13.1—17.26
(i)	The Arrest	14.43–52	18.1–11
(j)	The Passion and Resurrection[3]	14.53—16.8	18.12—20.29

It is to be noted further that the cleansing of the Temple (Mark 11.15–17) also occurs in John, but at a different point (2.14–16).

We have here quite a striking chain of very significant events. (b) and (f) have special significance because John does not retain Mark's simple framework of one visit to Jerusalem, and the sequence of (c)

---

[1] *N.T.S.* 9 (1963), 317–36.
[2] The transposition does of course weigh against the argument that John was aware of the Marcan order, but each incident remains in the same order in relation to the other members of the list, and a reason for the transposition can be suggested (see p. 409).
[3] Within the passion and resurrection narratives there are many parallels between Mark and John, in which John seems frequently to be dependent on Mark; see the commentary on chs. 18, 19, 20 *passim*.

and (*d*) is not readily explicable except on the hypothesis of literary relationship.

Within several of the passages mentioned there are close verbal resemblances. The following examples (again, the list is not exhaustive) may be given.

(*a*) Mark 1.7: ἔρχεται ὁ ἰσχυρότερός μου ὀπίσω μου, οὗ οὐκ εἰμὶ ἱκανὸς κύψας λῦσαι τὸν ἱμάντα τῶν ὑποδημάτων αὐτοῦ.

Mark 1.8,10,11

(*c*) Mark 6.37,38,43,44: ἀπελθόντες ἀγοράσωμεν δηναρίων διακοσίων ἄρτους; . . . πέντε [ἄρτους], καὶ δύο ἰχθύας . . . ἦραν κλάσματα δώδεκα κοφίνων πληρώματα . . . πεντακισχίλιοι ἄνδρες.

(*d*) Mark 6.50: θαρσεῖτε, ἐγώ εἰμι· μὴ φοβεῖσθε.

(*e*) Mark 8.29: σὺ εἶ ὁ χριστός.

(*g*) Mark 11.9f.: ὡσαννά· εὐλογημένος ὁ ἐρχόμενος ἐν ὀνόματι κυρίου· εὐλογημένη ἡ ἐρχομένη βασιλεία τοῦ πατρὸς ἡμῶν Δαυίδ.

Mark 14.3: ἔχουσα ἀλάβαστρον μύρου νάρδου πιστικῆς πολυτελοῦς.

Mark 14.5: ἠδύνατο γὰρ τοῦτο τὸ μύρον πραθῆναι ἐπάνω δηναρίων τριακοσίων καὶ δοθῆναι τοῖς πτωχοῖς.

Mark 14.7f.: πάντοτε γὰρ τοὺς πτωχοὺς ἔχετε μεθ' ἑαυτῶν, καὶ ὅταν θέλητε δύνασθε αὐτοῖς εὖ ποιῆσαι, ἐμὲ δὲ οὐ πάντοτε ἔχετε. ὃ ἔσχεν ἐποίησεν· προέλαβεν μυρίσαι τὸ σῶμά μου εἰς τὸν ἐνταφιασμόν.

(*h*) Mark 14.18: ἀμὴν λέγω ὑμῖν ὅτι εἷς ἐξ ὑμῶν παραδώσει με.

Mark 14.30: ἀμὴν λέγω σοι ὅτι σὺ σήμερον ταύτῃ τῇ νυκτὶ πρὶν ἢ δὶς ἀλέκτορα φωνῆσαι τρὶς με ἀπαρνήσῃ.

John 1.27: . . . ὁ ὀπίσω μου ἐρχόμενος, οὗ οὐκ εἰμὶ ἐγὼ ἄξιος ἵνα λύσω αὐτοῦ τὸν ἱμάντα τοῦ ὑποδήματος.

John 1.26,32,33,34

John 6.7,9,10,13: διακοσίων δηναρίων ἄρτοι . . . πέντε ἄρτους κριθίνους καὶ δύο ὀψάρια . . . οἱ ἄνδρες τὸν ἀριθμὸν ὡς πεντακισχίλιοι . . . δώδεκα κοφίνους κλασμάτων . . .

John 6.20: ἐγώ εἰμι· μὴ φοβεῖσθε.

John 6.69: σὺ εἶ ὁ ἅγιος τοῦ θεοῦ.

John 12.13: ὡσαννά, εὐλογημένος ὁ ἐρχόμενος ἐν ὀνόματι κυρίου, καὶ ὁ βασιλεὺς τοῦ Ἰσραήλ.

John 12.3: λαβοῦσα λίτραν μύρου νάρδου πιστικῆς πολυτίμου.

John 12.5: διὰ τί τοῦτο τὸ μύρον οὐκ ἐπράθη τριακοσίων δηναρίων καὶ ἐδόθη πτωχοῖς;

John 12.7f.: ἄφες αὐτήν, ἵνα εἰς τὴν ἡμέραν τοῦ ἐνταφιασμοῦ μου τηρήσῃ αὐτό· τοὺς πτωχοὺς γὰρ πάντοτε ἔχετε μεθ' ἑαυτῶν, ἐμὲ δὲ οὐ πάντοτε ἔχετε.

John 13.21: ἀμὴν ἀμὴν λέγω ὑμῖν ὅτι εἷς ἐξ ὑμῶν παραδώσει με.

John 13.38: ἀμὴν ἀμὴν λέγω σοι, οὐ μὴ ἀλέκτωρ φωνήσῃ ἕως οὗ ἀρνήσῃ με τρίς.

(i) Mark 14.47: εἷς δέ τις τῶν παρεστηκότων σπασάμενος τὴν μάχαιραν ἔπαισεν τὸν δοῦλον τοῦ ἀρχιερέως καὶ ἀφεῖλεν αὐτοῦ τὸ ὠτάριον.

John 18.10: Σίμων οὖν Πέτρος ἔχων μάχαιραν εἵλκυσεν αὐτὴν καὶ ἔπαισεν τὸν τοῦ ἀρχιερέως δοῦλον καὶ ἀπέκοψεν αὐτοῦ τὸ ὠτάριον τὸ δεξιόν.

(k) Mark 15.26: ὁ βασιλεὺς τῶν 'Ιουδαίων.

John 19.19: 'Ιησοῦς ὁ Ναζωραῖος ὁ βασιλεὺς τῶν 'Ιουδαίων.

It must be repeated that this is not a complete list of the verbal coincidences that can be found in parallel passages which occur *in the same order* in John and Mark. It cannot be said that the data that have now been collected amount to proof that John knew and used as a source our second gospel, but they do seem sufficient to make plausible the view that John had read Mark, thought that it contained a suitable gospel outline and often—perhaps involuntarily—echoed Mark's phrases when writing about the same events. It is true of course that there are differences, historical and theological, between John and Mark. They will be discussed later (pp. 46–54 below), but it seems that they can be adequately accounted for by John's peculiar interests and presuppositions, and therefore do not invalidate the literary conclusions that have been drawn. Moreover, it seems that sometimes John deliberately amends or corrects a tradition embodied in Mark; for example, cf. Mark 1.14f. and John 3.24, Mark 15.21 and John 19.17 (ἑαυτῷ).

It is certain that John did not 'use' Mark, as Matthew did. The parallels cannot even *prove* that John had read the book we know as Mark. Anyone who prefers to say, 'Not Mark, but the oral tradition on which Mark was based', or 'Not Mark, but a written source on which Mark drew', may claim that his hypothesis fits the evidence equally well. All that can be said is that we do not have before us the oral tradition on which Mark was based; we do not have any of the written sources that Mark may have quoted; but we do have Mark, and in Mark are the stories that John repeats, sometimes at least with similar or even identical words, sometimes at least in substantially the same order— which is not in every case as inevitable as is sometimes suggested. Gardner-Smith's rather lame comment on the sequence of the feeding miracle and the walking on the lake remains as an implied criticism of his own position: 'they go well together, and they were no doubt associated in oral tradition' (p. 33). The fact is that there crops up repeatedly in John evidence that suggests that the evangelist knew a body of traditional material that either was Mark, or was something much like Mark; and anyone who after an interval of nineteen centuries feels himself in a position to distinguish nicely between 'Mark' and 'something much like Mark', is at liberty to do so. The simpler hypothesis, which does not involve the postulation of otherwise unknown entities, is not without attractiveness.

45

The resemblance between John and Luke is much slighter than that between John and Mark; but it is at least a plausible hypothesis that John had read Luke. The evidence is best set out by Creed.[1] The following points only may be noted here.

Persons. Only Luke and John mention the sisters Mary and Martha. Only John mentions their brother Lazarus, but the name occurs in Luke 16.19f. John mentions a disciple called Judas, other than Judas Iscariot (14.22); this man is presumably the 'Judas of James' who appears only in the Lucan lists of the Twelve. Only Luke and John refer to Annas.

Details. The betrayal is due to the possession of Judas by Satan (Luke 22.3; John 13.2,27; cf. 6.70). In both Luke and John the prediction of Peter's denial is made at the Supper, and not after it, as in Mark; and the language of John 13.38 is closer to Luke 22.34 than to Mark 14.30. At the arrest it was the right ear of the high priest's servant that was struck off, and at the tomb on Easter morning there were two angels, not one, as in Mark. The details of the Johannine anointing story recall the Lucan as well as the Marcan narrative.

It would no doubt be possible to ascribe these agreements to coincidence, or to common use of an oral tradition; but it seems equally possible, and, it may be, preferable, to explain them as due to the fact that John had read Luke. Certainly there is no good reason why he should not have read this gospel, or some early draft of it.[2]

(ii) *Historical*. A superficial comparison of John and Mark (whose outline is substantially reproduced by Matthew and Luke) presents a contrast between two widely divergent accounts of the ministry of Jesus. In Mark, Jesus, after his baptism, begins his ministry by a preaching tour in Galilee. Occasionally he leaves the territory of Herod Antipas for a journey in the direction of Tyre and Sidon, or Decapolis, but he remains in the north of Palestine until at length he travels southward to Jerusalem to meet his death after no more than a week's work in the capital. In John, on the other hand, Jesus begins his ministry in Judaea and Jerusalem, and the narrative is punctuated at several points (2.13; 5.1; 7.10) by visits to Jerusalem made for the purpose of attending Jewish feasts in Jerusalem. Jerusalem, indeed, rather than Galilee, is the centre of Jesus' ministry. This apparent contradiction between two witnesses to the story of Jesus is mitigated by the following considerations. (*a*) Neither Mark nor John was primarily interested in chronology. Mark's outline was probably based upon the primitive apostolic preaching, which dealt in the most summary manner with the biographical material that intervened between the baptism and the death of Jesus. John for his part seems to have been governed in his

---

[1] J. M. Creed, *The Gospel according to St Luke* (1930), 318–21.
[2] See further J. A. Bailey, *The Traditions common to the Gospels of Luke and John* (1963). That John knew Matthew is argued by H. F. D. Sparks, *J.T.S.* 3 (1952), 58–61; there is a reply by P. Gardner-Smith, *J.T.S.* 4 (1953), 31–5.

grouping of the material, to an even greater extent than Mark, by topical considerations. His incidents are often accompanied by discourses which are theological commentaries, and the order of the gospel is, at least in part, dictated by the theological subjects dealt with. On this, see pp. 13ff. above. (b) There are hints in Mark which have been held to indicate that Jesus visited Jerusalem more frequently than Mark himself records. Thus, for example, Jesus has no difficulty in finding an ass and a furnished supper room when these are needed (Mark 11.1–7; 14.12–16). (c) Similarly, John seems to be aware of decisive journeys, first into Galilee, then into Judaea, and at each point there appear to be contacts with the Marcan narrative. At 3.24 John, it has been held, intentionally corrects Mark's reference to the arrest of John the Baptist (Mark 1.14), while the secrecy of John 7.10 corresponds to Mark 9.30.

If John corrects Mark on the arrest of the Baptist there are also other divergences in their treatment of him. Mark 9.13 seems to mean that John the Baptist was Elijah, who had returned to prepare the way for the Messiah; certainly this identification is explicitly made by Matthew (11.14; 17.13). In John (1.21) it is denied outright. John is not Elijah. It seems very probable that John is here correcting, for reasons which will be discussed elsewhere (below, pp. 51, 170f., and on 1.21), an earlier belief. In the same way his omission of the story of the baptism of Jesus himself, which plays an important part in Mark, seems to be intentional. It will be necessary to return to these matters in the treatment of the theological relationship of John to the synoptic tradition.

An important historical difference between John and Mark (followed by Matthew and Luke) lies in the motive which is suggested by the two evangelists for the final and successful plot of the Jewish authorities against the life of Jesus. In Mark 11.18 it is stated that when the chief priests and scribes heard of the cleansing of the Temple they sought how they might destroy Jesus. This bold challenge provoked their hostility and brought about the final crisis. But in John the cleansing of the Temple is described in ch. 2, and can therefore have had nothing to do with the final plot of the Jews. John, on the other hand, narrates at length the raising of Lazarus, an incident not mentioned by any of the synoptists but treated by him as decisive in the machinations of the Jews against Jesus (11.53, ἀπ' ἐκείνης οὖν τῆς ἡμέρας). There is a contradiction here which cannot be completely resolved. It does not seem probable that there were two cleansings of the Temple, one at the beginning and the other at the end of the ministry. It may be urged against Mark's dating of the incident that, since he has only one visit to Jerusalem and since the cleansing must have taken place there and nowhere else, he was bound to place it in the last week of the ministry, regardless of chronology, whereas John, if we suppose his account of several visits to be correct, was free to put it in the right place. On the other hand, if it be true that John's arrangement of his material is topical, it may be argued that he would regard the cleansing as a suitable and impressive foreshadowing of the work of Jesus and of his relations with Judaism. The only grounds for a decision are general probabilities regarding the incident itself, and general views of the comparative reliability of the two sources. It seems preferable to accept Mark's dating, but, if this is done, grave doubt is cast upon the historicity of the Lazarus story as it stands in John, and this not simply because the narrative is miraculous, but because no room can be found for it in the Marcan narrative. See further pp. 387ff. below.

John differs from the Synoptic Gospels also in the date which he gives for the crucifixion. According to Mark (followed by Matthew and Luke) the last supper was a Passover meal; that is, it was eaten in the early hours of Nisan 15; the arrest and trial took place in the same night and in the course of the next (solar) day Jesus was crucified. All these events took place on Nisan 15 (which extended, in the year of the passion, from about 6 p.m. on a Thursday to 6 p.m. on Friday). According to John (see 13.1; 18.28; 19.14,31,42 and the notes) the crucifixion happened on Nisan 14, the day before the Passover; the last supper must have been eaten the preceding evening. Thus the events are set a day earlier than in Mark, and the last supper is no longer the Paschal meal; Jesus died at the time when the Passover sacrifices were being killed in the Temple. Here again is a real contradiction; it seems impossible to reconcile the dates.

It is in fact often claimed that the synoptic narrative contradicts itself, and that John's dating is therefore to be preferred. The synoptic error is accounted for as due to the belief that, since the eucharist was interpreted as a Christian Passover, the last supper must have been a Passover meal. The arguments by which this view is sustained will not bear the necessary weight. The difficulties found in the synoptic narrative are described by Bernard (cvii) as follows: 'According to Mark 14.2, the Sanhedrim had decided *not* to arrest Jesus during the Paschal Feast, and yet they actually did so (Mark 14.43). The carrying of arms during the Feast was, at any rate, unlawful. ... To hold a formal trial before the high priest on the Feast day would, again, be unlawful (Mark 14.53). And the purchase of a linen cloth (Mark 15.46), and the preparation of spices and ointments (Luke 23.56) during such a Festival would be strange, if not forbidden. Finally, the language of Luke 22.15 (even though Luke regards the supper as the Passover Feast) implies that, although Jesus eagerly desired to celebrate one more Passover with his disciples, yet in fact he did *not* do so.' These arguments rest partly on supposed inner contradictions within the Synoptic Gospels, partly on alleged contraventions of the Jewish Law implied by the synoptic narratives.

The inner contradictions amount to little. There is nothing in the wording of Luke 22.15 itself to show whether the wish expressed there (ἐπιθυμίᾳ ἐπεθύμησα) was a fulfilled or unfulfilled desire. It is certain, as Bernard admits, that Luke himself took the words as a fulfilled wish, since, following Mark, he represents the last supper as a Passover; consequently it seems idle to deny that they could bear this meaning.[1] Mark 14.2 presents greater difficulty, but the difficulty is not insuperable. (i) Judas' offer to betray Jesus may have caused a change of plan on the part of the authorities. (ii) It is possible to give the sense of Mark 14.1f. as follows: They sought to seize and kill him by stealth (ἐν δόλῳ is in a position of emphasis), because people were saying (taking ἔλεγον as an impersonal use of the third person plural, as several times in Mark), Nothing can be done during the feast. (iii) ἐν τῇ ἑορτῇ may mean not 'During the feast' but 'In the presence of the festival crowd'. It would then correspond to ἐν δόλῳ in 14.1 and to ἄτερ ὄχλου in Luke 22.6. This use of ἑορτή is found in John (2.23; 7.11).

The alleged contraventions of Jewish law seem to rest upon misunderstandings of Jewish texts. The carrying of arms during a festival was not, *in the time of Jesus*, unlawful. The primary text is *Shabbath* 6.4. Here the mishnaic *halakah* runs: A man may not go out with a sword, or a bow or a shield or a club or a spear. The rule applies primarily to the Sabbath, but indirectly to festival days also, since the only difference between a festival day and a Sabbath is that on the former food may be prepared (*Betzah* 5.2). But the *halakah* of the Mishnah (c. A.D. 200) was not necessarily the *halakah* of the first century; and here the Mishnah itself goes on to quote the much earlier (first century) opinion of R. Eliezer ('the Great', b. Hyrcanus) that weapons are a man's adornments and may therefore be carried.

It is true that to hold a trial on a festival was normally illegal (*Betzah* 5.2: On a festival day . . . none may sit in judgement). It was also, however, illegal to hold a trial on the eve of a festival (*Sanhedrin* 4.1: Trials may not be held on the eve of a Sabbath or on the eve of a Festival-day), so that the Johannine narrative conflicts as seriously with the Mishnah as does the Marcan. The law also required that capital cases should be tried during the day time, and that a verdict of conviction should not be reached until the second day of the trial at the earliest (*Sanhedrin* 4.1). Thus the proceedings against Jesus were not carried out in strict form of law, whether we follow the account of Mark or that of John. The explanation is that special circumstances were regularly allowed to modify the course of the law. For example, Simeon b. Sheṭaḥ (*fl.* 104–69 B.C.) caused to be hanged 80 women (witches) in one day, though it was against the law to judge more than two. 'The hour demanded it' (*Sanhedrin* 6.4, *Y. Sanhedrin* 6,23c,58). Nisan 15, so far from being an unlikely day, was one of the best possible days for the execution of Jesus. The regulation for the condemnation of a 'rebellious teacher' runs: 'He was kept in guard until one of the Feasts (Passover, Pentecost, or Tabernacles) and he was put to death on one of the Feasts, for it is written, And all the people shall hear and

---

[1] This is, in fact, almost certainly their meaning. See *J.T.S.* 9 (1958), 305ff.

fear, and do no more presumptuously (Deuteronomy 17.13)' (*Sanhedrin* 11.4). There was only one day on which 'all the people' were gathered together in Jerusalem for the Passover; it was Nisan 15, the Marcan date for the crucifixion.

The argument regarding the purchase of the linen cloth and the preparation of spices and ointments may be subjected to a similar criticism. These activities were quite as unlawful on the date implied by John as on the later Marcan date. 'In Judaea they used to do work until midday on the eves of Passover, but in Galilee they used to do nothing at all' (*Pesahim* 4.5). Here also, however, the circumstances were exceptional. In view of the hot climate it was customary in Palestine to bury a corpse on the day of death. If that day were the Sabbath all preparations for burial might be made (*Shabbath* 23.5: They may make ready [on the Sabbath] all that is needful for the dead, and anoint it and wash it, provided that they do not move any member of it), but the burial itself would be deferred until the next day. If however two rest days occurred consecutively (as here, Passover followed by Sabbath) the situation would be intolerable and a rule would have to be broken;[1] and there was the additional motive for burying the body of Jesus that it was not permitted to leave a criminal's body hanging on a tree overnight (Deuteronomy 21.23). It is evident further from the action of Joseph of Arimathaea that there was in the Sanhedrin a minority that resisted the action of the majority and would doubtless take the quick action necessary to save Jesus from the usual fate of executed persons, who were buried in one of two burying places kept by the court, for those who were beheaded or strangled and those who were stoned or burnt.

So far there seems to be no reason why Mark should not be right in describing the last supper as a Passover meal. His narrative is intelligible. and is not inconsistent. It also contains a number of indirect indications that the supper was a Passover.[2] Before this conclusion is drawn, however, attention must be given to the suggestion of Mlle A. Jaubert,[3] who holds that Jesus and the disciples (followed in the Synoptic Gospels) used the 364-day calendar of *Jubilees*, according to which Passover was always celebrated on Tuesday/Wednesday, the meal being eaten on the Tuesday evening. This was not the official Jerusalem calendar, which John follows when he says that Jesus died on a Friday afternoon which was the eve of Passover. Thus Jesus celebrated *his* Passover on Tuesday, and died, when the people were slaughtering the 'official' lambs, on Friday. This double statement has the double advantage of reconciling the gospels and making the arrest, trial, and execution of Jesus, for

---

[1] See *Shabbath* 139a, b for a case where a Sabbath was followed by a festival day.
[2] See Jeremias, *Eucharistic Words*, 41–62.
[3] Especially *La Date de la Cène: Calendrier biblique et Liturgie chrétienne* (1957); also 'Jésus et le Calendrier de Qumran', in *N.T.S.* 7 (1960), 1–30, and 'Le Mercredi où Jesus fut livré', in *N.T.S.* 14 (1968), 145–64.

which nearly three days are now available, more credible.[1] The suggestion is attractive, but the patristic evidence which Mlle Jaubert uses bears witness not to historical tradition but to the fasting practice of the early church, and no source gives any positive hint that Jesus adopted a schismatic calendar; he was blamed for much but not for this. Moreover, all the evangelists, if they considered the matter at all, must have seen how difficult their story of arrest, trial, and execution within twelve hours was, and it seems unlikely that they would create this difficulty gratuitously. Probably Mark was right;[2] it is not difficult to see why John gives his alternative date. As early as Paul (1 Corinthians 5.7) Jesus was thought of as the true Paschal sacrifice. John repeats and emphasizes this theme (1.29; 19.36: see the notes on both passages). On his dating Jesus died on the cross at the moment when the Passover lambs were being slaughtered in the Temple. This may not be good history; but it does seem to be Johannine theology.

(iii) *Theological.* It has already been shown that some of the historical differences between John and the Synoptic Gospels are not unrelated to John's theological interests.[3] Indeed, if John knew the other gospels (or at least Mark) every serious divergence between them must mean either that John had fresh historical information, or, as is often more probable, wrote from a different point of view with a different intention. Thus John's treatment of the Baptist shows an abandonment of the apocalyptic belief according to which it was necessary to equate the Baptist with Elijah.[4] Again, the Johannine date of the last supper and crucifixion seems to be due to John's determination to make clear that Jesus was the true Paschal Lamb of God.

What is perhaps most striking in a comparison of John and the Synoptic Gospels is that several of the most important synoptic incidents are omitted by John, though he seems to show indirectly knowledge of some of them. These incidents are the virgin birth of Jesus, his baptism by John, the temptation, the transfiguration, the words explanatory of the bread and wine at the last supper, and the agony in the garden of Gethsemane. If we are right in supposing that John had read Mark and Luke, or if he merely knew the traditions on which these gospels are based, he must have been aware of all these events; and John 1.32–4 suggests that the baptism, John 12.27–30 and 18.11 that the agony, were in his mind as he wrote, while there may be an allusion to the virgin

---

[1] See also M. Black, 'The Arrest and Trial of Jesus, and the Date of the Last Supper', in *New Testament Essays*, ed. A. J. B. Higgins (1959), 19–33.

[2] On this question see especially S.B. II, 812–53; G. Dalman, *Jesus-Jeshua* (English translation, 1929), 86–184; Jeremias, *Eucharistic Words*. The last of these works is of fundamental and (it seems to me) decisive importance, but see the criticism in V. Taylor, *The Gospel according to St Mark* (1952), Note K, 664–7.

[3] On John's treatment of the Synoptic Gospels see especially Hoskyns, 56–92.

[4] On the position of the Baptist in John see on 1.19–34, and *J.T.S.* old series 48 (1947), 165.

birth in 1.13. It is unthinkable that he dismissed such incidents as unimportant; in fact, it seems that he regarded them as far more important than mere 'incidents'. The narratives as they stand in the Synoptic Gospels are in general readily detachable from their contexts; this followed inevitably from the mode in which the traditional material out of which the gospels were made was handed down. For this reason even the most significant events could easily become incidental, and could even, if removed from their proper setting, be dangerously misunderstood. John safeguards their meaning by stripping them of their historical individuality and building them into the theological framework of his gospel.

Thus the Matthaean and Lucan narratives of the virgin birth of Jesus, widely as they differ, agree in asserting the uniqueness of Jesus, the fact that he was the Son of God, in all things dependent upon and obedient to the Father's will, and the consequent faith that his entry into the world marked the beginning of God's new creation. That each of these themes is central in the Fourth Gospel is so manifest that documentation is unnecessary; every chapter of the gospel could be quoted. John incorporates the theological substance of the infancy narratives into his gospel. But there is in Matthew and Luke much more than theological substance. There is some questionable history; and (much more important, since it is unlikely that John considered the earlier tradition with the eye of a historical critic) there are unfortunate contacts with discreditable pagan mythology. Later, Justin and other apologists were to use these contacts in support of the credibility of the Christian story; but John, who came to his work with a far more biblical mind than they, cannot have found them so congenial.

Mark, who has no account of the birth of Jesus, sets at the head of his gospel the narrative of the baptism of Jesus. He does so with the intention of defining the person and work of Jesus; he was Messiah and Son of God, and upon him rested the Spirit. John has a clear allusion to this narrative in 1.32–4, but he omits to say that Jesus was baptized. To explain this as John's share in a controversy with those who rated the Baptist too highly in comparison with Christ is probably true as far as it goes, but is inadequate. The fact is that Mark's narrative, though in its own way a profound piece of theology, is not satisfactory from the Christological standpoint. It could too easily be interpreted in favour of the adoptionist view, that Jesus was born an ordinary man and that at his baptism a divine *dynamis* descended on him, making him Christ. For John, both the baptism and the birth were points too late for the opening of a gospel. It was necessary to begin with the pre-existence of the Logos, and so to exclude every suggestion of adoptionism. Further, the descent of the Spirit in the Marcan baptism story could be thought of as a flash of inspiration; to counter this John finds it necessary to add, what could be neither observed nor described, that the Spirit abode (ἔμεινεν) upon Jesus (1.32). Once more, John dispenses with the narrative in order to deal more satisfactorily with the theological fact.

In Mark, and in Matthew and Luke (perhaps in Q), the baptism is followed by the temptation. Here the Messiah is shown in decisive and victorious conflict with Satan, just as later in the Synoptic Gospels he does battle with Satan's subordinates in the exorcisms. Both temptation and exorcisms are wanting in John, though the conflict of Jesus with the prince of this world is a prominent Johannine theme (12.31; 14.30; 16.11). Again, John's motives seem clear. The temptation narrative conveyed truth in mythological form but it had also the power to mislead. The conflict between Jesus and Satan was not limited to forty days; its climax was not the fast in the desert but the cross. 'Now is the judgment of this world; now shall the prince of this world be cast out', says Jesus (12.31) as he prepares for death. The exorcisms, too, as handled in the synoptic tradition (Mark 3.22–7; Matt. 12.24–30; Luke 11.15–23; *et al.*) are highly significant. But exorcism was a very common art in the ancient world. Jesus the exorcist might be no more than Jesus the common magician. Accordingly the exorcisms are dropped, because John was concerned, not to invent a fresh narrative but to draw out with greater clarity the conflict between the Son of God and the forces of Satan.

The transfiguration is not recorded in John, and of the agony in Gethsemane there remain only traces in 12.27–30; 18.11. Here perhaps most clearly of all we see how Marcan incidents have been developed by John into major themes of his gospel. Throughout the gospel run the twin themes of the glory of Jesus, manifested not once only on the holy mountain but—for those who had eyes to see—continuously throughout his incarnate life (cf. 1.14, ἐθεασάμεθα τὴν δόξαν αὐτοῦ), and of his obedience to the Father's will, even in humiliation and suffering (cf. e.g. 4.34). It is a definition of the person of Jesus as described in John that he is at once glorious and humiliated.

John's understanding of the eucharist is discussed below (Introduction, pp. 82–5; also 281–5, 297–301). It would not be profitable to attempt a brief summary here, but this is perhaps John's own point. A swift passing reference to a loaf and a cup would have made clear neither the positive nor the negative views that appear in the discourse on the Bread of Life.

John thus probes into the meaning of the synoptic narratives and expresses it in other terms. It follows on the one hand that the differences between John and the Synoptic Gospels must not be exaggerated. John does not so much import foreign matter into the gospel as bring out what was already inadequately expressed in the earlier tradition. On the other hand, the consequences of this process for the question of the historicity of the Fourth Gospel must be understood and faced. It is of supreme importance to John that there was a Jesus of Nazareth who lived and died in Palestine; but to give an accurate outline of the outstanding events of the career of this person was no part of his purpose. The critical and scientific writing of history was no common art in the ancient world, and it was certainly not a primary interest with John. He sought to draw out, using in part the form and style of narrative, the true meaning of the life and death of one whom he believed to be the Son of God. It is for this interpretation, not for accurate historical data, that we must look in the Fourth Gospel.

It follows from these observations that John's representation of Jesus is superficially different from, but at a deeper level strikingly akin to that of the Synoptic Gospels. John's Christology is discussed later (pp. 70–5); here the contrast between John and the other gospels may be briefly summed up in two points. (a) John clarifies the relation of Jesus to God. Apart from his use of the word Logos he introduces no fresh terminology, but by liberating his thought from the apocalyptic pattern of early Christianity he is able to give to the title Son of God a more comprehensive meaning. It now implies an ontological relationship. Jesus in the Fourth Gospel can declare, 'I and the Father are one' (10.30), even though beside this proposition there stands as a necessary balance, 'The Father is greater than I' (14.28). In the Synoptic Gospels Jesus is not defined in terms of deity, but in terms of his work, and his relation to the kingdom of God (e.g. Matt. 12.28; Luke 11.20). John's thought about Jesus moves from the functional into the ontological, so that it is true both that Jesus is known in what he does, and that what he does arises out of what he is. (b) John universalizes the manhood of Jesus. In the Synoptic Gospels Jesus is a man; his personal feelings, his compassion for the poor and diseased, his anger at hard-heartedness in high places, shine out continually. John equally with the synoptists would repudiate with horror a docetic Christology;[1] but in the Johannine Christology (and here the orthodoxy of the fifth century is anticipated) the emphasis is upon the Logos, the Son of God, who takes upon himself humanity—perfectly real in its ignorance, hunger, and weariness—rather than upon Jesus as an individual human being. The gospel story loses, it may be, in human attractiveness, but it undoubtedly gains in theological clarity and force.[2]

2. PAUL AND THE PRIMITIVE CHURCH

The reader of the New Testament cannot fail to be impressed by the considerable measure of agreement between John and Paul in their presentation of Christian theology. For both, the distinctive Christian faith rests upon the solid foundation of an Old Testament doctrine of God. 'Salvation is of the Jews' (4.22), John declares, agreeing with Paul's assertion that to Israel belong the promises, the covenants, and

[1] See however p. 74.
[2] See the profound observations of H. Scott Holland in *The Fourth Gospel* (1923), 1–37.

the temple-worship, and that from them according to the flesh comes the Christ (Rom. 9.4f.). For both, God is the One Lord of the *Shema* (Deut. 6.4), a living God, transcendent in holiness, infinitely near in redeeming love. He is the Creator, and his sovereign will is the beginning and end of salvation (John 6.44; 15.16; Rom. 9.14–18). Jesus of Nazareth is the divinely appointed Messiah of Israel. Paul (though unlike John he makes no attempt to write a narrative of the earthly life of Jesus) knows equally well that this Messiah lived a human life of poverty, meekness, and love, and died on the cross in order to deal with sin; that he was buried and on the third day rose from the dead. Both describe Jesus as the Son of God, finding in this title perhaps their most characteristic definition of his person. John, retaining an old Semitic term, speaks of Jesus as the Son of man (see below, pp. 72f.; also on 1.51); Paul abandons the phrase, which would no doubt have been unintelligible to many of his readers, but describes Jesus as the Man from heaven (1 Cor. 15.47) and as the last Adam (1 Cor. 15.45; cf. Rom. 5.14). Both John and Paul lay much greater stress than any of the synoptic writers upon the person and work of the Holy Spirit, and for them both the Holy Spirit has the same essential function. His coming intervenes between the two appearances of Jesus, his incarnation in lowliness and obscurity and his manifestation in the glory of the Father, in order to anticipate the future salvation of Christians. He is the means by which eschatology is 'realized' (see below, pp. 67–70, 88–92).

Not only do John and Paul represent the basic truths of the Christian revelation in the same way; for them both the Christian life moves about the same foci of faith and love. Evidence need not be given for the centrality of πίστις in Paul's teaching; John never uses the noun but has the cognate verb πιστεύειν frequently, and finds it so significant that he is able to sum up his purpose in writing in the words 'that you may believe . . . and by believing may have life' (20.31). Again Paul teaches that to have love is to fulfil the law (Rom. 13.8–10); in John, Jesus gives his disciples the single commandment, 'that you love one another' (13.34).

This is an extensive and significant area of agreement, but it must not be allowed to mislead. It does not amount to evidence that John was in any way dependent on Paul or even that he was familiar with his works. The doctrines we have noted might all be derived by independent drawing on the common stock of primitive Christian tradition. So far John is shown to be not necessarily a Paulinist but, like Paul, merely a Christian. Moreover, it remains to be asked whether common terminology is used by the two authors in the same sense (see below, p. 58). There is however one point of Christology which has not yet been noted and might be held to prove more than this. In Col. 1.15–19 Paul[1] in dependence on the Jewish concept of σοφία

[1] Since the first edition of this Commentary the Pauline authorship of Colossians has come under stronger attack, and I am less confident that Paul wrote the epistle.

(Wisdom) develops a Christology which is practically a Logos-Christology, though the word Logos itself is not used. It could well be argued that John in the Prologue has done little more than add the technical term λόγος to a Christology which he took ready made from Paul. This is indeed possible, and cannot be disproved. But the conclusion, though possible, is not necessary. Paul's Wisdom-Christology was evolved in contact with a primitive form of gnosticism; John was also profoundly affected in his exposition of Christianity by gnosticism (see pp. 38–41), and there is in addition good reason to believe that he, like Paul, was familiar with that kind of Jewish speculation which hypostatized such concepts as Sophia and Torah. Hence it must be allowed that the Pauline Christology of Col. 1.15–19 and the Johannine Christology of 1.1–18 could have been independently drawn out from similar materials in similar controversial circumstances.

If the relationship between Paul and John is to be investigated, it will be necessary to exclude those points where the two writers are simply reproducing the common beliefs of the church and to compare their distinctive doctrines. Here much greater difference is found. One of the primary themes of the Pauline epistles is that of the divine righteousness, and justification. The language in which Paul expresses his theme is rare in John: δίκαιος occurs three times, δικαιοσύνη twice, and δικαιοῦν (the really characteristic Pauline *word*) not at all. It corresponds with this fact that there is little or nothing in John about the relation of faith, works, and the law. Circumcision is mentioned (7.22f.) but there is no hint that it was, in John's day, a threat to Christian liberty. So far is John from repeating the Pauline antithesis of faith and works that he can say that the work (ἔργον) God requires from men is that they should believe (have faith) in Jesus (6.29). This does not mean that John contradicts Paul, rather that they express themselves differently. In fact, John has a close equivalent to the Pauline doctrine of justification in the statement that the believer εἰς κρίσιν οὐκ ἔρχεται (5.24; cf. 3.18, ὁ πιστεύων . . . οὐ κρίνεται). See the notes, and cf. Rom. 8.1. See also the essay 'Justification in Johannine Thought' by Théo Preiss (in *Life in Christ* (1954), 9–31). The Law is several times referred to, but it is the Law 'of the Jews'. As such it has its proper significance, but we do not hear of Jewish Christians who wish to impose the obligation of observing the Law upon their Gentile brothers. In John as in Paul 'the Jews' (see on 1.19) stand over against the church, but the contrast is viewed quite unemotionally. To Paul the unbelief of Israel was an unceasing grief; he would gladly himself have fallen under a curse if thereby his compatriots might have been saved (Rom. 9.1–3). Indeed, they would be saved. It was unthinkable that God should prove faithless to the age-old call and the special benefits

---

On balance, the evidence seems to suggest that he did; and, if he did not, the argument in the text can easily be modified.

that had been showered upon the unresponsive people. The faith of the Gentiles would provoke Israel to jealousy and in the end (for Paul, no distant end) all Israel would be saved (Rom. 11.25). With all this John forms a marked contrast. The Jews are no children of Abraham, but of the devil (8.44); their sin abides (9.41). For both John (see on 1.19) and Paul (see especially Rom. 3.19) the Jews are a microcosm, in which both the universal love of God and the crisis of faith and unbelief are displayed. Again, a considerable bulk of Paul's writing arose out of the 'care of all the churches'. It was continually necessary for him to give practical moral advice, regarding, for example, marriage and other social relationships, and also relationships within the church itself. The gifts bestowed by the Spirit had to be disciplined and controlled in order that the church's worship and life might be conducted decently and in order. Of all this we see nothing in John. There is, as has been noted, the general command of love, but there is no attempt to work it out in detail; and we should never suspect the existence of the χαρίσμ-ατα of the primitive church if we had no other source than John.

One contrary point must be observed. One of the most characteristic Pauline phrases is ἐν Χριστῷ. Similarly, in John, and especially in the last discourses, Jesus bids the disciples to 'abide in' him, as he promises to 'abide in' them. Here the parallelism is close.

Several distinctive features of Johannine thought have only the slightest parallels in Paul. John's Logos-Christology may be mentioned again, because, though, as we have seen, Paul has the substance of this doctrine without the technical term which expresses it, the very absence, or presence, of that term is itself significant. It is John, not Paul, who selects and uses the word which, for all its biblical associations, remains a word proper to Greek philosophy. Nor does Logos stand alone in this respect. John seems to make a practice of employing words which have at least a double (Jewish and pagan) background (see e.g. on 1.1; 8.12; 10.9,11). Paul, though he worked, and was at home, in the Hellenistic world, and shows traces of the environment into which he had passed, does not make the same systematic, even sophisticated, use of its language. Another highly characteristic feature of the Fourth Gospel is its handling of eschatology (see pp. 67–70). Futurist eschatology is not abandoned, but it does not play the same dominant role that it has in Paul (e.g. 1 Thess. 4.13–18; 1 Cor. 15.20–28, 50–55; Rom. 13.11–14; Phil. 4.5—to quote material from various stages in Paul's career). Finally we may note John's insistence on the fact that the suffering and death of Jesus actually were his glorification, the path by which he ascended to the Father and to the glory he enjoyed before the world was. It is, of course, denied nowhere in the New Testament that the love of the cross is the glory of God, but the common pattern of speech in the New Testament refers to τὰ εἰς Χριστὸν παθήματα καὶ τὰς μετὰ ταῦτα δόξας (1 Peter 1.11). Paul frequently mentions the crucifixion and the resurrection together, viewing the latter as the glorious complement of the former; that is, he does not share the characteristic attitude of John.

Since then, almost without exception, neither Paul nor John shows the special characteristics of the other, it is natural to suppose that John, the later writer, was not closely dependent on Paul. This conclusion is reinforced when it is observed that sometimes when they do speak of the same thing they do so in quite different terminology. For example, Paul describes baptism as dying with Christ and rising in union with him to new life (Rom. 6.4). John on the other hand (3.3,5) connects baptism with 'birth from above' (ἄνωθεν). There is no great difference in substance between what the two writers mean to convey; but they use different terms. Another example is John's use of the word Paraclete (see on 14.16) to describe the Spirit, and a third the different words and metaphors used by Paul and John to explain the death of Jesus. John speaks of him as the Lamb of God, and of his death as the means by which the scattered children of God are gathered together. Paul uses an astonishing wealth of language about the cross, but nowhere does he use the two expressions adopted by John. Perhaps the most important example of all may be found by pressing beyond a piece of evidence already used. It is true that both Paul and John make much of faith as the basis of the Christian life, but it is by no means clear that each means the same thing in his use of πιστεύειν. For Paul, faith is primarily trust in a person, and involves the closest possible union with Christ. For John, faith seems often to include, if it is not exhausted in, the acceptance of a fact or doctrine. Thus at 20.31, the source of eternal life is not simply believing in Jesus, but believing that 'Jesus is the Christ, the Son of God'.

When all these differences, which of course are by no means sufficient to outweigh in importance the substantial similarities between Paul and John, are borne in mind, it seems easier to believe that Paul and John wrote independently of each other than that John was expressing Pauline theology in narrative form. John was not one of the deutero-Pauline writers; both he and Paul were dependent upon the primitive Christian tradition. It may however be added that the Johannine theology presupposes the existence of the Pauline. When John wrote some at least of the great controversies of the early church were past; they had already been won by Paul. In particular the controversy with Judaizing Christianity was over. Paul had fought for the freedom of the Gospel, and in John's day it was no longer necessary to discuss whether Gentiles might be admitted to the church, and if so, on what terms. The Jews remained, but as an enemy; the Jewish mission field was closing. Most important of all, the new situation of the followers of Jesus in the period after his resurrection had been grasped. Paul had recognized that this new development in world history made possible a new life in communion with Christ, and promised a future salvation, already guaranteed by his Spirit in a life on earth of growing holiness; and this recognition had opened the book in which the history of Christian doctrine was to be written. Albert Schweitzer (in *The Mysticism of Paul the Apostle*, 1931) oversimplifies when he claims that Paul did not himself hellenize the Gospel, but gave it a form (eschatological mysticism) in which John, Ignatius, and others were able to hellenize it; but there is much truth in his view. Even in the presence of John, Paul remains the most fundamental of all Christian theologians, but John is the first and greatest of the reinterpreters.

3. THE JOHANNINE LITERATURE

In our New Testament there are found, in addition to the gospel, four books which bear the name of John—three epistles and an apocalypse. The epistles are anonymous, but the apocalyptist speaks of himself as John (Rev. 1.1,4,9; 22.8), without however claiming any status other than that of prophet. A first glance at these books suggests a very close resemblance between the gospel and the epistles, and a very marked difference between the gospel and the apocalypse. Further examination however results in a lower estimate of both the resemblance and the difference.

The second and third epistles are too short to permit detailed comparison; but the first resembles the gospel so closely that the common authorship of the two has not frequently been disputed. Phrase after phrase in 1 John recalls the language of John.[1] A long list is given by A. E. Brooke (*A Critical and Exegetical Commentary on the Johannine Epistles* (1912), ii–iv); here only very few examples may be exhibited.

John 1.18: Θεὸν οὐδεὶς ἑώρακεν πώποτε	1 John 4.12: Θεὸν οὐδεὶς πώποτε τεθέαται
5.24: μεταβέβηκεν ἐκ τοῦ θανάτου εἰς τὴν ζωήν	3.14: μεταβεβήκαμεν ἐκ τοῦ θανάτου εἰς τὴν ζωήν
8.34: πᾶς ὁ ποιῶν τὴν ἁμαρτίαν	3.4: πᾶς ὁ ποιῶν τὴν ἁμαρτίαν

Further we meet in 1 John the same interest in light, life, and love as in the gospel, the same concern with the Word become flesh. The literary and theological resemblances between John and 1 John must not be underestimated; yet there must be set against them notable differences.[2] Once more, only a selection of the most important can be given.

---

[1] A. Feuillet, *Biblical Theology Bulletin* 3 (1973), 194–216, maintains that the resemblance extends not only to phraseology but to structure. The argument hardly takes sufficient account of the fact that the structure of the gospel, but not of the epistle, is, if not determined by considerations of narrative, at least cast in narrative form.

[2] For the opinion that John and 1 John were written by different authors see C. H. Dodd, *J.R.B.* 21 (1937), 129–56; *The Johannine Epistles* (1946), xlvii–lvi; For the contrary opinion see A. E. Brooke, op. cit., i–xix; R. H. Charles, *A Critical and Exegetical Commentary on the Revelation of St John* (1920), xli f.; W. F. Howard, *J.T.S.* old series 48 (1947), 12–25 (reprinted in *The Fourth Gospel in Recent Criticism and*

(i) *Prepositions.* 1 John uses 14 prepositions and prepositional adverbs. Of these the gospel uses 13 (all but χάριν), and in addition 10 more. This is a considerable number but it need not in itself be significant, since John is longer than 1 John and also contains considerable narrative sections which call for additional linguistic resources; yet it is not insignificant, and special note should be taken of παρά, used in the gospel 25 times with the genitive, and 9 times with the dative, and not at all in 1 John. It is particularly noteworthy that παρὰ θεοῦ, θεῷ (or other divine name) is a usage very characteristic of John.

(ii) *Adverbial particles.* A similar observation is in place. It is not merely that John has 35 such words, against 9 in 1 John; missing from the epistle is the group ἄνω, ἄνωθεν, ἐντεῦθεν, κάτω, πόθεν, all dealing with the questions where? or whence?—that is, the questions answered by παρά with dative or genitive. This linguistic observation corresponds to a very characteristic feature of the evangelist's thought.

(iii) *Other particles.* οὖν is used *c.* 190 times in the gospel; it is not used at all in the epistle.

(iv) *Compound verbs.* In 1 John, 11 compound verbs are used; in John, 105. This observation might in itself be misleading, since many of the compound verbs are narrative verbs; but if we confine our attention to John 14—17 (a passage comparable in length and subject matter to 1 John) we find in this part of the gospel 8 of the 11 compound verbs of the epistle, together with 12 more, a total of 20 compound verbs, used altogether 45 times.

(v) *Style and constructions.* The following points should be noted. Rhetorical questions are characteristic of the epistle (2.22; 3.12,17; 5.5); there are none in the gospel (? 18.37), though much of it is rhetorical and argumentative in style. Illogical conditional sentences, where the apodosis is not really contingent upon the protasis, occur in the epistle (1.9; 2.1; (3.20); 5.9); there are none in the gospel. Many passages in the gospel have been held to be Semitisms (see above, pp. 8–11); in the epistle only 2.21 and 5.9 are possibly, and by no means certainly, Semitisms.

(vi) *Vocabulary.* Here great caution is necessary; vocabulary far more than syntax is determined by subject matter. Nevertheless, the total vocabulary of John and 1 John is so small that it is notable and impressive that word groups so characteristic of John as the following are not represented in 1 John: σώζειν, σωτηρία, ἀπολλύναι, ἀπώλεια; γραφή, γράμματα, γράφειν, νόμος (used of Scripture); δόξα, δοξάζειν; πέμπειν; ζητεῖν; κρίνειν, κρίμα, κρίσις (κρίσις occurs once in 1 John, in the phrase ἡ ἡμέρα τῆς κρίσεως, an expression not found in John).

There appears then to be a small but quite definite linguistic difference between John and 1 John. It must be taken with the great general

---

Interpretation (4th edn, 1955), 282–96). The arguments on both sides are reviewed by E. Haenchen, *Die Bibel und Wir* 1968), 238–42.

resemblance, and the resulting problem is akin to the synoptic problem, in which also both difference and resemblance must be accounted for. The explanation might be found in some change in the habits of a single writer—the maturing of his style, for example, in the gospel; or in imitation, or in the natural affinities between two writers trained in the same atmosphere and under the same models. If more data are sought, the thought of the two books must be compared. Here also the resemblances are evident; the differences must be looked for. But they do exist, and they are difficult to account for on the hypothesis of common authorship. (a) In 1 John the primitive Christian eschatological hope is fully alive. The appearance of anti-Christs proves that already it is the last hour; at any moment the looked-for end may come (2.18,28; 4.17). Eschatological considerations are used as a motive for Christian ethics (3.2f.). Eschatological language is by no means absent from John (see pp. 67–70 below); but it is not this kind of eschatology, and it is not used in this way. The evangelist is not dominated by the thought of a manifest historical 'second coming'. Here, and in its presentation of the Holy Spirit as the spirit of prophetic inspiration (4.1–6; 5.6–8), the epistle gives the impression of being nearer to the primitive forms of the Christian faith. (b) On the other hand, there are passages where 1 John seems to have moved further than John in the direction of gnosticism. Thoroughly Hellenistic notions are found in 1 John 1.5 (God is light; contrast John 8.12) and 3.2 (transformation, even deification, through perfect knowledge of God). Possibly the references in the epistle to χρῖσμα (2.20,27) and σπέρμα (3.9) should be explained in the same way.

These observations cannot be regarded as completely convincing, but, for what they are worth, they suggest that the writer of the epistle was a man of less profound mind than the evangelist, capable of setting down side by side the old and the new, but not able (as the evangelist was) to fuse them into a unity. There remains, of course, a close connection between epistle and gospel; but exactly what this relation is can now only be guessed (see below, p. 62).

The Apocalypse presents problems perhaps as complicated as those of any book in the New Testament. We may be certain that the author of this book, written as it is in a unique kind of Greek,[1] has left us no other literary memorial; he wrote neither the gospel nor the epistles.[2] The Apocalypse itself is not a unity. The book as we have it was not compiled earlier than the principate of Domitian; but parts seem to require a date in the time of Nero, and must have been drawn by the final compiler from sources. The book, with its preoccupation with the

[1] See R. H. Charles, op. cit., cxvii–clix.
[2] See however E. Lohmeyer, 'Die Offenbarung des Johannes', Handbuch zum Neuen Testament 16 (1926), and the useful summary of opinion in P. H. Menoud, L'Évangile de Jean d'après les recherches récentes (1947), 73f. There is an interesting discussion of the question in Austin Farrer, The Revelation of St John the Divine (1964), 37–50.

catastrophic end of history, seems widely different from John; but in fact numerous parallels exist. In Revelation Jesus is called the 'Word of God' (19.13); and the σκηνή of God is said to be with men (21.3), just as according to John 1.14, the Word ἐσκήνωσεν ἐν ἡμῖν. In both books Christ is the Lamb of God, though in John (1.29,36) the word used is ἀμνός, while in Rev. (5.6 and 27 times) it is ἀρνίον. In both Christ has come to glory through suffering; he summons the thirsty (ὁ διψῶν ἐρχέσθω, Rev. 22.17; ἐάν τις διψᾷ ἐρχέσθω, John 7.37), and bids men keep (τηρεῖν) his words or commands (Rev. 3.8,10; 12.17; 14.12; 22.7,9; John 8.51f.; 14.15,21,23f.; 15.10,20; cf. 1 John 2.3ff.; 3.22,24; 5.3).

We may say that some relation exists between the two books, though it is not identity of authorship. A positive statement could only be a guess. Since however we are reduced to guessing, the conjecture may be hazarded here (it will be considered again at pp. 133f. below, when an attempt is made to locate the gospel in Christian history) that the evangelist, the author—or authors, since it must not be assumed that all three come from the same hand[1]—of the epistles, and the final editor of Revelation were all pupils of the original apocalyptist. They developed his work on similar lines, but it was the evangelist who saw most clearly how eschatological Christian theology could be re-expressed in the language of Hellenistic thought, and indeed saw this so clearly as to be far ahead of his time. This will appear in the next section.

4. THE GOSPEL IN THE DEVELOPMENT OF THEOLOGY[2]

To trace the influence of the Fourth Gospel upon Christian theology would be more than the task of a lifetime; to trace its influence upon the thought of the first half of the second century is easy, for it had none. The question of the literary relationships of the gospel is dealt with below (pp. 110–14); we are here concerned with kinship of thought. No early Christian writer seems to have shared John's attitude to the problems of Christian theology.

(i) *Ephesians and the Pastorals*.[3] Ephesians, though in form entirely different, reveals a number of points of contact with John. A primary emphasis in Ephesians is on the unity of the church (e.g. 1.10; 2.13–22; 3.6; 4.3–6); this is also one of the themes of John (e.g. 10.16; 11.52; 17.21). Christ is he who descended and ascended (Eph. 4.8–10); there is a close parallel in John 3.13, and in many other passages which speak of Christ's return to the Father. Eph. 2.18 (προσαγωγὴν . . . ἐν ἑνὶ πνεύματι πρὸς τὸν πατέρα) recalls the worship of the Father in Spirit

[1] On the authorship of 2 and 3 John see, in addition to commentaries and works cited above (pp. 59f.), R. Bergmeier, *Z.N.T.W.* 57 (1966), 93–100.

[2] See the literature cited on p. 110.

[3] These should be regarded as contemporary with, or possibly earlier than the Fourth Gospel, and therefore as not in a position to be influenced by it; they may however show a common background of thought.

and in truth which is spoken of in John 4.24. The use in Ephesians of ἀλήθεια, δόξα, ἐλέγχειν, καρπός, σκότος, and φῶς is similar to that of John; Eph. 5.8–13 is a particularly instructive passage. The use of ἀληθεύειν (Eph. 4.15) resembles the Johannine ποιεῖν τὴν ἀλήθειαν (3.21), and Eph. 5.26 (the sanctification of the church) recalls John 17.17,19. The Holy Spirit in Ephesians reveals the truth (1.17; 3.5) as in John does the Paraclete. Eph. 5.26 (καθαρίσας τῷ λουτρῷ τοῦ ὕδατος ἐν ῥήματι) alludes to baptism in terms not widely different from John 3.5. Finally, it may be said that the eschatological problem of early Christianity is solved in Ephesians, as it is in John. Ephesians maintains the tension of a future hope, while it makes no claim that the *parousia* is near.

The Pastoral Epistles are in many ways further removed from John than is Ephesians, but they approach it in two directions. (i) They contain the closest New Testament approach to the sacramental allusion of John 3.5. Baptism is a λουτρὸν παλιγγενεσίας καὶ ἀνακαιν-ώσεως πνεύματος ἁγίου (Tit. 3.5; for the notion of regeneration cf. 1 Peter 1.3,23). (ii) They presuppose the danger due to gnostic propaganda in Christian circles (1 Tim. 1.6f.; 4.1–7; 2. Tim. 2.16–18; 4.3f.; Tit. 1.10f. and many other passages). John also is aware of the danger of gnosticism, but he rebuts it not by the reiteration of orthodox formulae (πιστοὶ λόγοι, 1 Tim. 1.15; 3.1; 4.9; 2. Tim. 2.11; Tit. 3.8; cf. 1 Tim. 1.10; 6.3; 2 Tim. 1.13; 4.3; Tit. 1.9; 2.1,8) but by absorbing as much of its terminology as was compatible with the Christian faith.

There is at least some probability in the view that Ephesians and the Pastorals were written at or near Ephesus; and it may be said that they do something to illuminate the area of Christian life and thought in which the thought of the Fourth Gospel was born. Ephesians lies on or near a line drawn between Paul and John; the Pastorals represent a different route through the same country.

(ii) *Ignatius*.[1] The difference in atmosphere between the epistles of Ignatius and the Fourth Gospel is very great. The former are the fervent, unpremeditated and unplanned utterance of a man on the road to death; the latter bears all the marks of long, calm, and profound medita-tion. The difference in temperament (and in all probability in circum-stances) between John and Ignatius is so striking that it is possible to be confused about the relation between them. In fact they are men seeking similar goals and travelling over similar paths, but working independently; and John is far more successful than Ignatius, though this must not be taken to imply that he wrote at a later date. Apart from their common Christian faith, the two men were subject to similar

---

[1] Bishop of Antioch, martyred in Rome, c. A.D. 115. For the literary relationship between Ignatius and John see below, pp. 110f. See also Hoskyns, 110–18; C. Maurer, *Ignatius von Antiochien und das Johannesevangelium* (1949). Some points are discussed further, and other literature is cited, in my essay, in *Jews, Greeks and Christians* (ed. R. Hamerton-Kelly and R. Scroggs; 1976), 220–44.

influences: both were engaged in controversy with Judaism, and with incipient docetism, and both used the language of contemporary Hellenistic religion to express their faith. These impulses naturally led to similarities; like John, Ignatius insists upon the historical reality of the man Jesus—if Jesus were not truly man, of flesh and blood, his own sufferings would be meaningless (Ignatius, *Trall.* 10; perhaps Ignatius —like John, if Käsemann is right—protests too much); he asserts that Judaism has now been entirely superseded by the new religion— Christians who live as Jews avow that they have not received grace (*Magn.* 8.1; perhaps Ignatius has not fully understood Judaism); Jesus Christ is the Word of God proceeding from silence (*Magn.* 8.2), and he bestows incorruption upon the church (*Eph.* 17.1), feeding it with the medicine of immortality (in the eucharist, *Eph.* 20.2; but whether 'medicine of immortality' forms a parallel with John or a contrast is a good question—see on 6.35,51). But along with, and, as I have indicated, within, these similarities, differences abound. Thus for Ignatius it is the ministry of the church that guarantees the carnal reality of Jesus (*Magn.* 6.1; *Trall.* 3.1; *Philad.* 7; *et al.*). His acquaintance with the Old Testament is slight, and he by no means grasps all that John conveys when he says, Salvation is of the Jews (4.22). His use of Hellenistic concepts leads him to the verge of magic (e.g. *Eph.* 19.2f.). His eschatology is characteristic of the second-century movement towards chiliasm; these are the last times, and repentance and faith are urgent necessities (*Eph.* 11.1). And, generally speaking, the form of his work (so far as it may be said to have form) is determined by the example of Paul, though it is doubtful whether Ignatius fully understood his model.

(iii) *Barnabas.* F. M. Braun (*N.T.S.* 4 (1958), 119–24) thinks that the thought of Barnabas was influenced by the Fourth Gospel, whether as a written text or in earlier oral form. The contacts alleged, however, are not convincing.

(iv) *Polycarp.*[1] Little need be said here about Polycarp's letter (or letters) to the Philippians. To an even greater extent than those of Ignatius it is modelled on the epistles of Paul, who certainly is Polycarp's apostle *par excellence*. He emphasizes some of the points made by Ignatius (e.g. the reality of the incarnation (7.1, recalling 1 John 4.2f.), the eschatological hope (5.3)), but in a more restrained and biblical, and less Hellenistic, manner.

(v) *Justin.* With Justin we reach the middle of the second century, and a responsible Greek apologist and exponent of the Christianity of his age. He is capable of carrying to extremes the principles which are combined and held together in equilibrium in John. (*a*) Like other second-century writers he is a chiliast, with a high regard for the Apocalypse, which he

---

[1] Bishop of Smyrna, martyred *c.* A.D. 156. On his 'epistle' see P. N. Harrison, *Polycarp's Two Epistles to the Philippians* (1936). For the date of Polycarp's martyrdom, also for additional bibliographical references, see also *J.T.S.* 3 (1952), 79–83 (W. Telfer), 18 (1967), 433–7 (T. D. Barnes).

declares to be the work of John the Apostle (*Trypho* 81). (*b*) He develops a Logos-theology, a fact which might at first seem to argue dependence upon John. In fact, however, this first impression is misleading; Justin's theory of the Logos differs markedly from John's; it is more philosophical and less biblical.[1] (*c*) Justin teaches a more mechanical view of sacraments than is implied in John, where neither Christian baptism nor the eucharist is explicitly described.

In Justin, as in Ignatius, we see the working of factors that were operative in the composition of the Fourth Gospel also, but were in the gospel held under firm control by the primitive Christian faith, whereas Justin allowed them to lead him too far.

(vi) *The Odes of Solomon.* For certain verbal parallels between the Odes and John see below, pp. 112f.; also the commentary, *passim*. The relation between the evangelist and the Odist is much discussed, and there is little agreement on the subject. Even the date of the Odes has not been settled. A balanced and cautious view, with which I should substantially agree, is given by Schnackenburg, I, 143ff.; see also however J. H. Charlesworth, *The Odes of Solomon* (1973), and the same author's essay, 'Qumran, John and the Odes of Solomon', in *J. & Q.*, 107-55. There is much to be said for the view that the Odes in their present form originated in Syria towards the middle of the second century. That Qumran, and possibly, early pre-Johannine traditions current in Syria, were entangled in their roots seems probable. The author was touched with gnostic ideas and especially perhaps with gnostic imagery, without being deeply committed to gnosticism in a heretical sense. If these views are correct it is not surprising that there should be parallels between the Odes and John—though indeed the parallels noted on pp. 112f. hardly go beyond what might reasonably be expected in two Christian writers who use a variety of images to express union with Christ and the blessings that flow from that union. Both writers, John and the Odist, were expressing their faith partly through the terminology of Oriental-Hellenistic religion. The Odist is much less down-to-earth than John. He may have read the gospel; if he did, he will have found it congenial and borrowed a little from it. Further than this it would be rash to go.

(vii) *The Gnostics.*[2] In the first edition of this book there occurred at this point the statement, 'It cannot . . . be claimed that their use of the gospel notably affected their systems; and it is doubtful whether this would appear to be so even if more of their works had been preserved

---

[1] See Sanders, *Early Church*, 20-7, especially his conclusion: 'This brief sketch of the Christian Gospel as presented by the Apologists suggests that their teaching is in origin independent of the fourth gospel'(27). For the literary relation between Justin and John see below, p. 111. See also E. F. Osborn, *Justin Martyr* (1973), especially 86-98.

[2] By 'the gnostics' are meant here the Christian heretics of the second century usually designated by that term; of whom the best known are perhaps Valentinus and Basilides.

to us.' Gnostic works of the first importance had been discovered shortly before these words were written and have since been published.[1] These confirm the use of the gospel in gnostic circles. For allusions to John in the *Gospel of Truth*, for example, see pp. 113f.; for allusions in the *Gospel of Thomas* see the commentary *passim*. These and other works have to some extent broadened an interest that had seemed almost wholly confined to cosmology, and to concentrate on the Prologue (1.1–18). But it remains substantially true that the gnostics used John because out of it, by exegesis sound or unsound, they were able to win support and enrichment for preconceived theories and mythologies. We should not be justified in speaking of second-century gnosticism as in any sense a creation of John. To this however must be added the observation that John must be seen as one stage in the development of full-blown gnosticism. This is not the place for an attempt to describe the genesis of gnosticism, or even to list the various elements that contributed to it. Oriental, Greek, Jewish, and Christian factors all played their part, and all these factors are already to be seen in John. Their proportions and blending were not, in John, such as to produce a truly gnostic result, but when other writers used the same ingredients genuine gnosticism—in the sense of a Christian heresy—was sure sooner or later to emerge. Such a later gnosticism is to be seen in the Mandaean literature,[2] which is best regarded not as supplying (in any direct sense) a source of Johannine thought but as a later form of gnosticism which made some use of Johannine material.

The influence of John in the first half of the second century may perhaps seem far less substantial than might be expected. The reason for this is partly that the gospel remained to a great extent unknown; it did not enter the main stream of the church's life till later in the century. But it remains a striking fact that the Christian writers of this period were able to handle the problems that evoked the Fourth Gospel, and yet show no indication that they were aware of the immense and unique contribution John had made to their solution. Chiliasm, anti-Jewish polemic (for example in Justin's *Dialogue with Trypho*), sacramentalism, the Hellenized Logos-philosophy of the Apologists, all show that the circumstances in which John was written persisted; but all were one-sided exaggerations, and no Christian thinker before Irenaeus was capable of appropriating and interpreting the Johannine synthesis.

[1] The best short account is by R. McL. Wilson, *Gnosis and the New Testament* (1968).
[2] See especially K. Rudolph in W. Foerster, *Gnosis II, Coptic and Mandaean Sources* (E.T. edited by R. McL. Wilson, 1974), 121–319.

4

THE THEOLOGY OF THE GOSPEL

THE theology of the Fourth Gospel, though cast in the form of a miscellaneous account of the life and teaching of Jesus of Nazareth, is the result of a serious attempt to evaluate and restate the apostolic faith in a situation differing, in some respects considerably, from that in which it was first grasped and proclaimed. John was not a theologian who worked from hand to mouth, reassessing and adapting this or that doctrine as occasion arose; he seized upon the earlier tradition as a whole, and refashioned it as a whole (see pp. 97ff.). The result of this is that any attempt to itemize his theology and present it in neat compartments is bound to misrepresent it. Eschatology is bound up with Christology, salvation with faith and knowledge, miracles with sacraments; if any of these themes is isolated from the rest, indeed if any is discussed in isolation from the rest, distortion becomes inevitable. It is therefore with considerable hesitation that the following analysis[1] is presented, in the hope that it may be of use to some who are beginning their study of the gospel. The reader is urged not to confine his attention to one section only but to read each in conjunction with the rest, and to give special attention to the concluding section which deals with Johannine theology as an organic and living whole.[2]

1. ESCHATOLOGY[3]

The books of the New Testament, almost without exception, seek in various ways to express the conviction that in Jesus Christ there entered the world of human experience something which may be described in such terms as 'the absolute', 'the ultimate', or 'the suprahistorical'; more simply, as God. Since all human experience, and still more all human language, are relative, the inevitable result of such an intrusion is a strain upon the forms of expression used in describing it. When, for example, the Christian faith is expressed, as it very early was expressed, purely in terms of temporal eschatology violence is done to the tenses of the verbs used; the future tenses normal in eschatological

---

[1] Retained in outline from the first edition of this Commentary.

[2] I have discussed the movement of John's theology in a number of articles: *Prologue*; 'Dialectical Theology'; 'The Father is greater than I'; 'Menschensohn'; 'Theocentric'. See, in addition to the many valuable commentaries and monographs, S. S. Smalley, *N.T.S.* 17 (1971), 276–92; also M. L. Appold, *The Oneness Motif in the Fourth Gospel* (1976), 2–8.

[3] See M. E. Boismard, *R.B.* 68 (1961), 507–24.

speech are constrained to become present tenses in order to make clear that the end of history is in fact being experienced in the midst of its course. Yet, true as this is, the future tenses do not altogether disappear from the New Testament, since the 'end' of which the New Testament speaks remains a true end, and history was not brought to a conclusion with the appearance of Jesus. This clash and paradox of tense is characteristic of the New Testament, but it is nowhere expressed more clearly than in John. 'The hour cometh and now is', a phrase which carries with it a superficial contradiction, occurs twice (4.23; 5.25). The time when men shall worship the Father as he seeks to be worshipped is coming, and it is now here (4.23). There is a partial explanation of the paradox in the fact that John wrote from two standpoints, changing rapidly from one to the other. From a standpoint placed in the period of the ministry of Jesus, 'the hour is coming'; from John's own natural standpoint within the life of the church after the resurrection and Pentecost, 'the hour now is'. But this is only a partial explanation, for (see the commentary ad loc.) the basis of John's thought is that true worship can exist only in and through Jesus, and that worship in and through him is true worship. Consequently it is correct to say that, wherever Jesus is, there worship in Spirit and truth is possible; but this possibility is necessarily qualified by a future, or its equivalent ('the hour cometh'), because, and as long as, the person of Jesus himself is qualified in this way: he is the Messiah and he will be the Messiah; he has come and he will come. The worship of Christianity is an anticipation of the worship of heaven, but it is not yet the worship of heaven.

The contrast of 5.25 with 5.28 brings out the point even more clearly because in these verses John handles the characteristically eschatological notion of resurrection. In 5.28 it is said that the hour is coming when the dead will come out of their tombs to judgement. This might have been written in any Jewish apocalypse; the belief was common property. But 5.25 runs, 'The hour is coming *and now is* when the dead shall hear the voice of the Son of God, and those who hear shall live.' There may be here a glance forward to the resurrection of Lazarus in ch. 11, but it will be remarked that there is no reference to the tombs, and it is plain that John is not saying the same thing as in 5.28. A different kind of death and resurrection, of which the death and resurrection of the body are a parable, is in mind. There is a sense in which the word of the Son of God in the present world brings to life those who are dead (cf. 11.25f.); the promise is already being fulfilled, but is being fulfilled in such a way as to leave over something of itself for a future fulfilment also.

It is not true that John has abandoned the common New Testament eschatology.[1] This can be affirmed only if a quantity of material, such

---

[1] See especially W. F. Howard, *Christianity according to St John* (1943), 106–28, 201–4; also Schweizer, *Jesus*, 165 (quoting 14.2f.; 17.24; 12.25f.; 11.21–7).

as a set of references to the last day in 6.39,40,44,54, is omitted as the work of a redactor, who disapproved of an eschatology that appeared to him to be wholly realized. In fact it was John himself who disapproved of such an eschatology; see the notes on the verses in question. John has emphasized the truth of futurist eschatology, and at the same time its problems and inadequacies, perhaps more strongly than any other writer. Eschatology is least inadequate in figurative description of the final end and goal of history. It gives a tolerable account of the work and person of Jesus, which in any case are paradoxical.[1] It is least satisfactory in dealing with the age of the church, the interval which lies between the adumbration of the end in Jesus and the end itself. This age however is the age which John was primarily concerned to explain, and it was the necessity of explaining it which, more than any other factor, led to the development of his theology. Johannine theology is not so much the imposition of alien forms and terminology upon primitive Christian thought (though it is expressed partly in new forms and terminology), as the spontaneous development of primitive Christian thought under the pressure of inner necessity and the lapse of time.

John essays to describe the age of the church (as we may call it) in quasi-eschatological terms; at 14.23, for example (see the notes), he speaks of a twofold *parousia* of Christ and of the Father to the man who becomes a Christian, and of their abiding with him. But it is clear that he was not satisfied with this expedient, just as he was not satisfied with an account of Jesus himself in simply apocalyptic eschatological terms. It was necessary to find a new way of expressing the fundamental Christian affirmation of the Christian faith, that in Jesus Christ the new age had come, but had done so in such a way that it still remained to come, so that Christians live both in this age and in the age to come. Paul had already laid the foundations for this task by the development of 'eschatological mysticism'[2] but much remained for John to do. What he did will be briefly surveyed in the remaining sections of this chapter. In Christology both Jewish and Greek metaphysics were laid under contribution. In the description of the Christian life the resources of mysticism and of sacramentalism were employed. But the other side of the process is equally important. If John used non-eschatological terms and concepts to express that which the older eschatological language could express only with difficulty, he also used eschatology in order to prevent the errors that could arise from mysticism and sacramentalism uncontrolled by reference to the future. There is no feeding on the flesh of the Son of man, whether by mystical union or in the eucharist, that makes the believer an autonomous, self-sufficient source of life. At the last day, and every day, he will live only if he is raised up.

[1] The use of this word is questioned by Käsemann (*Testament*, 12, 17). On this see 'The Father is greater than I', 158.
[2] See Schweitzer, especially 101–40, 334–75.

The eschatological element in the Fourth Gospel is not accidental; it is fundamental. To have abandoned it would have been to abandon the biblical framework of primitive Christianity, and to run all the risks to which a purely metaphysical Christianity, divorced from history, is exposed. The dangers of mysticism, perfectionism, and antinomianism are, in this gospel, held in check by the constraint of the primitive Christian eschatology, which is a constant reminder that the church lives by faith, not by sight, and that it is saved in hope.

2. CHRISTOLOGY

John shares the conviction expressed in the first sentence of Section 1 of this chapter, but develops it in a more sophisticated way than the synoptic writers. In the Synoptic Gospels the primary concern is with the kingdom of God which began to be realized through the advent and ministry of Jesus; Jesus proclaimed the Gospel of the kingdom. What John perceived with far greater clarity than any of his predecessors was that Jesus *is* the Gospel, and that the Gospel *is* Jesus. It was through the life, and especially through the death and resurrection, of Jesus that men had been admitted to the blessings of the messianic kingdom, and the highest blessing of that kingdom was, as Paul had already seen, the life of communion with Christ himself: 'for me, to live is Christ' (Phil. 1.21). That is, when the Gospel was offered to men it was Christ himself who was offered to them, and received by them. It was intolerable therefore that the person of Christ should remain undefined. Paul who had recognized the same truth, evidently felt something of the same obligation.

None of the Synoptic Gospels presents a developed and systematic Christology, but they are all full of the raw material of Christology. In particular, they all affirm, in predominantly eschatological terms (see the previous section), that it was in Jesus that God caused the life and activity of the 'other' world to break through into this world. They use the technical language of Judaism in order to characterize him: he is (in his own words) Son of man, (in the words of others) Messiah. He is the Son of God. This language is retained and developed by John, who also adds to it from other sources and from long and deep Christian reflection.

The synoptic language of the messianic hope is not abandoned; on the contrary it is more common in John than elsewhere. In John alone is the transliterated form of the Hebrew or Aramaic מָשִׁיחַ, מְשִׁיחָא (*mashiaḥ, mᵉshiḥa'*) used (Μεσσίας, 1.41; 4.25); the word Χριστός is used seventeen times, and in addition the compound title Ἰησοῦς Χριστός twice. The question of Messiahship in general holds a prominent place in the gospel: the Baptist emphasizes that he is not the Christ (1.20; 3.28); the Jewish authorities (7.52), the common people (7.25–31,40–3; 12.34), and the Samaritans (4.29f.) discuss Messiahship; the earliest disciples confess the Messiahship of Jesus (1.41; cf. 4.29; also 6.69, where ὁ ἅγιος τοῦ θεοῦ is probably a messianic title), although to do so is an offence punishable with excommunication (9.22; cf. 16.2).

But what does John mean by representing Jesus as Messiah? In the Synoptic Gospels the Messiahship of Jesus is concealed. He nowhere claims the dignity for himself, and discourages the proclamation of it by demons, just as he keeps secret the miracles which he performs, though he accepts Peter's confession (Mark 8.29 and parallels), and in Mark (14.62)[1] answers in the affirmative the high priest's question, Are you the Christ, the Son of the Blessed One? In other words, the synoptic, and especially the Marcan, presentation of Messiahship is governed by the theme of the messianic secret: Jesus is truly Messiah, but a Messiah as bound to humility and obscurity as he is obliged in the end to suffer. This theme is not absent from John; the Jews ask Jesus to tell them plainly whether he is the Christ (10.24), and, as in Mark, the unescapable necessity of suffering drives the narrative forward (e.g. 12.24,27). The secret of the person and work of Jesus was one men could not grasp (12.39, οὐκ ἠδύναντο πιστεύειν, with reference to Isa. 6.9, the passage alluded to in Mark 4.12 and parallels). So far John runs parallel to Mark; but the parallelism is far from complete. Other facts must be taken into consideration. There is an element of concealment in Jesus' Messiahship, but it is also openly confessed from the beginning of the gospel (1.41, εὑρήκαμεν τὸν Μεσσίαν; 1.45,49). The fact is that in John the Messiahship of Jesus is both hidden and revealed. It is hidden from the unbelieving and revealed to the believer whom God has called. The Marcan dualism of time, which contrasts a present obscurity with a future glory, is partially replaced by a different kind of tension, which exists in the present and is also continued into the future (14.22f.); Christ is not manifested to the world, but he is manifested to his own (as indeed he is in Mark). In a similar way John deals with the problem raised at 12.34; it is true that the Messiah should abide for ever, but he makes his abiding place (μονή) with those who receive him. With them he does abide for ever; with the rest he does not abide at all. We may see here the roots of that twofold presentation of Jesus that is characteristic of John, who asserts both the equality of Jesus with the Father as God (1.10; 10.30; 20.28), and his subordination (14.28); see 'The Father is greater than I', 185f.; also P. Borgen in *Religions in Antiquity* (Festschrift E. R. Goodenough, 1968), 137–48.

It is clear that John, though he retains messianic language, restates its content. This is true also of his treatment of the other principal synoptic descriptions of Jesus—Son of God and Son of man. Superficially it might seem that the two are almost reversed in meaning, for while in

---

[1] Matthew and Luke, though they use less explicit terms, also seem to presuppose that the question has been answered in the affirmative.

the Synoptic Gospels 'Son of God' draws attention to Christ's obedience to God and 'Son of man' means a heavenly being, in John 'Son of God' means at times one who shares the nature of God, 'Son of man' one who shares the nature of man. To draw the contrast so sharply would however be misleading.

For John, Jesus' sonship does indeed involve a metaphysical relationship with the Father; it is not simply messianic (see on 20.31). The charge that Jesus, by claiming to be the Son of God and to work continuously with him, makes himself equal to God, is never rebutted. John does not mean to rebut it. He is aware of the Stoic doctrine of a son of God who is a son of God in virtue of a divine spark, a fragmentary logos, which dwells within him, and of such conceptions of union with God as are expressed in the Hermetic literature (see above, pp. 35f., 38f.). Undoubtedly he believes that the Son of God who was incarnate in Jesus of Nazareth inhabited eternity with the Father. But these notions are always qualified by the thought of a fundamentally moral relationship, in which the Son is obedient to the Father. The Son does nothing of himself, but only repeats and reproduces the actions of the Father (5.19f.). So completely does he reflect the Father's character that to see Jesus is to see the Father (14.9). By thus showing its two aspects John brings out more clearly than the synoptists the meaning of sonship: both moral likeness and essential identity are included.

The use of the term Son of man in the Synoptic Gospels is one of the greatest puzzles of New Testament theology and criticism. Jesus as Son of man lives a humble human life (e.g. Matt. 8.20; Luke 9.58); will suffer and die (e.g. Mark 8.31); will appear in glory (e.g. Mark 13.26). These are the most characteristic synoptic uses of the title. John has few parallels to the eschatological use (but see 5.27, and below.) Five passages, possibly six, refer to the passion (3.14; 6.53; 8.28; 12.23,34; ? 13.31); 6.27 goes closely with 6.53 and 3.13 with 3.14. Death is thus a central feature of John's Son of man doctrine, but it will be remarked that for him the death of Jesus is at the same time his glory; note for example the close parallel to Mark's δεῖ τὸν υἱὸν τοῦ ἀνθρώπου πολλὰ παθεῖν (Mark 8.31) in ὑψωθῆναι δεῖ τὸν υἱὸν τοῦ ἀνθρώπου (John 3.14), where ὑψοῦν means both 'to lift up on the cross' and 'to exalt in glory'. A few other Son of man passages remain, and they are particularly significant for John's use of the expression. These are 1.51; 3.13; 6.27,62; on each see the notes. Putting together 3.13 and 6.62 we learn that the Son of man was (? pre-existent) in heaven, descended from heaven, and ascended into heaven. Of no other can this be said (3.13). In 1.51 the Son of man himself is the way of angelic traffic between heaven and earth, and in 6.27 it is he who gives to mankind the true food of eternal life. All this means that the Son of man is the one true mediator between heaven and earth; he passes from the one to the other, and through his earthly sojourn he bestows upon men the revealed knowledge and the eternal life in virtue of which they in turn come to the life of heaven. This function of the Son of man is by no means inconsistent with his death, since John understands his death to represent at once his plunge into the depths of humanity and his ascent to the glory of the Father; and it is certainly not inconsistent with his eschatological functions. So much is in fact predicated of Jesus as the Son of man that it is doubtful whether the title as such has any distinctive significance.[1] There are some contacts, but it would not be easy to trace any direct relation between John and Daniel, the Similitudes of Enoch, 4 Ezra, or the Synoptic Gospels. The last Adam and the Man from heaven in Pauline usage provide no close parallel. To say this is not to deny an eschatological element in John's understanding of Son of man (this is indeed explicit at 5.27, and at least hinted in 1.51), or the notion of representative humanity. But John is far less dependent on a myth of the primal or archetypal man, which appears elsewhere in apocalyptic and gnostic or Platonic expressions, than on the fundamental Christological conviction that in Jesus deity and manhood are united in an indissoluble unity. The Son of man is the man who is also God, who is simultaneously on earth and in heaven (3.13); but this he is said to be, not in virtue of a ready-made myth, but because John as a Christian knew that this was what Jesus was.

The idea of mediation involves a further relation of Jesus Christ to men: he is a revealer. It is at this point that John's characteristic description of Jesus as the Logos may be introduced. The origins of this Christological expression, in Jewish and Greek thought, and in Christian usage, are discussed in the commentary; here it is sufficient to indicate that, having regard to the whole background, the term Logos is seen to describe God in the process of self-communication—not the communication of knowledge only, but in a self-communication which inevitably includes the imparting of true knowledge. The Logos is a Word of God which at the same time declares his nature and calls into being a created life in which a divine power circulates. Unlike Philo,[2] who equates the Logos with an archetypal Man in whose image the whole human race was made, John conceives the relation between the Logos and the human race soteriologically. Men are not in their own nature born of God, but those are so born who receive the Logos in his incarnate mission; these become a new humanity of which the Logos, or Son of God, is the source and pattern.

The Logos is thus related to mankind, and to the new redeemed humanity, in his own proper being; yet he is God, not man, and his relationship with man is not a Platonic relationship of type and antitype, but that of incarnation. Not only in the Prologue but constantly

---

[1] See E. D. Freed, *J.B.L.* 86 (1967), 402-9; also Lightfoot, 104f. ('The term . . . has more in common with Hellenistic than with purely Jewish thought. To Hellenistic readers the term would suggest an ideal humanity . . . the glory of the Son of man is His revelation . . . of the being and character of God . . .'); contrast R. Maddox, in *Reconciliation and Hope* (Festschrift Leon Morris; 1974), 186-204.

[2] For this contrast see 'Theocentric', 368-71.

John insists on the fact that the Word became flesh, that the Son of man was not only a heavenly but also an earthly man. He insists in the plainest terms on the human ignorance, weariness, and sorrow of Jesus (4.6; 11.34f.), who, in spite of his heavenly origin and status, was nothing if not human.[1] There is a superficial parallel between John's notion of the descent of his redeemer God and corresponding features in certain eastern religions (see further on Salvation, pp. 78–82 below); but there seems to be no true parallel to the true humanity of the Redeemer, which, to John, was essential if salvation was to be secured for men.

Two other attempts to estimate Johannine Christology must be briefly noted. Some features of the gospel recall the Hellenistic figure of the θεῖος ἀνήρ, or divine man.[2] The most persuasive account of these features sees them as representing the Christology of a source (probably the Signs Source[3]—see pp. 18f.) which John himself rejected, or at least corrected, regarding it as inadequate. The source presented Jesus as a wonder-worker, whose mighty acts were such as to evoke faith; John himself regarded faith based on signs as unsatisfactory—perhaps hardly as genuine faith at all. It is possible to see in John a criticism of θεῖος ἀνήρ Christology without believing that John had found this inadequate Christology in a source; cf. pp. 77f. Another Christological type that has been found in John is that of the prophet-king, which Judaism found in Moses.[4] That this figure plays some part especially in the background of John 6 is probably true; that it is the major constituent in John's Christology is a proposition much harder to prove.

The synoptic Christology lacks clarity of definition, both regarding the relation between Christ and God and regarding the relation between Christ and men. 'Son of God' does not necessarily align Jesus with God, nor does 'Son of man' declare him to be true and complete man. This is not to say that the synoptists are either Ebionite or docetic in intention; they simply view Jesus in the light of the eschatological crisis which he precipitated, and they describe the whole situation in appropriate terms. John releases himself from a purely apocalyptic interpretation of Jesus, while he continues to use eschatological language (though not exclusively). Jesus is the beginning and the end, the first creator and the final judge; also he is the ultimate truth both of God and of humanity. Being truly God and truly man, and being also the image of God and the archetype of humanity, he is

[1] Käsemann (Testament, 26 and elsewhere) thinks, on the contrary, that John himself manifests a 'naive docetism'. On this see Bornkamm, III. 104–21; also 'The Father is greater than I', 151f., 158f.
[2] See L. Bieler, ΘΕΙΟΣ ΑΝΗΡ I, II (1935, 1936); also the excellent account by Elwyn Jones, The Concept of the θεῖος ἀνήρ in the Graeco-Roman World with special reference to the first two Centuries A.D. (unpublished Durham Ph.D. thesis, 1973).
[3] See J. Becker, N.T.S. 16 (1970), 130–48.
[4] See Meeks; also T. F. Glasson, Moses in the Fourth Gospel (1963).

an ontological mediator between God and man; he is no less a mediator of true knowledge, and of salvation.

3. MIRACLES

It would not be impossible for the casual reader of the Synoptic Gospels to pick out from them miracle narratives which he could regard simply as the work of a strolling magician.[1] It would be much more difficult to do this in the Fourth Gospel. With the miracles, as with other elements of the tradition, John has seized the Christological interpretation which is implicit in the synoptics, clarified it, and stamped it upon the material in such a way that the reader is not allowed to escape it. The miracles of this gospel are a function of its Christology. Rightly to understand them is to apprehend Christ by faith (10.38; 14.11). The miracles once grasped in their true meaning lead immediately to the Christology, since they are a manifestation of the glory of Christ (2.11).

The miracles of Jesus are described as his works (ἔργα). As such, they are also the works of God himself; there is a complete continuity between the activity of Jesus and the activity of the Father (see, e.g., 5.36; 9.3; 10.32,37f.; 14.10). On the one hand, Jesus accomplishes the Father's work (ἔργον) because he is an obedient son (4.34), and, on the other, the miraculous power of God is manifested in him because he shares by nature in the Godhead (14.10): hence the further proposition that the works of Jesus bear witness to him (5.36, αὐτὰ τὰ ἔργα ἃ ποιῶ μαρτυρεῖ περὶ ἐμοῦ; similarly 10.25; cf. 10.38; 14.11). The works make visible both the character and the power of God, and at the same time that in Christ he is active in a unique way.[2]

The miracles are also described as signs (σημεῖα). This is one of the most characteristic and important words of the gospel. It has a history which must be noted. In classical Greek it means a distinguishing mark, a token, or a signal. It may be a device on a shield or a signet on a ring. It has special uses in logic. With Aristotle it means a probable argument over against a τεκμήριον, or certain proof; with the Stoics and Epicureans it is an 'observable basis of inference to the unobserved or unobservable' (L. S., s.v. II, 3b). In the LXX σημεῖον generally translates אוֹת ('oth), sometimes with τέρας (a combination attested in non-biblical Greek also) as a rendering of אות ומופת ('oth umopheth). Apart from the simple meaning 'mark', the most primitive sense seems to have been miraculous; so e.g. Exod. 4.8 (J): ἐὰν δὲ μὴ . . .

---

[1] See H.S.G.T. 69–93, where the 'implicit Christological interpretation' of the synoptic miracle narratives is also investigated.

[2] The rabbinic literature refers to certain persons, notably R. Ḥanina ben Dosa, as אנשי מעשה (literally, men of deed, or work), and G. Vermes, Jesus the Jew (1973), 79, takes this expression to refer to the working of miracles. It seems more probable owever that it refers to good deeds (done in obedience to Torah); see especially A. Büchler, Types of Jewish-Palestinian Piety from 70 B.C.E. to 70 C.E.: The Ancient Pious Men (1922), 79–91; also S.B. II, 211.

εἰσακούσωσιν τῆς φωνῆς τοῦ σημείου τοῦ πρώτου. . . . But the word acquired other, and quite non-miraculous, meanings. Thus Isaiah and his specially named son ἔσται σημεῖα καὶ τέρατα ἐν τῷ οἴκῳ 'Ισραήλ (Isa. 8.18). When Ezekiel took a stone and drew on it a picture of Jerusalem besieged σημεῖόν ἐστιν τοῦτο τοῖς υἱοῖς 'Ισραήλ (Ezek. 4.3). A sign is a part of the proclamation of the glory of God to the Gentiles: And I will leave a sign upon them (καταλείψω ἐπ' αὐτῶν σημεῖον), and I will send some of them, having been saved (σεσωσμένους), to the Gentiles . . . which have not heard my name nor seen my glory, and they shall proclaim (ἀναγγελοῦσιν) my glory among the Gentiles (Isa. 66.19). The אות—σημεῖον thus becomes a special part of the prophetic activity; no mere illustration, but a symbolical anticipation or showing forth of a greater reality of which the σημεῖον is nevertheless itself a part. A σημεῖον calls the attention of the people of God to the fulfilment of his purposes, and, finally, a σημεῖον draws the attention of the Gentiles to the glory of God.[1]

In the Synoptic Gospels the word is most frequently used of a sign which the adversaries of Jesus wrongfully seek from him and he refuses (Matt. 12.38,39; 16.1,4; Mark 8.11,12; Luke 11.16,29; 23.8). False prophets and false Christs work signs (Matt. 24.24; Mark 13.22). To this generation will be given only the sign of Jonah (Matt. 16.4; Luke 11.29f.). Signs (portents) may be expected to foreshadow the coming of Christ in glory (Matt. 24.3,30; Mark 13.4; Luke 21.7,11,25). Plainly the synoptic writers were unwilling to apply the word σημεῖον to the miracles (though it is certain that they regarded them as highly significant); they preferred to use it of eschatological events. John's usage is in marked contrast. The first sign, a miracle, creates faith in the disciples (2.11); at 12.37 John notes the unbelief of the people in spite of the signs which had been done; and at 20.30f. he says that he has made his selection of signs in order that his readers may believe that Jesus is the Christ, the Son of God. Jesus himself uses the word twice only (4.48; 6.26), and of these uses 4.48 reflects the synoptic situation; but for John himself σημεῖον exactly describes the things that Jesus did. They were σημεῖα in the Old Testament sense, special demonstrations of the character and power of God, and partial but effective realizations of his salvation. In this John differs from the synoptists rather in terminology than in thought, and the cause of the difference is probably not simple. In the first place, John (as elsewhere; see above, pp. 27–30) is using Old Testament language with a full awareness of its theological meaning, but he has carefully selected an Old Testament word which has non-biblical associations. σημεῖον, as we have seen, has interesting and significant Stoic associations; it is not unknown in popular Greek religion (e.g. Dittenberger, *Syll.* 709.24f. (*c.* 107 B.C.)

---

[1] Josephus, *Bel.* VI, 285 (σημεῖα τῆς σωτηρίας) is not, in its context, a very helpful parallel. See McNamara, *T. & T.*, 143, for the use in the Targums of נס and סימן in the sense of miracles; for נס in this sense see also *Berakoth* 4a.

προεσάμανε μὲν τὰν μέλλουσαν γίνεσθαι πρᾶξιν [διὰ τ]ῶν ἐν τῶι ἱερῶι γενομένων σαμείων). But, in the second place, a characteristic difference between John and the Synoptic Gospels, which has already been noted, comes to light once more at this point. The synoptists evidently preferred to reserve the word σημεῖον for those eschatological events which mark the near approach of the end; for John the miracles themselves are eschatological events. It would be proper to rejoin that for the synoptists also they are eschatological events (see, e.g., Matt. 12.28; Luke 11.20); but for them the eschatological significance of the ministry of Jesus is a hidden thing, which will be understood only in the eschatological future; thus the signs (in the sense of miracles) are for the present secret signs. Even the disciples fail to understand them (Mark 8.17,18, 21). John, as has been said, conceives the secret differently. To those who do believe, the miracles are signs which feed their faith; to those who do not, signs may be multiplied indefinitely without producing faith (12.37). John's reinterpretation of the synoptic eschatology releases the word σημεῖον for his use, and he uses it to the full because it is one of the words common to his biblical tradition and his Hellenistic environment.

It is often supposed that the word σημεῖον is to be connected with a special source used by John (the 'Signs Source'; see pp. 18f.). The evidence is against this view. The word is used in the gospel 17 times; in 13 (12) of these the word is in the plural, and refers to the actions of Jesus (e.g. 3.2; 4.48; 12.37). One of the occurrences in the singular refers to John the Baptist (10.41). Only three such occurrences remain. At 2.18 it is asked, What sign do you show? and at 6.30 there is the almost identical question, What sign do you do? This leaves only 4.54 to refer to a specific miracle (but cf. 2.11, though here the noun is plural). The evidence thus suggests at most a 'Cana source' for the two miracles wrought there; there is nothing to suggest a more extended source based on signs.[1] This does not lessen the significance of σημεῖον; it means that the word is John's own choice, his general interpretative term for the actions, especially the miraculous actions, of Jesus.

We have already touched upon the division produced by the signs among the beholders. They regularly in John (chs. 5, 6, 9, 11) give rise to controversy, and the controversial point specially selected by John from the synoptic material is the question of Sabbath observance (chs. 5, 9). This was chosen not because John found it necessary to liberate the Christians of his day from the bondage of Jewish legalism; that battle had long ago been fought and won. John raises the matter again because by means of it he is able to point to the true meaning of the miracles and the character of the miracle-worker. 5.16–18 is particularly important here (see the notes). The fact that the Father rested on the seventh day and hallowed it did not mean that on that day he ceased

---

[1] Bultmann's 'Signs Source' has been developed notably by R. T. Fortna, *The Gospel of Signs* (1970). But see also Conzelmann, *Theology*, 345.

to be what he had been hitherto, a beneficent Creator. On the contrary, the completion of God's work which is signified made it possible to use the Sabbath as a type of the messianic rest reserved for the people of God, a time of blessing for men introduced not by the cessation of God's activity but by an unprecedented outflowing of his creative power. The miracles of Jesus, then, are not merely, as in the Synoptic Gospels, signs that the kingdom of God is at hand, but also clear indications that he by whom the signs are wrought is the Son of God and equal to God himself. Hence the resistance of the Jews, who, however, in condemning Jesus on this issue show their own blindness and condemn themselves (9.41; 12.47f.).

After 12.37 the word σημεῖον does not occur until 20.30. As in Mark, there is no miracle in the passion narrative. This is not because the story of Jesus ceases to have the value of revelation; in fact the death and resurrection are the supreme revelation. Like the σημεῖα it is explained in discourse material (chs. 13—17; see pp. 14f., 454ff.), and the event is then narrated in quite simple language. Like the other σημεῖα it is a declaration of the character of God, and of the salvation he brings to men. Yet it is not a σημεῖον and is not called a σημεῖον,[1] because it is not merely a token of something other than itself; this event is the thing which it signifies, perhaps, in Johannine language, not a σημεῖον but ἀλήθεια. The miracles are set in a context of human need which ranges from the comparative triviality of a deficiency of wine at a wedding feast to the death of a beloved friend and brother; but the death of Jesus is itself a real event in which the suffering and sin of the world are everywhere apparent and are dealt with in their totality. The matter may be expressed by saying that throughout the gospel the course of events has taken place, as it were, in front of a mirror, and on a line intersecting the mirror. As the events themselves move nearer to the mirror, the images of the events, which we may take to represent the eternal realities portrayed by them, correspondingly move nearer to the mirror, and become clearer and clearer. Finally, object and image coincide in the surface of the mirror. So, in the death and resurrection of Jesus, sign and its meaning coincide.

4. SALVATION

God did not send his Son into the world to judge it but to save it (3.17; 12.47); those who believe in Jesus as the Christ, the Son of God, have life in his name (20.31); to receive Christ is to become a child of God (1.12). That salvation was in fact effected by Jesus Christ, and could be offered through him to men, is a point John scarcely troubles to demonstrate; the history he records is the history of God's saving

---

[1] So that R. T. Fortna's claim (*J.B.L.* 89 (1970), 151–66) that, in John's transformation of the Signs gospel, the chief sign becomes not the resurrection but the death of Jesus, is beside the point.

activity, directed to the need of men, and he never thinks of it in other terms. But what did he mean by salvation?

In the world in which Jesus lived more than one notion of salvation was current (see above, pp. 36–9). For example, within Judaism there was more than one form of the hoped-for messianic salvation. It might occur within the present world order as a reversal of political and military fortunes; or it might be a purely apocalyptic event taking place on the boundary between this world and the unseen other world. The elect might become prosperous rulers of a fruitful land; they might become as the angels in heaven. There is much variety here, but there is within Judaism a general tendency (not without exceptions) to regard salvation as the fruit of a future act of God, for which men may hope, in which they may believe, but upon which they cannot at present set their eyes. Outside Judaism the futurist, eschatological, outlook was not unknown, but it was not prevalent. Salvation was a present experience given by God to men, either through sacraments or through knowledge, γνῶσις. Each of these non-Jewish lines of thought was likely to include the descent of a redeemer God into the otherwise abandoned world of flesh, sin, ignorance, and death. On his return to the heavenly world from which he came, he left behind him means (sacramental or intellectual) by which men might follow him and so escape through the circle of destiny into the upper divine world. This was salvation.

There is good reason to conclude that John was acquainted with both worlds of thought, the Jewish and the pagan. He also makes clear the provenance of his own doctrine of salvation: Salvation is of the Jews (4.22). This dictum occurs in a controversial setting and means primarily a vindication of the Jewish tradition over against the Samaritan; but its full consequences must not be shirked. If Jerusalem rather than Gerizim is the seat of salvation it is also to be preferred to Athens and Phrygia. The Old Testament furnishes the essential thought-forms, and the essential language too, for the conceiving and expressing of salvation.

John, then, takes a decidedly Jewish viewpoint, and takes his stand upon the Old Testament. This fact must not, however, be allowed to obscure the complementary fact that he also uses language akin to that which we have noted as proceeding from Hellenistic and gnostic sources. 'This is eternal life, that they should know (γινώσκωσι) thee, the only true God, and him whom thou didst send, Jesus Christ' (17.3). Through knowledge comes salvation. There is also a sacramental interest in the gospel, though it needs careful definition (see pp. 82–5). It is beyond doubt that a non-Jewish flows beside the Jewish stream. This is no accident, nor is it due simply to the fashionable eclecticism which sought to make the best of all religions. We have reached again, from a different angle, the point that was made in the first section of this chapter. The old eschatological notion of salvation was not adequate for Christian use, because the promised salvation was now partly fulfilled, and could no longer be described as purely future. Moreover,

79

it was really true that the Redeemer had come down from heaven to earth, and had wrought his saving work and returned to heaven. It was true that to know him (though not precisely in the gnostic sense of knowing; see on 1.10) was to have eternal life; and John belonged to a community that believed that Jesus had left behind him rites in which he was able still to communicate himself to his own. The partial realization of the Jewish eschatology opened to John a field of thought and vocabulary that was closed to orthodox Judaism. Consequently John's description of the Christian salvation is richer than the synoptic presentation not because he has enriched it from non-Christian sources but because he has used non-Christian, and non-Jewish, terminology to bring out what was from the first implicit in the primitive faith.

Salvation is the fruit of the whole incarnate life of Jesus Christ, including his death and resurrection; consequently it is revealed in all his actions. The miracles in particular show figuratively what salvation is—the curing of the sick, the feeding of the hungry, the giving of sight to the blind, and the raising of the dead. Salvation, that is, means the healing of the ills of mankind, and the imparting of light and life; in other words, Jesus deals with sin, and gives men knowledge and life. These aspects of salvation are seen from time to time in the course of the gospel, but appear pre-eminently in the death and resurrection of Jesus.

(i) *Salvation and sin.* In the opening scene of the gospel Jesus is declared by John the Baptist to be the Lamb of God who takes away the sin of the world (1.29). Before taking it away, however, he reveals the existence and nature of sin. His coming into the world is like the shining of light (1.5; 3.19–21; 8.12; 9.5; 12.35f., 46; cf. 11.9f.); those who do good come to the light since there is nothing to fear in the exposure of their deeds; those who do evil shun the light. Their turning away from Christ is both the result of their sin and an indication of what sin means. When the Spirit exposes the sin of the world (16.8f.) it is revealed that sin consists in not believing in Christ. To reject him is in fact to commit what the Synoptic Gospels speak of as sin against the Holy Spirit (see Mark 3.28–30 and thereon *H.S.G.T.* 103–7; and cf. John 8.21; 9.41), yet this supreme sin is one to which every act of wickedness contributes since it is because of sin that men commit the sin of rejecting Christ. The consequence of sin is bondage (8.34) from which men are liberated not by physical descent from Abraham but by the truth of Christ. Since sin is concentrated into the rejection of Christ[1] it is clear that sin can be removed only by Christ; indeed John here runs into a difficulty which cannot readily be resolved since it springs out of the absolute theological terminology that he uses. He gives at times the impression that the world is divided into two groups, those who when the light shines come to the light, and those who avoid the light. He

---

[1] Conzelmann (*Theology*, 327) notes that John, like Paul, uses ἁμαρτία mostly in the singular; also that he avoids μετάνοια and ἄφεσις ἁμαρτιῶν.

seems to imply that the predestined groups of righteous and sinners must ever remain what they are; the righteous must be righteous, and the filthy must be filthy still. But this language is crossed by the belief that Jesus took away the sin of the *world*, and that none who comes to him will be rejected by Christ (6.37). This tension of predestination and choice[1] is of course not peculiar to John but is characteristic of New Testament theology as a whole, and its source has already been indicated. Jesus is both the judge and the redeemer of men, the light that exposes and the light that illuminates. He asserts that he has not come to judge but to save; yet he is bound to add that if he does judge his judgement is true (8.16). Judgement is the obverse of salvation; it is the form salvation takes for men who will have none of it.

To describe Jesus as the Lamb of God (see the notes on 1.29) is to draw special attention to his sacrificial death, but, although in the passion narrative John is at pains to draw out the analogy between Jesus and the paschal sacrifice (18.28; 19.36),[2] he does not explain the death of Jesus in sacrificial terms, and this is not his characteristic thought. The crucifixion is the means by which the scattered children of God are gathered together (11.52), by which all men are drawn to Christ (12.32). The Old Testament parallel is the serpent lifted up (ἐπὶ σημείου—‎סנ, not ‎אות[3]—Num. 21.8f.) in the wilderness, by which the people were cured. On this parallel see the commentary (at 3.14); the cross becomes, as it were, a focal point of faith, at which men's trust in God is concentrated and God's saving power is made known.

(ii) *Salvation and knowledge.* The word γνῶσις does not occur in the gospel. On the use of kindred verbs see on 1.10. To know God is to have eternal life (17.3); to know the truth is to be set free (8.32). Knowledge, then, is a way of entrance into salvation and life. Jesus himself knows the Father, and his ministry may be summed up as the communication of this knowledge (1.18; 17.26). The Johannine picture of Jesus corresponds in these respects with that of the gnostic redeemer; but important differences remain. The key of knowledge is not used for unlocking the various doors of the surrounding heavens so that man may escape from his prison house, nor does John give any indication that he shares the belief that man's wretchedness is due simply to ignorance; it is due rather to sin. Man cannot be saved by the acquisition of cosmological secrets; no such secrets are given in the gospel.[4] In fact the parallelism between the Johannine and gnostic language may be misleading; in John as in Paul the real medium of salvation is faith.[5]

---

[1] See *Essays*, 62–5.

[2] See the note on Christ as the Passover in Lightfoot, 349–56.

[3] See above, pp. 75ff.

[4] Cf. the profound remark of Bultmann (*Theology*, II, 66): 'Jesus as the revealer of God reveals nothing but that he is the revealer'.

[5] Bultmann, 489, rightly quotes Schlatter: 'By only giving us Jesus' word to the disciples in the form of farewell discourses, John has made very clear where the most important question of faith lies for him, i.e. in the fact that the community is separated from Jesus and has to believe in one whom it does not actually know or see'.

The verb πιστεύειν is used almost synonymously with γινώσκειν (e.g. 6.69; and cf. 17.3 with 3.15 and many other passages),[1] and knowledge itself implies relationship in addition to cognition: to know God is to be united with him (see the note on γινώσκειν and εἰδέναι cited above). On eternal life, to which faith and knowledge lead, see on 1.4; 3.15.

5. SACRAMENTS

Unlike the Synoptic Gospels, the Fourth contains no specific command of Jesus to baptize, and no account of the institution of the eucharist; neither rite is explicitly mentioned. Yet it has been held that there is more sacramental teaching in John than in the other gospels. John uses regularly categories of thought that might seem favourable to the development of sacramental theology. We find not only a notable use of symbolism, but also an insistence upon the significance not of the material as such but of the material circumstances of Jesus. The Word became flesh; flesh became the vehicle of spiritual life and truth, and history became charged with a supra-historical meaning. The incarnation was itself sacramental in that it visibly represented truth and at the same time conveyed that which it represented. This thought, fundamental as it is with John, needs only to be compared for a moment with the messianic categories of the Synoptic Gospels in order to appear at once as a promising soil for sacramental thought. Yet, paradoxically, the opposite conclusion might be drawn. If it is true that the Word of God became flesh, what room is left for minor manifestations of the divine in the material? Will not the great, the ultimate, sacrament drive out the minor ones? If John's thought provides suitable categories for the development of sacramentalism is it not the more striking that he does not refer to Christian baptism (in the sense of a rite to be performed after the resurrection of Jesus) or to the Lord's Supper? May it turn out to be true that John's thought so far from being favourable to the development of sacramental theology is in fact the negation of it?

It is not surprising that the place of the sacraments in Johannine theology has been evaluated in very different ways. According to some, sacramentalism is the essence of his thought. 'The Logos-Christ points in the clearest words to baptism and the eucharist, and declares that the rebirth from water and the Spirit, and the eating and drinking of the flesh and blood of the Son of man, are necessary to salvation' (Schweitzer, 352). Others hold that while John was 'affected with the sacramental ideas, against which, in their crude and unreasoned form, he makes his protest,' his own was a 'higher, more spiritual view'.[2] That is, though John could not escape the weight of the church's sacramentalism, he

---

[1] Cf. Bultmann, 435: 'γινώσκειν is nothing less than a factor in the structure of faith itself, namely faith in so far as it understands itself'.

[2] E. F. Scott, *The Fourth Gospel, its Purpose and Theology* (1920), 125.

did his best to spiritualize what he found, to emphasize in the sacraments the work of the Holy Spirit and to minimize that of the water, bread, and wine. More recently, Bultmann[1] has taken the view that genuine Johannine thought has no room for sacraments; where they appear to be alluded to (especially 3.5; 6.51c–58), the work of an ecclesiastical redactor, concerned to make the gospel more palatable to sacramentally minded readers, is to be inferred. Dr Cullmann,[2] on the other hand, sees allusions to sacraments in many places, and thinks them central in John's Christian belief. W. Michaelis[3] takes a middle way, and many writers since have said, in effect, that John is more of a sacramentalist than Bultmann allows, less than Dr Cullmann. It may be doubted whether any of these lines, even the middle one, is exactly right.

If it is true that 19.34 in its account of the effusion of blood and water from the side of Jesus contains an allusion to baptism and the eucharist (and the allusion is not certain), the verse provides a good illustration of John's attitude to the sacraments. These do not spring from religious experience, even from the exalted experience of Jesus himself, but from the historical scene of human obedience, suffering, and death which manifested the humble and ministering love of Jesus for his own. It is hardly too much to say that all the reasonably certain allusions to the sacraments in John spring from this context of the real humanity and the real humility of Jesus.

For baptism we must look primarily at 3.1–15, where the reference to a birth from above which takes place ἐξ ὕδατος καὶ πνεύματος[4] suggests awareness of the Christian rite. If the double reference to water and Spirit is authentically Johannine it must be set in the light of the whole paragraph, which continues past the description of the life begotten from the Spirit, and past Nicodemus' incredulous objection, to the basis of the doctrine of rebirth in the descent and ascent of the Son of man; it is in him (v. 15) that men have eternal life, and to that end he must be lifted up both upon the cross and to heaven. That is, baptism as a life-giving rite arises out of and depends upon the incarnation and death of the Son of man. Again, there may be an allusion to baptism in the feet-washing of 13.1–11; if this is so, it must be noted that the feet-washing represents the humble love of Jesus for those whom he had called; having loved his own, he loved them εἰς τέλος (13.1). It is possible that 20.23 refers to the remission of sins in baptism. The charge given in this verse is indeed given by the glorified Jesus after

---

[1] *Theology*, ii, 58f.; but note the often unobserved qualification in the Commentary (472): 'If the Evangelist did come to terms with the sacraments, he can only have understood them in the sense that in them the word is made present in a special way.' See also below.
[2] See especially *Early Christian Worship* (1953): *Les Sacrements dans l'Evangile Johannique* (1951).
[3] *Die Sakramente im Johannesevangelium* (1946).
[4] For the authenticity of the reference to πνεῦμα see the note, pp. 208f.

his resurrection, but it must be recalled that at the beginning of the paragraph he shows to the ten disciples his hands and his side (20.20), indicating that it was by the suffering of death that he came into his glory. Baptism, then, though he did not himself practise it (4.2), was rooted in the real human existence, and hence especially in the real death, of Jesus.

The most certain allusions to the eucharist are found in chs. 6 and 15. In ch. 6 the feeding of the multitude is recounted in language substantially Marcan. Later, the incident is recalled (6.26) and its meaning discussed and debated at some length. After reference to the manna eaten by Israel in the wilderness Jesus speaks of the true bread that comes down (καταβαίνειν) from heaven which men must eat if they are to live. With the notion of the bread that 'comes down' from heaven is interwoven the fact that Jesus came down' (καταβαίνειν) from heaven. Thus (6.33) the bread of God *is* he that comes down out of heaven and gives life to the world. Jesus is the bread of God not in his heavenly but in his incarnate life. Moreover, he came down in order to be obedient to the Father's will (6.38 . . . οὐχ ἵνα ποιῶ τὸ θέλημα τὸ ἐμὸν ἀλλὰ τὸ θέλημα τοῦ πέμψαντός με). The sacrifice of obedience offered by Jesus to the Father includes his sacrificial death: ὁ ἄρτος δὲ ὃν ἐγὼ δώσω ἡ σάρξ μού ἐστιν ὑπὲρ τῆς τοῦ κόσμου ζωῆς (6.51). The sacrificial sense of ὑπέρ is reinforced by the mention of the blood of Christ which appears immediately afterwards (6.53).

The treatment of the vine, in ch. 15, which may also have eucharistic significance, moves in a similar direction. This allegory of incorporation into Christ might seem at first to bear a purely mystical interpretation: μείνατε ἐν ἐμοί, κἀγὼ ἐν ὑμῖν (15.4). But it soon appears that union with Christ and in Christ cannot be adequately expressed without the use of ethical terms, and the key term is love. Nor is the thought allowed to rest here; the greatest love is shown when a man lays down his life for his friends (15.13), and it is precisely this love that Jesus shows. There is no communion, whether sacramental or mystical, that is independent of this.

The sacraments, then, so far as they appear in John, are means by which Christians are incorporated into the saving work of Christ, sharing thus in the descent of the Redeemer to an obedient death, and in his ascent through death to the glory he enjoyed with the Father before the creation. There is thus a close relation between the Johannine teaching and Paul's baptismal doctrine of crucifixion, burial, and resurrection with Christ, and his eucharistic doctrine of a rite based upon the proclamation of the Lord's death and continued in hope of his return in glory, though there is no literary ground for supposing that John had heard of Paul's terminology. The correspondence with Paul may be taken further. We owe Paul's treatment of the Supper (1 Cor. 11) to the fact that Christians in Corinth were profaning the common meal by gluttony and party spirit; also, at a deeper level (cf. 1 Cor.

10.1–13), by their belief that, with baptism, it supplied them with immunity for whatever kind of behaviour they chose to indulge in. This perversion Paul corrected by bringing the common meal into relation with the supper Jesus ate with his disciples in the night in which he was betrayed. He accepted the familiar Christian practices, but not uncritically. It is a similar critical acceptance that may be discerned in John, though, perhaps four decades later than 1 Corinthians, it not unnaturally takes a different form. The association of the common meal with the Last Supper is no longer the cure of abuse; it may rather have become a source of abuse. Men suppose that a rite recalling that solemn moment must be automatically salutary. It may be that Ignatius reflects even if he did not himself share such a view. Hence John detaches his eucharistic allusions from the Supper (which in other respects he describes in much circumstantial detail), and incorporates them in a discourse which, using in part Wisdom language and midrashic exegesis, describes Jesus as the Bread of Life. Jesus lived and died to give men not a solemn rite, but himself; and nothing less than the whole Christ is the life of men. Similarly it is easy to see behind 3.5 a situation in which men believed that baptism in water was itself sufficient to convey the new birth; no, John argues, water without the Spirit is of no avail, and birth of water and Spirit, is effective only because behind it lies the work of the Son of man.

John, then, who, like the other New Testament writers, has no word for sacrament, and can therefore hardly be supposed to have a sacramental theology or even a theology of the sacraments, does not reject or decry the practice of dipping in water or the taking together in a common meal of bread and wine; but his acceptance of them, is, in the proper, theological, sense, critical.

6. Mysticism

Of mysticism in the proper sense ('a tendency of religious feeling marked by an effort to attain to direct and immediate communion with God', *Chambers' Dictionary*) there is nothing in John. There is no communion with or knowledge of God save that contained in the Old Testament tradition and mediated through Jesus Christ. This is stated in the baldest terms: οὐδεὶς ἔρχεται πρὸς τὸν πατέρα εἰ μὴ δι' ἐμοῦ (14.6); θεὸν οὐδεὶς ἑώρακεν πώποτε· ὁ μονογενὴς υἱὸς ... ἐξηγήσατο (1.18); but it is also implied throughout the gospel. John permits no such flight from the material to the spiritual as is characteristic of mysticism; the way to God, the truth, and the life are nowhere to be found if not in the historic, carnal reality of Jesus. No one has ascended into heaven but he that came down from heaven, the Son of man (3.13); upon Jesus as ladder moves the shining traffic between heaven and earth (1.51, see the commentary ad loc.). The gospel does indeed offer communion with God, but the communion is never immediate, but always mediated through Jesus Christ.

A similar point may be made if, with Rudolf Otto, we say that 'essentially mysticism is the stressing to a very high degree, indeed the overstressing, of the non-rational, or supra-rational, elements in religion'.[1] John, on the contrary, shows a marked concern for the intellectual content of the Christian faith. The gospel as a whole is an attempt to restate Christian truth in a new intellectual idiom (see pp. 67–70, 134–144), and it is highly argumentative and controversial in form. John takes pains to emphasize the historical reality of what he describes, and insists that while the disciples were slow of heart during the ministry of Jesus (12.16) they were subsequently led by the Paraclete into all the truth (14.26; 16.13). Certainly he would not have held that the Gospel could be exhausted in rational categories; yet, equally certainly, he would have refused to set aside rational criteria and processes.

A third non-mystical feature of the gospel may be noted here. John insists forcibly upon the ethical aspect of the Christian life. The distinguishing mark by which Christian disciples may be recognized is their love for each other (13.35). It is to those who keep the word of Jesus that he and the Father manifest themselves (14.23). It is above all things imperative that men should choose to do the will of God (7.17), as Jesus himself does it (4.34). That which a disciple does in regard to Christ is to follow (ἀκολουθεῖν, 1.43, et al.), and following is, fundamentally, obedience (though it is interesting to note that ὑπακοή, ὑπακούειν do not occur in John). The life to which men are called in John is a life of obedience, conformed in love to the example of Jesus himself, an ethical life. Yet, though it would be untrue to say that ethical strenuousness is incompatible with mysticism, it is true that such a life is not characteristic of mysticism.

This threefold stress, on the mediation of Christ, on the intellectual content of Christianity, and on its ethical expression, makes it necessary to examine closely what may be meant by the term Johannine mysticism. It is certainly different from the mystical religions which flourished in the environment of the gospel. In them the final aim of mystical religion was deification; the mystic becomes so closely united with God as to become himself divine (e.g. τοῦτό ἐστι τὸ ἀγαθὸν τέλος τοῖς γνῶσιν ἐσχηκόσι, θεωθῆναι, C.H. 1, 26). A consequence of this radical change of nature is that he also becomes immortal (μεταλάβετε τῆς ἀθανασίας, ibid., 28). John on the other hand does not speak of immortality, though he almost does so at 11.25f.; here however the stress on resurrection (rather than immortality) is noteworthy. Moreover, Jesus himself is the resurrection. This is very far from an immortality in which man partakes in his own right. Still more does John

---

[1] The Idea of the Holy (1931), 22.

revolt from the language of apotheosis (in spite of 3.6; 10.34—see the notes). Man remains man, not God, even when he receives from God the gift of life.

For many reasons it is impossible to classify John with the mystics of his age, or of any age; but at the same time it must be admitted that there are mystical elements in his thought. In particular, he teaches the abiding of the Father and the Son with the believer (e.g. πρὸς αὐτὸν ἐλευσόμεθα καὶ μονὴν παρ' αὐτῷ ποιησόμεθα, 14.23) and of the Spirit with and in him (e.g. παρ' ὑμῖν μένει καὶ ἐν ὑμῖν ἔσται, 14.17); conversely the abiding of the believer in Christ is emphasized in the allegory of the Vine (15.1–6). The relation is in fact reciprocal (15.4: μείνατε ἐν ἐμοί, κἀγὼ ἐν ὑμῖν, et al.), and of course is essential to the conception of salvation which is taught in John; but it remains controlled by the notions of faith and knowledge referred to above (pp. 81f.; see also on 1.10). John knows no special class of 'mystic' Christians any more than he knows a special class of 'gnostic' Christians. The state which is described in this semi-mystic terminology is simply the state of Christian salvation, perhaps most simply represented by the ἐνεφύσησεν of 20.22. Jesus sends his apostles as he has himself been sent by the Father; he breathes into them the Spirit that has rested upon him.

John's 'mysticism' does not closely resemble, though it may be said to presuppose (see above, pp. 69f.), Paul's 'eschatological mysticism', in which being 'in Christ' means that the believer shares in the messianic kingdom inaugurated by the suffering and triumph of the death and resurrection of Jesus. Paul's mysticism rests upon a Christ who is primarily the eschatological redeemer, standing upon the boundary of this age and the age to come. The Johannine Christ may rather be described as himself the one true mystic. He is essentially one with the Father (ἐγὼ καὶ ὁ πατὴρ ἕν ἐσμεν, 10.30); he is the Son of God (υἱός, men being always τέκνα θεοῦ), and thus makes himself equal with God (ἴσον ἑαυτὸν ποιῶν τῷ θεῷ, 5.18). His communion with God is so constant and so close that no worded prayer is necessary (ἐγὼ δὲ ᾔδειν ὅτι πάντοτέ μου ἀκούεις· ἀλλὰ διὰ τὸν ὄχλον τὸν περιεστῶτα εἶπον, 11.42). He is truly immortal, since no one can take away his life; if he is to die he must lay it down of himself (10.18). If John has borrowed from contemporary mystical thought he has done so not in his description of Christians but in his portrait of Christ. The 'mystical' life of Christians (the word is misleading) is derivative and rests upon the essential relation of Jesus with the Father: ἐγὼ ἐν αὐτοῖς καὶ σὺ ἐν ἐμοί (17.23). Through his incarnate life and ministry the Son of God offers himself to faith, and those who, by this free act of divine love, come to be in him are thereby related to the Father and receive the Spirit.

7. The Holy Spirit: the Trinity

The superficial contrast and underlying unity which exist between John and the Synoptic Gospels appear perhaps most markedly in their treatment of the Holy Spirit. It is well known that in the Synoptic Gospels (especially in Mark) references to the Spirit are very few; in John they are numerous and striking. In this John stands no doubt nearer to the belief and interests of early Christian piety, but it is not for this reason alone that doubt is cast upon the genuineness of the sayings about the Spirit which he ascribes to Jesus. The question is not so much whether the Jesus who is presented in the Synoptic Gospels did speak them as whether he could have spoken them. They presuppose a considerable perspective of continuing Christian history, and it must be asked whether room for this can be found in the eschatological thought and teaching of Jesus himself.

John's doctrine of the Holy Spirit may not be reconcilable with the oldest Christian eschatology, but it is certainly integrated into his own. The sequel to the earthly life of Jesus was his return to the glory he had enjoyed before the creation of the world, and the earthly counterpart of this heavenly event was the gift of the Spirit. Previously the Spirit had not been at work (except in Jesus himself, 1.32, and, as John would no doubt have added, in the prophets; 7.39); now he became the means by which the eternal life which is God's gift to his own is realized, and herein is John's equivalent for the 'realized' eschatology which (along with futurist eschatology) is found in the Synoptic Gospels. All the Johannine statements about the Spirit are thrown into the period after the death and resurrection of Jesus, either by simple future tenses (as in chs. 14–16) or by association with elements of later church life (e.g. baptism 3.5, the eucharist 6.63). The only exception is that already during the ministry the Spirit rested upon Jesus (1.32; 3.34, though here too there is a future reference in that Jesus is the one who will baptize with the Holy Spirit; see below). These points must now be analysed.

Jesus himself is the bearer of the Spirit. This is said, not frequently, but very plainly. John does not record the baptism of Jesus, but it seems certain that he knew of it, and in the Marcan or some very similar form (see above, pp. 51f., and on 1.32). The Spirit descends upon Jesus and—a Johannine addition—abides upon him. It is unnecessary for John to record the ecstatic features which occur in some particular synoptic narratives; the Spirit rests permanently, not occasionally, upon Jesus. Like Mark, John mentions the sonship of Jesus in the same context as the descent of the Spirit upon him (1.34, if υἱός is the original reading), but no attempt is made to bring out a connection between the two relationships. It is probable that there is another allusion to Jesus' possession of the Spirit at 3.34, possible that there is another at 7.38, and conceivable that there is a fourth at 19.30. On each passage see the commentary.

Jesus is the bearer of the Spirit; he also bestows the Spirit. This is predicted directly at 1.33 (another synoptic passage), and duly takes place at 20.22 (possibly at 19.30); it is the theme of the Paraclete sayings (see below). It is of course always qualified, as we have seen, by the condition that only in the future, that is, after the death and resurrection, can the Spirit be given. The following points are worthy of note.

(i) References to the Spirit form part of what was described above as John's critical acceptance of baptism and the Lord's Supper. At 3.5 it is pointed out that not water only but the Spirit is needed for rebirth; at 6.63 that flesh alone is of no avail since it is the Spirit that gives life. In each case there is a reference back to the Baptist's perception that Jesus is the one on whom the Spirit rests, the one therefore who is able to bestow the Spirit. It is he who baptizes in Holy Spirit (1.33); his flesh is that which the Logos became (1.14) and is therefore flesh that stands not in contrast but in union with the Spirit. The Spirit is the means by which eschatological blessings (the kingdom of God, 3.5; eternal life, 6.63) are given in the present age.

(ii) Allied to this sacramental context in which John places the gift of the Spirit is the more general context of Christian worship. Christians worship God, who is Spirit, in Spirit and truth (4.23 f.; see the commentary).

(iii) The Spirit is the power at work in the church's mission and the source of its authority (20.22). The sending of apostles, a sending strictly parallel to the sending of Christ by the Father, is a central feature of the gospel (see on 20.21), but though the sending is several times alluded to in the course of the gospel, and especially in the last discourses, when it actually takes place it is preceded by the direct imparting of the Spirit by Jesus to those whom he sends. Only after they have received the Spirit can they fulfil their mission.

(iv) A number of important references to the Spirit may be collected from the last discourses, characterized by the use of the terms παρά-κλητος (on the origin and significance of this word see on 14.16)[1] and Spirit of truth. The passages are 14.16f.,26; 15.26; 16.7-15. It has been held that they are all to be regarded as insertions, that they interrupt the contexts in which they are placed, and introduce matter which, however appropriate in substance, is in form and expression out of place in the last discourses. This view can hardly be considered well founded. In the first place, it must be acknowledged that a simple consecutiveness of thought is not to be looked for in John's writings. His habit is to view a subject successively from a number of different standpoints. Thus it cannot be argued that the Paraclete passages are inconsistent with those which speak of the coming of Christ himself,

[1] Cf. H. Riesenfeld, *Ex Orbe Religionum I* (*Numen*, Supplement 21; 1972), 266-74.

and of the Father, to those who believe. The fact is that John's basic conviction is of a divine presence abiding with the Christians, and he views this basic conviction first from the eschatological standpoint of the *parousia* of Christ, and next from the standpoint of the Spirit. In the second place, if the Paraclete passages were removed there would remain not one reference to the Holy Spirit in the last discourses. It is, of course, conceivable that John should have written a set of discourses without speaking of the Spirit, but it does not seem probable. In the third place, the Paraclete passages stand where they do without the smallest evidence of textual dislocation, and no convincing hypothesis of their origin, and of the reason and method of their insertion, is forthcoming. It seems then on the whole best to treat these passages as genuine parts of the last discourses.

For a fuller exposition of the Paraclete passages reference must be made to the commentary. Here however two general, but not un-related, remarks may be made. First, John uses a good deal .of eschatological language when speaking of the Paraclete. This appears most clearly in ch. 16. The Paraclete will convict (ἐλέγξει) the world. ἐλέγχειν means 'to expose', 'to bring to the light of day', 'to show a thing in its true colours'. It is the activity of a judge and prosecuting counsel in one. The Spirit, that is to say, places the world in the position which it will occupy at the last judgement. The questions at issue are the questions reserved by the apocalypses for treatment at the last day: sin, righteousness, and judgement. It is in accordance with this that John adds, He shall announce to you the things to come (τὰ ἐρχόμενα ἀναγγελεῖ ὑμῖν, 16.13); the Spirit already proclaims the truth that will one day be manifest, and the judgement that will then be executed. In doing this the Spirit does not act independently of Christ, as if he were taking up a task which Christ had begun and had now relinquished. The life, death, and resurrection of Jesus themselves constitute an eschatological event, and a manifestation of the complete truth of God. It was for judgement that he came into the world (9.39); he could already announce the judgement of the prince of this world (12.31), faith in him (or its absence) is the criterion of sin, and his ascension is the pledge of righteousness. The Spirit's work is to bear witness (15.26) to Christ, to make operative what Christ had already effected. The Spirit is thus the eschatological *continuum* in which the work of Christ, initiated in his ministry and awaiting its termination at his return, is wrought out.

It follows from this that, secondly, the Paraclete sayings have a second *Sitz im Leben*, namely, the church, which might also, in another sense, be described as the eschatological *continuum* in which the purposes of God are being worked out. How, we may ask, does the Spirit in fact convince the world of sin, righteousness, and judgement? The answer is, primarily through the witness which the church bears to Christ, in particular, its preaching. The Spirit bears witness, and you bear witness (15.26f.); and it is through this conjoint witness that the conscience of the world is touched. The Spirit works, moreover, by revealing the truth; true notions of sin, righteousness, and judgement are brought to light over against the false notions entertained by the world; hence it is that the world is judged. But the true notions are not projected upon space. They are made known within the church, the proper sphere of the Spirit's activity (14.17). The Spirit thus relates the church positively to the truth upon which it stands, and by so doing reacts negatively upon the world, which is judged. The division between men produced by the presence of Jesus (e.g. 7.43) is perpetuated.[1]

The noun παράκλητος (unlike πνεῦμα, which is neuter) is masculine; thus in its grammatical form alone it tends to remove the Spirit from the sphere of abstract, impersonal force into that of personality. 7.39 forms a marked contrast; there πνεῦμα means not the Spirit in his personal existence (since it cannot be said that the Holy Spirit in his proper person did not exist before Jesus was glorified) but manifestations of the Spirit given to Christians. None of the earlier references in the gospel to the Spirit show the same measure of personalization as do the last discourses. It is true that even in these no doctrine of the Trinity is formulated; but the materials are present out of which the doctrine eventually grew. The three divine Persons are mentioned side by side, distinct from one another, yet akin to one another as they are not akin to man. The coming of Christ and the coming of the Spirit can scarcely be distinguished. The Spirit proceeds from the Father (παρὰ τοῦ πατρὸς ἐκπορεύεται, 15.26; cf. ὁ λόγος ἦν πρὸς τὸν θεόν, 1.1). He not only takes up the task of Christ (ἔτι πολλὰ ἔχω ὑμῖν λέγειν . . . ὅταν δὲ ἔλθῃ ἐκεῖνος . . ., 16.12f.), he may be described with Christ in mind as ἄλλος παράκλητος (14.16).

John emphasizes both the humanity of Jesus (see above, pp. 74f.) and his inferiority to the Father (5.19; 7.16; 10.29; 14.28). The latter passages are not to be simply explained away as having reference only to the humanity or incarnate life of our Lord.[2] The eternal Son (not the incarnate Jesus merely) was sent by the Father (3.17 and often), to speak the Father's words (14.10; 17.8) and to perform the Father's works (14.10). That is to say, Jesus reveals the Father; the object of his mission is to bring men to the supreme God. John's thought is paradoxical,[3] as perhaps all Christological thought must be. Since Jesus Christ reveals (not himself but) the Father, the Father is greater than he. Yet since to see Jesus is to see the Father (14.9), he is one with the Father (10.30) and equal to him (5.18); the Word shares the divine nature (θεὸς ἦν ὁ λόγος, 1.1). The incarnation, further, meant a real abating of the power and authority of the Logos. This is not to say that

---

[1] For an elaboration of some of the points in this section see *J.T.S.*, new series 1, (1950), 1–15; also G. Johnston, *The Spirit–Paraclete in the Gospel of John* (1970).
[2] See 'The Father is greater than I', 158f.
[3] See 'The Father is greater than I', 151f., 158.

John authorizes any particular modern form of kenotic theory; it means simply (and this is much more significant) that John takes seriously the sacrificial love of Christ which, though it was most clearly demonstrated in the cross, informed the whole earthly mission of the Son of God. This, however, is a veiled manifestation of something truly present (see on 1.14).

It may be that some of John's language is unguarded; the Arians found 14.28 very useful; but more than any other New Testament writer he lays the foundations for a doctrine of a co-equal Trinity.

8. THE CHURCH AND ITS LIFE[1]

Like Mark and Luke, John does not use the word ἐκκλησία. This is appropriate enough, for the church, though it may be said to have arisen out of the words and acts of Jesus, did not come into existence in any full sense until after his death and resurrection. John does, however, show, more clearly than any other evangelist, an awareness of the existence of the church. At times this awareness becomes quite explicit. At 17.20 Jesus prays not for the Twelve only but also for those who should believe through their word; and at 20.29 he pronounces a blessing upon these believers who have not seen. In these passages John writes in terms of his own time. There are other indications of conditions which did not come into being until after the crucifixion and resurrection. The Christians are assumed to exist as a body standing over against Judaism (note the use of οἱ 'Ιουδαῖοι; see on 1.19). This is a contrast which John brings out more frequently from a theological than from a historical standpoint. The Jews, for example, are not true descendants of Abraham but children of the devil (8.44); they were Christ's 'own', to whom he came, but they did not receive him, and in consequence there arose a new generation of the children of God, begotten by no human agency but of God himself (1.11–13). The old church of Israel was rejected, or rejected itself, and a new church was brought into existence. This two-fold theme constantly recurs throughout the gospel and is one that helps to bind together the Prologue and the rest of the book. The great controversies end in division. For example, at 3.19–21 the discourse on birth from above resolves itself in a judgement, a distinction between ὁ φαῦλα πράσσων and ὁ ποιῶν τὴν ἀλήθειαν; ch. 9, with its sign, leads up to the distinction between the blind who are made to see, by Christ, and those who claim to see and are blinded—by Christ. Here also judgement is stressed: εἰς κρίμα ἐγὼ εἰς τὸν κόσμον τοῦτον ἦλθον (9.39). The origin and progress of the Gospel consist in the supplanting of the Jewish church by the Christian.

This point is expressed by John theologically; but there is good

---

[1] See G. Baumbach, *Kairos* 14 (1972), 121–36; K. Haacker, *Theologische Zeitschrift* 29 (1973), 179–201.

evidence that he was also aware of it as a historical fact. It is probable that the controversial dialogues in the gospel reflect the course of Christian anti-Jewish polemic; Jewish objections to Christian theology, and especially to Christian views of the person of Christ, are stated, and strongly, sometimes fiercely (e.g. 8.39–59), rebutted. Clearer still are references to Jewish excommunication of Christians (ἀποσυνάγωγος, 9.22; 16.2; see the notes and p. 127, below), and to persecution. There can be little doubt that John has in mind here the situation of the church at, and before, his time.[1]

The church, presupposed in the writing of the gospel, had its origin in the mission of the apostles by the Lord himself. They were to be witnesses (15.27); they were chosen and appointed to bear fruit (15.16); they were intended to speak of Christ and by their speech (τοῦ λόγου αὐτῶν) to cause others to have faith in him (17.20). The authority given them to remit and retain sins (20.23) implies the existence of a community of pardoned sinners called into being by the apostolic testimony. In 21.15–17 Peter is given a special commission to tend the flock of God. The Paraclete's work of convincing the world (16.8) is doubtless thought of as effected, at least in part, by the apostles' preaching. It was no longer necessary for John (as it had been necessary for Paul) to argue that the apostolic mission should be directed not to Jews only but also to Gentiles. The Gentile mission is presupposed in the rejection of the Jews, and though John on the whole retains the historical perspective of the ministry of Jesus he lays great stress on Jesus' work among the Samaritans (4.4–42), concluding his account with the Samaritans' pronouncement that Jesus is the *Saviour of the world*, and also uses the arrival of the Greeks who wish to see Jesus (12.20f.) as the dramatic cue for the climax of the ministry. Moreover, a universal mission is implied in the use of the Logos-Christology.

We may say then that John writes with an awareness of the church which was born of the passion and glorification of Jesus. Earlier the church could not exist, since its scattered members were drawn together by the death of Jesus (11.52; cf. 12.32), and only by the gift of the Spirit, which was subsequent to the earthly ministry (7.39), could they understand and appropriate what Jesus had done. Yet John constantly, and rightly, finds the church prefigured in the period of the ministry. Primarily it is prefigured by the disciples. Of the last supper it is true that 'the Twelve[2] sat that evening as representatives of the Ecclesia at large' (Hort, 30); and the remark could be generalized. The disciples are primarily believers (2.11), men who have found that Christ has the words of eternal life (6.68). No more than the church do they exhibit a

---

[1] The best attempt to provide a specific *Sitz im Leben* for the gospel is that of Martyn; see pp. 137f. It may be questioned, however, whether it does justice to the range of the evangelist's background and intention.

[2] So Hort. John does not say explicitly that it was only the Twelve who shared the last supper with Jesus. See p. 438.

uniform perfection. They are slow of understanding (14.9), they forsake their Master (16.32), and one of them is a devil (6.70). They are accompanied by groups of believers who also prefigure the church, especially the Samaritans, who are first converted by the report of the Samaritan woman and with whom Jesus subsequently abides (4.39–42).

It must however be added that the disciples, while they prefigure the church, also occupy a special position within it. It has already been remarked that the church had its origin in the mission of the apostles. It is also true that the church inherited the mission, but not true that the later church could exercise it in the same way as those who became the apostles. They were witnesses ὅτι ἀπ' ἀρχῆς μετ' ἐμοῦ ἐστε (15.27). This qualification could not be inherited. A blessing is rightly pronounced upon those who, not having seen, nevertheless believe (20.29); but necessarily these later believers can believe only through the word of those who had both seen and believed (17.20). The Eleven (with Mary Magdalene) were the witnesses of the resurrection, and to them (see 20.19,26) Jesus committed the Spirit with the authority to remit and retain sins. On the relation between the mission of the Son from the Father, and the mission of the disciples from the Son, see on 20.21.

So far the apostles form a distinguished and important company, but it would be quite wrong to view them only in this light. Their own personal significance is nothing, or even negative. It has been said that Mark 'hates the Twelve'. The same remark (with the same necessary qualification and explanation) could be made about John. The disciples did not choose to be followers of Jesus; he chose them (15.16). No man, indeed, is able to come to Christ unless he be drawn by the Father (6.44). In spite of their long companionship with Jesus they fail even at the end to perceive the true subject of his revelation (14.9); and when at length they triumphantly proclaim their confident faith they are met by the devastating reply: Ἄρτι πιστεύετε; ἰδοὺ ἔρχεται ὥρα καὶ ἐλήλυθεν ἵνα σκορπισθῆτε ἕκαστος εἰς τὰ ἴδια κἀμὲ μόνον ἀφῆτε (16.31f.). The only meaning John will allow to apostleship is a strictly theological meaning. If the apostle ceases to be in as completely obedient a subjection to Jesus as Jesus was to the Father, if his own personality rather than the Spirit of God assumes dominance, he at once forfeits his position and, like Judas, goes out into the night. The word ἀπόστολος occurs once only in John (13.16), and there only in the warning that a 'sent man' is not greater than the one who sent him; he must therefore be prepared to fulfil his mission in humiliation and rejection. It is in this sense that the apostles are witnesses, qualified and equipped for a specific mission. The fact to which they witness is the foundation of the church through the work of Christ; and their mission, which is in effect the manifestation of the divine life in the world, constitutes the existence of the church.

The church itself, like the apostolic group to which it is heir, consists of the gathered children of God (τὰ τέκνα τοῦ θεοῦ τὰ διεσκορπισμένα,

11.52). It is beside the point to ask whether these persons were from the beginning of time children of God in virtue of some divine Logos residing in them, or only became children through the death of Jesus. John lays down clearly that the right to become a child of God can be given only by God and has nothing to do with natural human properties (1.12), and that rebirth as a child of God comes by water and Spirit (3.5). Sonship then is a gift which men receive from God, and which has been made possible by Jesus alone. But, equally, their becoming sons is not the haphazard chance of a moment. There are those who are Christ's sheep, even though they must be brought by him into the flock (10.16); there are those who are of the truth and therefore hear his voice (18.37). He comes to Christ who is drawn by the Father (6.44); he chooses Christ who has already been chosen by him (15.16). John does not employ Paul's predestinarian language, but that very vigour with which he thrusts the person of Christ back into eternity carries back also into the infinite depths of the divine mind the redemption of the church.[1] According to John as well as 1 Peter, Christians are 'elect according to the foreknowledge of God the Father' (1 Peter 1.2).

The Christians are thus elected and called in order that they may offer to God a pure worship in Spirit and in truth (4.23f.). This pure worship consists in the unity of men in Christ, and thus both with one another and with God, and in obedience to God through Christ. This unity is the object of the prayer of Jesus (17.22f.). In ch. 4, soon after the saying about God's search for true worshippers, Jesus himself says, Ἐμὸν βρῶμά ἐστιν ἵνα ποιῶ τὸ θέλημα τοῦ πέμψαντός με καὶ τελειώσω αὐτοῦ τὸ ἔργον (4.34); and when (6.28) men ask how they may work the works (ἔργα) of God, he replies Τοῦτό ἐστιν τὸ ἔργον τοῦ θεοῦ, ἵνα πιστεύητε εἰς ὃν ἀπέστειλεν ἐκεῖνος (6.29). To have faith in Christ is to offer to God the perfect sacrifice of perfect obedience. He himself is the centre and the means of the worship of God. When he declared (2.19), Destroy this temple and in three days I will raise it up, he was speaking, John notes (2.21), of the temple of his body. It is not easy to say (see the notes ad loc.) whether this means the physical body of Jesus or his body the church; on either view he substitutes himself for the Temple; he is man's access to God (14.6) and by him men offer worship to God.

The life of Christians thus described is necessarily ethical. It is true that the 'work of God' as defined in John is not the achievement of moral qualities but faith in Christ; but faith in Christ, since it means acceptance of the light, cannot fail to have ethical implications. The only command stressed by John as unavoidably and unequivocally imposed upon Christians is the command of love (see especially 13.34; 15.12); but even here it is important to observe that this love must be shown within the Christian body not simply because it is good in itself

[1] J. & Q. 95, 116 oversimplify the problem of Johannine predestination; on this see Essays, 62–5.

but primarily because to show it is part of the task of manifesting the divine life to the world. Just as love is the inward nature of, as well as emanates from, the Godhead, so love must be the mutual relation of Christians within the church. John has been accused of narrowing the scope of Christian love in that he speaks of love for one's friends, for one another, rather than for enemies (see Käsemann, *Testament*, 59f.). There is some formal substance in the charge, but it is in the end superficial. One of the objects of the special mutual love of Christians is that the world may thereby recognize their discipleship to Jesus, come to believe, and so be incorporated in the circle of love. See the notes on 13.34; 15.12. It may however be said that John's understanding, and especially his expression, of love was such as might lead to an exclusiveness that reversed the attitude of Jesus himself. Further movement in this direction may be seen in the Johannine epistles.

Finally, it should be noted that John's doctrine of the church is summed up in the two great symbolic discourses, that of the Shepherd (10.1–16) and that of the Vine (15.1–6). For full expositions see the notes on the passages. Here it must suffice to indicate that they bring out clearly and vigorously the facts that have been collected from the gospel as a whole. Everything rests upon Christ: the good shepherd lays down his life for the sheep (10.11); he came that they might have life (10.10). The life Christians enjoy exists only in him; apart from him they can do nothing (15.5). The sheep are brought by the shepherd into the fold as the Christians are gathered by Christ to himself; here the Gentile mission is represented (10.16). Christians who are all so closely united to Christ must be united in love to one another. They obey Christ, follow him, love him, and trust him. Since the Vine symbolism may have a special eucharistic background, it may be that John sees a special crystallization of the church's unity in God through Christ in an action wherein God imparts himself to men, who can live only in him, and men offer themselves to God in an obedience which can become operative and fruitful (15.8,16) only through the gift which God has already given.

9. JOHANNINE THEOLOGY[1]

It is possible to extract from the gospel John's views about various theological topics. It did not, however, occur to John himself to offer his readers a work in the form of a Systematic Theology, with chapters on Eschatology, Christology, Salvation, the Holy Spirit, and so forth. The systematic theologians of later years have done well to draw heavily on the Johannine literature,[2] but John himself is not one of their num-

---

[1] See pp. 139–44; also *Prologue; Essays*, 49–69; 'The Father is greater than I'; 'Menschensohn'; 'Theocentric', and, among other works not cited elsewhere, the two volumes by F. M. Braun, *Jean le Théologien: Sa Théologie I* (1966) and *II* (1972).

[2] See T. H. L. Parker's paper on Barth's use of John (*Studies in the Fourth Gospel*, ed. F. L. Cross (1957), 52–63).

ber. In him we find theology still in the classically formative stage of its development. It is therefore not surprising that interpretation of the gospel should pass from one phase to another, none of them to be dismissed as simply erroneous and misleading.[1] A generation ago Bultmann gave unsurpassable expression to an interpretation of Johannine thought in terms of existential anthropology. The gospel was a historicization and Christianization of a gnostic myth which presents the truth about human existence *coram Deo*. There is in this exposition much of permanent value which no student of John can afford to ignore. Since Bultmann's *Commentary* and *New Testament Theology* Johannine interpretation has moved in the direction of Christology; of this an extreme example occurs in the work of Dr Käsemann. That the figure of Jesus Christ is central in John's thought needs no demonstration; again, attention has been rightly drawn to an important Johannine theme. Yet it is also true, and of fundamental importance, that Jesus, central as he is, constantly points away to one other than himself. He, as the Son, does nothing of himself but only what he sees the Father doing. His words are not his; they come from one who sent him. On this one he is dependent, to this one he is obedient. The gospel is about Jesus, but Jesus (if one may put it so) is about God. The gospel is in the fullest sense of the term a *theological* work. John was concerned to confront his readers through Jesus with God.[2]

From the earliest days of Christianity two traditional streams may be distinguished. There was a historical tradition of things done and said by Jesus of Nazareth; we meet this in a relatively late and developed form in the Synoptic Gospels. There was also a theological tradition of beliefs, expressed in a variety of ways, about one who was the Lord in heaven, Redeemer and eschatological Saviour; the earliest traces of this tradition are to be found in the Pauline epistles. The traditions may be distinguished but they were never wholly separate, for the fundamental Christian proposition was that Jesus of Nazareth was the Lord, the Lord was Jesus. The Synoptic Gospels are theological works expressing faith in the risen, glorified, exalted Lord Jesus, and Paul, though he has next to nothing to say about the historical Jesus, clearly believed in his existence: no one can die (and the death of Jesus is central in Paul's preaching and theology) unless he has first lived. It is a not unfamiliar assertion, and it is certainly true, that John once for all clamped the traditions together; it may be worthwhile to look at his reasons for doing so, and the way in which he accomplished his task.

The historical tradition was inevitably open to non-theological

---

[1] For what follows see 'Theocentric', 361ff., also M. L. Appold, *The Oneness Motif in the Fourth Gospel* (1976), 2–8.

[2] It was the great achievement of E. C. Hoskyns in his posthumous commentary, and of his editor, F. N. Davey, to have grasped this truth and given it classical expression.

interpretation. This does not mean that anyone in the first century adopted anything like the kind of attitude that is familiar in modern rationalistic and liberal treatments of the figure of Jesus. He may well have been viewed, almost certainly was viewed by some, as a θεῖος ἀνήρ, a supernatural figure endowed by uncritical credulity with the power to work all sorts of miracles. He could equally be regarded as a Messiah conceived in political rather than theological terms. There is little evidence, apart from the use of the word Rabbi and its equivalents, that he was thought of simply as one of the great company of the doctors of the Law, but there may have been some who so estimated him. More will have looked back to a great supernatural figure of the past, founder and head of a new religion, a fountain head of saving gnosis. This view is not far removed from the corresponding opposite tendency to give a non-historical interpretation to the theological tradition. This does not mean a denial that events such as those reported in the gospels took place; no one, even those who adopted a docetic Christology, denied the historical reality of these events—at least in the sense that they appeared to beholders to happen. It was however held that their significance was purely symbolic; it did not matter whether they happened in history or not. The truth they represented was non-historical truth, which could be manifested in history but did not belong within history or affect history.

Over against this attitude, which cannot here be demonstrated in relation to the sources, John insisted upon the history of Jesus and upon interpreting it in terms of God. This is not an affirmation of the historical accuracy of John's account; the Fourth Gospel in fact adds little to our knowledge of the historical Jesus. It recognizes the facts that, according to John, the Word became flesh—historical human existence—and that the Word that became flesh was God. This again is not an affirmation in simple terms that Jesus the carpenter was God. Inevitably John was caught in the dilemma referred to above (see p. 71). 'The Father is greater than I'; 'I and the Father are one'. There is no straightforward, clearcut Christology in John (though the gospel is full of Christological material) because John was not setting out to produce a Christology: he was writing about Jesus in terms of God, and, correspondingly, about God in terms of Jesus. He adopted the standpoint of 2 Cor. 5.16:[1] Christ is not to be estimated κατὰ σάρκα. He existed as σάρξ, but to estimate him on the basis of σάρξ is to err. He pronounces ἐγώ εἰμι,[2] not to identify himself with God in any exclusive and final sense, but to draw attention to himself as the one in whom God is encountered and known.

In the last paragraph 2 Cor. 5.16 was quoted. In this verse Paul not only declares that he will henceforth no longer know Christ κατὰ

---

[1] See the note on this verse in my *Commentary on the Second Epistle to the Corinthians* (1973).
[2] See on 6.35; 8.24; and above all Bultmann, 225f.

σάρκα; he knows, understands, no man κατὰ σάρκα. His theological understanding of Christ opens to him the possibility of a new under-standing of human, and especially of Christian, existence as a whole. This universal point of view John also shared. He has acquired, and in his gospel sets out, a theological understanding of Jesus; he has also acquired, though he can set forth only indirectly, a theological under-standing of the church and of Christian existence. Dr Käsemann (see pp. 138f.) believes that the Johannine circle consisted of a coterie of enthusiasts, united by and insisting on a common spiritual experience as the foundation of their religion and the basis of their unity, and standing over against the developing catholic church, organized and disciplined as an institution. Here are two views of the church, of each of which it may be said that it interprets the church in terms of itself. Whatever may be said about the Johannine epistles, which probably did not come from the evangelist's hand (see pp. 59–62), the gospel represents neither of these interpretations, but insists on knowing no man κατὰ σάρκα, in an inward-looking, self-contained way. Even the κόσμος, which comes as near as anything in John to being thought of as an anti-God, makes sense only in that it is the object of God's love; it is the God whom no one has ever seen who is seen when men look at Jesus, and heard when they listen to his word. Theme after theme is taken up and set in this light: the figure of Christ himself (He that has seen me has seen the Father, 14.9); his teaching and his works of compassion (The word that you hear is not mine, but the Father's who sent me, 14.24; The Father who abides within me does his own works, 14.10); his call of disciples (Thine they were and thou gavest them me, 17.6); baptism and the Lord's Supper (see above), with images such as bread (My Father gives you the true bread from heaven, 6.32) and vine (My Father is the husbandman, 15.1); Jewish rites such as Sabbath (My Father is at work up to this moment, and so am I, 5.17); the issues of life and death (Father, I thank thee that thou heardest me, 11.41); crucifixion and resurrection (Father, the hour has come; glorify thy Son, that the Son may glorify thee, 17.1). Should we say that John's theological understanding has been quickened by his grasp of the Jesus of history, or that his grasp of Jesus has been illuminated by his theology? If we could put the question to him John would probably de-cline each alternative, on the ground that each implies a separation between two inseparable elements which cohere in a single apprehen-sion of truth. The story of Jesus requires that, just as God must be understood in terms of Jesus, so the humanity of Jesus, and with that the humanity of the race, must be seen and understood in terms of God. For God and for man the future lies only in the unity of the two, a unity to which the figure of Jesus points.

5

THE ORIGIN AND AUTHORITY OF
THE GOSPEL

1. John the Apostle

THE traditional account of John's later life and literary activity first appears in the writings of Irenaeus, bishop of Lugdunum in Gaul (c. A.D. 130–200). Two of the most important passages are quoted by Eusebius (*H.E.* III, xxiii, 3f.); the original sources are *adv. Haer.* II, xxii, 5, and III, iii, 4.

The former [Irenaeus] in the second book of his work *Against Heresies*, writes as follows: 'And all the elders that associated with John the disciple of the Lord in Asia bear witness that John delivered it [the gospel] to them. For he remained among them until the time of Trajan.' And in the third book of the same work he attests the same thing in the following words: 'But the church in Ephesus also, which was founded by Paul, and where John remained until the time of Trajan, is a faithful witness of the apostolic tradition.'

Adv. Haer. III, iii, 4 is given more fully in Eusebius, *H.E.* IV, xiv, 3–8, where Irenaeus gives his authority.

But Polycarp also was not only instructed by apostles, and acquainted with many that had seen Christ, but was also appointed by apostles in Asia bishop of the church of Smyrna. We too saw him in our early youth; for he lived a long time, and died, when a very old man, a glorious and most illustrious martyr's death, having always taught the things which he had learned from the apostles, which the Church also hands down, and which alone are true. To these things all the Asiatic churches testify, as do also those who, down to the present time, have succeeded Polycarp, who was a much more trustworthy and certain witness of the truth than Valentinus and Marcion and the rest of the heretics. He also was in Rome in the time of Anicetus and caused many to turn away from the above-mentioned heretics to the Church of God, proclaiming that he had received from the apostles this one and only system of truth which has been transmitted by the Church. And there are those that heard from him that John, the disciple of the Lord, going to bathe in Ephesus and seeing Cerinthus within, ran out of the bath-house without bathing, crying, 'Let us flee, lest even the bath fall, because Cerinthus, the enemy of the truth, is within.' And Polycarp himself, when Marcion once met him and said 'Knowest thou us?' replied, 'I know the first born of Satan.'

The sentence quoted above follows.

The relation between Irenaeus and Polycarp is treated more explicitly in Irenaeus' letter to Florinus (quoted by Eusebius, *H.E.* v, xx, 4–8). Irenaeus is rallying Florinus on his divagations from orthodoxy. His gnostic doctrines were not those which he received from his earliest teachers. Irenaeus proceeds:

For when I was a boy, I saw thee in lower Asia with Polycarp, moving in splendour in the royal court, and endeavouring to gain his approbation. I remember the events of that time more clearly than those of recent years. For what boys learn, growing with their mind, becomes joined with it; so that I am able to describe the very place in which the blessed Polycarp sat as he discoursed, and his goings out and his comings in, and the manner of his life, and his physical appearance, and his discourses to the people, and the accounts which he gave of his intercourse with John and with the others who had seen the Lord. And as he remembered their words, and what he heard from them concerning the Lord, and concerning his miracles and his teaching, having received them from eyewitnesses of the 'Word of life', Polycarp related all things in harmony with the Scriptures. These things being told me by the mercy of God, I listened to them attentively, noting them down, not on paper, but in my heart. And continually, through God's grace, I recall them faithfully. . . .

Thus Irenaeus appears to claim a direct contact with the apostle, mediated only by the venerable Polycarp of Smyrna, when he writes: 'Afterwards [*sc.* after the writing of the other gospels] John, the disciple of the Lord, who also reclined on his bosom, published (ἐξέδωκε) his gospel, while staying at Ephesus in Asia' (*adv. Haer.* III, i, 1; quoted in Eusebius, *H.E.* v, viii, 4).

This testimony of Irenaeus is simple and complete: John the son of Zebedee (for no other John can be meant) was the beloved disciple; he lived to a great age in Ephesus, and there published the Fourth Gospel. Along with this evidence drawn from Irenaeus may be placed a statement by Polycrates, bishop of Ephesus, A.D. 189–98. He writes to Pope Victor (*apud* Eusebius, *H.E.* III, xxxi, 3, also v, xxiv, 2f.):

In Asia also great lights have fallen asleep, which shall rise again on the last day, at the coming of the Lord, when he shall come with glory from heaven and shall seek out all the saints. Among these are Philip, one of the twelve apostles,[1] who sleeps in Hierapolis, and his two aged virgin daughters, and another daughter who lived in the Holy Spirit and now rests at Ephesus; and moreover John, who was both a witness (μάρτυς) and a teacher, who reclined upon the bosom of the Lord, and being a priest wore the sacerdotal plate (πέταλον).[2] He also sleeps at Ephesus.

[1] Polycrates appears to confuse Philip the Apostle with Philip the Evangelist—an error which does nothing to increase confidence in his other remarks.

[2] πέταλον occurs in the LXX (e.g. Exod. 28.32(36)) as the rendering of ץיצ (*tsits*), '*shining thing*', plate of gold, constituting the diadem on front of high priest's mitre' (B.D.B. *s.v.*). What Polycrates meant by the word is uncertain. It is conceivable that he thought that John had been high priest (or perhaps a priest); he may have used the word with reference to the Christian priesthood; or he may have used it in some sense which now escapes us. Various suggestions are reviewed by J. V. Andersen (*St. Th.* 19 (1965), 22–9, who himself connects the term with the Nazirite institution.

Polycrates, like Irenaeus, tells us that the beloved disciple was John, and that he resided in Ephesus. A similar tradition is attested by a legend concerning John which is narrated by Clement of Alexandria in the tract *Quis Dives salvetur?*, 42 (see Eusebius, *H.E.* III, xxiii, 6–19). Later writers frequently repeat this tradition, but add to it nothing that seems reliable, and do not strengthen its authority. For passages in Clement of Alexandria and the Muratorian Canon on the writing of the gospel see pp. 114f.

What authority has the tradition preserved by Irenaeus? The New Testament knows nothing of the residence of the apostle John in Asia. 1 John is anonymous; 2 and 3 John profess to have been written by an 'Elder' (2 John 1; 3 John 1). Revelation, clearly a work which had its origin in the province of Asia, was written by a person called John, but he seems to distinguish himself from the apostles (see 18.20; 21.14). In Galatians John is found in Jerusalem (Gal. 2.9). Perhaps more important is the fact that neither Ephesians nor Acts shows any awareness of the presence of John in Ephesus. In particular, there is nothing in the speech attributed to Paul in Acts 20.18–35 (that addressed to the Ephesian elders at Miletus) to suggest that the compiler of Acts, who, no doubt, was responsible for the present form of the speech, knew that John had subsequently lent his stabilizing influence to that church. Clement of Rome, writing to the Corinthians *c.* A.D. 95, makes no mention of John. This is not surprising; but it may be true, as has been argued, that his references to the apostles imply that when he wrote they were all known to be dead (see e.g. 42, 44). This however cannot be regarded as certain. Much more important is the evidence of Ignatius, who wrote to the church of Ephesus. On the relation between John and Ignatius see further pp. 63f., 110f. Here it must be noted that in writing to the Ephesians, though Ignatius is at pains to bring out their close relation with the apostle Paul (they are 'co-initiates of Paul' who 'mentions them in every epistle', 12.2), he never refers to John; nor does he do so in any other epistle. It is very probable that if Ignatius had known of John's residence in Ephesus he would have referred to it; and it is probable that if John had indeed resided in Ephesus only a few years previously Ignatius would have known of it. This is no common argument from silence. Not only Ignatius' silence must be explained, but also the fact that he wrote to the Ephesians as he did. It is worthy of note that in the interpolated edition of his epistles, made when the later tradition was current, John is duly mentioned in the Ephesian letter (11). Polycarp, in spite of the connection between him and John alleged by Irenaeus, says nothing about the apostle in his (admittedly quite short) epistle to the Philippians; Papias mentions John, a disciple of the Lord (see below, pp. 105–9), but does not, so far as our knowledge of his writings goes, say that he lived in Asia. Justin, who may possibly have known the Fourth Gospel (see below, p. 111), has nothing to say about its author, though he attributes the Apocalypse to the apostle John, without however communicating any further information about him.

Only one piece of evidence for the Ephesian residence of John can be found which antedates Irenaeus. This is the Acts of John, written by Leucius Charinus, probably about A.D. 150–60.[1] This work came evidently from gnostic circles, and is legendary and fantastic in style. It represents John as carrying on a widespread evangelistic and pastoral ministry in Asia, including Ephesus. The material contained in the Acts is of little historical value; but it is of some importance that there were in Asia in the middle of the second century Christians (though heretical Christians) who found it at least credible that the apostle John had worked in their country.

The tradition handed down by Irenaeus has little support earlier than his own; there are, further, traces of a divergent tradition concerning the fate of John. The evidence for this alternative tradition may be briefly set out as follows:

(i) Mark 10.39. This is apparently a prophecy that the sons of Zebedee should share the sufferings of their Lord; probably that they should suffer martyrdom. It matters not at all (so the argument might run) whether the prophecy is to be regarded as a genuine prediction made by Jesus or as a *vaticinium ex eventu*; it would not have been recorded had it not been fulfilled by the time Mark was written (*c.* A.D. 70). The martyrdom of James is recorded in Acts 12.2; it may be supposed that evidence for the martyrdom of John was suppressed in the interests of the tradition given by Irenaeus.

(ii) An epitomist of the historian Philip of Side (*c.* A.D. 430) gives the following quotation: 'Papias in his second book says that John the Divine (ὁ θεόλογος) and James his brother were killed by Jews (ὑπὸ 'Ιουδαίων ἀνηρέθησαν).'[2] It cannot be held against the reliability of this quotation that the title ὁ θεόλογος is an anachronism in the mouth of Papias; such a title might easily be inserted into earlier tradition by a later writer who thought it appropriate.

(iii) Georgius Monachus (Hamartolus) (ninth century) gives a similar reference to Papias: 'Papias, bishop of Hierapolis, who was an eye-witness of him (*sc.* of John), in the second book of the Oracles of the Lord, says that he was killed by Jews (ὑπὸ 'Ιουδαίων ἀνηρέθη).'[3] Then follows a reference to Mark 10.39.

(iv) Two martyrologies suggest that James and John suffered a similar fate, perhaps at the same time.

A Syriac martyrology, drawn up at Edessa *c.* A.D. 411, commemorates Stephen the first martyr on 26 December; 'John and James the apostles

[1] See M. R. James, *The Apocryphal New Testament* (1924), 228–70; also Hennecke-Schneemelcher, II, 144–76; text in Lipsius-Bonnet, II, i, 151–216.

[2] Codex Baroccianus 142 (Oxford). See C. de Boor, *Texte und Untersuchungen* V, 2 (1888), 170. This MS. is sometimes said to date from the seventh or eighth century; M. R. James (*J.T.S.* 22 (1921), 389) ascribed it to the fourteenth.

[3] *Chronicle* III, cxxxiv, 1, according to one MS., *Codex Coislinianus* 305.

in Jerusalem' on 27 December; Paul and Simon Cephas on 28 December.[1]

The Calendar of Carthage (c. A.D. 505) probably bears a similar interpretation. It contains two references to John the Baptist, one of which must certainly be a mistake for John the apostle. Probably the error is in the entry (under 27 December) 'Commemoration of St John the Baptist, and of James the apostle, whom (quem) Herod slew.'[2]

On the basis of the evidence which has now been reviewed it has been held that it was once known in the church that John the apostle had died an early martyr death, and that the later tradition, found in Irenaeus and Polycrates, arose in circles which backed the Fourth Gospel and desired to support the theory that it was written by an apostle. It is however extremely doubtful whether the evidence is strong enough to bear the weight of this hypothesis. It is impossible to feel confidence in the witness of the epitomist of Philip and of George to the text of Papias. Neither was an accurate historian. We know that both Irenaeus and Eusebius, who adopt the view that John lived to old age in Ephesus, had read, as we have not, the whole of Papias' works. If they read there the tradition that Philip and George record they must have suppressed it in the interests of their own opinion. In fact, we are almost compelled to choose between the veracity of Irenaeus and Eusebius on the one hand, and the intelligence and accuracy of Philip and George on the other. It is a comparison which does credit to the earlier writers. If however Philip and George are discredited, the other evidence falls to the ground. The martyrologies can hardly stand as independent witnesses. Mark 10.39 must be read along with Mark 8.34; 9.1; 13.12; it is scarcely precise enough to be taken as clearly implying a martyr's death already suffered when Mark was written. It is true that the tradition of John's martyrdom solves some problems; but it is not the only possible solution, and in any case we cannot martyr the apostle for our convenience in handling critical problems. The martyrdom tradition may have arisen simply on the basis of Mark 10.39; but it is worth noting that John might have been killed by Jews in Asia as well as in Jerusalem (cf. the death of Polycarp), and it is not impossible that the tradition is so far correct.

Even if the martyrdom tradition be rejected, difficulties remain in the alternative account of John. There is no evidence for his residence in Ephesus in any orthodox Christian writer earlier than Irenaeus. It cannot but appear probable that if John had been alive in Ephesus (a great centre of Christian life and letters) in or near A.D. 100 some trace of the fact would have survived from the literature of the first half of the second century. That no such trace remains is a grave difficulty, and means that we are forced back upon the statement of Irenaeus, made on the basis of his contact with Polycarp. Is this statement as reliable

---

[1] H. Lietzmann, Die drei ältesten Martyrologien (Kleine Texte 2; 1911), 7f.
[2] H. Lietzmann, op. cit. 5f.

as it appears at first sight to be? The following considerations diminish the confidence that can be placed in it.

(i) Irenaeus made about Papias a claim similar to that which he made about Polycarp. He says (*adv. Haer.* v, xxxiii, 4, cited in Eusebius, *H.E.* iii, xxxix, 1): 'These things are attested in writing by Papias, an ancient man who was a hearer of John and a companion of Polycarp.' But this remark, as Eusebius himself shows, is contradicted by the content of Papias' own work. Papias' relations with the apostle John were (at best) second hand (see below, pp. 105–9). Now it is true that Irenaeus does not claim to have known Papias personally, as he claims to have known Polycarp; but he speaks of Papias as a companion of Polycarp, and a notable error in his account of the one Father does not inspire confidence in his report of the other. On his own showing Irenaeus was young and Polycarp very old when Irenaeus heard some of Polycarp's sermons; and while one may admit the truth of Irenaeus' views on youthful memory as regards vividness, they may well be questioned as regards accuracy. That Irenaeus, in good faith, made a mistake is a possibility to be taken very seriously.

(ii) A life of Polycarp is extant, written under the name of Pionius.[1] This work was undoubtedly written later than the time of Irenaeus, and in general its value is not great; it contains features which are certainly legendary. Yet though it seems, at least in places, to be dependent on local Smyrnaean traditions, it nevertheless says nothing of any contact between Polycarp and John. Like most hagiographs it magnifies its subject as far as possible; but it describes Polycarp as the third bishop of his see (the first having been appointed not by John but by Paul), chosen by the people, appointed by the priesthood, and ordained by bishops (22f.). It is impossible to doubt that a local biographer would have recounted Polycarp's association with John if he could have found a shred of evidence to suggest it.

(iii) Polycarp, though he quotes 1 John, shows no knowledge of the Fourth Gospel (see p. 64).

The evidence of Irenaeus must not be uncritically accepted. It must be admitted that we have no certain knowledge of the movements of John in his later years; this however does not mean that the stories of his Asiatic ministry are pure invention; some truth may lie behind them.

2. JOHN THE ELDER

In the first half of the second century Papias was bishop of Hierapolis, in Phrygia, in the province of Asia, and wrote a work in five books called 'Expositions of the Lord's Oracles', which is no longer extant as a whole. It is not easy to determine precisely the date at which this work was composed; the passage which will presently be discussed

---

[1] Text and translation in J. B. Lightfoot, *The Apostolic Fathers* ii, ii, 2 (1885), 1005–47, 1068–86.

itself bears on the question, and the other considerations do not permit a confident conclusion. The main points are the following. (*a*) Irenaeus says that Papias was a hearer of John the apostle. In this Irenaeus was probably mistaken (see above, p. 105), and his statement cannot be used in dating the 'Expositions'. (*b*) Irenaeus also describes Papias as a companion of Polycarp; this is in no way improbable, but Polycarp's life covered so wide a span that the statement is not helpful. (*c*) Papias as an opponent of gnosticism seems to presuppose a developed gnostic doctrine—perhaps a date such as that of Basilides' *Exegetica* (*c.* A.D. 130) would serve as a *terminus a quo*. (*d*) Papias' chiliasm has been held to have affected Justin. (*e*) Papias seems not to have referred to Luke. This suggests that the Marcionite heresy was not known to him when he wrote. When these arguments are kept under consideration, a date *c.* A.D. 140, with a margin of at least ten years on either side, seems as likely as any.

Some passages from the 'Expositions' are quoted by Eusebius, among them the following (Eusebius, *H.E.* III, xxxix, 3f.):

But I shall not hesitate also to put down for you along with my interpretations whatsoever things I have at any time learned carefully from the elders and carefully remembered, guaranteeing their truth. For I did not, like the multitude, take pleasure in those that speak much, but in those that teach the truth; not in those that relate strange commandments, but in those that deliver the commandments given by the Lord to faith, and springing from the truth itself. If, then, anyone came who had been a follower of the elders, I inquired into the sayings of the elders (τοὺς τῶν πρεσβυτέρων ἀνέκρινον λόγους)—what Andrew, or what Peter said (τί ᾽Ανδρέας, ἢ τί Πέτρος εἶπεν), or what Philip, or Thomas, or James, or John, or Matthew, or any other of the disciples of the Lord (ἢ τις ἕτερος τῶν τοῦ κυρίου μαθητῶν) said—and the things which Aristion and the Elder John, the disciples of the Lord, were saying (ἅ τε ᾽Αριστίων, καὶ ὁ πρεσβύτερος ᾽Ιωάννης, οἱ τοῦ κυρίου μαθηταί, λέγουσι) For I did not think that what was to be had from the books would profit me as much as what came from the living and abiding voice.

It appears at once that Papias here refers to two groups of men, and in particular to two men both of whom bore the name John, one of them being included in a list of apostles, the other mentioned in company with a person called Aristion, and distinguished by the title ὁ πρεσβύτερος. The contrast between the two groups is brought out not only by the sense but also by the grammatical construction of Papias's sentence. For the former group he uses the interrogative pronoun and a past tense (τί ... εἶπεν); for the latter, the relative pronoun and a present tense (ἅ ... λέγουσι). This distinction cannot be accidental unless Papias was a much more careless writer than we have any reason to suppose him to have been. It seems that ἅ τε ᾽Αριστίων καὶ ... ᾽Ιωάννης ... λέγουσι must mean the same as τοὺς τῶν πρεσβυτέρων ... λόγους. Into these words Papias made inquiry in the hope of finding out (indirect question) what the apostles said (τί ... εἶπεν).

The difference between Papias' two groups may now be understood. There were, first, the apostles (though Papias does not use that term), who included Andrew, Peter, John, and others; and there were, secondly, Aristion (of whom we know nothing more) and the Elder John. This latter group was valued because it was the source of information concerning the former.

It is clear that Papias stood at several removes from the apostles. He drew his information from travelling Christians who had been in contact with Aristion and the Elder John. From these travellers Papias learned the words of the elders. These words in turn enlightened him with regard to what the apostles had said. The relation may be set out in a diagram.

The apostles, Andrew, Peter, etc.

|

The elders, Aristion, John (? and perhaps others)

|

παρηκολουθηκώς τις

|

Papias

The links in this chain are clear; it remains to ask what chronological intervals they represent. Do the apostles represent the first generation of Christians, the elders the second, and Papias the third? Or does some other temporal relation obtain? It will be recalled that other evidence regarding the date of Papias is inconclusive, so that the present material may be treated on its own merits.

The key-words in this passage are ἀνέκρινον, εἶπεν, and λέγουσι, and it is important to note their tenses. ἀνέκρινον can only mean that Papias conducted his inquiries at some earlier time than the writing of his 'Expositions'. εἶπεν and λέγουσι are both dependent upon ἀνέκρινον, and, unless Papias wrote in defiance of the rules of grammar, λέγουσι must refer to speech taking place at the same time as the action of ἀνέκρινον, and εἶπεν to speech completed before it.[1] That is to say, the παρηκολουθηκότες were able to report what the elders were saying at the time of their journey and their meeting with Papias; the witness of the apostles lay then in the past. Thus it appears that (approximately) a full generation intervened between the apostles and the elders; perhaps half a generation between the elders and their followers (παρακολουθεῖν is used by Papias (*apud* Eusebius, *H.E.* III, xxxix, 15) to describe the relation between Peter and Mark), and an indeterminate period, which might well be as much as half a lifetime or more, between Papias' inquiries (made while the elders were still alive) and the writing of his book. On these grounds we may plausibly think of the

[1] See e.g. J. B. Lightfoot, *Supernatural Religion* (1889), 143; T. Zahn, *Forschungen zur Geschichte des neutestamentlichen Kanons*, VI, i, *Apostel und Apostelschüler in der Provinz Asien* (1900), 124.

generation of the apostles as coming to an end *c.* A.D. 70, that of the elders *c.* A.D. 100, the time of Papias' inquiries into the witness of the 'living and abiding voice', while his writing of the 'Expositions' may well be placed *c.* A.D. 140, as previously suggested. It must be emphasized that all these dates are to be regarded as no more than approximations.

This seems to mean that, about A.D. 100, there was living an elder[1] by the name of John, whom Papias describes, with Aristion, as a disciple of the Lord, and who was able to report the traditions of the apostles (it may have been the same elder who was the source of Papias' information about Peter and Mark). The real difficulty in this statement is the description of the elder as a disciple of the Lord. Is it conceivable that a personal disciple of the Lord lived to so great an age? It is not impossible, and indeed the lateness of the period referred to may account for the fact that while Papias' former group contains several names, and could be expanded (καὶ εἴ τις ἕτερος τῶν τοῦ κυρίου μαθητῶν), his latter contains only two names: perhaps only Aristion and John survived. If however this seems unlikely, or if, as is possible, the date of the elders ought to be brought down still further so as to make personal discipleship impossible, one of the following suppositions may be made. (*a*) Papias is simply in error: these men were not disciples of the Lord. This view is by no means impossible. (*b*) The text is corrupt. In the description of the elders we should either omit οἱ τοῦ κυρίου μαθηταί, or read instead οἱ τουτῶν μαθηταί—that is, the elders were disciples of the apostles. (*c*) μαθητής does not mean 'personal follower', but simply 'Christian'. This however is a very weak rendering, and if μαθητής is to be given a different meaning from that which it evidently has when used of Andrew, Peter, and the other apostles, perhaps the best would be 'martyr'; see Ignatius, *Eph.* 1.2; *Rom.* 4.2. Each of these suggestions is possible, but none seems decisively preferable to the view that two personal disciples of Jesus lived till *c.* A.D. 100.[2]

It is to be observed that Papias does not say where the elder John lived. It is an attractive conjecture that his home was in Ephesus, and that it was through confusion between the elder and the apostle who bore the same name that Irenaeus (wrongly) described Polycarp as a hearer of John (the apostle). But, attractive as this hypothesis may be, it would be entirely fallacious to use the statement of Papias as evidence that John the elder lived in Ephesus. Indeed, one slight but positive indication suggests the contrary. The journey between Hierapolis and

[1] It is not likely that the word πρεσβύτερος is in this connection (as often elsewhere) the title of a church official. Evidently it suggests something distinctive. 'Christians of this province [Asia] seem to have spoken of 'the Elders' (Presbyters) in referring to a group of teachers who formed a link between the apostles and the next generation (Eusebius, *H.E.*, III, xxxix, 3f.)' (C. H. Dodd, *The Johannine Epistles* (1946), 155). One might refer also to Irenaeus; see Lightfoot, op. cit., 194–202.

[2] For the text, and the meaning of μαθητής, see Zahn, op. cit., 138ff., though Zahn draws a different conclusion.

Ephesus was not great (Hierapolis was only a few miles from Laodicea, whence one of the great trade routes of antiquity ran down the valley of the Meander and turned off to reach the coast at Ephesus), and one might have expected Papias to take the trouble to visit the elder and hear for himself rather than to depend on the reports of chance travellers. But the manner in which he expresses himself in the fragment preserved in Eusebius makes it seem unlikely that Papias had met the elder.

Eusebius himself says that Papias claims to have been a hearer not of the apostles but of Aristion and the elder John, but he at once qualifies his statement, adding, 'At least (γοῦν), he [Papias] mentions them frequently by name, and gives their traditions in his writings' (Eusebius, *H.E.* iii, xxxix, 7). This is no proof at all of personal acquaintance, as Eusebius was too honest not to admit. He was however seeking support for the opinion that two Johns had lived in Ephesus, because he did not wish to admit the apostolic authorship of Revelation. He adds at this point the statement that 'there were two tombs in Ephesus, each of which, even to the present day, is called John's. It is important to notice this. For it is probable that it was the second, if one is not willing to admit that it was the first, that saw the Revelation, which is extant under the name of John' (*H.E.* iii, xxxix, 6). The tradition of the two tombs is given again in the course of a long quotation from Dionysius of Alexandria, who argued on literary grounds that the Fourth Gospel and the Revelation came from different authors (*H.E.* vii, xxv, 16: 'But I think that he [the author of Revelation] was some other one of those in Asia; as they say that there are two monuments in Ephesus, each bearing the name of John'); it reappears in Jerome, *de Vir. Ill.* 9; but it is historically worthless. Even Dionysius quotes it only as hearsay, and even if two monuments were now uncovered, both bearing the name of John, it would be necessary to prove that they both were tombs, that they commemorated different persons, and that the two persons were these two Johns.

That there was an 'Elder John' need not be doubted. There is no reason to question the integrity of Papias, and even if there were it is hard to see what he would have gained by the fabrication of such a person. But equally there seems to be no convincing ground for the belief that this elder lived in Ephesus; nor is there any positive evidence in favour of the view that he wrote the Fourth Gospel, or was in any way connected with it. It should however be remembered that the author of 2 and 3 John describes himself as 'The Elder' (ὁ πρεσβύτερος); see below, pp. 133f.

3. THE GOSPEL IN THE CHURCH

The material here may be set out in two sections: (i) evidence of the existence and use of the gospel; (ii) early statements about the way in which the gospel was composed.

(i) Early quotations of the gospel are very few, but have been supplemented by the discovery of two papyrus documents, both of which are dated[1] on palaeographical grounds not later than A.D. 150, and may well be some years earlier. Rylands Papyrus 457 is a fragment of a MS. of the gospel, containing 18.31–3,37,38. Egerton Papyrus 2 is much more extensive and contains part of what appears to have been a gospel, different from our four canonical gospels and from all other known apocryphal gospels. The question of its relation to John cannot be regarded as closed, but there seems to be good reason[2] for the view that the author of the papyrus gospel used John as one of his sources; John therefore was in existence some little time before the date of the papyrus. These two papyri were both discovered in Egypt, and it is possible to feel confident that John was known there at least ten or twenty years before the middle of the second century, and possibly a good deal earlier.

There is no other satisfactory evidence of the existence of the Fourth Gospel before A.D. 150, though other papyri (see p. 145) confirm its early circulation. For a full consideration of possible allusions to John in the apostolic fathers see *The New Testament in the Apostolic Fathers* (1905), and Sanders, *Early Church*. The latter useful book also covers the Apologists, the gnostic heretics, and Irenaeus.[3]

Only in Ignatius among the apostolic fathers are there passages which may be seriously claimed as references to John. The most important of them may be set out. On the relationship of thought between Ignatius and John see above, pp. 63f.

Mag. 7.1: ὥσπερ οὖν ὁ κύριος ἄνευ τοῦ πατρὸς οὐδὲν ἐποίησεν.

John 5.19: οὐ δύναται ὁ υἱὸς ποιεῖν ἀφ' ἑαυτοῦ οὐδέν.
8.28: ἀπ' ἐμαυτοῦ ποιῶ οὐδέν.

The resemblance here cannot of course be denied; but is it necessary to suppose that Ignatius could have learned the Son's dependence on the Father only from John? ἄνευ is not a Johannine word.

Mag. 8.2: εἷς θεός ἐστιν ὁ φανερώσας ἑαυτὸν διὰ 'Ιησοῦ Χριστοῦ τοῦ υἱοῦ αὐτοῦ, ὅς ἐστιν αὐτοῦ λόγος ἀπὸ σιγῆς προελθών, ὅς κατὰ πάντα εὐηρέστησεν τῷ πέμψαντι αὐτόν.

John 1.1: ἐν ἀρχῇ ἦν ὁ λόγος.
8.29: ἐγὼ τὰ ἀρεστὰ αὐτῷ ποιῶ πάντοτε.
7.28 (and frequently): ὁ πέμψας με

Again, there is nothing necessarily Johannine in the statement that Jesus pleased God who sent him. Other theologians used the term λόγος,

---

[1] See C. H. Roberts, *An unpublished Fragment of the Fourth Gospel in the John Rylands Library* (1935); H. I. Bell and T. C. Skeat, op. cit.

[2] See C. H. Dodd, *J.R.B.* xx (1936), 56–92; cf. G. Mayeda, op. cit.

[3] In recent years the later use of the gospel has been much discussed. See e.g. M. F. Wiles, *The Spiritual Gospel* (1960); T. E. Pollard, *Johannine Christology and the Early Church* (1970); E. H. Pagels, *The Johannine Gospel in Gnostic Exegesis* (1973).

and the words ἀπὸ σιγῆς (very characteristic of Ignatius) are not drawn from John; nor does John use φανεροῦν in the way in which it appears here.

Philad. 7.1: εἰ γὰρ καὶ κατὰ σάρκα μέ τινες ἠθέλησαν πλανῆσαι, ἀλλὰ τὸ πνεῦμα οὐ πλανᾶται, ἀπὸ θεοῦ ὄν· οἶδεν γὰρ πόθεν ἔρχεται καὶ ποῦ ὑπάγει, καὶ τὰ κρύπτα ἐλέγχει.	John 3.8: τὸ πνεῦμα ὅπου θέλει πνεῖ, καὶ τὴν φωνὴν αὐτοῦ ἀκούεις, ἀλλ' οὐκ οἶδας πόθεν ἔρχεται καὶ ποῦ ὑπάγει. 16.8: ἐλέγξει τὸν κόσμον περὶ ἁμαρτίας καὶ περὶ δικαιοσύνης καὶ περὶ κρίσεως.

With undoubted similarity there goes difference. In John, we hear what men do not know, in Ignatius what the Spirit does know. With τὰ κρύπτα ἐλέγχει cf. Rom. 2.16; 1 Cor. 4.5; 14.25; 2 Cor. 4.2; Eph. 5.11. There is nothing in these (or any other) passages to prove that Ignatius had read John; but there is a good deal to confirm the general kinship of thought which was remarked earlier (pp. 63f.).

In his relation to the Fourth Gospel Justin closely resembled Ignatius. There are undoubted similarities, but no convincing evidence of literary dependence (see Sanders, *Early Church*, 27–32, and above, pp. 64f.). The following passages deserve consideration.

1 *Apol.* 61: καὶ γὰρ ὁ Χριστὸς εἶπεν· Ἂν μὴ ἀναγεννηθῆτε οὐ μὴ εἰσέλθητε εἰς τὴν βασιλείαν τῶν οὐρανῶν.

Cf. John 3.3,5. Here it can only be said that, if Justin is using the Fourth Gospel and not some other source for the words of Jesus, he is paraphrasing rather than quoting.

Trypho 63: . . . ὡς τοῦ αἵματος αὐτοῦ οὐκ ἐξ ἀνθρωπείου σπέρματος γεγεννημένου ἀλλ' ἐκ θελήματος θεοῦ.

Cf. John 1.13. It may be that Justin should be regarded as a witness for the reading ὃς . . . ἐγεννήθη in this passage; but this reading is probably incorrect and Justin diverges from John in other respects also.

Trypho 88: πρὸς οὓς καὶ αὐτὸς ἐβόα· Οὐκ εἰμὶ ὁ Χριστός, ἀλλὰ φωνὴ βοῶντος. . .

Cf. John 1.20. The Baptist explicitly denies that he is the Christ, and himself refers to Isa. 40.3, as at John 1.23.

Trypho 91. The brazen serpent in the wilderness is a type of Christ, as at John 3.14. A similar use is made of this Old Testament figure in Barnabas 12.7; it was probably common homiletical property.

These passages do not prove that Justin had read John; yet they are sufficient to give some plausibility to that hypothesis. 'Justin's writings illustrate rather the first tentative use which was made of the Fourth Gospel by an orthodox writer, and this tentativeness makes it difficult to believe that Justin regarded the Fourth Gospel as Scripture or as the work of an apostle' (Sanders, *Early Church*, 31).

Similar allusions are found in the Homily on the Passion by Melito bishop of Sardis, writing probably A.D. 160–70.[1] There can be no doubt that Melito was familiar with gospel material peculiar to John. He alludes to the raising of a man four days dead (*Homily* 78; cf. John 11.39–44). In a description of the crucifixion in *Homily* 95 he uses the word τίτλος (John 19.19 and in no other canonical gospel), and, still more important, says that Jesus ὑψοῦ[ται ἐ]πὶ ξύλου ὑψηλοῦ; on John's characteristic use of ὑψοῦν see on 3.14. Most significant of all is the recurrence of Johannine theological themes, especially that of the Paschal lamb. *Homily* 7 brings together this and other themes: καὶ γὰρ ὁ νόμος λόγος ἐγένετο, καὶ ὁ παλαιὸς καινός, συνεξελθὼν ἐκ Σιὼν καὶ Ἰερουσαλήμ, καὶ ἡ ἐντολὴ χάρις, καὶ ὁ τύπος ἀλήθεια, καὶ ⟨ὁ⟩ ἀμνὸς υἱός, καὶ τὸ πρόβατον ἄνθρωπος, καὶ ὁ ἄνθρωπος θεός; cf. *Homily* 5, 70f.

After the time of Melito there is little difficulty in finding references to the gospel. Theophilus of Antioch, for example, writes (*ad Autolycum* II, 22; date, *c.* A.D. 180) of spirit-inspired men, ἐξ ὧν Ἰωάννης λέγει· ἐν ἀρχῇ ὁ λόγος· καὶ ὁ λόγος ἦν πρὸς τὸν θεόν (cf. John 1.1). He is the first orthodox writer to ascribe the gospel to 'John', though it must be observed that he does not say (though he may have believed) that the evangelist was an apostle. By this time, however, we have reached the age of Tatian's *Diatessaron* and of Irenaeus himself, who uses the gospel freely as the inspired and authoritative work of John the apostle, the son of Zebedee, the beloved disciple.

Echoes of the gospel have also been found in the Odes of Solomon. The theological relation between John and the Odes (as well as the date and provenance of the Odes) is discussed above (p. 65; also p. 41); here we are concerned only with coincidences or parallelisms in language, and the evidence is hardly sufficient to justify direct dependence. The following are among passages that have been adduced.

6.11f. All the thirsty upon earth were given to drink (of it): and thirst was done away and quenched: for from the Most High the draught was given. Cf. John 4.14; 7.37.

7.6. Like my nature He became, that I might learn Him, and like my form, that I might not turn back from Him. Cf. John 1.14.

8.14. I do not turn away my face from them that are mine; for I know them. Cf. John 10.14.

8.22. Pray and abide continually in the love of the Lord. Cf. John 15.7,10.

10.5. The Gentiles were gathered together who had been scattered abroad. Cf. John 11.52.

11.19. (They) have changed from darkness to light. Cf. John 8.12.

12.7. (The Word) is the light. Cf. John 1.4.

12.12. The dwelling-place of the Word is man. Cf. John 1.14.

16.19. The Worlds were made by His Word. Cf. John 1.3.

18.6. Let not the luminary be conquered by the darkness; nor let truth flee away from falsehood. Cf. John 1.5.

---

[1] See the edition by Campbell Bonner, *Studies and Documents*, XII, 1940.

30.1f. Fill ye water for yourselves from the living fountain of the Lord: for it
has been opened to you: and come all ye thirsty and take a draught; and
rest by the fountain of the Lord. Cf. John 4.10; 6.35; 7.37f.
31.5. His face was justified; for thus his Holy Father had given to Him. Cf.
John 17.1,5; 12.28.
33.4. (He) drew to him all those who obeyed him. Cf. John 12.32.
41.11–15. And His Word is with us in all our way, the Saviour who makes
alive and does not reject our souls: the man who was humbled, and was
exalted by his own righteousness; the Son of the Most High appeared in the
perfection of His Father; and light dawned from the Word that was beforetime in Him; the Messiah is truly one; and he was known before the foundations of the world, that He might save souls for ever by the truth of His
name. Cf. John 1.1–5, 14; 6.33,37; 17.5,24.[1]

The resemblances are not unlike those found in Ignatius (see above,
pp. 110f.), and prove no more than they. Community of conviction and
background seems to account for them adequately. This does not lessen
the importance of the Odes for the student of John; but the (Syriac)
Odes do not prove the existence of John as a Greek document.

The orthodoxy of the Odes may be open to question; they certainly
have contacts with gnosticism. It is the gnostic heretics themselves who
are the first to show certain traces of knowledge of John. For a full
discussion of the subject see Sanders, *Early Church*, 46–66; also Pagels,
op. cit. A fundamental piece of evidence is an exposition of the prologue
of the gospel by Ptolemaeus, a disciple of Valentinus. Into the (often
unconvincing) details of the exegesis it is unnecessary here to enter;
Sanders' conclusion may be quoted.

One may admit that the Prologue to the fourth gospel and the later, more
developed, gnostic systems have this much in common, that they employ the
same religious and philosophical or theosophical terminology. This was seen
by the Gnostics (by the Valentinians especially), and they tried to use the
fourth gospel as a mine from which to extract proof-texts. By doing this they
showed that they cannot have felt that it was anti-gnostic propaganda. They
tended to make increasing use of the fourth gospel, as is shown by a comparison of Basilides, Valentinus, Ptolemaeus and Heracleon—whose Valentinian-
ism was profoundly modified by his understanding of the fourth gospel.
Moreover, they tried by this means to vindicate their own systems as having
apostolic authority (65).

Ptolemaeus (*apud* Irenaeus *adv. Haer.* I, viii, 5) ascribes the gospel to
'John the disciple of the Lord' ('Ιωάννης ὁ μαθητὴς τοῦ κυρίου), and
Heracleon wrote a commentary on the gospel (known through Origen's
quotations). It is possible that Valentinus himself was the author of
the *Gospel of Truth*, one of the Coptic texts found at Nag Hammadi
and certainly an early Valentinian work which shows more definite

---

[1] For convenience I have used the translation in R. Harris and A. Mingana, *The
Odes and Psalms of Solomon II* (1920); slightly different renderings might occasionally
be preferable.

connection with John than do the Odes of Solomon. The following passages may be noted:

18.8. They did not know the Father. Cf. John 16.3.

18.20. The way is the truth which he taught them. Cf. John 14.6.

19.25. They hated him. Cf. John 7.7; 15.18.

21.25. Those whose names he knew in advance were called at the end. Cf. John 10.3.

22.21. He goes before them to the places which are theirs. Cf. John 10.4.

26.7. The Word was not only a sound but had taken on a body (σῶμα). Cf. John 1.14.

27.7. He revealed that of him which is hidden, he explained it. Cf. John 1.18.

30.15. Blessed is he who has opened the eyes of the blind. Cf. John 11.37.

30.34. He breathed into them that which is in the mind. Cf. John 20.22.

37.21. Nothing happens without him, nor (οὐδέ) does anything happen without the will of the Father. Cf. John 1.3.

38.10. . . . whom he has begotten as Son. He has given him his name, the name that belongs to him, the Father. . . . Cf. John 17.12.

It seems probable, though perhaps not quite certain, that the author of the *Gospel of Truth* had read John.[1]

Finally we may note that there were persons who rejected the Fourth Gospel on account of its teaching regarding the Holy Spirit (Irenaeus, *adv. Haer.* III, xi, 9). Perhaps they were opponents of Montanism,[2] perhaps they were the same as those persons whom Epiphanius (*Panarion haer.* LI, 2f.) names 'Alogi', who, he says, ascribed the gospel (and the Apocalypse) to Cerinthus (a gnostic). That there was opposition to the gospel is certain, since Hippolytus wrote a defence of the gospel and apocalypse, which is mentioned in the inscription on the statue of him erected probably in A.D. 222, discovered in 1551, and now in the Lateran Museum.

(ii) Early statements about the composition of the gospel will now be considered. Only the following are old enough to be of value.[3]

(a) *The Muratorian Canon.* This early fragment of barbarous Latin was discovered in 1740 by L. A. Muratori; it may be dated c. A.D. 180–200, and has been conjecturally ascribed to Hippolytus. The section dealing with the Fourth Gospel runs as follows:

The fourth gospel is by John, one of the disciples. When his fellow-disciples

---

[1] See my article, 'The Theological Vocabulary of the Fourth Gospel and of the Gospel of Truth', *Current Issues in New Testament Interpretation*, ed. W. Klassen and G. F. Snyder, 1962.

[2] See K. Aland, 'Der Montanismus und die kleinasiatische Theologie', in *Z.N.T.W.* 46 (1955), 109–16.

[3] At this point the first edition of this Commentary mentioned the so-called Anti-Marcionite Prologue to the Gospel, adding however that its evidence must 'be used only with the greatest caution'. For references to the literature in which it is shown that the Prologues are neither early nor, in the direct sense, anti-Marcionite see W. G. Kümmel, *Introduction to the New Testament* (1966), 341ff., or, better, the German edition of 1973, 428–31.

and his bishops exhorted him he said, Today fast with me for three days, and let us recount to each other whatever may be revealed to each of us. That same night it was revealed to Andrew, one of the apostles, that John should write down all things under his name, as they all called them to mind (*recogniscentibus cuntis*, for *recognoscentibus cunctis*; perhaps 'revised', or 'certified'). So although various points are taught in the several books of the gospels, yet it makes no difference to the faith of believers, since all things in all of them are declared by one supreme Spirit, concerning [our Lord's] nativity, his passion, his resurrection, his converse with his disciples, and his twofold advent, the first in despised lowliness, which has taken place, and the second glorious with kingly power, which is yet to come. What wonder then if John so boldly sets forth each point, saying of himself in his epistles (*in epistulis*, for *in epistolis*; perhaps 'in his epistle'), What we have seen with our eyes and heard with our ears, and our hands have handled, these things we have written (*scripsimus*)? For so he avows himself to be not only an eye-witness and hearer (reading *se et auditorem*) but also a writer of all the wonderful works of the Lord in order.

According to this narrative, the Fourth Gospel had the authority not of one apostle only but of all the apostles and there is no reason why its difference from the other gospels should trouble the believer.[1]

(*b*) Clement of Alexandria, *apud* Eusebius *H.E.* vi, xiv, 7: 'But, last of all, John, perceiving that the external facts (τὰ σωματικά) had been made plain in the gospel, being urged by his friends, and inspired by the Spirit, composed a spiritual gospel (πνευματικὸν . . . εὐαγγέλιον).' It will be noted that Clement, like the writer of the Muratorian Canon, allowed some scope to colleagues of John in the inception of the gospel.

(*c*) A third, negative, point must be added. The Leucian Acts of John, which, as has already been observed, is an early, though heretical, legendary, and prolix life of John, says nothing whatever about any literary activity on his part, though it contains what appear to be echoes of the language of the gospel (89f., 95–8, 100f., 109; Latin remains, xiv, xvii; see M. R. James, op. cit. 251–7, 261, 268).[2]

The evidence that has been briefly sketched in these pages will be briefly discussed below (pp. 123–34). It may however be said here that the reception accorded to the Fourth Gospel in the early part of the second century makes it impossible to believe that it had been published with the full authority of apostolic authorship. If it was written by an apostle, it was not known to have been so written. The narrative recorded in the Muratorian fragment is frankly incredible. It is not hereby proved that the gospel was not written by an apostle; but it is hard to see why, if it was, it was not published under his name.

---

[1] On the Muratorian Canon see A. Ehrhardt, *The Framework of the New Testament Stories* (1964), 11–36.

[2] Mrs Lieu points out to me that the Acts of John 87, 93 come near to asserting that John did *not* write a gospel.

4. DIRECT INTERNAL EVIDENCE

The gospel, headed in the earliest MSS, κατὰ ’Ιωάν(ν)ην, is itself anonymous. It mentions only one John: the Baptist, who is clearly not intended as the author. If the gospel was, or was represented as being, the work of an eye-witness, it is natural to look for the evangelist among the characters who appear in it. A difficulty at once arises, in that neither John the son of Zebedee, who is named by tradition as the writer, nor his brother James is mentioned by name; the 'sons of Zebedee' (οἱ τοῦ Ζεβεδαίου) are mentioned in 21.2, but it is possible that ch. 21 should be regarded as an appendix, from a different hand from that of chs. 1—20; see below, pp. 576f. The anonymity of the gospel, and its silence with regard to any John who might have written it, make it necessary to look into the identity of certain disciples mentioned in the course of the narrative but not named.

Of these the most important is the man described as 'the disciple whom Jesus loved'. He is mentioned in five places. At 13.23; 19.26f.; 21.7,20ff. he is the disciple ὃν ἠγάπα (ὁ ’Ιησοῦς); at 20.2 he is the disciple ὃν ἐφίλει ὁ ’Ιησοῦς. No difference is implied by the change of verb (see on 5.20; 20.2; 21.15–17); on each passage see the commentary. If in the first place we exclude the passages in ch. 21 the following observations may be made.

(i) The beloved disciple is present at the last supper. John nowhere states that only the Twelve were present at this meal, but this is suggested by his narrative, and also in the Synoptic Gospels. Accordingly it is probable that we should look for the beloved disciple among the Twelve. (ii) He is mentioned twice in close contact with Peter, and once with the mother of Jesus. (iii) There seems no good ground for the view that the beloved disciple is merely an 'ideal' figure. The information given him at the last supper, for example, is a simple fact and not a piece of esoteric doctrine. These three points are all satisfied by the hypothesis that the beloved disciple was John the son of Zebedee. Further observations, however, must be made. (iv) All three passages, regarded from the historical point of view, have secondary features. The first, at the supper, looks like an attempt (see the notes) to square the Matthaean tradition that the traitor was unmasked at the supper with the Marcan tradition that he remained unknown to the Eleven. It is both intrinsically improbable that friends and relatives of Jesus would be allowed to stand near the cross, and inconsistent with the Marcan tradition that all the disciples fled (cf. John 16.32). Moreover, in the early chapters of Acts, Mary is found not with John but with the brothers of Jesus (Acts 1.14). The visit of Peter and John to the tomb is prompted by a message brought to them by one of the women; but in the earliest tradition the women said nothing to anyone (Mark 16.8). Since however Mark certainly did not intend to represent the women as permanently disobedient to their commission the last point is not important. (v) The beloved disciple appears only in Jerusalem, whereas the sons of Zebedee were men of Galilee. (vi) In some respects the beloved disciple seems to be ranked higher than Peter; for example, it is to him that the care of the mother of Jesus is entrusted; it is he who, when he sees the empty tomb, believes and thus becomes the foundation of the believing church. Thus it must be admitted that, while the beloved disciple seems to be a designation of John the son of Zebedee, there is no evidence that the references to him were derived from him, and indeed no evidence that they rest on good historical tradition.

So much may be deduced from the first three references to the disciple whom Jesus loved. It is confirmed in ch. 21. The two incidents contained in this chapter may well have been originally separate; in any case they may be considered separately. From the first we learn that the beloved disciple was one of the group of disciples mentioned in 21.2: Peter, Thomas, Nathanael, the sons of Zebedee, and two other disciples who are not named. It is therefore at least possible, though not necessary, that the beloved disciple was John. Once more we find him in association with Peter, and gifted with keener insight, since it is he who recognizes the Lord as he stands on the shore (21.7; cf. 20.8). The same superiority to Peter appears in the second incident, since it is pointed out that this disciple was 'following' (ἀκολουθῶν, 21.20), which was what the too curious Peter had been bidden to do. Most important however is the saying attributed to Jesus (21.22), which had (wrongly, as John comments) been understood to mean that the beloved disciple would survive till the *parousia*. Clearly by this title the author of John 21 must mean a disciple who lived long enough for this legend about him to develop. On 21.24, which connects the beloved disciple with the writing of the gospel, see below, pp. 118f. We may for the present say, not with certainty but with at least some assurance, that the author of the gospel, whoever he may have been, described as the disciple whom Jesus loved, John, the son of Zebedee and one of the Twelve. The balance of probability is that a man would not so refer to himself; if this is true, the evangelist was not the son of Zebedee.

Two passages which refer to disciples who are not named must now be examined.

The first is 1.35–42. After the Baptist bears public witness to Jesus two of his disciples leave him to follow Jesus. One of the two, Andrew, next brings his brother to Jesus. Who was the unnamed companion of Andrew? It is impossible to answer this question with certainty unless the reading πρῶτος (in v. 41) be accepted. If it is, we must suppose that the unnamed disciple was one of a pair of brothers, that is, that he was either James or John. Reason is given however in the commentary for preferring the reading πρῶτον, which allows no such inference, though of course it remains possible, and indeed probable, that the evangelist did mean, by the unnamed disciple, John the son of Zebedee.

The second passage is 18.15f., where a disciple is mentioned who was γνωστὸς τῷ ἀρχιερεῖ. He is in close contact with Peter, and this lends some weight to the view that he was the disciple whom Jesus loved, though not here described by that title. This view can be neither proved nor disproved; but it can be said that if the beloved disciple, the son of Zebedee, be intended, the description gives no ground for reliance upon the author's accuracy. It is highly improbable that the Galilean fisherman was γνωστὸς τῷ ἀρχιερεῖ.

In addition to these passages which refer to disciples, any of whom might conceivably be the author of the gospel, three others which deal more or less directly with the question of authorship must be examined. They are 1.14; 19.35; 21.24. On each see the commentary.

It has been held that the use of the first person plural (ἡμῖν ... ἐθεασάμεθα) in 1.14 proves that the writer was himself an eye-witness of the ministry of Jesus. It must be admitted that this is a possible interpretation of the words in question; but it is not a necessary, nor the best, interpretation of them. Their meaning will be considered below (p. 143, and ad loc.); for the present it is sufficient to point out that John throughout the Prologue speaks primarily of the dwelling of the incarnate Logos among *men* (not among a few particular persons in Palestine), and of the witness borne to him by the apostolic church.

19.35 is more significant, and also more difficult. It must first be considered without reference to 21.24. The most probable meaning of the verse as intended by the author of the gospel is that the beloved disciple (mentioned at 19.26f.) beheld the blood and water which flowed from the side of Christ, and bore witness to what he had seen and knew to be true (see the commentary). It is not stated that the witness was the author, and though this is not ruled out by the use of the third person (ἐκεῖνος οἶδεν) it does not seem probable. It is more likely that the evangelist appeals to the witness (whom he probably identifies with the beloved disciple) as the reliable source of his information. The incident is of doubtful historicity; this is in harmony with what has been observed about the passages which explicitly mention the beloved disciple. The author of the gospel venerated the disciple as a source of information for the gospel history; but the material which he drew from this source, at least in the form in which he handed it on, was not as reliable as he suggests.

21.24, like 19.35, refers to a witness; here the witness is explicitly stated to be the beloved disciple. The 'things' to which he witnesses may be the contents of ch. 21, or the last few verses of ch. 21, or the whole gospel; probably the last is (rightly or wrongly) intended. His witness is certified by the persons responsible for the verse: '*We* know that his witness is true.' According to this verse, the beloved disciple not only bore witness concerning the matters recorded in the gospel; he wrote them (ὁ γράψας ταῦτα). This means that the beloved disciple was the evangelist, unless we are to translate ὁ γράψας as 'who caused to be written'. This translation is not impossible, and if it be accepted, 21.24

says no more than 19.35. Moreover, if 21.24 be from the same hand as the gospel as a whole, this translation is required, and the verse may be paraphrased, 'We, who are actually publishing the gospel, recognize that the authority and responsibility for it are both to be found in the beloved disciple, who gave us the necessary information, and thus virtually wrote the gospel.' If however ch. 21, or even if only 21.24f., be an appendix added by representatives of the church in which the beloved disciple laboured and the Fourth Gospel was written and used, it is quite possible that the present note means, 'The beloved disciple wrote (or was responsible for the writing of) 1—20 (and perhaps the whole or part of 21.1–23) and we hereby certify his veracity.' The crucial points are the meaning of ὁ γράψας, and the origin and relation to the rest of the gospel of ch. 21.

The effect of 19.35 and 21.24 is to focus attention even more closely upon the beloved disciple, who, as we have seen, is probably to be identified with John the son of Zebedee. It is a plausible interpretation of 21.24 that this disciple himself wrote the gospel, or at least 1—20; but many other data seem to rule out this conclusion as impossible. It is very difficult to attribute the gospel as it stands to a Galilean disciple (see below, pp. 125ff.). Accordingly, the second possible meaning of 21.24 (that the beloved disciple was responsible for the gospel only in an indirect sense) may be accepted; or his responsibility may be limited to the incident described in 21 (just as 19.35 refers only to the single incident of the effusion of water and blood from the side of Jesus); or 21.24 may be simply an error, or an exaggeration of some more remote connection between the beloved disciple and the gospel.

The direct internal evidence afforded by the gospel, which seems in some lights so explicit and valuable, under examination loses definiteness. It raises at least as many problems as it solves. At every point difficulties of interpretation arise, and it is impossible to do better than speak in terms of probabilities. What does emerge from the evidence is, not that the gospel as it stands is a first-hand historical document but that those responsible for it were seriously concerned about the meaning and authority of the apostolic witness to the history of Jesus. See below, pp. 134–44.

5. INDIRECT INTERNAL EVIDENCE

At first sight less tangible than the direct evidence that has now been reviewed, the indirect evidence nevertheless yields more solid, though admittedly neither extensive nor conclusive, results. Much of it has already been set out in the chapters on the background of the gospel, and on its characteristics and purpose. Here the results of these chapters so far as they bear directly on the question of authorship may be summarized; more important aspects of the matter will be developed later in this chapter (pp. 123–34). John shows the influence of both

Jewish and Hellenistic thought, but the whole of his equipment is subordinated to the needs of a creative understanding and exposition of the specifically Christian content of the primitive tradition. Already the outlines of a picture of the evangelist begin to appear. First and foremost he is a Christian theologian with a profound and penetrating understanding of his material. He is a Jew, but has not, it seems, a first-hand knowledge of conditions in Palestine in the time of Jesus, though he has at his command material with a Palestinian stamp. He is well acquainted, as many Jews of his time were, with the movement of Hellenistic religious-philosophical thought, and moved in circles where this thought was understood and accepted. This sketch of the evangelist seems to be justified by the data, but it must be added that it would be assailed on several sides by various students of the gospel.

It is maintained that the gospel contains sufficient evidence to show that its author was a Palestinian Jew, and an eye-witness of the events he records. That there are points of contact between the thought of the gospel and Palestinian Judaism is not in dispute. For some of the evidence see above, pp. 31–4. When all has been reviewed it is difficult to resist the impression that the Palestinian material has been disposed according to the demands of a dominant non-Jewish partner. The question of John's Greek style has also been discussed (see above, pp. 5–11); there is no proof that John was translating Semitic sources, nor is his own mode of expression distinctively Semitic. There remain for discussion here the three assertions, (i) that the topographical references in the gospel show that John had a personal knowledge of Palestine; (ii) that his allusions to Jewish feasts and customs points to the same knowledge; and (iii) that many details of the narrative must have come from an eye-witness of the events described.

(i) The following places, not mentioned in the Synoptic Gospels, are referred to:

1.28, Bethany (or Bethabara or Betharaba) beyond Jordan.
2.1, Cana in Galilee. Cf. 4.46.
3.23, Aenon near Salim.
4.5, Sychar.
5.2, The sheepgate, or sheep-pool.
      The pool Bethzatha (or Bethesda or Bethsaida, etc.).
6.1, The sea of Galilee is the sea of Tiberias. Cf. 6.23; 21.1.
9.7, The pool of Siloam.
10.23, Solomon's porch.
11.54, Ephraim.
18.1, The garden beyond the brook Kedron.
18.28, The Praetorium.
19.13, The pavement, in Hebrew Gabbatha.

On each of these passages the commentary must be consulted; some have little weight. It must have been common knowledge that Roman headquarters in any provincial capital, or sub-capital, might be called the Praetorium; the sheepgate (if this be the meaning of ἡ προβατική), the pool of Siloam, and Kedron might be known from the Old Testament; Solomon's porch is mentioned in Acts (3.11; 5.12). There remain nine names. Of these six refer to southern Palestine (Bethany, Aenon near Salim, Bethzatha, Ephraim, Gabbatha) while only three (Cana, Sychar, Tiberias) refer to the north, and it is doubtful whether the use of the name Tiberias can be used as evidence of the work of an early resident in Palestine, since the town in question did not receive that name till A.D. 26. John's special knowledge, then, applies to the south rather than the north (which does not suggest a close dependence of the gospel on John the son of Zebedee).[1] Its value cannot be checked, but it may be observed (a) that tradition tends to add, even without authority, the names of places as of persons; (b) that the peculiar Johannine names may be due to the use of Palestinian sources by an author himself of different origin.

(ii) Jewish customs, etc. The following are the most noteworthy pieces of evidence:

1.46. Can any good thing come out of Nazareth? This may have been a popular proverb, but there is no evidence that it was. In any case, if the saying was in existence at all it was probably widely used by Jews in anti-Christian polemic, and is no evidence that John was a native of Palestine.

2.6. The reference to Jewish purifications proves nothing. That Jews used water for purificatory lustrations was known to many—for example, to Epictetus (*Discourses* II, ix, 19ff.).

4.9,20. The relation of Jews and Samaritans, Jerusalem and Gerizim. Only a general knowledge of Judaism is implied here. The Samaritan schism was well known, and Jews had good reason to be aware of the rival worshippers on Mount Gerizim. The technical use of συγχρᾶσθαι (see the commentary) might be known to a diaspora Jew, since Samaritans as well as Jews were dispersed in the Mediterranean world; see e.g. Josephus, *Ant.* XII, 7 (Ptolemy, after taking many captives both from the hill country of Judaea and the district round Jerusalem and from Samaria and those on Garizein, brought them all to Egypt and settled them there). The passage continues (XII, 10) with an account of a quarrel in Alexandria, 'those from Jerusalem saying that their temple was the holy one, and requiring that the sacrifices be sent there, while the Shechemites wanted these to go to Mount Garizein'. It must however be allowed that 4.9c is more probably of Palestinian origin.

5.10; cf. 7.22f.; 9.14. It does seem probable that John knew the

---

[1] R. D. Potter ('Topography in the Fourth Gospel', in *Studia Evangelica*, Texte und Untersuchungen 73 = V. 18 (1959), 331) rightly observes that the material in ch. 4 does not relate to Southern Palestine, but this does not affect the balance of interest. Cf. Dodd, *Tradition* 244f.

sabbath and circumcision laws from within; but, once more, this only proves that he was a Jew, not that he was a Palestinian Jew.

7.2. In addition to the Passover Feast, which all the evangelists know, John mentions also the σκηνοπηγία (*Sukkoth*, Tabernacles). The mere reference to it is of no significance. It was one of the three great pilgrim feasts, and indeed, 'The feast' *simpliciter* generally meant Tabernacles.

7.37. If it is correct (see the commentary) to see in the words attributed to Jesus an allusion to the water-drawing ritual celebrated at Tabernacles we have perhaps reason to think that John (or his source) was acquainted with Jerusalem and its customs before the Jewish War. This piece of evidence however may not be pressed too far since it is possible that knowledge only of the connection between Tabernacles and prayers for rain might account for what we find in the gospel. Similarly, the imagery of 8.12 (I am the light of the world) may perhaps be satisfactorily explained on the basis of the Old Testament without reference to the lamp-lighting at Tabernacles; or knowledge of the Jerusalem practice may be ascribed to the author of a source.

7.52. As at 1.46 it is superficially attractive to suppose that John is quoting a Judaean proverb; but not only can no trace of the supposed proverb be found, it would contradict (see the commentary) a very early saying. It seems more probable that in both passages John quotes arguments coined for anti-Christian use.

10.22f. In addition to Tabernacles, John knows the feast of Dedication (τὰ ἐγκαινία, *Ḥanukkah*). But every Jew in the Empire knew that there was a feast called Dedication and that it fell in the winter; and doubtless every Jew who had visited Jerusalem (and there were many), or who knew another who had done so, would know Solomon's porch in the Temple, as well as a modern American who had visited or heard of London would know Henry VII's Chapel in Westminster Abbey.

11.44; cf. 19.40; 20.7. See the commentary. It is not quite so easy as might be expected to parallel within Judaism the burial customs given by John. Certainly one cannot argue from them to a personal acquaintance with Palestine.

11.49: high priest that year; cf. 18.13. This statement has been used to prove that John was and that he was not familiar with Palestine before A.D. 70. In theory the high priest was not appointed for a year but for life; but the Romans deposed so many high priests that the office became at times almost annual. See the commentary.

It cannot be said that these passages taken together prove that John was so familiar with the customs of Palestine that he must himself have been a native of Palestine; they do not even prove that the author of any source used by him was a native of Palestine, though there is no reason why this should not be true. Any material in any way connected with Jesus may be expected to show traces of its Palestinian origin; such traces, and hardly more, are found in John. Accordingly we turn (iii) to the evidence adduced in favour of John's having been an eye-witness of the events he relates, with some scepticism. The main points are as follows:

(a) Several persons are named who do not appear in the synoptic gospels, for example, Nathanael, Nicodemus, Lazarus, Malchus. There is little force in this argument. The apocryphal gospels contain yet more names, but we do not therefore accept them as eye-witness authorities. There was in fact a tendency to insert names into the tradition on no authority at all. It has also been held that John adds life-like details of characterization to the figures that appear in his story; but they are not perceptible to every reader.

(b) The evangelist often records the exact time at which an event took place, and the intervals between events. This is true; see, for example, 1.29,35,43; 2.2; but by itself it does not amount to proof of the point in question.

(c) Certain details, such as numbers, are given, which could only be derived from an eye-witness. For example, at Cana there were six water-pots (2.6); the disciples had rowed twenty-five or thirty furlongs when Jesus came to them on the lake (6.19); Jesus' tunic was without seam, woven from the top throughout (19.23). It may be replied first that these details may have been taken by the evangelist from sources, and secondly that such features are precisely what a writer adds to his work in order to give it verisimilitude. An interesting example is to be found at 6.1–13, the feeding of the multitude, where John is in all probability following Mark. Some striking details are drawn from the source, others are elaborating additions to it.

The most the evidence that has now been surveyed can prove is that here and there behind the Johannine narrative there lies eye-witness material. It is certainly not proved, and is perhaps not provable, that the gospel as a whole is the work of an eye-witness. And the evidence already given of the Hellenistic side of John's thought suggests that the final editor of the gospel was not an eye-witness.

6. Date, Place, and Authorship

When all the evidence regarding the origin of the gospel is put together it amounts to a disappointingly small total. In several particulars, evidence, which at first appears clear and impressive, melts under critical examination and yields a quite inconclusive result. It will be necessary briefly to review this process in order to discover what residuum of fact, or probability, may be derived from the data that have been examined.

The post-biblical evidence regarding the life and work of John the apostle seems at first explicit and irrefutable. Polycarp spoke of his connection with John, and Irenaeus, who heard Polycarp, testified that John the son of Zebedee was the beloved disciple, that he wrote the gospel, that he lived in Ephesus, and that he survived till the principate of Trajan (that is, until at least A.D. 98). Polycrates and later writers support this almost first-hand tradition. It is exposed however to criticism of three kinds. First, it is in conflict with positive statements of a variant tradition, according to which John the apostle shared the martyrdom of his brother James, and therefore could neither have lived in Ephesus nor written the gospel. This variant tradition cannot be accepted as it stands; but it must mean at least that there were quarters in the early church (perhaps the Syriac-speaking church, as attested by its martyrology; see above, pp. 103f.), where the Ephesian residence of the son of Zebedee was not known, or not believed. Secondly, the tradition of Irenaeus is challenged by the silence of some whom we should have expected to confirm it. The silence of Ignatius is especially significant; that of Justin hardly less so. Little can be made of the fact that Polycarp in his extant epistle makes no mention of John; the epistle is short and does not call for personal references (though Polycarp does mention the example of Paul). Papias also, described by Irenaeus as a companion of Polycarp and hearer of John, seems, if we may judge from Eusebius, to have had no information about John. Thirdly, the tradition that the apostle wrote the gospel was assailed directly by those who rejected it as uncanonical and unapostolic. In the Muratorian Canon, and in the so-called anti-Marcionite prologue, whatever that may be worth (see above, p. 114), there is a rather nervous and over-anxious support of the apostolic authorship, in the latter a curious insistence that the gospel was written while John was *adhuc in corpore constituto*, which implies that there were those who held that John was dead before the gospel was composed. Hippolytus' *Defence* (see above, p. 114) also implies an attack. The question for consideration here, and unfortunately it is a question which it is impossible to answer with confidence, is whether these adversaries, including Marcionites and anti-Montanists, were motivated simply by a dislike of the theology of the gospel, or possessed positive information to the effect that John the son of Zebedee did not live to a great age in Ephesus and did not write the gospel.

It cannot be said that the Irenaeus tradition is disproved by these considerations, but it is impossible to place in it the confidence of earlier generations. To the question what elements of truth may be contained in the conflicting traditions we shall return later.

The witness of Irenaeus regarding the existence and use of the gospel is as clear and forceful as his witness regarding the apostle. The gospel is one of the four divinely appointed pillars of evangelical truth. He quotes it constantly, as do all later ecclesiastical writers. But as soon as the student pursues his investigation into the earlier writings of the second century a completely different picture appears. Orthodox Christian writers seem unaware, or scarcely aware, of the existence of the gospel, perhaps even suspicious of it; and this is true even of those who might with the greatest probability be expected to know and use it. Even Polycarp, according to Irenaeus the hearer of John, shows no knowledge of the gospel, though his epistle contains a possible allusion to 1 John. It is among gnostic heretics that John can first be proved to have been used. Only in the last third of the second century (perhaps from Tatian's use of it in the *Diatessaron*—and even here it must be remembered that the origins of the *Diatessaron* are shrouded in some obscurity, and that Tatian was not orthodox—does John come into clearer and less ambiguous light. The new papyrus fragments do not really disperse the shadows which surround the origin of the gospel. They prove its existence in the first half of the second century; but they do nothing to confirm (though they do not necessarily come into conflict with) the tradition that the gospel was written in Ephesus, and it remains quite uncertain whether Rylands Papyrus 457 was in orthodox or gnostic hands, and in what relation Egerton Papyrus 2, itself a mildly gnostic work, stood to the gospel.

It is clear that the confident testimony of Irenaeus is not valid for the period before him. The history of the Fourth Gospel in the second century is extremely difficult to read, and is certainly no plain tale of unquestioned reverence unhesitatingly accorded to a book known from the beginning to have been written by an apostle.

We have already seen that the gospel itself yields no simple answer when it is interrogated regarding its origin. The beloved disciple stands out as a figure of evident importance; but who was the beloved disciple? We are forced to the conclusion that he was either an unidentified, and unidentifiable, figure, or John the son of Zebedee, represented by an author with much more admiration for his hero than sound historical information. Was the beloved disciple the author of the gospel? The very title by which he is known bears on this question, but while to some it seems that it would be an intolerable arrogance to style oneself the 'disciple whom Jesus loved', to a few the designation seems a modest anonymity. 21.24 may assert (it is by no means certain) that the beloved disciple was the author of the whole gospel; but what is the provenance and authority of this verse? We are on much safer (but by no means undisputed) ground in suggesting that, in view of his use of sources and certain inaccuraries, the evangelist was not an eyewitness of the events he narrates. It is difficult to decide whether he himself knew the scenes of the ministry of Jesus. There are several indications that he did; but not a few points when closely examined show ignorance rather than knowledge of Palestinian conditions and affairs. That the data are contradictory may be admitted; but if this be admitted, the conclusion must be drawn. The gospel contains Palestinian, as well as other, material; but it was drawn up, edited, and published by persons who had no personal historical contact with Jesus, and perhaps no contact with Palestine; certainly not by an apostle.

The only safe affirmations that may be made about John must be made on the objective but impersonal ground of the contents of the gospel. Here two points come under consideration. First, it is widely held, and, though not capable of proof, is probably true, that John used sources; in this Commentary the view is taken that he knew at least one of the Synoptic Gospels and drew material from it. Yet—and this is why it is so difficult to make confident statements about sources—he was able to view these sources in perspective, to handle them freely and to arrange them in such a way as to bring out the themes he wished to emphasize. His method may be contrasted with that of Tatian, who, in compiling the *Diatessaron*, was always the servant of his material. John was the master of his material, using it for his own purpose with very great skill; he was not a mere compiler, but an author with a thesis to maintain. Secondly, the affiliations of the Johannine material may be traced with some confidence. The gospel stands in some relation, by no means easy to define, with Judaism.[1] The Jews provide the stage on which the drama of salvation is played (4.22); at the same time they are the enemy, chosen by John to typify the world (see on 1.19). The controversies reported in the pages of the gospel are not all controversies which find their historical setting in the ministry of Jesus, but they are Jewish controversies, not Greek. The key-words of the gospel can be traced in the Old Testament and in the documents of later Judaism. John knew the Old Testament and handled it in the same confident way as his literary sources.[2] Together with this Jewish material we find in the gospel unmistakable evidence of a different kind of thought, especially of that kind of religious-philosophical thought, which in the absence of Christian influences was later to find expression in the Hermetic literature. It seems that even those Hebraic thoughts and words to which reference has been made were selected by John because they awakened echoes in Hellenistic language and speculation. So far it may be said that John is simply treading the well-worn path of Hellenistic Judaism, the path which many Jewish missionaries had marked out in their attempt to commend the Jewish faith to the Hellenistic world without making it purely a philosophy or reducing it to the level of a mystery religion. John was essaying a task similar to Philo's, and it is for this reason (not because John had read his works and borrowed from them) that knowledge of Philo is valuable to a student of the Fourth Gospel. But to speak only of the Jewish and Hellenistic affiliations of John's thought is to leave out its most vital element, the fact (already hinted at) that he stands as a masterful figure in the Christian tradition, absorbing its essence and transmitting it in forms chosen in accordance with his own purpose. John used the methods of Hellenistic-Jewish propaganda in order to transmit the, originally Semitic, content of primitive Christianity to the Greek world. He was

[1] See *Judaism*.
[2] See B. Noack, *Zur johanneischen Tradition* (1954), especially 71–89, 89–109.

more however than a translator, more even than a translator of idioms. A theological task had to be accomplished before the primitive eschatological proclamation could be established as the constitutive faith of a church destined to last for a long time in an unlimited number of different environments. It was in the performance of this task that John, with his gospel, entered the realm of gnosticism and contributed to its evolution. If it is true (see p. 59) that Paul did not hellenize Christianity but put it into a form in which it could be hellenized, it is perhaps equally true that John was not himself a heretic (as Dr Käsemann says; see pp. 138f.), but put Christianity into a form in which it could easily be turned into a heresy. Orthodoxy and heresy are indeed terms that must be used with caution;[1] but the church was not wrong when, at a later time, it bestowed on John the title θεόλογος.

These are the most positive, significant, and certain statements that can be made about the Fourth Evangelist; and they are both positive and significant. It is more important to understand the theological task achieved by him than to know his name, and more important to know the materials with which he worked, and the way he used them, than to know the date and place at which he wrote. In fact, with the evidence at present at our disposal, it is impossible to determine name, date, and place with any confidence; yet a further investigation of the historical circumstances in which the gospel was composed is justifiable, and may be illuminating.

It will be convenient to begin with the question of date. A *terminus post quem* may easily be fixed if it is true that John knew Mark,[2] and not only knew it but had thoroughly mastered its contents, and expected his readers also to be familiar with them. There is wide agreement that Mark was written either not long before, or soon after, A.D. 70. We must allow time for Mark to reach the place in which John was written, and to be studied and absorbed. This brings us to a date certainly not earlier than A.D. 80; 90 would perhaps be a safer estimate. We are not dependent on Mark; this *terminus post quem* is confirmed by a second argument. John seems undoubtedly to envisage circumstances in which Jewish Christians were 'put out of the synagogue' (9.22; 16.2; ἀποσυνάγωγος). We are able, fortunately, to give with some exactness the date at which the well-known 'Test Benediction' (ברכת המינים, *birkath ha-minim*) was introduced into the synagogue service with the express intention of excluding heretics (Jewish Christians among them). It was drawn up by R. Simeon the Less, at the request of R. Gamaliel II, at about A.D. 85–90. Once more we arrive at A.D. 90 as *terminus post quem*. The *terminus ante quem* is given by the first use

---

[1] See W. Bauer, *Rechtgläubigkeit und Ketzerei im ältesten Christentum* (1934; E. T., *Orthodoxy and Heresy in Earliest Christianity*, 1971); also below, p. 139.

[2] See above, pp. 42–5. An example of the alternative view is given by J. L. Cribbs *J.B.L.* 89 (1970), 38–55 (cf. 90 (1971), 422–50), who, maintaining John's independence of the synoptics, thinks that the gospel was written by a Jew of Judaea in the late 50s or early 70s.

of the gospel. If we could be certain that Valentinus himself used John this could be given as *c.* A.D. 130. This, however, though possible and even probable, cannot be proved, and the next piece of evidence is the Rylands papyrus, which cannot be dated more precisely than the middle of the second century. It is of course very improbable that the papyrus should be the autograph copy of the gospel, and we may safely push the *terminus* back as far as A.D. 140, especially since the papyrus may have been written earlier, perhaps twenty or thirty years earlier, than A.D. 150. If the author of Egerton Papyrus 2 was dependent on John, as he probably was, the *terminus ante quem* must be fixed somewhat earlier.

The wide limits of A.D. 90–140 have now been reached, and it seems impossible to narrow them further without recourse to a hypothesis regarding authorship. John itself is a quite credible product of any date between 90 and 140. None of the attempts made to shift either date is successful. It is, for example, very improbable that the allusion in 5.43 to 'one who comes in his own name' refers to the messianic claim of Bar Cochba (A.D. 132). The errors combated are present in germ in the 'heresy' refuted by Paul in Colossians, long before A.D. 90. The fact that Ignatius does not quote John can prove at the most that Ignatius had not read John; it cannot prove that John was not in existence when Ignatius wrote. On one point however caution must be observed. The gospel was not written before A.D. 90 (it appears), nor was the date of its publication later than 140; it must not be assumed that the date of writing and the date of publication were identical; the gospel may have been slow in coming to the notice of the Christian public. Indeed, we cannot be certain that the gospel was *widely* known in A.D. 140. It must be emphasized that the dates 90 and 140, especially the latter, are extreme limits. The traditional date of *c.* A.D. 100 is probably very near the truth.

The question of the place where the gospel was written will be taken next. The traditional place of writing is Ephesus; and undoubtedly Ephesus was a great centre of Christian activity in the early second century. Nevertheless it must be recognized that the tradition rests upon the all-important evidence of Irenaeus. The validity of this evidence has already been called in question, and it has been shown to be at least far less certain than at first appears. We may ask what evidence remains to point to Ephesus. There is first the Irenaeus tradition. It must be admitted that this is gravely weakened when the Ephesian residence of the apostle, and his authorship of the gospel, are questioned or denied; but it is not wholly destroyed. The tradition which Irenaeus repeats so confidently, and which finds some support in the testimony of Polycrates, did not grow out of nothing, and among its roots may well be a genuine connection of the gospel with Ephesus. In fact the Ephesian origin of the book may be the primary tradition from which the rest developed.[1]

[1] Cf. A. Ehrhardt, *The Framework of the New Testament Stories* (1964), 14ff.

Second, there are the traces of the gospel which occur in Asiatic authors, notably Melito of Sardis and Leucius Charinus, the author of the Leucian Acts of John. These writers furnish some evidence of the early appearance of John in Asia.

The case for Ephesus as the place of origin of the gospel is not strong, though perhaps a little stronger than has recently been allowed. One alternative is Alexandria. Undoubtedly there is evidence pointing in that direction. The earliest certain use of the gospel is found in Egypt (the Rylands and Egerton papyri, and the Valentinians). Internal evidence (it has been held) confirms the external. Alexandria, 'the home of Philo and of the authors of the Corpus Hermeticum, . . . was a likely place for the development of a Christian Logos-doctrine' (Sanders, Early Church, 40). The hypothesis that John was written in Alexandria, the home both of gnostics and of a large Jewish population, would account for the twofold polemic of the gospel against both docetic and Judaizing tendencies, and perhaps also for the polemic against followers of John the Baptist. Finally, since it seems that the church of Alexandria was not in its earliest days strictly orthodox, it is easy to understand that a gospel proceeding from such a source should at first be looked upon with suspicion by orthodox Christians.

Of these arguments only that derived from external evidence carries weight, and that less than has been supposed. Only in Egypt are climatic conditions favourable for the preservation of papyrus, and in consequence the great majority of the papyri known to scholars are of Egyptian origin. It is quite possible that in the year A.D. 150 there were as many copies of John in Asia as in Egypt; but they had no chance of survival. The argument drawn from the kinship between John's Logos-theology and the thought of Philo depends upon the view taken of the relationship between the two authors. If it be held (as in this Commentary) that John was not directly dependent on Philo and perhaps had never read any of his works, the argument has no weight and may even be reversed. Surely, it might be urged, a theologian resident in Alexandria could not have failed to show more traces of his distinguished predecessor. As regards the Hermetica, it must be remembered (i) that the Tractates were not written down till a date certainly later than that of the Fourth Gospel; and (ii) that they represent a blending of several strains of philosophical and religious thought, some of which (for example, the thought of Posidonius) were not native to Alexandria. Again, gnostics were not confined to Alexandria. As early as Paul's writing of Colossians we find them in the Lycus valley (not far from Ephesus); and while there may have been disciples of John the Baptist in Alexandria we have at least the testimony of Acts that there were such men in Ephesus (Acts 19.1–3).

It cannot be said that the case for Alexandria has been made out. It remains to examine certain contacts between John and Syria, and in particular Antioch.

First, there are several parallels between 1 John and Matthew, which was probably written either in or near Antioch. The passages are set out in full by Professor C. H. Dodd (*The Johannine Epistles* (1946), xxxix–xli); the references are 1 John 2.17—Matt. 7.21; 1 John 3.1–3—Matt. 5.8f.; 1 John 4.1; 2.18—Matt. 24.11; 7.15,20; 24.24; 1 John 3.7—Matt. 5.48 (cf. Luke 6.36); 1 John 3.22—Matt. 7.8 (Luke 11.10); 1 John 4.17—Matt. 10.25 (cf. Luke 6.40); 1 John 5.3— Matt. 11.30. These parallels will of course carry most weight with those who believe that John and 1 John were written by the same author; but since it is at least beyond dispute that John and 1 John proceed from the same school of thought and tradition, they suggest in any case the presence of Johannine teaching in the neighbourhood of Antioch. Secondly, there is the general relationship between the theology of Ignatius and that of John. This resemblance, together with the absence in Ignatius' letters of specific quotations from the Johannine literature, could be plausibly accounted for if we could suppose that teaching akin to that of the Fourth Gospel was given orally in Antioch, the city of which Ignatius became bishop; John might first have lived in Antioch before moving to Asia. Thirdly, there is the somewhat similar relation between John and the Odes of Solomon. As we have seen (pp. 112f.), there is no clear ground on which to posit a literary relation between the two works, but there is a measure of theological resemblance, even though the framework of piety in which the Odes are conceived is different from John's. It is very improbable that the two works are to be traced back to a common origin in the Qumran sect, but that they share to some extent a common background is probable. A fourth consideration is the fact that Theophilus of Antioch wrote the first orthodox commentary on John.

These points come far short of proof that John was written in Antioch; but they do constitute evidence that the characteristic Johannine theology was not a product peculiar to the province of Asia. In particular a good case can be made for the view that the mingling of Jewish, Hellenistic, and Christian elements, which eventually resulted in the gnosticism that appeared in the middle of the second century as a rival to 'orthodox' Christianity, began in Syria—or, rather, had one of its beginnings in Syria, for it seems to have sprung up in the Lycus valley too. The origins of Christian orthodoxy make a complicated story—too complicated for us at so remote a time to be able to unravel it completely—and how developments in different places interacted can only be conjectured. It would be an oversimplification to suggest that 'Johannine theology' must have been carried from Antioch to Ephesus by one person, namely John. Johannine theology arose in response to needs felt within the theological and practical structure of the church, and if the needs were felt in more than one place kindred theologies may have arisen independently in those places.

It is impossible to make out a satisfactory and conclusive case for any of the three great cities, Ephesus, Alexandria, and Antioch, as the place of origin of the Fourth Gospel. The fact that John was claimed as a support for the Quartodeciman position in regard to Easter by the bishops of Asia, who alone were recalcitrant in the matter, has been claimed as decisive proof of the Asiatic origin of the gospel. But in point of fact, whatever oral traditions under the name of John the apostle may have been current, the gospel does not really bear on the question, which was (it seems) whether the fast of Lent should end on the Jewish Paschal day or on the Christian Sunday corresponding to it.[1] Our understanding of the Paschal question is however so uncertain that no valid arguments can be drawn from it. It is quite impossible to deny that John could have written at any of the places mentioned. Ephesus remains, perhaps, the best choice because of the residue of weight in the Irenaeus tradition. At least, on the hypothesis that the gospel was written at Ephesus it is possible to go on to make a conjectural attempt to deal with the question of authorship. If the gospel was written in Alexandria or Antioch we know nothing whatever about the evangelist (except what can be deduced from his gospel), and we are even deprived of the means of guessing.

It is certainly impossible to combine into one rational hypothesis all the data, internal and external, bearing on the question of authorship. It will be well to begin with the acceptance of John into the church's fourfold gospel canon, of which canon there is no certain trace before the time of Marcion.[2] There is no evidence that John was used by other than heretical Christians before the middle of the second century, and its ultimate acceptance recalls the inclusion of the fuller form of the heretic Marcion's gospel (Luke). The fourfold canon, when it was made (perhaps principally as a counterstroke to Marcion), was an inclusive canon. Whatever was suitable of the heretics' own literature was taken over and used against them; thus Luke and John were added to Matthew and Mark, for which we have the earlier authority of Papias. The strong claims made in the latter half of the second century on behalf of the authority and apostolicity of John—by Clement of Alexandria and Irenaeus, in the Muratorian canon, and probably by Hippolytus—are to be seen as part of this process. It is by no means impossible that 21.24 reflects the same interests. There was a similar tendency to emphasize the (indirect) apostolicity of Luke. This later history of the gospel tells us little, however, of its origins. The fact that it was accepted into the canon as the work of John the apostle does not prove that it was written by him; its early disuse by orthodox writers and use by gnostics show that it originated in circles that were either gnostic or obscure, or, perhaps more probably, both. It was gnostic, not in that it was docetic,[3]

---

[1] See also B. Lohse, *Das Passafest der Quartadecimaner* (1953), especially 136f.
[2] See especially J. Knox, *Marcion and the New Testament* (1942), 140–57.
[3] As Käsemann, *Testament*, thinks. See p. 74.

but in that its author took seriously the new movements of thought that agitated his intellectual environment,[1] and obscure in that he stood apart from the ecclesiastical developments in which Ignatius, for example, played so combative a part. His work was therefore unlikely to become quickly and widely known.

The crux of the problem of the origin of John lies in (i) the moral certainty that the gospel was not written by John the son of Zebedee;[2] (ii) the probability that the tradition (which seems to begin as early as 21.24) that the gospel was written by John the son of Zebedee, interested as it doubtless was, was not pure fiction but had some foundation. Closely related to this second point is the necessity of giving some account of the report of Polycarp handed down by Irenaeus. Here it is most important to notice exactly what statement Irenaeus ascribes to Polycarp, and it is noteworthy that, although Irenaeus himself sincerely believed that the apostle John had written the Fourth Gospel, he did not make Polycarp say so. In the Epistle to Florinus Polycarp is made to speak of 'his intercourse with John and with the others who had seen the Lord'. When he adds: 'And as he remembered their words, and what he had heard from them concerning the Lord, and concerning his miracles and his teaching, having received them from eye-witnesses of the "Word of Life", Polycarp related all things in harmony with the Scriptures', Irenaeus does nothing to suggest that Polycarp possessed a gospel written by the John he mentions. This may mean that Polycarp was speaking of John the Elder (if we suppose that he had seen the Lord, which is possible but not certain); or it may mean that he was speaking of John the apostle without asserting that John the apostle had written a gospel. There is nothing impossible in the latter suggestion; Polycarp was born c. A.D. 70, and it is not incredible that John should have lived till a later date than this.

It is also to be noted that Polycarp does not say where he had seen John. It is generally assumed that their contact took place in Ephesus, or at least in Asia; but this need not be so. The Pionian *Life* of Polycarp, which admittedly contains much untrustworthy matter, ascribes to Polycarp an eastern origin, and it does not say (as other traditions did) that Polycarp was consecrated bishop of Smyrna by John; Paul is the

---

[1] See 'Theological Vocabulary'.

[2] Apostolic authorship has been defended at length and with learning by L. Morris (in *Studies in the Fourth Gospel* (1969), 139–292, and in his commentary), and his arguments should be carefully considered. It must be allowed to be not impossible that John the apostle wrote the gospel; this is why I use the term 'moral certainty'. The apostle may have lived to a very great age; he may have seen fit to draw on other sources in addition to his own memory; he may have learnt to write Greek correctly; he may have learnt not only the language but the thought-forms of his new environment (in Ephesus, Antioch, or Alexandria); he may have pondered the words of Jesus so long that they took shape in a new idiom; he may have become such an obscure figure that for some time orthodox Christians took little or no notice of his work. These are all possible, but the balance of probability is against their having all actually happened.

apostolic founder of that church, and Strataeas its first bishop. It is at least possible that the *Life* is correct, and that Polycarp had met John in Palestine or Syria. This would agree with the fact that Papias (of Hierapolis) apparently did not know John at first hand, and with the silence of Ignatius and others regarding an Ephesian residence of John. Over against this however must be set the fact that in the last decades of the first century there lived a John in Ephesus—the John of the Apocalypse. He may not have been the apostle; certainly there are difficulties in the way of supposing that he was.[1] But the external evidence regarding the Apocalypse is very good, and the apostle may have been the author of at least part of it. If he was, the silence of Ignatius regarding his presence could still be readily explained, for (i) the earliest parts of the Apocalypse were written as much as fifty years before Ignatius, and (ii) Ignatius cannot have found the Apocalypse entirely congenial doctrine.

In the first edition of this Commentary I suggested a hypothesis that seemed to meet most of the few known facts; others have taken it further,[2] sometimes, it may be, further than the facts warrant. Undoubtedly, it was, and is, open to correction. It is repeated here in more or less the original terms, and will in some respects be developed in the next part of this chapter. I hope to return to it elsewhere. The solid fact behind it, in addition to the traditions just sketched, is that the Johannine literature exists, and is marked by differences, which forbid the view that all the works concerned come from the same hand, and similarities, which demand some kind of interrelation.

John the Apostle migrated from Palestine and lived in Ephesus, where, true to character as a Son of Thunder, he composed apocalyptic works. These, together with his advancing years, the death of other apostles, and predictions such as Mark 9.1, not unnaturally gave rise to the common belief that he would survive to the *parousia*. A man of commanding influence, he gathered about him a number of pupils. In course of time he died; his death fanned the apocalyptic hopes of some, scandalized others, and induced a few to ponder deeply over the meaning of Christian eschatology. One pupil of the apostle incorporated his written works in the canonical Apocalypse; this was at a date about the close of the life of Domitian—*c.* A.D. 96. Another pupil was responsible for the epistle (probably 1 John came from one writer, 2 and 3 John from another). Yet another, a bolder thinker, and one more widely read both in Judaism and Hellenism, produced John 1—20. Comparison with 1, 2, and 3 John shows at once that the evangelist stood apart from the busy and quarrelsome ecclesiastical life of the age. Probably he was not popular; probably he died with his gospel still unpublished. It was too

---

[1] See R. H. Charles, *A Critical and Exegetical Commentary on the Revelation of St John* (1920), xliii f.

[2] See the excellent article by D. Moody Smith in *N.T.S.* 21 (1975), 222–48, which has the additional virtue of referring to most of the literature.

original and daring a work for official backing. It was first seized upon by gnostic speculators, who saw the superficial contact which existed between it and their own work; they at least could recognize the language John spoke. Only gradually did the main body of the church come to perceive that, while John used (at times) the language of gnosticism, his work was in fact the strongest possible reply to the gnostic challenge; that he had beaten the gnostics with their own weapons, and vindicated the permanent validity of the primitive Gospel by expressing it in new—and partly gnostic—terms. The gospel was now edited together with ch. 21; the narratives of the final chapter were probably based on traditional material; perhaps material which the evangelist had left but had not worked into the main body of his work. The evangelist, perhaps, after Paul, the greatest theologian in all the history of the church, was now forgotten. His name was unknown. But he had put in his gospel references to the beloved disciple— the highly honoured apostle who years before had died in Ephesus. These were now partly understood, and partly misunderstood. It was perceived that they referred to John the son of Zebedee, but wrongly thought that they meant that this apostle was the author of the gospel. 21.24 was now composed on the model of 19.35, and the book was sent out on its long career as the work of John, foe of heretics and beloved of his Lord.

7. The Purpose, Historical Value, and Authority of the Gospel

The question, 'With what purpose was the Fourth Gospel written?' is often answered by the quotation of 20.31, 'These [signs] are written, that you may believe that Jesus is the Christ, the Son of God, and that believing you may have life in his name.'[1] It is not always observed that this verse, important as it is, raises more questions than it answers, and provides no more than a starting point for a discussion of the purpose of the gospel; for merely to say that John was written in the interests of faith is to say nothing at all, beyond that it is a Christian book, which is hardly in dispute. One major problem is suggested by the variant reading (πιστεύητε or πιστεύσητε; see the note) which occurs in the verse: Was the gospel written to deepen, instruct, and confirm the faith of believers, or to convert unbelievers? A solution of the textual problem (which cannot in any case be achieved with certainty) could not solve this problem, since John may have used his tenses inaccurately;

---

[1] The quotation of this passage is certainly justifiable, but it could be usefully supplemented. For example, the Prologue (1.1–18) provides important clues to John's purpose (see pp. 149ff.), and 4.23 in stating what the Father seeks (that is, seeks in the work of his Son) must at the same time show what John (who no doubt desired to see the will of God as he understood it done) intended as the outcome of his work (see 'Theocentric', 374 f.).

it remains one of the most important of those that confront the reader of John. A second problem arises out of the ὅτι clause which follows and gives content to πιστεύητε. The faith of which John writes has evidently an intellectual content; how far was this intellectual content a primary concern of his? Was it his conscious purpose that men should believe that Jesus was the Christ, the Son of God, rather than some other proposition about his person which they might conceivably prefer? How far was the purpose of the gospel polemical? Again, when taken with v. 30, 20.31 recalls, what has already been noted (above, pp. 42–54), that John in his gospel handled freely and selectively the earlier gospel tradition. This is acknowledged by those who do not think that John knew Mark as a written book. What was the motive of this apparently high-handed treatment?

It must not be assumed that the questions which 20.31 provokes, and those that would have arisen had we begun from some other passage, have all of them simple and precise answers; indeed it would be a mistake to press too far the question of the purpose of the gospel. For example, it need not be assumed that John formulated in his own mind before writing alternative kinds of gospel, a gospel intended to confirm the faith of the church, and a gospel written to impress with the claims of the Christian faith intelligent Gentiles versed in the religious and philosophical thought of their day. On the one hand, the profundity of the gospel is such that it seems very doubtful whether anyone, however intelligent, who had not a good grounding in the gospel tradition and elementary Christian theology would appreciate it to the full; but on the other, there were doubtless very many simple Christians among John's contemporaries who were content to hold the faith without in the least concerning themselves with the theological problems which he raised. There are other considerations (see p. 132 *et al.*) which suggest that the gospel had an obscure origin; it may not have been published during the author's lifetime; and it may be doubted whether he was very interested in its publication. It is easy, when we read the gospel, to believe that John, though doubtless aware of the necessity of strengthening Christians and converting the heathen, wrote primarily to satisfy himself. His gospel must be written: it was no concern of his whether it was also read. Again, it is by no means necessary to suppose that he was aware of the historical problems imposed upon later students by his treatment of the traditional material. It cried aloud for rehandling; its true meaning had crystallized in his mind, and he simply conveyed this meaning to paper.

It seems right to emphasize a certain detachment of the gospel from its immediate surroundings; no book ever was less a party tract than John. Yet the gospel and its author certainly did not stand in complete isolation from the world of thought to which they belonged, and without consideration of that world a full historical understanding of them can hardly be achieved. The last few decades have in fact witnessed a number of attempts to locate John and his interests precisely, and some of these must be briefly considered.

C. H. Dodd took the view that the gospel was a missionary work, addressed to Gentiles. 'We are to think of the work as addressed to a wide public consisting primarily of devout and thoughtful persons . . . in the varied and cosmopolitan society of a great Hellenistic city such as Ephesus under the Roman Empire' (*Interpretation*, 9). This belief was based on the parallels, which perhaps no one has set out and discussed with greater learning and insight, between John and such Hellenistic writings as Philo and the Hermetica. These contain a similar compound of religious and philosophical thought, and Philo, like John, was an apologist and propagandist in the Greek intellectual world for an originally Semitic religion. Dodd's perception of a dominant Hellenistic element in John is related to but must be distinguished from the belief that the gospel is gnostic in its conceptual background and presentation. This has been maintained by many, though its classical statement is still Bultmann's. Gnosticism is too simply described as the 'acute hellenization of Christianity'. There was if not gnosticism at least a 'gnosis'[1] or pre-gnosticism that was anterior to and therefore independent of Christianity, and gnosticism proper was not simply an amalgam of Christianity, Judaism, other oriental elements, and Hellenism, even in the right proportions.[2] Gnosticism (even as gnosis) involved a dualistic element that was not intrinsic to Hellenism as such.

More recently the tide seems to have turned against the belief that John's background has to be sought in the Hellenistic, or at least non-Jewish, world. The most important factor in this change of view has been the discovery of the so-called Dead Sea Scrolls,[3] which, like John, manifest a kind of dualism in which there is a vivid sense of the opposition between good and evil, life and death, light and darkness, God and the world, that never however goes to the length of positing an evil anti-God capable of standing on the same level as God, and sharing on equal terms in the government of the universe. If there is in the Qumran literature a war between the sons of light and the sons of darkness there is never any doubt who will win it. It is now possible to take a more balanced view of the Dead Sea Scrolls, which confirm the view (already expressed in the first edition of this Commentary) that Hellenism had already in the first century penetrated into Palestinian life. Some of John's Hellenism may have come to him neither direct nor by way of Philo but from Palestinian sources. This possibility can be affirmed more confidently now than thirty years ago, but this does not make John Qumranite, or even exclusively Jewish.

[1] There is something to be said for reserving 'gnosticism' for the Christian heresies and using 'gnosis' to denote 'the whole complex of ideas belonging to the Gnostic movement and related trends of thought' (R. McL. Wilson, *Gnosis and the New Testament* (1968), 9).

[2] See Wilson, op. cit., 10.

[3] See pp. 33f.

Some writers have placed John in a more precise Jewish setting, believing that he wrote specifically for the Diaspora. W. C. van Unnik,[1] for example, lays much stress on 20.31: John's intention was to prove that Jesus was the Jewish Messiah (for Son of God is to be understood in a messianic sense). Comparison with Acts enables us to determine the *Sitz im Leben* of this assertion: it was made by Christians in debates in the synagogue. To such a setting the apologetic, quasi-legal use of words such as μαρτυρεῖν and σημεῖον corresponds. The debate whether Jesus was the Messiah or not began in Palestine, and John is Palestinian; yet not wholly so, and the non-Palestinian element in the gospel shows that the scene of the Johannine debate was the Diaspora synagogue. J. A. T. Robinson[2] concludes somewhat similarly: the gospel is composed 'of material which took shape as teaching *within* a Christian community *in Judea* and under the pressure of controversy with "the Jews" of that area. But in its present form it is . . . an appeal to those *outside* the Church, to win to the faith that Greek-speaking *Diaspora Judaism* to which the author now finds himself belonging.' These two authors do not set out to develop at length the theology of the gospel and are therefore not to be blamed for failing to do so; but it should be noted that J. W. Bowker,[3] taking up Dr Robinson's conclusions, asks, What does Judaism become if Jesus is the Messiah? He argues that it is from this question that the outline of the gospel has developed: Jesus in terms of his antecedents (1.1—2.11); Jesus and Judaism in general (2.12—4.54); Jesus and special questions in Judaism (5.1—8.59); the Jesus-community in relation to Judaism (9.1—12.50).

Falling roughly under this heading but more detailed and comprehensive is the book by J. L. Martyn (*History and Theology in the Fourth Gospel* (1968)), in which is propounded the view that the gospel was written on two levels. One of these, which Dr Martyn describes as *einmalig*, relates incidents and sayings in the setting of the historical life of Jesus. The other depicts circumstances and events belonging to the time of the evangelist. Chapter 9 provides a particularly clear example. On the *einmalig* level we meet Jesus and his disciples, a blind man, his parents and acquaintances, and the Jewish authorities. But behind these familiar figures, and on a different level of writing, we may discern the cure and conversion of a Jew, living in the Jewish quarter of John's own city; the discussion of the matter by the man's neighbours and acquaintances; and a gathering of the local Jewish council, which is divided. It interviews the man, then his parents (who are frightened because they know of a previous resolution of the council that anyone confessing the messiahship of Jesus should be put out of the synagogue), then the man again. We leave the courtroom, and there is a new encounter between the Christian healer and preacher and

---

[1] *Studia Evangelica I* (Texte und Untersuchungen 73; 1959), 382–411.
[2] *N.T.S.* 6 (1960), 117–31.
[3] *N.T.S.* 11 (1965), 398–408.

the formerly blind man, who is now led to faith in Jesus. Finally Jesus, through his preacher-disciple, declares the judgement that his mission means, and proceeds with a sermon (chapter 10). There is no other chapter that provides Dr Martyn with so clear a contact and contrast of the *einmalig* and the contemporary; but that does not mean that he has not rightly seized upon the correct approach to John's method. His book has the great merit of going on from literary and historical observations to consider the theological task that John carried out. John accepts that Jesus is the prophet-messiah 'like Moses', but denies the ultimate validity of the midrashic methods needed to prove this proposition. He pushes beyond this to the conviction that Jesus is the Son of man who still through the Paraclete confronts men.[1]

Others have seen in the gospel a special relation with the Samaritans. This has been argued by, among others, J. Bowman.[2] Chapter 4 is sufficient to show an interest on John's part in the Samaritans. Jesus rejects the accusation that he has a devil, not that he is a Samaritan (8.48). 'The Jews' are his opponents, but Israel (the northern kingdom, now represented by the Samaritans) is spoken of more favourably, and Jesus shows special concern for his 'other sheep' (10.16). Perhaps the most convincing form of this hypothesis is Dr Cullmann's suggestion[3] of a triangular relationship between heterodox Judaism (including the Samaritans), Stephen's speech (Acts 7), and John, though here much remains hypothetical.

Another area of controversy in which John is believed by some to have played a part is that concerning John the Baptist. It is certain that John resists—perhaps exaggeratedly—any tendency to over-emphasize the significance of the Baptist: at 1.20,21 the Baptist declares that he is neither the Christ nor even Elijah; at 3.29f. he distinguishes himself from Jesus as the groomsman from the bridegroom, and acknowledges that Jesus must increase, he decrease.

So far only possible relations between John and various non-Christian circles have been considered. Attempts have also been made to relate the gospel to tendencies and movements within Christianity itself. Here it must suffice to mention the view of E. Käsemann,[4] who sees John as the product of a group of 'enthusiasts' who stood outside the main structures of the church and had as their leader the 'presbyter' (2 John 1; 3 John 1) who fell foul of Diotrephes. The group was heretical, maintaining a Christology that was in fact docetic, though

---

[1] This brief account is necessarily inadequate; I hope it is not misleading. Of all attempts to relate John to a Diaspora background this seems to me the best.

[2] *J.R.B.* 40 (1958), 298–308; *Samaritanische Probleme* (1967); also, e.g., Meeks (pp. 216–57 are very important); G. W. Buchanan, in *Religions in Antiquity, Essays in Memory of E. R. Goodenough* (1968), 149–75; E. D. Freed, in *Nov. T.* 12 (1970), 241–56.

[3] O. Cullmann, *Circle*, 52f.

[4] In addition to *Testament* see 'Ketzer und Zeuge', *Exegetische Versuche und Besinnungen I* (1960), 168–87. See also the important article by G. Klein, *Zeitschrift für Theologie und Kirche* 68 (1971), 261–326.

so advanced, in that it saw in Jesus God masquerading as a man, that it was in the end accepted by the main body of the church. So many questions are raised here—canon, 'orthodoxy' and 'heresy' in early Christianity, the development in the church of ministry and of discipline—in addition to Johannine Christology (see pp. 70–5) that they can only be mentioned in this Introduction. I hope to return to them elsewhere.

The last few paragraphs constitute an inadequate account of a remarkable body of learning and insight. The best comment, however, on John's relation to these currents of thought and life is Dr Cullmann's:[1] 'In the Fourth Gospel theology is not used in the service of polemics, but, on the contrary, polemics are obliged to appear in the service of the author's theological concerns.' John's primary concern was to bring out the theological meaning of the story of Jesus on the basis of the existing traditions about him. This is a task that no responsible theologian of any age can perform in a vacuum, and the evangelist knew a good deal about the religious world of his day. But he did not draw on the gospel tradition in order to write polemical tracts against the Baptists, or the Jews; or to write evangelistic tracts for Greeks, Samaritans, or Diaspora Jews. His position within the church will seem different (a) if Dr Käsemann's account of his Christology is challenged, and (b) if the epistles are ascribed to a different author. The latter point will be taken up below. For the present we may be content with a brief assessment of John's theological method and achievement. In the first edition of this Commentary it was said that the church of John's day was confronted by two urgent problems. This was an oversimplification, but in outline it may be allowed to stand.

One problem was that of Christian eschatology.[2] It seems clear from the epistles of Paul (e.g., 1 Thess. 4.15; 1 Cor. 15.51) that the earliest Christians expected the *parousia* of Christ to take place suddenly and soon, at least within their own lifetime. Paul himself (it appears) never changed radically the character of his expectation for the future, though more and more death pressed upon him as a real and even urgent possibility. It pressed upon the church too, and in the seventh decade the deaths of Peter and Paul, and of Nero's unknown victims, aroused an apocalyptic enthusiasm which is reflected in Mark 13. It was necessary above all to endure to the end; the end was not yet, but the time was running out and could not be much further extended—indeed, in mercy for the elect the Lord had cut it short. Perhaps the fall of Jerusalem (A.D. 70) had happened before Mark was written; if not, it no doubt fomented apocalyptic enthusiasm yet further. But it is clear that in the next decades a problem was emerging. For some fifty years the church had been living in expectation of the end of the world, and the

---

[1] O. Cullman, *V. und A.*, 175.
[2] See *J.T.S.* new series 1 (1950), 1–3; *S.J.T.* 6 (1953), 136–55, 225–43; *Jesus and the Gospel Tradition* (1967), 68–108.

time of reprieve had been constantly extended. Clearly this process could not be indefinitely prolonged. Apart from the fact that the first generation was rapidly disappearing, the whole aspect of Christian life was changing. In the thirties it was possible to think of the present as an almost insignificant interim, a mere interlude between the last two acts of a great drama. It was no longer possible to think in this way in A.D. 100. The mere extension of the interim in time had given it a different valuation. It was not merely something to be patiently endured; it must have a positive meaning in the purpose of God. No less than the points between which it intervened it must be the scene of a character-istic divine activity. But how could room be found within the church's primitive eschatological faith for such a development? Could the faith be seriously maintained at all, except by the shallower kind of chiliast who was prepared to postpone from one crisis to another the fulfilment of his hopes? That Christianity was in the end able to survive, and to maintain its unique and authentic tension of realization and hope, was due in no small measure to John's contribution to eschatological thought; see above, pp. 67–70.

The other problem was the problem of gnosticism (see above, pp. 38f.). The mystery religions, though in various ways they left their mark on early Christianity, were never in themselves a serious rival to it. For this, the moral difference was too marked, and Christians had no difficulty in convincing themselves that the cults were imitations of the Christian rites that resembled them, cunningly, but not cunningly enough, devised by the devil. Gnosticism was a much more formidable danger, precisely because, at least in some of its forms, it stood so much closer to Christianity, and because it was possible to accommodate the two religious systems to each other in various proportions. It is often (though not always) possible for a student of the history of doctrine to draw with some precision the line between orthodoxy and heresy. It was not so easy in the first half of the second century, and it is not always recognized how nearly 'gnostic Christianity' triumphed over the faith of the New Testament.[1] Thoughtful Christians in that period must have asked themselves how far it was legitimate and expedient for them to use the language of their religious contemporaries, and how far the gnostics, who spoke of one God, of knowledge, of a Saviour and salva-tion, of a divine Word and a heavenly Man, meant by these terms the same thing as they did themselves. In this problem, and in the con-

---

[1] These words were written in the first edition before I had read W. Bauer's *Rechtgläubigkeit und Ketzerei im ältesten Christentum* (1934), which sharpens the question about the relation between orthodoxy and heresy. Bauer's views have been discussed with reference to John in an interesting but hitherto unpublished dissertation by D. J. Hawkin (McMaster University, 1974); I have myself made some reference to the problem (e.g., *N.T.S.* 20 (1974), 229–45), and hope to return to it. In the time of John several attempts were being made to define and defend 'right' Christian belief, and it had not yet become apparent which were culs-de-sac, and which provided a way forward. See S. S. Smalley, *N.T.S.* 17 (1971), 276–92.

troversy that raged over it, the influence of John seems to have been thrown in at first on the gnostic side (see above, pp. 65f., 112ff.); but in the second half of the century, and chiefly through Irenaeus, it took its place as the sheet-anchor of orthodoxy, and as the sign-post not only to the Christian gnosticism of Origen but also to the biblical theology of Athanasius.

It is no doubt true that John himself could not have spoken in this way of an 'eschatological problem' and a 'gnostic problem'. Such problems do not always appear clear cut to those who are involved in them, and when they do appear clear cut it is often because vital aspects of them are being ignored. Yet it is impossible to doubt that John made, and hard to doubt that John knew he was making, a contribution to the church's struggle in the critical situation in which it found itself. He wrote to reaffirm the fundamental convictions of the Christian faith in the full light of new circumstances, new terminology, and new experiences.

These conclusions with regard to the purpose of the gospel cannot but bear upon the question of its historical reliability. It is evident that it was not John's intention to write a work of scientific history. Such works were extremely scarce in antiquity, and we have seen that John's interests were theological rather than chronological. Moreover, his treatment of the only source (Mark) we can isolate with any confidence from his gospel is very free; and there is no reason to think that he followed other sources more closely. He did not hesitate to repress, revise, rewrite, or rearrange. On the other hand there is no sufficient evidence for the view that John freely created narrative material for allegorical purposes. His narratives are for the most part simple, and the details generally remain unallegorized. This means that the chronicler can sometimes (though less frequently than is often thought) pick out from John simple and sound historical material; yet it may be doubted whether John would approve of the proceeding, for he wrote his gospel as a whole, combining discourse material with narrative, in order to bring out with the utmost clarity a single presentation, an interpreted history, of Jesus. Neither of these factors, history and interpretation, should be overlooked; nor, for a full understanding of what John intended, should they be separated. From one point of view John is a reaffirmation of history. Both apocalypticism and gnosticism may be regarded as a flight from history. The apocalyptist escapes from the past and present into a golden age of the future; the gnostic escapes from the past and present into a world of mysticism and fantasy. Over against these John asserted the primacy of history. It was of supreme importance to him that there was a Jesus of Nazareth who lived and died in Palestine, even though to give an accurate outline of the outstanding events in the career of this person was no part of his purpose. He sought to draw out, using in part the form and style of narrative (and that he did use this form is itself highly significant), the true meaning of the life and death of one whom he believed to be the Son of God, a being from beyond history. It is for this interpretation of the focal point of all history, not for accurate historical data, that we must look in John. Yet at every point history underlies what John wrote. The reader is reminded of ancient Egyptian figure drawing, where the artist has tried to give a full impression of his subject by incorporating both full-face and profile in one picture. The result is inevitably like (from the 'photographic' point of view) no man on earth, but it cannot be said that the general effect is unsuccessful; in some respects it is more successful than a straightforward photograph would have been. In the same way John presents in his one book both history and interpretation. The result is not a biography; it is impressionistic rather than photographically accurate in detail, but it cannot be denied that the total effect is impressive and illuminating.

By writing in this way John compels us to face one more question: What was his authority? Those who believe that the evangelist was the son of Zebedee, the apostle John, will of course have no difficulty in finding an answer. Those who do not will find themselves confronted also by a wider question of even greater importance: What is the nature of authority in the Christian church? For (if the view suggested in this commentary is right) John assumes a state of affairs in which all the apostles were dead. The natural authority of those who from the beginning had been eye-witnesses and ministers of the Word had been removed;[1] what authority, if any, could take its place? To this question the gnostics had an answer. Authority rested with the natural *élite* of the Church, the γνωστικοί *par excellence*, those who were supremely endowed with the charisma of theosophical speculation. It was an authority at once of the intellect and of religious experience; we may compare Dr Käsemann's cell of 'enthusiasts', and the authority they may have conceived themselves to have. In effect, this means no authority at all, and the church—represented by Diotrephes, if Dr Käsemann is right—did well to reject it. But what alternatives were available? And was this the only kind of authority that John could and would claim?

The history of Christian thought in the second century may be regarded as to some extent the record of the various attempts that were made to understand, establish, and apply the principle of authority. In the latter part of the century, after Marcion, rapid strides were made towards the fixing of a New Testament canon. Throughout the century, indeed, from New Testament times, we can dimly trace the progressive formulation of a *regula fidei* or *regula veritatis*, which enshrined the essentials of Christian belief. A third line of development in the defining of the authority was the growth, which also goes back to New Testament times, of a permanent ministry, by means of which, as by the

---

[1] 1 Clement, written probably at about the same time as John, seems to presuppose that the apostles are now dead: 5.3; 42.1; 44.1–3.

Scriptures and the Rule of Faith, apostolic truth was to be preserved and applied. John did nothing to further any of these lines of development. Instead, he asked, and causes his reader to ask, what was the nature of the authority of the apostles themselves; and the answer to this question follows two lines.

First, the authority of the apostles lies in their ability to bear witness to the gospel history. On this, for all his freedom with the details of history, John insists most strongly. See especially 19.35; cf. 21.24. The faith of the church rests upon the historical testimony borne by eye-witnesses.

Secondly, the authority of the apostles rests upon the commission given to them by Jesus. This appears most clearly in 20.21, but the parallelism between the mission of Jesus from the Father and the mission of the disciples from Jesus is brought out repeatedly and in the strongest terms. It is a parallelism not only of mission but of knowledge, and even of being (10.14f.; 14.20). Together with this mission of the apostles must be taken the mission of the Holy Spirit, 'whom the Father will send in my name' (14.26), 'whom I will send unto you from the Father' (15.26). It is clear from 20.22 that the mission of the apostles is dependent on the mission of the Spirit. The combined mission of the Spirit and the apostles results in the formation of a further company of believers (17.20; cf. 20.29); and these also enter into the unity and mission of Christ himself (17.21). We reach there the point of transition from the apostles and their authority to the authority under which Christians continued to live, an authority which was in fact perpetuated in the life of the church. For the evangelist places not only himself but also his readers beside the apostles both as eye-witnesses and as emissaries. 1.14 is a crucial verse for the understanding of the gospel. It was among 'us' that the incarnate Word tabernacled; it is 'we' who beheld his glory. This first person plural is to be taken with full seriousness. It does not mean 'we men', for it simply was not true that all men (even all who looked upon his person) beheld the glory of Christ; and it cannot mean 'we apostles', unless the author was himself an apostle. It remains possible only that it should mean 'we, the church', 'we Christians': we beheld the glory of Christ when he abode with us. There is a similar 'we' in 21.24, which emphasizes the importance of the testimony of a veracious eye-witness, and adds 'we know that his witness is true'—the church sets its seal upon the veracity of its spokesman. The church itself is thus the heir of the apostles and of their authority. It is clear that if this statement were left unqualified a door would be left open to a worse anarchy than that of gnosticism; but it is not left unqualified; and the gospel itself is a sufficiently radical qualification, for it is one of those documents in which that which calls itself the church is constantly encountered by him who alone can constitute it as the church. This, is, in essence, the answer to the question (raised above) about the canon. The Fourth Gospel is not canonical because it was written by an apostle or because it is a factually accurate record of the life and teaching of Jesus; it is canonical simply because of this encounter, which takes place through the apostolic word and its reception in faith (17.20). By this means the really historical Jesus meets men and makes real to them the divine love (3.16) and the divine judgement (9.39); and those who receive him become the children of God (1.12f.). 'Church' has no other valid meaning than this: they are disciples who hear and keep the word of Jesus (8.31; 13.35; 15.7f.),[1] in whom and with whom the Paraclete abides, leading them into all truth by declaring the things of Christ (14.17,26; 16.13ff.), who witness as the Spirit witnesses (15.26f.) and thus continue the mission of Christ (20.21). The gospel itself ensures that those who take it seriously shall direct their attention to the Word made flesh, and to the Holy Spirit, by whom the presence of the Word continues to be effected; by this they are related, not to a bygone past or to a particular kind of religious experience, but to God.

[1] 'Thank God, a child of seven years old knows what the church is—the holy believers and the lambs who hear the Shepherd's voice' (M. Luther, Schmalkaldic Articles; Weimar Edition, 50, 250; cf. John 10.27).

6

THE TEXT

IN the first edition of this Commentary I quoted, usually though not always with approval, the text of B. F. Westcott and F. J. A. Hort, *The New Testament in the Original Greek* (1881). This edition of the New Testament text is now seldom used, and I have substituted the more familiar Nestle—though indeed this applies consistently only to the *lemmata*; elsewhere I use what seems to me to be the correct text.

The textual notes are far from being complete. As a rule I have discussed only those variants which bear upon the interpretation of John's thought or contain some other point of special interest (lexical, grammatical, or historical). Further, I have kept to a minimum the number of authorities cited. This has been done of set purpose, for I believe it to be much more important that the student should have a thorough grasp of the principles of textual criticism than that he should commit to memory a large number of sigla. It must never be assumed (unless it is explicitly stated) that the authorities cited for any reading are all that attest it; those who desire fuller information will know where to look for it. In preparing the textual notes I have found help in many books, especially in WH's *Introduction* (Notes on Select Readings); A. Merx, *Die vier kanonischen Evangelien nach ihrem ältesten bekannten Texte*; II, ii, 2: *Das Evangelium des Johannes* (1911); and F. C. Burkitt, *Evangelion da-Mepharreshe* (1904); and in the apparatus in C. Tischendorf, *Nouum Testamentum Graece* (1869); in H. von Soden, *Die Schriften des Neuen Testaments* II: *Text mit Apparat* (1913), and in the smaller editions of Souter, Nestle, Kilpatrick, and of the United Bible Societies; but as far as possible every reading quoted has been verified, from facsimiles or standard editions.

The MSS. and other authorities quoted in the notes are the following:

UNCIAL CODICES

P⁵	A third- or fourth-century papyrus; in London.
P⁴⁵	The Chester Beatty Papyrus of the Gospels and Acts; third century; at Dublin and Vienna.
P⁶⁶	A papyrus of about A.D. 200; at Geneva.
P⁷⁵	An early third-century papyrus, at Geneva.
ℵ	Codex Sinaiticus; fourth century; in London.
B	Codex Vaticanus; fourth century; at Rome.
D	Codex Bezae; fifth or sixth century; at Cambridge.

W   The Washington (Freer) Codex; fourth or fifth century; at Washington.

Θ   The Koridethi Gospels; ninth (?) century; at Tiflis.

MINUSCULE CODICES

33   Ninth or tenth century; at Paris ('the queen of the cursives').

565   Ninth or tenth century; at Leningrad.

λ   denotes the reading of the family 1–118–131–209, etc. (the 'Lake Group').

φ   denotes the reading of the family 13–69–124–346–543, etc. (the 'Ferrar Group').

VERSIONS

Latin

it   The Old (pre-Vulgate) Latin version, of which the following MSS. are quoted:
a Codex Vercellensis; fourth or fifth century; at Vercelli.
b Codex Veronensis; fourth or fifth century; at Verona.
d The Latin text of D (a bilingual MS.; see above).
e Codex Palatinus; fourth or fifth century; at Vienna.

vg   The Vulgate Latin version, made by Jerome towards the close of the fourth century. The text of Wordsworth and White (W.W.) (1889–98) is quoted.

Syriac

sin   The Sinaitic Syriac (Old Syriac).

cur   The Curetonian Syriac (Old Syriac).

pesh   The Peshitta Syriac (the Syriac Vulgate).

hl   The Harclean Syriac (hl^{mg} signifies a marginal reading).

Coptic

sah   The Sahidic version (Southern Coptic).

boh   The Bohairic version (Northern Coptic).

FATHERS AND OTHER WRITERS

Heracleon	Second century
Irenaeus	Second century.
Tertullian	Second and third centuries.
Origen	Third century.
Eusebius	Fourth century.
Ambrosiaster	Fourth century.
Augustine	Fourth and fifth centuries.
Chrysostom	Fourth and fifth centuries.

The symbol ω is used as in Souter's *Nouum Testamentum Graece* to represent '*codices plerique*'.

WH signifies Westcott and Hort, and also the Westcott and Hort text.

COMMENTARY
AND NOTES

I. THE PROLOGUE

1.1-18

Each of the evangelists begins his work by tracing back the activity of Jesus to its origin (ἀρχή): Mark to the work of the Baptist and the baptism of Jesus, with the descent of the Spirit and the divine pronouncement, Thou art my Son; Matthew and Luke to the birth of Jesus from a virgin; John to the creation, and beyond it. Each intends to prepare his readers for understanding the ensuing narrative; Jesus can be understood only as Messiah, as Son of God, and as Logos. John alone, however, gives the narrative about Jesus an absolute theological framework, and, though he alludes to the starting-points used by Mark (vv. 6–8, 15) and by Matthew and Luke (v. 13, see the note), he must have regarded them as inadequate, and as possibly misleading. Mark's baptism story was capable of an adoptionist interpretation, and the notion of the virgin birth recalled pagan myths too clearly. The only perspective in which the work of Jesus, and his relation to the Father, could be truly seen and estimated was that of eternity. John's use of a cosmogony as a background for his message of salvation is paralleled in other Hellenistic literature, e.g. the *Hermetica* (see *C.H.* 1, 4–11), but his treatment of the theme is unique, not least in its combination of the characteristics of the hellenistic or gnostic revelatory discourse (see e.g. Becker, *Reden*, 14–59) and of Targumic exposition (see especially P. Borgen in *N.T.S.* 16 (1970), 288–95, which will be referred to below, and the same author in *Nov. T.* 14 (1972), 115–30).

The unity and construction of the Prologue have been keenly debated (see *Prologue*, and *Judaism*, 20–35, where a very small amount of the discussion is referred to; also S. Schultz, *Komposition und Herkunft der Johanneischen Reden* (1960), 7–69; H. Zimmermann, in *Neues Testament und Kirche* (Festschrift R. Schnackenberg, 1974), 249–65). The following analysis rests upon detailed exegesis, a sketch of which is given in the notes, with some reference to alternative views. In the analysis the most important question is: At what point does John first refer to the entry of the Word upon the human scene? See the notes on verses 5, 9, 14. The following divisions seem best to represent John's intention.

1. vv. 1–5, *Cosmological*. The eternal divine Word, God's agent in creation, is the source of light and life for men. The light is surrounded by darkness, from which it is absolutely and eternally distinguished, and by which it can never be quenched.

2. vv. 6–8, *The Witness of John*. The eternal truth about the Word having been stated, the evangelist begins to move towards his account

of its manifestation in time. In accordance with the Christian tradition, he first introduces the Baptist, carefully distinguishing him from the true Light, but bringing out his importance as bearing witness to it.

3. vv. 9–13, *The Coming of the Light*. The coming of the Word, or Light, is now reached; a coming which was an almost unmitigated failure. Even those who were most privileged did not believe when they saw the light; though John is careful to note and allow for the few who heard, believed, and received, and so constituted the church, whose spokesman he was. This account of the coming of the Word is less explicit than the pronouncement that follows in v. 14, and it is worth noting that Dodd (*Interpretation*, 281–4) thinks that this paragraph was written on two levels, relating both to the cosmic and to the incarnate being of the Word, and that Bultmann believes that whereas John's source spoke in vv. 1–5, 9–12 of the pre-existent Logos, John himself thought of the incarnation from v. 5 onwards.

4. vv. 14–18, *The Economy of Salvation*. The coming of Jesus the Word is dealt with in more detail, and for clarity accompanied by further reference to the Baptist. The earthly life of Jesus, though humble, was the scene in which the glory and mercy of God were displayed. The reader is now prepared to turn to, and understand, the story proper.

These divisions are of roughly equal length, but it does not seem possible to split them up further into poetic structure, either in Greek or in a conjectured original Aramaic. Greek poetry they certainly are not; and it is doubtful whether they can legitimately be described as a rendering into Greek of Semitic verse. (1) The Hebrew verse of the Old Testament was 'discovered' by Robert Lowth in the eighteenth century; most earlier users of Hebrew, for example in the New Testament period, do not seem to have been aware of it. Prose and verse, for example the Shema, the Eighteen Benedictions, and the Hallel Psalms, were all sung in the synagogue in the same way (S.B. IV, 394). (2) Josephus and Philo did not recognize what we call Hebrew verse as having a distinctive pattern and principle of its own; nor did the LXX translators. (3) The case for a Semitic original of the Prologue will not stand; see the detailed discussion in the notes. The Prologue is better described as rhythmical prose. If this is true, it is impossible to strike out certain passages as prose insertions into an original 'logos-ode'. This is confirmed by the fact that the whole passage shows, on careful exegesis, a marked internal unity, and also a distinct unity of theme and subject-matter with the remainder of the gospel; and by the variety of the attempts which have been made to restore the original form of the Prologue. To take two examples only, we may note that Burney (40f.) supposes that the original prologue was written in Aramaic couplets as follows:

1a } 1b }	1c } 2a }	3a } 3b }	4a } 4b }	5a } 5b }	10b } 10c }	11a } 11b }	14a } 14b }	14c } 14d }	14e } 16a }	17a 17b

It will be observed that vv. 6–10a, 12, 13, 15, 16b, 18 are here regarded as prose comments or insertions by an editor. J. Weiss (*The History of Primitive Christianity* (E.T., 1937) 790) divides the Prologue into quatrains and sets it out thus:

1a	3a	5a	11a	14ab	17ab
1b	3b	5b	11b	14cd	18a
1c	4a	10ab	12a	14e	18b
2a	4b	10c	12b	16ab	18c

Here vv. 10a, 12, 16b, 18 (discarded by Burney) are included, and, further, the rhythmical arrangement is entirely different. Other arrangements are given by other scholars; see Brown, 22. These differences cannot of course disprove the proposition that the Prologue was originally written in, or based upon, verse; they must however breed scepticism in the ability of scholars to distinguish between 'verse' and prose. It may be possible to reject certain verses as parts of the original Prologue on the ground of their content, and most students have in fact regarded vv. 6–8, 15 (which deal with John the Baptist) as insertions; this question will be dealt with in the notes. In fact, the references to John the Baptist help to make clear the present purpose of the Prologue. The Evangelist may have drawn to some extent on existing material—what writer does not? But the Prologue stands before us as a prose introduction which has not been submitted to interpolation and was specially written (it must be supposed) to introduce the gospel —and, it may be added, to sum it up. Many Introductions and Prefaces serve this dual purpose.

Only in the Prologue is the term λόγος used in a Christological sense. This fact must not be given undue emphasis. Many of the central ideas in the Prologue are central also in the body of the gospel; see, e.g., the notes on ζωή, φῶς (v. 4), μαρτυρία (v. 7), ἀληθινός (v. 9), κόσμος (v. 10), δόξα, ἀλήθεια (v. 14). If the Prologue was intended to express in eighteen verses the theological content of twenty chapters a good deal of condensation was necessary; and much of John's Christology is condensed in the word λόγος.

1. ἐν ἀρχῇ. Cf. Gen. 1.1, ἐν ἀρχῇ (בראשית, *bᵉreshith*) ἐποίησεν ὁ θεός, and Prov. 8.22, κύριος ἔκτισέν με ἀρχὴν ὁδῶν αὐτοῦ (דרכו) (*reshith*) (יהוה קנני ראשית). Cf. also Mark 1.1, ἀρχὴ τοῦ εὐαγγελίου Ἰησοῦ Χριστοῦ. That John's opening verse is intended to recall the opening verse of Genesis is certain; that it reflects the opening of the earliest gospel is probable. In view of the parallel between Logos and Wisdom (see below) an allusion to Prov. 8.22 is also probable. Similarly the existence of the Torah (see below) is thrown back to the 'beginning'; thus *Gen. R.* 1.2: There is no beginning (ראשית, *reshith*) but Torah; also *Pesahim* 54a: Seven things were created before the world was created—Torah, repentance, the Garden of Eden, Gehinnom, the throne of glory, the temple, and the name of the Messiah (in this *baraitah* Prov. 8.22 is quoted in proof of the pre-existence of the Torah). The soterio-

logical work and position of Jesus, being universal in scope, are represented against a cosmological background. It is a comparable fact that in (e.g.) *C.H.* salvation is given its shape by cosmology; Cullmann (*Christology*, 265), however, is right in saying that to understand v. 1 one must have v. 14 in his ear; that is, the Christology even of John is primarily functional, or, in other words, for John salvation has priority over cosmology. It is true that ἐν ἀρχῇ means that in Jesus one encounters what is beyond the world and time (Bultmann), but it might be even better to say that what is beyond the world and time is known in Jesus.

ἦν. The continuous tense is to be contrasted with the punctiliar ἐγένετο of v. 3 (creation), v. 6 (the appearance of the Baptist), and v. 14 (the incarnation). It indicates that by ἀρχή is meant not the first point in a temporal sequence but that which lies beyond time.

ὁ λόγος. By introducing this theological term without explanation John indicates that it was not unfamiliar to his readers. It is not common in the New Testament as a designation of Christ (apart from the Prologue it occurs at Rev. 19.13 and possibly at 1 John 1.1), but in Col. 1.15–20 Paul reaches a similar Christological position without using the word. An extended discussion of the word is called for and is now given; see also the notes on vv. 1 (ἐν ἀρχῇ, above), 2, 3, 4, and the Introduction, pp. 73f.

A. *Background.* (i) λόγος is a Greek word of many meanings (see L.S. *s.v.*), most of which can be summarized under the two heads of inward thought, and the outward expression of thought in speech. In a theistic system it could therefore naturally be used in an account of God's self-revelation: his thought was communicated by his speech. Early philosophical use of λόγος is questionable; it is probably wrong to claim that Heraclitus had a 'logos-doctrine' (T. F. Glasson, *J.T.S.* 3 (1952), 231–8). The word however lent itself to pantheistic use, and the earlier Stoics had no other god than λόγος, the rational principle in accordance with which the universe existed, and men, endowed in varying degrees with σπερματικοὶ λόγοι, were bound to frame their lives. In the fusion of Stoicism and Platonism which forms a diffuse but significant element in the background of early Christianity (see Introduction, p. 36) a compromise was reached; the rational principle of the Stoic universe was the λόγος of God. That John had some familiarity with thought of this kind is probable, but it must be remembered that common Greek usage (quite apart from philosophy) made λόγος a very convenient term for describing any kind of self-expression.

(ii) It has been claimed that gnosticsim makes a significant contribution to the background of John's use of λόγος. This is a proposition (see below) which cannot be made in simple terms since the word λόγος cannot be quoted from pre-Johannine gnostic texts as it can be quoted from pre-Johannine Stoic texts. It involves consideration of the character of the Prologue as a whole. Its source (it is said) 'belongs to the sphere of a relatively early oriental Gnosticism, which has been developed under the influence of the Old Testament faith in the Creator-God. This development has taken the following direction: the mythology has been severely pushed into the background; the Gnostic cosmology has been repressed and has given way to the belief in Creation; and the concern for the relation of man to the revelation of God, that is to say the soteriological concern, has become dominant. The Odes of Solomon prove to be the most closely related.—The figure of the Logos, as Creator and Revealer, is to be understood in terms of this Gnosticism, on the basis of a characteristically modified dualism' (Bultmann, 30f.). The question is thus not one that can be answered by quoting passages; it relates rather to the context of thought in which the Johannine λόγος is set in the Prologue as a whole. See further below on 'The Christian Word'.

(iii) λόγος is naturally a very frequent word in the Greek Old Testament; here special attention may be drawn to two groups of passages. In the former the word of God is creative; cf. Gen. 1.3,6,9, etc., the creating words of command, summarized in Ps. 33.6, By the word of the Lord (בדבר יהוה) were the heavens made (32.6, τῷ λόγῳ τοῦ κυρίου οἱ οὐρανοὶ ἐστερεώθησαν). In the latter, the word of the Lord is the prophet's message, that is, the means by which God communicates his purpose to his people; see e.g. Jer. 1.4, Now the word of the Lord came unto me (ויהי דבר יהוה אלי, καὶ ἐγένετο λόγος κυρίου πρὸς αὐτόν); Ezek. 1.3; Amos 3.1. In all the passages in each group the word is not abstract but spoken and active. Both creation and revelation are in mind in the Johannine Prologue, and the rest of the gospel encourages us to suppose that the influence of the Old Testament may be found here. It does not suffice to reply that 'word' in the Old Testament signifies event, whereas John's λόγος is timeless; it is precisely John's assertion that the timeless (ἐν ἀρχῇ) Word became an event (σὰρξ ἐγένετο).

(iv) In the Targums of the Old Testament frequent use is made of the Aramaic word מימרא (memra, word). It has sometimes been supposed that this מימרא is a divine hypostasis capable of furnishing a true parallel to John's thought of a personal Logos incarnate in Jesus. מימרא however was not truly a hypostasis but a means of speaking about God without using his name, and thus a means of avoiding the numerous anthropomorphisms of the Old Testament. One example will show both the true meaning of מימרא, and also the way in which it might erroneously be taken as a hypostasis: Gen. 3.8: for, They heard the voice of the Lord God (את קול יהוה אלהים), Targ. Onqelos reads, They heard the voice of the memra of the Lord God (ית קל מימרא דיי אלהים). Memra is a blind alley in the study of the biblical background of John's logos doctrine. A different view is taken by McNamara, T. and T., 101–4.

(v) A much more important line of approach is given by the Jewish concept of Wisdom (חכמה (hokhmah), σοφία). Already in Proverbs (see 8.22 quoted above) the Wisdom of God has ceased to be merely the quality of being wise; Wisdom has an independent existence in the presence of God, and also bears some relation to the created world. She remains also a blessed gift to man (8.34). In the later Sapiential books (it is unnecessary here to consider under what influences) this tendency is maintained, and Wisdom becomes, more and more, a personal being standing by the side of God over against, but not unconcerned with, the created world. See e.g. Wisd. 7.22 (ἡ γὰρ πάντων τεχνῖτις . . . σοφία) and 7.27 ([σοφία] εἰς ψυχὰς ὁσίας μεταβαίνουσα φίλους θεοῦ καὶ προφήτας κατασκευάζει), which illustrate both the cosmological and soteriological functions of Wisdom. Further references are given in the notes on vv. 1–4.

(vi) In speculative Judaism Wisdom found two successors. Philo found here a means of introducing the Stoic–Platonic Logos into Judaism. No simple or even consistent doctrine of the Logos can be drawn from his writings; the

Logos may be identified, for example, with persons in the Old Testament, such as the High Priest, allegorically interpreted. Philo's Logos, broadly speaking, takes the place Sophia had occupied in earlier Hellenistic Judaism, and in particular exercises a cosmological function. The ideal world, of which the phenomenal world is but a copy, can be called ὁ θεοῦ λόγος (*Op.* 24f.); but particularly the Logos is the ideal, primal Man, the image of God from whom spring and decline all empirical men. The real substance of Philo's thought is Greek (derived especially from the *Timaeus* of Plato); a more characteristically Jewish development of the figure of Wisdom is Torah (Law) in rabbinic Judaism. Passages will be quoted at the appropriate points which show that Torah could be fancifully described in personal terms, and thought of in cosmological and soteriological roles. There is here a truly Jewish line of thought which is of the first importance for the understanding of John; though it is necessary to remember that the Rabbis were not carefully elaborating a metaphysic but using startling metaphors, often in an undisciplined way.

B. *The Christian Word.* Of no less importance than the Greek and Jewish background is the Christian. In the New Testament the Word of God is frequently the Christian message of salvation, the Gospel (e.g. Luke 8.11; 2 Tim. 2.9; Rev. 1.9; cf. especially 1 John 1.1). It was spoken by Paul (e.g. Acts 13.5; 1 Thess. 2.13), by other apostles (e.g. Acts 6.2), and by Jesus himself (Luke 5.1; cf. Mark 2.2 and many similar passages). But the Gospel Paul proclaimed was Christ himself (e.g. 1 Cor. 1.23; 2 Cor. 4.1–6; Gal. 3.1); so it was with other apostles (e.g. Acts 2.36; 4.12); and while the synoptists are doubtless right in suggesting that Jesus proclaimed the approach of the kingdom of God (cf. τὸν λόγον τῆς βασιλείας, Matt. 13.19) John represents the kernel of Jesus' message as—himself, and in doing so does no more than take the last step of a process hinted at, and, it may be added, justified, by the rest of the New Testament (on this point see especially Hoskyns, 162–4). There was further development on this line, and on kindred but distinct lines, in somewhat later Christian literature, notably Ignatius, *Magnesians* 8.2, and a number of the Odes of Solomon, especially 7.7; 9.3; 12.11f.; 16.20 (cf. 1 QS 11.11); 41.13f. On the relation between John, Ignatius, and the Odes, see Introduction, pp. 63ff., 110–13; also my essay, cited on p. 63.

C. *The Johannine Conception of the Word* was thus preceded by more than one other in which similar thoughts are expressed without the use of the word λόγος. Col. 1.15–20 shows as clearly as does John 1.1–18 the use of language drawn from Jewish speculations about Wisdom. Paul (or the author of Colossians) was not content with the cosmic dignity to which Christians (gnostics?) in Colossae had elevated Jesus but insisted as John does upon his historical role, and found the work of creation and of salvation suitably combined in the figure of Wisdom; Hebrews (see especially 1.1–4) regards Jesus in a fundamentally similar way; but no other New Testament writer shows such mastery of the material as does John, who holds together Jewish, Hellenistic, and primitive Christian strands of thought in a consistent unity. That John was familiar with the Old Testament and with Judaism seems clear; yet it is also highly probable that in developing Sophia and Torah speculation he intentionally chose for employment those aspects of Jewish thought which had Hellenistic parallels. The question whether John's use of λόγος is in any way indebted to gnosticism is disputed. Jeremias (*Z.N.T.W.* 59 (1968), 82–5) argues that this can be proved by none of the passages cited (Irenaeus, *Adv. Haer.* III. xi, 1, for Cerinthus; Ignatius, *Magnesians*, 8.2; the Odes of Solomon); the source of the term is to be sought in Hellenistic Judaism, in which it is freely used by Philo (and hinted at by earlier writers). This argument is not wholly satisfactory, in that Philo himself must be reckoned among the witnesses to an early form of gnosis, which developed into gnosticism as primitive Christianity was added to the syncretism of Hellenism with Judaism and other oriental movements. It would however be wrong to suggest that John accomplished his task by making a neat amalgam of earlier notions of mediation and applying it to Christ; he begins with Christ, the eschatological fulfilment of God's purposes, and with the fundamental conviction that Christ himself is the Gospel, the Word which God has spoken. The Prologue, which can be read as Hellenistic philosophy and as rabbinic mysticism, and no doubt in other speculative terms, can also be read as history: He came to his own, and his own received him not. The Johannine Logos has a cosmological function similar to that described by Philo—but he became flesh. The Johannine Logos is parallel to the Sophia-Torah figure of Judaism; but John is quick to point out that as the Torah was historically given through Moses so grace and truth came by Jesus Christ (1.17). The Logos exists, but is unknown and incomprehensible apart from the historical figure of Jesus; creation is evidently so perverted (vv. 10f.) that it fails to manifest its Creator—John finds no place for natural theology (v. 18). Conversely, the events of the gospel narrative are comprehensible only in the light of the conviction that the chief actor was no mere man but the eternal Word of God. In this respect, as in others, the Prologue and the rest of the gospel are complementary to each other. Like Logos in the one Jesus in the other is pre-existent, the Son of God, the light of the world; he is rejected by those who should receive him, but gives to his own the grace and truth which are the life of the children of God.

ὁ λόγος ἦν πρὸς τὸν θεόν. πρός with the accusative can hardly mean 'in the presence of' in classical Greek, but this meaning is unquestionable in New Testament Greek (e.g. Mark 6.3, οὐκ εἰσὶν αἱ ἀδελφαὶ αὐτοῦ ὧδε πρὸς ἡμᾶς;), and the Hellenistic usage makes it unnecessary to see here the influence in translation of the Aramaic לות. For Wisdom as 'with God' cf. Prov. 8.30; I was by him, as a master workman (אצלו אמון, παρ' αὐτῷ ἁρμόζουσα). For Torah, cf. *Gen. R.* 8.2, where R. Simeon b. Laqish, commenting on Prov. 8.30 in the light of Ps. 90.4 (יום יום in the former passage is equal to 2,000 years) and identifying Wisdom and Torah, says that Torah preceded the creation of the world by 2,000 years. There are several other passages where the same identification is made, and others again where Torah is said to be pre-existent, creative, and divine. Such notions are the root of John's statement; it is therefore unnecessary to take πρός in a strict classical sense; no clear meaning is obtained by saying that the Word existed 'in relation to' God, and to render 'the word was addressed to God' (F. C. Burkitt, *Church and Gnosis* (1932), 95), with reference to Gen. 1.3, etc., raises more difficulties than it solves.

καὶ θεὸς ἦν ὁ λόγος. No equally high claim is made for Wisdom (but cf. Wisd. 7.25, ἀτμὶς γάρ ἐστιν τῆς τοῦ θεοῦ δυνάμεως, καὶ ἀπόρροια τῆς τοῦ παντοκράτορος δόξης εἰλικρινής). Torah is said to be the daughter of God (e.g. *Sanhedrin*

101a (a *baraitah*); *Lev. R.* 20.7; *Song of Songs R.* 8.13. θεός, being without the article, is predicative and describes the nature of the Word. The absence of the article indicates that the Word is God, but is not the only being of whom this is true; if ὁ θεός had been written it would have been implied that no divine being existed outside the second person of the Trinity; see M. III,183 (if Turner's observation about word-order is correct it takes away the relevance of Haenchen's reference to 11.25 (*Die Bibel und Wir* (1968), 218)). θεός can be a title for the 'divine man' (Betz, 102), but it is not in this sense that John uses it.

John intends that the whole of his gospel shall be read in the light of this verse. The deeds and words of Jesus are the deeds and words of God; if this be not true the book is blasphemous.

Sanders places a full stop after θεὸς ἦν, and begins a new sentence with ὁ λόγος οὗτος. . . . The variation is possible, but makes no serious difference to the meaning of vv. 1,2.

2. οὗτος ἦν ἐν ἀρχῇ πρὸς τὸν θεόν. V. 1a, b are resumed in combined form. This is not mere repetition. The Word does not *come to be* with God; the Word *is* with God in the beginning. Cf. 17.5; at the ascension Jesus returns to the position of glory he occupied before creation.

3. πάντα δι' αὐτοῦ ἐγένετο. This belief can be paralleled in Jewish, Hellenistic, and Christian sources. (*a*) For wisdom see Prov. 8.30 (quoted above). (*b*) For Torah see, e.g., *P. Aboth* 3.15: Beloved are Israel, for to them was given the precious instrument; still greater was the love, in that it was made known to them that to them was given the precious instrument by which the world was created (שבו נברא העולם: the context, with a quotation from Prov. 4.2, shows that Torah is meant). 1 QS 11.11, All that is he establishes according to his plan (במחשבתו), and without him nothing happens, presents a close formal parallel to both parts, the positive and the negative, of this verse, but it is not said of the *Word*, and when applied to God is a familiar biblical commonplace. (*c*) The Stoic Logos is *ex hypothesi* the ground of creation (cf. also Lucretius, *de Rerum Natura* 1, 4f., 21ff.). On the cosmological role of the Logos in Philo see above, pp. 153f. (*d*) Cf. 1 Cor. 8.6, δι' οὗ τὰ πάντα; Col. 1.16; Heb. 1.2. There are later parallels in the Odes of Solomon, 6.3; 12.10; 16.8–14,18. John's emphasis upon the role of the Word in creation brings out that he is not an occasional or accidental mediator.

χωρὶς αὐτοῦ. The same truth is now stated negatively. There was no other demiurge.

The division of words between vv. 3 and 4 is uncertain. We may read (*a*) χωρὶς αὐτοῦ ἐγένετο οὐδὲ ἓν ὃ γέγονεν. ἐν αὐτῷ ζωὴ ἦν, or (*b*) χ. αὐ. ἐγ. οὐδὲ ἕν. ὃ γέγονεν ἐν αὐτῷ ζωὴ ἦν. With this uncertainty must be taken the variant ζωή ἐστιν (not ἦν), supported by ℵ D it cur Gnostics. This variant should probably be rejected, since the second ἦν (ἡ ζωὴ ἦν τὸ φῶς) seems to require the first. The strongest argument in favour of (*b*) is that it is the interpretation of the earliest fathers (and heretics); only when the danger that lay in the heretical use of (*b*) was perceived did patristic exegesis swing over to (*a*). It is maintained further that (*b*) is to be preferred to (*a*) because it gives a better parallel structure to the clauses, because οὐδὲ ἕν is a frequent sentence ending when greater emphasis than a simple οὐδέν is required (e.g. Josephus, *Ant.* VI, 266), and because after οὐδὲ ἕν, ὤν (rather than ὃ) γέγονεν would be expected. None of these reasons is convincing, and against them may be set (1) John's very frequent use of ἐν at the beginning of a sentence; (2) his frequent repetitiousness (nothing was made that has been made; cf. e.g. vv. 1f.); (3) such passages as 5.26 (τῷ υἱῷ ἔδωκεν 3ωὴν ἔχειν ἐν ἑαυτῷ); 5.39; 6.53 which give a similar sense; (4) the fact that it makes much better, and more Johannine, sense to say that in the Word was life, than to say that the created universe was life in him, and that this life was the light of men. The alternative ways of rendering (b) (That which came into being—in it the Word was life; That which came into being—in the Word was its life) are almost impossibly clumsy. After a detailed discussion Schnackenburg comes to the same conclusion. K. Aland in an important article (*Z.N.T.W.* 59 (1968), 174–209) disagrees.

4. ἐν αὐτῷ 3ωὴ ἦν. On the reading see above.

ἡ 3ωὴ ἦν τὸ φῶς τῶν ἀνθρώπων. The words life and light are among the most characteristic of the gospel. Later Jesus claims that he is the life (11.25 si v. l.; 14.6) and that he is the light of the world (8.12; 9.5; cf. 12.46). The Prologue claims no more than the rest of the gospel, but sets first in a cosmological aspect what later will appear in a soteriological. The background of John's thought is here at its maximum width. Life and light are essential elements in the Old Testament creation narrative. God gives life (e.g. Ezek. 37.1–14; Dan. 12.2) and is the source of light and wisdom (e.g. Ps. 119.130). Old Testament teaching is summed up in Ps. 36.10 (35.10, παρὰ σοὶ πηγὴ 3ωῆς, ἐν τῷ φωτί σου ὀψόμεθα φῶς), a verse which has probably influenced John. Wisdom herself is ἀπαύγασμα . . . φωτὸς ἀιδίου (Wisd. 7.26). She declares αἱ ἔξοδοί μου ἔξοδοι 3ωῆς (Prov. 8.35), and her disciple will have (Wisd. 8.13) δι᾽ αὐτὴν ἀθανασίαν . . . (8.17) ὅτι ἔστιν ἀθανασία ἐν συγγενείᾳ σοφίας. Torah equally is the means of life for men; e.g. Ecclus. 17.11, νόμον 3ωῆς ἐκληροδότησεν αὐτοῖς; *P. Aboth* 2.7: The more study of the Law the more life (ascribed to Hillel). Torah is also said to be light; e.g. *Siphre Numbers* 6.25 §41: The Lord lift up the light of his countenance upon you—that is the light (מאור) of the Torah (cf. Prov. 6.23); *Deut. R.* 7.3: As oil is life for the world, so also are words of Torah life for the world; as oil is light for the world, so also are words of Torah light for the world. Life and light both have an apocalyptic connotation. The present age is darkness and death; e.g. *Mekhilta* Exod. 14.31 (בשלח §7): This world (העולם הזה) is altogether night; cf. 4 Ezra 14.20; but the age to come is light and life: e.g. *Gen. R.* 91.13; The age to come (העולם הבא) is altogether day; 2 Baruch 48.50: In that world to which there is no end, ye shall receive great light; Ps. Sol. 16.6(10): The pious of the Lord shall inherit life in gladness. See also 1 Enoch 58.3; 2 Enoch 42.5; Ps. Sol. 3.12. Braun notes that *life* (חיים) is not particularly common in the vocabulary of Qumran.

The words life and light are almost equally characteristic of Hellenistic religious and philosophical thought. Many of the popular religions were in some degree based upon mythologies treating of the conflict of light with darkness; light was thus inevitably an element in both cosmogony and redemption. The collocation of life and light is particularly characteristic of the first and thirteenth Hermetic tractates. Thus (1, 9) the god Νοῦς is 3ωὴ καὶ φῶς; the archetypal man shares the same attributes, ὁ δὲ Ἄνθρωπος ἐκ 3ωῆς καὶ φωτὸς ἐγένετο εἰς ψυχὴν καὶ νοῦν, ἐκ μὲν 3ωῆς ψυχήν, ἐκ δὲ φωτὸς νοῦν (1, 17); the man who has received salvation bears witness, εἰς 3ωὴν καὶ φῶς χωρῶ (1, 32). It is of course a fundamental principle of gnostic thought that only the bestowal of light (knowledge) can give life (salvation). The Odes of Solomon also refer frequently to light and life.

Even more significant for John than this varied background was the fact that Jesus, according to the earlier tradition, had, by his miracles, resurrection, and continued power in the supernatural life of the church, proved himself to be the life of the world, and the frequent use in the tradition of images drawn from light (e.g. Matt. 5.14; Mark 4.21f.; Luke 17.24). Jesus was life and light in himself, and he was the agent by whom God bestowed life and light upon the world. This John proceeds to set forth in a variety of ways; see especially (for life) 3.15f.; 4.14; 5.24-30; 6.35,63; 10.10; 17.3, and (for light) 8.12; 9; 12.35f., and the notes on each passage. The effect of the coming of Jesus into the world as light was that the world was judged; this thought appears in the Prologue (vv. 5, 10) and recurs in the gospel (3.19-21; 9; 12.46). For 'light' in John see further on 8.12.

The life *was* the light. The life was the essential energy of the Word. The Word signified the communication of the knowledge of God; hence the life was the light of men, which gave them true knowledge and by shining in their midst submitted them to judgement.

5. τὸ φῶς ἐν τῇ σκοτίᾳ φαίνει. σκοτία is as characteristic a word in John as φῶς; see 8.12; 12.35,46 (also 1 John 1.5; 2.8,9,11; σκότος, John 3.19; 1 John 1.6). The contrast of light and darkness seems inevitably to arise whenever theological use is made of 'light'. John's thought is not without contact with the fields mentioned in the note on v. 4, but it is governed throughout by his identification of Jesus with the light of the world. 'Darkness' in consequence takes on a corresponding ethical quality. See S. Aalen, *Die Begriffe 'Licht' und 'Finsternis'* (1951); also G. Klein, *Zeitschrift für Theologie und Kirche* 68 (1971), 269-91.

The present tense φαίνει distinguishes this statement from v. 6, ἐγένετο ἄνθρωπος, and v. 11, εἰς τὰ ἴδια ἦλθεν. No particular manifestation of divine light is meant; it is as much an eternal property of the Light to shine in the darkness as it is of the life to be the light of men, and of the Word to have life in himself. The light cannot cease to do this without ceasing to be light. Käsemann (1, 166, and elsewhere) and Conzelmann (*Theology*, 335f.) believe that the present verse already describes as an historical event the coming of the Logos who is light; for the views of Bultmann and Dodd see above, p. 150. The parallels with v. 9 and 1 John 2.8 (which describes the *state* initiated by the coming of the Word) do not suffice to give historical significance to John's φαίνει.

ἡ σκοτία αὐτὸ οὐ κατέλαβεν. καταλαμβάνειν, 'to seize', may mean 'to overcome', or, especially in the middle, 'to grasp with the mind', 'to understand'. Here it seems probable that John is (after his manner; see on 3.3) playing on the two meanings (as Lucian did; see *Vitarum Auctio* 27; *Verae Historiae* II, 18, and cf. *E.T.* 53 (1942), 297). Since the Greek word itself bears both meanings there is no need to resort to the hypothesis of an Aramaic original and confusion between קבל and אקבל. The darkness neither understood nor quenched the light. The thought here is primarily cosmological, but corresponds closely to what John is about to say of the historical mission of Jesus. Cf. Odes of Solomon 18.6: Let not the luminary be conquered by the darkness; nor let truth flee away from falsehood.

Sanders thinks there is a reference here to the failure of persecution to suppress the Gospel, but if it is unlikely that there is a reference here to the story of Jesus it is even less probable that there should be a reference to later Christian history.

6. ἐγένετο ἄνθρωπος. The second division of the Prologue begins and for the first time the stage of history is reached. The aorist ἐγένετο is to be contrasted with the continuous tenses of vv. 1–5. Like Mark, John (after his reference to creation and eternity) takes John the Baptist as the beginning of the gospel (cf. Acts 10.37); see on 1.19–34. There is no need to suspect interpolation here; John occupies an important place in the gospel, and it is quite natural that he should be introduced into the Prologue. On the references in the Prologue to John the Baptist see M. D. Hooker, *N.T.S.* 16 (1970), 354–8; also *Prologue*.

ἀπεσταλμένος παρὰ θεοῦ, sent and commissioned from God; like Moses (Exod. 3.10–15) and the prophets (e.g. Isa. 6.8); like Jesus himself (3.17 and many other passages); also like the Hellenistic philosopher (e.g. Epictetus, III, xxii, 23, ἄγγελος ἀπὸ τοῦ Διὸς ἀπέσταλται). On the use of ἀποστέλλειν (and πέμπειν) in John see on 20.21. The work of John the Baptist derives significance only from the fact that he is sent.

ὄνομα αὐτῷ ’Ιωάννης. The clause is parenthetical; cf. 3.1. There are Old Testament parallels to this phrase (as to ἐγένετο ἄνθρωπος), but there are Hellenistic parallels too; there is no ground for suspecting translation (*Judaism*, 24).

7. εἰς μαρτυρίαν, for the purpose of witnessing. 'Witness' (μαρτυρεῖν, μαρτυρία) holds an important place in the thought of the gospel. The Baptist (1.7f., 15,32,34; 3.26; 5.33), the Samaritan woman (4.39), the works of Jesus (5.36; 10.25), the Old Testament (5.39), the multitude (12.17), the Holy Spirit and the apostles (15.26f.), God the Father himself (5.(32),37; 8.18) all bear witness to Jesus. Jesus himself, who, knowing all things, has no need that witness concerning man should be borne to him (2.25), bears witness to the truth (18.37, cf. 3.11), in conjunction with the Father (8.13–18), whose consentient testimony validates his own. Witnesses in turn testify to the truth of the gospel record (19.35; 21.24). In 18.23 the accusers of Jesus are invited to bear witness regarding the evil he is alleged to have done, that is, to establish by their testimony the fact alleged. This is normal Greek usage, it corresponds sufficiently to the use of the root עוד in the Old Testament (which also supplies the notion of God's testifying to, or against, his people), and is the common meaning of the words in John. See further the notes on the passages referred to.

ἵνα μαρτυρήσῃ. Epexegetic of εἰς μαρτυρίαν.

περὶ τοῦ φωτός, the divine Light incarnate in Jesus, as vv. 8f. show. At 3.26; 5.33; μαρτυρεῖν when used of John is constructed with a dative.

ἵνα πάντες πιστεύσωσιν. The second ἵνα clause is dependent on the first. The purpose of John's witnessing, though not its actual result, was that all should believe in Jesus. πιστεύειν (cf. Hebrew האמין) corresponds closely to μαρτυρεῖν; it means to accept the testimony as valid, and the fact thereby attested as fact. Cf. 1.35–7; the two disciples heard John's witness and believed.

δι' αὐτοῦ must refer to John; men do not believe *through* Jesus but *in* him.

8. οὐκ ἦν ἐκεῖνος τὸ φῶς. For the repetition in negative form cf. v. 3. 'Such an assertion has meaning only if there were people who held that John really was "the light"' (Cullmann, *V. & A.*, 270f.). There is some force in this argument (cf. 3.25ff.); but the negative assertion is intended to prepare the way for v. 9.

ἀλλ' ἵνα. The sentence is elliptical; supply ἦλθεν. It is quite unnecessary to suppose, and is indeed improbable, that ἵνα is a mistranslation of the Aramaic ד in a passage where that particle should have been rendered as a relative; 'he was not the light, but one who bore witness . . .'. The words in Greek are readily intelligible as they stand, and no conjecture is needed. It is not likely that ἵνα is imperatival (M. III, 95).

9. With the opening of the third section of the Prologue John's thought moves, in gradual stages, from the eternal to the temporal and particular.

ἦν τὸ φῶς τὸ ἀληθινόν. On Jesus Christ as the light see on 8.12 (cf. 1.4; 3.21; 9.5). In John's usage, ἀληθινός is to be distinguished from ἀληθής, which is applied only to opinions and statements, and those who hold or make them (at 6.55 ἀληθῶς not ἀληθής, should be read—see the note), and means simply 'veracious'. ἀληθινός is capable of bearing this meaning (4.37; (7.28); (8.16); 19.35), but it is more characteristically applied to light (1.9), worshippers of God (4.23), bread from heaven (6.32), the vine (15.1), and to God himself (17.3; cf. 7.28). The meaning is brought out most clearly by the present passage (1.9). The Baptist might be supposed a light (indeed, in a sense he was a light, 5.35), but he was not τὸ ἀληθινὸν φῶς, the Word. That is, ἀληθινός means 'real', 'genuine', 'authentic'; cf. T. Asher 4.3, τὸ δοκοῦν καλὸν μετὰ τοῦ ἀληθινοῦ καλοῦ. ὁ ἀληθινὸς θεός is the true God over against idols; οἱ ἀληθινοὶ προσκυνηταί are the true worshippers over against idolaters. Whatever is described as ἀληθινός corresponds to the truth: what this means must be considered in the note on ἀλήθεια (see on 1.14). The thought is thus akin to but not identical with Philo's ἀρχέτυπον φῶς (*Som.* 1,75), akin because both writers are thinking in terms of true being, different because John's thought originates in and is determined by history whereas Philo's is speculative.

ἐρχόμενον εἰς τὸν κόσμον. ἐρχόμενον may be taken as either (*a*) neuter nominative, agreeing with φῶς, or (*b*) masculine accusative, agreeing with ἄνθρωπον. (*a*) gives a periphrastic imperfect, ἦν τὸ φῶς . . . ἐρχόμενον, presumably a reference to the incarnation; if the construction (*b*) is adopted we must render '. . . every man who comes (*or*, as he comes) into the world.' In favour of (*b*) is the fact that כל באי העולם, 'all who come into the world,' is a common rabbinic expression for 'every man'; cf. e.g. *Lev. R.* 31.6; Thou enlightenest (מאיר ל) those who are on high and those who are beneath and all who come into the world (i.e. all men, כל באי עולם). In favour of (*a*) may be reckoned (i) in the next verse the light is in the world; it is therefore natural to suppose that it should previously be described as coming; (ii) in other passages (6.14; 9.39; 11.27; 16.28) Jesus 'comes into the world', and at 12.46 he declares, ἐγὼ φῶς εἰς τὸν κόσμον ἐλήλυθα; (iii) the periphrastic imperfect is in accordance with John's style (1.28; 2.6; 3.23; 10.40; 11.1; 13.23; 18.18,25). These arguments seem to outweigh the parallel which stands on the other side—and is indeed not a true parallel, since the Hebrew is not כל איש (every *man* . . .). Construction (*a*) is thus to be preferred, and is to be taken as a reference to the incarnation (The true light was coming . . .) rather than as a further definition of the light (The real light was that which lights every man as it comes into the world—Sanders).

ὁ φωτίζει πάντα ἄνθρωπον. φωτίζειν may mean (*a*) 'to shed light upon', 'to bring to light', 'to make visible', or (*b*) 'to illuminate inwardly', 'to instruct', 'to give knowledge'. (*b*) is a common, though secondary use of the word. It is found in the LXX (Ps. 19(18).9, ἡ ἐντολὴ κυρίου τηλαυγής, φωτίζουσα ὀφθαλμούς—מאירת עינים); in the *Hermetica* (e.g. 1, 32, φωτίσω τοὺς ἐν ἀγνοίᾳ τοῦ γένους, μοῦ ἀδελφούς, υἱοὺς δὲ σοῦ), and in the New Testament (e.g. Eph. 1.18, πεφωτισμένους τοὺς ὀφθαλμοὺς τῆς καρδίας ὑμῶν). Cf. Heb. 6.4; 10.32; Justin 1 *Apol.* 61, 65; also Wisd. 9.9–18 (Lindars). When the Prologue is interpreted in terms of Hellenistic religion, and the Logos thought of in the Stoic manner, it is natural to see in the present verse a reference to a general illumination of all men by the divine Reason, which was subsequently deepened by the more complete manifestation of the Logos in the incarnation. (Cf. a similar view of the Law; T. Levi 14.4 (β), τὸ φῶς τοῦ νόμου . . . τὸ δοθὲν . . . εἰς φωτισμὸν παντὸς ἀνθρώπου.) Whether John's words do in fact bear this meaning is, however, open to doubt. (i) In the next verse he emphasizes that ὁ κόσμος αὐτὸν οὐκ ἔγνω—there was no natural and universal knowledge of the light. (ii) It was those who received Christ who received authority to become children of God. (iii) In the rest of the gospel the function of light is judgement; when it shines, some come to it, others do not. It is not true that all men have a natural affinity with the light. In view of these facts it is well to understand φωτίζειν in sense (*a*)—the light shines upon every man for judgement, to reveal what he is. For this usage cf. e.g. Polybius xxii, v, 10; and in the New Testament 1 Cor. 4.5, φωτίσει τὰ κρυπτὰ τοῦ σκότους, 2 Tim. 1.10, φωτίσαντος δὲ ζωὴν καὶ ἀφθαρσίαν. Render, therefore, '. . . which shines upon every man' (whether he sees it or not).

10. ἐν τῷ κόσμῳ ἦν. κόσμος is a common and important word in John. In general the κόσμος is not the totality of creation (11.9; 17.5,24; 21.25 are exceptions) but the world of men and human affairs. Even in 1.10 the world made through the Word is a world capable of knowing, or of reprehensibly not knowing, its Maker. The word is sometimes (8.23; 9.39; 11.9; 12.25,31; 13.1; 16.11; 18.36) further defined as ὁ κόσμος οὗτος. This expression is not simply equivalent to the rabbinic העולם הזה (ὁ αἰὼν οὗτος, 'this age') and contrasted with a future world, but is contrasted also with a world other than this but already existing; this is the lower world, corresponding to which there is a world above (see especially 8.23; 18.36). John seems to combine these ideas deliberately, so that Jesus appears both as the means by which an eschatological future is anticipated (as in the Synoptic Gospels) and also as an envoy from the heavenly world. The definition of the world as 'this world' necessarily involves a measure of dualism, which is at times very strongly expressed (1.10; 7.7; 14.17,22,27,30; 15.18f.; 16.8,20,33; 17.6,9,14ff., in addition to the places where ὁ κόσμος οὗτος is used). The world hates Jesus and his disciples. Yet the world into which he comes is also the scene of the saving mission of Jesus (1.9f.; 3.17,19; 6.14; 8.26; 10.36; 12.46; 16.28; 17.13,18; 18.20,37), and his mission to the world is grounded in the love of God for the world (3.16). It is noteworthy that in 3.16 the κόσμος is immediately split up into its components (πᾶς ὁ πιστεύων). It is this process

which accounts for the apparently contradictory things said about the relation between Christ and the world. On the one hand, he is the Saviour of the world (4.42; cf. 1.29; 3.17; 6.35,51; 8.12; 9.5) and it is emphatically repeated that he did not come to judge the world (3.17; 12.47); on the other hand, Jesus did come to judge the world (9.39; 12.31; cf. 3.18; 5.30; 8.16,26; 12.48) and overcame it (16.33). The enemy who is overthrown is the ἄρχων τοῦ κόσμου τούτου (12.31; 14.30; 16.11); those who choose to remain under his power convert salvation into judgement. Thus it can be said both that the outcome of the ministry of Jesus was that the world did not recognize him, or the Father, or the Spirit (1.10; 14.17; 17.25), and at the same time that its aim was that the world should know and believe (17.21,23). At 12.19; 18.20 ὁ κόσμος means *tout le monde*, 'everyone'. With this verse cf. *Thomas* 28 (I took my stand in the midst of the world (κόσμος) and in flesh (σάρξ) I appeared to them); also *P. Oxy.* 1.

ὁ κόσμος δι' αὐτοῦ ἐγένετο. This is not a mere repetition of v. 3 (πάντα δι' αὐτοῦ ἐγένετο). The κόσμος (see note above) is not the sum total of creation but the organized and responsible world. Thus it is not correct to say that in this verse κόσμος is used in two senses, as equivalent to τὰ πάντα (v. 3) and to ἡ σκοτία (v. 5), though this is maintained by G. Baumbach in *Kairos* 14 (1972), 121–36 (a fine article).

ὁ κόσμος αὐτὸν οὐκ ἔγνω. Cf. 1 Cor. 1.21, οὐκ ἔγνω ὁ κόσμος . . . τὸν θεόν. The world neither recognized nor responded to him. Though the noun γνῶσις does not occur in John, 'knowledge', represented by the verbs γινώσκειν and εἰδέναι, is an important feature of John's thought. On the relation between John and gnosticism see Introduction, pp. 38f. *et al.* The verbs γινώσκειν and εἰδέναι seem to be used synonymously; see especially 7.27; 8.55; 13.7; 14.7 (if γνώσεσθε be read); 21.17. Both words are used simply of human cognition of matters of fact; e.g. 7.51; 11.57; 9.20; 18.2. John's characteristic use, however, concerns knowledge of divine persons, of the relation between them, and especially of the mission of Jesus to the world. Behind this use lies a twofold background. In Greek thought, knowledge regularly implies observation and objectivity. It is closely (in εἰδέναι, etymologically) connected with vision, whether by the eye of the body or the eye of the soul. In the Old Testament, however, knowledge (√ידע) is a much less intellectual and more comprehensive term. God's knowledge of Israel includes his election of and care for his people (e.g. Amos 3.2), and for man to know God implies not only perception of his existence but also a relation with him of humble obedience and trust (e.g. Jer. 31.34). This Old Testament usage constitutes the decisive, though not the only, factor in John's conception of knowledge. (1) Jesus himself knows the Father, and this knowledge issues in a relation of love, obedience, and mutual indwelling (e.g. 10.15; 17.25: 7.29; 8.55). (2) When men know God through Jesus a similar relation is brought into being (e.g. 8.32; 17.8,25: 10.4; 13.17; 15.15). When, however, John goes on to add (3) that knowledge of God and Christ confers, or rather is, eternal life (17.3), he is treading ground that is common to both Hellenism and the Old Testament. Further, it will be noted that (4) very little is said in John of God's knowledge of man (1.48; 2.24f.; 10.14,27; (16.19): 6.64 and 13.11 are exceptional and even so not really analogous to the Old Testament use mentioned above), that (5) knowledge, as in Greek usage, is sometimes connected with seeing (e.g. 14.7f., 17), and that (6) verbs of knowing are often followed by a ὅτι clause, which gives a less personal and more intellectual content to knowledge. For the close connection between knowledge and faith see the Introduction, pp. 81f., and on 6.69. See also *T.W.N.T.* 1, 711–13 (R. Bultmann), and J. Painter, *John: Witness and Theologian* (1975), 86–100.

11. εἰς τὰ ἴδια ἦλθεν. He came to his own property (cf. Thucydides 1, 141), his home. The aorist points to a unique coming, the incarnation, and the 'home' to which Jesus came was Israel. But it must be observed that it would be possible to speak of a coming of the Logos in the Platonic sense to the created world, which was his natural counterpart, or in the Stoic sense to rational men, who were peculiarly λογικοί. Further, the Law had been given to Israel and found there its proper dwelling place. For the relation and the distinction between the use of τὰ ἴδια and οἱ ἴδιοι in this verse and gnosticism, see J. Jervell in *St. Th.* 10 (1956), 14–27.

οἱ ἴδιοι αὐτὸν οὐ παρέλαβον. As in the former part of the verse we have what may be taken as a simple historical statement, amply justified by the earlier tradition. The masculine οἱ ἴδιοι is now used: Jesus came to the framework of life to which as Messiah he belonged, and the several men who within that framework should have received him did not do so. The wider references alluded to in the previous note are again relevant. It was the world that rejected Jesus.

12. ὅσοι δὲ ἔλαβον. The simple verb is equivalent to παρέλαβον (v. 11); for the omission of the compounded preposition cf. M. 1, 115. The relative clause thrown to the beginning of the sentence as a *nominativus pendens* and resumed by αὐτοῖς is characteristic of John's style; see Introduction, p. 10. To receive Christ is to accept him in obedience and faith as the envoy of the Father. Cf. Odes of Solomon, 9. 7: . . . that those who have known him may not perish, and that those who receive him may not be ashamed.

ἔδωκεν αὐτοῖς. Men are not by nature the children of God, as for example by virtue of an indwelling σπερματικὸς λόγος. Only by receiving Christ do they gain the right to *become* children of God.

ἐξουσίαν τέκνα θεοῦ γενέσθαι. ἐξουσία is on the whole accurately used by John (1.12; 5.27; 17.2; 19.10f.), and means 'authority', 'right'. δύναμις does not occur in John. For τέκνα θεοῦ cf. 11.52, also 3.3,5 (γεννηθῆναι). In this gospel the word υἱός is always reserved for Christ, τέκνα for Christians. For illuminating comparison and contrast *C.H.* 1, 28 may be referred to. The Hermetic prophet asks why men have given themselves over to death, ἔχοντες ἐξουσίαν τῆς ἀθανασίας μεταλαβεῖν, when they have the right to partake of immortality. He bids them repent, and μεταλάβετε τῆς ἀθανασίας. The language is decidedly similar (so that it is wrong, as some have suggested, to omit ἐξουσίαν), especially since to have immortality is to be made divine (θεωθῆναι, cf. τέκνον θεοῦ γενέσθαι), but here the resemblance ends, for in the *Hermetica* men, who are compounded of mind and flesh, possess in themselves the right to partake of immortality, and need only to be told to exercise it. In John life is a gift from Christ, received by faith. For the idea of those who become sons through the Son Schweizer (*Beiträge*, 103) compares Philo, *Agric.* 51; *Conf. Ling.* 145–8; *Sobr.* 56.

τοῖς πιστεύουσιν εἰς τὸ ὄνομα αὐτοῦ. To receive Christ is to believe on his name.

This construction of πιστεύειν with εἰς τὸ ὄνομα is found at 1.12; 2.23; 3.18 (20.31 is not parallel, see the note). It may be distinguished from πιστεύειν with the dative, which generally means 'to give credence to', but not from πιστεύειν with εἰς and the accusative. Allegiance as well as assent is intended; cf. Dodd, *Interpretation*, 184. ὄνομα is not enough to suggest that John has baptism in mind. He mentions only faith, not knowledge, as the means of life and regeneration.

13. οἳ . . . ἐγεννήθησαν. This birth is conditional upon receiving Christ and believing on his name. The aorist is not pluperfect in sense; John does not mean that there existed a number of persons born in the manner described who in virtue of their birth were able to receive Christ when he came.

οὐκ ἐξ αἱμάτων. This and the two following phrases serve to accentuate ἐκ θεοῦ. No human agency is or can be responsible for such a birth as this. In ancient thought blood was sometimes considered the means of procreation; cf. Wisd. 7.2, Philo, *Op*. 132. The plural, 'bloods', is unusual but cf. Euripides, *Ion* 693, and the common use of דמים in Hebrew. Probably the blood of father and mother is meant. Hoskyns (143) suggests that it would have been impossible for John to write οὐκ ἐξ αἵματος (singular) because Christians are begotten of God through the blood of Christ.

οὐδὲ ἐκ θελήματος σαρκός. σάρξ in John is not evil in itself (see the next verse— only if v. 13 is regarded as an interpolation by a different writer is it reasonable to think that the word will bear a different meaning here from that which it has in v. 14), but stands for humanity over against God, as in the Old Testament expression (used also in later Jewish literature) בשר ודם, flesh and blood. It does not lie within man's will to become, or make, a child of God; cf. Rom. 9.16, οὐ τοῦ θέλοντος . . . ἀλλὰ τοῦ ἐλεῶντος θεοῦ.

οὐδὲ ἐκ θελήματος ἀνδρός. A more particular expression of the previous phrase. ἀνήρ is an adult male, frequently a husband. See below.

ἀλλ᾽ ἐκ θεοῦ ἐγεννήθησαν. On divine begetting see on 3.3,5. John boldly employs a new metaphor to describe the newness of the Christian life.

In place of the plural (οἳ . . . ἐγεννήθησαν) the singular (*qui . . . natus est*) · is read by b Irenaeus (lat.) Tertullian. This combination of early Western authorities is strong, but not strong enough to overthrow the plural reading, which is demanded by τοῖς πιστεύουσιν in the previous verse, and by the sense of the passage. The origin of the text of b is readily understandable; the threefold negation (not of blood, nor of the will of flesh, nor of the will of a husband) seemed to correspond exactly with the church's belief about the birth of Jesus, and since the Virgin Birth is nowhere expressly mentioned in John it was natural to introduce a reference to it here. The reading which refers explicitly to the birth of Jesus is to be rejected; but it remains probable that John was alluding to Jesus' birth, and declaring that the birth of Christians, being bloodless and rooted in God's will alone, followed the pattern of the birth of Christ himself. It is unnecessary to suppose (with Torrey, 151, 153) that explicit reference to the Virgin Birth has been lost through faulty translation of Aramaic. See M. II, 436.

14. καί, beginning the third section of the Prologue, resumes v. 11, and opens a statement of the incarnation in more theological terms.

ὁ λόγος σὰρξ ἐγένετο. On λόγος see on v. 1. σάρξ, as in v. 13, represents human nature as distinct from God, but expresses this in the harshest available terms, harsher than those of v. 6, where John the Baptist is described as ἄνθρωπος. Cullmann's suggestion that ἄνθρωπος is avoided because the Logos was already the (heavenly) ἄνθρωπος is not convincing (*Christology*, 187). John does not say this of the Logos, and if vv. 14–18 reflect Son of man ideas they do so very faintly. Cf. Odes of Solomon 7.4–6; 41.11f.; also *Thomas* 28, quoted on v. 10. Since the Word was described in v. 1 as θεός, John's statement is a full, and perhaps the most succinct, expression of the paradox of the person of Christ. It is difficult to determine precisely the meaning of ἐγένετο. It cannot mean 'became', since the Word continues to be the subject of further statements—it was the Word who 'dwelt among us', and whose glory 'we beheld'; the Word continued to be the Word. The meaning 'was born'—the Word was born as flesh, man—would be tolerable were it not that γεννηθῆναι has just been used in this sense, and a change of verb would be harsh. Perhaps ἐγένετο is used in the same sense as in v. 6: the Word came on the (human) scene—as flesh, man. It is part of the paradox of this statement that the same word should be used of the eternal Word as of the Baptist. Bultmann is right in pointing out the kinship of this σάρξ ἐγένετο with mythology, right also in pointing out the offensive difference. 'Men expect the Revealer to appear as a shining, mysterious, fascinating figure, as a hero or θεῖος ἄνθρωπος, as a miracle worker or mystagogue . . . All such desires are cut short by the statement: the Word became flesh. It is in his sheer humanity that he is the Revealer. True, his own also see his δόξα (v. 14b); indeed if it were not to be seen, there would be no grounds for speaking of revelation. But this is the paradox which runs through the whole gospel: the δόξα is not to be seen *alongside* the σάρξ, nor *through* the σάρξ as through a window; it is to be seen in the σάρξ and nowhere else. If man wishes to see the δόξα, then it is on the σάρξ that he must concentrate his attention, without allowing himself to fall a victim to appearances. The revelation is present in a peculiar *hiddenness*.' The whole of Bultmann's profound exposition should be read. For Käsemann's different understanding of this verse see *Prologue*, 10f., 27; for Athanasius' interpretation (which should be compared with Bultmann's) see G. D. Dragas, in Θεολογια (1976), 5–30.

καὶ ἐσκήνωσεν ἐν ἡμῖν. σκηνοῦν means properly 'to live in a tent', hence 'to settle', 'to take up one's abode'. The latter meaning is to be adopted here; ἐν ἡμῖν does not mean that the Word dwelt in our human nature as in a tent, though the Old Syriac rendering (*ban*, in us) might be held to suggest this. Rather, he took up residence in our midst. It has been thought that the word σκηνοῦν was chosen here with special reference to the word δόξα which follows. It recalls, in sound and in meaning, the Hebrew שכן, which means 'to dwell'; the verb is used of the dwelling of God with Israel (e.g. Exod. 25.8; 29.46; Zech. 2.14), and a derived noun שכינה (*shechinah*) was used (though not in the Old Testament) as a periphrasis for the name of God himself. Further, the bright cloud settled down (שכן) upon the Tabernacle (Exod. 24.16; 40.35), and since this cloud was the visible manifestation of the presence of God (cf. ὀφθήσομαι, Exod. 25.7 LXX) the abiding presence of God suggested his glory (כבוד, δόξα; see below). For further Jewish parallels see Bousset-Gressmann, 346; and see Sidebottom, 37–40. It must however be recalled that (*a*) שכינה (*shechinah*) means not the glory of God but his presence, and (*b*) שכן is not regularly represented by (κατα)σκηνοῦν. Probably John means no more than that the Word took up a temporary residence among men. Cf. Ecclus. 24.8 (κατέπαυσεν τὴν σκηνήν μου . . . Ἐν Ἰακὼβ κατασκή-νωσον), 10 (ἐν σκηνῇ ἁγίᾳ); 1 Enoch 42.2 for the temporary dwelling of Wisdom among men. See also Odes of Solomon 12.12, For the dwelling-place (*mashkᵉna*) of the Word is man.

ἐν ἡμῖν . . . ἐθεασάμεθα. This first person plural does not necessarily imply that the gospel was written by an eye-witness. It is the apostolic church that speaks. See Introduction, p. 143.

καὶ ἐθεασάμεθα τὴν δόξαν αὐτοῦ. The faith of the church rests upon a real beholding of one who, however glorious, was a historical person. For the connection between seeing and believing see also 14.11,29; 20.8,27ff. with the notes; and cf. C. Traets, *Voir Jésus et le Père en lui selon l'Evangile de Saint Jean* (1967). δόξα, δοξάζειν, are important words in John's vocabulary. In Classical and Hellenistic Greek δόξα means commonly 'opinion', 'repute', δοξάζειν 'to think', 'to imagine'; in the LXX, in certain other Hellenistic religious literature, and in the New Testament, the noun and verb respectively mean 'glory', 'to glorify'. In the LXX δόξα often renders כבוד, and denotes particularly the visible manifestation (often of light) accompanying a theophany (e.g. Exod. 33.22; Deut. 5.21; 1 Kings 8.11; all כבוד, δόξα). It acquired in the Old Testament an eschatological significance (e.g. Isa. 60.1; Hab. 2.14; both כבוד, δόξα), which it retained in the New Testament (e.g. Mark 8.38; 13.26; Rom. 8.18; 1 Peter 4.13), though in the New Testament the eschatological δόξα occasionally appears, by anticipation, in the present (2 Cor. 3.18; Eph. 3.21). The clearest example of this proleptic δόξα is the Transfiguration (Mark 9.2–8 and parallels), an incident which is not re-counted in John (see Introduction, pp. 51, 53). John nevertheless asserts that the glory of God was manifested in Jesus (1.14). It was shown in his miracles (2.11; 11.4,40); but in particular he enjoyed a position of glory before the Incarnation, and subsequently returned to it (17.5,24). Jesus did not enjoy this glory because he sought it for himself, but because he sought only God's glory (5.41; 7.18; 8.50), whereas other men sought their own (5.44; 12.43). The glory of Jesus is thus dependent upon both his essential relation with God (1.14) and his obedience. To this corresponds the special use of δοξάζειν as a description of the death of Jesus (7.39; 12.16,23; 13.31f.); Jesus dies as Son of God and as an obedient servant; he is thereby lifted up on the cross and exalted to heaven. His glory is to be manifested in χάρις and ἀλήθεια (see below). D. Hill (*N.T.S.* 13 (1967), 281–5) argues that John may have re-flected on the use of δόξα in Mark 10.35ff.—glory to be reached only through suffering and death.

ὡς μονογενοῦς παρὰ πατρός. μονογενής (1.18; 3.16,18; 1 John 4.9) and πατήρ are words too characteristic of the Johannine writings, and too theological in use, to permit us to render in general terms, 'the glory as of a father's only son'. Moreover, though μονογενής means in itself 'only of its kind', when used in relation to *father* it can hardly mean anything other than only(-begotten) son (cf. Dodd, *Interpretation*, 305). For παρά cf. v. 6; the Son (it is not the δόξα which is said to be παρὰ πατρός) not merely is his Father's Son, but proceeds from him in personal though never independent existence.

πλήρης, indeclinable (M. 1, 50; 11, 162; according to 111, 315, πλήρης is indeclinable only when followed by a genitive); it refers to Christ, and looks back to μονογενοῦς and αὐτοῦ.

χάριτος καὶ ἀληθείας. The same words (with articles) recur in v. 17. χάρις occurs four times only in John, and only in the prologue (1.14,16,17); ἀλήθεια is very common. The pair recalls the Hebrew pair חסד ואמת (*ḥesed weʾemeth*, e.g. Exod. 34.6, cf. 33.22, δόξα, in the same context). The two Hebrew words are closely related in meaning (signifying God's loyalty and faithfulness to his covenant and covenant people), but in the LXX חסד is most often rendered ἔλεος, and has the meaning 'grace', 'undeserved favour'; it is in this sense that it underlies the New Testament use of χάρις. ἀλήθεια retains in John more of the meaning of אמת. Sometimes, as in ordinary Greek usage, it means simply that which corresponds to fact, is not false (5.33; 8.40,44ff.; 16.7); but more characteristically it means the Christian revelation brought by and revealed in Jesus (1.17; 8.32; 16.13; 17.17; 17.19 (unless here ἐν ἀληθείᾳ=ἀληθῶς); 18.37: 1.14; 4.23f. should perhaps he added). This revelation arises out of the faithfulness of God to his own character, and to his promises, of which it is the fulfilment. It is saving truth (8.32); it is perceived only through the work of the Spirit (16.13), and by those who are predestined in conformity with it (3.21, ὁ ποιῶν τὴν ἀλήθειαν). Further, this truth is Jesus himself, who being God (1.1) is the fulfilment and revelation of God's purposes (14.6). 18.38 is to be taken closely with 18.37 (see the note); on πνεῦμα τῆς ἀληθείας (14.17; 15.26; 16.13) see on 14.17. On ἀλήθεια see Schnackenburg II, 265–81; also S. Aalen, in *Studia Evangelica II* (1964), 3–24; on the adjectives ἀληθής, ἀληθινός, see on 1.9.

It will be observed that when John begins to speak of the Word as incarnate his language takes on a more biblical colouring. δόξα, χάρις, and ἀλήθεια can indeed be paralleled elsewhere, but John's usage is controlled by biblical precedents. The glory of God is shown by his acting in faithfulness to his own character, and by his character's revealing itself in mercy. This however points back to the mythologically expressed theme of the Word who appears as man among men, and in his own being communicates to them the truth; John continues to combine Old Testament and Hellenistic terms, but his thought continues also to be dominated by the fact of Jesus.

15. Ἰωάννης. Cf. vv. 6–8. It is true that v. 16 can be read without difficulty immediately after v. 14, but it is unnecessary for that reason to suppose that v. 15 is an interpolation. John the Baptist represents the Old Testament, and vv. 15–17 are intended to make clear the Old Testament setting in which the work of Jesus is to be understood. See further below.

μαρτυρεῖ . . . κέκραγεν. The tenses are remarkable. The perfect κέκραγεν is used with the force of a present (see M. 1, 147, where weighty LXX evidence in support of this view is adduced; cf. Lucian, *De Morte Peregrini*, 31; 33, where the pluperfect is used with the force of a simple past tense); consequently both verbs speak of the testimony of John as having present significance. John (like the Old Testament) remains as a permanent witness to Christ. On μαρτυρεῖν see on v. 7; κράζειν is used again at 7.28,37; 12.44 to introduce important pronouncements of Jesus.

οὗτος ἦν ὃν εἶπον: P⁶⁶ P⁷⁵ אᶜᵇ B³ D Θ Ω *uerss.* οὗτος ἦν ὁ εἰπών: אᵃ B* Origen. The latter reading in spite of its early attestation seems to be an attempted correction of the former; but the construction of ὃν εἶπον is Johannine; cf. 8.27; 10.35. ἦν is superficially difficult but there is no need to suppose (with Torrey, 117f.) that an Aramaic הוא has been wrongly pointed *haʷaʾ*, 'was', instead of *hu'* 'is'. It must be remembered that present (perfect) tenses have been used, and John's witness at the time of writing can only be 'This Jesus *was* the person I spoke of'. The reference is to 1.30; see the note there. An important clue to the meaning of the Prologue as a whole is given by the fact that John makes two references to the Baptist (see *Prologue*, 26f.). The earlier reference (vv. 6–8) gives his witness to the pre-existent light and its coming into the world, the later deals neither with pre-existence nor with incarnation, but with the glorification of the Word. This rests upon pre-existence (πρῶτός μου ἦν), but what is now claimed is that he who first appeared as a successor, perhaps as a disciple (this may be suggested by ὀπίσω), of John the Baptist has now taken rank before him. Vv. 1–13 describe in theological terms how the pre-existent Logos or light came to the world that he had created, and was rejected in it, though in such a way that those who did receive him found in him regeneration as the children of God. But neither rejection nor regeneration is the last word. The humble follower of John was exalted to a position of pre-eminence. This recalls the old tradition of the resurrection and *parousia* of the Son of man who had been obedient unto death. For John however the relation between sacrificial service and glory is not simply chronological; each is the other. *Glory* means to be full of *grace and truth*. It is this point John develops in the remaining part of the Prologue.

16. ὅτι may continue the words of the Baptist in v. 15; more probably it is to be connected with v. 14.

ἐκ τοῦ πληρώματος. The word occurs here only in John. It was a gnostic term, taken over in something like its gnostic sense by some early Christian writers; see Col. 1.19; 2.9; Eph. 1.23; 3.19; 4.13. It is not used in this sense by John (cf. his non-technical use of πληροῦν). It looks back to v. 14 where it is said that Christ was 'full of grace and truth'; of this full complement of grace and truth 'we' have all received. The partitive use of ἐκ is common in John; see Introduction, p. 8. 1 QS 4.4 (ברוב חסדו) is at best a remote parallel.

ἡμεῖς πάντες. If John the Baptist is speaking 'we' must be the prophets. Otherwise, the reference is to the apostolic church; see Introduction, pp. 143f.

χάριν ἀντὶ χάριτος. The meaning of this phrase seems to be that Christian life is based at all points upon grace; as it proceeds one grace is exchanged only for another. For the sense, and for this use of ἀντί, see Philo, *Post.* 145, . . . ἑτέρας (*sc.* χάριτας) ἀντ' ἐκείνων (*sc.* τῶν πρώτων χαρίτων) καὶ τρίτας ἀντὶ τῶν δευτέρων καὶ αἰεὶ νέας ἀντὶ παλαιοτέρων . . . ἐπιδίδωσι. Cf. also Rom. 1.17,–ἐκ πίστεως εἰς πίστιν; 2 Cor. 3.18, ἀπὸ δόξης εἰς δόξαν. Three other interpretations may be mentioned. (i) The grace of the old covenant under Moses is exchanged for the grace of the Gospel; v. 17 is used to explain v. 16. But the point of the present passage is that grace did not come by Moses; nor is the grace of God available in two grades. (ii) Underlying the Greek is an Aramaic word-play, חסדא הלף חס(ו)דא, grace (*ḥisda*) in place of shame (*ḥisuda*, or *ḥisda*), which escaped the translator's notice (M. Black, *J.T.S.* old series 42 (1941), 69f.). This interpretation is not open to the objection brought against (i); but it presupposes the existence of the Prologue in Aramaic, which is not proven; and the hypothesis of a translation error would be acceptable only if the Greek were much more difficult than it is.

Moreover, though the Old Testament is represented as subordinate to the New Testament it cannot be said that John regards it as a matter of shame or reproach. (iii) Turner (M. iii. 258) thinks of the Spirit who comes *in place of* Jesus; but it is scarcely legitimate to read a reference to the Spirit into the text.

17. ἐδόθη. The Law is regularly regarded in Jewish sources as a gift of God to Israel; so e.g. Josephus *Ant.* VII, 338, τὰς ἐντολὰς αὐτοῦ καὶ τοὺς νόμους οὓς διὰ Μωυσέος ἔδωκεν ἡμῖν; *P. Aboth* 1.1: Moses received the Law from Sinai and committed it to Joshua . . .; *Siphre Deut.* 31.4 §305; Blessed be God who gave the Law to Israel through Moses (עַל יְדֵי מֹשֶׁה) our teacher.

ἡ χάρις καὶ ἡ ἀλήθεια. See on v. 14. In this verse the main emphasis lies on the contrast between Moses and Christ, Law and Gospel. The Law (according to John) did bear witness to Christ (5.39), but Moses is primarily an accuser (5.45). Glory is expressed not so much in deeds of power as in acts of grace and in the communication of truth, and grace is expressed, as by Paul, in contrast with law. Cf. J. Jervell, *Imago Dei* (1960), 191, 'χάρις and ἀλήθεια correspond to the Pauline Dikaiosyne'. For John, Jesus is certainly not a new Moses.

18. θεὸν οὐδεὶς ἑώρακεν πώποτε. That God is invisible, or at least that it is irreverent and unsafe to see him, is a general Old Testament assumption; see e.g. Deut. 4.12; Ps. 97.2. This idea was developed in later Judaism, and periphrases removed some of the unguarded anthropomorphisms of the Old Testament (e.g. Isa. 6.5, Mine eyes have seen the King, the Lord of hosts: Targum . . . the glory of the *shekhinah* of the King of the ages, the Lord of hosts). Cf. Josephus, *Bel.* VII, 346, ἀόρατος . . . τοῖς ἀνθρωπίνοις ὄμμασιν; *Lev. R.* 4.8 . . . he who sees and is not seen. The notion belongs equally to Greek speculative thought. John, however, is not thinking so much in terms of the attributes of God as of the fact that it is in Jesus Christ that God has chosen to reveal himself. Cf. 6.46; 1 John 4.12,20. The negation contained in this clause emphasizes that the fundamental theme of the gospel is the revelation of God. To say that 'in faith the idea of God's invisibility has become not a negative, but a positive concept; it has become the expression of man's true knowledge of himself' (Bultmann, 81; see the whole of 80f.), is true, but not the whole truth. See 'Theocentricity'.

μονογενὴς θεός (P⁶⁶ P⁷⁵ ℵ B C 33 boh pesh Gnostics, Irenaeus, Clement, Origen *al.*) has better MS. support than the alternative μονογενὴς υἱός (all other Greek MSS.; cur Eusebius, Athanasius, Chrysostom; most Latin VSS. and Fathers), and is received by many (for the patristic material see especially F. J. A. Hort, *Two Dissertations* (1876), 1–72; M. F. Wiles, *The Spiritual Gospel* (1960), 121; T. E. Pollard, *Johannine Christology and the Early Church* (1970), many passages indexed under 1.18); the added evidence of the two recently discovered papyri may seem to swing the verdict this way. Yet υἱός seems to be required by the following clause, and is in conformity with Johannine usage (3.16,18; 1 John 4.9; cf. John 1.14). This however may simply make it *lectio facilior*. The sense is substantially unaltered by the textual variation. The Son is the Word, and the Word has already been declared to be θεός; John may be deliberately returning, at the end of the Prologue, to this proposition stated in v. 1.

εἰς τὸν κόλπον. εἰς is used for ἐν, a Hellenistic usage (M. I, 235; B.D., §§ 206,

218); as at, e.g., Acts 2.5, ἦσαν δὲ εἰς Ἰερουσαλήμ. Cf. 13.23. The Father and the Son enjoy the most intimate communion.

ἐκεῖνος resumes the subject in a characteristically Johannine manner.

ἐξηγήσατο. Cf. Ecclus. 43.31, τίς ἑόρακεν αὐτὸν καὶ ἐκδιηγήσεται; Elsewhere in the New Testament (Luke 24.35; Acts 10.8; 15.12,14; 21.19) ἐξηγεῖσθαι means 'to rehearse facts', 'to recount a narrative'. This corresponds to one major Greek use of the word (L.S., *s.v.*, III). The word is also used of the publishing or explaining of divine secrets, sometimes by the gods themselves. It is this usage that appears in John; and it is not without significance that the Prologue closes with this word, characteristic as it is of Hellenistic religion. The notion of revelation is of course biblical as well as Hellenistic (though in the Bible, and not least in John, revelation is as much through action as through speech); but clearly John means to use language intelligible and even familiar to readers accustomed to Greek literature rather than to the Bible. The invisible God has now in Christ been manifested in his glory, grace, and truth.

2. THE WITNESS OF JOHN (I)

1.19–34

In John as in the Synoptic Gospels (cf. Acts 10.37) an account of John the Baptist introduces the ministry of Jesus. The Jewish authorities send a deputation to investigate John's intentions and personal claims. Refusing all attempts to identify his person he sums up his mission by bearing witness to a mightier one, as yet unknown, who is to come after him. This testimony is later amplified in the declaration that Jesus is (*a*) the Lamb of God, (*b*) one who, being equipped with the Spirit, is able to baptize with the Spirit, and (*c*) the Elect One (or Son) of God. It resumes in narrative form the more purely theological statements of the Prologue.

Behind this paragraph lie the synoptic traditions regarding the Baptist, and particularly his prophecy of the Coming One (Mark 1.7f.; Matt. 3.11; Luke 3.16), his baptism of Jesus (Mark 1.9–11; Matt. 3.13–17; Luke 3.21f.), and the question later addressed by him from prison to Jesus (Q, Matt. 11.2–6; Luke 7.18–23). In Matt. (3.14f.), as in John, the Baptist is made to recognize the authority of Jesus at a very early point in the ministry, but in view of the question from prison (Q) this seems improbable; Matthew and John, it may be supposed, thought they had good reason for altering the Marcan narrative. The synoptic traditions are constantly hinted at by John (for the numerous parallels see the notes), but in several further details his narrative differs from them. The identification of John the Baptist with Elijah is expressly repudiated; the baptism of Jesus is not mentioned; whereas in the synoptic account of the baptism a voice from heaven declares that

Jesus is the Son of God, in John this assertion is made by the Baptist himself.

John's rewriting of the synoptic material (F. E. Williams, *J.B.L.* 86 (1967), 311–19, thinks that vv. 19–28 are a dramatization of Luke 3.15f., with reference to Mark 8.27–30; Luke 7.18–30, Mark 1.3) may have been due in part to a desire to counteract an excessive veneration of the Baptist. In Ephesus there were persons who knew only the baptism of John (Acts 18.25; 19.3; cf. Justin, *Trypho* 80), and it is possible that they made exaggerated claims for their master (cf. *Clem. Recog.* 1, 54, 60). John emphasizes the Baptist's inferiority in the present passage and also at 1.8,15; 3.28–31, possibly with the intention of rebutting the assertions of his followers. A weightier motive for his action, however, is to be found in the desire to concentrate attention upon the Person to whom the Baptist bore witness, and to bring out certain fundamental definitions of his work. In the Synoptic Gospels the Baptist's own character and office are emphasized because his proclamation of the imminent judgement and his baptism of repentance in preparation for the judgement supply the eschatological framework in which the work and person of Jesus were first understood and proclaimed. John, who means to supply a new framework for the understanding of Jesus (see Introduction, pp. 67–70, 134–41), no longer finds it necessary to equate the Baptist with Elijah and to lay such stress on his work. John himself, however, remains, marked out even more clearly as the representative of the Old Testament (1.23; cf. 1.31, Jesus is manifested to Israel), and his work retains significance. In the synoptic tradition John the Baptist stands as the last term of a historical sequence (see especially Matt. 11.11–14; Luke 16.16), the immediate forerunner of the Messiah. In John, it is emphasized that, though in point of time Jesus follows the Baptist, in truth he is 'before' him (v. 30), being the Son of God and the bearer of the Spirit. John, in comparison, is but a voice (v. 23). In the same way, John's baptism has no independent significance, but serves to point to what it cannot itself achieve, the taking away of the world's sin by the Lamb of God.

For the relation between this section and the Qumran literature see Braun. There is an article on the redaction of the section by B.M.F. van Iersel in *Nov. T.* 5 (1962), 245–67.

19. καί. The opening narrative is linked very closely with the allusions to John the Baptist in the Prologue. He came εἰς μαρτυρίαν (1.7), and his μαρτυρία on a crucial occasion is now given. The parallel between John and Samuel, who bore witness to Saul, is not close (Daube, *N.T.R.J.*, 17ff.). John is the first in a sequence of witnesses to Jesus.

ἀπέστειλαν. No such sending as this is mentioned in the Synoptic Gospels, but cf. Mark 1.5; Matt. 3.7.

οἱ Ἰουδαῖοι (the singular is used only at 3.25; 4.9; 18.35) is the title regularly given by John to Judaism and its official leaders, who stand over against Jesus and (here) John. Their headquarters are at Jerusalem, where their conflict with Jesus reaches its height. They defend the letter of the Law (e.g. 5.16), refuse to accept the authority of Jesus and his messianic status (e.g. 9.22), and, denying their true king, finally deny their own status as the people of God (19.14f.). John's use of the title shows that he (like most Christian writers at and later than the end of the first century A.D.) was well aware of the existence of the church as a distinct entity, different from and opposed by Judaism, which it claimed to have supplanted. A similar use is found in the Gospel of Peter (e.g. 1: But of the Jews no man washed his hands . . .). 'The Jews' represent the world viewed from the religious point of view. It does not seem that John means 'the Judaeans' (as distinct from the Galileans), or that it is possible to use different senses of οἱ Ἰουδαῖοι to distinguish between the author and the redactor (C. Dekker, N.T.S. 13 (1966), 66–71). Schnackenburg points out that there were historical reasons for John's choice of 'the Jews' to represent the world.

ἱερεῖς καὶ Λευίτας. Only at this point are priests and Levites mentioned by John. The connection is too common in the Old Testament to constitute a parallel with Qumran. Brown suggests that they were sent to John as 'specialists in ritual purification'; but they do not begin by inquiring about baptism. The distinction between them in the service of the Temple appears in Ezekiel and in the Priestly Code but not earlier. It is maintained in the rabbinic literature, where the Levites form an intermediate class between priests and Israelites; thus *Horayoth* 3.8: A priest precedes a Levite, a Levite an Israelite, an Israelite a bastard, etc. Their main functions were to assist in the Temple worship (principally as musicians) and to act as police; see among many passages *Tamid* 7, *Middoth* 1f. We may suppose that it is in the latter office that they are here presented by John, but in view of 1.24 it seems doubtful whether John was intimately acquainted with the levitical institutions, and it may be that he has simply borrowed a familiar Old Testament phrase (e.g. 2 Chron. 23.4) to describe Jewish functionaries.

ἵνα ἐρωτήσωσιν, for infinitive, as often.

Σὺ τίς εἶ; Cf. 8.25; 21.12; and for the form of the question 6.9; 16.18. It recalls the ἐγώ εἰμι of Jesus; see on 6.35; 8.24.

20. καὶ ὡμολόγησεν καὶ οὐκ ἠρνήσατο, καὶ ὡμολόγησεν. The rather ponderous and repetitive style gives the effect of solemnity, as often in John. Cf. Josephus, *Ant.* VI, 151, ἀδικεῖν ὡμολόγει καὶ τὴν ἁμαρτίαν οὐκ ἠρνεῖτο. If v. 19 is punctuated as in the Nestle text the construction, though clumsy, is clear. It is however possible to place a stop after Ἰωάννου (19a), and construct 20 with 19b. If this is done v. 20 opens with a redundant καί—a probable mark of Semitic style. But there seems to be no necessity thus to import difficulty and Semitisms into the text. ὁμολογεῖν and ἀρνεῖσθαι suggest confessing and denying *Christ* both in John (9.22; 12.42; 13.38; 18.25,27) and elsewhere in the New Testament; and the Baptist proceeds at once with what may be called a negative confession of Christ.

ἐγὼ οὐκ εἰμὶ ὁ Χριστός. The sending of messengers, and the form of this negative statement, suggest that the possibility had been considered, perhaps even urged, that John was the Messiah. This John denies categorically. Possibly the ἐγώ is emphatic (and so throughout this narrative): *I* am not the Christ—but there is a Christ at hand. It may be that this denial owes something to polemic against those who rated the Baptist too highly; so e.g.

Cullmann, *Christology*, 29. See *Clementine Recognitions* 1,60: One of the disciples of John asserted that John was the Christ.

21. τί οὖν; Ἡλίας εἶ σύ; The position of σύ is variable, and it is omitted by ℵ a. It may have entered the text by assimilation to v. 19. The punctuation also is uncertain.

οὐκ εἰμί. In the Synoptic Gospels the Baptist is declared to be Elijah. The identification is made very clear in Matt. (11.14; 17.12), and accepted by Mark (9.13), though Matthew (see the parallel) goes out of his way to make the point more emphatically. Mark 1.6 in the shorter and probably original text does not suggest Elijah, and Luke 1.17 hardly amounts to an identification. John sharply contradicts the earlier, and apparently growing tradition, returning perhaps to a pre-synoptic stage of Christian belief, before apocalyptic necessity called for the discovery of Elijah in some forerunner of Christ. That Elijah should return before the appearance of the Messiah was a firm element in messianic speculation, based on Mal. 3.23; see further on v. 31. John, unfettered by the apocalyptic framework of thought, was free to handle the tradition in a new way. (See *J.T.S.* old series 48 (1947), 165ff.; for a different view, see Dodd, *Tradition*, 266.)

ὁ προφήτης εἶ σύ; Since it has already been ascertained that John is not the Christ (v. 20) ὁ προφήτης cannot here be a title of the Christ; cf. 7.40f., where *some* think Jesus to be the prophet, *others* the Christ. It is hard to see on what grounds Hahn, *Titles*, 364, 383, objects to the distinction drawn between these passages and 6.14. We may compare 1 QS 9.11, where (as Hahn himself observes) the title משיח is not applied to the coming prophet. There are other indications of a belief, or hope, that a new prophet, or one of the prophets of old, would be sent to the assistance of Israel; thus 1 Macc. 4.46; 14.41 . . . until there should arise a faithful prophet; 4 Ezra 2.18, For thy help will I send my servants Isaiah and Jeremiah; cf. 2 Macc. 15.15; *et al.* In the New Testament see Mark 6.15; 8.28 and parallels.

καὶ ἀπεκρίθη· οὔ. John's denial is complete. He corresponds to no known character within the framework of Jewish religion.

22. ἵνα ἀπόκρισιν δῶμεν . . . The expression is elliptical. Understand some such words as λέγε ἡμῖν.

23. John the Baptist corresponds to no known person; he is no more than a voice (Cullmann, *Christology*, 260, contrasts φωνή and λόγος); but his work had been foretold in the Old Testament (Isa. 40.3). The quotation agrees with the LXX text except in the use of εὐθύνατε, where the LXX (followed by Mark 1.3—the difference leads Dodd, *A.S.*, 40, to infer John's independence of the synoptics) has ἑτοιμάσατε (Aquila and Theodotion have ἀποσκευάσατε, Symmachus εὐτρεπίσατε). It may be that John made his own translation of the Hebrew (פנו), but this cannot be inferred with certainty, for he may have been influenced by the LXX in one or both of two ways: (i) he may have been influenced by the sound of εὐθείας which in the LXX immediately follows his quotation; (ii) he may have recalled the use of εὐθύνειν with ὁδός in Ecclus. (2.6; 37.15; 49.9). εὐθύνατε does not appear in any other early Christian quotation of Isa. 40.3. For the use of this quotation in 1 QS 8.13–16 see Fitzmyer, *Essays*, 34ff., but C. F. D. Moule (*N.T.S.* 14 (1968), 294) is right when he says that in the scroll the quotation is used 'as an injunction or authorization, whereas in the Gospels it is treated as a prediction'. John the

Baptist, though a true witness, is not simply to be identified with some character in the eschatological movement of history; nor is his testimony an independent opinion of his own. It possesses the only authority that can be recognized within Judaism, the authority of Scripture. The words are those of the un-named crying voice, but they are identifiable Scripture—καθὼς εἶπεν Ἡσαΐας ὁ προφήτης—indeed, they summarize the meaning attached by the church to the Old Testament. Cf. 5.33,39,46. John is the spoken word, whereas Jesus is the incarnate Word.

24. καὶ ἀπεσταλμένοι ἦσαν. οἱ is added before ἀπεσταλμένοι by some MSS. (including W Θ vg). It gives a slightly different sense: those who were sent, not the senders, are said to belong to the Pharisaic party. The shorter reading should be accepted; it is possible that the longer may be an 'improvement' intended to palliate the difficulty mentioned in the next note. The difficulty is dealt with differently by Dodd (*Tradition*, 263f.),who thinks John is using old material here.

τῶν Φαρισαίων. This parenthetical verse casts grave doubt upon the author's familiarity with Judaism before A.D. 70. The Pharisees, the truly progressive party in Judaism (Bernard's note *ad loc.* is misleading), stood over against the priests and Levites (v. 19), whom they would have no authority to send (though it is true that some priests were Pharisees). Many of the more influential priests were Sadducees, a party not mentioned by John, probably because they were no longer of any importance in the Judaism of his day, and perhaps also because, for that reason, he knew little about them.

25. τί οὖν βαπτίζεις . . .; It must not be inferred from the form of this question that either the Messiah, or Elijah, or 'the prophet', was expected to baptize. The question rather means, Why do you perform what appears to be an official act if you have no official status? This is the first reference to baptism; it is assumed that the readers will have been able to make the necessary connection.

26. ἐγὼ βαπτίζω ἐν ὕδατι. Cf. Mark 1.8 (and parallels), ἐγὼ ἐβάπτισα ὑμᾶς ὕδατι. The change of tense probably corresponds to John's belief that the Baptist and Jesus were at work at the same time, but it is probably mistaken to compare 1.30; 10.8 and argue that John intended to make an important theological point. The corresponding promise, that Christ should baptize with Spirit, is not given in John till v. 33; it was not revealed to the Baptist till he saw the Spirit descend upon Jesus.

μέσος ὑμῶν (cf. 19.18) στήκει ὃν ὑμεῖς οὐκ οἴδατε. There is nothing corresponding to these words in the Marcan narrative. The late verbal form στήκει (from στήκειν) is found twice only in John, here and at 8.44. In each verse there are variants. Of parallels adduced from *Thomas* (Quispel, *J. & Q.*, 145) only 91 (. . . him who is before your face you have not known) is at all close. Note (with Schnackenburg) the complete estrangement of Jesus' contemporaries; but historically John's words recall 7.27 and Justin, *Trypho* 8.4. Up to the present the Baptist himself had been unable to recognize Jesus for what he was; see v. 31 and note. The Revealer is known only when he wills to be known, but will at the right time be manifested to Israel.

27. ὀπίσω μου . . . ὑποδήματος. Cf. Mark 1.7 (and parallels), ἔρχεται ὁ ἰσχυρό-τερός μου ὀπίσω μου, οὗ οὐκ εἰμὶ ἱκανὸς κύψας λῦσαι τὸν ἱμάντα τῶν ὑποδημάτων

αὐτοῦ. John's words are probably dependent upon Mark's. He substitutes the more appropriate ἄξιος for Mark's ἱκανός, drops the vivid but unnecessary κύψας, and, as often, has ἵνα and the subjunctive for the infinitive (for the correct construction with ἄξιος see Luke 15.19). The repetition of αὐτοῦ after the relative οὗ, though it may be paralleled in Classical, Hellenistic, and Modern Greek, is probably to be regarded as a Semitism, but it has been taken over by John from Mark and cannot therefore be taken as a mark of his own style. The article ὁ before ὀπίσω is omitted by B ℵ*, probably rightly; though read by P[66] and accepted by Sanders it may have been added to form (with ἐρχόμενος) what was a recognized Christian title of the Messiah. Cf. 1.15. For the principle that a disciple should do for his master everything that a slave would do—except take off his shoes, see Daube, *N.T.R.J.*, 266f.

28. Βηθανίᾳ. There are several variants.
   (a) Βηθανίᾳ P[66] P[75] ℵ* B Θ ω it vg pesh hl boh Heracleon
   (b) Βηθαβαρᾷ λ 33 cur sah Origen Eusebius
   (c) Βηθεβαρᾷ φ sin
   (d) Βηθαραβᾷ ℵ[cb] hl[mg]

(c) is certainly no more than an orthographical variant of (b); so probably (by metathesis) is (d); there are other less significant variations. If our choice lies, as appears, between (a) and (b), it is clear, especially when the evidence of Origen (*In Evangelium Joannis* vi, 40) is examined. Origen knew that Βηθανίᾳ stood σχεδὸν ἐν πᾶσι τοῖς ἀντιγράφοις, and was read by Heracleon; but on his travels in Palestine he was unable to find a Bethany by the Jordan. There was however a Bethabara, where John was said by local tradition to have baptized. This, Origen concluded, must determine the locality of John's baptism, and at the same time the original reading. The readings of the Old Syriac VSS. probably represent the same tradition independently. The reading (a) must accordingly be received. John's first geographical statement is incapable of verification, and was already so at a date given by the agreement of Origen and the Old Syriac—that is, not more than a hundred years after the probable date of the gospel. At 10.40; 11.1ff. Jesus is said to remove from the place where 'John was baptizing at the first' to Bethany, the home of Mary, Martha, and Lazarus. This may have suggested to early readers of the gospel that the place where John baptized cannot have been Bethany, and so have helped to support the reading Bethabara; but in fact 11.1,18 seem carefully worded so as to distinguish Bethany near Jerusalem from the other Bethany. Jeremias, *Theology* 1, 43, prefers Bethabara. W. H. Brownlee, (*J. & Q.*, 167–74) argues at length but unconvincingly that Bethany should be understood in the sense of Batanaea.

ἦν . . . βαπτίζων. Periphrastic imperfect; see Introduction p. 10.

29. τῇ ἐπαύριον. Cf. 1.35,43; 2.1, and see on 2.1 for John's purpose in grouping a cycle of events in days.

ἐρχόμενον πρὸς αὐτόν. This cannot be the occasion of the baptism of Jesus since already (v. 32) John is able to bear witness to the descent of the Spirit upon Jesus. The baptism has already taken place (whether or not before v. 26 must remain obscure), and John has been convinced that Jesus is he that shall baptize with the Holy Spirit. Apparently this conviction carries with it also that which is expressed in this verse.

Ἴδε ὁ ἀμνὸς τοῦ θεοῦ ὁ αἴρων τὴν ἁμαρτίαν τοῦ κόσμου. It is certain that this phrase has an Old Testament background, less certain what that background is. We should note particularly the Paschal lamb (Exod. 12, *et al.*), the lamb of Isa. 53.7 (where the word ἀμνός is used), and the goat which bore away the sins of the people on the Day of Atonement (Lev. 16.21f.); yet none even of these provides an entirely satisfactory explanation (see *J.T.S.* old series 48 (1947), 155f.). The most frequent of all Jewish sacrifices, the תמיד (*tamid*) or daily burnt offering, consisted of a lamb, but this was not an expiatory sacrifice. References to a lamb in T. Joseph 19.8; T. Benjamin 3.8 are probably Christian additions; in any case, that in T. Joseph 19.8 recalls the conquering lamb of Revelation (e.g. 14.1) rather than the present passage.

Probably John's primary reference is to the Paschal lamb (cf. 19.33,36 and the notes); but the reference cannot have been drawn directly from Judaism, since in Judaism the lamb sacrificed at Passover does not take away sins. The probable source of John's thought and language is the Paschal interpretation of the last supper and the eucharist. The eucharist is a Paschal meal and in it the death of Christ for the remission of sins is portrayed. In the present context, the two propositions (*a*) Christ was the Passover lamb, (*b*) Christ bore, or took away, sins, though originally unconnected, are combined. This conclusion is not seriously shaken by two further suggestions. Dodd (*Interpretation*, 230–8) argued that the Lamb must be understood in the sense of Rev. 14.1 (and other apocalyptic passages): he is not a sacrificial lamb but an apocalyptic leader—the Messiah—who would purge his people of evil. On this see *N.T.S.* 1 (1955), 230–8; evidence for lamb as a title in this sense is very shaky, and that John did think of Jesus as the Passover seems fairly certain. G. Vermes (*Scripture and Tradition in Judaism*, 1961, 224f.) sees here an allusion to the Binding (*Akedah*) of Isaac; on this see G. Delling, *Der Kreuzestod Jesu in der urchristlichen Verkündigung* (1971) 98, and notes 566, 600 (making the point that in vv. 29–34 the Baptist makes the three great Johannine propositions about Jesus—his death, sonship, and pre-existence); there may however be a reference to the Lamb which God himself provides (Gen. 22.8, 13, 14). 1 QH 3.10; 8.10f. have also been quoted, but, as Braun points out, neither passage is messianic, and in the former the suffering is not atoning or expiatory.

It has been suggested (Burney 104–8; *T.W.N.T.* 1, 343 (J. Jeremias)) that a reference to the suffering servant of the Lord in Isa. 53 has been obscured here by mistranslation of Aramaic. The Aramaic טליא (*talya*) can mean 'servant' as well as 'lamb', and it is conceivable that when the present Greek text of John was made this word was misunderstood. But there is no other evidence to suggest that the present passage was translated directly from an Aramaic document, the natural Aramaic equivalent of the Hebrew עבד (*'ebed*, servant) is not טליא but עבדא (*'abda*), and to speak of Christ as a lamb is by no means foreign to the thought of the New Testament (e.g. Acts 8.32; 1 Pet. 1.19; Rev. 5.6). Nevertheless, the thought that Christ bore τὴν ἁμαρτίαν τοῦ κόσμου (the totality of sins, universal sinfulness) is present as well as the belief that, as a sacrificial victim, he took them away and secured forgiveness, and here Isa. 53.12, He bore the sin of many (חטא רבים נשא, ἁμαρτίας πολλῶν ἀνήνεγκεν) may well be in mind. The removal of guilt is a conception frequently found in the Old Testament; cf. Exod. 28.38; 34.7; Num. 14.18; 1 Sam. 15.25; Ps. 32.5; 85.3; Mic. 7.18. In all these passages the verb is

נשא (nasa'), often followed by עָוֹן ('awon, 'iniquity, guilt, or punishment of iniquity'—B.D.B.), and translated by a compound of αἴρειν, except in the Psalms, where it is rendered by ἀφιέναι. For the same word in later Hebrew see Zad. Frag. 5.5, וישא לפשעם. For ἁμαρτία as guilt, cf. John 9.41; 15.22,24; 19.11; 20.23. Another suggestion based on an ambiguity in Aramaic is made by A. Negoitsa and C. Daniel (*Nov. T.*, 13 (1971), 24–37). The word אמרא ('imm*ra, 'imra) may mean both lamb and word: John could thus be proclaiming Jesus as at once the Lamb and the Word of God. But John's double meanings seem to have been used for the benefit of his Greek readers, and though 'imra may occasionally mean *speech* it seems scarcely ever to mean *word*. See also B. Gärtner, *Svensk Exegetisk Årsbok* 18–19 (1953–4), 98–108.

By his amalgamation of Old Testament ideas John indicates that the death of Jesus was a new and better sacrifice. All the ordinances and institutions of Judaism were perfected by Jesus (cf. 2.19; 4.21; 5.17,39,47; 6.4; 10.1; 13.34). No longer are the sins of ignorance of the Jewish people removed by sacrifice, but the sin of the world.

30. ὀπίσω μου. Cf. vv. 15, 27; 1.26.

ὃς ἔμπροσθέν μου γέγονεν, who has now taken rank in front of me.

ὅτι πρῶτός μου ἦν, because his existence was prior to mine. For the contrast between γίνεσθαι and εἶναι see vv. 1, 6. πρῶτος is incorrectly used for πρότερος; see M. 1, 79, 245. For the general sense cf. 1 Esdras 3.7, δεύτερος καθιεῖται Δαρείου. At first Jesus was an unknown character in comparison with John's fame, but the time has now come for him to step forward and take the place which his pre-existence calls for—he must increase, John must decrease (3.30).

31. κἀγὼ οὐκ ᾔδειν αὐτόν. It need not be inferred that John did not know Jesus at all, only that he did not know that he was ὁ ἐρχόμενος.

ἀλλ' ἵνα... διὰ τοῦτο. διὰ τοῦτο more frequently precedes a clause which explains it; for this construction in which διὰ τοῦτο is preceded by its explanation cf. 15.19 (ὅτι... διὰ τοῦτο).

φανερωθῇ τῷ 'Ἰσραήλ. For the Jewish belief that the Messiah will be an obscure person until presented to Israel by Elijah see Justin, *Trypho* 8, 49, and cf. *Sotah* 9.15; *Eduyoth* 8.7. That the Targums speak of the Messiah as being revealed (McNamara, *T. & T.*, 140) adds little to this. The word φανεροῦν is characteristic of John (1.31; 2.11; 3.21; 7.4; 9.3; 17.6; 21.1,14). The word 'Ἰσραήλ, which occurs only four times in John, does not carry with it the bad connotation often attached to οἱ 'Ἰουδαῖοι in this gospel (see on v. 19). John denies the identification of the Baptist with Elijah, but emphasizes that the purpose of John's baptism was the public manifestation of Jesus; it was fulfilled therefore in the descent of the Spirit upon Jesus, and this event at the same time made possible the new Christian baptism with the Spirit. Like John himself, his baptism has no independent significance; both exist in order to bear witness (v. 7) to Christ, who alone truly takes away sin and confers the Spirit as well.

32. τεθέαμαι τὸ πνεῦμα καταβαῖνον. For the perfect τεθέαμαι, cf. v. 15, κέκραγεν. For the verse as a whole cf. Mark 1.10 and parallels. John assumes knowledge of the synoptic baptism story. He does not himself record that Jesus was baptized; see the introduction to this section. A further difference between John and Mark is that, in Mark, Jesus sees the Spirit descending as a dove;

in John, the Baptist sees. John removes the possibility of taking the story as merely the record of a private experience without objective significance. The event is no longer important to Jesus, but only to the Baptist, for identification (Bultmann).

ὡς περιστεράν. On the symbolism of the dove see *H.S.G.T.* 35–9; but in John the dove is only a piece of traditional imagery taken over from the earlier gospels, and has no independent meaning.

καὶ ἔμεινεν ἐπ' αὐτόν. The use of μένειν is characteristic of John, and does not suggest that he is using any other source than Mark. The Spirit abides permanently upon Jesus; the Baptism was not a passing moment of inspiration. The work of Jesus as a whole must be understood as accomplished in communion with the Spirit of God. Too much, however, should not be built upon the word μένειν; it was said by the Rabbis that the Holy Spirit, and the *shekhinah* (or presence) of God, abode (שרה, שרי) upon men, especially the prophets. Cf. Isa. 11.2 (ἀναπαύσεται ἐπ' αὐτόν).

33. κἀγὼ οὐκ ᾔδειν αὐτόν. Cf. v. 31.

ὁ πέμψας με. This phrase is often on the lips of Jesus; but John also had been sent from God (v. 6).

ἐκεῖνός μοι εἶπεν. The resumption of a distant subject by a pronoun is in John's style. The Baptist had received a divine warning how he should recognize the Coming One.

ἐν πνεύματι ἁγίῳ. Jesus has the Spirit in order that he may confer it; and it is the gift of the Spirit that pre-eminently distinguishes the new dispensation from the old (cf. vv. 26f.); it belongs neither to Judaism nor even to John. It is neither said nor implied that Christians will not use water in baptism; see 3.5. For the gift of the Spirit in John see further 7.39; 14.16f.; 20.22. 1 QS 4.20f. deals with cleansing by the Spirit and is thus not strictly parallel.

34. ἑώρακα καὶ μεμαρτύρηκα. For the perfect tenses cf. v. 15. According to Bornkamm II, 192 the words introduce a baptismal confession.

οὗτός ἐστιν ὁ υἱὸς τοῦ θεοῦ. Cf. Mark 1.11 (and parallels), Σὺ εἶ ὁ υἱός μου ὁ ἀγαπητός. The Nestle text of John gives a close parallel to the Marcan words, but instead of υἱός should perhaps be read ἐκλεκτός (P⁵ ℵ* e cur sin Ambrose). A conflate reading ἐκλεκτὸς υἱός (a (b) sah) is certainly secondary but bears witness to the existence of the reading ἐκλεκτός. ἐκλεκτός is thus a reading of very great antiquity and, especially in this gospel, it is much easier to understand the change of ἐκλεκτός into υἱός than the reverse. If the reading ἐκλεκτός be accepted (and it is weakened by the fact that P⁶⁶ and P⁷⁵ both have υἱός), cf. the Lucan form of the transfiguration saying (Luke 9.35), οὗτός ἐστιν ὁ υἱός μου ὁ ἐκλελεγμένος; also Isa. 42.1, Ἰσραὴλ ὁ ἐκλεκτός μου, ... ἔδωκα τὸ πνεῦμά μου ἐπ' αὐτόν. John does not use the word ἐκλεκτός elsewhere, and its meaning here is probably not greatly different from υἱός, save that it points more clearly than υἱός would to the messianic status of Jesus. Jeremias, accepting ἐκλεκτός, finds an allusion to the Servant (*Theology*, 1, 53ff.). For a discussion of 4 QMess ar, which contains the expression בחיר אלהא (God's elect one), see Fitzmyer, *Essays*, 127–60. In this important study Fitzmyer questions whether the words refer directly to a Messiah; they may, he thinks, refer to Noah. On Jesus as Messiah, and as Son of God, see Introduction, pp. 70ff.

3. THE DISCIPLES

1.35–51

John the Baptist repeats his witness to Jesus in the presence of two disciples. They detach themselves from their master and begin to follow Jesus, and abide with him. To this small nucleus of believers in the Messiahship of Jesus others are added. Jesus knows them, their past and their future, before they join him: Simon, who is renamed Peter, and Nathanael (again, perhaps, a symbolic name), whose ready faith evokes the promise that disciples of Jesus will come to see in Jesus a unique contact between heaven and earth.

Accounts of the calling of disciples appear also in the Synoptic Gospels: Mark 1.16–20 (Matt. 4.18–22; cf. Luke 5.1–11); Mark 2.13f. (Matt. 9.9; Luke 5.27f.). For the naming of Simon cf. Mark 3.16 (Luke 6.14); Matt. 16.18. It is impossible to harmonize the Johannine and synoptic narratives. It has often been suggested that the Johannine call was a preliminary one; the disciples were challenged to give their obedience to Jesus, permitted to return home to Galilee, and then decisively called to full-time discipleship in the manner recorded by Mark. But John leaves no room for a second call; from the first his intimate disciples follow Jesus closely and there is no need for them to be called again. Further, the Marcan story loses the force it was intended to have if the immediate response of the fishermen and of Levi is given a psychological explanation. That John knew the Marcan story is probable in view of his other contacts with the second gospel, but his own is quite different, not only in narrative content but also in theological implication, described by Schweizer (*Beiträge*, 222ff.) as follows: (1) It is not Jesus who calls men, but his witnesses; (2) the witnesses give a dogmatic description of his person; (3) those called must leave not boats and nets but other religions—e.g., John the Baptist. The variety of the narratives we possess (Mark, Luke, John) suggests that there was no generally accepted tradition of the 'call', though it is by no means unlikely that some of John the Baptist's disciples may have subsequently followed Jesus. It was natural that the church should wish to know something of the way in which its best-known leaders first came to be disciples and the growth of diverse legends of their call is therefore not surprising; nor is it surprising that the Johannine narrative should reflect the situation of the church after Easter.

The present passage occupies the position of a bridge in John's narrative, and we see the first disciples moving over from Judaism (v. 47) and from John the Baptist (v. 35) to Jesus and his fulfilment of what Judaism and the Baptist meant. So far they have not reached faith in or even an understanding of this fulfilment. The stage they have reached is represented by 'Come and see' (vv. 38, 46), and 'You shall see' (v. 51). The immediate goal of this movement is reached at 2.11, when the glory of Jesus is manifested and the disciples believe; but v. 51, with its reference to the Son of man and the angels, already applies the resources of apocalyptic to the definition of the position and meaning of Jesus. This plays a more fundamental part in the development of John's Christology than the figure of the Divine Man.

35. τῇ ἐπαύριον. See on 2.1.

εἱστήκει. Cf. 7.37; it is possible that in these two places the word lends a certain dignity and emphasis to the pronouncement.

ἐκ, partitive; see Introduction, p. 8. For disciples of John, cf. 4.1. The present verse does not suggest an active polemical interest on the part of the evangelist; see p. 171.

36. See v. 29. The testimony of the Baptist is repeated in order to furnish a motive for the action of the two disciples. Cf. 5.33,36. As soon as John has borne his witness he disappears from the scene; he has no other function (1.7f.).

37. It has been suggested that this narrative is based upon the Q account of the mission of two of the Baptist's disciples to Jesus (Matt. 11.2; Luke 7.18f.); in Q the disciples are charged with a question and return to their master with Jesus' answer. John (it is suggested) derived his incident (including the number 'two') from this source, changing the Baptist's question into an appropriate affirmation, and making his disciples transfer their allegiance to Jesus. This is possible; but on the other hand it is by no means incredible that some of Jesus' disciples may have been previously followers of John; and the evangelist may be following independent tradition, though it is perhaps more probable that he is working out in narrative form the substance of the note on v. 36.

ἠκολούθησαν. Elsewhere in John (1.44; 8.12; 10.4,27; 12.26; 21.19,20,22) ἀκολουθεῖν means 'to follow as a disciple'; but it also has a neutral meaning (e.g. 11.31). It is probable, and characteristic of his style, that here, and in vv. 38,40,43, John is playing on both meanings. Cf. 13.36f. 'Following' is the appropriate consequence of John's μαρτυρία.

38. στραφείς ... There is a striking parallel to these words in 21.20, ἐπιστρα-φεὶς ὁ Πέτρος βλέπει τὸν μαθητὴν ... ἀκολουθοῦντα; see on this verse.

τί ζητεῖτε; The question is quite intelligible as a straightforward piece of narrative. It is possible to compare Philo, Det. 24: This challenger (οὗτος ὁ ἔλεγχος, used of the 'real man', ὁ πρὸς ἀλήθειαν ἄνθρωπος; cf. John 16.8) inquired of the soul when he saw it wandering, τί ζητεῖς; (cf. Gen. 37.15). It seems probable (Fenton) that John wishes to show the Logos-Christ confronting men and challenging their intentions: What is it that man seeks in life? Cf. the double meaning of ἀκολουθεῖν noted above.

'Ραββί. This word (1.39,49; 3.2; 4.31; 6.25; 9.2; 11.8; at 3.26 it is addressed to John the Baptist) is put by John on the lips of imperfect or mistaken disciples; yet at 1.49 it is apparently not inconsistent with the titles Son of God and King of Israel. It transliterates רבי, the common title of a scholar and public teacher. It could hardly be applied to one of whom the accusation of 7.15 was true. For the question whether the use of the term is an ana-chronism, see Brown.

ὃ λέγεται μεθερμηνευόμενον (λέγεται ἑρμηνευόμενον, א* Θ ω; ἑρμηνεύεται, λ it). John commonly translates Hebrew and Aramaic words (1.38,41,42; 4.25; 9.7; 11.16; 19.17; 20.16,24; 2.12), and (as here) does so correctly.

ποῦ μένεις; Once more the question is intelligible as it stands; but the use of μένειν is so characteristic of John's theology (e.g. 15.4) that a deeper meaning may be intended. Nothing is more important than to know where Jesus abides and may be found.

39. ἔρχεσθε καὶ ὄψεσθε (the variant ἴδετε is well attested but is probably due to assimilation to v. 46). The phrase is common in rabbinic literature, but probably has no special significance here, though Fenton notes that for John coming to Jesus (6.35) is important and 'to see' is equivalent to 'to know' (14.9).

παρ' αὐτῷ ἔμειναν. Once more, it may be that John intends us to see a more than superficial meaning in the use of μένειν. These disciples did what all are bidden to do; e.g. 15.3.

ὥρα ἦν ὡς δεκάτη. Customary usage in the gospels, including John, is to reckon a twelve-hour day from dawn to sunset—very roughly, from 6 a.m. to 6 p.m. On this mode of reckoning the incident took place at 4 p.m.—not a natural point for the beginning of a day's stay. The time scheme is affected by the variant in v. 41; see the note. N. Walker (*Nov. T.* 4 (1960), 69–73) thinks that here and elsewhere John uses the modern reckoning—the time was 10 a.m. For Bultmann the number ten signifies the hour of fulfilment.

40. Ἀνδρέας ὁ ἀδελφὸς Σίμωνος Πέτρου. This pair of brothers is introduced in Mark 1.16–20, but John is not at this point using Marcan material. The double name Simon Peter is that most commonly used in John. Simon is a common Jewish name (שמעון, shim'on); on the name Peter see on v. 42. The name Andrew is of Greek origin, but it appears (as אנדרי, אנדראי) in the Talmud and consequently cannot be used to prove any Greek connections on the part of his family. In any case, it may have been, like Peter, a 'Chris-tian name'.

41. πρῶτον: so Nestle, but the reading is in doubt.
   (a) πρῶτον   P⁶⁶ P⁷⁵ אᶜ B Θ φ it vg Origen
   (b) πρῶτος   א* W
   (c) *mane*   b e
   (d) *on that day* sin, cur omits.
The reading (c) evidently corresponds to a Greek πρωΐ. It seems impossible to say whether (d), if not original, arose out of (a) or (c). It is difficult to accept it, and it is probably best to leave it out of account in discussing the other readings. If (c) is accepted we must suppose that Andrew and the other disciple spent a night with Jesus; Simon Peter is found early next morning; 1.43 brings us to the day after this, and so another day is introduced into the reckoning—see on 2.1. If (b) is chosen it may be taken to imply that after Andrew had found his brother the other disciple found his; he therefore belonged to another pair of brother disciples, and must have been one of the sons of Zebedee, James or John. If (a) is accepted these inferences are denied to us, and the text means no more than that Andrew found Simon before

he did anything else (taking πρῶτον as neuter accusative, used adverbially), or that he found his brother before he found anyone else (taking πρῶτον as masculine accusative). Adverbial πρῶτον is common in John (2.10; 7.51; 10.40; 12.16; 15.18; 18.13; 19.39), (a) is well attested textually, and it will probably be best to accept it. The use in this verse of τὸν ἴδιον does not bear upon the textual question, though it has been held to support (b) (. . . first finds his *own* brother). In spite of Moulton's opinion (M. 1, 90) that the emphasis of ἴδιον here is 'undeniable' it seems more probable that the word is used in its exhausted sense ('his' not 'his own'; B.D., § 286). It often has this meaning in late Greek, and in the LXX sometimes represents pronominal suffixes. See, however, for both text and ἴδιος, Turner, *Insights* 135ff. If πρῶτον is read it must be noted simply that an unnamed disciple appears here; it is of course in any case possible (though beyond proof) that one of the sons of Zebedee is intended; the two pairs of brothers are called in Mark 1.16–20.

τὸν Μεσσίαν. Only John among the New Testament writers transliterates the Hebrew (or Aramaic) term (here and 4.25). On Jesus as the Christ in John see Introduction, pp. 70f. No attempt is made in John to avoid the eschatological language of primitive Christianity, though that language is supplemented. The present section contains a remarkable sequence: Lamb of God (v. 36); Rabbi (v. 38); Messiah (v. 41); the one who was foretold by Moses and the prophets (v. 45); Rabbi, Son of God, King of Israel (v. 49); the Son of man (v. 51). In Mark the Messiahship of Jesus is not recognized by men till 8.29 and then is kept secret; in John also there is a messianic secret, but the Messiahship is neither obscured nor unfolded in the same way as in Mark. In εὑρήκαμεν τὸν Μεσσίαν Martyn, 45, sees the message of the first missioners in the synagogue.

ὅ ἐστιν μεθερμηνευόμενον χριστός. John, according to his custom (see v. 38), explains the Semitic term.

42. ἐμβλέψας. The same understanding gaze as John had directed upon Jesus (v. 36; cf. v. 29). Jesus knows at once the character and destiny of Peter. There is some resemblance to the characteristics of the θεῖος ἀνήρ; see Introduction, p. 74.

Σίμων ὁ υἱὸς Ἰωάννου. B³ λ φ ω, with various VSS. and Fathers, read Ἰωνᾶ, assimilating to Matt. 16.17. The father's name is mentioned again in 21.15,16, 17. It does not appear elsewhere in the New Testament except Matt. 16.17, Σίμων Βὰρ (=Aramaic בר, son of) Ἰωνᾶ (perhaps taken to be a variant spelling of Ἰωάννης). For an alternative meaning of Bar-Jonah, which would align Peter with the Zealots, see S. G. F. Brandon, *Jesus and the Zealots*, 1967, 204 note 2, with his references.

σὺ κληθήσῃ Κηφᾶς. The future means that Simon will from this moment bear the name Cephas; Peter's new name is thus, according to John, bestowed at this his first meeting with Jesus. In Mark it first appears at 3.16 (ἐπέθηκεν ὄνομα τῷ Σίμωνι Πέτρον), at the appointment of the Twelve, though we cannot be sure from Mark's words that the name had not been given earlier. Matt. 16.18 (κἀγὼ δέ σοι λέγω ὅτι σὺ εἶ Πέτρος, κτλ.) would make an admirable occasion for the giving of the name, but it is not so taken by Matthew himself. John explains that Κηφᾶς (=Aramaic כיפא (perhaps in Galilean Aramaic קיפא—Schlatter, 56), 'a rock', Greek πέτρα) is the equivalent of Πέτρος, but he gives no interpretation of the name, neither Matthew's (Peter the foundation-stone of the Church), nor that commonly accepted here (a prospective change in Peter's character). Perhaps he was aware that Peter's subsequent career would bear out neither interpretation. See further Fitzmyer, *Essays*, 105–12, with the references to C. Roth.

43. Τῇ ἐπαύριον. See on 1.19 (Saul), 29; 2.1. The subject of ἠθέλησεν is probably Jesus, not Simon or Andrew. Schnackenburg wishes to omit v. 43, noting that if this is done the πρῶτον of v. 41 will point forward to Philip. See also Schweizer, *Jesus*, 161 note 62; Dodd, *Tradition* 309f.; and the reference to *J. & Q.* on 1.28.

ἐξελθεῖν εἰς τὴν Γαλιλαίαν. Since the location of Bethany (v. 28) is uncertain no precision is obtainable with regard to the route envisaged (if John envisaged any route). By Galilee is meant the area to the west of the lake of that name, governed in the time of Jesus by the tetrarch Herod Antipas (Luke 3.1), and separated from Judaea by Samaria. According to Mark 1.14 the public ministry of Jesus began in Galilee after the arrest of John the Baptist: see on 3.23.

Φίλιππον. Philip is mentioned in the synoptic lists of the Twelve (Mark 3.18 and parallels). His name is Greek, but it appears (in various forms, e.g. פליפא) as the name of an Amora, and cannot therefore be held to prove Greek ancestry. Since he was a native of Bethsaida it may be inferred that he was in Bethany as an adherent of the Baptist. He is noticed in a more personal way in John than in the Synoptic Gospels (see, apart from this passage, 6.6ff.; 12.21f.; 14.8f.). It is possible, though far from certain, that there is some connection between this interest in Philip and Polycrates' statement (*apud* Eusebius *H.E.* III, xxxi, 3) that Philip, one of the Twelve, was buried in Hierapolis in Asia. It is however possible that Polycrates confused Philip the Apostle and Philip the Evangelist; see Introduction, pp. 101f.

ἀκολούθει μοι. The same word of command appears in Mark 2.14 (cf. Mark 1.17, Δεῦτε ὀπίσω μου). Those who think that the Marcan 'call' of Simon and Andrew can be made more credible by the use of the Johannine narrative do not always observe that the Johannine 'call' of Philip raises all the difficulties of the Marcan story. On ἀκολουθεῖν, see on v. 37.

44. Βηθσαϊδά. Cf. 12.21. Bethsaida Julias, built at the north-eastern extremity of the lake as his capital by Philip the tetrarch (Luke 3.1), was not in Galilee but in Gaulanitis; but it lay on the eastern bank of the Jordan, and though Philip's tetrarchy as a whole was not Jewish there may well have been a Jewish element in Philip's city since it was not a new foundation. Consequently it might naturally though inaccurately be thought of as belonging to Jewish territory. There is, further, reason to think that during and after the war of A.D. 66–70 the whole territory round the lake was described as 'Galilee' (see G. A. Smith, *E. Bib.*, 566); since only John among the evangelists describes Bethsaida as 'of Galilee' (12.21) it is natural to think that he follows later usage. According to Mark 1.29 the home of Simon and Andrew was at Capernaum, at the north-western end of the lake.

ἀπό ... ἐκ. There is here no difference in meaning between the prepositions. For their synonymous use see 7.17 (cf. 12.49); 11.1.

45. Ναθαναήλ, נתנאל, *God gives*, or *has given*. This name is purely Semitic. It is not found in the Synoptic Gospels and it has often been suggested that the

Nathanael of John is the Bartholomew of Matthew, Mark, and Luke. There is no real evidence for this conjecture. Nathanael appears again only in 21.2. It is possible that an ideal rather than a real person is meant; see on v. 47— Nathanael is an ideal Israelite. The name is rare in rabbinic writings, and this supports the view that its meaning is significant; cf. the description of the disciples as those whom the Father has *given* to Jesus (6.37 *et al.*). On the other hand, R. Simeon b. Nathanael was a Tanna of the second generation (i.e. *fl.* A.D. 80–120), and accordingly it is quite possible that there should have been a Nathanael among the disciples of Jesus. The paragraph however is apologetic rather than historical (Dodd, *Tradition*, 310ff.).

ὃν ἔγραψεν Μωϋσῆς ἐν τῷ νόμῳ καὶ οἱ προφῆται—i.e. the Messiah. For the Old Testament as a witness to Christ see 5.39. Here no passages are specified. There is probably no genuinely messianic passage in the Pentateuch; for a list of passages messianically applied by the Rabbis see A. Edersheim, *The Life and Times of Jesus the Messiah* (1892), II, 710–15; see especially Gen. 49.10. In the present context (v. 51) material from Gen. 28 is referred to. There is no specific reference here to the 'writings', but it would be unwise to draw any inference regarding the development of the Old Testament canon.

εὑρήκαμεν. The plural probably does not mean 'Andrew and I', but refers to the testimony of Christian preachers.

υἱὸν τοῦ Ἰωσήφ. At 6.42 the disbelieving Jews speak of Jesus as the son of Joseph, a relationship which discredits his claim to have come down from heaven. On the question of John's belief in the virgin birth of Christ see on v. 13. It is in accord with his ironical use of traditional material that he should allow Jesus to be ignorantly described as 'son of Joseph' while himself believing that Jesus had no human father.

τὸν ἀπὸ Ναζαρέτ. Cf. 12.21, τῷ ἀπὸ Βηθσαϊδά. Nazareth is not mentioned in the Old Testament or in the Talmud, but various strands of New Testament tradition speak of it as the home of Jesus. See G. Dalman, *Sacred Sites and Ways* (E.T., 1935), 57–78.

46. ἐκ Ναζαρὲτ δύναταί τι ἀγαθὸν εἶναι. The words are a scornful question: Can there be any good thing (τι ἀγαθόν is good Hellenistic Greek and quite unsemitic) which has Nazareth for its origin? They sound like a proverb, but no other evidence exists for such a saying. The suggestion that, since Nathanael came from Cana (21.2), the rivalry of two neighbouring towns might have produced the proverb, has little to commend it. Cf., however, 7.41,52. For the belief that the Messiah would be unknown till publicly manifested to Israel see on v. 31.

Ἔρχου καὶ ἴδε. See v. 39.

47. ἀληθῶς Ἰσραηλίτης. Jesus has supernatural knowledge of Nathanael's character; cf. v. 42, and 2.24f. Nathanael is one who truly is an Israelite. ἀληθῶς always has this meaning in John (4.42; 6.14,55; 7.26,40; 8.31; 17.8): cf. the note on ἀληθής, ἀληθινός, at v. 9. For the thought, cf. Rom. 2.28f.; the man who is ἀληθῶς Ἰσραηλίτης is ὁ ἐν τῷ κρυπτῷ Ἰουδαῖος. The word Ἰσραηλίτης is used here only in John; but the gospel abounds with Jews (Ἰουδαῖοι, see on v. 19) who if they were true Jews and listened with understanding and obedience to their own teacher Moses would believe in Jesus. It may be intentional that the word Ἰσραηλίτης is used in this passage, though, as

Schlatter notes (59), John, unlike Philo, gives no etymological interpretation of the name Israel. Yet Philo's interpretation of Israel is ὁρῶν τὸν θεόν (e.g. *Mut.*, 81), and in the present passage it is promised that Nathanael shall see heavenly sights (vv. 50f.). Cf. Num. 24.16, ὁ ἀληθινῶς ὁρῶν (*J. & Q.*, 176); but the parallel is not important.

ἐν ᾧ δόλος οὐκ ἔστιν. The true Israelite is further described. In view of the use in v. 51 of Gen. 28.12 it seems probable that there is here a reference to the cunning of Jacob (later called Israel) in robbing Esau of his blessing (cf. Gen. 27.35, ἐλθὼν ὁ ἀδελφός σου μετὰ δόλου ἔλαβεν τὴν εὐλογίαν σου). Nathanael is willing to put his prejudice to the test of experience (Sanders). Alternatively we may suppose that the reference to δόλος simply expands ἀληθῶς: you are truly an Israelite, with no pretence, seeming, dissimulation.

48. πόθεν με γινώσκεις; Whence comes your knowledge of me? That is, How do you know me? Cf. Mark 6.2, Πόθεν τούτῳ ταῦτα; This use of πόθεν (=How?) is Semitic in that it resembles the use of מנין, מאין (Whence? How?); but it is not a Semitism for it exists in Greek (e.g. Euripides, *Alcestis* 781, οἶμαι μὲν οὔ· Πόθεν γάρ; ἀλλ' ἄκουέ μου; Aristophanes, *Frag.* 532 (Dindorf)).

ὄντα ὑπὸ τὴν συκῆν εἶδόν σε. For such knowledge see above, and 4.17f.; 6.70; 9.3; 11.4,11; 13.10f.,38. In Philo the Logos is all-seeing (e.g. *L. A.* III, 171: ὁ θεοῦ λόγος ὀξυδερκέστατός ἐστιν, ὡς πάντα ἐφορᾶν εἶναι ἱκανός); but it is very unlikely that John is drawing on such ideas. To be under the fig tree may be a sign of peace and prosperity (e.g. 1 Kings 5.5), or of the study of the Law (e.g. *Ecclesiastes R.* 5.15, where R. Aqiba († A.D. 135) is mentioned; other trees were perhaps equally favoured for study), or indeed of nothing in particular—the supernatural knowledge of Jesus could not be brought out without reference to some landmark. C. F. D. Moule suggests (*J.T.S.* 5 (1954), 210f.) that 'Under what tree?' was a stock question, a proverbial expression meaning 'Can you tell me all about it?', but the evidence he cites is anything but conclusive.

49. Nathanael's faith is evoked by what is probably intended to appear (in view of μείζω τούτων, v. 50) a comparatively trivial exhibition of supernatural power.

ῥαββί. See on v. 38. The use of the word here is particularly striking; evidently John does not think it incompatible with the other epithets applied in this verse to Jesus.

σὺ εἶ ὁ υἱὸς τοῦ θεοῦ. On Jesus as the Son of God see Introduction, p. 72, and the next note. Nathanael's words may but need not reflect a baptismal confession (Bornkamm, II,192).

σὺ βασιλεὺς εἶ τοῦ 'Ισραήλ. The claim that this construction (in which βασιλεύς has no article) is Semitic cannot stand; the interposition of a word corresponding to εἶ between a construct and its governing noun is impossible. Further, this construction is characteristic of John; cf. 8.34; 9.5,28; 10.2; 11.9; 12.31; 18.17; 19.35. In chs. 18f. the title ὁ βασιλεὺς τῶν 'Ιουδαίων is used several times; Jesus never gives his assent to it as a description of him, just as he does not permit the Jews to make him a king (6.15). He is again represented as the king of Israel at 12.13. On οἱ 'Ιουδαῖοι in John, see on v. 19. Nathanael in his confession accepts the assertion of v. 45, which at first he had received with incredulity; both titles signify that Jesus is the Messiah.

This is certainly the meaning of 'king of Israel'; for the Messiah as Son of God, cf. 2 Sam. 7.14; Ps. 2.7; 1 Enoch 105.2; 4 Ezra 7.28f.; 13.52; 14.9; *Sukkah* 52a (a *baraitah* which interprets Ps. 2.7 of the Messiah); Mark 1.11; Rom. 1.3f., and other passages. If both titles have the same messianic meaning it follows that it is incorrect to suppose that the latter is a lower title than the former; there is no anti-climax. The latter title has however a peculiar aptness in this passage, which appears more clearly when the rarity in John of βασιλεύς, βασιλεία (outside the Passion Narrative) is remembered. Nathanael has been declared to be ἀληθῶς Ἰσραηλίτης; Jesus correspondingly is ἀληθῶς βασιλεύς—truly king of the true Israel. The former title, Son of God, is prefixed as the most general and comprehensive term used in John.

50. ὅτι εἶπόν σοι . . . πιστεύεις; The words might be better read as a statement than as a question. Cf. 9.35; 16.31; 20.29. Nathanael's faith is so far grounded only upon a miracle; such faith, though it is real faith, is inferior to the faith that needs no sign; cf. 4.48; 14.11.

μείζω τούτων ὄψῃ. Cf. 11.40; 14.12 (μείζονα τούτων [*sc.* τῶν ἔργων] ποιήσει); for the words, 4 Ezra 5.13, *audies iterato horum maiora*; 6.31. The 'greater things' are immediately explained, and are seen to go far beyond what might have seemed no more than the cheap trick of a clairvoyant.

51. ἀμὴν ἀμὴν λέγω ὑμῖν. This solemn formula of asseveration occurs 20 times in John; with σοι for ὑμῖν, 5 times more. ἀμήν is never used singly in John, or without λέγω ὑμῖν (σοι). In the Synoptic Gospels ἀμήν is never doubled, and is always followed by λέγω (except at Matt. 6.13, where there is doubt about the reading, and Mark 16.20). The origin of the characteristic New Testament use of ἀμήν to introduce a statement (over against its common use in affirming a prayer or similar formula) is obscure; see Daube *N.T.R.J.*, 388–93, but also J. Jeremias, *Abba*, 148–51, and *Z.N.T.W.* 64 (1973), 122f. John has merely taken it over from the earlier tradition, and employs it to give emphasis to a solemn pronouncement. In this passage σοι (rather than ὑμῖν) might have been expected, since Jesus is conversing with Nathanael. Probably John intends to make it clear that the prediction which follows is of more than private application; cf. 3.7.

ὄψεσθε τὸν οὐρανὸν ἀνεῳγότα. To these words, Θ ω λ φ e pesh Chrysostom Augustine prefix ἀπ' ἄρτι. The expression is used at 13.19; 14.7; but here it appears to have been imported into the passage from Matt. 26.64. If this is a correct judgement textually it has importance in regard to interpretation, for it means that the prediction of this verse was thought to be related to the eschatological prediction of Matt. 26.64. This may well be true; see below, also Jeremias, *Theology* 1, 263f. For the opened heaven, cf. Mark 1.10 (and parallels); also Isa. 64.1, ἐὰν ἀνοίξῃς τὸν οὐρανόν.

τοὺς ἀγγέλους τοῦ θεοῦ ἀναβαίνοντας καὶ καταβαίνοντας. Cf. Gen. 28.12, οἱ ἄγγελοι τοῦ θεοῦ ἀνέβαινον καὶ κατέβαινον. That the story of Jacob is alluded to seems certain, though neither in Genesis nor in John is it made clear what the angels are doing. McNamara (*T. & T.*, 146f.) quotes the Palestinian Targum on Gen. 28.12 (. . . the angels from before the Lord were ascending and descending and they observed him [Jacob]), but it does not seem adequate to say that the angels simply wished to *see* the Son of man. According to Schnackenburg they go up to God with his prayers and descend to serve him; but it may be best to see in them a relic of the old synoptic saying about the coming of the Son of man accompanied by the angels adapted to the new framework provided by the story of Jacob.

ἐπὶ τὸν υἱὸν τοῦ ἀνθρώπου. The passage in Gen. 28.12 concludes ἐπ' αὐτῆς, that is, the angels went up and down on the ladder (κλῖμαξ) of the vision. For the ladder John substitutes the Son of man. This substitution seems to arise from the use of the Hebrew text of Genesis (though it does not follow from this that John himself used the Hebrew), for the Hebrew corresponding to ἐπ' αὐτῆς is בו (since ladder, סלם, is masculine), and this, though certainly intended by the author to refer to the ladder, could, grammatically, be taken to apply to Jacob: the angels went up and down upon *him*. This misapplication of בו is known to have been made; see *Gen. R.* 68.18. Here R. Ḥiyya takes בו to refer to the ladder, R. Yannai to Jacob. The latter refers to Isa. 49.3, in which passage 'Thou' refers to the heavenly image איקונין ('*iqonin*, from the Greek εἰκόνιον) of Jacob (Israel) which remained on high while Jacob's body slept below. The movement of the angels certified the contact between the heavenly man and the earthly. See Dodd, *Interpretation*, 245ff.; but this material must be used with caution. The two rabbis are of the third generation of Amoraim and therefore much too late to have influenced John, though it is of course possible that R. Yannai's exegesis was known earlier. To say that Jesus as the Son of man is the 'second Jacob, i.e. the true Israel in his own person' (Sanders) goes too far; Nathanael is the 'Israelite indeed'. Nor is it justified by the text to say that the cross, on which the Son of man is lifted up (3.14; 8.28; 12.32, 34), is the ladder (Derrett, *Law*, 416). Philo has two interpretations of the ladder, neither of which seems relevant. In *Som.* 1, 133–5 the ladder is the air, the abode of incorporeal souls; in 146 it is the soul. Whether, by the analogy of microcosm and macrocosm, it may be inferred from the latter interpretation that the ladder may also symbolize the Logos, seems doubtful. It is probable that the starting point of John's thought is to be found in synoptic (and other Jewish apocalyptic) sayings about the Son of man (see especially Mark 13.26; 14.62 and the parallels). In primitive apocalyptic thought the Son of man was a heavenly being who, by descending from heaven at the last day, should set up contact between heaven and earth. John, returning to earlier speculations about a primal, archetypal, or heavenly Man (Adam), and, more particularly, reflecting upon the meaning of the incarnation, sees in Jesus, the Son of man, not merely an eschatological but an eternal contact between heaven and earth, God and man, and uses the ladder and the ascending and descending angels to express his conception. The Son of man is both in heaven and on earth (3.13); he descends to give life to the world (6.27,53); he ascends again to his glory (6.62), but this ascent and glorification are by way of the Cross (3.14; 8.28; 12.23,34; 13.31). 'It is no longer the place, Bethel, that is important, but the Person of the Son of Man' (Davies, *Land*, 298). On 'Son of man' in John see further Introduction, pp. 72f.; Hahn, *Titel* 39ff. (this passage is omitted in the E.T.); Higgins, *Son of man*, 157–61; Odeberg, 33–42. On this verse see S. S. Smalley in *Jesus und der Menschensohn* (Festschrift A. Vögtle, 1975), 300–13.

4. THE SIGN AT CANA

2.1–12

A wedding feast, attended by Jesus, his mother, and his disciples is the scene of the first miracle. Jesus, though he will not be hurried or dictated to, even by his mother, supplies handsomely a lack of wine by transforming the contents of six water pots. After the miracle, which is represented as taking place privately and as known only to a few servants and to the disciples, Jesus goes down to Capernaum to await the appropriate moment for beginning his public work.

No parallel to this incident is found in any of the Synoptic Gospels (but see below); non-biblical parallels, however, suggest themselves at once. The god Dionysus was not only the discoverer of the vine (εὑρετὴς ἀμπέλου, Justin, 1 *Apol.*, 54, *Trypho*, 69) but also the cause of miraculous transformations of water into wine (e.g. Euripides, *Bacchae* 704–7; Athenaeus 1, 61 (34a); Pausanias VI, xxvi, 1f.). That such 'miracles' took place in Dionysiac worship seems to be proved by archaeological evidence drawn from a temple (fifth century B.C.) at Corinth (C. Bonner, *American Journal of Archaeology*, 33 (1929), 368–75). There was thus an exact precedent for the benefaction of Jesus in a pagan worship doubtless known to some at least of John's readers. See further Dodd, *Tradition*, 224f., and Betz, 176; and, for the heretic Marcus, Irenaeus, *Adv. Haer.* 1, xiii, 2. The precedent was probably known to Philo, as the following evidence suggests. In *L. A.* III, 82, allegorizing the story of Melchizedek, he says: ἀλλ᾽ ὁ μὲν Μελχισεδὲκ ἀντὶ ὕδατος οἶνον προσφερέτω καὶ ποτιζέτω καὶ ἀκρατιζέτω ψυχάς, ἵνα κατάσχετοι γένωνται θείᾳ μέθῃ νηφαλιωτέρᾳ νήψεως αὐτῆς. In Genesis (14.18. ἐξήνεγκεν ἄρτους καὶ οἶνον) there is no reference to water; the substitution of wine for water is therefore a thought introduced by Philo himself (though the point may be simply that Melchizedek gave wine for the water the Ammonites and Moabites failed to supply—Guilding, 185). He goes on to speak of Melchizedek as Logos, probably because he saw an opportunity of showing the roots of Hellenistic religion in Judaism: not Dionysus but the Logos, of whom Melchizedek is a symbol, is the true miraculous dispenser of divine inspiration. This is confirmed by the fact that in *Som.* II, 249 he speaks of the Logos as οἰνοχόος τοῦ θεοῦ καὶ συμποσίαρχος. In this passage Philo makes it quite clear that he is using heathen models, for he goes on to say that the Logos is also the wine itself, 'the delight, the sweetening, the exhilaration, the merriment, the ambrosian drug whose medicine gives joy and gladness—ἵνα καὶ αὐτοὶ ποιητικοῖς ὀνόμασι χρησώμεθα'. See further on Philo's use of the theme Dodd, *Interpretation*, 298ff.

Thus there existed Jewish precedent for speaking of the Logos in pseudo-Dionysiac terminology, and John may have done this; it is even

conceivable that the miracle story had a non-Christian origin. In style
it stands a little apart from most of the Johannine material (Schweizer,
100; Introduction, p. 8) and may be extraneous matter lightly worked
over and incorporated by John. But it is also related to the earlier
gospel tradition. In Matt. 22.1–14; 25.1–13 (cf. Luke 12.36) a wedding
feast is used in parabolic description of the kingdom of God. At Mark
2.19 (Matt. 9.15; Luke 5.34) the disciples in the presence of Jesus are
said to be like guests at a wedding: they cannot be expected to fast.
Most important of all, in Mark 2.22 (Matt. 9.17; Luke 5.37f.) the
parable of wine and wineskins is used; over against Judaism the message
of Jesus is essentially new. The Johannine narrative may have simply
been made up out of these elements; or John may have taken an already
existing story and, treating it as a σημεῖον (v. 11), used it to bring out
these points. F. E. Williams (*J.B.L.* 86 (1967), 311–9) thinks that the
story was based on Luke 5.33–9 together with the tradition of Jesus'
mother and brothers; Dodd, *Tradition*, 227, that it developed out of a
parable. See also Daube, *N.T.R.J.*, 44f. In any case it seems clear that
John meant to show the supersession of Judaism in the glory of Jesus. It
is possible that in doing so he drew material from Dionysiac sources;
but it was Jewish purificatory water which stood in the water pots and
was made the wine of the Gospel. It is, however, far too characteristic
of John to use material with a twofold, Jewish and pagan, background,
for us easily to set aside the parallels to the miraculous transformation
of water into wine which have been noted in Hellenistic sources. His
main emphasis is the eschatological glory revealed in the fulfilment of
Judaism—note e.g. the use of the figure of an abundance of wine in
Amos 9.13f.; Hos. 14.7; Jer. 31.12; 1 Enoch 10.19; 2 Bar. 29.5 (Brown).
It remains quite uncertain whether any allusion to the eucharist is
intended. For a discussion of the place of the mother of Jesus see J.
McHugh, *The Mother of Jesus in the New Testament* (1975), 362–70,
388–96; 462–6.

Jesus as the fulfiller of Judaism, as the bearer of supernatural power,
becomes henceforth an object of faith to his disciples (v. 11). It is
natural to compare this verse with 4.54, which refers to a second sign at
Cana, but not necessary to infer that both narratives were drawn from a
'Signs Source' (see Introduction, pp. 18f.). In each case the word
σημεῖον occurs in an editorial verse and probably represents John's
own terminology and interpretation.

1. τῇ ἡμέρᾳ τῇ τρίτῃ. In spite of the chapter division there is no break with
what precedes, and this note of time is the last of the series 1.29,35,43, all
of which deal with the summoning of the disciples. The series of incidents
concerning them is brought to a close at 2.11 (ἐπίστευσαν εἰς αὐτὸν οἱ μαθηταὶ
αὐτοῦ), after which, and the intervening verse 2.12, the public ministry
opens at 2.13. 2.1–11 is a 'private' miracle (cf. v. 9). The series of dated
events runs as follows:

(a) John's statement in reply to his questioners, 1.19–28.

(b) τῇ ἐπαύριον—his pronouncement, Behold the Lamb of God, 1.29–34.

(c) τῇ ἐπαύριον—renewed declaration; two disciples and Simon follow Jesus, 1.35–42.

(d) τῇ ἐπαύριον—ἠθέλησεν ἐξελθεῖν; Philip and Nathanael, 1.43–51.

The miracle at Cana follows τῇ ἡμέρᾳ τῇ τρίτῃ; this means in Greek usage 'the day after the morrow (αὔριον)' and is probably to be reckoned from the day last mentioned, that of 1.43–51. We may thus count six complete days, the fifth being occupied, presumably, in travelling. This reckoning is probable, but not quite certain. If at 1.41 (see the note) πρωΐ is read another day is introduced into the series; and it is possible to count the 'third day' of 2.1 as the third day from the first call (first day, 1.35–42; second day, 1.43–51; third day, 2.1–11). The six-day interval, if, as seems probable, it should be accepted, is followed (2.13) by reference to the first Passover of the ministry, at which the meaning of the ministry as a whole is shadowed forth; a similar period of six days is defined with even greater clarity (12.1) before the last Passover, at which the ministry is consummated. Sanders thinks that 'on the third day' implies a vacant day which will have been the Sabbath. The first miracle therefore happens on the first day, which is also the third day—the day of resurrection.

γάμος here clearly means 'wedding' (see v. 9), though in this sense the plural γάμοι is more frequent in the New Testament. For marriage customs see S.B. 1, 500–17; 11, 372–99.

Κανὰ τῆς Γαλιλαίας. The defining genitive is not superfluous; the Cana (קנה, Κανά or Κανθάν) of Josh. 19.28, which was not far from Tyre, is excluded. Josephus (Vita, 86) speaks of a κώμη τῆς Γαλιλαίας, ἣ προσαγορεύεται Κανά. This village was a night's march from Tiberias (ibid. 90). At the present time there exist three villages, Kefr Kenna, Qanat el Gelil, and 'Ain Qana, all of which roughly satisfy the requirements of our text. Little is to be gained by an attempt to decide between them. John's τῆς Γαλιλαίας is intended not merely to identify the Cana in question, but also to indicate that the first miracle took place not in Judaea but in Galilee.

ἡ μήτηρ τοῦ Ἰησοῦ. The mother of Jesus is never named in this gospel, but is mentioned here and in 2.12; 6.42; 19.25ff. In all except the last of these passages it seems certain that John has in mind a historical character, and that he intends no veiled allusion to the Israel from which the Messiah sprang. The earlier passages probably carry 19.25ff. with them; see the notes ad loc.

οἱ μαθηταὶ αὐτοῦ. In 1.35–51 we learn of the call of Andrew, Simon, Philip, Nathanael, and an unnamed disciple. No more 'calls' are described, but in 6.67 we hear of 'the Twelve', and it is probably this complete group to which John here refers.

The text of this verse of simple narrative is curiously corrupt. In ℵ* it runs καὶ οἶνον οὐκ εἶχον, ὅτι συνετελέσθη ὁ οἶνος τοῦ γάμου· εἶτα λέγει ἡ μ. τ. Ἰ. π. α., οἶνος οὐκ ἔστιν. In the variant in the first part of the verse ℵ* is supported by several VSS., including a b, cf. e hlᵐᵍ. The reading of ℵ* is probably a gloss, though an early one; it is however accepted by Sanders. The use of ὑστερεῖν in the sense given it in this verse (the wine had run out) is late, and a copyist may have wished to make it quite clear that no wine at all was left. The second variant in ℵ* (οἶνος οὐκ ἔστιν for οἶνον οὐκ ἔχουσιν) is doubtless due to the same motive, and to the desire not to duplicate the clause οἶνον οὐκ εἶχον. We are probably intended to infer that the mother of Jesus brought him this information in the hope that he would remedy the deficiency. That the deficiency was caused by the presence of Jesus and his associates without the customary wedding gift of a contribution to the feast (Derrett, *Law*, 228–46) is speculation. John is not interested in the question why the wine failed.

4. Τί ἐμοὶ καὶ σοί, γύναι; There is no harshness or even disrespect in the vocative γύναι, as abundant examples, most significantly perhaps 19.26, show. But τί ἐμοὶ καὶ σοί; (a LXX rendering of מה לי ולך) is abrupt and draws a sharp line between Jesus and his mother. In these words the demons address Jesus (Mark 1.24; 5.7), and Matt 8.29 (ἦλθες ὧδε πρὸ καιροῦ βασανίσαι ἡμᾶς;) is particularly instructive: You have no business with us—yet. Similarly the reply of Jesus seems to mean: You have no claims upon me—yet. In the same way Jesus refuses to act upon the instructions of his brothers (7.6); his decisions are his own, and depend only on the Father's will. Cf. also 11.6.

οὔπω ἥκει ἡ ὥρα μου. The hour of Jesus refers to his death on the cross and exaltation in glory (7.30; 8.20—the 'hour' not yet come; 12.23,27; 13.1; 17.1—the 'hour' in immediate prospect). It is unthinkable that in this verse ἡ ὥρα should have a different meaning, such as 'the hour for me to supply them with wine', yet it is legitimate to compare the use of similar expressions in Hellenistic miracle and magical literature, e.g. Eunapius, *Vita Iamblichi*, p. 549, οὐκ ἐπ' ἐμοί γε τοῦτο (*sc.* the performance of requested miracles,) ἔλεγε, ἀλλ' ὅταν καιρὸς ᾖ (Bultmann, 117). The essential movement of the life of Jesus is described in Hellenistic as well as Old Testament language. The hour when men may expect to see the divine glory manifested in the creative activity of the Son of God has not yet come, though they may see anticipations of it (v. 11). Cf. 7.6,39. Cf. also 1 John 2.18, and see G. Klein, *Zeitschrift für Theologie und Kirche* 68 (1971), 291–304.

5. Clearly Jesus' mother does not regard his words as a direct refusal of the favour she has implicitly asked. Miracles may precede the supreme miracle; signs may foreshadow the glorifying of Jesus. Already prompt and complete obedience to his commands is required. Cf. Gen. 41.55, ὃ ἐὰν εἴπῃ ὑμῖν, ποιήσατε.

διάκονοι is not the most natural word for household servants. It may have been used here because the servants in bearing the wine to the guests at the feast recalled the activity of 'deacons' in pagan and Christian cultus (for the pagan use of διάκονος, see L.S. *s.v.*).

6. λίθιναι ὑδρίαι, *stone* waterpots, because stone, unlike earthenware, did not itself contract uncleanness. This is explicitly stated by Maimonides, and seems to be borne out by earlier evidence (see S.B. II, 406). Stone vessels are accordingly especially suitable for water used for purificatory purposes.

ἕξ. It is possible though by no means certain that the number six is symbolic; cf. on 21.11. Six, being less by one than seven, the number of completeness and perfection, would indicate that the Jewish dispensation, typified by its ceremonial water, was partial and imperfect. Perhaps it should be noted that the event took place on the sixth day (see on 2.1); on the other hand, no numerical interpretation of the miracle can be entirely satisfactory since Jesus does not create a seventh vessel.

κατά. Either, in accordance with, or for the purpose of. The latter alternative gives perhaps the simpler and more satisfactory sense.

τὸν καθαρισμὸν τῶν Ἰουδαίων. The genitive is of course subjective, and almost equivalent to an adjective—'for the purpose of Jewish purification'. If a single 'purification' is in mind it will doubtless be that of the ritual washing performed before and after a formal meal; but it may be questioned whether John intends any particular purification; cf. 3.25. As very frequently in this gospel, the Jews stand over against Christ and the church. John deals with water (e.g. 1.26; 3.5; 4.10; 7.38), both in purification and for the satisfaction of thirst, and this incident illustrates at once the poverty of the old dispensation with its merely ceremonial cleansing and the richness of the new, in which the blood of Christ is available both for cleansing (1.29) and for drink (6.53). The initial reference is to the supersession of Judaism, but Bultmann is right to generalize: the water 'stands for everything that is a substitute for the revelation, everything by which man thinks he can live and which yet fails him when put to the test' (120). There is no need to see here, on the ground that the Qumran sect assiduously practised ritual purifications, a special anti-Qumran intention; though it is a correct observation that whereas Qumran stood for a stricter application of existing institutions John represented Christianity as a transformation of the old.

κείμεναι is omitted by ‭א‬ a e; it may be a gloss, but the periphrastic tense (ἦσαν . . . κείμεναι) is a mark of Johannine style (Introduction, p. 10).

ἀνά, distributive, as frequently in the papyri.

μετρητὰς δύο ἢ τρεῖς. In classical usage the μετρητής was a measure equivalent to the ἀμφορεύς, a liquid measure of '1½ Roman *amphorae* or nearly nine gallons' (L.S. *s.v.* ἀμφορεύς). In the LXX μετρητής renders the Hebrew בת (*bath*), an almost identical measure. Each waterpot therefore contained 18–24 gallons; say 120 gallons in all. See above, p. 189.

7. This verse makes it impossible to regard v. 4 as a refusal to take any action. Jesus has not changed his mind in the interval, though he has indicated his independence.

ἕως ἄνω. Cf. v. 10, ἕως ἄρτι; but ἕως is much more commonly used with an adverb of time than an adverb of place. Cf. however Matt. 27.51 (ἀπ' ἄνωθεν ἕως κάτω).

8. ἀντλήσατε νῦν. ἀντλεῖν is properly used of drawing water from a well (as in 4.7,15), and it has accordingly been suggested (Westcott, 37f.) that the servants were bidden to fill the purification vessels from the well first, and that the water drawn subsequently and carried direct from the well to the feast was miraculously transformed into wine. This explanation avoids the difficulty caused by the huge volume of the water pots; but it is better to suppose that the 'water become wine' (ὕδωρ οἶνον γεγενημένον) was drawn from the pots, and that John used the word ἀντλεῖν either loosely, or (Hoskyns, 197) under the influence of his thought of Christ as the well of living water.

τῷ ἀρχιτρικλίνῳ. The word may mean 'head-waiter'; but the man seems perhaps a little too familiar with the bridegroom and a little too unfamiliar with the servants and their movements for this, and we may suppose that he was one of the guests appointed as *arbiter bibendi*, toast-master, or 'president of the banquet' (L.S.). It is idle to argue that the vulgarity of v. 10

points to a waiter rather than an honoured guest; but we lack Jewish evidence for any office corresponding to the title ἀρχιτρίκλινος (see S.B. ad loc.), and the question must remain unsolved; Sanders suggests an 'old family slave', but the story may be of Hellenistic origin.

9. *Ignorantia architriclini comprobat bonitatem uini; scientia ministrorum, ueritatem miraculi* (Bengel). It is rightly divined that this verse (like many features in the synoptic miracle stories) was intended to substantiate the truth of what had taken place. On ἀντλεῖν see on v. 8. Except the proper meaning of this word, there is nothing in this verse to suggest how the miracle (τὸ ὕδωρ οἶνον γεγενημένον—the accusative after γενέσθαι is unclassical, Radermacher, 98) was effected, nor is there any indication that John was interested in its mechanism. He records no act of Christ; his creative word alone was sufficient (cf. e.g. 4.49f.). It is, however, mistaken to see a Christological allusion in πόθεν.

10. We have no evidence for the custom alluded to by the ἀρχιτρίκλινος, and, though it is readily understandable, the usual practice seems to have been the opposite (H. Windisch, *Z.N.T.W.* 14 (1913), 248–57; Bultmann 118). The ἑωλοκρασία ('mixture of dregs, heel-taps, etc., with which the drunken were dosed at the end of a revel by their stronger-headed companions', L.S.) is hardly an exact parallel. There is of course no ground here for conclusions regarding the degree of intoxication of the guests at this wedding; John finds the remark a neat way of emphasizing the superior quality of the wine provided by Jesus—the new faith based on the eschatological event is better than the old.

11. Ταύτην ἐποίησεν ἀρχὴν τῶν ... For the construction cf. Isocrates, *Panegyr.*, 38, ἀλλ' ἀρχὴν μὲν ταύτην ἐποιήσατο τῶν εὐεργεσιῶν, τροφὴν τοῖς δεομένοις εὑρεῖν. 'Jesus did this as the first of his signs.' The noun is a predicate of the pronoun (M. III, 192). In both Isocrates and John ἀρχή may mean more than the first of a series; not merely the first sign but 'a primary sign', because representative of the creative and transforming work of Jesus as a whole.

σημείων. On the word σημεῖον see Introduction, pp. 75–8. The present sign is clearly a manifestation of the glory of God (see the next note); cf. T. Levi 8.11, σημεῖον δόξης. The intention of the signs is that men should believe; whether or not one accepts the theory of a 'Signs Source' (Introduction, pp. 18f.) the present verse points forward to 20.30f.

ἐφανέρωσεν τὴν δόξαν αὐτοῦ. φανεροῦν is a Johannine word (9 times in all, including 3 in ch. 21), but it is not used elsewhere in the gospel with δόξα. On δόξα see the note on 1.14. ἐφανέρωσεν corresponds to ἐθεασάμεθα. It belongs preeminently to the existence of the Word before the Incarnation, and to his return through suffering to the Father. Manifestations of δόξα during the incarnate life are exceptional (but cf. 11.4) and are not granted to all; Jesus οὐδέπω ἐδοξάσθη (7.39). Here we may compare v. 4 (οὔπω ἥκει ἡ ὥρα μου). The hour had not come for manifesting his glory; yet, as indeed in all the signs, a partial and preliminary manifestation was granted that the disciples might believe.

ἐπίστευσαν εἰς αὐτὸν οἱ μαθηταὶ αὐτοῦ. For the various constructions of πιστεύειν in John see on 1.12. It is implied that the disciples believed because of the manifestation of the glory of Jesus in the sign; cf. 1.50. The first episode of the gospel closes with the seeing and believing of the disciples, precisely as does the last and supreme sign, by which faith becomes a far wider possibility (20.29, ὅτι ἑώρακάς με πεπίστευκας; μακάριοι οἱ μὴ ἰδόντες καὶ πιστεύσαντες; cf. 20.8). Faith is indeed the purpose of the signs (20.31).

12. μετὰ τοῦτο (2.12; 11.7,11; 19.28)· and μετὰ ταῦτα (3.22; 5.1,14; 6.1; 7.1; 19.38; 21.1) are frequent, and synonymous, indications of the transition from one narrative to another. It is impossible to tell (unless further evidence is given) whether a long or short interval is intended. Cf. 4.43; 20.26.

κατέβη εἰς Καφαρναούμ. Capernaum (the modern Tell-Ḥum—see Dalman, *Sacred Sites and Ways* (E.T., 1935), 133–59, and S.B. 1, 159f.) is by the sea of Galilee, and to go there from Cana naturally meant a descent; cf. 4.47, 49. Jesus remains for a little while in the company of his mother and brothers, but from this point will do so no longer. His mother will not appear again until she stands with the beloved disciple at the foot of the cross; the brothers are mentioned only in 7.1–10, where it is said that they did not believe in Jesus. Jesus continues a few days longer in the obscurity that was only partially and privately disturbed by the 'sign'. He will open his ministry with due *éclat* at Passover, and at Jerusalem. Capernaum is no doubt chosen as the scene of his short delay in deference to the synoptic tradition. Dodd, *Tradition*, 235f., compares Matt. 4.13; Luke 4.31; John, he thinks, is not directly dependent on these passages, but they bear witness to a common tradition that at some stage in his ministry Jesus fixed his residence in Capernaum.

καὶ οἱ μαθηταὶ αὐτοῦ is omitted by ℵ it; and for ἔμειναν, ἔμεινεν is read by a few Greek MSS. (including P⁶⁶ᶜ) and b boh. These two variants probably arose with the intention of emphasizing that the mother and brothers of Jesus remained permanently in Capernaum while he, when the hour struck, left to begin his public ministry. The omission may well give the original text; in any case the interpretation appears to be correct.

5. THE CLEANSING OF THE TEMPLE

2.13–25

At Passover time Jesus made the customary pilgrimage to Jerusalem (Exod. 12.14–20,43–9; Lev. 23.4–8; Deut. 16.1–8; Josephus, *Bel.* II, 10 (among many passages)). The usual commercial activity was taking place in the Temple, but he forcibly interrupted it, clearing the courts of traders and bankers, in actions which (subsequently) recalled Old Testament scripture. The Jews not unnaturally asked for proof of the outstanding authority which alone could justify what Jesus had done; his answer was a dark saying which the Jews misunderstood and the disciples understood only after the resurrection, to which event, in covert fashion, it referred. By this reply Jesus in effect refused a sign; yet v. 23 implies that signs had taken place in Jerusalem, and that they had led to a superficial faith on the part of many beholders. Jesus, however, being omniscient, rated this faith no higher than its true worth.

A narrative of a Temple cleansing occurs in the synoptic tradition (Mark 11.15–18; Matt. 21.12–17; Luke 19.45f.). This also is dated at the Passover season, but the Passover is the last of Jesus' life (the only Passover Mark records), not the first of several in his ministry (as in John). In spite of this difference, considerable agreement in wording makes it probable that John knew Mark; see the notes on vv. 14–16. Further the challenge of v. 18, τί σημεῖον δεικνύεις ἡμῖν, ὅτι ταῦτα ποιεῖς; may be compared with both Mark 11.28, ἐν ποίᾳ ἐξουσίᾳ ταῦτα ποιεῖς; ἢ τίς σοι ἔδωκεν τὴν ἐξουσίαν ταύτην ἵνα ταῦτα ποιῇς; and Mark 8.11, ζητοῦντες παρ' αὐτοῦ σημεῖον. It seems very probable that John used Marcan material; it is therefore the more striking that he placed the incident in an entirely different setting. It is improbable that there were two cleansings, one at the beginning and one at the end of the ministry; this is both unlikely in itself and also quite without evidence if the literary connection between John and Mark is accepted. We may suppose either that John was in possession of an independent chronological tradition which he rated more highly than that of Mark, or that his placing of the incident was dictated by reasons theological rather than chronological. The latter supposition is more probable. An act of overt rebellion against the authorities of the nation is more readily understandable at the climax than at the beginning of the ministry (see on 11.53), and the disposition of John's material is often controlled by the development of thought (see Introduction, pp. 11–15). Cullmann (V. & A., 288) thinks that John placed the Cleansing at the beginning of the story because for him worship was a particularly important theme, Lindars that he removed it from ch. 12 to make room for the Lazarus story, Eisler that he did so to obscure the connection between the act of violence in the Temple and the crucifixion.

The Cleansing certainly occupies a position of great importance. After the section devoted to the calling of the disciples, in which the glory of Christ is foreshadowed (2.11), John begins to develop his main theme, that in Jesus the eternal purposes of God find their fulfilment. Since the historic ministry of Jesus was set in the context of Judaism it was necessary first to set forth Christ as the fulfilment of the religion of the Jews. He reveals himself authoritatively in the Temple, but his authority appears even more clearly in the words attributed to him than in his acts. His own body, first destroyed and then raised from the dead is to be the true Temple, the house of prayer for all the nations. John does not in the present section work out the implications of this claim, but they constantly recur in the gospel. Jesus is the place where God and human nature are joined in one (e.g. 1.14,51; 17.21); the church is the new People of God which includes Gentiles as well as Jews (10.16; 11.52).

John's interpretation of the Cleansing involves some modification of the original story. It would be rash to suggest that Mark presents us with the primitive form of it (see 'The House of Prayer and the Den of Thieves', in *Jesus und Paulus, Festschrift für W. G. Kümmel*, ed. E.E. Ellis and E. Grässer (1975), 13–20). He has made a prediction of the destruction of the Temple out of what at an earlier stage in the tradition was the complaint that what had been intended as a place of international prayer had been turned into a nationalist stronghold. The λησταί against whom Mark 11.17 is directed have disappeared in John with the historical setting, and nothing is left to complain of but relatively innocent trading. John retains however and makes more explicit the Marcan prediction that the Temple will be destroyed. Cf. Mark 13.2; 14.58; 15.29; also Acts 6.14. Moreover, a Q saying (Matt. 12.39; Luke 11.29) suggests that the only sign to be given to 'this generation' is the resurrection; an opinion with which John 2.18f. agrees precisely. This Johannine narrative, at first sight artless and simple, is in fact a very striking example of the way in which John collects scattered synoptic material and synoptic themes, welds them into a whole, and uses them to bring out unmistakably the true meaning of the synoptic presentation of Jesus, who acts with an authority he will not, and cannot, explain, and focuses this paradoxical authority upon his death and resurrection.

The position of the present section in relation to the gospel as a whole should be noted. 2.13—4.54 forms a whole, in which we see Jesus first as the fulfilment of all that the Temple represented; next as the fulfilment of apocalyptic and Pharisaic Judaism (3.1–21), and of what the Baptist foretold (3.22–36); then in relation to heretical Judaism (4.1–42) and to the Gentile world (4.43–54). See the introductions to these sections. Miss Guilding (205f.) goes further and sees chs. 1—4 as portraying not so much the opening year or so of Jesus' ministry as the history of the church 'from the incarnation and the call of the earliest disciples to the spread of the Gospel to the Gentiles through the missionary labours of the Church. In other words, chapters 1—2 cover Jesus' ministry from his birth to the cleansing of the Temple at the *last* Passover, while in chapters 3—4 the Evangelist is speaking from the standpoint of the post-resurrection Church, through whose agency Jesus continues the evangelization of Jerusalem, Judaea, Samaria, and the uttermost ends of the earth'. This explains the displacement (which is not really a displacement) of the Cleansing. She also connects this passage with lections read in Adar, Exod. 7 and 1 Sam. 2.25ff. (185ff.).

Lightfoot sees here a triple depth of meaning. 'First, the Lord performs an act by which He condemns the methods and the manner of the existing Jewish worship. Secondly, this act . . . is a sign of the destruction of the old order of worship . . . and its replacement by a new order of worship. . . . And thirdly, intermediate between the old order and the new order is the "work"—the ministry, death, and resurrection—of the Lord, which alone makes possible the inauguration and the life of the new temple' (114).

13. καὶ ἐγγὺς ἦν . . . καὶ ἀνέβη. The sentence recalls a well-known Hebrew construction (cf. M. II, 422): When the feast was near Jesus went up. John several times announces the arrival of a feast with the word ἐγγύς; see 2.13; 6.4; 7.2; 11.55. ἀνέβη indicates the ascent to the hill country of Judaea; but ἀναβαίνειν had become almost a technical term for pilgrimage to the capital.

τὸ πάσχα τῶν 'Ιουδαίων. The connection with the feast is traditional. For the ritual and significance of the Passover see on 1.29; 12.1; 13.1. John mentions three distinct Passovers (2.13; 6.4; 11.55; four if we add 5.1, on which see the note). Twice he calls the feast τὸ πάσχα τῶν 'Ιουδαίων, once τὸ πάσχα ἡ ἑορτὴ τῶν 'Ιουδαίων. The feast is so defined partly because it is John's habit to set 'the Jews' as a body over against Jesus and the church (see on 1.19), partly also, perhaps, because he knows of a Christian Passover. Cf. however 7.2.

14. On trade in the Temple see Abrahams, Studies 1, 82–9. It is true that the opportunities for buying and selling were not always abused; yet we have little first-hand information with regard to the practices that obtained before A.D. 70, and this narrative (or rather, the synoptic narrative on which it is based) may suggest that the proceedings were not entirely unobjectionable.

τοὺς πωλοῦντας βόας καὶ πρόβατα καὶ περιστεράς—for the purpose of sacrifice. It was convenient for worshippers coming from a distance to be able to rely upon finding suitable animals in the Temple market. For a detailed account of the complicated system of purchase see Shekalim 5.3–5. Cf. Mark 11.15, τῶν πωλούντων τὰς περιστεράς.

τοὺς κερματιστάς. Temple dues had to be paid in the Tyrian coinage; supplies were obtainable in the Temple and it seems that usually only a moderate charge (2–4 per cent) was made for the service. κερματιστής seems to be restricted to this and dependent passages; κερματίζεσθαι belongs to late Greek, and means to change money, generally from larger into smaller coins. Here of course one coinage is changed into another. Cf. Mark 11.15, τῶν κολλυβιστῶν.

15. φραγέλλιον, from the Latin flagellum, a whip or scourge, 'more severe than scutica' (Lewis and Short). But flagellum was also used to describe a whip for driving cattle, and this may be the sense here. The word was also transliterated into Hebrew (פרגול, פרגיל), with the meaning 'whip' or 'scourge'. To φραγέλλιον the word ὡς is prefixed by P⁶⁶ P⁷⁵ W 33 565 it vg hl^{mg}, perhaps correctly. On the dissimilation between Latin and Greek (l–ρ) see M. II, 103.

σχοινίων, cords. The diminutive form is not to be pressed. Neither φραγέλλιον nor σχοινίων occurs in the synoptic narratives. Berakoth 9.5 forbids the carrying of a staff (מקל, maqqel) in the Temple, and some find in this the reason why Jesus made an improvised whip (but σχοινίον need not suggest a cord roughly twisted out of rushes); the prohibition however can hardly have applied to those in charge of the animals.

πάντας ἐξέβαλεν . . . τά τε πρόβατα καὶ τοὺς βόας. πάντας (masculine) indicates that Jesus drove out all the men engaged in trade; if τά τε . . . βόας (regarded by many as an editorial addition) had been intended as a merely epexegetical phrase we should have had πάντα not πάντας. ἐκβάλλειν had weakened in Hellenistic usage, but here derives force from φραγέλλιον: 'he drove them all out, the sheep and the oxen as well'. With ἐξέβαλεν cf. Mark 11.15, ἤρξατο ἐκβάλλειν. John may have in mind the thought that animals are no longer needed for sacrifice in the presence of Jesus as the Lamb of God (1.29) (Fenton).

κολλυβιστῶν. Cf. Mark 11.15 (same word). Like κερματιστής it is a late word, and it is condemned by Phrynichus (CCCCIV; Rutherford, 499), who rightly prefers ἀργυραμοιβός. The meaning of the word is none the less clear.

ἀνέτρεψεν, P⁶⁶ B W Θ; κατέστρεψεν, ℵ; ἀνέστρεψεν, P⁷⁵ Ѡ. κατέστρεψεν is clearly due to assimilation to Mark 11.15, and ἀνέστρεψεν is probably to be ascribed to a similar cause; ἀνέτρεψεν, in itself quite appropriate and capable of explaining the other variants, is left in possession of the field.

16. τοῖς τὰς περιστερὰς πωλοῦσιν. Cf. Mark 11.15, τῶν πωλούντων τὰς περιστεράς. μὴ ποιεῖτε, cease to make. On the force of the present imperative see M. 1, 124f.

τὸν οἶκον τοῦ πατρός μου. The use of οἶκος may have been suggested by Mark 11.17, though it could be used independently. For 'the house of my Father' cf. Luke 2.49, ἐν τοῖς τοῦ πατρός μου, which should be translated 'in my Father's house'; see Creed, ad loc. Jesus' reference to God as his Father does not provoke the same reaction as in 5.17f. (Sanders). John takes one thing at a time. Here (v. 18) the Jews look for the authority behind Jesus' actions; his person will be discussed at a later stage.

οἶκον ἐμπορίου. ἐμπόριον itself means a place of trade and it was unnecessary to use οἶκος as well; the genitive may be described as in epexegetical apposition. 'House of trade' matches 'house of my Father'. There may well be a reference here to Zech. 14.21 (Dodd, Interpretation, 300). In the Synoptic Gospels Jesus, with a reference to Jer. 7.11, accuses the traders of making the house of prayer into a den of thieves. There is no such accusation in John; the trading itself, though perhaps honestly conducted, was wrong, and deprived the Temple of its right to be regarded as a house of prayer. John, however, 'remembering' (see next note) the event at a later date will have seen it in the light of v. 19; the Father's house is disclosed only in Jesus (14.2), and he fulfils the Temple so radically that it cannot itself continue to exist (cf. 4.21).

ἐμνήσθησαν οἱ μαθηταὶ αὐτοῦ. They remembered the Psalm (69 (68).10) at the time, and presumably perceived its messianic significance; contrast v. 22 where, after the resurrection, the disciples recall the whole incident with fuller apprehension and faith. Cf. 12.16. The Psalm is one that is used elsewhere of the Passion. 'Just as the Righteous Sufferer of the Psalm paid the price of his loyalty to the temple, so the action of Jesus in cleansing the temple will bring him to grief' (Dodd, Interpretation, 301). But John is not thinking in terms of analogy; the Psalmist actually speaks of Jesus.

ὁ ζῆλος τοῦ οἴκου σου καταφάγεταί με. The Psalmist traces his affliction to his zeal for the Temple; John reads his words as a prophecy of the messianic action of Jesus. καταφάγεται is read by P⁶⁶ P⁷⁵ ℵ B Θ Ѡ sah Origen; κατέφαγεν by φ it vg sin pesh boh Eusebius. A like variation occurs in the LXX texts of the Psalm. The Hebrew verb is in the perfect tense (אכלתני). It seems most probable that the original reading in John was καταφάγεται; the aorist in the predominantly Western texts may have been due in the first place to the retroversion into Syriac, where naturally the Semitic perfect was resumed. The texts of the LXX (made by Christians) must have experienced two opposite influences: that of the gospel text, where the future tense was useful in facilitating a prophetic interpretation of the Psalm, and that of the underlying Hebrew. The former would be much stronger. Most commentators see in καταφάγεται an allusion to the death of Jesus; his zeal for God will be (humanly speaking) his downfall. There seems however to be no good reason why the Psalmist and John should not both have spoken of consuming zeal.

18. ἀπεκρίθησαν reflects the common Hebrew ויען (Aramaic ענה), which may introduce a speech that is in no sense a response to another. It is not however necessarily due to translation from Hebrew or Aramaic. οἱ 'Ιουδαῖοι are not the traders but the representatives of the Jewish people; see on 1.19.

τί σημεῖον δεικνύεις ἡμῖν, ὅτι ταῦτα ποιεῖς; Cf. the question which almost immediately follows the Marcan cleansing narrative, ἐν ποίᾳ ἐξουσίᾳ ταῦτα ποιεῖς; (Mark 11.28). These words were probably in John's mind, and he has combined them with the request of Mark 8.11, ζητοῦντες παρ' αὐτοῦ σημεῖον ἀπὸ τοῦ οὐρανοῦ. Cf. also the Q version of this request, Matt. 12.38f. = Luke 11.29, where the reply, as in v. 19 here, is that the sign for this generation will be the resurrection. On σημεῖον see Introduction, pp. 75–8. Here, and at 6.30, it is used in a familiar synoptic way; adversaries of Jesus wrongfully seek a sign as proof of his claims and their request is rejected. There is a similar use in 4.48; 6.26. It may be inferred that this somewhat derogatory use of the word σημεῖον is proper to the original tradition, which still shows itself in John, while the characteristic Johannine use is the work of the evangelist himself.

19. No immediate sign of authority is granted. Instead an enigmatic saying is uttered, and no explanation is given. Even the disciples failed to understand what Jesus had said until after his resurrection (v. 22).

λύσατε. The construction is that in which an imperative is used to express a condition: If you destroy . . . I will build. Or the imperative may be ironic, as sometimes in the prophets, e.g. Amos 4.4, Come to Bethel, and transgress; Isa. 8.9f.; Jer. 7.21; Matt. 23.23. λύειν is quite regularly used for the destruction of a building; cf. e.g. Iliad XVI, 100, . . . ἱερά . . . λύωμεν; in the New Testament, Eph. 2.14, τὸ μεσότοιχον τοῦ φραγμοῦ λύσας. It is clearly intended by John that the primary (though not the only) reference of this verse should be to the destruction of the Temple buildings. Cf. the use of καταλύειν in Mark 13.2; 14.58; 15.29 and parallels.

ναός (which occurs only in this context in John) does not in general seem to be distinguished from ἱερόν in the New Testament. If a distinction is to be made, ναός must refer to the central shrine or sanctuary, not the whole Temple precincts (cf. Matt 23.35, and see L.S. s.v.).

ἐν τρισὶν ἡμέραις ἐγερῶ αὐτόν. ἐγείρειν, like λύειν, may properly be used of a building (e.g. Josephus Ant. VIII, 96, στοὰς ἐγείρας μεγάλας—of Solomon's Temple). ἐν τρισὶν ἡμέραις is used only in Mark 15.29 and parallels. In speaking of the resurrection Mark commonly has μετὰ τρεῖς ἡμέρας, Matthew and Luke τῇ τρίτῃ ἡμέρᾳ. John's expression must mean 'within the space of three days', but the form is not classical, and probably shows contact with the taunt in Mark. The Marcan accusation may well be more substantial than Mark himself suggests, but it is doubtful whether John adds to it any strictly independent confirmation. His form is weaker than Mark's 'I will . . .' (Haenchen, *Weg*, 509). There is a similar saying in *Thomas* 71: I shall destroy this house and no one will be able to build it again; but John is nearer to the synoptics than to *Thomas* (G. Quispel, *J. & Q.* 145). 'Jesus' reply means . . that whoever asks for a σημεῖον will receive a σημεῖον—but not until it is too late' (Bultmann).

20. As we have seen, the saying of Jesus in v. 19 is (apart from the space of time mentioned) entirely applicable to a building. The Jews take the superficial meaning of the words and naturally remark their absurdity: so great a building could not be erected in so short a time. The interpretation may be secondary (Bultmann), but it is John's. Such misunderstandings are very characteristic of John (see on 3.3) and are often, as here, more than a literary trick employed by a writer given to irony. They represent in miniature the total reaction of Judaism to Christ; the Jews perceived only what was superficially visible in Jesus and naturally rejected as absurd the suggestion that he should be the Son of God; if they had penetrated beneath the surface they would have seen its truth.

τεσσεράκοντα καὶ ἓξ ἔτεσιν οἰκοδομήθη ὁ ναὸς οὗτος. 'This sanctuary was built in forty-six years.' It seems impossible to translate otherwise. For the construction cf. Ezra 5.6. The dative (ἔτεσιν) is partly locative, the whole period regarded as a unit of time, and partly instrumental, time 'by the lapse of which anything is brought about' (Robertson, 527, cf. 523). The aorist (οἰκοδομήθη— unaugmented (M. II, 191); corrected to ᾠκ. in the majority of MSS.) is constative (Robertson, 833); the whole process is summed up and viewed as a single act. The grammar of this clause then is plain; but the history is difficult. The building of Herod's Temple was begun in 20/19 B.C. (see Josephus, *Ant.* xv, 380, in the eighteenth year of Herod; *Bel.* 1, 401 gives the fifteenth year of Herod, either in error, or with reference to the first planning of the Temple). Forty-six years from this date brings us to A.D. 27/28 (see Schürer 1, i, 410; Goguel, *Introduction* IV, i, 84ff.; G. Ogg, *Chronology of the Public Ministry of Jesus* (1940), 151–67), which would fall within some, but not all, estimates of the duration of the ministry. But we know that the Temple was not completed until *c.* A.D. 63 (Josephus, *Ant.* xx, 219). From these facts one of the following inferences must be drawn:

(*a*) Grammar must be strained and the sentence translated, 'Building, which is still in progress, has been going on forty-six years'.

(*b*) Building had temporarily come to a halt; possibly something which might be called ναός (over against ἱερόν) had been completed, though Josephus' account of the building operations does not suggest this.

(*c*) John mistakenly supposed that the Temple had been completed, either calculating or conjecturing the period since it had been begun.

Of these possible inferences, (*c*) seems to be the most probable.

21. ἐκεῖνος (Jesus; as at 5.11; 7.11; 9.12,28,37; 19.21; and see the note on 19.35) δὲ ἔλεγεν περὶ τοῦ ναοῦ τοῦ σώματος αὐτοῦ. John of course knows the true meaning of Jesus' words; this kind of explanatory remark is characteristic of him; cf. 2.24b,25; 6.6,64,71; 7.5,39; 9.7; 11.13, 51f.; 12.6, 33; 20.9

(Schnackenburg, who also refers to 1QS 5.5f.; 8.7–10; 1QH 6.25–8; cf. 7.7–9; 4QpPs37 2.16 for the use of building or temple as metaphors for a community). Elsewhere in John σῶμα is used only of the dead body of Jesus (19.31,38(bis),40; 20.12—there is doubt about the text of 19.38 which does not however affect the point). For the thought of a human body as a shrine cf. 1 Cor. 6.19; 3.16ff. Philo speaks of the first made man (Gen. 2.7) as οἶκός τις ἢ νεὼς ἱερός ... ψυχῆς λογικῆς, ἣν ἔμελλεν ἀγαλματοφορήσειν ἀγαλμάτων τὸ θεοειδέστατον (Op. 137). Elsewhere in Philo the soul itself is the house of God (e.g. Som. 1, 149, σπούδαζε οὖν, ὦ ψυχή, θεοῦ οἶκος γενέσθαι ἱερὸν ἅγιον), and the body is the prison of the soul (e.g. Ebr. 101, ὃς [sc. νοῦς] ἐν μὲν τῇ πόλει τοῦ σώματος ... περιεχόμενος ἔσταλται ... ὥσπερ ἐν δεσμωτηρίῳ καθειργμένος). For the Stoics also the body was the dwelling-place, though scarcely an honourable one, of a divine element (e.g. Epictetus II, viii, 11f., ... ἔχεις τι ἐν σεαυτῷ μέρος ἐκείνου [sc. τοῦ θεοῦ] ... θεὸν τρέφεις, θεὸν γυμνάζεις, θεὸν περιφέρεις ...). John's thought however is quite different, since it rests not upon general observations or speculations about the relation of the human soul to God but upon the unique mutual indwelling of the Father and the Son (14.10 and often); the human body of Jesus was the place where a unique manifestation of God took place and consequently became the only true Temple, the only centre of true worship; cf. 4.20–4. John thus shares with the Qumran sect an opposition to the Jerusalem Temple, but Braun rightly points out that whereas the sect was concerned with ritual purity John's concern was with spiritual worship. In the saying of v. 19 the two verbs, λύσατε and ἐγερῶ, have the same object, τὸν ναὸν τοῦτον and αὐτόν. It cannot therefore be maintained that the body that is raised up is the church, understood in terms of the familiar Pauline image (Rom. 12.5; 1 Cor. 12.12–27 et al.). It is however not unreasonable to suppose that John was aware of this image, and there may be a secondary reference to it. It was his own body, killed on the cross, that Christ raised up, but in doing so he brought the church into being.

22. ἐμνήσθησαν οἱ μαθηταὶ αὐτοῦ. During the ministry the disciples, in spite of their call and their belief in Jesus, evoked by his signs (2.11), understood his words little more than his adversaries. It was only his resurrection, and the gift, contingent upon it, of the Paraclete, which called his sayings to mind and enabled them to be understood (14.26; 16.14). The several incidents of the ministry could be understood only in the light of the completed whole; and of the inspired corporate recollection of the church John is itself the most striking monument.

ἐπίστευσαν τῇ γραφῇ. In John, when πιστεύειν refers to a thing, the dative is generally used—4.50; 5.47; 10.38; 12.38 (Isa. 53.1): 12.36 (εἰς τὸ φῶς) is only an apparent exception since τὸ φῶς = Christ. See further on 1.12. ἡ γραφή (singular) generally refers to a particular passage of Scripture, but none is quoted here (the quotation of v. 17 can be intended only if καταφάγεται refers to the destruction of Christ's body in death, which is a very strained interpretation). A close parallel to this use of ἡ γραφή is that in 20.9, where also the resurrection is in question. Perhaps John means that the Old Testament in a general way predicts the vindication of the Messiah.

23. ἐν τῷ πάσχα. Cf. v. 13. Jesus as a good Jew, remains in the city for Passover. There is no contradiction with 4.54, which refers to a sign done on Jesus' return to Galilee.

ἐν τῇ ἑορτῇ. These words are usually taken as parallel to ἐν τῷ πάσχα. This would however be a most awkward way of defining the feast, and the meaning is probably 'in the festival crowd' (see L.S. *s.v.*, 4; also Jeremias, *Eucharistic Words*, 71ff.). The same use occurs at 7.11 (and perhaps at Mark 14.2).

ἐπίστευσαν εἰς τὸ ὄνομα αὐτοῦ. For this construction cf. 1.12 (and note), and contrast v. 22.

θεωροῦντες αὐτοῦ τὰ σημεῖα. Cf. v. 18. No signs in Jerusalem have been described. For miracles performed at the time of the cleansing of the Temple see Matt. 21. 14f. (no parallel in Mark or Luke).

24. αὐτός is probably not due to the influence of the redundant Aramaic pronoun הוא; it emphasizes the contrast between the two uses of πιστεύειν.

οὐκ ἐπίστευεν αὐτόν, did not entrust himself. πιστεύειν is comparatively rare in this sense in the New Testament (Luke 16.11; Rom. 3.2; 1. Cor. 9.17; Gal. 2.7; 1 Thess. 2.4; 1 Tim. 1.11; Titus 1.3), the specifically Christian sense having excluded it.

διὰ τὸ αὐτὸν γινώσκειν πάντας. Cf. 1 Sam. 16.7; Jesus has divine knowledge and is not misled by appearances, even by the appearance of faith. For his knowledge cf. 1.47-50 (πόθεν με γινώσκεις; 1.48).

25. καὶ ὅτι with a finite verb continues διὰ and the articular infinitive. It is an unusual but readily understood construction *ad sensum*, and there is no need for conjecture (e.g. καθότι for καὶ ὅτι).

ἵνα τις μαρτυρήσῃ. The gospel is full of witness concerning Jesus (see on 1.7); witness to Jesus concerning man is unnecessary since he already possesses the knowledge man lacks. Qumran parallels are given by Schnackenburg, but they are as needless as he says the Hellenistic parallels are—the Old Testament often refers to God's knowledge of man.

αὐτὸς γὰρ ἐγίνωσκεν resumes v. 24b in John's manner; cf. 1.2. In Jewish literature knowledge of what is in man belongs to God (*Mekhilta* Exod. 16.32 (ויסע §6): There is no man who knows what is in his neighbour's heart, מה בלבו של חבירו). This knowledge is however possessed by the supernatural being Metatron (3 Enoch 11). See Odeberg, 43-7.

6. NICODEMUS

3.1-21

Narrative is in this section reduced to a minimum. Nicodemus appears before Jesus but never even states the purpose of his coming. As the discourse proceeds he is quickly forgotten, and, further, the conversation speedily moves out of the singular number into the plural: 'We speak', 'You (pl.) must be born again.' We are made to hear not a conversation between two persons but the dialogue of church and synagogue, in which (according to the Christian view) the former completes and fulfils the latter, which is in consequence superseded. The discourse thus falls into its place (a very important place) in the movement of thought in the gospel.

Judaism cannot simply move forward over a level plain to achieve its goal in the kingdom of God. This goal cannot be reached either by learned discussions between its distinguished teachers (such as Jesus and Nicodemus), or by waiting for an apocalyptic *dénouement* in which the kingdom should suddenly appear. This is emphasized not merely because human nature needs divine renewal before it can experience the kingdom of God, but primarily because, the kingdom of God being in part realized already, such a renewal becomes an immediate possibility which must not be neglected. The contrast between Jesus and John the Baptist (which is hinted at in 3.5 and developed in 3.22–36) brings out the point very clearly. John prepared men for the coming kingdom by means of a baptism with water; but Jesus was able to baptize with Holy Spirit (1.33) because in him the kingdom was already operative. 'Born of water' (for a fuller discussion of this expression see below), may suggest John's baptism and his disciples; Jesus' disciples were born of the Spirit and were thus a stage nearer to seeing and entering the kingdom of God—indeed they had in part experienced it in the gift of the Spirit. John's language confessedly belongs to his own age, not to that of the ministry of Jesus, when the Spirit was not (7.39); it was after the resurrection and glorification of Jesus that the gift of the Spirit and birth from above became generally available.

Nicodemus is uncomprehending and incredulous in spite of his professional knowledge of the Old Testament which should have prepared him for its fulfilment. It is consequently impossible to proceed to disclose heavenly secrets to him (v. 12). These he could receive only through Jesus, who, as the Son of man, links heaven and earth (for the Johannine use of the title 'Son of man' see on 1.51). Jesus, who has descended from heaven, must ascend to heaven, but his ascent will be by way of the cross. This revelation leads to a further statement, couched in more general terms and divorced from the particular situation to which Nicodemus belongs, of the purpose and method of the incarnation. Its motive is God's love, and its purpose, the gift of eternal life; only incidentally does it result in judgement, for it resembles the shining of light into the world. There are some who come to the light, that is, they believe in Jesus. There are some who do not; that is, they reject him. It is to be noted that the two groups seem thus to be determined before the coming of Jesus and to disclose their identity by their reaction to him. Not to believe in Jesus is equivalent to incurring condemnation, since in him only is salvation; cf. Mark 3.29f.; 4.11f.

The sources of the thought of this discourse are examined in detail in the notes. It is particularly instructive to note their variety, and the subtlety with which John has combined them. Jesus is portrayed as the fulfilment of Judaism, but in the portrayal concepts drawn from the Hellenistic world are employed, and through the whole there runs a thread drawn from the synoptic tradition (see the notes), and especially the eschatology of the earlier gospels. The whole is worked up into a revelatory discourse of a kind not uncommon in the environment of the gospel; cf. in particular *C.H.* XIII, περὶ παλιγγενεσίας, *On Rebirth.* It seems however that this discourse (like other compounds of dialogue and discourse in the gospel) should be viewed as the result of theological and literary processes working upon primitive Christian material rather than as the taking over and Christianizing of an existing gnostic work (see Introduction, pp. 38f, 65f., 112ff.). The gospel thus has its place in the development of the gnostic movement, and shows how Christians might participate in that movement. Some contacts with the earlier gospel tradition will be observed in the detailed notes that follow; it can hardly be doubted that John also shows awareness of the Christian institution of baptism. Whether the historical process behind the discourse can be made more precise than this is questionable. Martyn (75) sees in Nicodemus a figure typical of those of the local Jewish Gerousia who secretly believed; he compares the account in Acts 5 of Gamaliel (155ff.). This leads Martyn to a very suggestive analysis of the paragraph (110f., 122–7), but though he may have divined correctly the starting-point of the literary and theological process the end (as his own analysis may suggest) goes far beyond this. No book is less of a local party manifesto than John, and no part of John less so than this discourse.

Schnackenburg divides the discourse, and reads the chapter in the order 1–12, 31–6, 13–21, 22–30.

1. ἐκ τῶν Φαρισαίων. Cf. 1.24; it seems doubtful whether John was able to distinguish clearly between the Jewish parties. In this verse he goes on to describe Nicodemus as an ἄρχων τῶν Ἰουδαίων (that is, probably, a member of the Sanhedrin); but in 7.48; 12.42 the Pharisees are distinguished from the ἄρχοντες. Nicodemus is also (v. 10) a διδάσκαλος; John seems to be collecting titles in order to portray Nicodemus as a representative Jew, but it must be acknowledged that it is not impossible that one man should have been at the same time a Pharisee, a teacher, and a member of the Sanhedrin. That John instead of using τις introduces Nicodemus by the word ἄνθρωπος may reflect Old Testament usage (e.g. Judg. 13.2; 17.1) or look back to 2.25—Jesus knew what was in Nicodemus.

Νικόδημος. A quite common Greek name, adopted and transliterated by the Jews (נקדימון, Naqdimon). A certain wealthy and generous Naqdimon is known to have been in Jerusalem at the time of the siege (A.D. 70); it is possible, though by no means certain, that he may have been in Jerusalem as a young man (though hardly as an ἄρχων) forty years earlier. See C. G. Montefiore and H. Loewe, *A Rabbinic Anthology* (1938), 372f., 420, 687 (with references to *Gittin* 56a, *Ketuboth* 66b, *Taanith* 19b–20a). Nicodemus has sometimes been thought to be identical with the Buni mentioned in *Sanhedrin* 43a as a disciple of Jesus; but see Klausner, 30.

2. νυκτός. Rabbis are reported to have studied and conversed till late at night (S.B. II, 419f.; also 1 QS 6.7). Elsewhere, however (9.4; 11.10; 13.30), νύξ is used with more than its literal signification, and, though John may have meant simply that Nicodemus visited Jesus by night for reasons of secrecy

(cf. 19.38f.), it is perhaps more probable that he intended to indicate the darkness out of which Nicodemus came into the presence of the true Light (cf. vv. 19–21).

ῥαββί. See on 1.38, and cf. P. *Eg.* 2.45ff., διδάσκαλε ιη οἴδαμεν ὅτι [ἀπὸ θυ̅] ἐλήλυθας· ἃ γὰρ ποιεῖς μα[ρτυρεῖ] ὑπὲρ το[ὑ]ς προφας̅ πάντας. See Introduction, p. 110.

οἴδαμεν. See on 20.2. It seems, however, that Nicodemus speaks on behalf of others as well as himself. The 'we' may be the Pharisees, or the ἄρχοντες, or both; but it is (in view of the following words) more probable that it refers to the πολλοί of 2.23 who believed because they beheld the signs done by Jesus.

ἀπὸ θεοῦ ἐλήλυθας διδάσκαλος. διδάσκαλος takes up the title Rabbi. Nicodemus is willing to acknowledge Jesus as a teacher, equal with himself (v. 10). Contrast 7.15, where Jesus is dismissed as an unlearned person. The words ἀπὸ θεοῦ are in a position of emphasis, and probably imply that Jesus is more than a teacher, perhaps a prophet.

ταῦτα τὰ σημεῖα. Nicodemus' acceptance of Jesus as a teacher is based on the signs; cf. 2.23. The only sign narrated up to this point is that at Cana, but there is no need to conjecture displacement in the gospel; John assumes that his readers are familiar with the synoptic tradition and the many miracles described there.

ἐὰν μὴ ᾖ ὁ θεὸς μετ' αὐτοῦ. These words, though true, are to John an inadequate expression of faith. They treat Jesus as having essentially the same significance as e.g. Moses (Exod. 3.12, ἔσομαι μετὰ σοῦ) or Jeremiah (Jer. 1.19, μετὰ σοῦ ἐγώ εἰμι τοῦ ἐξαιρεῖσθαί σε). God is indeed no less with Jesus than with the Old Testament prophets, but to class him with them does not express the fact that Jesus is the Son of God, that the Son is one with the Father and that he that has seen the Son has seen the Father. Before Nicodemus can understand the person of Jesus, and the kingdom of God, further steps must be taken, and in the ensuing paragraph Nicodemus' presuppositions on both these subjects are radically probed and shaken.

3. γεννηθῇ. The verb γεννᾶν occurs here and at vv. 4a, 4b, 5, 7, 8 in all Greek MSS. In each of these places some old Latin MSS. (including a in every one, e in all but v. 8) have the verb *renascor* (ἀναγεννᾶσθαι). In vv. 3, 4a, 7 the Sahidic VS. uses a similar expression. In v. 5 the old Latin is joined by the Vulgate, and at both vv. 3 and 4b, the Sinaitic Syriac has a phrase meaning 'to be born again' (... *men d^erish*). Examination of the variants indicates that they have arisen out of attempts to render ἄνωθεν (see below); thus the Latin MSS. show *nascor*, *nascor denuo*, *renascor*, *renascor denuo* (and other variants). In v. 5 *renascor* (ἀναγεννᾶσθαι) is found rather more widely—Justin, Irenaeus, Eusebius, the Clementine Homilies, Chrysostom, Tertullian, Cyprian, Augustine are quoted. Here again the cause is evident, and is already so with Justin (see 1 *Apol.* 61—it cannot be regarded as quite certain that Justin used the Fourth Gospel; see Introduction, p. 111). Justin, and the other Fathers, no doubt rightly, connect this passage with baptism, and in such a setting 'regeneration', both in Latin and Greek, was a technical term.

ἐὰν μή τις γεννηθῇ ἄνωθεν. ἄνωθεν is capable of two meanings and here it probably has both. It may mean 'from above', but also 'afresh', 'again'.

The birth which is here required is certainly a second birth, but it is not (see v. 4) a mere repetition of man's first birth, but a begetting from above, from God. This, in view of 3.31, must be regarded as the primary meaning, though Nicodemus' understanding of it (4) is neither unnatural nor altogether wrong: it does denote a second birth (though of a different kind from the first). Sidebottom (206) rightly draws attention to Wisd. 9.17 (ἀπὸ ὑψίστων); Conzelmann, *Theology*, 354, compares the use of ἐκ in such phrases as ἐκ τοῦ θεοῦ, ἐκ τοῦ διαβόλου; there is an interesting verbal parallel (it is no more) in Lucretius II, 991 (*Denique caelesti sumus omnes semine oriundi*). The parallels in *Clementine Homilies* XI,26, *Recognitions* VI,9 are unlikely to be independent. γεννᾶν is commonly used of the father's act, 'to beget', and this is probably the right sense here; but it is occasionally used of the mother also, 'to bring forth', 'to bear'.

The notion of supernatural begetting plays a very important part in this passage (vv. 3–8); it occurs in the Prologue (1.12f.), and perhaps also in 11.52. It is not found in Paul, who prefers the metaphor of death and resurrection, but is used in 1 Peter (1.3,23, ἀναγεννᾶν), and in the Pastorals (Titus 3.5, λουτρὸν παλιγγενεσίας). It recurs frequently in 1 John (2.29; 3.9; 4.7; 5.1, 4,18). It seems not to be present in the Apostolic Fathers, but in Justin it is firmly established in Christian usage, in unmistakable connection with baptism (1 *Apol.* 61f.—the candidate for baptism is ὁ ἑλόμενος ἀναγεννηθῆναι). It seems possible to infer that it was especially in Asia that regeneration by divine power was used in explanation of the Christian life. Such language was not drawn directly from the Old Testament or from Judaism. The statement, which occurs here and there in the rabbinic sources, that a newly baptized proselyte is like a new-born child, is not a relevant parallel since it refers to the legal status of the convert, nor can we legitimately quote the view that the daily sacrifices have the effect of making Israel like a one-year-old child. The idea of generation is absent. (For this and other Jewish material see S.B. II, 421ff.; also E. Sjöberg in *St. Th.* 4 (1951), 44–85; 9 (1956), 131–6; 'In dem Sinne kann man tatsächlich von einer Wiedergeburtsvorstellung reden, dass der Mensch in gewissen Situationen etwas erlebt, was seinem ersten Eintritt ins Leben, seiner Schöpfung im Mutterleib und seiner Geburt—vor allem das erstere—entspricht' (4.82)). The novelty of John's thought when compared with Judaism is not accidental, since the point of this paragraph is to bring out the fact that the Old Testament religion and Judaism, which Nicodemus, the Pharisee and ruler of the Jews, the teacher of Israel, represents, is inadequate; it cannot move forward continuously into the kingdom of God. A moment of discontinuity, comparable with physical birth, is essential. Man as such, even the Israelite, is not by nature capable of the kingdom of God. 'By the term *born again* He means not the amendment of a part but the renewal of the whole nature. Hence it follows that there is nothing in us that is not defective' (Calvin). The novelty and discontinuity are admirably enforced by the new terminology.

The point of departure for the evolution of the new terminology is primarily the primitive gospel tradition; see especially Matt. 18.3 (cf. Mark 10.15; Luke 18.17). Together with these sayings about entering and receiving the kingdom of God must be taken (as even more important than any isolated parallel saying) the fundamental New Testament assertion about the kingdom of God, namely, that not merely is it to be expected in its fullness in the age to come, but it has already been manifested, germinally or potentially, in the person and work of Jesus. This belief (which distinguished primitive Christianity from Judaism) made possible the development of the traditional material in Hellenistic religious terminology, where rebirth and supernatural begetting are by no means uncommon. Language of this kind Judaism had rigidly avoided because it spoke in direct terms of the invasion of present human life by the power of God and thus annihilated the distinction between this age and the age to come. For Christians this distinction had already been modified by the incarnation, and of this modification one consequence was a greater freedom in dealing with Hellenistic religion. For a full illustration of pagan beliefs about divine begetting and rebirth see Bauer, 51ff., and cf. Introduction pp. 36–9, 78ff. Both gnostic and sacramental religions offered rebirth to men. Among gnostic writings it must be sufficient to notice here the Hermetic tractate (XIII) on Rebirth. The disciple (like Nicodemus) asks puzzled questions, and we learn (XIII, 2) that ἄλλος ἔσται ὁ γεννώμενος θεοῦ θεὸς παῖς. It is the will of God (τὸ θέλημα τοῦ θεοῦ) that acts as father; the seed is the true Good (τὸ ἀληθινὸν ἀγαθόν); the mother is Wisdom of the Mind (σοφία νοερά; ibid.). The experience cannot be communicated in rational terms (οὐ διδάσκεται, XIII, 3); it must be shared. References to sacramental regeneration are not to be dismissed (as has sometimes happened) as too late to have affected the New Testament. The *taurobolium* referred to in *C.I.L.* x, 1596 is to be dated A.D. 134, and since the rite there mentioned was the second which the subject had undergone we may without hesitation accept the inscription as proof (collateral with other evidence) that the ideas in question were current at the time when John was written; and the genuineness of such experiences as are described by Apuleius (*Metamorphoses* XI) cannot be questioned.

It is not suggested in this note that John plagiarized the notions of salvation and regeneration current in the Hellenistic world of his day, or that he effected a syncretism of Jewish and pagan ideas. He set out from an exceptionally clear perception of the two 'moments' of Christian salvation, that of the work accomplished and that of the work yet to be consummated; and he perceived that the language of Judaism (the kingdom of God) and the language of Hellenism (γεννηθῆναι ἄνωθεν) provided him with a unique opportunity of expressing what was neither Jewish nor Hellenistic but simply Christian.

οὐ δύναται ἰδεῖν τὴν βασιλείαν τοῦ θεοῦ. It is impossible to distinguish between ἰδεῖν τ. β. τ. θ. and εἰσελθεῖν εἰς τ. β. τ. θ. in v. 5. 'To see' means 'to experience'; cf. 3.36, οὐκ ὄψεται ζωήν; also Mark 9.1. John often uses synonymous pairs of words, e.g. γινώσκειν, εἰδέναι; ἀγαπᾶν, φιλεῖν. Cf. Wisd. 10.10, ἔδειξεν αὐτῷ βασιλείαν θεοῦ. The kingdom of God is mentioned only here and at v. 5 in John. At 18.36 we hear of the βασιλεία of Jesus, and βασιλεύς occurs frequently in the passion narrative, where one of the main themes is the kingship of Jesus. βασιλεύς is also used at 1.49; 6.15; 12.13,15. 'Kingdom of God' calls to mind that apocalyptic Judaism which John seems for the most part to avoid. Perhaps this general avoidance, and the mention of the kingdom of God at this point, suggest not so much John's use here of a traditional saying (Bultmann, 135) as his criticism of that Judaism which was content to await the miraculous vindication of Israel in the kingdom of God and to ignore the necessity for inward conversion or rebirth. It is perhaps possible to connect this interpretation with the appearance in the gospel of a class of Jews who believe but only partially and inadequately. For these persons see 2.23f.; 3.2; 4.(45),48; 6.2,15,26,30,60,66; 7.12,31,40f.,46,50ff.; 8.30,31 (and the following discourse, expecially v. 44); 9 (the whole story with its various contrasts of faith and unbelief); 11.24; 12.11,42; (? 19.38f.). It is very probable that John knew such Jews not only in the historical tradition but also in his own environment (perhaps cf. Acts 19.1–7; and see Sidebottom, 123—the kingdom of God points forward to the ἐπουράνια of v. 12). The dialogue proceeds by way of Nicodemus' misunderstanding of the requirement γεννηθῆναι ἄνωθεν. This kind of progression is common in John. Among words of double or doubtful meaning (other than simple metaphors) are: ἄνθρωπος (19.5), ἄνωθεν (3.3,7), ἀποθνήσκειν ὑπέρ (11.50f., cf. 18.14), βασιλεύς (19.14f., 19, 21), εὐχαριστεῖν (6.11,23), καθίζειν (19.13), καταλαμβάνειν (1.5), ὕδωρ (4.10), ὑπάγειν (8.21; 13.33), ὕπνος (11.13), ὑψοῦν (3.14; 8.28; 12.32,34). These several times give rise to misunderstandings which (as here) provide a step on which the discourse mounts to a further stage: 3.4; 4.11; 8.22; 11.13; 13.36ff.; cf. 7.35; 7.41f.; 8.56f. See O. Cullmann, 'Der johanneische Gebrauch doppeldeutiger Ausdrücke als Schlüssel zum Verständnis des vierten Evangeliums', *Th. Z.* IV (1948), 360–72; *V. & A.*, 176–86.

4. Πῶς δύναται ἄνθρωπος γεννηθῆναι γέρων ὤν; Cf. the incredulous questions of the Hermetic tractate on Rebirth: ἀγνοῶ . . . ἐξ οἴας μήτρας ἄνθρωπος ἐγεννήθη, σπορᾶς δὲ ποίας (XIII, 1; read perhaps ἄνθρωπος ἂν ἀναγεννηθείη); τὸ γὰρ σύνολον ἀπορῶ . . . αἴνιγμά μοι λέγεις (XIII, 2). γέρων undoubtedly means 'old', and the most natural conclusion to draw is that Nicodemus himself was an old man; this would agree with his being an ἄρχων. But if this conclusion is accepted he can be identified neither with the 'rich young ruler' (as has been suggested) nor with the Nicodemus who was prominent in A.D. 70 (see on v. 1). It is of course possible that Nicodemus was speaking generally without special reference to himself; and again that he was not intended as a historical but rather as a representative character.

μὴ δύναται . . . καὶ γεννηθῆναι; Nicodemus correctly understands part, but only part, of the meaning of ἄνωθεν. So far as that word means 'again' it is aptly paraphrased by δεύτερον; but to think of a second entry into, and a second emergence from, the womb of a human mother is to ignore the fact that ἄνωθεν means also 'from above'. Nicodemus understands what has been said to him in purely human terms (cf. v. 12, ἐπίγεια); and therefore misunderstands it. To be born again in his sense would mean only to re-enter the world of weakness and sin (Fenton).

5. ἐὰν μή τις γεννηθῇ ἐξ ὕδατος καὶ πνεύματος. 'Of water and spirit' is substituted for the ἄνωθεν of v. 3. It is reasonable to assume that John is still speaking of the same begetting, that is, that the adverb and the adverbial phrases are substantially equivalent to each other, though the introduction of 'water and spirit' suggests fresh, and more precise, ideas. There is no textual ground whatever for the omission of ὕδατος καί as an interpolation; they are undoubtedly the work of the writer who published the gospel, and must therefore be interpreted as part of the text. The juxtaposition of water and spirit (cf. Ezek. 36.25–7) calls to mind the Baptist's prediction (1.26, cf. 1.33) and also the latter part of this chapter (3.29–34), where the relation

and the contrast between Jesus and John seem to drive home this part of the dialogue. The preaching of John suggested that men might see and enter the kingdom of God not now but when it arrived, as it surely would, and that soon. This was essentially orthodox Judaism, though with an exceptionally urgent apocalyptic note. To it John added the declaration that men must prepare for the coming of the kingdom by means of his water-baptism. Jesus, in the present verse, is represented as going further still; preparation by means of water-baptism only is inadequate for the kingdom he preaches; men must be prepared by a radical renewal of themselves, a new birth effected by the Spirit who comes (as it were) as the advance guard of the new age. Such seems to be the background of this verse; but it seems probable that John in speaking of water had in mind not only John's baptism but also Christian baptism, which is often (though not always) represented in the New Testament as the means by which the Spirit is conferred. It was the addition of 'Spirit' which transformed John's into Christian baptism (cf. Acts 19.1–7). It is from this stand-point that John's attitude to Christian sacraments may be understood (cf. Introduction, pp. 82–5, and on 6.51,52, 63). As we have seen, there is no reason why ὕδατος καί should not be taken as part of the gospel as published; and it is probable (but see below) that it included a reference to Christian baptism. But Christian baptism so far as it was a washing with water was no more significant than John's; each was in itself an outward act which guaranteed no inward meaning. Only if washing with water signified and was accompanied by the action of the Spirit could Christian baptism introduce one into the kingdom of God. That is, John neither ignores nor repudiates the Christian rite, but sees it as a rite that is separable from its meaning, an outward that is separable from its inward, and thus issues the warning against a sacramentarian misapprehension of baptism comparable with his warning in ch. 6 against similar misapprehension of the eucharist. It is possible to interpret the word 'water' without reference to baptismal rites. Birth 'from water' might be held (on the basis of the use in rabbinic Hebrew of טיפה (a drop; *P. Aboth* 3.1 and other, later, passages; cf. 3 Enoch 6.2) for semen) to mean physical birth; the καί is then ascensive: a man must of course be born of water in the ordinary course of nature, but born also of the Spirit. Another interpretation is based upon the same possible meaning of water (=semen), but takes water and Spirit closely together: man must be born not of earthly but of spiritual semen (cf. vv. 8–12; 1 John 3.9; 1 Peter 1.23). This spiritual semen may be compared with (perhaps equated with) the primal heavenly water, which is life-creating (Gen. 1.2; *C. H.* 1, 17; Acts of Thomas, 52). The evidence does not seem to be sufficient to support an interpretation of this kind; but see Odeberg, 48–71. At Qumran, water and Spirit were connected with cleansing rather than regeneration. The following parallels have been adduced, but none is really close to John: 1QS 3.7; 4.20ff.; 1QH 7.21f.; 9.32; CD 19.9.

οὐ δύναται εἰσελθεῖν εἰς τὴν βασιλείαν τοῦ θεοῦ. See on v. 3b. There is no essential difference in meaning. 'Entering the kingdom of God (heaven)' is however a more common expression in the Synoptic Gospels (Matt. 5.20; 7.21; 18.3; 19.23f.; 23.14; Mark 9.47; 10.15,23ff.; Luke 18.17,25). See also Hermas, *Sim.* IX, xvi, 2 (ἀνάγκην . . . εἶχον δι' ὕδατος ἀναβῆναι, ἵνα ζωοποιηθῶσιν· οὐκ ἠδύναντο γὰρ ἄλλως εἰσελθεῖν εἰς τ. β. τ. θ.) and Justin, 1 *Apol.* 61 (ἂν μὴ ἀναγεννηθῆτε, οὐ μὴ εἰσέλθητε εἰς τ. β. τ. οὐρανῶν) for important parallels, in which baptism is connected with entry into the kingdom. This does not mean that Mark 10.15 was understood to refer to baptism. For 'entry-formulas' see Jeremias, *Theology* 1, 154.

6. τὸ γεγεννημένον ἐκ τῆς σαρκὸς ... τὸ γεγ. ἐκ τοῦ πνεύματος. The contrast is between flesh and spirit, not, as at Qumran (1QS 3.19) between two spirits. *Thomas* 29 (If the flesh has come into existence because of the spirit, it is a marvel; but if the spirit has come into existence because of the body, it is a marvel of marvels) also does not illuminate the Johannine contrast. This Dodd (*Interpretation*, 295) takes to be between two orders of being (e.g. σάρξ refers to 'the phenomenal order of being'). Schnackenburg thinks that John did not have in mind the Platonic dualism within man but refers to a contrast 'between the transitory existence of the human creature on earth and the inviolable power of the absolute, spiritual life of God' (372). An existential interpretation may be more attractive than any form of idealism: 'σάρξ refers to the nothingness of man's whole existence; to the fact that man is ultimately a stranger to his fate and to his own acts; that, as he now is, he does not enjoy authentic existence, whether he makes himself aware of the fact or whether he conceals it from himself. Correspondingly πνεῦμα refers to the miracle of a mode of being in which man enjoys authentic existence, in which he understands himself and knows that he is no longer threatened by nothingness' (Bultmann, 141). But essentially the two words point respectively to man and God (cf. 4.24). They are not the lower and higher sides of human nature (e.g. the physical and the spiritual); they refer respectively to human nature as a whole (cf. 1.14, ὁ λόγος σὰρξ ἐγένετο) and to the divine action and its orbit. Each produces results corresponding to itself. Flesh is flesh and not spirit; yet it remains true that flesh—and in particular fleshly generation—supplies a parable by which begetting from the Spirit may be apprehended. Cf. the more explicit discussion of flesh and spirit at 6.53–63 (... ἡ γὰρ σάρξ μου ἀληθῶς ἐστι βρῶσις ... τὸ πνεῦμά ἐστιν τὸ ζωοποιοῦν, ἡ σὰρξ οὐκ ὠφελεῖ οὐδέν), and the notes there.

The Western revisers make in this verse unnecessary explanatory additions; after σάρξ ἐστιν the Old Latin and cur add *quia (quoniam) de carne natum est*; after πνεῦμά ἐστιν some Old Latin MSS. and sin add *quia (quoniam) deus spiritus est*, while a Tertullian and cur have *quia deus spiritus est et ex (de) deo natus est*.

7. μὴ θαυμάσῃς. The present (instead of the aorist) would perhaps be expected; the idiom is perhaps 'colloquial or idiomatic, with an effect of impatience' (see M. 1, 126). The injunction is too commonplace for rabbinic parallels (Schlatter, 90) to be significant. Nicodemus ought not to be surprised (v. 10). δεῖ ὑμᾶς. Cf. the plural οἴδαμεν in v. 2. Nicodemus speaks and is addressed, as a representative of the half-believing Jews (see on v. 2; 2.23). Moreover, the requirement of rebirth is not one that is directed to one man only; it is universal. It is, further, a real requirement (δεῖ). It is impossible for flesh (human nature as such) simply to evolve upwards into the kingdom of God.

8. τὸ πνεῦμα ὅπου θέλει πνεῖ. The word πνεῦμα in Greek (like רוח, *ruaḥ*, in Hebrew) may be rendered either 'wind' or 'spirit' (or 'breath'). The allegory in this verse is therefore so close that it depends not upon a symbolical meaning attached to a word or group of words but upon different meanings properly belonging to one word. We may translate either: The wind blows

where it wills and you hear the sound of it, but you do not know whence it comes and whither it goes; or, The Spirit breathes where he wills and you hear his voice, but you do not know, etc. Each of these translations taken by itself is wrong; the point of John's Greek is that it means both, and the double meaning cannot be simply reproduced in English. The Spirit, like the wind, is entirely beyond both the control and the comprehension of man: It breathes into this world from another.

οὐκ οἶδας πόθεν ἔρχεται καὶ ποῦ ὑπάγει. Cf. Ignatius, *Philad.* 7.1, τὸ πνεῦμα οὐ πλανᾶται ... οἶδεν γὰρ πόθεν ἔρχεται καὶ ποῦ ὑπάγει. On these passages Lightfoot (Ignatius, ad loc.) comments: 'The coincidence is quite too strong to be accidental.' It should be noted however that whereas in John the point is man's ignorance, in Ignatius it is the perfect knowledge of the Spirit himself. It cannot be regarded as certain that Ignatius had read John, though a common saying may lie behind them both (see Introduction, p. 111). Cf. Eccles. 11.5. Lucretius (1, 270–98) notes the existence and force of invisible things, such as winds.

οὕτως ἐστὶν πᾶς ὁ γεγεννημένος ἐκ τοῦ πνεύματος. Men cannot in themselves fathom the operation of the Spirit, but the Spirit himself is able to bring them within the sphere of his own activity, and impart his own properties to them. Through the Spirit men live not in this age but in the age to come, and though active in the world they are not confined to the range of the senses. Such men have their 'origin and destiny in the unseen God' (Fenton).

For ἐκ τοῦ πνεύματος, ℵ it sin cur Ambrosiaster substitute ἐξ ὕδατος καὶ τοῦ πνεύματος; the long reading seems to be due simply to assimilation to v. 5.

9. Πῶς δύναται ταῦτα γενέσθαι; Not, How can these things be? but, How can these things happen?

10. ὁ διδάσκαλος τοῦ Ἰσραήλ. The article emphasizes the status of Nicodemus: the great, universally recognized, teacher. Cf. *Mart. Pol.* 12.2, ὁ τῆς Ἀσίας διδάσκαλος. Nicodemus therefore as the representative of the people of God (τοῦ Ἰσραήλ, not τῶν Ἰουδαίων; see on 1.19) ought above all men to have understood the meaning of the Spirit and birth from above, since his own authoritative book, the Old Testament, itself bears witness to these themes.

11. σοι. Contrast λαμβάνετε (plural) at the end of the verse and cf. v. 7 (ὑμᾶς). The conversation with Nicodemus remains at best a form under which a wider public is addressed. These second person plurals make it unlikely that the first person plurals should be regarded simply as a Semitism (cf. Jeremias, *Theology* 1, 305; also 20.2).

ὃ οἴδαμεν ... ὃ ἑωράκαμεν. The object is the life and activity of the Spirit, of which Nicodemus is ignorant. The verbs are plural. Jesus no longer addresses a single person (see the preceding note), and no longer speaks as a single person. Nicodemus represents the half-believing Jews who were impressed by Jesus' signs but had not reached an adequate faith in him (see on v. 2). Jesus, on the other hand, it seems, associates with himself his disciples who have seen, believed, and known. The perspective, however, is not that of the historical ministry (cf. 7.39—the work of the Spirit was not at that time knowable), but that of the church. The community of those who have been born of water and Spirit addresses the synagogue. The final assertion (τὴν μαρτυρίαν ἡμῶν οὐ λαμβάνετε) refers both to the ministry of Jesus (1.10f.;

12.36–50, and other passages) and to the witness of the church (15.17–21). Cf. Dodd, *Interpretation*, 328.

λαλοῦμεν . . . μαρτυροῦμεν. Like 'knowing' and 'seeing' these are characteristic Johannine terms. λαλεῖν occurs 60 (58) times; on μαρτυρεῖν, μαρτυρία, see on 1.7.

12. τὰ ἐπίγεια . . . τὰ ἐπουράνια. It is not easy to determine precisely the contrast conveyed in this verse. The best possibilities among those usually suggested are the following. (a) The ἐπίγεια are events, such as the new birth, which take place on earth though they are of divine origin and meaning, while the ἐπουράνια are the events of heaven itself, such as the Father's sending of the Son into the world. To this it may be objected that begetting ἄνωθεν is essentially an ἐπουράνιον. (b) The ἐπίγεια are earthly events, such as physical birth, while the ἐπουράνια are the heavenly events, such as begetting ἄνωθεν, which the earthly may parabolically represent. Here the very strong objection may be made that no one disbelieves (καὶ οὐ πιστεύετε) in such common facts as physical birth. It seems possible however to combine these two lines of interpretation in a way which is not open to strong objection, if we note in the first place that in John πιστεύειν (when not used with a dative) means not 'to believe in' in a general sense, but 'to have faith in' God or Jesus. τὰ ἐπίγεια may then be events in the physical universe (such as birth, or the blowing of the wind), not regarded as complete in themselves but as pointing parabolically to Christ and to God's activity in him, and intended to promote faith. Jesus has spoken parables which should have evoked in Nicodemus faith (in Jesus himself); they failed in their purpose and it will therefore be useless to speak directly, without parable, of τὰ ἐπουράνια; cf. Mark 4.11f. For somewhat similar exegesis see H. Sasse, *T.W.N.T.* 1, 680; for a comparable statement about the miracles of Jesus see 12.37–43.

13. οὐδεὶς ἀναβέβηκεν. This negative statement reinforces the interpretation of v. 12 that has just been given. It is futile for men to think that they can dispense with earthly parables (τὰ ἐπίγεια) and mount directly to heaven, thereby attaining a knowledge really independent of faith. There is a similar polemic against mysticism in Judaism; see Wisd. 9.16, μόλις εἰκάζομεν τὰ ἐπὶ γῆς . . . τὰ δὲ ἐν οὐρανοῖς τίς ἐξιχνίασεν; 4 Ezra 4.2, *Excedens excessit cor tuum in saeculo hoc, et comprehendere cogitas uiam altissimi?* *Sanhedrin* 39a: Rabban Gamaliel said to the Emperor: That which is on earth you do not know; should you know what is in heaven? *Sukkah* 5a: R. Jose (b. Halaphta) said: Neither did the presence of God come down to earth, nor did Moses and Elijah ascend on high; for 'The heavens are the heavens of the Lord; but the earth hath he given to the children of men' (Ps. 115.16). See further Odeberg, 73.

εἰ μή . . . ὁ υἱὸς τοῦ ἀνθρώπου. On John's use of the title Son of man see Introduction, pp. 72f., and on 1.51; also Higgins, *Son of Man*, 171ff., and S. S. Smalley, *N.T.S.* 15 (1969), 289f. On this passage, E. Ruckstuhl, in *Jesus und der Menschensohn* (Festschrift A. Vögtle, 1975) 314–41. It is as Son of man that Jesus forms the connecting link between the earthly and heavenly spheres; his earthly existence is the place where heavenly things become visible, and also the place where heavenly things are rejected by mankind (see next verse). The description of Jesus as ὁ καταβάς causes no difficulty; this refers to the incarnation. The Son of man descends from heaven to earth in order to convey ἐπουράνια to men. Cf. 6.41 *et al.* For the combination of ἀναβαίνειν and καταβαίνειν cf. Eph. 4.9. This comparison however brings out the difficulty of the verse, which lies in the tense of ἀναβέβηκεν. It seems to imply that the Son of man had already at the moment of speaking ascended into heaven. It is legitimate here to compare 1 Enoch 70.2; 71.1 where Enoch ascends into heaven there to be identified with the heavenly Son of man, but very doubtful whether the comparison really illuminates John's thought which has no room for such an ascent. The Word was the Word, and the Word was with God, ἐν ἀρχῇ (1.1.). It seems necessary to suppose that this verse is a comment made from the same standpoint as v. 11; it is not a saying which can be placed within the setting of the historical ministry of Jesus but is the testimony of the church after his death and ascension. The Ascent like the Descent is a fundamental element in the church's proclamation, and it is the totality of Christ's work that constitutes the Gospel. Sidebottom (120) suggests the rendering, 'No one has ascended into heaven, but one has descended.' Cf. Rev. 21.27. This avoids the difficulty, but is a questionable, and certainly not the most natural, way of taking the Greek. A similar suggestion is worked out at length by E. Ruckstuhl, op. cit.

After the words 'Son of man', ὁ ὢν ἐν τῷ οὐρανῷ is added by Θ Ω it vg (cur has 'who *was* in heaven'). A similar addition (ὁ ὢν ἐκ τοῦ οὐρανοῦ) is made by sin and a few Greek MSS. It seems probable that John wrote these additional words as they appear in Θ, etc. It is clear that they present in an acute form the difficulty that we have already noted in ἀναβέβηκεν. The Son of man at the moment of speaking was on earth. The complete omission of the clause (by P⁶⁶ P⁷⁵ ℵ B W, among others), and the 'improvements' in the two Old Syriac VSS., were intended to remove the difficulty. If the words are read it must probably be concluded that John is again speaking from the standpoint of the post-resurrection church; see however Hoskyns, 235f.

14. The chronological point of reference shifts; the ascent of the Son of man now lies in the future. This verse emphasizes the unique manner of his exaltation, which is not to be in clouds of glory but upon the cross. Jesus manifests heavenly things (ἐπουράνια) but they are rejected by those to whom he reveals them, and the rejection of the revelation is most clearly expressed by the rejection, and crucifixion, of Jesus himself. Here, according to Martyn (126), John affects the transition from Mosaic prophet–Messiah to Son of man.

καθὼς Μωϋσῆς ὕψωσεν τὸν ὄφιν ἐν τῇ ἐρήμῳ. Contrast 6.58 (οὐ καθώς) and see Martyn, 108f. The reference is to the narrative of Num. 21.4–9, where the people are cured of the bites of the fiery serpents by looking at a brazen serpent (נחש נחשת, ὄφιν χαλκοῦν) made by Moses and put upon a 'standard' (נס, ἐπὶ σημείου—in *Berakoth* 4a *nes* is taken to mean a miracle). Jewish tradition, aware of the end of the serpent (2 Kings 18.4), emphasized that the serpent did not itself cure the bites. Wisd. 16.6f.: Having a token of salvation (σύμβολον σωτηρίας), to put them in remembrance (εἰς ἀνάμνησιν) of the commandment of thy law: for he that turned toward it was not saved because of that which was beheld, but because of thee, the Saviour of all. *Rosh ha-Shanah* 3.8; But could the serpent slay or the serpent keep alive?—it is, rather, to teach thee that such time as the Israelites directed their thoughts on high and kept their hearts in subjection to their Father in heaven, they were healed; otherwise they pined away. McNamara, 147f., quotes the Fragment Targum: When anyone bitten by a serpent lifted up his face in prayer to his Father who is in heaven, and looked upon the brazen serpent, he lived. Philo makes use of the incident of the serpent, but his treatment (*L. A.* II, 79–81, *Agr.* 95–9) does not illuminate John's. Later Christian writers (e.g. Barnabas, 12.5–7; Justin, 1 *Apol.* 60; *Trypho* 94, 112 (on Justin see Dinkler, *Signum*, 38f.); Tertullian *Adv. Marc.* III, 18) treat the serpent as a type of Christ (Μωϋσῆς ποιεῖ τύπον τοῦ 'Ιησοῦ, Barnabas, 12.5), but this is not, it seems, John's intention. For him the point of comparison is not the serpent but the lifting up. As in the old Jewish interpretation the uplifted serpent drew the hearts of Israel to God for their salvation, so the uplifted Jesus drew men to himself and so gathered to God those who were his children (cf. 12.32; 11.52). See Derrett, *Law*, 148.

ὑψωθῆναι δεῖ. Cf. Mark 8.31, δεῖ τὸν υἱὸν τοῦ ἀνθρώπου πολλὰ παθεῖν ... καὶ μετὰ τρεῖς ἡμέρας ἀναστῆναι. Suffering, though it lead to glory, is (according to the gospels) the inescapable destiny of the Son of man. In Mark the suffering and glorification are chronologically distinguished; in John one word is used to express both. ὑψοῦν has this double meaning at each place in the gospel in which it is used, and further is always used of the Son of man (8.28, 12.32,34); on the suggested derivation of this use from the Aramaic אזדקף ('ezd*e*qeph) see Introduction, p. 9. Other suggestions include אשתלק ('est*e*laq), to be lifted up, but also to depart, die (McNamara, *T. & T.*, 143, 163), and ארים ('arim), to lift up, and to remove. It is possible, especially in view of John's use of the verb δοξάζειν (for which see on 1.14), that he has been influenced by Isaiah's description of the lot of the Servant of the Lord (Isa. 52.13, ὑψωθήσεται καὶ δοξασθήσεται σφόδρα). The connection of thought in the present passage is as follows. The Son of man alone is he who descends from heaven, and again ascends thither. Viewed in the conditions of his earthly life he is under necessity of being lifted up (exalted to glory); but his lifting up will be in the manner suggested by the serpent of the Old Testament. He will be lifted up on the cross (cf. especially 12.32f.), and his lifting up will result not only in glory for himself but also in healing for mankind. This result is immediately emphasized in the next verse.

15. The purpose of the Son of man's exaltation is the salvation of those who believe.

ἐν αὐτῷ. Apart from this verse πιστεύειν is never in John followed by ἐν, consequently it is probable that here ἐν αὐτῷ should be constructed not with πιστεύων but with ἔχῃ ζωὴν αἰώνιον—'... might in him have eternal life'. See Moule, *Idiom Book*, 80f. Cf. 6.47; 20.31, where πιστεύειν is used absolutely as the ground of eternal life; cf. 1.4, ἐν αὐτῷ ζωὴ ἦν. There are several textual variants.

ζωὴν αἰώνιον. Cf. Num. 21.8, ζήσεται. On ζωή see on 1.4. The adjective αἰώνιος is in John used only in the expression ζωὴ αἰώνιος (3.15,16,36; 4.14,36; 5.24,39; 6.27,40,47,54,68; 10.28; 12.25,50; 17.2,3). On the use of the noun αἰών see on 4.41. ζωὴ αἰώνιος derives from the phrase חיי עולם (literally, life of 'eternity') in Dan. 12.2, which is rendered both in the LXX and Theodotion, ζωὴ αἰώνιος. Its meaning is brought out in the perhaps more common rabbinic formula, חיי העולם הבא, literally, life of the age to come. In this sense the phrase appears in the Synoptic Gospels (e.g. Mark 10.30). It is noteworthy that in John eternal life is first mentioned after the only references in the gospel to the kingdom of God (3.3,5). It is clear from consideration of the passages enumerated above, in which eternal life is mentioned, that the concept retains something of its original eschatological connection, but also that it may equally be thought of as a present gift of God; in this, ζωὴ αἰώνιος in John resembles 'kingdom of God' in the Synoptic Gospels. That which is properly a future blessing becomes a present fact in virtue of the realization of the future in Christ. This observation is, however, complicated by the fact that John writes within and for, and from the standpoint of, the post-resurrection church. In this verse the argument is that the Son of man has been, by his death, exalted to heaven; those therefore who are in him (ἐν αὐτῷ) enjoy by anticipation the life of the age to come.

16. Mention of the death and exaltation of Christ, and of the eternal life given thereby to believers, suggests consideration of the general setting of the work of Christ in the love and judgement of God. This theme is pursued through the rest of the paragraph, up to v. 21.

οὕτως . . . ὥστε. For the construction cf. 1 Cor. 9.24, οὕτως τρέχετε ἵνα καταλάβητε, which, if the action were past instead of future, would run οὕτως ἔδραμον ὥστε κατέλαβον. ὥστε may be followed by an indicative or an infinitive; the former lays stress on the fact that the consequence mentioned did in fact ensue, the latter on its relation with the preliminary action; but it would be unwise in New Testament Greek to emphasize this distinction (for which see M. 1, 209f., and, with some exaggeration, Turner, *Insights*, 142ff.).

οὕτως γὰρ ἠγάπησεν . . . ὥστε . . . ἔδωκεν. The mission of the Son was the consequence of the Father's love; hence also the revelation of it. ἀγαπᾶν, ἀγάπη, are among the most important words in John. There is little in profane Greek, or in the LXX, to illuminate their meaning in the New Testament. In John the words are used much more frequently in chs. 13—17 than elsewhere (ἀγαπᾶν, 37 times altogether, 25 times in 13—17: ἀγάπη, 7 times altogether, 6 times in 13—17). This corresponds to the fact that while God loves the world (as is stated in this verse) his love only becomes effective among those who believe in Christ. For the rest love turns, as it were, to judgement. Love seems to be, for John, a reciprocal relation. The Father loves the Son (3.35; 10.17; 15.9f.; 17.23f., 26), and the Son loves the Father (14.31); Jesus loves his own (11.5; 13.1,33,34; 14.21; 15.9(f.), 12; 21.7,20), and his own love, or should love, one another (13.34f.; 15.12f., 17; 17.26). They must also love him (14.15,21,23f.,28; 21.15f.). Only occasionally do we hear of a love of the Father directly for the disciples (14.21,23; 17.23), and it is made clear that men in general do not, and cannot, love God (3.19; 5.42; 8.42). John's use of these words is perhaps too comprehensive to be always clear, or always consistent (see A. Nygren, *Agape and Eros* 1 (1937), 108–17). He uses the same words both for God's spontaneous, gracious, love for men, and also for the responsive relation of the disciple to God, to which man is moved not by free unmerited favour to God (which would be impossible), but by a sense of God's favours to him. John, however, more than any other writer, develops the conception of love as the nature of God himself and as the means by which the divine life, the relation of the Father and the Son, is perpetuated and demonstrated within the community (13.35). For God's gift of his Son cf. Rom. 8.3,32; Gal. 4.4; 1 John 4.9. Behind ἔδωκεν Cullmann (*Christology*, 70) sees παρέδωκεν and an allusion to Isa. 53. This reads too much into the text.

τὸν κόσμον. See on 1.10. The world as a whole is the object of God's love, but that very fact causes the distinction drawn in v. 18 between ὁ πιστεύων and ὁ μὴ πιστεύων.

τὸν υἱὸν τὸν μονογενῆ. On μονογενής see on 1.14. It underlines the uniqueness of the relation of the Son to the Father (in John υἱός is used of Christ only, never of Christians). Cf. Rom. 8.32 (ὑπὲρ ἡμῶν πάντων παρέδωκεν αὐτόν [*sc.* τὸν ἴδιον υἱόν]). In Romans, and perhaps also in John, there may be an allusion to Gen. 22.2,16.

ἵνα... μὴ ἀπόληται ἀλλ' ἔχῃ 3ωὴν αἰώνιον. The immediate, 'internal', consequence of the love of God is the sending of the Son; its ultimate purpose is the salvation of believers. For πιστεύειν εἰς see on 1.12. ἀπολλύναι is another characteristic Johannine word (the accumulation of such words in this passage shows its importance; John is summarizing his message). The verb is used transitively in the active, with a corresponding intransitive use supplied by the middle. For the transitive use see 6.39. The intransitive use is twofold: (*a*) 'to be lost' (6.12), (*b*) 'to perish', 'to suffer destruction' (3.16; 6.27; 10.28; 11.50). The same ambiguity applies also to the cognate noun ἀπώλεια (17.12 only). Destruction is the inevitable fate of all things and persons separated from God and concentrated upon themselves (cf. 12.25); this is a corollary of the fact that only in God the Father, the Word, and the Spirit does life exist. There is no neutral ground between ἀπόληται and ἔχῃ 3ωὴν αἰώνιον; they are absolute alternatives. On ἔχῃ 3ωὴν αἰώνιον see on v. 15.

17. οὐ γὰρ ἀπέστειλεν. The meaning of ἀπέστειλεν is substantially the same as that of ἔδωκεν in the previous verse, but the word is significant; see on 20.21. The idea of mission, or apostolate, is one of the most important in the gospel. The sending (of the apostles, as well as of Christ—cf. 17.18) is εἰς τὸν κόσμον; so in many gnostic and other pagan systems the divine redeemer penetrates the various circles of the heavens in order to reach sinful and corporeal humanity; but the sense of mission is found also in the synoptic accounts of the ministry of Jesus (e.g. Mark 1.38 interpreted by Luke 4.43; Mark 9.37; Matt. 15.24; Luke 4.18). On *sending* see E. Schweizer, in *Z.N.T.W.* 57 (1966), 199–210. In the present verse stress does not lie on the theological relations between Father and Son implied by the process of sending, but on the purpose of the mission.

ἵνα κρίνῃ τὸν κόσμον. Cf. Cornutus 16 (Ed. Lang (1881) p. 21, ll. 9f.), οὐ γὰρ πρὸς τὸ κακοῦν καὶ βλάπτειν, ἀλλὰ πρὸς τὸ σώζειν μᾶλλον γέγονεν ὁ λόγος. Later (5.27) John declares that Jesus as Son of man has authority to judge, and indeed (9.39) that he came into the world for the purpose of judgement. The apparent contradiction in fact illuminates the meaning of 'judgement' in this gospel. κρίνειν is used here (cf. 12.47) with the meaning 'to condemn'. Its opposite is σώζειν. To this corresponds the statement that the believer 'is not judged' (3.18), 'does not come into judgement' (5.24), while the unbeliever has already been judged, or condemned (3.18, cf. 16.11; 12.31). John speaks of a final judgement at the last day (5.27–9; 12.48), but his primary thought is that the ministry of Jesus (as later the ministry of the

Paraclete, 16.8,11) had the effect of judgement. More accurately, those who believed in Christ, who 'came to the light', escaped judgement (condemnation) altogether, while those who did not believe by that very fact sentenced themselves. The process of judgement is an inseparable concomitant of salvation; no real contradiction is involved when Jesus says that he came both not to judge, and to judge. See further on the passages cited in this note; also O. Cullmann, *Christus und die Zeit* (1962), 90f. (E.T., 1951; 89f.). Bultmann's 'To be judged is simply to shut our hearts to grace' (*P.C.*, 195) is nearly but not quite adequate. See further below.

ἀλλ' ἵνα σωθῇ ὁ κόσμος. σώζειν is not very common in John (3.17; 5.34; 10.9; 11.12; 12.27,47); for σωτήρ see on 4.42; for σωτηρία see on 4.22. The parallelism here (cf. 10.9; 11.12; 12.27) shows that the meaning of σώζειν is substantially the same as that of ζωή αἰώνιος. No stress is laid here upon anything from which the world is saved; it is in fact saved from being itself. Schnackenburg, citing *C.H.* 1.22f., notes the contrast between salvation designed for the world and the gnostic notion of salvation for a relatively small company of the elect; but the following verses take some of the force out of this contrast.

18. For the Johannine theme of judgement see on v. 17. The present verse may be regarded as a statement of the negative aspect of the doctrine of justification by faith. The believer (though a sinner) does not come under condemnation; but the absence of faith calls down condemnation upon itself, or, better, is itself an aspect, the subjective aspect, of condemnation. The reason for this is shown in the next verse; cf. Rom. 14.23: Whatsoever is not of faith is sin.

κέκριται, perfect tense: the judgement is already past, but the sentence remains.

ὅτι μὴ πεπίστευκεν. μή with an indicative is rare; contrast 1 John 5.10, ὅτι οὐ πεπίστευκεν εἰς τὴν μαρτυρίαν. 'The former (John 3.18) states the *charge*, *quod non crediderit*, the latter (1 John 5.10) the simple *fact*, *quod non credidit*' (M. 1, 171). Moule, *Idiom Book*, 155, however, properly observes that 'all this could have been expressed grammatically instead of by this solecism. ὁ μὴ πιστεύων, however, just before makes it sound less harsh.'

19. αὕτη ... ὅτι. For the construction of 15.12; 17.3, where an explanatory ἵνα (instead of ὅτι) is used.

κρίσις, like κρίνειν in v. 17, has the sense of condemnation, or, perhaps, of 'the decisive criterion—which in the given case results in condemnation'. Men are judged by their reaction to the work and person of Jesus. Those believe in him who are fit to be acquitted and saved; those who reject him do so because they are worthy of condemnation. Cf. 1QS 4.24ff.; but, as Braun observes, at Qumran judgement belongs to the future whereas in John it has already begun.

τὸ φῶς. See 1.4f. and the notes. See also 8.12, and ch. 9, especially 9.39–41. When a light shines in a dark night men who have nothing to be ashamed of make their way to it, seeking illumination; those who are about the deeds of darkness move away from it, lest their deeds should be disclosed.

20. ἐλεγχθῇ. The word is used at 16.8 of the activity of the Paraclete, and signifies a convincing exposure. It is important to note the parallel between

the work of Christ and the work of the Spirit; see the note on 16.8. See the important note by A. R. C. Leaney (*J. & Q.*, 45) on the use of יכח in the Scrolls.

21. ὁ δὲ ποιῶν τὴν ἀλήθειαν. On ἀλήθεια see the note on 1.14. In the Old Testament ποιεῖν (τὴν) ἀλήθειαν (עשה אמת, '*asah* '*emeth*) means 'to keep faith'. But in John, though the Hebrew word אמת ('*emeth*) is not far off in the background, the specifically Christian sense is dominant: 'he that practises the true (Christian) faith and life'. Such a man naturally comes to the light. His deeds have been wrought in God (for ἔργα ἐργάζεσθαι cf. 6.28; 9.4), and when he comes to the light he only returns to his own origin. According to J. H. Charlesworth (*J. & Q.*, 77), John's use is paralleled only in 1QS 1.5; 5.3; 8.2. But see also Gen. 32.10; 47.29; Isa. 26.10; 2 Esdr. 19.33; Tob. 4.6; 13.6; Targ. Hos. 4.1 (עבד קושתא). As Braun says, it is *allgemein-jüdisch*, not specifically Qumranite. Turner's argument (*Insights*, 11) that it means 'to worship' or 'to be a disciple of the truth' is unconvincing. Dodd (*Interpretation*, 210) thinks that both ἐν θεῷ εἰργασμένον and ποιεῖν τὴν ἀλήθειαν mean 'belongs to the realm of reality'; see below.

In vv. 19–21 (cf. 12.46ff.) the predestinarian teaching of this gospel comes clearly to light. See on this subject Introduction, pp. 8of., and on 12.36–43. Men are divided into two classes, those who do evil and those who do the truth. The former inevitably reject Christ and are rejected; the latter as inevitably accept him. The distinction between the two groups appears to exist before they are confronted with Christ himself; there seems to be no question of those who do evil being changed into men who will do the truth. If this were the whole of John's meaning 'the seriousness of the basic idea of ch. 3 and indeed of the whole Gospel would have been forfeited, and all that would be left would be a mythologically embellished moralism. This is certainly not what is intended. Rather what is meant is that in the decision of faith or unbelief it becomes apparent what man really is and what he always was. But it is revealed in such a way that the decision is made only now' (Bultmann, 159).

Like many important features of John this predestinarian teaching has a threefold background and origin: the Old Testament, where the doctrine of election is central; Hellenistic religion—see e.g. *C.H.* 1, 22f. (παραγίνομαι αὐτὸς ἐγὼ ὁ Νοῦς ὁσίοις ... τοῖς δὲ ἀνοήτοις ... πόρρωθέν εἰμι); and the primitive Christian faith, e.g. Mark 4.10–12. John does not however offer a mere amalgam of these constituents. The gospel is a factor in developing gnosticism rather than a simple product of it, and John is not describing a static condition (though his words might suggest this) but circumstances set and kept in motion by the Word (and Spirit—cf. 16.8–11) of God. 'His own received him not' is always crossed by 'as many as received him' (1.11f.), and to receive him means to recognize not that one's works are inherently good (in a moral sense; or ideal, in Dodd's Platonic sense) but that they have meaning only in God. Thus 'in the decision man makes when faced with the question put to him by God, it becomes apparent, in his very act of decision, what he really is. Thus the mission of Jesus is the eschatological event in which judgement is made on all man's past. And this mission can be the eschatological event, because in it God's love restores to man the freedom which he has lost, the freedom to take possession of his own authenticity' (Bultmann, 159f.; see also the excellent short note in Fenton, 56). If this means that the historical event of the mission of Jesus is the place where and the means by which man receives eternal life, whatever his past, it may be accepted as a restatement of John's meaning.

7. THE WITNESS OF JOHN (II)

3.22–36

The theme of John and his relationship with Jesus is resumed (cf. 1.19–34). The evangelist represents Jesus and the Baptist as pursuing their work simultaneously. This may be a correct representation, but it is not necessary to suppose that it was given because John possessed a historical tradition divergent from that of Mark; it was rather his intention to bring out the truth expressed in 3.30, possibly with some polemical intention against the adherents of the Baptist. The scene is introduced by reference to a discussion of which no details are given (v. 25) but which has the effect of representing John and his baptism as lying within the Jewish system of purifications. Jesus is superior to this system, the person to whom the system points, as the guests and bride at a wedding point to the existence of a bridegroom. He holds this position because, unlike John and the Jews, he is not of the earth but from above. He speaks the words of God and God has put all things into his hand. It follows from this that men's relation with him means either that they enjoy life eternal or that they incur the wrath of God.

It has often been supposed that this section, or part of it, is out of place. Three conjectural improvements are worthy of consideration. (*a*) vv. 22–30, which interrupt the connection between vv. 21 and 31, should be removed from their present position and read after 2.12. (*b*) vv. 22–30 and vv. 31–6 should be transposed. V. 31 is thus brought into immediate connection with v. 21 and v. 30 with the next chapter, the connections being improved in each case. (*c*) Vv. 31–6 should be placed between 3.12 and 3.13, and thus integrated into the dialogue and discourse initiated by the coming of Nicodemus. A case can be made for each of these suggestions (see the notes on v. 22 and v. 31) in that the sequence of verses as they stand is in some respects imperfect (Sanders explains this by the suggestion that a new source begins at v. 22). These respects, however, are not those with which John was primarily concerned, and the passage makes sense as a whole and its present position. Vv. 22–30 as well as vv. 31–6 follow suitably after vv. 1–21; see in particular on 3.5 where, it appears, the inferior baptism of John is alluded to; we now learn wherein and to what John's baptism was inferior; and vv. 31–6 continue and generalize the theme of the comparison between John and Jesus.

On the whole section see Dodd, *Tradition*, 279–87. It is probably correct to see some traditional elements, notably v. 23, in it. What is important, however, is that Jesus has now, in three paragraphs (2.13–25; 3.1–21; 3.22–36), been set forth as the fulfiller of Judaism (see p. 196). John will turn next to the world on and beyond the borders of Judaism.

22. Μετὰ ταῦτα. See on 2.12. The previous incident is now closed.

εἰς τὴν Ἰουδαίαν γῆν. The natural implication is that Jesus had come from Galilee; but the Nicodemus incident, which follows directly upon 2.23–5, seems to require a scene in or near Jerusalem. The difficulty is eased if vv. 22–30 are transferred from their present context and read after 2.12; for this suggestion see the Introduction to the present passage. Otherwise we must suppose either that εἰς τ. Ἰ. γ. means 'out of Jerusalem [where the interview with Nicodemus may be supposed to have taken place] and into the surrounding district' (for this use of γῆ Bultmann compares Aeschylus, Eumenides 993, καὶ γῆν καὶ πόλιν), or that John assumes events to have taken place in Galilee between 3.21 and 3.22, or that he is not interested in the locality, simply taking over the reference from a source.

καὶ ἐβάπτιζεν. Cf. 4.1f. and the notes; only in this gospel is it even hinted that Jesus baptized.

23. Though Jesus had begun to baptize John did not cease.

ἐν Αἰνὼν ἐγγὺς τοῦ Σαλίμ. Salim cannot be identified with certainty; Aenon cannot be identified at all. Two localities have been suggested for Salim. (a) Ancient tradition (Eusebius, Onomastica Sacra 40.1–4 (Ed. Klostermann)) found a Salim about six miles south of Bethshan (Scythopolis), in the extreme north-east of Samaria. (b) There exists today a Salim about three miles east of Shechem. It is possible to find in the neighbourhood of each of these localities places which might have been called Aenon since they have 'many springs' (ὕδατα πολλά). The name Aenon is probably derived from עין ('ayin), a spring. In addition, the Madeba map (sixth century) notes an Aenon in Peraea. It may be observed that the name Salim occurs only twice in the Old Testament (Gen. 14.18; Ps. 76.3). As early as Josephus (Ant. 1, 180) it was taken to mean Jerusalem, and it seems not impossible that John may also have used the word in this sense; but there is no need to suppose (as does Cheyne, E. Bib. s.v. Salim) that τοῦ Σαλίμ is a corruption of Ἱερουσαλήμ. Some have thought that Salim was intended to signify the Hebrew שלום (shalom), peace; John's baptism brought men near to the peace of God but could not confer that peace. The names, however, were probably drawn from tradition (see also Jeremias, Theology 1, 45f.); also M. E. Boismard, R.B. 80 (1973), 218–29. If the locality was in the neighbourhood of Samaria John makes nothing of the fact.

παρεγίνοντο καὶ ἐβαπτίζοντο. The verbs are impersonal: people came and were baptized. The popular baptist movement continued.

24. οὔπω γὰρ ἦν βεβλημένος εἰς τὴν φυλακὴν Ἰωάννης. Contrast Mark 1.14, μετὰ τὸ παραδοθῆναι τὸν Ἰωάννην ἦλθεν ὁ Ἰησοῦς εἰς τὴν Γαλιλαίαν.... It is often supposed that John is here silently correcting the synoptic tradition on a matter of chronology, but this is by no means necessarily so. It is equally possible that he may have intended to indicate that the events recounted in his first three (four) chapters are to be thought of as having taken place before the point at which Mark begins his account of the ministry with

Jesus' public appearance in Galilee. It is however true that John portrays what the synoptic writers do not suggest—parallel ministries of John and Jesus. There is nothing inherently improbable in this; but it seems probable that John's aim is not to furnish an interesting piece of historical information but to provide a background for v. 30 (ἐκεῖνον δεῖ αὐξάνειν, ἐμὲ δὲ ἐλαττοῦσθαι); cf. v. 26; 4.1.

25. ἐγένετο οὖν ζήτησις ἐκ τῶν μαθητῶν. ἐκ is not here used in the partitive sense characteristic of John (see Introduction, p. 8); the dispute arose from, originated with, the disciples of John (cf. e.g. Herodotus v. 21, ζήτησις ... μεγάλη ἐκ τῶν Περσέων ἐγίνετο). Most commentators agree that here too there is old tradition; but the evangelist's interest in it is that it provides a suitable occasion for the Baptist's renewed testimony to Jesus.

μετὰ Ἰουδαίου, P75 אᶜ B W ω: Ἰουδαίων, P66 א* Θ λ φ it vg cur sah boh. Each of these readings is unquestionably ancient, but the singular is unique in John, and is more likely to have been changed into the plural than *vice versa*. It is true that with the singular form τινος might have been expected, but true also that with the plural the article might have been supplied. The textual uncertainty lends a little weight to the suggestion that corruption has occurred, and that instead of Ἰουδαίου (or Ἰουδαίων) there should be read Ἰησοῦ, or τοῦ Ἰησοῦ, or τῶν Ἰησοῦ: the dispute was between the disciples of John and the disciples of Jesus, or Jesus himself. The conjecture (in all its forms) is attractive because in the following verses purification in general is not discussed but the significance and relative worth of Jesus and John; but it cannot stand since neither of the readings which are well attested by the MSS. is so difficult as to be impossible.

περὶ καθαρισμοῦ. Cf. 2.6. The reference is not to the baptism performed by John, or to that performed by Jesus, but to Jewish purification in general. For this reason it is not made precise; John cares (and perhaps knows) little about the details of Jewish ablutions. His intention (still with v. 30 in view) is to show that John the Baptist, great though he is, nevertheless belongs within the world of Judaism, which Jesus will supersede (Among them that are born of women there hath not arisen a greater than John the Baptist: yet he that is but little in the kingdom of heaven is greater than he—Matt. 11.11; Luke 7.28). Neither John nor the Jew is ὁ ἄνωθεν ἐρχόμενος (v. 31), and their καθαρισμός can at best point forward to the life-giving activity of the Son of God (v. 36).

26. ἦλθον ... εἶπαν. The subject may be the disciples of John, mentioned in v. 25; or it may be impersonal, 'people came and told John'; 'he was informed ...'.

Ῥαββί. See on 1.38. The title is nowhere else applied to John; it does not seem very appropriate.

ὃς ἦν ... μεμαρτύρηκας. See 1.26-34. John is now to repeat his testimony in fresh terms. The words of John's disciples are often taken to be complaining and resentful, but since they draw attention to John's own prophecy they may equally be taken as a joyful announcement of the fulfilment of their master's word. The evangelist's intention is to introduce the sayings that follow.

πάντες ἔρχονται πρὸς αὐτόν. Cf. Mark 1.45; 3.7f., and parallels. This verse leads up to v. 30; John does not share any bitterness his disciples may have felt at the success of Jesus because he recognizes in it the purpose of God. There is doubtless some historical exaggeration in the πάντες; but cf.11.48; 12.19.

27. For a discussion of parallelism, and word-play in a conjectured Aramaic original, in vv. 27–36, see Black, 146–9. His conclusion is, 'It is clear that the Fourth Gospel is, in the sayings it attributes to the Baptist, a Greek translation of an Aramaic poem or prophecy; and it is equally certain that the Fourth Evangelist is not entirely inventing sayings for the Baptist, as a comparison of vv. 23–8 in his first chapter with their Synoptic parallels shows. Perhaps a Greek sayings-group, translated from Aramaic sayings of the Baptist, was used by St John' (149). It will be noted that Black preserves the traditional order and position of vv. 27–36; see Introduction to this section. The cases of parallelism which are adduced (see the notes in detail below) are not sufficient evidence to prove the theory of an Aramaic original: it is possible to write rhythmical 'Old Testament' Greek without translating. For the word-play see the notes on vv. 29f., 31f.

ἦ δεδομένον, perfect subjunctive: unless it has been given; all the initiative lies with God. This is a general principle (ἄνθρωπος means 'any man'), but it may be applied to the contrasting ministries of Jesus and John. If the work of the former is eclipsing that of the latter, the will of God must require that it should do so. If this is the meaning it will follow that the two questions, (a) What is it that is given, truth (or grace), or the capacity to receive it? and (b) To whom is the gift given, Christ or the believer? are both unnecessary.

ἐκ τοῦ οὐρανοῦ, from God. Cf. 19.11, ἦν δεδομένον σοι ἄνωθεν. For the use of 'heaven' as a reverential periphrasis see G. Dalman, *The Words of Jesus* (E.T. 1909), 217–20.

28. αὐτοὶ ὑμεῖς, probably the disciples of John, though others may be included (v. 26).

οὐκ εἰμὶ ἐγὼ ὁ Χριστός. See 1.20.

ἀπεσταλμένος εἰμὶ ἔμπροσθεν ἐκείνου. See 1.26–34.

Vv. 27f. form 'two lines in synthetic or constructive parallelism, followed by other two which might be regarded as either synthetic or antithetic' (Black, 146):

A man can receive nothing,
Except it be given him from heaven.
I am not the Christ,
But . . . I am sent before him.

It seems very doubtful whether this goes beyond the range of balanced prose.

29. This verse may be taken simply as a parable. At a wedding, the 'best man', important though his functions may be, naturally and gladly gives place to the bridegroom; similarly John, important as his work in preparing the way has been, must give way to Jesus, and to do so is no pain but joy to him. It is possible however that though this interpretation is true it is not complete. John can hardly have been unaware that in the Old Testament Israel is occasionally regarded as the bride of God (e.g. Isa. 62.4f.; Jer. 2.2; 3.20; Ezek. 16.8; 23.4; Hos. 2.21); in the New Testament the church is the bride of Christ (2 Cor. 11.2; Eph. 5.25–7,31f.; Rev. 21.2; 22.17). The Baptist

is made to indicate that not he but Christ is the head of the New Israel. John may have drawn his metaphor from the synoptic tradition; see Mark 2.19f. and parallels (where however it may well be that nothing more than metaphor is intended). If καθαρισμός in v. 25 is a cross-reference to the miracle at Cana (2.1–11) the marriage metaphor in this verse may be another. It goes too far, however, to see here an allusion to the priestly Messiah, notwithstanding Isa. 61.10 (Targum: . . . he hath covered me with the robe of righteousness, as a bridegroom who is happy in his bridechamber, and as the high priest (כהנא רבא) that is adorned with his garments . . . (Stenning); cf. 1Q Is^a). The main point is still the comparison between Jesus and John.

ὁ ἔχων τὴν νύμφην, as Jesus by his teaching and baptizing is assembling his church.

ὁ δὲ φίλος τοῦ νυμφίου. The expression is not a technical term in Greek, but corresponds to the Hebrew (שׁוֹשׁבִין (shosh^e bin). Cf. Sanhedrin 3.5: A friend or an enemy (is disqualified from acting as witness or judge). By friend is meant a man's groomsman (אוהב זה שׁושׁבינו). . . . For the custom see Abrahams, Studies II, 213. The shosh^e bin was the friend who acted as agent for the bridegroom. It appears that in Judaea it was customary (S.B. 1, 45f., cf. 502) to have two groomsmen, one representing each family; cf. 1 Macc. 9.39, ὁ νυμφίος ἐξῆλθεν καὶ οἱ φίλοι αὐτοῦ. The saying in this verse either envisages a different custom (possibly Galilean), or, more probably, is an adaptation of custom to conform to the situation in which only John and Jesus are involved.

ὁ ἑστηκὼς καὶ ἀκούων αὐτοῦ. John often uses ἱστάναι where it is not strictly necessary; see on 1.35 and cf. 6.22; 12.29. Here however it may not be redundant. If ἀκούειν means (as often in the New Testament, perhaps in dependence on the Hebrew שׁמע) 'to hear obediently', 'to obey', ἑστηκὼς will describe the attitude of a servant; cf. e.g. 1 Kings 17.1, Before whom I stand; if however ἀκούειν means 'to hear the joyful shout of the bridegroom', or 'to hear the bridegroom in converse with the bride', as the next clause suggests, ἑστηκὼς will describe the attitude of one waiting for an expected sound.

χαρᾷ χαίρει is unusual but not impossible Greek. It resembles the use in Hebrew of the infinitive absolute to emphasize the verb, and some of the attempts made in the LXX to represent this usage; but since Semitic influence is to be seen 'only in the extension of such expressions in the New Testament' (M. II, 444), and since the construction occurs nowhere else in John, it cannot be regarded here as a mark of translation. Imitation of the LXX is a more likely cause. For joy at marriage feasts see S.B. 1, 504–17.

αὕτη οὖν ἡ χαρὰ ἡ ἐμὴ πεπλήρωται. The use of πληροῦν with joy is characteristic of John: 15.11; 16.24; 17.13; cf. 1 John 1.4; 2 John 12. The supersession of his ministry by that of Jesus completes John's joy, because it means that his task is complete.

30. Behind this verse may lie the synoptic comparison of John with him that is least in the kingdom of God (Matt. 11.11; Luke 7.28). The verse means only what it says; it is absurd to find astrological significance (a rising and a declining star) in it, though the words are used in this connection, and it may add something to the imagery.

δεῖ. Cf. the δεῖ of v. 14. This also is the will of God.

Vv. 29f. may, if certain transpositions are made, be set out in two triplets, each consisting of 'two antithetic lines followed by a concluding climactic line', as follows (Black, 147):

He that hath the bride (kall*e*tha) is the bridegroom:
He that standeth and heareth him (is) the friend of the bridegroom.
(And) rejoiceth greatly because of the voice (qala) of the bridegroom.
      He must increase
      But I must decrease (q*e*lal);
This my joy therefore is fulfilled (k*e*lal).

The words in brackets are Aramaic equivalents. 'The word-play ... is maintained throughout the simile and supports the proposed reconstruction of the last three lines' (Black, ibid.). It is however only in the second triplet that the parallelism is convincing, and here it will be noted that emendation of the text is necessary. V. 30 as it stands is at least as Greek as Semitic; cf. e.g. ... ἤδη ὥρα ἀπιέναι, ἐμοὶ μὲν ἀποθανουμένῳ, ὑμῖν δὲ βιωσομένοις (Plato, *Apology* 42a). The word-play detected by Dr Black is striking, but it must be remembered that φωνή and πληροῦν (with joy) are characteristic of John's Greek, and that the simile could not be used at all without the word νύμφη. It is possible then that the word-play is fortuitous.

31. This verse carries on the thought of vv. 22–30—Jesus and John are now contrasted as 'He that is from above' and 'He that is of the earth'; but it also looks back to the Nicodemus dialogue (vv. 1–21). The main theme of that dialogue was the new birth from above (ἄνωθεν) by which alone man can enter the new world of the kingdom of God. From this point the discourse moves towards the person of Jesus, the means of judgement and salvation, the Son of man who descends from and ascends to heaven. At this point the Baptist intervenes to indicate the relation between Jesus and himself, and, *a fortiori*, the relation between Jesus and all humanity outside the kingdom of God. Now John returns to the main theme with his customary confidence that Jesus himself *is* the Gospel. There is a birth ἄνωθεν because Jesus is ὁ ἄνωθεν ἐρχόμενος. Schnackenburg is not wrong in the view that v. 31 continues the thought of 3.12, but it does so with greater force and clarity when vv. 13–17, 27–30, are allowed to intervene.

ὁ ἄνωθεν ἐρχόμενος. Cf. the synoptic phrase ὁ ἐρχόμενος (Matt. 11.3; 21.9; 23.39 (cf. 3.11); Mark 11.9; Luke 7.19f.; 13.35; 19.38); and, in John, 1.15, 27; 11.27; 12.13 (cf. 6.14). The messianic phrase is here brought by John into relation with his theme. There can be no question here that the meaning of ἄνωθεν is 'from above'; cf. the parallel in this verse, ἐκ τοῦ οὐρανοῦ. Jesus as the Son of man (cf. v. 13) is ἐπάνω πάντων, the supreme ruler of the human race.

ὁ ὢν ἐκ τῆς γῆς. There is only one who comes from above (cf. v. 13), but this contrasting designation. has not the same uniqueness of reference. The primary application is doubtless to John, who, unlike Jesus, can baptize only with water, not Spirit; but man as such is ἐκ τῆς γῆς; he is γεγεννημένον ἐκ τῆς σαρκός, and is σάρξ (v. 6). Cf. 1 Cor. 15.47, ὁ πρῶτος ἄνθρωπος ἐκ γῆς χοϊκός, and the passage to which both Paul and John allude, Gen. 2.7, καὶ ἔπλασεν ὁ θεὸς τὸν ἄνθρωπον χοῦν ἀπὸ τῆς γῆς. Unlike κόσμος, γῆ implies no opposition to God; it signifies creation over against the Creator.

ἐκ τῆς γῆς ἐστίν. Unless this statement is purely tautologous, which is un-likely, it means: 'He that is earthy in origin is earthy also by nature.' For Black's suggestion see below; but Schnackenberg rightly draws attention to the two meanings of ἐκ, describing origin and kind.

ἐκ τῆς γῆς λαλεῖ. Cf. v. 12, εἰ τὰ ἐπίγεια εἶπον ὑμῖν. John in particular has spoken in terms of acts restricted to this world: he could summon men to repentance and wash their bodies, but so far as he spoke of the Spirit it could be only by way of promise to be fulfilled by another. He could not offer rebirth from the Spirit, eternal life.

31b, 32. The text from ἐπάνω to τοῦτο is in doubt. ἐπάνω πάντων ἐστίν om. P⁷⁵ ℵ* D λ 565 it cur Origen, Eusebius, Tertullian. τοῦτο om. ℵ D λ 565 it cur pesh hl Origen, Eusebius, Tertullian. The effect of these omissions (which, for practical purposes, may be taken as one variant) is to combine the two verses so that we must translate: 'He who comes from heaven testifies that which he has seen and heard.' The short reading has very good early attesta-tion and may well be correct. It is rightly remarked that v. 31c merely re-peats v. 31a: but this is in fact perhaps the strongest argument in favour of the longer reading. John's style is marked by repetition (see on 1.2), and the repetitiousness which here offends the modern reader may have already offended the ancient copyist, and perhaps especially the ancient translator. The variant makes no substantial difference to the sense of the passage as a whole. If τοῦτο be read it is an example of *casus pendens*: Introduction p. 10.

ὃ ἑώρακεν καὶ ἤκουσεν. It does not seem possible to distinguish between the perfect and the aorist. For an attempt to do so see B.D., §342, where it is argued that the difference of tense shows that greater stress is laid on the seeing; contrast 1 John 1.1,3, where equal stress is laid on seeing and hearing. The subject of both verbs is, of course, Christ. The object corresponds to the ἐπουράνια of v. 12, the subject is he who descended and ascended (3.13ff.). Cf. also 3.11, ὃ ἑωράκαμεν μαρτυροῦμεν.

τὴν μαρτυρίαν αὐτοῦ οὐδεὶς λαμβάνει. Cf. v. 11, τὴν μαρτυρίαν ἡμῶν οὐ λαμβάνετε. The whole of this verse is a generalization of what was said in the Nicodemus dialogue; see also the initial statements of the same theme in the Prologue, 1.5,10f. This gospel brings out most clearly the rejection of Jesus by Judaism; for the predestinarian ideas involved, which run through the chapter as a whole, see on 3.20f.

For traces of an Aramaic original in vv. 31f. see Black, 147ff. Black, arguing that v. 31b, ὁ ὢν ἐκ τῆς γῆς ἐκ τῆς γῆς ἐστίν, is tautologous and meaningless, conjectures that the second ἐκ τῆς γῆς is due to a misreading of an original Aramaic. What was translated was מן ארעא (*min 'ar'a*); but for this there should be restored מלארעיה מן לארעיה (מלארעיה), *min le'ar'ayeh* (*mille'ar'ayeh*), with the meaning 'inferior to him'. We now obtain the following poetical form:

      ᵃ   ᵇ
He that is of the earth is inferior to Him,
  (He that is from beneath is beneath Him)

          ᶜ
And speaketh of the earth

      ᵃ   ᵇ
He that cometh from above (*mille'el*) is above all ('*ilawe kulla*),

And what he hath seen and heard that he testifieth;
And (But) no man receiveth his testimony.

It will however be noted here that it is possible (see above) without emendation to find an intelligible meaning in ὁ ὢν ἐκ τῆς γῆς ἐκ τῆς γῆς ἐστίν, and that the word-play noted between *mill^e'el* (from above) and *'ilawe* (above) exists already in the Greek (ἄ ν ω θεν, ἐπ ά ν ω).

33. ὁ λαβὼν αὐτοῦ τὴν μαρτυρίαν. The negative (οὐδείς) of the preceding verse is not without exception; cf. 1.11ff. (οὐ παρέλαβον. ὅσοι δὲ ἔλαβον . . .). To receive the testimony of Jesus is to believe what he says.

ἐσφράγισεν. The man who does so believe has given his attestation to the truth of what Jesus says. σφραγίζειν is used again at 6.27 (these two places only in John); there God seals, that is to say accredits, Jesus as his trustworthy messenger; here man gives his assent to the same fact. L.S. quote no strictly parallel usage of σφραγίζειν in Greek, but cf. the use of חתם 'to sign, subscribe (as witness, judge etc.)' (Jastrow *s.v.*).

ὅτι ὁ θεὸς ἀληθής ἐστιν. One might have expected, 'that Jesus is true'. But Jesus is not his own messenger; to reject him is to make God a liar (1 John 5.10; John 12.44–50 and the notes), and conversely to receive his testimony is to recognize that in him God is fulfilling his purposes (see on ἀλήθεια, 1.14; on ἀληθής, 1.9). For Black's suggestion see below.

34. ὃν γὰρ ἀπέστειλεν ὁ θεὸς τὰ ῥήματα τοῦ θεοῦ λαλεῖ. The γάρ is to be noted: to accept the testimony of Christ means to attest the truth of God *because* Jesus as God's accredited envoy speaks the words of God. On ἀποστέλλειν see on 20.21. Jesus comes not in his own name but God's, not with his own words but with God's. This theme is constantly repeated in the gospel; see e.g. 5.19. Thus we have in v. 33 '. . . that God (not the testimony) is true' (Bultmann).

οὐ γὰρ ἐκ μέτρου δίδωσι τὸ πνεῦμα. The text is in some doubt. A subject for δίδωσι is supplied as follows:

ὁ θεός, D Θ ω a vg pesh hl sah boh Origen.

ὁ πατήρ, cur.

θεὸς ὁ πατήρ, sin.

τὸ πνεῦμα is omitted by B* sin.

The addition of God as subject to the verb is probably correct interpretation; cf. v. 35. To take either Jesus (understood) or τὸ πνεῦμα as the subject is to import alien ideas into the passage. It is however not impossible that the addition of τὸ πνεῦμα, though very widespread, is also interpretation. On this point certainty cannot be attained, but the general sense of the passage remains clear: it is because God gives (the Spirit) to Jesus in no measured degree but completely that Jesus speaks the words of God.

ἐκ μέτρου is not a Greek expression; μετρίως or μέτρῳ or κατὰ μέτρον would have been better. In rabbinic Hebrew במדה and שלא במדה (by measure, and not by measure) are a common contrasting pair (see S.B. II, 431), but they cannot account for John's ἐκ. The saying of R. Aha (*Lev. R.* 15.2), Even the Holy Spirit, who rests on the prophets, rests on them only by weight (or measure—במשקל); one of them prophesied one book, another two, is not strictly relevant. Ecclus. 1.10 (of Wisdom) in closer, though not in wording. The Spirit abides (μένει) upon Jesus (1.32, where also the statement connecting Jesus and the Spirit is put into the mouth of John the Baptist).

Black (148f.) restores connection between vv. 33 and 34 by a conjecture. ἀληθής (v. 33) presumably renders שרירא (shᵉrira); but this may have been a misreading of שדריה (shaddᵉreh), which means 'sent him'. If this emendation is made we have the following lines, ending with a climactic line:

> He that hath received his testimony
> Hath set to his seal that God *sent him*;
> For he whom God *hath sent*
> Speaketh the words of God:
> For God giveth not the Spirit by measure.

Alternatively the last line may be transferred to the end of v. 35:

> The Father loveth the Son,
> And hath given all things into his hand,
> For God giveth not the Spirit by measure.

These suggestions are attractive but not compelling, for, as was noted above, there already exists a sufficient connection between vv. 33 and 34.

35. ὁ πατὴρ ἀγαπᾷ τὸν υἱόν. The relation between the Father who sends, and the Son who, vested with the Father's authority, obeys, is one of love; for this relation see among other passages 10.17; 15.9; 17.23f.,26; on John's use of ἀγαπᾶν, ἀγάπη see on 3.16.

πάντα δέδωκεν ἐν τῇ χειρὶ αὐτοῦ. See on 5.19–47. Jesus has complete authority to act in the Father's name. For the expression cf. 13.3, where the εἰς is more natural in Greek; but it is hardly possible to distinguish between these prepositions in Hellenistic Greek; see B.D., §218—there is no need to suppose that John was influenced by the Hebrew נתן ביד. If this idiom is relevant εἰς and ἐν must be regarded as alternative renderings of the Hebrew preposition; Sanders' translation (. . . has given all things by his means, literally, by his hand) is not justified.

36. ὁ πιστεύων εἰς τὸν υἱὸν ἔχει ζωὴν αἰώνιον. This is the climax of the chapter, and a final indication that it is right to read it in the order in which it stands in the MSS. Because of the truth stated in v. 35 the hearer of Jesus encounters the absolute possibilities of faith (which leads to eternal life—unlike Paul, John does not mention righteousness as a middle term) and unbelief; hence the theme of judgement in 3.18,19ff.

ὁ δὲ ἀπειθῶν. ἀπειθεῖν means properly 'to be disobedient'; but John (who uses it here only) seems to use it in the sense 'not to believe'; see the parallel expression in v. 18, ὁ μὴ πιστεύων.

οὐκ ὄψεται ζωήν. 'Life' for 'eternal life'; 'see' as at v. 3.

ἡ ὀργὴ τοῦ θεοῦ μένει ἐπ' αὐτόν. Cf. 9.41. The wrath of God is mentioned here only in John. Elsewhere in the New Testament it is primarily an eschatological conception. John uses with it a present tense (cf. Rom. 1.18), as he does with ζωὴ αἰώνιος; cf. also v. 18, ἤδη κέκριται, where the meaning is substantially the same. Judgement is pronounced upon men in terms of, and through, their relation to Jesus, and when that relation has been established (ὁ πιστεύων—ὁ ἀπειθῶν) the judgement abides, either for eternal life, or for wrath. Cf. 5.24–9; a future judgement is not excluded by the fact that its decision—and in part its effects—are already realized. 1QS 4.12 (לשחת עולמים באף עברת אל) contains a partial verbal parallel, but the idea of

God's wrathful vengeance is too common in apocalyptic to constitute ground for direct contact between John and Qumran.

8. THE SAMARITAN WOMAN

4.1–42

This section is linked with the preceding sections in two ways: (*a*) by their common theme that in Jesus Judaism and the Old Testament find their fulfilment (though in the present section Jesus crosses the boundaries of orthodox Judaism); (*b*) by the use of the term 'water'. In 2.6 water is an agent of ritual cleansing; in 3.5 also it is a material element in a religious rite. In each case it is transcended, in the first by being transformed, in the second by the association with it of Spirit. In the new chapter Jesus gives 'living water' (cf. 7.39—a reference to the Holy Spirit is intended) for men to drink. Several themes, however, are compounded in this section, and it will be well at first to consider separately vv. 1–30, 39–42, which deal directly with the Samaritans, and vv. 31–8, an interlude in which Jesus converses with his disciples.

The greater part of the Samaritan story consists of a dialogue between Jesus and a Samaritan woman—itself, as John means to emphasize, an unusual conversation, since it is between man and woman, Jew and Samaritan. Jesus' request for a drink serves to bring out a double contrast and parallelism, first between the 'living' (flowing) water of the spring and the living water which is given by Jesus and is so called because it confers eternal life, and second between Jesus and Jacob as givers of water. The woman does not know, as readers of the gospel do (and the irony of the situation is characteristic of John), that Jesus is greater than Jacob because he gives water better by far. A disclosure of the woman's past life (which may or may not have allegorical significance—see on v. 18) reveals to her that Jesus is a prophet, and she properly raises one of the outstanding questions between Jews and Samaritans, that of the rival merits of Jerusalem and Mount Gerizim. The theme of 2.13–22 (see pp. 194–7) is thus reopened in a wider context; Jesus brings the fulfilment of all the Old Testament offered by way of worship. This he can do because God is Spirit and he, Jesus, brings the Spirit ('living water'), and so supplies the necessary medium and vehicle of worship. The woman recognizes the significance of the subjects that have been raised; only the Messiah can give full information upon them. Upon this, Jesus declares that he is the Messiah. The woman, half convinced, goes into the city; relying on her report, some believe, and the population of the city in general comes out to see Jesus; now on this first-hand acquaintance they confess that he is not the Messiah of Jews or Samaritans only but the Saviour of the world.

In the intervening section, vv. 31–8, the thought moves from the metaphor of food to that of harvest. Jesus has no need of the supplies brought by the disciples because to do the will of God is his food. Nor is there need to wait for harvest; even as he sows the seed the crop springs up, and the time is ripe for the disciples to enter upon their work as harvesters.

There is no parallel to the Samaritan incident in the Synoptic Gospels, though Luke's special interest in Samaritans and women (as in other despised classes) may be compared. It does not seem possible to isolate a pre-Johannine nucleus of the story, which is carefully written as a whole, and, further, is written from the standpoint of one who looks back on the gospel story from a later time. It is probably correct to say (Cullmann, *V. & A.*, 234) that the woman is a traditional figure, but is treated by John symbolically—better, perhaps, representatively. Dodd (*Tradition*, 325ff.) finds in vv. 31–4 a traditional dialogue akin in form to e.g. Mark 3.31–5 (where family relationships are sublimated) and to Matt. 4.1–4 = Luke 4.1–4 (where again there is sublimation but this time, as in John, of food). In vv. 35–8 Dodd (*Tradition*, 391–405) finds a sequence of traditional sayings whose original setting was the Mission charge and whose theme was realized eschatology. In substance the sayings addressed to the disciples recall Matt. 9.37f., and all the parables of seed and harvest (see especially Mark 4.3–9,26–9,30–2). The key to the whole section is perhaps to be found here. The Synoptic Gospels point forward to a near and great harvest, which, however near, remains always a future event; the kingdom of God though present during the ministry of Jesus is present only in germinal form. But for John the four-month interval between seed-time and harvest disappears. Nothing is said of the kingdom of God; but 'the hour cometh and now is' when men may be united in the Spirit to God who is Spirit; hence also the offer of living water can be made.

The process of modification which the synoptic material has undergone at John's hands must not be over-simplified. He is not simply writing of the time in which he lives and thereby introducing foolish anachronisms into his gospel, nor is he removing the futuristic eschatology from the gospel tradition. It is rather the 'realized eschatology' which he reinterprets. He no longer speaks of the kingdom of God as seed in the ground but, in language coloured by Hellenistic vocabulary, he re-expresses the gift with which Jesus challenged his contemporaries: it is living water, eternal life, and worship in the Spirit.

For the form of the section, in which the main narrative is split into two and made to enclose a second block of material, cf. several Marcan sections, e.g. Mark 3.20–35; 5.21–43; 11.12–25. For an interpretation in terms of structural analysis see B. Olsson, *Structure and Meaning in the Fourth Gospel*, 1974. For the connection between John and the Samaritans see Introduction, p. 138, and detailed notes below. For a short but sensitive exposition of the incident as a whole see Bornkamm II, 235f.; it will be referred to below.

1. ὁ κύριος. This is the reading of P⁶⁶ P⁷⁵ B ω sin sah and a few Old Latin MSS.; א D Θ λ it vg cur pesh hl boh read [ὁ] Ἰησοῦς. The latter reading is certainly ancient and is perhaps to be preferred, since in view of the recurrence of Ἰησοῦς in the same verse it would be natural to choose a different name. On the other hand κύριος is rare in narrative in John, and might perhaps for that reason have been altered to Ἰησοῦς. A further possibility suggested by the equal division of the witnesses is that no substantive stood in the original text (as in one MS., 047), and that both ὁ κύριος and ὁ Ἰησοῦς are conjectural supplements. As v. 3 shows, there is in any case no doubt that Jesus is intended as the subject of the verb. Cf. 3.30.

According to this verse, while John was still at work, Jesus was engaged upon his ministry, and his disciples were baptizing. The latter, but not the former, of these statements is contradicted by Mark 1.14,16–20. Mark leaves room for a Judaean ministry of Jesus before his appearance in Galilee, but places the call of the first disciples after John's arrest.

οἱ Φαρισαῖοι. See on 1.24.

2. καίτοι γε is *hap. leg.* in the New Testament (but cf. the *textus receptus* of Acts 14.17); the clause, which interrupts the sequence of vv. 1 and 3, may be an insertion by an editor who was anxious to distinguish between Jesus and John; so Jeremias, *Theology* 1,45, also Dodd, *Tradition*, 237,285f., who argues that it cannot have been written by the evangelist who wrote 3.22. No other gospel states that Jesus or his disciples baptized during his ministry, but it is not impossible that they did so, especially if the mission of Jesus was (as the synoptics also suggest) closely connected in its origin with that of John. On the possible connection between this baptizing and the later practice of Christian baptism see W. F. Flemington, *The New Testament Doctrine of Baptism* (1948), 30f., especially 'If... baptism were practised with the approval of Jesus, it becomes easier to explain why, immediately after Pentecost, baptism took its place as the normal rite of entry into the Christian community' (31). It should however be added that baptism practised during the ministry (even if historical) cannot be regarded as a sufficient explanation of the later rite.

3. ἀφῆκεν, Jesus *left* Judaea. Only at 20.23 does John use ἀφιέναι with the meaning 'to forgive'.
πάλιν. Cf. 2.1–12.

4. Ἔδει δὲ αὐτὸν διέρχεσθαι διὰ τῆς Σαμαρείας. John's statement is confirmed by Josephus: *Ant.* xx, 118: It was the custom of the Galileans (ἔθος ἦν τοῖς Γαλιλαίοις), when going, at festivals, to the holy city, to journey through the land of the Samaritans (cf. *Bel.* ii, 232—the same passages well illustrate the unpopularity of the Jews with the Samaritans); *Vita*, 269: Samaria was now under Roman rule and, for rapid travel, it was essential (ἔδει) to take that route (*sc.* through Samaria), by which Jerusalem may be reached in three days from Galilee. John's ἔδει probably conveys no more theological significance than Josephus'; he may however intend to suggest also that God willed that Jesus should take this route in order that he might meet the Samaritan woman (cf. Cullmann, *Heil*, 255).

τῆς Σαμαρείας. The name was applied by Omri to his new capital (1 Kings 16.24). The Hebrew is שֹׁמְרוֹן, Shomᵉron; the LXX at this verse transliterate (Σεμερών, Σαεμηρών, B; Σομηρών, A); but in 16.28 the usual form, Σαμάρια,

Σαμάρεια, followed in the New Testament, is adopted. The name was transferred to the district in which the city was situated, and used of the Northern Kingdom (e.g. Ezek. 16.46). Samaria was captured by the Assyrians in 721 B.C. (2 Kings 17.6; 18.10), the Israelites were deported and their place filled by foreigners (2 Kings 17.24ff.), who nevertheless preserved to some extent the religion of the previous occupants of the land, not a few of whom were doubtless left behind. It is clear that at some date after the exile a decisive break occurred between the returning Jews and the inhabitants of middle Palestine, but the details are far from clear; there are divergent accounts of the 'Samaritan Schism' in Neh. 13 and Josephus, *Ant.* XI, 297–347. It is certain, however, that in the first century, as at the present time, there was a distinct religious group whose centre was Mount Gerizim. In the time of Jesus Samaria had no independent political existence, being united with Judaea under one Roman procurator.

5. εἰς πόλιν τῆς Σαμαρείας λεγομένην Σύχαρ. This town is commonly, though not certainly, identified with the modern Askar, which lies close to the site identified by continuous tradition with the 'Jacob's Well' of antiquity. Sychar is not mentioned in the Old Testament, but a *Suchar* or *Sichar* is referred to in the Talmud. Askar is very close to Shechem, and stands on the road that runs through Samaria from Jerusalem to Galilee. Schnackenburg and Lindars accept this identification, but Brown rejects it, in this following W. F. Albright, who adopted the reading (Sychem) of sin (alone); so also Davies, *Land*, 298.

τοῦ χωρίου ὃ ἔδωκεν Ἰακὼβ τῷ Ἰωσήφ. The reference is apparently to Gen. 48.22 (cf. Gen. 33.19, and Josh. 24.32): I have given to thee one portion above thy brethren. The Hebrew for portion is שכם, literally 'shoulder', but also the proper noun Shechem. It seems that John (like the LXX who transliterate, σίκιμα) understood שכם as a piece of land given to Joseph. This is consistent with the identification of Sychar with Askar.

6. πηγὴ τοῦ Ἰακώβ. See above on Sychar. The absence of article with πηγή has been held to be Semitic; it is, however, correct Greek to omit the article with place names, and 'Jacob's Well' may have been so understood. McNamara (*T. & T.*, 145f.) finds targumic traditions behind this incident and location.

κεκοπιακώς. In the New Testament κοπιᾶν generally means 'to labour' (as at v. 38), but the meaning found here ('to grow weary'), is, from the time of Aristophanes, the more common in non-biblical Greek. To Käsemann (*Testament*) such notices of the humanity of Jesus seem artificial and forced. So perhaps they are; this underlines the fact that the evangelist intended to emphasise Jesus' humanity, however unskilfully.

οὕτως: either 'in this tired condition', or, more probably, 'at once', 'without more ado'. See L.S. *s.v.* IV; cf. Sophocles, *Philoctetes* 1067, ἀλλ' οὕτως ἄπει (Bauer, 67). See also Field, 87f.

ὥρα ἦν ὡς ἕκτη. The same words occur at 19.14; cf. also 1.39; 4.52. It is impossible to settle with complete certainty the method of enumerating the hours employed by John. If, as is probable, by the sixth hour he meant noon, the tiredness and thirst of Jesus are readily understandable.

7. ἔρχεται γυνὴ ἐκ τῆς Σαμαρείας. ἐκ τ. Σ. is to be taken adjectively with γυνή, not adverbially with ἔρχεται; i.e. the woman is a native of the district of

Samaria (cf. 11.1, Λάζαρος ἀπὸ Βηθανίας); she does not come out of the city of Samaria, which lay some miles to the north-west of Sychar-Schechem.

8. This stage direction removes the disciples till v. 27. Some see in it an insertion by the evangelist, who thus combined a traditional story about a Samaritan woman with the traditional sayings of vv. 31–8. In any case the story is neatly contrived dramatically. Jesus opens the conversation with his request for water; John as in all his narratives makes it clear that the initiative lies with Jesus.

9. 'Ιουδαῖος ὤν. It appears that (unless this verse is to be attributed to a redactor) John did not use 'Ιουδαῖος to mean 'Judaean'; see on 1.19. As Bornkamm (loc. cit.) observes, the Samaritans call Jesus a Jew, just as the Jews call him a Samaritan (8.48); in this world he is never anything but a stranger.

γυναικὸς Σαμαρίτιδος. On conversation with women see on v. 27; on the relation between Jews and Samaritans see the next note.

οὐ γὰρ συνχρῶνται 'Ιουδαῖοι Σαμαρίταις. These words are omitted by ℵ* D a b e, and it is possible that they are an explanatory addition to the original text; cf. 5.4, where, however, the evidence for omission is much stronger. The sentence if genuine is in any case to be regarded as a gloss; it is not part of the woman's speech. For the meaning of the sentence see Daube, N.T.R.J., 373–82, an article which corrects all previous interpretations. συνχρᾶσθαι does not mean 'to have dealings with'; for such a sense there is no evidence whatever. The passage from Diogenes of Oenoanda referred to by Sanders is fully discussed by Daube and shown to be no exception. The word should rather be rendered according to its etymology, 'to use together with'. If this rendering be adopted the passage is seen to reflect a regulation of A.D. 65 or 66, when it was laid down that, from the point of view of the laws of purity, 'the daughters of the Samaritans are menstruants from their cradle' (Niddah 4.1). One could never be certain that a Samaritan woman was not in a state of uncleanness, and therefore the only safe practice was to assume that she was. This uncleanness would necessarily be conveyed to the vessel she held, especially if she had drunk from it (Kelim passim). Accordingly the principle is reached (and stated in the text), 'the Jews do not use [sc. vessels] together with Samaritans'—a principle which Jesus manifestly ignores. The question of the authenticity and historicity of the saying is difficult. It seems on the whole more probable that John himself should have known and written down the regulation than that it should have been known and added by a later Christian editor; but the regulation did not apply to the time of the ministry of Jesus, and it is difficult to save the historicity of John's note on the ground that some of the strictest Shammaites among the Pharisees may have kept the regulation forty years before it was generally enacted, since John says explicitly that Jews do not use vessels with Samaritans. On the whole it is best to suppose that John has added to his material an editorial note applicable to his own day. The gloss is not (as is generally supposed) an explicit statement about general relations between Jews and Samaritans, but it does in fact attest the common attitude of Jews to their neighbours, which was one of suspicion. The Samaritans were (not exactly enemies but) seceders and non-conformists. The ritual cleanness of their women, for example, could not, as we have seen, be assumed; on the other hand, it is laid down (Berakoth

7.1) that if three Jews have eaten together they must say the common grace; if one of the three was a Samaritan, the same obligation holds. Later, and especially after the second Jewish revolt (A.D. 132–5), when the Samaritans stood aloof, feeling hardened and became embittered.

10. The story here takes a fresh turn. Contrast the story (cited by Bultmann) of Ananda who in similar circumstances said to a girl of the Candala caste, who hesitated to draw water for him, 'My sister, I do not ask what your caste or your family is; I am only asking you for water, if you can give it to me'. See also L. Schotroff in Z.N.T.W. 60 (1969), 199–214.

εἰ ᾔδεις. As frequently in John (see on 3.3), the thought turns upon a misunderstanding, here a misunderstanding of the person of Jesus. He is in appearance a thirsty and helpless traveller; in fact he is the Son of God who gives living water. The phrase ἡ δωρεὰ τοῦ θεοῦ is perhaps not a 'technical term' (Odeberg, 150), but at least it has important associations. Within Judaism the 'gift of God' *par excellence* is the Torah; see e.g. *Gen. R.* 6.7 (and several other references in Odeberg, loc cit.); for the significance of this see the note below on 'living water'. In gnostic thought also the gift of God is the life-giving revelation; e.g. *C.H.* IV, 5, ὅσοι δὲ τῆς ἀπὸ τοῦ θεοῦ δωρεᾶς μετέσχον, οὗτοι... ἀθάνατοι ἀντὶ θνητῶν εἰσι.... Such divine gifts are, invisibly, in the hands of Jesus. It is unlikely that the δωρεά should be taken to mean Jesus himself.

ὕδωρ ζῶν, fresh, flowing water; but also water creating and maintaining life. Living water as a metaphor for divine activity in quickening men to life occurs in the Old Testament, e.g. Jer. 2.13: They have forsaken me the fountain of living waters (πηγὴ ὕδατος ζωῆς); Zech. 14.8: It shall come to pass in that day, that living waters (ὕδωρ ζῶν) shall go out from Jerusalem; and cf. Ezekiel's description of the river flowing out of Jerusalem, especially 47.9: Everything shall live (ζήσεται) whithersoever the river cometh. '*Living* water' is a metaphor not commonly used in the rabbinic literature, but the simple metaphor 'water' is frequent (S.B. II, 433–6). Sometimes it stands for the Holy Spirit, more often for Torah. The same uses of the image are found at Qumran. At CD 3.16f.; 6.4–11; 19.34 it refers to Torah—but see especially 6.4, הבאר היא התורה, the well (Num. 21.18) is the Torah; at 1QS 4.20ff. it refers to the Holy Spirit. In CD the water gives life, in 1QS it effects cleansing. As Braun observes, in John the latter theme is wanting. In 1 Enoch (especially 48.1; 49.1) 'water' is Wisdom; for the connection between Wisdom and Torah see on λόγος, 1.1. See further on v. 14. The 'water' metaphor is used by Philo also, though it appears that he does not speak of ὕδωρ ζῶν. He comments on Jer. 2.13 thus: ὁ δὲ θεὸς πλέον τι ἢ ζωή, πηγὴ τοῦ ζῆν, ὡς αὐτὸς εἶπεν, ἀέννασος (*Fug.*, 198). Here God, as the fountain of life, is contrasted with matter, ἡ μὲν γὰρ ὕλη νεκρόν. Philo speaks of the divine Word (θεῖος λόγος) as 'full of the stream of wisdom' (*Som.* II, 245, πλήρη τοῦ σοφίας νάματος). For a similar notion in Hellenistic thought cf. *C.H.* I, 29, ἔσπειρα αὐτοῖς τοὺς τῆς σοφίας λόγους καὶ ἐτράφησαν ἐκ τοῦ ἀμβροσίου ὕδατος; but the metaphor of 'water' is perhaps less common in the West because it is in the waterless spaces of the East that the value of water is most clearly apparent. The image is used in the Odes of Solomon; see 6.8–18; 11.6ff.; 28.15; 30.1–7. Life-giving water appears in several important passages in John: 3.5; 4.10–15; 7.38; 19.34. See the notes on all these verses. The 'water' is pre-eminently the

Holy Spirit, which alone gives life (cf. 6.63). It proceeds from the side of the crucified Jesus; it is the agent of the generation of Christians; and it forms the fountain of life which for ever springs within Christians, maintaining their divine life. John uses the expression no doubt partly because it aptly conveys what he wishes to say, partly because of its twofold, Jewish and Greek, background, and partly because its double meaning conformed to his ironical style; see the next verse.

11. The woman duly misunderstands the word that has been spoken to her, supposing that ὕδωρ ζῶν means running water from the spring.

οὔτε *simpliciter* is rare in the New Testament (only Luke 20.36; James 3.12; 3 John 10; Rev. 9.20 in some MSS.) and elsewhere (see L.S. *s.v.*). It may have been used here in anticipation of an inverted form of the sentence: 'Neither have you a vessel, nor is the well a shallow one.'

φρέαρ may be distinguished from πηγή as an artificially constructed well over against a natural spring, perhaps supplying it; but it is probable that John intended no difference between the words. The use of synonyms is characteristic of his style.

12. The irony (for John and for most of his readers Jesus is of course greater than Jacob) is continued and is characteristically Johannine; cf. 7.42; 8.53. In the latter of these passages the wording is identical, but the 'father' is Abraham. πατήρ, like the Hebrew אב ('ab), is commonly used of ancestors, but its use as a title for one of the patriarchs seems to be rare outside the New Testament.

αὐτὸς ἐξ αὐτοῦ ἔπιεν . . . καὶ τὰ θρέμματα αὐτοῦ. This refers to no known incident; perhaps to local tradition. θρέμματα is *hap. leg.* in biblical Greek; the rendering 'slaves' is not impossible, but 'cattle' is more probable. That Jacob himself drank of the well lends it distinction—even he needed no better water; that his cattle did so indicates the copiousness of the supply, also that Jacob's well provided no more than material water, appropriate only to the animal life of man. See A. Jaubert in *L'Homme devant Dieu* (Mélanges offerts au Père H. de Lubac, 1963), 63–73.

13. τοῦ ὕδατος τούτου. Jesus begins to clear up the misunderstanding (v. 10). He is not speaking of ordinary water, 'this' water, which must be drunk day by day.

14. πίῃ. The aorist subjunctive must be translated. 'Whosoever shall drink . . .', not 'Whosoever drinks . . .'. A single draught of the water of life is contrasted with the necessarily frequent drinking of ordinary water. The variant ὁ δὲ πίνων (א* D), which misses this point, is perhaps due to the influence of Ecclus. 24.21.

οὐ μὴ διψήσει εἰς τὸν αἰῶνα. Cf. the description of the time of salvation in Isa. 49.10, οὐ πεινάσουσιν, οὐδὲ διψήσουσιν, quoted in Rev. 7.16. See also Isa. 44.3 (Dodd, *A.S.*, 90), and Ecclus. 24.21, οἱ ἐσθίοντές με ἔτι πεινάσουσιν, καὶ οἱ πίνοντές με ἔτι διψήσουσιν, where the meaning is that he who has tasted Wisdom will desire ever more Wisdom. Jesus makes an even higher claim than the divine Wisdom (see on λόγος, 1.1). Those who accept him and his gifts are thereafter permanently supplied, and their needs are inwardly met. With only one exception (9.32), αἰών occurs in John only in the phrase εἰς τὸν αἰῶνα. In this phrase, and at 9.32 (ἐκ τοῦ αἰῶνος), it refers always to unlimited time. On αἰώνιος see on 3.15. There is a somewhat remote parallel in *Thomas* 28 (I found them all drunk, I found none among them athirst; cf. *P.Oxy.* 1.14–17; Fitzmyer, *Essays*, 396). See also Bornkamm, loc. cit.: Jesus awakens the woman's conscience by no accusation but by the free offer of the spring of life from God.

γενήσεται ἐν αὐτῷ πηγὴ ὕδατος. On the metaphor of 'living water' see on v. 10. The well, or spring, of water is within man (cf. 7.38, but see the note there). It is possible that a contrast is intended between the old Law, expressed in external ordinances, and a new inward law inaugurated by Jesus. Cf. Jer. 31(38).31–4.

15. The woman continues to misunderstand and a fresh approach is made. Jesus appears as, in Jewish terms, a prophet, in Hellenistic terms, an omniscient θεῖος ἀνήρ. But neither of these is for John an adequate Christological category; see Introduction, p. 74.

18. ἔσχες ... ἔχεις. ἔχειν is sometimes used in this way, without a second accusative (ἄνδρα, γυναῖκα); see L.S. *s.v.* A 1 4; and e.g. 1 Cor. 5.1. 'There is no Greek for *possessed*, the constative aorist, since ἔσχον is almost (if not quite) exclusively used for the ingressive *got, received*. ... There is not one place where ἔσχον *must* be constative: John 4.18 may be rendered "thou hast espoused"' (M. 1, 145). But ἔσχον could be constative; cf. e.g. Herodotus III, 31, ἔσχε ἄλλην ἀδελφεήν.

πέντε ... ἄνδρας. It is possible (*a*) that the woman had had five legal husbands who had died or divorced her, and that she was now living with a man to whom she was not legally married; (*b*) that she was now living with a man who was legally her husband, according to Mosaic law but not according to Christian standards (Mark 10.11f. and parallels). It is to be noted that the Rabbis did not approve of more than three marriages, though any number was legally admissible (S.B. II, 437). It does not seem probable that John's intention is to show that, though both are now transcended, the Samaritans are morally inferior to the Jews. In fact, it is quite possible, and may well be right, to take these words as a simple statement of fact, and an instance of the supernatural knowledge of Jesus (cf. 1.48); this view is supported by v. 29 (πάντα ἃ ἐποίησα). Many commentators however have regarded them as symbolic. This would not be out of accord with John's manner and method. The woman represents Samaria peopled by five foreign tribes each with its god. The one who is 'not a husband' represents either a false god (Simon Magus has been suggested) or the Samaritans' false worship of the true God (v. 22). This interpretation meets with the difficulty that, according to 2 Kings 17.30–2,41, the Samaritans had not five false gods but seven; but since Josephus (*Ant.* IX, 288) reckoned five gods the difficulty is not insuperable. That John was referring to the Samaritans' acceptance of the five books of Torah as alone canonical is improbable since the Samaritans had not abandoned these books and it would be difficult to identify the one who is not a husband. Possibly under the influence of 2 Kings 17, but more probably under that of his own system of thought, Heracleon instead of πέντε read ἕξ, and took the six husbands to signify all material evil (τὴν ὑλικὴν πᾶσαν κακίαν, *apud* Origen, *In Evangelium Joannis*, XIII, 11). The reading is unsupported, and to be regarded rather as an example of Heracleon's exegesis than as a witness to John's text. 'The revelation is for man the disclosure of his own life' (Bultmann). This may be accepted if it refers to the effect of the revelation. In the present conversation Jesus has previously declared God's offer of the gift of the water of life.

19. κύριε. The vocative need mean no more than 'Sir', and has this meaning in vv. 11, 15; in this verse it seems to be on the way to its deeper religious meaning, 'Lord'.

προφήτης. Jesus' knowledge of the past convinces the woman that he is inspired. Or perhaps, although προφήτης is anarthrous, the woman is thinking of 'the prophet' (cf. 1.21), giving a messianic interpretation to Deut. 18.15. In view of v. 25 this is not likely, unless John is alluding to the fact that the Samaritans gave a messianic interpretation to Deut. 18.15 and saw their Messiah (Taheb) as a prophet. See p. 138; it does not however seem probable that John could assume much knowledge of Samaritan theology on the part of his readers. To suppose that in the following verses the woman is raising a knotty problem in theology with a view to avoiding an embarrassing discussion of her marriages is to psychologize the story in a way John did not intend.

20. ἐν τῷ ὄρει τούτῳ προσεκύνησαν. The transition to the theme of worship is perhaps less sudden if in the 'five husbands' there is a veiled reference to the idolatry of the Samaritans, but this does not suffice to prove the allegorical interpretation of the husbands. The Samaritans took the Deuteronomic law of one sanctuary to apply not to Jerusalem but to Mount Gerizim, in whose interest they also read other Old Testament passages. They continued to use this mountain in northern Palestine for their rites even after the destruction of their temple by Hyrcanus (c. 128 B.C.; Josephus, Ant. XIII, 255f.).

ὁ τόπος. The Temple; cf. 11.48.

21. πίστευέ μοι. The phrase is without parallel in John (but cf. 14.11). On πιστεύειν with the dative see on 1.12; 2.22; the word has here no special significance but is simply an asseverative. It serves as an alternative to the frequent ἀμὴν ἀμὴν λέγω ὑμῖν, the meaning of which is thereby fixed. It has been pointed out (e.g. J. & Q., 134) that John, the Odes of Solomon (6; 12.4; 20.1–4), and the Qumran writings (1QS 9.3–5) are all critical of the sacrificial worship of the Temple; they are all, however, critical on different grounds.

γύναι, vocative, as at 2.4; 19.26. In itself it is of neutral colour, 'Madam' rather than 'Woman'.

ἔρχεται ὥρα. ὥρα is used with the present tense of ἔρχομαι at 4.21; 5.28; 16.2,25 (cf. 16.4). In each of these passages the reference is to a time in the future, in the time beyond the crucifixion and resurrection; here, for example, it is said that true worship will become possible within the church (cf. 2.13–22). For a different and more complicated use of ὥρα with a verb of coming see v. 23.

προσκυνήσετε τῷ πατρί. In view of the ὑμεῖς of the next verse this second person plural must be taken seriously: You Samaritans who are about to believe (vv. 39, 41) will worship; but John no doubt thinks also of his readers, the Christians of his day. προσκυνεῖν, used absolutely in v. 20, here takes the dative, as it does in v. 23 and 9.38. In vv. 22, 23, 24 it is used with the accusative. John intends no difference in meaning; this is clearly proved by

v. 23 (προσκυνήσουσιν τῷ πατρί . . . προσκυνοῦντας αὐτόν); this is probably one of his means of varying his style. See however M. 1, 66 for the contrary opinion. πατήρ is the most characteristic Johannine term for God; so described he is (primarily) the Father of the Son; thus by the use of πατήρ the way is prepared for Jesus to speak of his own unique position₁ (v. 26).

22. ὃ οὐκ οἴδατε. Here, if not already in v. 18, the unsatisfactory religion of the Samaritans is brought to light. Religion without, or apart from the main stream of, revelation, may be instinctive but can be neither intelligent nor saving. Dodd, *Interpretation*, 314, notes that Samaria was traditionally the home of gnostic sects; the Valentinians worshipped the unknowable Βυθός, the Basilidians the Non-Existent. If however there is an allusion to this fact it will imply that the Gnostics, who prided themselves on their knowledge, were ignorant of the true God. 'In Jewry is God known' (Ps. 76.1).

ὅτι ἡ σωτηρία ἐκ τῶν 'Ιουδαίων ἐστίν. On salvation see on 3.17. Notwithstanding 1QH 5.12; 1 Q Isᵃ 51.4f. it seems improbable that σωτηρία should be regarded as a name of the Messiah. The saying does not mean that Jews as such are inevitably saved, but rather that the election of Israel to a true knowledge of God was in order that, at the time appointed by God, salvation might proceed from Israel to the world, and Israel's own unique privilege be thereby dissolved. As the next verse shows, this eschatological salvation is in the person of Jesus in process of realization and the Jews are losing their position to the church.

There is no need to suppose either part of this verse to be a gloss upon the narrative in which the church speaks (as at 3.11), contrasting its true worship with that of Jews and Samaritans alike. In v. 22a the We–You contrast is that which recurs throughout the discourse from v. 9 onwards; in v. 22b there is nothing inconsistent with John's usual attitude to the Jews. It is true that 'his own' rejected Jesus, but John never doubts that it was to them that he came, or that they were his own. The Old Testament scriptures, though not themselves able to confer eternal life, nevertheless testified to Christ (5.39). Cf. Cullmann, *Salvation*, 287; the ἀλλά with which v. 23 begins confirms that v. 22 is not a gloss (Lindars, Schnackenburg).

23. ἔρχεται ὥρα καὶ νῦν ἐστίν. Cf. and contrast v. 21. This curious expression, apparently contradictory, occurs at 4.23; 5.25. At 16.32 is the similar ἔρχεται ὥρα καὶ ἐλήλυθεν; at 12.23; 13.1; 17.1 a simple past tense (ἦλθεν, ἐλήλυθεν) is used alone. These last three, however, refer to the hour of the suffering and glorification of Jesus in its immediate approach; 16.32 similarly refers to the hour in which the disciples are about to desert Jesus and be scattered to their homes. 4.23 and 5.25, in which the simple continuous present is used along with νῦν ἐστίν, seem to stand by themselves. Each refers to events which seem on the surface to belong to a later time—a pure and spiritual worship of the Father, and the resurrection. Indeed John does not mean to deny that they do truly belong to a later time, but he emphasizes by means of his oxymoron that in the ministry, and above all in the person, of Jesus they were proleptically present. True worship takes place in and through him (cf. 2.19–22), just as he is himself the resurrection (11.25). 'Any cultic worship is only true worship if the eschatological event is realised in it' (Bultmann).

ἀληθινοί . . . ἀληθείᾳ. On ἀληθινός see on 1.9, on ἀλήθεια see on 1.14. The 'true' worshippers are those who do in truth worship God, whose worship realizes all that was foreshadowed but not fulfilled in the worship of the Jews at Jerusalem and of the Samaritans on Mount Gerizim, not because a higher level of worship has been reached in the course of man's religious development, in which the material aids of holy places can be dispensed with, but because Jesus is himself the 'truth', the faithful fulfilment of God's purposes and thus the anticipation of the future vision of God. Schnackenburg cites a number of Qumran texts (1 QS 4.20f.; 3.6ff.; 9.3–6; 8.5f.; 1 QH 16.11f.; 17.26; cf. 7.6f.; 12.11f.; 13.18f.; 14.25), and concludes, 'Thus praise of God and a perfect life are made possible by the holy spirit which the speaker believes he has received; but they are also a response to the grace of God'. This however does not seem to be quite what John has in mind.

ἐν πνεύματι in Paul may mean 'in a state of inspiration' (e.g. 1 Cor. 12.3); so also *Didache* 11.7. Similarly in John 11.33; 13.21 the simple dative (τῷ πνεύματι) is used in expressing emotion (with ἐνεβριμήσατο, ἐταράχθη). The only other use of ἐν πν. in John is 1.33, ὁ βαπτίζων ἐν πνεύματι ἁγίῳ, a technical term of early Christian theology. The meaning of ἐν πν. in the present verse must depend upon the force of the word πνεῦμα in the next verse; see the note. The connection here of πνεῦμα and ἀλήθεια recalls that one of the characteristic Johannine titles of the Holy Spirit is τὸ πνεῦμα τῆς ἀληθείας (14.17; 15.26; 16.13).

ὁ πατὴρ τοιούτους ζητεῖ. This clause has perhaps as much claim as 20.30f. to be regarded as expressing the purpose of the gospel. Such worshippers are what God seeks in sending his Son into the world. See below, and 'Theocentric', 374f.

24. πνεῦμα ὁ θεός. John's phrase recalls both pagan philosophic and Jewish religious polemic against anthropomorphic views of God. πνεῦμα itself was a Stoic term (φασὶ ... εἶναι τὸν θεὸν οἱ Στωικοὶ ... πνεῦμα κατ' οὐσίαν, Clem. Alex., *Strom.* v, 14), but similar notions were expressed elsewhere by other words, e.g. νοῦς; all meant that God was not corporeal in the human sense (though the Stoic πνεῦμα was in a sense material; see the context in Clement). This Hellenistic language was taken over into Judaism by Philo (e.g. *Op.* 8, τὸ μὲν δραστήριον (the active Cause in creation) ὁ τῶν ὅλων νοῦς ἐστιν). The rabbinic literature is not on the whole metaphysical, and anthropomorphisms abound in it, but in passages such as *Lev. R.* 4.7f. (other passages are referred to in S.B. II, 437f.) the relation of God to the world is compared with that of the soul to the body. There is little corresponding teaching in the Old Testament (cf. however Isa. 31.3: The Egyptians are men, and not God; and their horses flesh (בשר, *basar*), and not spirit (רוח, *ruah*); significantly this contrast does not appear in the LXX). Spirit in the Old Testament is regularly not an order of being over against matter, but life-giving, creative activity, and there are passages (e.g. 7.38f.) where John uses the word in this sense. Here however a better parallel is 3.8. 'πνεῦμα is invisible, known only through its sound (φωνή) and its effects. The proposition "God is Spirit" means that he is invisible and unknowable (cf. 1.18). The hour for disclosure however has now come, and God is known through his sound, his speech (for the word φωνή cf. 1.23; 5.25,28,37f.; 10.3,4,5,16,27; 11.43; 12.28,30; 18.37). God, then, is πνεῦμα: the invisible God whom no one has ever seen, but who has uttered his voice and sent his word into the world, so that to all who are of the truth the Word may make him known. It is here that the other sense of πνεῦμα makes itself felt, for the Spirit, the Paraclete, brings home to

men the truth revealed in Jesus (14.26; 16.14). God is πνεῦμα, and men must worship him ἐν πνεύματι καὶ ἀληθείᾳ’ ('Theocentric', p. 374, shortened). It is impossible to separate the two notions (note that neither in v. 24 nor in v. 23 is ἐν repeated before ἀληθείᾳ). ἐν πνεύματι draws attention to the supernatural life that Christians enjoy, and ἐν ἀληθείᾳ to the single basis of this super-natural life in Christ through whom God's will is faithfully fulfilled. That true worship is set over against idolatry, and over·against a cult restricted to one sanctuary, is not more than incidental. Ps. 145 (144).18 (τοῖς ἐπικαλου-μένοις αὐτὸν ἐν ἀληθείᾳ (באמת, be'emeth)) is not a true parallel, for there 'in truth' is adverbial. *Thomas* 69a (Blessed are those who have been persecuted in their heart; these are they who have known the Father in truth) is not a close parallel. But cf. Bornkamm, loc. cit.: 'God is Spirit! That means, once and for all: He is there, present, he is waiting for us; indeed he is not only waiting, he has run towards us with open arms, as the father ran to meet the prodigal son.'

25. οἶδα ὅτι Μεσσίας ἔρχεται. The woman is not merely catching at a straw to divert the argument; she grasps the messianic bearing of the reference to worship in Spirit and truth. The Samaritans seem to have expected the advent of a Messiah (see on v. 19), though it does not appear that they used that word. The Coming One was called by them Taheb, He who returns, or, He who restores.

ὁ λεγόμενος χριστός. John as usual translates; see on 1.38,41.

ἀναγγελεῖ. The Messiah is to be a revealer, who will declare all that men desire to know. There is some evidence (S.B. II, 348) for Jewish belief that the Messiah would teach the Gentiles, little that he would teach his own people; teaching is·not a characteristic function of the Messiah. In the Qumran literature we may note CD 6.11, though 'one who teaches right Torah' is an overtranslation of יורה הצדק, nor is it certain that the one who rises up to teach in this way is the Messiah, though he works באחרית הימים, at the end of the days. It is more important that the Samaritans, who, as has been noted, made messianic use of Deut. 18.15,18, appear to have thought of the Taheb as a teacher (but also as a political leader). The *Memar Markah* (third or fourth century A.D.) IV,12 says that he will reveal the truth; see Schnackenburg, also for bibliography; add J. Bowman, *Samaritanische Probleme*, 1967. More important however than these parallels is the fact that John constantly sets Jesus forth as the Revealer—indeed, as himself the truth (14.6).

The word ἀναγγέλλειν, which is apparently accepted by Jesus as a description of his work, frequently renders הגיד in the Old Testament, but has also important cultic associations, especially in Asia Minor (see *T.W.N.T.* I, 61f. (J. Schniewind)). It seems probable that here John is combining Jewish messianic with Hellenistic ideas. The Messiah is the supernatural person who will declare divine truth to men. Cf. 16.13 where the same word is used of the Paraclete. For ἀναγγελεῖ, sin has 'will give'.

26. ἐγώ εἰμι, ὁ λαλῶν σοι. On the special uses of ἐγώ εἰμι in John see on 6.35; 8.24. Here the meaning is simply, 'I (who am speaking to you) am the Christ you speak of'; therefore, I will reveal all things to you. W. Manson's attempt (*J.T.S.* 48 (1947), 141 = *Jesus and the Christian* (1967), 178f.), to make ἐγώ εἰμι mean, 'The Messiah is here', is unconvincing.

27. ἐθαύμαζον ὅτι μετὰ γυναικὸς ἐλάλει. The disciples return to the narrative. Cf. v. 9; it was considered undesirable that a Rabbi should speak with women. *P. Aboth* 1.5: Jose b. Johanan (*c.* 150 B.C.) said: Let thy house be opened wide and let the needy be members of thy household; and talk not much with womankind. They said this of a man's own wife: how much more of his fellow's wife! Hence the Sages have said: He that talks much with womankind brings evil upon himself and neglects the study of the Law and at the last will inherit Gehenna. *Sotah* 3.4: R. Eliezer says: If any man gives his daughter a knowledge of the Law it is as though he taught her lechery (but the contrary opinion is expressed in the same passage by Ben Azzai). For Jesus' contacts with women cf. 7.53—8.11; 11.5; in the Synoptic Gospels especially Luke 7.36–50; 8.2f.; 10.38–42.

οὐδεὶς μέντοι εἶπεν. It is not for disciples to question the actions of their Master.

28. ἀφῆκεν οὖν τὴν ὑδρίαν. ἀφιέναι as at v. 3; ὑδρία as at 2.6f. The woman left the waterpot presumably in order that Jesus might drink—thereby incurring uncleanness (Daube, loc. cit.). He did not regard the levitical regulations as binding. Others take the point to be simply that the woman forgot her pot in her haste to report what had happened; or that she is making a complete break with the past. The last suggestion seems very improbable.

εἰς τὴν πόλιν. Sychar; see v. 5. εἰς ('into') is here used correctly; incorrectly at v. 5.

29. μήτι introduces a hesitant question (M. 1, 170, 193): Can this perhaps be the Christ?

31. ἐν τῷ μεταξύ. The adverbial use of μεταξύ is rare in the New Testament; cf. Acts 13.42. The scene between the disciples and Jesus (vv. 31–8) takes place between the departure of the woman and the arrival of the men of Sychar. Cf. in the folk-tale the 'rule of two', the principle according to which in simple story-telling not more than two actors (or groups of actors) appear in one scene (see B.T.D. Smith, *The Parables of the Synoptic Gospels* (1937), 35f.).

ἠρώτων. ἐρωτᾶν (properly 'to question') is used in its late sense, as a synonym of αἰτεῖν.

32. ἐγὼ βρῶσιν ἔχω φαγεῖν. βρῶσις (etymologically the process of eating) is used synonymously with βρῶμα (food). φαγεῖν is epexegetic. As the woman failed to understand the living water, which is the gift of God, so even the disciples were ignorant of the food by which Jesus lived. The argument moves on (v. 33) by means of their misunderstanding, as often in John (see on 3.3).

34. ἐμὸν βρῶμά ἐστιν ἵνα ποιῶ. 'Doing God's will is my food.' The use of ἵνα and the subjunctive, with no final significance, which has now become regular in Greek, is already common in John.

ἵνα ποιῶ τὸ θέλημα ... καὶ τελειώσω αὐτοῦ τὸ ἔργον. Jesus came to do the will of God (4.34; 5.36; 6.38); his works are the works of God (4.34; 5.36; 9.3f.; 10.25,32,37f.; 14.10; 17.4). Cf. Deut. 8.3, and the use of it in Matt. 4.4 = Luke 4.4; it is possible that John is here dependent on the Q temptation narrative. Jesus does what Israel of old should have done. See also John

6.27,55 where he offers the food of eternal life. The creative will of God, realized in obedience, sustains life.

τοῦ πέμψαντός με. God is often so described in John (4.34; 5.23f.,30,37; 6.38f., 44; 7.16,18,28,33; 8.16,18,26,29; 9.4; 12.44f.,49; 13.20; 14.24; 15.21; 16.5), and the thought of the mission of Jesus from the Father is central (see on 20.21). The ministry of Jesus has no significance apart from the will of the Father; it is not the independent achievement of humanity but the fruit of submission. See especially 5.19–47 and the notes.

35. οὐχ ὑμεῖς λέγετε; ὑμεῖς is emphatic; 'Is it not *your* saying . . .?'

ἔτι τετράμηνός ἐστιν καὶ ὁ θερισμὸς ἔρχεται. The paratactic construction suggests Hebrew (cf. e.g. Jer. 51.33, עוד מעט ובאה; LXX (28.33), ἔτι μικρὸν καὶ ἥξει); but see *P. Paris* 18.14f., ἔτι δύο ἡμέρας ἔχομεν καὶ φθάσομεν εἰς Πηλούσι (quoted M. I, 12). 1 QS 10.7 does not explain the period. It has been suggested that the saying placed on the lips of the disciples was a current rural proverb; but there is no evidence that such a proverb existed. Again, the saying has been used to date the incident in which it occurred—it was four months before harvest time; but this is to read chronology where it was not written. It is best to suppose that the words mean, 'On the common reckoning (ὑμεῖς λέγετε), there is a four month interval (τετράμηνος, *sc.* χρόνος) between sowing and harvest.' This estimate corresponds to the rather scanty data we possess. According to a tradition preserved in *T. Taanith* 1.7 (215) and going back to R. Meir (*c.* A.D. 150), seed-time covered half of the month Tishri, Marcheshwan, and half of Chislev (S.B. II, 440). The firstfruits of harvest were offered at Passover time (on Nisan 16). Reckoning four months back from this date we reach Chislev 16, so that it may be said that between the end of sowing and the beginning of harvest four months intervened. Guilding, 207, reckons back from harvest to Shebat, and thus arrives at Gen. 24; Exod. 1.1—2.25; Josh. 24; Isa. 27.6ff.; Ezek. 20 as lections on which the paragraph was based. All this is very questionable. Dodd (*Tradition*, 394) points out that the clause ἔτι . . . ἔρχεται forms an 'iambic trimeter, with the initial foot resolved into a tribrach'. This is probably accidental.

θεάσασθε τὰς χώρας, ὅτι λευκαί εἰσιν. For the construction, in which τὰς χώρας is attracted out of the ὅτι-clause into the principal sentence, see M. II, 469. It is not stated that the harvest is already reaped: the fields are white; the harvest may immediately begin. Jesus has come to complete (τελειώσω) the work of God, and 'cette œuvre est déjà plus avancée qu'il ne semble' (Loisy, 188). In this crop there will be no interval between sowing and harvest. 'You reckon four months between sowing and harvest; I reckon no interval at all.'

ἤδη. Textual evidence (א D 33 b e sin cur) and Johannine usage (4.51; 7.14; 11.39; 15.3) alike require that ἤδη should be taken with v. 36, not with v. 35. A doubtfully significant mark in P75 may however suggest the opposite.

36. μισθὸν λαμβάνει, receives his wages, rather than, receives a reward. Both meanings ('wages' and 'reward') are attested for μισθός in the New Testament but the former is the primary meaning and is demanded here. The reaper cannot be rewarded for the sower's work. For the metaphor of God's workmen as harvesters cf. *P. Aboth* 2.15, if, with Abrahams (*Studies* I, 100), we read קצר as *qatsir*, not *qatser*: R. Tarfon (*c.* A.D. 130) said: Today is harvest

and the task is great and the labourers are idle and the wage is abundant and the master of the house is urgent.

συνάγει καρπὸν εἰς ζωὴν αἰώνιον. συνάγειν καρπόν is an Old Testament expression —Lev. 25.3. ζωὴ αἰώνιος is not the reaper's wage but that for (εἰς) which the crop is gathered; that is, the crop represents the converts (in the first instance, the Samaritans) to the Christian faith, who will receive eternal life.

ἵνα ὁ σπείρων ὁμοῦ χαίρῃ καὶ ὁ θερίζων. Cf. Amos 9.13. The exegesis of this verse depends in large measure upon the view that is taken of John's manner of writing. If it is parabolic we may paraphrase: The harvest is at hand; the reaper has overtaken the sower. This is the promised age of fulfilment (cf. the Q saying of Matt. 9.37 = Luke 10.2, of which this passage is quite probably an interpretation). If however John is writing allegorically we must seek a precise meaning for the terms ὁ σπείρων, ὁ θερίζων. It does not seem possible to find simple equivalents for them that will yield good sense throughout vv. 36–8 (but see Fenton), and accordingly it is best to accept as the basis of exegesis the parabolic interpretation (which corresponds to v. 35—seed-time and harvest paradoxically coincide), though it is not wrong to see here and there (as in the synoptic parables) fleeting allegorical allusions. Thus in this verse sower and reaper are identical; Jesus himself has sown the seed in conversation with the woman, and the believing Samaritans (v. 39) are his harvest (though, as v. 38 may suggest, the disciples will help him to reap it). The 'joy of harvest' is of course known in all agricultural communities; it appears in the Old Testament (e.g. Deut. 16.13f.), and is also used as an eschatological symbol (e.g. Isa. 9.2; Ps. 126.5f.).

37. ἐν ... τούτῳ may refer to what has gone before (v. 36) or to what follows (v. 38). In similar passages ἐν τούτῳ usually (so 9.30; 13.35; and 15.8; 16.30 is the single exception) points to a following statement and it probably does so here. It is difficult to see how v. 36 demonstrates the truth of the proverb; it is v. 38 that distinguishes sower and reaper.

ὁ λόγος, 'proverb', as often in Greek (L.S. s.v. VII, 2).

ἀληθινός. See on 1.9.

ἄλλος ... ἄλλος. The proverb is Greek rather than Jewish. Deut. 20.6; 28.30; Micah 6.15; Job 15.28 (LXX); 31.8 have been suggested as Old Testament parallels, but in each one the failure of the sower to reap is due to special punishment or misfortune. Better parallels are to be found in Greek sources, e.g. Aristophanes, *Equites* 392, ἀλλότριον ἀμῶν θέρος (several others are given by Bauer, 74). Philo (*L. A.* III, 227) may therefore be dependent on Greek rather than Jewish sources, and so may John. Sanders disagrees, citing Matt. 25.24 = Luke 19.21, but here the point is different: a grasping man deliberately seizes that to which he is not entitled. As ordinarily used the proverb doubtless expresses the sad inequality of life: one sows, and has no reward for his toil, while when in due course the harvest appears another reaps it who has not shared in the labour of sowing (Bultmann, 198). This principle, which expresses the common observation and wisdom of mankind, has been contradicted by v. 36, according to which sower and reaper rejoice together, the interval between sowing and reaping being annihilated in the eschatological circumstances envisaged; yet there is a limited (ἐν τούτῳ) sense in which it remains true.

38. ἐγὼ . . . ὑμᾶς . . . ὑμεῖς . . . ἄλλοι. This verse in particular requires some measure of allegorical interpretation (see on v. 36). It is however impossible to give a simple and precise interpretation, not because there are no allusions but because there are several. It may be said (a) that the disciples are sent to gather in the harvest of the Samaritans (cf. Acts 8.4–25), though nothing is said in the context of their activity in this matter; ἄλλοι represents Jesus (perhaps together with the Baptist, or the Old Testament writers, though again there is nothing to suggest this); (b) that the reference is generally to the mission (ἀπέστειλα, see on 20.21) of the apostles to the world, the ἄλλοι again meaning Jesus (perhaps with the Baptist and the Old Testament writers); (c) that there is a wider outlook to the church of John's own day (ὑμεῖς), which inherits the mission of Jesus and the apostles (ἄλλοι: Loisy, 190; Bauer, 74; Hoskyns, 271). In any case the force of εἰσεληλύθατε is to maintain both distinction and identity between sower and reaper, and thus to enforce the fact that in the person and work of Jesus a unique eschatological activity is, once for all, taking place. General interpretations such as these are more probable than Cullmann's view (V. & A., 232–40; Circle, 15f.) that the verse refers to the priority in the Samaritan mission of the Hellenists, whose work was subsequently assimilated by the apostles (Acts 8.14–7). For criticism of this view see Braun.

κεκοπιάκατε. κοπιᾶν has here a meaning different from that of v. 6; it signifies first the labour of producing the harvest, and secondly (as often in the New Testament—(Luke 5.5); Rom. 16.6,(12); 1 Cor. 15.10; 16.16; Gal. 4.11; Phil. 2.16; Col. 1.29; 1 Thess. 5.12; 1 Tim. 4.10; 5.17; cf. 2 Tim. 2.6) the labour of Christian proclamation.

39. πολλοὶ ἐπίστευσαν. There is no other evidence for a large body of Samaritan disciples before the crucifixion. Acts 8.4–25 (in spite of Luke's interest in Samaritans—9.51–6; 10.30–7; 17.11–19) treats the evangelization of the Samaritans as a fresh venture. Through the woman's testimony the Samaritans believed; they could do no more when they heard Jesus' own word (v. 41). Human testimony is by no means disparaged (cf. 17.20); see R. Walker, Z.N.T.W. 57 (1966), 49–54. Yet it is hard to doubt that v. 42 is intended to represent a transcending of merely human witness. See Bornkamm, loc. cit.

μαρτυρούσης. To bear witness (see on 1.7) is the task of a disciple. The woman joins with John the Baptist as witness, and in fact precedes the apostles.

40. ἠρώτων. As at v. 31.

μεῖναι, ἔμεινεν. The word is quite appropriate to simple narrative, but in John it often has a rich theological content (e.g. 14.10; 15.4), and this may be not altogether out of mind here; yet this 'dwelling' is but the temporary dwelling of Christ (cf. 14.25), since before his glorification and the coming of the Spirit he can remain only a short and limited time—as here, two days.

42. λαλιάν] μαρτυρίαν ℵ* D b. This western variant is probably due to assimilation to v. 39 (μαρτυρούσης). The word is not used disparagingly (chatter); see however the quotation from Bultmann below.

ἀκηκόαμεν καὶ οἴδαμεν. . . . Cf. 1 John 4.14, τεθεάμεθα καὶ μαρτυροῦμεν ὅτι ὁ πατὴρ ἀπέσταλκεν τὸν υἱὸν σωτῆρα τοῦ κόσμου. The Samaritans speak the language of Johannine Christology. Cf. Jer. 31.34. See above, the note on v. 39. All human testimony has its value, yet it is also secondary. 'The believer . . . must perceive, through the proclaimed word, the word of the Revealer himself. Thus we are faced with the strange paradox that the proclamation, without which no man can be brought to Jesus, is itself insignificant, in that the hearer who enjoys the knowledge of faith is freed from its tutelage, is free, that is, to criticize the proclamation which brought him himself to faith. That is why it is impossible ever to give a definitive dogmatic statement of the proclamation, because every fixed form of words, in that they are human words, becomes λαλιά. The eschatological word becomes a phenomenon within the history of ideas' (Bultmann).

ὁ σωτὴρ τοῦ κόσμου. Jesus is the Saviour of the world because it is through him that God wills to save the world (3.16); this is not a rank enjoyed by him independently of his action in obedience to God's will. In the Old Testament God is characteristically a God who saves his people, and sometimes he is called Saviour (מוֹשִׁיעַ, moshia', the Hiphil participle of ישׁע, not a title and not always, though sometimes, rendered σωτήρ; also גאל, go'el, the Qal participle of גאל, not a title and not translated σωτήρ). In later Jewish literature the Messiah is sometimes described as he who saves Israel (the word גאל, go'el, is used by the Rabbis), but especially in the Christian period there is a tendency to emphasize that God, not the Messiah, is the one Saviour (see S.B. 1, 67-70). In Greek sources however σωτήρ is freely used as a technical term describing divine or semi-divine deliverers. It was applied to the Roman Emperors, and the full expression σωτὴρ τοῦ κόσμου is very frequently applied in inscriptions to Hadrian (A.D. 117-38, a period in all probability not far removed from the writing of John). Many gods were distinguished by the title σωτήρ; so pre-eminently Zeus, and the divine healer, Asclepius; so also the gods of the mystery cults, e.g. Isis and Serapis. It is striking that Josephus does not use the word of God (Bauer, *Wörterbuch s.v.*); 'there is in the *Hermetica* no trace of a "Saviour" in the Christian sense—that is, of a divine or supracosmic Person, who has come down to earth to redeem men, has returned to the world above, and will take up his followers to dwell there . with him' (W. Scott, *Hermetica 1* (1924), 13). It seems very probable that John's terminology is drawn from Greek sources, as is in part his doctrine of salvation (see on 3.16f.), but he has behind him the Old Testament conception of, and hope for, salvation, and the primitive Christian conviction that the hope was fulfilled in Jesus. John does not hestitate, in this chapter (vv. 25f.), to represent Jesus as the Messiah of Judaism; but he insists here that this term, and all others, must be understood in the widest sense.

9. THE OFFICER'S SON

4.43-54

Jesus remained only two days in Samaria, and then moved on into Galilee (cf. 4.3) where he was warmly received by the Galileans who had witnessed the signs (mentioned at 2.23 but nowhere described) which he had accomplished in Jerusalem. In Galilee he came again to Cana, where he had first demonstrated the creative power of the

Gospel. An army officer asked him to go down to Capernaum to heal his son; Jesus did not go, but pronounced 'Your son is alive'. Satisfied with this assurance, the officer returned home and found that his son had recovered at the moment when Jesus had spoken. Upon this he and his household believed in Jesus—that is, became Christians.

Two synoptic incidents are recalled. First, v. 44 recalls Mark 6.1–6 (Matt. 13.54–8; the Marcan story is elaborated in Luke 4.16–30). In these passages, Jesus when he is unfavourably received in his own country (πατρίς) declares that this is no surprising or unusual fate for a prophet. Second, the miracle recalls a cure worked at the request of a centurion (Matt. 8.5–13, of his παῖς, Luke 7.1–10; 13.28f., of his δοῦλος). There are several close verbal parallels, for which see the notes on vv. 47, 50, 53. It seems very probable that the synoptic tradition (or a tradition very closely akin to it) lies immediately behind the Johannine narrative, and it is therefore the more important to note the differences between the two accounts, since they are significant of John's purpose.

A third synoptic narrative, the cure of the Syro-Phoenician woman's daughter (Mark 7.24–30; Matt. 15.21–8), may also be relevant; in this story as in John the petitioner is met with what at least appears to be a rebuff.

Most striking is the fact that, whereas in Mark (and in Matthew and Luke) the πατρίς of Jesus, in which he is rejected, lies in Galilee (Luke 4.16, Ναζαρά, οὗ ἦν τεθραμμένος), in John the πατρίς seems to be Judaea, or Jerusalem—ἐδέξαντο αὐτὸν οἱ Γαλιλαῖοι (v. 45). This view is by no means universally held; see the note on v. 44. Next, it must be observed that, while in Matthew and Luke the centurion's faith receives the highest praise, in John, it seems at first to be decried (ἐὰν μὴ σημεῖα καὶ τέρατα ἴδητε, οὐ μὴ πιστεύσητε, v. 48), but is subsequently emphasized (ἐπίστευσεν . . . τῷ λόγῳ, v. 50; ἐπίστευσεν, v. 53). John wishes to show, it seems, both that Jerusalem is the proper scene of the Messiah's ministry, where he teaches, performs signs, and dies, and also that the further he moves from Jerusalem the more warmly is he welcomed; for the officer (who in the end believes without signs and portents) is a Gentile. He believes the word of Jesus and is therefore superior even to the Galileans, who had seen signs in Jerusalem. This seems to be the point of the paragraph, but it must be recognized (see the note on v. 46) that the man in question is not plainly stated to be a military officer, and thus a Gentile.

On the history of the tradition of this paragraph see in addition to the commentaries Haenchen, *Weg*, 98. The reference to Cana in v. 46, and the description of this as a *second sign* (v. 54; cf. 2.11), even though other signs have intervened (2.23), suggests that this narrative once formed a pair with the wedding miracle at Cana; there is no occasion to deduce a more extensive 'Signs Source', since after this point there is no further enumeration. This two-miracle source must have been like many that were drawn upon by the synoptic writers; in addition John may have known Luke (see p. 46) and thus the form of the story that appears in Luke 7.1–10, but this was not his only source. It is reasonable to think that chapters 2, 3, and 4, beginning and ending with numbered signs, formed a unit in the structure of the gospel. Jesus fulfils the meaning of Jewish law and worship, speculation and eschatological hope. His home is Jerusalem, for salvation is of the Jews; yet he is the Saviour of the world, and in him do the Gentiles hope. In every scene he is the giver of life. In 2.1–11 he meets a relatively minor human need, and transcends the practices of Jewish ritual. In 2.13–22 he promises to raise up his body, the living Temple; in 3.1–21 he offers new birth and eternal life; in 3.22–36 the same theme is renewed (v. 36); in 4.1–42 Jesus offers living water, and in 4.46–54 he gives life to one who is at the point of death (v. 50, ὁ υἱός σου ζῇ). With the theme of life goes that of faith, for in 2.11 his nearest disciples believe, and in 4.53 so does a Gentile (at least, a Jewish 'outsider'). Neither of these themes however is complete in itself, and inevitably the next chapter opens a discussion of the person who claims to offer such exceptional gifts, and challenges men's trust.

43. μετὰ δὲ τὰς δύο ἡμέρας. See v. 40 and cf. John's use of μετὰ τοῦτο (ταῦτα), for which see on 2.12. The interrupted journey of v. 3 is resumed. For ἐξῆλθεν ἐκεῖθεν cf. Mark 6.1; this Marcan narrative of the rejection of Jesus in his own country is probably in mind here; see v. 44.

44. προφήτης ἐν τῇ ἰδίᾳ πατρίδι τιμὴν οὐκ ἔχει. There are parallels to this proverb-like saying in the Synoptic Gospels: Mark 6.4, οὐκ ἔστιν προφήτης ἄτιμος εἰ μὴ ἐν τῇ πατρίδι αὐτοῦ καὶ ἐν τοῖς συγγενεῦσιν αὐτοῦ καὶ ἐν τῇ οἰκίᾳ αὐτοῦ (Matt. 13.57 omits reference to the συγγενεῖς); Luke 4.24, οὐδεὶς προφήτης δεκτός ἐστιν ἐν τῇ πατρίδι αὐτοῦ. In addition, the saying occurs in P.Oxy. I (οὐκ ἔστιν δεκτὸς προφήτης ἐν τῇ πατρίδι αὐτ[ο]ῦ, οὐδὲ ἰατρὸς ποιεῖ θεραπείας εἰς τοὺς γιγώσκοντας αὐτόν), and in Thomas 31 (No prophet is acceptable in his village, no physician heals those who know him). It is very probable that the saying circulated as an isolated logion, and Mark 6.1–6 may well be a narrative framework constructed by Mark to accommodate it. This makes John's reinterpretation of it a more natural process. His is closest to the Marcan form, but like Matthew he abbreviates it. In the Synoptic Gospels the saying is used to explain a rejection of Jesus in Galilee (in Luke, at Nazareth), in John the reception of Jesus (οὖν, v. 45) by the Galileans after his rejection in Jerusalem. That is, for John, Jerusalem, not Galilee, is the proper scene on which the Messiah must teach, work, and die. Bultmann and others consider this interpretation impossible in view of 1.46; 7.41,52, which show that John knew that Jesus' home was in Galilee. The true πατρίς of the Logos is in heaven—'the bosom of the Father' (Lightfoot). But cf. 1.11; it is true that the Logos is at home in heaven, yet the world is his own; Judaea and Jerusalem represent the world in this sense. Martyn (58) thinks that the unwelcoming πατρίς points to the Jewish quarter of John's own city (cf. 7.1); but this does not seem to be the way John uses symbolism.

45. καὶ αὐτοὶ γὰρ ἦλθον εἰς τὴν ἑορτήν. Many Jews, including Galileans, made the pilgrimage to Jerusalem for Passover; cf. among many passages Josephus, Bel. II, 10, κάτεισι μὲν ἐκ τῆς χώρας λαὸς ἄπειρος ἐπὶ τὴν θρησκείαν.

46. βασιλικός. D a boh (codd) have βασιλισκός. This variant ('petty king', 'princelet') is often said to be due to assimilation to the old Latin and Vulgate *regulus*. Sanders questions this because the reading is implied by Heracleon; it is not easy however to follow him in thinking that βασιλικός may be due to assimilation to the Synoptic Gospels (which do not in fact contain it); βασιλικός should probably be accepted. βασιλικός means either a 'person of royal blood' or a 'royal official', 'person in the service of a king'. Josephus uses the word of troops in the service of a king, generally (as at *Bel.* 1, 45), and especially of forces serving the Herods (as at *Vita*, 400f.). If, as is probable, this βασιλικός is to be identified with the centurion of Matt. 8.5–13 = Luke 7.1–10 we may think of him as an officer under Herod Antipas (who was not strictly a king but was a member of the royal Herodian house and was sometimes popularly referred to as a king—e.g. Mark 6.14). It is probable that John draws the word from a tradition differing slightly from that in Matthew and Luke, but possible that he preferred βασιλικός for some reason of his own (note that in Matt. 8.12 the unbelieving Jews, who are to be rejected in favour of believing Gentiles, are called οἱ υἱοὶ τῆς βασιλείας; it is possible that the use of βασιλικός indicates that the officer, though not a Jew, is truly a 'son of the kingdom'). It is not impossible that the βασιλικός is a civilian in the service of 'king' Herod Antipas; if this is so he may not have been a Gentile.

οὗ ὁ υἱὸς ἠσθένει. In Matthew the sick person is the centurion's παῖς (it is not made clear in Matthew whether παῖς means 'servant' or 'child'), in Luke, the centurion's δοῦλος.

Καφαρναούμ. This is the scene of the Matthaean and Lucan stories. See on 2.12.

47. ἀπῆλθεν πρὸς αὐτόν. Matt. 8.5, προσῆλθεν αὐτῷ; in Luke the man does not venture to approach Jesus.

ἠρώτα ἵνα καταβῇ καὶ ἰάσηται αὐτοῦ τὸν υἱόν. Cf. Luke 7.3, ἐρωτῶν αὐτὸν ὅπως ἐλθὼν διασώσῃ τὸν δοῦλον αὐτοῦ ... 7.7, ... ἰαθήτω ὁ παῖς μου (Matt. 8.8 ἰαθήσεται ὁ παῖς μου). The incorrect use of ἐρωτᾶν (as if it were αἰτεῖν, 'to request') would be a more striking hint that John knew Luke if the same use had not already appeared twice in this chapter (vv. 31, 40). ἵνα and the subjunctive instead of an infinitive is also not unusual in John, and both constructions were spreading in late Greek.

ἤμελλεν γὰρ ἀποθνῄσκειν. Cf. Luke 7.2, ἤμελλεν τελευτᾶν.

48. ἐὰν μὴ σημεῖα καὶ τέρατα ἴδητε, οὐ μὴ πιστεύσητε. The plural shows that the remark is not addressed only to the officer (cf. 3.7b,11); the sharpness of the implied rebuke is thus blunted (so that there is no need to put a question mark after πιστεύσητε; this would be unusual (M. 1, 187–92), but cf. 11.56), though not removed; cf. 2.4. A faith based on miracles (though not negligible —14.11) is inadequate (2.23). The man must not seek the miracle as the ground of faith. σημεῖα καὶ τέρατα is a regular LXX rendering of the Hebrew אותות ומופתים (e.g. Exod. 7.3). It is a traditional expression (8 times in Acts) and therefore to some extent stands apart from John's characteristic use of σημεῖον (for which see Introduction, pp. 75–8). For the present use of σημεῖον cf. 2.18; 6.26; also Wisd. 8.8; 10.16. The suggestion that vv. 48f. are a redactional gloss, expressing John's point of view in contrast with that of the source (which seems to approve the officer's faith—vv. 50,53) is a natural one, but it is incorrect to suppose that we have here two irreconcilable opinions. John's view of signs is complex. 'Blessed are those who believe

without seeing' does not imply 'Cursed are those who believe because they have seen', for this would damn the apostolic testimony which the gospel claims to represent. See in addition to the discussion of miracles in the Introduction the quotation from Bultmann on v. 53.

49. The officer is in fact actuated by motives of compassion for his child (τὸ παιδίον] τὸν παῖδα ℵ it: τὸν υἱόν φ vg).

50. His request is granted—ὁ υἱός σου ʒῆ. For ʒῆν in the sense of 'recover from disease' cf. e.g. Num. 21.8, πᾶς ὁ δεδηγμένος ἰδὼν αὐτὸν ʒήσεται. Here and elsewhere in the Old Testament ʒῆν has this meaning in dependence on חיה (B.D.B. *s.v.* '2. be quickened, revive: a. from sickness').

ἐπίστευσεν . . . τῷ λόγῳ, before the intervention of any sign. For πιστεύειν with the dative see on 1.12; 2.22; the man is not yet a Christian believer; contrast v. 53. He believes that what Jesus has said is true. Cf. Matt. 8.8; Luke 7.7, εἰπὲ λόγῳ.

51. αὐτοῦ καταβαίνοντος . . . αὐτῷ. The improperly constructed genitive absolute is not rare in the New Testament, or in contemporary Greek.

For παῖς, υἱός (P⁶⁶ᶜ D 33 it vg cur pesh) is well supported but probably due to assimilation to vv. 46, 47 and especially 50, 53. G. D. Kilpatrick, *J.T.S.* 14 (1963), 393, argues for υἱός on the ground that παῖς is an assimilation to Matthew and Luke; E. D. Freed, *J.T.S.* 16 (1965), 448f., replies. For αὐτοῦ (giving indirect speech in the ὅτι-clause), σου (giving direct speech) is read by P⁶⁶ᶜ D Θ ω it cur pesh. This is also probably due to assimilation.

52. κομψότερον ἔσχεν. κομψῶς ἔχειν is a Hellenistic expression meaning 'to be well'. With the aorist it means 'to get better'; cf. *P. Tebt.*, 414.10, ἐὰν κομψῶς σχῶ, and see M. 1, 248.

ὥραν ἑβδόμην, point of time expressed by the accusative (instead of the dative, as correctly in the next verse); the use seems to have grown up in late Greek. See M. 1, 63, 245.

ἀφῆκεν αὐτὸν ὁ πυρετός. The same expression at Mark 1.31 (=Matt. 8.15).

53. ἐκείνῃ τῇ ὥρᾳ. Supply κομψότερον ἔσχεν, or some similar phrase. Cf. Matt. 8.13, ἰάθη ὁ παῖς ἐν τῇ ὥρᾳ ἐκείνῃ.

ἐπίστευσεν. The absolute use of the word (cf. 1.7,50 *et al.*) means 'he became a Christian'. Cf. v. 50, which may prefigure the conversion of the Gentiles by the hearing of the word of the Gospel but certainly does not describe the conversion of the officer.

καὶ ἡ οἰκία αὐτοῦ ὅλη. Cf. Acts 10.2; 11.14; 16.15,31; 18.8. We can only guess what the conversion of the officer's house implied; in fact John has probably imported into this gospel narrative an event of a kind familiar to him (as to the author of Acts) in the later mission of the church. 'The miracle to which man has no right, since he may not require the Revealer to give proof of his authority, is nevertheless on occasions granted to man in his weakness so long as man is aware of his own helplessness. For where it is granted it can lead man on beyond the faith that is based on miracles' (Bultmann).

54. πάλιν δεύτερον is pleonastic; cf. 21.16. The whole verse refers back, through vv. 3, 43, to the miracle at the marriage feast at Cana. The second sign, like the first, ends a division of the gospel; see pp. 189, 196.

For the whole narrative cf. *Berakoth* 34 b; Once a son of Rabban Gamaliel (II) was ill. He sent two disciples to R. Hanina b. Dosa, that he might pray for mercy for him. When he (b. Dosa) saw them, he went up into the attic and implored mercy for him. When he came down he said to them, 'Go (cf. πορεύου, v. 50), for the fever has left him' (cf. ἀφῆκεν αὐτὸν ὁ πυρετός, v. 52). They said to him, 'Are you a prophet then?' He answered them, 'I am no prophet, nor am I a prophet's son; but thus have I received tradition: When my prayer runs freely in my mouth I know that the person concerned has been accepted; but if it does not, I know that he will be carried off.' They returned and noted the hour in writing. When they came back to Rabban Gamaliel he said to them, 'By the Temple service! You have said neither too little nor too much; it happened exactly so that in that hour (vv. 52f.) the fever left him and he asked for water to drink.'

10. SIGN AND CONTROVERSY ON THE SABBATH DAY

5.1-18

For the view that ch. 6 has been misplaced and originally preceded ch. 5 see Introduction, p. 23, and on 6.1. A variation of this opinion is that ch. 6 was not part of the original gospel but was subsequently added, thus disturbing the sequence (Lindars).

Jesus left Galilee in order to attend a feast, which is not named, in Jerusalem, and found himself by a notable public pool. The indications both of time and place are extremely vague (see the notes); evidently John was not interested in them. At the pool Jesus cured a man of a longstanding disease, bidding him rise, take up his pallet, and walk. It was, however, the sabbath day, and the man, who did as he had been told, was rightly accused by the Jews of contravening the sabbath law by carrying his pallet. At first he was unable to identify the person who had cured him and bidden him carry the pallet, but when Jesus disclosed himself to warn the man to sin no more, the man revealed his identity to the Jews. In the closing verses of this section the way is prepared for the ensuing discourse, for Jesus defends his action not by discussing the law but by placing himself and his work on the same level as God.

This miracle is not narrated in the Synoptic Gospels, but a few phrases recall the miracle of Mark 2.1-12 (see the notes on vv. 8, 14). These may be due to a recollection of the Marcan miracle, but are not necessarily so. The story itself (vv. 2-9, omitting 3b, 4) is similar in form to many synoptic miracles, and there is no need to suppose that its origin is other than traditional. See Dodd, *Tradition*, 174-80.

The accusation of illegal activity on the Sabbath recalls many synoptic controversies, but there is no parallel to the reply made by Jesus (v. 17). In the Synoptic Gospels several arguments are brought

against the rigorous enforcement of the law of rest, notably the humani-
tarian argument (e.g. Luke 13.10–17; 14.1–6), and the argument that,
since with the coming of Jesus something 'more than the Temple'
has arrived (Matt. 12.5f.), and since Jesus and his followers form a
Davidic, messianic, community (Mark 2.23–8), the Sabbath is being
fulfilled in the new age. In the present passage, however, which is
expanded in the ensuing discourse, Jesus argues that as the Son of
God he does what God does; as the Father is unceasingly at work, so
also is the Son. It may be held that this argument is implicit in the
claim to forgive sins (Mark 2.5,7,10) and in the messianic conception
of the Synoptic Gospels; there also, Jesus acts on behalf of God, and it
is in virtue of the breaking in of the new age in which God's will is
more perfectly known and done that the law must be abrogated; but in
John the argument is given a Christological significance which is not
expressed in the earlier gospels.

This chapter (like ch. 9; see p. 355) provides particularly good
evidence for those who see the gospel as written on two 'levels'. Martyn
(54f.) treats the movement from v. 16 to v. 18 as a move from one level
to the other—in effect, from the controversy between Jesus and his contemporaries to that between end-of-the-century Christians and the
Jews of their day. There is important truth in this view (see pp. 137f.),
but it may reasonably be asked whether both verses do not belong to
both levels. Almost the whole of Martyn's theory is cautiously anticipated by Bultmann in a note on this passage so important that it must
be quoted entire. 'Manifestly the two stories in chs. 5 and 9 must be
understood against the same historical background. Both reflect the
relation of early Christianity to the surrounding hostile (in the first
place Jewish) world; in a peculiar way they reflect, too, the methods of
its opponents, who directed their attacks against men who did not yet
belong to the Christian community, but who had come into contact
with it and experienced the power of the miraculous forces at work in it.
These men were interrogated and in this way their opponents attempted
to collect evidence against the Christian community. Such stories provided the Evangelist with an external starting-point, and at the same
time they were for him illustrations of the world's dilemma, as it was
faced by the revelation, and of the world's hostility. The world attempts
to subject to its own κρίσις the event which is, in fact, the κρίσις of the
world; it brings the revelation, as it were, to trial' (239). The theological
significance of the paragraph is both unitary and universal. 'The
revelation-event means the disruption and negation of traditional
religious standards, and their protagonists (*sic*; German, Vertreter)
must become enemies of the Revealer' (Bultmann, 247).

1. ἑορτή, P66 P75 B D W Θ cur: ἡ ἑορτή, ℵ ω λ 33 sah boh. The agreement of
P66 P75 B D W Θ and the old Syriac (sin is not extant at this point) is a strong
argument in favour of the reading without the article; so also is the fact that
nowhere else in the gospel is ἑορτή anarthrous. It would be natural to assimi-

late this passage to, e.g., 6.4; 7.2. Moreover, if we translate 'a feast', the rendering corresponds with the fact that neither in this verse nor in the ensuing narrative is there anything to indicate what feast is meant. Those who transpose chapters 5 and 6 (see Introduction, p. 23, and on 6.1) take the feast referred to in this verse to be the Passover which is said in 6.4 to be near, but it is more probable that Passover is mentioned in ch. 6 in order to provide an appropriate setting for the discourse on the Bread of Life. Guilding, who transposes chs. 5 and 6, says that this feast must be either Pentecost or Rosh ha-Shanah, and concludes for the latter (69–72). So too does Lightfoot, referring to H. St J. Thackeray, *The Septuagint and Jewish Worship*, 1921, 80–111. It seems however that John here introduces a feast simply in order to account for the presence of Jesus in Jerusalem. The article was added out of the desire to supply further definition and precise information (as were the further supplements contained in isolated MSS.—τῶν ἀζύμων, ἡ σκηνοπηγία). If the article is read, the reference might be to the Passover or to Tabernacles, which was often known as 'the Feast' (החג).

ἀνέβη. See on 2.13.

2. The text of this and of the two following verses is in some disorder. There is no doubt that vv. 3b, 4 are no part of the original text, and it seems probable that their insertion was accompanied by some disturbance of the earlier verses, which copyists have also attempted to free from difficulties. On the whole question see the indispensable discussion by Dr J. Jeremias, *Die Wiederentdeckung von Bethesda* (1949), 5–8. The first variant is

(a) ἐπὶ τῇ προβατικῇ κολυμβηθρα, P⁶⁶ P⁷⁵ B ω
(b) ἐν τῇ προβατικῇ κολυμβηθρα, ℵᶜ D Θ
(c) προβατικὴ κολυμβήθρα, ℵ* e Eusebius
(d) κολυμβήθρα, 1 cur pesh Irenaeus (lat.)

In (a) and (b) κολυμβηθρα is intentionally left unaccented; the most ancient MSS. do not make it clear whether the nominative or the dative is intended; see below. (c) and (d) may with probability be set aside as attempts to ease a harsh construction. Between (a) and (b) it seems impossible to decide on external or internal grounds; the difference between them hardly affects the sense of the passage. It remains to decide how κολυμβηθρα should be taken. (i) If it is taken as a nominative the adjective προβατική is left without a noun. It is natural to think of ἡ πύλη ἡ προβατική, mentioned at Neh. 3.1; 12.39, and to supply πύλη. We should then translate 'There is in Jerusalem, by the Sheep (Gate), a pool, which in Aramaic is called ...'. (ii) If it is taken as a dative it is the noun qualified by προβατικῇ, and the following phrase, ἡ ἐπιλεγομένη ..., is left without a substantive. We should translate 'There is in Jerusalem, by the Sheep Pool, that which in Aramaic is called ...'. There are grammatical difficulties in both (i) and (ii), but (ii) is favoured, perhaps decisively, by the fact that the whole ancient tradition takes together προβατικῇ κολυμβήθρᾳ, and that no ancient writer (none in fact before A.D. 1283) supplies πύλη with προβατικῇ (see Jeremias, op. cit., 6). The name of the pool is variously given.

(a) Βηθεσδα, Θ ω cur pesh hl^{mg}.
(b) Βη(θ)ζαθα, ℵ 33 e Eusebius.
(c) Βελζεθα (or similar forms), D a b.
(d) Βηθσαιδα, P⁷⁵ B W vg hl sah boh Tertullian; Βηδσαιδα, P⁶⁶.

None of these variants can be easily dismissed, though (c) is probably a variant spelling of (b). If this is so the combined testimony for (b–c) is very strong, including as it does Eusebius' *Onomastica* 58.21-6 (ed. Klostermann). In discussions of this reading much has been made of the meaning of the Aramaic words which underlie the Greek forms given in the MSS. These considerations seem however to be out of place; when John finds meaning in a Semitic term he draws attention to it explicitly; note especially his interpretation of the name of the pool Siloam (9.7). We must suppose that he is simply naming the place in question and not allegorizing it, though of course it is possible that his copyists found allegorical meanings where the writer intended none; thus there might well be a tendency, especially in the Syriac-speaking church, to prefer the form Bethesda, since this might be connected with בית חסדא, 'House of mercy'—a name evidently suitable for the place in which Jesus cured a lame man. (d) is far too strongly supported to be excluded as merely an assimilation to the well-known Bethsaida on the Lake of Galilee, which appears frequently elsewhere in the gospels. In fact, none of the readings (a), (b–c), (d) can be dismissed on external grounds. If we turn from the variants themselves to consider the locality of the 'Five Porches' (see below), it appears that the site whose name is in question lay to the north-east of the city in the region known as Bezetha. This region is mentioned several times by Josephus, and its name given in Greek as Καινόπολις (*Bel.* II, 530), or Καινὴ Πόλις (*Bel.* v, 151). In the latter passage he says that Bezetha is *translated* 'New City'; this is inaccurate if Bezetha is a transliteration of בית זית (*beth zaith*), since this means 'house of olives', but this need not be assumed. Bezetha may possibly be a corrupt form of בית חדש (*beth ḥadash*), 'New House' (cf. the עיר חדשה, *'ir ḥᵃdashah*, 'New City', mentioned in *Erubin* 5.6). The variants in John show how easy it was for the sound of θ to disappear, and the Greek ζ readily arises out of—and passes into—both *ds* and *sd*. On the basis of these observations it may be suggested that either (a) or (d) was the original reading. One could easily have arisen out of the other; αι and ε are very frequently interchanged in Greek MSS., and while some copyists may have written Bethsaida under the influence of the frequently mentioned lakeside town others may have recognized the difficulty of a 'Bethsaida' in or near Jerusalem, and perhaps have been attracted by the possibility of seeing in Bethesda a 'house of mercy'. The forms Bethzatha, Belzetha, and the like, may have come into the textual tradition through the influence of Josephus, or of traditions of the name of the Jerusalem suburb similar to his. It would be tempting to ascribe them to the personal influence of the great historian Eusebius were it not that he cannot be supposed to have affected the old Latin VS. to any great extent. The objection (Jeremias, op. cit., 7) that the name of a suburb would not have been applied to one building within it—the 'Five Porches'—does not seem cogent. It is even possible that the building 'New House' existed before the suburb, just as more recently old country houses have often given their names to new housing estates which have sprung up around them. These considerations must be supplemented by the fact that the so-called 'Copper Scroll' (3Q15), discovered at Qumran, appears to attest the existence of a pool called בית אשדתין (*beth 'eshdathayin*), a name that might be derived from the root אשד, to flow, and could give rise to the Greek Βηθεσδά, with the sense, not 'House of mercy' but 'House of springs', or indeed 'House of the two springs' (since the form is dual; see the note below on the double pool of St Anna). For the text of the Copper Scroll see M. Baillet, J. T. Milik, R. de Vaux, *Discoveries in the Judaean Desert of Jordan III: Les petites grottes de Qumran*, 1962. This discovery adds weight to the view that the pool John referred to was called Bethesda (reading (*a*)); but (1) the transcription of the scroll is not certain; (2) we cannot be sure that the pool referred to in the scroll is that which John had in mind—if indeed John was interested in the topography at all; (3) the scroll may be in code (see G. R. Driver, *The Judaean Scrolls* (1965), 376). On this matter see Jeremias, *Wiederentdeckung*, and the same author's 'Die Kupferrolle von Qumran und Bethesda', in *Abba* (1966), 361–4; also D. J. Wieand, 'John v. 2 and the Pool of Bethesda', in *N.T.S.* 12 (1966), 392–404. Wieand thinks 'that Bethesda was the reading of the autograph of the Fourth Gospel, and that Bethesda was changed to Bethsaida by the author of chapter xxi in the interest of fish symbolism' (404). There is a full account of recent discussion in Davies, *Land*, 302–13 ('The healing at Bethesda by Christ implies a critique of a "holy place", be it pagan or Jewish', 313).

Ἑβραϊστί, as at 19.13,17,20; 20.16, probably means 'in Aramaic'. Elsewhere in the New Testament the word occurs only at Rev. 9.11; 16.16.

πέντε στοὰς ἔχουσα. This description permits the probable identification of the building with remains found between the two portions of the double pool of St Anna. See Jeremias, op. cit., 9–26. This identification excludes the view, otherwise improbable, that by the 'five porches' John intended to signify the five books of Moses, which were ineffective for salvation. When John employs symbolism he does so less crudely.

3a. After ξηρῶν, παραλυτικῶν is added by D a b; a good example of the Western text's inability to know when to stop.

3b, 4. The whole of this passage is omitted by P⁶⁶ P⁷⁵ ℵ B W 33 cur sah. In addition, v. 3b is omitted by a few MSS., and v. 4 by D vg boh (v. 4 is also obelized by other MSS.). There can be no doubt that the verses were added (possibly on the basis of old tradition) to explain v. 7 (on which see the note); v. 3b being added first, v. 4 as the textual tradition developed. A further argument against the authenticity of vv. 3b, 4 is that they appear in different MSS. in varying forms. The form translated in the RV mg is: '. . . waiting for the moving of the water: for an angel of the Lord went down at certain seasons into the pool, and troubled the water: whosoever then first after the troubling of the water stepped in was made whole, with whatsoever disease he was holden.' A sacred pool visited by the goddess Hera, is described by Lucian, *de Syria dea* 45–8, but the resemblance this passage bears to John's account is even less than Betz (152) allows.

5. τριάκοντα καὶ ὀκτὼ ἔτη ἔχοντα. The same construction occurs in the next verse and at 11.17; cf. 8.57; 9.21,23. It is a mark of John's style. It is very improbable that the number thirty-eight is symbolic, though some have seen in it an allusion to Deut. 2.14. In the *Acts of Pilate* 6.1 a man claims to have been cured by Jesus after being ill thirty-eight years. His story shows traces both of the present narrative and of the miracle of Mark 2.1–12. The author of the *Acts* cannot however be regarded as an independent witness; he wrote not earlier than the fourth century, and was probably dependent on both Mark and John. John does not specify the man's illness.

6. γνούς. John no doubt thinks of supernatural knowledge, not inference from observation. Cf. 1.47f. He offers no reason why Jesus should choose this man out of the crowd of sick persons. Jesus acts by his own choice (cf. 2.4; 4.47f.). As will appear, there are parallels and some contrasts between this story and that of the paralytic in Mark 2.1–12; perhaps here also a contrast is intended. In Mark the paralytic, let down through the roof, is set before Jesus, whose choice is therefore to some extent restricted, as it is not in John. A response from the man however is also sought: θέλεις ὑγιὴς γενέσθαι; The point however is overstressed by Dodd (*Interpretation*, 319) who, having allegorized the pool as the law writes, 'The law might show the way of life; it was powerless to create the will to live'. John has not yet begun to interpret the incident, and when he does so will look in a different direction.

7. ἄνθρωπον οὐκ ἔχω. The paralytic in Mark 2.3,5 had four men who carried him on a pallet and had faith; this man is utterly friendless, and there is no word of faith on his part or on any other's. His κύριε need mean no more than 'Sir'.

ἵνα ... βάλῃ. βάλλειν of course has its late, weakened, sense, 'put'. The construction has been claimed as the result of the mistranslation of the Aramaic particle ד, which, intended as a relative, has been taken as a final particle. But this is in fact another example of John's custom of using ἵνα and the subjunctive where correct Greek usage demands the infinitive.

ὅταν ταραχθῇ τὸ ὕδωρ. These words presuppose some such visitation as is described in v. 4, but we have no other evidence of such a legend in connection with any pool in Jerusalem, nor do the excavations at the St Anna pool yet afford any explanation, though there is some ground to hope that further work may do so (Jeremias, op. cit., 25). Evidently the curative powers of the water were operative for only one sick man after each disturbance. We are not told how often the disturbances took place.

8. For the whole verse cf. Mark 2.11, σοὶ λέγω, ἔγειρε ἄρον τὸν κράβαττόν σου καὶ ὕπαγε εἰς τὸν οἶκόν σου. The parallelism is striking, and some reminiscence is probable (especially when other evidence that John knew Mark is taken into account; see Introduction, pp. 42–5). The use of κράβαττος must not however be taken as a special indication of literary relation between John and Mark; the word is not good Greek, but there is no reason whatever to think it uncommon in colloquial Greek. For bed-carrying as a motif in miracle stories see Betz, 158.

9. Just as the thirty-eight years prove the gravity of the disease, so the carrying of the bed and the walking prove the completeness of the cure.

ἦν δὲ σάββατον ἐν ἐκείνῃ τῇ ἡμέρᾳ. John in the fewest possible words states the fact which forms the basis of the discourse that follows. Haenchen takes vv. 9b–13 to be a supplement, introducing the sabbath theme. The tradition however contained not a few stories of which this theme was an original part. Mark 2.1–12 (the paralytic) is the first of a series of controversy stories (2.1—3.6), of which two others (2.23–8 the cornfields, 3.1–6 the withered hand) deal with the question of the Sabbath.

10. οὐκ ἔξεστίν σοι ἆραι τὸν κράβαττον. The complaint is justified by the Mishnah law. *Shabbath* 7.2: The main classes of work are forty save one: ...taking out aught from one domain into another; 10.5: (If a man took out) a living

man on a couch he is not culpable by reason of the couch, since the couch is secondary. (It is implied that if there were no man on the couch the carrier would be culpable.) Jesus himself is not here accused of breaking the Sabbath (contrast v. 18); he has only given a command which has led another man into transgression.

11–13. The man however will not accept responsibility for his deed. He could hardly be blamed for obeying the man who cured him, ignorant though he was of that man's identity. There is both similarity and contrast between this sick man and the blind man of ch. 9; the latter takes a sturdy part in the proceedings, and eventually comes to complete faith in Jesus, whereas the former is a mere pawn.

ἐξένευσεν; properly, 'to turn the head aside', 'to dodge'. The extension of usage required here is quite natural. Jesus had taken advantage of the presence of a large crowd to depart unobserved.

14. μηκέτι ἁμάρτανε. It is neither said nor implied that the man's illness was the consequence of sin; probably it would be true to say here (as at 9.3; 11.4) that it occurred that God might be glorified in his works; μηκέτι certainly implies that the man has not been chosen on the ground of his merits! The bidding recalls the words of the Marcan story of the paralytic ἀφίενταί σου αἱ ἁμαρτίαι (Mark 2.9). In John nothing is said of forgiveness, but the whole chapter implies a treatment of evil too radical to be exhausted in the healing of physical disease, and the command to sin *no more* suggests that sins up to this point have already been dealt with.

ἵνα μὴ χεῖρόν σοί τι γένηται. Again a synoptic passage is recalled: Luke 13.1–5. Just as in Luke it is not said that the Galileans who suffered at the hands of Pilate, and those upon whom the tower of Siloam fell, were pre-eminently deserving of their fate, so here it is not implied that the thirty-eight years of illness were a punishment for an exceptionally sinful man. Both Luke and John point to the inevitable fate of unrepentant humanity. The χεῖρόν τι can hardly be anything other than the Judgement (cf. v. 29), though Martyn (55) gives it a more precise meaning. He notes the contrast (see above) with 9.35f.: this man is not led to a confession of faith; on the contrary, the *Christian* senses his instability—he might become an informer. He is therefore warned not to fall into *that* sin. The verse however does not say this; moreover this sin has already been partly committed (v. 11), and when it is completed (v. 15) no dire consequence is seen to follow.

16. διὰ τοῦτο is explained by the ὅτι-clause which follows. The first count of the Jews' accusation against Jesus appears at once—it is illegal activity on the Sabbath. The second count arises out of Jesus' reply to the first. His illegal actions (ταῦτα ἐποίει) are not however defined. The only action specifically objected to is the cured man's carrying his pallet, an act which Jesus had commanded but not himself done. John refers generally, and without precise application of detail, to the healing ministry of Jesus (note the imperfect, ἐποίει) and to his attitude to the sabbath law. John's method may be contrasted with that of the synoptic evangelists.

17. ὁ πατήρ μου ἕως ἄρτι ἐργάζεται, κἀγὼ ἐργάζομαι. For the construction cf. 15.27; Greek uses the present where English would use the perfect: My Father has been working. . . . ἕως ἄρτι means 'up to the present', with no implication that the time has now come, or soon will come, for work to stop

255

(cf. however Cullman, *Salvation*, 277; *V. & A.*, 187–91). The Greek may represent the Hebrew עוד—so C. Maurer. The Son's time is limited (9.4), but in the present verse ἕως ἄρτι is not applied to him. The present verse is the seed out of which the discourse which fills the rest of the chapter grows. According to Gen. 2.2f., God rested (שבת, *shabath*) on the seventh day of creation, an anthropomorphism which caused trouble to thoughtful exegetes. Philo, relying on the LXX rendering of *shabath*, κατέπαυσεν (not ἐπαύσατο), denies outright that God has ever ceased his creative activity: παύεται γὰρ οὐδέποτε ποιῶν ὁ θεός ... εὖ μέντοι καὶ τὸ φάναι 'κατέπαυσεν', οὐχὶ 'ἐπαύσατο' ... οὐ παύεται δὲ ποιῶν αὐτός (*L. A.* 1, 5f.; cf. *Cher.*, 87). Similar exegesis appears in the rabbinic literature: e.g. when Rabban Gamaliel II, R. Joshua, R. Eleazar b. Azariah, and R. Aqiba were in Rome (*c.* A.D. 95) they rebutted the objections of a sectary by the arguments that God might do as he willed in the world without breaking the sabbath law since (*a*) the whole world was no more than his private residence (Isa. 6.3), and (*b*) he fills the whole world (Jer. 23.24), (*Ex. R.* 30.6; cf. *Gen. R.* 11.10). It may be said then that when John was written there was a current exegesis of God's sabbath rest sufficient to support the argument of the evangelist. God is essentially and unchangeably creative (ἐργάζεται); what God does Jesus also does (v. 19); therefore Jesus also ἐργάζεται. That God is ceaselessly active is also a Greek thought; see Sanders, and Dodd, *Interpretation*, 20f., with the quotation from *C.H.* 11.5, οὐ γὰρ ἀργὸς ὁ θεός; but Bultmann rightly claims that God's work is understood here on Jewish, not Greek, lines.

18. The Jews are not slow to see the implications of Jesus' argument, and are when they see them the more anxious to kill him. The κἀγώ of v. 17 places Jesus on a level with God. Sabbath-breaking, though important, was a comparatively trivial offence (οὐ μόνον ἔλυε τὸ σάββατον—the imperfect may imply that Jesus habitually broke the Sabbath or that he was seeking to destroy it; at least it generalizes beyond the present incident. Jesus had called God his *own* father (πατέρα ἴδιον; cf. the use of ἀββά in Mark 14.36, on which see J. Jeremias, *Abba* (1966), 15–67; also his *Theology*, 1, 61–8), a form of speech which did not arise out of liturgical custom or the notion of Israel as God's child (see however Wisd. 2.16); and the assumption of a uniform activity common to Jesus and to God could only mean that Jesus was equal to God. This inference John of course himself admits, but rightly presents it as extremely provocative to the Jews. Cf. Mark 2.7; S.B. II, 462–5—God may make some (notably Moses) like himself, but the four who made themselves as God were Hiram (Ezek. 28.2), Nebuchadnezzar, Pharaoh, and Joash; Philo, *L. A.* 1, 49 (φίλαυτος δὲ καὶ ἄθεος ὁ νοῦς, οἰόμενος ἴσος εἶναι θεῷ); 2 Thess. 2.4; and for more material see Dodd, *Interpretation*, 320–8. Jewish theology and piety bore in mind that God is in heaven, and man upon earth (Eccles. 5.2), and reacted strongly against any confusion between the two. The sense in which Jesus' equality with God is to be understood is explained in the rest of the chapter. Cf. Phil. 2.6, οὐχ ἁρπαγμὸν ἡγήσατο τὸ εἶναι ἴσα θεῷ; John's ἴσον is perhaps a Christological advance upon Paul's adverbial neuter plural. 'The Jews can only conceive equality with God as independence from God, whereas for Jesus it means the very opposite, as is brought out immediately in v. 19' (Bultmann). We see Christology developing here in a controversial setting. Martyn (56) puts into the mouth of the Jews; 'We persecute Christians because they worship Jesus as a second god'.

256

11. JESUS AND THE FATHER

5.19-47

The occasion of this discourse is the miracle of 5.2-9, the Jewish objection to what Jesus had done and commanded on the Sabbath, and the reply of Jesus, 'My Father worketh hitherto, and I work', which was rightly understood by the Jews as a claim to equality with God. It was imperative that John should handle this claim without further delay. Already (even if the Prologue be excluded) he had made extensive claims on behalf of Jesus. He is greater than John the Baptist; he is the Lamb of God, the Son of God, the Messiah, the Son of man, the saviour of the world. In the following chapters the great 'I am' sayings occur: I am the bread of life, the light of the world, the good shepherd, the way, the truth, the life, etc. In what sense are these divine claims made? Is Jesus a man who exalts himself to a position of divine authority? A demi-god, half human and half divine? Do his assertions imply any rivalry with the Creator, the God of Israel and the Old Testament?

The present discourse makes the position clear. It is rightly described by Lightfoot as a 'defence of Christian monotheism'. Jesus is what he is only in humble obedience to and complete dependence upon the Father. He has no independent status; he even has no independent will or judgement. He does only what he sees the Father do. This is at once a humble acknowledgement and a lofty claim. Simply because his one aim is to be obedient men may see in him the character and activity of God himself. If he sought his own glory (as men do), this, his supreme glory, would instantly disappear. It is in this light, and not in that of human or demonic arrogance, that all his claims must be understood. Humility and obedience however do not exhaust what John has to say about Jesus, who is also the one whom God has sent (v. 30) and who represents and reveals God because as Son he shares his being (vv. 23, 37). Jesus differs from the rest of men not only because he is (as they are not) obedient, but also because he is the divine envoy. In addition to the language of moral relationships John uses also the language of myth; Jesus is the one in whom the true God is encountered.

The discourse may be divided into three sections.

In vv. 19-30 the main theme is solemnly, constantly, almost wearisomely, repeated. As v. 17 foreshadowed, there is complete unity of action between the Father and the Son, and complete dependence of the Son on the Father. Whether equality with God is the best way of describing this relation may be questioned. Dodd after discussing the matter at length (*Interpretation*, 320-8) decides that John would conclude that ἴσος was an improper term. Whatever be the right term, John applies his theme in two particular matters. The Father is the one true spring of life and of righteous judgement, but he has committed both the bestowal of life and the responsibility of judgement to the Son. These are mentioned partly because they are signs of the manifest power which will lead men either to honour Christ as they honour the Father or to reject him and so condemn themselves, and partly because life and judgement are two of the main themes of the gospe as a whole. Life and judgement are characteristically treated as both present and future in their scope. Brown distinguishes perhaps a little too neatly when he maintains that life and judgement are set forth in vv. 19–25 as realized eschatology, in vv. 26–30 as fina' eschatology.

In vv. 31–40 the discourse turns to the theme of witness, and the new paragraph is a good example of the complex relation to his environment in which John stands That it reflects a missionary situation, in which claims made for Jesus (such as those of the preceding paragraph) need to be substantiated, is certainly true; yet John is evidently concerned to question, or qualify, the various kinds of testimony—from John the Baptist, from miracles, from the Old Testament—that a missionary would be inclined to use. As Jesus does not seek his own glory, so he does not bear testimony to himself, being content that God should bear testimony to him in the various ways he has appointed. There is the witness of the Baptist, the witness of the works done by Jesus in the Father's name, and the witness of the Old Testament. These all are derived testimonies, of real but secondary authority. The tragedy of the Jews is that they are content to enjoy the testimony of these witnesses without attending seriously to that to which they testify. There is also the witness of God himself, the divine self-authentication of the mission of Christ to those who accept him; this alone is satisfactory testimony because here only the observer cannot be tempted to linger in the testimony without attending to that to which it testifies.

In vv. 41–7 the subjects already touched upon are brought to a head with direct reference to the specific situation of unbelief in which Jesus found himself. In complete contrast with Jesus, the Jews are utterly estranged from God, and therefore cannot believe. Faith and unbelief are not each equally possible for them (cf. 12.37–41 and the notes there); the way of faith is closed because they have denied its presuppositions. They do not love God, and do not seek glory from him alone. And—a notable example of Johannine irony—it is Moses himself who accuses them, for they have failed to see in Moses a witness to Christ and have treated him as himself an object of hope. Judaism is rightly understood as a ministry of hope when it is allowed to point to Christ; when viewed as closed and self-sufficient system it is a ministry of condemnation.

The whole passage is reminiscent of Pauline passages, both in its Christology (cf. e.g. Phil. 2.5–11, especially 2.8, ὑπήκοος μέχρι θανάτου) and in its treatment of Judaism and the Old Testament (cf. e.g. Rom. 2.17–24; 3.1f.; 9—11; Gal. 4.21–31). But primarily it is an independent rewriting, lit up by acute theological insight, of the historical situation disclosed by the earlier gospel tradition. The Son of man did fulfil his vocation in obedience, obscurity and suffering (e.g. Mark 10.45) and came to his death in the midst of Jewish unbelief. The Messiah was rejected; his ministry separated men into two groups (Mark 4.11f.). John, employing in this chapter primitive Christian rather than any other terminology, and starting from the well-known fact of sabbath disputes, hardly does more than develop, with attention to the question of Christology and the phenomenon of unbelieving Judaism, the historical situation to which the work of Jesus gave rise. Thus John not merely asserts that the humble figure of Jesus, who is obedient to God at the cost of life itself, is equal to God in that in him men truly encounter God himself, in his most characteristic activities of giving life and judging, hearing in Jesus the word of God, seeing in Jesus the God whom no one has ever seen; he asserts also that this is the true meaning of the old historical tradition about Jesus of Nazareth.

19. ποιεῖν ἀφ' ἑαυτοῦ οὐδέν, 'to do nothing without prompting', a common Johannine idiom; see, in various connections, 7.18; 11.51; 15.4; 16.13; 18.34. ἂν μή τι βλέπῃ. ἂν for ἐάν; rare in the New Testament, but cf. 20.23; Robertson, 190: 'unless he sees . . .'. The activity of Jesus the Son of God (after ὁ υἱός, τοῦ ἀνθρώπου is added by D φ; this reading may be due to such passages as 3.13 which speak of the Son of man in heaven) can only be claimed as a revelation of the Father on the ground that Jesus never acts independently of him. What he does is always a reflection of God's own work. With this may be compared (Odeberg, 204f.) remarks made in 3 Enoch about Metatron; see 3 Enoch 10.4f.; 11.1-3; 16; 48C.10f.,20.

ἐκεῖνος, that is, the Father. οὗτος is required by grammar, but ἐκεῖνος lays stress on the separate divine Person, pointing the contrast with ὁ υἱός. The positive statement in the second part of the verse stands in antithetic parallelism with the negative; there is no need, however, to conjecture translation from a Semitic poem.

20. φιλεῖ. φιλεῖν is used by John interchangeably with ἀγαπᾶν. With this verse cf. 3.35, ὁ πατὴρ ἀγαπᾷ τὸν υἱόν, where there is no difference in meaning whatever. Cf. also 11.3,36 with 11.5; and see on 20.2; 21.15-17.

πάντα. The activity of Jesus is not merely a reflection of God's activity but a complete reflection, since the Father shows the Son all that he does.

C. H. Dodd (*More New Testament Studies* (1968), 30-40) and P. Gaechter (in *Neutestamentliche Aufsätze, Festschrift für Prof. J. Schmid*, ed. J. Blinzler, O. Kuss, F. Mussner (1963), 65-8) suggest that in vv. 19,20a we have a parable: a son (generic use of the article) apprenticed to his father does only what he sees his father doing, but his father shows him all the processes that belong to his craft. Cf. Matt. 11.27 = Luke 10.22 (and see J. Jeremias, *Theology* 1, 58). Bultmann argues that ἀφ' ἑαυτοῦ (v. 19a) cannot be intended in a purely moral sense since this would apply to all men; it must refer to the authorization of the Son's mission, and hence to the gnostic myth. The activity of the Father and the activity of the Son are identical. Neither of these views is entirely satisfactory. 'The Son' is in John an established Christological term (see Schnackenburg, II,150-68), but John insists that the 'godlikeness' of the

Son is a matter of historical fact, and though in expressing this he uses the language of the gnostic myth his starting-point is the historical tradition.

μείζονα . . . ἔργα. As the next verse shows, the argument takes a step forward. The Son will do more than remedy men's diseases (vv. 1–9); he will assume the prerogative of God himself in giving life to the dead. Those who take the view (see above) that vv. 19,20a are a parable see here the beginning of its interpretation. Bultmann on the other hand writes, 'His "showing" consists in his speaking to us and challenging us to believe'. Again, neither view is satisfactory. There is a clear reference back to the miracle, and though John does insist on the central importance of Jesus' speech he also represents him as performing significant acts which can be seen and seen to be significant. Cf. 1.50. The total historical phenomenon of Jesus of Nazareth is the place where God is known.

21. ὥσπερ . . . οὕτως. Cf. v. 26. This expression, denoting exact parallelism between the Father and the Son, is the key-note of this paragraph.

ὁ πατὴρ ἐγείρει τοὺς νεκροὺς καὶ 3ωοποιεῖ. To raise the dead was a prerogative of God himself: 2 Kings 5.7, Am I God, to kill and to make alive (τοῦ θανατῶσαι καὶ 3ωοποιῆσαι)? For the continuance of this thought in later Jewish literature see e.g. Taanith 2a: R. Johanan said: Three keys are in God's hand which are given into the hand of no representative (שליח, shaliah), namely the key of the rain (Deut. 28.12), the key of the womb (Gen. 30.22), and the key of the resurrection of the dead (Ezek. 37.13). Elijah is sometimes recognized as an exception to this rule (S.B. 1, 523f., 737, 895); see also T.W.N.T. 1, 419 (K. H. Rengstorf). There is no evidence until very late for the belief that the Messiah would be entrusted with authority to raise the dead. Further, even God was believed not to raise the dead (with few exceptions) in this age; the resurrection was a phenomenon that belonged to the age to come. See on 11.24.

ὁ υἱὸς οὓς θέλει 3ωοποιεῖ. The authority that no human representative could possess is enjoyed by the Son in complete freedom (οὓς θέλει)—as he chose the sick man out of the multitude (5.6). Since he sees all that the Father does and is able himself to do all that he sees, he also gives life. It appears from the context that three thoughts are in John's mind. (a) The resurrection at the last day will be through Jesus (vv. 28f.; cf. 1 Thess. 4.16, οἱ νεκροὶ ἐν Χριστῷ ἀναστήσονται); (b) Jesus raises men from the spiritual death of sin and corruption (v. 25; cf. Rom. 6.4); (c) in this gospel, as a parable of (a) and (b), Jesus raises Lazarus (11.43f.).

22. One eschatological theme leads to another. Just as it is a fundamental Jewish belief that in the last days God will raise the dead, so also is it that at that time all men shall be judged. But God has handed over the office of judgement to the Son, (23) that the Son may receive equal honour with the Father. Men are bound to respect their judge. The judgement, like the resurrection, belongs to both the present and the future.

23. ὁ μὴ τιμῶν τὸν υἱὸν οὐ τιμᾷ τὸν πατέρα τὸν πέμψαντα αὐτόν, an expression in negative form of a principle that dominates John's Christology; see especially on 20.21. So complete is the identity in function and authority between the Father and the Son that it is impossible to honour God while disregarding Jesus. The point is here mentioned incidentally, but it is fundamental to the discourse, and is in fact implicit in v. 17, which supplies its 'text'.

24. ἀμὴν ἀμήν (see on 1.51) here introduces a very important saying which summarizes the paragraph. The related eschatological themes of resurrection and judgement are developed. The distinction between a present realization of these events and their full future realization is made quite clear; note especially vv. 25 and 28: ἔρχεται ὥρα καὶ νῦν ἐστίν, and ἔρχεται ὥρα. The Christian believer has eternal life (see on 3.15), and he is not judged (adversely; see on v. 29, where ἀνάστασις κρίσεως is contrasted with ἀνάστασις ζωῆς).

The believer is described as ὁ τὸν λόγον μου ἀκούων καὶ πιστεύων τῷ πέμψαντί με. The absence of a second article shows that the two participles are co-ordinate features of a single, twofold, description. John lays some stress on *seeing* as the ground of believing (e.g. 20.8), but he makes it clear that seeing (of this kind) was a privilege contributed by the apostles to the church (20.29); believing is also by *hearing* (cf. Rom. 10.17) and accordingly John emphasizes also hearing, believing and keeping the word of Jesus; see 2.22; 4.(41),50; 5.24; (6.60); 7.40; 8.43,51f.,55; 14.23f.; 15.20; 17.6. Cf. also among other passages 12.48 where the word of Jesus judges the man who rejects it (and him) at the last day, and 8.47, ὁ ὢν ἐκ τοῦ θεοῦ τὰ ῥήματα τοῦ θεοῦ ἀκούει. This corresponds to the synoptic teaching, e.g. Matt. 7.24-7 = Luke 6.47-9. To hear the word of Jesus is to have eternal life, since his sayings (ῥήματα) are the words of eternal life (6.68); that is, they are Spirit and life (6.63). ἀκούειν is used, as שמע is often used in the Old Testament, with the meaning 'to hear and do', 'to be obedient'. Correspondingly, the word of Jesus includes precept (for this meaning see especially 15.20), but it is far more. It is an active thing, which has almost an independent existence, and judges, gives life, and cleanses (15.3). Jesus does not in this context speak of believing in himself, though on occasion (e.g. 14.1) he does so. The theme of this discourse is the co-ordinate activity of the Father and the Son, and the complete dependence of Jesus upon the Father. Consequently faith is said to be directed through Jesus to him that sent him.

εἰς κρίσιν οὐκ ἔρχεται. The meaning is that of 3.18, οὐ κρίνεται. κρίσις includes the future judgement, and also the judgement that was in process throughout the ministry of Jesus (and that of the Holy Spirit, 16.8,11). The thought is closely akin to the Pauline doctrine of justification, according to which the believer does indeed come into judgement but leaves the court acquitted.

μεταβέβηκεν ἐκ τοῦ θανάτου εἰς τὴν ζωήν. For μεταβαίνειν cf. 13.1 and 1 John 3.14 where the same words are used (with the verb in the first person plural). For the thought cf. also *C.H.* 1, 32, εἰς ζωὴν καὶ φῶς χωρῶ. The believer has already passed out of the world ruled by death and entered the realm of eternal life; that is, his future reward has been anticipated, and is consequently assured to him. Does John here fall into the error of Hymenaeus and Philetus (2 Tim. 2.18; see on 11.26)? No, for Bultmann is right in saying that 'the elimination of the future judgement does not mean the complete elimination of the future in a mystical present', and we are not justified in omitting vv. 28f. in order to make John a heretic. It is his intention to assert both present and future aspects of eschatology. It is doubtful whether there is much relevance in the fact that resurrection and judgement are the main themes of Rosh ha-Shanah (Guilding, especially 83; see on 5.1), or in Philo's account of the ποιητική (creative) and βασιλική (ruling, judging) powers of God (Dodd,

Interpretation, 322ff.). The themes in question are fundamental enough to have parallels in most theological literature.

25. John begins to restate the content of v. 24 in more detail.

ἔρχεται ὥρα καὶ νῦν ἐστιν. See on 4.23; as there (see 4.21) the longer phrase is contrasted with a simple ἔρχεται ὥρα, and the contrast is not accidental. John distinguishes between the resurrection of the physically dead and the quickening of those who are raised from spiritual death. For the life-giving power of the voice, or word, of Jesus, which gives both spiritual and physical life, see on 6.63,68, and cf. 11.43. That the dead referred to in this verse are not the physically dead is confirmed by the fact that they are not (like those of v. 28) said to be in the tombs; the aorist participle ἀκούσαντες suggests those who at the time of writing have been vivified by the word of Christ.

26. ὥσπερ . . . οὕτως. See vv. 19–21. John returns to the central theme of the discourse, the complete continuity between the work of the Father and the work of the Son. The life however of the Son is dependent upon that of the Father. This does not contradict the words of the Prologue (1.4, ἐν αὐτῷ ζωὴ ἦν), since the giving (ἔδωκεν) is not a temporal act but describes the eternal relation of the Father and the Son.

27. As with life, so with judgement, the other eschatological factor under discussion. This verse takes up v. 22; such repetitions are in John's manner; cf.1.2.

ὅτι υἱὸς ἀνθρώπου ἐστίν. It is very unlikely that we should write ὅ, τι υἱὸς ἀνθρώπου ἐστίν, authority to pass judgement *on what man is*, equally unlikely that ἀνθρώπου should be regarded as an editorial addition designed to prepare for the supposed interpolation of vv. 28f. On Son of man in this passage see Higgins, *Son of Man*, 165–8, and Hahn, *Titel*, 40f. (apparently not in E.T.). Everywhere else in John both articles are used—ὁ υἱὸς τοῦ ἀνθρώπου. Because the phrase is here anarthrous it has been suggested that its meaning is not 'the Son of man' but 'man'; Jesus is qualified and authorized to judge because he has shared the experiences of men as one of themselves. It seems probable that the title is used 'qualitatively' (M. II, 441; emphasized by Sidebottom, 92f.); but it seems also wholly improbable that precisely at this place, where judgement—the characteristic function of the apocalyptic Son of man—is in mind, John would turn his back on the common Christian (and his own) usage. He may even be returning to the wording of Dan. 7.13, (ὡς) υἱὸς ἀνθρώπου. Note also Dan. 7.14, ἐδόθη αὐτῷ ἐξουσία, and cf. in this verse ἐξουσίαν ἔδωκεν αὐτῷ. It is unnecessary here to use the articles because 'in this context his uniqueness is perfectly clear. It arises out of the uniqueness of his status as Son of God. In relation to God the μονογενής is not a, but the, Son of man. But here the emphasis lies upon the fact that he belongs to humanity as he who took the measure of life appointed to men' (Schlatter, 152). Smalley (*N.T.S.* 15 (1969), 292) rejects Sidebottom's 'Jesus judges by virtue of his manhood', commenting that he judges '*as* vindicated Son of man'. There is however an aspect of truth in both views. Jesus does not judge *simply* because he is a human being; if this were so all men would be at liberty to judge. He judges because he is humanity restored and vindicated (Ps. 8.4–8) by its union with God.

28. μὴ θαυμάζετε τοῦτο. These words begin a fresh sentence. Chrysostom

(*Hom.* xxxix, 3) connected them with ὅτι υἱὸς ἀνθρώπου ἐστίν in the preceding verse, but the saying about the Son of man goes with what precedes it, not with μὴ θαυμάζετε τοῦτο. The question remains whether the ὅτι after τοῦτο means 'for', or explains the content of τοῦτο. The meaning may be either (*a*) Do not marvel at what I have just said (that the Son of man even now judges and quickens the spiritually dead), for he will be the agent of the final resurrection and judgement; or (*b*) Do not marvel at this, namely that the Son of man will be the agent ... (*a*) gives the better sense, gives the argument a cumulative force, and should be accepted. The sense is not much affected if we read μὴ θαυμάζετε not as a prohibition, but as a question: You are not surprised at this, are you? See B.D. §427. If (*a*) is accepted, it must be recognized that John has not so radically transformed the synoptic eschatology that he ceases to regard the final judgement as the supreme act of Jesus the Son of man. There is no reason whatever for regarding vv. 28f. as a supplement to the original Johannine discourse unless it is held incredible that John should have thought of resurrection and judgement under both present and future aspects. The combination of the two, however, is one of John's principal theological affirmations. See Introduction, pp. 67–70.

ἔρχεται ὥρα. Cf. v. 25. John does not now add 'and now is'; he is speaking of a real future.

πάντες οἱ ἐν τοῖς μνημείοις. John means the physically dead (contrast v. 25), and all of them, good and bad, in distinction from the elect (v. 24) who have already been raised by Jesus to the divine life. It is possible that he also alludes to the symbolic narrative of the raising of Lazarus, who was ἐν τῷ μνημείῳ (11.17).

ἀκούσουσιν τῆς φωνῆς αὐτοῦ. Cf. v. 25; also 11.43. There are similar words in a different setting at 10.3,16.

29. οἱ τὰ ἀγαθὰ ποιήσαντες ... οἱ τὰ φαῦλα πράξαντες. Cf. Rom. 2.6–9; also Matt. 25.35f.,42f. Paul and John adhere to the notion of a judgement on the basis of works; but such a judgement draws its meaning from the context of thought. Here it must be remembered that the believer neither is dead nor comes into judgement (v. 24). It is unbelievers who appear in this judgement, and their judgement at the last day rests upon precisely the same principles as those which direct the judgement that takes place in the presence of Jesus (3.17–21). It seems unlikely that John intends any difference between ποιεῖν and πράσσειν; he is fond of using pairs of synonyms.

ἀνάστασιν ζωῆς. They rise to share in the life of the age to come the ζωὴ αἰώνιος which those who believe already enjoy (v. 24). With this phrase and that which follows cf. Dan. 12.2: Many of those who sleep in the dust of earth shall arise (ἀναστήσονται), οἱ μὲν εἰς ζωὴν αἰώνιον, οἱ δὲ εἰς ὀνειδισμόν.

ἀνάστασιν κρίσεως. They rise to come under the adverse judgement that believers escape (v. 24). For κρίσις as adverse judgement, condemnation, see on 3.17, and cf. *Eduyoth* 2.10: He (R. Aqiba, † c. A.D. 135) used to say: ... the judgement (מִשְׁפָּט, mishpaṭ) of the generation of the Flood endured twelve months; the judgement of Job endured twelve months; the judgement of the Egyptians endured twelve months; the judgement of Gog and Magog which is to come shall endure twelve months; and the judgement of the unrighteous in Gehenna shall endure twelve months.

30. The opening paragraph (vv. 19–30) is summed up in this last verse. 'A oneness of essence exists because there is a complete oneness of will' (Cullmann, *Christology*, 300).

οὐ δύναμαι ἐγὼ ποιεῖν ἀπ' ἐμαυτοῦ οὐδέν. On the expression ποιεῖν ἀφ' ἑαυτοῦ οὐδέν see on v. 19. In both places the order of words lays great stress on οὐδέν. If he were to act independently of God (supposing such a thing to be possible) Jesus would be completely powerless. The whole meaning and energy of his work lie in the fact that it is not his work but God's.

καθὼς ἀκούω κρίνω. Cf. vv. 19f., 22. The Father has committed all judgement to the Son, but the Son judges according to the word of the Father. It follows that the judgement that he gives is just; all that he does proceeds not from his own will but from God's, who sent him. His mission is perfectly fulfilled in virtue of his perfect obedience. Cf. vv. 41, 44, where a contrast is drawn between seeking glory from men and seeking the glory of God.

31. This verse, and the following paragraph, arise out of v. 30. Just as Jesus seeks God's will, not his own, so he is content that God should bear witness to him.

ἐὰν ἐγὼ μαρτυρῶ περὶ ἐμαυτοῦ. On the important theme of witness see on 1.7. In this verse there is a formal contradiction with 8.14, while in 8.13 the Jews allege σὺ περὶ σεαυτοῦ μαρτυρεῖς· ἡ μαρτυρία σου οὐκ ἔστιν ἀληθής. In each place the speech is *ad hominem* and the meaning is sufficiently plain; yet it may be questioned whether a writer who had fully revised his work would have left the two statements in their present form. Here John means that it is impossible for Jesus, who acts only in conjunction with the Father, to pose as an independent, self-authenticating authority.

32. ἄλλος ἐστὶν ὁ μαρτυρῶν περὶ ἐμοῦ. The witness is not the Baptist (who is dealt with in vv. 33–6) but the Father. For the idea of God as witness cf. *P. Aboth.* 4.22 and especially *Ex. R.* 1.20, where he bears witness to Abraham; also Wisd. 1.6. John returns to the theme of God's witness to Jesus at v. 37.

οἶδα] οἴδατε, ℵ* D a e cur. The variant is strongly attested but probably secondary. Superficially the argument reads better if the Jews are forced to admit that they know the evidence of Jesus' 'Witness' to be true; but in fact they do not recognize the truth of his witness, or even hear his voice (v. 37). It is Jesus, not his opponents, who hears the voice and knows the mind of God.

33. μεμαρτύρηκε. See 1.20–7; also 1.29,32ff. (ἐμαρτύρησεν ... μεμαρτύρηκα)'. It was for witness that John came into the world (1.7.) The effect of the perfect tenses is to present his testimony as an established datum. For the relation of this gospel to surviving disciples of John the Baptist see pp. 138, 172f.

τῇ ἀληθείᾳ, in this context the truth concerning Jesus, that he is the Son (or Elect) of God, the Lamb of God, he that baptizes with the Spirit, etc. The Council of the Qumran sect were witnesses to truth (1 QS 8.6, עֵדֵי אֱמֶת; better perhaps, true witnesses). The thought is too commonplace for the parallel to be significant.

34. ἐγὼ δὲ οὐ παρὰ ἀνθρώπου τὴν μαρτυρίαν λαμβάνω. The witness of John is plain, valid, and true; but Jesus, who knows the witness of the 'Other', is

independent of human witness. He has mentioned the testimony of John, but explains that he has not done so because he himself relies upon it.

ταῦτα λέγω ἵνα ὑμεῖς σωθῆτε. Men are saved by believing in Jesus, so that the appeal to John, since it may cause them to believe, is justified, and may lead to salvation. There is no need (with Torrey, 135, 137) to emend; the verse makes quite satisfactory sense.

35. ἐκεῖνος. John the Baptist; his office is further defined. This verse and the next place John on a very high, but definitely human, level. It is conceivable, though far from certain, that they were directed against some who overestimated the Baptist's rank.

ὁ λύχνος, an ordinary portable lamp. Cf. 1.8, οὐκ ἦν ἐκεῖνος τὸ φῶς. John is distinguished from the true self-kindled light, just as his witness is secondary to and derived from (1.33) that of the Father. David was ὁ λύχνος Ἰσραήλ (2 Sam. 21.17), and Rabban Johanan b. Zakkai was addressed as 'Light of Israel' (נר ישראל, Berakoth 28b; the parallel in Aboth de R. Nathan 25 has נר עולם, Light of the world). More important however is the reference made by F. Neugebauer (Z.N.T.W. 52 (1961), 130) and A. T. Hanson (Studies in the Pastoral Epistles (1968), 12ff.) to Ps. 132 (131).16b,17: Her saints shall shout aloud for joy (ἀγαλλιάσει ἀγαλλιάσονται). There will I make the horn of David to bud: I have ordained a lamp for mine anointed (λύχνον τῷ χριστῷ μου). The lamp becomes a witness to the Messiah. Cf. also Ecclus. 48.1, where it is said of Elijah (the Forerunner) that his word ὡς λαμπὰς ἐκαίετο. The evangelist begins from primitive messianic concepts, but is aware of their inadequacy.

ὁ καιόμενος, not 'burning' but '(the lamp) which is kindled'; that is, John's light is derived from a higher source.

φαίνων. φαίνειν is used intransitively of any source of light, often of heavenly bodies but also of lamps, e.g. 1 Macc. 4.50 (lamps in the Temple).

ὑμεῖς δέ. You—who sent your inquiry to John, and to whom I now speak.

ἠθελήσατε ἀγαλλιαθῆναι πρὸς ὥραν. The aorist ἠθελήσατε, which would not otherwise be expected, corresponds to the short space of time signified by πρὸς ὥραν, which recalls the Hebrew לשעה (lᵉshaʿah). It may also point to the notion of preference which is sometimes contained in θέλειν. This comes out most clearly when θέλειν is followed by ἤ (see 1 Cor. 4.21; 14.19; and other examples given in T.W.N.T. iii, 46, n. 29 (G. Shrenk), and in M.M. s.v.). If θέλειν has this force here the meaning will be: You preferred the brief religious excitement of John's ministry to faith in him whom God sent (v. 38) and to whom John bore witness, and the eternal life which he offered. This would correspond exactly to what is said (vv. 39f.) about the witness of the Scriptures. ἀγαλλιᾶσθαι is a strong word, 'to rejoice greatly', 'to exult'; it is used elsewhere in John only at 8.56, of Abraham, who exulted to see the day of Christ. Possibly John refers to the exultant hope of the Jews in prospect of the messianic kingdom, but this must be regarded as quite uncertain, though there is evidence in Josephus as well as the New Testament that the work of John the Baptist provoked a good deal of messianic excitement.

ἐν τῷ φωτὶ αὐτοῦ. John was no more than a kindled lamp, yet as a lamp he gave a real light.

36. ἐγὼ δὲ ἔχω τὴν μαρτυρίαν μείζω τοῦ 'Ιωάννου. μείζω (masculine or feminine accusative) is read by the majority of MSS.: μείζονα (D) is simply an alternative form. μείζων occurs in P⁶⁶ B W φ; this is apparently a nominative and would require the rendering, 'I who am greater than John have the witness'. This however gives a false antithesis; Jesus is not here comparing himself with John but comparing different kinds of witness. Consequently it is better to take μείζων as another variant form of the accusative with the 'irrational addition of ν, which seems to have been added after long vowels almost freely as the equally unpronounced ι' (M. 1, 49). When this point has been settled the sentence remains ambiguous. μείζω is certainly predicative and may be taken in two ways: (a) I have testimony which is greater than John had; (b) I have testimony greater than the testimony John gave. Of these (b) undoubtedly suits the context better and should be preferred (though for this meaning μείζω ἤ τοῦ 'I. (B. D. §185) would have been better; see however Black, 116). Dodd (Tradition, 299) deduces that the appeal to John the Baptist no longer carried weight; groups of disciples such as those in Ephesus (Acts 19.1–7) had ceased to exist. If however this consideration had weighed with the evangelist he would simply have dropped the now pointless reference to the Baptist; he is less concerned with the immediate practical usefulness of a reference to John than with his theological significance (see especially 1.6ff.). The witness greater than John's is twofold, and is dealt with in vv. 36a, 37b.

τὰ γὰρ ἔργα. First is the witness of the works which Jesus himself performs; cf. 14.11. The works are the gift of the Father to Jesus; cf. v. 20.

ἵνα τελειώσω αὐτά. ἵνα and the subjunctive for infinitive, as frequently in John. τελειοῦν is characteristic of John, especially with ἔργον (elsewhere in the singular; 4.34; 17.4). Both sides of the activity of Jesus are brought out: his works are in origin not his own but the Father's; yet because of his complete obedience the Father's works are through him brought to a unique completeness. What had been done partially by the servants of God is finally accomplished by his Son.

αὐτὰ τὰ ἔργα ἃ ποιῶ. The subject is repeated after the relative clause which interrupts the flow of the sentence, but another relative is added to balance the former: God gives the works and Jesus does them. Cf. the passage in P. Eg. 2 quoted on 3.2.

μαρτυρεῖ περὶ ἐμοῦ ὅτι ὁ πατήρ με ἀπέσταλκεν. The works of Jesus are not merely such as to prove that he is a notable person, or even that God is with him, as Nicodemus allowed (3.2); he is able to perform distinctively divine works (see v. 21 and note), so that he is manifestly sent from God, with a delegated divine authority. On the mission of Jesus from the Father see on 20.21.

37. ὁ πέμψας με πατήρ (a common Johannine formula), ἐκεῖνος μεμαρτύρηκεν. Reference has already been made to the witness given by John the Baptist and by the works. It is also given directly by the Father. It is not clear to what witness John refers at this point. It seems unlikely that he is anticipating the reference to the Scriptures, which comes explicitly at v. 39, nor is there adequate reason for seeing here an allusion to the voice from heaven at the Baptism (Mark 1.11 and parallels), which John omits from his gospel (see on 1.32–4). The clue to this passage may be found in 1 John 5.9f. (on which see Dodd, ad loc.). The witness of the Father is granted to those who believe in

the Son. Those who do not believe in Jesus do not hear the voice of God (cf. 12.29), nor have they seen him (1.18); but he who has truly seen Jesus as the Son of God has seen his Father also (14.9); so also in Jesus himself the believer encounters the Word of God. The witness of the Father is thus not immediately accessible and assessable; the observer cannot sit in judgement upon it and then decide whether or not he will believe in Jesus. He must believe in Jesus first and then he will receive the direct testimony from God. John's expression of this belief is obscure, and the obscurity is not due simply to his brevity (Bernard, ad loc.), but also to the fact that he is driven to use negative language. The witness he speaks of is real and well understood within the church for which he writes; but in the context in the gospel it does not exist, since the Jews to whom Jesus speaks do not believe. What John means is that the truth of God in Jesus is self-authenticating in the experience of the believer; but no such convenient phrase lay to his hand.

38. τὸν λόγον αὐτοῦ οὐκ ἔχετε ἐν ὑμῖν μένοντα. God's word is his testimony, and it does not dwell within the unbelieving Jews who refuse to receive it; see the note on v. 37. But, as the parallelism with the next clause suggests, the thought was probably not absent from John's mind that the true Word of God was Jesus, who did not abide (μένειν) with these unbelievers as he did with his own (e.g. 15.3).

ὅτι. This may mean (a) You have not the word of God because you do not believe his Son; or (b) That you have not the word of God appears from the fact that you do not believe his Son. Neither alternative can be excluded; both are true. Rejection of the word of God is both the cause and the sign of unbelief. πιστεύειν is here used with the dative; the primary thought is that of giving credence to what Jesus says.

39. ἐρευνᾶτε τὰς γραφάς. The form of the verb may be indicative or imperative; the context shows that the indicative is meant; so also Dodd (*Interpretation*, 329f.), after a long discussion. Only this interpretation makes sense of the δοκεῖτε which follows, and of the whole context; and the indicative is parallel to the description of the Jews' veneration of John, the other witness (v. 35). Moreover, ἐρευνᾶτε as an indicative is a simple statement of undoubted fact. ἐρευνᾶν (on the spelling see M. 1, 46, II, 86; M.M. *s.v.*; B.D., §30) corresponds to דרש, the technical term for biblical study and exposition, which, with the study of the oral Torah, was the principal activity of rabbinic Judaism. In illustration of this (and of the following clause) see e.g. *P. Aboth* 2.7: (Hillel said): If a man has gained a good name he has gained (somewhat) for himself; if he has gained for himself words of the Law he has gained for himself life in the world to come.

ὅτι ὑμεῖς δοκεῖτε ἐν αὐταῖς 3ωὴν αἰώνιον ἔχειν. See the reference to *P. Aboth* 2.7 above. The words ἐν αὐταῖς are in a position of emphasis. The Jews regard their biblical studies as an end in themselves. Paul refers to and comments on the Jewish notion of a life-giving Law at Rom. 7.10 (εὑρέθη μοι ἡ ἐντολὴ ἡ εἰς 3ωὴν αὕτη εἰς θάνατον), and contradicts it flatly at Gal. 3.21 (εἰ γὰρ ἐδόθη νόμος ὁ δυνάμενος 3ωοποιῆσαι). It is Christ to whom the Father has given to have life in himself and to impart it (vv. 21, 26; 1.4 *et al.*). For the transference of attributes and powers from the Law to Christ cf. 1.1-4.

καί (and yet; a classical meaning of καί, so that Semitic influence need not be suspected) ἐκεῖναί εἰσιν αἱ μαρτυροῦσαι. The function of the Old Testament is precisely the opposite of that which the Jews ascribe to it. So far from being complete and life-giving in itself, it points away from itself to Jesus, exactly as John the Baptist did. 'The world's resistance to God is based on its imagined security, which reaches its highest and most subversive form in religion, and thus, for the Jews in their pattern of life based on Scripture. Their "searching" in the Scriptures makes them deaf to Jesus' word' (Bultmann). Yet, as Bultmann rightly deduces from the evangelist's note (ἐκεῖναί εἰσιν . . .), this is to pervert the Scriptures. The fact is that Jesus illuminates the Old Testament more than the Old Testament illuminates him. There is a close parallel to this verse in *P. Eg.* 2 (see Introduction, p. 110). The passage (lines 5–10) in the papyrus runs as follows: πρὸς [δὲ τοὺς] ἄ[ρ]χοντας τοῦ λαοῦ [στ]ρα[φεὶς εἶ]πεν τὸν λόγον τοῦτο[ν] ἐραυ[νᾶτε τ]ὰς γραφάς· ἐν αἷς ὑμεῖς δο[κεῖτε] ζωὴν ἔχειν ἐκεῖναί εἰ[σ]ιν [αἱ μαρτ]υροῦσαι περὶ ἐμοῦ. The differences between this form of the saying and that in John may be summarized thus. (*a*) The introduction differs. In John we hear nothing of the 'rulers of the people'. The difference is characteristic. In John the saying is worked up into a discourse; in *P. Eg.* 2 it appears almost in isolation, in the manner of the synoptic logia. (*b*) For the words which follow in *P. Eg.* 2 see on v. 45. (*c*) *P. Eg.* 2 has ζωήν for John's ζωὴν αἰώνιον. In this difference there is nothing inconsistent with direct literary relationship. (*d*) Before ἐκεῖναι *P. Eg.* 2 omits καί. This difference also is too slight to preclude literary relationship. (*e*) The most significant verbal difference is that where John has ὅτι . . . ἐν αὐταῖς, *P. Eg.* 2 has ἐν αἷς. A similar variation occurs in certain VSS. of John. a b cur have the following text: *illae* (b: *et ipsae*) *sunt quae testimonium dicunt* (b: *perhibent*) *de me, in quibus putatis uos uitam habere, hae* (b: *haec*) *sunt quae de me testificantur* (b: *testif. de me*). This variation, which in itself, notwithstanding the interesting combination of old Latin and old Syriac, could hardly be upheld as the true reading, must be considered with the claim that the current text of John arose out of a misunderstanding of an Aramaic original. ὅτι might represent the relative particle ד, which would be followed by the appropriate supplement 'in them'. There is no question that a piece of correct but ambiguous Aramaic can be thus reconstructed (Black, 72f.), and that the same Aramaic might be the base of both John and *P. Eg.* 2 (alternatively, *P. Eg.* 2, supposed directly dependent on John, preserves an extremely early text of the gospel). But it must be emphasized that the hypothesis of an original Aramaic, though not impossible, is in no sense whatever necessary. There is no difficulty in the Greek of either text. That of John gives perhaps the more forceful sense (You search the Scriptures with the motive of gaining eternal life), that of *P. Eg.* 2 (You search the Scriptures in which you suppose you have eternal life) the smoother Greek. The latter is probably secondary.

40. Just as the Jews chose to enjoy for a moment the temporary and secondary light of the Baptist (v. 35), so they prefer to pursue their studies and refuse to come to Jesus, who could in truth give them eternal life. 'Coming to Jesus' is a common Johannine phrase (e.g. 1.47; 3.2; 4.30,40,47); for its result in eternal life cf. 6.35; 7.37.

41. δόξαν παρὰ ἀνθρώπων οὐ λαμβάνω. For the words cf. v. 34, with μαρτυρία for δόξα. The connection of thought seems to be that Jesus does not upbraid the Jews for their unbelief because he wishes to enjoy the glory of human approbation. He states what is to him a manifest fact (ἔγνωκα).

42. ἔγνωκα ὑμᾶς ὅτι . . . οὐκ ἔχετε. The subject of the subordinate clause is attracted into the principal sentence as its object. This construction is common in Aramaic, but not unknown in Greek.

τὴν ἀγάπην τοῦ θεοῦ . . . ἐν ἑαυτοῖς. The genitive may be objective (You do not love God), or subjective (You are not men whom God loves). The former statement would be the sign of the Jews' unbelief, the latter the grounds of it. The former alternative is more probable: ἐν ἑαυτοῖς suggests an attribute or activity of the persons concerned. They are those who love the darkness rather than the light (3.19). Brown prefers the subjective genitive by analogy with 'his word' in v. 38. But love may be regarded as the response to the word.

43. ἐγὼ ἐλήλυθα ἐν τῷ ὀνόματι τοῦ πατρός μου. This resumes the whole section from v. 19. The immense claims made by Jesus for himself are conjoined with complete self-effacement; he comes to speak to men not of himself but God.

καὶ οὐ λαμβάνετέ με. καί as at v. 39; cf. 1.11, οἱ ἴδιοι αὐτὸν οὐ παρέλαβον. Just as the previous clause summarizes the divine mission of Jesus, so this summarizes the reaction of men to him.

ἄλλος. The form of the sentence leaves open the question whether such an 'other' would or would not come. The reference to Bar Cochba, the messianic claimant of c. A.D. 132, which some have found here, is very unlikely; see Introduction, pp. 127f., on the date of the gospel. Other historical persons have been suggested as the 'other', and so has Anti-Christ (Bousset-Gressman, 255); but it seems unnecessary, and perhaps wrong, to seek precise definition. The point lies in the contrast between ἐν τῷ ὀνόματι τοῦ πατρός μου and ἐν τῷ ὀνόματι τῷ ἰδίῳ. One who relies upon his own dignity and power, and seeks glory from men, will belong to the same world as the unbelievers (v. 44) and will therefore prove more attractive to them.

44. δόξαν παρὰ ἀλλήλων λαμβάνοντες. δόξα here means 'good repute', 'praise'. Men seek praise from their fellow men, and consequently understand others who do the like; and they would enjoy the flattery of one who, unlike Jesus, was more anxious to secure a good reputation for himself than to do the will of God. The participle λαμβάνοντες is co-ordinated with the finite verb ӡητεῖτε by means of καί; cf. 1.32. This might be due to Aramaic influence but is more probably the result of careless writing. Inferior MSS. correct ӡητεῖτε to ӡητοῦντες.

τὴν δόξαν τὴν παρὰ τοῦ μόνου θεοῦ. θεοῦ is omitted by P66 P75 B W a b sah boh Origen (sometimes), Eusebius. This is impressive evidence, but on the whole it seems more probable that the letters ΘΥ (contraction of θεοῦ) should have been accidentally omitted from ΤΟΥΜΟΝΟΥΘΥΟΥ than that they should have been intentionally added. John nowhere calls God ὁ μόνος; at 17.3 he has τὸν μόνον ἀληθινὸν θεόν. Turner, Insights, 6ff., thinks that the original text was τοῦ θεοῦ μόνου, from God only. That there is one only God is of course a commonplace in the Old Testament and in Judaism. The choice lies between seeking glory from a number of men, and from the one God. Since the Jews (denying their own vocation as the people of God—cf. 19.15, We have no king but Caesar) have chosen the former alternative it is impossible for them to believe (πῶς δύνασθε ὑμεῖς πιστεῦσαι;), for to believe means not merely to credit the existence of God, but, like Jesus, to offer him love and obedience, and to seek glory from him alone (cf. Rom. 2.29), recognizing the insecurity of all existence apart from him (see the note on v. 39).

45. God has committed all judgement to the Son (v. 22), but it is not the Son's office to lay accusations before the Father. It is unnecessary that he should do so.

ἔστιν ὁ κατηγορῶν ὑμῶν Μωϋσῆς. He that accuses you is Moses. The word κατή-γορος (or κατήγωρ) was transliterated into Hebrew and Aramaic and used in the rabbinic literature; e.g. *P. Aboth* 4.11: He that performs one precept gets for himself one advocate; but he that commits one transgression gets for himself one accuser (קטיגור, *qaṭegor*; see further on 14.16). In Rev. 12.10 ὁ κατήγωρ . . . ὁ κατηγορῶν is the devil; accusation was the traditional office of the Satan. In John (not as in *P. Aboth*) the ground of the accusation is not that men have transgressed a commandment but that they have failed to understand the commandments, have taken them as ends in themselves. See below.

εἰς ὃν ὑμεῖς ἠλπίκατε. For the construction cf. 2 Cor. 1.10; for the thought, v. 39. For Moses as the Mediator between God and Israel see, e.g., Bonsirven I, 81f., 253f. It was through Moses that there came to the people the saving knowledge of God, and the Law in the performance of which was life (see on v. 39). It was because Moses thus became the author of a final system of religion, and not, as he wished to be, a witness to Christ, that he became also the accuser of his people, whose punctilious performance of the Law led to their rejection of Jesus (v. 16). The witness of Moses is explained (γάρ) in the next verse.

P. Eg. 2 (see on v. 39) contains a close parallel to this verse also. It runs (lines 10–14): μὴ δ[οκεῖτε ὅ]τι ἐγὼ ἦλθον κατηγο[ρ]ῆσαι [ὑμῶν] πρὸς τὸν π̄ρ̄ᾱ μου· ἔστιν [ὁ κατη]γορῶν Μ̄ω̄ εἰς ὃν [ὑμεῖς] ἠλπίκατε. The differences are very slight. (*a*) ἐγὼ ἦλθον κατηγορῆσαι for ἐγὼ κατηγορήσω; (*b*) τὸν πατέρα μου for τὸν πατέρα. These are very simple editorial changes, quite compatible with direct literary relationship. In the papyrus the Johannine vv. 40–4 disappear, and immediately after the present saying there follows a parallel to John 9.29 (on which see the note). We must probably choose between the hypotheses (*a*) that the author of the papyrus gospel took out of John such sayings as he desired to use; (*b*) John worked up sayings from the papyrus (or a kindred source) into his discourses.

46. εἰ γὰρ ἐπιστεύετε. In point of fact, though the Jews *hope* in Moses they do not believe what he says (πιστεύειν with the dative). The Law, rightly used, should lead men not to unbelief but faith.

περὶ γὰρ ἐμοῦ ἐκεῖνος ἔγραψεν. John mentions no particular Old Testament passages having reference to Christ; this is not his manner. But he is sure that the Old Testament generally is a witness to Christ (v. 39; on John's use of the Old Testament see Introduction, pp. 27–30, and *J.T.S.* old series 48 (1947), 155–69).

47. γράμμασιν . . . ῥήμασιν. The witness of Moses written in the Pentateuch is contrasted with the spoken words of Jesus. It is not probable that a disparagement of the oral Law is intended.

On the question whether this discourse is immediately continued in 7.15–24 see on 7.15.

12. THE FEEDING OF THE FIVE THOUSAND

6.1–15

The notes of time (v. 4) and of place (v. 1) given with this narrative raise considerable difficulty; on this difficulty see the notes on the verses mentioned. The scene depicted by John represents Jesus seated on a mountain (unnamed), surrounded by his disciples, and followed at a greater distance by a large multitude, attracted by his miracles of healing. In this scene, Jesus himself raises the question of supplying food for the multitude. The disciples prove unable to deal with so great a problem, but Andrew draws attention to a boy who has with him his own rough provisions. Over these few loaves and fish Jesus pronounces the blessing and distributes them to the seated crowd, who not only are satisfied but leave uneaten twelve baskets full of broken pieces. The miracle produces upon them a great impression, and Jesus withdraws to the mountain in order to escape their violent and misguided enthusiasm.

It has been argued (notably, and at great length, by Brown) that in this narrative John was independent of Mark. In the sense that John did not *copy* Mark (which is all that Brown may be said to prove) this may well be true, but many indications (for details, and for the view of Dodd and Sanders, see the notes below) suggest that John knew and recalled the two miracle narratives of Mark 6.35–44; 8.1–9 (Matt. 14.13–21; 15.32–8; Luke 9.10–17). Only minor differences, due to motives which can generally be clearly perceived, exist between the Marcan and Johannine narratives. Lindars thinks that John used a source intermediate between those represented by Mark 6 and Mark 8; a more probable view is that John knew and combined both Marcan narratives. In particular, John, in accordance with his custom, stresses the initiative of Jesus, and his freedom of action; see v. 5. A discussion of what may be supposed actually to have taken place in this incident belongs rather to a commentary on Mark than to one on John. The narrative of a miraculous multiplication of food has deep roots in the tradition (as is shown by the fact that already in Mark it appears twice), and John reproduced the tradition. There is no occasion for doubting that John believed that he was recording a real event, and a strictly miraculous one. It is certain that he did not invent this or the following story, since they were already in Mark, and a presumption is thereby created that his other (non-synoptic) miracle stories were received rather than created by him. Bultmann sees editorial insertions in vv. 4,6,14f.

John is probably right in ascribing eschatological significance to the event (see A. Schweitzer, *The Mystery of the Kingdom of God* (E.T., 1925), 168–74; Dodd, *Tradition*, 196–217; and below on vv. 14f.; H. W.

Montefiore, *N.T.S.* 8 (1962), 135–41, exaggerates its political importance). His own interpretation is given later, in 6.22–59. The question
whether this discourse on the Bread of Life may be described as sacramental, or eucharistic, will be discussed below, pp. 281–5, 310f. Very
different views of the story itself have been held. Bultmann, noting that
nothing is said in v. 11 about the breaking of the bread, thinks it does not
contain sacramental language. Guilding (60) thinks that the miracle
symbolizes the last supper. Lindars thinks that the story was valued as
a type of the eucharist and concludes that the event itself had quasi-
sacramental character—perhaps the eating was symbolic and non-
miraculous. Some points of detail will be mentioned below. Eucharistic
parallels, which do exist, were probably no more than incidental to
John. More important may be the analogy with Moses and the manna;
see 6.31f. and the notes; the feeding is one of the three signs of the Mosaic
prophet; see *Eccles. R.* 1.8; Martyn, 98ff.; and cf. p. 74.

1. μετὰ ταῦτα. John's usual expression for denoting the lapse of an undefined
period; see on 2.12.

πέραν. The last place mentioned (5.1) was Jerusalem. This is clearly an
impossible base for a crossing of the lake, and for this reason (among others)
it has been proposed by some scholars to reverse the order of chs. 5 and 6
(see Introduction, p. 23). In 4.46–54 Jesus is at Cana (see on 2.1), not
far from Tiberias and near the lake. This would furnish a suitable starting
point for 6, while 7.1 (or 7.15—see Bultmann, 203, 209f., where the order
advocated is 4.43–54; 6.1–59 (vv. 51b–58 being an insertion); 5.1–47; 7.15–
24; 8.13–20) might well take up the narrative after the opposition in Jerusalem described in ch. 5. These transpositions effect some improvements in
John's narrative; whether they should for that reason be accepted is another
matter which depends on the question whether the writing of good narrative
was a primary aim of the evangelist. It should be noted that the whole section
6.1–21 is very similar to the Marcan section 6.32–53, which contains (i) a
crossing of the lake (cf. especially Mark 6.32 with John 6.1, ἀπῆλθον–ἀπῆλθεν),
(ii) the miraculous feeding of the five thousand, (iii) an attempt by the
disciples, who have left Jesus behind alone, to cross the lake, and (iv) the
appearance to the disciples in the boat of Jesus, walking on the water. The
whole incident is followed in Mark by an assembly of the people and a debate
(Mark 6.54–6; 7.1–23), as in John. If, as is very probable, John was using
the Marcan (or some very similar) tradition, and wished to insert the
material at this point because on theological grounds he desired to present
next his discourse on the Bread of Life, the facts are explained without
recourse to purely hypothetical reconstructions. Brown finds the reversal of
chs. 5 and 6 attractive but not compelling. Sanders sees here a *non sequitur*, but
his own observation that μετὰ ταῦτα and the imperfects ἠκολούθει, ἑώρων,
ἐποίει (v. 2) imply an interval in which unrecorded signs were performed robs
his argument of much of its force. There is a full discussion in Schnackenburg
II, 6–11.

τῆς Τιβεριάδος. The second genitive is added as further explanation of τῆς
Γαλιλαίας. Cf. 21.1, τῆς θαλάσσης τῆς Τιβεριάδος. This name for the lake of
Galilee, which is not used elsewhere in the New Testament, was derived

from Tiberias (cf. v. 23), founded in A.D. 26 (or perhaps a few years earlier) by Herod Antipas and named in honour of the Emperor Tiberius. Josephus reports the foundation in *Ant.* XVIII, 36ff., and for the lake has ἡ πρὸς Τιβεριάδι (or Τιβεριάδα) λίμνη (*Bel.* III, 57) and ἡ Τιβεριέων λίμνη (*Bel.* IV, 456). It is doubtful whether the name 'Sea of Tiberias' would have come into general use as early as the ministry of Jesus, but this of course does not affect the historicity of John's account; he supplies the up-to-date term for the convenience of his readers. The effect of the two genitives is clumsy, and it is not surprising that a few MSS. omit τῆς Γαλιλαίας, while D Θ b e add εἰς τὰ μέρη before τῆς Τιβεριάδος—'across the sea of Galilee to the parts of Tiberias'. The clumsy text is no doubt the original.

2. ὄχλος πολύς. Cf. Mark 6.33f., including the words πολὺν ὄχλον. For the wording cf. 2.23, θεωροῦντες αὐτοῦ τὰ σημεῖα ἃ ἐποίει, and 6.14, ἰδόντες ὃ ἐποίησεν σημεῖον. There seems to be no other example of σημεῖον ποιεῖν ἐπί τινος; the word σημεῖον has almost acquired the specific sense of 'cure', 'miracle of healing'.

ἑώρων (P⁶⁶ ℵ ω) is the reading that should be adopted; ἐθεώρουν, though supported by P⁷⁵ B D W Θ and other MSS., is probably due to assimilation to 2.23.

3. ἀνῆλθεν (ἀπῆλθεν ℵ D) εἰς τὸ ὄρος. The reference to 'the mountain' (the use of the article is perhaps an indication that John is drawing on the synoptic tradition since he nowhere else (except 8.1, not a genuine part of the gospel) speaks of Jesus' withdrawing to a mountain) may be a substitute for Mark's εἰς ἔρημον τόπον (6.31). Jesus returns to the mountain at v. 15, as at Mark 6.46. Cf. also Matt. 5.1, which not only refers to a mountain but also says that Jesus sat down in the presence of his disciples. There is however no necessary implication that Jesus' intention was to teach. There seems to be no symbolic interest in the mountain, though it is not impossible that there is an allusion to Moses and Mount Sinai; cf. the reference to Moses in vv. 31f., with the quotation from *Ecclesiastes R.*

4. ἐγγύς. A Johannine formula; see on 2.13.

τὸ πάσχα. The authenticity of these words was suspected by Hort, though they are contained in all MSS. and VSS. and the only evidence against them is patristic. For a full statement of this evidence see WH, *Notes on Select Readings*, 77–81. Hort concludes 'The supposition that τὸ πάσχα formed no part of the original text must remain somewhat precarious in the absence of any other apparent corruption of equal magnitude and similarly attested by all known MSS. and VSS. But as a considerable body of patristic evidence points to the absence of the words in at least some ancient texts, and internal evidence is unfavourable to their genuineness, while the chronology of the gospel history is fundamentally affected by their presence or absence, it has seemed right to express suspicion, and to justify it at some length' (op. cit., 81). The objection cannot be sustained. The omission of the words by some of the Fathers, and by Hort, rests upon a view of the structure and intention of the gospel which cannot be maintained; the Passover is mentioned here not for chronological but for theological reasons. It is true that this is the second passover in John (cf. 2.13,23), and that only one is mentioned in the synoptics; it is true also that it is impossible to spread out the events of chapters 3—5 over the space of a year. The interesting observations of Abrahams (*Studies* 1, 10f.) do not justify the Johannine dating; 'everything points . . . to a date soon after the Passover'; but John says that the Passover 'was near', that is, had not yet come. He mentions the Passover primarily because, as will appear, some of the acts and words of this chapter have a eucharistic significance, and the eucharist, like the last supper (cf. 13.1), must be understood in the context of the Jewish Passover.

ἡ ἑορτὴ τῶν Ἰουδαίων. If τὸ πάσχα is omitted this phrase might well refer to the feast of Tabernacles; see on 5.1.

5. ἐπάρας οὖν τοὺς ὀφθαλμούς. Cf. 4.35; 17.1. The expression is Lucan—6.20; 16.23; 18.13. For Jesus' pity on the πολὺς ὄχλος cf. Mark 6.34.

ἔρχεται. In Mark the crowd have been with Jesus, and he has taught them. It is not easy to picture this 'coming' of the crowd as a whole; perhaps John thinks of 'coming' in more than a physical sense (see on 5.40).

λέγει πρὸς Φίλιππον. In Mark the disciples take the initiative, asking Jesus to dismiss the multitude. It is characteristic of John that Jesus should act on his own initiative; see 2.4 and the note. For Philip see 1.43; no disciple is mentioned by name in the Marcan narrative. Names are often added in the later forms of New Testament narratives (and in the apocryphal gospels); they sometimes lend an appearance of verisimilitude, but are in fact a sign of lateness; cf. 12.4; 18.10. Martyn (113) notes the parallel between Jesus' question to Philip and Peter's question to Jesus in 6.68 (Lord, to whom shall we go (for the bread, or word, of life)?), and adds, 'The theme of the chapter is "The Origin of Life", couched in terms of the tension between man's self-determination of his life and God's predestination to life. This theme is developed primarily, but not exclusively, with reference to the eucharist, and in such a way as to make the connection between the eucharist and predestination unmistakably clear.' This is well said; cf. also *Essays*, 62–9. Whether John intended his reader to see so much in this verse is another question; Martyn does not say that he does.

6. πειράζων. Elsewhere in the gospels πειράζειν has a bad sense; Jesus is tempted by Satan or by wicked men. The word in itself however is neutral, and may mean 'to try', 'to test' a person. Jesus wishes to test the extent of Philip's faith. At the same time, John forestalls 'any implication of ignorance' on Jesus' part (Brown).

7. διακοσίων δηναρίων ἄρτοι. The genitive is the genitive of price: 'loaves to the value of . . .'. Cf. Mark 6.37, ἀπελθόντες ἀγοράσωμεν δηναρίων διακοσίων ἄρτους. The coincidence in number is remarkable (see below vv. 9f., 13). It seems unlikely that all the numbers should be accurately preserved in oral tradition, and probable therefore that John used a written account of the miracle, similar to if not identical with Mark's. Philip answers Jesus' test (v. 6) 'at the level of the market-place' (Lightfoot); his words also serve to heighten the miracle (Lindars).

9. ἔστιν παιδάριον ὧδε. The youth is mentioned in no other gospel; the word παιδάριον, a double diminutive, occurs nowhere else in the New Testament (Matt. 11.16, *v.l.*), and its meaning is not certain. The grammatical form does not require extreme youth; at Gen. 37.30 Joseph at the age of seventeen is described as a παιδάριον (ילד); cf. Tobit 6.3 (B). The meaning 'young slave' is well attested, and occurs in *Mart. Pol.* 6.1; 7.1 (further references in

L.S., Bauer, *Wörterbuch*, M.M., *s.v.*). The meaning of the word here may be determined by the origin of this feature of the narrative. It is possible that this may have been drawn by John from independent tradition, and again that it may be an expansion of the ὑπάγετε ἴδετε of Mark 6.38. More probably it is due to recollection of the narrative of 2 Kings 4.42–4 (which may have influenced John's narrative again; see below). Here Elisha, in miraculously feeding one hundred men, is assisted by a servant. The latter is not here described as a παιδάριον but as a λειτουργός (משרת); but in the preceding narrative (4.38–41) Elisha's servant is twice described as a παιδάριον (in v. 38 נער, in v. 41 no Hebrew equivalent). It does not seem probable that John here intends to introduce into his narrative an equivalent to an item of eucharistic ritual. It is true that the offering of bread and wine early became a feature of the eucharist; see especially Justin, 1 *Apol.* 65,67 (ἄρτος προσφέρεται καὶ οἶνος καὶ ὕδωρ); 1 Clement 44.4 is earlier but vague (τὰ δῶρα τῆς ἐπισκοπῆς), Irenaeus (*adv. Haer.* IV, xxix, 5) later. But if John had intended to refer to this custom (supposing him to have known it) he (*a*) would have made the act of *offering* much clearer (in fact he omits to mention it), (*b*) would hardly have failed to make use of the LXX word λειτουργός, and (*c*) would not have omitted from Mark the interesting detail of the distribution of the food by the disciples (see on v. 11). Moreover, John is not, in his gospel, concerned with the details of ecclesiastical rites (hence his omission of all explicit reference to baptism and of the 'institution of the eucharist') but to set forth Jesus as the dispenser of life. Cf. however Sanders, and Richardson, *Theology*, 384f. (the offering is the people's, not the apostles').

πέντε ἄρτους κριθίνους καὶ δύο ὀψάρια. Cf. Mark 6.38, πόσους ἔχετε ἄρτους; ... πέντε, καὶ δύο ἰχθύας. As in v. 7, the coincidence cannot be fortuitous, and is with difficulty ascribed to oral tradition. John adds κριθίνους. In the Elisha story there were εἴκοσι ἄρτους κριθίνους (2 Kings 4.42); barley loaves were the cheap bread of the poorer classes (Philo, *Spec.* III, 57, says that barley is suitable for ἀλόγοις ζῴοις καὶ ἀτυχέσιν ἀνθρώποις). There may however be a eucharistic allusion here; for the use of barley bread in the eucharist see J. McHugh, *Studiorum Paolinorum Congressus Internationalis Catholicus 1961* (1963), 1–10. ὀψάριον is a diminutive of ὄψον, 'cooked food', with the special meaning of pickled fish; see M.M. *s.v.*, and cf. ὀψαριοπωλεῖον, fish-shop; ὀψαριοπώλης, fishmonger. According to Suidas, ὀψάριον τὸ ἰχθύδιον. In modern Greek ψάρι is fish, but M.M. derive this word from ψωρός and ψᾶν. The only other New Testament uses of ὀψάριον are in John 21.9f., 13.

10. ποιήσατε τοὺς ἀνθρώπους ἀναπεσεῖν. Cf. Mark 6.39, where the command is given in indirect speech, and the verb ἀνακλιθῆναι is used. John's editing of Mark (if this process be assumed) raises a difficulty here; Phrynichus (CXC, Rutherford, 293f.) explicitly condemns ἀναπεσεῖν as a substitute for ἀνακλιθῆναι, and rightly from the standpoint of Attic purism, with which of course John was little concerned.

χόρτος πολύς. Cf. Mark 6.39, ἐπὶ τῷ χλωρῷ χόρτῳ.

τὸν ἀριθμόν. Accusative of specification; this, the case of classical usage, was in Hellenistic times giving place to the dative (M. 1, 63).

ὡς πεντακισχίλιοι. Cf. Mark 6.44 (a note placed at the end of the story), πεντακισχίλιοι ἄνδρες: a significant agreement, as at v. 7.

11. Ἔλαβεν οὖν τοὺς ἄρτους . . . καὶ εὐχαριστήσας. Cf. Mark 6.41, καὶ λαβὼν τοὺς πέντε ἄρτους καὶ τοὺς δύο ἰχθῦας, ἀναβλέψας εἰς τὸν οὐρανὸν εὐλόγησεν καὶ κατέκλασεν. In Mark the food is next given (ἐδίδου) to the Twelve for distribution to the crowds; in John Jesus acts independently and without assistance (διέδωκεν τοῖς ἀνακειμένοις). In both Mark and John the words and actions of Jesus recall the last supper; cf. Mark 14.22, λαβὼν ἄρτον εὐλογήσας ἔκλασεν καὶ ἔδωκεν αὐτοῖς; 1 Cor. 11.23, ἔλαβεν ἄρτον καὶ εὐχαριστήσας ἔκλασεν. It will be noted that, in their miracle narratives, both Mark and John use the verb λαμβάνειν; John has the verb εὐχαριστεῖν but not the breaking of the bread, while Mark has the breaking but, instead of εὐχαριστεῖν, εὐλογεῖν. εὐχαριστεῖν is used at Mark 14.23 of the cup, and Paul (1 Cor. 10.16) calls the eucharistic cup, τὸ ποτήριον τῆς εὐλογίας ὃ εὐλογοῦμεν. εὐχαριστεῖν, used also at Mark 8.6, is more definitely a Christian technical term, but it would be wrong to seek any difference in meaning between it and εὐλογεῖν. Both find their origin in the thanksgivings, or blessings, pronounced by Jews at meals over bread and wine. The two blessings are: Blessed are thou, O Lord our God, King of the universe, who bringest forth bread from the earth; and, Blessed art thou . . . who givest us the fruit of the vine. It follows that there is nothing in the acts here ascribed to Jesus that would be out of place or even unusual in any Jewish meal, but there can be little doubt that eucharistic associations would be detected in the narrative both in John and in Mark. John does not however go out of his way to multiply sacramental allusions, and indeed does not narrate the breaking of the bread or the role of the disciples in distribution. Cf. v. 9, and the note. He is not concerned to teach any particular doctrine of the eucharist; the only effect of such details as are given is to point forward to the ensuing discourse (6.26–58). For εὐχαριστήσας διέδωκεν, א D it have εὐχαρίστησεν καὶ ἔδωκεν; this variant may have first arisen in Latin, where there was no convenient equivalent for the Greek aorist participle active. After (δι)έδωκεν, D Θ φ ω b e add τοῖς μαθηταῖς οἱ δὲ μαθηταί; this is an assimilation to Matt. 14.19.

ἐκ τῶν ὀψαρίων. The partitive use of ἐκ is characteristic of John's style; it is not clear why it is used of the fish and not of the loaves.

12. ἐνεπλήσθησαν. Cf. Mark 6.42, ἔφαγον πάντες καὶ ἐχορτάσθησαν; Dodd (A.S., 85) recalls Jer. 31.14, τῶν ἀγαθῶν μου ἐμπλησθήσεται. But by the words they use both Mark and John show that they believed a truly miraculous action to have taken place. The meal, though it may have been symbolic, was not merely symbolic.

συναγάγετε . . . ἵνα μή τι ἀπόληται. In Mark there is no command to gather up the broken pieces; but they are gathered up and as in John are called κλάσματα (Mark 6.43; in Mark 8.8 the word περισσεύματα is also used; cf. John's περισσεύσαντα). The two verbs συνάγειν and ἀπολλύναι are both used in John of persons as well as things. For συνάγειν see 11.52 and cf. 11.47. For ἀπολλύναι see 3.16; 6.39; 10.28; 11.50; 17.12; 18.9. In Didache 9.4 συνάγειν is used of the 'gathering' of the eucharistic bread, which is a symbol of the gathering of the church (ὥσπερ ἦν τοῦτο τὸ κλάσμα διεσκορπισμένον . . . καὶ συναχθὲν ἐγένετο ἕν, οὕτω συναχθήτω σου ἡ ἐκκλησία . . .). 1 Clem. 34.7 (ἐν ὁμονοίᾳ ἐπὶ τὸ αὐτὸ συναχθέντες . . .) has probably a eucharistic significance (perhaps cf. Ignatius, Poly. 4.2, πυκνότερον συναγωγαὶ γινέσθωσαν), and later σύναξις became a technical term for the gathering of the faithful at the eucharist. C. F. D. Moule (*J.T.S.* 6 (1955), 240–3), thinks that the passage in the *Didache* shows the influence of John. In view of the discourse that follows it is not impossible that John is here speaking symbolically of the gathering of Christian disciples, and of the will of Christ to preserve them all from destruction (17.12; on ἀπολλύναι see on 3.16), and that he does so with some reference to the eucharist. It is with the preservation from evil of human beings, not with the 'sacredness of the sacramental bread' (Guilding, 59) that he is concerned; and it may be that he represents no more than a desire not to waste food. For Jewish carefulness in this respect see E. D. Johnston, *N.T.S.* 8 (1962), 153f., and add *T. Berakoth* 6.4. On the whole see Daube, *N.T.R.J.*, 36–51, and the same author's suggestion (given in Dodd, *Interpretation*, 334) that the gathered bread represents the βρῶσις μένουσα of 6.27. John probably did see some symbolical significance in the details he recounted, but it is doubtful whether his thought went beyond that of the gathering by God of his elect.

13. δώδεκα κοφίνους. Cf. Mark 6.43, δώδεκα κοφίνων πληρώματα; in Mark 8.8 the word σφυρίς is used (cf. Mark 8.19f.).

14. οἱ οὖν ἄνθρωποι ... ἔλεγον. Comments by the onlookers frequently follow the synoptic miracle stories, and, in a manner paralleled in contemporary stories, bring out the impression created by the miracle worker. John however uses them in the interests of his own theological exposition.

οὗτός ἐστιν ἀληθῶς ὁ προφήτης ὁ ἐρχόμενος εἰς τὸν κόσμον. On a different use of ὁ προφήτης see on 1.21. Here the supplement ὁ ἐρχόμενος εἰς τὸν κόσμον (cf. the use of ὁ ἐρχόμενος at Matt. 11.3 = Luke 7.19f., and elsewhere), and the following verse make it clear that the prophet is understood not as a forerunner of the Messiah but as in some sense the Messiah himself. This identification is probably connected with a messianic interpretation of Deut. 18.15ff. known to have been current among Samaritans and Christians (see *Beginnings* 1, 404–8), and now attested also for the Qumran sect. The words of Deuteronomy are quoted in 4Q test 5–8, and may underlie also 1 QS 9.11, which speaks of the coming of a prophet (נביא) and the Messiahs of Aaron and Israel (i.e., the high-priestly and royal Messiahs). The Qumran material itself is sufficient to warn us against any neat systematization of messianic belief in first century Judaism, and Dodd (*A.S.*, 56) thinks that John, though acquainted with Deut. 18.15 as a testimonium for Jesus' Messiahship, did not accept it as such. According to Martyn, 98–101, the crowd understood the miraculous feeding as a repetition of the manna miracle, one of the Mosaic signs (see especially Meeks, 91–8; also Schnackenburg). The parallels and differences between Jesus and Moses are worked out in the discourse (especially 6.31f.). It is doubtful whether John should be thought of as defending the Mosaic prophetic understanding of Messiahship against the royal political understanding implied by v. 15. Neither is adequate for his Christological purposes, though each contributes something, both positively and negatively.

ὃ ἐποίησεν σημεῖον is the reading of the majority of MSS.; P75 B a boh have ἃ ἐποίησεν σημεῖα. It is not easy to decide between these readings; the plural might be due to assimilation to 2.23; 6.2, the singular might be an adaptation to the miracle of feeding which had just been witnessed. P75 B a is a strong combination, but it is probably better to adopt tentatively the reading of the vast majority of MSS. and VSS.

15. Ἰησοῦς οὖν γνοὺς (John probably thinks of supernatural knowledge; cf. 1.47f.) ... ἀνεχώρησεν (φεύγει ℵ a vg cur Tertullian Augustine, probably rightly; the notion of flight would be avoided as inconsistent with the dignity of Jesus). In Mark 6.45 Jesus compelled (ἠνάγκασεν) the disciples to cross the lake before him while he remained to dismiss the crowds. His action is unexplained; but the proposed *coup* by the multitude (mentioned, it should be noted, not by Mark but by John, who does not say that the disciples were compelled to leave in the boat) would account for it. John is probably dependent upon Mark at this point since he notes that Jesus withdrew alone to the mountain (cf. v. 3), εἰς τὸ ὄρος αὐτὸς μόνος, and Mark uses very similar words (6.46, εἰς τὸ ὄρος προσεύξασθαι, 6.47, αὐτὸς μόνος). The origin and historical value of John's note have been variously assessed, and a good deal of speculative reconstruction has been based on it; see the note on v. 14. Sanders, e.g., thinks that Jesus raised the messianic hopes of the crowd by 'an eschatological sacrament ... a foretaste of the Messianic banquet'. John interprets this in 6.26ff. 'because he is relying on a source with a better understanding of the situation than Mark had'. It is however historically perverse to argue from a Johannine discourse in this way. There is a somewhat similar, but more cautious and much more detailed interpretation in Dodd, *Tradition*, 196–217. In fact, as Bultmann notes, the events of vv. 14f. have no sequel and indeed no mention in 6.25ff. They are John's portrayal, based probably on hints in Mark, of mistaken reaction to a sign (v. 14; cf. 12.37). On Jesus' flight see Daube, *N.T.R.J.*, 19 (Saul as type of the Messiah).

ἁρπάζειν. The subject is not expressed, but it is presumably the ἄνθρωποι of v. 14 who had been impressed by the sign. ἁρπάζειν is a strong word—'to kidnap' (e.g. Herodotus 1, 2, ἁρπάσαι τοῦ βασιλέος τὴν θυγατέρα). At Matt. 11.12 (cf. Luke 16.16) it is what violent men do to the kingdom of heaven (βιασταὶ ἁρπάζουσιν αὐτήν); it is possible that John, with his constant insistence that Jesus himself is the Gospel, has transferred the verb from the kingdom to the King. But as the kingdom is God's gift and men cannot violently possess themselves of it, so Jesus, whom God gives (3.16) and who gives himself to men, cannot be violently constrained.

βασιλέα. The kingship of Jesus is one of the main themes of the Johannine Passion Narrative (see on 18.33ff.). There Jesus asserts that his kingship is not of this world (18.36); the kingship offered him here is one which he must renounce. Cf. his rejection of the kingdoms of the world, and the glory of them, in the Q temptation narrative (Matt. 4.8 = Luke 4.5). The connection between vv. 14 and 15 is not immediately clear. In the former, men take Jesus to be the prophet, in the latter he escapes an attempt to make him king. The explanation is probably to be found in the figure of Moses as the type of the Prophet-King (see Meeks, *passim*).

13. ON THE LAKE

6.16-21

The disciples in the absence of Jesus set out to cross the lake alone, but are surprised in the midst of the lake by a storm. While this is raging they see Jesus walking upon the water; he calms their fear by revealing his identity (which, at first, it seems, they had not perceived), and immediately the boat reaches port.

This short narrative, like the preceding, was probably derived by John from Mark (6.45–52; Matt. 14.22–34). For the many parallels, and for the differences, see the notes. The fact that in Mark as in John the two events stand side by side increases the probability of literary dependence. There are few touches of characteristic Johannine writing, but Brown's argument that John presents a 'relatively undeveloped form of the story' is not convincing.

In Mark the narrative is preceded by the perplexing statement that Jesus compelled (6.45, ἠνάγκασεν) the disciples to embark; in John by v. 15 and the threat to make Jesus a king. It is possible that these two notes explain one another; Jesus urgently sent away his closest friends lest they should be infected by the mistaken messianic enthusiasm of the crowds. This may be true; but it should be noted that neither Mark nor John says so; and that John, who adds to Mark the statement that the crowds were seeking to take Jesus, omits his ἠνάγκασεν. It may be doubted whether John was interested in such explanations. That he meant to record a miracle, and not that Jesus waded into the sea a few yards from the beach, seems certain.

Unlike the miracle of feeding, this miracle is not directly expounded by John (according to A. Richardson, *The Miracle Stories of the Gospels* (1941), 117f., it is expounded in chs. 13—17). That many early Christians saw in it an index both of the power of their Lord and of his saving presence with his people in all their affliction is doubtless true, but it has little to do with the Johannine context. It is probable that John included the narrative (a) because it was firmly fixed in the tradition along with the miracle of the five thousand, and (b) in order to bring Jesus and the disciples back to Capernaum, where the discourse on the Bread of Life was held (6.59). Lightfoot sees here the teaching of 14.5f.; 15.4f. presented in another form. The suggestion (Guilding, 58ff.) that as the feeding represents the last supper so the crossing of the lake represents the death (separation from the disciples) and resurrection of Jesus has little support in the text, but the Passover *haphtarah*, Isa. 51.6–16 corresponding to the Torah lection Exod. 15, contains some striking parallels; Brown adds Ps. 107 (especially vv. 4f.,9,23,25,27–30). Non-biblical parallels are relatively unimportant. If the paragraph is more than a traditional bridge it may be right (Borgen, 180) to contrast it with 6.15: Jesus escapes from those who would make him a political Messiah, but for the disciples there is a theophanic encounter with the Son of God. But again, unless an improbable interpretation is given to v. 20, it cannot be said that John does anything to make his meaning clear.

16. ὡς δὲ ὀψία ἐγένετο. Cf. Mark. 6.47, ὀψίας γενομένης.

17. ἤρχοντο. The durative, or perhaps the conative, force of the imperfect must be given weight: 'they were on their way', or perhaps, 'they were trying to go'.

πέραν τῆς θαλάσσης (cf. v. 1) εἰς Καφαρναούμ. We are not told the point from which the first journey was made. Capernaum (twice mentioned already—2.12; 4.46—without becoming the scene of any important event, but the place of the discourse that interprets the miraculous feeding, v. 59) is on the western shore of the lake, and the miracle may therefore be supposed to have occurred on the east—that is, in territory predominantly Gentile; but it must not be presumed that John intended to suggest this, or thought it significant. According to Mark 6.53 the stormy crossing of the lake ended at Gennesaret (εἰς Γεννησαρέτ), which was not a town but a district to the north-west of the lake (Josephus, *Bel.* III, 516–21).

καὶ σκοτία ἤδη ἐγεγόνει. According to Mark 6.48 it was περὶ τετάρτην φυλακὴν τῆς νυκτός (not long before dawn) that Jesus approached the disciples on the lake. For the text ℵ D write κατέλαβεν δὲ αὐτοὺς ἡ σκοτία, probably under the influence of 12.35. Fenton notes the symbolic use of darkness in this gospel (1.5; 8.12; 12.35,46; (20.1)).

18. ἀνέμου μεγάλου πνέοντος. Cf. Mark 6.48, ἦν γὰρ ὁ ἄνεμος ἐναντίος αὐτοῖς. Abundant evidence is available for the suddenness with which storms fall upon the lake (e.g. Klausner, 269).

19. ἐληλακότες. Cf. Mark. 6.48, βασανιζομένους ἐν τῷ ἐλαύνειν.

ὡς σταδίους εἴκοσι πέντε ἢ τριάκοντα. Cf. Mark 6.47; they were ἐν μέσῳ τῆς θαλάσσης. The singular noun is στάδιον, but for the plural both στάδια and στάδιοι are used by classical writers, apparently indifferently (see L.S. *s.v.*, M. II, 122). Here ℵ D have στάδια. The στάδιον was equal to 606¾ feet; hence the 'furlong' by which it is commonly translated in the English Bible (it is more nearly equal to one-eighth of a Roman than of an English mile).. According to Josephus (*Bel.* III, 506) the lake was 40 stadia broad by 140 long. In fact, its length is 109 stadia (12½ miles) and its greatest breadth 61 stadia (7 miles). The Johannine and Marcan statements therefore correspond with sufficient accuracy; but this need not be taken to mean that John's figures have the authority of recollection. The figures cannot be used to rationalize the miracle; they were probably intended to heighten it.

θεωροῦσιν τὸν Ἰησοῦν περιπατοῦντα ἐπὶ τῆς θαλάσσης. Cf. Mark 6.49, οἱ δὲ ἰδόντες αὐτὸν ἐπὶ τῆς θαλάσσης περιπατοῦντα. In Matt. 14.25 we have ἐπὶ τὴν θάλασσαν ('upon, or over, the sea'). It is true that ἐπί with the genitive could be translated '*by* the sea'; that is, Jesus walked on the shore, or in the shallow water on the beach. If this translation were adopted the story would contain no miracle. But it is to be noted that for John, as v. 16 shows, ἐπὶ τὴν θάλασσαν means '*to* the sea', and for ἐπί with the genitive cf. Job 9.8, Rev.

10.5. It also appears from 6.25 that something out of the ordinary course of nature has happened. There can be little doubt that both Mark and John, whether or not they used the best possible Greek, intended to record a miracle. It is highly improbable that this story was ever told otherwise than as a miracle story; though this must not be allowed to prejudice the question whether a miracle actually took place.

ἐφοβήθησαν. Cf. Mark 6.50, ἐταράχθησαν, the cause being given in v. 49, ἔδοξαν ὅτι φάντασμά ἐστιν. John has abbreviated, and conformed the emotion of the disciples more closely to Jesus' answer (v. 20, μὴ φοβεῖσθε). The suggestion that the disciples were afraid of being wrecked on the shore on which Jesus was walking misses John's point completely.

20. ἐγώ εἰμι· μὴ φοβεῖσθε. In Mark 6.50 the same words, with θαρσεῖτε prefixed. In this passage it is probable that ἐγώ εἰμι means simply 'It is I'. (i) John is probably following Mark, and it is unlikely that Mark meant anything more abstruse (cf. the use of אני, ἐγώ, in the Old Testament, e.g. 1 Kings 18.8). (ii) At John 9.9 there is a very similar use of ἐγώ εἰμι as pure identification; cf. also Luke 24.39. There are other passages in John where this simple meaning may not suffice (see on 6.35; 8.24); it would be wrong however to interpret this passage by the others—rather, the fact that John can use ἐγώ εἰμι as a simple self-identification should be borne in mind before elaborate theories based on occurrences of the words elsewhere are accepted. If in the present passage there is any hint of the epiphany of a divine figure it is not because the words ἐγώ εἰμι are used but because in the gospel as a whole Jesus is a divine figure.

21. ἤθελον οὖν λαβεῖν. Cf. Mark 6.48, ἤθελεν παρελθεῖν αὐτούς. It is possible but unlikely that John's unexpected ἤθελον is a reminiscence of the Marcan phrase. It does not seem necessary (with Torrey 105, 107f.) to mend the sense by postulating an underlying Aramaic בעו (ba'u) 'they rejoiced greatly' which was misread as בעו (bᵉ'u) 'they wished' (ἤθελον); the simplest way of taking the sentence is, 'They wished to take him into the boat, but (adversative use of καί, as often in John; see M. ii, 469) found immediately that they had reached the shore'.

καὶ εὐθέως ἐγένετο τὸ πλοῖον ἐπὶ τῆς γῆς. See on v. 19. If there ἐπὶ τῆς θαλάσσης means 'by the sea' these words may be regarded as confirmatory: the disciples were closer to land than they thought. But it is more probable that John is recording a second miracle (so already Origen; see Bauer, ad loc., and cf. 11.44 for another 'miracle within a miracle'), perhaps with reference to Psalm 107.23–32 (especially v. 30, So he bringeth them unto the haven where they would be). Here the narrative ends abruptly; the absence of interpretation confirms the view that John included this narrative primarily because it was in the source—in all probability, Mark—he used for the preceding narrative.

14. BREAD FROM HEAVEN

6.22–59

Philo (*Decal.* 15–17) declares that one reason why Moses delivered the Law in the midst of the wilderness and not in a city was that he intended to show that it was not his own invention but the oracles of God. To this end he led the people into a wilderness where their lack of water and food was miraculously supplied by God; this would convince them of the divine authority of what was said to them. John in a similar way moves from the miraculous satisfaction of hunger (6.5–13) to a discourse upon the Bread of Life, in which Jesus speaks of the true bread from heaven with an authority greater than that of Moses.

The present passage consists mainly of discourse, introduced and concluded with narrative, and interrupted here and there by comments from the hearers. It may be divided into four sections (vv. 22–7, 28–40, 41–51, 52–9) and summarized as follows.

Vv. 22–7. The opening verses of narrative are obscure; see the notes. In vv. 26f. the main theme is simply given out. Men are foolishly concerned not with the truth, but with food for their bodies. They must learn that there is a bread which conveys not earthly but eternal life, and earn it; yet they will not earn it, for it is the gift of the Son of man, whom God has avouched. The whole discourse is summarized here. Jesus is the Son of man, and it is in communion with him that men have eternal life.

Vv. 28–40. The next step is taken (as often in John) by means of a misunderstanding. The crowd hear the word ἐργάζεσθαι, and mistake it, because their own religion, which they take seriously, consists in 'working' works which (it is hoped) will be pleasing to God. In fact there is only one 'work' which God requires, and that (as will appear) is not a work in the ordinary sense; it is that men should put faith in Jesus. But why should they do so? The hearers require of him a sign (for synoptic parallels see the notes), thereby proving the truth of his own saying in v. 26. The request for a sign, however, serves to recall Moses and the Old Testament story of the manna, the bread from heaven, and from this point Jesus identifies the bread which comes down from heaven with himself, who as Son of man has come down from heaven. He is the Bread of Life, which delivers men from hunger and thirst; men take this bread by coming to him and believing in him. But this 'believing', and this 'coming', are not works which, like others, lie within the power and will of man. They do not exist apart from the power and will of God, upon whom they are completely dependent. Once more the discourse is summarized with the significant addition of reference to the will of God; it is his will that the believer should by his faith have eternal life.

Vv. 41–51. To all this that Jesus has asserted a radical objection is made. Jesus is a man among men, of well-known family and origin; how can he claim to have come down from heaven? Jesus no more denies his human than his heavenly origin, but simply repeats that coming to him, faith in him as the Man from heaven, are impossible without divine instruction; no wonder, then, that some should be offended. Much of the previous paragraph is repeated, but once more

there is a significant addition. Jesus continues to speak of himself as the
Bread of Life, but adds that the bread he will supply is his flesh, and his
flesh given for the life of the world. This is a plain reference to his
sacrificial death, and points forward to the reference, which is almost
explicit, to the eucharist in the final section.

Vv. 52–9. Once more the Jews, shocked by the word 'flesh', ask the
question, How? Once more the question is met, not by explanation, but
by reassertion and addition, this time by the addition of blood. This
lays further emphasis upon the death of Jesus, and makes allusion to the
eucharist. John makes it clear, however, that his main thought is of
the mission of Jesus from the Father, and of the reciprocal indwelling of
Christ and the believer.

The discourse thus outlined is essentially simple and contains few
distinct thoughts. It is only by coming to Jesus and living in union with
him that men may attain eternal life. This coming and this living,
however, are possible only in virtue of a twofold divine initiative: (a)
Jesus has come down from heaven as the Bread of Life, that which supplies life to those who, by appropriate means, assimilate it; (b) God
draws to Jesus all those who are to be united with him in eternal life.
The divine action runs throughout the whole process, from the initial
coming to the last day, when Jesus himself will raise up the believer
who is thus dependent on him from beginning to end. The means by
which the process is activated can be described both as the word of
Jesus, and as Spirit. So much seems clear, but closer analysis of the
chapter has raised profound problems (see *Essays*, 49–69, and the
admirable discussion by Lindars). It may be accepted that the chapter
manifests stylistic unity; it cannot be divided up on literary grounds
(see E. Ruckstuhl, *Die literarische Einheit des Johannesevangeliums* (1951);
C. Dekker's view, that it is an insertion by a Gentile author into a Jewish work (*N.T.S.* 13 (1966), 77f.), remains unproved). It has however
been maintained, notably by Bultmann but subsequently by others, that
it is not a theological unity; in particular, that the recurring formula
'I will raise him (it) up at the last day' is inconsistent with Johannine
eschatology (in this chapter see especially v. 50), and that the allusion
to the eucharist in vv. 51c–58 is inconsistent with the negative attitude
to sacraments manifested elsewhere in the gospel. The inconsistent
clauses were inserted, it is held, by an ecclesiastical redactor who wished
to harmonize the gospel with the futurist eschatology and sacramentalism current in his time. Johannine eschatology and sacramentalism
have been discussed above (Introduction, pp. 67–70, 82–5). The former
scarcely calls for further treatment here. It is true that the clauses
referred to can be excised without damage to the text, but this is not
true of all future references in the gospel as a whole, and it seems that
it was John's intention to retain just enough futurist eschatology to make
it clear that the believer never becomes independent of God's saving
activity. To the end (whatever precisely that may mean) he remains,

apart from God, in death. If this is so, it will follow that John did not understand the eucharist as a φάρμακον ἀθανασίας in (what is usually taken to be) the Ignatian sense (see Ignatius, *Ephesians* 20.2), and from this it will follow that most of the theological objections brought against the Johannine authorship of vv. 51c–58 will fall to the ground. On the interpretation of this passage see in addition to the commentaries the article by J. D. G. Dunn (*N.T.S.* 17 (1971), 328–38), which summarizes much recent discussion and makes its own significant addition. Here (see also the detailed notes) the following points may be made. (*a*) The new paragraph begins not at v. 51c but with the new Jewish objection in v. 52. This means that there is already a clear quasi-eucharistic allusion to the eating of the flesh of Jesus in the earlier part of the discourse. (*b*) It has been maintained that whereas the interpretation of the Bread of Life in vv. 35–50 is sapiential (p. 293; Brown, especially 285–91), in vv. 51–8 it is sacramental and that these interpretations are inconsistent with each other. To this it may be replied that the matter is not so simple. By placing the two interpretations side by side, and indeed intermingling them, for the sacramental element appears in vv. 35–50 (see, e.g., v. 35, shall never thirst) and the sapiential in vv. 51–8 (vv. 57f.), John guards against precisely that form of sacramentalism that is often attributed to him (see X. Léon-Dufour, *The Gospels and the Jesus of History* (tr. and ed. by J. McHugh, 1968), 91f.). The two passages are thus complementary rather than inconsistent, or alternative (as Brown thinks— his own analogy of word and sacrament suggests that they belong together). John is not in any crude sense anti-sacramental, but he does appear to be critical of sacramental tendencies prevailing in his day, and to lay such stress on the fundamental sacramental fact of the incarnation that the partial expressions of this fact, baptism and the eucharist, are relegated to a subordinate place. (*c*) It has been maintained (see especially G. Bornkamm, 'Die eucharistische Rede im Johannes-Evangelium', in *Geschichte und Glaube* 1 (1968), 60–7 (originally in *Z.N.T.W.* 47 (1956), 161–9; also *G. & G.* 11, (1971), 51–64) that vv. 60–71 refer back not to vv. 51–8 but to vv. 35–50, thereby showing that vv. 51–8 must be regarded as an insertion. It will however be shown in notes that vv. 60–71 refer to both the earlier passages. See also 'Menschensohn', and U. Wilckens, in *Neues Testament and Kirche* (Festschrift R. Schnackenburg, 1974), 220–48.

Strong support for the unity of ch. 6 was given by Borgen (cf. also Guilding, and B. Gärtner, *Jewish Passover*, 1959), who drew out parallels between this chapter and Philonic and midrashic exegesis of the miracle of the manna. The chapter as a whole could be regarded as an extended exegesis, by accepted methods, of Ps. 78.24. The argument is on the whole convincing (see detailed notes below, especially on v. 32), but it must be stated in such a way as to make due allowance for other influences upon John's method. If John knew what it was to preach in the synagogue (and to adopt appropriate methods) he also knew what it was to be thrown out of the synagogue (9.22; 16.2), and the structure of his theological thought, which is well exemplified in this discourse, is indebted also to pagan models, and to the earlier Christian tradition.

22–4. These verses are very confused. Some clarity is achieved if εἶδον (v. 22) is translated as a pluperfect 'they had seen' (it would be simpler to accept the reading ἰδών (W ὡ e cur), but the attestation is hardly sufficient since the reading looks like an attempt to solve a difficulty), and v. 23 is regarded as a parenthesis. The general sense is then seen to be as follows. Jesus had left the multitude on the eastern (see on v. 17) shore of the lake. They had seen (εἶδον), on the day of the feeding miracle, that only one boat was on the eastern shore where they stood, and they had seen the disciples embark in this without Jesus (א* D Θ cur makes this clearer by adding after ἕν, (ἐκεῖνο) εἰς ὃ ἐνέβησαν οἱ μαθηταὶ τοῦ Ἰησοῦ). Jesus had now (τῇ ἐπαύριον; cf. 1.29) disappeared, but manifestly not by boat, though certain vessels (v. 23) had now reached a spot near to the scene of the miraculous meal (blown out of harbour, it may be, from Tiberias, on the west coast). Convinced that Jesus must somehow have rejoined his disciples, the crowd now made use of the available boats, either guessing or informed that the disciples were making for Capernaum. Thither they come, and there the ensuing discourse takes place (v. 59).

ὁ ἑστηκώς. For John's redundant (sometimes solemn, but hardly so here) use of ἱστάναι see on 1.35.

πέραν, from the standpoint of v. 21.

πλοιάριον, πλοῖον. It seems certain that John uses πλοῖον and its diminutive synonymously. Cf. M.M. s.v., πλοιάριον '. . . hardly to be distinguished from the ordinary πλοῖον'.

ἦν. If εἶδον (see above) has a pluperfect sense so also has ἦν.

ἄλλα ἦλθεν πλοιάρια. πλοιάρια is the reading of most MSS. WH follow B (which is joined by P[75]) in reading πλοῖα, and the corrector who accentuates the first word ἀλλά. There are several variations, of which the most significant are ἄλλων πλοιαρίων ἐλθόντων (D (b) (cur)), ἐπελθόντων οὖν τῶν πλοίων (א it (vg)). The genitives absolute are probably attempts to improve the connection.

εὐχαριστήσαντος τοῦ κυρίου. These words are omitted by D a e sin cur. It is very difficult to see why they should have been left out if they stood in the original text, and accordingly the Western text may well be right (its omissions of course are always noteworthy). If these words did not stand in the original text of the gospel the main ground for the contention that v. 23 is a gloss inserted into the narrative (Bernard, 189) disappears. The narrative use of ὁ κύριος, and the precise reference to the eucharist contained in the repetition of the verb from v. 11, together with the singular ἄρτον (a reference to the eucharistic loaf?) and the mention of the lately founded Tiberias, are the proofs offered that this v. is a gloss; the last two are not in themselves sufficient.

ὅτε οὖν resumes v. 22 after the parenthesis.

25. πέραν τῆς θαλάσσης underlines the miracle of the walking on the water.

Ῥαββί. For the title see on 1.38. It is the title of a teacher and inconsistent with the attempt (v. 15) to make Jesus a king.

πότε ὧδε γέγονας; γέγονας is hardly expected after πότε. 'It is the combination of "When *did* you come?" and "How long *have* you been here?"' (M. 1, 146). Cf. Robertson, 896, '... has punctiliar and durative ideas'. ἐλήλυθας (D) and ἦλθες (ℵ) are evident corrections (cf. *uenisti* in the Latin VSS.). Like the ἀρχιτρίκλινος in 2.9f., the crowd provides unconscious confirmation of the miracle.

26. ἀμὴν ἀμὴν λέγω ὑμῖν. See on 1.51. Jesus does not answer the question. As the sequel will show, there is no advantage in the multiplication of miracles.

οὐχ ὅτι εἴδετε σημεῖα ἀλλ᾽ ὅτι ἐφάγετε. ... This does not on the surface correspond to what had happened; vv. 14f. suggest that the miracle, if not fully understood, had at least been understood to be a miracle, and Jesus had been recognized as, at least, an exceptional person. The crowd had also observed something mysterious in Jesus' crossing of the lake. The point is made clearer when a parallel in 4.15 is recalled. The Samaritan woman is willing, and indeed desires, to receive a constant supply of 'living water'— in order that she may no longer have to draw water from the well. In the same way the multitude are happy to obtain unexpected supplies of free bread, and willing to accord the highest honours to the supplier as a miracle worker; but they do not perceive the parabolic significance of what he does, that the loaves he distributes are the sign of heavenly food, the bread of eternal life. This distinction casts light on John's use of the word σημεῖον (see on 2.11); a sign is not a mere portent but a symbolic representation of the truth of the Gospel. See the note on 4.48; it is however fair to observe that 6.14f. seem to be lost to view in the later part of the chapter.

ἐχορτάσθητε. χορτάζειν is not used in the Johannine miracle, but it appears at Mark 6.42 (καὶ ἔφαγον πάντες καὶ ἐχορτάσθησαν) and at Mark 8.8 (καὶ ἔφαγον καὶ ἐχορτάσθησαν). The parallelism is close and supports the view that John knew Mark.

27. This verse supports the interpretation that has just been given of v. 26, since the food given by Jesus, though supernaturally produced, was nevertheless 'bread that perishes'. It is closely parallel to 4.13f. (πᾶς ὁ πίνων ἐκ τοῦ ὕδατος τούτου διψήσει πάλιν. ὃς δ᾽ ἂν πίῃ ἐκ τ. ὕδ. ... οὐ μὴ διψήσει εἰς τὸν αἰῶνα).

ἐργάζεσθε, 'earn by working' (L.S. *s.v.* II, 4, with examples); this meaning lies behind some (not all) of the Pauline uses of the word (e.g. Rom. 4.4f.).

τὴν βρῶσιν τὴν ἀπολλυμένην. βρῶσις (used again at v. 55) is for John synonymous with βρῶμα (see 4.32,34). On ἀπολλύναι (a Johannine word) see on 3.16, and cf. vv. 12, 39. For the sense cf. 1 Cor. 6.13; Col. 2.22. Physical food is not despised, but it must not be valued too highly. At the highest it is a parable of the life God gives.

τὴν μένουσαν εἰς ζωὴν αἰώνιον. Cf. 4.14, πηγὴ ὕδατος ἁλλομένου εἰς ζωὴν αἰώνιον. Though the food, being Christ himself (vv. 53-5 *et al.*), is eternal, the sense here is not that the food lasts to eternity, but that, since it is 'abiding' food, its result is to produce eternal life in the believer. On ζωὴ αἰώνιος see on 3.15. Many parallels to the notion of heavenly, or spiritual, food are given by Bultmann. Perhaps the greatest importance of them is their testimony to a universal desire, or need. Cf. the note on 6.12.

ἣν ὁ υἱὸς τοῦ ἀνθρώπου ὑμῖν δώσει. For the Son of man in John see Introduction, pp. 72f., and on 1.51. In the synoptics the phrase has a predominantly eschatological meaning, but here John's δώσει (‎‎א‎ D e cur read δίδωσιν, probably by assimilation to v. 32) is not an eschatological future. It refers to the time after the glorification of Jesus (7.39) when his gifts would be fully available to men; cf. 4.14, τὸ ὕδωρ ὃ δώσω αὐτῷ. The Son of man is a figure who moves from heaven to earth (3.13) and from earth to heaven (6.62) and thus is essential to the process of mediation; hence he conveys heavenly food to men. It is a more profound development of this thought that he himself is the food that he conveys (v. 53). Note that the ἐργάζεσθε of the first part of the verse is now complemented by δώσει; whatever men may do, life is the Son of man's gift.

τοῦτον γὰρ ὁ πατὴρ ἐσφράγισεν ὁ θεός. At 3.33 the word σφραγίζειν is used to indicate that the believer, by accepting the testimony of Christ, has attested the truth of God himself. Here the word has the same meaning, but it is God the Father who attests the authority and truth of Jesus. In view of the aorist it is natural to look to a particular act of sealing; this should probably be found in the baptism of Jesus, or rather, since John does not record the baptism itself, in the descent of the Spirit upon Jesus. See especially 1.33f. This suggestion is to some extent supported by the fact that σφραγίς, σφραγίζειν were early used to describe Christian baptism (e.g. 2 Cor. 1.22; Eph. 1.13; 2 Clem. 7.6; Acts of Paul and Thecla 25); Sanders, however, discounts this, on the ground that the usage is not Johannine. ὁ θεός is added in emphatic explanation of ὁ πατήρ. It is none other than God who validates the mission of the Son of man. This use of an attributive substantive is characteristic of John; Radermacher, 88, compares 7.2; 18.1,17; 11.11ff.

τί ποιῶμεν ἵνα ἐργαζώμεθα τὰ ἔργα τοῦ θεοῦ; The meaning of ἐργάζεσθαι shifts in this verse. It is now used as the cognate verb of ἔργον, 'to work a work', 'to perform a work'. Bauer (95) refers to 4.34, ἐμὸν βρῶμά ἐστιν ἵνα ποιήσω τὸ θέλημα. . . . Thus to do the works of God (i.e. the works willed by God, the works he wills that we should do; thus 1 QS 4.4, ‎מעשי אל‎, the works God does (as at Ps. 107(106).24), is not a parallel) is to have the food God gives. Cf. 9.3. It is possible, though on the whole not likely, that the ἔργα τοῦ θεοῦ are intended by the crowd to stand over against what the Son of man gives. (27) Work for the food which the Son of man gives—(28) But what shall we do to *God's* work (which surely is far more important)?—(29) It is God's work to believe in him whom he has sent, that is, the Son of man.

29. τὸ ἔργον τοῦ θεοῦ. Singular (contrast v. 28, τὰ ἔργα); only one 'work' is required by God.

ἵνα πιστεύητε εἰς. . . . ἵνα is explanatory of the preceding τοῦτο, a Johannine idiom. Cf. Rom. 3.28, δικαιοῦσθαι πίστει ἄνθρωπον χωρὶς ἔργων νόμου; John's thought is closely parallel to the Pauline doctrine of justification, though his formulation of it is quite different. He never uses the noun πίστις, and is able to use ἔργον as a description of faith. But for him ἔργον does not mean what Paul means by ἔργα νόμου; it is not a work that may be performed by human effort. It is the answer to the question, What does God look for in man?, but it cannot exist except as the act of God (e.g. v. 44, No man can come to me, except the Father . . . draw him). The present (continuous) tense of πιστεύητε is perhaps significant: not an *act* of faith, but a *life* of faith. πιστεύειν is constructed with εἰς; see on 1.12; trust in Christ is implied. See the next v.

ἀπέστειλεν ἐκεῖνος. ἐκεῖνος characteristically for God; on ἀποστέλλειν and the mission of Jesus see on 20.21. Both 'Son of man' (v. 27), and the 'one whom God sent' are significant terms; Jesus is the heavenly messenger who from heaven brings truth and life to men.

30. τί οὖν ποιεῖς σὺ σημεῖον; Cf. 2.18, and for σημεῖον generally see Introduction, pp. 75–8. Haenchen, *Weg*, 287 thinks that at an earlier stage the request for a sign was directly linked with the feeding miracle. Cf. v. 26; also 6.14f., but this episode is now almost forgotten. Since it is to be presumed (see above on v. 26) that the crowds acknowledge that Jesus has performed a miracle, they must now be asking for an even greater wonder than that performed by Moses (v. 31); he who makes greater claims than Moses must provide a more striking attestation of his right. John probably takes this request for a sign from Mark 8.11ff. (cf. 11.28), the debate which follows immediately upon the second miracle of feeding and is itself followed by a discussion of loaves (8.14–21). In Mark as in John the request is unanswered because it is unanswerable; no sign can prove (though many signs suggest) that Jesus is the messenger of God. Rigid proof would render impossible the work of God, which is to believe in Jesus. For the special significance of the sign in relation to Moses and the manna see on the next two verses.

ἵνα ἴδωμεν [*sc.* the sign] καὶ πιστεύσωμέν σοι. Contrast v. 29; πιστεύειν is no longer constructed with εἰς but with the dative; that is, the Jews contemplate no more than putting credence in the words of Jesus. ἵνα is not incorrectly used: the sign is to be done *in order that* we may see it. There is no need to postulate mistranslation of the Aramaic relative (Burney, 75; M. II, 436). Cf. *Thomas* 91: Tell us who thou art so that (ἵνα) we may believe (πιστεύειν) in thee.

31. οἱ πατέρες ἡμῶν. This description of the generation that left Egypt recurs in 1 Cor. 10.1; the whole paragraph is an important parallel to the Johannine discourse. אבות (*fathers*) is used generally in rabbinic literature for the fathers, ancestors, of the Jewish nation. See 4.12,20.

τὸ μάννα ἔφαγον ἐν τῇ ἐρήμῳ. For the story of the manna see Exod. 16. The word is not used in this chapter (16.15, מן הוא (*man hu'*) is rendered in the LXX τί ἐστιν τοῦτο;), but appears at Num. 11.6; Deut. 8.3; Josh. 5.12; Neh. 9.20; Ps. 77.24. Some of these passages show that 'manna' was used to represent moral and spiritual teaching. Neh. 9.20 brings together three Johannine terms; τὸ πνεῦμά σου ... ἔδωκας ... καὶ τὸ μάννα σου οὐκ ἀφυστέρησας ... καὶ ὕδωρ ἔδωκας αὐτοῖς. Philo several times allegorizes the story of the manna; the main passage is *L. A.* III, 169–76: the food of the soul (τῆς ψυχῆς τροφή) is God's word (λόγος θεοῦ). Later, the manna became a symbol of the new age. The rabbinic statements to this effect (e.g. *Mekhilta* Exod. 16.25 (ויסע, §5): In this age you shall not find it [the manna] but in the age to come you shall find it; *Ecclesiastes R.* 1.28: R. Berechiah (*c.* A.D. 340) said in the name of R. Isaac (*c.* A.D. 300): As was the first Redeemer so is the latter Redeemer ... as the first Redeemer brought down the manna, so will also the latter Redeemer bring down the manna; see further S.B. and Schlatter, ad loc.) are not early; but in 2 Baruch (perhaps not far from A.D. 100, and therefore roughly contemporary with John—see D. S. Russell, *The Method and Message of Jewish Apocalyptic* (1964), 64) we have: And it shall come to pass at that self-same time that the treasury of manna shall again descend from on high, and they will eat of it in those years, because these are they who have come to the consummation of time (29.8).

καθώς ἐστιν γεγραμμένον. This quotation formula occurs again at 12.14; it is not found elsewhere in the New Testament (καθώς γέγραπται is very common), but cf. Luke 4.17, τόπον οὗ ἦν γεγραμμένον.

ἄρτον ἐκ τοῦ οὐρανοῦ ἔδωκεν αὐτοῖς φαγεῖν. The source of this quotation is uncertain. Cf. Neh. 9.15, καὶ ἄρτον ἐξ οὐρανοῦ (לחם משמים) ἔδωκας αὐτοῖς; Ps. 78(77).24, καὶ ἄρτον οὐρανοῦ (דגן שמים) ἔδωκεν αὐτοῖς. The word φαγεῖν is missing from both lines but it occurs in the first half of Ps. 78.24 (ἔβρεξεν αὐτοῖς μάννα φαγεῖν), and this is perhaps in favour of the Psalm as source of the quotation, since φαγεῖν could easily be transferred, accidentally or intentionally, from one clause to the other. But John's ἐκ τοῦ is closer to Nehemiah's ἐξ than to the Psalm's genitive. φαγεῖν without reference to heaven occurs in Exod. 16.15. John may well have known and combined all these passages; on his use of the Old Testament (with which this would be in conformity) see *J.T.S.* old series 48 (1947), 155–69.

John's use of this Old Testament material has been given much greater precision and significance by the work of P. Borgen, who points out (59) 'several midrashic features which are common to parts of Philo, John and the Palestinian midrash: the systematic paraphrase of words from Old Testament quotations and fragments from haggadic traditions, and the use of a widespread homiletic pattern'. That this exegetical pattern can be traced through the chapter as a whole lends a great deal of weight to the view that the chapter is a unity. The texts on which Borgen bases his study are *Ex. Rabba* 25.2; 25.6; Philo, *Mos.* I, 201f.; *Mekhilta* Exod. 16.4; *Petirat Moses*; Philo, *Mos.* II, 267. The use he makes of them is on the whole convincing, but cannot be reproduced here. The main points, however, that he makes about John's exegesis of the basic text (He gave them bread from heaven to eat) will be noted. Martyn (108–19) broadly accepts Borgen's view of John's midrashic exegesis, but is not content with Borgen's view that John employed the midrashic method to counter docetism. Rather John is saying to the Jews, 'The issue is not to be defined as an argument about an ancient text. It is not a midrashic issue. By arguing about texts you seek to evade the present crisis. God is *even now* giving you the true bread of heaven, and you cannot hide from him in typological speculation or in any other kind of midrashic activity. You must decide now with regard to this present gift of God' (118). The crowds sought the specific manna sign as a proof that Jesus was the Mosaic Prophet-Messiah. 'But Jesus had just repeated this miracle! Clearly a subtle point is being driven home, and it is this: The crowd did not see the sign (6.26). If they had, they would have recognized that as God's self-authenticating emissary Jesus presides over the issue of the origin of life with complete sovereignty. *The* point of the sign is not the Moses-Messiah typology but rather God's gracious election' (115).

32. οὐ Μωϋσῆς δέδωκεν (so most MSS.; ἔδωκεν, read by B D Clement, may be due to assimilation to the quotation in v. 31) ὑμῖν τὸν ἄρτον ἐκ τοῦ οὐρανοῦ. This sentence may be taken in several ways. (i) It was not Moses who gave you the bread from heaven (but God). (ii) It was not bread from heaven that Moses gave you (but merely physical food, over against the true bread from heaven which the Father gives you). (iii) The sentence has been taken

(Torrey, 60–2) as a question: Did not Moses give you bread from heaven? (Yes, indeed. But the father gives you the true bread from heaven.) If only one of these possible ways of taking the sentence is to be chosen it should probably be (i). The name Moses is in an emphatic position, and the οὐ is placed so as to negative it. Moreover, it would be hard for John to deny what the Old Testament positively asserts, that the manna was bread from heaven, and the emphatic position in the next clause of ἀληθινός does not deny that the bread supplied by Moses was bread from heaven but asserts that as such it was a type of the heavenly bread given by Jesus. It is however doubtful whether John would have regarded (i) and (ii) as mutually exclusive; it is certain that he intends to make, and does make, the two positive statements implied by the negations in (i) and (ii): There is a true bread from heaven, and it is God's gift through Christ. The interpretation of the verse is further complicated by the fact that the Law is referred to figuratively as 'bread' (see S.B. II, 483f.). The proof text is Prov. 9.5 (Come, eat ye of my bread, לחמי); see e.g. Gen. R. 70.5. The bread given by Moses was not the true bread, and the Law given by Moses was not the true Law, though both were parables of the truth. True bread and true Law, that is, eternal life, are the Son of man whom God gives (vv. 35, 47–51, et al.). For further comparison between Jesus and the Law see especially 1.1–4.

δίδωσιν. The change in tense is to be noted. The contrasts John is working out result in a sentence almost too pregnant; not 'Moses did not give you bread from heaven, but God did', though this is part of the thought, but 'God now gives you what Moses could only foreshadow'.

τὸν ἀληθινόν. The word is emphatic: '. . . bread from heaven, I mean the true bread from heaven'. See on 1.9 and cf. especially 15.1. It does not imply that that which Moses gave was not 'bread from heaven'. The manna was in fact a valuable type of the bread of life; it came down from God to undeserving sinners who were preserved and nourished by it. But only in a comparatively crude sense could it be called 'bread from heaven'. It was itself perishable, and those who ate it remained mortal and liable to hunger. The Mosaic law also was a secondary and transient revelation. That which is given through Christ is the substance to which these figures point, the true bread from heaven. These notes on John's interpretation of the Old Testament fall into place when it is noted (Borgen, 61–7) that John has employed the Al-tiqri method of exegesis. This takes the form . . . אל תקרי . . . אלא (Do not read . . . but . . .). The most important points are: (1) The name Moses is negatived: Do not read Moses (gave you bread), but God (gave you bread). (2) The Hebrew is repointed: Do not read נתן (nathan, has given, δέδωκεν), but נותן (nothen, gives, or will give, δίδωσι, διδούς, or δώσει). (3) A haggadic variation is introduced: coming down instead of giving.

33. ὁ γὰρ ἄρτος τοῦ θεοῦ, the bread which God gives.

ὁ καταβαίνων ἐκ τοῦ οὐρανοῦ. This could be rendered, '. . . that which (i.e., the bread which) comes down out of heaven', and the rendering would not be entirely false. But especially in this chapter ὁ καταβαίνων is Christ the Son of man. Both present and aorist participles are used: καταβαίνων in vv. 33, 50, καταβάς in vv. 41, 51, 58 (and 3.13). There is no essential difference of reference, though there is a difference of emphasis. The present participles, in this verse both καταβαίνων and διδούς, are descriptive: Christ is one who descends and gives: the aorist puts the same fact with a greater stress on history: On a unique occasion in time Christ did descend.

ζωὴν διδούς. On ζωή (αἰώνιος) see on 1.4; 3.15. That Christ is the life-giving bread is constantly affirmed in this discourse; that Christ gives life to the world is the central thought of the gospel: 'bread', 'water', 'vine', 'birth', etc., are means by which it is conveyed. The parallel between Jesus and Law is here maintained, since the Law also was believed to give life, and in particular life in the age to come—eternal life; see *P. Aboth* 2.7, quoted above on 5.39.

34. The people take the words of Jesus in the manner mentioned above as grammatically possible though not representing John's thought to the full— The bread of God is that which comes down. . . . It does not yet occur to them that Jesus *is* the bread of God, though they perceive that he claims to give it. Cf. the request of the Samaritan woman, 4.15, Κύριε, δός μοι τοῦτο τὸ ὕδωρ, where a similar misunderstanding is apparent.

πάντοτε. They hope for continuous supplies (as the Samaritan woman hoped no longer to be obliged to come to the well; as Peter desired to be washed hands and head as well as feet, 13.9). But this is not necessary; what Jesus does for men he does once for all. Since πάντοτε is a misunderstanding characteristic of John's method (cf. e.g. 3.4) we cannot infer from it a reference to the eucharist as constantly available within the church. See Michaelis, *Die Sakramente im Johannesevangelium* (1946), 23f.; and the note on the next verse.

35. The two errors of the preceding verse are corrected. The bread of life is not a commodity which Jesus supplies—he *is* the Bread of Life; and to eat it does not mean hungering, eating, and hungering again.

ἐγώ εἰμι ὁ ἄρτος τῆς ζωῆς—the bread which gives life. The phrase ὁ ἄρτος ἐκ τοῦ οὐρανοῦ is not satisfactory since it could—quite properly as far as language goes—be understood simply as 'the bread which comes down out of the sky', like rain or dew. This would however be as inadequate a notion as the idea of being born ἄνωθεν by going back into one's mother's womb. The words of Ignatius, φάρμακον ἀθανασίας, ἀντίδοτος τοῦ μὴ ἀποθανεῖν (*Ephesians* 20.2) share this inadequacy, though Ignatius may not have intended them in the crude sense sometimes ascribed to him. Jesus is the means by which men have eternal life, but the means is personal, and is to be appropriated personally, not mechanically.

The frequent use of ἐγώ εἰμι coupled with a predicate such as ὁ ἄρτος τῆς ζωῆς is a striking characteristic of John's style (for ἐγώ εἰμι without a predicate see on 8.24). It occurs in the following passages:

6.35, ἐγώ εἰμι ὁ ἄρτος τῆς ζωῆς (cf. v. 48; v. 41, ὁ ἄρτος ὁ καταβὰς ἐκ τοῦ οὐρανοῦ; v. 51, ὁ ἄρτος ὁ ζῶν).

8.12, ἐγώ εἰμι τὸ φῶς τοῦ κόσμου.

[8.18, ἐγώ εἰμι ὁ μαρτυρῶν περὶ ἐμαυτοῦ.]

[8.23, ἐγὼ ἐκ τῶν ἄνω εἰμί.]

10.7,9, ἐγώ εἰμι ἡ θύρα (τῶν προβάτων).

10.11,14, ἐγώ εἰμι ὁ ποιμὴν ὁ καλός.

11.25, ἐγώ εἰμι ἡ ἀνάστασις (καὶ ἡ ζωή).

14.6, ἐγώ εἰμι ἡ ὁδὸς καὶ ἡ ἀλήθεια καὶ ἡ ζωή.

15.1,5, ἐγώ εἰμι ἡ ἄμπελος (ἡ ἀληθινή).

8.18,23, evidently differ in form from the other passages and are not considered here. In the other passages the predicates are metaphorical or symbolical titles; on these several titles see the notes on the verses concerned. The background of the ἐγώ εἰμι formula is varied. (i) In the Old Testament ἐγώ εἰμι is the divine word of self-revelation and of command. See especially Exod. 3.6, ἐγώ εἰμι ὁ θεὸς τοῦ πατρός σου, 3.14, ἐγώ εἰμι ὁ ὤν, 20.2, ἐγώ εἰμι κύριος ὁ θεός σου, ὅστις ἐξήγαγόν σε ἐκ γῆς Αἰγύπτου (the ten commandments follow). The same formula is found in the prophets; e.g. Isa. 51.12, ἐγώ εἰμι ἐγώ εἰμι ὁ παρακαλῶν σε. In Hebrew the speech of Wisdom in Prov. 8 several times emphasizes the word אֲנִי (I; elsewhere rendered ἐγώ εἰμι, here ἐγώ) and is in general cast in an 'egoistic' form; Wisdom proclaims her own virtues. Cf. Ecclus. 24. (ii) This manner of speech attributed to Wisdom may be due to the form of the Isis aretalogy (see W. L. Knox, *St Paul and the Church of the Gentiles* (1939), 55–89), and of magical formulas dependent on the Isis form. Only three examples of this form can be quoted here (see the texts conveniently collected in Deissmann, 133–40) (*a*) An inscription is quoted by Diodorus Siculus (1, 27): ἐγώ Ἶσις εἰμι ἡ βασίλισσα πάσης χώρας . . . ἐγώ εἰμι τοῦ νεωτάτου Κρόνου θεοῦ θυγατὴρ πρεσβυτάτη. ἐγώ εἰμι γυνὴ καὶ ἀδελφὴ Ὀσίριδος βασιλέως . . . κτλ. (*b*) An inscription at Ios, very similar to that recorded by Diodorus, contains the following (Dittenberger, *Syll.* 1267.4,16f.): Εἶσις ἐγώ εἰμι . . . ἐγώ εἰμι ἡ παρὰ γυναιξὶ θεὸς καλουμένη . . . κτλ. (*c*) *P. Lond.* 46.145–55, ἐγώ εἰμι ὁ ἀκέφαλος δαίμων . . . ἐγώ εἰμι ἡ ἀλήθεια . . . ἐγώ εἰμι ὁ γεννῶν καὶ ἀπογεννῶν. (iii) Possibly a special development of the Isis 'ego' is the declaratory and revelatory formula found in the opening tractate of the Hermetic Corpus (*Poimandres*), in which Poimandres reveals himself to Hermes. See especially *C.H.* 1, 2, ἐγώ μέν, φησίν, εἰμὶ ὁ Ποιμάνδρης, ὁ τῆς αὐθεντίας νοῦς; 6, τὸ φῶς ἐκεῖνο, ἔφη, ἐγώ Νοῦς, ὁ σὸς θεός. (iv) The declaratory 'I' also belongs to the synoptic Christological statements, though here, characteristically, instead of εἰμι we have a finite verb; e.g. Matt. 5.22,28,32,34,39,44, ἐγώ δὲ λέγω ὑμῖν; Mark 9.25, ἐγώ ἐπιτάσσω; Matt. 12.28 = Luke 11.20, ἐγώ ἐκβάλλω. But the 'ego' is veiled under parables, and we have more frequently 'The Kingdom of God (heaven) is (like) . . .' These parables are particularly notable because they provide much of the subject matter of the Johannine 'I-sayings'. The background of these sayings, then, proves to be multiple, but essentially simple. Synoptic sayings or incidents (see the notes on the several passages) have been concentrated upon the person of Jesus in a form of speech calculated to be impressive, and to suggest, to both Jews and Greeks, the presence of an active and self-revealing God. The point of attachment may be found in the midrashic exegesis that John employs in this passage (Borgen, 73). *Bread* is a term found in the fundamental text; it is interpreted and identified by the ἐγώ εἰμι. It is unfortunate that the passage Borgen cites (*Lamentations Rabba* 1.16, §45: Trajan found the Jews occupied with Deut. 28.49, . . . as the vulture (הַנֶּשֶׁר) swoopeth down; he said to them, I am the vulture (אֲנָא הוּא נִשְׁרָא) . . .) is of uncertain date; it is nevertheless illuminating. The exegetical basis of the expression should settle the controversy between Bultmann, who takes ἐγώ as predicate (e.g., Bread is not something else—it is I), and Conzelmann (*Theology*, 349–52), who takes it as subject (e.g., What I am is bread). On ἐγώ εἰμι see Bultmann's long footnote (225, n. 3); Schweizer, 5–45; L. Cerfaux, in *Coniectanea Neotestamentica*, XI (1947), 15–25; Schnackenburg, II, 59–70; and S. Schulz, *Komposition und Herkunft der Johanneischen Reden* (1960), 85–90.

The notion of heavenly bread is rooted in the Old Testament and Jewish thought, and arises out of the gift of the manna. It is not however purely Jewish; 'the idea of heavenly food, which nourishes unending life, with the Greeks goes back as far as Homer and is equally at home in the East' (Bauer, 100, with many references). It is however of primary importance that the manna was interpreted in the wisdom tradition of Israel in terms of word and instruction; that Torah is bread, and that (for Philo) the logos is food (see Dodd, *Interpretation*, 336f.). We have here what Brown and others have described as the sapiential interpretation of the bread of life. God feeds men by his word; Jesus is his word. The Jewish and pagan elements in the background are thus joined and cemented by the Christian tradition, especially in the form of the feeding miracle and the record of the last supper.

ὁ ἐρχόμενος πρὸς ἐμὲ οὐ μὴ πεινάσῃ. 'I am' with predicate reveals not Jesus' essence but his dealings with men (Brown). 'Coming to' Jesus is an expression that occurs frequently in John (see 5.40); in this chapter vv. 35,37,44,45, 65. Cf. *Essays*, 62–5. ὁ ἐρχόμενος πρὸς ἐμέ is not distinguishable in meaning from ὁ πιστεύων εἰς ἐμέ in the parallel clause (for the promise in both cf. 4.14, οὐ μὴ διψήσει εἰς τὸν αἰῶνα) and the primary reference is not to the eucharist but to union with Christ effected by faith, through which life is conveyed to men. It is nevertheless important that the image of thirst and drinking is included; this does not arise first in vv. 51–8, and there is no need to regard this later paragraph as a later insertion designed to introduce a sacramental note otherwise entirely wanting. If a man truly has life-giving contact with Jesus he never ceases to be dependent on him (see pp. 283f.) but the initial contact does not need to be repeated. The crowd's πάντοτε (v. 34) is therefore beside the point. Dodd (*A.S.*, 85) compares Jer. 31(38).12 (LXX), but the parallel is not close. For the parallelism between the two clauses cf. Ecclus. 24.21; Rev. 7.16 (in dependence on Isa. 49.10). It is unnecessary to hold that John translated a Semitic source. Note οὐ μὴ πεινάσῃ (with correct subjunctive); οὐ μὴ διψήσει (with incorrect indicative). John seems quite careless in handling this construction.

36. εἶπον ὑμῖν. See v. 26.

καὶ ἑωράκατέ με. με should be omitted, with ℵ a b e sin cur. The omission makes the reference to v. 26 much plainer; με assimilates in thought, not wording, to v. 40.

καὶ οὐ πιστεύετε. And yet (καί adversative; see 5.40) you do not believe. The sign of the loaves quickened the appetite but not faith.

37–40. This short paragraph is a unity the thought of which is made no clearer by the fact that some members of it are repeated several times over. It may be summarized thus:

> I have come down to do not my will but the will of God who sent me.
> It is God's will that none whom he has given me should perish, but that they all should receive life and be raised up at the last day.
> Therefore I will receive and raise up every one who 'comes to me', since he is the Father's gift to me and it is the Father's will that I should do so.

For the form of the section, in which the will of God (v. 38) is expounded in the two following verses, Borgen (75f.) compares 1QS 4.2f., where there are similar explanations, with the Hebrew ל corresponding to John's epexegetical ἵνα.

πᾶν ὃ δίδωσίν μοι ὁ πατήρ. πᾶν ὅ is used collectively where the masculine πάντες οὕς would be expected. Cf. 3.6; 6.39; 10.29; 17.2,24; see also 17.21. The effect of the neuter is to emphasize strongly the collective aspect of the Father's gift of believers.

πρὸς ἐμὲ ἥξει. ἥκειν is probably used synonymously with ἔρχεσθαι; John uses such pairs of synonyms (e.g. ἀγαπᾶν, φιλεῖν). It is true that ἥκειν is used particularly of worship (see T.W.N.T. s.v. (J. Schneider); and, e.g., Dittenberger, O.G.I.S. 186.6, ἥκω πρὸς τὴν κυρίαν Ἴσιν); but the decisive consideration here is the use of τὸν ἐρχόμενον in the same verse (see on v. 35).

οὐ μὴ ἐκβάλω ἔξω. ἔξω is wrongly omitted by אּ D a b e sin cur; it was no doubt thought pleonastic. For the thought cf. Matt. 8.12 and similar passages. The verse sums up the universalism, the individualism, and the predestinarianism of the gospel. Jesus rejects no one who comes to him, but in coming to him God's decision always precedes man's.

38. καταβέβηκα. See on v. 33. There is no difference in meaning between ἀπὸ τοῦ οὐρανοῦ and ἐκ τ. οὐ. used hitherto.

τὸ θέλημα τὸ ἐμὸν ... τὸ θέλημα τοῦ πέμψαντός με. Cf. Mark 14.36 (and parallels). The Gethsemane story is not found in John but the thought expressed in it governs the gospel as a whole; see Introduction, p. 53, and on 5.19–47.

39. πᾶν ... μὴ ἀπολέσω ἐξ αὐτοῦ. John's partitive use of ἐκ; see Introduction, p. 8. The odd construction is the result of the collective use of the neuter πᾶν: '. . . that I should not lose one of the whole company . . .'. Cf. 10.28f., and for the fulfilment of the implied promise 17.12. See also for parallelism in thought and language Matt. 18.14, οὐκ ἔστιν θέλημα ἔμπροσθεν τοῦ πατρὸς ὑμῶν τοῦ ἐν οὐρανοῖς ἵνα ἀπόληται ἐν τῶν μικρῶν τούτων.

ἀναστήσω αὐτὸν ἐν τῇ ἐσχάτῃ ἡμέρᾳ. Cf. vv. 40, 44, 54. Here ἀναστήσω is to be taken as an aorist subjunctive, dependent on ἵνα. For the view that these clauses are insertions made by an ecclesiastical redactor concerned to accommodate the discourse to the 'official' futurist eschatology, see p. 283. In fact there is no ground for thinking of them as anything other than a genuine part of John's thought and they must be interpreted as such. (ἐν) τ. ἐ. ἡ. occurs again at 11.24; 12.48 (and at 7.37 but not in an eschatological sense). The thought is expressed more fully in the next verse: the destiny of believers is to receive in this world eternal life (which clearly is not simply equivalent to unending life, cf. 5.24) and to be raised up at the last day. Here, as in 5.24–9, John balances exactly the two aspects of the Christian life, in present possession and future hope; and there is nothing to indicate that he thought one more important than the other.

40. θεωρῶν. θεωρεῖν is sometimes though not consistently used of a special, perceptive, beholding of Christ: 6.62; 12.45; 14.19; 16.10,16f., 19; cf. 20.14. Here we have both seeing and believing—contrast v. 36; but the contrast lies in the addition of πιστεύειν, rather than in the substitution of θεωρεῖν for ὁρᾶν.

ἀναστήσω may be rather loosely constructed with the same ἵνα as ἔχῃ (. . . that he should . . . and that I should . . .), or may be an independent future indicative; probably the former, as in v. 39, and because the final raising up is also dependent on the will of the Father.

41. ἐγόγγυζον οὖν οἱ Ἰουδαῖοι, as did the fathers in the wilderness, Exod. 16.2,8f. (noun γογγυσμός, verb διαγογγύζειν). For 'the Jews' see on 1.19. Again, as at vv. 28, 30, the discourse takes a further step through the misunderstanding or complaint of the Jews.

ὁ καταβάς. Vv. 33 and 35 are (rightly) combined. Earlier the present participle καταβαίνων was used, but the change is not significant.

42. οὐχ οὗτός ἐστιν Ἰησοῦς ὁ υἱὸς Ἰωσήφ . . .; A similar objection is brought in Mark 6.3 and parallels (only Luke names Joseph, in a closely parallel phrase, οὐχὶ υἱός ἐστιν Ἰωσὴφ οὗτος; 4.22). The argument is that one whose local parentage is known cannot have come down from heaven. John nowhere affirms belief in the virgin birth of Jesus, but it is probable that he knew and accepted the doctrine (see on 1.13) and that he here ironically alludes to it—if the objectors had known the truth about Jesus' parentage they would have been compelled to recognize that it was entirely congruent with his having come down from heaven. But cf. 7.42: no amount of information, even of correct information, would enable the Jews to evaluate Jesus and pass judgement upon him. See v. 44.

44. οὐδεὶς δύναται ἐλθεῖν πρός με. The complaint is pointless and the dispute in which the Jews are engaged must be fruitless; it cannot lead them to come to Jesus. Only the direct act of the Father—not the mere resolution of some problem—can effect this. 'So long as a man remains, and is content to remain, confident of his own ability, without divine help, to assess experience and the meaning of experience, he cannot "come to" the Lord, he cannot "believe"; only the Father can move him to this step, with its incalculable and final results' (Lightfoot, 160f.). The Synoptic Gospels are as emphatic as John that salvation apart from the initiative of God is quite impossible; see, Mark 10.23-7 (. . . παρὰ ἀνθρώποις ἀδύνατον, ἀλλ᾽ οὐ παρὰ θεῷ . . .). Hence Jesus merely reiterates the truth and does not seek to establish it by force of argument; those whom the Father gives to him will be drawn to him, with or without argument, and they will not be cast out; those whom the Father does not give will not come.

ἑλκύσῃ. Cf. 12.32 where Jesus draws all men to himself. The word is found in a similar connection in the Old Testament: Jer. 38(31).3, εἵλκυσά σε εἰς οἰκτείρημα. It may be relevant to compare the use of the Piel of קרב ('to bring near') for the conversion of proselytes, e.g. P. Aboth 1.12: Hillel said: Be of the disciples of Aaron, loving peace and pursuing peace, loving mankind and bringing them nigh (מקרבן) to the Law. It is interesting to compare (though it is quite impossible to restore and interpret with certainty) a papyrus fragment of a saying of Jesus (P. Oxy. 654.9f.) λέγει Ἰ [   ] οἱ ἕλκοντες ἡμᾶς [. . . . But see now Thomas 3, and Fitzmyer, Essays, 315f. The saying is irrelevant.

ἀναστήσω here (contrast v. 40) is probably future indicative; the coming takes place before the last day.

45. ἔστιν γεγραμμένον. Cf. v. 31 for this periphrastic perfect.

ἐν τοῖς προφήταις. John does not elsewhere use this vague reference; the suggestion, made in the first edition of this Commentary, that it may indicate uncertainty regarding the exact source of the quotation, should be abandoned. The parallel alleged from Matt. 2.23 where the difficult saying 'He shall be called a Nazarene' is said to have been given 'through the prophets' (διὰ τῶν προφητῶν) is hardly fair, since the source of this quotation constitutes in any case a problem, whereas John's quotation comes from what appears to have been a Passover *haphtarah*, and must therefore have been known to him. καὶ ἔσονται πάντες διδακτοὶ θεοῦ. From Isa. 54.12f., καὶ θήσω . . . πάντας τοὺς υἱούς σου διδακτοὺς θεοῦ (למודי יהוה). John gives a sufficiently exact paraphrase and is probably dependent on the LXX: he does not use διδακτός elsewhere. For the thought cf. also Jer. 31.33f. (a law written on the heart); this is particularly interesting in view of the use of ἕλκειν just before (31.3, see on v. 44), but it would be unwise to lay much stress on this concidence. There is also a hint of Ps. 78 (77), referred to at v. 31; this provides a link with Exod. 16, and so a further connection with Passover. The prophecy is given a personal reference to the Messiah in Ps. Sol. 17.32: καὶ αὐτὸς βασιλεὺς δίκαιος διδακτὸς ὑπὸ θεοῦ. The quotation is adduced in explanation of God's drawing men; this consists in teaching, the inward teaching which God gives to those whom he chooses and so directs to Jesus. For every one who has heard (ἀκούσας) what the Father says, and learnt (μαθών) from it, comes to Jesus.

46. The previous verse might be misleading. It must not be taken to mean that any man may enjoy a direct mystical experience of God and then, enlightened, attach himself to Jesus. Jesus only has immediate knowledge of God (τὸν πατέρα ἑώρακεν), and to others he is the mediator, since he has come forth from the presence of God (ὢν παρὰ τοῦ θεοῦ). See 1.18, which has probably caused (by assimilation) the reading of ℵ* D it (θεόν; sin has θεὸν πατέρα). Cf. also 14.7ff.; 21.18. A man is 'taught of God' by hearing Jesus; and the result of this is that he is drawn to Jesus. The process is circular, but John means to assert that it is set in motion not by man's volition but by Jesus, or rather, by God's initiative in Jesus. The parallel in *Thomas* 27 (If you fast not from the world, you will not find the Kingdom; if you keep not the Sabbath as Sabbath, you will not see the Father) is not close.

47. See on 1.51; 3.15.

48. See on v. 35.

These two verses are 'the natural conclusion of this pattern of exegetical debate' (Borgen, 86). If this is so, it will follow that v. 49 is the beginning of a new paragraph. Borgen draws this conclusion, and adds (87) that it 'marks a new beginning by repeating—with slight differences and a supplement (καὶ ἀπέθανον)—the haggadic fragment at the beginning of the homily in v. 31a'. His new paragraph runs to the end of the discourse in v. 58. Bultmann, on the other hand, thinks that the new section starts with the reference to the σάρξ of Jesus in v. 51c, and (see above, pp. 283f.) regards vv. 51c–58 as a eucharistic supplement added to the discourse by the ecclesiastical redactor. Neither of these views is satisfactory. Here, as elsewhere, John builds his discourse by ending one section with a provocative remark which elicits misapprehension or opposition on the part of the audience. Vv. 49–51 are a summarizing conclusion of what precedes, with the word σάρξ introduced into the restatement so as to lead to the strife of v. 52, with which the new treatment of the theme of the bread of life begins. See 'Menschensohn',

345ff.; also H. Schürmann, *Biblische Zeitschrift* (1958), 244–62, and *Trierer Theologische Zeitschrift* 68 (1959), 30–45, 108–18.

49–50. Borgen (87) rightly notes that the word *eat* is now taken up from the basic text for elucidation. Eating the manna was essential for life, yet the life it fostered was not eternal life: the eaters, in the end, died. The heavenly bread that Jesus gives, or rather is, is such that those who eat of it enjoy eternal life. *Not dying* is equivalent to hungering and thirsting no more (in v. 35): those so provided have enough for every spiritual need and therefore never die. Cf. 11.26. ἵνα in v. 50 is John's loose explanatory non-final ἵνα; it need not be regarded as a mistranslation of Aramaic (Burney, 76, M. ɪɪ, 436).

51. ὁ ἄρτος ὁ ζῶν is a synonym of ὁ ἄρτος τῆς ζωῆς; cf. ὕδωρ ζῶν in 4.10f. (and ὕδωρ τῆς ζωῆς in Rev. 21.6; 22.1,17).

καὶ ὁ ἄρτος δὲ ὃν ἐγὼ δώσω ἡ σάρξ μου ἐστίν. The position of δέ is unusual but by no means wrong (B.D., §475); it introduces a fresh thought. This of course is apparent on other than grammatical grounds. The first two clauses in this verse repeat what has already been said. The person of Jesus received by faith is the means by which eternal life is given and sustained. Further exegesis of the basic term *bread* identifies it with the flesh of Jesus (for the form, Borgen, 89, compares Philo, *L.A.* ɪɪ, 86, ἡ γὰρ ἀκρότομος πέτρα (Deut. 8.16) ἡ σοφία τοῦ θεοῦ ἐστιν, and CD 6.4, היא (Num. 21.18) הבאר התורה, the well is the Law). This identification recalls that of Mark 14.22 (Matt. 26.26; Luke 22.19; 1 Cor. 11.24), where Jesus says of the loaf used at the last supper τοῦτό ἐστιν τὸ σῶμά μου, and it is inevitable that the reader should think of the Christian supper as the context in which Jesus gives himself to the believer as his life. This impression is confirmed in the following verses, especially in v. 53 (see the notes), and few dispute that the eucharist is alluded to in this part of the discourse, whether it be regarded as John's own work or as a redactional gloss. On the unity of the discourse see above, pp 283f. To see in this part of it an allusion to the eucharist ('a transition to the eucharistic part'—Schnackenberg) does not in itself determine what John's eucharistic theology was; indeed, it is a fundamental mistake to assume that he (or the author of vv. 51c–58) understood the bread and wine to be a kind of medicine, conferring immortality by quasi-magical means. His removal of the eucharistic allusion from the last supper to this discourse proves precisely the contrary: it is his intention to set the eucharist in the context of the work of Jesus as a whole and to give it a strictly personal interpretation. By his stress throughout this paragraph on the divine initiative he avoids completely the magical notion of placing constraint upon God; the eucharist provides (as the feeding miracle did) a vivid picture of what it means to receive Christ by faith, but the fact that eucharistic and non-eucharistic statements stand in parallel shows that John is not concerned to argue for the uniqueness of the eucharist as a means of grace. Cf. J. E. L. Oulton, *Holy Communion and Holy Spirit* (1951), especially 69–99. For other views see G. Bornkamm, *Gesammelte Aufsätze* ɪɪɪ, 60–7; also ɪᴠ, 51–64; G. Richter, in *Z.N.T.W.* 60 (1969), 21–55. It was pointed out above that in Mark 14.22 the bread was identified with the σῶμα of Jesus; John uses not this word but σάρξ (cf. Ignatius, *Romans* 7.3; *Philadelphians* 4.1; 11.2; *Smyrnaeans* 6.2; Justin, 1 *Apology* 66). According to Lindars, σάρξ is a legitimate alternative to σῶμα as a rendering of בשר; Jeremias (*Eucharistic Words*,

198–201) thinks *flesh* the more original term, so that what Jesus said at the supper must be understood to refer to 'my flesh and blood', i.e., myself. This is not the place to discuss the words and events, and the original meaning, of the last supper (since it is illogical to argue back to Mark from John, who probably knew and reflected on Mark, and especially from a part of John possibly connected with the eucharist but not with the last supper). John probably substituted σάρξ for σῶμα partly because it corresponded with the use of his own church and partly because it fitted his theology of incarnation (see 1.14).

ὑπὲρ τῆς τοῦ κόσμου ζωῆς. These words (preceded by ἡ σάρξ μου ἐστίν) are the reading of P⁶⁶ P⁷⁵ B D it vg sin cur sah, and should very probably be accepted. Other readings are attempts to improve the run of the sentence: ἡ σάρξ μου ἐστίν ἣν ἐγὼ δώσω ὑ. τ. τ. κ. 3. (Θ λ ω pesh boh); ὑ. τ. τ. κ. 3. ἡ σάρξ μου ἐστίν (א Tertullian). The meaning however is not really obscure; cf. 1 Cor. 11.24, τοῦτό μού ἐστιν τὸ σῶμα τὸ ὑπὲρ ὑμῶν. Some word such as 'given' must be supplied; cf. Luke 22.19b, τὸ σῶμά μου τὸ ὑπὲρ ὑμῶν διδόμενον. For the use of ὑπὲρ in John see 10.11,15 (ὑπὲρ τῶν προβάτων), 11.50 (ὑπὲρ τοῦ λαοῦ; cf. 18.14), 11.51f. (ὑπὲρ τοῦ ἔθνους), 15.13 (ὑπὲρ τῶν φίλων αὐτοῦ), 17.19 (ὑπὲρ αὐτῶν ἐγὼ ἁγιάζω ἐμαυτόν), cf. 13.37f. These passages show conclusively that a reference to the death of Jesus is intended—he will give his flesh in death—and suggest a sacrificial meaning, but no precision about the mode or significance of the sacrifice can be obtained. The expression ἡ τοῦ κόσμου ζωή has no parallel in the New Testament. The meaning of the whole sentence is that of 3.15f.: God loved the world and provided in Christ the means by which it might have eternal life. ὑπὲρ τῆς τοῦ κόσμου ζωῆς is equivalent to ἵνα ὁ κόσμος ζῇ. Cf. 11.50: ἵνα εἷς ἄνθρωπος ἀποθάνῃ ὑπὲρ τοῦ λαοῦ καὶ μὴ ὅλον τὸ ἔθνος ἀπόληται.

52. ἐμάχοντο οὖν πρὸς ἀλλήλους. 'They disputed violently with one another.' The metaphorical use of μάχεσθαι is well established in Greek (e.g. *Iliad* 1, 304, μαχεσσαμένω ἐπέεσσιν). Presumably different opinions were current on the question that follows.

πῶς δύναται οὗτος (perhaps used contemptuously—this fellow) ἡμῖν δοῦναι τὴν σάρκα φαγεῖν; P⁶⁶ B lat sy have τὴν σάρκα αὐτοῦ, but this has been accommodated to the context, and the short text, which recalls more clearly the complaining of the Israelites (Num. 11.4) is better. John regularly uses this unintelligent kind of question as a means of building up his argument and underlining the contrast between Jesus and those who surround him; see on 3.4.

53. The truth is v. 51b is now put in negative form. The bread of heaven is the flesh of Jesus, which gives life to the world; and there is no life for the world in any other source. Two fresh points are made. (i) The title Son of man is introduced. On the use of this title in John see Introduction. pp. 72f., and on 1.51. Cf. also vv. 27, 63, in this chapter. There can be no doubt here that the Son of man is a person who has flesh and blood, i.e., the Son of man is Jesus; yet he is not simply man, for his flesh and blood are such that others may be said to eat and drink them. The Son of man is *a* man, a real man whom God has sealed; i.e., God has given him the seal of his approval, constituting him his messenger and accredited agent. He descends from heaven and returns thither (3.13; 6.63), for the salvation of the world.

(ii) To the statement about the flesh of the Son of man is added καὶ πίητε αὐτοῦ τὸ αἷμα. This unmistakably points to the eucharist. It seems to be the parallelism between flesh and blood that is insisted on here, though some have distinguished them, supposing that the blood emphasizes the necessity of death, and symbolizes the life which is given to the believer, while the flesh means the self-sacrifice in which the believer shares. But it is more probable that 'blood' is introduced in order to suggest the eucharist, and to emphasize that it is the whole incarnate life (note the common Hebrew phrase בשר ודם, flesh and blood) of the incarnate Son of God which is the lifegiving food. There may be an attack on Docetism; see E. Schweizer, *Evangelische Theologie* 8 (1952/3), 341–63.

54. No substantially new thought is added in this verse, though the parallel mention of flesh and blood seems to confirm the reference to the eucharist.

ὁ τρώγων. τρώγειν is used from the time of Homer for the eating of animals, especially herbivorous animals. From the time of Herodotus it is used of the eating of men; but the sense of eating with pleasure, or audibly, is not supported in L.S. *s.v.* It is very improbable that John saw any special meaning in the word and distinguished it from other words for eating. Up to this point he has used the aorist stem √φαγ; he now requires a present participle, and instead of using ἐσθίειν, the usual supplement of the defective √φαγ, he uses τρώγειν. ἐσθίειν is never used in John, though √φαγ is quite common. τρώγειν occurs four times in this paragraph, and at 13.18 (where it is substituted for the ἐσθίειν of Ps. 41.10).

ἀναστήσω αὐτὸν τῇ ἐσχάτῃ ἡμέρᾳ. Cf. vv. 39, 40, 44; here the verb is future indicative. Bultmann, though we should not follow him in attributing vv. 51c–58 to an ecclesiastical redactor (see pp. 283f.), is right in noting the combination of eucharistic and eschatological interests. These were associated from the beginning (cf. 1 Cor. 11.26), and John was capable of seeing that eucharistic theory and practice stand in particularly great need of the check supplied by futurist eschatology. See Introduction, pp. 82–5.

55. ἀληθής, P⁶⁶ P⁷⁵ B W: ἀληθῶς, ℵ* D Θ ω it vg sin cur pesh. Johannine usage confirms the ancient support for ἀληθῶς. With symbolical predicates such as βρῶσις ,πόσις, John uses not ἀληθής but ἀληθινός (see on 1.9), while the use of ἀληθῶς is quite in accord with his style (cf. 1.47; 4.42; 6.14; 7.40; 8.31). These passages show the meaning of ἀληθῶς here. My flesh and blood really are what food and drink should be, they fulfil the ideal, archetypal function of food and drink, that is in giving eternal life to those who receive them. καὶ τὸ αἷμα . . . πόσις is omitted by D, probably by homoeoteleuton.

56. The grounds for the preceding statement are now given, though there is no grammatical connection such as γάρ. The flesh and blood of Christ are truly food and drink to those who receive them because by means of them a complete and reciprocal indwelling of Christ and the believer is attained.

ἐν ἐμοὶ μένει κἀγὼ ἐν αὐτῷ. Cf. 15.4, μείνατε ἐν ἐμοί, κἀγὼ ἐν ὑμῖν (also in a possibly eucharistic context). μένειν is one of John's most important words. The Father abides in the Son (14.10), the Spirit abides upon Jesus (1.32f.); believers abide in Christ and he in them (6.56; 15.4). There are variations of the same thought: the word of Christ abides in Christians and they in it (5.38; 8.31; 15.7); Christ abides in the love of God and ·the disciples must abide in the love of Christ (15.9f.). What is meant is that the being of Jesus is completely determined by God, the being of disciples by Jesus. After this verse D (with some old Latin support, notably a) adds καθὼς ἐν ἐμοὶ ὁ πατὴρ κἀγὼ ἐν τῷ πατρί. ἀμὴν ἀμὴν λέγω ὑμῖν, ἐὰν μὴ λάβητε τὸ σῶμα τοῦ υἱοῦ τοῦ ἀνθρώπου ὡς τὸν ἄρτον τῆς ζωῆς, οὐκ ἔχετε ζωὴν ἐν αὐτῷ. It is not impossible that these words are genuine and were omitted from most MSS. by homoeoteleuton; but it is more probable that they are a homiletical Western addition, intended to make the eucharistic reference more explicit.

57. καθὼς ἀπέστειλέν με. On the sending of Christ see on 20.21.

ὁ ζῶν πατήρ. The meaning is that of 5.26; cf. ὁ ἄρτος τῆς ζωῆς, ὁ ἄρτος ὁ ζῶν above. 'The living Father' occurs in Thomas 3, 50. Of these sayings, the former occurs in P. Oxy. 654.19, where the words appear to be τοῦ πατρὸς τοῦ ζ[ῶντος . . .]. The ζ however has been variously read as τ and π. See Fitzmyer, Essays, 378.

κἀγὼ ζῶ . . . κἀκεῖνος ζήσει. The thought is that of 5.21,24–30 given in compressed form; see also 1.4. Life is the essential property of the primal God; it is transferred to the Son that as the Father gives life to whom he will so also may he. The life of the Son is entirely dependent upon the Father (διὰ τὸν πατέρα); he has no independent life or authority, and it is because he abides in the Father that men may live by abiding in him.

ὁ τρώγων με is now substituted for ὁ τρώγων μου τὴν σάρκα (v. 56); this supports the view that 'flesh and blood' signifies the whole person of Jesus.

δι' ἐμέ, corresponding to διὰ τὸν πατέρα. The Christian life is a mediated life. John, though he has been called a mystic, is unaware of any religious life which is not wholly dependent on Jesus. Cf. 1.18 and see Introduction, pp. 85ff.

58. No fresh thought is added in this rather confused verse, which sums up the teaching of the discourse.

οὗτος has no proper antecedent. 'What I am talking about, the true food which is given in my flesh and blood, which is I myself, is . . .'.

οὐ καθώς. The connection is muddled through too great compression but the meaning is clear. Once more the contrast is drawn between the manna (and the Law it was taken to symbolize) and the heavenly bread which is Christ. Only the latter confers eternal life. Martyn (108f.) compares 3.14, where, in a similar context, καθώς stands unnegated, and concludes that John's attitude to the Mosaic Prophet-Messiah was complex. This is no doubt true, and the insight valuable, but it may be better to see the major contrast between Torah and Jesus.

59. ἐν συναγωγῇ, 'in synagogue'. At v. 24 we learned that the scene was Capernaum, but the discourse with its interruptions suggests a less formal occasion than a synagogue sermon. For Jesus preaching in a synagogue cf. especially Mark 6.1–6 and parallels.

Καφαρναούμ. See on 2.12. The synagogue which has been excavated at Tell-Ḥum is certainly not earlier than the second century A.D., and is therefore not the synagogue referred to in the gospels, though it is not impossible that it was erected on the site of the previous building. See E. L. Sukenik, Ancient Synagogues of Palestine and Greece (1934; Schweich Lectures 1930), 7–21.

At the end of the verse σαββάτῳ is added by D a Augustine, an imaginative supplementary detail characteristic of the Western text.

15. REACTION AND CONFESSION

6.60–71

The present paragraph marks the close of the Galilean ministry of Jesus, and in it John presents, in summary form and in dependence upon certain significant synoptic incidents, the result of that ministry. Cf. 12.37–50, where the work of Jesus in Jerusalem, and indeed his whole public ministry, is similarly summarized. Bultmann places 6.60–71 immediately before 12.37–41, and after 11.55—12.33; 8.30–40. It seems to make satisfactory sense as it stands.

The synagogue discourse comes to its close, and not 'the Jews' only, who have already made objection, but also some of the disciples complain of what has been said. It cannot be accepted. Without being told, Jesus knows their thoughts, and at once volunteers the explanation. All that he has said about the bread of life must be viewed in the light of two facts, the ascension and the gift of the Spirit. All crude misunderstandings must be abandoned. The Son of man, whose 'flesh' all must eat, is one whose home is in heaven, to which he returns. Flesh as such is unprofitable: only the Spirit (who, it must be remembered, rested and abides upon Jesus—1.32) can give life. The substance of Jesus' discourse is the means by which Spirit, and thereby life, is conveyed. It is not surprising, however, that some should be offended; they lack faith, and only by faith can the truth of what Jesus has said be perceived, since he has spoken not of flesh as such, which all can see and understand, but of the flesh of the Son of man, and of the Spirit. Faith, moreover, is not a human achievement but the gift of God, and for this reason Judas, whatever the piety and ability which may have suggested his choice as an apostle, is marked out as the traitor.

Jesus next uses the defection of many disciples as a means of challenging the faith of the Twelve. They, being (with the exception of Judas) men whom God himself has drawn to Jesus, make their confession of faith: there is no other than Jesus to whom such men may go. The reply of Jesus emphasizes, with a trenchancy remarkable even in this gospel, both that he has chosen the Twelve (they have not chosen him—cf. 15.16) and that he well knows the future treachery of Judas. The frailty of man and his complete dependence upon the predestinating grace of God are alike brought out.

This passage, which is evidently of great importance in the movement and thought of the gospel, seems to rest upon a number of synoptic passages: the rejection of Jesus in the synagogue of his own πατρίς (Mark 6.1–6; Matt. 13.54–8; cf. Luke 4.16–30; see above on John

4.43–54), the confession of Peter in the neighbourhood of Caesarea Philippi (Mark 8.29; Matt. 16.16; Luke 9.20) and the prediction of the betrayal by Judas Iscariot (Mark 14.18; Matt. 26.21; Luke 22.21; cf. John 13.21). In Mark these are isolated units of tradition; in John they are worked up into a whole in which the reader is compelled to consider both the reaction to Jesus of representative persons in the past, and his own. It is not a matter of chance that in a certain synagogue Jesus marvelled because of men's unbelief (Mark 6.6), nor was the confession of Mark 8.29 either a lucky guess, or the result of profound human insight. Neither the unbelief nor the faith was independent of the power of God.

Jesus now, in John's narrative, leaves Galilee to make the offer of eternal life in Jerusalem.

For the relation of this paragraph to the rest of the chapter see p. 284, where it is noted that Bornkamm has argued that vv. 60–71 relate to vv. 35–50, and drawn the conclusion that vv. 51–8 are an interpolation. If this is true v. 63 will not refer to the eucharistic flesh of Christ (which, it is held, could hardly, after v. 53, be said to be of no avail) but to flesh as this is intended in 3.6, 'the natural principle in man which cannot give life' (Brown, 300). The difficulty in this view, and it seems insuperable, is that the word σάρξ does not occur in vv. 35–50; it occurs only (in this chapter) in vv. 51,52,53,54,55,56. Further, it will be noted that in all these verses the reference is to *my flesh*, or *the flesh of the Son of man*, with the exception of v. 52, where the uncomprehending crowd say, How can this fellow give us *flesh* to eat? They thus make precisely the mistake that is corrected in v. 63. *Flesh* as such will do men no more good than the quails in the desert, but the flesh of the Son of man is the vehicle of the Spirit and the mouthpiece of the Word of God (1.32; 1.14).

That this passage reflects the historical situation represented by the Johannine Epistles (Fenton) is true; John however is not absent-mindedly reading back contemporary events in a crudely anachronistic fashion, but using his historical material to make clear the nature of decision, confession, and the life of faith. Cf. 1 John 2.19.

60. ἐκ τῶν μαθητῶν. On John's partitive use of ἐκ see Introduction, p. 8. The disciples are here clearly distinguished from the Twelve; vv. 66f. Not only the crowd but the disciples too are to be tested. In 2.11,23; 4.39–42 signs led to faith; here they lead to unbelief. Miracles are an unsatisfactory ground of faith.

σκληρός, originally of physical objects, 'hard', 'harsh', 'rough', means 'hard' not in the sense of 'difficult to understand', but 'unacceptable, harsh, offensive'. It is parallel to ὑμᾶς σκανδαλίζει in the next verse. For the usage cf. Gen. 21.11; 42.7; Jude 15 (quoting 1 Enoch 1.9); Hermas, *Mandate* XII, iii, 4f.; iv, 4 (of ἐντολαί).

τίς δύναται αὐτοῦ ἀκούειν; John's usage is not decisive on the question whether αὐτοῦ refers to λόγος or to Jesus himself. ἀκούειν with an accusative always refers to a thing; with a genitive it refers 9 times to a person, 9 times to a thing, though of these last 7 are τῆς φωνῆς (or τῶν ῥημάτων) τινος, so that the personal source of sound is in mind. The balance of probability is therefore perhaps slightly in favour of 'who can hear (listen to) him?' ἀκούειν is here close to the meaning 'obey' (as שׁמע in the Old Testament).

61. εἰδὼς δὲ ὁ Ἰησοῦς ἐν ἑαυτῷ. John means a supernatural knowledge; see on 1.47f.

σκανδαλίζει. The verb is common in the Synoptic Gospels but in John occurs only here and at 16.1. The noun σκάνδαλον is not used at all. See Derrett, Law, 255f. What is it that offends crowds and disciples and so leads them into disbelief? It is natural, and probably correct, to answer: the thought of eating the flesh and drinking the blood of the Son of man (vv. 53–6). This would offend not only Jews but also John's Hellenistic public (Dodd, Interpretation, 341). V. 62 has suggested that the offensive thought is the descent of the Son of man: Does his descending offend you? What then if you see him ascending . . .? In fact these are both partial expressions of the total scandal, which is that 'a mere man, whose life ends in death, solemnly lays the claim that he is the Revealer of God! And this declaration, which demands of man the abandonment of all his securities, is clearly seen at the cross to be a demand for the surrender of life itself, a demand to follow right to the cross' (Bultmann, 445).

62. ἐὰν οὖν θεωρῆτε τὸν υἱὸν τοῦ ἀνθρώπου ἀναβαίνοντα ὅπου ἦν τὸ πρότερον; The sentence is evidently incomplete; it wants an apodosis. Commentators generally have adopted two kinds of supplement. (i) If the condition is fulfilled the offence will be greater. 'Clearly we have to understand: "Then the offence really will be great!"' (Bultmann, 445; but see below). (ii) If the condition is fulfilled the offence will be diminished or removed. 'Jesus by no means intends to heighten the σκάνδαλον, but rather to solve the riddle of his paradoxical speech. His ascension . . . will prove that he had not required anthropophagy' (Bauer, 101). (i) and (ii) are not however to be regarded as mutually exclusive. 'Each of these two interpretations appears to contain elements of the full meaning' (Westcott, 109). This becomes especially clear when it is recalled that the ascending (ἀναβαίνειν) of the Son of man means at once suffering and glory; he returns where he was before (cf. 1.1) by mounting upon the cross (see on 3.13–15). The whole process of the return of Christ to the glory of the Father, including as it did the crucifixion, was both the supreme scandal, and the vindication of Christ as the Bread of Life; and, at the same time, the proof that eating his flesh and drinking his blood was neither murderous nor magical. This allusion to the scandal of the cross also makes clear the nature of the offence given by Jesus in the course of his ministry. This verse asks indirectly the question asked directly in v. 67 (Bultmann, 445). The offence must be faced and the costly decision of faith made before man can eat and drink the flesh and blood of Christ and, being united with him in death, receive the gift of eternal life. It is impossible to say why John has left his sentence incomplete. The hypothesis is attractive that he did so in order to leave room for the twofold interpretation which he seems to have intended; but this could have been done equally well if he had written τί οὖν ἐὰν . . . . See however B.D. §482.

τὸν υἱὸν τοῦ ἀνθρώπου ἀναβαίνοντα. ἀναβαίνειν and καταβαίνειν (when used theologically) occur always in contexts dealing with the Son of man (except 20.17); and with Son of man belongs also the characteristic Johannine use of ὑψοῦν. These observations, particularly relevant in the present context, strongly reinforce the view that for John Son of man is a being who descends from heaven to the work of salvation and ascends to glory (and finally judgement). See on 1.51.

τὸ πρότερον, used adverbially. It implies, what John elsewhere explicitly states, the pre-existence of the Son of man.

63. The way is now open for a full understanding of the discourse. The ascension makes possible, both logically and chronologically, the work of the Spirit (cf. 7.39).

τὸ πνεῦμά ἐστιν τὸ ζωοποιοῦν. ζωοποιεῖν (also 5.21) is a Pauline word (7 times; see especially 1 Cor. 15.45, ὁ ἔσχατος ᾿Αδὰμ εἰς πνεῦμα ζωοποιοῦν; 2 Cor. 3.6, τὸ δὲ πνεῦμα ζωοποιεῖ). Though this word is not used in the earlier chapters of John (nor in the last discourses) the essential property of the Spirit is to give life: 3.5f.,8 the Spirit effects the new birth; 4.23f. the Spirit is brought into connection with the discourse on living water (see the notes); 7.38f. again the Spirit is living water. In the Old Testament also this is a fundamental concept regarding the Spirit; see H.S.G.T. 18-23, and especially Gen. 1.2; Ezek. 37.1-14. It is important to note the standpoint which is established by this reference to the Spirit. John is writing with the completed work of Christ (7.39) in mind, including his ascension and the gift of the Spirit, and the discourse of this chapter is incomprehensible except from this standpoint; otherwise the words of Jesus could have led only to a crude cannibalism. Moreover it was necessary that Jesus himself should be understood as the bearer of the Holy Spirit (cf. 1.32f.); otherwise his flesh and blood would lose all meaning. It is not as the supremely great man but as the obedient, Spirit-filled Son of the Father that he confronts men. The antithetical statement follows at once.

ἡ σάρξ οὐκ ὠφελεῖ οὐδέν. These words cannot be unrelated to the statement about the σάρξ of the Son of man in v. 53, but it would be wrong to suppose that this is the only context to which they belong. It is part of the truth that explicit reference to the inadequacy of the flesh as such was needed, with the reference in vv. 70f. to Judas' defection, to make clear that faith is essential in the eucharist (Guilding, 59), but it is also true (Martyn, 138) that John rejects the notion that the eucharist as a rite is in itself capable of solving the problem caused by the separation of Jesus from his disciples (as Martyn says, the discourses of chapters 13—17 deal with this issue). Quite apart from their bearing on the eucharist, however, the words are a problem: see 1.14. The offence 'arises when one's gaze is directed to the σάρξ' (Bultmann, 446). Neither devout participation in the eucharist, nor a historically exact account of the ministry of Jesus, even if it did full justice to his supposed winsomeness of character, wisdom, and piety, would constitute the revelation of God. There is no revelation apart from the Spirit and the Word, and no reception of revelation apart from the initiative of God himself (6.44). Lindars' true remark, 'In the composition of man it is the Spirit that gives life, and the flesh is of no avail', applies also to Jesus. It is worth noting (Charlesworth, J. & Q., 96) that here (and at 3.6) the dualism is between flesh and

Spirit, not, as at Qumran, between two spirits. See also the note on 6.39, and the introductory note to this section.

τὰ ῥήματα ἃ ἐγὼ λελάληκα ὑμῖν πνεῦμά ἐστιν καὶ ζωή ἐστιν. For the lifegiving word (λόγος) of Jesus cf. 5.24. The words of Jesus are the words (ῥήματα) of God. Cf. Isa. 40.6ff. (1 Pet. 1.24f.). It may be that the eucharist still forms part of the background of John's thought, not in that ῥήματα are the eucharistic words (not given by John, but presupposed), or that they (cf. the Hebrew דברים) should be understood as *matters* ('That which I have told you of, sacramental feeding, is Spirit and life'), or that the eucharist, like the miraculous feeding, is a σημεῖον, a *signum efficax* and thus a *verbum visibile* (Dodd, *Interpretation*, 342f.), but in that action and word are parallel as they are at 13.8–11 (feet-washing) and 15.3 (cleansing by the word) (Lightfoot). But the thought is wider. The words of Jesus are what men consume (Jer. 15.16; Ezek. 2.8—3.3; Rev. 10.9ff.; also *L.A.* III, 172f., where Philo, interpreting the manna says that what the Israelites ate was τὸ ἑαυτοῦ (sc. τοῦ θεοῦ) ῥῆμα καὶ τὸν ἑαυτοῦ λόγον). ῥήματα need not refer exclusively to the words of the preceding discourse; all the words of the incarnate Christ may be meant, and John no doubt does not forget that Jesus himself is the creative word of God (1.1). The ἐγώ is possibly though not certainly emphatic: *My* words are able to give life, whereas those of Moses were unable to perform what was promised. See Deut. 8.3; *Mekhilta* Exod. 15.26 (ויסע §1): The words of the Law (דברי תורה) which I have given you are life (חיים הם) for you; Gal. 3.21. Jesus supersedes Torah as the source of life. His visible flesh and his audible words (ῥήματα) bear witness to the Spirit and the Word through which he becomes revelation and salvation.

64. ἀλλ᾽ εἰσὶν ἐξ ὑμῶν τινες οἳ οὐ πιστεύουσιν. It is implied that the life contained in the words of Jesus is received on the basis of faith, and this knife edge inevitably divides the hearers of Jesus into two parties, which however do not necessarily correspond with visible groups, since even among those who are reckoned to be μαθηταί there are unbelievers.

ᾔδει γάρ. Cf. v. 61.

ἐξ ἀρχῆς, probably from the beginning of the ministry, but in this gospel, where all things are commonly traced back to their origin in the eternal counsels of God, not impossibly from the ἀρχή of 1.1.

τίνες εἰσὶν οἱ μὴ πιστεύοντες is omitted by P⁶⁶* e sin cur, μή alone by ℵ and a few other MSS. Both are probably accidental variants, though the latter may have been intended to bring out the fact that Jesus knew his own (rather than those who were not his own).

ὁ παραδώσων αὐτόν. Cf. v. 70.

65. διὰ τοῦτο. Jesus knew of the existence of faith and unbelief before these were manifested in the secession of disciples; he therefore, in order to prepare the true believers, explained the divine initiative which underlies faith.

εἴρηκα ὑμῖν. V. 44 . . . ἐὰν μὴ ὁ πατήρ . . . ἑλκύσῃ αὐτόν. There is no difference in meaning between the two clauses and they illuminate each other. Faith in Christ is not merely difficult; apart from God it is impossible (cf. Mark 10.27). Coming to Jesus is not a matter of free human decision, and the present circumstances will make clear (vv. 66ff.) the difference between opinion and faith.

ἐὰν μὴ ᾖ δεδομένον αὐτῷ ἐκ τοῦ πατρός. For both construction and sense cf. 3.27.

66. ἐκ τούτου, 'for this reason' or 'from this time'. There is a similar ambiguity at 19.12. Both meanings are applicable, and there is no reason why John should not have had both in mind.

ἀπῆλθον εἰς τὰ ὀπίσω, 'fell away'; the expression is curious; cf. 18.6; 20.14, and 1 Macc. 9.47, ἐξέκλινεν ἀπ' αὐτοῦ εἰς τὰ ὀπίσω. The Greek seems to rest upon a Hebrew construction, possibly נסוג אחור (nasog 'aḥor), which means sometimes 'to turn back' (Isa. 50.5), sometimes 'to be turned back', 'to be repulsed' (Isa. 42.17). In the group of passages where it bears the latter meaning the LXX rendering regularly includes εἰς τὰ ὀπίσω. Nevertheless the meaning in the present passage is 'fell away' rather than 'were driven back'.

οὐκέτι μετ' αὐτοῦ περιεπάτουν. 'No longer followed him as disciples'. This expression also is Hebraic; see Schlatter, 182f.

67. Jesus now challenges the Twelve, who appear to form a distinct group among the disciples. John assumes that his readers know, presumably from Mark or some other form of the synoptic tradition, who they are.

μὴ καὶ ὑμεῖς. . . . 'In a direct question μή either demands the answer No (as at Matt. 7.9, etc.), or puts a suggestion in the most tentative and hesitating way (John 4.29)' (M. 1, 193). The latter alternative applies here. καὶ ὑμεῖς emphasizes the distinction between the Twelve and the other disciples: '. . . you also, as well as they?'. That the question was a real one is shown by the presence of Judas among the Twelve; yet on the other hand, Jesus knew that none whom the Father had given him could be lost (vv. 37–39, 10.27–9).

68. Σίμων Πέτρος. See 1.42. In Mark the confession of Peter at Caesarea Philippi (8.29) takes place soon after the feeding of the Four Thousand; in Luke it is in even closer proximity to the feeding of the Five Thousand. In view of the many synoptic parallels in this chapter it seems probable that John is here reproducing the synoptic incident and order. John shows at this point no knowledge of the special Matthaean material (Matt. 16.17–19). On the relation between John and the synoptic tradition see, in addition to commentaries, F. Hahn, Titles, 231–4; E. Dinkler, Signum, 303ff. Cullmann (V. & A., 210) refers also to Luke 22.31ff.

ῥήματα 3ωῆς αἰωνίου, anarthrous; τὰ ῥήματα would imply a formula. Cf. v. 63. The words of Jesus are words which are in themselves living, deal with the subject of eternal life, and convey eternal life to those who believe. Those who have once become aware of the meaning and possibility of eternal life can take refuge with no other. John probably uses these words to link the tradition of Peter's confession with the context in which he has placed it.

69. πεπιστεύκαμεν καὶ ἐγνώκαμεν. The use of the perfects of πιστεύειν and γινώσκειν is characteristic of John; for πιστεύειν see 3.18; 6.69; 8.31 (participle); 11.27; 16.27; 20.29; for γινώσκειν, 5.42; 6.69; 8.52,55; 14.7 (pluperfect, with perfect as a variant); 14.9; 17.7. Here, as often, the sense is: 'We are in a state of faith and knowledge; we have recognized the truth and hold it.' For the relation between faith and knowledge see Introduction, pp. 81f., and on 1.10. Over a great range of their use the verbs πιστεύειν and γινώσκειν

seem to be used synonymously. Cf. 11.42; 17.8,21 with 17.3; 16.27–30 with 7.17; 11.27 and 20.31 with 6.69; and note the synonymous parallelism of 17.8. Several times πιστεύειν stands first (6.69; 8.31f., cf. 10.38); but it cannot be assumed that faith is the beginning of a process of which knowledge is the end since the reverse order is also found (16.30; cf. 1 John 4.16). The one certain distinction is that while Jesus is said to know God (7.29; 8.55; 10.15; 17.25) he is never said to believe in him. Faith (it may be inferred) includes the dependence of the created being upon the Creator; it is something which man as such can never outgrow (here John parts company with the gnostics). What follows is a genuine confession, since (1) it grows out of the situation and is therefore a decision, not general assent, and (2) it is an answer to the challenge of the revelation, not independent speculation (cf. Bultmann).

σὺ εἶ (cf. the ἐγώ εἰμι of Jesus himself) ὁ ἅγιος τοῦ θεοῦ. There is considerable textual variation, most of which can be ascribed to the desire to harmonize with Matt. 16.16 and Mark 8.29. The reading of the text, which is certainly to be preferred, is given by P⁷⁵ ℵ B D sah. The title ὁ ἅγιος τοῦ θεοῦ occurs in Mark 1.24 (=Luke 4.34), where it is the confession of the supernatural knowledge of a demon, and should be understood as a messianic title, though evidence for its use in this sense is wanting. There is no good ground for regarding it as equivalent to the Priestly Messiah of Qumran. Dinkler (op. cit., 303) takes the use of the term to be proof that John was not using Mark, since Mark's ὁ Χριστός would have been acceptable to John, who uses Χριστός 19 times, Μεσσίας twice; at this point however John is moving away from the technical language of Judaism into more universal categories (cf. 4.42). In 17.11 Jesus addresses God as πάτερ ἅγιε (elsewhere in John ἅγιος is applied exclusively to the Spirit), and the Johannine use of ἁγιάζειν is distinctive and important. Jesus is he ὃν ὁ πατὴρ ἡγίασεν (10.36), and for the sake of the disciples he sanctifies himself (17.19, ἁγιάζω ἐμαυτόν). Jesus is the emissary of God; in Jewish terms the Messiah, more generally, the Holy One of God, who comes from God and goes to God.

70. οὐκ ἐγὼ ὑμᾶς τοὺς δώδεκα ἐξελεξάμην; ἐγὼ ὑμᾶς takes up ἡμεῖς ... σύ in Peter's confession of faith, which is true so far as it goes but must not be allowed to suggest that the maker of it is in any sense conferring a benefit upon Jesus. The Twelve have not chosen him; he has chosen them (cf. 15.16). The Twelve are mentioned under that title only here (vv. 67, 70f.) and at 20.24; John has little or no interest in the number as such. This is perhaps because its original significance was eschatological (cf. Matt. 19.28=Luke 22.30), and because the Twelve as such played no important role in the history of the church. The number however remained in the recollection of the church and was convenient to use when it was desired to distinguish between the main body of disciples and an inner circle, and to point out that even in the inner circle chosen by Jesus himself one was a devil. John does not record the choice and appointment of the Twelve.

καὶ ἐξ ὑμῶν. καί is 'And yet', or 'And even'. No human virtue or privilege creates security.

διάβολος. Elsewhere in the New Testament (except where it is an adjective meaning 'slanderous') διάβολος means Satan, the prince of evil; so also John 8.44; 13.2; cf. Σατανᾶς at 13.27. The sense of the present verse is explained by 13.2: Satan has made Judas his ally, a subordinate devil. Cf.

Mark 8.33, where Peter after the confession is addressed as Satan (διάβολος is not used in Mark). Perhaps John is intentionally correcting Mark—the real devil is not Peter but Judas. Cf. Luke 22.3 where Judas' sin is ascribed to Satan, and 22.31 where Jesus prays that Peter may be strengthened against Satan's devices. See also E. Haenchen, *Die Bibel und Wir* (1968), 130, for the suggestion that the name Simon (v. 71) reflects the old tradition in which Simon Peter was a devil (Mark 8.33).

71. τὸν Ἰούδαν Σίμωνος Ἰσκαριώτου: Judas, (the son) of Simon Iscariot. This man is mentioned in eight places in the gospel. In four (13.29; 18.2,3,5) he is called simply (ὁ) Ἰούδας, twice with the addition of ὁ παραδιδούς. In one (12.4) he is Ἰούδας ὁ Ἰσκαριώτης; in three (6.71; 13.2,26) the longer title including the name Simon is used. In the last four passages there is considerable variation, which turns principally on two points: (i) the question whether the name Ἰσκαριώτης is to be attributed to Judas or to his father Simon (mentioned only in John); (ii) the interpretation of Iscariot as ἀπὸ Καρυώτου (at 6.71 in א Θ φ; at 12.4; 13.2,26—cf. 14.22—in D only). Of course, it is natural that father and son should bear the same surname, especially if Iscariot is derived from קריות איש (*'ish qᵉriyyoth*), 'man of Kerioth'. For this place cf. Jer. 48.24,41; Amos 2.2. The reading ἀπὸ Καρυώτου is no doubt based upon some identification and variant spelling of the Old Testament place, but we have no knowledge of its origin. In the present passage it is best to follow the Nestle text (P⁶⁶ P⁷⁵ B W cur; cf. vg *scariotis* and sin omitting Simon) against Ἰούδ. Σίμ. Ἰσκαριώτην (ω); Ἰούδ. Σίμ. Σκαριώθ (D it) and Ἰούδ. Σίμ. ἀπὸ Καρυώτου (א Θ φ). On the name, see B. Gärtner, *Die rätselhaften Termini Nazoräer und Iskariot* (1957), who after discussing other suggestions proposes to derive Iscariot from the root שקר (falsehood, deceit). But 'man of Kerioth' is not as difficult as Gärtner (and C. C. Torrey, whom he quotes) suggest.

εἷς ἐκ τῶν δώδεκα. Judas' status as one of the Twelve is emphasized (as in Mark 14.10,18,20), and with it Jesus' foreknowledge. He was not deceived by Judas, though he had chosen him. Psychological reconstructions of the character and motive of Judas are not profitable. For the question what Judas betrayed see on 18.2. 'Who will build on his own decision, or make of the consciousness of his election a sure possession?' (Bultmann).

16. TO JERUSALEM

7.1–13

The activity of Jesus in Galilee, which had proved a safer place of retreat than Jerusalem, was cut short by the arrival of the feast of Tabernacles. His brothers (whose foolish suggestion showed their unbelief) urged him to seek publicity among the great crowds who always assembled for this, the most popular of the pilgrim feasts. It was absurd, they said, for him to think that he could be a public figure while he restricted his activity to an obscure corner. To such an argument Jesus could not yield; it ignored the essential difference between himself and other men. In the first place, unlike others, he could not choose his own time for coming and going; his time was appointed by God. In the second place, his destiny was not popularity but the hatred of the world, a hatred such as no one else could experience, since he alone brought the world into judgement. Accordingly he remained in Galilee. Nevertheless, when his independence of human advice had been demonstrated, he did go up to Jerusalem, but secretly, without any attempt to attract attention. His failure to appear, however, provoked a covert discussion about him: Was he a good man or a deceiver?

In one respect this narrative invites serious historical objection. It is presupposed that Jesus had hitherto worked in obscurity, but this is by no means the impression conveyed by John himself. Both in Jerusalem (e.g. 2.23; 5.1–9) and in Galilee (e.g. 2.1–11; 6.1–15) Jesus' works had been witnessed by the people; indeed 7.11–13 implies that Jesus was a well-known public figure. The passage then has the appearance of an artificial construction, and it seems to be based on material drawn from the earlier gospel tradition. The visit of Jesus to his πατρίς (already hinted at in 4.44 and 6.59–61) supplies the reference to his brothers (Mark 6.3; Matt. 13.55); the secret journey to Jerusalem (7.10, οὐ φανερῶς ἀλλὰ ὡς ἐν κρυπτῷ) recalls Mark 9.30 (οὐκ ἤθελεν ἵνα τις γνοῖ). But, further, one of the main and most characteristic Marcan themes reappears in these verses, that of concealment and revelation (on this theme in Mark see, among other works, W. Wrede, *The Messianic Secret in the Gospels* (E.T., 1971); A. Schweitzer, *The Mystery of the Kingdom of God* (E.T., 1925), 180–218; *The Quest of the Historical Jesus* (E.T., 1911), 328–95; *H.S.G.T.*, 118–20, 154–7). It is natural that men should wish and plan for publicity, but the way of Jesus was rather the way of secrecy until the appointed time should arrive (ὁ καιρός, 7.6,8). On John's treatment of the 'messianic secret' see further Introduction, p. 71. For him, the moment of Jesus' manifestation to the world (τῷ κόσμῳ) never in fact arrives (14.22); the contrast between revelation and concealment is ultimately not chronological but theological. Jesus becomes manifest to those whom the Father draws to him (6.44), but to them only. The debate of 7.12 serves to introduce the arguments and discourses of chs. 7—12, in which this fact is made clear. Signs have evidently failed to convince the brothers, and will surely not convince Jerusalem. For the composition of chs. 7,8, see Lindars.

1. μετὰ ταῦτα. For this Johannine transition see on 2.12. It is not implied that the sequence of events is immediate, and accordingly there is no support here for the view (see pp. 23, 272) that the order of chs. 5 and 6 should be reversed.

περιεπάτει. Imperfect of customary action; περιπατεῖν is sometimes used by John symbolically (in light, or darkness), also with the meaning 'to conduct one's life', 'pass one's time'; cf. 11.54.

οὐ γὰρ ἤθελεν. This is the reading of the majority of MSS. οὐ γὰρ εἶχεν ἐξουσίαν is read by W a b cur Chrysostom Augustine, and is probably right, since (i) its early and widespread attestation is hard to understand if it was a merely local blunder or emendation, (ii) it canot be explained as having originated from the common text by accidental error, (iii) the change from εἶχεν ἐξουσίαν to ἤθελεν is much easier to understand than the reverse, and (iv) ἔχειν ἐξουσίαν 'to be able' is a Johannine idiom; cf. 10.18 (*bis*) and perhaps 19.10. Here, with the negative, it means 'could not', perhaps 'was not free to'. Martyn, 58f., suggests that references to Judaea and Jerusalem may suggest the danger to which Christians were exposed if they entered the Jewish quarter of the city in which the gospel was written. John may well have been aware of this danger, but his interests were too fundamentally theological for such covert allusions to be probable.

ἐζήτουν αὐτὸν οἱ 'Ιουδαῖοι ἀποκτεῖναι. Cf. 5.18, where the same words are used. This suggests a connection between chs. 5 and 7, but not that 7 ought necessarily to follow immediately after 5. (i) Similar language is common; see 7.19f., 25,30; 8.37,40; 10.39; 11.8, and cf. 18.4,7f. (ii) In vv. 1f. John is setting the scene for the ensuing chapter. He reminds the reader that Jesus 'was walking' in Galilee (6.59), and that the Jewish opposition had been fierce. The step taken in v. 10 was therefore both dangerous and decisive. On 'the Jews' see on 1.19; they represent 'the world' (cf. v. 7), but in such a way that the atmosphere of danger that pervades chs. 7,8 has a forensic element, which enables the dispute of these chapters to supply the place in the Passion Narratives of a Jewish trial; see pp. 334, 523f.

2. ἐγγύς. See on 2.13 for this formula.

ἡ σκηνοπηγία, the feast of Tabernacles, or Booths. For the basic institutions of the feast see Lev. 23.33–6,39–43; Deut. 16.13–15; cf. Exod. 23.16 (Ingathering); also the Mishnah Tractate *Sukkah* (see on vv. 37f.; 8.12). Miss- Guilding finds significance not only in the rites of water-drawing and lamp-lighting (referred to in the Mishnah) but also in the dwelling in huts (cf. 1.14, ἐσκήνωσεν) and the vintage festival (cf. 15.1—16.24). In Leviticus and Deuteronomy the word σκηνοπηγία is not used; the Hebrew חג הסכות (*hag ha-sukkoth*) is literally rendered ἑορτὴ σκηνῶν. Elsewhere, e.g. in Josephus, the word σκηνοπηγία (perhaps under the influence of Hellenistic religious terminology—see Deissmann, 116f.) is used. 'That it was called simply "The Feast" shows that Tabernacles was the most popular of all Jewish feasts. Josephus (*Ant.* VIII, 100) says that it was the holiest and greatest feast (ἑορτὴ ἁγιωτάτη καὶ μεγίστη) among the Hebrews. Tabernacles lasted seven days, from 15th to 21st Tishri (September–October); of these the first day was sabbatical. A special festival day with a festival assembly (עצרת, Lev. 23.36) marked the eighth day (22nd Tishri)' (S.B. II, 774; see also Bonsirven II, 123–5).

3. οἱ ἀδελφοὶ αὐτοῦ. The brothers of Jesus are briefly mentioned at 2.12; here only do they play a definite part in the gospel story (at 20.17 'my brothers' are the disciples). For a full account of the traditional views of the relationship of the 'brothers' to Jesus see J. B. Mayor, *The Epistle of St James* (1897), vi–xxxvi. It may be said here that there is nothing in the Fourth Gospel itself to suggest any other view than that the brothers were sons of Joseph and Mary. In this incident they appear as unbelievers (cf. Mark 3.21,31–5 and parallels; and perhaps 6.3 and parallels), and there is no indication of their subsequent conversion (except in the variant reading noted in v. 5).

ἵνα καὶ οἱ μαθηταί σου θεωρήσουσιν σοῦ τὰ ἔργα ἃ ποιεῖς. ἵνα with future indicative (not subjunctive or optative) is not classical, but occurs several times in the New Testament and elsewhere in Hellenistic literature. See B.D., §369.2, and for papyrus examples M.M. *s.v.* (1). The suggestion made by the brothers might seem to imply that the disciples of Jesus, or at least a majority of them, were to be found in Jerusalem. This would be contrary not merely to the synoptic tradition but also to 6.66–71. It has been suggested (Torrey 155, 158) that a mistake has arisen in the translation of a primitive Aramaic document through the omission of a single letter (ו). The restored Aramaic text would give the sense '. . . that they [the Judaean public] may see your disciples [accusative now] and your works. . . .' It is in favour of this view that v. 4 speaks of a manifestation not to disciples but to the world. The suggestion however is not necessary and arises out of too literal and rigorous a reading of the text. The defection of many disciples has just been mentioned (6.66), and the suggestion of the brothers (who also do not believe) is that by a public display of his power in the capital Jesus may recover his position. This explanation, which seems the simplest and best, not only renders linguistic emendation unnecessary but also makes it unnecessary to think of a distinct group of Judaean, or Jerusalem, disciples, or to draw the conclusion (Wellhausen) that John by modifying his source has produced nonsense. For ἔργα, see p. 75.

4. The words of this verse recall several synoptic sayings; cf. especially Mark 4.22 and Luke 8.17; Luke 12.2 and Matt. 10.26. For the linguistic contacts see Lindars. More important, they recall one of the fundamental themes of Mark, that of the messianic secret. An unescapable condition of the glory of Jesus was that he should first undergo a period of obscurity and humiliation. The same condition is implied here, since the unbelieving advice of the brothers is rejected. Their assumption is that a sufficient display of power will establish Jesus as Messiah, whereas his messianic vocation is suffering and death.

αὐτός is read by P⁶⁶ᶜ P⁷⁵ א Dᶜ Θ ω it vg cur pesh sah; the neuter αὐτό is in P⁶⁶* B D* φ. In these MSS. the position of the pronoun varies; it is omitted altogether by b e (boh), and perhaps by cur, but it is impossible to tell which Greek text is supported by the Syriac. It seems probable that John did not write the pronoun and that his text has been supplemented in various ways, correctly by א Dᶜ etc.

ἐν παρρησίᾳ. παρρησία is a Johannine word (9 times). It is used in two senses: (i) 'plainly', without the obscurity of parabolic utterance (10.24; 11.14; 16.25,29), (ii) 'publicly', 'openly' (7.13,26; 11.54; 18.20). There is no doubt that (ii) is the meaning intended here. For the word, see W. C. van Unnik, *J.R.B.* 44 (1962), 466–88, especially 482; also *De Semitische Achtergrond van* παρρησία *in het NT* (1962).

φανέρωσον σεαυτὸν τῷ κόσμῳ. The brothers, since they do not believe, represent the world; and the world naturally looks upon itself as the final bar of judgement. If Jesus is to vindicate his mission and authority he must therefore commend himself to the world. But Jesus does not receive glory from men (5.41), and it is the Father who seals the truth of his work (5.37; 6.27). He never manifests himself in glory to the world, either during the ministry or after it (14.22, see the note), since the world as such is incapable of apprehending him.

5. οὐδὲ γὰρ (introducing an explanatory comment—'for not even') οἱ ἀδελφοὶ αὐτοῦ ἐπίστευον. Unless they were challenging him to a show of power with a view to his embarrassment their unbelief did not include scepticism with regard to the power of Jesus to perform mighty works (cf. Mark 3.22—Jesus' enemies accept his power to exorcize but attribute it to black magic). They believed that Jesus might be able to dazzle Jerusalem with miracles but had not begun to perceive the meaning of what they had already beheld. Cf. the fact that in Mark the request for a sign (8.11f.) stands immediately after the miracle of the Four Thousand. Cf. also the reply of Jesus there.

εἰς αὐτόν: τότε is added by D it sin cur to mitigate the condemnation of the brothers and to harmonize with Acts 1.14, etc.

6. ὁ καιρὸς ὁ ἐμὸς οὔπω πάρεστιν. καιρός occurs in John only at 7.6,8; it is not distinguishable from the more common ὥρα; see on 2.4. χρόνος, on the other hand, always means extent, not a point, of time: 5.6; 7.33; 12.35; 14.9. On improper distinctions between the two words, see J. Barr, *Biblical Words for Time* (1962), 62f. For this refusal cf. 2.4; Jesus means that the moment has not come for him to manifest his glory; and when it does come it will not be such a manifestation as the brothers have in mind, for his glory will be manifested in crucifixion and exaltation. The point is sharpened by the use (vv. 8, 10) of ἀναβαίνειν, in itself a proper word for the festival pilgrimage to Jerusalem, but also John's word for the ascent of Jesus through death to the Father (3.13; 6.62; 20.17).

ὁ δὲ καιρὸς ὁ ὑμέτερος. Jesus because of his divine mission and unique destiny is compelled to await the predetermined moment; with his brothers this is not so. Their visit to Jerusalem has no particular significance and can therefore be made at any time. They are free to make their visit at any moment—καιρός—they please. Jesus is not, because he waits upon the Father's word. This (not because the word καιρός is used) is why his actions are significant.

7. The falsity of the presuppositions of v. 4 now appears. Jesus cannot commend himself to the κόσμος and win its favour; the κόσμος of necessity hates him. The world cannot hate his brothers, for they are of the world and the world loves its own (cf. 15.18f.). The world however hates to be convicted of sin (e.g. 3.19–21; 7.19; 8.31–59; 9.39–41; also 16.8f.; cf. Wisd. 2.14f.); hence its constant hatred of Jesus, and the fact that his only φανέρωσις (cf. on v. 4) to the world consists in his being lifted up on the cross.

8. οὐκ: so ℵ D it vg sin cur boh. οὔπω, though read by P⁶⁶ P⁷⁵ B W Θ pesh hl sah, is certainly wrong, being an attempt, based on the second part of the verse (οὔπω πεπλήρωται; cf. v. 6, οὔπω πάρεστιν), to remove what was felt, in view of v. 10, to be a difficulty.

οὐκ ἀναβαίνω. There is (as was noted by early copyists) a superficial contradiction with v. 10. It may be taken that John's own understanding of the words was not such as to suggest moral obliquity on the part of Jesus. There are parallels at 2.4, where Jesus apparently refuses to perform a miracle at the request of his mother on the ground that his hour has not yet come, and subsequently does what has been (implicitly) asked; and at 11.6, where Jesus, told of the illness of his friend Lazarus (again with an implicit request for a miracle), remains where he is two days and goes to the scene of need at what appears, by human standards, to be the wrong time. This need not however, mean (Bultmann) that 7.1–13 was originally the introduction to a miracle. The point is that John's οὐκ ἀναβαίνω merely negatives the request of the brothers, and does not negative absolutely the intention of Jesus to go to Jerusalem at the proper time. He refuses in the plainest terms to comply with human—and unbelieving—advice, acting with complete freedom and independence with regard to men, but in complete obedience to his Father. If this interpretation is satisfactory there is no need for the hypothesis (Torrey, 135, 137f.) of a slight misreading of an Aramaic original, which should have been rendered 'I will not go up yet, for my time...'. For the ambiguity in the word ἀναβαίνειν see on v. 6.

ὁ ἐμὸς καιρὸς οὔπω πεπλήρωται. The meaning is that of v. 6a; and there is perhaps a verbal echo of Mark 1.15, πεπλήρωται ὁ καιρός. John hints that the promised time was not fulfilled in the ministry of Jesus, but only at his death and exaltation.

9. αὐτοῖς. αὐτός is read by P⁶⁶ ℵ D* W b vg, and the pronoun omitted altogether by a few Greek MSS., and by e sin cur pesh. αὐτός is Johannine and probably to be preferred; the short reading would be preferable if any strong motive could be found for the addition of a pronoun in early copies.

10. ἀνέβησαν, aorist in the sense of the English pluperfect. When they had gone up.

οὐ φανερῶς ἀλλὰ ὡς ἐν κρυπτῷ. When Jesus did finally leave Galilee for Jerusalem it was in a manner the reverse of that recommended by his brothers (v. 4, οὐδεὶς γάρ τι ἐν κρυπτῷ ... φανέρωσον σεαυτόν ...). There are important parallels here with Mark. (i) Unlike Mark, John recounts several visits of Jesus to Jerusalem; it is the more striking that on this occasion he represents a decisive departure from the north for a ministry in Jerusalem and Judaea, precisely as does Mark (9.30; 10.1). (ii) This decisive departure is secret; cf. Mark 9.30. Undoubtedly, John's contrast of a concealed with a manifest departure and entry is theologically motivated: Jesus can be manifested as Son of God only to his own; no publicity can declare the truth about him. But it may be that John is also reproducing primitive tradition, for which there is no need to look further than Mark, even though the dates of arrival in Jerusalem are different (Mark, Passover; John, Tabernacles).

ὡς is omitted by ℵ D pc it syr cur, perhaps rightly; it may have been added to lessen the impression of contradiction and deceit.

11. οἱ οὖν 'Ιουδαῖοι ἐζήτουν αὐτόν. ζητεῖν is here used in its simple sense, 'to seek', 'to search for', not (as in v. 1) 'to seek means', 'to seek an opportunity'. Cf. 11.56. Nevertheless, the search is probably hostile. The 'Jews' (see on 1.19) are regularly in John the enemies of Jesus; it is among the ὄχλοι that some hold a good opinion of him (v. 12), and they are restrained from expressing it by fear of the Jews (v. 13).

ἐν τῇ ἑορτῇ, as at 2.23, where see the note.

ποῦ ἐστιν ἐκεῖνος; Cf. 9.12. It is possible that in these places (and at 9.28) ἐκεῖνος carries a derogatory sense—'that fellow'; but this is not always so, or necessarily so here.

12. γογγυσμός generally signifies a murmuring complaint, as of Israel in the wilderness (see on 6.41); but sometimes it means 'subdued debate', and must have this meaning here, since the crowds are divided and some of the murmurers say ἀγαθός ἐστιν, which however inadequate it may be as an opinion of Jesus is not a complaint.

ἐν τοῖς ὄχλοις. The multitudes (or multitude; the singular is read here by P⁶⁶ ℵ D latt syr) play an important part in this chapter (cf. v. 32), and in ch. 12. They stand as an independent but uninstructed party between Jesus and the Jews (or Pharisees). Their independence does not however qualify them to make a right judgement concerning Jesus, for this can only be made by faith, and to say simply ἀγαθός ἐστιν (cf. Mark 10.17) is beside the point.

οἱ μὲν ... ἄλλοι δὲ ... P⁶⁶ ℵ D ω omit δέ; it was probably added in an attempt to improve the construction, which should however have been οἱ μὲν ... οἱ δέ ...

πλανᾷ τὸν ὄχλον. For the Jewish opinion of Jesus as one who led the people astray see Justin, Trypho 69, καὶ γὰρ μάγον εἶναι αὐτὸν ἐτόλμων λέγειν καὶ λαοπλάνον; 108 ... ἀπὸ Ἰησοῦ τινος Γαλιλαίου πλάνου ...; Sanhedrin 43a (a baraitah): On the preparation of the Passover Jesus was hanged, and a crier went before him forty days proclaiming, 'He must be led away for stoning, because he has practised sorcery and led Israel astray. If anyone knows anything to justify him let him come and declare it.' But no one found anything to justify him, and he was hanged on the preparation of the Passover. It is probable that John knew this charge as one already circulating among the Jews in Asia in his day (cf. the complaint of the Jews against Polycarp, Mart. Pol. 12.2). He might have been expected to put it on the lips of 'the Jews', but evidently wishes to show division among the people as a whole. For the theme of 'leading astray' see Martyn, 60–8, 151–4; John's language may reflect charges against Christians.

13. παρρησίᾳ. See on v. 4 and contrast the γογγυσμός of v. 12. It is not quite impossible that the meaning here is 'plainly', 'unambiguously', but the opinions expressed in v. 12 are plain enough, and almost certainly what John means is that they were not expressed publicly.

διὰ τὸν φόβον τῶν Ἰουδαίων. The same phrase occurs in Esther 8.17 (Bauer, 109), but there is no reason whatever to think that John is alluding to this passage. 'The Jews' (1.19) have already set themselves against not only Jesus but his followers also. Cf. 9.22; 16.1f; John was doubtless personally aware of these conditions. The crowd also are Jewish; οἱ Ἰουδαῖοι must be for John a technical term.

17. CONTROVERSY IN JERUSALEM

7.14-52

This passage falls into four sections.

Vv. 14-24. Not at the beginning (cf. 7.8,10) but in the middle of the feast Jesus appeared in Jerusalem and taught in the Temple. That an uneducated person should do so provoked comment, and in turn the reply that though Jesus did not derive his doctrine from any earlier teacher he was nevertheless not speaking what were merely his own thoughts. His teaching came from God; and this could be recognized by any one who intended serious obedience to God. This however the Jews did not mean to give; they did not keep even their own Law, though this, had they understood it, would have pointed them to Christ and thus shown that he and his teaching were of God. The Law itself justified an act on the Sabbath which effected the physical and ceremonial perfection of man, and thereby justified the sabbath work of Jesus.

Vv. 25-36. The question however was raised whether Jesus could be the Messiah in view of his well-known human origin. This origin Jesus admitted, but dismissed the objection as irrelevant. He did not stand before his people as the distinguished representative of a famous or religious city, but as the envoy of God himself, whose true origin was in God. Along with the argumentative opposition to the claims of Jesus went an official attempt to arrest and kill him, which was necessarily unsuccessful because the time for his decisive work had not yet come. The attempt however served as the occasion for teaching complementary to that about his origin: he was going whither his hearers could not follow. He had come from God and was going to God (cf. 13.3).

Vv. 37-44. His relation to God, and thereby his authority, having been made clear, Jesus, taking advantage of a feature of the Temple ritual at Tabernacles, introduced a new theme into his teaching and made proclamation of the gift of God (cf. earlier references to water, 3.5; 4.14). Through him, and in consequence of his exaltation, the Spirit was to be given as never before. So bold an assertion renewed the division among his hearers. Some counted him 'the prophet'; others, still arguing from the known (or supposed) origin of Jesus in Galilee, alleged that he could not be the Messiah.

Vv. 45-52. The Jewish rulers, foiled in their attempt to arrest Jesus, reproached the constables who were responsible for the miscarriage of their scheme, and by pronouncing the ignorant multitude accursed, sealed their own doom (cf. 9.40f.). Nicodemus claimed for Jesus the common rights of the law, only to be met by a reiteration of the argument that nothing good could come out of Galilee.

The great Jerusalem debates now, at the volition of Jesus himself, begin, and there are no further substantial narrative parallels between John and the Synoptic Gospels till the feast and anointing at Bethany (12.1–8). John does, however, in the present chapter, make use of synoptic material, especially the fact that Jesus was known as Jesus of Nazareth (i.e. of Galilee), though according to the tradition contained in both Matthew and Luke he had been born in Bethlehem. The simple factual misunderstanding of vv. 41f. leads John to a more subtle and theological treatment of the origin of Jesus; the important question (which lies behind all the Christological material in this gospel) is whether or not Jesus comes from God (cf. Mark 11.27–33; Matt. 21.23–7; Luke 20.1–8). Whether he comes from Nazareth or Bethlehem is comparatively irrelevant. John's teaching about the death of Jesus (that is, his going to God) is only adumbrated here; it will be given more explicitly later, especially in the Last Discourses; but he makes in this passage one of his most explicit statements about the Holy Spirit (vv. 37–9). See Introduction, pp. 88–91; the Spirit is most intimately bound up with Jesus, and is (as elsewhere in the New Testament) thought of in eschatological terms; the gift of the Spirit is a consequence of the glorification of Jesus.

On the construction of the chapter see in addition to the Commentaries J. Schneider, *Z.N.T.W.* 45 (1954), 108–19. The material seems to fall into two cycles:

	Verses	Verses
Jesus teaches	15–24	37–39
His teaching evokes speculation among the people	25–31	40–44
Mission of the Jewish officials and its consequences	32–36	45–52

This pattern however reflects John's style rather than the use of sources; the chapter, which must be read in close connection with chapter 8, which is continuous with it, is as a whole coherent in its handling of the themes of judgement, division, and passion (Dodd). The discussions take place during the Feast of Tabernacles (7.2,14), but the argument that chapters 7—9, with 15.1—16.24, are determined by the lections for this season (Guilding, 98) is not convincing. As throughout the gospel, John, though willing to pick up and develop hints, including hints provided by the calendar (see on v. 37 and 8.12), is ultimately determined by his subject-matter. Here, as in chapters 5, 9, and 10 (see on these chapters, and Introduction pp. 137f.) Martyn sees John operating on two levels, telling a story about Jesus and also writing with reference to a concrete situation in his own environment; see the detailed notes below. If, however, this observation is correct (and it is at least partially true), John as a theologian concentrates his attention rather on the story of Jesus than on his own circumstances; with this chapter we enter upon the great debates which extend as far as chapter 10 and to a great extent replace the synoptic 'Jewish Trial' narratives.

See pp. 523f. On the question whether this chapter, or at least 7.15–24, should follow immediately after 5.47 see on v. 15, and p. 23.

14. τῆς ἑορτῆς μεσούσης (μεσαζούσης, P⁶⁶ D Θ; μέσης οὔσης, W it; μεσούσης is common and may possibly be an 'improvement' of one of these expressions). John may mean the fourth day of the feast; or, less precisely, some point between the beginning and the end; not the beginning, when his brothers urged Jesus to go, and not the end when he made the proclamation of vv. 37f.; possibly, in view of vv. 22ff., on a Sabbath, but John is more interested in the Sabbath as a theological factor than as a date.

ἀνέβη. On the ambiguity of this word see on v. 8. When finally Jesus does 'go up' he does so in conformity with neither custom nor good advice, but in free obedience to the Father.

εἰς τὸ ἱερόν. Cf. 2.13–22; 10.23 for Jesus' presence in the Temple. For the large crowds, and entertainments, in the Temple during the feast of Tabernacles see Sukkah 5.2–4 (for the presence of Hillel, Sukkah 53 ab). In the Temple pre-eminently Jesus came to his own (1.11), and his own did not receive him.

15. πῶς οὗτος γράμματα οἶδεν μὴ μεμαθηκώς; Those who take the view (e.g. Bernard, xixf., 258f.; Bultmann, 237ff.) that 7.15–24 should follow immediately upon 5.47 suppose that this question arose out of the reference to the γράμματα of Moses in that verse. The complaint (scornful rather than merely surprised; οὗτος contemptuously, 'this fellow') is however sufficiently introduced by the presence of Jesus teaching in the Temple (v. 14). Cf. Acts 4.13, where the Jewish authorities, perceiving that Peter and John ἄνθρωποι ἀγράμματοί εἰσιν καὶ ἰδιῶται, ἐθαύμαζον. In this context the question does not mean (though the words could mean), How is this man able to read? but, How is it that this man who has never been a disciple in the rabbinic schools can carry on a learned disputation? It would not be surprising that an ordinary man should be able to quote Scripture. Any reasonably intelligent man who heard the Law read through year by year in synagogue and recited the Shema daily would be able to quote parts. This is against a close connection between this verse and 5.47; in fact the question serves primarily to elicit the theme of the next verse, and indeed of the next two chapters—the relation of Jesus to, and his mission from, the Father. There is one other apparent cross-reference to ch. 5: 7.19 (τί με ζητεῖτε ἀποκτεῖναι;) recalls 5.18 (ἐζήτουν αὐτὸν οἱ Ἰουδαῖοι ἀποκτεῖναι); but this does not compel us to accept the hypothesis of a primitive disarrangement of the sheets of the gospel. It is possible that the echo is due to the fact that 5 and 7 were derived by John from one source into which he interpolated ch. 6. Cf. Martyn's analysis (49f.) of 5.1–47; 7.11–52 as parallel with chapters 8 and 9. It should be noted however that already in 7.1 John has reminded the reader that the Jews were seeking to kill Jesus, and continually returns to the theme (see references on v. 1). The teaching of chs. 7 and 8 demands this antagonism as its background. John's chronological connections are at least tolerable and his theological connections are in perfect order; the latter can hardly be mended, the former only slightly, and that at the expense of the latter.

16. ἡ ἐμὴ διδαχὴ οὐκ ἔστιν ἐμή. Jesus' answer is in part a direct reply to the scornful question of v. 15. He laid no claim to the teaching succession which

authorized the utterances of an ordained Rabbi, but he was not a self-taught upstart. If others drew their teaching from a rabbinic lecture room, he brought his from his Father (ὁ πέμψας με, a common Johannine formula). The answer is not however simply based upon the analogy of the authorization given by precedent to rabbinic pronouncements (*halakhoth*); throughout the gospel it is emphasized that Jesus proceeded from the Father, that his words and works were the words and works of the Father, and that his authority was not that of a learned, influential, or distinguished man, or of a θεῖος ἀνήρ, but the authority of God. See e.g. 5.19; 6.57; 8.26,38; 14.9f. Whether or not this claim is true cannot, however, be determined by intellectual analysis, but only by the kind of decision described in the next verse.

17. ἐάν τις θέλῃ τὸ θέλημα αὐτοῦ [*sc.* of God, who sent Jesus] ποιεῖν. A free human decision about the claims of Jesus is impossible (cf. 6.44). The only condition for understanding the claims of Jesus is faith. 'Doing the will of God' does not mean ethical obedience as a preliminary to dogmatic Christianity, but believing in him whom God sent (6.29; Bultmann, 274). Such faith enables the believer to perceive the congruence of the moral character of Jesus' mission with the divine will.

πότερον . . . ἤ, a classical construction, occurs here only in the New Testament. The alternatives are absolute; the extreme humility of the Johannine Christ is to be noted. He does not speak as a θεῖος ἀνήρ with authority of his own; his humility and obedience allow him to speak with the authority of God.

18. The only test applicable to the claims of Jesus cannot be applied by those who receive δόξα from one another (5.44) but only by those who, by believing, have renounced such δόξα. If Jesus were simply giving utterance, as other men do, to his own thoughts he would naturally seek his own glory and adopt the best means of making his own opinions prevail; but action of this kind he had deliberately eschewed (vv. 3–8; the sequence of thought here is another argument against transposing vv. 15–24 to the end of ch. 5); on the contrary his single-minded seeking of God's glory proves (to those who are able to apprehend it as proof) his freedom from ulterior motive and that he has come in God's name. 'In the Palestinian Targum the dutiful son is one "who has consideration for the glory ('*iqar* or 'honour') of his father" (Gen. 32: 7(8), 11(12), TJ1; Lev. 19.3, Neofiti)' (McNamara, *T. & T.*, 142). ἀληθής elsewhere in John is applied to a person only at 3.33; 8.26, in each passage to God. The truthfulness which characterizes God as a witness is naturally transferred to the Son who seeks his Father's glory.

Neither ἀδικία nor any of its cognates occurs elsewhere in John. Here it means the opposite quality to being ἀληθής, faithful and reliable; in the LXX it sometimes renders שקר (*sheqer*, falsehood).

19. οὐ Μωϋσῆς ἔδωκεν (so B D; many MSS., assimilating to v. 22, have δέδωκεν) ὑμῖν τὸν νόμον; If the paragraph 7.15–24 be taken to follow immediately after 5.47 the introduction of Moses at this point is easy to understand, and, as has been suggested, this may have been the original sequence of thought in a source used by John. In the present context however the reference to Moses arises out of the demand (v. 17) that those who would understand the origin of Jesus' teaching must do the will of God. For the Jew, the will of God is contained and expressed in the Law of Moses (Hoskyns,

357f., comparing Ps. 40.9: I delight to do thy will, O my God; Yea, thy law is within my heart). Why then does not the Jew, possessing the Law, recognize that the teaching of Jesus is from God? Because he does not even do the Law—καί ('and yet', καί adversative) οὐδεὶς ἐξ ὑμῶν ποιεῖ τὸν νόμον. They do not do the Law; they do not do God's will; no wonder then that they seek to kill Jesus. The inadequacy of the Law and the departure of Jesus are elucidated in the ensuing paragraphs.

ὑμῖν . . . ἐξ ὑμῶν. Jesus appears to distinguish himself more sharply from the Jews than is historically likely. It is true that the evangelist is concerned here, as Paul was, to fasten the Law upon the Jews as at once their pride and their condemnation; yet there is truth also in the view that he writes as one engaged in the later debates between church and synagogue, when the Christians had come to feel themselves a distinct body. Cf. Justin's *Trypho* where also the Jews are regularly ὑμεῖς, etc. Cf. in John 8.17; 10.34 'your law'. For the connection between Moses and the Law cf. 1.17, ὁ νόμος διὰ Μωϋσέως ἐδόθη. John is here probably thinking of the whole law as Moses' gift, and as transgressed by the Jews; in the source there may have been a special reference to the sabbath law. In the latter case the argument will be: In view of the exception I am about to cite (v. 22) it cannot be maintained that any Jew keeps the sabbath law. But more probably John connects the transgression of the Law (as a whole) with the attempt to kill Jesus (cf. 8.39f.). If this is so, it may be said with confidence that the paragraph 7.15-24 belongs not to ch. 5, where Jesus reveals the relation between himself and the Father and exposes the unbelief of the Jews, but to chs. 7 and 8, where he turns the tables upon his adversaries and attacks them vigorously.

20. The crowd, perhaps (see on v. 12) in contrast with the authorities, indignantly repudiate the charge that they are plotting against Jesus' life.

δαιμόνιον ἔχεις. Cf. 8.48,52; 10.20. The words do not seem to mean more than 'You are mad', but they recall the synoptic accusation (Mark 3.22 and parallels) that Jesus cast out demons in the power of Beelzebul. There is no theological treatment of the charge in John, just as there are no stories of the exorcism of demons.

21. ἓν ἔργον ἐποίησα. The reference is probably (see v. 23) to the miracle of 5.1-9. The use of ἔργον for the mighty works of Jesus is characteristic of John; see Introduction p. 75 and on 4.34. It is this usage that is in mind rather than the thought that *work* done on the Sabbath breaks the Law.

καὶ πάντες θαυμάζετε. Neither θαυμάζειν nor any synonym occurs in 5.1-18. It is contrary to Johannine usage to connect διὰ τοῦτο (v. 22) with θαυμάζετε, equating τοῦτο with ἓν ἔργον; and the suggestion of confusion in Aramaic (Torrey, 5) is not convincing.

22. διὰ τοῦτο. 'for this reason'; the reason however is not clearly stated—a fact that leads some (e.g. Sanders) in disagreement with the preceding note to connect διὰ τοῦτο with v. 21. Though not clearly stated a reason exists. It is probably not the negative one—Moses gave you command of circumcision in order that a precedent (see below) for breaking the law (of the Sabbath) might exist, but a positive one—Moses gave the command of circumcision to serve as a type of the complete renewal of human nature (ὅλον ἄνθρωπον ὑγιῆ ἐποίησα, v. 23) which Jesus effects.

ἐκ τῶν πατέρων, i.e. from the patriarchs. On this use of πατήρ see on 4.12,20; 6.31. Circumcision was practised by Abraham (Gen. 17.10), the heir of the promise, and, like the promise itself, was antecedent to the Mosaic Law, and took precedence of it (cf. Gal. 3.17).

ἐν σαββάτῳ περιτέμνετε ἄνθρωπον (a human being). The law of circumcision required that a child be circumcised on the eighth day (Lev. 12.3). It followed that if a child was born on the Sabbath its circumcision fell due also on the Sabbath. It was required that in these circumstances the circumcision should go forward, notwithstanding the law of the sabbath rest. See *Shabbath* 18.3; 19.2: They may perform on the Sabbath all things that are needful for circumcision; *Nedarim* 3.11: Great is circumcision which overrides even the rigour of the Sabbath. There are many sabbath controversies in the Synoptic Gospels, but the present argument is used in none of them. Dodd (*Tradition*, 332f.) sees here an indication of a Christian sabbath *halakah*, drawn on independently by the evangelists.

23. εἰ περιτομὴν λαμβάνει ὁ ἄνθρωπος ἐν σαββάτῳ. This is the customary fact which can be assumed as protasis to the argument.

ἵνα μὴ λυθῇ ὁ νόμος Μωϋσέως. For λύειν νόμον cf. 5.18. There might appear to be a contravention of the Law in the practice of circumcising on the Sabbath; in fact the practice has the opposite effect, and fulfils the Law, since it completes man's perfection. Cf. *Nedarim* 3.11: Rabbi (i.e. Judah the Patriarch, c. A.D. 165–200) says: Great is circumcision, for despite all the religious duties which Abraham our father fulfilled, he was not called 'perfect' until he was circumcised, as it is written, Walk before me and be thou perfect (Gen. 17.1). From such principles it was easy to draw further conclusions. Thus *T. Shabbath* 15.16 (134), R. Eliezer (c. A.D. 90) said: Circumcision overrides the Sabbath. Why? Because if one postponed it beyond the appointed time one would on its account render himself liable to extirpation. And does this not justify a conclusion *a minori ad maius* (קל וחומר, a very common rabbinic formula)? If he overrides the Sabbath on account of one of his members, should he not override the Sabbath for his whole body (if in danger of death)? Cf. *Yoma* 85 b: R. Eleazar (b. Azariah, c. A.D. 100) said: If circumcision, which concerns one of a man's 248 members, overrides the Sabbath, how much more must his whole body (supposed in danger of death) override the Sabbath? These extensions of the principle drawn from the practice of circumcision on the Sabbath refer only to cases where life is in immediate danger. This condition was not satisfied in the sabbath healings recorded in the gospels, certainly not in 5.1–9; a man who had waited thirty-eight years might well have waited one day more.

ἐμοὶ χολᾶτε (here only in the New Testament; for χολοῦσθαι; 'to be angry') ὅτι ὅλον ἄνθρωπον (cf. the rabbinic passages cited above) ὑγιῆ ἐποίησα ἐν σαββάτῳ; The reply might be: We are angry because it was not necessary that you should make this whole man well on the Sabbath (see Abrahams, *Studies* I, 135). But John carries the whole argument a stage further with the assertion that Jesus' action was not a transgression of the word of God in the Old Testament but a fulfilment of it; his action was not permitted, but demanded by the Law for its own fulfilment. This gives a striking and important turn to the sabbath controversy which plays so large a part in the Synoptic Gospels but is never really explained in them. Jesus' attitude is not a sentimental liberalizing of a harsh and unpractical law (comparable with but more extensive than that underlying the *'erub* regulations—see *Erubin passim*), nor the masterful dealing of an opponent of the Law as such; it is rather the accomplishment of the redemptive purpose of God towards which the Law had pointed. There is a similar, but by no means identical, controversial treatment of the practice of circumcision on the Sabbath in Justin, *Trypho* 27.

24. μὴ κρίνετε ('Cease to judge ...'; for the force of the present imperative in a prohibition see M. 1, 122–6) κατ' ὄψιν. The primary meaning of ὄψις is 'appearance', as here; at 11.44 it is 'face', as often in the papyri (M.M., Bauer, *Wörterbuch, s.v.*).

τὴν δικαίαν κρίσιν κρίνατε: so א Θ W. The present imperative κρίνετε in (P⁶⁶) P⁷⁵ B D has been shortsightedly conformed to that in the first part of the verse but is in fact less appropriate than the aorist—Stop judging by appearance, adopt a right judgement. For the contrast between a judgement based on appearance only and a right, fair judgement cf. among many passages Deut. 16.18f., ... κρινοῦσιν τὸν λαὸν κρίσιν δικαίαν· οὐκ ἐπιγνώσονται πρόσωπον ...; Lysias, *Orat.* XVI, 19 (147), οὐκ ἄξιον ἀπ' ὄψεως ... οὔτε φιλεῖν οὔτε μισεῖν οὐδένα, ἀλλ' ἐκ τῶν ἔργων σκοπεῖν. See also Zech. 7.9, κρίμα δίκαιον κρίνατε, and Isa. 11.3f., though the latter passage is more suitable to 8.16, since it refers to the righteous judgement of the messianic King. The Jews must not jump to the conclusion that Jesus is a Sabbath-breaker, but enter by faith (v. 17) into the true meaning of his mission. 'Since Jesus here alludes to things which took place at a considerably earlier time, and simply assumes that his hearers had witnessed the miracle at the Pool, it is natural to suppose that 7.15–24 should be transferred to and interpreted in the context of ch. 5, the original place of these verses being after 5.47. But they can also be understood in their present position, in which they are fixed by the reference of v. 25 to verses 19f. John thinks rather of his readers, who have only just learnt of these things, than of the hearers of the discourse' (Bauer, 111).

25. Ἱεροσολυμειτῶν. In the New Testament the word occurs only here and at Mark 1.5. It is possible, though far from certain, that John means to distinguish the local residents from the crowds who had come from Galilee for the feast. The reference is to 5.18; 7.19; the plot against the life of Jesus continues in the background of the whole chapter (and of the rest of the gospel). The suggestion that this verse originally followed v. 14 is possible, but is certainly not necessary.

26. παρρησίᾳ. See on v. 4. Jesus, recognized as a man whom the authorities desired to arrest, was at liberty and publicly pursuing his ministry. What could this mean?

μήποτε (a tentative suggestion; 'Can it possibly be that ...'?; M. 1, 192f.) ἀληθῶς ἔγνωσαν ('really have recognized', not in semblance or pretence) οἱ ἄρχοντες (see on 3.1; for the vagueness of John's terminology in describing Jewish parties and authorities see on v. 32) ὅτι οὗτός ἐστιν ὁ χριστός; One possible explanation of the fact that Jesus was at liberty presented itself at once: the authorities had changed their minds and recognized that he was the Christ. But this was improbable, for even the lay mind could think of an objection.

27. ἀλλὰ τοῦτον (not necessarily disrespectful here; attracted out of the ὅτι-clause into the principal sentence as object) οἴδαμεν πόθεν ἐστίν. Cf. v. 41 and 6.42. Jesus was well known to have been a resident in Nazareth; 1.45; 18.5,7; 19.19.

ὁ δὲ χριστὸς ὅταν ἔρχηται, οὐδεὶς γινώσκει πόθεν ἐστίν. The belief that the Messiah before entering upon his office would be hidden is attested in Justin, *Trypho* 8, Χριστὸς δὲ εἰ καὶ γεγένηται καὶ ἔστι που, ἄγνωστός ἐστι καὶ οὐδὲ αὐτός πω ἑαυτὸν ἐπίσταται οὐδὲ ἔχει δύναμίν τινα, μέχρις ἂν ἐλθὼν Ἡλίας χρίσῃ αὐτὸν καὶ φανερὸν πᾶσι ποιήσῃ; cf. 110. It is also presupposed by common rabbinic statements about the 'appearing' of the Messiah (see S.B. II, 489; Bousset–Gressmann, 230). This however does not amount to much more than saying: 'The Messiah will not be known until he is known', and is not a full parallel to the words in John, which imply that when the Messiah is known to be Messiah it will still not be known whence he has come. John (who uses the objection of this verse in order to lead up to the pronouncement of the next) probably used the well-known Jewish belief but adapted it to his own thought of a supernatural, heavenly redeemer. The Son of man, or heavenly Man, is hidden in his origin: 1 Enoch 48.6, And for this reason hath he (the Son of man) been chosen and hidden before him, before the creation of the world and for evermore; 4 Ezra 13.51f., Then said I, O Lord that bearest rule, shew me this: wherefore I have seen the Man coming up from the midst of the sea. And he said unto me, Like as one can neither seek out nor know what is in the deep of the sea, even so can no man upon earth see my Son, or those that be with him, but in the time of his day. John is not however simply saying: You are right; the origin of the Messiah will be mysterious, only more mysterious than you think. He is theologizing, or retheologizing, a concept that had become secularized. 'To admit the truth of the doctrine of the secret origin of the Messiah is, or should be, equivalent to the admission that all human judgement about it is, and is bound to be, inadequate; and this admission the Lord's opponents are not prepared to make' (Lightfoot; see also Bultmann, 296). Cf. also the biblical inquiry, Where shall Wisdom be found? (Job 28; (1) Bar. 3.14f.; Wisd. 6.12; Prov. 1.28f., referred to by Brown).

28. ἔκραξεν. κράζειν, used originally of a loud inarticulate cry, is used by John (1.15; 7.28,37; 12.44) to introduce solemn pronouncements. Jesus replies, though he has not been addressed. He is in fact speaking to the world (Bultmann; better, perhaps, to the Jews as representing the world) before God's tribunal.

ἐν τῷ ἱερῷ διδάσκων. Cf. v. 14.

κἀμὲ οἴδατε καὶ οἴδατε πόθεν εἰμί. Jesus admits, and indeed could not deny, the truth of the claim made by the Jerusalemites, in their own sense, though there is another sense in which his origin is quite unknown to them. It is possible that these words should be punctuated with a question mark. If this is done Jesus at once begins to cast doubt upon the confident knowledge of the men of Jerusalem. But it seems in closer accord with John's manner of thought and expression that the truth of the Jewish objection should be admitted before its inadequacy is exposed. (There is also factual error in what the Jews think about the parentage and birthplace of Jesus—see on vv. 41f., 8.41.)

καί ('and yet', καί adversative) ἀπ' ἐμαυτοῦ οὐκ ἐλήλυθα: I did not come by my own prompting, on my own authority, for my own purposes. Behind Jesus stands another who sent him and who alone gives meaning to his mission; it follows that his visible movements are an inadequate indication of his nature and authority.

ἔστιν ἀληθινὸς ὁ πέμψας με. ὁ πέμψας με is a common Johannine formula, but the words here carry their full weight: Jesus points away from himself to one who sent him (see on 20.21); this Sender, though invisible, is no figment of the imagination, but real and faithful to his own character. On ἀληθινός see on 1.9; it is here synonymous with ἀληθής; cf. 8.26.

ὃν ὑμεῖς οὐκ οἴδατε. The Jews claimed that, over against the heathen, they knew the true God (cf. Rom. 2.17–19; God was revealed in the Law, and only Israel among all the nations had received the Law; see also 4.22); but if they had really known him they would not have rejected Jesus (8.42). It is in fact no longer through the Law but through Jesus that God wills to be known, though the Law remains a valid testimony to Jesus and to the revelation given in him (5.46).

29. ἐγὼ οἶδα αὐτόν. Like all true knowledge (according to John) the knowledge Jesus has of God is based on relation; he has come forth from God. It is impossible to distinguish between ἀποστέλλειν in this verse and πέμπειν in v. 28.

30. ἐζήτουν οὖν αὐτὸν πιάσαι. The subject is still 'some of the Jerusalemites' (v. 25). This then appears to be a popular movement to seize Jesus, to be distinguished from the formal attempt at an arrest (vv. 32, 45); but it would be unwise to suppose that John meant the distinction seriously; he has already spoken of an attempt by 'the Jews' to kill Jesus (5.18, etc.). He doubtless thinks of a miraculous deliverance of Jesus from the hands of his assailants; cf. Luke 4.30.

οὔπω ἐληλύθει ἡ ὥρα αὐτοῦ. The hour is the hour of the death and glorification of Jesus (see on 2.4). Until the appointed time he may work unhindered. Cf. vv. 6ff.

31. ἐκ τοῦ ὄχλου δὲ πολλοὶ ἐπίστευσαν εἰς αὐτόν. The believers are drawn not from the ruling class but from the crowd (ἐκ τοῦ ὄχλου emphatic, standing before δέ), presumably the crowd of Jerusalemites. Cf. 8.30; they play no real part in the narrative or in history and serve to balance those who (v. 30) seek to seize Jesus. His words necessarily have this twofold effect; cf. 1.11f.; 3.18–21, et al.

μὴ πλείονα σημεῖα ποιήσει; Their faith is based upon signs; cf. 2.23; 4.48, et al., supposing that signs can be added up as mere portents. They do not ask the meaning of the signs, the thing signified. Martyn, in view of the fact that the Messiah was not expected to work miracles, raises (103) the question of the logical basis of this observation, and answers it by referring to the Johannine equation of the wonder-working Prophet with the Messiah. This is a shrewd remark, but it would be rash to affirm that it was only in Johannine circles that this equation was made, and that no Jews hoped for miracles from the Messiah; moreover, it would be natural for Jews, even though they had not been expecting a miracle-working Messiah, to wonder, if confronted by miracles, whether the miracle-worker might not be the Messiah.

ἐποίησεν] ποιεῖ, א* D Θ φ it vg, perhaps rightly.

32–6 is a separate paragraph not closely connected with the preceding verses. It is concerned with the search for Jesus, looks back to vv. 10–13, and is resumed at v. 45, where the messengers return to those who sent them. The intervening section, vv. 37–44, is no doubt intended to cover the lapse of time, but perhaps covers too much, since with v. 37 we reach a new day (v. 32 is still governed by the date of v. 14). John is however far more concerned with the flow of thought than of narrative.

32. γογγύζοντος. See v. 12, γογγυσμός. Here (as there) discussion or debate, not complaint, is meant.

οἱ ἀρχιερεῖς καὶ οἱ Φαρισαῖοι. Most of the chief priests (members of leading priestly families, the 'court' of the high priest) were Sadducees (Acts 5.17; Josephus, *Ant.* xx, 199); we should not in general expect to find them acting in concert with the Pharisees. They regularly appear together, however, in John (7.32,45; 11.47,57; 18.3). In Mark (14.1, and elsewhere in the passion narrative) the chief priests and the scribes (many, though not all, of whom were Pharisees) conspire to secure the death of Jesus. John has assumed that the combination, which represents hardly less than a general movement of the whole Sanhedrin, took place much earlier. This seems doubtful, and throws suspicion on John's supposed knowledge of Palestine in the time of our Lord. It seems that, either in ignorance or with no concern for accuracy in such matters, he simply takes οἱ 'Ιουδαῖοι as a general term for the enemies of Jesus, analysing it on occasion into οἱ ἀρχιερεῖς (or οἱ ἄρχοντες) together with οἱ Φαρισαῖοι. Cf. v. 48.

ὑπηρέτας ἵνα πιάσωσιν αὐτόν. The unofficial and unsuccessful attempt of v. 30 is now taken up by the hierarchy. Only the chief priests had ὑπηρέται at their disposal (cf. 18.3). Martyn (73f.) sees this as a two-level word (representing ḥazzanim), referring both to the Jerusalem police sent to arrest Jesus and to the synagogue officials who took action against Jewish Christians.

33. οὖν. αὐτοῖς is added by many MSS., but omitted by P⁶⁶ P⁷⁵ א B D W Θ, rightly; Jesus did not confine his remarks to the temple police sent to arrest him, but spoke generally. The comment of vv. 35f. is ascribed to οἱ 'Ιουδαῖοι who must therefore be taken to be the hearers of the original speech.

ἔτι χρόνον μικρὸν μεθ' ὑμῶν εἰμι. Jesus is unperturbed by the plot to arrest him because he knows that before his hour comes there must intervene a 'little while' (cf. 12.35; also 13.33; 14.19; 16.16–19, where μικρόν is used without χρόνον), in which he must accomplish the remainder of his ministry (9.4; 11.9f.). His lot is determined not by the Jewish authorities but by himself, in obedience to the will of God. This fact is expressed in time by the chronological limitation of his ministry. Faith is not a natural human possibility but is linked with the specific divine action in Jesus which thus, though in itself it has the nature of gift, and communicates life and truth, comes to have the effect of judgement (cf. 3.19ff.). In the presence of Jesus men are summoned (by God's gift) to decision, and the decision will not always be open.

καὶ ὑπάγω, and then I shall go: temporal parataxis, as at 2.13; 4.35; M. II, 422. ὑπάγειν is used for the departure of Jesus from this world here and at 8.14,21f.; 13.3,33,36; 14.4f.,28; 16.5,10,17. This choice of words is characteristic of John, who wishes to show that the death of Jesus was not merely physical dissolution but a going to the Father; cf. his use of ὑψοῦν (see on 3.14). Here John has chosen the word partly because it can be used appropriately with 3ητεῖν (vv. 1, 11, 19, etc.).

34. 3ητήσετέ με, that is, after the departure of Jesus to the Father. Now (v. 30) they were seeking to arrest him; there would be a time (the final judgement rather than a time of national necessity is meant) when, too late, they would seek his aid. Cf. 8.21; 13.33; *Thomas* 38 (Many times have you desired to hear these words which I say to you, and you have no other from whom to hear them. There will be days when you will seek me (and) you will not find me).

ὅπου εἰμὶ ἐγὼ ὑμεῖς οὐ δύνασθε ἐλθεῖν. This saying is, in John's manner, expressed ambiguously, so as to give rise to the misunderstanding of the next verse. The primary reference of course is to the death of Jesus; his adversaries also will die, but their death will not mean a departure to the Father. It is not impossible that ειμι should be accentuated εἶμι, 'whither I am about to go . . .'.

Notwithstanding Augustine's '*Nec dixit, ubi ero: sed ubi sum. Semper enim ibi erat Christus qùo fuerat rediturus: sic enim venit, ut non recederet*' (*Tract. in Joh.* XXXI, 9, quoted by Brown, but see the whole passage; and cf. Fenton) it does not seem right here to stress the continuous sense (for which see 8.58 and note) of ἐγὼ εἰμι; the present passage stresses rather the temporal limitation of Jesus' ministry (see on v. 33); he will not always be accessible as he now is.

35. πρὸς ἑαυτούς for πρὸς ἀλλήλους, as often in Hellenistic Greek. The Jews are puzzled by the saying; and it is clear (v. 36) that they are not satisfied with their own explanation (they attempt another at 8.21f.).

μὴ (cautious and tentative suggestion; cf. v. 26) εἰς τὴν διασπορὰν τῶν Ἑλλήνων μέλλει πορεύεσθαι; Perhaps Jesus' 'going away' means that he is leaving Palestine, so that Palestinian Jews will no longer be able to find him. 'διασπορά in the LXX frequently refers to the dispersion of the people among the heathen (Deut. 28.25; 30.4; Jer. 34(41).17), but also to the dispersed people as a whole (Isa. 49.6; Ps. 147(146).2; 2 Macc. 1.27; Ps. Sol. 8.34); it is further used, as here, to refer to the place in which the dispersed are found (Judith 5.19)' (Bultmann, 309). A genitive after διασπορά often denotes the persons scattered; here it is clearly a 'genitive of direction' (B.D., §166).

καὶ διδάσκειν τοὺς Ἕλληνας. This is a further step. Jesus will not merely visit the scattered Jews but will also teach those who by birth are not Jews at all. In John Ἕλλην occurs here and at 12.20. In the latter passage the Ἕλληνες may well be proselytes. The same meaning may hold here, but in view of the use of Ἕλλην in the phrase διασπορά τῶν Ἑλλήνων it is by no means impossible that John includes the heathen pure and simple: at least, if he does not ascribe this meaning to the Jews he probably held it himself, for, with characteristic irony, he makes the Jews utter incredulously and uncomprehendingly what is in fact the truth. Jesus, through the church, will go into the Dispersion, and will teach Gentiles, both heathen and proselytes. There may further be in his mind the thought of the Christian Dispersion (see 1 Pet. 1.1; also John 11.52; 10.16); so Hoskyns, 364. J. A. T. Robinson, though less confident about this passage than about 12.20, thinks it probable that here too Ἕλληνες means Greek-speaking Diaspora Jews. To others, e.g.

Sanders and Brown, this view seems improbable. See the note on 12.20, and *Judaism*, 11–14.

37. ἐν δὲ τῇ ἐσχάτῃ ἡμέρᾳ τῇ μεγάλῃ τῆς ἑορτῆς. Or the feast of Tabernacles and its duration see on v. 2. The question that arises here is whether by 'the last day' John means the seventh and final day of the feast itself, or the eighth day, that of the עצרת, or closing festival. On this day the *sukkah* (booth, or tabernacle) itself was taken down, the *Hallel* was recited and the rejoicing continued (*Sukkah* 4.1,8, see below). In favour of the seventh day it has been argued that (i) there is no sufficient ground for calling the eighth day (not strictly part of the feast at all) the 'great day' of the feast, and (ii) the rites of libation and lights (see below on 7.38; 8.12) seem to have ceased on or before the seventh day (see *Sukkah* 4.1, and 5.1 with Danby's note). For the eighth day it may be urged (i) The eighth day was a rest day (like a Sabbath) with special sacrifices (*Sukkah* 5.6). It was held in honour: *Sukkah* 4.8, 'The *Hallel* and the Rejoicing, eight days' [a reference to 4.1]—this is to teach us that a man is bound to recite the *Hallel* and observe the Rejoicing and give the honour [due to the Feast] on the last Festival-day [the eighth day] of the Feast as on all other days of the Feast. (ii) Josephus speaks of Tabernacles as an eight-day festival (*Ant.* III, 245, ἐφ' ἡμέρας ὀκτὼ ἑορτὴν ἄγοντας, 247). (iii) Jesus' sayings about water and light may not have been suggested by the festival ritual; and if they were there is no reason why Jesus should not have proclaimed the *true* water and light after the merely symbolic water and light had been withdrawn from the Temple. On the whole it seems that a better case can be made for the eighth day; but it is doubtful whether John was deeply concerned about the matter and possible that he was quite unaware of the question raised by his words.

εἱστήκει. See on 1.35. A public proclamation rather than conventional teaching is suggested.

ἔκραξεν. ἔκραζεν (א D Θ), the imperfect, seems less apt, and may well be right.

37b, 38. The punctuation of the words ascribed to Jesus is uncertain. (i) We may (with Nestle) place a stop after πινέτω, and a comma after εἰς ἐμέ. The phrase ὁ πιστεύων εἰς ἐμέ is then a *nominativus pendens* (see Introduction, p. 10, and cf. 6.39; 8.45; 15.2; 17.2), resumed in αὐτοῦ. The rivers of living water flow out of the belly of the believer, and to this the 'scripture' refers. (ii) We may (as e.g. Bultmann, 303, on account of the difficulty of finding an Old Testament text to satisfy (i), and the rhythm of the clause) place a comma after πρός με and a stop after εἰς ἐμέ. This gives a couplet in parallelism: If any man thirst let him come to me/He that believes on me, let him drink✗The reference to Scripture, καθὼς εἶπεν ἡ γραφή, may now be applied either to what precedes or to what follows; and in ἐκ τῆς κοιλίας αὐτοῦ the pronoun may refer to Christ or to the believer. It is not easy to decide between these complicated alternatives. Each yields not merely sense but Johannine sense (Hoskyns, 365–9). The question is made more difficult by the problem raised by the words καθὼς εἶπεν ἡ γραφή. ἡ γραφή (singular) generally refers to a particular passage of the Old Testament, but this quotation cannot be located with confidence (see *J.T.S.* old series 48 (1947), 156; and below). We cannot therefore say with certainty whether ἐάν τις ... εἰς ἐμέ or ποταμοί ... ζῶντος forms the quotation, and cannot therefore decide whether or not ὁ πιστεύων εἰς ἐμέ is to be connected with ποταμοί. The ancient authority for (ii) consists of some Western Fathers, the colometry of the old Latin MSS. d and e, and a possible allusion in the Epistle of the Martyrs of Vienne (*apud* Eusebius *H.E.* v, i, 22; the martyr Sanctus was refreshed and strengthened in his sufferings ὑπὸ τῆς οὐρανίου πηγῆς τοῦ ὕδατος τῆς ζωῆς τοῦ ἐξίοντος ἐκ τῆς νηδύος τοῦ Χριστοῦ–but the reference may be to 19.34, not to v. 38b). This does not weigh heavily against the majority of Greek Fathers, who take the alternative view. Certainty is not attainable, but (i) may be preferred because (*a*) the parallelism produced by (ii) is at best imperfect, and there is therefore no compelling reason for thinking that it was intended; (*b*) the invitation πινέτω is better connected with ἐάν τις διψᾷ than with ὁ πιστεύων; as thirsty, a man is properly summoned to come and drink; as a believer, who has come and drunk, he can be the subject of a statement. The fact that P[66] places a point between πινέτω and ὁ πιστεύων provides strong support for punctuation (i) which is not seriously weakened by the arguments of G. D. Kilpatrick (*J.T.S.* 11 (1960), 340ff.—If any man thirst, let him who believes in me come and drink) and N. Turner (*Insights*, 144f.), or by the one Coptic MS. that connects πινέτω ὁ πιστεύων (K. H. Kuhn, *N.T.S.* 4 (1957), 63ff.).

ἐάν τις . . .πινέτω. The thought is similar to that of 4.10–14; 6.35; cf. also 19.34, and see the note. There is similar language in Rev. 22.17, ὁ διψῶν ἐρχέσθω, ὁ θέλων λαβέτω ὕδωρ ζωῆς δωρεάν, and probably at least an indirect allusion to Isa. 55.1. There may also be a special allusion to the ritual of the feast of Tabernacles. On the seven days of the feast a golden flagon was filled with water from the pool of Siloam and used for libations in the Temple (*Sukkah* 4.9). This rite is not mentioned in the Old Testament (but see below on Zech. 14.8) or in Josephus, but there is no reason to doubt that it was carried out before the destruction of the Temple (cf. *Sukkah* 4.9 end, with Josephus *Ant.* XIII, 372; these passages suggest that the rite was as early as Alexander Jannaeus). It probably originated in a rain-making charm, but the crudity of the practice had been refined away, leaving the custom of beginning prayers for rain at Tabernacles (*Taanith* 1.1; according to R. Eliezer b. Hyrcanus (*fl.* A.D. 80–120) from the first day of the feast, according to R. Joshua b. Hananiah (*fl.* A.D. 80–120) from the last (eighth) day). This reference to rain is expressed in terms of the second of the Eighteen Benedictions ('the Power of Rain'), which also speaks of God as one who gives life to the dead, mighty to save (Singer, 44: מחיה מתים אתה רב להושיע). It seems probable that this feature of the festival suggested the form of the saying here ascribed to Jesus, especially in view of the similar facts to be adduced at 8.12. It is of course true (Hoskyns, 365) that the notion of Christ as the dispenser of the water of life has a far wider Old Testament and Johannine background than the feast of the Tabernacles would in itself suggest; but this is no reason why the celebration of the feast, with its allusion to 'water from the wells of salvation' (Isa. 12.3), should not have supplied the cue for the teaching here given on this subject. Lightfoot emphasizes the eschatological significance of Tabernacles, and Martyn (98ff.) quotes *Eccles. R.* 1.8 (Rabbi Berekiah said in the name of Rabbi Isaac: As the first redeemer was, so shall the latter Redeemer be. What is stated of the former redeemer? And Moses took his wife and his sons, and set them upon an ass (Exod. 4.20). Similarly it will be with the latter Redeemer, as it is stated,

Lowly and riding upon an ass (Zech. 9.9). As the former redeemer caused manna to descend, as it is stated, Behold, I will cause to rain bread from heaven for you (Exod. 16.4), so will the latter Redeemer cause manna to descend, as it is stated, May he be as a rich cornfield in the land (Ps. 72.16). As the former redeemer made a well to rise, so will the latter Redeemer bring up water, as it is stated, And a fountain shall come forth of the house of the Lord, and shall water the valley of Shittim (Joel 4.18)—translation as given by Martyn) and observes that we have here (cf. 12.14f.; 6.35;—also 4.14) one of the signs related to the Moses-Messiah typology (see further Meeks). In offering water Jesus fulfils this expectation. On 'coming' to Jesus see *Essays*, 62–5, and the notes on 6.44f.

38. ὁ πιστεύων . . . ὕδατος ζῶντος. Cf. 4.14. Christ is himself the fountain of living water, but it is a valid inference that the believer, being joined to him, is also, in a secondary way, a source of living water. The divine life is rooted within him. Cf. *Thomas* 108: Whoever drinks from my mouth shall become as I am and I myself will become he, and the hidden things shall be revealed to him. For ὕδωρ ζῶν see on 4.10.

ἐκ τῆς κοιλίας αὐτοῦ. κοιλία may represent (S.B. II, 492) the rabbinic גוף (*guph*, body), which could be used with the meaning 'person', 'self'; but גוף would naturally be represented by σῶμα, not κοιλία, which points rather to טבור (*ṭibbur*) or בטן (*beṭen*). The Greek word of course is used metaphorically, and signifies that the living water flows out of the man's personality (cf. ἐν αὐτῷ, 4.14); the choice of word however must be significant. See the next note.

καθὼς εἶπεν ἡ γραφή. On the punctuation of these verses that has been rejected in an earlier note the γραφή may state or imply (*a*) the invitation to the thirsty; (*b*) that living water flows from the belly of the believer; (*c*) that living water flows from the belly of Christ. On the punctuation accepted above, only (*b*) is admissible. (*a*), (*b*), and (*c*) can all be paralleled in a general sense in the Old Testament (see *J.T.S.*, loc. cit.), in that God is there represented as a fountain of living waters who supplies men's need of water. Further precision is difficult to attain, but it may be that special attention should be paid to Zech. 14, one of the prophetic *Haphtaroth* for the feast of Tabernacles (Abrahams, *Studies* I, 11f.; H. St. J. Thackeray, *The Septuagint and Jewish Worship* (1921), 64–7). Zech. 14.8 runs, Living waters shall go out from Jerusalem. Now in rabbinic tradition Jerusalem was the navel of the earth (e.g. Jubilees 8.19: Mount Zion—the centre of the navel of the earth; Ezek. 38.12; Sanhedrin 37a), and it is possible that John used this word as a means to transfer the prophecy from the city to a person. Other Old Testament passages (e.g. Isa. 58.11) may have made the transference easier. See also Deut. 8.11; Ps. 114.8; Isa. 43.20; 44.3; Jer. 2.13; Ezek. 47.1–12; Joel. 4(3).18. 1QH 8.16 speaks of a fountain of living water (מבוע מים חיים), but as Braun (ad loc.) points out this is a common Jewish conception; in 1QS 4.20–2 the water is for cleansing rather than for giving life. CD 3.16f.; 6.4–11; 19.34 are better parallels, but there the water is Torah, and this too is a common Jewish conception by no means peculiar to the Qumran sect. It is not necessary to suppose (Torrey, 108–11) that a mistake took place in the rendering of Aramaic, גוה (*gawwah*) 'the midst of her (Jerusalem)' being taken as גוה (*gawweh*) 'the midst (belly) of him'; neither in Aramaic nor in

Greek was the gospel interested in water flowing out of Jerusalem, but in water flowing out of believers (or Christ). For reference to other interpretations see M. II, 475, Bultmann, 303f., and Schnackenburg II, 215f.

39. τοῦτο δὲ εἶπεν περὶ τοῦ πνεύματος. Water, especially living water, was sometimes used as a symbol of the Holy Spirit; see S.B. II, 434f., and especially *Gen. R.* 70.8, where the water-drawing of Tabernacles is interpreted as drawing the Holy Spirit. It is the Spirit who mediates divine life to men. Cf. 1 Cor. 12.13.

ἔμελλον λαμβάνειν οἱ πιστεύσαντες εἰς αὐτόν. The comment is John's, and he is contemplating the age in which he himself lived. οἱ πιστεύσαντες are not the apostles only but also those who should believe through them (17.20; 20.29).

οὔπω γὰρ ἦν πνεῦμα, ὅτι Ἰησοῦς οὐδέπω ἐδοξάσθη. This is the simplest and probably the correct text. Various attempts were made to exclude the possible though unintelligent inference that the Holy Spirit did not exist before the glorification of Jesus. After πνεῦμα the Latin and old Syriac VSS., and some Fathers, add δεδομένον; the same reading, with the addition of ἅγιον, is in B e hl. D adds ἅγιον ἐπ' αὐτοῖς, and sah has 'they had not yet received Spirit'. These variants are almost certainly 'improvements', and we should probably reject also πνεῦμα ἅγιον (ω) in favour of Nestle's πνεῦμα. John does not mean to deny the earlier existence of the Spirit, nor indeed that he was active in the prophets; and he says expressly that the Holy Spirit descended upon Jesus himself at the beginning of his ministry (1.32). He means rather that the Holy Spirit was not given in the characteristically Christian manner and measure until the close of the ministry. This corresponds closely with the almost complete silence of the Synoptic Gospels regarding the Spirit; that John has so much more to say on the subject is due to the fact that he writes from a later standpoint (see *J.T.S.* new series 1 (1950), 1–15). He himself recognizes clearly the dependence of the gift of the Spirit upon the completed work of Jesus (see in addition to the present passage 20.22; also 19.34 with the note), and in this recognition he is in close touch with the eschatological roots of the Christian proclamation. The Spirit was a gift of the new age (see *H.S.G.T.*, especially 152–62); in John's idiom this is expressed by saying that after Christ's return to the Father, Father and Son send the Holy Spirit (14.16,26; 15.26). Jesus is glorified in and through his death; cf. 12.23; 17.1. See on 3.14 as well as the passages mentioned. Cf. also passages where it is said that the disciples are to understand *later*: 2.21f.; 12.16; 13.7; 16.4; 20.9.

Brown raises the question whether sacramental symbolism is to be found in these verses. Is the water the water of baptism? If the question is put in this crude form the answer must be No. John is not simply speaking of baptism in veiled terms. It is however proper to recall that though the water of baptism is not drinking water but water in which the convert is immersed and bathed yet Paul could write (1 Cor. 12.13), In one Spirit we were all baptized into one body . . ., and we were all given one Spirit as drink (ἐποτίσθημεν); and John was certainly not unaware of the rite of baptism. The fact remains that in these verses water is an image of the Spirit, not a means by which the Spirit is conveyed, and not a word conveys any positive indication that baptism is in John's mind. This silence, when a reference would have been easy, can hardly fail to be significant; see Introduction, pp. 82–5.

40. ἐκ τοῦ ὄχλου. The prepositional phrase is used as a substantive governing a plural verb; understand τινές, as at 16.17. The construction is probably Semitic in origin; B.D. §164.2.

οὗτός ἐστιν ἀληθῶς ὁ προφήτης. For ἀληθῶς cf. v. 26. For ὁ προφήτης cf. 1.21,25; 6.14; perhaps 4.19, not 9.17. Whatever this designation of Jesus may mean elsewhere it is here clearly distinguished from the claim, which follows, that he is the Messiah. We are therefore not dealing with the messianic interpretation of Deut. 18.15,18 which appears in Acts 3.22f., and among the Samaritans, but seems to have no parallel in Jewish literature, unless 1QS 9.11 and 4QTest 5-8 are to be cited, though in these passages the Prophet is not identified with the messianic King. John 1.21-5 shows equally clearly that 'the prophet' is not Elijah *redivivus*. Subsidiary eschatological expectations, based perhaps in part on texts such as Deut. 18.15,18 and Mal. 3.1 (where it is not necessary to identify the 'messenger' with the returning Elijah of 3.23f.), may however have existed. At 1 Macc. 4.46; 14.41 certain questions are deferred until the appearance of a prophet, but there is no evidence that this deferment ever became part of the eschatological hope (S.B. II, 479). See also the reference to Martyn on v. 37, and Introduction, pp. 74f. On the present passage Martyn (103) sees not a sharp distinction between the Mosaic Prophet and the Messiah but the 'easy modulation from the Mosaic Prophet to the Mosaic Prophet-Messiah'. That there was an 'easy modulation' need not, in an area where there were few if any precise definitions, be denied; it is not inconsistent with the plain fact that ἔλεγον ... ἄλλοι ἔλεγον makes a distinction—some said one thing, others another.

41. οὗτός ἐστιν ὁ χριστός. Others went further and held that Jesus was not a forerunner but the Christ himself; cf. Mark 8.28f. The claim of Jesus to supply the Spirit naturally gave rise to the belief.

οἱ δὲ ἔλεγον. ℵ D have again ἄλλοι ἔλεγον, to make it quite clear that another division of the multitude is meant. It is argued that a messianic interpretation of Jesus' words is impossible; the circumstances of his birth did not accord with prophecy.

μὴ γάρ. γάρ strengthens μή, which expects the answer No. 'What, does the Christ ...?'

42. (i) The scripture referred to is, for the place of the Messiah's birth, Micah 5.2, καὶ σύ, Βηθλέεμ οἶκος Ἐφράθα, ... ἐξ οὗ μοι ἐξελεύσεται τοῦ εἶναι εἰς ἄρχοντα τοῦ Ἰσραήλ. The use of this passage seems to be Christian; it is not quoted in rabbinic literature for the origin of the Messiah until late (see Bonsirven I, 378), and though it is used in Justin, *Trypho* 78, it is found on the lips of Justin, not his Jewish opponent. Several passages declare that the Messiah will be of the seed of David, e.g. Ps. 89(88).4f., ὤμοσα Δαυεὶδ τῷ δούλῳ μου, Ἕως τοῦ αἰῶνος ἑτοιμάσω τὸ σπέρμα σου, κτλ. Fitzmyer (*Essays*, 86) sees a reference to 2 Sam. 7.11-14, as in 4QFlor. Cf. Rev. 5.5; 22.16. (ii) We may feel confident that John was aware of the tradition that Jesus was born at Bethlehem (for the probability that he knew of the doctrine of the virgin birth see on 1.13); he writes here in his customary ironical style. The critics of Jesus ignorantly suppose that because he was brought up in Galilee he was also born there. For contemporary criticism of Galilee, see G. Vermes, *Jesus the Jew* (1973), 42-57. (iii) But John's irony goes far deeper than this. The

birth place of Jesus is a trivial matter in comparison with the question whether he is ἐκ τῶν ἄνω or ἐκ τῶν κάτω (8.23), whether he is or is not from God. Cf. 7.28 where though Jesus admits that his hearers know whence he came he emphasizes that human origins are irrelevant (ἀπ' ἐμαυτοῦ οὐκ ἐλήλυθα), and 8.14 where Jesus denies that the Jews (truly) know whence he came—they judge κατὰ τὴν σάρκα. See also 3.8—no one knows whence comes and whither goes one who has been born of the Spirit. This refers primarily to Christians, but *a fortiori* to Jesus himself. It follows that all disputes about the birth place of the Messiah, the heavenly Man, are far wide of the point. A preconceived and rigidly held dogma prevents men from coming to Jesus in faith (Bultmann); cf. 6.42 and the reference there to Conzelmann.

ὅπου ἦν Δαυείδ. See 1 Sam. 16.1, etc.

43. σχίσμα οὖν ἐγένετο, that is, between those who held that Jesus was the Prophet, those who held that he was the Christ, and those who rejected his Messiahship on the ground of his supposed Galilean origin. The word σχίσμα occurs in several important places in the gospel (7.43; 9.16; 10.19), and summarizes the result of the mission of Jesus, since the inevitable effect of his word was to create a division among his hearers: the shining of the light distinguished between those who loved and those who hated it (3.19–21). Cf. Mark 4.11f.; this division among men is, in the New Testament, an inseparable part of the mission of Jesus. See further 12.37–50.

44. This verse closely resembles v. 30; though it is not impossible that τινὲς ... ἐξ αὐτῶν refers to some of the ὑπηρέται of v. 32. The notes of action suggest that it would be possible to take together vv. 25–31 and 37–44, and vv. 32–6 and 45–52. It is not impossible that John has taken over and combined two sources, but that he himself did combine them is shown by the unity of thought. Elaborate rearrangements of the chapter are justifiable only if the material as it stands is unintelligible. Lightfoot, noting that the ὑπηρέται appear to return on the day after they are sent, observes that John is not interested in historical consistency.

45. ἐκεῖνοι, the chief priests and Pharisees, though strictly the word should mean 'the former'. For the sending of the ὑπηρέται see v. 32. From this point, according to Martyn (74), John concentrates on the contemporary situation of the church, not on the historical situation of Jesus. There is truth in this view, but it should not be taken to mean that John is simply describing his own affairs as it were in cypher.

46. οὐδέποτε ἐλάλησεν οὕτως ἄνθρωπος. The stress appears to lie on the last word. The speech of Jesus is not the speech of a *man*. The constables were cowed by his superhuman authority, though they draw no precise conclusion about his person. Cf. 18.6.

47. μὴ καὶ ὑμεῖς (You also, in addition to the crowds who believed) πεπλά-νηθε; V. 12 (πλανᾷ τὸν ὄχλον) suggests that the verb is passive rather than middle. Have you also been deceived, led astray? Behind πλανᾶν may lie the technical rabbinic use of סות, יסת (suth, yasath). The 'Jamnia loyalists' (Martyn, 104) interrogate their unsuccessful חזנים (hazzanim, see v. 32). The next verse, however is against Martyn's distinction (76) between ἄρχοντες and Φαρισαῖοι.

48. It is implied that Nicodemus (3.1, ἄνθρωπος ἐκ τῶν Φαρισαίων . . . ἄρχων τῶν ’Ιουδαίων; see the note) though an inquirer had not become a believer. The description of Nicodemus puts rulers (ἄρχοντες) and Pharisees side by side; this verse distinguishes them (unless John means very broadly 'the upper class of Jews', over against those mentioned in v. 49).

49. ὁ ὄχλος οὗτος ὁ μὴ γινώσκων τὸν νόμον. These persons correspond to the עַמֵּי הָאָרֶץ ('amme ha’arets), 'people of the land', of rabbinic literature. 'The term is in express or implied contrast to talmide ḥakamim, 'scholars'; the educated class sets itself over against the masses of the people' (G. F. Moore, in Beginnings I, 439; see the whole very useful short note, 439–45). Not to know the Law meant, the Law being what it was for Judaism, lack of both education and religion. The authorities, however, put their trust in the Law; hence 'it is among those who, according to the world's standards, are the most questionable, that we may in the first place expect to find a readiness to receive the word of the Revealer' (Bultmann).

ἐπάρατοί εἰσιν. There is abundant evidence of bad feeling between the 'people of the land' on the one hand and scholars and Pharisees on the other; the former were genuinely believed by the latter to be outside the limits of true religion. Thus P. Aboth 2.6: Hillel used to say: A brutish man (בור, bor, a very bad example of the 'am ha’arets) dreads not sin, an ignorant man ('am ha’arets) cannot be saintly (that is, in the technical sense of legal observance). Cf. P. Aboth 3.11, R. Dosa b. Harkinas (c. A.D. 90) said: Morning sleep and midday wine and children's talk and sitting in the meeting-houses of the 'amme ha’arets put a man out of the world (cause his death). A passage which shows both that this dislike was returned by the 'amme ha’arets and also that the gulf between the two classes was not impassable is Pesahim 49 b: R. Aqiba said of himself: When I was an 'am ha’arets I used to say, 'I wish I had one of those scholars, and I would bite him like an ass.' His disciples said, 'You mean like a dog.' He replied, 'An ass's bite breaks the bone; a dog's does not.'

50. ὁ ἐλθὼν πρὸς αὐτὸν πρότερον. Cf. 3.1f. There is much textual variation in these words, which are perhaps a gloss. They are omitted altogether by א*. Martyn (155ff.) rightly compares the role of Gamaliel in Acts 5.34–9. εἷς ὢν ἐξ αὐτῶν. Possibly John means that for all his good will and fair-mindedness, Nicodemus remains one of the Jews, not one of the disciples.

51. Cf. Exod. 23.1; Deut. 1.16; 17.4; Josephus, Ant. XIV, 167; Bel. I, 209; Ex R. 21.3: Men (literally, Flesh and blood) pass judgement on a man if they hear his words; if they do not hear his words they cannot establish judgement on him. The Law is here spoken of personally, as if it were judge. τὸν ἄνθρωπον is any man who is on trial. ἀκούειν παρὰ τινός is a classical expression for hearing a man's defence. Cf. v. 49; it is misuse of the Law that makes men deaf.

52. μὴ καὶ σὺ ἐκ τῆς Γαλιλαίας εἶ; If Nicodemus defends Jesus the Galilean it must be out of local patriotism. The Jerusalem authorities could not accept pleas from such a source.

ἐρεύνησον. Cf. 5.39. Search the Old Testament Scriptures.

καὶ ἴδε . . . We may punctuate either ἐρ. καὶ ἴδε· ὅτι . . . (Search and see; for out of Galilee . . .); or ἐρ., καὶ ἴδε ὅτι . . . (Search, and by doing so discover for

yourself that . . .). The former alternative is better. The argument ascribed
to the Pharisees seems to be without parallel in Jewish literature. Contrast
'R. Eliezer (c. A.D. 90) said: Thou hast no single tribe in Israel from which
a prophet has not come forth' (*Sukkah* 27 b); 'Thou hast no town in the
land of Israel in which there has not been a prophet' (*Seder Olam R.* 21;
quoted S.B. II, 519). In view of the fact that Jonah the son of Amittai (2
Kings 14.25) came from Gath-hepher in Galilee the point may be (Sanders):
Scripture gives no ground for supposing that a prophet will come from
Galilee in the future. This is however rather strained, and the verse must cast
some doubt on John's firsthand acquaintance with Judaism. The two early
papyri, however, P⁶⁶ and P⁷⁵, both read ὁ προφήτης, 'the Prophet', the
messianic prophet, will not come from Galilee. This is an attractive reading,
but Lindars is probably right in regarding it as due to assimilation to v. 40.

53. On 7.53—8.11 see pp. 589–92.

18. WHO IS JESUS? (I)

8.12–59

The controversy begun in the preceding chapter continues and is now
concentrated upon the person and authority of Jesus himself. These
questions turn upon one that has already been under discussion, namely
the Whence and Whither which determine the nature and work of
Jesus, but several new themes are introduced.

Vv. 12–20. The chapter opens with a pronouncement of Jesus about
himself (I am the light of the world), brought forward from ch. 9 (see
the introduction to that chapter and the notes on 9.4f.,39–41). The
pronouncement is not explained here, but is introduced merely to raise
the question of witness-bearing. It is objected that a man's claims for
himself are irrelevant, and untrustworthy, just as no man ought to sit
alone in judgement. Jesus refutes the objection by a twofold argument.
First, unlike other men, he knows his origin and destiny, and hence is
able to bear true and reliable witness about himself. Secondly, it is in
appearance only that he witnesses and judges alone; in fact, he is
inseparable from the Father, and their combined witness ought to be
acknowledged as valid by those who accept the Jewish Law. Thus the
origin and end of Jesus in God justify his activity in bearing witness to
the truth and in judging.

Vv. 21–30. In this paragraph also the basis of the argument lies in
the origin and destiny of Jesus. Unlike other men, he is not of this world,
not from below, but from above, that is, from God. Whither he goes
none can follow, for he goes to a death and to a glory neither of which
can be shared by other men. Because of these things Jesus is a revelation
of God; he teaches what the Father teaches, he acts always in obedience
to the Father, who consequently is heard and seen in all that Jesus says
and does. Thus Jesus can even describe himself in terms that recall

the eternal and self-existing God (vv. 24, 28, ἐγώ εἰμι; see the notes).

Vv. 31–59, 'a *locus classicus* of Johannine theology' (Dodd, *Tradition*, 330; see 330ff.; also *Revue d'Histoire et de Philosophie religieuses* 37 (1957), 5–17). The same theme is developed again, but in new terms (though, according to Guilding, 107, truth is equivalent to light). A fundamental affirmation is first made: through Jesus the truth is made known to men, and by the truth he sets men free. In the course of the ensuing argument it appears that it is from sin (v. 34) and from death (v. 51) that they are liberated. This affirmation leads to a development of the primary theme in which Jesus and his adversaries are contrasted. They claim descent from Abraham, but belie the claim by their evil works: Jesus (it is implied) is the true descendant of Abraham. But with such a narrow and nationalistic statement it is impossible for John to rest. Ultimately (as family resemblance shows) the Jews are descended from the devil, the agent of sin and death, even as Jesus is the Son of God. This is the reason for their unbelief when the truth is spoken to them.

For the most part this discourse is couched in Jewish terminology: the debate turns, for example, on the Law, Abraham, the devil. This is natural if the debates in this part of the gospel are John's equivalent for the trial of Jesus before the Jewish court (cf. pp. 523f.). Occasionally, however, the influence of Hellenistic thought breaks through (see the notes on vv. 12, 23, 32f.). There are cross-references to other parts of the gospel (e.g. vv. 48, 50). The contacts with the Synoptic Gospels are numerous, subtle, and instructive. The theme of light is related to synoptic sayings (Mark 4.21f.; Matt. 4.16; 5.14; Luke 2.32). John seems again (cf. 1.13) to show knowledge of the belief that Jesus was born of a virgin. He hints at this when the Jews are made to claim (v. 41) that they were not born of fornication but have God as their father. Probably slanders about the parentage of Jesus were already current. The argument about the descent of the Jews from Abraham recalls not only the language of Paul (Rom. 4, 9; Gal. 3, 4, especially 3.16) but also the saying of John the Baptist (Matt. 3.9; Luke 3.8). The Beelzebul controversy (Mark 3.22–30; Matt. 12.24–32; Luke 11.15–22; 12.10) is recalled by v. 48 (cf. 7.20). Jesus is greater than Old Testament worthies (v. 53); cf. Matt. 12.39–42; Luke 11.29–32. The treatment of descent from Abraham, a privilege which Jesus minimizes in comparison with something greater, recalls his question about the Messiah and David's son (Mark 12.35–7; Matt. 22.41–6; Luke 20.41–4).

John, it appears, is working with primitive Christian material, but he has deepened it, and sharpened its edge. Thus, in the first place, its Christological significance is brought out much more clearly; Jesus is unmistakably 'from above', the eternal Son of the eternal God. In the second place, there is revealed the sharpest antagonism to the Jews. This is due in part, no doubt, to the controversies between church and synagogue in Ephesus and its neighbourhood towards the end of the first century, controversies in which, it may be, John himself had played some part, and learnt thereby not a little about Judaism (on this possibility see especially Martyn); but it is primarily due to a genuine theological understanding, for if the Jews who rejected Jesus were not right they were very wrong indeed. In perceiving this John sees clearly; but it is difficult to think that the writer of v. 44 had ever felt towards Israel the love and longing of Rom. 9.1–3; 10.1.

Many attempts have been made to rearrange the contents of this chapter; Sanders for example thinks that vv. 12–20 would come better after 5; 7.15–24; he suggests 8.12–20;7.1–14;7.25–42 as the original sequence. For a discussion of Bultmann's radical rearrangement of the gospel see (in addition to his commentary) Smith. The chapter contains several possible allusions to Isa. 43, possibly because this may have been the *Haphtarah* for the first Sabbath of Tabernacles (Guilding, 107–10).

12. πάλιν οὖν αὐτοῖς ἐλάλησεν ὁ Ἰησοῦς λέγων. The discourse is continued from 7.52. There is no indication of a change of place, and 8.20 shows that Jesus is still in the Temple (as at 7.28); but in these central discourses John seems indifferent to details of sequence and movement. ἐλάλησεν . . . λέγων need not be a Semitism; see M. II, 454. It is not clear whom Jesus is here addressing. Since controversy immediately arises we may suppose the Jewish leaders rather than the crowd. This is Jesus' first utterance since 7.37f.

ἐγώ εἰμι. On these words, used with a predicate, see on 6.35.

τὸ φῶς τοῦ κόσμου. As with most of the great Johannine descriptions of Jesus, the background is complex; see for much detail G. P. Wetter, ΦΩΣ (1915). It may be briefly outlined as follows. (i) *The feast of Tabernacles* (see on 7.2, 37f.). In *Sukkah* 5.2–4 is described the ceremony of the first festival day of the feast. In the Court of the Women 'there were golden candlesticks . . . with four golden bowls on the top of them and four ladders to each candlestick. . . . They made wicks from the worn out drawers and girdles of the priests and with them they set the candlesticks alight, and there was not a courtyard in Jerusalem that did not reflect the light of the House of Water-drawing (בית השואבה, or בית השאובה; the pointing is uncertain; see Danby, 179, note 12). Men of piety and good works used to dance before them with burning torches in their hands, singing songs and praises. . . .' Also in the Tabernacles *Haphtarah* (Zech. 14) there is reference to light: 'It shall come to pass, that at evening time there shall be light (ἔσται φῶς)' (v. 7). If the allusion to 'living water' (7.37f.) was in part suggested by the ceremony of water-drawing it is equally possible that the ceremony of lights may have suggested the inclusion in the same context (it must be remembered that, since 7.53—8.11 is not part of the original text of the gospel (see pp. 589f.), the context is the same) of the saying 'I am the light of the world', and the two possibilities tend to confirm each other. (ii) *Pagan Religions.* That God is light is the basic assumption of most gnostic systems, and of the oriental religions which form their base. It was from the East, and especially from Persia, that the religion of the Sun (which took various forms, notably that of Mithraism) passed westward over the Roman Empire, leaving traces of the most diverse kinds, especially in the belief in divinized men, often portrayed as gods with rays emanating from their heads (see, e.g., H.P. L'Orange, *Apotheosis in Ancient Portraiture*, 1947). Macrobius (*Liber Saturnaliorum*, I, xxiii, 21) points out this attitude to the Sun, which became less and less *a* god, and more and more a symbol of cosmic light or truth: *Postremo potentiam solis ad omnium potestatem summitatem referri indicant theologi, qui in sacris hoc brevissima precatione demonstrant, dicentes:* ἥλιε παντοκράτορ, κόσμου πνεῦμα, κόσμου δύναμις, κόσμου φῶς. Light was especially the sign of God manifest. Lucian (*Pseudomantis*, 18) represents Glycon, the god preached by Alexander of Abonuteichos, as proclaiming himself: εἰμὶ Γλύκων, τρίτον αἷμα Διός, φάος ἀνθρώποισιν. A revealer-god was naturally a light to men, and in the Hermetic revelation we have (*C.H.* 1, 6) τὸ φῶς ἐκεῖνο, ἔφη [*sc.* ὁ Ποιμάνδρης], ἐγὼ νοῦς ὁ σὸς θεός. The light here brought into the process of revelation is the primal light, the beginning of the Hermetic cosmogony (1, 4). Poimandres continues (1, 6) ὁ δὲ ἐκ νοὸς φωτεινὸς λόγος υἱὸς θεοῦ. Here the writer refers again to his cosmological vision where (1, 5) ἐκ δὲ φωτὸς λόγος ἅγιος ἐπέβη τῇ φύσει (the primal moist nature—the formless mass out of which the universe was made). It is by the holy Word that creation is set in motion. When Tat (the disciple who receives the revelation) inquires the meaning of what he has been told, the answer is (1, 6) τὸ ἐν σοὶ βλέπον καὶ ἀκοῦον, λόγος κυρίου, ὁ δὲ νοῦς πατὴρ θεός. οὐ γὰρ διΐστανται ἀπ' ἀλλήλων· ἕνωσις γὰρ τούτων ἐστὶν ἡ ζωή. In this very important passage the following points are clear: (*a*) The Word is the agent of the Father, active in creation, standing in a cosmological relation to the world and men; (*b*) The Word is the immanent revealing activity of the Father, standing in an epistemological relation to men; (*c*) As Νοῦς is φῶς, so the Word is φωτεινός; they are Father and Son, so that the Word is (at least in part) personal; (*d*) The union of the two is ζωή. This collocation of light and life, of the cosmological and revealing functions of the Word, who is the Son of God and the light of men, is very close to John's thought. (iii) *Judaism*. In Genesis (1.3) light is the first created thing; it is not (as in the Hermetica) equated with God. Nevertheless, light frequently accompanies theophanies (e.g. Gen. 15.17), and is inevitably a symbol of divine instruction (e.g. Ps. 119(118).105: Thy word (νόμος) is a lamp unto my feet, and a light (φῶς) unto my path; cf. Prov. 6.23). Wisdom already comes within the range of the light metaphor at Prov. 8.22 (LXX, κύριος ἔκτισέν με ἀρχὴν ὁδῶν αὐτοῦ—the first creation was light), and at Wisdom 7.26 it is said explicitly, ἀπαύγασμα γάρ ἐστιν [*sc.* ἡ σοφία] φωτὸς ἀιδίου. At Ps. 27.1 the Hebrew text is, The Lord is my light (אוֹרִי) and my salvation, but the LXX, perhaps fearing an identification of God with impersonal light, in the Persian manner, rendered, κύριος φωτισμός μου κτλ., The Lord is my illumination. This point is missed by Philo (*Som.* 1, 75), who, after quoting the Psalm in the LXX form, goes on to speak of God as φῶς, and also of the Word, in precisely the Hermetic manner. 'God is light, for . . [reference to Ps. 27.1 follows]. And he is not only light, but the archetype of every other light, nay, prior to and high above every archetype, holding the position of the model of a model [adding a second παραδείγματος, with Colson and Whitaker]. For the model or pattern was the Word which contained all his fullness—light, in fact; for, as the Lawgiver tells us, God said, Let light come into being (Gen. 1.3).' The parallelism between John, Philo, and the *Hermetica* is very remarkable. The Rabbis naturally (in view of Ps. 119.105;

Prov. 6.23) spoke of the Law as a Lamp or light (Test. Levi 14.4: The light of the Law which was given for to lighten every man; *Ex. R.* 36.3 . . . What is the lamp of God? The Law (Prov. 6.23); further S.B. II, 521f., 552f.). But 'light' was also used in a specifically messianic sense. It is used of the light which shines upon the Messiah and is bestowed by him upon the righteous, and Light is a name of the Messiah; the messianic light is sometimes identified with the primal light of creation. See S.B. I, 67, 151, 161; II, 428; the evidence is not very early, but it may well be that Hellenistic and rabbinic Judaism were developing on parallel, and not unconnected, lines. There is confirmation for the interpenetration of Hellenism and Judaism in the Qumran material. The following passages have been noted as significant: I QS 2.3; 3.7,20f.; 4.11 (Charlesworth in *J. & Q.*, 101f. finds 3.13—4.26 particularly relevant to John; in addition the scroll dealing with the war of the sons of light against the sons of darkness must be borne in mind. Whether however these passages contribute anything to the understanding of the Fourth Gospel is doubtful; even 3.7, which contains the expression 'light of life' (אור החיים), betrays rather an affiliation with the Old Testament which John shares, and the contrast in 3.20f. (cf. 4.11) between light and darkness is hardly more dualistic than any moral philosopher who distinguishes between good and evil and is prepared to use metaphor in his exposition. John and the Qumran author share the conviction that right and wrong are and remain ultimately distinct; they have little more than this, and their acquaintance with the Old Testament, in common. (iv) In the *Synoptic Gospels* the metaphor of light is used several times. In the parable of the lamp (Mark 4.21f. and parallels), the lamp probably refers in some way to the revelation conveyed in the ministry of Jesus. At Matt. 4.16, Isa. 9.1 is quoted and finds fulfilment in the work of Jesus (ὁ λαὸς . . . φῶς εἶδεν μέγα); at Luke 2.32 Jesus himself appears to be the fulfilment of a light-prophecy of the Old Testament. Simeon's words (φῶς εἰς ἀποκάλυψιν ἐθνῶν) recall Isa. 49.6, ἰδοὺ δέδωκά σε . . . εἰς φῶς ἐθνῶν. At Matt. 5.14 the disciples are described in the words used by John (ὑμεῖς ἐστὲ τὸ φῶς τοῦ κόσμου). Jesus, with his followers, assumes and fulfils the destiny of Israel. Cf. *Thomas* 77: Jesus said: I am the Light that is above them all, I am the All, the All came forth from Me and the All attained to Me.

This brief review of the background of the phrase 'the light of the world' shows that John stands within the primitive Christian tradition (cf. also Acts 13.47; Phil. 2.15; Col. 1.12f.; Eph. 5.8; I Peter 2.9). Nevertheless, it remains very probable that in the formulation of his statement he was influenced both by Hellenistic religion and by Jewish thought about Wisdom and the Law; cf. pp. 152ff. Yet for John 'the light of the world' describes what is essentially a soteriological function rather than a cosmological status. Lindars rightly notes that 7.27f.,41,52 referred to the emergence of the Messiah from obscurity (Galilee); cf. Isa. 9.1f. Jesus (as the following words show) is light illuminating; and it is by being light, not by pointing to it, that he gives light.

ὁ ἀκολουθῶν μοι. ἀκολουθεῖν expresses the obedience of faith; see on 1.37.

οὐ μὴ περιπατήσῃ ἐν τῇ σκοτίᾳ, ἀλλ' ἕξει τὸ φῶς τῆς ζωῆς. Light in John is not merely a component of the universe; it is active and saving; the disciple is delivered out of the darkness of the world (1.5; 12.35,46). The light has life in itself and gives life (cf. 4.10,14; 6.35,51; also 1.4). 'He, and He only, irradiates human existence with the knowledge of its nature, meaning, and purpose' (Lightfoot). In 1 QS 3.7 'the light of life' probably refers to the Law and is thus a parallel only in that Jesus takes the place of the Law.

13. The subject of light is now dropped, and is not taken up again till 9.5. The real subject matter of ch. 8 is the authority of Jesus, viewed over against a Judaism that has betrayed its own origin, but the dialogue had to be set in motion by a pronouncement of Jesus about himself (σὺ περὶ σεαυτοῦ μαρτυρεῖς), and this one is anticipated from 9.5; it is however entirely suitable to its context, since light cannot but bear witness to itself and is authenticated by its source; '... it would no longer be God's Word if it demanded other authorities recognised by men to confirm its authenticity' (Bultmann). Cf. Guilding, 107.

ἡ μαρτυρία σου οὐκ ἔστιν ἀληθής. For the adjective (here 'veracious') see on 1.9. In the Old Testament it is expressly stated that one witness is inadequate on a capital charge (Num. 35.30; Deut. 17.6; cf. Deut. 19.15), but in the Mishnah the application of the principle is extended (Rosh Ha-Shanah 3.1; Ketuboth 2.9: None may be believed when he testifies of himself. ... None may testify of himself. These passages deal with particular cases but appear to apply to them a general principle).

14. ὅτι οἶδα πόθεν ἦλθον καὶ ποῦ ὑπάγω. Cf. 5.31, where there is an apparent contradiction, and see the note there. Here Jesus vindicates his right to make, in conjunction with his Father (v. 16b), statements about himself. Indeed if he did not make them the truth could never be communicated to men, who (as Bultmann says) are dependent on the self-knowledge of the Revealer. For the important question whence Jesus comes and whither he goes see also 7.27f., 34f.; 9.29f.; 13.36f.; 14.4ff.; 16.5; 19.9; cf. 3.8, but here John thinks of a unique property of Jesus, not of one shared by Christians. Man as such is a creature of the present; that is why his testimony about himself is unreliable. He does not know what brought him to the present hour or where the next moment will find him. Jesus on the other hand knows whence he came, and therefore fully understands himself, and whither he goes, and is therefore subject to no temptation to conceal or twist the truth; hence his own witness regarding himself is true. He is not as other men—ὑμεῖς δὲ οὐκ οἴδατε. The Jews are not in themselves qualified to bear true self-testimony; nor can they understand why Jesus is so qualified. The ensuing discourse traces their complete ignorance of the origin, destiny, and significance of Christ, and of their own.

15. ὑμεῖς κατὰ τὴν σάρκα κρίνετε. An observation arising out of the situation. In refusing the testimony of Jesus to himself the Jews judge him on the basis of what they see—his flesh, not allowing, or conceiving, that he is the Word become flesh. Cf. 2 Cor. 5.16, εἰ καὶ ἐγνώκαμεν κατὰ σάρκα Χριστόν; neither Paul nor John repudiates the true humanity (σάρξ) of Christ, but each insists that a judgement about him on a purely human basis, formed by appearance only, is necessarily a false judgement. John has κατὰ τὴν σάρκα (here only), Paul always (and frequently) κατὰ σάρκα (except possibly 2 Cor. 11.18). No other New Testament writer uses the phrase.

ἐγὼ οὐ κρίνω οὐδένα. Cf. 12.47; also 5.30; when Jesus does judge it is in the name and as the agent of God. It was perhaps on account, and in illustration, of these words that the Pericope Adulterae (7.53—8.11) was added by those

338

MSS. that contain it. Cf. on the other hand 5.22; 9.39. In both sets of passages however the stress lies on the complete unity of will and action that exists between the Father and the Son; and, as the next verse shows, John is able to emphasize from time to time whichever aspect of the truth seems to him important at the moment.

16. καὶ ἐὰν κρίνω δὲ ἐγώ. For the position of δέ cf. 6.51; 7.31. Here it has the effect of reversing the whole negative proposition of v. 15b. Jesus does not issue such judgements as do the Jews, but he cannot be made to deny altogether his right to judge; only his judgement is of a different kind. It is also ἀληθινή (see on 1.9; here synonymous with ἀληθής, unless the sense is that Jesus' alone is authentic judgement).

ὅτι μόνος οὐκ εἰμί. See above on vv. 13, 15. Cf. P. Aboth 4.8: He (R. Ishmael, late second century A.D.) used to say: Judge not alone, for none may judge alone save One. According to John, judgement, by the Father's will, belongs equally to the Father and the Son (and to the Holy Spirit, 16.8,11). In the Father is the eternal standard of rightness beyond which is no appeal; the Son, being the light of the world, is the occasion by which mankind is separated into the two groups of those who love, and do not love, the light (3.20f.). This process is continued in the ministry of the Holy Spirit.

ἀλλ' ἐγὼ καὶ ὁ πέμψας με. No verb is expressed, but the sense is clear: I am not alone, but I and the Father are together, and judge together. On the sending of the Son see on 20.21.

17. The conditions of the Law (Deut. 17.6; 19.15) are thus fulfilled. Jesus and the Father are two consentient witnesses. See J. P. Charlier, in R.B. 67 (1960), 503–15.

καὶ ἐν τῷ νόμῳ δὲ τῷ ὑμετέρῳ. δέ stands fifth (cf. v. 16), making the preceding words very emphatic. It is unlikely that Jesus himself, speaking as a Jew to Jews, would have spoken of your law. As at 7.19 (cf. 10.34; 15.25) John indicates the rift that had opened between synagogue and church, and also his intention to fasten upon the Jews the witness, disregarded by them, of their own Scriptures. Also 'Jesus stands in the same relation to the Torah as his Father' (Odeberg, 292).

18. ἐγώ εἰμι ὁ μαρτυρῶν. On John's use of ἐγώ εἰμι see on 6.35; the present use however is not identical with those in which a simple predicate (such as 'the light of the world') follows. The article with μαρτυρῶν is to be noted; the meaning is almost 'I am he that is in a position to witness'—for the reason given above. Cf. Isa. 43.10, LXX, γένεσθέ μοι μάρτυρες, καὶ ἐγὼ μάρτυς. Cf. Guilding, 108.

καὶ μαρτυρεῖ . . . ὁ . . . πατήρ. For the Father's witness to the Son cf. 5.37; comparison of the language of that verse with this suggests equivalence of function and status between the Father and the Son.

19. ποῦ ἐστιν ὁ πατήρ σου; As often in John (see on 3.4), a profound statement by Jesus is misunderstood by his hearers, and the misunderstanding leads to further teaching. Here the question, though for the moment left unanswered, leads up to the discussion in the remainder of the discourse of the origin and departure of Jesus, and of his parentage and that of the Jews. Bernard (297) thinks that the Jews understand that by his Father Jesus means God, and this is perhaps borne out by v. 41, where the Jews assert that it is they who

can claim divine parentage, whereas Jesus was not even born in wedlock. In any case, however, the request that Jesus should as it were, produce his Father remains a foolish and perhaps perverse misunderstanding of his meaning. Contrast the question of 14.8, which shows slowness of understanding, but not perversity.

οὔτε ἐμὲ οἴδατε ... The foolishness of the question about the Father proves that the questioners do not understand Jesus himself. They judge him κατὰ τὴν σάρκα (v. 15), and therefore entertain similar views about the Father. But if they had rightly understood him, had known whence he came and whither he went, they would have known the Father also (cf. 1.18; 14.7,9).

20. ἐν τῷ γαʒοφυλακείῳ. The sense in which γαʒοφυλακείον (cf. Mark 12.41,43) is used is not clear. In Josephus (Bel. v, 200) the plural is used to describe a number of chambers in the Temple used as strong rooms for the preservation of the Temple valuables (and also private property committed to them, cf. Bel. VI, 282; Ant. XIX, 294): similar rooms seem to be referred to in Middoth 4, 5. But no public teaching could have taken place in these rooms. There were also in the temple thirteen 'Shofar-chests' for the reception of offerings. The Shofar itself was the horn on which trumpet blasts were blown, and the receptacles may have been named from their shape. Each was inscribed with a name indicating the use made of the gifts placed within it. The Shofar-chests were in the Temple (Shekalim 2.1; 6.1,5; במקדש), but it is nowhere stated where in the Temple they were situated, though it is generally assumed that they were in the Court of the Women, since (according to a note in the Tosephta and Mark 12.41f.) women as well as men had access to them. It may be noted that the ceremony which may be alluded to in v. 12 took place in the Court of the Women. We may therefore think of Jesus as teaching in a certain part of the Court of the Women, but it is impossible to give precision to John's words, and possible therefore that he himself had no precise conception of the plan of the Temple in his mind. See however S.B. II, 37–45.

ὅτι οὔπω ἐληλύθει ἡ ὥρα αὐτοῦ. Cf. 7.30; 2.4.

21. As at v. 12, the discourse is resumed with πάλιν. The points raised in the short opening discussion are developed and combined with one another. (i) Whence Jesus comes: vv. 23; 26, 29 (ὁ πέμψας); 41f.; 48; 58 (ἐγώ εἰμί). (ii) Whither he goes: vv. 21f., 28, 35, 54. (iii) Who is the Father? vv. 26f., 38, 54f. (iv) Who is Jesus? vv. 23–6, 38, 54f. Each of these themes, moreover, is applied, as it were, in reverse, to the Jews. As Jesus is ἐκ τῶν ἄνω, they are ἐκ τῶν κάτω; whither he goes, they cannot come; God is his Father, they are of their father the Devil—even their descent from Abraham is misleading; he cannot but speak the truth, they cannot but speak falsehood.

ἐγὼ ὑπάγω καὶ ʒητήσετέ με. Cf. 7.33f. By ὑπάγω John generally refers to the death of Jesus, by which he departs to the Father. The Jews will seek him in vain; they cannot ascend into heaven where he will be and they do not offer to God an obedience unto death. Peter (13.33,36) can do no more than they; only by faith (v. 24) can any one be united with Jesus in his death and resurrection.

ἐν τῇ ἁμαρτίᾳ ὑμῶν ἀποθανεῖσθε. Cf. v. 24 (where the plural ἁμαρτίαις is used). The singular focuses attention upon the cardinal sin of rejecting Jesus. Cf. 9.41, ἡ ἁμαρτία ὑμῶν μένει, which belongs to the same context of thought;

those who in their self-sufficiency reject the light place themselves outside the scope of its salutary (though not its condemnatory) effect. Cf. Mark 3.28f. and parallels. ἐν is probably locative (in a state of sin), but may be instrumental (by reason of sin).

22. οἱ Ἰουδαῖοι are as usual the adversaries of Jesus (see on 1.19), and though in this chapter some of them believe, their faith is not satisfactory (vv. 31, 37).

μήτι ἀποκτενεῖ ἑαυτόν; For μήτι see on 4.29. Again (cf. 7.35) a wrong interpretation is given of the impending departure of Jesus. Both misunderstandings (see on 3.4), however, conceal a true, though unwitting (cf. 11.51), understanding of the intention of Jesus; through the church he will teach the Greeks, and he will lay down his own life (10.11,15). It is also true that *they* will kill *him*.

23. The parallelism is striking, but it arises rather out of the subject matter than out of a conscious attempt to write in the style of Semitic verse (or out of the translation of a Semitic original).

ὑμεῖς ἐκ τῶν κάτω ἐστέ, ἐγὼ ἐκ τῶν ἄνω εἰμί. For τὰ ἄνω cf. Col. 3.1f.; there is no corresponding New Testament parallel to τὰ κάτω. τὰ ἄνω (here as in Colossians) means the heavenly world; τὰ κάτω means (as the second part of the verse shows) this world; not hell, but all that is not contained in the heavenly world. Little can be learned from Greek usage: οἱ ἄνω are the living, οἱ κάτω the dead; there are οἱ ἄνω θεοί and οἱ κάτω θεοί. But the distinction is between this world and the underworld, not between this world and an upper world. There is a closer parallel in *Hagigah* 2.1: Whosoever gives his mind to four things it were better for him if he had not come into the world—what is above (מה למעלה)? what is beneath (מה למטה)? what was beforetime? and what will be hereafter? Such subjects, though forbidden, were discussed; see *Hagigah* 14 b (a *baraitah*): There are four who entered into Paradise (that is, engaged in speculation regarding the heavenly dwelling place of God— S.B. III, 798), and these are Ben Azzai, Ben Zoma (both *c.* A.D. 110), Aḥer (that is, the apostate Elisha b. Abuya, *c.* A.D. 120) and Aqiba († *c.* A.D. 135). There is thus no reason why the ultimate context of this verse should not be Judaism rather than Hellenism, though it has probably been shaped in a popular Platonic mould.

ἐκ τούτου τοῦ κόσμου. The Hebrew עוֹלָם (*'olam*, Aramaic עלמא) could mean 'world' as well as 'age'; here undoubtedly 'this world' is the lower world as opposed to heaven, whence Jesus has come. The thought in this verse is not so much that of a world of appearance and a world of reality, as of a primitive 'three-storey' universe, in which heavenly beings may come down from their proper abode (cf. 1.51) to visit the earth.

24. εἶπον, at v. 21. The change from singular to plural (ἁμαρτίαις) is significant only as pointed out on that verse. It is possible that there is an allusion to the fate of unbelieving Judaism in the disaster of A.D. 66–70; but this is not the primary thought.

ἐὰν γὰρ μὴ πιστεύσητε ὅτι ἐγώ εἰμι. Faith in Christ is the only escape from sin and its consequences. The difficulty lies in the clause which expresses the content of faith. ἐγώ εἰμι occurs several times in John with a predicate; for these uses see on 6.35. The absolute use of ἐγώ εἰμι at 6.20; 18.6 (see the notes) can be readily understood from the context; here however it seems impossible to supply an appropriate complement from the context. Moreover the question that follows (σὺ τίς εἶ; v. 25) suggests that the words were not plain to the hearers, that is, the expression here anticipates v. 28 with a view to raising in the sharpest terms the question who Jesus is.

ἐγώ εἰμι without complement (see also vv. 28, 58, and 13.19) is hardly a Greek expression, and it is therefore natural to look into its Jewish background. The words occur not infrequently in the LXX where they render אני הוא ('ani hu', literally 'I (am) he'), which occurs especially in the words of God himself, and there is a particularly close parallel to the present passage in Isa. 43.10, ἵνα γνῶτε καὶ πιστεύσητε καὶ συνῆτε ὅτι ἐγώ εἰμι (אני הוא). Similar passages occur at Deut. 32.39; Isa. 41.4; 43.13; 46.4; 48.12. In the Isaiah passages the meaning of the Hebrew is apparently 'I am (for ever) the same' with perhaps an allusion to the name יהוה (YHWH) given in Exod. 3.14-16; so G.K., 459, n. 1 and more recently K.B., s.v. הוא, 9. The context demands a similar meaning for the Greek, though ἐγώ εἰμι is in itself (as Greek) a meaningless expression. The Lord, the first and with the last, is the eternal one. The εἰμί, that is to say, is a properly continuous tense, implying neither beginning nor end of existence. This meaning is particularly appropriate to v. 58 (where see the note), and appropriate also to the present verse, where it reinforces the assertion that Jesus belongs to the eternal, heavenly world (ἐκ τῶν ἄνω). See G. Klein, *Der älteste christliche Katechismus und die jüdische Propaganda-Literatur* (1909), 44-55; cf. 55-61; Daube, *N.T.R.J.*, 325-9; Dodd, *Interpretation*, 93-6 (especially for the related phrase אני והוא, I and he); and Brown, Appendix IV, 533-8. It is not however correct to infer either for the present passage or for the others in which ἐγώ εἰμι occurs that John wishes to equate Jesus with the supreme God of the Old Testament (see E. Stauffer, *Jesus and His Story* (E.T., 1960), 102, 142-59; on this, Haenchen, *Weg*, 511). This is not demonstrated by the Jewish material (S.B. II, 797; see however Isa. 47.8; Zeph. 2.15 for the blasphemous use of the words by men), and is in the contexts impossible. Note that in v. 28 it is followed by 'I do nothing of myself, but as the Father taught me I speak these things ... I always do the things that are pleasing to him', and in 13.19 by 'He who receives me receives him who sent me' (13.20). Jesus is the obedient servant of the Father, and for this reason perfectly reveals him. ἐγώ εἰμι does not identify Jesus with God, but it does draw attention to him in the strongest possible terms. 'I am the one—the one you must look at, and listen to, if you would know God.' This open form of words is better than 'I am the Christ, the one who can save you' (Sanders; cf. Lindars), just because it is open. More satisfactory is Bultmann: 'He is everything he has claimed to be.'

ἀποθανεῖσθε. Cf. Isa. 43.25 (Guilding, 108).

25. σὺ τίς εἶ; The ἐγώ εἰμι of Jesus, though full of meaning, is formally no definition of his person; it is the kind of revelation that must bewilder unbelief (cf. the 'messianic secret' of the Synoptic Gospels; see Introduction pp. 70f.). Possibly this question should be regarded as an example of the misunderstandings which it is characteristic of John's style and method to relate (see on 3.4). The Jews fail to grasp the real force of what has been said, supposing the sentence to be unfinished. Cf. *C.H.* 1, 2, σὺ γὰρ τίς εἶ; (addressed to the Revealer).

τὴν ἀρχὴν ὅ τι καὶ λαλῶ ὑμῖν; Cf. Isa. 43.12 (Guilding, 108). The difficulty of this sentence has perhaps been exaggerated. It must be observed at the outset that (τὴν) ἀρχήν is used quite frequently in Greek adverbially (see L.S. *s.v.* ἀρχή I. 1, c). All now turns on whether the sentence is a question or a statement. If it is a question, τὴν ἀρχήν will have the meaning 'at all' and οτι must be written ὅτι and translated 'Why?'—'Why do I speak to you at all?' This meaning of ὅτι is quite possible (e.g. Mark 9.28), but taken as a whole this rendering goes so badly with the next verse (πολλὰ ἔχω περὶ ὑμῶν λαλεῖν), and seems so pointless, that it must be rejected and the sentence read as a statement, writing οτι as ὅ, τι and supplying ἐγώ εἰμι. τὴν ἀρχήν must now be rendered 'at first', 'at the beginning', 'in the beginning'; cf. e.g. Thucydides II, 74 (οὔτε τὴν ἀρχήν ... οὔτε νῦν); Gen. 41.21; 43.18,20 (in each place=בתחלה, *batteḥillah*, 'in the beginning'); Dan. 8.1 (Th. τὴν ἀρχήν = LXX τὴν πρώτην = בתחלה); 9.21 (LXX τὴν ἀρχήν = Th. ἐν τῇ ἀρχῇ = בתחלה). We must choose between the renderings (*a*) I am from the beginning what I tell you, and (*b*) I am what I tell you from the beginning. Of these (*a*) gives the better rendering of the present λαλῶ. It suits the sense of the whole discourse, and it follows up the ἐγώ εἰμι of v. 24 (as interpreted above) particularly well. It should probably be accepted. See however Turner, *Insights*, 140ff.

26. Cf. 12.49. The connection between the two parts of the verse is obscure. Perhaps it is best to take ἔχω in the sense of 'I can'. This is well attested in Greek (cf. 8.6; Heb. 6. 13; Sophocles, *Philoctetes* 1047, πολλ' ἂν λέγειν ἔχοιμι). We should then take the verse as follows: I can say and judge many things about you; (but in fact I forbear to speak my own words and pass my own judgements) preferring to speak the things I have heard from him that sent me; and they are true for he is true. For the sending of Jesus see on 20.21; on ἀληθής see on 1.9.

εἰς τὸν κόσμον. Perhaps, I address these words *to* the world; more probably εἰς with the accusative is, according to Hellenistic usage, used for ἐν with the dative (see M. 1, 63, 234f., 245).

27. It is not clear from the sentence as it stands whom the Jews can have thought Jesus meant. τὸν θεόν, added after ἔλεγεν by ℵ* D it (vg), though perhaps not the original reading, suggests the right sense. The Jews did not understand that Jesus had been sent from God.

28. ὅταν ὑψώσητε. On the double meaning of this verb see on 3.14. It is appropriate here: the exaltation of Jesus in glory proves that his claim ἐγώ εἰμι is true; and the fact that he was lifted up on the cross in death, though effected by the Jews (ὑψώσητε), proves his complete obedience to the Father who sent him.

τὸν υἱὸν τοῦ ἀνθρώπου. On John's use of this term see Introduction, pp. 72f. and on 1.51. Its use here is consistent with the synoptic tradition (cf. Mark 8.31), and with its double application to the heavenly origin and authority of Jesus (3.13) and his humble, earthly, human life. See Higgins, *Son of Man*, 168f.; also S. S. Smalley, *N.T.S.* 15 (1969), 295 and J. Riedl, in *Jesus und der Menschensohn* (Festschrift A. Vögtle, 1975) 355-70.

γνώσεσθε ὅτι ἐγώ εἰμι. On ἐγώ εἰμι see on v. 24. The subject of γνώσεσθε is apparently the Jews, who have lifted up the Son of man (by crucifying him).

John can hardly mean that they, after the crucifixion, will accept the heavenly status of Jesus, for he knew well that most of them had not done so, and he evidently regards 'the Jews' as the opponents of the church. Either John changes the subject awkwardly and addresses his readers—'You men will know'; or he means that the Jews will learn the truth too late. 'The Cross was the Jews' last and definitive answer to Jesus' word of revelation, and whenever the world gives its final answer in the words of unbelief it "lifts up" the Revealer and makes him its judge' (Bultmann).

For the latter part of the verse cf. 5.30; 6.38, etc.

29. Cf. v. 16. Because Jesus is constantly obedient to the Father he is never without God. It is unlikely that John is consciously correcting or contradicting Mark 15.34.

30. πολλοὶ ἐπίστευσαν εἰς αὐτόν. Cf. 2.23; 7.31; 10.42; 12.11,42. References to many believers strike an anachronistic note, but are not a crude displacement of post-resurrection circumstances into the ministry and a thoughtless interpolation (though vv. 30,31a may well have been John's addition to a now untraceable source). The discourse proceeds (see vv. 31,37) to manifest and discuss the inadequacy of faith that does not abide in the word of Jesus and recognize the truth (vv. 31f.).

31. τοὺς πεπιστευκότας αὐτῷ 'Ιουδαίους. Many commentators regard τοὺς πεπιστευκότας αὐτῷ as a gloss. On the change in construction with πιστεύειν see M. 1, 67f.; it can hardly be accidental, especially if the two clauses are John's insertion into a source. Merely to place credence in Jesus' words is not enough; men must abide in his word.

ἐὰν ὑμεῖς μείνητε ἐν τῷ λόγῳ τῷ ἐμῷ. Cf. T. Joseph 1.3, ἔμεινα ἐν τῇ ἀληθείᾳ κυρίου; also Thomas 19 (If you become disciples to me and hear my words . . .). There are several similar but not identical expressions in ch. 15. Those who have believed Jesus, that is, accepted his word, must continue in it if they are to be true disciples and to know the truth.

32. γνώσεσθε τὴν ἀλήθειαν. This expression is in close parallel with γνώσεσθε ὅτι ἐγώ εἰμι (v. 28). On ἀλήθεια in John see on 1.14; here it is closely related to the eternal existence and the saving mission of Jesus, and not far from the meaning 'Gospel' (cf. T.W.N.T. 1, 244f.; but Bultmann in this article takes ἀλήθεια to mean revelation).

ἡ ἀλήθεια ἐλευθερώσει ὑμᾶς. In Judaism the truth was the Law; and study of the Law made a man free. P. Aboth 3.5: R. Nehunya b. Ha-Kanah (c. A.D. 70–130—roughly contemporary with John) said: He that takes upon himself the yoke of the Law, from him shall be taken away the yoke of the kingdom and the yoke of worldly care; but he that throws off the yoke of the Law, upon him shall be laid the yoke of the kingdom and the yoke of worldly care. Cf. P. Aboth 6.2, which however is late. Josephus speaks similarly: in Ant. IV, 187, after speaking of the blessings secured by obedience to the Law, he adds τὴν τ' ἐλευθερίαν ἡγεῖσθε μὴ τὸ προσαγανακτεῖν οἷς ἂν ὑμᾶς οἱ ἡγεμόνες πράττειν ἀξιῶσι. Cf. also c. Apionem II, 183, 291f. The Stoics believed that man acquired freedom by living in accordance with Logos, the natural law that was the governing principle of all things. Philo developed this notion under a thin veneer of Judaism in the treatise Quod Omnis Probus Liber Sit (note, e.g., 44, ἆρ' ἄξιον τὸν προνομίας τοσαύτης τετυχηκότα (one who

344

like Moses worshipped the true God) δοῦλον ἢ μόνον ἐλεύθερον εἶναι νομίζειν;). The Rabbis and the Stoics, however, did not think of 'truth' and 'freedom' in the same way, and it must not be assumed that John's thought was either Stoic or rabbinic. ἐλεύθερος, ἐλευθεροῦν occur in this context (vv. 32f., 36) only in John, and it is clear (v. 34) that by them John means to express primarily the Christian liberation from sin; that is, being made free is nothing other than a synonym for salvation (cf. 17.3, where knowing God is the ground of eternal life). Again, knowledge does not stand over against faith as purely rational analysis (Bultmann, 435) but involves a relation of man to God (see Introduction, pp. 81f., and on 1.10). Ignatius, *Philad.* 8.1; Odes of Solomon 10.3; 17.9ff.; 42.15ff. may be compared, but the parallels are not close.

33. ἀπεκρίθησαν. Again the colloquy proceeds by means of a misunderstanding; the Jews fail to grasp what Jesus means by freedom, and that they can have it only as a gift, not as a moral or political achievement.

σπέρμα 'Αβραάμ ἐσμεν. Cf. Gen. 12.2, *et al.*; in the New Testament, Rom. 9.7; 11.1; 2 Cor. 11.22; Gal. 3.16; Heb. 2.16; also Matt. 3.8f.; Luke 3.8; cf. Dodd, *Tradition*, 331.

οὐδενὶ δεδουλεύκαμεν πώποτε. Cf. *Shabbath* 128a, All Israelites [being descended from Abraham, Isaac, and Jacob] are kings' sons (attributed to R. Aqiba and others). Cf. Josephus, *Bel.* vii, 323, Long ago, my brave men, we determined neither to serve (δουλεύειν) the Romans nor any other save God, for he alone is man's true and righteous Lord ... (336) ... we preferred death to slavery (θάνατον ἑλόμενοι πρὸ δουλείας). The true 'seed of Abraham' was reckoned through Isaac 'the son of the free woman', not through Ishmael 'the son of the bondwoman' (cf. Gal. 4.22–31). It is probable that the claim John puts into the mouth of the Jewish objectors is not that they have never been in political subjection (which would have been absurd), but that they have never lost their inward freedom of soul; but this very claim, uttered in human pride over against the representative of God himself, is an instance of the bondage referred to in v. 34. Bauer (125) aptly compares Mark 2.17 where the Jews are confident that they are well and have no need of a physician. Here they are confident that they are free men and have no need of a liberator; cf. also 9.40f. See the reference to Philo on v. 32.

34. ὁ ποιῶν τὴν ἁμαρτίαν. Cf. 1 John 3.4,8f.; also the corresponding expression, ποιεῖν τὴν ἀλήθειαν, John 3.21; 1 John 1.6. The use of the verb ποιεῖν insists upon the actual performance of sinful acts, and the meaning is twofold. He who actually commits sin demonstrates thereby that he is already the slave of sin; also, by the very sin he commits he makes himself still further a slave. Sidebottom, 94f., sees here a reference to the *Testament of Abraham*.

δοῦλός ἐστιν τῆς ἁμαρτίας. This notion is not characteristically Jewish. Cf. however a saying attribu ed to R. Aqiba († *c.* A.D. 135): In the beginning it (the evil *yetzer* or inclination) is like a spider's thread, but in the end it is like a ship's cable (*Gen. R.* 22.11). Cf. also T. Asher 3.2; T. Judah 19.4. In Greek thought the notion of bondage to and through sin is comparatively common. In the opening lines of his treatise (referred to above) *Quod Omnis Probus Liber Sit* Philo refers to a companion work περὶ τοῦ δοῦλον εἶναι πάντα φαῦλον. See also *C.H.* x, 8, ἡ κακοδαίμων [*sc.* ψυχή], ἀγνοήσασα ἑαυτήν, δουλεύει σώμασιν ἀλλοκότοις καὶ μοχθηροῖς. This last parallel is significant, but it must be observed that John does not say that the soul is the slave of the body, but that the man who practises sin is, body and soul, the slave of sin. Sin is not a concomitant of matter as such but an alien power which takes possession of the will and makes use of the whole man. Cf. Rom. 6.17, δοῦλοι τῆς ἁμαρτίας. The last words (τῆς ἁμαρτίας) are omitted by D b sin Clement; they may be an editorial supplement (rightly) giving the sense of the passage, provided that sin is understood not simply in moral terms but as the barrier between man and God.

35. The connection of this verse with its context is not immediately apparent. It must be remembered that in v. 33 there began a discussion, which continues to the end of the chapter, of the true descendants of Abraham. This recalls Gen. 21.9; Gal. 4.30. The free son, Isaac, remains in the household, while the slave-born son, Ishmael, is driven out. The Jews now claim to be the free sons of Abraham, but in truth they are not, being slaves (not of Abraham but of sin). Hence their status is lost; cf. Mark 12.9; Matt. 3.9; 8.11f., and many other passages. Who then is the son, who abides for ever? Not the Christian, it seems, but Christ himself, who in John is regularly υἱὸς τοῦ θεοῦ, while Christians are τέκνα. Jesus is both the true σπέρμα Ἀβραάμ (cf. Gal. 3.16) and the Son of God. He abides for ever. This εἰς τὸν αἰῶνα renders improbable the view (Dodd, *Tradition*, 379–82) that in this verse ὁ υἱός and ὁ δοῦλος are elements in a parable. The words ὁ υἱὸς μένει εἰς τὸν αἰῶνα are omitted by ℵ 33 and a few other MSS., probably by homoeoteleuton. On αἰών in John see on 4.14.

36. υἱός in this verse as in v. 35 is Jesus, free himself and the liberator of others. Cf. Gal. 5.1; Rom. 8.2. Alternatively, the parable of v. 35 is continued.

ὄντως. The Jews counted themselves free, but theirs was a false freedom. To be made free by the Son, who never acts except in harmony with the Father's will, is to be liberated by God himself, and thus to share the only true freedom. ὄντως is similar in meaning to ἀληθῶς; see on 1.9 for this group of words.

37. σπέρμα Ἀβραάμ ἐστε. Cf. v. 33. In the physical sense this was indisputable, and in this sense Jesus admits it. But the truth, hinted at in v. 35, appears in vv. 38b, 39f., 44.

ζητεῖτέ με ἀποκτεῖναι. Cf. 7.32; 8.20. The words follow oddly after v. 31, τοὺς πεπιστευκότας. Either John is writing very carelessly or he means that the faith of these Jews was very deficient.

οὐ χωρεῖ must mean 'has no place in', or perhaps, 'does not operate in'. Cf. 15.7.

38. The contrast between Jesus and the Jews in their different lines of descent is carried further, and the original point of departure abandoned (though it continues to influence the discourse). Descent from Abraham gives of the Jews a false, and of Jesus an inadequate, description. The father of Jesus is God, of the Jews the devil; he and they both draw their activity from their parentage. Jesus does not speak of himself, but reveals what he has seen in the Father's presence (παρά with the dative; he was—and is—with God; cf. 1.1, also 5.19). The Jews do the things they have heard from their father (the devil); here παρά is used with the genitive; their existence is purely human. M. 1, 85 suggests that τοῦ πατρός means ('God) the Father', not 'your father (the devil)'. If this translation be adopted ποιεῖτε must be taken as an imperative, as it must be (if read—see below) in v. 39. But it seems that this verse contains a statement rather than a command, and the true parallel is v. 41, where ποιεῖτε is an indicative.

ἠκούσατε] ἑωράκατε (with minor variations), P⁶⁶ ℵ* D ω it vg sin pesh hl sah Tertullian. This variant is doubtless due to assimilation, and a failure to perceive the difference between the direct seeing of supernatural things which Jesus enjoys, and the hearing which is possible for men.

39. τὰ ἔργα τοῦ ᾿Αβραάμ ποιεῖτε. 'Conduct is the clue to paternity' (Sanders). Descent from Abraham, in the only true sense, cannot be proved by a pedigree; see on vv. 33f. and cf. Rom. 2.28f.; 9.6f. The latter passage is so close to the Johannine that it (or some similar Pauline argument) may well have been known to John. Cf. also the Q passage (Matt. 3.9 = Luke 3.8) where John the Baptist bids the Jews not to claim descent from Abraham but to bring forth fruit worthy of repentance. Imitation of Abraham was of course commended in Jewish circles also; e.g. *P. Aboth* 5.19: A good eye and a humble spirit and a lowly soul—[they in whom are these] are of the disciples of Abraham our father.

The text of v. 39b has been transmitted in several forms. The chief variants are:

(i) ἐστε, P⁶⁶ ℵ B D vg Origen Augustine: ἦτε, Θ ω it sah boh.
(ii) ἐποιεῖτε, P⁷⁵ ℵ* B² D Θ it sah boh Origen: ποιεῖτε, P⁶⁶ B* vg: ἐποιεῖτε ἄν, ω.

Only two strictly 'correct' forms of this conditional sentence are possible: (a) ἐστέ... ποιεῖτε; (b) ἦτε... ἐποιεῖτε ἄν, though 'the addition of ἄν in the apodosis was no longer obligatory' (B.D., §360, 1; see 9.33; 15.22,24; 19.11; *P. Oxy.* 526.10ff., and other papyri). It is very probable on transcriptional grounds that the original text was neither (a) nor (b) and that the variants arose as attempts to improve the Greek. The weight of MS. evidence suggests that the original reading was ἐστέ... ἐποιεῖτε. This must be translated, 'If you were... you would do...'; the present tense (ἐστέ), and possibly the absence of ἄν, give greater vividness—'If you *really* were...' (cf. Luke 17.6, 'If you *only* had...'). The evidence of P⁶⁶ however strengthens the case for ποιεῖτε, and Sanders may be right in taking the sentence ironically: If (as you claim) you are Abraham's children, then (I suppose I must admit that) you were doing what Abraham used to do (when you attacked me).

40. νῦν δὲ ζητεῖτε. The adversative δέ supports the reading of the potential imperfect (ἐποιεῖτε) in v. 39. In fact the Jews show works very different from those of Abraham. The contrast is not only moral; Abraham's mind was not closed against the truth.

τὴν ἀλήθειαν ὑμῖν λελάληκα. ἀλήθεια, as the following relative clause shows, must be not simply 'what is true' but '*the* truth' revealed in the whole mission of Jesus from God.

41. τοῦ πατρὸς ὑμῶν. Cf. v. 38. The 'father' intended is of course the devil; v. 44.

ἡμεῖς ἐκ πορνείας οὐκ ἐγεννήθημεν (there are several variants, none significant, of the last word). The Jews find a fresh way of turning the argument against Jesus. The implication (especially of the emphatic ἡμεῖς) is that Jesus was born of πορνεία. This allegation is found in Jewish sources (the earliest probable—not certain—reference is *Yebamoth* 4.13: R. Simeon b. Azzai (*c.* A.D. 110) said: I found a family register in Jerusalem and in it was written, 'Such-a-one is a bastard through [a transgression of the law of] thy neighbour's wife'; see further R. T. Herford, *Christianity in Talmud and Midrash* (1903), 35-50) and also in the accusation of Celsus (*apud* Origen, *c. Celsum* I, 28).

ἕνα πατέρα ἔχομεν τὸν θεόν. Cf. vv. 33, 34, 39; also Matt. 23.9 (Dodd, *Tradition*, 331f.); the theme of fatherhood cannot stop short on the human level, and the Jews now trace their ancestry not to Abraham but to God. It is probable that John is subtly bringing out by implication what he believes to be the truth regarding the birth of Jesus, who, though the circumstances might to the uninitiated suggest fornication, was in fact born of no human act but of God (see on 1.13). His main contention however is not that the birth of Jesus was effected in a particular way, but that Jesus was from God: see the next verse.

42. Cf. v. 39; if appropriate behaviour may be expected from descendants of Abraham, much more should children of God love his Son. They above all should recognize that he had come from God (cf. 3.2; 1 John 5.1).

καὶ ἥκω. This word may suggest the arrival of a divine prophet; cf. Philostratus, *Vita Apollonii* I, 1, ὡς ἐκ Διὸς ἥκοντα; Origen, *c. Celsum* VII, 9, ἐγὼ ὁ θεός εἰμι, ἢ θεοῦ παῖς . . . ἥκω δὲ . . . ἐγὼ δὲ σῶσαι θέλω. But the word need not recall the connotation of such passages as these; it means simply 'I have come'. ἐξῆλθον denotes the departure of Jesus ἐκ τοῦ θεοῦ, ἥκω his arrival in the world.

οὐδὲ γὰρ ἀπ' ἐμαυτοῦ ἐλήλυθα, ἀλλ' ἐκεῖνός με ἀπέστειλεν. Once more the mission of Jesus is emptied of every suggestion of self-will or self-seeking. This is a very common and essential Johannine emphasis; see especially 5.19-30 and the notes. Jesus did not come into the world of his own accord; he came because he was sent. His ministry has significance not in any wisdom or virtue of his own (nor in a miraculous birth—see on v. 41), but in the fact that he is the delegate of God himself. His debates must not be understood as self-defence; they are a manifestation of the Father. For the 'sending' of Jesus see on 20.21.

43. λαλιάν . . . λόγον. The two words must be distinguished or the sentence is meaningless. λαλιά is audible speech, the spoken word (not, of course, 'chatter' or 'loquacity' as often in earlier Greek): the Jews fail to understand the sayings they hear (cf. their frequent misunderstandings, e.g. in this chapter vv. 19, 22, 25, 33, etc.). This is because they cannot grasp and obey (for the use of ἀκούειν see on 5.24) Jesus' *message*, the divine Word which he bears (and indeed is). See Dodd, *Interpretation*, 266.

οὐ δύνασθε must be given full weight; cf. 12.39.

44. ὑμεῖς ἐκ τοῦ πατρὸς τοῦ διαβόλου ἐστέ. It would be possible to translate 'You are of the father of the devil', but, though the last clause of the verse (see below) lends a superficial attraction to this rendering, and there are some gnostic parallels (see Bernard 313, Bauer, 127-9), it is unsatisfactory.

The contrast requires the sharpest contrast with God the Father of Jesus, and this is found in the devil, who destroys the life God creates (ἀνθρωποκτόνος) and denies the truth God reveals (ψεύστης). 1 John 3.8 puts the interpretation beyond doubt. Translate therefore '... your father the devil', though to express this unambiguously πατρός should not have had the article (B.D., §268, 2).

τὰς ἐπιθυμίας τοῦ πατρὸς ὑμῶν, the desires characteristic of your father, θέλετε ποιεῖν, you mean, intend, to do, are set upon doing. See Isa. 43.27 (Guilding, 108).

ἀνθρωποκτόνος ἦν ἀπ' ἀρχῆς, because he robbed Adam of immortality, Gen. 3, cf. Wisd. 2.24; Ecclus. 25.24; Rom. 5.12. Just as the Word is what he is in the beginning (1.1), so the devil is what he is from the beginning.

ἐν τῇ ἀληθείᾳ οὐκ ἔστηκεν. The variant οὐχ (P[75] ω) is to be rejected, but it is not impossible that we should read οὐκ ἔστηκεν (see M. II, 100). This would mean (perfect of ἵστημι with present intransitive meaning) 'does not stand in the truth'. It is however better to take the smooth breathing, and take ἔστηκεν as the imperfect of the late verb στήκειν (see on 1.26), 'did not stand', 'was not standing'. This would agree well with the ἀπ' ἀρχῆς of the preceding sentence; possibly a fall from truth ἐν ἀρχῇ is presupposed. The converse statement (οὐκ ἔστιν ἀλήθεια ἐν αὐτῷ), in which ἀλήθεια does not have the article (see Moule, *Idiom Book* 112), is intended to emphasize that the devil has nothing in common with truth. Cf. Eph. 4.21. ζωή and ἀλήθεια bestow authenticity of existence; hence the devil kills and lies (Bultmann).

τὸ ψεῦδος, what is false, takes the article in parallel with ἡ ἀλήθεια.

ἐκ τῶν ἰδίων, of his own substance or characteristics. Lying is his nature.

καὶ ὁ πατὴρ αὐτοῦ. The construction is very harsh but it seems that there is no acceptable alternative to the rendering 'he is a liar and the father of it [that is, of the lie, or falsehood]'. It has been suggested that the whole sentence be taken differently: 'When a *man* speaks a lie he speaks of his own, for he is a liar, and so is his father [the devil]'; but this is more difficult still. It also seems wrong to render '... and so is his [the devil's] father', though, as noted above, the first clause in the verse could be taken in a way consonant with this. On the grammatical problem see Bultmann's full note (318f.); also Turner, *Insights*, 148ff. The awkwardness is probably due to the fact that John is forcing the negative parallel with Jesus and his Father.

45. ἐγὼ δὲ ὅτι. The ἐγώ stands first for emphasis: 'But I, because I ...'. It is unnecessary to conjecture a false rendering of an Aramaic ٦ (Burney, 77, M. II, 436, Black, 74, 92). The ὅτι makes excellent sense.

οὐ πιστεύετέ μοι. It is because (ὅτι) Jesus speaks the truth that they do not believe. They have inherited falsehood from their father, and can therefore no more believe the truth than they will come to the light (3.19).

46. In this verse (omitted by D), and v. 47, the foregoing arguments are resumed.

τίς ἐξ ὑμῶν ἐλέγχει με περὶ ἁμαρτίας; For ἐλέγχειν περί cf. 16.8. Accusations are made against Jesus in this chapter and elsewhere; none can be proved. Cf. T. Judah 24.1, πᾶσα ἁμαρτία οὐχ εὑρεθήσεται ἐν αὐτῷ. There is a similar saying in *Thomas* 104: Which then is the sin that I have committed, or in what have I been vanquished?

εἰ . . . οὐ πιστεύετέ μοι; Cf. v. 45; the question is answered in v. 47.

47. Only he who is from God (cf. v. 42) hears the words of God. The Jews do not hear the word of Jesus (v. 43) because they are not from God but from the devil. Their reaction results from a condition prior to the historic mission of Jesus.

48. οὐ καλῶς λέγομεν ἡμεῖς. Cf. 4.17; 13.13; also Mark 7.6, καλῶς ἐπροφήτευσεν. In Modern Greek a corresponding expression καλὰ δὲ λέμε ἐμεῖς means 'Are we not right in saying?' (Pallis, 20), and this is the meaning here.

Σαμαρίτης εἶ σύ. For the relations of Jews and Samaritans see 4.9; for John's interest in Samaritans, see 4.40ff. The Samaritans were regarded as a mixed (cf. v. 41) and apostate race. It may however be noted that the two accusations receive but a single reply (v. 49, ἐγὼ δαιμόνιον οὐκ ἔχω) and this may mean that the charge of being a Samaritan was equivalent to the charge of possession. To this suggested equivalence the best parallel that can be offered is the fact that Dositheus and Simon Magus, the Samaritans who claimed to be sons of God, were regarded as mad (possessed). Alternatively, the charge is that Jesus is a heretic; but there is no evidence that 'Samaritan' was a regular term of abuse for heretics, and it is very doubtful whether Jesus held views peculiar to the Samaritans. Cf. Justin, *Trypho* 69, and the observations on this in Martyn 64f. Cf. also Origen, *c. Celsum* VI, 11; VII, 8.

δαιμόνιον ἔχεις. This charge is brought several times in John; 7.20; 8.48,52; 10.20. Cf. Mark 3.22 and parallels. In John the charge seems to imply little more than madness (see especially v. 52) and is simply dismissed; in the Synoptic Gospels it is vigorously refuted, and becomes the occasion of important teaching. This corresponds with the absence of exorcism narratives from John.

49. τιμῶ τὸν πατέρα μου. The claims of Jesus are not arrogant or demented self-assertion but (as John constantly emphasizes) mere obedience to the Father. ἀτιμάζετε, not so much 'you insult' as the antithesis of τιμᾶν, 'you fail to give me due honour as the Father's Son'. Cf. 5.23.

50. ἐγὼ δὲ οὐ ζητῶ τὴν δόξαν μου. The converse of τιμῶ τὸν πατέρα. ἔστιν ὁ ζητῶν καὶ κρίνων. For the construction cf. 5.45. The former part of the verse compels us to supply with ζητῶν, τὴν δόξαν μου; the forensic meaning of κρίνειν is not to be found in ζητεῖν also. It is the Father who seeks the glory of Christ (as Christ seeks his), and he also judges, vindicating the truth and at the same time condemning its adversaries.

51. For the thought of this verse cf. 5.24; 6.40,47; 11.25. It is suggested by the κρίνειν of the preceding verse. Those who keep Jesus' word (14.23f.; 17.6) will escape judgement because they have already passed from death to life. Cf. Mark 9.1.
θάνατον οὐ μὴ θεωρήσῃ (='experience', like ἰδεῖν at 3.3) must refer to the death of the soul.

52. The Jews however once more suppose that Jesus' words are meant literally, and therefore amount to proof that he is mad (has a demon).
'Αβραὰμ ἀπέθανεν. Cf. *Iliad* XXI, 107; Lucretius III, 1042ff. (Bultmann).
οὐ μὴ γεύσηται θανάτου for θάνατον οὐ μη θεωρήσῃ of the previous verse. It is

doubtful whether any variation in meaning is intended; John is fond of using pairs of synonyms. γεύεσθαι θανάτου is used of physical death at Mark 9.1, and it is possible that, if a distinction between the two verbs is intended, John is ascribing to the Jews the crude view that physical immortality was claimed, whereas the truth, which they misunderstood, was that Christians should not be overcome by death. Cf. *Thomas* 1 (whoever finds the explanation of these words will not taste death); Fitzmyer, *Essays*, 370.

53. μὴ σὺ μείζων εἶ; The question of course expects the answer No, like the question of the Samaritan woman (4.12). It expresses John's characteristic irony; the true answer (known to him and his readers) is the reverse of that presumed by the Jews.

πατρὸς ἡμῶν is omitted by D W it sin. The words may have been omitted because it has already been denied that the Jews had Abraham as father (vv. 39f., 44) or added in conformity with v. 56.

καὶ οἱ προφῆται ἀπέθανον. The construction is very loose—'and so did the prophets', almost an afterthought.

τίνα σεαυτὸν ποιεῖς; Cf. 5.18; 10.33; 19.7. Once more the Jews simply invert the truth. Jesus does not make himself someone: rather he empties himself of all personal dignity and emphasizes his obedience to and dependence upon God (vv. 28, 38, 42, 50), that God may be all.

54. What Jesus 'makes' himself is of no significance; such self-glorifying would be no glory. Cf. Heb. 5.5. On δόξα, δοξάζειν, see on 1.14.

ἔστιν ὁ πατήρ μου ὁ δοξάζων με. Cf. v. 50. Jesus glorifies the Father and the Father glorifies him; cf. 17.1,4f. But this is not a visible glorification that can be proved before spectators.

θεὸς ἡμῶν ἐστιν. For ἡμῶν (P66 P75 Θ ω), ὑμῶν is read by ℵ B D; but the direct speech of the former reading is to be preferred, since the more vivid clause might be toned down into the less colourful. The Jews, claiming the promises of the Old Testament (e.g. Gen. 17.7), think of God as theirs, unmindful of the fact that by their own behaviour they have disavowed the relationship (v. 42). Cf. 4.22.

55. καὶ (adversative—'Although you claim ... yet ...') οὐκ ἐγνώκατε αὐτόν. Cf. 7.28; 1 John 2.4. No difference is intended between the verbs γινώσκειν and εἰδέναι; see on 1.10. For the perfect ἐγνώκατε cf. 6.69.

ὅμοιος ὑμῖν. ὑμῶν (P66 ℵ) may be right; cf. the Latin *vestri similis*.

τὸν λόγον αὐτοῦ τηρῶ. Cf. 15.10; 17.6. Obedience is a characteristic feature of Johannine 'gnosis'.

56. Ἀβραὰμ ὁ πατὴρ ὑμῶν—as you claim (vv. 33, 39). The argument of these verses is *ad hominem*. For the continuing life of Abraham, see J. Jeremias, *Heiligengräber in Jesu Umwelt* (1958), 134f.; Derrett, *Law*, 86; McNamara, *T. & T.*, 144f.

ἠγαλλιάσατο (a strong word, here and at 5.35 only in John) ἵνα ἴδῃ τὴν ἡμέραν τὴν ἐμήν. The ἵνα is explanatory and introduces the ground of the rejoicing; this is a feature of John's style (see Introduction, p. 8). Bauer (131) compares *B.G.U.* 1081.3, ἐχάρην ἵνα σὲ ἀσπάζομαι; cf. also the Modern Greek, χαίρομαι νά σε θωρῶ ('I'm glad to see you', M. ii, 476). The belief that to Abraham were disclosed the secrets of the age to come is at least as old as

R. Aqiba. In *Gen. R.* 44.25 there is recorded a difference of opinion between him and R. Johanan b. Zakkai, the latter holding that God revealed to Abraham this world only, while R. Aqiba believed that the age to come also had been revealed to him. If he were shown the age to come this would include the days of the Messiah. (In *Tanhuma B.* חיי שרה, §6 (60a) (S.B. ii, 525) this is deduced from Gen. 24.1, בא בימים, literally, 'He went into the days'). 'Days' (plural) is the usual Jewish expression, but for the singular cf. Luke 17.22; John, with the ministry of Jesus within his knowledge, is able to make the moment of eschatological fulfilment more precise. Abraham's rejoicing may be derived from Gen. 17.17, already taken by Philo (*Mut.* 154–69) to signify rejoicing, not incredulity. Cf. also T. Levi 18.14, Then [in the days—ἐν ταῖς ἡμέραις (v. 5)—of the 'new priest'] shall Abraham and Isaac and Jacob exult (ἀγαλλιάσεται). There is thus no need for the suggestion (Torrey, 144, 148; cf. M. ii, 475f.) that an original Aramaic בעא אברהם ('Abraham prayed...') was corrupted by the loss of an א to בע אברהם ('Abraham rejoiced...') For Abraham's foresight of Jesus cf. Barn. 7.7 (προβλέψας). It is idle to ask whether by Jesus' 'day' John intended his ministry or the coming in glory of the Son of man. He meant that the work of salvation, potentially complete in Abraham, was actually complete in Jesus.

57. πεντήκοντα ἔτη οὔπω ἔχεις. Probably fifty is a round number, and no more is intended than to point the contrast between a short life-time and the great interval separating Jesus and Abraham; but quite early this passage with 2.20 was taken to prove that Jesus during his ministry was between forty and fifty years old (Irenaeus, *adv. Haereses* ii, xxii, 5f.). Contrast Luke 3.23. Such literalism is beside the point, and invites the extension of Bultmann's comment, 'The Jews remain caught in the trammels of their own thought'. Cf. however G. Ogg, *N.T.S.* 5 (1959), 291–8.

Ἀβραὰμ ἑώρακας; The reading suggested by v. 56, Ἀβραὰμ ἑώρακέν σε, is found in P75 א sin sah; it is doubtless a correction. The reply of the Jews (according to the better text) differs from the statement of Jesus because, assuming the superiority of Abraham (v. 53), they naturally think of Jesus seeing Abraham (if such a thing were possible).

58. πρὶν Ἀβραὰμ γενέσθαι. Before Abraham came into existence; perhaps, before Abraham was born, since γίνεσθαι can have this meaning. Cf. v. 56; Isa. 43.13 (Guilding, 108).

ἐγὼ εἰμί. On the absolute use of these words see on v. 24. The meaning here is: Before Abraham came into being, I eternally was, as now I am, and ever continue to be. Cf. *Thomas* 19: Blessed is he who was before he came into being. Cf. Ps. 90.2. Lindars is right in saying that there is no allusion here to Exod. 3.14.

59. λίθους. Cf. 10.31–3; 11.8. Stoning was the punishment for blasphemy (Lev. 24.16; *Sanhedrin* 7.4), but this does not mean that Jesus had claimed to be God. See the important note in Bultmann, 327f.

ἐκρύβη, reflexive, as ἐκρύβην at Gen. 3.10. Cf. 12.36; Jesus deliberately withdraws, but the concealment is only temporary; see 9.1. For Jesus' escape from arrest cf. 7.30,44; 8.20; also 18.6. Adversaries are powerless against him until he wills his own death at the appointed time. John probably intended to suggest a supernatural disappearance, comparable with the obscurity whence Jesus had come (7.4,10).

ἐκ τοῦ ἱεροῦ. Cf. v. 20. The text is expanded by the addition of (καὶ) διελθὼν διὰ μέσου αὐτῶν (ἐπορεύετο), καὶ παρῆγεν οὕτω in ℵ^{ca} Θ^c ω λ pesh hl boh; but the shorter text is almost certainly right. The longer text is an assimilation to Luke 4.30; there may be some traditional connection between the two narratives. Davies (*Land*, 290–6) assigns a special place to this verse in the development of John's presentation of Jesus. After Jesus has replaced the Sabbath (ch. 5), the manna (ch. 6), and the water and light ceremonies of Tabernacles (chs. 7 and 8), and before he is consecrated (at Dedication) as the replacement of Tabernacle and Temple (ch. 10), we see here 'the departure of the Divine Presence from the old "Holy Space"' (296).

[handwritten margin: "Replacement Theme" see Also Brown, "community"]

19. THE MAN BORN BLIND: JUDGEMENT AT WORK

9.1–41

The foundation of this chapter is twofold: a simple miracle story in which blindness is cured, and the saying, I am the light of the world (cf. 8.12). The miracle is an efficacious sign of the truth of the saying, and the divisive, judging effect of the light, alluded to elsewhere (3.19ff., cf. 12.35f.,46), is brought out in the narrative. The means of transition from the story of healing to the pronouncement of judgement is found in the fact that the miracle takes place on a Sabbath.

The narrative element is straightforward but skilfully handled. Jesus is not asked to cure the blind man; he acts entirely of his own volition, but uses means of cure not unknown to contemporary medicine and magic. An instructive parallel to the whole incident is found in Dittenberger, *Syll.* 1173.15–18 (Deissmann, 132). In this inscription a miraculous cure (probably by Asclepius) is recorded as follows:

To Valerius Aper, a blind soldier, the god revealed that he should go (ἐλθεῖν, cf. v. 7, ὕπαγε) and take the blood of a white cock, together with honey, and rub them into an eyesalve (cf. the use made of clay and spittle, v. 6) and anoint (ἐπιχρεῖσαι, cf. v. 11) his eyes three days. And he received his sight (ἀνέβλεψε, cf. v. 11), and came (ἐλήλυθεν, cf. v. 7, ἦλθεν) and gave thanks publicly to the god.

As in the inscription, the cure is not effected instantly; before it is completed the man must wash in a specified water. When however it is complete no small astonishment results, and doubt is cast on the identity of the man who professes to have been blind and to have been made to see. Sure of his sight, he knows only that his benefactor's name is Jesus, but nothing of his whereabouts. At this point, when the man is brought to the Pharisees, the sabbath question is raised and produces a dilemma. Jesus must be a sinner for he breaks the Sabbath: Jesus cannot be a sinner for a sinner could not work such a cure. Further inquiry only confirms the basic facts of the case, and the Jews are reduced to abuse. They contrast Jesus, who is of unknown origin and authority, with Moses through whom God gave the sabbath law; and they expel the blind man, who dares to question their assumptions. At this point Jesus re-enters the story in person. First, he discloses his identity to the man whom he has cured; the latter believes and worships him, thus showing that he has received spiritual as well as physical sight. Next, speaking in his character as the light of the world, he states the awful purpose of his mission: For judgement did I come into the world, that those who see not might see and those who see might become blind (v. 39). The Pharisees, interjecting a question, are met with a specific condemnation based on the general principle just stated.

This short chapter expresses perhaps more vividly and completely than any other John's conception of the work of Christ. On the one hand, he is the giver of benefits to a humanity which apart from him is in a state of complete hopelessness: it was never heard that one should open the eyes of a man born blind (v. 32). The illumination is not presented as primarily intellectual (as in some of the Hermetic tractates) but as the direct bestowal of life or salvation (and thus it is comparable with the gift of living water (4.10; 7.37f.) and of the bread of life (6.27)). On the other hand, Jesus does not come into a world full of men aware of their own need. Many have their own inadequate lights (e.g. the Old Testament, 5.39f.) which they are too proud to relinquish for the true light which now shines. The effect of the true light is to blind them, since they wilfully close their eyes to it. Their sin abides precisely because they are so confident of their righteousness.

The cure of the blind man has no precise parallel in the Synoptic Gospels (for similar stories cf. Mark 8.22-6; 10.46-52). There is no need to suppose it invented as a whole; it was probably drawn from the still-flowing stream of tradition. The charge that Jesus failed properly to observe the Sabbath is found several times in the Synoptic Gospels and has already occurred in the Fourth (see the Introduction to and notes on 5.1-18). For earlier traditional material bearing on the pronouncement 'I am the light of the world' see the note on 8.12. The divisive, critical effect of the ministry of Jesus upon his contemporaries is also deeply rooted in the earlier tradition. The allegation that Jesus casts out demons by Beelzebul is met (Mark 3.28ff.) by the pronouncement that such blasphemy against the Holy Spirit is never forgiven; it is an eternal sin (cf. v. 41, ἡ ἁμαρτία ὑμῶν μένει). The synoptic parables reveal at once a distinction between οἱ περὶ αὐτὸν σὺν τοῖς δώδεκα and ἐκεῖνοι οἱ ἔξω (Mark 4.10f.) and a few verses later in Mark we learn that to him that has shall be given, while from him that has not shall be taken away even that which he has (4.25). Jesus observes a hardening (πώρωσις, Mark 3.5; cf. 6.52; 8.17) in those who have eyes but fail to see (the πώρωσις in Mark 3.1-6, if understood as blindness, could have suggested the present sabbath story). And much of the syn-

354

optic material suggests that the ministry of Jesus constitutes the test by which men will stand or fall (such sayings as, e.g., Mark 8.38; Matt. 11.6, 21-4; Luke 7.23; 10.13-16, and many others). John has with unsurpassed artistry and with profound theological insight brought out one of the major themes of the Christian faith. (For the same theme in Paul cf. Rom. 9-11; 1 Cor. 1.18,23f.; 2 Cor. 2.15, and other passages.)

John's insight into the theological significance of the earlier tradition is the most important single factor in the shaping of this chapter, and, unlike other kinds of analysis, hardly a matter of conjecture. It may be, for example, that the Tabernacles lections Lev. 13, 2 Kings 5; Deut. 10, 2 Kings 13.23ff. affected the story and also account for parallels with John 15,16 (Guilding, 121-5), but the allusions are by no means explicit. Vv. 2-5 may be a Johannine interpolation into a traditional story (Dodd, *Tradition*, 184-8), but though v. 5 (and possibly v. 4) serve the useful purpose of a cross-reference to 8.12 this cannot be said of vv. 2,3. There is a clear break between v. 7 and v. 8, but to say that vv. 8-41 must be a dramatic expansion because miracle stories are interested only in the healer and not in the healed (Martyn, 5) overstates the matter. John may have intended to convey teaching on baptism (see especially Brown, 380ff.), often in the early church thought, and spoken, of as φωτισμός; there is no doubt (see also Hoskyns) that the chapter was early associated with baptism. But John himself never makes the association explicit (cf. his allusion to the eucharist in 6.51-6), and we impoverish his theology if we make it so. He is concerned with faith, conversion, light, darkness, judgement, rather than with particular settings for them, however important in their own way these may be. Cf. Schnackenburg II, 325-8.

This observation may lead to a reference to Martyn, whose book on the setting of John finds its starting-point in this chapter. (There is an important anticipation of it, to which unfortunately Martyn does not refer, by the late E. L. Allen, *J.B.L.* 74 (1955), 88-92.) The essence of Martyn's hypothesis (for which see further Introduction, pp. 137f.) is that John 'wishes to show how the Risen Lord continues his earthly ministry in the work of his servant, the Christian preacher' (9). John thus writes history on two levels, a simple historical level which gives a narrative of what was done and said by Jesus, but also a contemporary level which (though still in the form of a story about Jesus) describes the Christian mission to Jews and their response to it. Details will be brought out in the notes below. Many of Martyn's suggestions are convincing; it is certainly true that John's fundamental concern was to apply the traditional story of Jesus to the post-resurrection (and indeed end-of-century) period. He is however in some danger of narrowing the scope of John's work, which was rather to bring out the full theological content of the tradition than to adapt it to a particular diaspora setting.

See also Bornkamm IV, 65-72.

1. παράγων. Jesus is presumably still in Jerusalem, presumably not still in the Temple (8.59). The participle conveys only the vaguest indication of the circumstances; cf. Mark 1.16.

ἐκ γενετῆς. At Acts 3.2; 14.8 men are described as having been ill ἐκ κοιλίας μητρός. γενετή is not used elsewhere in the New Testament, but John's expression is good Greek for 'from the hour of birth'. This feature of the man's case is often used as evidence of John's 'heightening the miraculous', and v. 32 to some extent supports this view; but it seems probable that John also has in mind the fact that mankind is not by nature receptive of the light (cf. 1.5,10f.). Man is spiritually blind from birth. The present narrative, combined with Mark 10.46–52, is probably alluded to in the Acts of Pilate 6.2 (And another Jew came forward and said: I was born blind: I heard words but I saw no man's face: and as Jesus passed by I cried with a loud voice: Have mercy on me, O Son of David. And he took pity on me and put his hands upon mine eyes and I received sight immediately).

2. τίς ἥμαρτεν. It is assumed that sin, by whomsoever committed, was the cause of the blindness. This was the common belief in Judaism (not only in Judaism; for Lucian see Betz, 156); see e.g. Shabbath 55 a: There is no death without sin (proved by Ezek. 18.20) and no punishment (i.e. sufferings) without guilt (proved by Ps. 89.33). When a man has been blind from birth, the sin must be sought either in the man's parents, or in his own ante-natal existence. That the sins of parents could lead to physical defects in their children is attested in passages cited in S.B. II, 529, and ante-natal sin was regarded as possible; see the interpretation of Gen. 25.22 in Gen. R. 63.6; also Song of Songs R. 1.41 (when a pregnant woman worships in a heathen temple the foetus also commits idolatry). The continuation shows that more is involved here than a 'biblical conundrum' (Guilding, 124) based on 2 Kings 14.6. All history serves the glory of God and its manifestation in Jesus. ἵνα here expresses result.

3. οὔτε οὗτος ἥμαρτεν οὔτε οἱ γονεῖς αὐτοῦ. Not all sickness could be ascribed to sin. It was recognized that there were יסורין של אהבה, 'punishments of love'. 'If the sufferer accepted them willingly, long life, confirmation of his knowledge of Torah, and forgiveness of all sins were his reward' (S.B. II, 193). Such chastisements cannot however be in mind here, for they might be recognized by the fact that they did not hinder the study of the Law, as blindness certainly would do. Moreover John's positive account of the purpose of the man's suffering is different (see next note).

ἀλλ' ἵνα φανερωθῇ τὰ ἔργα τοῦ θεοῦ ἐν αὐτῷ. The expression is elliptical, but the meaning is clear: Neither his own sin nor his parents' was the cause of his being born blind; he was born blind in order that (or, with the result that— cf. the use of ἵνα in v. 2) ... Cf. 11.4; Lazarus's sickness is ὑπὲρ τῆς δόξης τοῦ θεοῦ. The question with regard to ἵνα is grammatically interesting but theologically less important than at first appears. In any case John would not suppose that the man's birth and blindness were outside the control, and therefore the purpose, of God. Cf. Exod. 9.16, ἕνεκεν τούτου διετηρήθης ἵνα ἐνδείξωμαι ἐν σοὶ τὴν ἰσχύν μου, καὶ ὅπως διαγγελῇ τὸ ὄνομά μου ἐν πάσῃ τῇ γῇ, quoted (with several variants) in Rom. 9.17. The ἵνα is too closely in accord with John's style and thought to make it necessary to suppose that ἵνα ... ἐν αὐτῷ misrepresents an Aramaic relative (J. Héring, Le Royaume de Dieu et sa

Venue (1937), 22, n. 2), or that it is used imperatively (Turner, *Insights*, 145f.). τὰ ἔργα τοῦ θεοῦ finds a parallel in 1QS 4.4 (מעשי אל), but, as Braun points out, John and Qumran are drawing independently on the Old Testament. Here the works of God are 'the works God wills me to do'. The same words are used in a different sense at 6.28. See further Introduction, p. 75, and on 4.34; 5.36.

4. ἡμᾶς δεῖ ἐργάζεσθαι τὰ ἔργα τοῦ πέμψαντός με. The singular pronoun is read throughout by Θ Ω it vg sin pesh, the plural by P⁶⁶ P⁷⁵ ℵ* and a few other MSS.; there can be little doubt that B D are right with ἡμᾶς ... με. This, the more difficult reading, corresponds to other passages (notably 3.11) where Jesus associates with himself the apostolic community which he has gathered about him. As the Father has sent him so he sends them (20.21—see the note), and therefore upon them as upon him there rests the obligation to do the work of God while opportunity lasts. It is not suggested that the disciples took any part in the miracle; but cf. 14.12. The ἡμᾶς is particularly important to Martyn (7f.) since it points to the 'continuation of Jesus' works ... in the deeds of Christian witnesses'. Dodd (*Tradition*, 186) however sees in 'We must work while it is day' a proverb which John adopts to his use by adding τὰ ἔργα τοῦ πέμψαντός με.

ἕως ἡμέρα ἐστίν. ἕως with the present indicative and meaning 'while' is used here only in John; at 21.22,23 it means 'until'. Cf. 12.35,36, where ὡς is used (so here also in W and a few other MSS.). Cf. *P. Aboth* 2.15: R. Tarfon (c. A.D. 130) said: The day (cf., however, pp. 241f.) is short and the task is great and the labourers are idle and the wage is abundant and the master of the house is urgent. Here 'the day' refers to the length of a man's life; it has the same meaning in John, with however special reference to the fact that Jesus' life is the appointed 'day of salvation', and that Jesus himself is the light of the world, whose departure means the coming of night—ἔρχεται νύξ. The same twofold imagery is continued in this phrase. νύξ is used with more than its literal meaning at 11.10; 13.30 (and perhaps 3.2, cf. 19.39), and doubtless here.

5. ὅταν ἐν τῷ κόσμῳ ὦ. It would have been better to repeat the ἕως of the previous verse. John does not mean 'As often as I am in the world' or 'When I am in the world' (implying some future uncertainty). To be 'in the world' (בעולם, *ba'olam*, in rabbinic Hebrew,) is to be alive—'in the land of the living'; but in view of the special use of κόσμος in John (see on 1.10) more than this must be intended here; because God loved the world Jesus was sent into the world to save it: 'While I live my human life, and while I carry out my earthly mission of salvation.'

φῶς εἰμι τοῦ κόσμου. See on 8.12. The statement here lacks the emphatic Johannine ἐγώ εἰμι (and thereby perhaps underlines the significance of that form when it does occur; pronouncements can be made without it). Even more clearly than at 8.12 it here appears that 'light' is not a metaphysical definition of the person of Jesus but a description of his effect upon the cosmos; he is the light which judges and saves it. In him only the world has its day in which men may walk safely (12.35); in his absence is darkness.

6. ταῦτα εἰπών. The connection with what goes before is very close. Having declared that his mission in the world is to be its light Jesus proceeds at

once to illustrate his words by giving light to the blind man, and by judging those who, confident in their own vision, turn their back upon the true light. At the same time, he is as an obedient man doing God's will while he has opportunity.

ἔπτυσεν χαμαί. In this miracle (contrast 2.3; 4.47; 11.3; cf. 5.6) Jesus takes the initiative. The blind man, introduced as the theme of a theological debate, becomes the object of divine mercy and a place of revelation. Spittle is used in two Marcan miracles (Mark 7.33; 8.23); not elsewhere in the New Testament. χαμαί is used only at 9.6; 18.6; it is used as here for χαμᾶζε by classical writers also. In antiquity spittle was believed to be of medicinal value; see, e.g., the well-known story of Vespasian at Alexandria (Tacitus, *Historiae* IV, 81 ... *precabaturque principem ut genas et oculorum orbes dignaretur respergere oris excremento ... caeco reluxit dies;* Suetonius, *Vespasian* 7; Dio Cassius LXV, 8). Tacitus rationalizes, but the use of spittle was in general accompanied by magical practices (cf. Betz, 150) which made it suspect in Judaism. Thus at *Sanhedrin* 10.1 R. Aqiba says that 'he ... that utters charms over a wound' has no share in the world to come, but the *Tosephta* (12.10 (433)) adds to the same saying, 'He that ... and spits' (ורוקק). In this case however the spitting is upon the wound, not upon the ground; but the practice recorded in John is reflected in a saying attributed to Samuel (died A.D. 254): One must not put fasting spittle on the eyes on the Sabbath (*Y. Shabbath* 14, 14d, 17f.). This was the application of a general principle: anointing on the Sabbath was allowed only with those fluids commonly used for anointing on weekdays. *Shabbath* 14.4: If his loins pain him he may not rub thereon wine or vinegar, yet he may anoint them with oil but not with rose-oil. King's children may anoint their wounds with rose-oil since it is their custom so to do on ordinary days. Irenaeus (*adv. Haer.* v, xv, 2 ... that which the artificer, the Word, had omitted to form in the womb, he then supplied in public) saw an allusion here to Gen. 2.7, but this is improbable.

For ἐπέθηκεν (B and a few other MSS.) ἐπέχρισεν is very well attested (P66 P75 ℵ D W Θ ω) but may be due to assimilation to v. 11; ἐπέχρισεν would have been followed by an accusative, not by ἐπί. For the act of anointing cf. the cure of the soldier recounted in the inscription quoted in the introduction to this section.

7. ὕπαγε νίψαι. The asyndetic juxtaposition of two imperatives may be a sign of Semitism (Black, 64). It is however possible that νίψαι should be omitted (with one MS.; see B.D., §205). If νίψαι is read, for the construction cf. Epictetus III, xxii, 71, ἵν᾽ αὐτὸ λούσῃ εἰς σκάφην. In John νίπτειν is used only in this chapter and in ch. 13. There it is always active (except at 13.10, νίψασθαι); in this chapter it is always middle. The double imperative does not occur at 2 Kings 5.10 (πορευθεὶς λοῦσαι), but there may be an allusion to the story of Naaman; see p. 355.

εἰς (unless νίψαι is omitted, used, as often in late Greek, for ἐν) τὴν κολυμβήθραν τοῦ Σιλωάμ (ὃ ἑρμηνεύεται Ἀπεσταλμένος). For John's manner of explaining non-Greek words see on 1.38. The Pool of Siloam (Isa. 8.6, cf. Neh. 3.15) was situated within the city walls, at the southern extremity of the Tyropoean valley. The Hebrew name is שלח (*shiloah*), derived from שלח, to send. At Isa. 8.6 (there is no rendering at Neh. 3.15) the Hebrew name is rendered by the LXX Σ(ε)ιλωάμ; Josephus customarily uses a declinable form Σιλωά.

John, with whom ἀποστέλλειν and πέμπειν are important words (see on 20.21), brings out the derivation of the name of the pool. Jesus himself is ὁ ἀπεσταλμένος, and he gives light to the blind, just as he is himself a spring of living water. In Isa. 8.6 it is said that the Jews refused the waters of Shiloah, just as in this chapter they refuse Jesus; and at Gen. 49.10 the similar but not identical name שׁילה (shiloh) appears, and was, rightly or wrongly, interpreted messianically by both Jews and Christians (thus *Gen. R.* 98.13; 99.10; *Targum of Onqelos*). It was from Siloam that the water used in the libations at the feast of Tabernacles (see on 7.37f.) was drawn.

ἀπῆλθεν οὖν. The man's obedience was complete and so was his cure.

8. τὸ πρότερον. For the adverbial use cf. 6.62; 7.50.

ὅτι προσαίτης ἦν. The subject of the ὅτι clause has been attracted into the principal sentence, where it becomes the object. Cf. 4.35, and see M. II, 469; there is no need to suppose (Burney, 78) that ὅτι is a misrendering of the Aramaic ד, which should here have been translated ὅτε.

9. ἐγώ εἰμι. I am he, the man you speak of. ἐγώ εἰμι is used in the same way in 4.26. This simple use of the words warns the reader against assuming that ἐγώ εἰμι was necessarily to John a religious formula. At this point he is writing simple narrative. Lightfoot's comment, 'Underlying these two verses [8 and 9] is the question whether a man after baptism and rebirth is the same person as before, or not', is too sophisticated.

10. ἠνεῴχθησαν. For the augment of ἀνοίγειν see Rutherford, 83, 85. John is not consistent.

11. ὁ ἄνθρωπος ὁ λεγόμενος Ἰησοῦς. The words are intended as a description of Jesus in purely human terms. The blind man has much to learn before he makes the confession and offers the worship of v. 38.

ἐπέχρισεν. In v. 6 ἐπέθηκεν is (probably) used; ἐπιχρίειν is not used elsewhere in the New Testament. See the inscription referred to on v. 6; cf. also the use of χρίειν at 2 Cor. 1.21 and the use of χρίσμα at 1 John 2.20,27.

ἀνέβλεψα. See again the inscription mentioned above. ἀναβλέπειν properly means 'to recover sight' (previously enjoyed and since lost); but its use to describe the cure of blindness (see, in the New Testament, Mark 10.51f.; Matt. 11.5 = Luke 7.22; *et al.*) would naturally lead to its employment even where the cured man had never previously seen.

12. ποῦ ἐστιν ἐκεῖνος; Cf. 7.11. The speakers (cf. vv. 8ff.) are the people generally. The Pharisees, as the official opposition, are not introduced till the next verse.

13. τοὺς Φαρισαίους. See on 1.24. Martyn (12) thinks of the Beth Din in Jamnia rather than of a Pharisaic Sanhedrin in Jerusalem. This sort of consideration may explain why the healed man was brought 'to the Pharisees'.

The redundancy αὐτὸν ... τόν ποτε τυφλόν (cf. v. 18, αὐτοῦ τοῦ ἀναβλέψαντος) recalls Aramaic usage (Burney, 85; M. II, 431).

14. ἦν δὲ σάββατον. It was forbidden to perform cures on the Sabbath unless life was in danger (see S.B. 1, 623–9); kneading was also forbidden (*Shabbath* 7.2), and making clay would fall under this prohibition. A passage in *Abodah Zarah* 28b (S.B. II, 533f.) reveals a division of opinion on the question whether

the eyes may be anointed on the Sabbath; for the use of spittle on the Sabbath see the passage quoted on v. 6. As at 5.9, Sabbath is mentioned not for its own sake but in order to lead to weightier theological matters.

15. See the introduction to this section. The examination of the blind man, and through him of Jesus, now begins. At the same time, for the discerning reader, the Pharisees themselves are being judged.

16. οὐκ ἔστιν οὗτος παρὰ θεοῦ ὁ ἄνθρωπος. The order of words is unusual, but οὗτος must be connected with ὁ ἄνθρωπος. The emphasis, if any is intended, might be rendered 'He is not from God—this man'; and certainly he is no more than man. Cf. Deut. 13.2-6: a prophet or dreamer of dreams, even though he succeed in performing signs and wonders, must not be believed but must rather be put to death, if he tend 'to draw thee aside out of the way which the Lord thy God commanded thee to walk in'.

ἄλλοι δέ—that is, of the Pharisees, who were divided in their opinion.

πῶς δύναται ἄνθρωπος ἁμαρτωλὸς τοιαῦτα σημεῖα ποιεῖν; The word ἁμαρτωλός occurs only in this chapter in John. The argument is repeated in v. 31 (cf. 3.2), but as just noted it is not a sound biblical argument; the New Testament as well as the Old Testament is aware of miracle workers who are able to lead astray even the elect. Nevertheless, John himself regards a faith based on signs as a true, though inferior, kind of faith; see especially 14.11. For the word σημεῖον see Introduction, pp. 75-8.

καὶ σχίσμα ἦν ἐν αὐτοῖς. For the word σχίσμα see also 7.43 (with the note); 10.19.

17. λέγουσιν, that is, the Pharisees.

τί σὺ λέγεις περὶ αὐτοῦ. The emphatic pronoun carries the investigation a step further; in effect, the man is provoked to align himself with Jesus (contrast the lame man of ch. 5).

ὅτι ἠνέῳξεν. Burney (76f.; cf. Black, 74, 92; M. ɪɪ, 436) found here a mistranslation of the Aramaic particle ᴅ, which should, he thought, have been rendered by a relative, not by ὅτι. This gives the form in which the sentence appears in the Vulgate (qui aperuit), 'What do you say of him who opened your eyes?' It would however be as easy, and more attractive, to render the presumed Aramaic, 'What do you say of him, you whose eyes he opened?' See M. ɪ, 94, where however it is argued that it is unnecessary to suppose that there is a Semitism in the text, since the Modern Greek ποῦ is used in a way similar to the Aramaic ᴅ and Hebrew אשר. But all these speculations are unnecessary: see L.S. s.v. ὅτι, IV: 'ὅτι sts. = with regard to the fact that': see e.g. Plato, Protagoras, 330 e: ὅτι δὲ καὶ ἐμὲ οἴει εἰπεῖν τοῦτο, παρήκουσας. This supplies exactly the sense required here. Cf. 1.16; 8.45.

προφήτης ἐστίν. This avowal is not the same as that of 6.14; 7.40, where the article is used (see on these verses). Cf. rather 4.19; the formerly blind man, like the Samaritan woman, is simply aware of the presence of an unusual person, who excites wonder and respect. No ordinary man could have given sight to the blind. Cf. v. 32.

18. οὐκ ἐπίστευσαν οὖν οἱ Ἰουδαῖοι. John speaks indiscriminately of 'the Jews' and 'the Pharisees', probably with no clear knowledge of conditions in Palestine before A.D. 70 (see on 1.24). The dilemma of v. 16 was real. A man who was good enough to perform the miracle would not have performed it on

the Sabbath. There was a mistake somewhere, probably in the man's story. αὐτοῦ τοῦ ἀναβλέψαντος may be an Aramaism; see on v. 13.

19. ὃν ὑμεῖς λέγετε ὅτι τυφλὸς ἐγεννήθη. A mixed construction; more natural would have been ὃν ὑ. λ. τυφλὸν γεννηθῆναι.

In this verse, and the two following, the circumstances of the cure as well as the gravity of the disease are brought out with the fullest clarity. This is a common feature of miracle stories, but the form of the present narrative is dictated primarily by the main theme of the trial of the man, and of Jesus through the man, and of the Jews through Jesus.

21. ἡλικίαν ἔχει is often followed by an infinitive expressing what the person in question is of fit age to do. Here the infinitive is to be supplied: either 'to respond rationally to inquiry' or 'to make legal response'. If the latter is meant, the age in Jewish law is at least thirteen.

22. ταῦτα εἶπαν. The whole of this circumspect speech, but (as v. 23 shows) especially the last sentence, is intended by the parents to throw back the whole responsibility upon their son.

ἤδη γὰρ συνετέθειντο. The agreement had already been made (pluperfect); but we have heard nothing of it in John, though there have been attempts to arrest Jesus himself (notably 7.32). The whole matter, including both the offence and the punishment, is anachronistic, See below. Behind συνετέθειντο Martyn (32) sees the verb תקן, used in *Berakoth* 28b, quoted below.

ἐάν τις αὐτὸν ὁμολογήσῃ χριστόν. This is the Christian profession of faith, corresponding to Paul's ἐὰν ὁμολογήσῃς τὸ ῥῆμα ... (Rom. 10.9). According to Mark Jesus was not during his ministry publicly confessed as Messiah (except by demons). That the synagogue had already at that time applied a test of Christian heresy is unthinkable—though Sanders thinks it not 'intrinsically improbable' that the Jews determined to silence the followers of Jesus during his ministry.

ἀποσυνάγωγος γένηται. The word is peculiar to John in the Greek Bible: 9.22; 12.42; 16.2. It is doubtful whether the ordinary synagogue 'excommunication' is meant. On this see a very full account in S.B. IV, 293–333; also J. Juster, *Les Juifs dans l'Empire romain* (1914) II, 159–61, and Schürer II, ii, 59–62. Martyn, 24, 148ff., reaches a conclusion similar to that proposed here. The matter is particularly important to him as indicating the setting in which the gospel took shape. There was a light, informal punishment called נזיפה (*neziphah*), and the regular punishment, called indifferently נדוי (*nidduy*) and שמתה (*shammattah*; there are other vocalizations of both these words). The latter was commonly imposed for a period of thirty days, but if this did not produce reform two further periods of thirty days might be added; after this the normal punishment gave place to the more severe חרם (*herem*), 'ban'. *Nidduy* was reckoned a more severe punishment than the synagogue flogging. Apart from the magical influences believed to be set in motion (which, being believed in by the victim, were a sufficiently real punishment), the person thus temporarily excommunicated was forbidden all dealings with Israelites except his wife and children. He was not however cut off from the religious practices of the community, and it is this which makes it doubtful whether John, by his word ἀποσυνάγωγος, refers, or at least refers accurately, to synagogue excommunication. There is a closer parallel to the situation presupposed by John in the twelfth of the Eighteen Benedictions (the so-called 'Heretic Benediction', ברכת המינים, *birkath ha-minim*). This Benediction has undergone much revision, but in its earliest form (as propounded by Samuel the Small for Rabban Gamaliel (A.D. 85–90); see *Berakhoth* 28 b and in particular J. Jocz, *The Jewish People and Jesus Christ* (1949), 51–7) it must have run somewhat as follows: For the renegades let there be no hope, and may the arrogant kingdom soon be rooted out in our days, and the Nazarenes (הנוצרים) and the *minim* (המינים) perish as in a moment and be blotted out from the book of life and with the righteous may they not be inscribed. Blessed art thou, O Lord, who humblest the arrogant (Jocz's translation of the form of this prayer given in a MS. from the Cairo Genizah). The Benediction was probably intended as a means of marking out Jewish Christians and excluding them from the synagogue community; it hardly amounts to the 'cursing' mentioned in Justin, *Trypho* 16, which is probably the result of a sharpening of feeling between Jews and Christians in the province of Asia, a sharpening of which John itself shows, probably, the early stages. It is probable that among the readers of John were Jewish Christians who had been put out of the synagogue, being regarded, not improperly, as apostates.

24. δὸς δόξαν τῷ θεῷ. Not 'Give the praise for your cure to God, and not to Jesus' but 'Admit the truth'. Cf. Josh. 7.19, δὸς δόξαν σήμερον τῷ κυρίῳ θεῷ 'Ισραήλ; 1 Esdras 9.8; 2 Esdras 10.11. At *Sanhedrin* 6.2 Josh. 7.19 is quoted in this sense.

ἡμεῖς οἴδαμεν. They speak with the responsibility and authority of Judaism, and correctly. There is no doubt (see above) that Jesus had transgressed the Law, and therefore was in the technical sense a ἁμαρτωλός.

25. ἓν οἶδα. The man will not however give up the other side of the dilemma stated in v. 16. It is also beyond question that he has received sight at the hands of Jesus. The only possible conclusion that could be drawn from the two given facts (the man's recovered sight, and the conviction of Jesus by the Law of sinfulness) was that the Law itself was now superseded—a conclusion Paul had long before drawn. The Law in condemning Jesus had condemned itself (Gal. 3.10–14); this theme forms the theological basis of the present chapter. The Law condemns itself, and so do its exponents, when they try and condemn Jesus.

27. μὴ καὶ ὑμεῖς θέλετε. The μή of 'cautious assertion' (M. 1, 192f.; cf. 4.29), here forming an ironical question: 'What? Don't tell me that you also wish . . .?'

28. σὺ μαθητὴς εἶ ἐκείνου, ἡμεῖς δὲ τοῦ Μωϋσέως ἐσμὲν μαθηταί. ἐκεῖνος is probably contemptuous, 'that fellow'; B.D. §291, 1. Jesus and Moses, with their disciples, are intentionally thrown into sharp contrast. For the importance of Moses in Judaism see the references given on 5.45. Martyn (14, cf. 88) thinks that the view expressed here must have come from Jews known to John, since his own view (5.46) was that Moses wrote about Jesus. Note however the contrast of 1.17. 'Disciples of Moses' was not a regular term for rabbinic scholars; see however Matt. 23.2 and a *baraitah* in *Yoma* 4a where the Pharisaic, as against the Sadducean, scholars are called תלמידיו של משה (disciples of Moses; S.B. II, 535). John uses the term to bring out the opposition, already revealed in the sabbath healing, between Jesus and the Law.

Men must now ally themselves with either the new authority or the old. This opposition runs deep into the gospel tradition, and is found in the Synoptic Gospels (e.g. Matt. 5.21f., 27f., 31f.,33f.,38f.,43f.). It appears also in rabbinic sources; e.g. *P. Aboth* 5.19: How do the disciples of Abraham our father (the Jews) differ from the disciples of Balaam the wicked (the Christians)? Cf. *Deut. R.* 8.6: Moses said to them (the Israelites), Lest you should say, 'Another Moses is to arise and to bring us another Law from heaven', I make known to you at once that it is not in heaven; there is none of it left in heaven (with reference to Deut. 30.11f.).

29. Μωϋσεῖ λελάληκεν ὁ θεός. So frequently in the Pentateuch; see especially Exod. 33.11, And the Lord spake unto Moses face to face, as a man speaketh unto his friend.

τοῦτον δὲ οὐκ οἴδαμεν πόθεν ἐστίν. τοῦτον is attracted out of its proper position in the indirect interrogative clause into the principal sentence. This verse is in formal contradiction with 7.27 where it is argued that Jesus cannot be the Messiah because his origin, in Nazareth, is known. Each allegation is however, to John, false, and each ironically true; they do not point to the use of different sources. The Christian revelation began not with an awe-inspiring theophany but with the incarnation of the Word, a process in which both the divine Word and the flesh which he took must be taken seriously. Cf. also 3.8; 8.14.

There is a close parallel to this verse in *P. Eg.* 2. The words follow upon the passage quoted above on 5.45 and are as follows. Lines 14–19; α[ὐ]τῶν δὲ λε[γόντω]ν ε[ὖ] οἴδαμεν ὅτι Μω ἐλά[λησεν] ὁ θς [·] σὲ δὲ οὐκ οἴδαμεν [πόθεν εἶ]. ἀποκριθεὶς ὁ Ἰη εἶ[πεν αὐτο]ῖς· νῦν κατηγορεῖται [ὑμῶν ἡ ἀ]πιστεῖ[α... On the connection between John and this papyrus see Introduction, p. 110, and on 5.39,45. All the passages hitherto quoted (they are consecutive) refer to Moses and the Old Testament.

30. ἐν τούτῳ. A Johannine phrase; cf. 4.37; 13.35; 15.8; 16.30.

ὑμεῖς οὐκ οἴδατε. Cf. 3.10; the leaders of Israel should know the credentials and authority of so notable a miracle-worker.

καὶ ἤνοιξεν. 'And *yet* . . .'.

31. ὁ θεὸς ἁμαρτωλῶν οὐκ ἀκούει. Cf. 16.23–7; 1 John 3.21f.; Isa. 1.15; Ps. 66.18; 109.7; Prov. 15.29; Job 27.9; 35.13. Naturally so simple an idea can be paralleled in extra-biblical sources also. In Jewish literature the biblical passages above are applied; for a Greek expression of the same thought cf. Philostratus, *Vita Apollonii* 1, 12, If you too really care for goodness (καλοκἀγαθίας), go boldly up to the god and tender what prayer you will (εὖχου, ὅ τι ἐθέλεις). It is of course not denied that the penitent prayer of a repenting sinner is heard; it is the hypocritical prayer of one who has no intention of offering obedience that is disregarded.

θεοσεβής occurs nowhere else in the New Testament (θεοσέβεια at 1 Tim. 2.10). It is common (with the meaning 'pious') in Hellenistic religious literature (for examples see Bauer, *Wörterbuch*); and perhaps was especially applied to Jews—see the inscription from Miletus quoted in Deissmann, 446f. (τόπος Ειουδέων τῶν καὶ θεοσεβίον [–ίων *lgd.*]). Cf. also the centurion Cornelius, described as εὐσεβὴς καὶ φοβούμενος τὸν θεόν (Acts 10.2), whose prayers and alms caused him to be remembered by God (10.4). The juxtaposition in John of the two phrases, the Hellenistic θεοσεβής and the Jewish τὸ θέλημα αὐτοῦ ποιῇ, is striking (Bultmann, 337) and very characteristic of John's theological and linguistic workmanship.

32. ἐκ τοῦ αἰῶνος. Cf. Isa. 64.4, ἀπὸ τοῦ αἰῶνος οὐκ ἠκούσαμεν. This renders the Hebrew מעולם, and in later Hebrew the phrase מעולם לא occurs frequently, meaning simply 'never' (see Jastrow, 1052b). But the expression is not necessarily translation Greek, or even a Semitism; see the examples given by M.M. (s.v. αἰών), and, e.g., a second century A.D. inscription from Olympia, which claims a record: ἦν μόνος ἀπ' αἰῶνος ἀνδρῶν ἐποίησα (Dittenberger, Syll., 1073.48f.).

33. See 3.2 and the note. For the omission of ἄν cf. 8.39; 15.22,24; 19.11.

34. ἐν ἁμαρτίαις σὺ ἐγεννήθης ὅλος. See on v. 2; the Jews find it convenient to believe that the man's blindness was due to sin. ὅλος (ὅλως is read by λ, a few other Greek MSS., and sin) is predicative; cf. 13.10.

ἐξέβαλον αὐτὸν ἔξω. This is presumably the fulfilment of the threat to put disciples of Jesus out of the synagogue; see v. 22. Contrast 6.37, also 10.4; when the good shepherd puts forth (ἐκβάλλειν) his sheep he leads them to pasture.

35. εὑρὼν αὐτόν. The story is not yet complete. The light has shone and it has created division between the children of light and the children of darkness. The Jews have cast out the man (and so have rejected Jesus); he for his part refuses to deny the light that has come to him in the opening of his eyes. But he has not yet understood what has taken place, or come to faith in Jesus. Jesus therefore, taking the initiative (cf. 5.14), as he must, *finds* the man. Martyn, 16, sees here the initiative of the Christian preacher.

σὺ πιστεύεις εἰς τὸν υἱὸν τοῦ ἀνθρώπου; The pronoun is emphatic: Do *you*, over against those who have expelled you, believe? τὸν υἱὸν τοῦ ἀνθρώπου (P66 P75 ℵ B D sin) is to be preferred to τὸν υἱὸν τοῦ θεοῦ (Θ Ω it vg); it is most improbable that the latter should have been changed into the former. Nowhere else in John is πιστεύειν used with 'Son of man'. There is however a close parallel to this passage in 12.34ff., where the question regarding the lifting up of the Son of man becomes acute and Jesus replies in terms of the light, which is in the world for a little while that men may believe, and goes on to quote the passage from Isa. 6 which is alluded to in vv. 39–41. In these verses Jesus appears as judge; hence perhaps the otherwise surprising use of the title Son of man (Martyn, 131–5). He is also (Bultmann) the eschatological bringer of salvation, at work in this age.

36. καὶ τίς ἐστιν. The words may be taken in two ways. (i) I do not know what Son of man means. Who is this person? What are his functions, etc.? (ii) I know sufficiently what Son of man means. But who among men is the Son of man? How can he be identified? The reply here suggests (ii); but cf. 12.34.

κύριε. If the word is to be interpreted as used in a historical dialogue it should be rendered 'Sir', though it must have a different sense in the confession of faith in v. 38. But it is doubtful whether John intended to make this distinction.

ἵνα πιστεύσω εἰς αὐτόν. It is unnecessary to suppose that ἵνα misrepresents the Aramaic ד, originally intended as a relative (Burney, 76; M. II, 435f.).

Cf. 1.22, and in each case supply '*Answer me (us)*, in order that I (we) may . . .'.

37. ἑώρακας αὐτόν. Contrast Mark 14.62 (ὄψεσθε τὸν υἱὸν τοῦ ἀνθρώπου) where seeing the Son of man is a future event. He will be manifested as a figure belonging essentially to the world of futurist eschatology. In John, while the eschatological background remains, the Son of man can be seen by faith (but only by faith—cf. 6.36) now and in the future, on earth or in heaven. Truly to see Jesus is to see God (14.9).

ὁ λαλῶν μετὰ σοῦ ἐκεῖνός ἐστιν. Cf. 4.26, ἐγώ εἰμι, ὁ λαλῶν σοι. The use here of the third person (ἐκεῖνός ἐστιν) seems to prove that ἐγώ εἰμι may well mean simply 'I am' with a predicate supplied from the context. Jesus asserts his identity with the Son of man. Cf. 1 Enoch 71.14, Thou art the Son of man (on the text of this verse see R. H. Charles, ad loc. (Text, 1906; Translation, 1893 and 1912); E. Sjöberg, *Der Menschensohn im äthiopischen Henochbuch* (1946), 154–9).

38. After the self-revelation of v. 37 the man's response is that of Christian faith and worship (προσεκύνησεν need mean no more than 'did him reverence', but in the Johannine context there is no doubt that it bears a deeper meaning). Cf. the reactions of men to theophanies in the Old Testament; e.g. Exod. 3.6. The sign and its interpretation are now both complete: the blind man has received physical sight, and has also, through Jesus the light of the world, seen the truth and believed in Jesus as the Son of man. But 'the immediate cause of the confession is neither a theophany, nor a straightforward demand that he should believe, compliance with which would be no more than an arbitrary act of will. But whereas man's experience would remain obscure to him without the intervention of the spoken word, so too the word itself is only intelligible because it reveals to man the meaning of his own experience' (Bultmann).

39. The narrative being now completed Jesus sums up its meaning. For synoptic parallels to vv. 39ff. see Dodd, *Tradition*, 327f. V. 38,39a are omitted by P75 ℵ* W b and a Coptic MS. C. L. Porter (*N.T.S.* 13 (1967), 387–94) argues convincingly that they are a liturgical addition to the text.

εἰς (for the purpose of) κρίμα. κρίμα occurs here only in John, though the verb κρίνειν and noun κρίσις are common (see 3.17). There is a superficial contradiction here with 3.17 (οὐ γὰρ ἀπέστειλεν ὁ θεὸς τὸν υἱὸν εἰς τὸν κόσμον ἵνα κρίνῃ τὸν κόσμον; cf. also 5.22; 8.15f.); but in fact the judgement inevitably implied by the presence of Christ is brought out at once in 3.18–21. The 'light and darkness' imagery of 3.19–21 lies behind and explains the present narrative.

ἐγώ . . . ἦλθον. The purpose of the mission of Jesus is often expressed in John in these and similar terms: 10.10; 12.46f.; 18.37; cf. 5.43; 7.28; 8.42; 12.27; 16.28; 17.8. The pre-existence of Christ, and the vital place of his mission in the eternal purposes of God, are presupposed.

εἰς τὸν κόσμον τοῦτον. For the contrast between the 'other world' which is the natural home of the Son of man and 'this world' see especially 8.23; cf. 9.39; 11.9; 12.25,31; 13.1; 16.11; 18.36. For κόσμος see on 1.10.

ἵνα οἱ μὴ βλέποντες βλέπωσιν καὶ οἱ βλέποντες τυφλοὶ γένωνται. The language is in part borrowed from a number of Old Testament passages, notably in Isaiah.

For the gift of sight to the blind cf. Isa. 29.18 (ὀφθαλμοὶ τυφλῶν ὄψονται); 35.5 (ἀνοιχθήσονται ὀφθαλμοὶ τυφλῶν); 42.7 (ἀνοῖξαι ὀφθαλμοὺς τυφλῶν); 42.18 (οἱ τυφλοί, ἀναβλέψατε ἰδεῖν); cf. Ps. 146.8. For the blinding of those who see, cf. Isa. 6.10; 42.19. John's words are also in part based upon the miracle itself: the physically blind man received sight, though it is not true conversely that those who could see were struck with physical blindness. But the primary intention of the saying is to bring out the underlying meaning of the miracle and 'trial', which is also the meaning of the ministry of Jesus as a whole. To receive Jesus is to receive the light of the world; to reject him is to reject the light, to close one's eyes, and to become blind. Cf. Mark 4.11f., where also reference is made to Isa. 6.10; and John 12.40, where the Isaiah passage is quoted; see especially on this verse for the predestinarian teaching of the gospel. It should be noted that in some sense men 'predestinate' themselves by their confidence, or lack of confidence, in their own spiritual vision. The man born blind emphasizes his ignorance throughout: he does not even know whether or not Jesus is a sinner (v. 25); he does not know who is the Son of man (v. 36); he emphasizes that he knows one thing only (v. 25). On the other hand the Jews make confident pronouncements about Jesus (vv. 16, 22—he is certainly not the Christ; 24—ἡμεῖς οἴδαμεν; 29—ἡμεῖς οἴδαμεν); they will not be taught (v. 34). They are in truth the instructed members of the community; they are οἱ βλέποντες, and, when the true light shines, they refuse to see it because they regard their own illumination as sufficient. Cf. their attitude to John the Baptist and the Old Testament (5.35,39). For the double meaning (Cullmann, V. & A., 183) of 'blind' cf. τυφλοὶ τῇ καρδίᾳ, P. Oxy. 1.20f. (Fitzmyer, Essays, 396).

40. ἐκ τῶν Φαρισαίων ... οἱ μετ' αὐτοῦ ὄντες. Cf. 11.31, οἱ οὖν 'Ιουδαῖοι οἱ ὄντες μετ' αὐτῆς. μετά does not imply any kind of alliance—see e.g. 3.25, ζήτησις ... μετὰ 'Ιουδαίου.

μὴ καὶ ἡμεῖς ...; 'What, are even we ...?' expecting the answer, No.

41. The reply of Jesus brings out the point that was anticipated in the note on v. 39. The blind have no sin; cf. Paul's οὗ δὲ οὐκ ἔστιν νόμος, οὐδὲ παράβασις (Rom. 4.15); ἁμαρτία δὲ οὐκ ἐλλογεῖται μὴ ὄντος νόμου (Rom. 5.13), and elsewhere. Those who are blind may be willing to obey the directions of Jesus (vv. 6f.) and so receive sight. Those however who enjoy the light of the Law are unwilling to leave it for more perfect illumination, and so become blind, losing the light they have. Cf. 15.22; also Prov. 26.12 (Sidebottom, 207).

ἡ ἁμαρτία ὑμῶν μένει. μένειν is one of John's characteristic words. Generally it is used in a good sense (e.g. of the abiding of Christ), but cf. 3.36, ἡ ὀργὴ τοῦ θεοῦ μένει ἐπ' αὐτόν. The blindness of such men is incurable; cf. the synoptic saying about blasphemy against the Holy Spirit, especially Mark 3.29 (see the parallels also), οὐκ ἔχει ἄφεσιν εἰς τὸν αἰῶνα, ἀλλὰ ἔνοχός ἐστιν αἰωνίου ἁμαρτήματος. Cf. also 1 John 5.16f., the sin 'unto death'. The blindness of such men is incurable since they have deliberately rejected the only cure that exists.

20. THE GOOD SHEPHERD

10.1–21

No break is indicated by John between chs. 9 and 10; but the present passage is rather a comment upon ch. 9 than a continuation of it. A signal instance of the failure of hireling shepherds has been given; instead of properly caring for the blind man, the Pharisees have cast him out (9.34). Jesus, on the other hand, as the good shepherd, found him (9.35, εὑρὼν αὐτόν) and so brought him into the true fold.

As often in the Johannine discourses it is difficult to pursue a simple thread of argument, and the treatment of the shepherd theme in particular lacks the form of the synoptic parables. As it stands, it is neither parable (so also Dodd, *Interpretation*, 134f.; but see below) nor allegory, though it is related to both forms of utterance. It is a symbolic discourse in which symbolism and straightforward statement alternate and stand side by side. This juxtaposition does not make for clarity; nor does the fact that two contrasts are worked out side by side, one between the good shepherd and thieves and robbers, and another between the good shepherd and hirelings. Again, the meaning assigned to the sheep seems to vary (see the notes), and beside the declaration 'I am the good shepherd' stands another, 'I am the door'. John's meaning as he goes from point to point is on the whole intelligible, and an attempt to bring it out is made in the notes on the several verses; that John combines more themes than one, and that his thought moves in spirals rather than straight lines, is not an adequate reason for rearranging the paragraph. The points so far mentioned are covered in the first sixteen verses; but already in v. 11 another theme is given out; Jesus will die for the sheep. The precise significance of his death is not shown, but it is mentioned in connection with the statements that Jesus knows his sheep as the Father knows him, and that he has 'other sheep' to bring.

The origin of the designation 'the good shepherd' is discussed in the notes on v. 11; here it is necessary to point out only the general dependence of the paragraph on the Old Testament, and upon the earlier gospel tradition (cf. Mark 6.34; Matt. 9.36; 18.12–14; Luke 15.3–7). That parables about sheep and shepherd should be crystallized by John into the great Christological affirmation 'I am the good shepherd' is characteristic of his style and method.

It has already been shown that the shepherd discourse follows naturally upon 9.41, and it is presupposed by 10.26–9; accordingly it seems unnecessary to transpose the order of the chapter as has been proposed (the order suggested by Bernard is vv. 19–29, 1–18, 30–42). The paragraph is also linked to the preceding chapter by 10.21 (τυφλῶν ὀφθαλμοὺς ἀνοῖξαι) and by the word σχίσμα (10.19) which sums up the effect of the cure of the blind man. Against such transpositions see Dodd, *Interpretation*, 353ff.; on the connection between ch. 9 and ch. 10, Guilding, 129f. ('The real reason for the transition of thought lies in the sequence of lectionary readings upon which the Fourth Gospel is framed, since on the sabbath nearest to the Feast of the Dedication [see 10.22] virtually all the *regular* lections for every year of the cycle contain the theme of sheep and shepherds and of God the Shepherd of Israel').

There have been several attempts to penetrate behind John's text to his sources. J. D. M. Derrett (*St. Th.* 27 (1973), 25–50) reconstructs a parable which, he suggests, John had in front of him. The evangelist "decoded" it by tracing back the biblical allusions, and based his chapter upon it' (50), using the methods of *halakah* and *haggadah* (27). There are acute observations in this article, but taken as a whole it must be described as fanciful. Sanders thought that vv. 1–5 contained an original parable in which the sheep represented Israel entrusted to the Messiah and under attack from false messiahs. Vv. 7–18 are an allegorical variation by a Christian prophet. J. A. T. Robinson (*Z.N.T.W.* 46 (1955), 233–40) finds in vv. 1–5 a fusion of two parables. The first, in vv. 1–3a, originally posed a 'challenge to the θυρωροί of Israel. Would they be prepared to recognize and open to him who came to them by the door of the sheep-fold and had the right to entry?' (237). The second is contained in vv. 3b–5; its original point may have been that Jesus' 'authority cannot be proved by signs: it is self-authenticating' (235). The fusion of the two has obscured the point of vv. 1–3a by taking emphasis away from the θυρωροί and laying it upon the shepherd. This analysis is, broadly speaking, accepted by Dodd (*Tradition*, 382–5); there are short but good notes on it in Lindars, and a full discussion in Schnackenburg. It seems in fact that the chapter as a whole contains more than two such pieces of synoptic or quasi-synoptic tradition, reworked in the Johannine idiom of language and thought. All however are focused on the figure of Jesus (this is true not least of vv. 1–3a) and have been unified by this process.

1. ὁ μὴ εἰσερχόμενος διὰ τῆς θύρας εἰς τὴν αὐλὴν τῶν προβάτων. The details in this account of shepherds and sheep agree well with what is known of shepherding in the east; see e.g. A. M. Rihbany, *The Syrian Christ* (1927), 207–16. But of course such details belonged not to Palestine only but to most of the Mediterranean (and indeed other) countries of a similar state of civilization. αὐλή is used as a 'steading for cattle' in Homer; later it becomes 'court' or 'hall' (so L.S.). Here presumably it means the enclosed courtyard of a house, used as a fold for sheep (αὔλιον is 'fold', 'stable', and so on).

ἀναβαίνων ἀλλαχόθεν, literally 'goes up from some other point'. It is not impossible (in view of the special use of ἀναβαίνειν in John—see on 3.13) that there is in the back of John's mind the thought of those who would ascend to heaven by some other means than the cross; but undoubtedly the main, and probably the only, thought is composite: 'climbs the wall (instead of going through the door)', and 'goes in from some other quarter (than the door)'.

κλέπτης ἐστὶν καὶ λῃστής. The words are not synonymous (though John may not have intended any clear distinction between them here). Judas, who pilfered money from the money-box, was a κλέπτης (12.6), Barabbas, who was implicated in murder and perhaps armed revolt (Mark 15.7), was a λῃστής (18.40). Perhaps καί means something like 'or'. The κλέπτης καὶ λῃστής is not to be precisely identified; John refers not to a person but to a class. Messianic pretenders may be in mind; perhaps more probably the many 'saviours' of the Hellenistic world (see further Bultmann, 371f.).

2. διὰ τῆς θύρας. At this point in the discourse the door and the shepherd are clearly distinguished; later Jesus is identified with both (see especially v. 7). This leads to some obscurity in the presentation of the material, and has given rise to attempts to improve its order. F. Spitta (Z.N.T.W. 10, (1909), 59–80; 103–27) thought that the original parable (of synoptic style) was contained in vv. 1–5, 11b–16a, 18c. For Bultmann's rearrangement see on 10.39; for the two parables found here by J. A. T. Robinson see the introduction to the section.

3. ὁ θυρωρός. Cf. ἡ θυρωρός, 18.16f. The use (= 'porter') at Mark 13.34 is more usual. The θυρωρός of a sheepfold was perhaps an under-shepherd; or possibly one fold served more than one flock (see below) and had an independent porter.

τὰ ἴδια πρόβατα φωνεῖ κατ' ὄνομα. Notwithstanding Rihbany (loc. cit.) this can hardly mean anything other than that each sheep has a name and that each name is called by the shepherd. Since the shepherd calls his own sheep it is implied that there are in the fold other sheep which are not his. Cf. v. 16, where it appears that the shepherd has other sheep which are not of the original fold. This, then, is the fold of Judaism, which contained the first disciples and also the unbelieving Jews, of whom the former were to be joined by Gentile believers.

καὶ ἐξάγει αὐτά. For this, and for the following verses, cf. Num. 27.17, . . . ὅστις ἐξελεύσεται πρὸ προσώπου αὐτῶν καὶ ὅστις εἰσελεύσεται πρὸ προσώπου αὐτῶν, καὶ ὅστις ἐξάξει αὐτοὺς καὶ ὅστις εἰσάξει αὐτούς, καὶ οὐκ ἔσται συναγωγὴ κυρίου ὡς πρόβατα οἷς οὐκ ἔστιν ποιμήν. It can hardly be doubted that this passage was given a messianic interpretation and alluded to in that sense, though such an interpretation does not appear elsewhere; but the fact that the required man is appointed in Num. 27.18 would equally prevent Jews from using the verse as a prophecy and suggest such a use to Christians, since the person appointed is Joshua (in Greek, Ἰησοῦς). Passages such as Mark 6.34 may have suggested to John's mind the use of the Old Testament passage.

4. This verse is not allegorical but simply parabolic; it describes what a shepherd does. The reading τὰ ἴδια πάντα ((P66) P75 ℵ B D Θ) is certainly to be preferred to τὰ ἴδια πρόβατα (ω); the omission of πάντα in ℵ* is probably accidental. ἐκβάλῃ recalls 9.34; see the note.

οἴδασιν τὴν φωνὴν αὐτοῦ. Cf. v. 27. It is most improbable that v. 27 should precede this verse; see the introduction to this section. Cf. 18.37, and see below on v. 14. The parabolic verses (1–5) provide material for the ensuing discourse.

5. ἀλλοτρίῳ. Presumably a thief or robber is in mind. The thought of the hireling is not introduced till v. 12. Those who truly are Christ's elect sheep cannot be deceived by the pretenders of v. 1. Jesus calls by name all those whom the Father has given him (6.37,39; 17.6,9,24; 18.9), and since they are his own they hear his voice and follow him (cf. 3.19–21, where the same truth is differently expressed—those who are children of the light, whose works are good, come to the light). There are others who are not Jesus' own sheep since they have not been chosen and given him by the Father (8.47; 10.26f.); these do not hear his voice; cf. v. 6, ἐκεῖνοι δὲ οὐκ ἔγνωσαν. Cf. Mark 4.11f. If vv. 1–3a, 3b–5, were originally separate ἀλλότριος will have meant simply 'a stranger'.

6. ταύτην τὴν παροιμίαν. παροιμία (on the background and usage of this word see, in addition to commentaries, E. Hatch, *Essays in Biblical Greek* (1889), 64–71; B. T. D. Smith, *The Parables of the Synoptic Gospels* (1937), 3–15; L. Cerfaux, 'Le thème littéraire parabolique dans l'évangile de saint Jean', in *Coniectanea Neotestamentica* XI (1947), 15–25) occurs again in 16.25,29, but nowhere in the Synoptic Gospels; nor does παραβολή, which is common there, occur in John. In biblical usage there is little or no distinction between the two terms. In the LXX, παραβολή is the usual rendering of מָשָׁל (mashal), and translates no other word. παροιμία is occasionally used for מָשָׁל (mashal), and seems to have increased in popularity in the later VSS. (see Hatch loc. cit.). What special flavour παροιμία may have had in biblical usage is accounted for by its use in Prov. 1.1: one of the meanings of מָשָׁל (mashal) is 'proverb', and this meaning παροιμία naturally acquired (cf. 2 Peter 2.22, the only other use of the word in the New Testament). But at 1 Kings 4.32 (=3 Kdms 5.12) the proverbs (מְשָׁלִים) of Solomon are παραβολαί, and it is impossible in John to translate παροιμία as proverb. In 16.25,29, speech ἐν παροιμίαις is contrasted with speech (ἐν) παρρησίᾳ; παροιμία must therefore mean some kind of veiled or symbolic utterance. The synoptic similitudes and the Johannine 'allegories' have often been contrasted; in fact, neither are the synoptic speeches pure similitude nor the Johannine pure allegory. The Christocentric tendency of the synoptic parables is accentuated by John, who composes symbolic discourses which bring out the fact that the death and exaltation of Jesus are the life of men.

ἐκεῖνοι δὲ οὐκ ἔγνωσαν. See on v. 5. 'They' are the Jews of ch. 9, who there and elsewhere (see on 1.19) are the adversaries of Jesus. They are not his sheep and therefore do not hear and understand what he says.

7. ἀμὴν ἀμὴν λέγω ὑμῖν. See on 1.51. At v. 1 this formula introduced the opening section of the parable. Here it introduces a second stage, not an interpretation of the first, but an interpenetration of its material with statements about Jesus in the first person singular.

ἐγώ εἰμι. On these words, used with a predicate, see on 6.35. This ἐγώ εἰμι (cf. 15.1) contrasts sharply with the common synoptic formula 'The kingdom of God is like . . .', and the contrast is significant. John finds in the person of Jesus himself that which the synoptists find in the kingdom of God.

ἡ θύρα (see further v. 9) τῶν προβάτων. This is a surprising identification; we should have expected Jesus to say 'I am the shepherd of the sheep' (this occurs in P⁷⁵ sah but cannot be other than a secondary correction of the more difficult text). That he does not shows that we have here not simply an interpretation but a development of the parable in characteristic Johannine style. The difficulty of the sudden introduction of θύρα is removed by the suggestion (Torrey, 108, 111–13, cf. Black, 259, n. 1) that the original Aramaic of the passage ran: אנא אתית רעהון די ענא (...'atheth ra'ehon..., I came as the shepherd of the sheep), and that the words were wrongly divided by the translator, as follows: אנא אתי תרעהון די ענא (... 'ithai tar'ahon ..., I am the door of the sheep). The suggestion cannot however be accepted. Torrey finds it necessary to dismiss v. 9 as an addition to the text designed to support the misreading of v. 7. This is an unwarrantable hypothesis; v. 9 in fact bears out the difficult reading of v. 7. And although v. 7 is unexpected it makes good sense and stands in no need of emendation.

8. πάντες (om. D, perhaps wishing to exclude Old Testament worthies from condemnation) ὅσοι ἦλθον πρὸ ἐμοῦ (πρὸ ἐμοῦ, om., perhaps rightly, P⁴⁵ P⁷⁵ א* it vg sin pesh, with some support from Θ, which has the order, πρὸ ἐμοῦ ἦλθον) κλέπται εἰσὶν καὶ λῃσταί (cf. v. 1). It is certainly not intended to dismiss the prophets and other righteous men of the Old Testament as thieves and robbers. The thieves and robbers of this verse must be the same as those of v. 1, who climb up 'some other way', false messianic claimants and bogus 'saviours'. It is most unlikely that there is a polemical reference to John the Baptist, or sectaries of his, though Cullmann (V. & A., 174) thinks this possible. Cullmann also thinks that there may be an allusion to the Qumran Teacher of Righteousness (in K. Stendahl, *The Scrolls and the New Testament* (1958), 31; against this see Braun, who points out that the messianic figures of Qumran are not called shepherds). See further on vv. 11, 18. Brown sees a reference to Pharisees and Sadducees. The suggestion (Odeberg, 329) that Abraham and the prophets cannot be referred to because πρὶν 'Αβραὰμ γενέσθαι ἐγώ εἰμι (8.58) is not satisfactory because in this sense there was no one πρὸ Χριστοῦ, and thus the whole sentence falls to the ground as meaningless. As in v. 1 it is not possible to single out particular persons whom John may have had in mind; it is rather his intention to emphasize the unique fulfilment of the Old Testament promises in Jesus, and within the framework of the parable his emphasis had to take this form. Bultmann thinks that the basis of John's thought is to be found not in the Old Testament but in gnosticism; he is certainly right in seeing that John's intention is to emphasize 'the exclusiveness and absoluteness of the revelation'.

ἀλλ' οὐκ ἤκουσαν αὐτῶν τὰ πρόβατα, that is, the sheep who were Christ's own (v. 3). They were predestinated as his, and could not be led astray by false Christs.

9. ἐγώ εἰμι ἡ θύρα. For the use of ἐγώ εἰμι with a predicate see on 6.35, and cf. especially v. 7, ἡ θύρα τῶν προβάτων, though it may well be (see J. Jeremias, *T.W.N.T.* s.v. θύρα) that the meaning is not identical in the two verses. In v. 7 it seems to be, 'I am the door *to* the sheep', by means of which the true shepherd will enter; in v. 9 it is rather, 'I am the door by means of which the sheep enter into the fold.' V. 7 is perhaps open to both meanings; such ambiguity would be in accordance with John's style. In any case it is quite unnecessary to suppose that this variety amounts to contradiction, and that the two verses are drawn from different sources, or that one is a supplement. There is much variety in this discourse—for example, on no interpretation can 'I am the door' and 'I am the shepherd' be made to fit neatly together.

The only unity in the discourse is Christological; Jesus draws to himself every epithet which the picture of sheep and shepherd suggests. The word θύρα calls to mind a very complicated background (see J. Jeremias, op. cit., and Bauer, 139, 144). (i) Ancient people who thought of a heaven situated above the earth naturally thought of it as entered by a door or doors; this idea appears in Greek literature from Homer onwards. In itself it is not important, but it formed the basis of gnostic mythologies, most of which included the descent of a redeemer from heaven to earth, and the ascent of the redeemed (see Introduction, pp. 36–41, 78ff.). From this the notion of a Redeemer who was himself the door between heaven and earth was not far removed. Cf. 1.51. (ii) The notion of a heavenly door appears also in Jewish sources. In the Old Testament itself we have 'the gate of heaven' (שער השמים, ἡ πύλη τοῦ οὐρανοῦ, Gen. 28.17), and 'the doors of heaven' (דלתי שמים, θύρας οὐρανοῦ, Ps. 78(77).23). In the apocalypses the gate of heaven appears frequently: e.g. 1 Enoch 72—5 (the Book of the heavenly Luminaries, e.g. 72.2, The luminary the sun has its rising in the eastern portals of the heaven and its setting in the western portals of the heaven); 3 Bar. 6.13 (The angels are opening the 365 gates of heaven). This apocalyptic use is of twofold significance: (a) the visionary receives a view of the eternal truth of heaven (cf. Rev. 4.1), and (b) it is out of heaven that the eschatological salvation descends. The doors of heaven (apart from being the entrances and exits of angels, luminaries, and so on) are the means by which knowledge and salvation are conveyed to men. Material such as this has been worked up into a characteristic piece of Johannine Christological writing, in which Jesus appears as the Mediator, or Revealer. Cf. John's use of the term Son of man (and see especially 1.51), and of Word, since the Word is the bringer both of knowledge and salvation. Cf. Odes of Solomon 17.6–11; 42.15–17. (iii) A third set of parallels is to be found in the Synoptic Gospels and earlier Christian theology. There come under consideration not only those passages in which words such as 'door' or 'gate' are used, but also the many sayings about entering the kingdom of God; see Matt. 7.13f. (=Luke 13.24); Luke 13.25; Matt. 25.10; Matt. 7.7 (=Luke 11.9); Mark 9.43,45,47 (=Matt. 18.8f., εἰσελθεῖν εἰς τὴν ζωήν). These synoptic passages have for the most part an eschatological reference, which John has characteristically transformed, using Old Testament material which the earlier tradition had already selected, but applying it with special reference to the person of Jesus (rather than to the kingdom) and in such a way as to make it appropriate to the intellectual atmosphere in which he lived. (iv) Two further points may be added here. (a) Ignatius (Philad. 9.1) speaks of Jesus as αὐτὸς ὢν θύρα τοῦ πατρός. It is not easy to say whether he is in conscious dependence on John (see Introduction, pp. 110f.); his meaning does not seem to be identical with John's. (b) In describing the death of James the Just, Hegesippus (apud Eusebius, H.E. II, xxiii, 8, 12) makes 'some of the seven sects' of the Jews inquire of James 'What is the door of Jesus?' (τίς ἡ θύρα τοῦ Ἰησοῦ;). The passage is possibly corrupt (see the note in M. J. Routh, Reliquiae Sacrae I (1846), 234–8, still the best source of information) and in any case obscure. Direct dependence on John (or vice versa) is improbable. It would be mistaken to suppose that this wealth of parallel material was consciously—or unconsciously—present to John's mind. He is, in the first instance, developing a parabolic picture in which God's elect are a flock of sheep. He uses it, as he uses most of his material, to magnify the figure of Jesus. There is only one means of entering the fold; there is only one source of knowledge and life; there is only one way to obtain spiritual nourishment; there is only one way to heaven. And the single means of access to all that is good is Jesus.

δι' ἐμοῦ ἐάν τις εἰσέλθῃ. Jesus is the only means of entry into the messianic community as he is the only bringer of salvation. See an outstanding note (dealing with 10.7–10) on 'The exclusiveness and absoluteness of revelation' (and the 'intolerance of revelation') in Bultmann, 375–80.

σωθήσεται (on σώζειν see on 3.17; cf. Jer. 31.10—Dodd, A.S., 85), καὶ εἰσελεύσεται καὶ ἐξελεύσεται καὶ νομὴν εὑρήσει. The believer is first of all delivered, then finds freedom in the fold (cf. 8.32,36), and finds also the means of sustaining life (mentioned in the next verse). With νομή cf. the 'water of life' (in ch. 4) and the 'bread of life' (in ch. 6).

10. ὁ κλέπτης, the unauthorized entrant (v. 1), whose purpose is clearly no good one.

θύσῃ. θύειν is not used elsewhere in John; θυσία is not used at all. ἀποκτείνειν is fairly frequent (twelve times), and θύειν was probably chosen here as particularly appropriate to the slaughtering of animals. This means that this word at least is still part of the parable-allegory, not the interpretation—the killing of Christians in persecution is not in mind.

ἀπολέσῃ. ἀπολλύναι, unlike θύειν, is an important Johannine word; see on 3.16. It is commonly used in a theological sense, and may here mean much more than θύειν. ἀπολέσαι is precisely what Christ will not do to any of his own (6.39; 18.9; cf. 3.16; 6.12; 10.28; 17.12).

ἵνα ζωὴν ἔχωσιν. The purpose of the mission of Jesus is to give (eternal) life to the world. This thought is fundamental in John and constantly recurs; see e.g. 3.16; 20.31. For ζωή see on 1.4.

καὶ περισσὸν ἔχωσιν (om. P⁶⁶* D, perhaps by homoeoteleuton), 'to have abundance, even superfluity' (of life). Cf. Xenophon, Oeconomicus XX, 1, οἱ μὲν αὐτῶν ἀφθόνως τε ζῶσι καὶ περιττὰ ἔχουσιν, οἱ δ' οὐδὲ τὰ ἀναγκαῖα δύνανται πορίζεσθαι.

11. ἐγώ εἰμι. See on 6.35.

ὁ ποιμὴν ὁ καλός. καλός corresponds to the Hebrew יפה (yapheh), used for example at Ex. R. 2.2. in describing David as a shepherd (רעה יפה, ro‘eh yapheh). It may be compared with ἀληθινός, used several times with the characteristic Johannine predicates of Jesus (see on 1.9); here Jesus is contrasted not with temporal human copies of an eternal reality, but with men (thieves, robbers, and hirelings) whose attitude to the sheep was the reverse of his own. Brown renders model, Lindars ideal; Betz, 103, notes that καλός is used of the θεῖος ἀνήρ. The background of the description of Jesus as Shepherd is closely akin to that of Door (see on v. 9); see especially Bauer, 143f. (i) In the Old Testament God is described as the Shepherd of his people: e.g. Ps. 23.1; 80.2; Isa. 40.11; Jer. 31.9; cf. Ps. 74.1; 79.13; 95.7; 100.3, where the same description is implied in the description of the people as sheep. David (or the Davidic Messiah) is spoken of as a shepherd in Ps. 78.70–2; Ezek. 37.24; Micah 5.3 (cf. Ps. Sol. 17.45), and in Jer. 2.8; 10.20; 12.10 we read of unfaithful shepherds who injure God's flock. Unfaithful shepherds and God as the true shepherd are found together in Zech. 11.4–9, and in Ezek. 34 passim (emphasized by Dodd, Interpretation, 358ff.; Sidebottom, 75, compares the use of Ezek. 15 in John 10) these two ideas are combined with that of David as God's shepherd. In Isa. 63.11 (LXX) Moses is the 'shepherd of the sheep'. This description is found also in rabbinic writings, e.g. *Ex. R.* 2.2 where it is said that Moses was first tested as a shepherd of sheep before being allowed to act as shepherd of God's people (for other examples see S.B. II, 209, III, 407). In the Qumran literature CD 13.9f. is not a good parallel since it refers not to a messianic figure but to the Overseer and contains only the analogy 'as a shepherd . . .' (. . . כרועה). (ii) In non-Jewish circles also gods and great men were described as shepherds; Bauer (loc. cit.) notes the following: Anubis, Attis, Yima, Zarathustra, Marduk, and the Phrygian god. Babylonian kings and Greek heroes (especially Agamemnon—see the discussion in Xenophon *Memorabilia* III, ii) were spoken of as shepherds of their people; Apollonius of Tyana (Philostratus, *Vita* VIII, 22) spoke of his disciples as his flock (ποίμνη). (iii) Important sayings in the synoptic tradition bear upon the subject. See especially Mark 6.34 (cf. Matt. 9.36); Matt. 18.12–14 (cf. Luke 15.3–7); Mark 14.27 (=Matt. 26.31); Matt. 25.32. In most of these passages the comparison between the ministry of Jesus and the work of a shepherd is general, but the messianic shepherding of God's people lies in the background. Cf. in the rest of the New Testament Heb. 13.20; 1 Peter 2.25; 5.4. (iv) Philo draws together the biblical and Hellenistic themes. Thus (in the manner of *Ex. R.* above) he argues that Moses was first trained and tested as a shepherd of sheep before being allowed to act as shepherd of God's people (*Mos.* 1, 60–2), since shepherding is the best preparation for rulership (διὸ καὶ ποιμένες λαῶν οἱ βασιλεῖς, 61). God is the Shepherd of his people and also employs as shepherd his firstborn Son or Word (*Agr.* 50–4). Dodd, *Interpretation*, 57, adds *Post.* 67f. Even more than Philo John is primarily dependent upon the biblical and messianic meaning of the shepherd imagery, but he is doubtless aware also of other ideas of divine kingship, and it is not wrong to say that the 'subject [*sc.* of John 10.1–18] is: the Divine-spiritual world and Jesus as the all-inclusive centre of that world by virtue of his unity with his Father' (Odeberg, 313), provided it is recognized that for John, guided as he was by the earlier tradition, these notions are focused upon the incarnate life and death of Jesus. A parallel to John's thought without this essential condition is found in Manda d⁶Hayye (also a 'good shepherd') in the Mandaean writings. The importance of these, and with them the essentially gnostic background of the Johannine concept of the shepherd, is stressed by Bultmann. It is however better to see John moving from an Old Testament base in a gnostic direction than assimilating gnosticism to the Old Testament.

τὴν ψυχὴν αὐτοῦ τίθησιν. A new thought is here introduced, suggested by the θύσῃ καὶ ἀπολέσῃ of v. 10. The thief takes the life of the sheep; the good shepherd gives his own life for the sheep. τιθέναι τὴν ψυχήν is peculiar to John and 1 John (10.11,15,17f.; 13.37f.; 15.13; 1 John 3.16); cf. δοῦναι τὴν ψυχήν (Mark 10.45). It may represent the rabbinic מסר נפשו (*masar naphsho*, 'to give one's life'; cf. מסר עצמו למיתה, *masar ʿatsmo lᵉmithah*, 'to give oneself up to death'); more probably it is a variant of διδόναι τὴν ψυχήν intended to emphasize the free action of Jesus in dying; see v. 18. Here and elsewhere the unusualness of the expression gave rise to variants; in this verse P⁴⁵ ℵ* D it vg sin have διδωσιν, Clement (2/4), ἐπιδίδωσιν. This feature of the parable is not derived from the Old Testament or any other source, nor does it enter into the synoptic shepherd parables; it is based specifically upon the crucifixion as a known historical event. For the prediction of the death of Jesus cf. Mark 8.31; 9.12,31; 10.33f.,38f.,45; 12.8; and the parallels.

ὑπὲρ τῶν προβάτων. In the Synoptic Gospels ὑπέρ is used of the death of Christ only at Mark 14.24 (and at Luke 22.19f., if these verses be counted part of the original text of Luke). But in John ὑπέρ nearly always carries the significance of death: 6.51; 10.11,15; 11.50ff.; 18.14 (and cf. 17.19 with the note)— the death of Jesus; 13.37f.—Peter promises to lay down his life for Jesus; 15.13—a man lays down his life for his friends. The word, however, though certainly suggesting a sacrificial (in no technical sense) death for the benefit of others, conveys no more precise shade of meaning.

12. ὁ μισθωτὸς καὶ οὐκ ὢν ποιμήν. On οὐ with the participle see M. 1, 231f.: 'In many of these examples [taken from the papyri] we can distinctly recognize, it seems, the lingering consciousness that the proper negative for a statement of a downright fact is οὐ. . . . Much the same principles may be applied to the New Testament.' Philo (*Post.* 98, *Agr.* 27–9) contrasts the shepherd (ποιμήν) with the inferior cattle-rearer (κτηνοτρόφος), but the point of his contrast is quite different from John's.

τὰ πρόβατα ἴδια. Cf. v. 3.

θεωρεῖ τὸν λύκον. For such attacks cf. 1 Sam. 17.34–6, and for the hireling's flight 4 Ezra 5.18 (. . . *sicut pastor gregem suum in manibus luporum malignorum* (*derelinquit*)).

καὶ ὁ λύκος ἁρπάζει αὐτὰ καὶ σκορπίζει. These words must, in view of the reading which must certainly be accepted in v. 13 (see below), be regarded as a parenthesis, adding vividness to the picture. ἁρπάζειν, 'to carry off', is used of wild animals from the time of Homer; σκορπίζειν, 'to scatter', is found in the LXX and late writers only; see especially Mark 14.27 (quoted from Zech. 13.7) πατάξω τὸν ποιμένα, καὶ τὰ πρόβατα διασκορπισθήσονται. There may be a recollection of Mark here, but more probably John was reconstructing a situation sufficiently familiar to him; cf. Acts 20.29—grievous wolves will harry the Ephesian flock.

13. Before ὅτι, many MSS. add ὁ δὲ μισθωτὸς φεύγει; these words are however omitted by P45 P66 P75 ℵ B D W Θ and other MSS., no doubt rightly. Without them the construction though not impossible is awkward; they were added to improve it. W also omits ὅτι μισθωτός ἐστιν; this too improves the construction and is a corruption.

οὐ μέλει αὐτῷ περί. For the construction of the impersonal verb cf. 12.6, and for the sense (in reverse) 1 Peter 5.7. The hireling's flight is due to his character and relation with the sheep; he cares for himself and his wages, not for the sheep.

14f. ἐγώ εἰμι. The repetition brings out the importance of the new theme of mutual recognition which is introduced in these verses. Jesus, the good shepherd and no hireling, owns the sheep; he knows them and they know him (cf. v. 3). This mutual knowledge is analogous to the mutual knowledge which exists between the Father and the Son; on this characteristic Johannine theme of knowledge see Introduction, pp. 81f., and on 1.10; 6.69. The present passage, which stresses the mutual knowledge of God and believer, raises acutely the problem of the origin of John's conception of knowledge. 'This profound conception is by no means peculiar to Christianity, but a common possession of oriental-hellenistic mysticism' (E. Norden, *Agnostos Theos* (1923), 287). This view is to some extent borne out by passages such as the prayer from the magical papyrus published by C. Wessely (*Denkschrift der kaiserlichen Akademie, Wien*, Phil.-Hist. Classe xlii (1893), 55; cf. R. Reitzenstein, *Poimandres* (1904), 20f.): ... οἶδά σε, ʿΕρμῆ, τίς εἶ καὶ πόθεν εἶ ... οἶδά σε, ʿΕρμῆ, καὶ σὺ ἐμέ. ἐγώ εἰμι σὺ καὶ σὺ ἐγώ. It seems very probable that John was not unaware of language of this kind, which bears so close a resemblance to his own. Yet the differences pointed out in the notes referred to above remain, and are indeed underlined by these verses, which conclude with the statement that Jesus lays down his life for the sheep. This makes any kind of identification between God and worshipper unthinkable; man is not deified but delivered. Moreover, knowledge here evidently implies and includes love; it is a moral relation between distinct persons. Cf. Matt. 11.27 = Luke 10.22; John's explicit reference to Jesus' sacrificial death however makes it clear that the relation is neither mystical nor pietistic (Bultmann). Mutual knowledge means mutual determination—of the shepherd to his sheep in love, of the sheep to the shepherd in gratitude, faith, and obedience.

16. ἄλλα πρόβατα ... οὐκ ... ἐκ τῆς αὐλῆς ταύτης. Cf. 11.51ff.; Isa. 56.8; and see O. Hofius in *Z.N.T.W.* 58 (1967), 289ff. For the αὐλή see v. 1. This verse reinforces the interpretation given at v. 5. The αὐλή is Israel and it contains some who are Christ's own sheep and some (the unbelieving Jews) who are not. The incarnation makes clear the predestined distinction between the two groups. Christ then has some sheep in the αὐλή of Judaism, but also others who are not of that αὐλή, that is, Gentiles. John was written in the context of the Gentile mission.

κἀκεῖνα δεῖ με ἀγαγεῖν. The Gentile mission is itself an activity of Christ, just as his ministry in Palestine was.

τῆς φωνῆς μου ἀκούσουσιν. Cf. v. 3, where the Jewish 'sheep' hear the shepherd's voice. There is no significance in the fact that in v. 3 ἀκούει (singular) is used, whereas here the plural is used. In this verse the neuter plural subject is further from the verb and the thought of the 'sheep' as individual persons takes precedence. Cf. in the first part of this verse ἃ οὐκ ἔστιν.

γενήσεται (P⁶⁶ P⁷⁵ ℵ* ω) μία ποίμνη, εἷς ποιμήν. There is much to be said for the plural verb, γενήσονται (P⁴⁵ B ℵ D Θ)—not 'there shall be' but 'they shall become'. John's thought is not identical with that of the Stoic view of the unity of mankind, although the Stoics sometimes used similar language (cf. Zeno quoted in Plutarch, *de Alex. virt.* 1, 6, ... εἷς δὲ βίος ᾗ καὶ κόσμος ὥσπερ ἀγέλης συννόμου νόμῳ κοινῷ συντρεφομένης). For John, the unity of the one flock is not a given unity naturally existing, but a unity created in and by Jesus; though it is not impossible that he wished to convey to his readers that the achievement of the Stoic ideal had been anticipated in the church. As is indicated by the first part of this verse, his primary thought is of the unity of Jew and Gentile in the church; cf. especially Eph. 2.11–22; 4.3–6. He also emphasizes again, as frequently, the unity of believers with Christ and of Christ with the Father. For the 'one shepherd' cf. Ezek. 34.23. For μία ποίμνη the Vulgate has *unum ouile*, 'one fold'. This is a mistranslation but not so misleading as is sometimes supposed; there is nothing to suggest that John thought of one flock lodged in a number of different folds.

17. διὰ τοῦτό με ὁ πατὴρ ἀγαπᾷ. The relation between the Father and the Son is essential and eternal; John does not mean that the Father loved Christ because the crucifixion took place. But the love of the Father for the Son is a love that is eternally linked with and mutually dependent upon the Son's complete alignment with the Father's will and his obedience even unto death. It is this that makes him the Revealer (Bultmann).

ἵνα πάλιν λάβω αὐτήν. It is possible, but, in view of the weakening of ἵνα in Hellenistic Greek, not certain, that *purpose* is intended and stressed: the resumption of life was the intention behind the suffering of Jesus; he died that the power of his resurrection might be manifested and released. Otherwise the clause means simply, 'with a view to taking it again'.

18. οὐδεὶς ἦρεν αὐτὴν ἀπ' ἐμοῦ. ἦρεν is the reading of P⁴⁵ ℵ* B; all other authorities read αἴρει. The aorist is the more difficult reading and is probably to be preferred. It does not refer to earlier unsuccessful attempts upon the life of Jesus, but to the crucifixion viewed as an event in the past—viewed, that is, from John's own standpoint. It is very unlikely that, in the production of the gospel in Greek, an Aramaic participle properly referring to present or future was wrongly given a perfect sense (Torrey, 114); the same tendency which led to the substitution of αἴρει for ἦρεν would have prevented such an error. It is also unlikely that there is an unfavourable comparison with the Qumran Teacher of Righteousness, where martyrdom (if it is rightly inferred from texts that are anything but explicit) was unwilling; cf. v. 8 and the note. To prove that Jesus accepted death voluntarily was an important point in early Christian apologetic.

ἐξουσίαν ἔχω in John means little more than *possum*; 7.1 (see the note); 19.10f.

ταύτην τὴν ἐντολήν. The words ἐντολή and ἐντέλλεσθαι are frequent in the latter part of John (and in 1 and 2 John). The Father gives a commandment to Jesus (10.18; 12.49f.; 14.31; 15.10) and he gives commandments to his disciples (13.34; 14.15,21; 15.10,12,14,17). The characteristic ('new') commandment of Jesus is that his disciples should love one another (13.34; 15.12,17). If they keep his commandments they abide in his love and show their love for him (14.15,21; 15.10,14). Similarly the love of the Father for the Son is bound up with the Son's voluntary acceptance of suffering in the work of salvation. The word ἐντολή therefore sums up the Christian doctrine of salvation from its origin in the eternal love of God, manifested in Jesus, to the mutual love of Christians in the church. Jesus himself found complete freedom of action in obedience (v. 18a); so will the disciples.

19. σχίσμα; for this word see 9.16. It is unnecessary (with Bernard—see the introduction to this section) to suppose that vv. 1–18 and vv. 19–29 have been displaced and that v. 19 should immediately follow 9.41, the σχίσμα being then the result of the healing of the man born blind. The σχίσμα is caused by τοὺς λόγους τούτους, that is, by the parable of the shepherd and the door. (It is true that sometimes in the New Testament λόγος (like the Hebrew דבר) means not spoken word but thing, fact, deed; but this usage never occurs in John.) In Mark also parables produce division (Mark 4.10–12); both miracles and parables are revelation, the shining of the true light, and it is this that distinguishes man from man (3.19–21).

20. δαιμόνιον ἔχει καὶ μαίνεται. There is one charge only here, not two; the madness is not distinct from but is regarded as the result of demon possession.

Cf. 7.20; 8.48; Mark 3.21f.,30. Cf. Wisd. 5.4, τὸν βίον αὐτοῦ [sc. τοῦ δικαίου] ἐλογισάμεθα μανίαν. Cf. also Justin, *Trypho* 38.1 (Martyn).

21. The words of Jesus, though possibly obscure (v. 6), are intelligent and searching, and some at least cannot view a beneficent miracle as a sign of madness. The section ends dramatically and appropriately with division and suspense, which are resumed in the next (v. 24). 1 QS 4.11 is not a significant parallel.

21. WHO IS JESUS? (II)

10.22–42

The middle section of the gospel (chs. 7—10) comes to an end with another section which is primarily Christological. The question who Jesus is is raised bluntly (v. 24), and answered not indeed in the terms in which it was asked but with equal plainness.

Although the material which begins in ch. 7 (when Jesus goes up to the feast of Tabernacles) is plainly a unit as regards thought, John places the conclusion at the feast of Dedication (v. 22). For conceivable connections between the themes suggested by the feast and those of this passage see the note on v. 22. In response to a demand that he should plainly declare who he is, Jesus (*a*) draws attention to the witness of his works, (*b*) explains that the objectors cannot believe because they are not of his sheep. Faith rests upon election, not upon human choice. Those however who are his enjoy the infallible protection of the Father. To be Christ's is to belong to the Father, since he and the Father are one. This claim provokes another murderous attack, the Jews (rightly) asserting that Jesus is claiming to be divine. Jesus counters by reference to an Old Testament passage in which men to whom the word of God came are said to be divine; why then should not the incarnate Word of God be so described? The touchstone of his claims lies in his works; if they are the works of God the reciprocal indwelling of God and Christ may be accepted. This argument proves, however, to have no effect. The works correspond to the words and have no automatic effect; they can be received only by faith.

This paragraph recalls the discourse on the good shepherd, and certain earlier Johannine incidents (v. 32). It has no direct parallel in the Synoptic Gospels (cf. however v. 39) but its substance is closely related to the Marcan theme of the messianic secret (see Introduction, pp. 70f.). Evidently it is not clear to the Jews whether Jesus is or is not claiming messianic status; evidently also he does not intend to give an unambiguous answer to their question (cf. 8.25). He will not say, 'I am the Messiah.' The two points of his answer, noted above, are found in Mark, and in other strands of the synoptic tradition. Thus, although it is wrong to seek from Jesus a sign from heaven (Mark 8.11–13; Matt.

12.38f.; 16.1–4; Luke 11.16; 12.54–6), the works he performs are nevertheless full of meaning to those who have eyes to see; indeed they are the clearest evidence he offers of his royal authority (Mark 4.41; 8.17–21; Matt. 11.4–6 = Luke 7.22f.; Matt. 12.28 = Luke 11.20). Further, men are divided in the Synoptic Gospels as in John into two classes, those who are Christ's sheep and those who are not, and it is recognized (though by no means so clearly stated as in John) that the ground of this distinction lies ultimately in the Father's will (Mark 4.11f.; Matt. 11.25ff.; 16.17; Luke 10.21f.). John brings out the point that the issue between Jesus and the Jews is in the last resort Christological, and makes clearer the absolute relation between Jesus and the Father. Lightfoot rightly points out a measure of parallelism between this paragraph and Mark 14.55–64 (note especially the high priest's question, Are you the Christ?), and Dodd, *Interpretation*, 361, observes that there is 'a movement from Jewish messianic categories to categories more akin to Hellenistic religious thought'.

At the close of the incident (which is also the close of the great central section of debates, chs. 7—10) Jesus withdraws to the place where John used to baptize. The purpose of this topographical note is twofold. First, Jesus is represented as retiring to a place of safety, whence, at the right moment and of his own free will (11.7), he will return to Jerusalem in order to give life to the world by his death. Second, he is once more brought into relation with the Baptist, and an opportunity is thereby given for reconsidering the Baptist's witness.

22. ἐγένετο τότε τὰ ἐνκαίνια—the Feast of the Dedication, or *Hanukkah* (חנוכה). On this feast see O. S. Rankin, *The Origins of the Festival of Hanukkah* (1930). It celebrated the rededication of the Temple (in 165 B.C.) after its profanation by Antiochus Epiphanes. It began on the 25th of the month Chislev (approximately, December), and lasted eight days. It was an occasion of great rejoicing. See 1 Macc. 4.36–59; 2 Macc. 1.9,18; 10.1–8; Josephus, *Ant.* XII, 316–25. No note of time has been given in John's narrative since the references (7.2,37) to the feast of Tabernacles, held in October, and it seems probable that here he has no other intention than that of indicating the lapse of a short interval; it does not seem possible to detect any symbolical correspondence between the conduct of the feast and the ensuing discussion (though according to Rankin (191–256) *Hanukkah* was the 'feast of the new age'). It is worth noting that though the lighting of lamps was so marked a feature of the feast that already in the time of Josephus it was called 'Lights' (φῶτα, *Ant.* XII, 325) Jesus is not here spoken of as the light of the world. See however on vv. 30, 34, 36. *Hanukkah* and Tabernacles resembled one another (in 2 Macc. 1.9 *Hanukkah* is referred to as 'the Tabernacles of the month Chislev'), but this fact does not seem to be significant.

χειμὼν ἦν, December. But χειμών may mean 'wintry weather', and this note may be intended to give the reason why Jesus was walking in Solomon's porch and not in the open.

23. ἐν τῇ στοᾷ τοῦ Σολομῶνος. Cf. Acts 3.11; 5.12. According to Josephus (*Bel.* v, 184f.; *Ant.* xv, 396–401; xx, 220f.) it was on the eastern side of the

Temple. It is not mentioned in the Mishnah tractate *Middoth*, and certainty regarding its location cannot be achieved. See *Beginnings* v, 483–6. In Mark 11.27 Jesus walks in the Temple immediately before the question about authority and the parable of the Vineyard owner's son (Lightfoot).

24. ἐκύκλωσαν. The word occurs repeatedly in Ps. 118(117).10ff., but it is very doubtful whether an allusion is intended. For οἱ Ἰουδαῖοι see on 1.19; they are the enemies of Jesus, and John does not find it necessary to specify any particular sect.

ἕως πότε τὴν ψυχὴν ἡμῶν αἴρεις; The words are generally understood to mean, 'How long do you [mean to] keep us in suspense?' But Pallis (23f.) quotes Pernot who on the basis of Modern Greek idiom translates 'Jusqu'à quand vas-tu nous tracasser [trouble, annoy, vex, pester] de la sorte?' The idiom is not wholly modern, for we may cite Sophocles, *Oedipus Rex* 914, ὑψοῦ γὰρ αἴρει θυμὸν Οἰδίπους; Euripides, *Hecuba* 69f., . . . αἴρομαι . . . δείμασι, φάσμασιν. This point is not unimportant, for if the meaning is suspense, we must think of not unfriendly Jews who simply wish to find out the truth; if it is annoyance we must think of Jesus' adversaries who are vexed by his not wholly explicit claims which give no adequate basis for attack. It is very unlikely that τὴν ψυχὴν ἡμῶν αἴρειν means 'take away our life', that is, destroy us.

εἰ σὺ εἶ ὁ Χριστός, εἰπὸν ἡμῖν παρρησίᾳ. For παρρησία see on 7.4. For the whole sentence cf. Luke 22.67, εἰ σὺ εἶ ὁ Χριστός, εἰπὸν ἡμῖν. John may be dependent upon Luke (see G. Delling, *Der Kreuzestod Jesu in der urchristlichen Verkündigung* (1971), n. 577), but the whole of the present section recalls the Marcan trial before the high priest, with its question, charge of blasphemy, and murderous attack. This challenge can be taken in two ways (see the preceding note): either as the request of puzzled men, or the attack of those who have already made up their minds that Jesus is not the Christ and are seeking an opportunity to accuse him. There is a 'messianic secret' in John, though it is expressed differently from Mark's (see Introduction, pp. 70f.). To 'his own sheep' Jesus is the good shepherd—the Messiah; the others cannot 'hear his voice' and believe (vv. 26f.). Jesus is at the same time a hidden and a manifest Messiah.

25. εἶπον ὑμῖν, καὶ οὐ πιστεύετε. Cf. Luke 22.67, ἐὰν ὑμῖν εἴπω, οὐ μὴ πιστεύσητε. The Jews are right, and yet Jesus is right also (Bauer, 145). Only to the Samaritan woman (4.26) has Jesus specifically declared himself to be the Messiah (cf. his avowal to the man born blind (9.37)· that he is the Son of man). Yet his teaching has so constantly enforced and illustrated his unique relation with the Father that there should have been no room for doubt— and indeed with the elect there is no doubt (6.69).

τὰ ἔργα ἃ ἐγὼ ποιῶ. The *nominativus pendens* is characteristic of John. This sentence extends the previous statement; Jesus has spoken (εἶπον), and his actions also have declared his status, precisely because he has not done them in his own authority but ἐν τῷ ὀνόματι τοῦ πατρός μου. On the ἔργα of Jesus, their testimony, and the faith generated by them, see Introduction, pp. 75–8, and on 4.34; 5.36.

26f. See on v. 24, and cf. vv. 3, 5, 14f.; and especially 12.39, οὐκ ἐδύναντο πιστεύειν, with the notes. At the end of this verse D ω it add καθὼς εἶπον ὑμῖν; this may be a gloss; in any case it shows decisively that vv. 1–18 must always have preceded vv. 19–29 (see on v. 19). The allegory merges into its application (Lindars).

28. κἀγὼ δίδωμι αὐτοῖς ζωὴν αἰώνιον. Cf. v. 10. On ζωή see on 1.4, on αἰώνιος on 3.15. That Christ gives his own eternal life is the constantly recurring theme of the gospel, here stated παρρησίᾳ, elsewhere expressed as water, bread, light, pasture, and so on.

οὐ μὴ ἀπόλωνται εἰς τὸν αἰῶνα, the negative result of receiving eternal life. In Johannine usage εἰς τὸν αἰῶνα simply strengthens the negative οὐ μή (cf. 11.26); not 'They shall not perish eternally' but 'They shall never perish'.

οὐχ ἁρπάσει τις. Cf. v. 12, ὁ λύκος ἁρπάζει αὐτά. But these sheep are under the care not of a hireling but of the good shepherd. Cf. also v. 29, the sheep will not be snatched out of the Father's hand. See the reference to the hand of the prophet and the hand of God in Ezekiel 37.17,19, a Dedication *haphtarah* (Guilding, 130f.). This virtual identification of Jesus with God leads to the charge of blasphemy; cf. Lev. 24.1—25.13, 'the seder for the second year of the cycle' (ibid.). The connections are not close enough to be quite convincing.

29. The text of the first part of this verse is in confusion. The words between μου and ἐστιν appear in these forms:

    (a) ὃ δέδωκέν μοι πάντων μεῖζον, B (it vg) boh;

    (b) ὃ δέδωκέν μοι πάντων μεῖζων, ℵ W sah;

    (c) ὃς δέδωκέν μοι μείζων πάντων, ω sin pesh hl (P⁶⁶, ὃς ἔδωκεν . . .);

    (d) ὃς δέδωκέν μοι μεῖζον πάντων, Θ;

    (e) ὁ δεδωκώς μοι πάντων μεῖζων, D.

The masculine ὅς thus appears in P⁶⁶ Θ sin pesh hl, the neuter ὅ in ℵ B W it vg; the masculine μεῖζων is in P⁶⁶ ℵ W syr, the neuter μεῖζον in B Θ it vg. The reading of D is either correct, or a radical attempt to clear up a muddle— probably the latter. The attestation of the neuters, though small numerically, is very strong; nevertheless, the masculines are far more suitable to the context. If we accept the masculine readings the argument runs: No one shall snatch them out of my hand; my Father who has given them to me is greater than all others; no one therefore can snatch them out of his hand. This is straightforward and makes good sense. If on the other hand we accept the neuter reading ((a) above), it is difficult to attach a meaning to the sentence and impossible to fit it into the context. The sentence will run: As to my Father, what he has given me is greater than all, and no one can snatch . . . The *nominativus pendens* is Johannine; but what is the Father's gift to the Son? The context suggests the sheep, but these cannot be said to be greater than all. The next possibility is the ἔργα of v. 25 (cf. 5.36); but this is four verses away. Augustine's interpretation (*Tractatus in Joh.* XLVIII, 6), that the Father's gift to Christ is the being Life, Logos, etc., is even more strained. Internal evidence seems therefore decisively in favour of the reading (c)—ὅς . . . μεῖζων; but it is impossible to explain how this excellent reading came to be changed into the difficult ὅ . . . μεῖζον. It may be that John wrote the text which has been preserved (perhaps accidentally) in Θ, that is, ὅς . . . μεῖζον. For the neuter adjective cf. Matt. 12.6; 12.41f. (=Luke 11.31f.), and especially the neuter ἕν of the next verse. This reading must be rendered: My Father who gave them to me is greater than any other power, and no one can snatch . . . This reading makes as good sense as (c), and in addition could easily give rise to ὅ . . . μεῖζον, ὅς . . . μεῖζων, and even (in course of time) ὁ ... μείζων (a very difficult reading which must presumably be translated: My Father in regard to what he has given me is greater than all). This seems to be the only satisfactory way of accounting for all the variants; the suggestion in M. 1, 50 ('. . . that the false reading in John 10.29 started from an original μείζω' (sic)) demands too much conjecture. It should be noted that in an important article (*J.T.S.* 11 (1960), 342ff.) J. N. Birdsall prefers reading (*b*); he agrees with the translation of it given above. He regards it as the reading that is capable of explaining the rest. It is probable that ὅς should be read rather than ὁ, since the relative follows the masculine πατήρ (but surely here Birdsall overlooks the principle *difficilior lectio potior*, on which elsewhere he properly lays some stress). In regard to the choice between μείζων and μεῖζον we must, he says, apply the criteria of syntax and style, context and exegesis. On these grounds he rejects μεῖζον, and claims that 'My Father in regard to what he has given me is greater than all' fits the context, where 'the subject is the unassailability of the flock of God because of his guardian power' (344). It must however be remarked that this sentence, with its relative clause treated as an accusative of respect, fits the context no better than (*d*), which simply declares that the Father who gave me my flock is greater than anything else in the world,—and is therefore able to defend his own. Suitability to the context, which turns out to be Birdsall's main criterion, thus proves not to favour his reading more than others. It seems, too, unsound to reject a reading contained in Θ on the ground that its scribe was not a native Greek speaker. The question, however, is an open one. Birdsall may be right; or μεῖζον in Θ may be an itacistic variant of μείζων; in this case P[66] D Θ ω sin pesh hl would be in essential agreement: The Father who has given (them) me is greater than all. It is a fair question whether any alternative to this is not so *difficilis* as to be *impossibilis*. ὅς δέδωκεν ... μείζων is the reading preferred by J. Whittaker (*Vigiliae Christianae* 24 (1970), 241–60), who not only gives a strong textual argument but offers a convincing Hellenistic setting for the reading he prefers.

30. ἐγὼ καὶ ὁ πατὴρ ἕν ἐσμεν. Cf. 1.1f.; 17.11. John is thinking in terms of revelation not of cosmological theory (Bultmann, 387). His meaning turns upon the belief that the actions and words of Jesus were veritably the actions and words of God, who thus uniquely confronted men in his incarnate Son. This unity is often expressed in moral terms: Jesus, who was sent by God, acts in such complete obedience to God's will that what he does is a complete revelation of that will (see e.g. vv. 17f.); here, as in the Prologue, John's language comes somewhat nearer to metaphysics, but even here the thought is by no means purely metaphysical and v. 17 is not far away: the oneness of Father and Son is a oneness of love and obedience even while it is a oneness of essence. The suggestion (Odeberg, 332) that ἐγώ means the *Shekinah* and that union of God with his *Shekinah* effects salvation is very fanciful. It may be somewhat more relevant to recall the privileged intercourse of Moses with God mentioned in Num. 7.89, the last verse of the Torah lection for the feast of Dedication (*Megillah* 3.6); cf. vv. 22, 34, 36. But it must be admitted that John gives no indication that this verse was in his mind. For the interpretation (including the patristic interpretation) of this verse, and its relation with 14.28, see further 'The Father is greater than I'.

31. ἐβάστασαν πάλιν λίθους. Cf. 8.59. The penalty for blasphemy was stoning,

but stoning was not a matter of lynch law, though that is what seems to be in operation here. An attempted lynching is, of course, not impossible, and Jewish practice in the first half of the first century may have differed from that which is codified in the Mishnah. Belief that John had first-hand knowledge of Palestinian Judaism must however be weakened by this verse. According to Delling (see on v. 24) it corresponds to Luke 22.71.

32. πολλὰ ἔργα ἔδειξα ὑμῖν καλὰ ἐκ τοῦ πατρός. The works were God's gift to Jesus (5.36). Not 'many' works have so far been described in the gospel—six, in fact; but John was well aware that many other signs had been done (20.30f.) and assumed that they were known. καλός is used five times in this chapter (three times of the shepherd, twice of works); elsewhere in the gospel in one verse only (2.10, of wine). It is impossible to find a single English word equivalent to the Greek, which suggests deeds of power and moral excellence, resulting in health and well-being. Their significance, however, lay in the fact that they proceeded from (ἐκ) God.

33. λιθάζομεν must, in view of v. 39, be described as conative. The word is not a common one, and is not the technical term used for stoning as a punishment. The only occurrences in the Old Testament are 2 Sam. 16.6,13.

περὶ βλασφημίας. It is difficult to comprehend the references in the gospels to blasphemy under what is known of the Jewish law of blasphemy. The only formal statement in the Mishnah (*Sanhedrin* 7.5) is that the blasphemer 'is not culpable unless he pronounces the name [the Tetragrammaton] itself'. Two sayings which recall the present passage are ascribed to R. Abbahu (*c.* A.D. 300). *Y. Taanith* 2, 65b, 59: If a man says to you, I am God, he lies; if he says, I am the Son of man, he will regret it in the end; if he says, I ascend into heaven—he has said it, but he will not perform it. *Ex. R.* 29.4: [Exod. 20.2 is quoted]—Compare a king of flesh and blood, who can rule as king, while he has a father or a brother or a son. But God says (Isa. 44.6), I am the first—therefore I have no father; and I am the last—therefore I have no brother; and apart from me there is no God—therefore I have no son. R. Abbahu lived in Caesarea and was no doubt engaged in anti-Christian polemic; his statements therefore cannot be taken as evidence for formulated views going back to the time of the ministry of Jesus. It is on the other hand very probable that such pronouncements were made whenever Jews and Christians came into conflict. The old midrash in the Passover Haggadah probably shows the same motive: [Deut. 26.8]—The Lord brought us forth out of Egypt, not by an angel, nor by a seraph, nor by a messenger (שליח, shaliaḥ, cf. v. 36), but the Holy One, blessed be he, in his glory and by himself, as it is said [Exod. 12.12]—I will go through the land of Egypt in that night, I myself and not an angel; and will smite all the firstborn in the land of Egypt, I myself and not a seraph; and against all the gods of Egypt I will execute judgements. I am the Lord, I am he (אני הוא), and not a messenger; I am the Lord, I am he (אני הוא, *'ᵃni hu'*; it is not inconceivable that there is here a retort to the ἐγώ εἰμι placed on the lips of Jesus in John—see D. Daube, *N.T.R.J.*, 325–9) and no other (or, and not another). Cf. also the prohibition against speaking with Christians mentioned by Trypho (Justin, *Trypho*, 38, . . . βλάσφημα γὰρ πολλὰ λέγεις). It is probable that John also reflects the controversy between church and synagogue (see e.g. on 9.22), but this is not to say that Jesus was not in his lifetime accused of blasphemy; see further on 19.7. The later humane regulations of the Mishnah are not decisive for the first century, especially for the Sadducees, who were in power in the Sanhedrin. See Klausner, 343f.; what to the Pharisees might have seemed no more than a 'rash fantasy' might have seemed far more serious to Sadducees. For a similar charge of blasphemy in the synoptic tradition see (apart from the trials) Mark 2.7 and parallels. See *Judaism*, 48f.

σὺ ἄνθρωπος ὢν ποιεῖς σεαυτὸν θεόν. See the preceding note and cf. 5.18. John reports the words ironically; he knows that Jesus, being God, has humbly accepted the form of a man.

34. οὐκ ἔστιν γεγραμμένον . . .; For the interrogative form of introduction cf. CD 9.5.

ἐν τῷ νόμῳ ὑμῶν. ὑμῶν is omitted by P⁴⁵ א* D Θ it sin, perhaps rightly, since it would occasion no difficulty to an early copyist, and its insertion (through assimilation to 8.17) would be natural. ὑμῶν, if read, impresses a modern reader as unnatural, since it is unlikely that a Jew would speak to Jews of '*your* law'. It is probable that John (whether or not he was Jewish by birth) was conscious of his membership of a community which when he wrote stood over against organized Judaism (see above on v. 33). Yet it must be remembered that the Old Testament was also the Bible of the church, and his purpose in using the word ὑμῶν (if he used it) was not to disavow the Old Testament but to press home upon the Jews the fact that the truth of the Christian position was substantiated by their own authoritative documents. 'Law' is used to cover the Psalter; cf. 12.34; 15.25; 1 Cor. 14.21. So also in rabbinic literature Torah sometimes covers the whole of the Old Testament. On the quotation that follows see A. T. Hanson in *N.T.S.* 11 (1965), 158–62; 13 (1967), 363–7.

ἐγὼ εἶπα· θεοί ἐστε. Ps. 82.6, אֲנִי אָמַרְתִּי אֱלֹהִים אַתֶּם. John quotes the LXX exactly. The next verse of the Psalm speaks of the 'princes' (ἄρχοντες) and it may be held to be possible that the use of the Psalm was suggested by the fact that Numbers 7 ('The Princes'—LXX, ἄρχοντες) was the Torah lesson for the feast of Dedication; but this is fanciful. According to *Tamid* 7.4 this Psalm was sung by the Levites in the Temple on the third day of the week; this fact seems to have no relevance, except to show that though this was a difficult passage for convinced monotheists to deal with it was not neglected. The most common interpretation (for the material see S.B. II, 543) seems to have been that the words were addressed to Israel when they received the Law at Sinai. Thus *Abodah Zarah* 5 a: R. Jose (*c.* A.D. 150) said: The Israelites have only received the Law that the angel of death may have no power over them, as it is written [Ps. 82.6]. Later passages make the same statement more explicitly, and in others the idea of receiving the Law and so becoming אֱלֹהִים, divine, is made personal rather than historical, but the active and decisive agent remains the Law. In the passage above it is Israel's sin (in the Golden Calf) that revokes the promise, in the words of Ps. 82.7 (Ye shall die like men); while in others the same notion is expressed in more general terms. For the interpretation of the Psalm see further J. A. Emerton, *J.T.S.* 11 (1960), 329–32.

35. πρὸς οὓς ὁ λόγος τοῦ θεοῦ ἐγένετο. For the construction cf. e.g. Hosea 1.1, λόγος κυρίου ὃς ἐγενήθη (הָיָה) πρὸς (עַל) 'Ωσῆε; but the persons intended here are probably not (as is often thought) the prophets, but, as is shown by the

above quotations, Israel constituted by the reception of the Law. This provides a more coherent argument than the suggestion (J. A. Emerton, op. cit., 330ff.) that angels are intended. This finds some support in the Qumran literature and leads to the argument that Jesus 'does not find an Old Testament text to prove directly that men can be called god. He goes back to fundamental principles and argues, more generally, that the word "god" can, in certain circumstances, be applied to beings other than God himself, to whom he has committed authority. The angels can be called gods because of the divine word of commission to rule the nations ... Jesus, however, whose commission is more exalted than theirs, and who is the Word himself, has a far better claim to the title' (332). See however M. de Jonge and A. S. van de Woude, *N.T.S.* 12 (1966), 312ff.

καὶ οὐ δύναται λυθῆναι ἡ γραφή, a parenthesis. For the use of λύειν cf. Matt. 5.19; John 7.23; also John 5.18 (λύειν τὸ σάββατον). The principle was an axiom both of Judaism and of primitive Christianity; the two differed only in their beliefs about the fulfilment of Scripture. It is possible that there is polemic here against the views just quoted, that the divine pronouncement θεοί ἐστε was annulled by the sin of the Golden Calf. The Jews are not to be allowed to escape the consequences of their own canonized literature—the argument is *ad homines*.

36. ὃν ὁ πατὴρ ἡγίασεν. The relative clause is an accusative of reference, governed by λέγετε, and explaining the ὅτι clause: Do you say of him whom ... You blaspheme? ἁγιάζειν is used in John only here and at 17.17,19, where Christ sanctifies himself for the sake of his disciples, and prays the Father to sanctify them. There is no real parallel in the New Testament (only at 1 Peter 3.15 is Christ said to be sanctified and there the meaning is quite different). ἁγιάζειν is used in its normal biblical sense—'to set apart for God's purpose'—and is an eminently suitable word to describe Jesus, who was appointed to fulfil on earth the Father's supreme purpose as his messenger. It is sometimes assumed that this 'sanctification' or 'consecration', especially as used at 17.19 (where see the note), implies a sacrificial meaning, but this is not so, though of course sacrificial ideas may be implied by the context. ἁγιάζειν and קדש do not refer specifically to sacrifices. Here the whole mission of Jesus, not his death only, is in mind. It is possible that the first verse of the Dedication lesson (Num. 7.1) may have prompted this statement, or affected the form of it. As Moses sanctified (ἡγίασεν, ויקדש) the Tabernacle and its contents for their holy purpose, so God sanctified (ἡγίασεν) Jesus for his mission.

καὶ ἀπέστειλεν εἰς τὸν κόσμον. For the sending of Jesus see especially on 20.21.

υἱὸς τοῦ θεοῦ εἰμι. Jesus had not used these words but verses such as 30 certainly imply their meaning. The *ad homines* argument of vv. 34–6 now comes to its close. In form it is naïve—though it cannot have been easy for Jews who took θεοί—אלהים in Ps. 82.6 at its face value to answer. If Scripture can describe men by such a word why should I not use it for myself? But behind the argument as thus formulated there lies no belief in the 'divinity' of humanity as such, but a conviction of the creative power of the word of God. Addressed to creatures it raises them above themselves; in Jesus it is personally present, and he may therefore with much more right be called divine. (This *a fortiori* kind of argument is found in the rabbinic writings; but it is so widespread wherever logical processes are used that to regard it as a sign of John's rabbinic knowledge is absurd.) τοῦ is omitted by P⁶⁶* ℵ D, perhaps rightly. Cf. Wisd. 2.18 (and, for υἱὸς ἀνθρώπου, John 5.27).

37. The crux of the argument is the character of Jesus' works. His sonship and apostleship could be disproved by deeds not congruent with them. Cf. 8.39f.—the ἔργα of Abraham and his descendants. Cf. 9.4.

38. τοῖς ἔργοις πιστεύετε. Cf. 14.11; also v. 25, and the references there. To recognize that the works of Jesus were the works of God would imply that God had sent Jesus, that Jesus was his ἀπόστολος (his שְׁלִיחַ, shaliaḥ; see on v. 33). In rabbinic Judaism prophets are not in general referred to as שְׁלִיחִים (sheliḥim) of God; this title is reserved for those who performed works specifically recognized as works guarded by the divine prerogative. Elisha was such a שְׁלִיחַ because he made conception possible for a barren woman, Elijah because he brought rain, and Elijah, Elisha, and Ezekiel because they raised the dead—these three works being all normally reserved for God's direct intervention (Midrash Ps. 78, § 5 (173b); S.B. III, 3f.). These considerations seem important here, but whether the rabbinic material on which they are based is early enough to make them truly relevant remains doubtful.

ἵνα γνῶτε καὶ γινώσκητε. The aorist subjunctive denotes the beginning of knowledge at a point in time—'that you may perceive'; the present subjunctive, the continuous and progressive state of knowledge. For καὶ γινώσκητε (P⁴⁵ P⁶⁶ P⁷⁵ B W Θ), ℵ ω vg read καὶ πιστεύσητε; the words are omitted altogether by D (it) sin.

ὅτι ἐν ἐμοὶ ὁ πατὴρ κἀγὼ ἐν τῷ πατρί. For the mutual indwelling of Father and Son cf. among many passages 14.10f.; 17.21; John here refers back to v. 30, the statement that provoked the debate of vv. 31–8.

'The charge to man to believe his works can only mean that man must allow himself to be questioned by Jesus' words, must allow the security of his previous understanding of himself to be shattered, and must accept the revelation of his true existence. The knowledge that he and the Father are one (v. 30), or as it is stated now, "that the Father is in me and I in the Father", stands not at the beginning but at the end of the way of faith. It cannot be blindly accepted as a dogmatic truth, but is the fruit of faith in the "works" of Jesus. When it is first heard it can only cause offence; but this causing offence is an integral part of the Revealer's "work"' (Bultmann, 391). The whole of Bultmann's interpretation of vv. 37ff. should be read. As an analysis of the impact of the revelation upon humanity it is convincing, but misses something of John's objective Christology.

39. ἐζήτουν οὖν αὐτὸν πάλιν πιάσαι. Cf. 7.30; 8.20,59. John no doubt intends his readers to think of a miraculous escape (cf. Luke 4.30). Jesus' hour was not yet come.

This verse marks the close of the third of the great divisions into which Bultmann divides the gospel ('The Revealer in conflict with the World'). This is a highly complicated block of material, and is constituted as follows: 7.1–13,14,25–9; 8.48–50,54f.; 7.30,37–44,31,32–6,45–52; 8.41–7,51,52f.,56–9; 9.1–41; 8.12; 12.44–50; 8.21–9; 12.34–6a,36b; 10.19–21,22–6,11–13, 1–6,7–10,14–18,27–30,31–9. On the question of dislocations in the text of the gospel see Introduction, pp. 21–4, and in the commentary passim.

40. ἀπῆλθεν πάλιν πέραν τοῦ ᾿Ιορδάνου. That is, to the east side, to Peraea. See 1.28, ἐν Βηθανίᾳ . . . πέραν τοῦ ᾿Ιορδάνου, ὅπου ἦν ὁ ᾿Ιωάννης βαπτίζων. Cf. Mark 10.1.

τὸ πρῶτον is used adverbially; for πρῶτον, πρότερον should perhaps be read, with P⁴⁵ א Θ it.

41. καὶ ἔλεγον. Bultmann puts the stop before this, and treats the third person plural verb as impersonal: Jesus stayed there and many came to him. And people were saying . . .

᾿Ιωάννης μὲν σημεῖον ἐποίησεν οὐδέν. Cf. 1.20ff.: the Baptist refused all titles and honours, and would be nothing but a voice announcing the presence of the Christ. Similarly his activity was in itself void of power, a mere washing with water (it is clear that σημεῖον must mean much more than 'symbol'); but like his words it had pointed forward to the living water, the Spirit, which Christ gave. John gives no account (except 1.26f.,29) of what the Baptist said about Jesus; he means in effect that Jesus fulfilled the Old Testament in the person and predictions of its last and greatest representative. 1.31 has been fulfilled, even though the authorities have not believed. E. Bammel, 'John did no miracle', in C. F. D. Moule (ed.), *Miracles* (1965), 179–202, argues that vv. 41,42 are likely 'to be an ancient fragment of tradition which represents the source's view of the Baptist more faithfully than does the present text-form of the introductory chapters. Its contents, based on a Jewish scheme, reflect the Christian–Jewish discussion rather than the Christian–Baptist one. The fact, that John was not reputed to have done miracles may have been used as a charge against the Christians, who claimed the Baptist as a witness for their Messiah' (200).

42. καὶ πολλοὶ ἐπίστευσαν εἰς αὐτὸν ἐκεῖ. Who were these 'many' and what were they doing at Bethany? Was the work of baptism still in progress in the absence of John? These questions cannot be answered, and it is doubtful whether they even presented themselves to John's mind. At the end of the great central section of the gospel he brings Jesus back to the place at which his ministry began. The next two chapters introduce the passion, and sum up the ministry as a whole—henceforth we hear no more of the water of life, the bread of life, the light of life; Jesus gives life itself. For the πολλοί cf. 2.23; 8.30. John tells us nothing further of these believers. They represent the abiding fruit of the ministry.

22. LAZARUS

·11.1–44

This, the most striking miracle story in John, is narrated in the plainest and most matter-of-fact style. The main points in the narrative may be indicated very briefly. A rather clumsy introduction (vv. 1f.) reveals the identity of a sick man, Lazarus. Jesus is summoned to care for him, but defers his help until Lazarus is dead. He then sets out for Bethany (near Jerusalem) and his disciples accompany him, though they know, in view of earlier plots, that he is going to his death. As Jesus approaches, one of Lazarus' sisters, Martha, goes to meet him; after conversation she returns to bring the other sister, Mary. There now forms round the grave of Lazarus a group consisting of Jesus, Mary and Martha, the disciples (as we may presume—they are not mentioned), and a body of Jews who have come to console the bereaved sisters. The love of Jesus for his dead friend is manifest, and the expectation of the reader is aroused by the orthodox resurrection hope of the sisters, the tentative faith of some of the onlookers, and a saying of Jesus (vv. 25f.). Nevertheless, Jesus' command to take away the stone which seals the grave causes surprise. He prays, thereby emphasizing his dependence on the Father, and bids the dead man come forth. Still in the trappings of death, Lazarus comes out alive. In the last miracle the last enemy is overthrown (Fenton); Dodd (*Interpretation*, 366) rightly says, 'the Hellenistic society to which this gospel was addressed was haunted by the spectacle of φθορά', but it is not only the Hellenistic world that has had to come to terms with death.

The meaning of this narrative for John is as simple as the narrative itself. Jesus in his obedience to and dependence upon the Father has the authority to give life to whom he will. The incident is a dramatic demonstration of the truth already declared in 5.21 (cf. 5.25,28), which is itself the best commentary on the incident. The raising of Lazarus is no piece of black magic, or even the supreme achievement of a saint; it is an anticipation of what is to take place at the last day. It means that the believer has eternal life; that he has passed from death into life.

What is the historical value of the story? This question depends mainly on the view taken of the sources and purpose of the gospel. It is of course possible to take an *a priori* view of miracle that rules out the possibility of such an event as this. If such an *a priori* view is taken there is clearly no further room for argument, and it is not within the province of this Commentary to discuss the philosophical aspects of miracle. If *a priori* opinions, whether negative or positive, be set aside, the chief argument against the historicity of the incident appears to be that there is no place for it in the synoptic tradition. The miracle is recorded by John not merely as a stupendous portent but also as the direct occasion of the fatal plot against Jesus (11.46,53). Mark, on the other hand (it is said), finds this direct occasion in the cleansing of the Temple (Mark 11.18). This argument is worth little, since Mark's notes on the reactions of the hearers of Jesus cannot always be taken seriously. For example, as early as Mark 3.6 the Pharisees and Herodians take counsel ὅπως αὐτὸν ἀπολέσωσι. This plot is then entirely lost to view in the Marcan narrative. It is also possible that the miracle story itself comes from early tradition though its connection with the death of Jesus may be a Johannine development (Brown). It is perhaps not so likely that John knew better than Mark the grounds for the Sanhedrin's action.

There is no parallel in any other gospel to the Johannine narrative as it stands (there are resurrection stories in Mark 5.21–43; Matt. 9.18–26; Luke 8.40–56; Luke 7.11–16); this, however, need not in itself mean that the narrative was created by John. There are suggestive parallels between the Johannine narrative and a Lucan parable (Luke 16.19–31). The conclusion of the Lucan parable is that, even should the poor man Lazarus rise from the dead, men will not be persuaded to repent. No such resurrection takes place, either in fact or in the fictitious narrative; but it is contemplated. It is probable, though not certain (see Introduction, p. 46), that John knew Luke, and therefore knew this parable. There is ground for thinking that elsewhere (notably Mark 11.12–14,20–5) 'miracles' may have developed out of parables; may this development not have taken place in the present chapter? It is indeed possible that this may have happened, though, as has already been said, it is also possible that John drew the narrative from tradition, where it may already have undergone some modification. Dodd, on the other hand, suggests that the name Lazarus may have come into the parable from the narrative tradition; it was known that the raising of a man called Lazarus had in fact failed to win men to faith (*Tradition*, 229). It is certain that John has himself edited the miracle to suit his own theological purposes. For the relation of these purposes to history, and for the relation of the gospel as a whole to history, see Introduction, pp. 141f. These questions are here raised in the most acute form, and there is no simple answer to the question, Did it happen?—except for those who can say either, Such things do not happen, or, Everything in the gospel must be taken at face value and in the most literal sense.

1. ἦν δέ τις ἀσθενῶν. For the construction cf. 5.5 (ἦν δέ τις ἄνθρωπος . . . ἔχων); also Judges 19.1; 1 Sam. 1.1; Esther 2.5 and especially Job 1.1 (ἄνθρωπός τις ἦν . . .), but John's words are less Hebraistic than any of these.

Λάζαρος. The name אֶלְעָזָר ('*El'azar*) had already in Hebrew been shortened to לְעָזָר (*Le'azar*), the form presupposed by the Greek. It is unlikely, though not impossible, that the etymological significance of the name ('God helps') was present to John's mind. Elsewhere in the New Testament the name occurs only in Luke 16.19–31, the parable of Lazarus and the rich man, in which the possibility of a resurrection of Lazarus is contemplated, though rejected.

ἀπὸ Βηθανίας. The construction is common (e.g. Acts 6.9). ἀπό is synonymous with ἐκ in ἐκ τῆς κώμης. Bethany is mentioned in all the Synoptic Gospels, and is here distinguished, by the reference to Mary and Martha and by the distance given in v. 18, from the Bethany of 1.28 (see the note there), which was in Peraea. The distinction was the more needful since, according to 10.40, Jesus was in Peraean Bethany when word was brought to him of the illness of Lazarus. Bethany in Judaea may probably be identified with El-'Azariyeh, S.E. of the Mount of Olives (the modern name is derived from Lazarus). W. H. Brownlee has a long discussion of Bethany and its significance in *J. & Q.*, 167–74.

Μαρίας (here even B, which usually has the indeclinable Semitic form Μαριάμ,

has the declinable Μαρία) καὶ Μάρθας. These sisters are mentioned only by
Luke (10.38–42) and John. Luke does not identify their home (εἰς κώμην τινά,
10.38). It seems on the whole probable that John knew Luke (see Introduction, pp. 46f.) and that he was able to locate the sisters at Bethany because
he identified Mary (see v. 2) with the woman who anointed Jesus at Bethany
(Mark 14.3–9; see further pp. 408–15).

2. John points forward to the incident which he describes in 12.1–8; but
it seems clear that he is able to presuppose that his readers were already
familiar with it; this implies that they were Christians, and knew the
synoptic tradition (or a tradition closely akin to it). The words used in this
allusion—μύρον, ἀλείφειν, ἐκμάσσειν, πόδες, θρίξ—are all used again in 12.3.
All of them are found in the Lucan anointing story, only μύρον in the Marcan.

ἦν δὲ Μαριάμ . . . ἧς ὁ ἀδελφὸς Λάζαρος ἠσθένει, 'it was Mary . . . whose brother
Lazarus was ill'. The construction is clumsy but not intolerable; the suggestion (Torrey, 144, 148f.) that John rendered a slightly corrupt Aramaic text
is unnecessary.

3. ἀπέστειλαν . . . λέγουσαι recalls the use of the Hebrew לֵאמֹר (cf. 2 Chron.
35.21), but there is no need to suspect translation. For the message cf. 2.3,
where the mother of Jesus also states a need, implying, without expressing,
a request for help. Here, as in ch. 2, Jesus makes no immediate response.

ὃν φιλεῖς ἀσθενεῖ. The antecedent of ὅν is expressed only in the verb. It seems
clear that, at least in this chapter, φιλεῖν and ἀγαπᾶν are synonymous; cf.
vv. 3, 36 (φιλεῖν), and 5 (ἀγαπᾶν). There is in these verses little ground for
the view that Lazarus was the 'beloved disciple'; see Introduction, pp. 116f.
and on 13.23. Cf. 15.14f.

4. οὐκ ἔστιν πρὸς θάνατον. This sickness will not end—finally—in death. For
the expression cf. 1 John 5.16f., ἁμαρτία πρὸς θάνατον. Cf. vv. 25f.

ἀλλ’ ὑπὲρ τῆς δόξης τοῦ θεοῦ. ὑπέρ with the genitive of a *thing* is not uncommon,
but the translation naturally depends upon the context; see Bauer, *Wörterbuch*, *s.v.* ὑπέρ, 1b. Here, 'for revealing', 'in order to reveal' the glory of
God. On δόξα see on 1.14. V. 40 shows that the meaning is not 'in order that
God may be glorified'; here as elsewhere the glory of God is not his praise,
but his activity.

ἵνα δοξασθῇ ὁ υἱός. The glory of God is however revealed in the glorification
of his Son. This sickness (ἵνα . . . is directly explanatory of ἡ ἀσθένεια) provides
an occasion upon which (in a proleptic manner, since his full glorification
lies in the future) God may bestow glory upon his Son. Cf. *P. Lond.* 121.503f.,
where a wonder-worker prays to Isis for a miracle in similar terms: Ἶσις . . .
δόξασόν μοι ὡς ἐδόξασα τὸ ὄνομα τοῦ υἱοῦς σου Ὥρος. The passage from death
to life, so vividly represented in this miracle, sets forth parabolically the
process by which Jesus himself returns to his glory with the Father.

5. ἠγάπα (ἐφίλει, D a e, is an assimilation to v. 3). This verse corrects a
possible misinterpretation of v. 6; Jesus' delay, and the consequent death
of Lazarus, were not due to lack of affection on his part.

6. τότε μέν looks forward to ἔπειτα μετὰ τοῦτο in the next verse, and lays
stress on the deliberate delay.

ἐν ᾧ ἦν (for these three words ἐπὶ τῷ, P[45] D, may well be correct) τόπῳ, attraction of relative and antecedent into the same clause, a construction fairly common in John.

δύο ἡμέρας. The motive for Jesus' delay is not stated. It is not likely (a) that Jesus was waiting for Lazarus to die, in order that a more glorious miracle might be effected. Lazarus was already dead at the time Jesus heard of his illness (cf. v. 39 (τεταρταῖος) and the fact that a journey of approximately one day was involved in each direction); and since in vv. 11, 14 it appears that Jesus was supernaturally informed of the death we may suppose that he knew of it as soon as it took place; consequently he must have known that if he had left Peraean Bethany as soon as the messengers arrived he would have had the opportunity of effecting a resurrection. It is possible (b) that Jesus waited in order that Lazarus might be *four days* dead (for the significance of this see on v. 39), but this seems far-fetched. A different kind of explanation has been found (c) in the situation in which the gospel was written, 'the problem raised in the Church by the continued delay in the promised coming of the Lord' (Guilding, 147): Jesus may delay, but he will come, and resurrection will follow. A more probable view is (d) that John wished to underline the fact that Jesus' movement towards Jerusalem, and so to his death, was entirely self-determined; no mere human affection led him into a trap he did not suspect. Cf. 2.3f.; 7.3–9 where Jesus refuses to act immediately at the request of his mother and brothers; here he refuses to be directed by his friends. For the 'two days' cf. 4.40.

7. ἔπειτα μετὰ τοῦτο. A pleonasm, but perpetrated with full consciousness, and for emphasis. 'Then, after the delay just mentioned'; see on τότε μέν above. Brown points out that vv. 7–10 have nothing to do with the Lazarus story.

ἄγωμεν. The use of this first person plural seems to have grown out of the classical ἄγε, ἄγετε, and to have developed in Hellenistic usage (e.g. Epictetus III, xxii, 55, ἄγωμεν ἐπὶ τὸν ἀνθύπατον).

εἰς τὴν Ἰουδαίαν πάλιν. For earlier visits to Judaea see 2.13; 5.1; 7.14. Lazarus is not mentioned by Jesus in this declaration, nor by his disciples in their reply; all the stress lies on the journey to the place of danger and death. It seems clear that John regarded this visit to Bethany as the cause and beginning of the final and decisive journey into Judaea.

8. νῦν, of that which has but lately happened; a classical use.

λιθάσαι. Cf. 10.31,39. The disciples perceive that to return to Judaea would bring the ministry of Jesus to a close; they do not perceive that to do so would bring its intended consummation. Jesus lays down his life for his friends (15.13). There may also be an allusion to the danger of missionary work among Jews (Martyn, 59).

9f. οὐχὶ δώδεκα ὧραί εἰσιν τῆς ἡμέρας; The Jewish day (for details see S.B. ad loc.), like the Roman, was divided into twelve equal 'hours' which occupied the whole period between sunrise and sunset, however long or short that period might be. During the hours of daylight movement was free and unhindered, but darkness brought an inevitable cessation of activity. Jesus' ministry is of limited duration, and he must therefore use such time as he has in doing God's will regardless of the consequences (cf. 9.4 for a very similar statement). Thus Jesus in this verse gives a clear and positive answer to the question of v. 8. The words used, however, especially 'hour' and 'light', suggest that more than a simple answer on these lines may be intended. Elsewhere in John the 'hour' of Jesus is specifically the hour of his death and exaltation (e.g. 8.20; 2.4); and Jesus speaks of himself as the 'light of the world' (8.12; 9.5; 12.46). The metaphor of this verse then, though a true parable (Sidebottom, 178), suggests not merely an argument which any man might use, but one which relates uniquely to the work of Jesus in illuminating the world through his death.

ἐάν τις . . . ἐὰν δέ τις . . . In addition to the surface meaning John intends to suggest that in the light given by Jesus men walk safely; apart from him is darkness, in which men plunge into sin (9.39–41).

προσκόπτει. The word is both biblical and Hellenistic. In the New Testament cf. Rom. 9.32; 14.21; 1 Peter 2.8; also the words πρόσκομμα (Rom. 9.32f.; 14.13,20; 1 Cor. 8.9; 1 Peter 2.8), προσκοπή (2 Cor. 6.3). The important passage Isa. 8.14 is referred to both in Rom. 9.32f. and 1 Peter 2.8. The stumbling block over which men fall is appointed by God himself. So in John, the light by which men walk, in the absence of which they stumble, is Christ, who, simply by being the light of the world, distinguishes between the children of light and the children of darkness (cf. 3.19–21 and many other passages).

τὸ φῶς οὐκ ἔστιν ἐν αὐτῷ (ἐν αὐτῇ, that is, in the night, D). Cf. Matt. 6.23 (=Luke 11.35). Ancient thought did not clearly grasp the fact that vision takes place through the entry of light into the eye, and a new point is accordingly introduced; absence of light without is matched by absence of light within. Cf. *Thomas*, 24: Within a man of light there is light and he lights the whole world. When he does not shine, there is darkness. There is some resemblance in language, but John's point is different: men must not follow a supposed inner light, but accept Jesus as the light of the world (8.12; 9.5).

11. Another pregnant saying, misunderstood by the hearers, follows. Jesus' words mean on the surface, 'Lazarus (now described as ὁ φίλος ἡμῶν, a friend of the whole company) has fallen asleep; but I am going (to Bethany) to awaken him.' The misunderstanding (implied by v. 12) is evident but artificial (for the use of this literary device in John see on 3.4). Cf. Mark 5.39; and see Radermacher, 88, and Cullmann, *V. & A.*, 185. Jesus' knowledge of Lazarus' sleep must in any case be supernatural, and the disciples might therefore have been prepared for a rather more than commonplace remark. The reader is intended to observe at once the true meaning of the words. φίλος is probably a technical term for 'Christian' (see 3 John 15; Luke 12.4; Acts 27.3; and especially John 15.13–15 and the notes there; also the valuable discussions in Bauer, *Wörterbuch s.v.* and *Beginnings* v, 379f., and the literature cited). κοιμᾶσθαι is often used of the death of Christians, in the New Testament (e.g. Acts 7.60; 1 Cor. 15.6) and in later Christian literature (e.g. Ignatius, *Rom.* 4.2; 1 Clement 44.2; Hermas, *Sim.* IX, xvi, 7). A similar usage cannot be demonstrated for ἐξυπνίζειν (a late word (e.g. M. Aurelius Antoninus 6.31), condemned by Phrynichus (CC; Rutherford, 305), who prefers ἀφυπνίζειν), but its use follows naturally from κοιμᾶσθαι, and such passages as Eph. 5.14 (ἔγειρε, ὁ καθεύδων, καὶ ἀνάστα ἐκ τῶν νεκρῶν) and Rom. 13.11 (ἐξ ὕπνου ἐγερθῆναι) may be compared. Probably John avoided ἐγείρειν and ἀνιστάναι because they were too closely linked with the Christian belief in the resurrection to suit his allusive style. It is clear to

the Christian reader that Lazarus is dead and that Jesus will raise him up; and the language used suggests the resurrection of all Christians at the last day.

12. εἰ κεκοίμηται σωθήσεται. The disciples, who fail to grasp the meaning of what Jesus has said, mean 'If he has fallen asleep he will recover; the sleep will benefit him'; they imply that he should not be wakened. 'To recover from illness' is a common meaning of σώзεσθαι; but John himself means to suggest that Christians sleeping in death will be saved. The disciples, ignorant as they are, may nevertheless unwittingly say what is true (like Caiaphas himself, vv. 50–2).

13. John himself points out the misunderstanding of the disciples. The resemblance between sleep and death has often been noted; e.g. T. Reuben 3.1, πνεῦμα τοῦ ὕπνου . . . εἰκὼν τοῦ θανάτου. At Ecclus. 46.19 κοίμησις is used for death. ἡ κοίμησις τοῦ ὕπνου is a clumsy, but sufficiently clear, expression.

14. παρρησίᾳ. For this word see on 7.4. Here without question the meaning is 'plainly', 'without obscurity or ambiguity of speech'; cf. 16.29.

ἀπέθανεν. Black (129) takes this aorist to be equivalent to a Semitic perfect; it could equally be the aorist of 'what has just happened' (M.1, 135, 139f., 247).

15. χαίρω δι' ὑμᾶς . . . ὅτι οὐκ ἤμην ἐκεῖ. The ὅτι clause is directly dependent upon χαίρω, the ἵνα clause being parenthetical. It is sometimes expedient for disciples that Jesus should be absent from them; cf. 16.7. If Jesus had been present Lazarus (it is presumed) would not have died, and the disciples' faith would not have been quickened and confirmed by his resurrection.

ἵνα πιστεύσητε. The grammatical connection of ἵνα is not clear; the clause loosely indicates the advantage the disciples would receive through the absence of Jesus from Lazarus. There is no specific note at the close of the miracle that the *disciples* believed as a result of it; but cf. vv. 42, 45, 48. Lazarus' illness was ὑπὲρ τῆς δόξης τοῦ θεοῦ ἵνα δοξασθῇ ὁ υἱὸς τοῦ θεοῦ δι' αὐτῆς (v .4); cf. 2.11, where Jesus' manifestation of his glory was the occasion of faith.

ἄγωμεν. See on v. 7, πρὸς αὐτόν—as if Lazarus were still a living person.

16. Θωμᾶς ὁ λεγόμενος Δίδυμος. The name Thomas (Hebrew תאום, *T^e'om*) does not seem to be attested in earlier literature; Δίδυμος in Greek, however, is. Both words mean 'twin', and Δίδυμος is rightly given by John as a translation (this is the meaning of λεγόμενος; cf. e.g. 4.25, and for John's translations of Semitic words see on 1.38). See however B.D. § 53 for the view that Θωμᾶς is a genuine Greek name chosen because it resembled the Hebrew (and Aramaic). The theory was early formed, perhaps in the Syriac-speaking churches, that Thomas was the twin of Jesus himself, and was to be identified with Judas (Mark 6.3). This view appears in, e.g., the Acts of Thomas (1, *et al.*, Judas Thomas; 31, I know that thou art the twin brother of the Christ), and in the variants at 14.22 (see the notes). See E. Nestle in *E. Bib. s.v.* Thomas; also many interesting observations and conjectures in J. R. Harris, *The Dioscuri in the Christian Legends* (1903); *The Cult of the Heavenly Twins* (1906); *The Twelve Apostles* (1927). See now, especially for the wording of P. Oxy. 654 and the (Coptic) *Thomas*, Fitzmyer, *Essays*, 369f. Elsewhere in the New Testament Thomas is mentioned only in lists of the Twelve (Matt. 10.3; Mark 3.18; Luke 6.15; Acts 1.13); in John he plays a much more important part; see 14.5; 20.24–9; 21.2.

συνμαθηταῖς. The word is *hap. leg.* in the New Testament; cf. *Mart. Pol.* 17.3.

ἄγωμεν (see on v. 7) καὶ ἡμεῖς ἵνα ἀποθάνωμεν μετ' αὐτοῦ. Thomas' remark looks back to v. 8, apparently ignoring, or mistaking, the answer given by Jesus in vv. 9f. His proposal, though it shows courage and devotion to the person of Jesus, shows also a complete failure to grasp the significance of Jesus' death as it is presented in John; it is unthinkable that such a death should be shared. It is unlikely that Thomas' proposal rests upon early tradition (cf. Mark 8.34, which, if the words are based upon an authentic utterance of Jesus, appears to mean that some or all of the disciples may die with Jesus), and much more probable that here Thomas (like the disciples as a whole at v. 12) is made to speak an unconscious truth: the journey into Judaea is for the purpose of death, and later dying with Christ will become the characteristic mark of Christian discipleship.

17. εὗρεν αὐτὸν τέσσερας ἤδη ἡμέρας ἔχοντα. The construction is Johannine; see 5.5f.; 8.57; 9.21,23. Cf. v. 39 and see on v. 6. The μνημεῖον is described in v. 38.

18. Βηθανία. See on v. 1. The geographical details of this verse are given primarily in order to account for the visit of many Jews (v. 19)—they could easily come out from Jerusalem; but also to draw attention to the fact that Jesus had, in coming to Bethany, almost arrived at Jerusalem for his passion.

ὡς (om. D W sin) ἀπὸ σταδίων δεκαπέντε. The use of ὡς with a number is characteristic of John (1.40; 4.6; 6.10,19; 19.14,39; 21.8). For the construction of the whole clause cf. 21.8; also 12.1. It resembles the Latin, e.g., *a millibus passuum duobus*. On the question whether John's phrase is to be regarded as a Latinism see M. 1, 100–2, Robertson, 424,469,575; according to B.D., § 161, it is 'genuinely Greek'; so also Radermacher, 100. There are parallels in Hellenistic writers.

19. ἵνα παραμυθήσωνται. The duty of consoling the bereaved has always been acknowledged and practised in Judaism. For a detailed account of injunctions and customs relating to it see S.B. IV, 592–607, A. Edersheim, *Life and Times of Jesus the Messiah* (1892) II, 320f. παραμυθεῖσθαι, a word of wide meaning (see L.S. *s.v.*), is rarely used of 'comfort' in Christian literature, where παρακαλεῖν and its cognates are preferred. Thus in the New Testament παραμυθεῖσθαι is used in John 11.19,31; elsewhere only in 1 Thess. 2.11; 5.14 where death is not in question, whereas in 1 Thess. 4.18, in regard to dead Christians, ὥστε παρακαλεῖτε ἀλλήλους. It would however be unwise to conclude that John here used παραμυθεῖσθαι to denote a non-Christian consolation, since (with the notable exception of παράκλητος) words of the παρακαλεῖν group are entirely absent from the gospel (and from the Johannine epistles). There is no need whatever to question the sincerity and good intentions of these Jews; John uses the term 'Jew' in a historical as well as a theological sense.

20. It is legitimate to cf. Luke 10.39f., where also Martha appears to be the more active of the two sisters. It is possible that Luke and John (or their sources) give an accurate historical picture of Mary and Martha; possible again that John drew his characterization from Luke; but it is impossible to infer either of these possibilities with certainty.

21f. κύριε is omitted, probably accidentally, by B sin (cur). Martha is confident that Jesus could and would have cured Lazarus had he been present; and indeed her faith goes further. She implies that if Jesus asks God for the life of his friend it will be granted.

καὶ νῦν, even now that Lazarus is dead and buried.

ὅσα ἂν αἰτήσῃ . . . δώσει. Cf. 2.5 ὅ τι ἂν λέγῃ . . . ποιήσατε.

23. ἀναστήσεται ὁ ἀδελφός σου. This short saying contains the truth of what is about to take place: Lazarus will shortly come out of his tomb alive. But the words, though they express this truth, suggest not falsehood but a more general truth, and are uttered not so much to inform Martha as to set in motion the ensuing conversation, in which the Christological basis and interpretation of the miracle are brought out. The use of words of double meaning is characteristic of John.

24. ἀναστήσεται ἐν τῇ ἀναστάσει ἐν τῇ ἐσχάτῃ ἡμέρᾳ. Belief in a final resurrection is a firm constituent of Pharisaic Judaism; see e.g. Acts 23.8, Josephus, *Bel.* II, 163 (in the Hellenized form, ψυχήν τε πᾶσαν μὲν ἄφθαρτον, Every soul is imperishable), *Sanhedrin* 10.1 (These are they that have no share in the world to come: he that says there is no resurrection of the dead prescribed in the Law . . .), *Sotah* 9.15, and the second of the Eighteen Benedictions (Singer, 44f., Thou, O Lord, art mighty for ever, thou quickenest the dead, thou art mighty to save; cf. *Berakoth* 5.2). The phrase ἡ ἐσχάτη ἡμέρα, though based on the Old Testament (Isa. 2.2, ἐν ταῖς ἐσχάταις ἡμέραις, cf. Micah 4.1), seems to be restricted to John (6.39f.,44,54; 11.24; 12.48); cf. ἐσχάτη ὥρα in 1 John 2.18, and ἔσχαται ἡμέραι several times; also the day of judgement, variously expressed by Paul. Martha's statement of her faith is thus orthodox Pharisaism. It was also the faith of the Christians among whom John wrote; of the dead in Christ it could only be said that they would rise in the general resurrection at the last day. Martha's belief is in no way discredited but rather confirmed by the extraordinary events that follow. These demonstrate two points. (*a*) The presence of Jesus effects an anticipation of eschatological events, and his deeds are therefore signs of the glory of God. Wherever he is, the divine power to judge and to give life is at work. Cf. 5.25; the whole passage 5.19–40 is the best commentary on this miracle. (*b*) The pattern of the life of all Christians is determined by the movement from death to life experienced by Lazarus. Christians have already risen with Christ (Rom. 6.4f.; Col. 2.12; 3.1). This movement, to be completed only at the last day, has already taken place in regard to sin; the resurrection of Lazarus therefore is an acted parable of Christian conversion and life.

25. ἐγώ εἰμι. See on 6.35. Resurrection and life are to be found only in Jesus.

ἡ ἀνάστασις καὶ ἡ ζωή. ἀνάστασις, ἀνιστάναι are not common in John; apart from this context they are to be found only in 5.29; 6.39f.,44,54 (all in ch. 6 are of the form ἀναστήσω . . . ἐν τῇ ἐσχάτῃ ἡμέρᾳ); 20.9 (the only use of these words in John for the resurrection of Christ, for which elsewhere ἐγείρειν (2.19f.,22; 21.14; used of God or Christ raising men from the dead in 5.21; 12.1,9,17) is used). ζωή, however, both with and without the adjective αἰώνιος, occurs frequently, especially in chs. 5, 6; see on 1.4; 3.15. Cf. especially 5.29, ἀνάστασιν ζωῆς; this verse conveys the fundamental notion of a dual resurrection, either to the life of the age to come, or to judgement (condemnation). Of this resurrection it is said (5.25) that the hour of its happening 'is coming and now is'; this is true solely in view of the presence of Jesus as Son of man. This theme is taken up here. Jesus is the resurrection and the life; apart from him there is no resurrection and no life, and where he is, resurrection and life must be. Jesus is always the realization, in this world, of eternal life in the experience of Christians; in order that this truth may be manifested in a sign he accomplishes the resurrection of Lazarus. The words καὶ ἡ ζωή are omitted by P⁴⁵ a sin; also by Cyprian and sometimes by Origen. (According to Clement, *Excerpta ex Theodoto* VI, 4, the Valentinians ascribed to the Lord the saying, ἐγώ εἰμι ἡ ζωή; it would however be unwise to take this as a definite quotation; it might be a shortened version either of the long text here, or of 14.6.) This short text may well be original; it is entirely suitable to the context, yet the addition is one which might easily be made by a copyist. It makes little difference to the sense, though the short text emphasizes more sharply the fulfilment of eschatology in Jesus himself. It would make more difference if ἀνάστασις were omitted, for, as Lightfoot points out, the life is life through resurrection, and this means life through death, which is presupposed by resurrection.

Jesus now states the truth which was implicit in his claim to be the resurrection, first in a form specially adapted to the present situation, and then more generally.

ὁ πιστεύων εἰς ἐμὲ κἂν ἀποθάνῃ ζήσεται. The meaning is not, 'If a man be dead (in sin) and believes, he shall be brought to life.' The aorist ἀποθάνῃ requires the rendering, 'If a believer die, he shall live (come to life again).' It is of course a fact that Christians die, but their death is followed by life. Cf. 6.40, where the sequence is clearly stated: ὁ ... πιστεύων ... ἔχῃ ζωὴν αἰώνιον, καὶ ἀναστήσω αὐτὸν ἐγὼ τῇ ἐσχάτῃ ἡμέρᾳ. So will it be with Lazarus, the last day being anticipated for the purpose of the sign. κἂν is not 'though' (ἐὰν καί), but 'even if'.

26. πᾶς ὁ ζῶν καὶ πιστεύων εἰς ἐμὲ οὐ μὴ ἀποθάνῃ εἰς τὸν αἰῶνα. Translate '... shall never die'. That this (and not '... shall not die eternally') is the meaning is clear from 4.14; 8.51f.; 10.28; 13.8, where also the construction οὐ μή (subjunctive) εἰς τὸν αἰῶνα recurs. The only death that is worth regarding cannot affect those who believe in Christ. The difference is thus not great; Sanders compares the 'second death' cf. Rev. 2.11; 20.6,14; 21.8. Bultmann, who identifies the propositions of vv. 25f., is thus more nearly right than Dodd, who distinguishes them. The question is 'whether a man is ready to let life and death as he knows them be unreal' (Bultmann), that is, whether he is ready to accept Jesus as the truth (as well as the life) against apparent reality. Is John here repeating the heresy of Hymenaeus and Philetus (2 Tim. 2.17f.), who taught that the resurrection had already happened? Cf. John 5.24, and see the note there. Käsemann (*Testament*, 75) suggests that he is, but in the same book (15) writes rather more cautiously. John did not take over this inheritance (which goes back to Hellenistic enthusiasm) without modification, but uses it in the interests of Christology. 'The *praesentia Christi* is the centre of his proclamation. After Easter this means the presence of the Risen One' (*Testament*, 15). The Christological significance of Martha's faith becomes explicit in the next verse; see the note. In v. 26, πᾶς ... οὐ μή should not be regarded as a Semitism; see M. II, 434.

27. ναί, κύριε. Martha does believe what has just been stated, but this does not imply the belief that Lazarus will presently come out of his tomb. The

confession of faith in Christ, or rather the confessional statement about his person, which follows is not a loose variation of v. 26. It is by true belief in Jesus as Christ and Son of God that men have life (see especially 20.31 ... ἵνα πιστεύοντες ζωὴν ἔχητε). Martha's reply takes the discourse a step forward, to 'the climax of this theological section of the chapter' (Lindars). She 'drops the "I", and speaks only of "Thou"'—the genuine attitude of faith (Bultmann).

πεπίστευκα. For John's characteristic use of the perfect of πιστεύειν see on 6.69. It is noteworthy that there and in this passage this grammatical form introduces what looks like a primitive confession of faith, or creed. Bornkamm (II,192) suggests that the present passage is a baptismal confession. The confessional implication is less obvious at 16.27; 20.28f., while at 3.18; 8.31 the perfect is readily explicable on the grounds of common usage. The present however appears with similar formulae (1.49f.; 4.42), and it would be wrong to lay great stress on this observation, though the creed-like form of Martha's words should be noted. They consist of three unco-ordinated elements.

ὁ χριστός. On Jesus as the Messiah see Introduction, pp. 70f., and on 1.41.

ὁ υἱὸς τοῦ θεοῦ. On Jesus as the Son of God see Introduction, pp. 71f., and on 1.49.

ὁ εἰς τὸν κόσμον ἐρχόμενος. It is perhaps best to take these words as the third of three parallel titles: the Christ, the Son of God, he that comes into the world; cf. 6.14 where this participial clause is used with ὁ προφήτης. εἰς τὸν κόσμον corresponds with the description of 3.31 (ὁ ἄνωθεν ἐρχόμενος, ὁ ἐκ τοῦ οὐρανοῦ ἐρχόμενος). See also the note on 'coming into the world' on 1.9. Jesus is the Son of man who comes down from heaven to earth for the salvation of the world (for κόσμος see on 1.10). John has taken over the expression from the primitive tradition (e.g. Matt. 11.3 (=Luke 7.19f.), Mark 11.9 and parallels, used in John 12.13), and used it to express his own fundamental conception of the mission of Jesus from the Father. See however Schnackenburg.

28. The conversation breaks off. If Jesus is what Martha believes him to be there is no more to say; and all things are possible to him that believes.

λάθρᾳ (σιωπῇ, D it vg sin, may well be right). It is not clear why Martha should act so; probably the motive was to conceal from the Jews who were with Mary the fact that Jesus was at hand, but to suppose that they were his enemies is to assume too much, and is not warranted by the remainder of the narrative. We have not been told that Jesus had called for Mary.

ὁ διδάσκαλος. The description is surprising after the exalted terms of Martha's confession of faith (v. 27); yet Mary Magdalene uses it at 20.16. The word remained in occasional use as a Christological title: Mart. Pol. 17.3 (along with Son of God and King), Ep. Diog. 9.6 (along with Saviour, Physician, Mind, Light, and other titles); cf. Ignatius, Eph. 15.1; Mag. 9.2.

πάρεστιν. Is it conceivable that this word is intended to remind the reader of the παρουσία (a cognate word) of the Son of man at which the dead would be raised? It seems not impossible, but more cannot be said.

29. ἤρχετο πρὸς αὐτόν. The words are of course to be taken in their literal meaning; but the reader of the gospel cannot fail to remember that 'coming to Jesus' is an important thought with John; cf. among many passages 6.35,37.

30. That Jesus should, after the departure of Martha, remain where he was instead of going into the village is another inexplicable feature of the narrative. It may be that this verse, and λάθρᾳ in v. 28, are marks of the secrecy which is characteristic of the miracle narratives in Mark; see on v. 33. ἔτι is omitted, perhaps rightly, by P⁴⁵ D Θ ω.

31. οἱ οὖν ᾿Ιουδαῖοι. See v. 19. Nothing is said of these Jews to suggest hypocrisy in either their consolation or their grief.

ἰδόντες τὴν Μαριάμ. τὴν Μαριάμ is attracted out of the ὅτι clause into the principal sentence. This 'prolepsis of the substantive' is a 'rather common idiom' (Robertson, 1034; see W.M. 781f. for a fuller list of references).

ταχέως; cf. ταχύ in v. 29. No difference in meaning is intended. ταχέως is the more usual form, though in the New Testament ταχύ slightly preponderates (12 to 10; but 6 uses of ταχύ are in Revelation). Neither word is used elsewhere in John, but cf. τάχειον in 13.27.

εἰς τὸ μνημεῖον. In Hellenistic Greek εἰς encroaches upon the use of ἐπί and πρός (Robertson, 596; B.D., § 207); they think that Mary is going to not into the tomb.

ἵνα κλαύσῃ ἐκεῖ. Cf. Wisd. 19.3, προσοδυρόμενοι τάφοις νεκρῶν.

32. ἔπεσεν. Mary acts with greater devotion, or with less reserve, than Martha, but her words are almost identical; the changed position of the pronoun μου is probably not significant. The repetition emphasizes the confidence of the two women, which, partial though it is, is contrasted with the hesitant question of the bystanders (v. 37).

33. ὡς εἶδεν αὐτὴν κλαίουσαν καὶ τοὺς ... ᾿Ιουδαίους κλαίοντας. It is clearly the presence and grief of Mary and of the Jews which form the occasion of the anger of Jesus (see below), but it is far from clear why the sight of lamentation should have moved him to anger. We may at once set aside the explanation that Jesus was provoked by the sorrow of the Jews because it was, in contrast with that of Mary, *hypocritical*. No ill is spoken of these Jews, who had voluntarily come out of Jerusalem to comfort the sisters (v. 19); their sorrow is not contrasted with, but, as it were, added to Mary's; moreover John (unlike the synoptists) does not attribute hypocrisy to the Jews (ὑποκριτής and cognates are absent from John). We must consider more seriously the suggestion that it was the *unbelief* of the Jews and of Mary that provoked the indignation of Jesus. The possibility did not occur to them that Jesus should awaken Lazarus from the sleep of death; they sorrowed as those who had no hope. It is pointed out that Jesus is again indignant at v. 38, immediately after the sceptical remark of v. 37. But it is not necessary to regard v. 37 as a sceptical utterance (see the notes) and it is therefore not necessary (though not impossible) to take unbelief as the cause of Jesus' anger. The suggestions that Jesus was stirred with deep emotion at the concrete fact of death (and sin), or sternly repressed the natural human feelings which sprang up within him, do not meet the statement that it was ὡς εἶδεν ... that Jesus ἐνεβριμήσατο .... See the next note.

ἐνεβριμήσατο τῷ πνεύματι. Cf. v. 38, ἐμβριμώμενος ἐν ἑαυτῷ; τῷ πνεύματι has no reference to the Holy Spirit, but is synonymous with ἐν ἑαυτῷ. Cf. 13.21. According to Sanders, τῷ πνεύματι 'seems to exclude any external expression'; but that Jesus suppressed his emotions is not suggested by v. 35.

It is beyond question that ἐμβριμᾶσθαι (on the spelling see below) implies anger. This is suggested by biblical (e.g. Dan. 11.30, ἐμβριμήσονται αὐτῷ . . . ὀργισθήσονται ἐπὶ τὴν διαθήκην) and other (e.g. Lucian, *Menippus* 20, ἐνεβριμήσατο ἡ Βριμὼ καὶ ὑλάκτησεν ὁ Κέρβερος) usage of the word itself, by the use of the simple form βριμᾶσθαι (see L.S. *s.v.*), of which ἐμβριμᾶσθαι is here only an intensive, and by the usage of the cognates (e.g. Lam. 2.6, ἐμβριμήματι ὀργῆς). Some false or misleading interpretations of the anger of Jesus were discussed in the preceding note. ἐμβριμᾶσθαι is used again in this context (v. 38); elsewhere in the New Testament only in Mark 1.43 and Matt. 9.30 (and in Mark 14.5 where the subject is not Jesus). Cf. *P. Eg.* 2.51. In both of these passages the word occurs in miracle stories, in which Jesus charged the person or persons cured not to divulge what had taken place; that is, it reinforces in the strongest terms the Marcan theme of the 'messianic secret'. It seems plausible to suggest that it may be used in a similar way in John. (For the existence of a 'messianic secret' in John see Introduction, pp. 70f.) Jesus perceives that the presence and grief of the sisters and of the Jews are almost forcing a miracle upon him, and as in 2.4 the request for miraculous activity evokes a firm, almost rough, answer, here, in circumstances of increased tension, it arouses his wrath. This miracle it will be impossible to hide (cf. vv. 28, 30); and this miracle, Jesus perceives, will be the immediate occasion of his death (vv. 49-53). Cf. 4.48; 6.26. This interpretation is supported by the following words. See however Hoskyns, 473.

ἐτάραξεν ἑαυτόν. Jesus is troubled, as in 12.27; 13.21, at the prospect of the *dénouement* of his ministry. In John ταράσσειν always means such a fearful perturbation (cf. 14.1,27), except in 5.4,7 where its use is physical, not psychological. Jesus is said to have 'troubled himself'. If this is not a mere variation in the Johannine manner of similar expressions (e.g. ἡ ψυχή μου τετάρακται, 12.27; ἐταράχθη τῷ πνεύματι, 13.21) it must be intended to underline the contention that Jesus was always master of himself and his circumstances.

Hitherto the text of v. 33 has been expounded as it stands in Nestle; it appears to yield an intelligible meaning, and this is an argument against resort to conjecture. The reading of P⁴⁵ (P⁶⁶) D Θ sah (ἐταράχθη τῷ πνεύματι ὡς ἐμβριμούμενος) is an easier text, since it avoids the statement that Jesus ἐνεβριμήσατο, and should be rejected as an editorial 'improvement' made in reverence for the person of Jesus. (It presupposes the form ἐμβριμέομαι (or -όομαι), as do some texts at v. 38, Mark 14.5; on the variation between the form in -άομαι and that in -έομαι (or -όομαι) see B.D., § 90.) The difficult Greek of this verse has attracted conjecture regarding an original Aramaic. It has been noted (Torrey, 39, 41-3) that the root רגז (r-g-z) is ambiguous; it often means 'to be angry', sometimes 'to be deeply moved'. The translator of John 11.33,38 selected the wrong meaning. To this simple proposal it is objected, 'If *rᵉgaz* was the original, why did a translator go out of his way to select so unusual an expression in Greek?' (Black, 240). The whole of Black's discussion (240-3) is very important, but only its conclusion can be quoted. 'The assumption of an Aramaic source of which the two expressions [ἐνεβριμήσατο τῷ πνεύματι and ἐτάραξεν ἑαυτόν] are "translation-variants" can account for the Johannine Greek. The Aramaic equivalent of ἐτάραξεν ἑαυτόν is a reflexive form of the verb *za*ʻ; in Esther 4.4, when Esther heard of the decree of Haman against the Jews, ". . . then was the queen exceedingly grieved"; the verb here is a very strong one in Hebrew; it **means** literally "she writhed with anxiety"; it is rendered in the Targum by the equally strong and expressive verb za'; the LXX renders ἐταράχθη. The latter was selected by a Greek translator of the Aramaic of John 11.33, but he set alongside it the Syriac expression ἐνεβριμήσατο τῷ πνεύματι, an even more expressive equivalent of the Aramaic, and rendered the same verb za' in v. 38 by the Greek equivalent of the corresponding Syriac 'eth'azaz. Clearly the translator of the Lazarus story came from a bilingual circle such as Syrian Antioch where Greek and Syriac were both well known' (242f.). This, though somewhat complicated by the introduction of Syriac as well as Aramaic, is probably the best solution of the problem, if any linguistic problem really exists. If the interpretation given above is correct, the Greek itself makes sense and no 'solution', however ingenious, is called for. The same may be said of the suggestion (Torrey, 76, 80) that, in ἐτάραξεν ἑαυτόν, ἑαυτόν represents the Aramaic ethic dative (za' leh).

34. ποῦ τεθείκατε αὐτόν; τιθέναι is used of the disposal of a body in 19.41f.; 20.2,13,15 (ποῦ ἔθηκας αὐτόν); similarly Matt. 27.60; Mark 6.29; 15.46f.; 16.6; Luke 23.53,55; Rev. 11.9; cf. Acts 9.37. This use of the verb is classical (e.g. Sophocles, Ajax, 1108–10, τόνδε . . . ἐς ταφὰς ἐγὼ θήσω δικαίως) and so frequent that no word for 'grave' need be expressed (e.g. Iliad XXIII, 83, μὴ ἐμὰ σῶν ἀπάνευθε τιθήμεναι ὀστέα). Accordingly we may here translate, 'Where have you buried him?'

ἔρχου καὶ ἴδε. The same words as in 1.46 (cf. 1.38). S.B. (II, 371) draw attention to a very common rabbinic idiom, but no such reference is necessary here.

35. ἐδάκρυσεν ὁ Ἰησοῦς. δακρύειν (see L.S. s.v.) means 'to shed tears', generally at some misfortune, or in lamentation. The word is different from that (κλαίειν) used of Mary and the Jews. The aorist probably means 'burst into tears' (so Sanders). The emotion here expressed is different from that of v. 33, and it is not more legitimate to say that Jesus wept than that he was angry at the unbelief implied by the lamentations of Mary and the Jews; rather he took part in them. Jesus' tears call forth two comments from the Jews, who several times in this gospel, of which irony is so striking a feature, are made to express the truth without perceiving it (see especially Caiaphas' statement in v. 50, and cf. 3.2; 7.35; 8.22,53; 10.33, et al.). Here also the Jews' comments, rightly understood, provide a sufficient explanation of the scene.

36. πῶς ἐφίλει αὐτόν. Cf. v. 3 (φιλεῖν), v. 11 (φίλος). The Jews suppose that Jesus' grief, like their own and that of Mary and Martha, is due to human affection. This indeed is not untrue, but it is only part of the truth, for the love Jesus has for his own is far more than this; see e.g. 15.9, καθὼς ἠγάπησέν με ὁ πατήρ, κἀγὼ ὑμᾶς ἠγάπησα.

37. ὁ ἀνοίξας τοὺς ὀφθαλμοὺς τοῦ τυφλοῦ. See 9.1–7; cf. 9.32; 10.21. The reality of the cure is assumed, and no doubt is cast upon it.

ποιῆσαι ἵνα. Cf. Col. 4.16; Rev. 3.9; 13.12,16; and the Latin facere ut.

These words of 'some of them' are often taken to imply scepticism. If Jesus were what he claims to be he would have acted so as to prevent Lazarus' death (they still do not entertain the possibility of a resurrection). He does not act because he is not able to do so. It is however far from certain that this is their meaning. They do not doubt Jesus' power as so far manifested. They say no more than Mary and Martha have already said (vv. 21, 32), but they express themselves more hesitantly, and show a faith which we are not justified in dismissing as dissembled though it certainly was inadequate and even erroneous. They think of Jesus not as the Son of God who is light and life (though this is the unintended truth contained in their saying; cf. v. 36) but as a thaumaturge whose capacities, authenticated by the cure of the blind man, might conceivably have been expected to rise to this extremity.

38. πάλιν ἐμβριμώμενος ἐν ἑαυτῷ. Again—cf. v. 33. ἐν ἑαυτῷ interprets τῷ πνεύματι in v. 33. It is not unbelief but inchoate faith in v. 37 which causes Jesus' wrath. He sees that a public miracle of decisive character will be required.

μνημεῖον is a general term, signifying (in late Greek) a tomb, of any kind. It requires further description.

σπήλαιον (cf. Heb. 11.38; Rev. 6.15) is a 'cavern'; there is epigraphical evidence for its use as 'grave', and there is ample Jewish evidence for the use of natural caves (further prepared by artificial means, *Baba Bathra* 6.8) for burial (see a detailed account in S.B. 1, 1049–51). It is not stated here whether the shaft of the cave is vertical or horizontal, but the latter is suggested by archaeological evidence and by many regulations in the Mishnah (especially the passage just referred to).

λίθος ἐπέκειτο ἐπ' αὐτῷ, the usual means of sealing a tomb, e.g. *Oholoth* 2.4. Cf. John 20.1. If the shaft was vertical, ἐπί will mean 'upon', if horizontal, 'against'.

39. ἄρατε τὸν λίθον. From this point the narrative moves with highly dramatic speed. John uses αἴρειν of the stone sealing the tomb of Jesus (20.1); the other evangelists use ἀνακυλίζειν, ἀποκυλίζειν.

ἡ ἀδελφὴ τοῦ τετελευτηκότος (these four words are omitted by Θ it sin; they may well be a gloss) Μάρθα. Cf. v. 44, ὁ τεθνηκώς. John does not speak of Lazarus as νεκρός; but it is doubtful whether this is significant. Martha has now rejoined her sister; we have been told nothing of her movements since she spoke to Mary in v. 28.

ἤδη ὄζει. To these words sin prefixes, Lord, why are they taking away the stone? The addition appears to contradict the statement of v. 40 that the stone was then taken away; it may be original. Martha's belief that putrefaction would already have begun suggests that the body had not been embalmed, though v. 44 suggests the contrary: see on that verse.

τεταρταῖος γάρ ἐστιν. Cf. vv. 6, 17; also Herodotus 11, 89, τεταρταῖος γενέσθαι, 'to be four days dead'. 'A state of death beyond the third day meant, from the popular Jewish point of view, an absolute dissolution of life. At this time the face cannot be recognized with certainty; the body bursts; and the soul, which until then had hovered over the body, parts from it (*Eccl. R.* 12.6; *Lev. R.* 18.1)' (G. Dalman, *Jesus-Jeshua* (E.T., 1929), 220). Other passages could be cited, and though Lagrange (307) doubts whether this belief existed in the time of Jesus it is probably in mind here. Martha's words both heighten the dramatic feeling of the story and prove that Lazarus was truly dead. In spite of vv. 21–7 she still does not hope for an immediate resurrection.

40. οὐκ εἶπόν σοι. Jesus had declared to the disciples that Lazarus' illness was ὑπὲρ τῆς δόξης τοῦ θεοῦ (v. 4), but in the conversation with Martha the word 'glory' is not used. The reference is to v. 26: the raising to life of one who has died is nothing less than a manifestation of the glory of God.

ἐὰν πιστεύσῃς. The change of dependent subjunctives in indirect speech into optatives was not essential in classical Greek, and tends to disappear in Hellenistic. Here faith is made a condition of seeing the glory of God; in 2.11 faith is the result of seeing the glory of Christ. There is no contradiction; both statements are true. On δόξα see on 1.14. Dodd (A.S., 40, 84) suggests a reminiscence of Isa. 40.5 (ὀφθήσεται ἡ δόξα κυρίου . . .).

41. ἦρεν τοὺς ὀφθαλμοὺς ἄνω—in the attitude of prayer; cf. 17.1; also Mark 6.41; Luke 18.13; Acts 7.55. The Jewish custom seems to have been to face the Holy Place of the Temple in Jerusalem (S.B. II, 246f.; E. Peterson, Th. Z. 3 (1947), 1–15); but cf. Ps. 120 (121).1, ἦρα τοὺς ὀφθαλμούς μου εἰς τὰ ὄρη.

πάτερ. 'Father' is the term by which Jesus frequently and characteristically speaks of God in John. The vocative in prayer recurs in 17.1; in 17.11 we have πάτερ ἅγιε, and in 17.25 the nominative for vocative, πατὴρ δίκαιε. In the Lucan form of the Lord's Prayer (Luke 11.2) the address is πάτερ, in the Matthaean (Matt. 6.9) πάτερ ἡμῶν. Cf. also the use of Abba (Mark 14.36; Rom. 8.15; Gal. 4.6), and on this J. Jeremias, Abba (1966), 15–67. John however is a Greek book; there is nothing extraordinary in the use in prayer of the vocative of a divine title, and conclusions based on Aramaic usage must not be read into John's Greek.

εὐχαριστῶ σοι. Elsewhere in John εὐχαριστεῖν is used only (6.11,23) with reference to the miracle of the Five Thousand, where it was no doubt intended to call to mind the eucharist (see the notes). Here its sense is simply 'to give thanks'. This simple usage persisted in Christian literature along with the technical.

ἤκουσάς μου. No prayer of Jesus has been recorded earlier in the chapter; perhaps we should think that it was offered at the time of great emotional disturbance (vv. 33, 38). But much more probably, in view of the next words (see below), no specific moment of prayer is in mind; Jesus is in constant communion with his Father, who always 'hears' even the unspoken thoughts of his heart, and therefore has already 'heard' his petition for Lazarus. If this is true we need not deduce from the aorist ἤκουσας that the miracle has already taken place and that at this moment Lazarus is alive in the tomb; the aorist rather expresses the absolute confidence of Jesus that his prayer will be granted.

42. In view of the complete unity between the Father and the Son there is no need for uttered prayer at all.

ἀλλὰ διὰ τὸν ὄχλον τὸν περιεστῶτα. So far it is true to say (Loisy, 353), 'en apparence, il prierait pour la galerie'; the spoken word conveys no advantage to either Jesus or the Father, but only to the multitude. But it is not correct to infer that Jesus uttered the prayer in order to gain glory for himself; in fact its intention is the reverse of this. We have already observed (see especially the notes on vv. 33, 37) a tendency, familiar in the Synoptic Gospels, to think of Jesus as a wonder-worker who, in virtue of supernatural knowledge and power, is able to perform extraordinary deeds. The purpose of the prayer is to show that this is not true. Jesus has no authority independent of the Father; it is because the Father has sent him and given him authority that he can quicken the dead; 'he is no magician, no θεῖος ἀνήρ, who works by his own power and seeks his own δόξα' (Bultmann). This belief, that God is seen in the self-effacement of Jesus, is fundamental to the thought of the gospel; see Introduction, pp. 97f., and 'Theocentric'. See also 5.19–30, a discourse which, with its two themes, that Jesus can do nothing of himself and that he does whatever things he sees the Father doing, is a most important commentary on the present story. The vital truth which the bystanders must believe is:

ὅτι σύ με ἀπέστειλας. The thought of the mission of the Son, whereby he derives his authority, is central in John; see on 20.21. Once the complete dependence on God, and the consequent absolute authority of Jesus have been made clear, the miracle proceeds at once and is described in simple and matter-of-fact language.

43. δεῦρο ἔξω. δεῦρο is an adverb, commonly used in the New Testament, but here only in John, with the force of an interjection or command: Here! See 5.28f.; also 10.3 (he calls his own sheep by name).

44. ὁ τεθνηκώς. Cf. τοῦ τετελευτηκότος in v. 39, and the note.

δεδεμένος τοὺς πόδας καὶ τὰς χεῖρας κειρίαις. Cf. 19.40; 20.5,7. κειρία (here only in the New Testament and not common in non-Christian Greek) must here bear the meaning, attested in the papyri, 'bandage' (in Prov. 7.16 the meaning is 'bed-clothes'). Such winding strips seem to have been in use in Jewish practice (e.g. *Shabbath* 23.4, ... a corpse ... its coffin and wrappings (תכריכין, *takhrikhin*). In view of this and similar passages the statement (S.B. II, 545) that 'Strips of linen, κειρίαι, for the binding up of the hands and feet of the corpse, do not appear to be mentioned in the rabbinic literature' must be supposed to refer specially to the hands and feet, and not to other parts. Before the time of Rabban Gamaliel II (*c.* A.D. 90), who set a better example, the dead were dressed with great luxury.

καὶ ἡ ὄψις αὐτοῦ σουδαρίῳ περιεδέδετο. The construction recalls that of a Hebrew circumstantial clause. At 7.24, ὄψις means 'appearance'; here, as perhaps at Rev. 1.16, 'face'. σουδάριον is a transliteration of the Latin *sudarium*, 'a napkin' (literally 'a cloth for wiping off perspiration'). It is not to be confused with the rabbinic סודר (*sudar*, 'scarf', 'turban'), which is not a transliteration. There is some reason to think (S.B. II, 545) that at the time of the gospels only the faces of the poor were covered in this way.

It is difficult to visualize the emergence of Lazarus thus bound. Hoskyns (475), following Basil, suggests that we have a 'miracle within a miracle'.

ἄφετε αὐτὸν ὑπάγειν. Lazarus came out of the tomb alive under the bandages. It is unlikely that John saw allegorical significance in this statement. The story ends here, abruptly; there is no more to say.

23. THE PLOT AGAINST JESUS

11.45–54

This short section is very characteristically Johannine, and no doubt comes from John's pen, though some points may rest upon earlier tradition. It falls into three parts.

Vv. 45f. The first verse describes the effect of the raising of Lazarus. Miracles in John regularly lead either to faith, or to the reverse of faith; see e.g. on σχίσμα, 7.43. The Pharisees are informed. Here John links to the story of Lazarus material which he uses to interpret it.

Vv. 47–53. The Sanhedrin is convoked in order that the situation brought about by Jesus' popular activity may be discussed. Plans are made for his arrest and death. John writes in his most ironical vein. The unfortunate results which the Jews seek to avoid are results which in fact followed (as John and most Christians believed) from their rejection of Jesus. Caiaphas is made to prophesy against himself and his own people, just as their own law is elsewhere made to bear witness against them (e.g. 5.45). In this paragraph Dodd (especially *Interpretation*, 367f.) sees traditional material attached by John as a pendant to the story of Lazarus. See also X. Léon-Dufour, *The Gospels and the Jesus of History* (ed. J. McHugh; 1968), 101. As such it could be historical, or alternatively (as Lindars suggests) the justification for the arrest of Jesus subsequently accepted by Jews and used in debates with Christians. It is however so characteristically Johannine that it is best to regard it as John's own work.

V. 54. The plot is known to Jesus, who withdraws to the wilderness.

John uses the present section for two purposes, historical and doctrinal. Historically, he shows the final decision of the Jews to kill Jesus, apparently substituting the present narrative for the synoptic accounts of a trial of Jesus before the high priest. This raises the dramatic tension of the gospel to a climax which is resolved only in the passion narrative, but is of dubious historical value. Theologically, John brings out the true significance of Jesus' death, which he is about to narrate. Jesus, as the story of Lazarus has shown, gives life to the dead, but he can do so only at the cost of his own life, which he surrenders that others may not perish.

45. οἱ ἐλθόντες πρὸς τὴν Μαριάμ. See 6.19. This participial clause, strictly understood, means that the Jews who came to Mary were the many who believed. This is immediately qualified in v. 46, but we have here not so much a loose construction (Brown, Lindars; cf. the reading of D, τῶν ἐλθόντων) as a Johannine idiom. It is characteristic of John to make a sweeping statement and then qualify it; cf. 1.11f. (His own did not receive him; but those who did receive him . . .); 12.37,42 (They did not believe in him . . . Nevertheless, many . . . did believe in him).

ἐπίστευσαν. Cf. 6.15. For such belief, based on signs, see 2.23. Fenton distinguishes between v. 45, ὅ (singular) ἐποίησεν, the unity of the revelation, which leads to faith, and v. 46, ἅ (plural) ἐποίησεν, a multiplicity of disconnected actions, which is meaningless.

46. τινὲς δέ. As usual, the effect of the miracle is to divide the beholders into two groups. The report of the miracle to the Pharisees forms a decisive point in the unfolding of the Johannine story. Cf. Mark 11.18, where the cleansing of the Temple seems to hold a similar place, and on the difference between John and Mark see Introduction, pp. 47f.

τοὺς Φαρισαίους. On the Pharisees see on 1.24. Here John seems to speak of them as an official body, like priests, magistrates, or councillors. If he did so speak of them he was ignorant of Judaism as it was before A.D. 70. This judgement is only partially palliated by the observation that the scribes formed one element in the Sanhedrin and that most of the scribes were Pharisees.

47. οἱ ἀρχιερεῖς καὶ οἱ Φαρισαῖοι. The 'chief priests' were members of the leading priestly families, most of them Sadducees. See on 3.1; also Jeremias, *Jerusalem*, 160–81.

συνέδριον. That is, probably, they convoked a meeting of the Sanhedrin, the governing council and chief court of the Jewish nation. On the Sanhedrin see Schürer II, i, 163–95.

τί ποιοῦμεν ὅτι . . . It would be better to write the question mark after ποιοῦμεν. This is to be distinguished from the deliberative subjunctive (What are we to do?). It means, 'What are we *now* doing?' and implies the answer 'Nothing'. ὅτι will then mean 'for', 'because'; we ought to be active (as in fact we are not), for this man is doing . . . A deliberative use of the indicative is not, however, impossible; see B.D. § 366 and Radermacher, 155; also Brown, with references to Schlatter and Lagrange.

πολλά . . . σημεῖα. For πολλά, D it read τοιαῦτα; this is more awkward than πολλά and may be original, though possibly an assimilation to 9.16. It may also reflect the fact that John can hardly be said to have recounted *many* signs. It has been suggested that these signs may, at an earlier stage in the development of the Johannine tradition, have included the triumphal entry and the cleansing of the Temple. σημεῖα on the lips of the Jews cannot have its full Johannine meaning (for which see Introduction, pp. 75–8. It means here simply 'miracles'; cf. the use at 3.2; 7.31; 9.16.

48. οὕτως. If we leave him as he is (at liberty). Cf. 4.6.

πάντες πιστεύσουσιν . . . ἐλεύσονται οἱ Ῥωμαῖοι. A striking example of Johannine irony. The Jews did not leave Jesus alone, but crucified him; and the consequence was precisely that which they desired to avoid. When this gospel was written, throughout the world men were coming to Jesus by faith (12.32, πάντας ἑλκύσω) and the Romans had destroyed the Temple and subjugated the Jews.

τὸν τόπον means primarily the Temple, the holy place. Cf. Jer. 7.14; Neh. 4.7; 2 Macc. 5.19; John 4.20; Acts 6.14; 21.28. Possibly a wider meaning, Jerusalem, may be included. The same ambiguity occurs in *Bikkurim* 2.2: (Second) Tithe and First-fruits require to be brought to the Place (מקום,

that is, Jerusalem, as most interpreters suppose, or the Temple (so Schlatter, 257)). The destruction at least of the Temple is envisaged—a theme that plays an important part in the synoptic trial narrative (Mark 14.5f.; 15.29).

τὸ ἔθνος, the Jewish nation. In its present form this double prediction is doubtless a *uaticinium ex euentu*; yet in the generation before A.D. 70 it must have been apparent to many clear-sighted persons that undue provocation, such as messianic disorders, would result in decisive action by the Romans. There is therefore no reason why the Sanhedrin should not have regarded Jesus as in this way a danger to the state. There are interesting verbal parallels between this verse and those that follow and Esther 3.8,9; 4.1 (Guilding, 168f.), but it is very doubtful whether John found them significant.

49. Καϊαφᾶς, mentioned again at 18.13f.,24,28. He is not named in Mark but cf. Matt. 26.3,57; Luke 3.2; Acts 4.6. Caiaphas was appointed high priest by the Roman procurator Gratus, probably in or near A.D. 18; Vitellius, proconsul of Syria, removed from office both Pilate and Caiaphas in A.D. 36. Only John (18.13) mentions his relationship to Annas; for the other details see Josephus, *Ant.* xviii, 35, 95.

τοῦ ἐνιαυτοῦ ἐκείνου. Caiaphas, as has just been seen, was high priest for about twenty years. Moreover, the high-priesthood was not an annual office but was, in Jewish law, held for life. It is true that some of the Roman procurators made and deposed high priests with a frequency that made the appointment seem annual; yet even so no Jew could have written in such a way as to contradict the fundamental principles of the national religion. If John by his words in this verse (repeated emphatically in v. 51 and 18.13) means that a high priest was appointed every year we must conclude that he was not a Jew. His words however do not necessarily bear this meaning. Probably he meant only that Caiaphas was high priest in that memorable year of our Lord's passion. This will no doubt account for his unconscious prophecy (v. 51).

ὑμεῖς οὐκ οἴδατε οὐδέν. The last word is emphatic. Bernard (404) aptly compares Josephus, *Bel.* ii, 166, The Sadducees ... are, even among themselves, rather boorish in their behaviour, and in their intercourse with their peers are as rude as to aliens. This of course was written by a Pharisee. The reasons advanced (Torrey, 61, 63) for regarding this and the following sentences as questions are not convincing.

50. οὐδὲ λογίζεσθε ὅτι ..., nor do you take into account the fact that ...

συμφέρει ὑμῖν. ὑμῖν is read by P45 P66 B D (it) and some vg MSS.; ἡμῖν is in Θ λ φ ω sin pesh and other vg. MSS.; the pronoun is omitted altogether by ℵ and a few other MSS. The omission is supported by the variation and may perhaps be right; otherwise ὑμῖν should be preferred. In a sense not intended by Caiaphas the departure of Jesus was advantageous: 16.7 (συμφέρει—Fenton). Double meanings continue to mark the paragraph (Cullmann, V. & A., 185).

ἵνα εἷς ἄνθρωπος ἀποθάνῃ ὑπὲρ τοῦ λαοῦ. Cf. *Gen. R.* 94.9: It is better that this man be put to death than that the community should be punished on his account. Johannine irony scarcely reaches a higher point. Jesus was put to death; and (politically) the people perished. Yet he died ὑπὲρ τοῦ λαοῦ and those of the nation who believed in him did not perish (καὶ μὴ ... ἀπόληται) but received eternal life (3.16). There is no adequate textual ground for omitting ὑπὲρ τοῦ λαοῦ, and that the (formally) correct theology comes from the lips of Caiaphas accords with John's manner. See further Derrett, *Law*, 418–23; but it is unlikely that John meant that the Jewish suggestion was that Jesus was innocent and that his death, as one of the righteous, would benefit the people.

51. ἀφ' ἑαυτοῦ οὐκ εἶπεν. For the expression cf. 14.10. God is able to speak through an unwilling agent (Caiaphas) as well as through a willing one (Jesus).

τοῦ ἐνιαυτοῦ ἐκείνου. Cf. v. 49. It is Caiaphas' connection with Jesus and his passion, rather than his high-priesthood, that makes him prophesy (but see below); we should therefore not follow the few authorities that omit τοῦ ἐνιαυτοῦ ἐκείνου.

ἐπροφήτευσεν. Caiaphas was made an unconscious vehicle of truth. 'Prophecies made without the knowledge and intention of the speaker are often mentioned in the rabbinic literature' (S.B. ii, 546; examples are given). For unwitting prophecy see Philo, *Mos.* 1, 274,277,283,286. For the high priest as prophet see Josephus, *Bel.* 1, 68f.; *Ant.* xi, 327; xiii, 299f.; Philo, *Spec. Leg.*, iv,192 (ὁ πρὸς ἀλήθειαν ἱερεὺς εὐθύς ἐστι προφήτης); *Tos. Sotah* 13.5,6; also Dodd, in *Neotestamentica et Patristica* (Festschrift O. Cullmann, 1962), 134–43.

ὑπὲρ τοῦ ἔθνους. Cf. v. 50. ἔθνος and λαός are evidently used as synonyms.

52. ἵνα καὶ τὰ τέκνα τοῦ θεοῦ τὰ διεσκορπισμένα συναγάγῃ εἰς ἕν. In a Jewish work this would naturally mean the gathering together of the dispersed Israelites to their own land in the messianic age. Cf. (among many passages) Isa. 43.5, ... ἀπὸ δυσμῶν συνάξω σε; Jer. 23.2f., ... διεσκορπίσατε τὰ πρόβατά μου ... εἰσδέξομαι τοὺς καταλοίπους τοῦ λαοῦ μου; Ezek. 34.12, ἐκζητήσω τὰ πρόβατά μου ... οὗ διεσπάρησαν ἐκεῖ; 37.21, ... συνάξω αὐτούς; Ps. Sol. 8.34, συνάγαγε τὴν διασπορὰν 'Ισραήλ; 4 Ezra 13.47 *multitudinem collectam cum pace.* See also Philo, *Praem.*, 163–72. Other Old Testament passages that may have been in mind are Isa. 49.5; Jer. 31.10; and, for the gathering of the Gentiles to Zion, Isa. 2.3; 56.7; 60.6; Zech. 14.16. The New Testament writers were not slow to appropriate the language of dispersed Judaism for their own use (e.g. James 1.1; 1 Peter 1.1). It is however unlikely that John was thinking of the gathering of dispersed Christians at the last day, but rather the gathering of men into the church, the *one* body of Christ (cf. 17.21, ἵνα πάντες ἓν ὦσιν). There may be a metaphorical allusion to this, with the use of the same verb (συνάγειν), in 6.12f.

The question now arises what is meant by the scattered children of God. We may think that the death of Christ effects the gathering together in one of those who by nature *are* children of God, or that the death of Christ in the first place makes men children of God and thus unites them in the church. The former view accords well with the Stoic belief in a σπερματικὸς λόγος, which is believed by some to underlie John's thought, and with gnostic language, which is almost certainly recalled here (Dodd, *Interpretation*, 108, aptly quotes Clement, *Exc. ex Theodoto*, XLIX, 1: ὅταν συλλεγῇ τὰ σπέρματα τοῦ θεοῦ); but only the latter is compatible with the gospel itself. 1.12f.; 3.3,5 make it clear that men *become* children of God only by receiving Christ, by birth of water and Spirit. There are however some who are predestined as his; cf. 10.16 (see the note). Jesus collects those who belong to him within and without Judaism, and lays down his life for them. The unity of the church thus constituted on earth is to be fully consummated in heaven; John retains this eschatological hope. This verse is probably reflected in Odes of Solomon 10.5f.: And the Gentiles were gathered together (אתכנשו) who had been scattered abroad (מבדרין) ... and they became my people for ever and ever.

53. ἀπ᾽ ἐκείνης οὖν τῆς ἡμέρας. For the expression cf. 19.27; and, for the whole verse, Matt. 26.4.

ἐβουλεύσαντο. Cf. 12.10. The process set in motion at v. 46 soon bears fruit. From the meeting of v. 47 plans emerged. It may be noted once more that John suggests that the notable miracle of the resurrection of Lazarus was the immediate occasion of Jesus' death.

54. παρρησίᾳ, a common word in John, see on 7.4; here, 'openly'.

περιεπάτει ἐν τοῖς ᾽Ιουδαίοις. Cf. 7.1. He had come (11.17f.) to Bethany, near Jerusalem. ἐκεῖθεν, from Bethany.

χώραν. D adds Σαμφουρειν (d sapfurim). This name has been conjectured to be a corruption of שמה אפרים (shᵉmeh 'ephraim, 'whose name was Ephraim'). In some Semitic form of the gospel (whether an original Aramaic or a Syriac VS.) dittography took place, and the dittograph was thus corrupted in D. 'Samphurim' would thus have no claim to be an original part of the text but would reveal something about the origin of D. An alternative suggestion, that 'Samphurim' is Sepphoris, seems less probable. Sepphoris is in Galilee, on the road between Nazareth and Ptolemais; it is not a district (χώρα) but a town.

᾽Εφραΐμ. Cf. Josephus, Bel. IV, 551, where a πολίχνιον Ephraim is mentioned. It is near Bethel and thus ἐγγὺς τῆς ἐρήμου. It is probably to be identified with the modern Et-Taiyibeh, 4 miles NE. of Bethel; Albright, however, prefers Ain Samieh. For details see Brown. The name Ephraim serves no allegorical or other purpose, and is probably traditional.

κἀκεῖ ἔμεινεν. διέτριβεν (P⁴⁵ P⁶⁶ D Θ it vg) may be due to assimilation to 3.22. The aorist ἔμεινεν is constative. Jesus now waits in retirement for his hour, which will strike at Passover.

24. THE ANOINTING

11.55—12.11

The scene is now set for the final Passover of the ministry of Jesus, and interest is roused by the expectation of the people. Six days before the feast Jesus took a meal with Lazarus, whom he had raised from the dead, and with Mary and Martha, the sisters of Lazarus. The occasion is represented by John as being at least semi-public, and the presence of Lazarus attracted great attention (v. 9). In the course of the meal Mary anointed the feet of Jesus with perfume; when complaint was made at her extravagant use of the ointment Jesus defended her. The incident ends with a note of the belief in Jesus caused by the raising of

Lazarus, and the determination of the chief priests to kill not Jesus only but Lazarus also.

In Luke 10.38-42 Jesus is entertained in the house of Mary and Martha (there is no mention of Lazarus). An anointing story is given by Mark (14.3-9; Matt. 26.6-13), and another by Luke (7.36-50). Reminiscences of both appear in John; see the notes on vv. 3, 4, 5, 7, 8. For a very valuable discussion of the relation of the anointing stories to each other and to the narratives of the burial of Jesus see D. Daube, *N.T.R.J.* 301-24, where it is argued that behind all these narratives there lies a desire to show that the body of Jesus was decently and reverently treated; it was duly anointed, either in the normal way at the time of burial (John 19.39f.), or by anticipation while Jesus was still alive (Mark 14.8, προέλαβεν μυρίσαι). That this motive was operative in the formulation of the tradition seems beyond reasonable doubt; it does not however apply directly to the Johannine anointing, since John provides otherwise for the anointing of the body (19.39f.). John has, it appears, compiled a narrative out of traditional material, and though (see pp. 42-6) the matter is incapable of rigid proof there is no more economical hypothesis than that the tradition reached him by way of Mark and Luke. Those who bring to bear against this view the observation that it means that John has by this compilation of material produced a confused narrative tend to overlook the fact that John's narrative is confused wherever it came from, and one source of confusion is not necessarily preferable to another. It is not necessary here to discuss the question (answered affirmatively by Brown and Lindars) whether the Lucan narrative records a distinct incident, but the peculiarly Johannine features seem secondary. John's interest lies not so much within the limits of Jewish thoughts and customs as in the anointing as a means of expressing the royal dignity of Jesus in preparation for his triumphal entry into Jerusalem (12.12-16). It is particularly significant that John reverses the Marcan order of these two events. It is as anointed king that Jesus rides into Jerusalem, and as anointed king that he dies (18.33-40; 19.1-6,12-16,19). It is true that the theme of Messiahship is not explicitly mentioned, and that Mary anoints not Jesus' head but his feet (v. 3, contrast Mark 14.3). This is because the Johannine King is glorified in death, and is anointed with the spices of burial; hence John's alteration of Mark; cf. the comment of Heitmüller, quoted by Bultmann: the dying Jesus must be presented before the triumphant Jesus. See also Schnackenburg II, 464-7.

55. ἦν δὲ ἐγγὺς τὸ πάσχα. Cf. 2.13. This is John's normal method of referring to the arrival of a feast. This Passover is the third named by John (2.13, 23; 6.4); if the unnamed feast of 5.1 is a Passover, it is the fourth of the ministry. ἀνέβησαν, as at 2.13, a word of pilgrimage. Passover was one of the three 'pilgrim feasts'.

ἐκ τῆς χώρας. Either the district referred to in v. 54, or, more probably, 'the country', 'the provinces', generally.

ἵνα ἁγνίσωσιν ἑαυτούς. Cf. Josephus, *Bel.* 1, 229 (at a festival time the provincials were purifying themselves, ἁγνεύοντας τοὺς ἐπιχωρίους), VI, 290 (the people were assembling for Unleavened Bread (= Passover) on the 8th of Xanthicus (treated by Josephus as equivalent to Nisan), that is, a week before Passover). See Num. 9.6–12, interpreted in *Pesahim* 9.1.

56. ἐζήτουν. Cf. 7.11, 13. The parallel suggests to Brown that John may have been re-using traditional material in order to effect the transition to the new paragraph. Vv. 55ff. are in any case an editorial link.

ἐν τῷ ἱερῷ ἑστηκότες. The Temple was a popular place for meeting and talking.

τί δοκεῖ ὑμῖν; should be so punctuated: 'What do you think?'

ὅτι pursues the question '. . . that he will not come to the feast?' (in view of the plot to kill him). It is difficult to estimate the force of μή. It may introduce an element of doubt: 'He will not come, will he?' Or, taken closely with οὐ, it may form a very strong denial. The former is more probable.

57. δεδώκεισαν, pluperfect without augment. This is usual in the New Testament and common in Koine Greek (and in some other authors, such as Herodotus, but not in Attic); M. II, 190; B.D., § 66,1.

οἱ ἀρχιερεῖς καὶ οἱ Φαρισαῖοι. See on v. 47, and cf. 7.11,32; 9.22.

ἵνα. Explanatory ἵνα, 'to the effect that'.

πιάσωσιν. Cf. 7.30,32,44; 8.20; 10.39.

1. πρὸ ἓξ ἡμερῶν τοῦ πάσχα. For the construction see M. 1, 100f.; Moule, *Idiom Book*, 74. There is no need to regard it as a Latinism, based on (e.g.) *ante diem tertium Kalendas*, though such renderings as πρὸ δέκα δύο καλανδῶν Δεκενβρίων can be quoted (Dittenberger, *Syll.* 866.38ff.). Other native Greek passages can be quoted, e.g. Dittenberger, *Syll.* 736.70 (92 B.C.), πρὸ ἀμερᾶν δέκα τῶν μυστηρίων (ten days before the mysteries); *P. Fay.* 118.15f. (second century A.D.), πρὼ δύο ἡμερῶν ἀγόρασον τὰ ὀρνιθάρια τῆς ἑορτῆς [*sic*] (buy the fowls two days before the feast, or perhaps, buy the fowls for the feast two days beforehand).

John represents the Passover as beginning on the following Friday evening (13.1; 18.28; 19.31,42). Reckoning six days before this brings us to the preceding Saturday (see below on v. 2). The hour of Jesus now strikes (v. 23). The Jews have determined to put him to death (11.53,57), and the whole of this chapter reviews the ministry as an episode now past and looks forward to the crucifixion. This John places emphatically in the context of Passover and it is probable that John saw in this connection a significant interpretation of the death of Jesus (cf. 1.29), as sacrificial, and as effecting the deliverance of the people of God. For the six-day interval during which the final events took place cf. the notes of time in 1.29,35,43; 2.1,13, and the discussion on 2.1. It is possible that some liturgical motive may lie behind these divisions of significant weeks; if so, it will have been a concern not of John but of his source, for John does nothing to indicate it.

ἦλθεν εἰς Βηθανίαν, ὅπου ἦν Λάζαρος. See on 11.1. The reduplication of references is awkward, and suggests to Brown that the Lazarus story was brought rather late into its present chronological sequence. A more probable conclusion is that John derived the Anointing story from Mark, the raising of Lazarus from a different source; the present note co-ordinates the two. Cf. Mark 14.3; it will appear probable in the consideration of the next few verses

410

that John was familiar with the Marcan anointing story; if he was not familiar with Mark's story he was certainly dependent upon a tradition which placed the event at this point, and at Bethany. Contrast Luke 7.36–50, where the anointing takes place in quite different circumstances. After the name Lazarus, ὁ τεθνηκώς is added by P⁶⁶ D Θ ω vg; this is a gloss. It is not impossible that ὂν ἤγειρεν ἐκ νεκρῶν 'Ιησοῦς is another, since the repetition of the name Jesus is awkward; but this is not good enough ground for the deletion of the clause.

2. ἐποίησαν οὖν αὐτῷ δεῖπνον. For δεῖπνον ποιεῖν cf. Mark 6.21; Luke 14.12,16. In John δεῖπνον is used elsewhere only of the last supper (13.2,4; 21.20); here also it probably means 'supper'. Outside the New Testament, Greek usage is not decisive what meal is meant by the word—it can mean a morning, afternoon, or evening meal; in Luke 14.12 it stands beside ἄριστον, signifying, presumably, a later meal. If δεῖπνον is 'supper', we have here the Saturday (see on v. 1) evening meal, which was connected with the *Habdalah* (הבדלה), or service denoting the separation (הבדיל, *habdil*, 'to make separation') of the Sabbath from the rest of the week. This service was probably connected with a meal as early as the time of Jesus since there was a controversy between the school of Hillel and the school of Shammai on the question whether the order should be the lamp, the spices, the food, and the *Habdalah*, or the lamp, the food, the spices, and the *Habdalah*; also over the form of the benediction over the lamp (*Berakoth* 8.5). See also Singer, 216f. Legends about Elijah, connected with the bringing in of the Messiah at the beginning of a week, came to be associated with the *Habdalah* (I. Abrahams, *Annotated Edition of the Authorised Daily Prayer Book* (1914), clxxxii), but we do not know their age; the use of spices however is evidently ancient, and may possibly be not unconnected with the anointing. It must be added that John himself shows not the smallest knowledge of or interest in the *Habdalah* ceremony, and may well have been unaware of its existence.

ἐποίησαν has no subject, and it is therefore not clear who gave the supper. That Lazarus was sitting at table does not mean that he was not host, and that Martha served does not mean that she was not hostess (cf. Luke 10.38–42); the most probable view is that Lazarus, Mary, and Martha should be thought of as providing the meal. John simply drops the Marcan 'Simon the leper' and the Lucan 'Simon the Pharisee', and takes it for granted that the reader will let the brother and sisters take their place.

ἡ Μάρθα διηκόνει. Cf. Luke 10.40, ἡ δὲ Μάρθα περιεσπᾶτο περὶ πολλὴν διακονίαν. This feature, and the contrasted notice of Mary, suggest strongly that John was aware of Luke. On the augment of διηκόνει see Rutherford 83, 86; M. II, 192, 303; B.D. § 69.

ὁ δὲ Λάζαρος εἷς ἦν. Lazarus plays no part in the story, and is not mentioned again till v. 9. This suggests that John had no independent narrative here, but simply identified the characters of the Marcan story, which was placed at Bethany, with the family he had already mentioned as resident there.

3. ἡ οὖν Μαριὰμ λαβοῦσα λίτραν μύρου νάρδου πιστικῆς πολυτίμου. Cf. Luke 7.37, κομίσασα ἀλάβαστρον μύρου; also the much more striking parallel in Mark 14.3, γυνὴ ἔχουσα ἀλάβαστρον μύρου νάρδου πιστικῆς πολυτελοῦς. Most striking of all is the use of the word πιστικός, which occurs only in these passages and in writers certainly dependent on them. Its derivation and meaning are

uncertain, a fact which probably accounts for its omission in Mark by D and a few other MSS. The omission by P⁶⁶* D of νάρδου in John is hardly to be taken seriously; if it were the dependence of John on Mark would be as good as proved for there would be no other way of accounting for the feminine πιστικῆς. L.S. derive this word from πίνειν, and so render *liquid*. An alternative Greek derivation is from πιστός; the meaning will then be *genuine* (Pliny, *Historia Naturalis* XII, 43 (26), refers to the possibility of adulterating nard). It is very unlikely that both in Mark and John the text suffered corruption and originally read some form of the Latin *spicatum*, though this appears in the Vulgate of Mark 14.3. To suppose that πιστικός is a local or trade name (so that we should transliterate, 'pistic nard') is a counsel of despair, but not necessarily wrong. Probably the best solution is that John simply took the word over from Mark, perhaps understanding it to mean *genuine*, but that in Mark it was a transliteration of the Aramaic פיסתקא (*pistaqa*), the pistachio nut (Black, 223ff., following J. Lightfoot, *Horae Hebraicae* on Mark 14.3 (edition of 1699 (Utrecht) II, 456)). The ointment would then be that known as *myrobalanum*. See further M. II, 379f.; M.M. *s.v.* λίτρα in the papyri, and no doubt here, is equivalent to the Roman *libra*, that is, about 12 oz. νάρδος is the Old Testament נרד (*nerd*, LXX νάρδος, Song of Solomon, 1.12; 4.13f.), an eastern ointment. For further details see *E. Bib. s.v.* Spikenard.

ἤλειψεν τοὺς πόδας. Cf. Mark 14.3, κατέχεεν αὐτοῦ τῆς κεφαλῆς; Luke 7.38, στᾶσα ὀπίσω παρὰ τοὺς πόδας αὐτοῦ . . . καὶ ἤλειφεν τῷ μύρῳ [*sc.* τοὺς πόδας τοῦ 'Ιησοῦ]. Here John follows the Lucan rather than the Marcan narrative. ἀλείφειν means merely 'to smear with oil', as after the bath, or for gymnastics; cf. Matt. 6.17.

ἐξέμαξεν ταῖς θριξὶν αὐτῆς. Cf. Luke 7.38, ταῖς θριξὶν τῆς κεφαλῆς αὐτῆς ἐξέμασσεν. There is no parallel in Mark, and John omits the Lucan details that the woman wet Jesus' feet with her tears, and kissed them. By this omission the wiping is made unintelligible. Further it should be noted that the woman's unbound hair, and her anointing the feet (rather than the head) of Jesus, are much more easily explicable in the Lucan context, where the woman is a penitent sinner, than in John, where she is the sister of Lazarus (and apparently joint hostess with Martha). John has combined the Marcan and Lucan narratives with each other, and with material of his own, and there is some confusion. John may have abandoned the anointing of Jesus' head, as recounted in Mark, because it suggested too crudely the anointing of a messianic king of a kind inconsistent with his understanding of Jesus, and adopted a suggestion provided by his other source, Luke.

ἡ δὲ οἰκία ἐπληρώθη ἐκ τῆς ὀσμῆς τοῦ μύρου. For ἐκ meaning 'with' cf. Matt. 23.25; Rev. 8.5. Origen (*Ev. Ioannis* I, 11) saw in this detail a reference to the prediction in Mark (14.9, not reported by John) that the woman's deed should be universally reported. This is to some extent supported by the use of the metaphor of scent in rabbinic sources: *Ecclesiastes R.* 7.1: Good ointment spreads from the bedroom into the dining room; but a good name spreads from one end of the world to the other. *Song of Songs R.* 1.22 (on 1.3) explains the verse with reference to Abraham. Before his call (Gen. 12.1) Abraham was like a jar of ointment lying in a corner, whose odour was unknown. When God called him to go forth his good works became known and the name of God was magnified, as when the jar is brought out and men become aware of its scent. Whether John was aware of these (late) rabbinic passages is highly doubtful, and whether he intended to say more than that Mary's deed quickly became known is questionable, though it may be right to see here an answer to Brown's argument that John cannot have known the Marcan story, for had he known it he would not have omitted Mark 14.9. Lindars thinks that the filling of the house with perfume underlines the extravagance of the woman's deed. There is a possible allusion to this verse in Ignatius, *Eph.* 17.1., διὰ τοῦτο μύρον ἔλαβεν ἐπὶ τῆς κεφαλῆς αὐτοῦ ὁ κύριος, ἵνα πνέῃ τῇ ἐκκλησίᾳ ἀφθαρσίαν. μὴ ἀλείφεσθε δυσωδίαν … The allusion would seem probable if on other grounds it were certainly established that Ignatius used John; but this is not so (see Introduction, pp. 110f.).

4. Ἰούδας ὁ Ἰσκαριώτης. On Judas, his name, and the textual variants that occur when it is mentioned, see on 6.71. In Mark 14.4 the complaint is made by τινές; in Matt. 26.8 by οἱ μαθηταί. See on v. 6.

εἷς … παραδιδόναι. Cf. the similar description in 6.71, also Mark 3.19; 14.10,18,20,43 and parallels. All the gospels emphasize that the traitor was one of the inner group of disciples.

5. Cf. Mark 14.4f., εἰς τί ἡ ἀπώλεια αὕτη τοῦ μύρου γέγονεν; ἠδύνατο γὰρ τοῦτο τὸ μύρον πραθῆναι ἐπάνω δηναρίων τριακοσίων καὶ δοθῆναι τοῖς πτωχοῖς. The parallelism is very close and the coincidence in the numbers (διακοσίων in φ seems to be an accidental error) is particularly striking. It seems very probable that John knew Mark. The priority is clearly with Mark; in Mark the '300 denarii' is given as an estimate; in John it is assumed as the value of the ointment.

6. περὶ … ἔμελεν αὐτῷ. Cf. 10.13 for the construction and also for the sense; among the true shepherds Judas is a hireling—and worse. The verse may be John's composition.

κλέπτης ἦν. We have no other ground for regarding Judas as a thief, though he is said to have received money for his treachery. John may have an independent tradition, but more probably he represents the traditional and progressive blackening of Judas' character.

τὸ γλωσσόκομον. Phrynichus (LXXIX, Rutherford, 181; see further M. II, 272) notes that the 'correct' form is γλωττοκομεῖον, and that the word should be used only for a box employed as a receptacle for the mouthpieces (γλῶτται) of flutes, but adds that it was also—wrongly—used for other receptacles, containing books, clothes, money, and so on. The papyri amply attest the meaning 'money-box'. The word is used again at 13.29, where also Judas appears as treasurer.

τὰ βαλλόμενα ἐβάσταζεν. Both verbs have secondary meanings. βάλλειν. originally 'to throw', is often weakened in Hellenistic Greek 'to put', βαστάζειν is originally 'to carry'; hence, 'to lift', 'to carry away', 'to pilfer'. This last meaning is well attested in the papyri; see G. A. Deissmann, *Bible Studies* (E.T. 1901), 257.

7. Cf. Mark 14.6,8, ἄφετε αὐτήν … προέλαβεν μυρίσαι τὸ σῶμά μου εἰς τὸν ἐνταφιασμόν. The Marcan words are much clearer than the Johannine. Mark means 'Leave the woman in peace … she has anticipated the anointing of my body for burial'. The body of Jesus is not in Mark anointed after the crucifixion, and this act of love forms the only substitute for the last rite which the friends of Jesus were prevented by his resurrection from performing.

The Johannine narrative is confused by the fact that the evangelist later records an elaborate anointing of the dead body of Jesus by Joseph of Arimathaea and Nicodemus (19.38–42). There is thus no room in John for a merely anticipatory anointing, which accomplished the rite by a legal fiction. The confusion however is best explained as due to John's continuing to follow his Marcan source, and thus proves to be a strong argument for his use of Mark. Two difficulties arise, though each bears upon the other. (i) with regard to the construction; (ii) over the meaning of τηρεῖν. (i) In Hellenistic Greek ἄφες, ἄφετε had become almost auxiliaries introducing a first person subjunctive in the sense of an imperative. Possibly a similar usage is to be accepted here, and if so we should translate 'Let her keep it . . .'. See M. 1, 175. Alternatively we may render (a) (with substantially the same sense) 'Let her alone in order that she may keep it . . .' (b) (taking the ἵνα as imperatival —M. 1, 178f., 248) 'Let her alone; let her keep it . . .'; (c) 'Let her alone; (this was) that she might keep it . . .'; (d) hesitantly Dodd suggests the possibility that we should construe τηρήσῃ as if it were τετηρηκυῖα ᾖ, 'Allow her to have kept it.' None of these can be dismissed on purely grammatical grounds, and the construction remains uncertain and obscure. (ii) It is even more difficult to understand the meaning of τηρεῖν. In what sense can the woman 'keep' the ointment which she has already used? (The variant τετήρηκεν is a manifest attempt to alleviate the difficulty.) To suggest that only a small part of the ointment had been used and that the rest might be preserved is not only to miss the spirit of the narrative but also to ignore v. 3c. It is equally inconsistent with the narrative to suppose that John thought of a miraculously unfailing supply of ointment. The simplest suggestion is that here τηρεῖν means not 'to keep', but 'to keep in the mind', 'to remember'. We should then translate '. . . let her remember it (the ointment, or the act of anointing) on the day of my burial'. As the gospel now stands this would mean, 'Let her, when Joseph and Nicodemus anoint my body, remember that she has foreshadowed this act of piety and thus shared in it'; but it may reflect a pre-Johannine stage of the tradition in which the anointing by Joseph and Nicodemus was not mentioned (see Daube, loc. cit.), and in this stage it would presumably mean, 'Let her remember, when my body is consigned to the grave without due care, that she has anointed it by anticipation'. The objection to this rendering, and it is serious, is that τηρεῖν does not mean 'to remember'. It is especially frequent in John and means 'to keep' (e.g. good wine), or 'to observe' (e.g. the word or command of Jesus; or the Sabbath); cf. however Luke 2.19,51 (συνετήρει . . . διετήρει, where however 'in her heart' is added). One further alternative must be noted: a possible Aramaic original of the Greek (Torrey, 61–3) could be taken as a question, 'Let her alone; should she keep it till the day of my burial?' This is a not unattractive hypothesis, but no explanation is given, or can be given, of the folly of the translator in thus reversing the meaning of his text. The best possibilities are (a) that we should disregard the lexical evidence and render 'Let her remember . . .'; (b) that we should adopt the not very natural view that αὐτό refers to the act of anointing and translate, 'Let her observe the last rite *now* with a view to the day of my burial'; (c) that we should look back to v. 5 and fill up the sentence thus: 'Her failure to sell the ointment and give the proceeds to the poor was in order that she might keep . . .'. It cannot be said that any of these is wholly satisfying.

414

8. Cf. Mark 14.7, πάντοτε γὰρ τοὺς πτωχοὺς ἔχετε μεθ᾽ ἑαυτῶν, καὶ ὅταν θέλητε δύνασθε αὐτοῖς εὖ ποιῆσαι, ἐμὲ δὲ οὐ πάντοτε ἔχετε. This verse in Mark stands between the command to leave the woman alone, and the saying about burial. In John the verse is omitted altogether by D sin, perhaps rightly, since here it has no direct connection with the context (v. 5 being answered by v. 7, and v. 6 intervening), and may be due to assimilation. For the poor cf. Deut. 15.11, The poor shall never cease out of the land; for the care of the dead as a good work superior to almsgiving cf. *T. Peah* 4.19 (24); *Sukkah* 49b.

9. ἔγνω. Cf. 11.56. ὁ ὄχλος πολύς. These are apparently not the ruling Jews (see the next verse, ἀρχιερεῖς), though generally in John οἱ ᾽Ιουδαῖοι are the enemies of Jesus (see on 1.19). ὁ ὄχλος πολύς (with the article) occurs again in John only at v. 12, where it denotes the great multitude which came up to Jerusalem for the feast; at v. 9 it must have the same meaning though otherwise the suggestion would be natural that the common people (עמי הארץ, *'amme ha'arets*; see on 7.49) were meant.

10. ἐβουλεύσαντο δὲ οἱ ἀρχιερεῖς. The chief priests are mentioned (along with the Pharisees) as having plotted the arrest of Jesus at 7.32,45; but their plans mature in 11.47–53. Lazarus proves to be a ground of faith in Jesus and it therefore becomes necessary to remove him also.

11. ὑπῆγον. ὑπάγειν is a common word in John. Here it means that many Jews *left* their former Jewish allegiance and way of life to become disciples; cf. 6.67 where many disciples similarly went away from Jesus and walked with him no more. There is thus no need for the hypothesis (Torrey, 30, 39f., 43f.) that 'went and believed' represents אזלין ומהמנין, which should have been translated 'believed in increasing numbers'. Even if the conjectured Aramaic were accepted it should probably be translated 'believed more and more'. For the belief of large numbers of Jews cf. 2.23, for the evidential value of signs cf. 20.30f.

25. THE ENTRY INTO JERUSALEM

12.12–19

The narrative of the entry of Jesus into Jerusalem, riding on an ass and acclaimed by the crowds, occurs also in the Synoptic Gospels (Mark 11.1–11; Matt. 21.1–11; Luke 19.29–38). The narratives are indeed not identical, but it can hardly be said that John's differs from Mark's more seriously than do those of Matthew and Luke. If John introduces (v. 15) an explicit reference to Zech. 9.9, so also does Matthew (21.5); if he has Jesus hailed as King (v. 13), so also does Luke (19.38). The most important difference between John and Mark is that in Mark Jesus initiates the proceedings by arranging for the procurement of an animal to ride on, whereas in John it is after he has received the plaudits of the crowd that he 'finds' (v. 14) a young ass and rides on it; for this point see below. The essential content of John's narrative is the same as Mark's, and though it cannot be proved that John had read Mark there is no simpler and more economical hypothesis than that he had done so, and modified it in the light of his theological interests; see Introduction, pp. 42-5. Whether based on Mark or not, the substance of the narrative is traditional and John does not vary it greatly. He does however lay stress on two theological themes which have special importance for him. (a) He emphasizes that Jesus is ὁ βασιλεύς τοῦ 'Ισραήλ (v. 13), the messianic king, who is received in a manner befitting his state. John knows that the charge on which Jesus was in fact executed was his claim, misinterpreted by the Roman governor, to be a king; this point he develops fully in the passion narrative (18.33-40; 19.1-6,12-16,19), and uses the present incident to introduce it. (b) He notes that, though the disciples later understood the royal significance of the entry, they did not do so at the time (v. 16; see the note). The glorification of Jesus was the necessary condition of their understanding —another main theme of the gospel.

John does not perceive that his expression of these two themes is hardly possible as history; or, if he perceives it, he is too little concerned with the details of history to correct the contradiction he appears to have introduced into his narrative. If the disciples did not understand the messianic significance of the entry, then *a fortiori* neither did the crowd (cf. Matt. 21.11); but if they did not understand the occurrence in this way they would not have hailed Jesus as the king of Israel. ὁ ἐρχόμενος may originally have had a different meaning (cf. 6.14, ὁ προφήτης ὁ ἐρχόμενος εἰς τὸν κόσμον).

It may be (see above) that John deliberately reversed the order in which the acclamation and the reference to the ass occur in the narrative. In the view of several recent commentators (e.g., Dodd, Sanders, Brown, Lindars) his motive was to show that Jesus could and would accept the designation King (cf. 6.15) only when this was defined in terms of Zechariah's Prince of Peace, who rides not on a warhorse but on an ass. This is certainly more probable than the view (see the note on v. 13) that the entry was intended as the cue for a nationalist rising. Even if (as is unlikely) this was the original intention of the event, John does not countenance it. It is probable that he had no interest in Mark's circumstantial narrative, and introduced the ass as briefly as possible when it was needed to prepare for the quotation from Zechariah.

The Pharisees note the enthusiastic welcome given to Jesus, and comment, in words full of Johannine irony, on their failure to deal with the situation. 'The world is gone after him.'

12. τῇ ἐπαύριον. For the note of time cf. 1.29. This looks back to 12.1; the interval between the day of this verse (five days before Passover) and 13.1 (one day before Passover) is accounted for by v. 36 ('Ιησοῦς ἀπελθὼν ἐκρύβη). In Mark the triumphal entry precedes the anointing (11.1-11; 14.3-9). After ἐπαύριον sin adds 'He went forth and came to the Mount of Olives; and ...' This recalls Mark 11.11,19; Luke 21.37; but the origin of the reading remains obscure.

ὁ ὄχλος πολὺς ὁ ἐλθὼν εἰς τὴν ἑορτήν. Passover was one of the three annual Pilgrim Feasts, and very large crowds assembled in Jerusalem. Josephus (*Bel.* VI, 422–5) speaks of a census held under the orders of Cestius Gallus (governor of Syria at the time of the outbreak of the Jewish War), when the number taking part in the Passover was estimated at 2,700,000. It is difficult to believe that quite so large a number was accommodated within the confines (even though enlarged for the purpose) of the city; but undoubtedly immense multitudes were present.

ἀκούσαντες is constructed *ad sensum* with ὄχλος. Cf. v. 9.

13. τὰ βαΐα τῶν φοινίκων. βάϊον (so accented, L. S., new edition) is derived from the Coptic *ba(i)*, 'branch of the date-palm'. The more usual form is βαΐς (βάϊς), but John's is attested in the papyri (see M.M. *s.v.*), and also at 1 Macc. 13.51 (but nowhere else in the Greek Bible), though here the form βαιων (genitive plural) could possibly be derived from βάϊς. In 1 Maccabees as in John the palm-branches are used in a triumphal procession. φοῖνιξ, sometimes used of palm-branches (e.g. Rev. 7.9), will here mean 'palm-tree', so that the full expression, βαΐα τῶν φοινίκων, is pleonastic, though it occurs (without the articles) in T. Naph. 5.4. The use of the palm-branches probably signifies no more than a jubilant welcome accorded to a notable person; so Mark 11.8, ἄλλοι δὲ (ἔστρωσαν) στιβάδας κόψαντες ἐκ τῶν ἀγρῶν. It is however not impossible that John may have intended to represent the לולב (*lulab*, literally 'palm-branch'), which was a bundle made up of palm, myrtle, and willow (*Sukkah* 3), in fulfilment of Lev. 23.40 (note . . . κάλλυνθρα φοινίκων . . .), and used at the Feast of Tabernacles. These *lulabs* were shaken at the occurrence of the word Hosanna when Psalm 118 was sung at Tabernacles (*Sukkah* 3.9). According to 2 Macc. 1.9; 10.6 the Feast of Dedication (see on 10.22) was celebrated in a manner similar to Tabernacles; and for a suggestion that the entry of Jesus into Jerusalem had the significance of a new Dedication see F. C. Burkitt, *J.T.S.* old series 17 (1916), 139–49, with C. G. Montefiore, *The Synoptic Gospels* (1927) 1, 259f. See further, in addition to the commentaries, W. R. Farmer, *J.T.S.* new series 3 (1952), 62–6, and B. A. Mastin, *N.T.S.* 16 (1969), 76–82. Experts appear to disagree on the question whether palms grew and were readily available in the city of Jerusalem; it is probably safe to say with J. Jeremias, 'If we recall that there are a few palm trees in Jerusalem even today and that Pseudo-Aristeas 112 enumerates dates among the products of Jerusalem . . ., John's account appears to be within the bounds of possibility' (*Jerusalem*, 43). The element of premeditation will then be confined to ἔλαβον and the article τά, which may however be overtranslated as 'they took *the* palm-branches', i.e., those that had been brought (perhaps from Jericho) for the purpose. Palms alone, even if not as a constituent of the *lulab*, give something of a nationalist air to the scene, but nationalism and religion often went hand in hand in the first century. The details in John do not suffice for more than speculation, and may in the end be best explained, like those in Mark, as the signs of a spontaneous ovation, though as symbols palms are consistent with the words heard on the lips of the crowd; see below.

ἐξῆλθον εἰς ὑπάντησιν. This suggests that the crowd was in Jerusalem already and came out to meet Jesus. Vv. 17f. suggests two crowds, one accompanying Jesus, the other going out of the city to meet him.

ώσαννά. A transliteration of the Hebrew הושיעה נא, or, more probably, of the corresponding Aramaic, הושענא, Ps. 118.25. The LXX translate accurately, σῶσον δή, 'Save now, we pray'. In John the difficulties are absent which arise in the Marcan use of the word (11.10). The Psalm was the last of the *Hallel* group sung at Passover; but it was also a special part of the Tabernacles festival; see *Sukkah* 3.9; 4.5. It may be that the word had already lost much of its original meaning and become little more than a jubilant shout of praise.

εὐλογημένος ὁ ἐρχόμενος ἐν ὀνόματι κυρίου. So also Mark 11.9. Ps. 118.26 runs ברוך הבא בשם יהוה, Blessed be he that comes in the name of the Lord, where 'in the name of the Lord' should certainly be taken with 'blessed'. John, however, like Mark before him, meant, 'Blessed be he that comes in the name, that is, to the work and with the authority, of the Lord.' The LXX here have the same words as John and Mark, so that we cannot say whether John has translated the Hebrew, borrowed from Mark, or quoted the LXX. It is possible but unlikely that there is a reference to Elijah (Daube, *N.T.R.J.*, 20–3).

καὶ ὁ βασιλεύς (καὶ ὁ β. P75 B א; ὁ β. P66 D Θ; β. ω) τοῦ 'Ισραήλ. Cf. Mark 11.10, εὐλογημένη ἡ ἐρχομένη βασιλεία τοῦ πατρὸς ἡμῶν Δαυίδ. Luke 19.38 has εὐλογημένος ὁ ἐρχόμενος, ὁ βασιλεὺς ἐν ὀνόματι κυρίου. Here *King* is certainly an interpretation of *the Coming One*; this is doubtless true in John also, for καί (if read) will mean 'that is to say', co-ordinating the two titles in one: *the Coming One* is (not Elijah but) the Messiah. The reference, which is probably John's own interpretative gloss, is a clarification of Mark based on Zech. 9.9 (cf. Zeph. 3.15), which is to be quoted in v. 15. On Jesus as the king of Israel (not of the Jews; cf. 18.33,39; 19.3,14,19) see 1.49; 18.37; 19.19 and the notes.

14. εὑρὼν δὲ ὁ 'Ιησοῦς ὀνάριον. Cf. Mark 11.1–7, where the securing of the ass is described in much greater detail. It is unnecessary to suppose that John intended to correct Mark; εὑρών could mean 'to find after search', 'to find by the agency of others', and cuts short a story in which John found no special significance; he has for Jesus higher categories than that of the θεῖος ἀνήρ with second sight (see Introduction, p. 74). It is however a valid observation that, unlike Mark, John places the finding of the animal after the ovation, and it may be that he intended the selection of the ass as a correction of the nationalistic enthusiasm of the crowd. It is however equally possible (see above) that he is simply straightening out the story in terms of its Old Testament components: Jesus is greeted as the coming King in the language of Ps. 118; next he finds an ass and so fulfils Zech. 9. ὀνάριον, *hap. leg.* in the New Testament, is John's abbreviated equivalent of πῶλον ὄνου in v. 15.

καθώς ἐστιν γεγραμμένον. Cf. 6.31.

15. John's quotation of Zech. 9.9 differs from both the Hebrew and the LXX in two points. (i) John has μὴ φοβοῦ; Hebrew גילי מאד, Rejoice greatly; LXX, adequately representing the Hebrew, χαῖρε σφόδρα. The source of John's version is obscure, and there is no evidence of its earlier existence, whether in a full translation of the Old Testament or in a Testimony Book. No better explanation is at hand than that John quoted loosely from memory. A passage such as Isa. 40.9 (μὴ φοβεῖσθε ... ἰδοὺ ὁ θεὸς ὑμῶν) may have in-

fluenced his recollection (cf. Isa. 44.2; Zeph. 3.16). (ii) John's quotation ends καθήμενος ἐπὶ πῶλον ὄνου. The Hebrew has רכב על חמור ועל עיר בן אתנות, Riding upon an ass, even upon a colt the foal of an ass; the LXX, ἐπιβεβηκὼς ἐπὶ ὑποζύγιον καὶ πῶλον νέον. Here again John may be quoting carelessly; or perhaps he was aware of the misunderstanding which the Hebrew parallelism invited (and may have caused in Matthew) and rewrote the difficult words simply and clearly, caring more for the sense than for verbal accuracy. John uses Old Testament *testimonia* more frequently in narrative than in discourse; here, of course, he is reproducing traditional material. Martyn (98ff.) points out that we have here one of the three messianic signs of *Eccles. R.* 1.8, where Zech. 9.9 appears as a counterpart to Exod. 4.20; cf. 6.1–14; 7.37f.; 4.13. In the Midrash the Messiah is being compared with Moses, but this comparison does not appear in the present passage in John.

θυγάτηρ Σιών. This expression (the LXX uses the vocative but is otherwise identical) arises out of the Hebrew use of the feminine in collectives (G.K., 414).

16. ἔγνωσαν. D Θ read ἐνόησαν. νοεῖν occurs elsewhere in John only at 12.40 (a quotation) and may well be original; it would be natural to change it to the very common γινώσκειν. For the thought of the verse cf. 2.22; 13.7; for ἐδοξάσθη cf. 7.39; 12.23 *et al.* For the Spirit (see 7.39) explaining the ministry of Jesus see 15.26; 16.13f. Sometimes (though not invariably) the disciples seem in John to be as slow of perception as they are in Mark; cf. especially 16.29–32. Here they fail to see the messianic, royal, significance of the entry into Jerusalem, upon which John himself evidently laid some stress. They do not recognize in Jesus' use of the ass the fulfilment of prophecy. By emphasizing their failure John probably intended to bring out the necessity of the glorification of Jesus (and by implication the gift of the Spirit) before even his closest followers could understand him. It is probable also that, in doing this, John reproduced, intentionally or unintentionally, old and reliable tradition, and that the disciples did in fact fail to understand what they saw. If however this view is correct its consequences must be noted and accepted. If the disciples did not see in the entry of Jesus the entry of the Messiah it is very unlikely that the crowds did so; why should they be quicker to see the Old Testament allusion? Yet John represents them as hailing Jesus as ὁ βασιλεὺς τοῦ Ἰσραήλ (v. 13). The narrative is really self-contradictory. It may well be that the crowds greeted Jesus as ὁ ἐρχόμενος *without* giving that phrase a messianic interpretation; that is to say, without regarding Jesus himself as Messiah. But John (*a*) introduced the title ὁ βασιλεὺς τοῦ Ἰσραήλ under the influence of Zech. 9.9 and because it was his plan to represent Jesus as the true king of Israel, and (*b*) remarked—probably quite truly—that, before the completion of the work of Christ, the disciples did not understand the proceedings, not perceiving the contradiction he thereby introduced.

ταῦτα ἐποίησαν. Only in the Synoptic Gospels, not in John, had they (the disciples) contributed to the event; John's words show awareness of the older tradition, probably Mark.

17. ἐμαρτύρει. They proclaimed what had been done as testimony to the power of Jesus. Cf. the witness borne by the signs themselves, e.g. 5.36.

ὅτε]ὅτι, P⁶⁶ D it sin pesh. This is probably an attempt to simplify the scene; see on the next verse.

18. διὰ τοῦτο καὶ ὑπήντησεν αὐτῷ ὁ ὄχλος. Cf. v. 13. The words suggest a crowd accompanying Jesus and proclaiming the miracle, and another crowd coming out of Jerusalem because they had heard what was proclaimed.

τοῦτο αὐτὸν πεποιηκέναι τὸ σημεῖον. τοῦτο is brought into a position of emphasis. This miracle as John suggests elsewhere (especially 11.45f.) was of fundamental and decisive importance.

19. οἱ οὖν Φαρισαῖοι εἶπαν πρὸς ἑαυτούς. Cf. at 11.47, οἱ ἀρχιερεῖς καὶ οἱ Φαρισαῖοι. It is doubtful whether John clearly distinguished between the two groups. Black (103) suggests that πρὸς ἑαυτούς represents the Aramaic ethic dative, and Sanders translates 'for their part'. But see B.D. § 287; ἑαυτούς is used for ἀλλήλους.

θεωρεῖτε (probably indicative but possibly imperative) ὅτι οὐκ ὠφελεῖτε οὐδέν. Cf. 11.49. For the use of ὠφελεῖν cf. Matt. 27.24; John 6.63: You are doing no good, effecting nothing.

ὁ κόσμος. D Θ φ it vg sin pesh add ὅλος, or the like, perhaps rightly; omit, P⁶⁶ P⁷⁵ ℵ B. כל העולם (like similar expressions in Aramaic) is a common idiom in the sense of 'every one' (*tout le monde*). The usage is Semitic, not Greek. Cf. in this gospel 7.4; 14.22; 18.20. The Pharisees need mean no more than 'Every one is on his side'. Yet John is writing his own characteristic Greek, and implies ironically in the words he ascribes to the Jews the two truths (*a*) that Jesus was sent into the world to save the world (3.17), (*b*) that representatives of the Gentile world were at the moment approaching (v. 20), the forerunners of the Gentile church. Cf. also 11.52; 12.32. Universalism is already implied in Zech. 9.9. Lindars believes that this passage was originally followed by the Cleansing of the Temple (now transferred to 2.13–25) and 11.47f.

26. THE GREEKS AT THE FEAST

12.20–36

The approach of the Greeks, who come to Philip with the request, Sir, we would see Jesus, marks the end of the first part of the gospel and the fulfilment of 12.19. The world is gone after him. John is writing for Greeks (Gentiles); he knows that the Christian message has reached them and that the Christian church includes them, but they appear only on the fringe of the gospel material itself. It is not the result of accident or of bad writing that the Greeks who desire to see Jesus never appear in his presence, nor is this due to a careful regard for accurate history. They cannot see Jesus yet, but their presence is an indication that the hour of Jesus' death and glory is at hand, since it is only after the crucifixion that the Gospel compasses both Jew and Gentile. Jesus now has no further place in Judaism, which has rejected for itself its place in the purposes of God. Blessed are those who have not seen, yet have believed (20.29). Paul did not in this way give up the belief that Israel retained a special vocation (Rom. 9—11).

The material introduced by the coming of the Greeks is based mainly upon the synoptic tradition. The reference to the seed which must die before it can bear fruit (v. 24) recalls the synoptic parables about seeds and sowing (Mark 4.3–9,26–9,30–2; Matt. 13.3–9,24–30,31f.; Luke 8.4–8; 13.18f.). The sayings that follow (vv. 25f.), on losing and saving one's life, are taken with little modification from Mark (8.34f.; Matt. 10.39; Luke 9.23f.; 17.33). Vv. 27–30 are derived from the synoptic narratives of the agony of Jesus in Gethsemane (Mark 14.32–42; Matt. 26.36–46; Luke 22.40–6), and the closing section deals with the title Son of man, and returns to the imagery of light and darkness. For the former, see Introduction, pp. 71ff., and the note on 1.51; for the latter the note on 8.12. It is important to notice the material which John has thus selected for this significant point in his gospel; it is in harmony with the main trend of the gospel as a whole. The central point is the complete obedience of Jesus to the Father. This theme, stressed again and again, alone makes possible the revealing of God which takes place in his ministry. It is illustrated here by the Geth-semane material, but this is deliberately put in more general terms than in the Synoptic Gospels. The 'hour' of suffering and death finds Jesus prepared, because he has lived for no other purpose than the complete offering of himself to God. The death of Jesus, seen as the climax of his obedient life, means (a) the judgement of this world (v. 31); (b) the exaltation of the Son of man (vv. 23, 32); (c) the climax and harvest of the whole ministry (v. 24) and (d) a challenge to Israel (vv. 35f.). These points are all highly characteristic of John's thought.

The paragraph ends with stress upon the urgency of the situation with which the Jews are confronted. For them, the light shines only for a little while. Soon Jesus will hide himself (v. 36), and when the light shines again it will do so in order to 'lighten the Gentiles' but to judge Israel. The point however is of permanent validity and applies also to John's readers; it is important that they too should accept the light without delay.

20. Ἕλληνές τινες. The word Ἕλλην signifies not one strictly of the Greek race but one of non-Jewish birth. Cf. 7.35 and see Mark 7.26, where a woman first described as a 'Greek' (Ἑλληνίς) is further defined as a Syro-Phoenician. According to J. A. T. Robinson (N.T.S. 6 (1960), 120, 'these Greeks are *not* Gentiles. They are Greek-speaking Jews'. On this view it is hard to see why John called them Ἕλληνες. These 'Greeks' are mentioned here and in the next verse, and then heard of no more; the narrative proceeds without them. They speak as representatives of the Gentile church to which John and his readers belonged.

ἐκ τῶν ἀναβαινόντων ἵνα προσκυνήσωσιν. On ἀναβαίνειν as a technical term see on 2.13. It is possible that ἀναβαινόντων (not ἀναβάντων) has frequentative force; not 'those who had gone up for that feast', but 'those who used to go up for the feast'. It cannot be inferred for certain that these men were proselytes, though they may have been. Cf. Acts 8.27; the Ethiopian eunuch (who could never be a proselyte) ἐληλύθει προσκυνήσων. See also Josephus, *Bel.* VI, 427, . . . τοῖς ἀλλοφύλοις, ὅσοι κατὰ θρησκείαν παρῆσαν; these persons were evidently not full proselytes since they were not allowed to partake of the Passover. There is however no need to suppose that John had clearly defined the status of the men in his own mind; it was sufficient that they were not Jews.

21. Φιλίππῳ τῷ ἀπὸ Βηθσαϊδὰ τῆς Γαλιλαίας. On Philip, his Greek name, and his place of origin, see on 1.44. The fact that Bethsaida was really situated not in Galilee but in Gaulanitis is not relevant as a reason why John should have represented Gentiles as approaching Philip among the Twelve, since John evidently thought (wrongly) that it was in Galilee. It was, indeed, only just on the other side of the frontier. There is thus no point in conjecturing another, otherwise unknown, Bethsaida in Galilee. John may have had Isa. 9.1–7 in mind (Lightfoot).

κύριε—here of course to be translated 'Sir'.

θέλομεν τὸν Ἰησοῦν ἰδεῖν. For ἰδεῖν 'to have an interview with' cf. Luke 8.20; 9.9; Acts 28.20. The usage is classical; see L.S. *s.v.* εἴδω, A.1.b. The interview, it seems, did not happen, and was not indispensable (20.29).

22. λέγει τῷ Ἀνδρέᾳ. Like Philip, Andrew (see on 1.40) bears a Greek name, and was perhaps the only other of the Twelve to do so. Bartholomew's name seems to be half Greek and half Semitic: Son of (Aramaic, *bar*) Ptolemy. The only reasons for mentioning these two disciples in what appears to be a symbolical story are (*a*) the Hellenistic background suggested (but by no means proved) by their names, and possibly (*b*) a connection existing or supposed to exist between them and the church in or for which the gospel was written. For the connection of Philip with the province of Asia see Introduction, p. 101. For Andrew see Eusebius *H.E.* III, i, 1 (Ἀνδρέας δὲ [*sc.* εἴληχεν] τὴν Σκυθίαν) and McGiffert's note in loc.; also the Acts of Andrew (M. R. James, *The Apocryphal New Testament* (1924), 337–63).

23. ὁ δὲ Ἰησοῦς ἀποκρίνεται. Jesus replies not so much to the particular statement that certain Greeks wished to see him as to the situation thereby created. It is his death about which he speaks (see the next note). The evangelization of the Gentiles does not belong to the earthly ministry of Jesus (cf. Matt. 10.5f.); the way to it lies through the crucifixion and resurrection, and the mission of the church. The movement of thought is comparable with that of Rom. 9—11. Israel as a whole (a small remnant excepted) first rejects the Messiah; then by his death and exaltation those who stood outside the earlier covenant (the sheep who are not 'of this fold') are brought near. Here John does not represent Jesus in direct conversation with the Greeks; this however is not careless writing, for the rest of the chapter winds up the ministry of Jesus to the Jews in order that the true and spiritual 'conversation' of Jesus with the Greeks may begin—on the other side of the crucifixion.

ἐλήλυθεν ἡ ὥρα. For the use of ὥρα in John see on 2.4; 4.21,23. Here, as at 2.4; 7.30; 8.20 (where the hour has not yet come), and at 12.27; 13.1; 17.1 (where it is in immediate prospect) the hour is the hour of the death of Jesus.

ἵνα δοξασθῇ. But the death of Jesus means his glorification. Cf. v. 16, and for δόξα, δοξάζειν see on 1.14. Cf. also the use of ὑψοῦν, and cf. T. Joseph 10.3, ὑψοῖ καὶ δοξάζει αὐτόν. ἵνα is used as a temporal particle, defining the ὥρα. This Burney (78) regarded as a Semitism, but see M. II, 470 ('. . . This usage is therefore at most a secondary Semitism, and can quite as easily be explained by the writer's strong partiality for this particle, which had already gained great flexibility in the κοινή'). Dodd (A.S., 92) sees here a reference to Isa. 52.13: the Servant δοξασθήσεται. It is not however of the Servant but of the Son of man that John speaks.

ὁ υἱὸς τοῦ ἀνθρώπου. On this title see Introduction, pp. 71ff., and on 1.51. In pre-Christian usage the glory of the Son of man, and his function as the being who should unite heaven and earth, are conceived in predominantly apocalyptic-eschatological terms; so also in the earlier Christian tradition. But John, while not altogether abandoning this usage, prefers to see the Son of man as one whose glory is achieved in his humiliation, which effects the reconciliation of God and man. See Higgins, Son of man, 177ff.; also S. S. Smalley, N.T.S. 15 (1969), 296.

24. ὁ κόκκος τοῦ σίτου. The use of the article is generic—a representative grain; but perhaps not without a touch of allegory—the grain which dies and bears fruit is Christ. The imagery of sowing and seeds is found in the Synoptic Gospels (Mark 4.3–9,26–9,31f.; Matt. 13.24–30); also in Paul (1 Cor. 15.36–8), where the parallelism is especially close. John was no doubt aware of both uses of the metaphor; he certainly connects it with the resurrection, and the synoptic teaching about the kingdom of God recurs with a characteristic emphasis upon its Christological significance—for John the rule of God is concentrated into the person of the king. Dodd (Tradition, 366–9) points out the formal resemblance between this saying and the synoptic parables; the context is sufficient to give it a characteristically Johannine emphasis.

ἐὰν δὲ ἀποθάνῃ, πολὺν καρπὸν φέρει. The cycle of the seasons, with the death and renewal of nature, formed the basis of many local fertility religions, and of some mystery religions, in antiquity. The cycle was reproduced in a myth of the death and resurrection of a god. It is quite unnecessary to suppose that John was directly dependent on such sources—the earlier Christian tradition with the facts of the death and resurrection of Jesus which he was expounding is sufficient to account for his language; but it is not unlikely that here as elsewhere he chose to use imagery which was meaningful to his (Hellenistic) readers. For καρπὸν φέρει cf. 15.1–8.

25. A synoptic saying, found in both Mark and Q (Mark 8.35 and parallels; Matt. 10.39=Luke 17.33; cf. Luke 14.26). Dodd (Tradition, 338–43), rightly stresses the multiple attestation of the saying. In Mark however as in John it immediately follows a prediction of the passion and it is very probable that John had the Marcan form of the saying in mind, for he proceeds (v. 26) with a parallel to Mark 8.34. V. 24 forms a suitable transition to these sayings about discipleship because, though it is specially applicable to Jesus himself, it is stated in general terms and is of universal scope. In the Synoptic Gospels predictions of the sufferings of Jesus are not infrequently accompanied by predictions of sufferings for the disciples (e.g. Mark 8.34; 10.39); cf. also Paul's ἀνταναπληρῶ τὰ ὑστερήματα τῶν θλίψεων τοῦ Χριστοῦ (Col. 1.24). An

interesting rabbinic parallel (*Taanith* 32a) is adduced by Daube (*N.T.R.J.* 137).

ὁ φιλῶν τὴν ψυχὴν αὐτοῦ. ψυχή, like נפשׁ (*nephesh*), combines the meaning of life itself with soul, that part of man which, over against his flesh, is really alive. In the synoptic passages quoted above the original meaning of ψυχή, which has been subjected to some reinterpretation, is *life*, and Mark 8.35 might be rendered idiomatically 'He that wishes to save his skin ...'. V. 24 determines a similar but slightly extended meaning for John: 'He that wishes to live (in and for himself) shall die'.

ἀπολλύει αὐτήν, is the cause of his own perdition. For ἀπολλύναι and cognates see on 3.16. Mark 8.35 characteristically has the future (ἀπολέσει), but in view of John's future φυλάξει it would be wrong to stress this difference.

ὁ μισῶν τὴν ψυχὴν αὐτοῦ, i.e. regards his life as of secondary desirability and importance. This use of 'hate' is Semitic. Cf. the use of שׂנא at, e.g., Deut. 21.15; Gen. 29.31,33.

ἐν τῷ κόσμῳ τούτῳ. Cf. Mark 10.30, νῦν ἐν τῷ καιρῷ τούτῳ ... μετὰ διωγμῶν, καὶ ἐν τῷ αἰῶνι τῷ ἐρχομένῳ ζωὴν αἰώνιον. The primary meaning of John's phrase, as of the Hebrew העולם הזה (*ha‘olam ha-zeh*), is temporal—the present age; but it is not without a quasi-spatial element (cf. 8.23).

εἰς ζωὴν αἰώνιον φυλάξει αὐτήν. On ζωὴ αἰώνιος see on 1.4; 3.15. It is primarily the 'life of the age to come', and corresponds therefore to 'this world' (see above). The meaning of εἰς is accordingly temporal, though again not exclusively so. It means not only 'with a view to' (in the future) but also 'for the purpose of'. The man will keep his ψυχή not indeed for physical life, which he may well surrender, but for eternal life, of which he can never be robbed.

26. Cf. Mark 8.34 and parallels, also Mark 9.35; 10.43–5; Luke 22.26f. As with v. 25, Dodd (*Tradition*, 352f.) stresses that this saying belonged to more than one stream of tradition. The accumulation of parallels to vv. 34, 35, 36 in Mark 8 remains significant. What kind of service may be implied by this διακονία may be seen from the fact that it follows and explains the saying about hating one's life. To serve Jesus is to follow him (for the important word ἀκολουθεῖν see on 1.37), and he is going to death.

ὅπου εἰμὶ ἐγώ, that is, in life or death, humiliation and glory. Cf. 14.3; 17.24.

τιμήσει αὐτὸν ὁ πατήρ. John nowhere else uses τιμᾶν with God as subject, but cf. 5.23. Probably there is allusion to Mark 10.30, the reward of following; and 10.35–45, where (10.43) the reward of being great among the disciples is given to the διάκονος.

27–30. This passage corresponds to the synoptic story of the agony in Gethsemane, to which there is no more exact parallel in John (see also 18.11, τὸ ποτήριον). See Mark 14.32–42 and parallels. The 'Agony' is taken at this point not because John feared that such human anxiety would spoil the effect of ch. 17 but because in the present chapter he was summing up the ministry of Jesus in terms of service and death. No synoptic narrative better illustrates the devotion of one who hates his life in this world, and John's form of the story illustrates also God's strength made perfect in weakness; he thus presents the combined humiliation and glory of the earthly life of

Jesus, both of which were to be consummated together in the cross. Dodd (*Tradition*, 69ff.) draws attention to differences between these verses and the Marcan narrative which, he argues, shows John's independence. The differences are real, but most of them can be explained in terms of Johannine usage and interest, and they do not override the general resemblance.

27. νῦν—now that the hour has come and death is at hand.

ἡ ψυχή μου τετάρακται. Cf. Mark 14.34, περίλυπός ἐστιν ἡ ψυχή μου ἕως θανάτου. John has perhaps gone independently to Ps. 42(41).6f., 12, ἵνα τί περίλυπος εἶ, ἡ ψυχή, καὶ ἵνα τί συνταράσσεις με; . . . πρὸς ἐμαυτὸν ἡ ψυχή μου ἐταράχθη. Cf. also John 11.33, ἐτάραξεν ἑαυτόν. ταράσσειν is a Johannine word, and Mark's reference to the Psalm will have been sufficient to turn John's attention to the whole. Even for Jesus obedience unto death is costly; but the cost, being expressed in the language of the Old Testament, does not lie outside God's calculation.

τί εἴπω, deliberative subjunctive. The petition which is offered in the synoptic narrative (Mark 14.36, qualified there by 'Howbeit not what I will, but what thou wilt') is here introduced only with hesitation.

πάτερ, σῶσόν με ἐκ τῆς ὥρας ταύτης. It is possible to punctuate either with a full stop (so Nestle; the prayer is then a real petition, though instantly reconsidered), or with a question mark (the petition is considered only to be dismissed). The deliberation of τί εἴπω perhaps suggests the latter, but little difference is made. 'Father' as Jesus' term for God is very common in John; but there may be a recollection here (and in v. 28) of the striking use of Ἀββὰ ὁ πατήρ in Mark 14.36. For the 'hour' see v. 23. McNamara, *T. & T.*, 143f., refers to Pseudo-Jonathan on Gen. 38.25, but the parallel is not close. X. Léon-Dufour (Cullmann Festschrift, 1972; 157–65) translates: Bring me safely through this hour; with this, Glorify thy name, is in synonymous parallelism.

διὰ τοῦτο, that is, that I might lay down my life. Prayer for deliverance is therefore impossible. The Marcan narrative gives the impression that even at the last moment there might have been an alternative to crucifixion, though if crucifixion should be the will of the Father Jesus would not refuse it.

28. πάτερ. See on v. 27.

δόξασόν σου τὸ ὄνομα (τὸν υἱόν, λ φ boh, seems to be an assimilation, probably accidental, to 17.1). Up to this point δοξάζειν has been used of the Son; afterwards most commonly of the Father (13.31f.; 14.13; 15.8; 17.1,4; 21.19). In this prayer Jesus merely repeats the principle that has guided his life—7.18; 8.50. As Bultmann observes, one might have expected σῶσον and δόξασον to be synonymous; but in fact God is glorified in the complete obedience of his servant, and the servant who does not his own will but the will of him that sent him desires only the glory of God.

ἦλθεν οὖν φωνὴ ἐκ τοῦ οὐρανοῦ. The introduction of the 'voice' recalls the way in which a בַּת קוֹל (*bath qol*), or divine voice, makes itself heard in numerous rabbinic stories. On this phrase see *H.S.G.T.* 39f. It should be noted that whereas in the rabbinic literature these voices are looked upon as a sort of inferior substitute for prophecy the New Testament commonly represents them as the directly heard voice of God—that is, *bath qol* (which means 'echo') is not a strictly accurate description of them.

καὶ ἐδόξασα, notably in the signs (e.g. 11.40), καὶ πάλιν δοξάσω, in the death and exaltation of Jesus. An alternative interpretation takes ἐδόξασα to include the completion of Jesus' work in death (cf. 19.30, τετέλεσται) and δοξάσω to refer to his subsequently drawing all men to himself. Cf. also 13.31f.

29. ὁ οὖν ὄχλος ὁ ἑστώς. For this use of ἱστάναι cf. 1.35; 3.29; 6.22; 7.37; 11.56. It is not exactly redundant, but it is very characteristic of John's style.

βροντὴν γεγονέναι. Some, not all, of the crowd failed to recognize that words had been spoken. Misapprehensions are very common in John; see on 3.4.

ἄγγελος αὐτῷ λελάληκεν. Presumably those who made this comment recognized that the sound was speech, not mere noise; but they did not recognize its source. This makes the remark of Jesus in the next verse difficult, for it is hard to see how a voice could be said to come for the sake of men who did not understand it, and did not even know who was speaking. In the Lucan Gethsemane story (at 22.43, which is omitted by B W φ sin sah boh), ὤφθη δὲ αὐτῷ ἄγγελος. It is just possible that John's words are based on a recollection of this statement.

30. Jesus needed no reinforcement of his faith, but the crowd needed to be convinced of his unity with the Father. But how they could be convinced of this if they thought they had heard thunder or even the voice of an angel does not appear. Possibly John has in mind a third group (perhaps the disciples) who did recognize the origin and meaning of the voice; or the thunder may have been taken to be the voice of God (cf. Exod. 19.19; Ps. 29.3ff.; Sanders adds Vergil, *Aeneid* II, 692f.).

31f. In these verses John brings to a head the teaching that has been given about the passion. It signifies (*a*) the judgement of the world, (*b*) the overthrow of evil, (*c*) the simultaneous death and glorification of Jesus, and (*d*) the drawing together of all men to him.

31. νῦν. Cf. v. 27. The repetition of the word in this verse gives it great emphasis: *Now*, in the all-important crisis of the crucifixion. In vv. 24–8 we become aware of the moral struggle in which Jesus was engaged as he faced crucifixion; this history at least John was concerned to record. He interprets it by setting beside it here a mythological struggle between Jesus and the prince of this world. The moral victory secures the mythological victory and the redemption of the world from the power of evil.

κρίσις ἐστὶν τοῦ κόσμου τούτου. Judgement is treated at length in 5.22–30. For the word κρίσις see also 3.19; 7.24; 8.16, and the note on 3.17. 3.19 makes it clear that while judgement also takes place later (at the 'last judgement') it is effected by the coming into the world of Christ as the shining of a light, which men according to their works will either love or hate. It is in this sense that the cross means the passing of judgement; those who are not drawn to it (see v. 32) are repelled by it (cf. for a close parallel 1 Cor. 1.18–31). As in ch. 9 the Jews passed judgement on themselves by casting out the man born blind, so the world by crucifying Jesus passed judgement on itself. ὁ κόσμος οὗτος is the whole organized state of human society, secular and religious; see on 1.10.

Though Jesus appears to have been cast out this is in fact not so: ὁ ἄρχων τοῦ κόσμου τούτου ἐκβληθήσεται ἔξω. The devil is meant and is so described again at 14.30; 16.11. The exact phrase is peculiar to John, but similar expressions are common: Eph. 2.2; 6.12; 2 Cor. 4.4; Matt. 4.8f. (=Luke 4.6f.); Ignatius, *Eph.* 17.1; 19.1; *Magn.* 1.3; *Trall.* 4.2; *Philad.* 6.2; *Rom.* 7.1; Ascension of Isaiah 1.3; 10.29; Martyrdom of Isaiah 2.4. The word κοσμοκράτωρ is transliterated into Hebrew (קוזמוקרטור) to designate the Angel of Death, and in rabbinic writings שׂר העולם ('Prince of the world') is frequent but does not refer to Satan. J. E. Bruns, *J.B.L.* 86 (1967), 451ff. thinks that (the Angel of) Death may be intended here. He is right in seeing Jesus as depicted as the divine victor—one might add, as the true ἄρχων τοῦ κόσμου. John is here close to gnostic thought. 'That the ascent of the Messenger means the destruction of the world and its Ruler (or Rulers) is the doctrine of the gnostic myth' (Bultmann, 330, n. 3 of the German edition—the E.T. is at this point incorrect; see further evidence here and in Bauer ad loc.). But the defeat of Satan by Jesus is also an essential element in the older Christian tradition; for the synoptic tradition see *H.S.G.T.* 46–68, and cf. 1 Cor. 2.6–8. For ἐκβληθήσεται ἔξω cf. 6.37; 9.34f.; also 14.30; 16.11. The devil will be put out of office, out of authority. He will no longer be ἄρχων; men will be freed from his power. Nothing is said of his subsequent fate. From what appears to be the original reading, ἐκβληθήσεται ἔξω, two variants have been derived. (*a*) βληθ. ἔξω (P⁶⁶ D) is a simplification—a compound verb is unnecessary before ἔξω; (*b*) βληθ. κάτω (Θ it sin) is derived from (*a*). ἔξω is no longer held fast by the prefix ἐκ, and is changed to κάτω under the influence of Luke 10.18; Rev. 12.7–12; 20.3.

32. κἀγὼ ἐὰν ὑψωθῶ. For ὑψοῦν see on 3.14; the word is ambiguous and was chosen by John for that reason. Jesus was lifted up in execution on the cross and thereby exalted in glory. For the collocation of ὑψοῦν and δοξάζειν (v. 28) cf. Isa. 52.13, ὑψωθήσεται καὶ δοξασθήσεται σφόδρα (of the Servant of the Lord). ἐκ τῆς γῆς underlines the ideas both of the death on the cross and of the ascension. The conviction expressed here is the reason (though John does not stop to point it out) why Jesus engages in no conversation with the Greeks. It is by being lifted up that he draws men to himself.

πάντας ἑλκύσω. Elsewhere (6.44; see the note at this place for the word itself) ἑλκύειν has the Father as subject. No difference in thought is intended. The act is that of both the Father and the Son (5.19). πάντας (cf. e.g. Mark 16.15) means 'not to Jews only', and is anticipated by the inquiry of the Greeks (v. 20).

33. ποίῳ θανάτῳ, what kind of death. The ascension of Jesus was to be accomplished only through suffering and death; but the language used by Jesus would be quite inappropriate if applied to death by stoning. Cf. 21.19.

34. ἐκ τοῦ νόμου, that is, out of Scripture, the Old Testament. For this wider use of νόμος see on 10.34. No passage of the Old Testament however is specified. Ps. 110.4; Isa. 9.6 may be suggested; Ps. 88(89).37 is better still (W. C. von Unnik, *Nov. T.* 3 (1959), 174–9). It is however doubtful whether John himself was thinking of particular passages so much as of the common messianic *theologia gloriae* which had to be corrected by the *theologia crucis*. There was a sharp division between earlier and later Jewish opinion on the point mentioned in this verse. According to the earlier, the messianic age itself brought the period of fulfilment, so that the Messiah could be thought of as abiding for ever (1 Enoch 49.1; 62.14; Orac. Sib. III, 49f.; Ps. Solomon 17.4); according to the later, the messianic age was to come to an end before

the final period. The earlier period certainly lasted until the time of John; Justin, *Trypho* 32 (Trypho speaks), These and similar scriptures compel us to expect ἔνδοξον καὶ μέγαν ... τὸν παρὰ τοῦ παλαιοῦ τῶν ἡμερῶν ὡς υἱὸν ἀνθρώπου παραλαμβάνοντα τὴν αἰώνιον βασιλείαν.

δεῖ ὑψωθῆναι. See on 3.14. 'As usual in John, the bystanders are represented as understanding the Johannine idiom' (Sidebottom, 72). They rightly understand Jesus' saying as a prophecy of death but fail to perceive that it is at the same time a prophecy of glory. 'The ὄχλος stands for the desires and imaginings of Jewish apocalyptic' (Bultmann).

τὸν υἱὸν τοῦ ἀνθρώπου. On the meaning of 'Son of man' in John see Introduction, pp. 71ff., and on 1.51. Here he is—at least for the moment—assuming the identity of Son of man and Messiah, an identification which raises difficulty in the minds of the hearers.

τίς ἐστιν οὗτος ὁ υἱὸς τοῦ ἀνθρώπου; Do you really mean Messiah when you say Son of man? What do you mean? The dilemma may be set out thus:

(*a*) The Messiah is to abide for ever.
(*b*) The Son of man is to die (be lifted up).
(*c*) But the Son of man is the Messiah.

Since (*a*) is established ἐκ τοῦ νόμου, (*b*) and (*c*) may be queried. It should not be inferred that Son of man was (in John's mind) a strange or obscure title. He does not intend to shed (and does not shed) light on Jewish usage and terminology, but emphasizes that the work of Jesus, though truly the fulfilment of the Old Testament, was inconsistent with current Jewish messianic presuppositions.

35. The relevance of Jesus' reply is not immediately apparent. It must be taken as another summary of the ministry, comparable with vv. 31f., and a reply not so much to v. 34 as to the Jewish opposition as a whole; the whole chapter, as has been remarked, is an extended summary and conclusion.

ἔτι μικρὸν χρόνον. For the expression cf. 16.16–19. Here the 'little while' evidently refers to the ministry, in which decision is urgently required.

τὸ φῶς ἐν ὑμῖν ἐστιν. Again, the reference is to Jesus in his ministry; cf. 1.14, ἐσκήνωσεν ἐν ἡμῖν. On Jesus as the light of the world see on 8.12; here however we have similitude, not metaphorical definition.

περιπατεῖτε ὡς τὸ φῶς ἔχετε. Both for the use of ὡς (replacing ἕως; Radermacher, 164) and for the thought cf. 9.4; also Isa. 50.10. The light is soon to be withdrawn. It is notable that whenever in John περιπατεῖν is used in a sense not strictly literal it is used in connection with light and darkness (8.12; 11.9f.; 12.35). περιπατεῖν is clearly connected at 8.12 with following Jesus, just as it is here connected with believing (see next verse). This command then is to be regarded as a last appeal (v. 36b) to the Jews who had witnessed the ministry. The appeal can be cast in this form not because John thought it impossible to believe in Jesus after his death and resurrection—such belief was that with which he himself was most immediately concerned (17.20; 20.29,31)—but (*a*) because it suits the historical perspective of a gospel, and (*b*) because the gospel narrative as a whole is regarded as a paradigm of the presentation of Christ to the world, and the urgency of that presentation is expressed by the limited duration of the ministry.

ἵνα μὴ σκοτία ὑμᾶς καταλάβῃ. See on 1.5. Cf. 1QS 3.20f. (In the hand of the angel of darkness is all authority over the sons of wickedness, and they walk in the ways of darkness); 4.11.

ὁ περιπατῶν . . . ὑπάγει. Cf. 11.10; also 3.8; only the man born of the Spirit has the light, and knows whence he comes and whither he goes.

36. πιστεύετε εἰς τὸ φῶς; that is, Receive the light, and proceed by its illumination.

ἵνα υἱοὶ φωτὸς γένησθε. To believe in the light is to become a son of light. For the Hebrew expressions 'son of . . .' (. . . בֶּן), cf. G. Dalman, *The Words of Jesus* (E.T. 1909), 115f.; B.D.B. *s.v.* בֵּן, 8; K.B., 133f.; G.K., 437f. Cf. Luke 16.8; 1 Thess. 5.5. At Eph. 5.8 occurs the similar τέκνα φωτός (also with περιπατεῖτε; on this *Filii Lucis* as an element in the primitive Christian catechetical tradition see E. G. Selwyn, *The First Epistle of St Peter* (1946), 375–82). Those who believe in Jesus themselves take on the quality of light and so never walk in darkness; cf. 4.14 where it is said that the believer has a well springing up within himself, so that his supply never fails. The phrase 'sons of light' (בְּנֵי אוֹר) occurs at 1QS 1.9; 2.16; 3.13,14,25; 1QM 1.1,3,9,11,13, and refers to the members of the Qumran community.

ἐκρύβη. The word is also used at 8.59 (cf. 10.59f.; 11.54), but it is especially appropriate here. The light shines, giving men one last chance to believe and to 'walk'; then is hidden. The public ministry of Jesus is now ended. It is unnecessary to place vv. 44–50 between vv. 36a and b. Vv. 44–50 are not a continuation of the earlier speech. They are no longer couched in the second person plural, a direct address to the Jews. Rather, they are a final judicial summing up of evidence which has now been completely presented. See further (on v. 43) the account of Bultmann's rearrangements. On the use of passive (ἐκρύβη) for reflexive see on 8.59. Some commentators attach v. 36b to the next paragraph; in fact it is both the conclusion of 12.20–36 and the beginning of 12.37–50.

27. THE CONCLUSION OF THE PUBLIC MINISTRY

12.37–50

The public ministry of Jesus is now over; he returns into the obscurity out of which he emerged (12.36b is at once the end of the preceding paragraph and the beginning of this; cf. 11.54; 12.1) to utter his last words to the world. Henceforth he holds only private intercourse with his disciples. Vv. 37–43 are a comment by the evangelist; the speech of vv. 44–50 is an epilogue rather than a speech within the main structure of the play.

The whole section, which may be said to correspond to 1.10f. in the Prologue, is a comment on the unbelief of Judaism. This unbelief was not fortuitous; it had been foretold in the very Scriptures upon which the Jews had set their hope. Once more the predestinarian element in the teaching of John comes to light: 'they could not believe' (v. 39). They could not truly believe even when a superficial impulse moved them to do so, for they preferred the praise of men to the praise of God. The full significance of faith and unbelief in Jesus is next brought out. Jesus does not speak of himself; he speaks only the words of God his Father, who sent him. Thus to believe in Jesus is to believe in God, since God sends eternal life into the world through Jesus who utters his, God's, command; to see Jesus is to see God, since Jesus in his perfect obedience reveals God. Conversely, to reject Jesus and his words, or to hear and not to keep them, is inevitably to incur judgement. Jesus himself came not to judge but to save; but the divine word he speaks (and the thought is not far distant of the divine Word he is) cannot but judge those who reject it. The judgement is as sure and clear as the distinction between light and darkness.

All this material is cast in characteristically Johannine form. It may to some extent reflect the circumstances in which Jesus wrote (see the notes below), but its substance is common to the Synoptic Gospels and to Paul. In Mark (4.11f.) the crucial words of Isa. 6.9f. are used to similar effect. Those who 'are without', to whom the 'mystery of the kingdom of God' has not been given, will neither perceive nor understand. To hear and keep the word of Jesus is the all-important criterion by which men are judged (Matt. 7.24-7; Luke 6.47-9). Behind Jesus and his mission stands the Father who sent him (e.g. Matt.10.40; Luke 9.48; 10.16). So also for Paul faith is no human activity, and the attempt to establish one's own righteousness implies the rejection of God's. Once more, and with the greatest dramatic emphasis and artistry, John sets forth the central and decisive significance, in mercy and in judgement, of the ministry of Jesus in the whole activity of God. On predestination in John see Schnackenburg II, 328-46.

37-43. The unbelief of the Jews is now fully declared, together with its causes, and also with the few partial exceptions to it. Underlying the declaration are two historical facts—the actual outcome of the ministry in rejection and crucifixion, and the apparent rejection and punishment of the Jews (cf. Rom. 9—11); the conviction that this unexpected failure on the part of the people of God was in fact an element in God's eternal purpose, and as such had been written in the Old Testament; and a perception of the nature of the choice in which the Jews had erred, the choice between man's pursuit of his own glory or of the glory of God.

37. τοσαῦτα δὲ αὐτοῦ σημεῖα πεποιηκότος, 'although he had done ...'. For faith based upon the signs (or 'works') see on 2.11; 14.11. τοσαῦτα refers back to the gospel as a whole with its convincing selection of signs (20.30f.). See also Deut. 29.2ff., to which Brown draws attention. Signs do not suffice if God does not give men eyes to see.

38. ἵνα ὁ λόγος ... πληρωθῇ. If ἵνα be given its full purposive force, this verse signifies predestination (to condemnation) of the most absolute kind. Grammatically it would be possible to take this ἵνα as ecbatic ('the result of their so disbelieving was the fulfilment of the word ...'). The non-purposive use of ἵνα is attested elsewhere in John (e.g. 1.27; 17.3), but that it is impossible here is shown by v. 39 (οὐκ ἠδύναντο πιστεύειν ὅτι ...). It can

hardly be questioned that John meant that the hardening of Israel was intended by God. That on the other hand his words were not the cut and dried statement of a philosophical theology appears at once from the exceptions immediately introduced at v. 42 (ὅμως μέντοι), and indeed the existence of Jewish Christians, such as Peter and the beloved disciple. See also the almost immediately preceding affirmation of 12.32, πάντας ἑλκύσω πρὸς ἐμαυτόν. The form of expression used here (an absolute statement followed by a qualification) is characteristically Johannine, cf. e.g. 1.11f. John's treatment of the bulk of Israel was historically justified by the events recorded in the Synoptic Gospels, and sharpened no doubt by the continued antagonism between church and synagogue. Theologically it conveys the truth which the whole gospel teaches; the historic Israel was unable to move forward on its own level and so enter the kingdom of God (see on 3.3–5). It had to be regenerated through the Word of God and the Spirit; and this regeneration it refused. Hence the old Israel came to stand under the judgement of God (cf. 9.41), and henceforth this was its significance.

κύριε, τίς ... ἀπεκαλύφθη; John accurately follows the LXX of Isa. 53.1, which (except in the opening word κύριε) represents the current Hebrew text with sufficient accuracy. Cf. Rom. 10.16. In the quotation, ἀκοή represents the discourses of Jesus, βραχίων his actions. Neither has been effective, or could be effective in itself; see above on v. 37.

39. διὰ τοῦτο, as elsewhere in John, is taken up and explained by the ὅτι clause. They could not believe for this reason, namely, that Isaiah had said. ... With this reason for unbelief must be set that given in v. 43. The divine predestination works through human moral choices, for which men are morally responsible.

40. The quotation is from Isa. 6.10. John, the Hebrew, and the LXX are all different, but John seems to be nearer to the Hebrew than to the LXX. His version lacks the characteristic words—ἐπαχύνθη, ἐκάμμυσαν, συνῶσιν— of the LXX, and differs little from the Hebrew except in the omission of the reference to ears and hearing (this is of course a difference from the LXX also), and in the mood and person of the verbs השמן—ἐπώρωσεν, and השע—τετύφλωκεν. The simplest hypothesis is that once more John was quoting loosely, perhaps from memory, and adapting his Old Testament material to his own purpose. The reference to 'ears' he might well omit since he was at this point speaking especially (see v. 37) of the signs done by Jesus and seen by the Jews. The changes mentioned above (perfects for imperatives) might have been accidental (since both forms could be written with the same consonants); but it is more likely that 'the alterations are best explained by the intention of the writer of the gospel to emphasize the judgement as the action of God'—so Hoskyns (502), who however thought that John's καὶ ἰάσομαι αὐτούς indicated dependence on the LXX. John may have made use of these words with an allusion to the inner meaning of Jesus' miracles of healing. The importance in the New Testament of the quotation from Isa. 6 can hardly be exaggerated. It is used or alluded to at Mark 4.11f. (and the parallels); 8.17f.; Acts 28.26f. Not once only, in the ministry of Jesus, but again and again throughout its history, Israel had been confronted with the necessity of birth from above, only to reject the prophetic message and the Spirit of God. This recurring pattern, detected by the first Christians

in the Old Testament, was brought out with unique clearness in the ministry and death of Jesus. There was in the divine Word something which necessarily offended the natural man.

ἐπώρωσεν is read by B Θ; ἐπήρωσεν (P⁶⁶ P⁷⁵ ℵ W) is an attempt to find a somewhat more suitable verb, πεπώρωκεν (ω) to find a more suitable tense, and to assimilate to τετύφλωκεν.

41. ὅτι εἶδεν τὴν δόξαν αὐτοῦ. ὅτι is the reading of P⁶⁶ P⁷⁵ ℵ B Θ λ e sah boh Origen. ὅτε is in D ω it vg sin pesh; ἔπει in W. The difference in meaning is slight; it was in any case the vision of Isa. 6 that initiated Isaiah's speech and ministry. ὅτε is perhaps the easier reading, and ὅτι may therefore be preferred; but ὅτι is not so difficult as to make probable the opinion that it is a mistranslation of the Aramaic ד, intended as a temporal particle (M. II, 469). John's words are plain and need no explanation; the theophany as described in Isa. 6 could well be termed the 'glory of God'. But it is to be noted that in the Targum to Isa. 6.5 Isaiah declares that he has seen not 'the King, the Lord of hosts' but 'the glory of the *shekinah* of the King of the ages' (יקר שכינת מלך עלמיא). It is possible that John was aware of some such version, but not likely that it was the reference to the *shekinah* of God that made him say that Isaiah saw the glory of *Christ* and spoke of him. To John as to most of the New Testament writers all the Old Testament spoke of Christ. Cf. 8.56 (Abraham), and see A. T. Hanson, *Jesus Christ in the Old Testament* (1965), especially pp. 104–8. Cf. Philo, *Som.* I, 229f. (For αὐτοῦ, Θ φ sah read τοῦ θεοῦ, D, τοῦ θεοῦ αὐτοῦ.)

42. ὅμως μέντοι. See on v. 38. As had happened before in Jewish history there remained a believing remnant, though a weak and faint-hearted remnant.

καὶ ἐκ τῶν ἀρχόντων πολλοὶ ἐπίστευσαν. 'Many even of the rulers...'. Cf. 19.38f., and for John's treatment of imperfect faith, among other passages, 2.23; 4.48; 8.30; 11.36f.; 12.29. For John's use of ἄρχοντες, and his apparent failure to distinguish between the sects and groups of first century Judaism, see on 3.1; 1.19,24. For the faith of a large number of priests cf. Acts 6.7; both statements are of doubtful historicity. Possibly John was intentionally covering a statement for which he knew there was no direct evidence by the addition of οὐχ ὡμολόγουν. For a similar use of ὁμολογεῖν see 9.22; here it is necessary to supply αὐτὸν χριστὸν (εἶναι).

ἀποσυνάγωγοι γένωνται. See on 9.22. A detailed reconstruction of the historical background of this passage has been attempted by Martyn, who suggests as a paraphrase of this verse (76): 'Many of the members of the Gerousia (ἄρχοντες) believed. But they did not confess their faith. For the Pharisaic apostles (οἱ Φαρισαῖοι = השלוחים) came from Jamnia with the reworded Benediction against Heretics, and the majority of the Gerousia (οἱ Φαρισαῖοι) employed it as was intended: to excommunicate Christians from the synagogue.' See also Martyn, 21f.,24,105. This reconstruction may well be correct, though it is evident that it contains a substantial measure of conjecture. It should in any case be added that by placing the circumstances of his own time within the framework of the ministry of Jesus John is not simply perpetrating a thoughtless anachronism but giving them an absolute theological setting and thereby a theological interpretation; he is not sniping in a passing controversy but writing theology of permanent significance. See Introduction, pp. 137–44.

43. ἠγάπησαν γὰρ τὴν δόξαν τῶν ἀνθρώπων. There is doubtless an allusion to the glory of Christ seen by Isaiah (v. 41; cf. also 5.44). But, with ἀγαπᾶν (here 'to take pleasure in', with ἤπερ, 'to prefer'), δόξα with the genitive must be the glory (praise) which comes from men or God; hence, since these rulers preferred praise from men, they chose not to offend the Pharisees (see on 1.24). This is to love darkness rather than light (Dodd, *Interpretation*, 380); it is also to allow the decision of faith to be affected by a desire for personal security. Cf. Matt. 6.1–21; Rom. 2.29. The desire for the praise of men is a form of idolatry.

ἤπερ]ὑπέρ (P⁶⁶) ℵ λ 565. The two words were almost identical in pronunciation.

This verse marks the close of the fourth of the great divisions into which Bultmann divides the gospel ('The hidden victory of the Revealer over the World'). Like the third, this is a highly complicated block of material, and is constituted as follows: 10.40–2; 11.1–44,45–54; 11.55—12.19; 12.20–33; 8.30–40; 6.60–71; 12.37–43. Bultmann places vv. 44–50 in the discourse on the light of the world (8.12; 12.44–50; 8.21–9; 12.34–6). On the question of dislocations in the text of the gospel see Introduction, pp. 21–4, and in the commentary *passim*.

44–50. In vv. 35f. Jesus made his last appeal to the Jews; the present speech is not a continuation of it but an independent piece, which is not an appeal but a summary of the results of the ministry, and of its motives and themes. Almost all the thoughts, and indeed almost all the words, which appear in these verses have already been used in the gospel. They include (*a*) the mission of Jesus from the Father; (*b*) the revelation of the Father; (*c*) the light of the world; (*d*) judgement; (*e*) eternal life. Lightfoot however rightly notes that some of the best parallels are to be found in chs. 13—17 (e.g., with 12.45 cf. 14.9; with 12.50 cf. 14.31), where Jesus addresses those who did receive him. Notes on these verses may to a considerable extent be confined to cross-references, but it is hardly fair to say that, being a summary, they are on a lower level of composition than the rest of the gospel; it is important to note the points that are selected and the way in which they are combined. They make unmistakable the theological significance of the story of Jesus.

44. ἔκραξεν. Cf. 1.15; 7.28,37. Dodd (*Interpretation*, 382) argues that, since κράζειν and κηρύσσειν are alternative LXX renderings of קרא, what follows may be regarded as the kerygma of Jesus. The conclusion is correct but the argument unconvincing because קרא is more often translated by other words, notably καλεῖν. For the content of the verse cf. Matt. 10.40; the thought is as much synoptic as Johannine. On Jesus as the envoy of God, and his authority as such, see on 20.21.

οὐ πιστεύει εἰς ἐμέ. Faith in Jesus is not faith in a particular man, however holy. It is faith in God directed by a particular revelation. Otherwise it is not faith at all.

45. ὁ θεωρῶν ἐμὲ θεωρεῖ τὸν πέμψαντά με. Precisely because Jesus is the obedient Son and envoy of the Father, to see him is to see the Father, just as to believe in him is to believe in God. Cf. 1.18; 14.9.

46. ἐγὼ φῶς εἰς τὸν κόσμον ἐλήλυθα. Cf. 8.12, though there the equation was absolute—I am the light—whereas here we have similitude—I came as light

433

(cf. v. 35). There is thus no substantial difference between the two expressions 'I am the light of the world', and 'I have come as light into the world'.

ἵνα πᾶς . . . ἐν τῇ σκοτίᾳ μὴ μείνῃ. Cf. v. 36 (υἱοὶ φωτὸς γένησθε), where the same truth is put positively. The believer passes from darkness to light; cf. 8.12; 9.39. Cf. also *C.H.* 1, 32, πιστεύω καὶ μαρτυρῶ· εἰς ζωὴν καὶ φῶς χωρῶ. The thought is characteristic of Hellenistic religion. πᾶς . . . μή is not a Semitism; M. II. 434. Cf. 6.39; 11.26.

47. ἐὰν τίς μου ἀκούσῃ τῶν ῥημάτων καὶ μὴ φυλάξῃ. Cf. Matt. 7.24–7 (=Luke 6.47–9); again, the thought is familiar in the Synoptic Gospels. The word of Jesus must be not only heard but kept; obedience is essential. P⁶⁶ D omit μή; presumably the copyists were unwilling to write that Jesus would not judge those who did not keep his words (which they probably understood as commands).

ἐγὼ οὐ κρίνω αὐτόν. In different passages in John it is said that Jesus acts as judge (5.22,27; 8.16,26), and that he does not judge (3.17; 8.15). It is hardly credible that John should have been unaware of this apparent contradiction, or that it should have been undesigned. It appears in Paul (cf. e.g. Rom. 8.33f. with 2 Cor. 5.10). The meaning in both Paul and John is that justification and condemnation are opposite sides of the same process; to refuse the justifying love of God in Christ is to incur judgement.

ἵνα κρίνω . . . ἀλλ' ἵνα σώσω. Infinitives would have been expected, but already in Hellenistic Greek ἵνα with the subjunctive had begun to take the place of the object infinitive; in Modern Greek the process is complete. For the thought cf. 3.17; Luke 9.56 (long text). On κόσμος see on 1.10.

48. ὁ ἀθετῶν ἐμέ. Cf. Luke 10.16, ὁ ἀθετῶν ὑμᾶς ἐμὲ ἀθετεῖ· ὁ δὲ ἐμὲ ἀθετῶν ἀθετεῖ τὸν ἀποστείλαντά με. As vv. 49f. show, this thought is present in John also; the word of Jesus is the Father's word.

μὴ λαμβάνων τὰ ῥήματά μου. The ῥήματα are the λόγος, which Jesus bears, as it is split up into particular utterances; λόγος is a kind of collective noun for the ῥήματα.

ὁ λόγος . . . κρινεῖ αὐτόν. There seems to be no precise parallel to this statement; contrast 5.45. There is a similar expression at 7.51 (μὴ ὁ νόμος ἡμῶν κρίνει . . .), and this may point to the origin of the present saying. It goes without saying that, in Jewish thought, judgement was according to the Law; and sometimes the Law seems to take a more active and personal part in the process of judging. See 2 Bar. 48.47, And as regards all these [the sinners] their end shall convict them, and thy Law which they have transgressed shall requite them on thy day; 4 Ezra 13.38 (Syriac, not Latin), Then shall he destroy them without labour by the Law which is compared unto fire. At Wisd. 9.4, Wisdom (often equated with the Law) is described as τὴν τῶν σῶν θρόνων πάρεδρον, which seems to mean that Wisdom is an assessor with God in judgement. Philo uses a similar expression (ἡ πάρεδρος τῷ θεῷ) of δίκη (*Mos.* II, 53). Thus, though John's phrase may well be a development of a synoptic expression such as Mark 8.38, ὃς γὰρ ἐὰν ἐπαισχυνθῇ με καὶ τοὺς ἐμοὺς λόγους . . . καὶ ὁ υἱὸς τοῦ ἀνθρώπου ἐπαισχυνθήσεται . . ., yet it may also be true that the development took place under the influence of a tendency to view the words of Jesus as a new Law. For the connection between λόγος as a Christological title and the Law see on 1.1.

49. ὅτι. The word of Jesus will prove to be judge at the last day because it is not the word of Jesus only but equally the word of the Father. Cf. 5.22: Jesus will judge because the Father has given all judgement to him.

ἐγὼ ἐξ ἐμαυτοῦ οὐκ ἐλάλησα. The aorist looks back upon the ministry as a completed whole. Elsewhere John has, with no difference of meaning, ἀπ' ἐμαυτοῦ; see especially 7.17.

ὁ πέμψας με πατήρ. A common Johannine phrase: 5.23,37; 6.44; 8.16,18; 14.24.

ἐντολὴν δέδωκεν. Cf. 10.18 and other passages.

τί εἴπω καὶ τί λαλήσω. The use of synonyms is characteristic of John's style; it is impossible to distinguish between the two verbs.

50. ἡ ἐντολὴ αὐτοῦ ζωὴ αἰώνιός ἐστιν. For the Law of Moses as, in Jewish belief, the source of life see on 5.39, and cf. Deut. 32.45ff.; this view is echoed in the teaching of Jesus (Luke 10.28; Mark 10.17f.). Here however the command of God which Jesus bears, and himself executes, takes the place of the old Law. Jesus himself draws life from his obedience to God's command (4.34), and this even though the command is that he should lay down his life (10.18).

ἃ οὖν ἐγὼ λαλῶ (λαλῶ ἐγώ, Θ ω; λαλῶ, D a; ἐγώ may well be a secondary addition) ... οὕτως λαλῶ. Cf. 8.26,28, and the whole of the present context. It is particularly striking that John ends his final summary of the public ministry on this note. Jesus is not a figure of independent greatness; he is the Word of God, or he is nothing at all. In the first part of the gospel, which here closes, Jesus lives in complete obedience to the Father; in the second part he will die in the same obedience.

28. THE SUPPER TO THE DEPARTURE OF JUDAS.

13.1-30

The day before Passover Jesus and his disciples took supper together. The meal was not the Passover meal, nor any identifiable in the Jewish calendar. During (or after—see the note on v. 2) supper Jesus washed the feet of his disciples, and there followed conversation on washing, and on humility and love. The unity of the small group of friends, though close, was not perfect; Jesus foretold that Judas, though he had eaten with him, would betray him. This intelligence he communicated to the disciple 'whom he loved'.

The narrative which may be thus briefly outlined raises noteworthy critical and historical difficulties. It contains on the one hand material closely parallel to the synoptic narratives—the fact that a supper was taken on the last night of Jesus' life, and the prediction of the betrayal by Judas. This material probably reflects the synoptic tradition, though both supper and betrayal are attested by 1 Cor. 11.23ff., and were thus to be found in non-synoptic tradition too. On the other hand, John places the supper on a different day from that given by the synoptists, omits altogether the synoptic words in explanation of the bread and wine eaten and drunk at the supper (the 'Institution of the eucharist'), and includes the narrative of the feet-washing, which is contained in no other gospel. On the date of the last supper and crucifixion see Introduction, pp. 48–51; on the omission of the eucharistic passage see Introduction, pp. 53, 84f.; the feet-washing is probably to be regarded as a Johannine construction based on the synoptic tradition that Jesus was in the midst of his disciples as ὁ διακονῶν (Luke 22.27). The humble service of the Son of man is thus brought out in a telling narrative. It is not impossible that the incident was already to be found in pre-Johannine tradition; but in its present form it bears unmistakably the imprint of John's thought. This is indeed true of the section as a whole, in which the rejection of Jesus described in chs. 1—12 is balanced by an exhibition of the blessedness of those who believe (Dodd, *Interpretation*, 403). This observation, though illuminating, needs qualification, since the belief presupposed in these chapters is partial and inadequate; see, especially 13.21,38; 14.9; 16.12,31f. It is better to say, with Lindars, that the chapters are about discipleship—with, we may add, its blessedness and its shame.

For the form of the present incident—action, question, and interpretation—see Daube, *N.T.R.J.*, 182. There is no ground for connecting the feet-washing with purifications preparatory to the Passover (11.55).

It has already been suggested (p. 14; see also pp. 454ff.) that chs. 13—17 are to be regarded as explanatory of the passion narrative which follows them. In this explanation 13.1-30 plays a special part. There stands first a symbolic narrative, the washing of the disciples' feet, which prefigures the crucifixion itself, and in doing so points the way to the interpretation of the crucifixion. The public acts of Jesus on Calvary, and his private act in the presence of his disciples, are alike in that each is an act of humility and service, and that each proceeds from the love of Jesus for his own. The cleansing of the disciples' feet represents their cleansing from sin in the sacrificial blood of Christ (1.29; 19.34). When the significance of what is taking place is explained to him, Peter exclaims, Lord, not my feet only, but also my head and my hands (v. 9); so Jesus being lifted up on the cross draws all men to himself (12.32). Just as the cross is the temporal manifestation of the eternal movement of Christ from the Father who sends him into the world, and again from the world to the Father, so the feet-washing is enacted by Jesus in full recognition of the same fact (vv. 1, 3). Perhaps, in a secondary way, the sacraments of baptism and the eucharist are also prefigured; see the notes on vv. 10, 18. In any case, the act of washing is what the crucifixion is, at once a divine deed by which men are released from sin and an example which men must imitate. A full list of sacramental and non-sacramental interpretations of the feet-washing is given by Brown. Whether or not sacramental ideas are present there can be no question that in the paragraph as it stands the washing

is represented as both efficacious and exemplary. This twofold interpretation of the one act may be regarded as due to redactional combination of two sources. Thus Boismard (*R.B.* 71 (1964), 5–24) finds a
Moralizing Account in vv. 1,2,4,5,12–15,17,18,19 and a Sacramental
Account in vv. 3,4,5,6–10(11),21–30, vv. 16,20 being redactional. That
John used two sources is undoubtedly possible, but the source-critical
question (which is probably insoluble) does not exhaust the expositor's
task, for the combination of the two themes is a characteristic piece of
Johannine theology.

Out of this twofold significance of the feet-washing and of the death
of Jesus two further points arise. (i) Through the work of Christ God
has cleansed a people for himself; yet the people are not all cleansed.
Satan finds in Judas, one of the Twelve, a tool ready to his hand. John,
as was noted above, uses synoptic material here, but he welds it into
his own scheme of thought (vv. 10f., 18f.). Sin, even the ultimate
apostasy of Judas, remains possible (cf. 1 John 5.16). (ii) The apostles,
the disciples and servants of Jesus who is teacher and lord, must
follow his example: they must show the same humility, must, in fact,
take up the cross and follow Jesus. So far as they do so, they share his
authority. To receive a man sent by Christ is to receive Christ; to
receive Christ is to receive God (v. 20). Thus the church is the responsible envoy of Christ, sharing his dignity and obliged to copy his
humility and service. Notwithstanding its authority, it enjoys no absolute
security, since even one of the Twelve may prove to be a traitor.

At the end of this section Judas goes out into the darkness; from this
point Jesus is alone with the faithful. They are slow of heart, and their
loyalty is about to be shaken to the foundations, but to them the
mystery of God may be unfolded.

1. πρὸ δὲ τῆς ἑορτῆς τοῦ πάσχα. Cf. 12.1. That John means in fact the day
before the Passover is shown by 18.28; 19.14,31,42. By this note he clearly
distinguishes between the last supper and the Jewish Passover; in doing so he
contradicts the synoptic narrative, according to which the last supper was
the Passover meal, and Jesus died a day later than John allows. On this
difference, and the date of the crucifixion, see Introduction, pp. 48–51. By
this alteration, and by his omission of any reference to the bread and wine
of the supper, John emphasizes that the eucharist was not simply a Christian,
or Christianized, Passover. He may also have been influenced by a *disciplina
arcanorum*, and unwilling to betray factual details about the origin and conduct of the Christian rite; this, however, cannot be regarded as certain, and
is perhaps improbable.

εἰδώς. There is no reason whatever for supposing that this is a mistranslation
of an Aramaic participle (which has the same consonants as the perfect;
see Torrey, 44f., 47f., translating *had known*). In the clash between εἰδώς here
and εἰδώς in v. 3, and in the awkwardness of an apparent timing of Jesus' love
(πρὸ δὲ τῆς ἑορτῆς . . . ἠγάπησεν), Bultmann sees confusion of the text,
and argues that 13.1 (or part of it) originally introduced the prayer of
17.1–26.

ἦλθεν (ἐλήλυθεν, ω; παρῆν, D; ἧκει, P⁶⁶) αὐτοῦ ἡ ὥρα, the hour of his death and exaltation. See on 2.4.

ἵνα μεταβῇ. The explanatory ἵνα is characteristic of John; there is no need to regard it as a misrendering of the Aramaic ד, here intended as a temporal particle (M. II, 470). μεταβαίνειν is well chosen to express transference from one world to another; it is equally applicable to the thought of death as a departure, and to ascension into heaven. Cf. 5.24.

ἐκ τοῦ κόσμου τούτου. On κόσμος see on 1.10. The word is common throughout the gospel, but ὁ κόσμος (οὗτος) occurs 40 times in the last discourses. The emphasis lies on the distinction between the world, and the disciples (representing the church), who are chosen out of it. This distinction is naturally a qualitative one; yet it is not forgotten that in the primitive Christian tradition ὁ κόσμος (αἰών) οὗτος, representing העולם הזה (ha'olam ha-zeh, this age), is an eschatological expression, and behind the qualitative distinction there remains a temporal. In the eschatological terminology it had been said that the full manifestation of Jesus and his own lay in a real chronological future. John does not lose sight of this future, but his stress upon the centrality of the incarnate life of Jesus, and particularly of his death and exaltation, makes possible an ontological distinction between Jesus and his own on the one hand, and the world on the other. It is in view of his own imminent departure from the sphere of this world that Jesus regulates the life of his own who, since they belong to him and will for ever be united to him yet continue to live in the world, will henceforth live a twofold existence.

ἀγαπήσας τοὺς ἰδίους τοὺς ἐν τῷ κόσμῳ. See the last note. For οἱ ἴδιοι cf. 1.11, where however the expression is used in a different sense. 10.3f.,12 form a closer parallel, but the meaning is perhaps best brought out by 15.19; Jesus loves his own, and the world similarly loves its own (τὸ ἴδιον) and hates those who belong to Jesus. John emphasizes the contrast between Jesus and the world and thereby prepares the way for the whole of chs. 13—17. The disciples, though belonging to Jesus, are nevertheless ἐν τῷ κόσμῳ, where their Master leaves them, both united with him and separated from him. 'Of course the love of the Son, like that of the Father, is directed towards the whole world, to win everyone to itself; but this love becomes a reality only where men open themselves to it. And the subject of this section is the circle of those who have so opened themselves. In the actual situation as it was, this circle was represented by the twelve (eleven); but the use of the term ἴδιοι here, and not μαθηταί, is significant; it shows that they are the representatives of all those who believe' (Bultmann).

εἰς τέλος ἠγάπησεν αὐτούς. εἰς τέλος may in Hellenistic Greek be an adverbial phrase with the meaning 'completely', 'utterly' (see M.M. s.v. τέλος). This would yield a satisfactory sense here: Jesus' love for his own was capable of any act of service or suffering. But it is probable that here (and at Mark 13.13 and parallels; 1 Thess. 2.16) τέλος retains something of its primary significance of 'end'. Jesus loved his own up to the last moment of his life. Moreover τέλος recalls the eschatology of the earlier gospels; the 'hour' of Jesus, the hour of his suffering, was an anticipation of the last events. It would be characteristic of John to see a double meaning in εἰς τέλος.

2. δείπνου γινομένου. For δεῖπνον see on 12.2. Here it undoubtedly means an evening meal (v. 30), supper. At 1 Cor. 11.20 it is used with reference to the

agape or eucharist. For γινομένου, γενομένου is fairly well attested ((P⁶⁶) ℵᶜ D Θ λ it vg pesh sah boh); it is not however so appropriate to the context as γινομένου, since the supper was still in progress (v. 26). Since it is evident that John leaves out intentionally the events connected with the 'Institution of the eucharist' there is no point in asking at what points they might be fitted into his narrative.

τοῦ διαβόλου ἤδη βεβληκότος εἰς τὴν καρδίαν ἵνα παραδοῖ αὐτὸν 'Ιούδας. 'The devil had already made up his mind that Judas should betray him [Jesus].' The translation of R.V. (The devil having already put into the heart of Judas ... to betray him) can be maintained only if the genitive of the name Judas is read, with D Θ ω a e sin pesh sah. This however is probably a simplifying gloss, and should be rejected. On the other hand it should be noted that the Old Latin has *cum diabolus se misisset* (or, *misisset se*) *in cor*. ... For the construction cf. Job 22.22, ἀνάλαβε ... ἐν καρδίᾳ σου (בלבבך ... שׂים, literally, Put ... in thy heart), and 1 Sam. 29.10, μὴ θῇς ἐν καρδίᾳ σου (no corresponding Hebrew). See also Luke 21.14 (and parallels adduced in *H.S.G.T.*, 131). For the thought cf. v. 27, and 6.70, ἐξ ὑμῶν εἷς διάβολός ἐστιν; also Luke 22.3, εἰσῆλθεν δὲ Σατανᾶς εἰς 'Ιούδαν (Luke is the only other evangelist to connect Judas' treachery directly with Satan). παραδοῖ is the form of the verb that appears in ℵ B, 'An obviously vernacular form—as its papyrus record shows—it may safely be assumed right. ... Though a late form of the optative coincides with it, there is not the slightest syntactical reason for doubt that in the New Testament it is always subjunctive' (M. II, 211). Cf. Mark 14.10; that this parallel also deals with Judas' treachery may not be purely fortuitous. For the textual tradition of the name of Judas see on 6.71.

3. εἰδὼς ὅτι πάντα ἔδωκεν αὐτῷ ὁ πατὴρ εἰς τὰς χεῖρας. The construction is awkward; either αὐτῷ or εἰς τὰς χεῖρας would have sufficed alone. The primary intention here and in the next clause is to emphasize the humility of the Lord and Master, who stoops to serve his servants. Jesus washes their feet in full knowledge that he is the Son of God. Cf. *C.H.* 1,12, the Father παρέδωκε τὰ ἑαυτοῦ πάντα δημιουργήματα to the Heavenly Man whom he had begotten. ἔδωκεν, aorist: the Father gave the Son authority for his mission (vv. 16,20). Cf. 3.35, ὁ πατὴρ ... πάντα δέδωκεν ἐν τῇ χειρὶ αὐτοῦ, and the less general statements of 5.22,26.

ὅτι ἀπὸ θεοῦ ἐξῆλθεν καὶ πρὸς τὸν θεὸν ὑπάγει. 'Knowing ... that he had come from God and *was going* to God'. Cf. v. 1; the hour of departure was at hand, and in fact Jesus was going to his eternal glory with the Father through the humiliation of the cross, of which the humiliation of the feet-washing was an intended prefigurement. This glory in humiliation is one of the major themes of chs. 13—17, and the opening acted parable states it very clearly. Ignatius, *Magn.* 7.2, referred to by Brown, is not a close parallel.

4. ἐκ τοῦ δείπνου, from the supper table. τίθησιν τὰ ἱμάτια. ἀποτιθέναι would have been a more natural word. Cf. the use of τιθέναι (with ψυχήν) at 10.11, 15, 17f.; 13.37f. When Jesus lays aside his garments in preparation for his act of humility and cleansing he foreshadows the laying down of his life. Cf. 19.23; also Luke 12.37.

λέντιον, here, and v. 5, only in the New Testament. It is a Latinism, a transliteration of *linteum*, but not uncommon in later Greek (see L.S. *s.v.*).

439

Caligula insulted senators by causing them to wait on him so attired (Suetonius, *Caligula*, 26).

5. βάλλει is of course used in the weak sense common in Hellenistic Greek; the addition of λαβών by D φ sin is due to assimilation to λαβών λέντιον in v. 4.

τὸν νιπτῆρα. The word is *hap. leg.* in the New Testament, and not attested elsewhere (except in ecclesiastical Greek). It is regularly formed from νίπτειν (for the classical νίζειν); substantives in -τηρ 'are chiefly names of agents and instruments' (Palmer, 108). The word ποδανιπτήρ is found.

ἤρξατο. This word brings out the force of ἔρχεται in the next verse; he proceed to wash each in turn. This is therefore not the redundant Semitic use of 'to begin' as an auxiliary.

νίπτειν τοὺς πόδας τῶν μαθητῶν. The washing of the master's feet was a menial task which was not required of the Jewish slave (in distinction from slaves of other nationalities; *Mekhilta* Exod. 21.2 (מכילתא §1)). The degrading character of the task should not however be exaggerated. Wives washed the feet of their husbands, and children of their parents. Disciples were expected to perform acts of personal service for their rabbis (e.g. *Berakoth* 7b: R. Johanan († A.D. 279) said in the name of R. Simeon b. Yochai (*c.* A.D. 150): The service of the Law [that is, of teachers of it] is more important than learning it. See 2 Kings 3.11: Elisha the son of Shaphat is here, which poured water on the hands of Elijah. It does not say 'who learnt' but 'who poured'; that teaches that the service is the greater of the two). The point in the present passage is that the natural relationship is reversed in an act of unnecessary and striking (as Peter's objection, vv. 6, 8, shows) humility. In John's understanding the act is at once exemplary, revelatory, and salutary. The disciples must in turn wash each other's feet (vv. 14f.); the act of loving condescension reveals the love of Jesus for his own (v. 1), just as the mutual love of the disciples will reveal their relationship with Christ (v. 35); and the feet-washing represented a real act of cleansing which did not need to be repeated (vv. 8, 10).

6. λέγει αὐτῷ. Many MSS. indicate the change of subject: ἐκεῖνος, D Θ ω; Simon, the Syriac VSS.; Petrus, the Latin. For the objection cf. Matt. 3.14.

σύ μου. The pronouns are placed together in a position of emphasis: Do *you* wash *my* feet? For a different view see B.D. §473.

7. σὺ οὐκ οἶδας ἄρτι, γνώσῃ δὲ μετὰ ταῦτα. Cf. 2.22; 12.16, where it is noted by John that only after the death and resurrection did the disciples perceive the full meaning of the cleansing of the Temple and the triumphal entry. This failure to understand is emphasized by John, and its reason is brought out at 7.39; 14.26; 16.13. Only by the Spirit can men understand Jesus at all; and his disciples no less than the Jewish opposition are included here. The equivalence in this verse of the synonymous words εἰδέναι, γινώσκειν, should be noted.

8. D Θ prefix to Peter's speech the vocative κύριε, assimilating to v. 6.

οὐ μὴ νίψῃς ... εἰς τὸν αἰῶνα. For the construction cf. 11.26; the negation is very strong. Peter's sense of what is fitting for his master is completely outraged; cf. Mark 8.32 (and parallels). John has no direct equivalent to this Marcan saying; it is possible that he intentionally supplied the want here, since (as has been noted) the feet-washing prefigures the crucifixion. Both in the Marcan passage and here we may see 'the refusal to see the act of salvation in what is lowly, or God in the form of a slave' (Bultmann).

ἐὰν μὴ νίψω σε, οὐκ ἔχεις μέρος μετ' ἐμοῦ. Cf. Mark 8.33 (the reply to Peter's remark quoted above), ὕπαγε ... Σατανᾶ, ὅτι οὐ φρονεῖς τὰ τοῦ θεοῦ ἀλλὰ τὰ τῶν ἀνθρώπων. Peter for all his apparent devotion to Jesus is in danger of taking the wrong side. His objection to receiving Jesus' love and service is in fact Satanic pride. For μέρος ἔχειν cf. Matt. 24.51 (=Luke 12.46); also Acts 8.21. If Peter is not washed he will have no share in the benefits of Jesus' passion, and no place among his people. A reference to the practice of Christian baptism has often been seen here; cf. 3.5, and see Schweitzer, 360-2. See also Introduction, p. 83. That John was familiar with baptism is hardly open to doubt, and it is likely that he would see some connection between this initiatory washing and the washing of the disciples' feet, but this connection must not be construed too rigidly, as though John argued: All Christians must be baptized; the apostles were Christians; therefore the apostles must have been baptized, and if not in the ordinary way then by some equivalent. Rather, John has penetrated beneath the surface of baptism as an ecclesiastical rite, seen it in its relation to the Lord's death, into which converts were baptized (cf. Rom. 6.3), and thus integrated it into the act of humble love in which the Lord's death was set forth before the passion. Cf. John's treatment of the eucharist in ch. 6; see pp. 283ff.

9. μή. νίψῃ s must be supplied. If washing is to be the only way to have fellowship with Christ, Peter would be washed entirely, no part of him being left unwashed.

10. There are in this verse two major forms of textual tradition (with minor variations which need not here be noted); (a) a long text, ὁ λελουμένος οὐκ ἔχει χρείαν εἰ μὴ τοὺς πόδας νίψασθαι, he that has been bathed has no need save to wash his feet; (b) a short text, ὁ λελ. οὐκ ἔχει χρ. νίψασθαι, he that has been bathed has no need to wash. The former is supported by the majority of MSS., including B W (P66 D Θ) and most of the VSS. The latter is supported only by ℵ vg (the original text—see W.W.), together with some old Latin texts and Origen. The textual question cannot be settled apart from the interpretation of the verse as a whole; both readings are unquestionably ancient, and that must be preferred which is more intelligible in the context. It must be noted first that while the two verbs used are not identical in meaning (λούεσθαι, 'to take a bath'; νίπτεσθαι, 'to wash') John's fondness for pairs of words (e.g. εἰδέναι, γινώσκειν) makes it impossible to feel certain that he distinguished clearly between them; this of course applies only in (b); in (a) the additional words make a clear distinction. Secondly, it should be noted that v. 8b makes it impossible to suppose that what Jesus has just done can be regarded as trivial; it is of fundamental importance and indispensable—that is, it is not a secondary 'washing' subordinate to an initial 'bath'. Thirdly, it seems to have been customary at least in some quarters for guests at a meal to take a bath before leaving home, and on arrival at their host's house to have their feet, but only their feet, washed. Knowledge of such a custom as this might have caused the expansion of (b) into (a). Fourthly, the verb λούειν, though not common in the New Testament, is connected with religious washing. This is true in non-Christian Greek (see Bauer, Wörterbuch s.v.). In Heb. 10.22 there is a probable allusion

to Christian baptism (λελουσμένοι τὸ σῶμα ὕδατι καθαρῷ); cf. the use of the noun λουτρόν in Eph. 5.26; Tit. 3.5.

If these facts are borne in mind it seems probable that the meaning of the verse is as follows. John wrote the text in the form (b). He introduced the verb λούειν as a synonym of νίπτειν, but as a word which also suggested rather more definitely a background of religious washings, and thus the rite of baptism. The intention of the saying was to point out the foolish misunderstanding of Peter, who supposed that, because Jesus' act in washing his feet represented the humble ministry of his death, he would get more good by having his hands and head washed also, as if washing with water were in itself a religious benefit. Against this Jesus points out that once one has received the benefit of his love and death ('has been baptized into his death') he is 'entirely clean' (καθαρὸς ὅλος); further washings are pointless. The disciples have now been initiated into his death and there is no more to do. This statement was however misunderstood, partly because it was not grasped that λούειν and νίπτειν were synonyms, and partly because of the social custom mentioned above. The text was then expanded, regardless of the fact that it introduced the implication that the feet-washing was a comparatively unimportant addition to the process of bathing. Against this view Sanders makes the point that a reference to feet (as in the long text) is necessary since Jesus is persuading Peter to allow him to wash his feet; but this is not so—Jesus is answering Peter's mistaken desire that he should wash not his feet only but also his hands and head. Lightfoot compares 12.3, where the anointing of the feet is a sufficient symbolical anointing for the whole body. The opinion that the feet-washing represents the eucharist, while the 'bathing', being apparently unrepeatable, represents baptism, is very far-fetched, and implies a much too rigid sacramental interpretation of the acted parable; see above. It is also unlikely (see Braun) that John is engaging in polemic against washings practised by the Qumran sect; his intention is (as usual) to bring out the full theological significance of Christian tradition and practice. The true cleansing agent is the word that Jesus speaks, and is; see 15.3. Cf. 6.63; both the eating and drinking of the flesh and blood of the Son of man, and the washing in water (even that which he himself performs), derive efficacy not through the *opus operatum* but from the word spoken.

καθαρὸς ὅλος. ὅλος means here 'in every part' (as feet, head, hands, and so on) of the body. For καθαρός cf. 15.3, the only other passage in John (in addition to v. 11) where it is used.

οὐχὶ πάντες. The reference is of course to Judas, as the next verse points out. Judas has been washed with the other disciples; all possibility therefore of a merely mechanical operation of salvation, whether by baptism or otherwise, is excluded. Cf. 6.63f.; also the Matthean parables (13.24–30,36–43, the wheat and the tares; 13.47–50, the dragnet) which stress the mixed quality of those who are gathered into the kingdom, and 1 Cor. 10.1–13. Judas' feet were washed, but he did not enter into the meaning of Jesus' act of humility and love.

11. διὰ . . . ἐστε. These words are omitted by D. As an explanation they are somewhat otiose, and may possibly have entered the text as a marginal gloss.

12. ἔλαβεν τὰ ἱμάτια αὐτοῦ. See on v. 4 (τίθησιν τὰ ἱμάτια), and cf. 10.17f., λαμβάνειν ψυχήν.

ἀνέπεσεν. See on 6.10.

γινώσκετε τί πεποίηκα ὑμῖν; Cf. v. 7. The interpretation of the act of Jesus seems now to change. In the preceding verses it was a symbolical action (like those of the Old Testament prophets), indicative of the purification effected by Jesus in men's hearts. Here it becomes an example of humility. The two interpretations do not however exclude but rather imply each other. The purity which Jesus effects consists in an active and serviceable humility. Those who have been cleansed by him do in fact love and serve one another, and there is no other test of their having been cleansed than this (v. 35; cf. 1 John 3.16f.,23; 4.11 et al.). The death of Christ is at once the means by which men are cleansed from sin, and the example of the new life which they must henceforth follow. Moreover, so far as the feet-washing represents the whole redemptive work of Jesus the disciples must enter into this work. 'Jesus is not the ὑπόδειγμα for an Imitatio; but by receiving his service a new opportunity of existence together is disclosed to the disciple' (Bultmann). It will follow too that 'the only kind of impurity which is recognized by this fellowship is selfishness, represented here by Judas' (Fenton).

13. ὁ διδάσκαλος καὶ ὁ κύριος. These words are nominative, not accusative (second object of φωνεῖτε); they are therefore the articular nominative used for the vocative; cf. M. 1, 70; B.D., §§143, 147. διδάσκαλος represents the title Rabbi (Rabboni); see on 1.38; 20.16. κύριος is a frequent designation of Jesus in John. Hahn (Titles, 73–89) is right to point out that, as a title, κύριος originated in address to Jesus as teacher (cf. the address of a rabbinic pupil to his teacher, רבי ומרי—S.B. II,558), but it is unthinkable that a Christian author writing at the end of the first century should mean no more than this. A rabbi might expect his feet to be washed by his disciples (see on v. 5); a κύριος, a potentate whether divine or human, might expect any service from his inferiors (the word correlative to κύριος is δοῦλος).

14. καὶ ὑμεῖς ὀφείλετε. Arguments of this kind a minori ad maius are very common in rabbinic writings (and are there known as קל וחומר, 'light and heavy'). It would however be ridiculous to claim this as a Jewish, or rabbinic, feature of John's style. Such arguments are used wherever men think and speak logically; and the Jewish קל וחומר is not unrelated to Hellenistic logic and rhetoric (D. Daube, H.U.C.A. 22 (1949), 251–7). 1 Tim. 5.10 shows that, at the time when John wrote, 'washing the feet of the saints' had become an accepted metaphor for Christian service. The Johannine incident may have grown out of the metaphor, but the metaphor itself must have had some origin, and this may have been the tradition used by John.

15. ὑπόδειγμα. For the word cf. Heb. 4.11; 8.5; 9.25; James 5.10; 2 Peter 2.6. It means both 'pattern' and 'example' or 'instance', and it is interesting to note the occurrence of the phrase ὑπόδειγμα ἀρετῆς in inscriptions (see L.S. s.v.). ὑπόδειγμα was well established in Koine Greek, but incurred the condemnation of Phrynichus (IV; Rutherford, 62; the classical παράδειγμα is to be preferred).

ἵνα is John's common 'explanatory' ἵνα, indicating both the purpose and the content of the example.

16. οὐκ ἔστιν . . . τοῦ πέμψαντος αὐτόν. This corresponds to the argument of v. 14. Cf. Matt. 10.24, οὐκ ἔστιν μαθητὴς ὑπὲρ τὸν διδάσκαλον οὐδὲ δοῦλος ὑπὲρ τὸν κύριον αὐτοῦ. On the general question of the sending of Jesus by the Father and

of the apostles by Jesus, and of the relations between sender and sent, see on 20.21. The meaning here is plain.   The disciples are not to expect better treatment than their Lord received, nor are they to think themselves too important to perform the acts of service which he performed. ἀπόστολος is used here only in John, though the cognate verb ἀποστέλλειν is common, as is πέμπειν. It is not here a technical term (as it often is in the New Testament), but is used simply as a passive verbal noun, almost equivalent to ἀποσταλείς or ἀπεσταλμένος. The fact that it is used with τοῦ πέμψαντος αὐτόν shows clearly that John did not distinguish between the two roots and groups of words.

17. εἰ ταῦτα οἴδατε. It is not clear to what ταῦτα refers. It appears at first to refer to the fact that a servant is not greater than his master, nor a person sent than the sender; but it is impossible to speak of 'doing' (ποιῆτε) these things. Probably the construction is *ad sensum* and John means, 'If you know that, in view of these considerations and of what you have seen, it is a good thing to wash one another's feet, happy are you if you do it'. V. 16 is almost parenthetical. John elsewhere (12.47f.) emphasizes the necessity of doing as well as hearing the word of Jesus: so indeed does the New Testament as a whole, e.g. Matt. 7.21,24–7. In this verse sin has 'If you know these things and do them, blessed are you'; e has *haec scientes beati eritis*. It seems not improbable that e is right and that the reference to 'doing' was introduced by analogy with other passages, but introduced in different places.

18. οὐ περὶ πάντων ὑμῶν λέγω. The discussion of the significance of the feet-washing is interrupted by the thought of the traitor, who has separated himself from the community which is united in the love of Jesus. The words just spoken are not applicable to him. Yet Jesus has not blundered in admitting him to the circle of the Twelve; he has rather acted in such a way as to fulfil Scripture and thus promote rather than weaken faith.

ἐγὼ οἶδα τίνας ἐξελεξάμην. The bearing of these words and their connection with the following sentence are not clear. They may mean (*a*) I know whom I have really chosen, and of course I have not really chosen Judas; or (*b*) I know (the characters of) those whom I have chosen, and therefore know that Judas, though I have chosen him, will betray me. The interrogative τίνας suggests (*a*) rather than (*b*), but correspondence with 6.70 (which Brown thinks suggests that John, like the Synoptists, believed that only the Twelve were present at supper) suggests (*b*), and probably outweighs the grammatical argument (οὕς, which is more suitable to (*b*), is read by P⁶⁶ D Θ ω). If (*b*) is accepted, a considerable ellipse must be supplied before ἀλλ' ἵνα: I know whom I have chosen: *therefore I know that Judas is a traitor, but I have chosen him* in order that . . . An alternative, but less probable, explanation of ἀλλ' ἵνα ἡ γραφὴ πληρωθῇ is that ἵνα with the subjunctive is used as a substitute for the imperative—'But let the Scripture be fulfilled'. So Turner, *Insights*, 147f. See M. 1, 178f., 248.

ὁ τρώγων μου (μετ' ἐμοῦ, P⁶⁶ ℵ D Θ ω it vg sin boh—possibly right, since μου might be an assimilation to the LXX) τὸν ἄρτον ἐπῆρεν (ἐπῆρκεν, ℵ W Θ λ) ἐπ' ἐμὲ τὴν πτέρναν αὐτοῦ. The quotation is from Ps. 41 (40). 10. On the whole John is nearer to the Hebrew (אוכל לחמי הגדיל עלי עקב) than to the Greek of the LXX (ὁ ἐσθίων ἄρτους μου ἐμεγάλυνεν ἐπ' ἐμὲ πτερνισμόν), though he departs from the Hebrew where the LXX renders it literally (ἐμεγάλυνεν for הגדיל). Probably John was rewriting freely; τρώγειν is a word of his own used in the discourse on the Bread of Life (6.54,56ff.), and the singular ἄρτον not only corresponds to the Hebrew (as pointed by the Massoretes, *laḥmi*) but also suggests the eucharistic loaf of which, it may be presumed, Judas had unworthily partaken. The last four words of the LXX clumsily render an idiom meaning 'to scorn'; John's substitute suggests to Hoskyns (518) the sudden kick of a horse; perhaps better the action of one who 'shakes off the dust of his feet against' another. Other suggestions may be found in Brown and Lindars. λάκτισμα δείπνου (Aeschylus, *Agamemnon*, 1601) is an interesting coincidence of language, no more. On the use of the quotation see Dodd, *A.S.*, 100.

ἀπ' ἄρτι. Here, and at 14.7 (but cf. the variant at 1.51) only in John. In this place the meaning must be 'now', as the parallel in 14.29 (νῦν εἴρηκα ὑμῖν πρὶν γενέσθαι) shows. The words of Jesus are not understood as he utters them (cf. v. 7), but later they will be remembered (under the influence of the Spirit, 14.26) and become an occasion of faith.

πρὸ τοῦ γενέσθαι. The subject is the betrayal of Judas, which is also the subject of γένηται.

ὅτι ἐγώ εἰμι. Cf. 14.29 where in a similar saying we have simply ἵνα... πιστεύσητε. For ἐγώ εἰμι without a predicate see on 8.24, to which, as to this passage, there is a very close parallel in Isa. 43.10 (... ἵνα γνῶτε καὶ πιστεύσητε καὶ συνῆτε ὅτι ἐγώ εἰμι), where the speaker is God.

20. The thought in this passage oscillates rapidly between the intimate union which exists between Christ and his faithful disciples, and the prophecy of the traitor. For the present saying cf. Matt. 10.40 and parallels. It may be suggested by the claim implied in the use of ἐγώ εἰμι (v. 19). Men do truly meet God in the person of Jesus.

ἄν τινα πέμψω. For the construction of 20.23.

ὁ λαμβάνων . . . τὸν πέμψαντά με. Cf. the converse statement in v. 16. On the mission of Jesus from the Father, and of the disciples from Jesus, see on 20.21. The exact parallelism between the two commissions is to be particularly noted; similar but by no means identical parallels are made by Ignatius (*Mag.* 6.1; *Trall.* 3.1; *Smyrn.* 8.1.) As at 12.45,50, the effect is to give to the mission of Jesus and the mission of the church an absolute theological significance; in both the world is confronted by God himself. The activity of Jesus is coextensive with that of the Father (5.19), and to see him is to see the Father (1.18; 14.9); the disciples will in their turn do greater works than Jesus (14.12) and their mutual love will reveal the unity of the Father and the Son (13.35; 15.9f.).

21. The thought moves back to the presence of unfaithfulness among the Twelve; now however the act of betrayal is specifically mentioned.

ἐταράχθη τῷ πνεύματι. The reference is not to the Holy Spirit, but to the human spirit, the seat of emotion, within Jesus. Cf. the use of ψυχή in 12.27, and especially 11.33, ἐνεβριμήσατο τῷ πνεύματι καὶ ἐτάραξεν ἑαυτόν; see the note on this passage. Dodd sees here a reference to Ps. 42.6. Bultmann says that Jesus speaks as a prophet.

ἐμαρτύρησεν. μαρτυρεῖν and its cognates are common and important words in John (see on 1.7); here however it seems to be used in the sense of making an important and solemn declaration (cf. 1.32; 4.44).

ἀμὴν ἀμὴν λέγω ὑμῖν ὅτι εἷς ἐξ ὑμῶν παραδώσει με. For the whole sentence cf. Mark 14.18, ἀμὴν λέγω ὑμῖν ὅτι εἷς ἐξ ὑμῶν παραδώσει με, ὁ ἐσθίων μετ᾽ ἐμοῦ (cf. Matt. 26.21; Luke 22.21). John has already given more fully the Marcan allusion to Ps. 41.10 (see v. 18). It seems probable that he is here dependent upon Mark.

22. Cf. Mark 14.19.

23. ἐν τῷ κόλπῳ τοῦ Ἰησοῦ. Persons taking part in a meal reclined on the left side; the left arm was used to support the body, the right was free for use. The disciple to the right of Jesus would thus find his head immediately in front of Jesus and might accordingly be said to lie in his bosom. Evidently he would be in a position to speak intimately with Jesus, but his was not the place of greatest honour; this was to the left of the host. The place occupied by the beloved disciple was nevertheless the place of a trusted friend; cf. Pliny, *Epist.* IV, xxii, 4, *Cenabat Nerua cum paucis*; *Ueiento proximus atque etiam in sinu recumbebat*. The expression ἐν τῷ κόλπῳ is not however exhausted by this simple observation. At 1.18 the only begotten Son is described as ὁ ὢν εἰς τὸν κόλπον τοῦ πατρός. 13.20, emphasizing the relationship between God, Christ, and those whom Christ sends, points forward to the special case in which the specially favoured disciple is represented as standing in the same relation to Christ as Christ to the Father. It is further to be noted that the fact that Jesus and the disciples reclined at table (and did not sit) is an indication that the meal in question was the Passover meal, for which reclining was obligatory (see Jeremias, *Eucharistic Words*, 22–6). That is, this detail (and cf. vv. 26, 29f.) contradicts the general Johannine dating of the supper (see v. 1) and supports the Marcan. See Introduction, pp. 48–51. This point is however less convincing in John than in the synoptists. The custom of reclining at the Passover meal was probably a borrowing from the Roman world, and John, familiar with that world, may simply have described what he thought must have taken place at any meal, independently of any historical tradition about the last supper. Or, again, John may simply be dependent on the synoptic material. In any case, so far as historical value is attached to his statement that Jesus and the disciples reclined and did not sit, so far value must be deducted from his statement (v. 1) that the supper took place *before* the Passover.

ὃν ἠγάπα ὁ Ἰησοῦς. The 'beloved disciple' is here mentioned for the first time. See also 19.26f.; 20.2 (where the verb is φιλεῖν); 21.7,20; and on the general question see Introduction, pp. 116–19. Here the following points may be noted. (*a*) The disciple is present at the last supper. John nowhere says that none but the Twelve were present at the supper, but this is explicitly stated by Mark (14.17), whose account John probably knew and does not contradict. The disciple was therefore probably one of the Twelve. Note however the view of Schweizer (*C.O.N.T.* 11, i) that the beloved disciple supersedes the Twelve; also the rather fanciful suggestion (*J. & Q.*, 193) that the beloved disciple replaces Judas. (*b*) The part of the narrative which includes special reference to this disciple has a secondary appearance. It combines the Marcan account of a general prediction with the Matthean tradition (a difficult one) that the traitor was named in the hearing of the whole company. John says, The man was named but only to a specially intimate disciple. He does not however make clear why that disciple took no action. (c) The disciple occupies a higher place than Peter. It has been pointed out that the place of highest honour was that to the left of the host, but Peter cannot have taken it, for if he had he would not have been able to make signs to the disciple to ask his question for him, nor would he have needed to do so. The suggestion that the supper is 'described in the style of the communal meal of the Essenes' (K. G. Kuhn in Stendahl, *Scrolls*, 69; cf. 1 QS 6.10, No man shall interrupt the speech of the other before his brother has finished speaking. Nor shall he speak out of his rank) breaks down when the manner of the conversations in chs. 14, 15, 16 is considered. Moreover, 13.12–16 forbids such considerations of rank (Braun). Speculation on the question who did occupy the place of honour at Jesus' left hand is therefore fruitless. (d) There is in this passage no ground whatever for supposing that the beloved disciple is to be thought of as a purely 'ideal' disciple, corresponding to no historical character. It is no special revelation which is accorded to him but a plain statement of fact.

24. νεύει. Cf. Acts 24.10. Evidently Peter was not in a position to ask his own question; he could only beckon to the beloved disciple.

καὶ λέγει αὐτῷ· εἰπὲ τίς ἐστιν ... is much simpler and more characteristic of John's style than the alternative, πυθέσθαι τίς ἂν εἴη (οὗτος, D) contained in (P⁶⁶) (D) (Θ) ω (sin). א combines the readings.

25. ἀναπεσών (ἐπιπεσών P⁶⁶ א D Θ ω). See on 6.10. By throwing back his head the disciple would be able actually to touch the chest (στῆθος) of Jesus, and then to speak very quietly. For οὕτως cf. 4.6.

26. ᾧ ἐγὼ βάψω τὸ ψωμίον καὶ δώσω αὐτῷ. αὐτῷ is redundant and corresponds to Semitic usage (Hebrew אשֶׁר ... לֹו). Translation must not however be assumed; see B.D., §297; M. II, 435. Cf. Mark 14.20; Matt. 26.23. ψωμίον, a diminutive of ψωμός, need not refer to bread; in the Synoptic Gospels it refers most naturally to the dipping of the bitter herbs of the Passover meal in the *ḥaroseth* sauce: לוקחין כזית מרור מטבילין אותו בחרוסת מברכין (Passover *Haggadah*: Take an olive's bulk of bitter herbs, dip it in the *ḥaroseth* and say the blessing). John represents the supper as taking place before the Passover, and therefore cannot have been thinking of the bitter herbs and *ḥaroseth*, but his use of βάπτειν and ψωμίον (suggesting טבל and מרור) may be regarded as a trace of the earlier synoptic tradition in which the supper was a Paschal meal (cf. v. 23). In the Passover *Haggadah* the Passover supper is distinguished from all other meals in several ways including 'on all other nights we do not dip (מטבילין) even once, but on this night twice'.

λαμβάνει καί is omitted by P⁶⁶ א* D Θ ω it vg sin pesh, perhaps rightly. λαμβάνει may have been added to recall the notable action of Jesus at the last supper, repeated in the eucharist, of *taking* the bread before distribution.

'Ιούδᾳ Σίμωνος 'Ισκαριώτου. On the name and the text see on 6.71. It is plain from the narrative that the beloved disciple must have understood that Judas was the traitor. To say that he failed to grasp the meaning of the sign is to make him an imbecile. His subsequent inactivity is incomprehensible, and, as was suggested above, casts doubt on John's narrative.

27. τότε εἰσῆλθεν εἰς ἐκεῖνον ὁ Σατανᾶς. Cf. v. 2; Luke 22.3. Wrede, cited by Bultmann, speaks of a kind of Satanic sacrament. The name Satan is not used elsewhere in John; διάβολος at 6.70; 8.44; 13.2. The crucifixion, though

within the purpose of God, was yet compassed by Satan; τότε marks the precise moment when, in fulfilment of his plan (v. 2), Satan took control of Judas (this is not quite consistent with 6.70). μετά states a temporal but not a causal relation; receiving the morsel did not make Judas Satan's tool. Cf. T. Simeon 2.7, I set my mind against him to destroy him [Joseph], because the prince of deceit (ὁ ἄρχων τῆς πλάνης) sent forth the spirit of jealousy and blinded my mind (ἐτύφλωσέ μου τὸν νοῦν).

ὃ ποιεῖς ποίησον τάχιον. ποιεῖς is either an inchoative present ('Do what you are about to do'), or means 'What you are bent on doing', 'cannot leave undone'. For the latter meaning cf. (Bauer, 175) Epictetus IV, ix, 18 . . . ποίει ἃ ποιεῖς· οὐδὲ θεῶν σέ τις ἔτι σῶσαι δύναται. For τάχιον see M. II, 164f.; B.D., §§61, 244. It took the place of the Attic θᾶττον (θᾶσσον). Its meaning here is not certain. It may be elative, and mean 'quickly'; it may mean 'as quickly as possible'; but it is perhaps best to take it as a simple comparative, 'more quickly (than you are at present doing)'. Cf. 20.4, where the word is a simple comparative.

28. τοῦτο δὲ οὐδεὶς ἔγνω. τοῦτο is the direct object of εἶπεν. πρός τί is 'to what purpose', 'for what end', or simply 'why'. None of the company understood (for γινώσκειν in this sense cf. v. 7) what Jesus said; this presumably includes the beloved disciple and Peter (though the former at least must have understood the act of Jesus). The weakness in the narrative suggests its secondary value; John is exonerating the Eleven from complicity in Judas' sin.

29. The Eleven had however heard what Jesus said, and had to account for it. Judas' financial duties supplied the most natural explanation.

γλωσσόκομον. See on 12.6.

εἰς τὴν ἑορτήν. This is consistent with John's representation of the last supper as taking place twenty-four hours before the Passover, inconsistent with the synoptic tradition. The question whether work (such as this would be) was permitted on the night of which John writes was in dispute. Pesahim 4.5: The Sages say: In Judaea they used to do work until midday on the eves of Passover, but in Galilee they used to do nothing at all. In what concerns the night [between the 13th and 14th of Nisan], the School of Shammai forbid [any work], but the School of Hillel permit it until sunrise.

ἢ τοῖς πτωχοῖς ἵνα τι δῷ. The construction changes abruptly. λέγει introduces first direct speech (ἀγόρασον . . .), then an indirect command (ἵνα . . . δῷ). This explanatory use of ἵνα is common in John. Not only the construction changes but also the historical setting. The supposed command to give to the poor would be particularly appropriate on Passover night (see Jeremias, Eucharistic Words, 54, 82); cf. v. 23, and contrast the last note.

30. ἐκεῖνος ἐξῆλθεν εὐθύς. Cf. v. 27. Judas was now simply and entirely a servant of Satan. Even so, and though he no longer holds his place with the Eleven, he is instantly obedient to the word of Jesus and goes out as he is bidden. Black (N.T. Essays in Memory of T. W. Manson, 32) suggests that Judas may have carried off the sop to the Jewish authorities as evidence that an illegal Passover had been held. This is not impossible, but reads a good deal into the text.

ἦν δὲ νύξ, the night that puts an end to Jesus' work (9.4; 11.10; 12.35).

When Judas goes out it is into the outer darkness (Matt. 8.12; 22.13; 25.30). It is the hour of the power of darkness (Luke 22.53). John was of course aware that the hour was evening (see on v. 2, δεῖπνον, and cf. 1 Cor. 11.23, ἐν τῇ νυκτί); but his remark is far from being merely historical. In going into the darkness (see on 1.5, and elsewhere) Judas went to his own place. So far as the remark is historical it suggests that the event took place on Passover night (in agreement with the Marcan tradition). Normally in Palestine the main meal was taken in the late afternoon, not in the evening 'but the Passover-offering could be eaten only during that night and only until midnight' (*Zebahim* 5.8). Cf. v. 23, and see Jeremias, *Eucharistic Words*, 44, 54.

29. TRANSITION TO THE LAST DISCOURSES

13.31–8

With the departure of Judas the long looked for hour of the departure and glorification of Jesus strikes, and he immediately declares, νῦν ἐδοξάσθη ὁ υἱὸς τοῦ ἀνθρώπου (v. 31). The disciples would be left to show to the world their relation to him by means of their mutual love. Even Peter could not follow Jesus at once; indeed he was to deny Christ that night.

In this paragraph the distinctive Johannine theme of departure and glory, which is developed throughout the last discourses, is united with the synoptic prediction of Peter's denial, which is introduced in highly dramatic form, being contrasted with the perfect obedience of Jesus. Peter still shows the attitude to Jesus which he expressed in 13.8; he is himself too proud to countenance the humility of Jesus. By laying down his life he means to accompany Jesus in suffering and glory. The inadequacy of his good intentions must be exposed before he can follow Jesus where he goes (21.15–22). What is said in this short paragraph to Peter is repeated for the whole body of disciples; see 16.29–32, where the confidence of the disciples is met by the prediction that they are about to desert their Master. The present paragraph thus anticipates the themes, and even the form, of chs. 14—16; in this it constitutes an argument for the unity of chs. 14—16 in their present form. See however pp. 454f. Brown points out that the components of the present passage have parallels and contacts with other parts of the gospel; thus vv. 31,32 = 12.23,27–8; 33 = 7.33; 8.21; 34–5 = 15.12; and we may add 36 = 7.35; 8.21. It was probably constructed by John on the basis of this material together with the (probably synoptic) tradition of Peter's denial.

31. The action of the supper is now completed and the final discourse begins. The difficulty of time, setting, and interpretation which marks this discourse as a whole appears at once in this verse and the following, in the use of νῦν and in the tenses—ἐδοξάσθη, δοξάσει. The true setting of these chapters is the Christian life of the end of the first century, but from time to

time John, whose intention it is to bind the life of the church in his own age to the history upon which it was founded, consciously brings back his narrative to what is ostensibly its original setting, the night in which Jesus was betrayed.

λέγει. Fitzmyer, *Essays*, 371f., notes that the sayings of Jesus are introduced in the same way as those given in *P. Oxy.* 1.

νῦν ἐδοξάσθη . . . καὶ ὁ θεὸς ἐδοξάσθη. See on v. 1; the hour which has now struck is both the hour of Jesus' departure in death, and the hour of his glory. The aorist ἐδοξάσθη will undoubtedly refer to that which has just happened, but this will be not the decisive departure of Judas (G. Delling, *Der Kreuzestod Jesu in der urchristlichen Verkündigung*, 1971, n. 574) but the action of Jesus. The passion is regarded as already worked out (it has been visibly expressed in the feet-washing), and the glory of Jesus has thereby been revealed (cf. 12.23). For Bultmann, who rearranges the text, the νῦν follows immediately upon the prayer of ch. 17, but since this too in a different way represents the passion the interpretation is not essentially different. Cf. Isa. 49.3; Dodd, *A.S.*, 91. As Jesus has been glorified, so also God has been glorified in Jesus, by his offering of perfect obedience. This statement is discussed in an article by G. B. Caird (*N.T.S.* 15 (1969), 265–77); he concludes (p. 277) that it is reasonable 'to suppose that a Jew, searching for a Greek word to express the display of splendid activity by man or God, which in his native Hebrew could be expressed by the niphal נכבד, might have felt justified in adapting the verb δοξάʒεσθαι to this use, with every expectation that his Greek neighbour would correctly discern his meaning. Thus when John put into the mouth of Jesus the words ὁ Θεὸς ἐδοξάσθη ἐν αὐτῷ, he could confidently expect his readers, whether Jews or Greeks, to understand that God had made a full display of his glory in the person of the Son of Man'.

ὁ υἱὸς τοῦ ἀνθρώπου. On the use of this title in John see Introduction, pp. 71ff., and on 1.51. Outside the New Testament the Son of man is regularly a figure of glory (Dan. 7.13; 1 Enoch *passim*). The distinctive synoptic contribution is that he must suffer. John combines the two notions, bringing together into one composite whole experiences of suffering and glory which in Mark are chronologically distinguished.

32. Before this verse the following words are inserted by Θ ω vg and Origen: εἰ ὁ θεὸς ἐδοξάσθη ἐν αὐτῷ; they are omitted by P⁶⁶ ℵ* B D W it sin. They make no addition to the sense of the passage; their addition could be explained by dittography, their omission by haplography. In the circumstances it seems inevitable to follow the majority of the earlier authorities and accept the short text. The longer probably owes its popularity to Origen. For the opposite view see Sanders and Lindars.

καὶ ὁ θεὸς δοξάσει αὐτὸν ἐν αὐτῷ. The aorist ἐδοξάσθη now changes to a future as John reverts to the historical position of the last night of Jesus' life; this will be fully resumed in the next verse. Jesus would be glorified (so common belief had it) in his resurrection, ascension, and *parousia*. ἐν αὐτῷ (so αυτω must be accentuated; ἑαυτῷ is read by D Θ ω) must mean 'in God'. The glory achieved by Jesus in his death on the cross (see next note) is sealed by his exaltation to the glory which he had with the Father before the world was (17.5). God was glorified in Jesus' temporal act of self-consecration; Jesus is glorified in the eternal essence of God the Father, which, in a sense, he re-enters at the resurrection and ascension. Torrey (75, 77f.) transfers ἐν αὐτῷ to the end of the next clause and supposes that it represents בנפשה (bᵉnaphsheh) 'at the cost of his life'. Jesus 'was to glorify the Father by the supreme act of yielding up his life'. There is little to be said for this suggestion.

εὐθύς. It will not be necessary to wait for the *parousia* before Christ enters the glory of the Father. His glory appears at once in the resurrection, the gift of the Spirit, and his abiding presence with his own; it appears also, for those who have eyes to see, in the crucifixion itself. This fact is worked out in the next three chapters.

33. τεκνία. This address is used nowhere else in John; it is frequent in 1 John (7 times; also Gal. 4.19, *si v.l.*). It is a probable inference that John is thinking of his readers. He uses παιδία at 21.5 (twice in 1 John).

ἔτι μικρὸν μεθ᾽ ὑμῶν εἰμι. For the 'little while' cf. 14.19; 16.16–19: 7.33; 12.35. For the departure of Christ and the fruitlessness of search for him cf. 8.21. The words plainly in their present context look forward to the departure of Christ in death, but they are equally applicable to his departure in the ascension. The disciples cannot yet share either the death or the glory of Jesus.

ζητήσετέ με. ζητεῖν is a frequent word in John 1—12; in the last discourses it occurs only here and at 16.19. The change in frequency seems adequately accounted for by the change in subject matter.

καθὼς εἶπον. Cf. 7.33; 8.21; also Prov. 1.28. There may also be an allusion to the fruitless search for the body of Jesus on Easter Day (20.15; Fenton).

ὑπάγω. See on 7.33. The word is relatively much more common in the last discourses than in the rest of the gospel (in ch. 17 it naturally gives place to ἔρχεσθαι). There can be no doubt that it is intended to cover both the departure of Jesus in death and his ascent to the glory of the Father. The use of the word arises out of John's characteristic thinking about the death of Jesus, not from translation or imitation of the Semitic root אזל, though it is true that this root is much more frequently used with the meaning 'to depart out of this life' (='to die') than is ὑπάγειν in Greek. Cf. however Mark 14.21; Matt. 26.24.

οὐ δύνασθε ἐλθεῖν. The ambiguity is maintained. The disciples are incapable (as appears in the next verses) of following Jesus to death; equally they cannot accompany him at once into the presence of the Father.

καὶ ὑμῖν λέγω ἄρτι. The disciples must not suppose that they are better than the Jews. Their faith and knowledge are both inadequate; they are still of this world.

34. The disciples cannot accompany Christ in his death; they are to be left to live in this world (cf. v. 1). For the direction of their life in this new situation (a messianic community living between the advents of the Messiah) Jesus leaves one new commandment.

ἐντολὴν καινήν. The word ἐντολή is especially characteristic of the Johannine epistles (1 John, 14 times; 2 John, 4 times; many of these relate to the command of love), and of the last discourses (John 13—17, 7 (or 6) times; the rest of John, 4 times). The command that men, especially within the nation of Israel or a group of disciples, should love one another, was not 'new' in the sense that it had never previously been promulgated. Cf. Lev. 19.18, and

P. Aboth. 1.12: Hillel said: Be of the disciples of Aaron, loving peace and pursuing peace, loving mankind and bringing them nigh to the Law. Bultmann gives examples illustrating the same kind of precept in other, non-biblical and non-Jewish, areas. The commandment is new, however, in that it corresponds to the command that regulates the relation between Jesus and the Father (10.18; 12.49f.; (14.31); 15.10); the love of the disciples for one another is not merely edifying, it reveals the Father and the Son. See below on 15.12f. The command of Jesus was new also in that it was delivered in and for the new age which was inaugurated by his life and death. Cf. 1 John 2.8, ἐντολὴν καινὴν . . . ὅτι ἡ σκοτία παράγεται καὶ τὸ φῶς τὸ ἀληθινὸν ἤδη φαίνει, and see G. Klein, *Zeitschrift für Theologie und Kirche* 68 (1971), 304–7. There may be a specific reference to the fact that at the supper a new covenant (1 Cor. 11.25; cf. Luke 22.20) was inaugurated (Lindars); but since the Johannine narrative omits not only the reference to covenant but also the synoptic and Pauline mention of wine no stress can be laid on this. See also below on καθὼς ἠγάπησα ὑμᾶς. The old—to some extent prudential—command that fellow-members of a community should love one another is now given a new basis.

ἵνα introduces the content of the ἐντολή.

ἀγαπᾶτε ἀλλήλους. Cf. T. Simeon 4.6f.; Benjamin 4.3; Gad 6.1. Josephus, *Bel.* II, 119, observes that the Essenes are specially φιλάλληλοι; cf. 1 QS 8.2, To walk in merciful love (אהבת חסד) and modesty (צנע) each man with his neighbour. See also *Thomas* 25, Love thy brother as thy soul, guard him as the apple of thine eye. Lev. 19.18 is probably the more or less direct source of all these passages. It has been held (e.g. Fenton, 27) that John contracts the universal love of the Sermon on the Mount, which extends even to enemies, to something more like a narrow sectarian affection. This is hardly a fair judgement. Cf. 3.16; 4.42; 17.9; God loves the world, the Son is the Saviour of the world, yet he does not pray for the world, because when the world is brought within the circle of love it ceases to be in the world. The mutual love of Christian disciples is different from any other; it is modelled upon, and in some measure reveals, the mutual love of the Father and the Son. The Father's love for the Son, unlike his love for sinful humanity, is not unrelated to the worth of its object, since it is a part of the divine excellence of both Father and Son that each should love the other. Similarly, it is of the essence of the Christian life that all who are Christians should love one another, and in so far as they fail to do so they fail to reproduce the divine life which should inspire them and should be shown to the world through them. The disciples do not exist (see v. 35) if they fail to love one another, since the faith that accepts what Jesus does for men (13.8, 10) is necessarily accompanied by love (13.14f.). For a general note on ἀγαπᾶν, ἀγάπη, in John see on 3.16.

καθὼς ἠγάπησα ὑμᾶς. The immediate reference is to the feet-washing (cf. vv. 14f.); but since this in its turn points to the death of Christ this last must be regarded as the ultimate standard of the love of Christians (cf. 15.13). But καθώς denotes not the degree or intensity but 'the basis of the ἀγαπᾶν' (Bultmann). Faith which has accepted the service of love can only be fulfilled in love.

35. ἐν τούτῳ is taken up by the clause introduced by ἐάν; elsewhere in John by ἵνα or ὅτι; but by ἐάν at 1 John 2.3.

γνώσονται πάντες ὅτι ἐμοὶ μαθηταί ἐστε. Mutual love is the proof of Christian discipleship, and its evident token. See above, and on 15.12f.,17. 'Love is the only criterion by which the believer can know that he has ceased to belong to the old world' (Bultmann, *P. C.*, 205). Cf. 1 John 3.14.

36. Dissatisfied with the command of love, Peter takes up v. 33 in his desire to follow Christ at once. Knowledge and religious experiences are more attractive than obedience.

ποῦ ὑπάγεις; Peter, like the Jews at 7.35 (cf. 8.21), fails to understand Jesus' saying about his departure; though, as v. 37 shows, he has some idea that death may be involved. For the problem raised by 16.5 (None of you asks me, Where are you going?) see on that verse.

οὐ δύνασαί μοι νῦν ἀκολουθῆσαι, ἀκολουθήσεις δὲ ὕστερον. The characteristic ambiguity of ὑπάγειν is maintained and, perhaps, made even clearer. Peter is not at present ready, in spite of his confident assertion, to give his life for Christ, though eventually he will do so (21.18f.). Neither can he at present enter into the presence of God in heaven, yet this also will eventually be granted him (cf. 14.3). ἀκολουθεῖν is an important Johannine word; see on 1.37. 'Following' is the basic requirement of one who would be a disciple of Jesus, and to follow Jesus must mean in the end to follow him both to death and glory.

37. κύριε (omitted by ℵ* vg sin) was probably added by assimilation to v. 36.

διὰ τί οὐ δύναμαί σοι ἀκολουθεῖν ἄρτι; Peter is unwilling to abide by the distinction of 'now' and 'then', the eschatological distinction which for John is also a spiritual distinction. Cf. 3.3–8; following Jesus, like entering the kingdom of God, is not a simple human possibility, waiting only upon a human decision. It can take place only in a future guaranteed by the Spirit. Peter's intentions are excellent, but he remains within the world of sin, ignorance, and unbelief.

τὴν ψυχήν μου ὑπὲρ σοῦ θήσω. For Peter's boast cf. Mark 14.29 and parallels. The language (ψυχὴν τιθέναι) however is Johannine (cf. 10.11); that is, John makes Peter assume language which is peculiarly applicable to Jesus. But this is absurd; to lay down one's life in the sense in which Jesus lays down his means complete obedience to the Father and perfect love for men, neither of which does Peter possess (though later Christians will lay down their lives for one another, 15.13). In fact, the truth is the reverse of what Peter thinks.

38. οὐ μὴ ἀλέκτωρ φωνήσῃ. Mark (14.30, not Matt. or Luke) adds δίς. Phrynichus (CCVII; Rutherford, 307f.) advises the use not of ἀλέκτωρ· but of ἀλεκτρυών.

ἕως οὗ ἀρνήσῃ με τρίς. The prediction is fulfilled in 18.17f., 25–7; this incident, like the prediction itself, is synoptic. In Matthew and Mark the prediction is made after the supper; in Luke (22.34) and John at the supper itself. This may be a sign that John knew Luke; on this question see Introduction, p. 46. John 'spares the Twelve' perhaps even less than does Mark; cf. 16.31f.

453

30. THE DEPARTURE OF JESUS A GROUND OF HOPE AND CONFIDENCE

14.1–31

In view of his death, now so close at hand, Jesus sums up the meaning of his life and ministry, and explains that his departure to the Father is for the benefit of his disciples. It will not mean complete separation, for they will continue to enjoy the divine presence, though in another mode.

It is strongly suggested by vv. 30f. that this chapter contains the whole of the words spoken by Jesus to the disciples in the room where they had supped, and in view of the continuation of the discourse through three more chapters (15—17) considerable difficulties are raised, of which various solutions have been offered. (*a*) It has been suggested that the material contained in chs. 15—17 should be thought of as spoken in the streets of Jerusalem, or in the neighbourhood of the Temple, as Jesus made his way to the garden mentioned in 18.1. This seems incredible, even when allowance is made for the fact that John's primary interest is in his discourses rather than in their settings. (*b*) It is suggested that the words of Jesus ἐγείρεσθε, ἄγωμεν ἐντεῦθεν do not mean, Rise from the supper table, let us leave the house, but Arise, let us go to the Father; or, Arise, let us go to face the prince of this world. But these proposals are exegetically unacceptable (see the notes). The difficulty is removed by the ingenious proposal of C. C. Torrey (see the note on v. 31), but only by incurring two further difficulties, viz., the assumption of an Aramaic original of the gospel, and the ascription of a considerable measure of stupidity to the translator. (*c*) A more popular view is that the chapter has been displaced, and that the material in chs. 13—17 should run as follows: 13.1—31a; 15; 16; 13.31b–8; 14; 17 (so Bernard; Bultmann suggests 13.1–30; 17; 13.31–5; 15; 16; 13.36—14.31; other suggestions have been made). This view avoids the difficulties that have been already mentioned, and also that of 13.36; 16.5 (on which see the notes), but it may be questioned whether it really improves the connections in the material. The questions, which are a characteristic feature of ch. 14 (vv. 5, 8, 22), are much less intelligible if we must suppose that chs. 15, 16 have already been spoken, and vv. 16f. read like the first introduction of the Paraclete. On the alleged displacements elsewhere in the gospel, and for general considerations bearing on the subject, see Introduction, pp. 21–4. (*d*) The most probable explanation is that in ch. 14 (or 13.31—14.31) and chs. 15—17 (16) we have alternative versions of the last discourse. This hypothesis is easily credible if we may suppose that the gospel material was collected over a period, and particularly so if some of it was first delivered orally. It is confirmed by a striking series of parallels between ch. 14 and chs. 15, 16 (for more details see the notes). In each set of material Jesus speaks of his relation to the Father (14.6f., 9ff., 28: 15.10,23f.; 16.15; 17.1f.,4f.,8,10,21–6); of his departure to the Father and of his coming again (14.2f., 18–20,22f.,28: 16.5–7, 16–22,28; 17.11,13); of his revelation of the Father (14.9: 17.6,26); of prayer in his name (14.13f.: 16.23f.,26, cf. 15.7); of keeping his commands (14.15, 21,23: 15.10,12–14,17); of the Paraclete (14.16f.,26: 15.26; 16.7–15); of the peace which he gives (14.27, cf. 14.1: 16.33), and of the judgement of the prince of this world (14.30: 16.11, cf. 16.33). The two passages cover substantially the same ground. The existence of these parallels must to some extent tell against the argument of J. Becker (*Z.N.T.W.* 61 (1970), 215–46) that the 'second' farewell discourse, in chs. 15—17, is also secondary.

To the discourse as a whole there is no parallel in the Synoptic Gospels (for occasional echoes of synoptic language see the notes). It stands at a point in John similar to, though not identical with, that of the eschatological discourse in Mark (13). This resemblance sheds light upon the intention and interpretation of the Johannine discourse. It is dominated by the thought of the departure and return of Jesus, but his return is no longer, as in Mark, conceived in apocalyptic terms. By his death Jesus enters at once into his glory with the Father, but subsequently returns, with his Father also, to manifest himself not to the world, as the Son of man upon the clouds of heaven, but to believers. The coming of Jesus is conceived in different ways: he returns to the disciples shortly after his crucifixion in the resurrection appearances (vv. 18ff.); he comes in the person of the Holy Spirit, the Paraclete (vv. 15ff.); he comes together with the Father to make his abode with those who love him (v. 23). Truly eschatological thought is not abandoned; Jesus prepares a place for his own in heaven and will receive them into the prepared abode. The eschatology is however modified; not so much 'realized' as individualized, for Jesus comes to the believer, presumably at his death, to take him into the heavenly dwelling. Whether this should be described (as by Bultmann) as gnostic eschatology is not clear; Jewish eschatology experienced a similar transformation after A.D. 70 (*Judaism*, 42–6). Martyn, 139, says that John modifies the hope of a home in heaven (v. 2) into the reality of a home on earth (v. 23), but it seems rather that John retains both notions side by side. The discourse permits a measure of analysis, as just described, but even so very important elements have been omitted: Jesus as way, truth, and life; the revelation of the Father; the term Paraclete. But, though Conzelmann (*Theology*, 355) describes the theme of the discourse as 'the community in the world', its main theme is the coming of Christ. The thought of the coming of Jesus to the believer is enriched by the conception of the Paraclete, by whom the divine presence is effected. The spiritual presence of Jesus, and the ministry of the Holy Spirit, are secured only through the departure of Jesus in death. His crucifixion, therefore, though it must at first be felt by his friends as a staggering blow, is in fact a blessing to them; by it the prince of this world is defeated, the Father is glorified, the revelation of God is consummated in the complete obedience of Jesus, and the disciples receive the gift of peace.

1. To this verse D a prefix καὶ εἶπεν τοῖς μαθηταῖς αὐτοῦ (sin, Jesus said). No doubt it was desired to make a suitable introduction to the last discourses as a whole (possibly for lectionary purposes; cf. the similar addition at the beginning of this passage in the Gospel for St Philip and St James' day).

μὴ ταρασσέσθω ὑμῶν ἡ καρδία. For the language cf. v. 27, and 4 Ezra 10.55, *Tu ergo noli timere, neque expauescat cor tuum.* At this point the discourse takes up and proceeds at once to elaborate the theme enunciated at 13.33, the departure of Jesus. He is about to leave the disciples, but they must not be afraid; the separation is a temporary one, and ultimately for their benefit. The distress they now feel will lead to more adequate faith.

πιστεύετε εἰς τὸν θεόν, καὶ εἰς ἐμὲ πιστεύετε. This sentence may be taken in several ways; we may take both verbs to be imperatives, or both to be indicatives; or we may take the former to be an indicative and the latter to be an imperative; or the former to be an imperative, the latter an indicative. These variations give rise to the following translations: (*a*) Believe in God and believe in me; (*b*) You believe in God and you believe in me; (*c*) You believe in God; believe in me also; or (Bultmann), Do you believe in God? Then believe also in me (for you can only believe in God through me!); (*d*), taking the former clause as an imperatival condition, the latter as an apodosis introduced by καί, (If you) believe in God (and) you (will) believe in me. None of these is entirely repugnant to the sense of the passage as a whole, but the imperative ταρασσέσθω suggests that the later verbs may be imperative also, and they are so taken in nearly all the Old Latin MSS., and by many early Fathers. πιστεύειν εἰς is the common Johannine phrase for *trust in* God or Christ; see on 1.12. The faith is to be based upon the relations between the Father and the Son, and upon the work of the Son, which the discourse proceeds to describe.

2. ἐν τῇ οἰκίᾳ τοῦ πατρός μου. Cf. Luke 2.49, ἐν τοῖς τοῦ πατρός μου, and John 2.16. Both of these passages refer to the Temple. See also 8.35. The thought of heaven as God's habitation is of course very widespread in most religions; see Eccles. 5.1, and many passages in the Old Testament. Cf. Philo, *Som.* 1, 256, οὕτως γὰρ δυνήσῃ καὶ τὸν πατρῷον οἶκον ἐπανελθεῖν, where the thought (of the return of the soul from exile in the flesh to heaven) is taken from current religious philosophy. Jesus speaks of God as his Father in a special sense, and his Father's home is also his own, to which he is now returning through death. See further in the next note.

μοναὶ πολλαί εἰσιν. μονή in Pausanias (e.g. x, xxxi, 7) means a 'stopping-place', or 'station' (for other evidence see L.S. *s.v.*, and cf. the Latin *mansio*); and some commentators, ancient and modern, take the word in this sense in this passage: the life of heaven includes progression. But this interpretation is almost certainly wrong; as v. 23 shows, μονή is the noun corresponding to the common and important Johannine verb μένειν, and hence it will mean a permanent, not a temporary, abiding-place (or, perhaps, mode of abiding). This is confirmed by the one use of μονή in the LXX (1 Macc. 7.38, πεσάτωσαν ἐν ῥομφαίᾳ ... μὴ δῷς αὐτοῖς μονήν), and by indications of a Jewish belief in compartments, or dwelling-places, in heaven (1 Enoch 39.4; cf. 2 Enoch 61.2). John however is not thinking of compartments or dwelling-places, but of the action, or state, of μένειν. This means that to speak of 'heaven' may, if the term is not carefully understood, misinterpret the 'Father's house'. Communion with God is a permanent and universal possibility.

εἰ δὲ μή; cf. v. 11. 'If there were not such abiding-places', that is, 'otherwise'; cf. Rev. 2.5,16; Mark 2.21f.; generally in the New Testament εἰ δὲ μήγε.

εἶπον ἄν ὑμῖν. The question is whether a stop should be placed after ὑμῖν, or the sentence should run on with ὅτι (wrongly omitted by P⁶⁶* Θ ω it). If no stop is made we may continue either with a statement of fact '. . . if not, I would have told you that I go to prepare a place for you'), or with a question ('if not, would I have told you that . . .?'). The former of these does not seem to make good sense; the latter encounters the difficulty that, in John's narrative, Jesus has not yet told the disciples that he is going to prepare a place for them. It seems best to take εἰ δὲ μὴ εἶπον ἄν ὑμῖν as a parenthesis, and to connect ὅτι with v. 2a: 'There will be many abiding-places (and if it had not been so I would have told you), for I am going to prepare a place for you.' Bultmann however thinks that to treat ὅτι as causal results in a 'triviality'.

πορεύομαι. Cf. ὑπάγω in 13.33. There is no difference in meaning. The journeying away of Jesus means (a) his death, and (b) his going to the Father's house, or, more simply, to the Father (17.11).

ἑτοιμάσαι τόπον ὑμῖν. Cf. 1 Enoch 42.1f., also Mark 10.40; but John is thinking here of the whole process of the passion and glorification of Jesus as the means by which believers are admitted to the heavenly life. Cf. also Heb. 11.16. Brown quotes Augustine, *In Joh.* LXVIII. 2, *Parat autem quodam modo mansiones, mansionibus parando mansores.* McNamara, *T. & T.,* 142f., notes that on Exod. 33.14 the Neofiti Targum has, The glory of my Shekinah will accompany amongst you and will prepare a resting place for you.

3. πάλιν ἔρχομαι καὶ παραλήμψομαι. The future παραλήμψομαι, with the explanatory clause ἵνα ... ἦτε, demands a future meaning for the present ἔρχομαι. Jesus promises to return to bring his disciples to the heavenly dwelling-places which he is about to prepare; the primary reference of ἔρχομαι therefore is to the eschatological advent of Jesus, or at any rate to his coming to the individual disciple at his death. This recalls the eschatological element in the synoptic supper narratives, and 1 Thess. 4.17, σὺν κυρίῳ. But the ensuing discourse, in which the theme of 'going and coming' is constantly repeated, shows clearly that John's thought of the advent is by no means exhausted in the older synoptic notion of the *parousia.* The communion of Jesus with his disciples, their mutual indwelling (μονή—μένειν) is not deferred till the last day, or even to the day of a disciple's death. It seems probable that here at the beginning of the discourse John generalizes the theme of the return of Jesus, though Lindars argues that since the going of Jesus is a departure in death his return must refer to the resurrection. On vv. 1–3 see R. H. Gundry in *Z.N.T.W.* 58 (1967), 68–72.

4. ὅπου ἐγὼ ὑπάγω οἴδατε τὴν ὁδόν. This is the reading of P⁶⁶ᶜ ℵ B W: it is ungrammatical and obscure (Bernard, ad loc.). But the longer reading (ὅπου ἐ.

ὑ. οἴδατε καὶ τὴν ὁδὸν οἴδατε, P⁶⁶* D Θ Ѡ it vg sin pesh sah boh) is a simplification and improvement and should be rejected. It is based upon Thomas' question in v. 5, which in any case however must be taken to give the sense of the shorter and more difficult text. The disciples ought to know that Jesus is going to the Father, and that the way lies through the shame and glory of the crucifixion and resurrection. Cf. *Thomas*, 12: The disciples said to Jesus, We know that thou wilt go away from us.

5. λέγει αὐτῷ Θωμᾶς. Thomas (see on 11.16 and cf. 20.24) appears in John as a loyal but dull disciple, whose misapprehensions serve to bring out the truth. Θωμᾶς]add ὁ λεγόμενος Δίδυμος, D (from 11.16).

πῶς]καὶ πῶς, ℵ D Θ Ѡ it vg; cf. v. 9.

6. ἐγώ εἰμι. See on 6.35.

ἡ ὁδός. The second half of the verse (οὐδεὶς ἔρχεται . . .) shows that the principal thought is of Jesus as the way by which men come to God; that is, the way which he himself is now about to take is the road which his followers must also tread. He himself goes to the Father by way of crucifixion and resurrection; in future he is the means by which Christians die and rise. The expression also calls to mind the description of the Christian faith and life as ἡ ὁδός (Acts 9.2; 22.4; 24.14); and the Jewish term *halakah*. Cf. also the claim of Isis (*I.G.* XII, v, 1, 14.17), ἐγὼ ἄστρων ὁδοὺς ἔδειξα. There is a good discussion in Brown, 629, of the use of דרך (*derek*) in 1 QS 9. 17f., 21; CD 1. 3. But Qumran contributes little to the interpretation of ὁδός; neither the Teacher of Righteousness nor the doctrine of the sect is described as the Way. By refusing to separate goal and way (for both are Jesus) John 'corrects the mythological thinking' (Bultmann) involved in coming and going. Cf. Sidebottom, 146.

ἡ ἀλήθεια καὶ ἡ ζωή. For ἀλήθεια in John see on 1.14 (nowhere else is it said 'I am the truth'); for ζωή in John see on 1.4 and 3.15, and especially 11.25, ἐγώ εἰμι ἡ ἀνάστασις (καὶ ἡ ζωή; see the note on the text). Both words are inserted here as explanatory of ὁδός. Because Jesus is the means of access to God who is the source of all truth and life he is himself the truth and the life for men (cf. vv. 7, 9). Life and truth are characteristic themes of the first and second parts of the gospel respectively (ζωή: ch. 1—12, 32 (31) times; chs. 13—21, 4 times; ἀλήθεια: chs. 1—12, 13 times; chs. 13—21, 12 times). For truth and life as characteristics of the Word see Odes of Solomon 8.8; 12.3, 12; 32.2; 38.1, and 10.2; 15.10; 41.11 respectively.

οὐδεὶς ἔρχεται πρὸς τὸν πατέρα εἰ μὴ δι' ἐμοῦ. If John, here and elsewhere, used some of the notions and terminology of the religions of his day, and there are many indications that he was not unfamiliar with them, he was quite sure that those religions were ineffective and that there was no religious or mystical approach to God which could achieve its goal. No one has ascended into heaven but the Son of man who came down from heaven (3.13); he alone is the link between God and men (cf. 1.51), and there is no access to God independent of him.

7. εἰ ἐγνώκειτε με, καὶ τὸν πατέρα μου ἂν ᾔδειτε. This is the reading of B; for ᾔδειτε, (Θ) Ѡ substitute ἐγνώκειτε, without substantial change. In P⁶⁶ ℵ D however the verbs are ἐγνώκατε, γνώσεσθε (without ἄν). The two readings give quite different senses to the verse. That of B utters a reproach: If you had known me, and though you ought to have done so you do not, you would

have known my Father also. That of P⁶⁶ ℵ D is a promise: If you have come to know me, as you have done, you shall know my Father also. V. 7b suggests the latter sense; the former reading may be due to assimilation to 8.19, or more probably to the fact that Philip's question, and the reply in v. 9 suggests that the disciples did know neither Jesus nor the Father. The reading of sin (If you have not known me, will you know my Father also ?) seems to be an accidental error, but may lend some support to that of P⁶⁶ ℵ D.

ἀπ᾽ ἄρτι refers to the moment when Jesus having completed the revelation of the Father departs in glory. The last discourses as a whole represent this 'moment' of completion (cf. also 19.30, τετέλεσται). Cf. 13.19; Sanders translates, At present you are getting to know him. But the discourses do not suggest such a continuous process of learning.

8. Φίλιππος. Only in John are special words and deeds ascribed to Philip; see on 1.44. His uncomprehending question here serves simply, according to John's method, to advance the argument. It implies separation between Jesus and the Father whereas in truth there is mutual indwelling.

δεῖξον ἡμῖν τὸν πατέρα, καὶ ἀρκεῖ ἡμῖν. Philip expresses the universal longing of the religious man. Cf. Exod. 33.18 (LXX), ἐμφάνισόν μοι σεαυτόν; C.H. 1, 27, where the revelation is described in the words διδαχθεὶς τοῦ παντὸς τὴν φύσιν καὶ τὴν μεγίστην θέαν [the vision of God]; ibid. VII, 2, ἀφορῶντες τῇ καρδίᾳ εἰς τὸν ὁραθῆναι θέλοντα; Berakoth 17a: In the world to come there is neither eating nor drinking, no marital relations, no business affairs, no envy, hatred nor quarrelling; but the righteous sit with their garlands on their heads, enjoying the splendid light of the Shekinah [the presence of God], as it is said: And they beheld God, and did eat and drink (Exod. 24.11). Nothing more can be desired than the vision of the true God; but just as there is no access to, so there is no knowledge of, God apart from Jesus. By this statement John prepares for his exposition of the work of Jesus as revealer. The form of the sentence is that of the imperatival condition; it is equivalent to 'If you will show ... it will suffice'. Sanders accentuates ἄρκει, imperative: 'Show us ... and satisfy us'. There is no substantial difference in meaning.

9. τοσοῦτον χρόνον]τοσούτῳ χρόνῳ, ℵ D. The accusative (which commonly expresses duration of time) is the easier reading and that of ℵ D should be preferred. The dative suggests (if we may suppose John to have been handling his cases with care) that the whole period of the ministry is regarded as a unity, a point in time.

ὁ ἑωρακὼς ἐμὲ ἑώρακεν τὸν πατέρα. Philip's question is otiose and rests upon failure to understand the person and work of Jesus, which are declared as early as the Prologue to be directed towards the revelation of God (1.18). To see Jesus is to see the Father, because the Father is in him and is in fact the agent of his works; see the following verses. Cf. 13.20; Jesus is God's envoy or agent (שליח, shaliaḥ), and 'a man's agent is like to himself' (e.g. Berakoth 5.5). See P. Borgen in Religions in Antiquity (Ed. J. Neusner, 1968), 137–48. Philip's question, natural as it is, has now lost its point, since all search for God must look to the decisive revelation in Jesus.

πῶς]καὶ πῶς, D Θ ω; cf. v. 5.

10. οὐ πιστεύεις; It is presumed that a disciple ought to have this faith.

ἐγὼ ἐν τῷ πατρὶ καὶ ὁ πατὴρ ἐν ἐμοί ἐστιν. Cf. 17.21, and other passages in the prayer of ch. 17. The relation between the Father and the Son is not completely reciprocal, yet each can (in slightly different senses) be said to be in the other. The Father abiding in the Son does his works; the Son rests from, and to, eternity in the Father's being.

τὰ ῥήματα . . . τὰ ἔργα αὐτοῦ. Cf. 12.49. John's exalted Christology never permits him to suggest that the activity of Jesus can be understood without reference to the transcendent God. Cf. 5.19. John is able to pass readily from the words to the works of Jesus since both alike are revelatory and both are full of power.

11. πιστεύετέ μοι, not 'believe in me' but 'accept the following statement as true'. See on 1.12.

εἰ δὲ μή (cf. v. 2), διὰ τὰ ἔργα αὐτά (αὐτοῦ, B—assimilation to v. 10) πιστεύετε (add μοι, B Θ ω). Men ought to believe what Jesus says; if they refuse to be convinced on these terms they should consider his works. Throughout this gospel the ἔργα or σημεῖα are presented as events which ought to and sometimes do elicit faith (e.g. 2.11). The contrast between this treatment and the refusal of Jesus in the Synoptic Gospels to grant signs is less striking than appears at first sight; see Introduction, pp. 52f., 75f., and on 2.11. Cf. also Matt. 11.21 = Luke 10.13.

12. ὁ πιστεύων εἰς ἐμέ. The construction with πιστεύειν changes; we now have εἰς with the accusative, indicating the true believer who trusts in Christ.

τὰ ἔργα ἃ ἐγὼ ποιῶ κἀκεῖνος ποιήσει, καὶ μείζονα τούτων ποιήσει. The power to work miracles was universally credited to the apostles and their contemporaries (cf. for example 1 Cor. 12.9f.), and seems to have continued, especially as the power of exorcism, till a late date. John, however, though he doubtless accepted the miracles of his day, thought of the ἔργα primarily as acts in which the power and character of God are made known; cf. 13.15,35. The greater works therefore are the gathering of many converts into the church through the activity of the disciples (cf. 17.20;20.29), which however is effective only through the continuing power of Jesus' word and the work of the Holy Spirit (15.26f.). See further the next note.

ὅτι ἐγὼ πρὸς τὸν πατέρα πορεύομαι. The death and exaltation of Jesus are the condition of the church's mission. Cullmann, Christology, 233, rightly compares Jesus' going to the Father with Matt. 28.18, All authority has been given to me. When Jesus is glorified the Spirit will be given (7.39); when he is in heaven he will hear and answer his disciples' prayers. Thus the 'greater works' are directly dependent upon the 'going' of Jesus, since before the consummation of the work of Jesus in his ascent to the Father all that he did was necessarily incomplete. The work of the disciples on the other hand lies after the moment of fulfilment. Cf. 16.8–15. Their works are greater not because they themselves are greater but because Jesus' work is now complete.

13. ἐν τῷ ὀνόματί μου. Cf. 15.16; 16.23. 'In my name' suggests 'with the invocation of my name'. See Beginnings v. 121–34, Note xi. But John's thought is by no means magical; cf. 1 John 5.14 (ἐάν τι αἰτώμεθα κατὰ τὸ θέλημα αὐτοῦ), and v. 15, where it is presumed that the disciples will love Christ and keep his commandments. The disciple will pray 'as his representative, while about his business' (Sanders).

τοῦτο ποιήσω. Christ himself will hear and answer prayer; cf. the passages just referred to, where God gives what is asked for. John would not have allowed that any contradiction was involved: the Father acts in and through the Son.

ἵνα δοξασθῇ ὁ πατὴρ ἐν τῷ υἱῷ. The Father is glorified in the Son's activity, both in himself and through his followers, since in all things the Son seeks (and achieves) his Father's glory; 5.41; 7.18; 8.50,54.

14. The whole verse is omitted by λ b sin, no doubt because it seemed redundant after v. 13. There are two other variants. (i) After αἰτήσητε, με is read by P⁶⁶ ℵ B W Θ vg pesh; it is omitted by D ω it sah boh. με ought to be retained; it may have been omitted with the intention of removing a contradiction with 16.23 (this might supply another motive for the omission of the whole verse). (ii) For τοῦτο ποιήσω (P⁷⁵ B φ it vg), ℵ D W Θ have ἐγὼ ποιήσω (so also P⁶⁶, τοῦτο being prefixed in the margin), and their reading should be accepted. τοῦτο harmonizes with v. 13, and also weakens the emphasis on the work of Jesus himself in answering prayer. This stress on the name of Christ, and on the fact that prayers are to be addressed to him and that he will answer them, is explained by and is to be understood in the light of the context (vv. 10–14) which emphasizes that the works of Christ are the works of God.

15. ἐὰν ἀγαπᾶτέ με. This protasis controls the grammar of the next two verses (15–17a), and the thought of the next six (15–21). The relation between Jesus and the disciples which is created by the Holy Spirit is expressed in their mutual love.

τὰς ἐντολὰς τὰς ἐμὰς τηρήσετε. Cf. vv. 21, 23; also 1 John 5.3, αὕτη γάρ ἐστιν ἡ ἀγάπη τοῦ θεοῦ, ἵνα τὰς ἐντολὰς αὐτοῦ τηρῶμεν; 1 Clem. 49.1, ὁ ἔχων ἀγάπην ἐν χριστῷ ποιησάτω τὰ τοῦ χριστοῦ παραγγέλματα. John never permits love to devolve into a sentiment or an emotion. Its expression is always moral and is revealed in obedience. This is true even of the love of the Son for the Father; cf. 15.10. See further on 3.16. τηρήσετε (B) suits the context better than the imperative τηρήσατε (D Θ ω). τηρήσητε (P⁶⁶ ℵ) continues the protasis, the apodosis beginning with κἀγώ. Brown accepts the reading of P⁶⁶ ℵ, but is obliged to insert an 'and' (and keep my commandments) which is not in the text.

16. κἀγὼ ἐρωτήσω. One consequence of the disciples' love for Christ will be their obedience to his commandments; another will be that Christ for his part will obtain for them the gift of the Paraclete. At this point the Paraclete is said to be given by the Father at the Son's request; at v. 26 the Father sends him in Christ's name; at 15.26 Christ sends him from the Father (παρὰ τοῦ πατρός), and he proceeds (ἐκπορεύεται) from the Father; at 16.7 Christ sends him. John intends no significant difference between these expressions.

ἄλλον παράκλητον. Either ἄλλον or παράκλητον may be taken adjectivally, and we may accordingly translate: He will give (a) another Paraclete, or (b) another person to be a Paraclete. (a) implies that Jesus himself is a Paraclete (cf. 1 John 2.1, the only use of παράκλητος, outside John, in the New Testament, παράκλητον . . . Ἰησοῦν Χριστὸν δίκαιον); this is nowhere else stated in the gospel. But the context (and that of the other uses of παράκλητος) suggests very strongly continuity between the offices of Jesus and the Paraclete, so that translation (a) may be accepted with little hesitation. On the place of the Holy Spirit in John's thought see Introduction, pp. 88–92.

On the word παράκλητος see *J.T.S.* new series 1 (1950), 7–15; also, among many contributions, N. Johansson, *Parakletoi* (1940); J. G. Davies in *J.T.S.* 4 (1953), 35–8; Bornkamm III, 68–89, 90–103; H. Riesenfeld in *N.T.S.* 18 (1972), 450; O. Betz, *Der Paraklet* (1963); G. Johnston, *The Spirit-Paraclete in the Gospel of John* (1970). The primary meaning of the Greek word is 'legal assistant, advocate' (L.S. *s.v.*), and with this meaning it was transliterated into Hebrew and Aramaic (e.g. *P. Aboth* 4.11: He that performs one precept gets for himself one advocate (פרקליט, *peraqliṭ*)). Many figures in Jewish history and belief were described by this term; see Johannsson and Betz. This meaning however does not seem to be prominent in John's usage; there is a forensic aspect of the Paraclete's work (16.8–11), but he is a prosecuting rather than a defending counsel. The meaning of παράκλητος in John is best arrived at by considering the use of παρακαλεῖν and other cognates in the New Testament. This is twofold. (a) παρακαλεῖν and παράκλησις both refer to prophetic Christian preaching (and to the same preaching communicated by apostolic letter); e.g. Acts 2.40; 1 Cor. 14.3. This corresponds to the normal Greek usage in which παρακαλεῖν means 'to exhort'. (b) Both words are used in another sense which seems to have little or no basis in Greek that is independent of the Hebrew Bible; they refer to consolation, and in particular to the consolation to be expected in the messianic age. This usage is common in the Old Testament (e.g. Isa. 40.1), recurs in the New Testament (e.g. Matt. 5.4; Luke 2.25), and is paralleled in the rabbinic נחמה (*neḥamah*, e.g. *Makkoth* 5b), and in מנחם (*menaḥem*; see Bousset-Gressmann, 227), used as a name of the Messiah. The two usages, (a) and (b), though distinct, are closely combined: the main burden of the παράκλησις (prophetic exhortation) is that men should enter, or accept, the παράκλησις (messianic salvation), which has been brought into being through the work of Jesus; cf. 1 Cor. 14.24,31.

Comparison with the verses in John 14—16 which speak of the Paraclete shows that his functions correspond closely with the points that have just been expressed. He witnesses about Christ; he takes 'the things of Christ' and declares them (15.26; 16.14; for the meaning of this declaration cf. 2.22; 12.16). He also declares τὰ ἐρχόμενα (16.13); he realizes the future eschatological judgement and thus reproves or exposes (ἐλέγχει, 16.8–11) the unbelieving world. He does so by the same means as the Christian preachers: he announces the departure of Christ to the Father (and for John this includes his death, resurrection, and ascension), the judgement of Satan, and the necessity of faith. The Paraclete is the Spirit of Christian paraclesis (cf. the very common rabbinic description of the Holy Spirit as the 'Spirit of prophecy'). See further on all the passages where παράκλητος is used (14.16f.,25f.; 15.26; 16.7–15), also the note below on τὸ πνεῦμα τῆς ἀληθείας. The view set forth here has been developed by both Johnston and Martyn; see especially Martyn, 135–42, where some of the most important conclusions of the book are to be found. 'The paradox presented by Jesus' promise that his work on earth will be continued because he is going to the Father is "solved" by his return in the person of the Paraclete. *It is, therefore, precisely the Paraclete who creates the two-level drama.*' This 'two-level drama makes clear that the Word's dwelling among us and our beholding his glory are not events which transpired only in the past . . .. These events to which John bears witness transpire on both the *einmalig* and the contemporary levels of the drama, or they do not transpire at all. In John's view, their transpiring on both levels of the drama is, to a large extent, the good news itself' (Martyn, 140, 142). This may perhaps underestimate the distinction between the persons. For consideration of the view that these Paraclete passages have been interpolated into the last discourses see Introduction, pp. 89f.

ἵνα ᾖ (μένη, P⁶⁶ D Θ ω vg) μεθ' ὑμῶν. There is no need to suppose that ἵνα ᾖ mistranslates an Aramaic relative clause, 'who shall be with you'. See E. Ullendorf, *N.T.S.* 2 (1955–6), 50 ff. The Spirit is given in order that the divine presence may be with the disciples continually, after the ascension.

17. τὸ πνεῦμα τῆς ἀληθείας. This expression is used three times (14.17; 15.26; 16.13), always in definition of the Paraclete. Already in this chapter (v. 6) Jesus has declared himself to be the truth (ἡ ἀλήθεια). The Spirit of truth will guide the disciples into all the truth (16.13) by bringing to their remembrance what Jesus had said and done. Cf. 1 John 4.6 (τὸ πνεῦμα τῆς ἀληθείας καὶ τὸ πνεῦμα τῆς πλάνης); 5.6 (τὸ πνεῦμά ἐστιν ἡ ἀλήθεια). T. Judah 20.1, 5 (The spirit of truth and the spirit of deceit . . . the spirit of truth testifieth all things, and accuseth all), which is sometimes quoted, is not relevant, since the 'spirits' seem to be the good and evil 'inclinations'. This applies also to the spirits of truth and wickedness (רוחי (ה)אמת ו(ה)עול) in 1 QS 3.18f.; 4.23. The Spirit of truth (רוח קודש = רוח אמת) in 1 QS 4.12 is (as Braun points out) an agent of cleansing, not of instruction, and there is nothing to connect the Prince of lights (שר אורים, 1 QS 3.20) with the Paraclete. τῆς ἀληθείας is not simply a defining genitive (equivalent, for example, to ἀληθινή at 15.1), nor is it simply a substitute for Jesus (the Spirit of Jesus, who is the truth). John means 'the Spirit who communicates truth'—a meaning closely parallel to that which has been ascribed above to παράκλητος, especially when it is borne in mind that in Jewish and early Christian literature ἀλήθεια often means the truth proclaimed by a missionary preacher and accepted by his converts (e.g. 2 Cor. 4.2). For ἀλήθεια generally in John see on 1.14.

ὁ ὁ κόσμος οὐ δύναται λαβεῖν. For κόσμος in John see on 1.10. Cf. 1 Cor. 2.14; the world means mankind over against God, and by definition the Spirit is alien to it. The contrast between the disciples and the world, a frequent theme in these chapters, is strongly brought out.

γινώσκετε . . . μένει (but the vg assumes μενεῖ) . . . ἔσται. The presents anticipate the future gift (ἔσται for ἐστίν (P⁶⁶ P⁷⁵ᵛⁱᵈ ℵ D² vg, against B D* it cur pesh), is probably a correction), and reflect the time at which John wrote. ὑμεῖς again emphasizes the contrast between the disciples and the unbelieving world. μένειν is used of the abiding of the Father in the Son and the Son in the Father, and of the Son in the disciples and the disciples in the Son. παρ' ὑμῖν, like μεθ' ὑμῶν (v. 16) suggests the presence of the Spirit in the church, ἐν ὑμῖν his indwelling in the individual Christian.

18. ὀρφανούς, literally, orphans, children left without a father; but the word was used also of disciples left without a master. Cf. Plato, *Phaedo* 116a, the friends of Socrates at his death ἀτεχνῶς ἡγούμενοι ὥσπερ πατρὸς στερηθέντες διάξειν ὀρφανοὶ τὸν ἔπειτα βίον; also Lucian, *de morte Peregrini* 6, the master has left ὀρφανοὺς ἡμᾶς. S.B. ii, 562, cite *Y. Hagigah* 1, 75d, 40.

ἔρχομαι πρὸς ὑμᾶς. In v. 3 the πάλιν ἔρχομαι of Jesus seemed to refer most naturally to his *parousia*, but it must not be inferred that the ἔρχομαι of this verse necessarily refers to the same coming. The alternatives are the coming of Jesus in the resurrection appearances (cf. 20.19, ἦλθεν ὁ Ἰησοῦς; 20.26, ἔρχεται ὁ Ἰησοῦς), and the coming of Jesus in the person of the Holy Spirit. Of these, the latter is improbable, since we ought not to suppose that John simple confounds Jesus with the Holy Spirit, and the former is supported by the following verses. It is however by no means impossible that John consciously and deliberately used language applicable to both the resurrection and the *parousia*, thereby emphasizing the eschatological character of the resurrection. See below, on ὅτι ἐγὼ ζῶ . . . There is no ground for seeing here (with Richardson, *Theology*, 372) a reference to the coming of Christ in the eucharist.

19. ἔτι μικρόν. Cf. 16.16–19 (without ἔτι). For the expression cf. Heb. 10.37 (ἔτι γὰρ μικρὸν ὅσον ὅσον—ἔτι added to Isa. 26.20), 12.26 (ἔτι ἅπαξ, from Hag. 2.6).

ὁ κόσμος με οὐκέτι θεωρεῖ, ὑμεῖς δὲ θεωρεῖτέ με. The simplest reference of these words, and one which is suggested by the context and by the parallel in 16.16ff., is to the crucifixion and resurrection. When Jesus is dead and buried the world will see him no more; but the disciples, to whom he will appear in his risen body, will see him. Nevertheless, the words are also applicable, and John, it seems, intended them to be applicable, to the whole of Christian history, throughout which the church is united to Jesus while the world does not know him. Cf. vv. 22f.

ὅτι ἐγὼ ζῶ καὶ ὑμεῖς ζήσετε. These words may be run on from the previous sentence—'. . . you behold me because I live and you shall live'; or they may be taken as an independent sentence—'because I live you shall live also'. The former interpretation suits the context better and is to be preferred. The latter introduces a fresh idea, that the life of Christians is dependent upon that of Christ, which, though thoroughly Johannine, is not in question here. On the other hand, with the former interpretation the thought is clear; even though Jesus dies the disciples will see him because he will be alive, risen from the dead, and they too will be spiritually alive and capable of seeing him. The interpretation of ἔρχομαι πρὸς ὑμᾶς (v. 18) is thus confirmed: the primary reference is to the Easter experience. But Bultmann is right in saying that the Easter experience is regarded as the fulfilment of the promise of the *parousia* (cf. 16.20ff.). The promise of the *parousia* is stripped of its mythological character, and the Easter experience is affirmed as the continuing possibility of the Christian life. Sanders takes θεωρεῖτέ με ὅτι ἐγὼ ζῶ to mean, 'You shall see that I am living' (cf. 9.8); καὶ ὑμεῖς ζήσετε then begins a new sentence, 'And you also shall live'.

20. ἐν ἐκείνῃ τῇ ἡμέρᾳ. Cf. 16.23. 'That day' is a phrase drawn from eschatological usage (cf. e.g. Mark 13.32); here however it looks back to ἔρχομαι πρὸς ὑμᾶς in v. 18. In both places the primary reference is to the resurrection, but the thought is extended (see especially v. 20b) to the permanent presence of Christ with his own. Here, as frequently in the last discourses, it is significant that eschatological language is borrowed to describe these events which fall within the time-sequence: they are events of eternal quality and significance. In the presence of Jesus with his own the full meaning of life is disclosed.

ἐγὼ ἐν τῷ πατρί μου. Cf. v. 11. What is there required as a matter of faith will clearly appear (to the disciple) when Jesus has overcome death and returned to his own.

ὑμεῖς ἐν ἐμοὶ κἀγὼ ἐν ὑμῖν. The unity of the Father and the Son could not be perceived except on the basis of unity between Jesus and the disciples; cf. v. 19b. The resurrection of Jesus and his presence with his own points unmistakably to the continuity of the divine life which flows from the Father, through the Son, and in the church.

21. ὁ ἔχων τὰς ἐντολάς μου. The thought resumes v. 15; ἔχειν here means 'to grasp firmly with the mind'. It is a not uncommon use; see e.g. Sophocles, *Philoctetes* 789, ἔχετε τὸ πρᾶγμα.

καὶ τηρῶν αὐτάς, observes them as well as knows and understands them.

ἐκεῖνός ἐστιν ὁ ἀγαπῶν με. Obedience is the mark of love. This is simply the converse of v. 15.

ἀγαπηθήσεται ὑπὸ τοῦ πατρός μου. John does not mean, though his language is such as might be taken to imply, that God's love is conditional upon man's obedience. He is not contradicting such passages as 3.16; 13.34; 15.9,12; 17.23. His thought is at this point (and frequently in the last discourses) concentrated upon the mutuality of the relation between Father, Son, and believers; see on 13.34. Because the disciples love one another they will appear to men as members of the divine family; their love for Christ, and union with him, means that the Father loves them in him. They enjoy the Father's love merely as his creatures (cf. 1 John 4.10); but as Christians they have entered into the same reciprocity of love that unites the Father and the Son.

κἀγὼ ἀγαπήσω αὐτὸν καὶ ἐμφανίσω αὐτῷ ἐμαυτόν. The love of Christ for his disciple is declared in self-manifestation. ἐμφανίζειν is used again in the next verse; nowhere else in John, and nowhere else in the New Testament in this sense. It is an appropriate word since it is used of theophanies: e.g. Exod. 33.13,18, ἐμφάνισόν μοι σεαυτόν (quoted by Philo, *L. A.* III, 101); Wisd. 1.2, [The Lord] ἐμφανίζεται δὲ τοῖς μὴ ἀπιστοῦσιν αὐτῷ; cf. Josephus, *Ant.* xv, 425, ἐμφάνεια τοῦ θεοῦ. The manner of the manifestation is not made clear in this verse. ἐμφανίζειν might refer to a resurrection appearance, or to a spiritual revelation of Christ; and it would not be inappropriate to the appearance of Christ in glory at the last day. Cf. the use of ἐπιφάνεια (2 Thess. 2.8; 1 Tim. 6.14; 2 Tim. 1.10; 4.1, 8; Titus 2.13).

22. Ἰούδας, οὐχ ὁ Ἰσκαριώτης (D: οὐχ ὁ ἀπὸ Καρυώτου). On Judas Iscariot (whose name is regularly given by D as here) see on 6.71. The Synoptic Gospels mention a Judas among the brothers of Jesus (Mark 6.3; Matt. 13.55; cf. Jude 1). Only Luke–Acts mentions an apostle of this name; see Luke 6.16 (Ἰούδαν Ἰακώβου, mentioned between Simon called Zelotes and Judas Iscariot, at the end of the list), and Acts 1.13 (Ἰούδας Ἰακώβου, mentioned last, after Simon Zelotes). There is no sufficient ground for identifying him with Thaddaeus in the Marcan list, or Lebbaeus in the Matthean. John probably had a non-synoptic list of the Twelve. For 'Judas, not Iscariot', sah has Judas Cananites, sin has Thomas, cur has Judas Thomas. On the apparent identification of Judas and Thomas in the Syriac-speaking church see on 11.16. In view of the fact that, in place of οὐχ ὁ Ἰσκαριώτης, b has *sed alius*, it seems not impossible that the original text read simply Judas. This

however cannot be concluded with certainty. See Cullmann, *V. & A.*, 217–20.

κύριε, τί γέγονεν ὅτι. See Radermacher, 159. P⁶⁶ᶜ ℵ read καί before τί. This may be original; cf. 9.36 for a similar construction. The καί adds vigour to the question: 'Yes, but how is it . . . ?' But καί may be due to dittography. κύριε would in an uncial MS. be written KE; if the letters KE were repeated they might well be taken as an equivalent for καί, since ε for αι is a very common itacism.

ἡμῖν μέλλεις ἐμφανίζειν (cf. Wisd. 1.2, above) σεαυτὸν καὶ οὐχὶ τῷ κόσμῳ. ἡμῖν stands first for emphasis, and in contrast with τῷ κόσμῳ at the end of the sentence. How is it that it is to *us* thou wilt manifest thyself, and not to *the world*? Cf. Acts 10.41, οὐ παντὶ τῷ λαῷ ἀλλὰ μάρτυσι τοῖς προκεχειροτονημένοις. In Acts the reference is undoubtedly to the resurrection appearances; only believers had seen the risen Christ. This meaning is suggested for John also by vv. 18f. (see the notes). But John's thought was neither simple nor static, and at this point a further stage has been reached. It was contrary to the earliest expectations of the church that a long interval should intervene between the death of Jesus and his appearance in glory before the eyes of the whole world (Mark 13.26; Rev. 1.7). This glorious appearance on the clouds of heaven had not taken place, and the question attributed to Judas is one which was doubtless asked by many perplexed Christians (cf. 2 Peter 3.4, ποῦ ἐστὶν ἡ ἐπαγγελία τῆς παρουσίας αὐτοῦ;). John here gives a solution of the problem. Part of the truth lies in the coming of Jesus to his followers at the resurrection; part lies in his coming, as expected, at the last day (John never denies and occasionally confirms this hope); but between these comings there is a different kind of *parousia* and manifestation.

23. ἐάν τις ἀγαπᾷ με, τὸν λόγον μου τηρήσει. Cf. vv. 15, 21. The word (singular) of Jesus is the whole saving message that he brought; cf. e.g. 5.24, ὁ τὸν λόγον μου ἀκούων . . . ἔχει ζωὴν αἰώνιον.

πρὸς αὐτὸν ἐλευσόμεθα. The plural alone (the singulars ἐλεύσομαι and ποιήσομαι, read by D cur, are an accommodation to better-known ideas) is sufficient to · show that John has in mind neither the resurrection appearances nor the *parousia* of the last day. To the man who becomes a Christian (for the notion of conversion cf. Wisd. 1.2 quoted on v. 21) both the Father and the Son (their equality is implied) will come. This is the *parousia* upon which John's interest is concentrated, and it is the interval, unforeseen by apocalyptic Christianity, between the resurrection and the consummation that he proposes to explain. The explanation is in terms of the 'mystical' abiding of God with the believer.

μονὴν παρ' αὐτῷ ποιησόμεθα. For the expression cf. Josephus, *Ant.* XIII, 41, Ἰωνάθης ἐν Ἱεροσολύμοις τὴν μονὴν ἐποιεῖτο. For μονή see on v. 2; it is simply the verbal noun derived from the characteristic Johannine μένειν. The Father and the Son will make their permanent dwelling with the Christian. The Old Testament is primarily concerned with the dwelling of God with man (cf., e.g., 1 Kings 8.27, ὅτι εἰ ἀληθῶς κατοικήσει ὁ θεὸς μετὰ ἀνθρώπων ἐπὶ τῆς γῆς; Zech. 2.10, ἐγὼ ἔρχομαι καὶ κατασκηνώσω ἐν μέσῳ σου); John, having stated the basic solution at 1.14, comes here to its personal outcome. Intimate mystical union with God was the goal of many religions in antiquity, not least the mystery cults and gnostic theosophies. The climax of the Hermetic religion is that elect souls δυνάμεις γενόμενοι ἐν θεῷ γίνονται (*C.H.* 1, 26); they are so closely united with God as to be deified (θεωθῆναι). In many places Philo speaks of God and also of the Word as dwelling in man (see for many references Bauer, 186). John's thought is distinguished from that of his contemporaries by (*a*) his insistence upon the historical framework of Christianity, (*b*) his insistence upon moral obedience and love as a prerequisite and accompaniment of the indwelling of God.

24. ὁ μὴ ἀγαπῶν με τοὺς λόγους μου οὐ τηρεῖ. The converse of v. 23a. It is possible that a contrast is intended between τὸν λόγον ... τοὺς λόγους—lack of love to Christ is manifested in transgression of his precepts; but the return to ὁ λόγος (singular) in the second half of this verse may suggest that no difference was intended.

ὁ λόγος ὃν ἀκούετε. Perhaps the message of Jesus as a whole; perhaps the word just spoken and heard. The speech of Jesus, like his actions, is not his own. For the complete unity of action of Father and Son see 5.19 and the gospel *passim*; it is essential to John's presentation of the Gospel.

25. ταῦτα λελάληκα. The reference is to the words of consolation which Jesus has spoken; but they will only have their effect through the future ministry of the Paraclete (v. 26).

παρ᾽ ὑμῖν μένων. The first μένειν of Jesus with his disciples is broken sharply by his death.

26. τὸ πνεῦμα τὸ ἅγιον; so the majority of MSS.; a few assimilate to the τὸ πνεῦμα τῆς ἀληθείας of v. 17; 15.26; 16.13, sin omits τὸ ἅγιον; this short reading may be original; it would account for the two variants. Cf. 1 QS 4.21 (on v. 17).

ὃ (ℵᶜ, ὃν) πέμψει ὁ πατὴρ ἐν τῷ ὀνόματί μου. See on v. 16, 'In my name' can hardly mean 'because you ask in my name'; perhaps, 'because I ask', or 'to act in relation to me, in my place, with my authority'. Cf. Mark 13.6, where those who claim to be Christ (ἐγώ εἰμι) are said to come ἐπὶ τῷ ὀνόματί μου.

ἐκεῖνος ὑμᾶς διδάξει πάντα. Cf. 15.26 (μαρτυρήσει); 16.13f. (ὁδηγήσει, λαλήσει, ἀναγγελεῖ). One of the primary functions of the Paraclete is to teach. For the words used cf. Ps. 25(24).5,9, ὁδήγησόν με ἐπὶ τὴν ἀλήθειάν σου, καὶ δίδαξόν με ... ὁδηγήσει πρᾳεῖς ἐν κρίσει, διδάξει πρᾳεῖς ὁδοὺς αὐτοῦ. Cf. also Neh. 9.20; 1 John 2.20, 27.

ὑπομνήσει ὑμᾶς. There is a parallel to the words in *C.H.* XIII, 2: τοῦτο τὸ γένος [the teaching about regeneration], ὦ τέκνον, οὐ διδάσκεται, ἀλλ᾽ ὅταν θέλῃ, ὑπὸ τοῦ θεοῦ ἀναμιμνήσκεται. But here it is the contrast rather than the parallel in thought which serves to bring out John's meaning. In the *Hermetica* the recollection is of the hidden origin and true nature of man and the universe, and it is called up from within; in John the Paraclete reminds the believer not of anything within himself but of the spoken, though not fully understood, words of Jesus. There is no independent revelation through the Paraclete, but only an application of the revelation in Jesus. The Paraclete recalls πάντα ἃ εἶπον ὑμῖν ἐγώ, and thereby recreates and perpetuates the situation of judgement and decision that marked the ministry of Jesus. The ἐγώ is very emphatic; it is omitted by P⁷⁵ ℵ D Θ ω. For εἶπον, D has ἂν εἴπω. This gives an entirely different meaning to the work of the Paraclete, who (according to this reading) receives fresh teaching from Jesus and transmits it to the church. This is contrary to the meaning of the passage as a whole.

27. εἰρήνην. Jesus is taking leave of his disciples and uses the conventional word of farewell, Peace, (שלום, shalom). εἰρήνη is used in John only here and at 16.33 (in a similar sense); and as a greeting at 20.19,21,26. But the word had already acquired much more than conventional depth; thus in the Old Testament, Num. 6.26; Ps. 28.11; Isa. 54.13; 57.19; Ezek. 37.26; and in the New Testament, Rom. 1.7; 5.1; 14.17 and many other passages. There is a similar use in Philo; see especially *Mos.* 1, 304, δωρησάμενος ὁ θεὸς Φινεεῖ τὸ μέγιστον ἀγαθόν, εἰρήνην, ὃ μηδεὶς ἱκανὸς ἀνθρώπων παρασχεῖν. The rest of this verse shows that peace means the absence of fear and perturbation of heart; and that it is the gift of Christ alone. As the chapter (and perhaps one form of the last discourses) moves to a close it takes up again the theme of the opening verses.

ἀφίημι ὑμῖν. For ἀφιέναι with the meaning 'to bequeath' (a meaning not quoted in L.S.) see Ps. 17 (16).14, ἀφῆκαν τὰ κατάλοιπα τοῖς νηπίοις αὐτῶν; Eccles 2.18; cf. Mark 12.22.

οὐ καθὼς ὁ κόσμος δίδωσιν. The peace of Christ (τὴν ἐμήν) is not the world's peace (since he has it at the moment of supreme peril and distress), and accordingly he gives it in a novel way. Cf. the synoptic promise of assistance in time of persecution (Mark 13.11, μὴ προμεριμνᾶτε).

μὴ ταρασσέσθω. Cf. v. 1. μηδὲ δειλιάτω—Let it not play the coward.

28. ἠκούσατε. Cf. vv. 2–4, 12, 18f., 21, 23. The discourse is recapitulated in the repetition of the key-words ὑπάγειν, ἔρχεσθαι. Jesus will return to the glory of the Father through death; yet he will come to his disciples and be closer to them than ever. The fact that the discourse is recapitulated in this way lends some weight to the view that ch. 14 is a discourse complete in itself. This cannot however be pressed in view of John's generally repetitive style.

εἰ ἠγαπᾶτέ με, ἐχάρητε ἄν. An unfulfilled condition. 'If you loved me (as you do not) you would...'. This is weakened in (D φ) to εἰ ἀγαπᾶτε, which implies nothing about the fulfilment of the condition. The sterner reading is original. True love for Jesus, which they did not yet possess, would have made the disciples rejoice in his exaltation just as true understanding would have enabled them to see that his departure was for their advantage.

ὁ πατὴρ μείζων μού ἐστιν. See 'The Father is greater than I'. The Father is *fons divinitatis* in which the being of the Son has its source; the Father is God sending and commanding, the Son is God sent and obedient. John's thought here is focused on the humiliation of the Son in his earthly life, a humiliation which now, in his death, reached both its climax and its end. For the patristic interpretation see M. F. Wiles, *The Spiritual Gospel* (1960), 122–5; T. E. Pollard, *Johannine Christology and the Early Church* (1970), (see index).

29. Cf. 13.19.

30. οὐκέτι πολλὰ λαλήσω μεθ' ὑμῶν. These words raise forcibly the question whether v. 31 was originally planned as the end of the discourse, that is, the question of the original order of chs. 14, 15, 16. See pp. 454ff. They do not however solve the question. With the gospel in its present state it can still be reasonably maintained that the words are valid since no more prolonged public teaching is given. πολλά is omitted by sin. It is not impossible that the

word was added to alleviate the apparent difficulty. The text without this word would suggest even more strongly that 14.31 was the original end of the discourse.

ἔρχεται γὰρ ὁ τοῦ κόσμου ἄρχων; that is, primarily, the events of the passion are about to begin (see the preceding note). For ὁ τοῦ κόσμου ἄρχων see on 12.31. For the devil as precipitating the death of Jesus cf. 6.70; 13.2,27. The passion itself may be regarded as a conflict between Jesus and Satan.

ἐν ἐμοὶ οὐκ ἔχει οὐδέν (οὐκ ἔχει οὐδὲν εὑρεῖν, D a; εὑρήσει οὐδέν is a further variant) recalls the Hebrew expression אין לו עלי 'he has no claim upon me'. Cf. 8.46. Since Jesus is not of this world (8.23, cf. 18.36) the ruler of this world can make no claim against him. It is not implied (as in some later theories of the atonement) that the devil was deceived. It is not certain whether we should punctuate with a comma or a colon after οὐδέν. The sentence may be taken thus: (a) ... has nothing in me, but [this happens] in order that the world may know.... Rise ... (b) ... has nothing in me. But that the world may know ..., rise ... Neither punctuation can be ruled out as impossible. (a) is perhaps to be preferred. See on the next verse.

31. ἀλλ' ἵνα. With the punctuation tentatively suggested above some supplement is needed before ἵνα. This is in accord with John's style; for similar elliptical constructions see 9.3; 13.18; 15.25; 1 John 2.19. It is easy to supply either 'These things are happening', or 'I am acting in this way'. A less probable alternative would be to regard the ἵνα as imperative: 'Let the world know ...'.

ἵνα γνῷ ὁ κόσμος ὅτι ἀγαπῶ τὸν πατέρα. Love is shown by keeping commandments (vv. 15, 21, 23); the Son keeps the Father's commandments and it is therefore demonstrated that he abides in the Father's love (15.10). The obedience and love of the Son find their supreme demonstration in his willing acceptance of the commandment that he lay down his life (10.17f.). ἐντολὴν ἔδωκεν is read by B and only a few other MSS.; the rest have ἐνετείλατο, probably rightly, since the reading of B assimilates the text to many passages in the context.

ἐγείρεσθε, ἄγωμεν ἐντεῦθεν. Cf. Mark 14.42, ἐγείρεσθε ἄγωμεν (spoken not in the supper room but in Gethsemane immediately before the arrest). It seems more probable that John is here echoing the Marcan words than that he refers to the ascent of Christ to the Father, though the latter view might be suggested by punctuation (b) of v. 30 (see above): Let me go to death and exaltation that the world may know. ... The problem of the construction of chs. 14, 15, 16 is raised again, since these words are most naturally read as the conclusion of the upper room discourse, immediately before the departure and arrest of Jesus. On this question see pp. 454ff. The difficulty can be removed by translation into Aramaic (Torrey, 135, 138–40). Only very slight alterations are required to turn '... thus I do. Rise, let us go hence' into '... thus I do. I will arise and go hence' (Present Greek text: כן עבד אנא קומו נאזל מכא; conjectured original: כן עבד אנא אקום ואזל מכא). But the hypothesis requires belief in a continuous Aramaic text underlying the Greek of John, and there is no good reason why the proposed mistake should have been made. Guilding, 89, explains the words in terms of the New Year lections. Dodd, Interpretation, 409, understands them as follows: 'The Ruler of this world is coming. He has no claim upon me; but to show the world that I love the Father, and do exactly as He commands,—up, let us march to meet him!' It remains a difficulty that chs. 15 and 16 follow; and ἐντεῦθεν means 'away from here', not 'to meet him'.

31. THE TRUE VINE

15.1–17

It was suggested above (pp. 454f.) that, in view of the problem caused by 14.31, ch. 14 and chs. 15—16 (17) might be regarded as alternative versions of the 'last discourse' of Jesus to his disciples. If this view is correct, the opening verses of ch. 15 must be thought of as standing in immediate connection with the supper described in ch. 13; in any case, unless we suppose that 14.31 means departure from the room where supper was held, ch. 15 is represented as taking place in the context of the supper. These connections must lend some support to the view that the symbolism of the vine is in part eucharistic. John's attitude to the sacraments has been discussed above (Introduction, pp. 82–5; also 281–5); it is certainly not such as to suggest that he would here intend to convey by symbolic language details of sacramental belief or practice. Moreover, as Bultmann observes, we hear nothing in this chapter of believers drinking the fruit of the vine (as wine is described in Matt. 26.29; Mark 14.25; Luke 22.18); Christ himself is the vine and they are branches—branches which will themselves bear grapes (v. 2) from which wine may be obtained. The truth is that John is speaking of the union of believers with Christ, apart from whom they can do nothing. This union, originating in his initiative and sealed by his death on their behalf, is completed by the believers' responsive love and obedience, and is the essence of Christianity. The problem of the continuing presence of Jesus after his departure is not handled in the same way as in ch. 14; the theme is no longer coming but abiding. A branch detached from the parent vine can bear no fruit; it is worthless and useless. The image in itself is a valid one; but John must have lived in complete isolation if he did not know that Christians met from time to time to eat bread (the flesh of the Son of man) and to drink the fruit of the vine (his blood). It is therefore reasonable to think that, as in ch. 6 he introduces eucharistic references into the discourse on the Bread of Life (see the commentary on ch. 6, especially pp. 297f.) so here he accepts the rather more remote allusions afforded by the image of the vine. But his theme is the union between the believers and Christ as manifested in his whole work in life, death, and resurrection. This union is the theme of the present and of the next section. Only in Christ can Christians live. In him there is the fruitfulness of true service to God, of answered prayer, and of obedience in love. All who are in him are his friends, and they are necessarily united with each other in love.

Symbolic speech based upon vines and vineyards is found in the

Synoptic Gospels; Mark 12.1–9; Matt. 21.33–41; Luke 20.9–16; Matt. 20.1–16; 21.28–32; cf. Luke 13.6–9. All these parables have in common the fact that the vineyard, or persons connected with it, represent Israel, or a section of Israel. A contrast is drawn between the fruit which ✳ Israel, as God's vineyard, or the labourers in his vineyard, ought to bear, or to produce by labour, and the scanty results which in fact appear. In pointing this contrast the New Testament follows in the steps of the Old Testament (e.g., Isa. 5.1–7; for many other Old Testament references see the notes below). What must be noted here is the twofold transformation of the traditional material which John has effected, and which is visible in both the form and the substance of the parable. (a) John withdraws the point of the parable from the eschatological crisis of the ministry of Jesus and applies it to the continuous life of the church. (b) The vine in his handling of the material ceases to represent Israel and becomes a Christological definition applied to Jesus himself. The change in the form of the parabolic material appears in the facts (a) that no clear story is told; we do not hear the fate of a particular vine or vineyard, but rather certain general observations on viticulture; (b) that the whole symbolism is governed by the opening words ἐγώ εἰμι: Jesus is all that the vine truly symbolizes.

The Old Testament and the Synoptic Gospels are not the only sources in which parallels to the Johannine symbolism of the vine can be found. 'A Hellenistic reader of the gospel would find the figure of God as γεωργός familiar enough' (Dodd, Interpretation, 137; see 136f.). Bultmann (see below) finds parallels in the Mandaean literature and the Odes of Solomon, and sees in the vine a reflection of the oriental myth of the tree of life (often identified with the vine). Miss Guilding thinks that the main connection of chs. 15, 16 is, as with chs. 7—9, with the Feast of Tabernacles. 'The Feast of Tabernacles sets forth God as the giver of abundance—the rainfall, the sunshine, and the fruit of the vine: at Tabernacles Jesus shows himself as the giver of living water, the light of the world, and the true vine. . . . The theme of the Supper Discourses is that Passover, Tabernacles, and Dedication are fulfilled in Jesus and his Church, and that the single Christian feast, the eucharist, is the fulfilment of the entire Jewish festal system. It is for this reason that we have in the Supper Discourses a recapitulation of the cycle of the Jewish feasts placed in the historical setting of the last supper. It follows that although the words of 15.1 "I am the true vine" may well refer to the eucharistic cup, they do so through the medium of the Feast of Tabernacles, and the primary allusion is to the vintage of the autumn feast and to the Tabernacles lections which speak of Israel as an empty vine' (Guilding, 118). None of these parallels however is as important as those in the Old Testament and the Synoptic Gospels. Brown argues that in form the material is neither parable nor allegory but מָשָׁל (mashal). It is simpler and better to see in it John's reflection upon the traditional image.

1. ἐγώ εἰμι. See on 6.35.

ἡ ἄμπελος ἡ ἀληθινή. John introduces abruptly one of his great symbols; cf. 10.1ff. for that of the shepherd. The vine is one of the most prized of plants and in allegorical usage naturally represents the most privileged among nations and men. This usage appears in the Old Testament where Israel is described as a vine. See e.g. Jer. 2.21, ἄμπελος ἀληθινή (שׂרק כלה), a passage the more important because it is the *haphtarah* to Deut. 9, which may have been a lection used at the time of Tabernacles (Guilding, 95); also Isa. 5.1–7; 27.2ff.; Jer. 12.10ff.; Ezek. 15.1–8; 17.5ff.; 19.10–14; Ps. 80.9–16. In these passages the pure and favoured origin, but often also the degeneration or danger, of Israel are described. The same use is to be found in rabbinic literature; the fullest example is *Lev. R.* 36.2 (quoted at length in S.B. II, 563f.). As the vine is the lowest of all plants and yet becomes the king of all plants, so the Israelites appear lowly in this world, but in the future (i.e. the messianic age) they will obtain possession from one end of the world to the other. In later Judaism Wisdom (Ecclus. 24.27) and the Messiah (2 Baruch 39.7) appear under the likeness of the vine. More important for the identification of the vine with Jesus rather than with the people is the occurrence of both vine and Son of man in Ps. 80. Philo gives a characteristically non-historical interpretation to the vine when, quoting Isa. 5.7 (The vineyard of the Lord Almighty is the house of Israel), he immediately explains that 'Israel' means 'seeing God' (θεὸν ὁρῶν), so that the soul, which houses the mind, which sees God, is 'that most holy vineyard which has for its fruit that divine growth, virtue' (*Som.* II, 172f.). Vine-symbolism has a prominent place in certain other non-Christian sources (e.g. the cult of Dionysus, and the Mandaean literature, though the latter seems here to be certainly dependent on Christian imagery), but these have no particular relevance here. It is more interesting to note that among the ornaments of Herod's Temple was a notable golden vine (*Middoth* 3.8; Josephus, *Bel.* v, 210; Tacitus, *Historiae* v, 5) and that the disciples of Johanan b. Zakkai at Jabneh (Jamnia) after A.D. 70 were called כרם ביבנה (*kerem bᵉyabhneh*, the vineyard of Jabneh; *Ketuboth* 4.6, *et al.*). This last point would be the more interesting if we followed Pallis (32) in taking ἄμπελος to mean 'vineyard'. 'In Modern Greek ἀμπέλι(ον) and κλῆμα are specific terms for *vineyard* and *vine* respectively' (loc. cit.). There is some papyrus support for this meaning of ἄμπελος; see M.M. *s.v.* Most important however is the Old Testament use of the vine as a symbol for Israel, and the connection of this chapter with the synoptic accounts of the last supper (it is possible that originally ch. 15 was planned to follow immediately upon the supper without the intervention of ch. 14; see pp. 454ff.). In the Marcan account one of the central features is the blessing of a cup of wine which is afterwards given to the disciples with the words 'This is my blood of the covenant which is shed for many' (Mark 14.24; cf. Matt. 26.28; also Luke 22.20, but this verse may not be part of the original text of Luke). In the next verse the wine is described as τὸ γένημα τῆς ἀμπέλου in the eschatological saying 'I will no more drink of the fruit of the vine until that day when I drink it new in the kingdom of God' (cf. Luke 22.18 '. . . until the kingdom of God come'). This recalls the usual Jewish benediction over wine, 'Blessed art Thou, O Lord . . . who createst the fruit of the vine' (פרי הגפן). In the synoptic narratives the fruit of the vine is thus at once the means by which the disciples are made sharers in the sacrificial death of Christ and an anticipation of the life of the age to come. Union with Christ (and contact thereby with the other world) forms the basis and theme of the whole of ch. 15. There is a mutual indwelling of Father, Son, and disciple. The historical foundation of this relation is in the call of Christ (ἐγὼ ἐξελεξάμην ὑμᾶς, v. 16), and its outcome is the mutual love of Christians for one another (v. 13). Conversely, the hatred of the world for the church arises out of its hatred for Christ (vv. 23f., cf. vv. 9f.). The mission of the Son provokes hatred as it provokes love, and the inevitable effect is a cleavage between the children of light and the children of darkness. This divine mission is continued in the witness of the Paraclete and of the church (vv. 26f., and ch. 16). For ἀληθινός see on 1.9. Here as often the adjective draws a contrast with some other object less real than that described by John. Thus Israel is called a vine; but the true vine is not the apostate people but Jesus, and those who are, as branches, incorporated in him. This corresponds with what was said above (pp. 291f.) about the 'I am' of Jesus; fragments of meaning, obscurely hinted at by other vines, are gathered up and made explicit by him. He is the *true* vine. For a different use of vine-symbolism cf. *Didache* 9.2; also Acts of Thomas 36; 146 (Lipsius-Bonnet II, ii, 154, 2f.; 253, 19–22). For a full list of Mandaean passages see Schweizer, 40f.

ὁ πατήρ μου ὁ γεωργός ἐστιν, is in supreme control of the whole process. Cf. 1 Cor. 3.6–9 (. . . θεοῦ γεώργιον . . . ἐστε). There is a different picture in the parable of Mark 12.1–12, where the owner of the vineyard lets it out to γεωργοί. Cf. Lucian, *Phalaris* II, 8, where God acts as γεωργός without the collaboration of men. Fenton points out that the relation of husbandman to vine teaches the same kind of 'subordination' as that of Father to Son.

2. πᾶν κλῆμα. The word κλῆμα, though it can be used generally, is particularly applied to vine-branches; see L.S. *s.v.* πᾶν . . . μή is not a Semitism; the order is not that of the characteristically Semitic לא כל; M. II, 434. The image of fruit and fruit-bearing is common in the Odes of Solomon: 1.2f.; 8.2; 10.2; 11.1f., 12, 23; 12.2; 14.17; 16.2; 17.13; 38.17; also Acts of Thomas 61 (Lipsius-Bonnet, II, ii, 178, 10, καρποὺς ἀληθινούς).

ἐν ἐμοί. The interpretation of the unfruitful branches may be twofold. The original branches in God's vine were the Jews; these, being unfruitful (unbelieving), God removed. Cf. Matt. 21.41, where the thought is very similar, and Rom. 11.17, εἰ δέ τινες τῶν κλάδων ἐξεκλάσθησαν. . . .; also Matt. 15.13, πᾶσα φυτεία . . . ἐκριζωθήσεται. This seems to have been the earliest Christian interpretation of the vine-symbolism, and it may well have been at the back of John's mind; but ἐν ἐμοί shows that his primary thought was of apostate Christians.

αἴρει . . . καθαίρει. The paronomasia suggests original Greek composition, not the translation of a Semitic original. καθαίρειν is equally suitable for agricultural processes and for religious purgation. It is used of cleansing corn by winnowing (Xenophon, *Oeconomicus* XVIII, 6) and of clearing weeds from the ground before sowing (ibid. xx, 11). It is used of religious ceremony (*Iliad* XVI, 228, purifying a cup for a libation), and in a moral sense (Plato, *Phaedo* 114c, οἱ φιλοσοφίᾳ ἱκανῶς καθηράμενοι). Philo uses the agricultural process in a moral allegory (*Som.* II, 64, . . . βλάσται περισσαί . . . ἅς καθαίρουσι καὶ ἀποτέμνουσι . . . οἱ γεωργοῦντες). But in John both καθαίρειν and μένειν are determined not by agricultural processes but by the Christian truth the evangelist is concerned to teach (Dodd, *Interpretation*, 136). For the means of purification see the next verse; its purpose is ἵνα καρπὸν πλείονα φέρῃ. The bearing of fruit is simply living the life of a Christian disciple (see vv. 5, 8); perhaps especially the practice of mutual love (v. 12).

3. ἤδη ὑμεῖς καθαροί ἐστε. The adjective καθαροί, like the cognate verb, is used in agriculture, and can be quoted in special connection with the growth of vines; Xenophon, *Oeconomicus* xx, 20, . . . ἵνα ὕλης καθαραὶ αἱ ἄμπελοι γένωνται. The disciples as the initial members of the new people of God have already undergone the process of purification. Cf. 13.10.

διὰ τὸν λόγον ὃν λελάληκα ὑμῖν. For the active power of the word of Jesus cf. 12.48 (κρινεῖ αὐτόν); also 15.7; 17.8 (ῥήματα). No particular word is in mind (contrast perhaps v. 7). There is no inconsistency with 13.10, nor in John's mind any wish to contrast a cleansing activated by physical means (baptism) with a cleansing wrought by the spoken word only. In both ch. 13 and ch. 15 he is thinking of the total effect of what Jesus was and did for his own. In the former the process of washing represents, as we have seen, the whole loving service of Jesus to men, culminating in his death; in the latter his 'word' is the message of salvation which he brings, and in himself is. Cf. 6.63, where John passes from the eating of flesh and the drinking of blood to the ῥήματα of Jesus as spirit and life. It would be as wrong (in John's view) to suppose that men are morally and spiritually cleansed by a formula as by the dipping in water called baptism. It is the speaking and acting Christ who cleanses, but the meaning of his action is revealed by his active word.

4. μείνατε ἐν ἐμοί, κἀγὼ ἐν ὑμῖν. This is the basic thought of the chapter; see on v. 1. The sentence may be taken in three ways. (*a*) καί introduces a comparison: abide in me, *as* I abide in you. (*b*) καί introduces the apodosis of a conditional sentence, the protasis of which is expressed by an imperative (Robertson, 948f.): if you abide in me, I will abide in you. V. 5 however suggests that (*c*) we should take the two balanced clauses very closely together: let there be mutual indwelling. The Christian life is unthinkable except in union with Christ. It is not however a static condition that John has in mind. 'Μένειν means holding on loyally to the decision once taken, and one can hold on to it only by continually going through it again. So too the words κἀγὼ ἐν ὑμῖν do not say that Jesus continues to be present in the Christian church and culture in the sense of being present within the history of the world and the history of ideas; they speak of the promise that he will always remain the ground and origin of the possibility of life' (Bultmann).

μένῃ, B ℵ: μείνῃ, P66 D Θ ω. Similarly, μένητε, B ℵ Θ*: μείνητε, D ω. The present (continuous) tenses are more suitable to the context, but for that very reason the aorists (if original) might have been changed. But they may be due to assimilation to v. 7, and it is probably best to accept the readings of B ℵ.

5. The thought of the previous verse is repeated in different words. Such repetitions are characteristic of John: see on 1.2.

6. ἐβλήθη ἔξω . . . καὶ ἐξηράνθη. For these 'timeless' aorists cf. Isa. 40.7 (ἐξηράνθη ὁ χόρτος καὶ τὸ ἄνθος ἐξέπεσεν) and see M. 1, 134, 247; B.D., §333. The usage is not unclassical; cf. Euripides, *Alcestis* 386, ἀπωλόμην ἄρ', εἴ με δὴ λείψεις. Radermacher, 124, and Moule, *Idiom Book*, 12f., think the aorists

point to immediate action (cf. Epictetus, IV, x, 27; Ignatius, *Ephesians* 5.3). Cf. Matt. 3.10; Luke 3.9; *Thomas* 40 (A vine has been planted without the Father and, as it is not established, it will be pulled up by its roots and be destroyed). The verbs that follow (συνάγουσιν ...) show how the aorists are to be taken. An unfaithful Christian suffers the fate of an unfruitful branch.

συνάγουσιν ... βάλλουσιν. The construction and tense change but not the sense; the third person plurals active are used for passives, in a manner recalling Hebrew and Aramaic usage. Cf. 20.2 and see M. II, 447f. Accordingly it is fruitless to ask who are the subject of the verbs. On the tense see the preceding note.

εἰς τὸ πῦρ ... καίεται. The words are primarily parabolic; that is, it is unfruitful branches which are cast into the fire and burned. Yet John would probably not have denied a similar fate for faithless Christians; cf. 5.29; Matt. 13.37–42. According to Brown, v. 6 is the counterpart of v. 5, not of v. 7; there seems to be no reason why it should not be taken as the counterpart of both, a negative statement between two positive ones.

7. ἐὰν μείνητε ἐν ἐμοὶ καὶ τὰ ῥήματά μου ἐν ὑμῖν μείνῃ. Cf. vv. 4f. for the mutual indwelling of Jesus and the believer, and v. 3 for the cleansing effect of his word (λόγος). Here ῥήματα are probably the specific sayings and precepts of Jesus (cf. v. 10); these must remain in the Christian's mind and heart.

ὃ ἐὰν θέλητε αἰτήσασθε (B φ it; αἰτησασθαι, P⁶⁶ A D, is to be taken as a variant spelling; αἰτήσεσθε, ℵ Θ vg). Cf. 14.13 (and note); 16.23. The prayer of a truly obedient Christian cannot fail, since he can ask nothing contrary to the will of God. For γενήσεται ὑμῖν cf. Mark 11.24, ἔσται ὑμῖν.

8. ἐν τούτῳ ἐδοξάσθη ὁ πατήρ μου. For the aorist cf. v. 6. In John it is usually the Son who is glorified, but cf. 12.28; 13.31; 14.13; 17.4. The Father is glorified in the Son—in his obedience and perfect accomplishment of his work. It is therefore but a short step to see the glorification of the Father in the obedience and fruitfulness of those who are united to the Son. ἐν τούτῳ is followed by an explanatory ἵνα in John's manner.

καὶ γενήσεσθε ἐμοὶ μαθηταί. This should be preferred as the rougher reading (Sanders); Lindars suggests that γένησθε (P⁶⁶ B D Θ it vg sah) may be due to assimilation to φέρητε. In any case, the difference in meaning is scarcely perceptible—Bultmann thinks that if the future indicative is read it must be taken as equivalent to an aorist subjunctive. Brown compares Ignatius, *Romans* 5.3 (νῦν ἄρχομαι μαθητὴς εἶναι—rightly?) and claims that fruit-bearing and becoming a disciple are not two separate things; they are indeed inseparable, but John seems to think of fruit-bearing as the outward and visible sign of being a disciple. Cf. 13.35, where mutual love is the sign of discipleship, and v. 12 where the same thought is resumed.

9. καθὼς ἠγάπησεν ... κἀγώ ... ἠγάπησα. κἀγώ introduces an apodosis, 'so also I ...'. The notion of a correspondence between the relation of Father and Son and that of Son and disciples is especially frequent in chs. 13—17. The aorist ἠγάπησα denotes the whole act of love lavished by Jesus upon his disciples and consummated in his death. The love of the Father for the Son is expressed by continuous tenses at 3.35; 5.20; 10.17; here, and at 17.24,26, the aorist is used, by analogy with the aorist used for the love of Jesus for the disciples, and also perhaps with reference to the pretemporal relations of

Father and Son. A different punctuation is adopted by WH, who place only a comma after ἠγάπησα. If this is followed we must translate, 'As my Father loved me and I loved you, abide (μείνατε) . . .'. This does not seem preferable to the interpretation given above.

μείνατε. The aorist imperative may be used for emphasis (Bernard, ad loc.); perhaps rather it is a summons to the disciples to enter into and so to abide in the love of Jesus.

τῇ ἀγάπῃ τῇ ἐμῇ, 'my love for you'. Cf. Odes of Solomon 8.22, Pray and abide continually in the love of the Lord; ye beloved ones, in the Beloved. What John understands by abiding in the love of Jesus, however, is shown in the next verse.

10. ἐὰν τὰς ἐντολάς μου τηρήσητε. Cf. 14.15, 21, and the notes.

καθώς . . . The parallel shows that love and obedience are mutually dependent. Love arises out of obedience, obedience out of love.

11. ταῦτα λελάληκα. Cf. 14.25.

ἵνα ἡ χαρὰ ἡ ἐμὴ ἐν ὑμῖν ᾖ. The joy of Jesus springs out of his obedience to the Father and his unity with him in love. The seal upon his obedience and love is his ascent to the Father, and this should make his disciples rejoice (14.28; 16.20–4; 17.13). But in addition they too may experience the joy of mutual love and obedience.

πληρωθῇ, may be complete. The expression is Johannine; 3.29; 16.24; 17.13; 1 John 1.4; 2 John 12.

12. αὕτη ἐστὶν ἡ ἐντολὴ ἡ ἐμή. The commandment (now become singular, summarizing all commandments, v. 10) which will keep in the love of Christ those who observe it is itself the commandment of love. Love is, as it were, the bond of existence within the unity of Father, Son, and believers (the Holy Spirit is not here in mind).

ἵνα ἀγαπᾶτε ἀλλήλους καθὼς ἠγάπησα ὑμᾶς. Cf. 13.34f., and for the latter clause v. 9. The whole ministry of Jesus, including his glorification in death (cf. Mark 10.45), is summed up as the service of love to those who by it are redeemed; every Christian owes the same service of love to every other. It is not said that they should love their enemies (cf. Matt. 5.44), and John has been accused of narrowing the Christian idea of love. See the note on 13.34. It cannot be said that, in John, God does not love the world (see 3.16); but his love for the world results in the separation from it of a group of φίλοι (v. 14). In a special sense the love of Jesus was lavished upon these 'friends' to the end that among them and in them love in turn might grow. Love for enemies, though one of the highest forms of ethical achievement, is not an exclusively Christian ideal; for a noble example see Sophocles, *Antigone*, 522f. Christian love is new in its origin and basis (see p. 96), and the mutual love of Christians is a reflection of Jesus' love for them, more, of the mutual love which exists eternally between the Father and the Son. The eternal divine love reached its complete and unsurpassable expression in the death of Christ, which was at the same time the death of a man for his friends.

13. μείζονα ταύτης ἀγάπην makes explicit the point just hinted at. It does not claim that love for friends is better than love for enemies; only that there is

nothing greater you can do for your friends than die for them. Life sacrificed in death is the supreme gift, and the mark of love. Brown quotes Plato, *Symposium*, 179b (καὶ μὴν ὑπεραποθνῄσκειν γε μόνοι ἐθέλουσιν οἱ ἐρῶντες).

ἵνα τις τὴν ψυχὴν αὐτοῦ θῇ. ἵνα and the subjunctive are explanatory of ταύτης. For ψυχὴν τιθέναι see on 10.11.

ὑπὲρ τῶν φίλων αὐτοῦ. John seems to draw no distinction between ἀγαπᾶν and φιλεῖν; accordingly we may render here, '... for those whom he loves' (for the common *passive* sense of φίλος see L.S. *s.v.*). The further, and specifically Christian, meaning of φίλος is brought out in the next verses. W. Grundmann (*Nov. T.* 3 (1959), 62–9) sees in φίλοι a eucharistic allusion; it is better to be less specific and note, with Conzelmann, *Theology*, 278, a particularly close relation between the command of love and the act of salvation.

14. ἐὰν ποιῆτε ὃ (B; ἅ, P⁶⁶ ℵ D; ὅσα, Θ ω) ἐγὼ ἐντέλλομαι ὑμῖν. It is clear that the status of friend is not one which precludes obedient service; this is rather demanded. Cf. v. 10 and the parallels noted there; there is no essential difference between being Christ's φίλος and abiding in his ἀγάπη.

15. οὐκέτι λέγω ὑμᾶς δούλους, ... ὑμᾶς δὲ εἴρηκα φίλους. The contrast is an evident one and occurs for example in Philo. See *Mig.* 45, καὶ γὰρ εὔηθες τοὺς δούλους οἰηθῆναι πρὸ τῶν φίλων τοῦ θεοῦ τὴν ἀρετῆς χώραν διανέμεσθαι. Here the friend of God is Moses. See also *Sob.*, 55, φίλον γὰρ τὸ σοφὸν θεῷ μᾶλλον ἢ δοῦλον. In *Sob.*, 56 Philo quotes Gen. 18.17 with the description of Abraham as τοῦ φίλου μου (LXX, τοῦ παιδός μου; no Hebrew equivalent); this reading may be dependent on Isa. 41.8. In Wisd. 7.27, Wisdom is said to make men friends of God: εἰς ψυχὰς ὁσίας μεταβαίνουσα φίλους θεοῦ καὶ προφήτας κατασκευάζει. In the LXX φίλος is sometimes used for a highly placed official at court (1 Macc. 2.18; 3.38; 10.65 *et al.*); it was similarly used in the Ptolemaic court (for the evidence see L.S. *s.v.* 1.1.d; possibly this Egyptian usage affected the Greek of the LXX). There is however no need to suppose (Deissmann, 383) that this usage strongly influenced John, with whom the most important factors are the connection of φίλος with φιλεῖν-ἀγαπᾶν, and the contrast between friends and slaves. For φίλος τοῦ θεοῦ see Epictetus, II, xvii, 29. According to John, the difference between a δοῦλος and a φίλος lies not in doing or not doing the will of God, but in understanding or not understanding it. The disciples are φίλοι because Jesus has declared to them the whole counsel of God (cf. 16.12). Cf. the contrasts between servants and sons at Gal. 4.1–7; Heb. 3.5f. It is characteristic of John that that which (according to him) distinguishes the friend from the slave is knowledge, and that knowledge should be very closely related to love. The existence of a superior group of φίλοι, distinguished from δοῦλοι, recalls both gnosticism and the mystery cults (cf. Clement of Alexandria, *Strom.* VII, 11, where the γνωστικός is τέλειος, φίλος, and υἱός); but it must always be remembered that for John the distinguishing marks of those who become φίλοι are the obedience and humility shown by Jesus himself. φίλος probably became a technical term for 'Christian'; see on 11.11.

ἐγνώρισα. The aorist contemplates the completed work of Christ. For γνωρίζειν cf. 17.26.

16. οὐχ ὑμεῖς με ἐξελέξασθε, ἀλλ᾽ ἐγὼ ἐξελεξάμην ὑμᾶς. The analogy with groups of initiated gnostics, superficially attractive as it is, again breaks down. The

initiates had chosen their way of life for themselves. Cf. *Stobaei Hermetica*, Excerpt xviii, 3 (W. Scott, *Hermetica* 1 (1924), 446), τὸ δὲ αἱρεῖσθαι ἔχομεν; *C.H.* iv, 6, ἡ αἵρεσις θατέρου καταλείπεται τῷ ἐλέσθαι βουλομένῳ; and many similar passages. In the gospel narrative, however (and this is as true of the Synoptic Gospels as of John), Jesus chooses, calls, and appoints his disciples. The initiative is entirely his ; the ἐγώ is emphatic. This emphasis governs the interpretation of the whole passage. Men are not Jesus' friends because they have a natural affinity with him, but because he has named them (εἴρηκα) his friends. If they lay down their lives in love, it is because he first laid down his life for them. For the element of predestination in John's thought see Introduction, pp. 8of.

ἔθηκα ὑμᾶς. This use of τιθέναι is probably Semitizing (Lindars); in Greek the object usually has a noun or adjective predicate in apposition. Cf. Acts 13.47; 20.28; Rom. 4.17; 1 Cor. 12.28; 1 Thess. 5.9; 1 Tim. 1.12; 2.7; 2 Tim. 1.11; Heb. 1.2; 1 Peter 2.8. In all these passages τιθέναι is used actively with a personal object, or passively with a personal subject. Two of them (Acts 13.47; Rom. 4.17) are quotations of the Old Testament (Isa. 49.6; Gen. 17.5), and in these places the Hebrew verb is נתן. This verb (or rather a recollection of it and of one of its Greek renderings) may underly the present passage; or possibly ἔθηκα is a rendering or echo of סמך, originally 'to close', 'to join', hence 'to lay the hands on (the head of)', that is 'to ordain' (the word commonly used of the ordination of a scholar or rabbi).

ἵνα ὑμεῖς ὑπάγητε καὶ καρπὸν φέρητε. The metaphor looks back to the metaphor of the vine with which the chapter opened. ὑπάγητε refers to the mission of the apostles to the world. It is sufficiently explained without recourse to the view (Torrey, 40, 44) that it is a mistranslation of a well-known Semitic idiom which should have been rendered, 'that you may bear more and more fruit'.

ὁ καρπὸς ὑμῶν μένῃ. Cf. 4.36. The fruits of the apostolic mission will be gathered in, and not be lost.

ἵνα . . . δῷ ὑμῖν. Cf. 14.13. Here the Father himself is the giver. This ἵνα clause seems to be co-ordinate with, not dependent upon, ἵνα . . . ὑπάγητε . . .

φέρητε . . . μένῃ. Bearing fruit, and prayer which is sure of its answer, are the twin privileges which flow from the appointment of Jesus.

17. This verse forms a transition to the next paragraph; it repeats the thought of vv. 10, 12, and other passages. If ἵνα is read, it explains ταῦτα (cf. v. 13), and the sense is, The commandments I give you are to the effect that you should love one another. But ἵνα is omitted by P66* D, perhaps rightly. It may be due to assimilation to v. 12, and without it the sentence is harsher, but stronger. 'These things I charge you: Love one another.'

32. THE HATRED OF THE WORLD

15.18–27

In the previous section the thought was concentrated upon the small group of the friends of Jesus, their union in love with each other and with him, their obedience, their prayers. John now looks outward to consider their surroundings. They live in the midst of the κόσμος (see the notes on 1.10; 3.16). To the love which flourishes within the circle of believers corresponds the hatred of the world, which first hated Jesus and naturally continues to hate those who are his, since the world can only love its own. It is as truly the nature of the world to hate as it is the nature of the Christians to love. Because the Christians are in Christ, hatred of them is hatred of Christ, and hatred of Christ is hatred of the Father who sent him. The unpopularity of Christians in the world is due ultimately to the attitude of the world to God. This truth John perceived on theological grounds. It is unlikely that Isa. 66.5 (part of a prophetic lection read at Tabernacles; Guilding, 54, 113f.) contributed much to his insight; Qumran (see *J. & Q.*, 33) offers no very significant parallel. Lightfoot (284f.) sees a parallel between ch. 9 (the resistance provoked by Jesus) and 15.18—16.11 (the resistance provoked by his disciples, who bear witness to him). This is a more important observation (which to some extent anticipates Martyn; see pp. 137f.).

The hatred of the world for Christians is a theme of the Synoptic Gospels also. It appears in the Marcan apocalypse: Mark 13.9–13. Some of the Matthean parallels to this material are in the mission charge (Matt. 10.17–22) and in the same context there is further material (Matt. 10.23–39) with parallels in Luke 12.2–9,51–3; 14.26f.; 17.33. Cf. also the sayings of Mark 8.34f.; Matt. 16.24f.; Luke 9.23f. In spite of rearrangements made by Matthew it seems probable that most (at least) of these sayings were originally eschatological predictions: the last days would be marked by the resistance of evil powers who would unleash their hatred against the Messiah and his servants. This eschatological expectation was taken by the synoptists to be fulfilled in the experience of suffering undergone by themselves and their contemporaries. Thus for example readers of Mark 13 would be able to understand and interpret such events as the Neronian persecution, giving to them a theological significance which had practical consequences: Roman Christians must hold the faith and endure to the end; if they do so they will be saved and will see the joy that is to follow the affliction. John also gives the prediction of persecution absolute significance, but he changes the setting. The hatred of the world for Christ's people is, as has already been noted, hatred of God himself. In this way John uses the gnostic concept of the conflict between light and darkness to interpret the primitive Christian eschatology.

At the close of the chapter the Paraclete is again introduced. The connection is that it is on account of their witness to Christ that the disciples incur the world's hatred; but their witness is continuous with that of the Spirit.

Many commentators take the present paragraph to run on into ch. 16, some to 16.4, others to 16.11, others to 16.15. There is indeed no break:

ch. 16 recognizes particular forms that the hatred of the world may take, and shows how the witness of the Paraclete and of the disciples bears upon the world. It is however convenient (though by no means necessary) to pause at the end of ch. 15 before the themes of hatred and judgement are elaborated.

18. εἰ ὁ κόσμος ὑμᾶς μισεῖ, as in fact it does. The hatred of the world was a known datum of Christian experience long before John wrote. Cf. Tacitus, *Annales* xv, 44, *per flagitia inuisos*. This is real hatred, and not, as in the Semitic idiom (cf. 12.25), a matter of liking less.

γινώσκετε may be either indicative or imperative. Either would make sense. The older VSS. give the imperative (e.g. it vg, *scitote*), and in default of other argument may well be followed.

ἐμὲ πρῶτον ὑμῶν. πρῶτος is incorrectly used in comparison (the omission by ℵ* D it of ὑμῶν somewhat improves this); but cf. 1.15. The point is that of 1 John 3.13; the disciples must not be surprised by the hatred they encounter. Cf. also Ignatius, *Romans* 3.3.

μεμίσηκεν. Cf. 7.7. The perfect brings out the enduring hatred of the world for Christ.

19. εἰ ἐκ τοῦ κόσμου ἦτε. This condition, unlike that of the previous verse, is not fulfilled. The disciples have been 'of the world' and they continue to be 'in the world' (17.11), but they have been chosen out of the world. Cf. 17.14.

τὸ ἴδιον, neuter, 'that which belongs to it'. For a neuter representing a group of persons cf. 6.37,39; 17.2, and perhaps 1.11, though here there seems to be a contrast between τὰ ἴδια and οἱ ἴδιοι.

ἐγὼ ἐξελεξάμην. Cf. v. 16 and the note. A further point of difference between John's thought and the gnostic systems is brought out. The disciples were not in themselves alien to the world, an essentially superior group; they were chosen out of the world.

διὰ τοῦτο resumes ὅτι, the usual Johannine order (διὰ τοῦτο ... ὅτι [or ἵνα]) being reversed.

20. μνημονεύετε τοῦ λόγου. Cf. 13.16. It may be that the present discourse should be thought of as a comment on the traditional material of ch. 13 (cf. Brown). The use of δοῦλος is somewhat surprising after 15.15, though it would be wrong to conclude from that verse that the disciples were no longer intended to render obedience and service to the Lord.

εἰ ἐμὲ ἐδίωξαν, καὶ ὑμᾶς διώξουσιν. A special application of the λόγος referred to. Doubtless John's readers knew its truth from experience, but the reference to persecution is too vague for us to use it in dating the gospel. See 16.1f., and for the theme of persecution cf. Odes of Solomon, 5.4; 23.20; 28.8ff.; 42.5,7.

εἰ τὸν λόγον μου ἐτήρησαν, καὶ τὸν ὑμέτερον τηρήσουσιν. John means, If there are some who persecute you, there will also be others who will keep your word. The mission of the church will result in the same twofold response as the work of Jesus himself (cf. especially 12.44–50). Cf. the work of the Old Testament prophets: the rejection of their message by the people as a whole and the formation of a remnant; no less, the work of the Hermetic prophets—

see especially *C.H.* 1, 29, καὶ οἱ μὲν αὐτῶν καταφλυαρήσαντες ἀπέστησαν, . . . οἱ δὲ παρεκάλουν διδαχθῆναι.

21. διὰ τὸ ὄνομά μου, 'because of me'. The disciples will be neither hated nor believed on their own account but on account of Christ who sends them. It is conceivable that there may be an allusion here to persecution 'for the name', but the general New Testament usage of τὸ ὄνομα (and the common Hebrew and Aramaic לְשֵׁם, לִשְׁמָא, 'for the name of' = 'for the sake of') does not favour this view. It is not inconsistent with this simple rendering to say that the name of Jesus is the challenge he presents as Revealer (Bultmann); it goes too far to say that the world will hate the disciples of Jesus because he bears the divine name (Brown).

ὅτι οὐκ οἴδασιν τὸν πέμψαντά με. Cf. 14.7; 17.3, and especially 16.3. To know God, that is, to recognize him in Jesus, is to transfer oneself from the world to the friends of Jesus, the church. ὁ πέμψας με is a very common Johannine description of the Father.

22. ἁμαρτίαν οὐκ εἴχοσαν (P⁶⁶ ℵ B; εἶχαν, D*; on the form εἴχοσαν, which is very common in the LXX and is to be preferred here and in v. 24, see M. I, 52; II, 194; Robertson, 335f.; B.D., §84). In this apodosis (after an unfulfilled condition in past time) ἄν would have been expected (as in v. 24); but in Hellenistic Greek 'the addition of ἄν in the apodosis is no longer obligatory' (B.D., §360). Cf. 8.39; 19.11. For the thought of the verse cf. 9.39–41 and the notes there. The coming of Jesus makes possible the ultimate and unmistakable manifestation of sin, which is disbelief in him (16.9); accordingly it passes judgement on the world. It is clear that by sin John means conscious and deliberate rejection of the light.

νῦν δὲ ('but now in fact', 'as it is') πρόφασιν οὐκ ἔχουσιν. πρόφασις is not used elsewhere in John, and the other New Testament uses (Mark 12.40 (= Matt. 23.13; Luke 20.47); Acts 27.30; Phil. 1.18; 1 Thess. 2.5) do little to explain the meaning here. The best rendering is 'excuse'; see L.S. *s.v.*, and cf. e.g. Xenophon, *Cyropaedia* III, i, 27, ἔχει μὲν προφάσεις τὰ ἡμέτερα ἁμαρτήματα. Those who have seen and heard Jesus are deprived of excuse because Jesus both exposes sin and is its remedy. The thought is taken further in 16.8–11.

23. ὁ ἐμὲ μισῶν καὶ τὸν πατέρα μου μισεῖ. Cf. 13.20 where the corresponding positive statement is made. John always insists that the work of Jesus is unthinkable apart from the constant activity of God. What Jesus does is done by God, and every attitude of men to him is an attitude to God.

24. τὰ ἔργα. On the works of Jesus and their value for faith see on 4.34; 5.36. In them divine activity was plainly visible; they therefore leave men without excuse for their unbelief. Cf. 9.32.

ἁμαρτίαν οὐκ εἴχοσαν. For the text, accidence, syntax, and meaning, cf. v. 22.

νῦν δὲ (cf. v. 22) καὶ ἑωράκασιν. In spite of the καὶ it seems best to supply, as the object of ἑωράκασιν, τὰ ἔργα μου.

μεμισήκασιν in tense follows ἑωράκασιν and also draws attention to the enduring hatred of the Jews.

καὶ ἐμὲ καὶ τὸν πατέρα μου—as follows from v. 23.

25. ἀλλ' ἵνα πληρωθῇ. Either the expression is elliptic ('These things are so happening in order that the word may be fulfilled') or ἵνα with the subjunc-

tive is used imperativally ('But let the word be fulfilled'—cf. Mark 14.49, and see Turner, *Insights*, 147f.). The ellipse is perhaps more probable; cf. 9.3; 13.18 and the references there given. For πληροῦν with a reference to Scripture cf. 12.38; 13.18; 17.12; 19.24,36. Explicit references to the verbal fulfilment of Scripture are comparatively rare in John (see *J.T.S.* old series 48, (1947), 155–69) and when they do occur are generally of special significance. Here the point (see next note) is that the Jews, who hate Jesus, are convicted out of their own Law.

ἐν τῷ νόμῳ αὐτῶν. For νόμος as including more than the Pentateuch, see on 10.34. Jesus distinguishes himself and his disciples from the Jews by speaking of '*their* Law'; see on 'your Law' at 10.34. The Jews' hatred of Jesus is referred to and described as causeless in their own Law; they are self-condemned and without excuse.

ἐμίσησάν με δωρεάν. The reference is either to Ps 35(34).19 or to Ps. 69(68).5. In both occur the words οἱ μισοῦντές με δωρεάν (שׂנאי חנם). Bernard (ad loc.) plausibly suggests that John had in mind the latter Psalm because it was regarded as messianic. Lindars adds the consideration that Ps. 69 is widely used in the New Testament. See J. Jocz, *The Jewish People and Jesus Christ* (1949), 43, for the statement in *Yoma* 9b that the Temple was destroyed 'because of undeserved hatred'.

26. ὅταν ἔλθη ὁ παράκλητος. For the word παράκλητος, and for the teaching connected with it, see on 14.16. In the synoptic persecution passages also there is reference to the Spirit; see e.g. Mark 13.11 (Brown).

ὃν ἐγὼ πέμψω (D, πέμπω) ὑμῖν παρὰ τοῦ πατρός. Cf. 14.26, ὁ πέμψει ὁ πατὴρ ἐν τῷ ὀνόματί μου. It is doubtful whether John intended any difference between the two statements, either in the gender of the relative or the subject of the verb.

τὸ πνεῦμα τῆς ἀληθείας. See on 14.16. Cf. 1 QS 3.18f.; 4.21,23.

ὃ παρὰ τοῦ πατρὸς ἐκπορεύεται. The mission of the Spirit is closely parallel to that of the Son; cf. 8.42, ἐγὼ γὰρ ἐκ τοῦ θεοῦ ἐξῆλθον; 13.3, ἀπὸ θεοῦ ἐξῆλθον; 16.27; ἐγὼ παρὰ τοῦ πατρὸς ἐξῆλθον, cf. vv. 28, 30; 17.8, παρὰ σοῦ ἐξῆλθον.

ἐκεῖνος. The gender changes; the occurrence in the previous clause of the neuter relative ὃ shows that this is not simply a matter of grammatical agreement with παράκλητος; the Spirit is thought of in personal terms.

μαρτυρήσει περὶ ἐμοῦ. Witnessing is one of the primary themes of the gospel; see on 1.7. Here only is the Spirit said to bear witness; his work in this respect is more fully expounded (though without the use of μαρτυρεῖν) in ch. 16. The connection with the context is important. Jesus testifies against the Jews, who hate him, and crowns his testimony with a reference to the Jews' own Bible. The Paraclete will continue to testify to Jesus. The disciples also bear witness (v. 27) and this introduces (16.1f.) the subject of persecution; and at 16.8 John returns to the convicting work of the Paraclete. The whole paragraph bears such strong marks of unity that it seems very improbable that the verses about the Paraclete have been inserted into already prepared material.

27. καὶ ὑμεῖς δὲ μαρτυρεῖτε. Cf. Acts 5.32. The Spirit and the disciples both continue the work of Jesus—naturally, not independently of each other.

'The Spirit is the power of the proclamation in the community' (Bultmann). Lightfoot compares the testimony of the blind man in ch. 9. Cf. Isa. 43.10.

ὅτι ἀπ' ἀρχῆς μετ' ἐμοῦ ἐστε. Their qualification is their long association with Jesus. Cf. Acts 1.22; 10.37. For this use of ἀρχή cf. 16.4; elsewhere in John ἀρχή refers not to the beginning of the ministry but the beginning of creation, or of time. ἐστε suggests continuity; the disciples have been and still at the moment of speaking are with Jesus; indeed their unity with him (as the last discourses constantly repeat) can never be permanently broken.

33. THE JUDGEMENT OF THE WORLD

16.1–15

It was pointed out above (pp. 479f.) that the preceding paragraph (15.18–27) is continued in the present one. Inevitably the church is separated from the world, and incurs the hatred of the world, which rejected the witness to the truth borne by Jesus and continues to reject the same testimony when it is presented by the disciples and by the Paraclete. This separation of the church from the world, and the world's hatred of the church, could be explained as a purely sociological phenomenon: an exclusive and somewhat mysterious group can hardly hope to be popular. The phenomenon however is not merely sociological; it is theological, and it is its theological significance that the new paragraph, after first restating the separation in historical terms (exclusion from the synagogue, and martyrdom), goes on to express. The real danger of the attack lies in the possibility not of death but of apostasy, and it is against this that Jesus proceeds to guard his disciples; the attack arises not out of dislike but out of refusal to recognize the revelation of God in Jesus. The world's attitude to the church's witness discloses its attitude to God; this means that the world itself is being judged. The synoptic apocalypses, already alluded to (see the introduction to 15.18–27), move to and culminate in the theme of judgement; and so do the Johannine discourses. Once more however the theme is transposed. The judgement is no longer primarily future (see however v. 13 and the note), but proceeds continuously through the operation of the Paraclete in the church. The Paraclete brings to bear, directly upon the church and mediately upon the world, the truth, the truth of God which was manifested in Jesus (1.18). Through him the ministry of Jesus is prolonged. The process of conviction in respect of sin, righteousness, and judgement serves as an analysis both of the ministry of Jesus and also of the mission of the church. The sin of the world, the righteousness of God, and the judgement which takes place when the two meet, are laid bare. But the seal is set upon the whole process by the departure of Jesus to be with the Father, and the gift, subsequent to his glorification, of the Spirit. This is why the departure of Jesus, painful though it may be, is nevertheless for the advantage of his disciples. This anticipation of the future takes place upon the stage of history, and it is therefore to some extent possible to reconstruct the historical circumstances implied (see especially Martyn's reconstruction); but John's thought is theologically rather than circumstantially motivated, and for that reason is relevant to more than one historical situation. The themes of this paragraph are developed further in the next.

1. ταῦτα λελάληκα ὑμῖν. Cf. 14.25. Here ταῦτα refers to the hatred of the world (15.18–27), which is mentioned again in greater detail in the next verse, while the judgement of the world by the Paraclete follows.

ἵνα μὴ σκανδαλισθῆτε. The only other use of σκανδαλίζειν in John (the word is especially characteristic of Matthew) is at 6.61; see the note. In both places it has considerable force, and means 'to cause to give up the Christian faith'. This use appears in later Christian writings, e.g. Didache 16.5, Hermas, Vis. IV, i, 3, Mand. VIII, 10 (in the passages in Hermas, however, the ἐσκανδαλισμένοι are waverers rather than apostates). John was undoubtedly thinking of the possibility that Christians might give up their faith under persecution; perhaps he had reason to know that the possibility was real. Such lapses took place: cf. Rev. 21.8; also, referring, it may well be, to defections made under persecution at about the same time, Pliny, Ep. x, xcvi, 6, [Christianos] fuisse quidem, sed desisse, quidam ante plures annos, non nemo etiam ante uiginti quoque (i.e. c. A.D. 92). The disciples are forewarned so that no surprise of persecution (cf. 1 Peter 4.12, μὴ ξενίζεσθε) may shake their faith. There is a somewhat similar warning, including the use of σκανδαλίζεσθαι, in Mark 14.27–31. This, like the present warning, is set in the context of the last supper, and John is probably developing traditional last supper material in the light of actual persecution (cf. Lindars). There is no good reason why he should not have known the tradition in its Marcan form.

2. ἀποσυναγώγους ποιήσουσιν ὑμᾶς. See on 9.22. It is fair to remark that the members of John's church are the ἀποσυνάγωγοι (Martyn, 20; cf. 24, 148).

ἀλλ'. For this pregnant use of ἀλλά ('and not only so, but further . . .') cf. 1 Cor. 3.2; 2 Cor. 7.11; Phil. 1.18. See B.D., §448.

ἔρχεται ὥρα. For this phrase see on 4.21,23. Here it refers to a real future; from the viewpoint of the last night of Jesus' life the time of persecution lies ahead. That the same word (ὥρα) is used with reference to the suffering of the disciples as with reference to the suffering of Jesus (e.g. 13.1) suggests that the former also is theologically significant.

ἵνα is explanatory; there is no need to suppose that it misrepresents the Aramaic ‫ד‬, intended as a temporal particle (cf. 12.23; 13.1; 16.32; see M. II, 470).

πᾶς ὁ ἀποκτείνας . . . τῷ θεῷ. Cf. the earlier threats to kill Jesus. Martyn (47f., 52) rightly points out that v. 2a takes up the move to 'excommunicate' Jesus (chs. 9, 10), v. 2b the attempt to kill him (chs. 5, 7). John may be given credit for perceiving the sincerity of motive which prompted the Jewish opposition to Christianity. Cf. Sanhedrin 9.6: If a man stole a sacred vessel or cursed by Kosem or made an Aramean woman his paramour, the zealots may fall upon him. If a priest served [at the Altar] in a state of uncleanness his brethren the priests did not bring him to the court, but the young men among the priests took him outside the Temple Court and split open his brain with clubs. Also *Num. R.* 21.4 (with reference to Num. 25.13): Did he then bring an offering, that power to make atonement should be attributed to him? This will teach you that every one who sheds the blood of the godless is like one who brings an offering. It would, of course, be a grave error to suppose that either of these passages gave general approval to indiscriminate bloodshed; or indeed was ever taken very seriously. John writes ironically here, as at 11.50–2. The death of the Christians in persecution truly is an offering to God. λατρεία occurs nowhere else in John, and in only four other places in the New Testament. In three (Rom. 9.4; Heb. 9.1,6) it refers to the worship of the Temple, and corresponds to the Hebrew עבודה (*'abodah*). For other references to Jewish persecution of (Jewish) Christians see (in the Synoptic Gospels) Matt. 5.10f.; 10.21f., 28; 24.8; Mark 13.12f.; Luke 6.22; 12.4; 21.12. Paul was a persecutor of such Christians (Acts 8.3; 1 Cor. 15.9; Gal. 1.13, 23; Phil. 3.6). It is unlikely that John's words arose merely out of imagination, but the evidence for the death of Christians at the hands of Jews is not extensive. See Acts 7.54–60; (12.2f.); Josephus, *Ant.* xx, 200; *Mart. Pol.* 13.1; Justin, *Trypho* 110.4; 131.2; 133.6; also D.R.A. Hare, *The Theme of Jewish Persecution of Christians in the Gospel according to St Matthew* (1967).

3. The whole verse is omitted by sin, perhaps through homoeoarcton. V. 4 begins *halen* (ἀλλά not being represented), and in the archetype v. 3 may have begun with *halen* (or *wᵉhalen*, as in pesh). After ποιήσουσιν, ὑμῖν is added by ℵ D a Augustine.

ὅτι οὐκ ἔγνωσαν . . . Cf. 15.21,23f. The aorist ἔγνωσαν if given its full force means that the Jews will persecute the Christians because they failed to recognize God in the person and work of Jesus.

4. Cf. v. 1. When the time of persecution comes the disciples will remember that Jesus had foretold it, and it will therefore not weaken but strengthen their faith, because they will see in it the fulfilment of his word and the confirmation of his supernatural knowledge.

ἡ ὥρα αὐτῶν. Cf. Luke 22.53, αὕτη ἐστὶν ὑμῶν ἡ ὥρα. Translate 'their hour' (of your persecutors), not 'the hour of these things' (which I have foretold). The 'hour' of Jesus appears to mean his failure but is in fact his exaltation and glory; that of his enemies appears to mean their victory but is in fact their defeat.

ἐξ ἀρχῆς, as at 6.64. Cf. ἀπ' ἀρχῆς, 15.27.

ὅτι μεθ' ὑμῶν ἤμην. There was no need to warn the disciples of danger while Jesus was with them for they were then under his immediate protection; cf. 18.8f., . . . ἄφετε τούτους ὑπάγειν . . . οὐκ ἀπώλεσα ἐξ αὐτῶν οὐδένα.

5. ὑπάγω . . . τὸν πέμψαντά με. The language is characteristically Johannine. For ὑπάγειν see especially 7.33; 13.33.

οὐδεὶς ἐξ ὑμῶν ἐρωτᾷ με· ποῦ ὑπάγεις; It seems both necessary and justifiable to emphasize the present tense ἐρωτᾷ; John does not write ἠρώτησε, which would involve a flagrant contradiction with 13.36; 14.5. Here he is dealing simply with the disciples' immediate reaction to the words of Jesus. The thought of his departure fills them with grief; but if only they had asked where he was going, and grasped that it was to the Father, they would not have grieved but recognized that his departure was for their advantage

(v. 7, συμφέρει ὑμῖν). The cause of their sorrow is their preoccupation with their own affairs (cf. 2 Kings 6.15); it must therefore be mastered by their coming to understand why they must be left alone (cf. Bultmann). Dodd (*Interpretation*, 412f.) has a different explanation of the apparent contradiction between this verse and 13.36; 14.5. He concludes, 'Jesus is reproaching them, not because they are not enquiring about His destination, but because in spite of knowing that He is going to the Father they are dismayed about the future' (413).

6. λύπη is characteristic of this chapter; see vv. 20, 21, 22.

πεπλήρωκεν. It is unusual for πληροῦν (active and transitive) to have as its subject that with which the object is filled. The effect is to give an almost personal force to λύπη: Grief has pervaded, taken possession of, your heart. Cf. Ps. 47.7 (LXX).

7. ἐγὼ τὴν ἀλήθειαν λέγω. On ἀλήθεια see on 1.14. It is quite possible that here ἀλήθεια means no more than truth as opposed to falsehood. 'It is no lie I am telling you; it is really true that my departure will be to your advantage.' It is however by no means impossible that the fuller meaning may have been intended. The Gospel itself consists in the fact that Jesus departs, for his departure means his death, his exaltation to heaven, and the coming of the Holy Spirit.

συμφέρει ὑμῖν. Cf. 11.50; 18.14 (the only other uses of συμφέρει in John). Both refer to the departure of Jesus in death and the consequent benefits, and though spoken by Caiaphas are regarded by John as unwittingly and ironically true. συμφέρει is usually followed by an infinitive (with or without article); John in accordance with his style substitutes an explanatory ἵνα clause.

ὁ παράκλητος οὐ μὴ ἔλθη (B; οὐκ ἐλεύσεται, ℵ D Θ ω). On παράκλητος see on 14.16. The thought is identical with that of 7.39; the coming of the Spirit waits upon the glorifying of Jesus. The Spirit is the agent of the creation of the church and the salvation of the world; in this sense the coming of the Spirit depends upon the completion of the work of Christ.

πέμψω αὐτόν. See on 14.16.

8. ἐλέγξει τὸν κόσμον. See Introduction, p. 90. ἐλέγχειν means 'to expose', for example, of sin, or error; hence 'to convict'. A. R. C. Leaney (*J. & Q.*, 45) points out that הוכיח (hiphil of יכח) is used in a somewhat similar sense ('to rebuke') in the Dead Sea Scrolls, and notes, in addition to passages where one man rebukes another, 1 QH 9.23, where God is the subject of the verb, and 1 QS 9.16, 17, where it appears (though this may be questioned) that the object of the process is not simply to prove an opponent wrong but to persuade him that he is wrong and so to change his mind. This use of the verb is however not confined to the Scrolls (see Jastrow), and does little to explain the meaning of John's Greek. ἐλέγχειν is used primarily by Greek moralists (e.g. Philo) of the conscience; many examples could be given. In some important passages Philo speaks of the Word (and kindred beings) as an ἔλεγχος; so e.g. *Det.*, 146 (though God punishes us he will of his mercy correct our faults), τὸν σωφρονιστὴν ἔλεγχον, τὸν ἑαυτοῦ λόγον εἰς τὴν διάνοιαν ἐκπέμψας; but it is to be noticed that Philo is speaking of those who are already συνειδήσει ... ἐλεγχόμενοι. The effect of God's Word is thus to intensify the work of conscience. It is accordingly natural in the present passage to see in the work

486

of the Paraclete an operation upon the conscience of the world, though John does not say in what way this operation will be effected. He has already said, however, at 14.17, that the world cannot receive the Paraclete, and we must therefore think of his work as mediated through the church, which alone can receive him, and in particular of the Spirit-inspired utterances of Christian preachers which convict the world. There may be a reminiscence here (and also in the word παράκλητος) of the synoptic sayings (Mark 13.11 and parallels) in which the assistance of the Spirit is promised to disciples when on trial. If so, John has characteristically (cf. chs. 9, 18f.) pressed home the idea so that the Spirit, not content with defending the believers, takes the offensive against the world. What this amounts to is 'a picture of the Church's evangelistic work in progress' (Sanders). There may elsewhere be hints (Johnston, Martyn) of the details of this progress, but here John is dealing with it in theological rather than circumstantial terms.

περὶ ἁμαρτίας καὶ περὶ δικαιοσύνης καὶ περὶ κρίσεως. On sin, righteousness, and judgement see the following verses in which John defines his meaning. In the present verse Sinaitic Syriac has 'concerning its sins, and concerning its (or his) righteousness, and concerning judgement'. This reading cannot be accepted as original, but is to be borne in mind when the interpretation of the nouns is considered.

9. περὶ ἁμαρτίας μέν, ὅτι . . . The structure of the sentence depends upon the way in which περί and ὅτι are taken. The main possibilities are three. (a) περί means 'in regard to'. The sentence may then be paraphrased 'He will convict the world (of its error) in regard to sin, showing it that sin consists in not believing in me'. If περί be translated in this way, ὅτι can hardly have any meaning other than that assigned to it in the paraphrase. (b) ἐλέγχειν περί means 'to convict of'. In this case two meanings of ὅτι are possible. One is 'because'. 'He will convict the world of its sin because that sin reached its complete demonstration in men's failure to believe in me.' (c) It is also possible to accept the rendering of ἐλέγχειν περί given in (b), and to give ὅτι the meaning 'that', 'in that'. We may then paraphrase, 'He will convict the world of its sin, in that men do not believe in me (or, namely, that they do not believe in me)'. None of these interpretations can be dismissed as impossible. (a) is particularly attractive because it is easily adaptable to the three words, sin, righteousness, and judgement. The world has wrong notions of all three. It believes that Jesus was a sinner, justly punished by crucifixion; it believes on the other hand that its own righteousness is all that can be required, and it believes that in these opinions it has rightly judged Jesus and itself, and that its judgement will receive divine confirmation. It is however the work of the Spirit to rectify these wrong notions, and to show that sin consists in the rejection of Jesus, that the only acceptable righteousness is that of Jesus, since he alone has been exalted to the Father's right hand, and that it is not Jesus but the prince of this world who has been judged. That this interpretation is sufficiently 'Johannine' cannot be disputed, but it is a grave objection to it that it requires us to give to ἐλέγχειν περί a sense different from that which it has at 8.46, where it must mean 'Which of you convicts me of sin (shows me to be a sinner)?' and cannot possibly mean 'Which of you convicts me of having wrong views of sin?' It will be necessary then to accept either (b) or (c). As has been noted,

these do not give as neat a connection with the next two verses as does (a), but the difficulty is not in fact great; see the notes on vv. 10f. The sense is, He will convict the world of the fact of sin (in men), of the fact of righteousness (in me), and of the fact of judgement, in which sin and righteousness stand side by side. The world will be compelled to admit these facts. (b) seems preferable to (c). John seems to be giving the fundamental ground of conviction of sin (and righteousness and judgement) rather than stating the content of sin (and righteousness and judgement). The present verse, then, will have the following meaning. The Spirit operating upon the conscience of men, through the witness of the church (which is not confined to preaching, though preaching is its plainest expression), will convince them of their sin. This finds some confirmation in the Sinaitic Syriac reading in v. 8 (see above); in the present verse the reading is 'sins' (possibly but improbably 'sinners'—Merx). It was perhaps natural yet mistaken to use the plural; the world's sins find their focus in its rejection of Jesus. The light shone in the darkness, but men preferred the darkness (3.19–21). The rejection of Jesus is not the only sin, but it is the type and crown of all sin, and ultimately the sin of the world amounts to the crucifixion of Christ.

10. See on v. 9. It is essential to remember the general significance in John of πρὸς τὸν πατέρα ὑπάγω, and of οὐκέτι θεωρεῖτέ με. They refer to the departure and disappearance of Jesus in an event which was at once truly death and truly a glorious exaltation. This compound event is throughout the New Testament regarded as setting the seal upon the righteousness of Jesus, and the righteousness of God; see especially Rom. 3.21–31. John does not separate the two elements in the compound event, but it may be said that Jesus' death proved his complete obedience to the will of God, and his exaltation proved that his righteousness was approved by more than human acclamation. The word δικαιοσύνη occurs only in this context in John; it is however, in a context determined by the theme of judgement, the necessary correlative of ἁμαρτία, and signifies in the first instance the innocence of Jesus (cf. the Hebrew רשע, צדק). The Syriac reading mentioned above (v. 8) probably makes this meaning explicit (though it could mean that the Paraclete proves that *the world's* righteousness is false). The possessive pronoun however is not original, and John may by the noun δικαιοσύνη mean justification (for the thought cf. Paul, and it may be some of the Qumran writings, e.g. 1 QH 4.30–7; 7.16–19, 28–31; 1 QS 11.10–15), the vindication of the believers whom the world attacks, thinking thereby to manifest its own piety (v. 2).

11. ὁ ἄρχων τοῦ κόσμου τούτου κέκριται. Cf. 12.31; 14.30, with the notes. The death of Jesus involved the downfall of Satan (the perfect κέκριται is written from the standpoint of the church). It is on the basis of this historical event that men may be convinced by the Spirit of the fact of judgement, and thus of their own judgement by God.

12. ἔτι πολλὰ ἔχω ὑμῖν λέγειν. Cf. v. 4b. There were things Jesus had not said during the course of his ministry; some he could not say even at the end. Yet in another sense he has said everything, for even the Paraclete adds nothing fresh but only brings to remembrance what Jesus has said (14.26; 16.13ff.). For the theme of the incompleteness of the ministry of Jesus see 'Theocentric', 364–8; also the essay by E. Bammel, in *Christ and Spirit in the New Testament* (Festschrift C. F. D. Moule, 1973), 199–217.

οὐ δύνασθε βαστάζειν ἄρτι. For βαστάζειν = 'to endure', 'support' cf. Acts 15.10; Gal. 5.10; Rev. 2.2f. This use of βαστάζειν is not common; see M.M. s.v. Cf. the Hebrew use of נשא (see B.D.B. s.v., Qal, 2.d). For the thought of truth which cannot be conveyed by teaching but only by the direct act of God cf. C.H. XIII, 2, (the truth about regeneration) οὐ διδάσκεται . . . ὑπὸ τοῦ θεοῦ ἀναμιμνήσκεται. See on 14.26.

13. τὸ πνεῦμα τῆς ἀληθείας. See on 14.16.

ὁδηγήσει ὑμᾶς. ὁδηγεῖν is a word characteristic of the Psalms. See e.g. Ps. 25(24).5, ὁδήγησόν με ἐπὶ τὴν ἀλήθειάν σου; 143 (142).10, τὸ πνεῦμά σου τὸ ἅγιον ὁδηγήσει με ἐν τῇ εὐθείᾳ. Cf. Philo. Mos. II, 265, . . . εἰ μὴ καὶ θεῖον ἦν πνεῦμα τὸ ποδηγετοῦν πρὸς αὐτὴν τὴν ἀλήθειαν. The (inspired) Hermetic prophet is summoned to become a καθοδηγός to the worthy, that they may through him be saved by God (C.H. I, 26; also 4.11; 7.2; 9.10; 10.21; 12.12). Cf. also Wisd. 9.11; 10.10,17. In some mystery religions there was a μυσταγωγός who led (ἄγειν) candidates for initiation into the mysteries. For ὁδηγήσει ὑμᾶς, the Vulgate and some Old Latin MSS. seem to have read διηγήσεται ὑμῖν; this seems to be an intended 'improvement'. There is no more than a remote parallel here with the work of the Qumran 'Teacher of Righteousness'. Cf. Isa. 43.19; 44.7, from the haphtarah corresponding to the Tabernacles lection Gen. 35.9 (Guilding, 115).

εἰς τὴν ἀλήθειαν πᾶσαν. This is the reading of B, which here has little support, though εἰς π. τ. ἀλ. is the reading of Ω. But ἐν τῇ ἀληθείᾳ πάσῃ has the best attestation (ℵ D W et al.—Θ has ἐν. π. τ. ἀλ.) and should probably be preferred. It need not be dismissed as a 'correction' to LXX usage, where ὁδηγεῖν is often followed by ἐν, since John himself certainly knew the LXX and may for that very reason have written ἐν. The difference in meaning between the two readings is slight, but whereas εἰς τ. ἀλ. suggests that, under the Spirit's guidance, the disciples will come to know all truth, ἐν. τ. ἀλ. suggests guidance in the whole sphere of truth; they will be kept in the truth of God (see on 1.14) which is guaranteed by the mission of Jesus. Brown however may well be right in saying that it is possible to make too much of the difference between the prepositions. According to Sanders, εἰς was original, and was removed because it was found theologically dangerous. According to 1QS 4.2, These are the ways in the world (of the spirits of light and of darkness): to illuminate the heart of man, and to make straight before him all the ways of true righteousness (צדק אמת). There is some parallelism here, but Braun rightly points out that the emphasis is on righteousness, and that truth (אמת) only qualifies it as genuine.

οὐ γὰρ λαλήσει ἀφ' ἑαυτοῦ, as Jesus had not spoken of himself (7.17; 12.49; 14.10). John never tires of emphasizing that the words and deeds of Jesus were not those of a wise and good man, or of a demi-god; they came from the only true God. Similarly the teaching of the Spirit is not merely inspiration in the ordinary sense; it is the teaching of God.

(a) ὅσα ἀκούει: ℵ b. (b) ὅσα ἀκούσει: B D* W vg. (c) ὅσα ἂν ἀκούσῃ: Ω a. (d) ὅσα ἂν ἀκούσει: Dᶜ Θ.

Of these readings (a) is that of Nestle, but (b) should be preferred. (d) is probably no more than an orthographical variant of (c): (c) is a grammatical improvement, and (a) a dogmatic improvement (the present tense suggests the eternal relations of the divine persons) of (b). The future in (b) is due to

John's careful emphasis upon the future operation of the Spirit; cf. 7.39 and the future tenses of 14.16 (δώσει); 14.26 (πέμψει, διδάξει, ὑπομνήσει), etc. The words conveyed by the Spirit to the church and to the world are the words of God; cf. 8.26, κἀγὼ ἃ ἤκουσα παρ' αὐτοῦ ταῦτα λαλῶ εἰς τὸν κόσμον.

τὰ ἐρχόμενα ἀναγγελεῖ ὑμῖν. ἀναγγέλλειν is used at 4.25; (5.15); 16.13,14,15 and perhaps at 16.25 (*v.l.* ἀπαγγέλλειν). At 4.25 (and 16.25) it is applied to the revelation of divine truth, and it is apparent that it is so used here. The difficulty lies in the identification of τὰ ἐρχόμενα. Two interpretations may be suggested. (*a*) From the standpoint of the night 'in which Jesus was betrayed' τὰ ἐρχόμενα are the events of the passion, which was about to take place, and include perhaps both the crucifixion and the resurrection. (*b*) From the standpoint of the evangelist τὰ ἐρχόμενα must be events still future, that is properly eschatological events. There can be little doubt that, if we view the last discourses as a whole, their standpoint appears to be that of the author. Accordingly, τὰ ἐρχόμενα are real future events. It does not follow from this that the work of the Spirit described here is simply that of inspiring predictive prophecy, though no doubt John (like Paul) would have accepted this as a genuine χάρισμα (cf. the fragment of the Preaching of Peter preserved in Clement, *Stromateis* VI, 6, where the apostles are said to have declared τὰ μέλλοντα in order that men might be without defence in the judgement). The final eschatological event is the unveiling of sin and righteousness, and hence of judgement; and it is precisely this function that John has just attributed to the Spirit. When the Spirit declares the things that are to come he declares them as already operative; the final judgement is anticipated in the conviction of the world by the Paraclete. It is not necessary, however, in accepting (*b*) to rule out (*a*); it is probable that John had both trains of thought in mind, since (as the language of going and coming, of seeing and not seeing, shows) he thought of the death and resurrection of Jesus as themselves eschatological events. The meaning of the last discourse, and especially of the Paraclete sayings, is that the interval between the last night of Jesus' life and the evangelist's own day is annihilated by faith. The whole church enters the supper room and participates in the glory of Christ, which was manifested in his death and resurrection and will be manifested eschatologically, as a present reality.

14. ἐκεῖνος ἐμὲ δοξάσει. Glory is the natural accompaniment of the Messiah in his coming at the last day; cf. Mark 13.26, and many other passages in Jewish and Christian literature. The Spirit, by realizing the eschatological functions of Christ, gives him this glory by anticipation. Cf. 7.39; ἐδοξάσθη in that verse refers to a simple fact, the exaltation of Christ before the coming of the Spirit, δοξάσει in this verse to the Spirit's work in bringing home the glory of Christ to the world. How this will be done is explained in the ὅτι clause.

ἐκ τοῦ ἐμοῦ λήμψεται καὶ ἀναγγελεῖ ὑμῖν. With ἐκ τοῦ ἐμοῦ cf. the plural form (ἐμά) in the next verse (which in turn gives place again to the singular). The meaning of ἐκ τοῦ ἐμοῦ is determined by the use of ἀναγγελεῖ, and by the contents of the preceding verses. It is the truth not simply of the teaching but of the mission and being of Christ which the Spirit declares to the world, as he puts into effect Christ's judgement of the world. The revelation apprehended by men is not however the whole sum of divine truth; hence the partitive ἐκ τοῦ ἐμοῦ, and the reminder in the next verse of the plurality of things which the Son shares with the Father.

15. πάντα ὅσα ἔχει ὁ πατήρ. Cf. 3.35; 5.20 and the notes.

λαμβάνει. The change of tense (cf. λήμψεται, v. 14) does not seem to be significant.

34. THE FUTURE, DISTANT AND IMMEDIATE

16.16–33

This paragraph gathers together the striking language of the last discourses—of going and coming, grief and joy, tribulation and peace, asking and receiving, seeing and not seeing, parable and open speech, unbelief and faith, the world and God. This fact confirms the paragraph in its present position; it would be wrong to place it elsewhere. Most of this characteristic language is marked by a studied ambiguity. For example, the sayings about going and coming can be interpreted throughout of the departure and return of Jesus in his death and resurrection; but they can equally well be interpreted of his departure to the Father at the ascension and his return at the *parousia*. By this ambiguity John means to convey that the death and resurrection were themselves eschatological events which both prefigured and anticipated the final events. The church of John's own day was living in the ἐρχόμενα (16.13) which it was the Spirit's work to declare. The connection with 16.8–15 is close and appropriate. Cf. 14.19–24 and the notes.

Vv. 25–33 bring the discourse back to the situation in the room of the supper in the hours immediately preceding the arrest and crucifixion. They do so, however, in such a way as to universalize the significance of these hours, which are so set forth as to represent the 'little while' of life in this age which becomes meaningful only in communion with God and Jesus, and in the light of eternity. John makes use of two synoptic themes—that of parables (cf. Mark 4.10–12) and that of the desertion of Jesus by the disciples (see the notes on vv. 29, 32). The two are closely related for they both signify that not even the Twelve were able to grasp the meaning of the life and teaching of Jesus and to adhere firmly to him, apart from the divine aid which was conditional upon the complete working out of God's purpose regarding Jesus—the glorification of the Son of man in death. In Mark, this theme is expressed in terms of the messianic secret; in these discourses John's main theological instrument is the doctrine of the Paraclete.

16. μικρόν. See on 14.19. See also Isa. 26.20, ἀποκρύβηθι μικρὸν ὅσον ὅσον, ἕως ἂν παρέλθῃ ἡ ὀργὴ κυρίου (and see the whole passage, Isa. 26.16–21, of which further parts are quoted at v. 21). The short spaces of time referred to here create a tension comparable with that of the imminent eschatology of other parts of the New Testament.

καὶ (regarded as Semitic by Torrey, 51) οὐκέτι θεωρεῖτέ με. Cf. 14.19; 16.10; 17.11. Clearly it is possible to take this disappearance of Jesus as that of his burial or that of his ascension.

ὄψεσθέ με. There is no doubt that the future of ὁρᾶν may here mean simply 'In two or three days, that is after my resurrection, you will see me again'. Cf. 20.18,15, where the seeing of the risen Jesus is described in the perfect tense. The future however recalls such passages as Mark 13.26; 14.62, where it is used of apocalyptic vision of the coming Son of man. Cf. also John 1.50f.; 11.40, where a beholding of glory strictly dependent upon Jesus is referred to in terms which are partly though not exclusively eschatological. So here, a second interpretation of the seeing of Jesus after 'a little while' arises. In addition to the resurrection as a historical event there is a coming that is beyond history. Cf. 14.23 where Jesus and the Father 'come' in a coming which is not simply that of the resurrection or that of the *parousia*. The vision of God, denied as a possible experience of the present life by Judaism as reflected in John (1.18, θεὸν οὐδεὶς ἑώρακεν πώποτε), is the goal of Hellenistic religion, and indeed of most religions. Cf. e.g. *C.H.* XIII, 13, πάτερ, τὸ πᾶν ὁρῶ καὶ ἐμαυτὸν ἐν τῷ νοΐ.—αὕτη ἐστὶν ἡ παλιγγενεσία, ὦ τέκνον. It is the peculiar Christian eschatology, which affirms the partial but not complete fulfilment of the conditions of the age to come, that enables John to use this Hellenistic language (see on 3.3); he retains the primitive Christian affirmations about the resurrection and the *parousia*, but fills in the period between them. See further on v. 21.

After this verse ὅτι (ἐγὼ) ὑπάγω πρὸς τὸν πατέρα (μου) is added by Θ ω vg sin pesh. It was probably added to prepare for the last part of the question in v. 17.

17. The question of this verse is a clear indication that, in John's own view, novel teaching has been given, and not unambiguously expressed.

ἐκ τῶν μαθητῶν, '*some* of . . .'. See on 7.40.

ὑπάγω πρὸς τὸν πατέρα. If the long reading in v. 16 is rejected we must look back to v. 5, and earlier in the discourse.

18. τί λαλεῖ] τί λέγει, (D) Θ: *om*. B. B is probably right; the omission is supported by the fact that two different supplements are found.

19. ἔγνω. Perhaps the use of γινώσκειν rather than ἀκούειν suggests that John thought of supernatural discernment on the part of Jesus; though since the disciples were speaking to one another there is no reason why Jesus should not have heard them. See v. 30; they had no need to ask.

ἐρωτᾶν. Cf. v. 23.

περὶ τούτου looks forward to and is explained in John's manner by the ὅτι clause.

20. κλαύσετε καὶ θρηνήσετε ὑμεῖς. θρηνεῖν is found here only in John; κλαίειν is used only in connection with death (11.31,33; 20.11,13,15). For the conjunction of the two verbs cf. Luke 7.32, ἐθρηνήσαμεν καὶ οὐκ ἐκλαύσατε. See also Jer. 22.10, in a context of mourning for the dead. The pronoun ὑμεῖς is emphatic, and brings out the contrast between the disciples and the world.

ὁ δὲ κόσμος χαρήσεται. On the κόσμος see on 1.10. Here it stands over against the believing Christians, and over against Christ himself, as rejoicing in his death.

ὑμεῖς (emphatic again—you, in contrast with the world) λυπηθήσεσθε. λύπη is *grief*, caused often, though not necessarily (cf. e.g. Rom. 9.2; 2 Cor. 2.1) by death, or the prospect of death; similarly λυπεῖν, λυπεῖσθαι. The primary reference is to the grief of the disciples at the death of Jesus (16.6), though they may well fear the threat to themselves (16.2).

εἰς χαρὰν γενήσεται. Cf. 20.15f.,20. γίνεσθαι εἰς is a construction common in the New Testament; e.g. Mark 12.10 (and parallels); Luke 13.19; Acts 5.36. It corresponds to the Hebrew ל היה. See M. 11, 462; B.D., §145.

21. ἡ γυνὴ ὅταν τίκτῃ λύπην ἔχει. There is no reference here to a specific woman (by way of 2.4; 19.25ff.; Gen. 3.15f.; or Rev. 12) or to the synagogue; the article is generic—any representative woman. See also below on ἄνθρωπος.

λύπην ἔχει. The parallel is in itself a simple one: the short travail pains give place to satisfaction at the birth of a child—the short sorrow of Good Friday and the following day give place to the joy of Easter. But the analogy has a deeper meaning. It belongs to the Old Testament; see especially Isa. 26.16–19 (... ὡς ἡ ὠδίνουσα ἐγγίζει τεκεῖν ... οὕτως ἐγενήθημεν ... ἀναστήσονται οἱ νεκροί, καὶ ἐγερθήσονται οἱ ἐν τοῖς μνημείοις, καὶ εὐφρανθήσονται οἱ ἐν τῇ γῇ ...); 66.7–14 (πρὶν τὴν ὠδίνουσαν τεκεῖν ... καὶ ὄψεσθε, καὶ χαρήσεται ἡ καρδία ὑμῶν ...). In these passages the messianic salvation which relieves the affliction of the people is compared to the relief and joy of childbirth, and from them (and like passages) was drawn the later Jewish doctrine of the חבלי המשיח (ḥeble ha-mashiaḥ, the 'travail pains of the Messiah'), a period of trouble which must intervene before the final consummation. The significance of these facts is that the death and resurrection of Jesus were described in a language which is properly eschatological; that is, John treats them as types and anticipations of eschatological events. The resurrection means, in an anticipatory way, the realization of the messianic salvation. It goes a little too far to say that 'by combining the terminology of Easter and the Parousia, the Evangelist shows that for him they mean the same thing' (Bultmann; he adds that, in view of the Paraclete passages, 'Pentecost belongs to Easter and the Parousia too'); John does not identify Easter and parousia, but sees their coherence and uses it to explain the period between them.

ὅτι ἦλθεν ἡ ὥρα αὐτῆς. Cf. the frequent references in John to the 'hour' of Jesus, e.g. 17.1, ἐλήλυθεν ἡ ὥρα. ἡμέρα (read by P⁶⁶ D it sin pesh) may attempt a more general reference to the 'day of the Lord'.

ἄνθρωπος is used in its proper sense, a *human being* (contrast ἀνήρ, an *adult male*). The expression is neither linguistically Aramaic nor messianic. The image of the travailing woman is used in 1QH 3.6–18; see especially 3.10, with its allusion to Isa. 9.6: (there shall come forth) out of the womb of the pregnant woman a wonderful counsellor, with his heroic power (פלא יועץ עם גבורתו; in 3.9 the word גבר (*man*) is used). But the reference is not messianic in a personal sense (see Lohse's note *ad loc.*; also Braun), and it is not relevant to John's analogy.

εἰς τὸν κόσμον. Cf. the rabbinic phrase 'those who come into the world'. for human beings; see on 1.9. But the phrase is a self-evident one and there is no ground here for the view that John's thought was formulated in a specifically Jewish way.

22. καὶ ὑμεῖς, 'you in the same way'.

νῦν ... ἔχετε. Cf. vv. 5f.; the mere prediction of Jesus' departure was sufficient to grieve the disciples. νῦν, however, refers primarily to the time of Jesus' departure, and also to the interval of waiting between the resurrection and the *parousia*. Cf. v. 33. ἕξετε (P⁶⁶ D W Θ it) is a pedestrian 'improvement' and should be rejected.

πάλιν δὲ ὄψομαι ὑμᾶς, καὶ χαρήσεται ὑμῶν ἡ καρδία. Cf. Isa. 66.14, ὄψεσθε, καὶ χαρήσεται ἡ καρδία ὑμῶν. John's allusion to the Old Testament seems beyond question, and the change from 'You shall see' to 'I shall see' can hardly be accidental. Cf. Gal. 4.9, νῦν δὲ γνόντες θεόν, μᾶλλον δὲ γνωσθέντες ὑπὸ θεοῦ; I Cor. 13.12. John's grasp of the eschatological situation of the church allows him to speak of 'seeing Christ' and so of 'seeing God in Christ' (see v. 16, 14.9; 1.18); yet he holds so surely the fundamental biblical faith in the invisibility of God (his self-disclosure in Christ excepted) that here he insists upon the prior truth: I shall see you (cf. 15.16, I chose you).

τὴν χαρὰν ὑμῶν οὐδεὶς αἴρει ἀφ' ὑμῶν. John's thought returns to the opening verses of the chapter, which dealt with persecution. The same thought recurs in v. 33.

23. ἐν ἐκείνῃ τῇ ἡμέρᾳ. In the New Testament 'that day' or 'those days' often refers to the last days, the end of the age; so, e.g., Mark 13.11,17,19, 24,32; 14.25; Acts 2.18; 2 Tim. 1.12,18; 4.8; Heb. 8.10; 10.16 (=Jer. 31(38).33); Rev. 9.6. John must have been aware of this Christian usage; see on 14.20. There is a similar transference of 'day' from an eschatological context to present experience in Odes of Solomon 41.4 (Bultmann).

ἐμὲ οὐκ ἐρωτήσετε οὐδέν. The interpretation here depends upon the meaning of ἐρωτᾶν. In classical usage it is distinguished from the partial synonym αἰτεῖν in that it means 'to ask a question', while αἰτεῖν means 'to ask for something'. In later Greek however ἐρωτᾶν, while retaining its original meaning, is sometimes used in the same sense as αἰτεῖν. (a) It is possible that this may be so here. John does use ἐρωτᾶν with the meaning 'to ask for something' (see 4.31,40,47; 14.16; 16.26; 17.9), and he also has the habit of working with pairs of synonyms (e.g. ἀγαπᾶν and φιλεῖν). If this view is accepted the point of the present verse lies in the contrast between ἐμὲ οὐκ ἐρωτήσετε ... αἰτήσητε τὸν πατέρα: you will bring your requests not to me but to the Father. The disciples will have immediate access to the Father, who himself loves them (v. 27) and will grant their requests. (b) It seems however more probable that in this verse ἐρωτᾶν and αἰτεῖν are to be distinguished. John always uses αἰτεῖν with the meaning 'to ask for something' (see 4.9f.; 11.22; 14.13f.; 15.7,16; 16.23f.,26) and does upon occasion use ἐρωτᾶν with the meaning 'to ask a question' (see 1.19,21,25; 9.2,19,21; 16.5,19,30). This is, in particular, the prevailing usage in this chapter. Moreover, John is drawing out a contrast between the present (the time of the ministry) and the future ('in that day'). The disciples have not asked Jesus for anything, but in chs. 13—16 they have asked many questions (13.24f.,37; 14.5,8,22; 16.17f.). John's meaning seems to be that in the time when the Holy Spirit is given and guides the believers in all the truth they will no longer ask such questions as, What is the meaning of the 'little while' of which Jesus speaks? Cf. 1 John 2.20, οἴδατε πάντες. The Christians are the true gnostics. John does not however reach this conclusion by a conventionally gnostic route. See the note on v. 21. 'That ... is the eschatological situation: to have no more questions!' (Bultmann). It is right to place a full stop after οὐδέν. The next words introduce a fresh point.

ἀμὴν ἀμὴν λέγω ὑμῖν. See on 1.51, and the last note. The formula usually introduces a fresh thought rather than a contrast.

494

ἄν τι αἰτήσητε τὸν πατέρα. For the construction and thought cf. 14.13f.; 15.16; for the construction (ἄν for ἐάν), 20.23.

24. ἕως ἄρτι οὐκ ἠτήσατε οὐδέν, 'You have made no petition'. It would not be true to say that they had asked no questions.

ἵνα ἡ χαρὰ ὑμῶν ᾖ πεπληρωμένη. Cf. 15.11, but the completion of joy is now more closely defined; it consists in the access to God which is described as asking and receiving.

25. ταῦτα ἐν παροιμίαις λελάληκα ὑμῖν. On ταῦτα λελάληκα ὑμῖν see on 14.25; on παροιμία see on 10.6. Here the contrast with παρρησία (see below) makes it clear that veiled speech, difficult of comprehension, is meant. This makes it unlikely that the reference is simply to the analogy of the woman in childbirth in v. 21. It is rather to the last discourses as a whole, or to all the teaching of Jesus, which John certainly represents as not having been understood (e.g. 14.9).

ἔρχεται ὥρα. See on 4.21,23. The 'hour' is not that of the immediately following sentences, but of the period after the resurrection, when the Spirit is given. The teaching of Jesus was necessarily obscure because of the veil which, until his work was complete, hung over his person. In comparison, the church's proclamation, focused upon the now crucified and glorious figure of Jesus, was plain, or at least was plain to those to whom the glorified Jesus was manifested (14.22).

οὐκέτι ἐν παροιμίαις . . . ἀλλὰ παρρησίᾳ. For παρρησία see on 7.4. The closest parallels to the present passage are 10.24; 11.14. This contrast recalls that of Mark 4.11 (ὑμῖν τὸ μυστήριον δέδοται τῆς βασιλείας τοῦ θεοῦ· ἐκείνοις δὲ τοῖς ἔξω ἐν παραβολαῖς τὰ πάντα γίνεται). In Mark a contrast is drawn between two groups; one is mystified by the teaching of Jesus, the other seizes upon the true meaning of the parables, because to it has been given the secret of the kingdom of God, which ultimately is the secret of the person of Jesus. John is well aware of this radical division brought about by the teaching and work of Jesus; but he is perhaps truer to the facts than Mark when he suggests that even the Twelve remained to the end among the mystified. For him the contrast is not between the multitudes on the one hand and the immediate circle of Jesus on the other, but between multitudes and disciples alike during the ministry, and the disciples after the resurrection. Cf. 2.22; 12.16; 13.7; and see in the next verses the horrifying emphasis laid by Jesus on the approaching desertion and denial. Only with the Spirit to teach them (when the 'hour' comes) will the disciples know and believe the truth.

περὶ τοῦ πατρὸς ἀπαγγελῶ ὑμῖν. All Jesus' incarnate life had been a revelation of the Father (1.18; 14.9); in the age of his glory there will be no new theme. ἀπαγγελῶ is read by P⁶⁶ B D W Θ and is almost certainly the true reading; ἀναγγελῶ (ω; ℵ has ἀπαγγέλλω, probably an accidental error) is due to assimilation to vv. 13, 14, 15. There is however no substantial difference in meaning.

26. ἐν ἐκείνῃ τῇ ἡμέρᾳ ἐν τῷ ὀνόματί μου αἰτήσεσθε. For both parts of the sentence cf. v. 23.

οὐ λέγω . . . There is no division between the Persons of the Godhead. Any thought of a merciful Son over against a just or wrathful Father is excluded: indeed, οὐ λέγω may suggest the combating of some such view as this. It would not however be true to say that John contradicts Rom. 8.34; Heb. 7.25, which speak of the heavenly intercession (ἐντυγχάνειν) of the Son, since these deal not with petitionary prayer but with the status of the Christian before God, a status which rests entirely upon the eternal consequences of the priestly work of Christ. Cf. 1 John 2.1.

27. αὐτὸς γὰρ ὁ πατὴρ φιλεῖ ὑμᾶς. It may be that αὐτός represents an Aramaic proleptic pronoun (on this usage see Black, 96–100), and is quite unemphatic. It is better, however, with Field (104), to compare the classical use of αὐτός, *proprio motu*—the Father himself, of his own accord, loves you, and needs no prompting from me.

ὅτι ὑμεῖς ἐμὲ πεφιλήκατε καὶ πεπιστεύκατε. These words taken as they stand might suggest that God's love is contingent upon the love and faith of men; only those who love and believe in Jesus are loved by God. This would contradict other passages, such as 3.16, and can hardly be John's intention, though his words are undoubtedly open to misunderstanding. He is in fact elaborating the language and thought of 15.13–15, where the disciples are called the φίλοι of Jesus since with him they form a unique circle of love. In the present passage the point is that the Father himself stands within this circle (as is indeed implied by 15.9f.).

The text at the end of this verse and the beginning of the next is in some confusion. The following points are worthy of notice. (*a*) ἐξῆλθον ἐκ τοῦ πατρός (v. 28) is omitted by D W b sin. The two verses are thus united: You have believed that I came forth from God and have come into the world. The attestation is strong and the reading may be original; cf. 14.4; here as there the shorter reading is somewhat clumsy and the expansion 'improves' it. The longer reading however finds support in the fact that repetition with slight variation is a Johannine characteristic (Lindars). (*b*) If the short reading in v. 28 is accepted, we should probably in v. 27 read παρὰ τοῦ πατρός (B D); otherwise παρὰ θεοῦ (P66 ℵ Θ; τοῦ θεοῦ, ω), the reading which differs from v. 28, would seem better. (*c*) Within the long reading in v. 28 there are the variants ἐκ τοῦ πατρός (B), παρὰ τ. π. (ℵ Θ ω); if the whole clause is not rejected, ἐκ, which differs from παρὰ in v. 27, should be preferred.

28. The long text of this verse (see above) is a complete summary, in John's manner, of the Christian faith. It expresses God's movement to the world in Christ; the moment of humiliation and revelation (ἐλήλυθα εἰς τὸν κόσμον); the return of Christ to the Father, which is both the consummation of his glory and the redemption of the world, since, as the discourses of chs. 13—16 have been designed to show, it was the condition and signal for the coming of the Spirit and the inauguration of a new dispensation of knowledge and life. If the shorter text (see above) is preferred, we have either such a summary, depending on πεπιστεύκατε; or (a break being made before πάλιν) a statement of the disciples' belief in the mission of Jesus from God, and a return to the theme of his going to the Father.

29. The chapter, and with it the last discourses, closes with a striking example of Johannine irony. In spite of Jesus' warning that the hour for plain speech was coming (and had not come, v. 25) the disciples leapt to the conclusion that, because they had acquired an orthodox faith (vv. 27f.), they fully

understood his meaning. They were answered by an unsparing disclosure of the truth about themselves.

ἐν παρρησίᾳ . . . παροιμίαν. On this contrast see on v. 25.

30. νῦν οἴδαμεν. νῦν is repeated emphatically from v. 29; the disciples are confident that now already, before the death and exaltation of Jesus, before the coming of the Spirit, they have reached the moment of knowledge. Their exposure (vv. 31f.) can therefore serve as the exposure of gnostic claims founded outside the Christian revelation.

οἶδας πάντα. This might be taken generally ('You have all knowledge'), but the next clause,

οὐ χρείαν ἔχεις ἵνα τίς σε ἐρωτᾷ, seems to necessitate a special reference to v. 19, Jesus had answered their question before they had asked it. Jesus knows the thoughts of men's hearts. (Cf. 2.24f.; it is attractive to conjecture that the original reading in the present verse was πάντας, πάντα being a corruption— cf. 1 John 2.20 for a similar corruption.) The context however requires generalization beyond v. 19. Jesus' disclosure of the truth was made upon his, and the Father's, initiative, and did not wait upon human inquiry; that is, it was motivated by spontaneous love (contrast the superficial sense of v. 27; see the note). 'Οἶδας πάντα means basically: "Thou art the Revealer," and it is the assent to Jesus' statement in v. 27. The answer to every question which can worry the believer has been contained in the revelation from the beginning' (Bultmann). ἵνα is explanatory, as often in John.

ἐν τούτῳ. This was a slight foundation for their (formally quite correct) belief. Cf. 1.48f.; 4.19,29 for faith grounded in Jesus' supernatural know-ledge. Whether ἐν is causal or local it may, but need not, represent the Semitic ב; M. II, 463.

31. ἄρτι πιστεύετε; The question does not perhaps deny the existence of some kind and measure of faith; but its complete inadequacy is shown in the next verse.

32. ἔρχεται ὥρα καὶ ἐλήλυθεν. The contrast with v. 25 is marked; the time of knowledge is future; the present is a time of offence and disaster. 'The eschatological hour is first of all an hour of dismay; before [man] can ap-preciate its χαρά he has to experience its λύπη' (Bultmann). This clause is followed as often by an explanatory ἵνα, which need not be thought to represent the Aramaic ד used as a temporal particle (M. II, 470).

σκορπισθῆτε ἕκαστος εἰς τὰ ἴδια. Cf. Mark 14.27, πάντες σκανδαλισθήσεσθε . . . πατάξω τὸν ποιμένα, καὶ τὰ πρόβατα διασκορπισθήσονται (quoting Zech. 13.7). The use of Zechariah in the interpretation of the passion is too widespread to permit us to infer use of Mark. The prediction finds a prompt fulfilment in Mark 14.50, καὶ ἀφέντες αὐτὸν ἔφυγον πάντες, which however has no parallel in John, where on the contrary the evangelist is at pains to represent as present at the crucifixion the beloved disciple (19.26f.) and a witness (perhaps identical with the beloved disciple, 19.35). 21.2 however seems to presuppose a return of the disciples, including the beloved disciple, to their homes in Galilee. A formal contradiction is avoided by the use of εἰς τὰ ἴδια at 19.27— the beloved disciple also went to his home; but it is difficult to avoid the conclusion that John is trying to represent two things at the same time: on the one hand the isolation of Jesus and the complete failure even of the

Twelve to understand and believe in him before the coming of the Spirit, and on the other the continuity between Jesus and the church which in the person of the ideal apostle was present at the supreme moment of the death and exaltation of the Lord. The former theme is almost certainly better history, and better theology too; crucifixion, resurrection, and the gift of the Spirit are the theological as well as the historical foundation of the church. At the time of the crucifixion Jesus was all the 'church' there was.

καί, 'and yet'. This meaning of καί is not necessarily Semitic, and based on ﬩ adversative.

ὁ πατὴρ μετ’ ἐμοῦ ἐστίν. Cf. 8.16,29. It is possible that John is here combating a misunderstanding of Mark 15.34. All Jesus' works, including the greatest, were wrought in harmony and communion with the Father; his isolation was apparent only.

33. ταῦτα λελάληκα ὑμῖν. Cf. 14.25. ταῦτα may refer simply to the preceding verse: I have foretold your desertion that you may know that it was not unforeseen, and may therefore not be tormented by remorse but have peace. More probably it refers to the whole of the discourse (especially from 16.1) which sets in its true context the θλῖψις the disciples will have to endure, and so ensures their peace.

εἰρήνην. Cf. 14.27 and the note. ἐν τῷ κόσμῳ. On the relation between the disciples and the κόσμος see especially 15.18–25.

θλῖψιν. Cf. v. 21. In the New Testament θλῖψις is used in two main senses: (a) of eschatological woes (e.g. Mark 13.19,24; Rom. 2.9), (b) of the afflictions, and especially the persecutions of the church (e.g. Mark 4.17; Acts 11.19; Eph. 3.13). These two senses are not to be sharply distinguished, for it seems certain that the primitive church regarded its sufferings as having eschatological significance (Rev. 7.14 is a particularly clear instance of the use of θλῖψις in both senses simultaneously). This is John's thought here, as v. 21 shows. Through the church, and especially through its love, its joy in the Spirit, and its persecutions, the eschatological salvation, anticipated in the crucifixion and resurrection and hoped for at the last day, is continually presented to the world.

ἐγὼ νενίκηκα τὸν κόσμον. νικᾶν occurs here only in John, but it is characteristic of 1 John (2.13f.; 4.4; 5.4f.). In 1 John 5.4f. we read of 'overcoming the world'; cf. 4.4, 'overcoming antichrists'. See also Wisd. 10.2; 1 Cor. 15.57; Odes of Solomon 9.11; 10.4. The humiliation of Jesus in the crucifixion is more truly seen as his departure in glory to the Father and the overthrow of the world, which, with a special clarity in chs. 13—17, is set forth as the opponent of Jesus and the church, as humanity organized apart from God (see further on 1.10). Usually it is the 'prince of this world' who stands out as the adversary of Jesus; see on 12.31. There are traces in the Synoptic Gospels also of the view that the death of Jesus was a struggle between him and evil powers (see H.S.G.T., 66ff.), but the thought becomes explicit in John. The present passage differs however from others in that it is not the 'prince' but the world itself that is defeated. What this means is not made clear. Superficially, John appears to distinguish the believers from the world so rigidly that (as in certain gnostic and similar systems) the final result can be only the complete destruction of the world by the victorious god. Yet clearly John thought that there would be (and doubtless was himself familiar with) conversions from the world to the church (17.20; 20.29). Nevertheless there remains within the world a principle of evil (17.15) which can only be defeated and destroyed. In fact the defeat and destruction have already taken place. Evil can no longer harm those who belong to Christ; it is exposed by the Paraclete; and in the end all the children of God will be safely gathered together in one.

35. THE PRAYER OF JESUS

17.1-26

This chapter falls into four divisions. In the first (vv. 1–5), Jesus addresses the Father, recalls his obedient completion of the work entrusted to him in the incarnation, and prays that the approaching hour (of his passion) may prove to be the decisive means by which he glorifies the Father and the Father glorifies him, the act at once of divine grace and of human obedience whereby he ascends to that state of glory which was his in the beginning with the Father. In the second (vv. 6–19), Jesus prays for the disciples who are gathered about him. They have been drawn together out of the world and they will be exposed to its attacks. Hitherto Jesus has himself preserved and enlightened them; he prays that in his absence they may be kept in the truth of God. They are to be kept in unity, with each other, in himself, and in God, and there is committed to them a mission to the world in which they continue to live. In the third section (vv. 20–4), the scope of the prayer is extended, not indeed to the world but to later generations of believers, who are dependent on the word of the apostles. They too must be one: and their unity will be the means of convincing and persuading the world. The final destiny of all believers is to live with Christ in the eternal world and to behold his glory. Lastly (vv. 25f.), Jesus reviews the result of his ministry. The world did not recognize God; but the believers have recognized the mission of Jesus from the Father, and therein have found, and will eternally find, knowledge and love.

As the gospel stands, the chapter intervenes between the Upper Room discourses and the arrest; Bultmann places it between 13.30 and 13.31 (with some words of 13.1 to introduce it), so that it precedes the discourses. In any case it is closely related to them. 'Almost every verse contains echoes' (of chs. 14—16) (Dodd, *Interpretation*, 417).In this there is nothing surprising: farewell discourses often end with a prayer in which the person taking his departure commends his friends, or his children, to God. Whether we can go further and add (with Dodd, *Interpretation*, 419) that the prayer is 'the spiritual and ethical reality of that ἀνάβασις or ὕψωσις of the Son of Man which is hereafter to be enacted in historical actuality on the cross' is another question. The prayer is not simply an interpretation of the crucifixion and resurrection (though it is this) but takes into account the circumstances that will follow them, just as it also fits into a specific place in the story of Jesus.

The Synoptic Gospels speak frequently of the prayers of Jesus (Mark 1.35; 6.46; 14.32–9; 15.34; Matt. 14.23; 19.13; 26.36–44; 27.46; Luke 3.21; 5.16; 6.12; 9.18,28f.; 11.1; 22.41–5; 23.(34),46), but only on rare occasions are we informed of the contents of his prayers. The most notable exceptions are the prayers in Gethsemane and those uttered from the cross. In John, Jesus offers a prayer at the raising of Lazarus, 11.41f.; at 12.27 (see the note) there is a prayer that recalls the Gethsemane story (Mark 14.35f.). The present prayer falls into roughly the same place in the story as the Gethsemane prayer, but (see especially Fenton for this) whereas the synoptic prayer brings out the meaning of the passion in terms of obedience at great cost the Johannine prayer makes no reference to cost, sorrow, or distress. It does however emphasize Jesus' obedience to the Father, obedience even unto death; the fact that his death is the means by which the glory of God is manifested; the choosing of the disciples out of the world; the revealing to them of God in the person of Jesus; their mission to the world; their ultimate unity in love, and their dwelling in Christ and in God. The effect of putting this summary into the form of a prayer is (as Dodd points out— see above) to consummate the movement of Christ to God which is the theme of the last discourses, and anticipates his lifting up on the cross. This is more important than the fact that certain other Hellenistic revelatory discourses, such as the first tractate (*Poimandres*) of the *Corpus Hermeticum*, also end in prayers (*C.H.* 1, 31f.). For the relevance and limitations of these Hermetic parallels see Dodd, *Interpretation*, 422f.

It will be seen from this account of the chapter that the common description of it as the 'High-priestly prayer' (already hinted at by Cyril of Alexandria), or the 'prayer of consecration', does not do justice to the full range of the material contained in it. It is a setting forth of the eternal unity of the Father and the Son in its relation to the incarnation and the temporary (and apparent) separation which the incarnation involved. Thus there arise the themes which have already been noted. They are dealt with elsewhere in the gospel, in teaching and in action; but here they are made to stand forth as they eternally are in the relation of the Son to the Father, for while the Son of God remains truly and visibly man it is in prayer that his union with God can be most clearly shown; this is part of, and also goes far towards explaining, the element of subordinationism that is to be seen in Johannine Christology (see 'The Father is greater than I'). At the same time, since the relation of the Son to the Father becomes known not by speculation but only through the divine act in history for the salvation of the world, the prayer reveals the nature and meaning of Christian life in the relation of the Christian to God and to the world.

It will be observed that there is in this chapter no reference to the

Holy Spirit (contrast chs. 14—16). It seems that for John the Holy Spirit remained a fundamentally eschatological concept (see Introduction, pp. 88–92), and was not yet expressed in terms of an eternal relationship within the Godhead (cf. 7.39).

The prayer is best read and interpreted in the context in which John has placed it—between the last discourses and the story of the passion. Other contexts are less important but may contain elements of truth. Thus there are parallels (see below) between the prayer of Jesus and the eucharistic prayer of *Didache* 10, and there is thus some plausibility in the view that the prayer developed in the setting of the liturgy of the eucharist. It is not however always observed that no celebrant could so identify himself with the Lord, and with the Lord's position in the night in which he was betrayed, as actually to say, in the first person singular, 'Glorify me . . . I have manifested thy name . . . I came forth from thee . . . I am coming to thee', and so on. There are parallels with the Lord's Prayer (Matt. 6.9–13 = Luke 11.2–4), but these are by no means extensive enough to cover the prayer as a whole; parallels also with the Odes of Solomon, especially 31.4f. (He lifted up his voice to the Most High, and offered to him the sons that were in his hands. And his face was justified; for thus his Holy Father had given to him), but these cannot do more than point to a common area of development (see *J. & Q.*, 128). There is not much to be said for the view (Guilding, 141f., 161f.) that the chapter is related to Gen. 48 (as a Hanukkah lection), or that it has a poetical structure (Brown, 748–51).

See further B. Rigaux, *Revue théologique de Louvain* 1 (1970), 289–319; J. Becker, *Z.N.T.W.* 60 (1969), 56–83; Käsemann, *Testament*.

1. ταῦτα ἐλάλησεν Ἰησοῦς. Cf. 14.25. ταῦτα refers to the discourses of chs. 13—16. John emphasizes that the address of Jesus to the disciples is over, and clearly distinguishes it from his address to the Father. For the connection between them, see above.

ἐπάρας τοὺς ὀφθαλμοὺς αὐτοῦ εἰς τὸν οὐρανόν. See on 11.41. For a number of references to the directions in which persons praying looked see A. D. Nock and A. J. Festugière, *Corpus Hermeticum* (1945), ΙΙ, 398f. (n. 342); but note also *C.H.* v, 10, where the author deprecates looking in any spatial direction (ἄνω, κάτω, ἔσω, ἔξω) for God.

πάτερ. Cf. 11.41; 12.27. This name for God is very frequent in John and the most natural for use in a prayer ascribed to Jesus. Cf. vv. 11 (π. ἅγιε), 25 (π. δίκαιε).

ἐλήλυθεν ἡ ὥρα. Cf. 2.4; 12.23. As in the latter passage, the hour which has been so long looked for and has now arrived is the hour of the Son's glory. Equally, it is the hour of his death. The gospel as a whole moves towards this point, and from this point John sees the possibility of the Christian faith and the Christian church emerge.

δόξασόν σου τὸν υἱόν. This is more explicit than 12.23; the glory of the Son proceeds from the Father, and is the consequence of the Son's obedience. Dodd (*A.S.*, 91) sees a reference to Isa. 49.3. For the connection between this clause and the next cf. Odes of Solomon 10.4 (I was strengthened and made mighty and took the world captive; and this became to me for the praise of the Most High and of God my Father).

ἵνα ὁ υἱὸς δοξάσῃ σέ. If the Father glorifies the Son by accepting his obedient suffering and through it exalting him to heaven, this is in order that the Son may by his obedience, thus ratified, glorify the Father. The religious papyrus quoted on 11.4 is valuable here (a) because it so strikingly illustrates the Johannine language, and (b) because it reveals precisely the opposite process of thought. In the papyrus a wonder-worker prays to be glorified *because* he has glorified the name of Horus; Jesus prays to be glorified *in order that* he may glorify the Father. See however vv. 4f., where John's thought approximates more closely to that of the papyrus.

2. Corresponding to (καθώς) the glorification for which Jesus prays, is the position he occupied, and the authority given him, before the incarnation.

ἔδωκας αὐτῷ ἐξουσίαν πάσης σαρκός. The Semitism πᾶσα σάρξ (כל בשר) occurs here only in John. For ἐξουσία see on 1.12 and for the gift of authority 5.27, ἐξουσίαν ἔδωκεν αὐτῷ κρίσιν ποιεῖν; but here the authority, as explained in the following words, is wider. Cf. Wisd. 10.2 (ἔδωκέν τε αὐτῷ ἰσχὺν κρατῆσαι ἁπάντων); also Matt. 28.18, and see Dodd, *Tradition*, 361ff.—but if John had been thinking in terms of 'Son of man' he would have used the title. The aorist may refer to a special empowering for the earthly ministry of the incarnate Son, or to a pre-temporal act proper to the constitution of the Godhead; the Son receives authority from the Father as *fons diuinitatis*. On the latter view the aorist would be in the strictest sense timeless. The former view however is to be preferred, and we should compare 1.32f.: the Son receives the Spirit that he may baptize with the Spirit. Cf. also *C.H.* 1, 27, where the prophet, having received the divine revelation, is sent forth to proclaim it δυναμωθεὶς καὶ διδαχθεὶς τοῦ παντὸς τὴν φύσιν καὶ τὴν μεγίστην θέαν.

ἵνα . . . δώσῃ. ἵνα is partly purposive ('. . . gave him authority . . . in order that he might give . . .'), partly explanatory ('. . . gave him authority to give . . .'). Alternatively, ἵνα may depend on δόξασον: Glorify him . . . that he may give. This seems more remote and therefore less probable. Brown suggests combining the alternatives. δώσει (B) is probably only an orthographical variant of δώσῃ; δώσω (ℵ) is an assimilation of person to that of the speaker. The aorist points to a specific gift—the gift of eternal life through the completed work of Jesus. The reading of D (ἔχῃ for δώσῃ αὐτοῖς) smooths the construction and is certainly secondary.

πᾶν ὃ δέδωκας αὐτῷ. The αὐτοῖς which follows shows that πᾶν, although neuter singular, refers to the disciples. Their unity is thus represented in the strongest possible way (not πάντες, 'all', but 'the whole'). Cf. v. 24. The theme of unity is constantly repeated in this chapter (vv. 11f., 20ff., 24, 26); here however the unity is assumed as a fact, whereas elsewhere it is the subject of prayer. It is also stated here and repeated later (vv. 6, 9, 24) that the disciples are men whom God has given to Christ; and in this way prominence is given in this chapter to the idea of predestination, which appears elsewhere in the gospel (e.g. 12.37–41; 15.16). The small group of disciples, previously selected by and known to God, stands over against the world. Two points distinguish John's conception from those of many gnostic systems in which a small circle of gnostics is foreordained to knowledge

502

and life: in John the status of believers rests entirely upon the act and gift of God, and upon the historic work and call of Jesus.

ζωὴν αἰώνιον. The completed work of Jesus thus means (a) the glorifying of the Father, and (b) the gift of eternal life to men. For ζωὴ αἰώνιος see on 1.4; 3.15. The phrase is very common in chs. 1—13; in chs. 14—17, only here and in the next verse (cf. 14.6, ζωή). The reason for this change is that in the earlier part of the gospel John represents the Gospel message to the world, the offer of eternal life to all who believe; in the final discourses he concentrates upon the group of believers who have been chosen out of the world and emphasizes the necessity of Christian love.

3. This verse must be regarded as parenthetical, but this does not mean that it is a gloss. John felt the necessity of a definition of eternal life, and being unable to use a footnote incorporated it into the prayer, to which it is grammatically attached (σὲ . . . ἀπέστειλας).

. . . ἡ αἰώνιος ζωὴ ἵνα γινώσκωσι (γινώσκουσι, D) σέ. On αἰώνιος ζωή see on 1.4; 3.15. The notion that knowledge of God is essential to life (salvation) is common to Hebrew and Hellenistic thought (see Introduction, pp. 32ff., 34f., 81f.). In the Old Testament knowledge is characteristic of the Wisdom literature (e.g. Prov. 11.9, Through knowledge (דעת) shall the righteous be delivered); but the use of the word in the prophets is even more important. See e.g. the prophecy of the good age in Hab. 2.14, The earth shall be filled with the knowledge (דעת) of the glory of the Lord (τοῦ γνῶναι τὴν δόξαν κυρίου), and the significant negative statement of Hos. 4.6, My people are destroyed for lack of knowledge (מבלי הדעת, οὐκ ἔχων γνῶσιν). Similar passages can be found in rabbinic Judaism. Thus Berakoth 63a Bar Qappara (c. A.D. 220) said: What is the smallest section of Scripture on which all the essentials of the Law hang? Prov. 3.6, Acknowledge him (literally, Know him דעהו), and he shall direct thy paths. Similarly Makkoth 24a; Amos came and reduced them [the commandments of the Law] to one, thus: (Amos 5.4) Seek ye me, and ye shall live [seeking God of course implies seeking to know him]. In Judaism, knowledge of God comes primarily through the Law and the Law is life (see on 5.39). For the equivalence of Law and Knowledge see e.g. Song of Songs R. 1.24 where Hos. 4.6 (Because thou hast rejected knowledge, I will also reject thee) is paraphrased, Thou hast forgotten the Law of thy God, therefore will I also forget thy children. From Qumran 1QS 2.2f.; 4.22; 9.3f.; CD 3.20 have been cited, but none of them provides a satisfactory parallel (Braun). Outside Judaism, the vision of God which the initiate received in the Hellenistic and oriental cults was the source of life and salvation. This notion in various forms reappears in, and indeed was the foundation of, gnosticism. It is found in a particularly refined form in the Corpus Hermeticum (see Introduction, pp. 38f., and note in particular C.H. 1, 3, μαθεῖν θέλω τὰ ὄντα καὶ νοῆσαι τὴν τούτων φύσιν καὶ γνῶναι τὸν θεόν; x. 15, τοῦτο μόνον σωτήριον ἀνθρώπῳ ἐστίν, ἡ γνῶσις τοῦ θεοῦ). Since the knowledge of God is central both in Judaism and in Hellenism it is not surprising to find it in Hellenistic Judaism also. See Philo, passim; e.g. Deus 143, τὸ δὲ τέρμα τῆς ὁδοῦ (the way of wisdom) γνῶσίς ἐστι καὶ ἐπιστήμη θεοῦ.

Clearly then the notion of knowledge as the ground of salvation is very widespread, but it must not be assumed that in all the sources quoted 'knowledge' means the same thing. For a discussion of this question see on 1.10

and Introduction, pp. 81f. The following points suggested by this verse may be noted here. (a) Knowledge of God and Christ gives life; but the same result follows from believing (20.31). Knowing and believing are not set over against one another but correlated. This suggests that John's conception of knowledge is close to that of the Old Testament. (b) Knowledge has also an objective, factual, side. Men must know the only true God (cf. 8.32, γνώσεσθε τὴν ἀλήθειαν). This objectivity is partly Greek but owes something to the native Jewish conception that God reveals himself, and is known, in concrete historical events. (c) Knowledge of God cannot be severed from knowledge of his incarnate Son; cf. 14.7; 20.31 and many other passages. This fact makes possible a unique fusion of the Greek and Hebrew conceptions of knowledge. Saving knowledge is rooted in knowledge of a historical person; it is therefore objective and at the same time a personal relation.

τὸν μόνον ἀληθινὸν θεόν. Cf. Philo. Spec. 1, 332, τὸν ἕνα καὶ ἀληθινὸν θεόν; Leg. ad Gaium 366, τὸν ἀληθινὸν θεόν; 3 Macc. 6.18, ὁ . . . ἀληθινὸς θεός; 1 Thess. 1.9; 1 John 5.20. The use of μόνος helps to explain the meaning of ἀληθινός (here and elsewhere). The God whom to know is to have eternal life is the only being who may properly be so described; he and, it must follow, he alone is truly θεός. See on 1.9.

ὃν ἀπέστειλας Ἰησοῦν Χριστόν. Parallelism with the previous phrase—σὲ τὸν μόνον ἀληθινὸν θεόν—suggests that ὃν ἀπέστειλας should be taken as the direct object, Ἰησοῦν Χριστόν being in explanatory apposition: '. . . that they should know . . . him whom thou didst send, that is to say, Jesus Christ'. For the mission of Jesus from the Father see on 20.21. To the thought of God and his envoy there is a parallel of sorts (noted by Betz, 129) in Lucian, Alexander 22, ἐγὼ καὶ Ἀλέξανδρος ὁ προφήτης μου.

4. ἐγώ σε ἐδόξασα ἐπὶ τῆς γῆς. The past tense contrasts with the forward-looking subjunctive of v. 1 (ἵνα . . . δοξάσῃ). A different kind of glorification is here in view. In v. 1 (cf. v. 2) the Son will glorify the Father by giving life to men; here the meaning of glorification is brought out by the next clause—

τὸ ἔργον τελειώσας. The participle should be translated "by finishing the work . . .". The Son glorifies the Father by his complete obedience and faithful fulfilment of his task. τελειώσας looks back upon the completed life of Jesus, and probably upon his death too (cf. 19.30, τετέλεσται). For ἔργον cf. 4.34. There is a close verbal parallel, probably dependent, in the Acts·of Thomas, 145, ἐπλήρωσά σου τὸ ἔργον καὶ τὸ πρόσταγμα ἐτελείωσα. Details of the 'work' Jesus has done are given in the following verses; cf. also 5.21f.— the work of the Son is κρίνειν and ζωοποιεῖν (Bultmann).

ἵνα ποιήσω. The 'explanatory' ἵνα, used for the infinitive.

5. καὶ νῦν δόξασόν με σύ. The νῦν, the aorist imperative, and the sharply juxtaposed pronouns are intended to bring out a contrast. In his obedient ministry Jesus has glorified the Father; now, in response to the death which sets the seal upon his obedience and his ministry, let the Father glorify him.

παρὰ σεαυτῷ, that is, by causing me to return to the position I enjoyed before the incarnation; cf. παρὰ σοί, and with both cf. 1.1, πρὸς τὸν θεόν. The glory, that is, is the heavenly glory of Christ; the prayer is a prayer for exaltation and ascension. After the crucifixion the Son of man will ascend where he was before (6.62). With πρὸ τοῦ τὸν κόσμον εἶναι cf. 8.58.

6. The thought now turns to the disciples, the first-fruits of the completed work of Christ.

ἐφανέρωσά σου τὸ ὄνομα. Cf. v. 26 (ἐγνώρισα). Revealing the name of God is a notion peculiar in John to this chapter. For the relation between revealing the name and glorifying God (v. 4) see Sidebottom, 40. Name and word are closely related (see Charlesworth, *J. & Q.*, 149–55), but not to be identified. The aorist ἐφανέρωσα sums up the work of the ministry (cf. ἐδόξασα, v. 4). Cf. Ps. 22 (21).23, διηγήσομαι τὸ ὄνομά σου τοῖς ἀδελφοῖς μου. For 'the name' as embodying the (revealed) character of God see B.D.B. 1028 a, b, and the references there given. Cf. Exod. 3.15, and especially Isa. 52.6, where knowledge of the name of God is promised for the future (ידע עמי שמי, γνώσεται ὁ λαός μου τὸ ὄνομά μου). In later Jewish literature the name of God commonly refers to the sacred tetragrammaton (יהוה, YHWH), which was no longer pronounced, except by the high priest in the Holy of Holies in the Temple. Sometimes 'the Name' (השם) was used as a reverential substitute for the word God. Jesus' manifestation of the name of God is his declaration of the invisible God (1.18). We are not to think of the revelation of a particular name (though Brown suggests 'I AM', and Dodd similarly אני הוא, or אני והוא—*Interpretation*, 417). The language is both biblical and gnostic.

ἐκ τοῦ κόσμου. See on 15.19.

σοὶ ἦσαν κἀμοὶ αὐτοὺς ἔδωκας. The disciples belonged to God from the beginning, because from the beginning he had predestinated them as his children. He gave them to Jesus to be his disciples as part of his gift of all authority (v. 2), and as contributory to his act of revelation. The love of Jesus for his own, shown in the fact that he laid down his life for them, and the mutual love of the disciples, are the true revelation of God in his essential activity of love.

τὸν λόγον σου τετήρηκαν. The third person plural perfect ending -αν (for -ασι) began to come into use in the second century B.C., and is undoubtedly the right reading here (cf. ἔγνωκαν in v. 7). See WH *Introduction*, Notes on Orthography 166; M. 1, 52; II, 221 (where Moulton's view is changed); B.D., §83. Nowhere else in John do we hear of men keeping the word of God. Jesus keeps it (8.55; cf. 15.10, ἐντολάς), and he bids his disciples keep *his* word (8.51f.; 14.23; cf. 14.24, λόγους; 14.15,21; 15.10, ἐντολάς). It is shown at 14.23f. that a distinction should be drawn between *word* (singular) and *words* (plural). The former means the divine message brought by Jesus taken as a whole, the latter is nearer in meaning to ἐντολαί, precepts. That the disciples have kept the word of God means that they have loyally accepted, and faithfully proclaimed, the truth of God in Jesus. This can hardly refer to the period of the ministry (especially in view of 16.31f. and similar passages). John is looking back (perhaps from the end of the first century) upon the work of the apostles.

7. νῦν. The meaning seems to be different from that of vv. 5, 13; not 'now, in the moment of glory', but 'now, at the end of the ministry'. Cf. 16.30. ἔγνωκαν seems to be the true reading. For this form of the verb see on τετήρηκαν, v. 6. There are several variants. ἔγνωσαν (φ 33) is probably due to assimilation to v. 8. ἔγνωκα (W) is probably an accidental error. ἔγνων (א it sin pesh sah) must not be lightly dismissed, but probably arose out of a mistaken following of the person of ἐφανέρωσα at the beginning of v. 6. In fact Jesus is still speaking of the disciples. The present verse and the next are explanatory of the last clause. The disciples have recognized that 'all things' have come to Jesus from God; 'all things' include ῥήματα, words; receiving the words of Jesus means keeping the word of God.

πάντα ὅσα δέδωκάς μοι παρὰ σοῦ εἰσιν. It would have been simpler, and less tautologous, if John had written 'Everything I have is from thee' rather than 'all things that thou hast given me are from thee'; but John, as ever emphasizes the dependence of Jesus, in his incarnate mission, upon the Father.

8. ὅτι. The disciples know the truth only because Jesus has given it to them and they have received it.

τὰ ῥήματα. In the incarnate mission of Jesus the λόγος of v. 6 is necessarily differentiated into numerous sayings, ῥήματα. The disciples have received the word of God in accepting (ἔλαβον) the sayings of Jesus. Cf. 6.63; by receiving the words of Jesus the disciples have received life (v. 2).

ἔγνωσαν ἀληθῶς. They have also, in the ῥήματα of Jesus, found knowledge, and learned the truth (and it is thus by receiving knowledge that they have received life). The truth is that Jesus has come not in his own name but from God. For the expression cf. 7.26. It may be that ἀληθῶς has been attracted away from ἐξῆλθον to the verb in the principal sentence.

ἐπίστευσαν. It is idle to seek a distinction between the two ὅτι clauses. 'Knowing' and 'believing' are used in the closest parallelism. On the relation between the two see on 17.3.

σύ με ἀπέστειλας. See on 20.21. As there, so in this prayer, the thought of the mission of the Son leads to the complementary thought of the mission of the disciples to the world (see especially v. 18).

9. ἐγὼ περὶ αὐτῶν ἐρωτῶ. After the introductory vv. 6–8 the prayer for the disciples begins, ἐρωτᾶν is here certainly synonymous with αἰτεῖν. The content of the prayer becomes explicit in the following verses; first, however, it is brought out by the contrast of the next clause.

οὐ περὶ τοῦ κόσμου ἐρωτῶ. The order of the words indicates the emphasis: It is not for the world that I pray. See on 15.19. It must be emphasized once more that John, having stated (3.16) the love of God for the κόσμος, does not withdraw from that position in favour of a narrow affection for the pious. It is clear (see especially v. 18) that in this chapter also there is in mind a mission of the apostolic church to the world in which men will be converted and attached to the community of Jesus. But to pray for the κόσμος would be almost an absurdity, since the only hope for the κόσμος is precisely that it should cease to be the κόσμος (see on 1.10).

περὶ ὧν δέδωκάς μοι. See v. 6.

ὅτι σοί εἰσιν. The world cannot be prayed for because, as the κόσμος, it has set itself outside the purpose of God. The disciples on the other hand belong to God as they do to Christ. The paradoxical predestinarianism of the gospel is brought out once more. The disciples belong to the Father and come to Jesus because the Father gives them to him (6.37,44); yet they become the Father's through their faith in Jesus and because they keep his word.

10. τὰ ἐμὰ πάντα σά ἐστιν καὶ τὰ σὰ ἐμά. For the change from masculine to neuter cf. v. 2. There seems to be here a definite intention of broadening the

thought. Not only are the disciples at once the Father's and the Son's; there is a complete mutuality of interest and possession between the Father and the Son. The Father and the Son are thus equal; yet their equality springs, as it were, from the Father's gift.

δεδόξασμαι ἐν αὐτοῖς. αὐτοῖς is most naturally taken as neuter, with reference to the πάντα held in common by the Father and the Son; it is however possible that καὶ τὰ ἐμά . . . ἐμά should be taken as a parenthesis, and αὐτοῖς will then look back to ὧν (v. 9, the disciples). The latter, the more personal, interpretation is perhaps the better in view of 13.31f.; 14.13. In these passages the Father is glorified *in* the Son, by the Son's obedient self-offering. In the former the stress lies upon the act of obedience, in the latter upon the fruit of that act (the prevailing prayer of the disciples). Here the disciples are the place (ἐν seems to be locative, though perhaps instrumental as well) where Christ is glorified, and, as the next verse shows, he will be glorified by their faithful fulfilment of their mission. The perfect tense δεδόξασμαι should be noted. Jesus had already in his ministry been glorified by the obedient trust of the Twelve, but the word also reflects the later standpoint of the evangelist.

11. Jesus once more, as very frequently in the last discourses, explains his approaching passion as going to the Father (ἔρχεσθαι, rather than ὑπάγειν or πορεύεσθαι, is used here because Jesus is speaking to the Father in prayer). The disciples are left in the world, in, that is, the position he himself occupied. They now, with the Holy Spirit, must bear witness to the world, and endure its hostility.

ἔρχομαι. After this word, D, with some Old Latin support, reads οὐκέτι εἰμὶ ἐν τῷ κόσμῳ καὶ ἐν τῷ κόσμῳ εἰμί. Cf. 3.14 (the longer text). This reading, though interesting, probably arose through accidental repetition of the first two clauses of the verse.

πάτερ ἅγιε. Cf. vv. 1, 5, 25; also the prayer in Singer, 36, and especially *Didache* 10.2, where πάτερ ἅγιε occurs in the eucharistic prayer. 'His holy Father' occurs in Odes of Solomon 31.5, quoted above. It is natural to suppose that the epithet 'holy' has special relevance to the petition that follows; and this is indeed so. The prayer for the disciples is that as Christ has sanctified himself, so they may be sanctified in unity with one another, in Christ, and for God. It is the original holiness of the Father which makes intelligible and possible the consecration of Jesus and the church. This is John's equivalent of the Old Testament 'Ye shall be holy for I am holy' (Lev. 11.44), which elsewhere in the New Testament is reproduced in a predominantly ethical sense (1 Peter 1.16, cf. Matt. 5.48). John, though no one could stress more strongly the ethical result of holiness in love, is careful to bring out the root of holiness in a relationship.

τήρησον αὐτοὺς ἐν τῷ ὀνόματί σου (D adds from v. 12, καὶ ὅτε ἤμην μετ' αὐτῶν ἐγὼ ἐτήρουν αὐτοὺς ἐν τῷ ὀνόματί σου); that is, preserve them as what they are, a group of men separated from the world as God's own possession. ἐν τῷ ὀνόματί σου may simply express this thought—'keep them as thine, as thy property'—or the ἐν may be instrumental. The name of God (see vv. 6, 26) is his revealed character.

ᾧ δέδωκάς μοι. And God's revealed character has been committed to Jesus.

Cf. 1.18; 14.9. Jesus himself has kept the disciples (see the next verse) and in so doing has acted in the character and with the authority of God. This is expressed by saying that God has given to Jesus his name. ᾧ must refer to ὄνομα, and it is doubtless the correct reading. οὕς and ὅ, which are attested by a few MSS., are 'corrections'; the former introduces again the notion that the disciples were given by God to Jesus (cf. vv. 2, 6, 9); the latter avoids the attraction of the relative. There is no need to suppose (Burney, 102f.) that ᾧ is a mistranslation of the Aramaic relative ד, which should have been rendered οὕς. It is true that οὕς gives a characteristically Johannine thought; but so does ᾧ.

ἵνα ὦσιν ἕν. The disciples are to be kept by God not as units but as a unity (ἕν, neuter). The unity of the disciples in love has already been stressed in the last discourses (13.34f.; 15.13), and will be stressed again in the prayer (vv. 21ff.); it is a demonstration of the truth of the Gospel.

καθὼς ἡμεῖς. It is such a demonstration because it is no merely human unanimity but is modelled upon, and springs from, the unity of the Father and the Son. Any body of men to be effective must be united, but the unity of Christians is thus differentiated from secular unity, including the unity or community (יחד, yaḥad) of Qumran, even where this is יחד אל, yaḥad 'el, God's unity (1QS 1 12). The thought is developed through the rest of the prayer; see below.

ᾧ . . . ἡμεῖς. These words are omitted by it sin, the last five words by P⁶⁶ The short text has much to commend it, since it is hard to find any good motive for the omission. Certainty, however, seems to be unattainable.

12. During the ministry Jesus himself watched over his own in the person of God.

For ᾧ, D Θ ω it vg read οὕς; see above. ᾧ δέδωκάς μοι is omitted altogether by ℵ* sin.

ἐφύλαξα is ordinarily a stronger word than τηρεῖν, but its military meaning is not to be pressed; cf. 12.25,47, the only other uses of the word in John. It is probably no more than a synonymous variation, in John's style, of τηρεῖν. The aorist sums up the process represented by the imperfect ἐτήρουν.

οὐδεὶς ἐξ αὐτῶν ἀπώλετο, none has been lost as a disciple. Cf. 18.9 for the fulfilment of Jesus' claim. On ἀπολλύναι, ἀπώλεια see on 3.16.

εἰ μὴ ὁ υἱὸς τῆς ἀπωλείας, Judas Iscariot. In the New Testament ἀπώλεια commonly means eschatological perdition, damnation (Matt. 7.13; Acts 8.20; Rom. 9.22; Phil. 1.28; 3.19; 1 Tim. 6.9; Heb. 10.39; 2 Peter 2.1; 3.7; (3.16); Rev. 17.8,11), and the same Semitic expression (υἱὸς τῆς ἀπωλείας =man destined for perdition) occurs in 2 Thess. 2.3, in an apocalypse in which it is foretold that the parousia of Christ will not take place 'except the falling away come first, and the man of sin (ὁ ἄνθρωπος τῆς ἁμαρτίας, v.l. ἀνομίας) be revealed, the son of perdition (ὁ υἱὸς τῆς ἀπωλείας)'. It seems probable that John saw in Judas this eschatological character who must appear before the manifestation of the glory of Christ (just as in 1 John 2.18,22; 4.3 heretical teachers are represented as Antichrist). It should be noted that the Semitism is traditional, not Johannine; it cannot be used to prove the existence of a Semitic source, or even of Semitic thought— rather the reverse.

ἵνα ἡ γραφὴ πληρωθῇ—probably the γραφή (Ps. 41.10) quoted in 13.18 rather than any prediction of Antichrist or Ps. 109.8 (Acts 1.20). Judas was thus 'a victim of teleological thinking' (Derrett, *Law*, 427), though how teleological thinking claimed its victim is explained neither by John nor by the modern writer.

13. νῦν δὲ πρὸς σὲ ἔρχομαι. Once more the movement of Jesus to the Father is underlined, here in order to bring out the contrast between the time when he was able in his earthly life to guard his own, and the time of his withdrawal.

ταῦτα λαλῶ . . . ἵνα ἔχωσιν . . . ταῦτα may refer to the content of the last discourses as a whole; in this case cf. 15.11. If ταῦτα refers to the prayer, cf. 11.42, where Jesus prays aloud διὰ τὸν ὄχλον. He himself, as the eternal Son in perpetual communion with the Father, has no need of the formal practice of prayer; but this human practice is the only means by which the communion he enjoys can be demonstrated to human observation, and forms the pattern for the communion which his disciples will subsequently enjoy. Hence it helps to convey to them his joy, which springs, as will theirs, from unsparing obedience to and unbroken communion with the Father. This can be looked at from either a gnostic or an eschatological angle. In the Odes of Solomon, where joy is a frequent theme, the former predominates.

πεπληρωμένην. For the expression cf. 16.24.

14. ἐγὼ δέδωκα αὐτοῖς τὸν λόγον σου. Cf. v. 6, and for the word of God which Jesus gave to his disciples see v. 17, ὁ λόγος ὁ σὸς ἀλήθειά ἐστιν. Jesus committed to them the truth of his relation to God, which they truly received (v. 8). To know this truth is to have eternal life (17.3; 20.31).

ὁ κόσμος ἐμίσησεν αὐτούς. Cf. 15.18f. for the inevitable hatred of the world for that which is intrinsically other than itself. The aorist ἐμίσησεν is written from the evangelist's standpoint. Force is lost if it is supposed (Torrey, 109, 114) to be due to the wrong pointing of שׂנא, read as *s*e*na'* (perfect, ἐμίσησεν) instead of *sane'* (participle, to be translated μισήσει).

καθὼς ἐγὼ οὐκ εἰμὶ ἐκ τοῦ κόσμου. The disciples share this 'otherness' of Jesus because he has chosen them out of the world (15.19), and because they have been born of the Spirit (3.3–8), not in any human way (1.13). On this correspondence see Käsemann, *Testament*, 69f. These words are omitted by P66* D it sin, perhaps because they seemed redundant in view of v. 16. This verse is omitted by a few MSS., perhaps for a similar reason.

15. ἵνα ἄρῃς αὐτοὺς ἐκ τοῦ κόσμου. ἵνα with the subjunctive replaces the infinitive that should follow ἐρωτᾶν (used here in the sense of αἰτεῖν); so at Mark 7.26; Luke 7.36; 16.27; John 4.47; 19.31,38; 2 John 5 (not elsewhere in the New Testament). The disciples, though not of the world, are in it (v. 11). It is their vocation to stay in it. It is possible that John intended to correct the apocalyptic view that the Christians would very shortly, at the *parousia*, be caught up from the earth (ἁρπαγησόμεθα, 1 Thess. 4.17; cf. ἁρπαγέντα, ἡρπάγη, 2 Cor. 12.2,4). 'No, the church's essential nature involves being the eschatological community in which the world is annulled *within* the world' (Bultmann). At the same time John opposes a gnostic kind of withdrawal of the elect from the world. Historically his words were no doubt intended in part as a warning to Christians not to fall back into the world.

509

ἀλλ' ἵνα τηρήσῃς αὐτοὺς ἐκ τοῦ πονηροῦ. Cf. vv. 11f. It is impossible to be certain whether John means ὁ πονηρός or τὸ πονηρόν. The only other uses of πονηρός in the gospel are 3.19; 7.7—both adjectival. But the use in 1 John (2.13f.; 3.12; 5.18f.) suggests strongly that John is thinking of the Evil One, not of evil. The death of Jesus means the judgement of the prince of this world (12.31; 14.30; 16.11), but he is not deprived of the power to harm the disciples, if they are left without divine aid. Cf. Matt. 6.13.

16. Cf. v. 14.

17. ἁγίασον αὐτούς. The ἅγιος group of words is of infrequent occurrence in John. ἁγιάζειν occurs at 10.36; 17.17,19; ἅγιος at 6.69; 17.11 (and at 1.33; 14.26; 20.22 with πνεῦμα). These uses, few as they are, are nevertheless important. The present verse is significant not least because whatever ἁγιάζειν means here, it can scarcely mean anything different in v. 19, where Jesus says ἁγιάζω ἐμαυτόν. At 10.36 God is said to have sanctified Jesus, clearly for his mission to the world. This is a normal and very common use of ἁγιάζειν; a person is set apart for a sacred duty. For example, Jeremiah was sanctified to be a prophet (Jer. 1.5, πρὸ τοῦ σε ἐξελθεῖν . . . ἡγίακά σε (הִקְדַּשְׁתִּיךָ), προφήτην εἰς ἔθνη τέθεικά σε); Aaron and his sons were sanctified to be priests (Exod. 28.41, καὶ ἁγιάσεις αὐτούς, וְקִדַּשְׁתָּ אֹתָם). The setting of the present verse is similar to that of 10.36; as there, the word ἀποστέλλειν is in the context. The disciples in their turn are to be set apart by God for a mission to the world. There is certainly no reason to think that they are consecrated to death. In other contexts ritual ablutions (Exod. 19.22) might be intended (Lindars). Cf. 1QS 4.20f.

ἐν τῇ ἀληθείᾳ. On ἀλήθεια in John see on 1.14. The article makes it difficult to translate simply 'in reality', 'in truth', as might otherwise be done. Here, as for example at 8.32, and as is required by the next clause, it means the saving truth revealed in the teaching and activity of Jesus. It is this truth which designates and separates the apostles for their mission.

ὁ λόγος ὁ σὸς ἀλήθειά ἐστιν. For the word of God cf. vv. 6, 14. Both λόγος and ἀλήθεια, 'message' and 'truth', approximate to the person of Jesus himself, who, as John emphasizes, is the Word and the Truth.

18. καθὼς ἐμὲ ἀπέστειλας . . . κἀγὼ ἀπέστειλα αὐτούς. The introduction of an apodosis by καί may be Semitic. For the thought see on 13.20; 20.21. Here the mission of the apostles is taken up into the supreme moment of the mission of the Son in which the task appointed him by the Father is completed. The aorist ἀπέστειλα is used of the sending of the disciples, although they are in fact not sent till 20.21 (πέμπω, present). John writes from the standpoint of his own age, but also regards the mission of the Son as virtually completed, and the mission of the church as virtually begun, at the last supper, in which the love, obedience, and glory of Jesus are fully represented.

εἰς τὸν κόσμον. Both Jesus and the apostles have a mission to the world. This fact must be set beside the limitation of Jesus' prayer to the disciples (v. 9) and to those who believe through their word (v. 20), the emphasis upon his love for his own (13.1 et al.), and the command that the disciples should love one another (13.34; 15.12f.). The world is to be invited, through the witness of the Holy Spirit and of the disciples, to enter this circle of prayer and love. Käsemann, Testament, 29f., argues that these words apply to all disciples and therefore presuppose the priesthood of all believers, which he is surprised to find at the end of the first century. But v. 20 must make it doubtful whether John has in mind more than the original witnesses; and cf. 1 Pet. 2.9; Rev. 1.6; 5.10; 20.6.

19. ὑπὲρ αὐτῶν ἐγώ (*om.* (P⁶⁶) ℵ W) ἁγιάζω ἐμαυτόν. See on v. 17, and on 10.36. There is nothing in the word ἁγιάζειν itself to make a reference to the death of Jesus necessary: this reference lies rather in the context, especially in the use of ὑπέρ; cf. 11.50–52; 15.13; 10.11; cf. also 1.29 and Mark 10.45, λύτρον ἀντὶ πολλῶν. If there is an allusion to Mark 14.24 (ἐκχυννόμενον ὑπὲρ πολλῶν) John is reinterpreting traditional eucharistic language in a non-eucharistic setting; in view of 6.51–8 this is not improbable. To consecrate oneself is the act of a servant of God, who makes himself ready for his divinely appointed task, and the task immediately ahead of Jesus was that of dying for his friends. The language is equally appropriate to the preparation of a priest and the preparation of a sacrifice; it is therefore doubly appropriate to Christ. Except as indicated in the note on v. 17, there is little Jewish material to illustrate the thought. The expression קַדֵּשׁ עַצְמְךָ ('sanctify thyself') occurs, but generally has an ethical sense. 1 QH 6.6–9 leads up to forgiveness, סליחה, and is thus not strictly relevant. Cf. *C.H.* 1, 32, ὁ σὸς ἄνθρωπος συναγιάζειν σοι βούλεται. The meaning of συναγιάζειν is not clear, but it is plain that the Hermetic prophet wishes in some sense to share the holiness of God. Festugière (in A. D. Nock and A. J. Festugière, *Corpus Hermeticum* (1945) 1, 19) translates; '. . . veut te prêter aide dans l'œuvre de sanctification'. Here apotheosis, or something of the kind, is in mind; and, though apotheosis strictly understood is foreign to John's thought, the present passage looks in the same direction. The Son who has prayed to be glorified now asks again in other terms that he may re-enter the divine life, in order that he may take his disciples with him and so, as it were, incorporate them into God.

ἐν ἀληθείᾳ. Here (contrast v. 17) there is no article, and if this verse stood alone the translation 'may be duly sanctified', 'may be sanctified indeed' would be necessary. But in view of the parallel in v. 17 it seems at least possible that John is restating the same thought, though he does not express himself without ambiguity.

20. οὐ περὶ τούτων, those gathered with Jesus at supper, probably (though this is never explicitly stated) the Eleven. There is a parallel to this verse in Deut. 29.13f. (LXX, 14f.)—I owe this reference to D. Daube.

ἀλλὰ καὶ περὶ τῶν πιστευόντων διὰ τοῦ λόγου αὐτῶν. John has already referred to the mission of the disciples εἰς τὸν κόσμον (v. 18). As their faith was itself the result of Jesus' mission to the world, so their mission will evoke faith. John now deliberately turns to view this process, the history of the church. For him there is no problem in the continued existence of an earthly society after the Lord's resurrection; Jesus himself willed it and prayed for those who should join it (cf. 20.29). The present participle πιστευόντων is timeless, and there is no need to see in it an Aramaism.

εἰς ἐμέ. πιστεύειν εἰς is a common Johannine idiom (see on 1.12) and εἰς ἐμέ should probably be constructed with πιστευόντων. Yet it must be admitted that the order of words would make it more natural to take εἰς ἐμέ with λόγου, and this is not impossible. For the use of such a prepositional phrase with λόγος cf. 2 Cor. 1.18, ὁ λόγος ἡμῶν ὁ πρὸς ὑμᾶς. If this construction is accepted the meaning will be 'their word of testimony to me'.

21. ἵνα πάντες ἓν ὦσιν. As at v. 15, ἵνα expresses the content of the request. Jesus prays that the whole church may be one, as he has already prayed that his own disciples may be one (v. 11). Sanders is probably right in deducing from John's stress on unity that this had already become a problem in the church. It is however clear that John has little interest in the church as an institution (Introduction, pp. 98f.), and, unlike Ignatius, he does not appeal for unity in institutional terms. The church's unity is not merely a matter of unanimity, nor does it mean that the members severally lose their identity. The unity of the church is strictly analogous to the unity of the Father and the Son; the Father is active *in* the Son—it is the Father who does his works (14.10)—and apart from the Father the deeds of the Son are meaningless, and indeed would be impossible; the Son again is in the Father, eternally with him in the unity of the Godhead, active alike in creation and redemption. The Father and the Son are one and yet remain distinct. The believers are to be, and are to be one, in the Father and the Son, distinct from God, yet abiding in God, and themselves the sphere of God's activity (14.12). Bultmann rightly points out that the kind of unity John has in mind, and the means by which it is to be secured, are given by the words of v. 20: τῶν πιστευόντων διὰ τοῦ λόγου. It is 'unity in the tradition of the word and of faith'. He continues: 'Such unity has the unity of Father and Son as its basis. Jesus is the Revealer by reason of this unity of Father and Son; and the oneness of the community is to be based on this fact. That means it is not founded on natural or purely historical data, nor can it be manufactured by organization, institutions or dogma; these can at best only bear witness to the real unity, as on the other hand they can also give a false impression of unity. And even if the proclamation of the word in the world requires institutions and dogmas, these cannot guarantee the unity of true proclamation. On the other hand the actual disunion of the Church, which is, in passing, precisely the result of its institutions and dogmas, does not necessarily frustrate the unity of the proclamation. The word can resound authentically, wherever the tradition is maintained'.

ἐν ἡμῖν. ἐν is repeated here by ℵ Θ ω vg pesh boh, but omitted, rightly, by P66 B D it.

ἵνα ὁ κόσμος πιστεύῃ ὅτι σύ με ἀπέστειλας. The unity of the church in God is the supreme testimony to the truth of the claim that Jesus is God's authorized emissary. The existence of such a community is a supernatural fact which can be explained only as the result of a supernatural cause. Moreover, it reveals the pattern of the divine activity which constitutes the Gospel: the Father sends the Son, and in his works the love of the Father for mankind is manifest, because the Son lives always in the unity of love with the Father; the Son sends the church, and in the mutual charity and humility which exist within the unity of the church the life of the Son and of the Father is reflected. The church's unity in word and faith means that the world is challenged to decide between faith and unbelief. It seems to be implied here that the κόσμος as a whole will believe, and therefore be saved. With this apparent universalism contrast 16.33. John retains the customary New Testament tension between universalism and the predestination of an elect remnant. In fact, the inevitable human imperfection of the church means inevitably an imperfect faith on the part of the world, and church and world alike must ever remain under the judgement and mercy of God.

22. In this and the next verses the theme of unity is repeated, but with variations of expression which introduce a number of new thoughts.

τὴν δόξαν ἣν δέδωκάς μοι. It is difficult to think that this statement does not presuppose the answer to the prayer of vv. 1, 5. John looks back upon the completed work of Christ, in which the glory of God has been bestowed upon him in his return to the Father.

δέδωκα αὐτοῖς. Christ has been glorified, and he has communicated his glory to the church, which, being in God, could not fail to share in the glory of God. This does not however teach a crude *theologia gloriae*. The glory is the glory of Christ, and the glory of Christ is acquired through, and is most completely expressed in, the crucifixion. The church receives glory on precisely the same terms, by unity in faith with the death and resurrection of Jesus, and expresses it in obedience, and pre-eminently in humiliation, poverty, and suffering. This is certainly not a promise of visible prosperity; cf. 16.33.

ἵνα ὦσιν ἓν καθὼς ἡμεῖς ἕν. See v. 21.

23. ἐγὼ ἐν αὐτοῖς καὶ σὺ ἐν ἐμοί. See on v. 21. It is impossible to draw any sharp distinction between 'I in them' and 'they in us'. It may be said with equal truth that Christ is in the Father and the Father in Christ, and the relation between the disciples and the Godhead is of a similar reciprocal kind.

ἵνα ὦσιν τετελειωμένοι εἰς ἕν, 'that they may attain perfect unity'. In John τελειοῦν is used at 4.34; 5.36; 17.4 of carrying out, or completing a task; at 19.28 of the fulfilment of Scripture. No other word of the τέλειος group is used in John. There seems to be reason for thinking (see Lightfoot on Col. 1.28) that Paul sometimes used these words with the initiatory rites of the mystery religions in mind, but there is no ground for such a view with regard to John. The idea of completeness is all that is involved here. Final completeness and unity can of course be achieved only when the number of the elect is accomplished at the time of the end, but these words do not exclude the notion that the church may be complete at every stage of its growth.

ἵνα γινώσκῃ ὁ κόσμος ... Cf. v. 21, ἵνα ὁ κόσμος πιστεύῃ ... On the relation between believing and knowing see Introduction, pp. 81f. and on 1.10; 17.3.

ἠγάπησας (*pr.*)] ἠγάπησα D φ a b sin pesh. The Western text may be due simply to accident—the dropping of a ς is an easy error, especially with another ἠγάπησας at hand. But it also repeats the scheme which has appeared so often in these discourses, the equivalence of the relation between the Father and the Son and the church. It is possible that John himself intended to repeat this scheme, and possible therefore that the Western reading is original. But the Western editor may well have hesitated to say that the Father loved the disciples as he loved the Son. Cf. however 16.26f.

24. πατήρ. The nominative (B) should probably be accepted, the vocative in the majority of MSS. being an assimilation to v. 1. It is however possible

that πατήρ should be regarded as a form of the vocative. See Robertson, 264, 461, and cf. v. 25, where πατήρ is combined with a vocative adjective (in v. 21 it would be possible to regard πατήρ as a real nominative).

ὅ (ℵ B D sin boh) is certainly to be preferred to οὕς. The tendency to alter the neuter into conformity with ἐκεῖνοι would be very strong, though the neuter is in fact Johannine (e.g. v. 2).

θέλω. The ordinary language of prayer breaks down because Jesus is speaking, as it were, within the Godhead. He expresses his will, but his will is identical with the Father's (4.34; 5.30; 6.38). After θέλω, ἵνα with the subjunctive is used for the infinitive to express the content of the wish; cf. the use of the same construction after ἐρωτᾶν (vv. 15, 21).

ὅπου εἰμὶ ἐγὼ κἀκεῖνοι ὦσιν μετ' ἐμοῦ. Contrast 13.33,36, where Jesus says that even the disciples cannot follow him, to be where he is, 'now'. To Peter he gives the promise, ἀκολουθήσεις δὲ ὕστερον. This prayer contemplates the time when such following becomes possible; that is, the thought of the last discourses comes finally to the eschatological hope that in the end the church will be with Christ in God. The way to this glory lies through suffering, for if Peter is to follow Jesus it will be in suffering before it is in triumph (cf. 21.18f.). Jesus is going to the Father's glory, through death; the disciples cannot follow him now because they are to be left in the world (v. 11); but they will follow, and see 'the δόξα that is freed from the veil of the σάρξ' (Bultmann).

ἵνα θεωρῶσιν τὴν δόξαν τὴν ἐμήν. This means the glory of Christ within the Godhead, his glory as God. In 2 Cor. 3.18 the Christians in this life behold the heavenly glory of Christ as in a mirror, and are themselves transformed by the vision from glory to glory. But this does not seem to be John's view; he thinks of the future consummation. With ἣν δέδωκάς μοι cf. v. 22.

ὅτι ἠγάπησάς με. The ultimate root of the final hope of men lies in the love of the Father for the Son, that is in the eternal relationship of love which is thus seen to be of the essence of the Holy Trinity.

πρὸ καταβολῆς κόσμου. Cf. v. 5, πρὸ τοῦ τὸν κόσμον εἶναι. The word is not used elsewhere in John, but is fairly common in the New Testament (Matt. 13.35; 25.34; Luke 11.50; Eph. 1.4; Heb. 4.3; 9.26; 1 Peter 1.20; Rev. 13.8; 17.8). The beginning and end of time are here brought together to find their meaning in the historical mission of Jesus and its results.

25. πατήρ (on this form see on v. 24) δίκαιε. Cf. v. 11, πάτερ ἅγιε. The short final section of the prayer begins. John applies the adjective δίκαιος to no other than God, and the whole group of words is of infrequent occurrence. It is significant here because it is by God's righteous judgement that the world is shown to be wrong, and Jesus and the disciples right, in their knowledge of God.

καὶ ὁ κόσμος . . . ἀπέστειλας. These words, with those of the next verse, summarize, and were no doubt intended to summarize, the substance of the Gospel. The world (see on 1.10) does not know God. There exists however a unique reciprocal knowledge between the Father and the Son. The Son alone, who from eternity has been in the bosom of the Father, knows him, as God knows all men. The disciples do not step into the place of Christ and know God as Christ knows him; but they know that God has sent Christ, and that accordingly Christ is the authorized agent and revealer of God. Their knowledge of God is mediated through Christ; and this, so far as John knows, is the only saving knowledge of God accessible to men. This thought is developed in the next verse. In this sentence the initial καί is obscure. It was probably intended to co-ordinate the statement about the world and the disciples: 'It is true *both* that the world did not know thee . . . *and* that these men knew . . .'. This involves treating ἐγὼ δέ σε ἔγνω as a parenthesis, though of course a very important one. Moule (*Idiom Book*, 167) doubts this way of taking the initial καί, but it seems preferable to Sanders' rendering ('although the world . . . yet I . . . and these . . .').

26. ἐγνώρισα αὐτοῖς τὸ ὄνομά σου. Cf. v. 6, ἐφανέρωσα; no difference in meaning is intended. γνωρίζειν is used at 15.15; not elsewhere in John. Jesus conveyed the revealed character of God to his disciples not only in his teaching but in his deeds and in his own person (14.9; 1.18).

καὶ γνωρίσω, in personal union, and through the work of the Holy Spirit. The two tenses of γνωρίζειν are mutually necessary lest the past become a mere historical record and the future lose the control of history.

ἵνα ἡ ἀγάπη . . . ἐν αὐτοῖς ᾖ. ἐν αὐτοῖς may be rendered either 'within them'. that is, 'within each one of them', or 'among them'. It is impossible to draw a sharp line between the two interpretations, and it may be said that each implies the other. If we take the former it means that the love of God as an active divine principle is at work within the heart of the Christian; but if this is so the same divine love cannot fail to be the relation existing between those who are so inspired. Because the love of God is in them it must needs be among them; and *vice versa*. The church is not a côterie of gnostics enjoying esoteric knowledge but a community of love.

ἣν ἠγάπησάς με. Cf. v. 24. The love which inspires and rules the church, and is its life, is the essential inward love of the Godhead, the love with which the Father eternally loves the Son (the love which God *is*, 1 John 4.8,16). See on 15.12–17.

κἀγὼ ἐν αὐτοῖς. Here also ἐν probably means both 'in' and 'among'. That God would dwell in the midst of his people was a regular feature of the messianic hope. The only proper object of the love with which the Father loves the Son is the Son, and it is because he is in the disciples, and in their midst, that they can be said to enjoy this love. Cf. 14.20, where the double relationship ὑμεῖς ἐν ἐμοὶ κἀγὼ ἐν ὑμῖν, is expressed. Cf. Matt. 28.20; the promise of the presence of Jesus is interpreted in the light of Paul's doctrine of the mutual indwelling of Christ and the believer. Jesus is leaving the world and going to the Father not that his disciples may be left solitary but in order that (ἵνα) he may abide in them and among them.

36. THE ARREST OF JESUS

18.1–11

The last supper ended, Jesus, accompanied by his disciples, went out, with no specified motive, to a garden (orchard, or plantation) beyond the Kedron, which was a common meeting place for them. Thither

Judas the traitor led a mixed company of Roman soldiers and Jewish police. Jesus, thus confronted with the power of this world, at once took the initiative. On his declaration of his identity his adversaries fell to the ground, and he secured the safe withdrawal of his friends. Peter, unwilling to be thus protected, struck off the right ear of a slave named Malchus, only to receive the rebuke of Jesus. Neither inward shrinking, nor outward force, nor the embarrassments of his friends could prevent him from laying down his life at his own time, in obedience to the Father and for the salvation of the world.

It was inevitable that the passion narrative should contain an account of the arrest of Jesus, especially because the arrest was bound up with the betrayal, but John in giving this account was probably dependent on the work of his predecessors, notably Mark. Detailed points of resemblance and difference between the Johannine and the earlier narratives are mentioned in the notes; here the following main tendencies in John's work may be observed.

(a) Topographical and other details are introduced. It is difficult to see how any theological purpose can be served by the names Kedron, Peter, and Malchus, and it may therefore be supposed either that John possessed other valuable sources of traditional material in addition to the Synoptic Gospels, or that with the lapse of time the earlier tradition came to be enriched with such personal details. Comparison with the apocryphal gospels (cf. e.g. Gospel of Peter 31; Acts of Pilate 1.1) suggests that the latter is the more probable alternative.

(b) The Romans are introduced at the opening of the passion narrative. This is historically improbable (see the note on v. 3) and seems to be due to John's desire to show that the whole κόσμος was ranged against Jesus. 'It becomes plain that the struggle between light and darkness cannot simply be played out in private, nor in the discussions that take place in fraternities and official religion. The world has been shaken to its foundations by Jesus' attack, so it seeks help from the power set over it to maintain order, and in this way the state too is drawn into the eschatological event. It cannot simply ignore the relevation' (Bultmann, 633).

(c) The synoptic narrative of the agony in Gethsemane is entirely omitted, though there is a plain allusion to it in v. 11 (cf. also 12.27–30 and the notes); we cannot suppose that John was ignorant of this tradition, but it did not accord with his purpose to represent the issue as in any sense doubtful.

(d) There is throughout the narrative an emphasis upon the authority of Jesus. He, not Judas or the tribune, is in command. He goes out (vv. 1, 4) to his arrest, identified by no treacherous kiss, but by his own act; he interrogates his captors, and fells them to the ground with a word; he rebukes and also preserves his own disciples.

(e) Jesus thus acts in defence of his disciples, that none of them may be lost, suffering on their behalf (cf. Mark 10.45).

These points have been fully brought out here because they recur throughout the Johannine passion narrative. It has been argued that in the omission of the Agony and the introduction of Roman soldiers John is following tradition older, and historically sounder, than that of the Synoptic Gospels. This is improbable. The omission of the Agony leaves the visit to the garden unmotivated; this means that John is not following a source but introducing modifications of his own into what could well have been the Marcan narrative.

1. ταῦτα εἰπών. By these words the passion narrative is bound to the discourses at the last supper; cf. 14.25; 16.1; 17.1; also 16.25.

ἐξῆλθεν, out of the room where the supper had been held; but see 14.31 and the note.

πέραν τοῦ χειμάρρου τοῦ Κεδρών. χείμαρρος (better, χείμαρρους) is an adjective meaning 'winter-flowing' which was used as a noun, meaning 'torrent', 'brook', or 'water-course' containing water perhaps only in the winter. Accordingly it represents the Hebrew נחל (naḥal). Thus נחל קדרון (naḥal Qidron) in 2 Sam. 15.23; 1 Kings 2.37; 2 Kings 23.6,12; 2 Chron. 15.16; 29.16; 30.14 is rendered χείμαρρος (more often χείμαρρους) Κεδρών; in these places (and in Jer. 31 (38). 40 where we have νάχαλ κεδρών) Κεδρών is clearly an undeclinable noun, transliterated from קדרון. In 1 Kings 15.13, however, we find ἐν τῷ χειμάρρῳ τῶν κέδρων, where the article shows κέδρων to be the genitive plural of κέδρος, a cedar. The same phrase is inserted by the LXX without any basis in our Hebrew texts in 2 Sam. 15.23, along with the transliterated form. The MSS. of John show an even greater variety at this point: (a) τῶν κέδρων, אᶜ B Θ ω boh Origen; (b) τοῦ κέδρου, א* D W a b sah; (c) τοῦ Κεδρών, A (Codex Alexandrinus) it vg sin pesh. Further small variations occur which need not be recorded. It seems clear that (c) in spite of its scanty Greek support is the original reading, and that copyists, detecting what they took to be a false concord, corrected either the article or the noun. This view is supported by the fact that no 'Cedar brook' is known in the neighbourhood of Jerusalem, while the brook Kedron was well known (e.g. to Josephus). It lay just to the east of Jerusalem, and was rarely filled with water. Cf. however M. II, 149; 'These [readings (a) and (b) above] would plausibly figure as independent attempts to regularize the reading of A, regarded as Greek; and so Lightfoot (Bibl. Essays, 174) actually read. But it seems better with WH to accept τῶν κέδρων as a Greek popular etymology of Kidron: it is needless with them to labour a proof that this etymology was correct. . . . An interesting parallel occurs in Ps. 82.10, where "some inferior MSS." (Lightfoot) have τῶν κισσῶν, making Kishon into "ivy brook".'

ὅπου ἦν κῆπος. John is the only evangelist to use κῆπος in narrative (cf. Luke 13.19). Mark and Matthew describe the scene of the arrest as a χωρίον and give the name Gethsemane, which is mentioned by neither Luke nor John. Luke says that Jesus went to the Mount of Olives (i.e. across the brook Kedron). κῆπος, if it means 'orchard' or 'plantation', will agree well enough with χωρίον. John says also, with less probability, that the crucifixion and burial took place in a κῆπος (19.41). εἰσῆλθεν, ἐξῆλθεν in vv. 1, 4, suggest a walled enclosure, and from v. 2 we learn that Jesus and his disciples frequented the place. It is not profitable to guess at its owner. The dropping of the name Gethsemane, and the addition of Kedron and κῆπος, are taken by Dodd to be strong evidence that John was not using Mark. These facts cannot, however, prove more than that Mark was not John's only source of information, which is certainly true.

οἱ μαθηταὶ αὐτοῦ. John omits the agony of Jesus (see on v. 11, and on 12.27) and consequently does not distinguish between the whole body of disciples and the three mentioned in Mark 14.33. As in Luke, all are present; here with a view to vv. 8f.

2. ᾔδει δὲ καὶ 'Ιούδας. This verse suggests that what Judas betrayed to the Jewish authorities was the place where Jesus might be found and conveniently arrested. Whether such a betrayal was necessary or even helpful has been doubted (see e.g. A. Schweitzer, *The Mystery of the Kingdom of God* (E.T. 1925), 214–18), but John does not help us to find any other explanation.

ὁ παραδιδούς. The participle has become almost a technical term in the gospels: Matt. 26.25,46,48; (27.3, *v.l.* παραδούς); Mark 14.42,44; Luke 22.21; John 13.11; 18.2,5. Cf. the other forms παραδούς, Matt. 10.4; John 19.11; παραδώσων, John 6.64; μέλλων . . . παραδιδόναι, John 12.4.

πολλάκις. This is possible if the Johannine account of the ministry is presupposed, but it is inconsistent with the one short visit to Jerusalem of the Marcan.

συνήχθη. The passive of συνάγειν is unusual in the singular (otherwise than with a collective noun). We must translate 'Jesus often met there with . . .'.

3. λαβὼν τὴν σπεῖραν. In the Synoptic Gospels Judas appears at the head of an ὄχλος (πολὺς ὄχλος, Matthew). The participation of Roman forces at this stage of the proceedings against Jesus seems improbable, since the first step was apparently for the Jews to frame a charge that might be brought before the Governor, and Roman soldiers would have taken Jesus at once to Pilate, not to the high priest. So, rightly, E. Haenchen, *Die Bibel und Wir* (1968), 187, with the observation that 18.29 implies that the Romans had not participated in the arrest; Winter's defence of the historicity of the Johannine account on the grounds that John would have no motive for inserting a reference to Roman troops is implicitly answered above. The suggestion (Guilding, 167) that John was influenced by Deut. 28.49 (as the eagle flieth) is unnecessary. σπεῖρα usually means a cohort, a unit of the Roman army containing (normally) 600 men; but it could also mean a maniple (200 men), and probably means a company no larger than this at Mark 15.16. If John was freely constructing his narrative he may well have meant cohort (this is supported by the appearance in v. 12 of the tribune, the commander of a cohort); but if there is any historical basis for his statement maniple is more probable; the larger detachment would have been unnecessary and might have left the city dangerously unguarded. It may well be asked what authority Judas had to 'take' a detachment of soldiers of any size; but since the commander was present John probably means no more than that Judas acted as guide (and, of course, as instigator of the proceedings).

ἐκ τῶν ἀρχιερέων καὶ ἐκ τῶν (א D a; τῶν B; *om.* Θ ω) Φαρισαίων ὑπηρέτας. For the construction cf. 1.24. See also 7.32 and the note. The two groups are several times mentioned together (7.32,45; 11.47,57; 18.3). By ἀρχιερεῖς John evidently means the priestly aristocracy. The Pharisees (see on 1.24) do not

518

appear again after this point. Clearly John regards the ἀρχιερεῖς as the official leaders of 'the Jews' who put Jesus to death; but it cannot be said that he wished to exonerate the Pharisees, or they would not have been mentioned at this decisive point. The Sadducees are not referred to in John. ὑπηρέται, in John, are always a sort of military police (7.32,45f.; 18.3,12,18,22; 19.6; cf. 18.36, the ὑπηρέται of Jesus); doubtless the Temple guard, acting under orders of the Temple officer (סגן הכהנים; cf. Acts 4.1), whose usual function was to watch the Temple at night (*Middoth* 1.2). Their arms and methods are recalled in a 'street-ballad' (Klausner, 337):

Woe is me, for the house of Boethus! woe is me, for their club!

Woe is me, for the house of Annas: woe is me, for their whisperings!

Woe is me, for the house of Kathros (Kantheras): woe is me, for their pen!

Woe is me, for the house of Ishmael (ben Phiabi): woe is me, for their fist!

For they are the high priests, and their sons the treasurers: their sons-in-law are Temple-officers, and their servants beat the people with their staves. (*Pesahim* 57a; *T. Menahoth* 13.21 (533).)

φανῶν καὶ λαμπάδων καὶ ὅπλων. Cf. Phrynichus XL (Rutherford, 131f.), φανὸς ἐπὶ τῆς λαμπάδος ἀλλὰ μὴ ἐπὶ τοῦ κερατίνου λέγε. τοῦτο δὲ λυχνοῦχον λέγε. This implies that while φανός and λαμπάς were synonymous in the older Greek, in the later φανός had come to mean a lantern. Lanterns and torches are mentioned only by John. They need not be thought out of place on the night of the paschal full moon; they may have been intended for use in case of an attempt at concealment, or the night may have been cloudy. It is not impossible however that John may have intended by means of these feeble lights to stress the darkness of the night in which the light of the world was for the moment quenched. For ὅπλων cf. the passage quoted in the preceding note.

4. For εἰδώς, ἰδών (D φ sin) may be correct, the common reading being an attempt to give the passage a more supernatural appearance. Lindars suggests that ἰδών may be due to the influence of Luke 22.49, and the theme of supernatural knowledge is Johannine; cf. 1.47f. One of John's Christological methods may be to depict Jesus as a θεῖος ἀνήρ (cf. p. 74), but he. is certainly an unusual member of the species; contrast Philostratus, *Life of Apollonius* VIII, 5, where Apollonius conveniently vanishes from the Emperor's court.

τὰ ἐρχόμενα ἐπ' αὐτόν, the things that were about to befall him. Cf. 16.13, the only other place in the gospel where ἐρχόμενα is used in the sense of 'things to come'.

ἐξῆλθεν. Out of the κῆπος; Jesus gives himself up to death of his own will; cf. 10.18.

5. Ἰησοῦν τὸν Ναζωραῖον (Ναζαρηνόν, D it vg). Apart from this context John uses the adjective once only (19.19, in the *titulus* on the cross). It is found twice in Matt. (2.23; 26.71), once in Luke (18.37) and six times in Acts (and once more of the Christians, 24.5). John once describes Jesus as ὁ ἀπὸ Ναζαρέθ (1.45). Mark uses Ναζαρηνός four times, Luke twice. The meaning of Ναζωραῖος in John has been disputed; for a full list of views see Brown. That in other contexts the word had other meanings is certain (see Gärtner, 5–36),

but John appears to have used it as a patrial as if it meant ὁ ἀπὸ Ναζαρέθ (1.45; see the full and still valuable note by G. F. Moore in *Beginnings* I, 426–32). The word seems not to have been much used in the Greek-speaking church (not in the New Testament epistles, Revelation, the Apostolic Fathers, or the Apologists) and its appearance in John may probably be taken as a proof that the evangelist was familiar with traditional gospel material other than that contained in Mark.

ἐγώ εἰμι. I am Jesus of Nazareth, whom you seek. Cf. 9.9, ἐγώ εἰμι, I am the man who was born blind; also Mark 14.44, αὐτός ἐστιν. The predicate of ἐγώ εἰμι is thus to be supplied from the context; but it is possible that there is a reminiscence of words spoken (13.19) before the departure of Judas, . . . ἵνα πιστεύητε ὅταν γένηται ὅτι ἐγώ εἰμι. For the meaning of the words see on 13.19, and on 8.24; cf. 6.35 and note. After εἰμι the word Ἰησοῦς is added by B (a) It was probably added by dittography of the following letters. εἱστήκει was often spelt ἱστήκει (indeed it is so spelt by WH); the first two letters might easily be written twice; but I͞C was the common contraction of the name Ἰησοῦς. It is of course not impossible that the reverse process took place, and that I͞C was accidentally omitted. If this was so there is no question about the meaning of ἐγώ εἰμι. But there is no variant in v. 8, and there if not here the simple ἐγώ εἰμι must be explained.

εἱστήκει δὲ καὶ Ἰούδας. In John the traitor does not identify Jesus by a kiss (cf. Mark 14.44f.); Jesus identifies himself, and gives himself up. Bultmann's reference to Euripides, *Bacchae*, 434–40, where the god Dionysus gives himself up without resistance, is interesting, but does little to explain John's meaning. Judas remains standing with his followers. The ancient interpretation that he was blind, or paralysed and unable to move, goes perhaps too far, but it rightly conveys the thought, which John means to suggest, of the complete impotence of all but Jesus, who now stands alone over against the world.

6. ἀπῆλθαν εἰς τὰ ὀπίσω καὶ ἔπεσαν χαμαί. The thought is stressed further. The mere speech of Jesus (perhaps because expressed in language proper to God himself—see on 8.24) is sufficient to repel his adversaries. ἐγώ εἰμι is not itself (though some have said so) the divine name, which is יהוה, not אהיה or אני הוא, but it recalls the way God speaks. The language describing the recoil of Jesus' opponents may have been modelled upon Ps. 55(56).10, ἐπιστρέψουσιν οἱ ἐχθροί μου εἰς τὰ ὀπίσω, ἐν ᾗ ἂν ἡμέρᾳ ἐπικαλέσωμαί σε ἰδοὺ ἔγνων ὅτι θεός μου εἶ σύ. Cf. Ps. 26(27).2. εἰς τὰ ὀπίσω is an unnecessarily long way of saying ὀπίσω; it is found several times in the New Testament. ἀπῆλθαν εἰς τὰ ὀπίσω occurs at 6.66, and consequently cannot here be given a violent meaning. χαμαί is peculiar to John in the New Testament (9.6; 18.6); properly it means 'on the ground', but it is often used in place of χαμᾶζε, 'to the ground'. For such reaction to theophanies cf. Dan. 10.9; Acts 9.4; 22.7; 26.14; Rev. 1.17 (Lindars).

7f. Question and answer are repeated, and the independence and authority of Jesus underlined.

ἄφετε τούτους ὑπάγειν. Jesus purchases the safety of the disciples at the cost of his own life. It is by no means impossible that an apologetic motive may be detected in this ascription of the disciples' flight to the intention of Jesus himself, but, especially in view of the clause that follows, it seems to be John's primary intention to show, in an acted parable, that the 'good shepherd lays down his life for the sheep' (10.11); cf. Mark 10.45. He also sets the disciples in a more favourable light; they do not as in Mark (14.50) simply run away, but escape at Jesus' own bidding.

9. ἵνα πληρωθῇ. The phrase ἵνα (ὅπως) πληρωθῇ is several times used in John and often elsewhere in the New Testament, of the fulfilment of prophecy; only in John (here and 18.32) is it used of the fulfilment of words of Jesus (cf. however Mark 13.31). The reference here is to 17.12 (cf. 6.39); the exception (ὁ υἱὸς τῆς ἀπωλείας) is not mentioned here because Judas had already taken his place with the powers of darkness (v. 5b). This verse has been taken to be a redactional gloss, exhibiting a crassly materialist and prosaic misunderstanding of 17.12. This view is rightly rejected by Dodd; the escape of the disciples is an illustration of, not a substitute for, their eternal salvation. See the previous note. Brown notes that the notion of fulfilment puts Jesus' words on the same level as the Old Testament; but see already Mark 13.31.

οὓς δέδωκάς μοι. This clause forms a *nominativus pendens* taken up by ἐξ αὐτῶν. This construction is very characteristic of John's style; cf. e.g. v. 11.

10. Σίμων οὖν Πέτρος. The double name is common in John. The incident here described is found in the Synoptic Gospels (Mark 14.47 and parallels), but none of them names the aggressive follower of Jesus. It is characteristic of the later tradition to add names and make identifications which are not in the earlier sources (cf. 12.4). See Lagrange and Taylor on Mark 14.47, who suggest that εἶς τις means 'a certain person known to me'. Mark knew (it is suggested) that the man who struck the blow was Peter, but for reasons of security or respect did not mention his name.

ἔχων μάχαιραν. Cf. Luke 22.38. The word means knife, or dagger, rather than sword, and the anarthrous participle means no more than 'he happened at that moment to have with him a dagger'. It is often said that to carry such a weapon on Passover night was forbidden. On this question see Dalman 96f., Jeremias, *Eucharistic Words*, 75f.; on the general question of the date of the last supper see Introduction, pp. 48–51. In any case regulations would be dispensed with by men who foresaw real and imminent danger. To carry a weapon for self-defence does not in itself make a man a Zealot.

τὸν τοῦ ἀρχιερέως δοῦλον. The article seems to draw attention to the particular slave named, Malchus; but it appears also in the Synoptic Gospels where no name is given, so that it is not impossible that some particular official of the high priest is referred to. We have however no information on this score.

ἀπέκοψεν. Matthew, Mark, and Luke have ἀφεῖλεν.

ὠτάριον. This diminutive is used by Mark; Matthew has ὠτίον (read in John by D Θ ω), Luke οὖς. Brown translates *earlobe*, but the diminutive is probably equivalent to the original οὖς (L.S.). D. Daube (*J.T.S.* 11 (1960), 59–62) compares *Tos. Parah* 3.8 (632); Josephus, *Ant.* xiv, 366; *Bel.* i, 270, and suggests that the act was an insult; physical mutilation would involve disqualification from the priesthood. This would be intelligible in an attack on the high priest himself, but would there have been any point in mutilating his slave, who may not even have been a Jew (see the note below on his name)?

τὸ δεξιόν. This detail is added by Luke also (not by Matthew and Mark). It is possible that both Luke and John were independently embroidering the Marcan narrative (which ἔπαισεν and ὠτάριον strongly suggest was known to John), but perhaps more probable that John was familiar with Luke as well as Mark (on the general question see Introduction, p. 46). It is true that John omits the healing of the slave's ear (found in Luke only); but from this we should probably infer not that Luke was unknown to John, but that the latter thought it inappropriate that such a cure should have been performed; the gulf between Jesus and his adversaries, between light and darkness, was now unbridgeable.

Μάλχος. The man is named only in John. The name is probably derived from the common Semitic root m-l-k (e.g. Hebrew מלך, melek, king). Other sources connect the name chiefly with Arabs; see e.g. 1 Macc. 11.39 ('Ιμαλκουε, א V; Μάλχος, Josephus, Ant. XIII, 131). The suggestion (Guilding, 164ff., 232f.) that the name reflects Zech. 11.6 (in the Haphtarah for Tebeth), into the hand of his king (מלכו), seems very improbable.

11. βάλε τὴν μάχαιραν εἰς τὴν θήκην. Cf. Jer. 47.6. Among the synoptists only Matthew (26.52, ἀπόστρεψον τὴν μάχαιράν σου εἰς τὸν τόπον αὐτῆς) has a parallel to this saying, but since there are no words in common (except μάχαιρα) it would be unwise to infer knowledge of Matthew on the part of John. No moral generalization such as Matthew's follows. As always, John's attention is focused on the Christological significance of his material. Peter must sheathe his sword not because if he fails to do so another sword will smite him but because nothing may hinder the destiny appointed by the Father for the Son. βάλλειν is used here in the weakened sense of 'put'; θήκη may be any receptacle into which a thing is put (τιθέναι); it is used for a sheath of a sword by Pollux and in a papyrus (see L.S. and M.M. s.v.).

τὸ ποτήριον. For the nominativus pendens cf. v. 9. In John the word ποτήριον is used nowhere else, either literally or metaphorically. Cf. Isa. 51.22. In Mark (followed in the main by Matthew and Luke) it is used (a) of the cup of suffering which Jesus must drink and the sons of Zebedee may share (Mark 10.38f.); (b) of the sufferings of Jesus contemplated by him in his agony (Mark 14.36); (c) of the cup at the last supper, which is clearly connected with his death (Mark 14.24, τοῦτό ἐστιν τὸ αἶμά μου τῆς διαθήκης τὸ ἐκχυννόμενον . . .). John, who omits the prayer in Gethsemane before the arrest, shows his knowledge of it, but emphasizes two further points. (a) He uses the expression not in a prayer that the cup may pass but in a calm determined acceptance of it (cf. 12.27, διὰ τοῦτο ἦλθον εἰς τὴν ὥραν ταύτην). (b) The cup is the Father's gift; Jesus' suffering is not the arbitrary and unfortunate result of circumstances but the work appointed him by the Father. It is right to note the freedom with which John handles the synoptic material, but also his faithfulness to its meaning, and the fact that behind the peculiarly Johannine language there lies the common vocabulary of the primitive tradition.

οὐ μὴ πίω αὐτό; οὐ μή is not commonly used in questions; elsewhere in the New Testament only at Luke 18.7. See Radermacher, 137.

Before τὸ ποτήριον Θ inserts πάντες γὰρ οἱ λαβόντες μάχαιραν ἐν μαχαίρᾳ ἀπολοῦνται, an assimilation to Matt. 26.52.

37. THE JEWISH TRIAL: PETER'S DENIAL

18.12–27

After his arrest Jesus is immediately handed over to Annas, the father-in-law of the high priest Caiaphas. In examination Jesus is questioned regarding his disciples and teaching, and refuses to answer, alleging that evidence should be brought in proper form. The proceedings descend from the illegal to the abusive, and Jesus is sent in custody from Annas to Caiaphas. Interwoven with this narrative is another which deals with two disciples who follow Jesus. One, who has the *entrée* at least to the courtyard of the high priest's house, brings in with him Peter, who is thus exposed to the scrutiny and challenge of the high priest's household. Under this challenge he thrice denies Christ before cockcrow.

It has been possible to give a fairly coherent outline of this piece of narrative, but only by means of omissions and glosses. In John's own account great difficulties appear at once. The most notable is the impossibility of combining the statements made about the high priest; why should Jesus be sent to Caiaphas (v. 24) when the high priest (who, John tells us (v. 13), was Caiaphas) has already questioned him (v. 19)? Why is Jesus first of all brought to Annas, if Caiaphas is to question him? Why do we hear nothing at all of the result of the examination before Caiaphas? It was doubtless to alleviate these difficulties that the variant discussed at v. 13 arose; the variant must be rejected, but the fact that it exists shows that the difficulties are real.

In spite of marked variations John seems to be at least partially dependent on Mark. Numerous verbal coincidences (see the notes) make this probable. That the denials of Peter should be separated into two sections is easily explicable (the Marcan narrative falls into two parts: Mark 14.54, 66–72), and it will be recalled that Mark seems to represent two Jewish trials, at night and in the early morning (Mark 14.53; 15.1). It is probably out of this Marcan narrative that the two 'trials', before Annas and Caiaphas respectively, arose. Benoit, however, reverses this argument, holding that the similar narratives of Luke and John should be accepted rather than those of Matthew and Mark, who have turned a private investigation before Annas into a general and official session of the Sanhedrin (1,298–306). It is striking that before neither Annas nor Caiaphas is there anything corresponding to the taking of evidence and the interrogation of Mark 14.53–64. The Jewish trial is in John glossed over with extreme rapidity; in fact there is really no trial narrative at all. This may be due to two reasons: (i) John wished to avoid the strongly apocalyptic tendency of the Marcan narrative; (ii) he had already given with great fullness his account of the controversy between Jesus and the Jews in chs. 7–10, which chapters (especially ch. 9—see the introduction and notes) in a sense anticipate the trial, and bring out the theological themes that are implicit in the conflict between Jesus and the Jews but are not dealt with in the present narrative. It is however assumed at 18.31 that the Jews have at some time decided that Jesus must be put to death.

Some recent writers have taken a much higher view of John's historical independence and trustworthiness. Dodd (*Tradition*, 95f.) concludes '(*a*) that for the hearing before the High Priest John is entirely independent of the Synoptic form of Passion narrative, although (*b*) at two points we recognize traits which belong to the common tradition underlying all our accounts; and (*c*) his account of the interrogation is drawn from some source, almost certainly oral, which was well informed about the situation at the time, and had contact with the Jewish tradition about the trial and condemnation of Jesus'. See also Brown's detailed discussion. But 18.33; 19.7 presuppose the synoptic trial tradition and we must (with Lindars) infer that John deliberately omitted the trial story, though he knew it. It would be perverse to maintain that he had no non-synoptic material at his disposal, but there is little in his story that cannot be explained as Johannine modification of a narrative not unlike Mark's. On the general question of John's knowledge of the Synoptic Gospels, see Introduction, pp. 42–6. On the composition of this passage see further J. Schneider in *Z.N.T.W.* 48 (1957), 111–19; also M. A. Chevallier, *Neues Testament und Geschichte* (Festschrift O. Cullmann, 1972), 179–85.

12. ἡ οὖν σπεῖρα καὶ ὁ χιλίαρχος καὶ οἱ ὑπηρέται. See on v. 3. χιλίαρχος is properly 'captain of a thousand' (and so represents שר אלף), but it was especially a technical term in the Roman army, *tribunus* (*militum*), the commander of a cohort; for a non-technical use see Mark 6.21.

13. The paragraph vv. 13–24 presents, as will appear below, very great difficulties in sequence and arrangement. Probably for this reason variant orders appeared. Sin has the verses in the order: 13, 24, 14, 15, 19–23, 16–18; the MS. 225 has 13a, 24, 13b, 14–23. But the 'improvements' are manifestly secondary and are themselves not free from objection (see especially Bultmann, 643f.; also Benoit, 1, 299).

ἤγαγον πρὸς Ἅνναν πρῶτον. Annas is mentioned only by Luke (3.2, cf. Acts 4.6) and John among the evangelists. John however, clearly recognizes that Annas was not high priest, whereas Luke seems to confuse Annas and Caiaphas in this office, or at least to express himself obscurely.Annas had been high priest from A.D. 6–15 (Josephus, *Ant.* XVIII, 26–35) and was succeeded not only by his son-in-law Caiaphas but also by five sons (*Ant.* xx, 198), so that Luke and John are doubtless correct in suggesting that he retained great influence, especially since his deposition by the Roman procurator Gratus could have no validity in Jewish opinion. Accordingly there is no historical difficulty in the statement that Jesus first appeared before him (Klausner, 340, referring to Josephus, *Ant.* IV, 186 (this seems to be the passage intended but the reference is obscure), *Horayoth* 3.4, *Megillah* 1.9, *Makkoth* 2.6, *T. Yoma* 1.4 (180)). John's πρῶτον distinguishes two examinations; cf. v. 24. In the former Jesus is interrogated about his disciples and his teaching, and struck for his answer, but the narrative is complicated by the fact that it is the high priest (Caiaphas, not Annas) who questions Jesus; cf. vv. 19, 22. No information is given about the latter. Mark also mentions two judicial meetings, a 'trial' (14.53–64) held before the high priest (who is not named) and ending in a verdict of guilty, and secondly an action on the part of the whole Sanhedrin by which Jesus was handed over to Pilate (15.1). Matthew follows Mark (adding the name Caiaphas); Luke retains only one examination. The legal basis of the Jewish action in John is quite incoherent. No charge is brought against Jesus, much less proved. The Jews bring him to Pilate with the incredible remark, If he had not been an evil doer we should not have delivered him to you (18.30); they are however convinced that it is necessary to put him to death (18.31). Only in 19.7 is a charge formulated: υἱὸν θεοῦ ἑαυτὸν ἐποίησεν, a charge of which no Roman official could have taken cognizance. In 18.33; 19.12,14f.,19, the charge of pretended kingship, which certainly would have been of greater interest to Pilate, is assumed, but it is nowhere explicitly stated. On the absence of a Jewish 'trial' in John see the introduction to this section. It is difficult to resist the conclusion that the trial narratives have been rewritten by John in order to bring out what, in his opinion, were the points at issue, and that no reliance can be placed on his version of the story (though probably numerous historical details remain in it).

ἦν γὰρ πενθερὸς τοῦ Καϊάφα. For this statement we have no authority other than John's. It is in itself entirely credible.

ἀρχιερεὺς τοῦ ἐνιαυτοῦ ἐκείνου. See on 11.49. Dodd (Tradition, 94) thinks John confused and wrong, but the explanation given above seems adequate.

14. See on 11.50. Lightfoot compares 18.8,9—Jesus is giving himself for those who are his people.

15. ἠκολούθει δὲ τῷ Ἰησοῦ Σίμων Πέτρος. All the evangelists narrate Peter's denial. Mark's language at this point (and later) is strikingly similar to John's: ὁ Πέτρος . . . ἠκολούθησεν αὐτῷ ἕως ἔσω εἰς τὴν αὐλὴν τοῦ ἀρχιερέως (Mark 14.54). The inference is that John is altering Mark (where necessary) in the interests of theology rather than using independent tradition.

καὶ (add. ὁ, Θ ω) ἄλλος μαθητής. The singular verb covers both subjects in the Hebrew manner (G.K. 489–92) but is by no means without precedent in Greek. The 'other disciple' is not mentioned by Mark and his identity is obscure. It is quite possible to identify him with the disciple 'whom Jesus loved' (see Introduction, pp. 116–19, and on 13.23), but there is no definite ground for doing so. In view of the description of him which follows (see the next note) it is very improbable that he was John the son of Zebedee. It is not impossible that John was aware of an objection to the traditional narrative, that Peter would not have been admitted to the scene of the trial, and introduced the other disciple to answer it. See Haenchen, Weg, 506f.

γνωστὸς τῷ ἀρχιερεῖ. The precise force of γνωστός is not certainly known. In the LXX it sometimes represents the Puʽal participle of ידע ('to know'; מידע, meyuddaʽ), which seems to be used for 'familiar friend'; see 2 Kings 10.11, and especially Ps. 54(55).14, It was thou, a man mine equal, my companion, and my familiar friend. The collateral form, γνωτός, may mean 'kinsman' or even 'brother' (e.g. *Iliad* xv, 350, γνωτοί τε γνωταί τε, 'brothers and sisters'). It would therefore be unwise to dismiss the acquaintance between the disciple and the high priest as slight (see however on the contrary Schlatter, 332), and it is very difficult to see how any such acquaintance as γνωστός suggests could exist between a Galilean fisherman and Caiaphas. It is not inconceivable that this verse is itself the foundation of the statement of Polycrates (see Introduction, pp. 101f.) that John was himself a priest and wore the πέταλον; but this view cannot be more than conjecture. The same is true of the suggestion that we have here the source of John's supposed interest in high priesthood.

εἰς τὴν αὐλὴν τοῦ ἀρχιερέως. αὐλή has a wide range of meanings (see L.S. *s.v.* and cf. 10.1), and its sense here will be determined by the general view that is taken of the examinations as John records them (cf. Mark 14.54,66; 15.16). If we are to think (see on v. 13) of a preliminary and informal investigation held by Annas before the formal trial by the Sanhedrin under Caiaphas, αὐλή will probably mean the *atrium* of Annas' house; if however the examination presided over by Annas was held before the Sanhedrin, the scene may have been within the Temple (see on v. 24).

16. ἔξω. Naturally the proceedings were private. We do not know Peter's motive in following Jesus. He can hardly have hoped to renew profitably the violence John ascribes to him in v. 10, though the possibility of escape may still have seemed open. Perhaps he expected a divine intervention. But it is unlikely that questions of this kind were in John's mind.

τῇ θυρωρῷ. For woman porters cf. 2 Sam. 4.6 (not Hebrew); Acts 12.13 and references in M.M. *s.v.* θυρωρός. If this is an accurate report the scene must be a private house (Annas'), not the Temple; but it may be simply a construction on the basis of Mark 14.66 (see on v. 17): the Marcan narrative includes a παιδίσκη; the story of admission requires a θυρωρός. Use of Mark provides a much more satisfying explanation than dittography in a conjectural Aramaic original (Black, 258).

εἰσήγαγεν τὸν Πέτρον. The subject may be the 'other disciple' or the θυρωρός; 'he introduced' or 'she admitted'.

17. λέγει . . . ἡ παιδίσκη ἡ θυρωρός. In Mark (14.66,69) it is μία τῶν παιδισκῶν τοῦ ἀρχιερέως who challenges Peter. John seems to be dependent on Mark at this point, and apparently uses Peter's entry into the court as an appropriate moment for the first recognition and denial. The reference to ἡ θυρωρός may be based on nothing more than Mark's παιδίσκη. This word meant in later Greek 'female slave'; earlier it was equivalent to νεανίς (see Phrynichus CCXVI; Rutherford, 312f.).

μὴ καί σύ. μή in direct questions commonly expects the answer 'No'. But καί σύ—'you also in addition to the man recognized as both a disciple and a friend of the high priest's'—suggests that the answer expected is 'Yes'. Probably here μή is the 'μή of cautious assertions' (M. 1, 192f.). The question does not seem to have been put in a hostile manner: 'You have come with X, whom we know; perhaps you too are a disciple.' Haenchen however thinks that καί σύ cannot mean 'in addition to the other disciple', for he is known as γνωστός τῷ ἀρχιερεῖ. Rather it must mean, 'You too, like many others'.

οὐκ εἰμί. Cf. the use of ἐγώ εἰμι without predicate at v. 5, and elsewhere.

18. In this verse John seems to show dependence on Mark. See Mark 14.54, ἦν συγκαθήμενος μετὰ τῶν ὑπηρετῶν καὶ θερμαινόμενος.

οἱ δοῦλοι καὶ οἱ ὑπηρέται. The personal slaves of the high priest and the Temple guard (see on v. 3).

ἀνθρακιὰν πεποιηκότες. Cf. 21.9; only in these two passages in the New Testament is ἀνθρακιά found. In the Temple a fire was kept burning in the Chamber of Immersion for the comfort of priests who had to immerse themselves during the night (*Tamid* 1.1); but this would not have been available for others than priests; nor would it have been said to have been specially made (πεποιηκότες).

ὅτι ψῦχος ἦν. This might be an indication that the narrative is based on the account of an eye-witness who himself remembered the cold night (cf. 10.22f.); but it may equally well be an inference from the fire mentioned, but not explained, in Mark.

Peter joined the group by the fire in the courtyard (κάτω, according to Mark 14.66) while the interrogation described in the next verses took place within. We hear no more of the 'other disciple'.

19. ὁ οὖν ἀρχιερεύς. The high priest was Caiaphas; but the prisoner had been taken to Annas (v. 13), and was subsequently sent to Caiaphas (v. 24). It is uncertain whether John was loosely but understandably referring to Annas as high priest (cf. Luke 3.2; Acts 4.6), or thought that Caiaphas was present and conducted the former examination. It is true that ἀρχιερεύς in the plural could denote members of the priestly aristocracy (Jeremias, *Jerusalem*, 181–98), so that Dodd (*Tradition*, 94) can render, 'the said member of the hierarchy'. But in the singular the word must suggest first *the* high priest.

ἠρώτησεν τὸν Ἰησοῦν. This interrogation is the only feature of the Jewish 'trial' in John. In Mark (14.55–9) the proceedings begin with the taking of testimony. This is not merely not mentioned by John but seems to be excluded by v. 21, ἐρώτησον τοὺς ἀκηκοότας. On the legality of the procedure see on v. 21. Here it may be observed that John completely omits the two points on which the synoptic trial turns: the question regarding the messiahship of Jesus, and the accusation of blasphemy. The high priest's question is put in a surprising form, since he inquires about Jesus' disciples and teaching, but not about his person, which, according to the Jews both in John (19.7) and in the other gospels, was the real centre of dispute and accusation.

περὶ τῶν μαθητῶν αὐτοῦ. This question is not followed up and its bearing consequently remains obscure. If it be read in the light of the synoptic narratives it may be taken to indicate apprehension of an armed rising with Jesus at its head: 'Why do you gather followers? How do you propose to exercise the authority you have over them?' Cf. 18.36. But it is doubtful whether John had this in mind; probably he simply states a general inquiry. In view of v. 17 it is an ironical one (Fenton).

περὶ τῆς διδαχῆς αὐτοῦ. This takes the place of the more precise Marcan question about messiahship (see above). Possibly it reflects questions put to Christians on trial for their faith; see especially *Acta Martyrii S. Iustini et Sociorum* 2, Ῥουστικὸς ἔπαρχος εἶπε· Ποῖόν ἐστι δόγμα; and cf. *Mart. Poly.* 10.1 and

Eusebius, *H.E.* v, i, 31 (Pothinus, bishop of Lugdunum); also Pliny's discovery by the examination of deaconesses that Christianity was *nihil aliud quam superstitionem prauam immodicam* (*Ep.* x, xcvi, 8).

20. παρρησίᾳ. See on 7.4. The contrast with ἐν κρυπτῷ proves that the meaning here is 'publicly'. Cf. Mark 14.49, if καθ' ἡμέραν means by day (and not by night). Brown cites Plato, *Apology* 33b; but it is unbelief that makes Jesus' words cryptic.

τῷ κόσμῳ. ὁ κόσμος in the sense of *tout le monde* occurs in late Greek; e.g. Dittenberger, *O.G.I.S.* 458.40f., ἦρξεν δὲ τῷ κόσμῳ τῶν δι' αὐτὸν εὐαγγελί[ων ἡ γενέθλιος] τοῦ θεοῦ (9 B.C.); *P. Oxy.* 1298.8, ἐ λέσχε [*sic*] τοῦ κόσμου (fourth century A.D.). But the special Johannine use of κόσμος should be recalled; see 1.10 and the note there. Here, as often in John, the world is represented by the Jews (Fenton).

πάντοτε. This word, and the next sentence, cannot be intended to exclude all private teaching, of which there is a good deal in John.

ἐδίδαξα ἐν συναγωγῇ. Cf. 6.59.

ἐν τῷ ἱερῷ. Cf. 7.14,28; 8.20. The article is used with ἱερόν (not with συναγωγή) because there was one Temple, but many synagogues. Cf. *Pesahim* 26a (R. Johanan taught in the temple; Bousset–Gressmann, 167).

ὅπου πάντες οἱ 'Ιουδαῖοι συνέρχονται; clearly an editorial note. Probably the whole reply was composed by John, perhaps on the basis of Mark 14.49, καθ' ἡμέραν ἤμην πρὸς ὑμᾶς ἐν τῷ ἱερῷ διδάσκων.

ἐν κρυπτῷ takes up παρρησίᾳ; cf. 7.10, where it is contrasted with φανερῶς. Cf. Isa. 48.16 (Guilding, 165). Braun, referring to Stauffer, rightly contrasts the Qumran preference for secret teaching.

21. τί με ἐρωτᾷς; It seems to have been regarded in rabbinic law as improper to attempt to make an accused person convict himself. This principle is not explicitly stated before Maimonides (on *Sanhedrin* 6.2; 'Our true Torah does not inflict the penalty of death upon a sinner either by his own confession or by the declaration of a prophet that the accused had done the deed'), and it was argued by H. Danby (*J.T.S.* old series 21 (1920), 51–76) that it should not be accepted as ancient. But Abrahams has shown (*Studies* II, 132–4) that Maimonides' was a legitimate inference from the texts. It was therefore incorrect procedure for the high priest to open a trial (if the examination was so formal) by interrogating Jesus himself. If however this was an informal inquiry direct questions might well be in place.

ἐρώτησον τοὺς ἀκηκοότας. 'Ask them what I have said'; that is, take testimony in the legal manner. This was done (though the witnesses were false witnesses) in the synoptic account of the 'first trial'.

22. ῥάπισμα. Cf. 19.3 (the soldiers at the Johannine 'mockery'); Mark 14.65 (the ὑπηρέται—as here—at the 'first trial'). Cf. Matt. 26.67, ἐράπισαν. The word is used in the sense condemned by Phrynichus (CLII; Rutherford, 257–65) of a blow on the face with the flat of the hand. John may well show knowledge of Mark; but both may depend on Isa. 50.6 (Dodd, *Tradition*, 93).

οὕτως ἀποκρίνῃ τῷ ἀρχιερεῖ; Cf. Exod. 22.27; Acts 23.4f.; also Josephus, *c. Apion.* II, 194, ὁ τούτῳ (*sc.* τῷ ἀρχιερεῖ) μὴ πειθόμενος ὑφέξει δίκην ὡς εἰς θεὸν αὐτὸν ἀσεβῶν. Jesus had in fact refused to answer what might well be regarded as an improperly put question.

23. The truth is always objectionable to those who are concerned to establish a case at all costs. It is easier and more effective to answer it with blows than with arguments.

24. Cf. Mark 15.1, and see the note on v. 13. It is very probable that John was aware of a tradition of two 'trials', since he has nothing to say about that which he represents as taking place before Caiaphas. It may be that his introduction of the two names, Annas and Caiaphas, is due to the fact that two inquiries have to be accounted for. It is not clear *where* Jesus was sent; see on vv. 13, 15. 'Sending' need not imply movement from one building to another, perhaps no more than remission from one court-room in the Temple to another. Cf. Benoit 1, 309ff. πρὸς Καϊαφᾶν means not to the house but to the person of Caiaphas, wherever he may have been. This would probably be, for a meeting of the Sanhedrin, the לחכת הגזית (*liḥkath ha-gazith*). The specific mention in this verse of Caiaphas as high priest underlines the difficulty of vv. 19, 22; if Caiaphas had already been present at the first inquiry why should Jesus be *sent* to him?

25. θερμαινόμενος. See on v. 18. There follow the second and third denials of Peter; the first was separated from them because the παιδίσκη who challenged him was identified with the θυρωρός.

εἶπον—the group standing by the fire (v. 18).

μὴ καί σύ. Their words are almost identical with those of the doorkeeper (v. 17).

ἠρνήσατο. The word was not used in v. 17, but it is repeated in v. 27. Cf. Mark 14.68,70. It calls to mind the saying of Jesus about those who deny (ἀρνεῖσθαι) him before men (Matt. 10.33=Luke 12.9); John seems however to mean no more by the word than that Peter said he was not what he had been alleged to be (οὐκ εἰμί).

26. συγγενὴς ὤν. Only John knows the name of the man who was struck (see on v. 10); he only knows of this relationship. We must conclude either that behind the Johannine passion narrative there stands a first-hand source, or that John is himself elaborating details in the manner of the apocryphal gospels. The general lack of coherence in the narrative does not confirm the former alternative.

ὠτίον. In v. 10, ὠτάριον (but ὠτίον occurs as a textual variant).
ἐν τῷ κήπῳ. See v. 1; but v. 4 suggests that Jesus came out of the garden before the arrest.

27. John does not mention the oaths and curses with which (Mark 14.71 and parallels) Peter denied Jesus.

ἀλέκτωρ ἐφώνησεν. Cf. 13.38 where the denial is predicted. John's abrupt ending is more dramatic and effective than Mark's explanation (14.72) that Peter remembered what Jesus had said. Peter now disappears from the story till 20.2. The story 'should be read in the light of the words of Jesus to Peter ... (13.36); Peter cannot follow Jesus, until Jesus has died for him' (Fenton).

38. JESUS, PILATE, AND THE JEWS

18.28—19.16

This long continuous piece includes conversation between Jesus and Pilate, and between Pilate and the Jews; Jesus no longer has direct converse with representatives of his own nation. For the most part he remains within the Praetorium; Pilate goes outside to speak to the Jews, who refrain from entering in order to avoid ceremonial pollution. The Jews constantly seek Pilate's condemnation of Jesus (on the ground that they have not the power to put anyone to death), alleging first in general terms that he is an evil-doer (18.30), secondly that he made himself Son of God (19.7), and finally that by making himself a king he was engaging in rebellion, which Pilate, if he released him, would be abetting (19.12). In their first conversation (18.33–7), Pilate questions Jesus about his kingship, and Jesus speaks of the truth to which he bears witness; in the second (19.8–11) the theme is authority (which is closely related to the previous theme of kingship). The Jews are constantly malevolent, and seek the blood of Jesus (18.30,40; 19.6,15), even at the cost of denying their own faith (19.15); Pilate on the other hand declares three times that Jesus is innocent (18.38; 19.4,6), seeks to release him (18.39 (the Jews however choose Barabbas); 19.12), and is compelled to crucify him only by the threat of 19.12. Into this sequence the scourging and mockery (carried out by Pilate's subordinates) are rather oddly inserted (19.1–3; see the notes).

Most of this material is based upon the Marcan narrative, which supplies not only the basic fact of an examination before Pilate, his unwillingness to condemn Jesus, the reference to Barabbas and the custom of releasing one prisoner at the feast, the scourging, the mockery, the clamour for the death of Jesus, and the ultimate handing over of Jesus to crucifixion, but also the main theme of the conversations between Pilate and Jesus—that of kingship. John's additions and alterations do not inspire confidence in his historical reliability. Details are given in the notes, but it may be observed here in general that it is highly improbable that reliable information respecting private conversations between the prisoner and the judge (if any took place) should have reached the evangelist. It is surprising that when the Jews first approach Pilate no accusation is brought against Jesus; it is assumed in 18.33 that Pilate knows the charge. That the charge on which the governor in fact acted was one of alleged kingship is probably true; but the discussions of this subject, and of true authority (18.33–7; 19.10f.) are unmistakably in the Johannine idiom, and the theology is not the eschatological thought on which the synoptic teaching about the kingdom of God is based. The scourging and mockery are as they stand (19.1–3) incomprehensible, since at this point Pilate intends not merely to release Jesus (cf. Luke 23.16) but to acquit him altogether. The mockery is probably retained however in order to provide for the dramatic effect of 19.5. John seems to have been uncertain on points both of Roman and of Jewish law (see 18.28,31,39; 19.1–3,6,16, and the notes). His only topographical addition to the earlier tradition is the name Gabbatha. The discovery of a paved space in what may be the relevant area (the Antonia; see on 19.13) does little or nothing to confirm the accuracy of the narrative. Light has been thrown on Roman procedures in the trial narrative by A. N. Sherwin-White (see the detailed notes), and Dodd (*Tradition*, 96–120) argues at length for John's use of an independent tradition of considerable historical value. He seems, however, to underestimate John's use of Mark, and the theological content and interest of the purely Johannine sections. A more moderate view is expressed by Brown (861): 'With all its drama and its theology, John's account of the trial is the most consistent and intelligible we have.' But this too seems on examination to overrate not only John's historical achievement but his historical intention. See also E. Haenchen, *Die Bibel und Wir* (1968), 190–205. The real core of the paragraph is the discussion of βασιλεία and ἐξουσία, though it is hardly possible to derive from it (as Bultmann does) a theology of church and state. Guilding (49, etc.) cannot be said to be successful in demonstrating in this paragraph the themes of Purim.

The historical value of John's account is lower than Mark's (on the conflicting dates ascribed by the two evangelists to the crucifixion see Introduction, pp. 48–51). But it must be repeated that John has with keen insight picked out the key of the passion narrative in the kingship of Jesus, and has made its meaning clearer, perhaps, than any other New Testament writer.

28. ἀπὸ τοῦ Καϊαφᾶ—to whom he had been taken in v. 24. Cf. Mark 15.1; but John has said nothing whatever about Caiaphas' dealings with Jesus. a, with several other Old Latin MSS. and many MSS. of the vg, reads *ad caipham*; this reading is probably due to the difficulty which has just been mentioned; cf. the rearrangement of verses given in sin (see on v. 13).

εἰς τὸ πραιτώριον. The praetorium was the official residence of a governor of a province; here, Pilate's residence. The governor of Judaea normally lived at Caesarea (where there was another praetorium, Acts 23.35), but came to Jerusalem for the great feasts, to quell disturbances. The Jerusalem residence here referred to is probably not the Antonia but Herod's Palace; see Benoit, I, 332f. This view accords better with the account of Pilate's movements in the rest of the paragraph. εἰς is loosely used; it appears later in the verse that though the Jews went *to* (πρός) the Praetorium they would not go *into* (εἰς) it.

ἦν δὲ πρωΐ. The last two watches of the night (on the Roman reckoning) were ἀλεκτοροφωνία and πρωΐ. Cockcrow was now past, and early morning (before 6 a.m.) had arrived.

καὶ αὐτοί—the subject of ἄγουσιν, the Jews responsible for transferring the case from the local court to the Governor's.

ἵνα μὴ μιανθῶσιν. Cf. *Oholoth* 18.7,9: The dwelling-places of Gentiles are unclean. . . . The rules about the dwelling-places of Gentiles do not apply to colonnades. In ordinary circumstances a Jew would enter a Gentile's house, but he would become unclean—technically unclean (see Bonsirven II, 262, and the article by A. Büchler (*J.Q.R.* 17 (1926-7), 1–81) there cited; also S.B. II, 838ff.). On the day before the Passover therefore (for a comparison of the Johannine with the Marcan dating of the last supper and crucifixion see Introduction, pp. 48–51) the Jews remained outside ἵνα . . . φάγωσιν τὸ πάσχα. The irony of this intention is characteristically Johannine: those who plot the murder of the Son of God mind to the last detail their formal religious punctilio. Whether the implication of John's statement, that the uncleanness acquired was of a major degree, lasting seven days, is correct has been disputed (see especially Morris). The alternative view is that the uncleanness the Jews would have incurred by entering the Praetorium would last only till the end of the day when it could be removed by a bath; in the immediately ensuing evening (the beginning of the next day) the Passover could be eaten. It may be well to preface the discussion with the observation that 'we do not know how the laws of ritual cleanness were interpreted at the time of Jesus' (J. B. Segal, *The Hebrew Passover* (1963), 36, n. 2; Segal also notes, ibid., that according to Matt. 27.11f.; Mark 15.2f.; Luke 23.1f. the priests did enter the Governor's Court). The controlling biblical passage is Num. 9.7–10: a man unclean by reason of a dead body (which means uncleanness for seven days; Num. 19.11,16; 31.19) must keep Second Passover (a month later). The question now arises whether the uncleanness incurred by entry into Gentile premises was this kind of uncleanness. The Mishnah quoted above gives no reason for regarding Gentile dwelling-places as unclean; the context however suggests that this was because Gentiles were supposed to dispose of abortions (corpses) within them. So far the evidence suggests that one who entered a Gentile dwelling would be obliged to wait seven days before he could take part in religious acts. The evidence however is not simple, and it is complicated by a division of opinion between the School of Hillel and the School of Shammai. An important text is *Pesahim* 8.8: He that mourns his near kindred may, after he has immersed himself, eat the Passover-offering in the evening, but he may not eat of other Hallowed Things. If a man heard of the death of one of his near kindred or caused the bones of his dead to be gathered together, he may, after he has immersed himself, eat of Hallowed Things. The School of Shammai say: If a man became a proselyte on the day before Passover he may immerse himself and consume his Passover-offering in the evening. And the School of Hillel say: He that separates himself from his uncircumcision is as one that separates himself from a grave. That the more lenient Shammaite practice prevailed in the earlier period is shown by a story contained in *T. Pesahim* 7.13 (167); *Y. Pesahim* 8, 36b, 47 (quoted in Jeremias, *Jerusalem*, 321). It was the Hillelite view that ultimately prevailed, being in the end accepted by the Shammaites. This fact could account for anachronism in John's account. Note also that only a small number of priests was concerned, and 'if the congregation or the greater part thereof contracted uncleanness, or if the priests were unclean but the congregation clean, the Passover may be kept in uncleanness' (*Pesahim* 7.6; the Mishnah adds that if a minority of the congregation are unclean they must keep the Second Passover). John's statement therefore that the Jews acted as they did in order that they might be able to eat the Passover is questionable. What seems at first sight to be a straightforward historical note may be due rather to John's sense of irony, perhaps also to his desire to use the dramatic device of two stages (Dodd, *Tradition*, 96). There is a balanced discussion of the matter in Brown, ad loc.

29. ἐξῆλθεν οὖν ὁ Πιλᾶτος. It is assumed that the reader will know who Pilate is—an indication that the evangelist expects the reader to know if not Mark some similar account of the passion. Pilate was prefect (the term procurator must now be abandoned in view of the inscription [PON]TIUS PILATUS [PRAE]FECTUS IUDA[EAE]: *J.B.L.* 81 (1962), 70) of Judaea c. A.D. 26–36. Josephus' account of him does not lead the reader to expect such accommodating compliance. Yet it is not impossible. A Roman governor would show wisdom in being no more provocative than necessary, especially at Passover time. This verse, however, does not add to the historical probability of the incident.

30. εἰ μὴ ἦν... This remark reveals either extraordinary and almost incredible impudence, or an understanding between the Jews and Pilate. The latter alternative is excluded because Pilate in referring the case back to the Jews shows that he did not understand that a capital sentence was required. Since the former alternative also strains the imagination we may suppose that we have here an attempt on the part of John (or of earlier tradition on which he depended) to fasten the guilt of the condemnation of Jesus yet more firmly upon the Jews and to exonerate the Romans—a tendency frequently visible in early Christian literature.

κακὸν ποιῶν. Probably the charges brought against Christians in early persecutions were general rather than specific; cf. 1 Peter 2.12; 3.17; 4.15; also Tacitus, *Annales* xv, 44, ... *per flagitia inuisos ... haud perinde in crimine incendii quam odio humani generis* ...

31. λάβετε αὐτὸν (om. ℵ* W c) ὑμεῖς. The last word is emphatic; Pilate like Gallio was not minded to be a judge of Jewish quarrels. Whether a provincial governor would have allowed to pass out of his hands a disturber of the peace must be regarded as doubtful. Pilate's action, however, places all the responsibility on the Jews.

ἡμῖν οὐκ ἔξεστιν ἀποκτεῖναι οὐδένα. Evidently the Jews have already decided that Jesus must be put to death, but John has not told us when, where, or by what authority. The synoptic account, or something very much like it, is presupposed. The question whether the Jews had or had not the right (under the prefects and procurators) to carry out capital sentences is very difficult, and is still disputed among scholars. Still an invaluable discussion of the question is that in J. Juster, *Les Juifs dans l'Empire romain* (1914) II, 127–49. (a) The following are among the arguments brought in support of John's statement that the Jews in this period had not the right to carry out executions. (i) Josephus (*Bel.* II, 117) says that the first governor, Coponius, was sent by Augustus μέχρι τοῦ κτείνειν λαβὼν παρὰ Καίσαρος ἐξουσίαν; but a governor could hardly have been appointed without this authority and it by no means follows that the competent local courts were deprived of it. (ii) The same author says (*Ant.* xx, 202) οὐκ ἐξὸν ἦν Ἀνάνῳ [the high priest] χωρὶς τῆς ἐκείνου [the governor's] γνώμης καθίσαι συνέδριον; but this can hardly have been a general regulation. (iii) in *Y. Sanhedrin* I, 18a, 34; 7,

24b, 41 it is stated that the right of pronouncing sentences of life and death was taken from Israel forty years before the destruction of the Temple (in A.D. 70). It is suggested that though the forty-year period may be a mistake the statement itself may be accepted; during the interval A.D. 6–70 (that is, under the governors) the Jews could not pronounce capital sentences. According to Juster (II, 133, note 1), however, the statement in *T. Sanhedrin*, loc. cit., is no more than a deduction from the statement (*Abodah Zarah* 8b) that forty years before the destruction of the Temple the Sanhedrin migrated thence, and the belief that capital sentences could be passed only in the Temple (cf. *Sanhedrin* 41a). (iv) It has also been argued that the very fact that Jesus was handed over to the Romans for crucifixion proves that the Sanhedrin itself had no authority to stone him; but this argument carries no weight. A popular court can only carry out sentences that have the backing of popular opinion; if only the priestly aristocracy (and perhaps the Pharisaic theologians) seriously wished the death of Jesus the simplest means of achieving their end was to hand him over to the Roman governor on a charge (such as sedition) that would be certain to secure his condemnation. (*b*) the following arguments may be brought against John's statement. (i) The Mishnah tractate *Sanhedrin* contains full regulations regarding the different kinds of capital sentence—burning, stoning, strangling, and beheading. It is difficult to believe that all the details given are either imaginary, or have been preserved from the period before A.D. 6. (ii) At least one crime is known to have been punishable with death at the hands of Jewish authorities—that of a Gentile who trespassed within the inner part of the Temple (see the Temple inscription discovered in 1871 by Clermont-Ganneau, most conveniently accessible in Deissmann, 75; also Josephus, *Bel.* v, 193f.; vi, 124–6; *Ant.* xv, 417). For this offence even Romans were liable to punishment; it is therefore not improbable that Jews who were not Romans could be punished by the Sanhedrin for other religious offences. (iii) Several executions in the relevant period are known to us. In the New Testament there is the death of Stephen (Acts 6, 7; parts of the narrative read like the story of a lynching rather than a judicial act, but a session of the Sanhedrin is described); Paul's refusal to be tried by a Jewish court should also be noted (Acts 25.9ff.). Josephus gives an account of the stoning of James the brother of Jesus (*Ant.* xx, 200; see also Eusebius, *H.E.* II, i, 4; xxiii, 4–18). In the Mishnah there is *Sanhedrin* 7.2: R. Eliezer b. Zadok said: It happened once that a priest's daughter committed adultery and they encompassed her with bundles of branches and burnt her [this was not the proper method of carrying out the death sentence of burning]. They said to him: Because the court at that time had not right knowledge. The *Tosephta* (9.11 (429)) adds that Eliezer himself had seen the event as a child, so that its date must fall within the period of the governors. The *Gemara* (52b) adds that the ill-instructed court was composed of Sadducees; its method of execution is criticized, but its right to execute is not questioned. A few other probable examples may be found in the Talmud. Juster concludes that John is mistaken; the Sanhedrin did possess the right to execute capital sentences. This view has been contested, notably by Sherwin-White (op. cit., 36–43), whose main argument is that it was not Roman practice to allow such extreme powers to local tribunals. J. Jeremias (*Z.N.T W.* 43 (1950/51), 145–50) finds further support in the story of the woman taken in adultery (7.53—8.11; see pp. 591f.) and in *Megillath*

Taanith 6, which he takes to mean that the Jews resumed the right of carrying out death sentences five days after the expulsion of the Romans in A.D. 66. Cf. T. W. Manson in *Z.N.T.W.* 44 (1952–53), 255f. On Sherwin-White's book see T. A. Burkill in *Nov. T.* 12 (1970), 321–42; also Burkill's article in *Vigiliae Christianae* 10 (1956), 80–96; 12 (1958), 1–18. Like Burkill, P. Winter concludes that the Sanhedrin did have the right in question; see *The Trial of Jesus* (1961), also *Z.N.T.W.* 50 (1959), 14–33, 221–51, especially 14–18. Winter refers to Philo, *Leg. ad Gaium* 307, where, in a letter purporting to have been written by Herod Agrippa I, the claim is made that 'if any priest, to say nothing of the other Jews, and not merely one of the lowest priests but of those who are ranked directly below the chief, goes in either by himself or with the High Priest, and further even if the High Priest enters on two days in the year or thrice or four times on the same day death without appeal is his doom', and to *Sanhedrin* 48b (The property of those executed by the State (מלכות) falls to the king; the property of those executed by the Law Court (בית דין) belongs to their heirs). These passages, especially the latter, seem at first conclusive. There is however a close parallel in *T. Sanhedrin* 4.6 (421), which instead of מלכות (the State) reads מלך (the King); this reflects the fact that in both Talmud and Tosephta the passage turns upon the interpretation of 1 Kings 21. It is therefore possible that we have here no more than an imaginative reconstruction of conditions the Rabbis believed to have obtained in the time of Ahab. Even if this is true, their reconstruction may well bear some relation to conditions with which they were themselves familiar, so that though these rabbinic passages may be less conclusive than Winter thought they are nevertheless not unimportant. [I have had the privilege of discussing the passages with my colleague Dr J. W. Rogerson.] It does not seem probable that this question will ever be finally settled; it may well be that one governor allowed more latitude than another (for probable constitutional changes see E. Bammel, in *Studies in Jewish Legal History*, 35–49), and that in the words John puts on the Jews' lips there was an element of flattery. It may be too that we should see in them a reference to Jewish rights and their limitations not in Jerusalem but in the city in which the evangelist lived and wrote (Martyn, 57). The equivocal evidence suggested to Hoskyns (616f.) that it may be 'legitimate to find in the phrase *put to death* [ἀποκτεῖναι] a subtle reference to shedding blood as distinct from stoning". It is their own Law which does not permit (this is the usual reference of ἔξεστιν in the New Testament) the Jews to shed blood, and the shedding of blood is the point of vital significance for John. 'It is of little importance to him whether the formal accusation be blasphemy or sedition; both are equally false. It is, however, vital to him that the blood of Jesus should be poured out for the salvation of the world. . . . Crucifixion, therefore, not stoning, fulfils the divine plan of salvation and the prophecies of the Lord.' It is strongly in favour of this interpretation that it makes much better sense of v. 32 than the view that the Sanhedrin was incapable of inflicting death by any means. But, as we have seen, we are not compelled by the evidence to accept this view; and it must be observed further that there is no evidence for the belief that ἀποκτείνειν means to kill with rather than without bloodshed, and that it can hardly be said that John in the rest of the gospel lays special stress on the blood of Jesus.

32. See 12.32f. Lindars rightly says that this verse is not redactional but the

point of the paragraph—at least, the fulfilment of the word of Jesus is one of its main points.

33. εἰσῆλθεν οὖν πάλιν; that is, he went back where he had been before.

σὺ εἶ: either there is a scornful stress on σύ—'You, a prisoner, deserted even by your friends, are a king, are you?'—or the expression is an interrogative correlative of the Johannine ἐγώ εἰμι (for which see on 6.35; 8.24).

ὁ βασιλεὺς τῶν 'Ιουδαίων. The reader has not been prepared for the introduction of this title, but it plays a large part in the ensuing narrative and dialogue (18.33–7,39; 19.3,12,15,19–22). The Jews are not reported to have brought any formal accusation (see v. 30), but it must be understood from v. 35 that they made a charge similar to that implied by the Marcan narrative (see Mark 15.2, σὺ εἶ ὁ βασιλεὺς τῶν 'Ιουδαίων; . . . σὺ λέγεις). John's narrative indeed at this point follows Mark closely. Pilate's opening question is the same, and vv. 34–7 may be regarded as a Johannine expansion of Mark's σὺ λέγεις. The phrase ὁ β. τ. 'Ιουδαίων has not been used earlier in the gospel, but cf. 1.49 (σὺ β. εἶ τ. 'Ισραήλ), and 3.3,5. What is meant by the kingship of Jesus is brought out in the following verses.

34. ἀφ' ἑαυτοῦ. This, the harder reading (cf. ἀπὸ σεαυτοῦ), should be preferred. In Hellenistic Greek ἑαυτῶν is commonly used for the second person plural of the reflexive pronoun; but ἑαυτοῦ for σεαυτοῦ is much less common. The only other possible usage in the New Testament is 1 Cor. 10.29. See M. II, 181; B.D., §64. It is impossible for Jesus to answer the question until he knows what it means. It is conceivable that Pilate is inquiring because he has himself apprehended the true and unique royalty of Jesus; but if, as is much more probable, he is merely testing a political charge brought by the Jews further explanation is necessary (v. 36).

35. μήτι ἐγὼ 'Ιουδαῖός εἰμι; Such questions are nothing to me. Your own national authorities have brought the charge; what is its basis? (τί ἐποίησας;) Of what seditious activities are you guilty? Here μήτι clearly expects the answer No; contrast 21.5.

36. ἡ βασιλεία ἡ ἐμὴ οὐκ ἔστιν ἐκ τοῦ κόσμου τούτου. Jesus admits that he is a king, but proceeds at once with such a definition of his kingship as removes it from the sphere of sedition and rebellion. On κόσμος in John see on 1.10. The Johannine idiom partly corresponds to the synoptic (and apocalyptic) 'this age' (ὁ αἰὼν οὗτος). In the Synoptic Gospels the kingdom of God is essentially not of this age but of the age to come; it is possible to speak of it as present just in so far as it is true that in the ministry of Jesus the age to come broke into the present age. In the Johannine transposition of the synoptic ideas this belief tends to become the conviction that the kingdom is not ἐκ τοῦ κόσμου τούτου (cf. 8.23), that is, of the field (rather than period) in which humanity and the spiritual world are organized over against God. That the metaphor is spatial rather than temporal is confirmed by the use at the end of the verse of ἐντεῦθεν; the last clause duplicates the first and ἐντεῦθεν is equivalent to ἐκ τοῦ κόσμου τούτου. It must be remembered that the Hebrew עוֹלָם means not only age but world, and that apocalyptic closely relates the world above and the world to come.

οἱ ὑπηρέται οἱ ἐμοὶ ἠγωνίζοντο ἄν. ἄν is omitted altogether by B* (and perhaps by P⁶⁶), and variously placed by other MSS.; it was probably inserted to regularize the grammar. Dodd (*Tradition*, 112) notes the tense of ἠγωνίζοντο (imperfect), 'are not in arms'. The disciples are described by the same word as the Temple police (v. 3); but the word had already been taken over into Christian usage (Luke 1.2; Acts 13.5; 26.16; 1 Cor. 4.1), and John doubtless availed himself of it as a means of practising his customary play on words. Kings of this world naturally fight for supremacy; that Jesus and his followers do not do so shows that his kingdom is of a different order.

παραδοθῶ; this may refer to the betrayal, or to 19.6,16.

37. οὐκοῦν βασιλεὺς εἶ σύ; The argumentative particle οὐκοῦν seeks a definite answer: 'Very well; so you are a king?' Sanders prefers to accentuate οὔκουν, and translates You are a king then, are you not? The difference in overall meaning is not great.

σὺ λέγεις. Cf. Mark 15.2. Jesus himself will neither affirm nor deny his kingship. If it is to be spoken of it must be on the lips of others. Pilate is clearly pressing (not necessarily in a hostile manner) for an answer in terms of kingship in 'this world'; such an answer Jesus refuses to give (he cannot give an outright 'No' since, though his kingship is not 'of this world' he has been sent 'into this world' (3.16; 17.18)), but proceeds to define his mission in fresh and more suitable language. The punctuation σὺ λέγεις. ὅτι β. εἰμι ἐγώ εἰς . . . has little to commend it except that it makes Jesus' answer in John agree exactly with that in Mark. In fact John is probably expounding, and thereby attaching more precise meaning to, the obscure Marcan words. 'It is you who will talk about kingship. A better way of expressing the purpose of my mission is to say that I came to bear witness to the truth.' John is not satisfied with, though he does not abandon, the term βασιλεία in his understanding of the work of Jesus.

εἰς τοῦτο is taken up and explained in the Johannine manner by ἵνα.

γεγέννημαι. The birth of Jesus is nowhere else explicitly mentioned (see on 1.13); it is synonymous with his entry into the world (ἐλήλυθα εἰς τὸν κόσμον). The description of birth as an entry into the world is not in this context accidental. Jesus himself, like his kingdom, is not of this world, not ἐντεῦθεν. He does not originate in the world; yet he has entered this world for the purpose of witnessing (for this important Johannine theme see on 1.7) to the truth (τῇ ἀληθείᾳ; see on 1.14), that is, to the eternal reality which is beyond and above the phenomena of the world, and, in particular, to the true and eternal kingdom of God which is the fount and pattern of all human authority (19.11). For this reason truth is not to be taken in a purely intellectual sense. It is active truth, and constitutes the Gospel. Cf. 1QS 8.6, cited on 5.33.

πᾶς ὁ ὢν ἐκ τῆς ἀληθείας. This sentence prepares the way for Pilate's uncomprehending inquiry, What is truth? The witness of Jesus to the truth can be grasped only by those who are themselves related to the truth (cf. 3.3,21). For ὁ ὢν ἐκ τῆς ἀληθείας 'it would be difficult indeed to cite any Old Testament or Hebrew parallel. It is parallel to such Johannine expressions as ἐκ τοῦ πνεύματος, ἐκ τοῦ θεοῦ, ἐκ τῶν ἄνω, all of which are applied to those who partake of the higher order of being, as opposed to those who are ἐκ τῆς σαρκός, ἐκ τῶν κάτω, ἐκ τοῦ κόσμου τούτου, ἐκ τοῦ διαβόλου. 'Αλήθεια therefore stands here for the realm of pure and eternal reality, as distinct from this world of transient phenomena. Similarly, in the former part of the verse Jesus says that He has come to bear witness to "the truth", i.e. to the divine reality as now revealed to men. There is the same movement of meaning between "reality" and "knowledge of reality" that we find in Greek philosophical language from Plato onwards' (Dodd, *Interpretation*, 176). It is impossible not to feel the force of this argument, difficult not to feel that Dodd has somewhat overstated it. ἐκ τῆς ἀληθείας points back (as indeed Dodd observes) to ἐκ τοῦ κόσμου τούτου. Jesus stands not for 'reality' if that means a static kind of supramundane existence, but for a kingdom that comes into this world from without, bearing with it a new understanding of the will of God; he himself is this kingdom as he is the truth (14.6). *Truth* is, as it were, truth in motion, entering the world, addressing the world, liberating (8.32) those who are capable of hearing it. It relates not to a world of timeless forms, but to an enacted plan of salvation. So much may be implied by Dodd's footnote ('With the very drastic revision of the idea of what *is* real which we shall have to observe in the development of Johannine thought'), but it is well to make it explicit.

ἀκούει μου τῆς φωνῆς. Cf. 10.3,16,27. What is lacking in Pilate is the personal attachment of the sheep to their own Shepherd, who is the Word (1.14) and the Truth (14.6) incarnate. Deut. 18.15 is of doubtful relevance here.

38. τί ἐστιν ἀλήθεια; As in the Synoptic Gospels, Pilate is represented as not unfriendly to Jesus; he does not wish to put him to death, and he sees that he is the victim of a Jewish plot. Yet sympathy is, in John's mind, a quite inadequate attitude to Jesus; like Nicodemus (7.50f.), Pilate for all his fair play and open-mindedness is not of the truth; he is of this world. This is John's point; E. Haenchen (*Die Bibel und Wir* (1968), 196f.) gives an illuminating account of over-subtle theological and psychological interpretations of this famous question.

ἐγὼ οὐδεμίαν εὑρίσκω ἐν αὐτῷ αἰτίαν. Like the earlier evangelists John does not lose the opportunity of emphasizing the political innocence of Christianity. For the wording cf. Luke 23.4,14,22.

39. ἔστιν δὲ συνήθεια ὑμῖν. Cf. Mark 15.6 and parallels. There is no direct extra-biblical evidence for this custom, and the parallels that have been adduced are of little value. The releases at the Roman *Lectisternia* (Livy v, 13; Dionysius of Halicarnassus XII, 9) are irrelevant; the papyrus quoted by Deissmann (266f.; *P. Flor.* 61.59–62) is closer but differs in important particulars. The prefect of Egypt in A.D. 85, G. Septimius Vegetus, declares to a prisoner, ἄξιος μὲν ἦς μαστιγωθῆναι . . . χαρίζομαι δέ σε τοῖς ὄχλοις. It will be observed that this is a single act of grace, not a custom, and that the prisoner is not on a capital charge. The custom mentioned by John is not however impossible, and it may be that there is an allusion to it in *Pesahim* 8.6: They may slaughter the Passover . . . for one whom they have promised to bring out of prison (להוציאו מבית האסורים). The Mishnah continues in such a way as to suggest that doubt remained about the release, and this would hardly have been so if a Jewish court had been involved. A special promise of release, at Passover time, by the foreign authority, may therefore be in mind; and unless this happened with some regularity it would be unlikely to become the subject of legislation.

βούλεσθε οὖν ἀπολύσω ὑμῖν τὸν βασιλέα τῶν Ἰουδαίων; Cf. Mark 15.9, θέλετε ἀπολύσω ὑμῖν τὸν βασιλέα τῶν Ἰουδαίων; For the construction see M. II, 421; B.D., §366; the subjunctive immediately after the second person of θέλειν, βούλεσθαι, is classical. There is no question of Semitism. Pilate, who wishes to release Jesus, determines to take advantage of the custom; perhaps the Jews will accept Jesus as the prisoner to be released under its terms. It is not clear however why Pilate describes him as the 'King of the Jews'. (a) He has apparently himself decided that Jesus is not a king in the ordinary sense of the word. (b) Since the Jews were using the charge that Jesus was or desired to be king of the Jews as a means of getting rid of him it was hardly a title likely to commend him to them. John has probably taken the title straight out of the earlier tradition; though it also suits his purpose, which is to portray Jesus in his humility as in fact the true king of Israel.

40. ἐκραύγασαν. A strong word, suitable for a mob; cf. 19.6.

πάλιν ((P⁶⁶) א B), though the Old Latin and a few Greek MSS. substitute πάντες, should probably be read. It is out of place here, and borrowed from Mark 15.13. The two readings are conflated—πάλιν πάντες—by Θ ⲱ vg.

μή (sc. ἀπολύσῃς) τοῦτον ἀλλὰ τὸν Βαραββᾶν. The unexplained introduction of Barabbas presupposes knowledge of an earlier narrative, probably the Marcan. Βαραββᾶς might represent בר־אבא (bar-'abba', son of the father), or בר־רבן (bar-rabban, son of the master). The former, a common name, is much more probable. On the occurrence of Abba as a name see Abrahams, Studies II, 201f. In some MSS. of Matt. 27.16,17 the name occurs as Jesus Barabbas, and Pilate asks whether he should release Jesus Barabbas or Jesus called the Christ. It has been suggested that misunderstanding of this alternative led to belief that there existed the custom mentioned in v. 39; discussion of this suggestion belongs rather to a commentary on Matthew than to one on John.

ληστής is a very brief description of Barabbas in comparison with Mark 15.7 and parallels. According to Mark he had been involved in a στάσις in which murder had been committed. He was thus a political prisoner, whose position was therefore comparable with that of Jesus, since the latter was accused of a messianic rebellion. There is some evidence that ληστής was used of a guerrilla (see L.S. s.v.; in Mark 14.48 Jesus asks those who are arresting him, ὡς ἐπὶ ληστὴν ἐξήλθατε;), so that (pace Dodd) John may well have been summing up Mark's meaning in a single word. Cf. also the λῃσταί of 10.1,8.

1. ἐμαστίγωσεν. μαστιγοῦν 'is the regular term for punishment by scourging' (M.M. s.v.; cf. the papyrus quoted above on 18.39). Scourging normally preceded crucifixion (see e.g. Josephus, Bel. v. 449, μαστιγούμενοι . . . ἀνεσταυροῦντο; Livy XXXIII, 36, alios uerberatos crucibus affixit). If, as appears, the scourging preceded the verdict, it was of course irregular; but John does not make clear when the formal sentence was passed. In Mark (15.15, φραγελλώσας) the scourging takes place after the sentence; in Luke there is no scourging, though one is threatened (23.16,22). Sherwin-White (op. cit., 27f.) notes that Luke uses the word (παιδεύειν, rather than Mark's φραγελλοῦν) denoting the less severe kind of beating appropriate to the dismissal of the prisoner with a warning. Unfortunately he does not comment on John's μαστιγοῦν.

2. πλέξαντες . . . αὐτόν. It is very probable that John is here dependent on Mark 15.17, ἐδιδύσκουσιν αὐτὸν πορφύραν καὶ περιτιθέασιν αὐτῷ πλέξαντες ἀκάνθινον στέφανον. See *J.T.S.* new series 3 (1952), 66–75 (H. St. J. Hart). The crown was probably intended not as an instrument of torture but as a crude imitation of the radiate crowns worn by supposedly divine oriental and Hellenistic rulers, and thus as part of the mockery. There are further references in Brown; see also Guilding, 169.

3. καὶ ἤρχοντο πρὸς αὐτόν: omit, ω. The words might well seem superfluous, but in fact they contribute to a vivid picture of the mocking approach of the soldiers pretending to do reverence to the king.

Χαῖρε, ὁ βασιλεὺς τῶν Ἰουδαίων. Cf. Mark 15.18, Χαῖρε, βασιλεῦ τῶν Ἰουδαίων. See M. 1, 70f.: '*Descriptiveness* is . . . the note of the articular nominative of address in the New Testament: so in . . . John 19.3, where we may represent the *nuance* by . . . 'Hail, you "King"!' In the latter passage [John 19.3] we can easily feel the inappropriateness of the βασιλεῦ found in ℵ, which would admit the royal right, as in Acts 26.7. Its appearance in Mark 15.18 is merely a note of the writer's imperfect sensibility to the more delicate shades of Greek idiom.' Robertson, 465, thinks that Moulton may be guilty of 'slight overrefinement' here. βασιλεῦ is found also in P⁶⁶.

ἐδίδοσαν αὐτῷ ῥαπίσματα (on this word see on 18.22). Cf. Mark 15.19, ἔτυπτον αὐτοῦ τὴν κεφαλὴν καλάμῳ; also (at the trial before the high priest, 14.65) οἱ ὑπηρέται ῥαπίσμασιν αὐτὸν ἔλαβον (with a parallel in John 18.22). Cf. Luke 22.63–5. The details of this mockery are clear in themselves, and so are their theme and motive: Jesus is mocked as the king of the Jews. The probable inference is that the charge brought from the Sanhedrin and preferred before Pilate was that of claiming to be the king of the Jews, that is, the Messiah. It is thus with excellent historical justification that John brings out the theme of kingship in his passion narrative. Further details are added in the Gospel of Peter, 6–9: And they having taken the Lord pushed him as they ran, and said: Let us hale the Son of God, now that we have got authority over him. And they put on him a purple robe, and made him sit upon the seat of judgement, saying: Give righteous judgement, thou King (βασιλεῦ) of Israel. And one of them brought a crown of thorns and set it upon the Lord's head; and others stood and did spit in his eyes, and others buffeted his cheeks; and others did prick him with a reed, and some of them scourged him, saying: With this honour let us honour (*or* at this price let us value) the son of God. See below on v. 13. Other passages, such as Philo, *In Flaccum* 36–42, Dio Chrysostom, *de Regno* IV, 66–70, have been quoted in explanation of the mockery. They in fact explain nothing, and there is nothing for them to explain. See M.-J. Lagrange, *Évangile selon Saint Marc* (1920), 393–5. More significant is the occurrence of the language (μάστιγες, ῥαπίσματα) of Isa. 50.6, but if the fulfilment of Scripture had been, at this point, more than a secondary interest John would have drawn attention to it.

4. ἴδε ἄγω ὑμῖν αὐτὸν ἔξω. This act is introduced in preparation for the dramatic pronouncement of v. 5. The situation is highly dramatic but equally improbable. A Roman judge would have released or executed his prisoner.

οὐδεμίαν αἰτίαν εὑρίσκω ἐν αὐτῷ. Cf. 18.38.

5. ἀκάνθινον. The adjective is not used in v. 2, but it is used in Mark 15.17.

Ἰδοὺ ὁ ἄνθρωπος. The article is omitted by B, probably by accident. The whole clause is omitted by P⁶⁶. This is one of the most dramatic moments in the gospel; cf. v. 14 (and, for the use of ἰδού in an announcement, 1.29). A series of striking contrasts is involved. (i) Jesus is dressed as a king, and is announced as the man. (ii) In v. 7 his claim to be the Son of God is mentioned; the claimant to divine honours is announced as the man. (iii) The man announced by Pilate with mingled pity and contempt was to the readers of the gospel their Lord and their God. Reference to the גבר (man) of 1QS 4.20; 1QH 3.10 seems most improbable. A more important comparison is with Zech. 6.11f. (Thou shalt take silver and gold and shalt make crowns (στεφάνους) and set them on the head of Jesus (Ἰησοῦ) the Son of Josedek the high priest, and thou shalt say to him, Thus saith the Lord Almighty, Behold a man (Ἰδοὺ ἀνήρ), Branch (Ἀνατολή) is his name, and he shall rise up (ἀνατελεῖ) from beneath, and shall build the Lord's house), though it would be hard to affirm that John was referring directly to this passage. ὁ ἄνθρωπος also recalls the term Son of man (on this term in John see Introduction, pp. 72f., and on 1.51), and John may have wished to evoke this while feeling that he could not place such a barbarism as ὁ υἱὸς τοῦ ἀνθρώπου on Pilate's lips. Besides, ὁ υἱὸς τοῦ ἀνθρώπου would have lacked the ambiguity that marks Pilate's words (on John's use of ambiguity see on 3.3). Pilate hits the truth accidentally (as Caiaphas did, 11.50ff.). No comment on this verse sets out the truth more clearly and succinctly than Bultmann's, 'The declaration ὁ λόγος σὰρξ ἐγένετο has become visible in its extremest consequence (in seiner extremsten Konsequenz)'. See also R. Schnackenburg, in Jesus und der Menschensohn (Festschrift A. Vögtle, 1975), 371–86.

6. On ἀρχιερεῖς see on 7.32; on the ὑπηρέται, on 18.3; on ἐκραύγασαν, on 18.40.

σταύρωσον. Cf. Mark 15.13. The demand for this kind of punishment implies the recognition that the case has passed into Roman hands. See however the next note.

λάβετε αὐτὸν ὑμεῖς. The pronoun is emphatic: Take him yourselves. This of course the Jews could not do; according to 18.31 they were not allowed to inflict capital punishment; and even if they had done so they would have inflicted death by stoning, not by crucifixion; moreover, a Roman official could not have transferred his own responsibility to any local court. If the words were spoken by Pilate they must have been a taunt; probably they were intended to fasten responsibility for the death of Jesus on the Jews rather than the Romans. E. Stauffer (Jerusalem und Rom (1957), 123–7) adduces cases of alleged crucifixion by Jews, but Winter (op. cit., 62–6) seems to be right in concluding that 'crucifixion was not a punitive measure used by Jews or adopted by Jewish judicial institutions at any time in history' (66).

7. ἡμεῖς νόμον ἔχομεν. νόμος is here used in the sense of a particular statute (הוק), not in the general sense of Torah. The law of blasphemy is meant; cf. Lev. 24.16 and Sanhedrin 7.5; Kerithoth 1.1f. The question of blasphemy is not raised in the very short account of the Jewish 'trials' in ch. 18, but it is central in Mark 14.55–64, and in earlier chapters in John (e.g. 5.18; 10.33,36).

κατὰ τὸν νόμον. The addition of ἡμῶν (Θ ω) misses the fact that νόμος in this verse has the meaning pointed out above.

υἱὸν θεοῦ ἑαυτὸν ἐποίησεν. Cf. 5.18; 10.33; also perhaps Wisd. 2.18. ποιεῖν here means 'make out to be'; cf. 1 John 1.10. It is far from clear in Mark on what the charge of blasphemy is founded; in John there is no difficulty; Jesus blasphemes in claiming for himself essential equality with God. The anarthrous phrase υἱὸν θεοῦ has perhaps a qualitative sense; see on 5.27.

8. μᾶλλον ἐφοβήθη. Pilate's fear is aroused by Jesus' reported claim to supernatural dignity. Dodd, *Tradition*, 114, says that Pilate understands Jesus to be claiming to be a θεῖος ἄνθρωπος; hence his question, πόθεν εἶ σύ; Do you indeed claim to be such a person? This gives the sense, even if θεῖος ἄνθρωπος is not a term Pilate would have used. For the place of this concept in Johannine Christology see Introduction, p. 74. The translation 'he was the more afraid' may be justified if 18.38 is held to imply fear (the word φοβεῖσθαι itself is not used before the present verse); but it is probably better to suppose that μᾶλλον (the comparative of μάλα) is here elative (see L.S. *s.v.* μάλα, II): 'he was very much afraid'.

9. τὸ πραιτώριον. See on 18.28. Presumably he brought Jesus in with him, since at v. 5 Jesus had been brought out.

πόθεν εἶ σύ; The form of the question recalls Luke 23.6, ἐπηρώτησεν εἰ ὁ ἄνθρωπος Γαλιλαῖός ἐστιν, and may be based upon a recollection of it. If this is so, the meaning has been transformed in Johannine style; or rather, a characteristic double meaning has been attached. John does not think primarily of the province of Jesus' birth but of the fact that, being Son of God, he is 'from above'. His origin is both known and not known; see 3.8; 8.14; 9.29 and the notes. It is for this reason that

ὁ δὲ Ἰησοῦς ἀπόκρισιν οὐκ ἔδωκεν αὐτῷ. This question (like the question 'Art thou a king?') is not capable of a simple answer. In Mark the silence of Jesus is mentioned at 14.60f.; 15.5. In Luke Jesus does not answer Herod (23.9). The silence of Jesus is much less prominent in John than in the other gospels because much more conversation is introduced into the story.

10. ἐμοὶ οὐ λαλεῖς; The silence of Jesus disturbs Pilate, who desires to release him. By provoking the next question the silence continues the conversation as effectively as a reply.

ἐξουσίαν ἔχω. For ἐξουσία see on 1.12; 7.1; 10.18. What Pilate has is *potestas;* it rests entirely with him to release or to execute Jesus. Cf. *Digest,* L, xvii, 37, *Nemo, qui condemnare potest, absoluere non potest.* Cf. Josephus, *Bel.* II, 117: the first governor, Coponius, was sent μέχρι τοῦ κτείνειν λαβὼν παρὰ Καίσαρος ἐξουσίαν.

11. οὐκ εἶχες (P⁶⁶ B Θ ω; א W, ἔχεις) ἐξουσίαν κατ' ἐμοῦ οὐδεμίαν. Pilate's assertion is radically (οὐδεμίαν is very emphatic) qualified. The reading εἶχες is probably to be preferred, though the verb ought to be accompanied by ἄν; for its absence cf. 8.39. This verse shows one of John's common literary devices in reverse. Several times (e.g. 3.3–8) a theological word used by Jesus is misunderstood when the hearers take it in a literal sense; here Pilate uses the word 'authority' in an un-theological sense; Jesus takes the word out of his mouth and uses it absolutely, speaking of the authority not of Rome but of God. The discussion of ἐξουσία provides a counterpart to the discussion of

βασιλεία in 18.33–8. Jesus, who is not backed by servants who fight (18.36), and indeed has no earthly power to show, nevertheless holds and exercises βασιλεία, kingship, in bearing witness to the truth. Pilate, supported by an army and wearing the trappings of authority, is incapable of recognizing truth, and has only such ἐξουσία as is lent him for the performance of his office.

εἰ μὴ ἦν δεδομένον σοι ἄνωθεν. All human authority is derived from God's (cf. Rom. 13.1). For ἄνωθεν see on 3.3. It is implied primarily that in condemning and crucifying Jesus Pilate acts with divine consent—the crucifixion does not contravene the authority of God but lies within his purpose; perhaps also that the Roman authority in general is of divine appointment and consent. Cf. 8.20; authority to arrest Jesus was not given until the moment appointed by God had come. It should however be noted that the participle δεδομένον is neuter and does not agree with ἐξουσία; the meaning is, Unless it had been granted you to have authority.

διὰ τοῦτο—because your authority is not your own.

ὁ παραδούς μέ σοι. The use of παραδιδόναι (6.64,71; 12.4; 13.2,11,21; 18.2,5; 21.20), and the singular number of the participle, suggest Judas; but Judas did not deliver Jesus to Pilate (σοι), and παραδιδόναι is also used of the act of the Jewish authorities (18.30,35). Nevertheless, Judas, the devil (6.70), the tool of Satan (13.2,27), is probably intended. Sanders and Brown are among those who think that Caiaphas is intended; Lindars thinks of the people as a whole.

μείζονα ἁμαρτίαν ἔχει. ἁμαρτίαν ἔχειν is a Johannine phrase (9.41; 15.22,24; 1 John 1.8; nowhere else in the New Testament). Here ἁμαρτία plainly means 'guilt'.

12. ἐκ τούτου, 'for this reason' or 'from this time'. See on 6.66. If the causal sense be adopted the present verse is parallel to v. 8. The theme of ἐξουσία is continued, and the frailty of Pilate's authority is exposed.

φίλος τοῦ Καίσαρος. Cf. 15.15. E. Bammel (*Th.L.Z.* 77 (1952), 205–10) has shown that the title *amicus Caesaris* is very probably old enough to have been used in this conversation as at least a semi-technical term. E. Stauffer (*Jesus and His Story* (E.T. 1960), 108ff.) goes further and connects Pilate's status as *amicus Caesaris* with Sejanus; it is because of the fall of Sejanus (18 October 31) that Pilate finds himself compelled to be so subservient to the Jews. He dare not face the *renuntiatio amicitiae*. Haenchen (op. cit., 202) is right in claiming that John would not have been aware of these political entanglements, and that the words should be understood in a simple way as the counterpart of ἀντιλέγει τῷ Καίσαρι. Anyone who sets himself up as a king, or even tolerates such a rebel, is an enemy, and no friend, to the Emperor (regularly in the Greek-speaking world, βασιλεύς).

ἀντιλέγει τῷ Καίσαρι. For the verb cf. e.g. Isa. 65.2, λαὸν ἀπειθοῦντα καὶ ἀντιλέγοντα. Bauer (219) cites evidence of the significance and frequency of the charge of *maiestas* in the time of Tiberius; it is perhaps more to the point to note that similar conditions prevailed under Domitian (for a summary see *C.A.H.* xi, 27–33), when this gospel was probably taking shape. Yet in allowing the theme of kingship (and *maiestas*) to govern the decisive stages of the narrative up to v. 16 John is probably true to history. These arguments rather than any others would compel Pilate to act. For the Jewish pressure on Pilate cf. Philo, *Leg. ad Gaium*, 301f.

13. βήματος. Cf. Matt. 27.19. The word is used in Hellenistic Greek for the tribunal of a magistrate, and in the New Testament for the judgement-seat of God (or Christ); cf. Rom. 14.10; 2 Cor. 5.10. For a judgement-seat out of doors in Jerusalem cf. Josephus, *Bel*. II, 301: Florus lodged at the palace, and on the following day had a tribunal (βῆμα) placed in front of the building and took his seat; the chief priests, the nobles, and the most eminent citizens then presented themselves before the tribunal (βήματι).

It is not easy to determine who sat upon the βῆμα. ἐκάθισεν may be intransitive —Pilate sat upon the tribunal; or transitive—he caused Jesus to sit upon the tribunal. In favour of the latter rendering the following points may be urged. (i) It gives great dramatic force to Pilate's words in v. 14, ἴδε ὁ βασιλεὺς ὑμῶν. (ii) In doing so it provides a parallel to vv. 2, 3, 5. (iii) If Pilate sat on the judgement-seat it must have been to pronounce sentence; but no sentence is recorded. (iv) There are traces elsewhere of a similar tradition. See Justin 1 *Apol.*, 35, διασύροντες αὐτὸν ἐκάθισαν ἐπὶ βήματος καὶ εἶπον· κρῖνον ἡμῖν; Gospel of Peter 7 (see on v. 3), ἐκάθισαν αὐτὸν ἐπὶ καθέδραν κρίσεως λέγοντες· δικαίως κρῖνε, βασιλεῦ τοῦ Ἰσραήλ. Against the transitive rendering the following arguments may be brought. (i) In the only other place in John in which καθίζειν occurs (12.14; cf. 8.2) it is intransitive; and so it commonly is in the rest of the New Testament. This is a strong argument. (ii) Such an act as is suggested would not have been becoming to a Roman governor. It will however be recalled that (according to Luke 13.1) Pilate had committed the grim jest of mingling the blood of worshippers with their sacrifices; and it may be that the deed is not historical. (iii) The Johannine narrative suggests that Pilate was afraid (v. 8), and more anxious to release Jesus than to mock him (v. 12). This also is a good argument. It is not easy to decide between these alternatives; both are supported by good arguments. Probably John was conscious of both meanings of ἐκάθισεν. We may compare his habit of playing on words of double meaning (see on 3.3) and also his subtle presentation of the investigation in ch. 9, where ostensibly the blind man is examined while through him Jesus himself is being tried, only to turn the tables on his accusers by judging them. We may suppose then that John meant that Pilate did in fact sit on the βῆμα, but that for those with eyes to see behind this human scene appeared the Son of man, to whom all judgement has been committed (5.22), seated upon his throne.

λεγόμενον introduces a proper name, as e.g. at 4.5.

Λιθόστρωτον. As an adjective the word means 'paved with stones'; it may mean a tessellated or mosaic pavement. For attempts to identify the site see below.

Ἑβραϊστί. Cf. 5.2; 19.17,20; 20.16. Here the form of the word Gabbatha shows clearly that Aramaic is meant.

Γαββαθά. This should represent גבתא (*gabbᵉtha'*). John does not say that the Greek name translates the Hebrew (Aramaic); contrast his different expression at 1.38 (where see the note). The derivation of גבתא is obscure. It may be a variant of גובתא (*gubta'*), which appears in several spellings, and means a hill or a pit, and is used as the name of several places (see Jastrow *s.v.*). A similar meaning ('raised place') would result if we accepted the

544

suggestion that Γαββαθά represents גבחתא (*gabbahta'*, 'a high forehead'). Dodd, *Tradition*, 108, proposes גבעתא (*gib'etha*), equivalent to the Hebrew גבעה (*gib'ah*), from the root גבע, high, projecting. In the Palestinian Syriac Lectionary at Matt. 26.23 גבתא renders τρυβλίον, 'a dish'; but, even though it has been pointed out that the Arabic word for 'dish' may mean also 'an enclosed place open to the sky', this does not seem relevant. Another suggestion is that Γαββαθά should be split up into גב ביתא (*gab baitha'*, 'hill of the house', that is, Temple mound, or Temple ridge); but this does not give good sense. The attempt to make Gabbatha (by way of the root גבב, *g-b-b*, 'to collect') mean 'mosaic' fails to grasp that Λιθόστρωτον is not intended as a *translation* of Gabbatha. A paved area has been found in a building identified as the Antonia (see on 18.28), and it has been argued that this must be Gabbatha, the place where Jesus was exposed by Pilate to the crowd. Additional interest has been awakened by the discovery of scratched lines, suggesting that soldiers had played there a 'king game' (cf. 19.2f.). It has been concluded that the Praetorium of 18.28 must be the Antonia; that a scene from the last hours of Jesus has been positively located; that John's historicity has been vindicated. None of these conclusions will stand. There are good reasons for thinking that the Praetorium was Herod's Palace, and it is hard to think that none of its external and internal floor surfaces was paved (and could therefore be described as λιθόστρωτον); it is therefore anything but certain that the newly discovered site is the scene of John 19.13f. (and very improbable that the soldiers would play their game over the βῆμα); and even if it were known that the site was called Gabbatha this could not prove the historicity of John's narrative. On the whole question, and for bibliography, see P. Benoit in *H.T.R.* 64 (1971), 135–67. The buildings and paving in question belong to the second century and have nothing to do with the events of the gospel.

14. ἦν δὲ παρασκευὴ τοῦ πάσχα. The use of παρασκευή for a date is not Greek (see L.S. *s.v.*); it represents the Hebrew ערב (*'ereb*), here ערב הפסח. The meaning of this phrase in Jewish literature is quite clear. It does not mean Friday (ערב שבת, 'eve of Sabbath') in Passover week, but 'eve of Passover', Nisan 14. For the significance of this date, and the conflict with the Synoptic Gospels, see Introduction, pp. 48–51. See *Sanhedrin* 43a (quoted on 7.12): On the eve of Passover (בערב הפסח) Jesus was hanged. *PASSOVER = SABBATH*

ὥρα ἦν ὡς ἕκτη. Another conflict with the Synoptic Gospels; contrast Mark 15.25, ἦν δὲ ὥρα τρίτη καὶ ἐσταύρωσαν αὐτόν. The disagreement may have arisen by accident, through the confusion of the Greek numerals Γ (3) and F (6); or through the use of a Hebrew sign which in square character is *waw* (6), but on some old coins *gimel* (3). Or there may have been a conscious change. Mark's 'third' may have arisen because he was anxious ·at 15.33 to depict darkness 'at noonday'; John's 'sixth' may have arisen because he wished to represent the death of Jesus as that of the true Paschal lamb (the passover sacrifices were killed in the course of the afternoon). This is in fact probably John's motive for inserting the note of time; or he may have wished to show in the simplest terms that the 'hour' of Jesus (see on 2.4) had now come.

ἴδε ὁ βασιλεὺς ὑμῶν. In the dramatic narrative the clever argument of the Jews is thrust back upon them with bitter irony; the helpless prisoner of

Rome is the only king they are likely to have. It is now they who are mocked, not Jesus. But throughout the passion story John works so frequently with the theme of kingship (see on 18.33) that it seems likely that here he has intentionally put into the mouth of Pilate an unintended truth. Just as Pilate inscribes on the cross (vv. 19, 22) the royal title of Jesus, so here, in spite of all appearances, he truly proclaims Jesus as the king of Israel. The title recalls the messianic claim, and the charge on which Jesus was no doubt prosecuted in the Roman court. Cf. v. 5; the representative Man is also the true king of the human race.

15. ἆρον. 'Away with him!' The parallel, quoted by most commentators and by M.M. *s.v.*, in *P. Oxy.* 119.10, in which the mother of a tiresome schoolboy says ἀναστατοῖ με· ἆρρον αὐτόν ('he upsets me; away with him!'), is poor (since the circumstances are so different); but it is hard to find a better. 'We may think it possible that the Jews, in thus crying "Hoist Him up! Hoist Him up!", unconsciously ask for his exaltation as the Son of man [3.14; 8.28; 12.32,34]' (Lightfoot). Possible perhaps, but hardly probable.

τὸν βασιλέα ὑμῶν σταυρώσω; Pilate resumes his irony, and leads up to the Jews' blasphemy.

οὐκ ἔχομεν βασιλέα εἰ μὴ Καίσαρα. Cf. Judges 8.23; 1 Sam. 8.7, and many other passages of the Old Testament, where it is insisted that the only true king of Israel is God himself, and that even a Jewish king can be tolerated only on condition of his obedience to God and fidelity to the national religion. In denying all claims to kingship save that of the Roman Emperor Israel abdicated its own unique position under the immediate sovereignty of God. In the language of vv. 10f., it now becomes clear that true ἐξουσία resides neither in Pilate nor in the Jews, nor in what these represent, but in God only.

16. παρέδωκεν. This is the nearest approach to a sentence of death that John gives. It is far from clear how it can be intended. Pilate could not hand Jesus over to the Jews for crucifixion, which was a Roman punishment and must have been carried out by Roman troops. Either John uses παρέδωκεν loosely—Pilate gave Jesus up to the fate the Jews demanded (as at Luke 23.25, τὸν δὲ Ἰησοῦν παρέδωκεν τῷ θελήματι αὐτῶν); or (and this would be required by a strict interpretation of αὐτοῖς) he mistakenly supposed that the Jews did crucify Jesus (but vv. 23,25, οἱ στρατιῶται). Cf. Mark 15.15, where nothing is amiss; probably John simply borrowed the word παρέδωκεν from this source, not noticing the effect of the addition of αὐτοῖς (possibly from Mark 15.15a).

39. THE CRUCIFIXION AND DEATH OF JESUS

19.17-30

Jesus, now delivered over to death, carries his own cross to Golgotha and is there crucified between two others, his cross bearing the legend, Jesus of Nazareth the king of the Jews, a legend to which the Jews object in vain. His clothing is, in fulfilment of Scripture, shared among the soldiers, who cast lots for his tunic. In the presence of certain women Jesus presents his mother and the beloved disciple to each other as mother and son. In fulfilment of another passage of Scripture Jesus is given vinegar to drink; then, with the declaration that the work of God is completed, he dies.

Again, the essential events are paralleled in Mark: the journey to Golgotha, the royal title on the cross, the division of the clothes, the presence of the women, the vinegar, and the death. John makes additions and omissions. Simon of Cyrene (Mark 15.21) disappears, and Jesus carries the cross for himself. The fulfilment of prophecy is stressed in both the division of the clothes and the drink offered to Jesus. The committing of the mother and the beloved disciple to each other is peculiar to John, as is the objection of the Jews to Pilate's notice of condemnation. There is no mockery (cf. Mark 15.29–32). Jesus dies not as in Mark 15.34 with a cry of dereliction but with an affirmation of fulfilment, and the words (παρέδωκε τὸ πνεῦμα, v. 30) by which his death is described recall the words of commendation (παρατίθεμαι τὸ πνεῦμά μου) of Luke 23.46. John's narrative is probably based on Mark's (see Introduction, pp. 42–5), but either he, or intermediate tradition, has modified the source considerably. That John was independent of Mark is maintained by e.g. Dodd (*Tradition*, 121–36) and Brown who (915) argues (1) that in material common to John and the Synoptists there are often notable differences in vocabulary and sequence, and (2) that the properly Johannine details may as well be traditional as imaginative addition. There is substance in these points, but some answer to them may be found in Brown's own analysis (911) of the structure of John 19.16b–42. If John did indeed force his narrative into this elaborate chiastic pattern differences in vocabulary and sequence are to be expected; and Brown's estimate of the historical value of the incidents peculiar to John is not wholly convincing.

Every one of the differences between John and Mark is at least connected with a dogmatic motive. Once more John brings out the theme of the royalty of Jesus (see above on 18.33, *et passim*), and the fact that the crucifixion was the fulfilment of prophecy, and the perfect performance by Jesus of the Father's will. He does not allow himself even to suggest that Jesus was deserted by God. The men crucified with Jesus are forgotten as soon as mentioned. They are not introduced by John for their own sake, but in order to make possible the narrative of 19.31–7. The incident regarding the mother and the beloved disciple is a crux in the Johannine problem. It is most naturally explained as simple historical reminiscence due to the beloved disciple himself. Against this view however must be ranged the historical difficulties mentioned in the notes; it cannot be regarded as satisfactory. On the other hand, the theological interest of the incident is too slight to make it seem plausible that the whole matter was created for this purpose. The probability must remain that John was using what was already in his day traditional material which was of questionable historical value but caught his eye on account of its theological suggestiveness.

17. βαστάζων ἑαυτῷ τὸν σταυρόν. The dative ἑαυτῷ is emphatic; according to Radermacher (106) the usage is Hellenistic and must here be translated 'alone'. Black (102) thinks that the word represents the Aramaic ethic dative. Contrast the Marcan account (15.21) of Simon of Cyrene, who was compelled to carry the cross. It is of course possible to harmonize the Marcan and Johannine narratives by supposing that Jesus began to carry the cross himself, fainted under the burden, and was relieved by the forced assistance of Simon; yet, if it is true that John knew Mark, his words read like a correction, and its motive must be sought. The Fathers (e.g. Chrysostom, *In Joh. Hom.* LXXXV, 1) saw a type of Christ bearing the cross in Isaac, who (Gen. 22.6) carried the materials for the sacrifice of himself. Philo had already commented on this incident (*Abr.*, 171) αὐτὸ δικαιώσας τὸ ἱερεῖον τὰ πρὸς τὴν θυσίαν ἐπηχθίσθαι; and it seems not impossible that John also may have had in mind some such typology, and conformed the narrative to it. This connection is perhaps reinforced by the fact that the comment on Gen. 22.6 in *Gen. R.* 56.4 is '. . . as one bears the cross (צלוב) on his shoulder'. On the significance of the 'Binding of Isaac' in Judaism see G. Vermes, *Scripture and Tradition in Judaism* (1961), 193–227; Vermes sees a reference to this in John 1.29 (see the note) but not in the present passage. Had one been intended John would probably have made it clearer. Barnabas 7.3 however already takes Isaac to be a type of Christ. An alternative explanation is that John wished to avoid the possibility of the view adopted by some Docetists that at the last moment a substitution was effected so that Simon of Cyrene was crucified instead of the impassible Son of God (Irenaeus, *adv. Haer.* 1, xix, 2). But most probable is the view that John wished once more to emphasize the all-sufficiency of Jesus; he needed no help in effecting the redemption of the world.

εἰς τὸν λεγόμενον Κρανίου τόπον. For this use of λεγόμενον to introduce a proper name cf. v. 13. The place was probably called 'Skull-place' from its appearance. On the tradition that it was the place where Adam's skull was buried see G. Dalman, *Sacred Sites and Ways* (E.T. 1935), 347, and, for much detail, Brown.

ὃ (א B; Θ ω, ὅς) λέγεται Ἑβραϊστὶ Γολγοθά: the Aramaic is גולגלתא or גולגולתא, a *skull* or *head*.

18. καὶ μετ' αὐτοῦ ἄλλους δύο. Cf. Mark 15.27, δύο λῃστάς; John gives no hint that he knows the Lucan tradition of the penitence of one of these malefactors (Luke 23.40–43). They are mentioned only in order that it may later (vv. 31–7) be emphasized that no bone of *Jesus* was broken, and that from his side there flowed blood and water. From the fact that the two are described neither as λῃσταί nor as κακοῦργοι (Luke) it is not to be inferred that the Johannine tradition understood them to be disciples (Zealot followers of a Zealot king). John omits the description partly because he has no use to make of it (he offers no allusion to Isa. 53.12), partly in order to avoid the suggestion that such company was appropriate to Jesus.

ἐντεῦθεν καὶ ἐντεῦθεν suggests a Semitic construction (cf. Num. 22.24 (φραγμὸς ἐντεῦθεν καὶ φραγμὸς ἐντεῦθεν, inaccurately represented by L.S. *s.v.* ἐντεῦθεν); Dan. 12.5 (Theod.); 1 Macc. 6.38; 9.45), but does not exactly represent one.

Delitzsch properly renders מזה אחד ומזה אחד. The expression indicates a Semitic mind, but not translation from a Semitic original.

μέσον δὲ τὸν Ἰησοῦν, 'and Jesus as the middle one'.

19. ἔγραψεν δὲ καὶ τίτλον ὁ Πειλᾶτος. Here γράφειν clearly means 'cause to be written'; cf. 21.24 and the note. τίτλος is a transliteration of the Latin *titulus*. For the custom of exposing such a notice cf. e.g. Suetonius, *Caligula* 32, *praecedente titulo qui causam poenae indicaret.* See however E. Haenchen, *Die Bibel und Wir* (1968), 206.

Ἰησοῦς ὁ Ναζωραῖος ὁ βασιλεὺς τῶν Ἰουδαίων. The charge against Jesus appears in similar forms in the other gospels: Mark 15.26, ὁ βασιλεὺς τῶν Ἰουδαίων; Matt. 27.37, οὗτός ἐστιν Ἰησοῦς ὁ β. τῶν Ἰ.; Luke 23.38, ὁ β. τῶν Ἰ. οὗτος. Of all these forms the Marcan is probably the oldest; but no evangelist adds any significant, or misleading, point. It has already been pointed out that the charge of claiming to be king (Messiah) must almost certainly have been that which compelled the Roman governor to act, and that kingship is a fundamental theme of John's theological treatment of the passion narrative. The title 'suggests on the one hand the price paid by the Jews for the rejection of their King, namely the condemnation and destruction of Judaism and of its age-long hopes. On the other hand the reader knows that, precisely because of the crucifixion, the Lord is King indeed; the cross is the manner of His exaltation and glorification' (Lightfoot). 'The condemnation of Jesus is at the same time the judgement of Judaism, which had surrendered the very hope that gave its existence its meaning—and so the judgement of the world, that for the sake of its security in the present gives up its future (Bultmann). See also E. Dinkler, *Signum*, 305ff.

20. ἐγγὺς ἦν ὁ τόπος. See on v. 17; the place is unknown.

Ἑβραϊστί, Ῥωμαϊστί, Ἑλληνιστί. For the first word, see vv. 13, 17, above. The second, and related words, are not uncommon in late Greek; Ἑλληνιστί is used as early as Plato. For the adverbial suffix see M. ii, 163. Polyglot notices in the Hellenistic age were probably almost as common as they are in continental railway carriages today. Cf. e.g. Josephus, *Ant.* xiv, 191, βούλομαι δὲ καὶ Ἑλληνιστὶ καὶ Ῥωμαϊστὶ ἐν δέλτῳ χαλκῇ τοῦτο ἀνατεθῆναι; *Bel.* vi, 125; and the well-known Latin and Greek inscriptions of the *Res Gestae Diui Augusti.* See also Esth. 8.8ff. (Guilding, 169). If John saw any theological significance in the trilingual inscription—the universal condemnation of those who thus condemned Jesus, and the universal offer of salvation to the universally condemned—he does nothing to indicate it.

21. The Jews' objection to the *titulus* was natural. In the first place, they had just declared that they had no king but Caesar, and the *titulus*, if they accepted it, was tantamount to an admission of sedition; and in the second place, to suggest that a powerless, condemned, and dying outcast was the king of their nation was a studied insult. To state only that the crazy fellow had claimed to be king would be harmless.

μὴ γράφε. Moule (*Idiom Book*, 21) notes that the present tense is surprising. Turner's (M. iii. 76) 'Alter what you have written' (i.e., Do not go on writing (what you have written)) probably gives the sense.

22. Pilate, no doubt anxious to avenge himself upon the Jews who had forced him to act against his will, refused to alter what he had written. Accordingly

Jesus went to his death under a title unintentionally but profoundly true. Cf. v. 14. Another consummate dramatic touch of the evangelist's reaches its mark.

23. Cf. Mark 15.24. The clothes of an executed criminal were a recognized perquisite of the executioners (*Digest* xlviii, xx, 6).

τὰ ἱμάτια. τὸ ἱμάτιον (singular) means always the *outer* garment; but the plural when used generally (as here) is equivalent to our 'clothes' (see L.S. *s.v.* ἱμάτιον, 1, 2).

τέσσερα μέρη. There were therefore four soldiers. Probably they formed a military unit; cf. the τετράδια of Acts 12.4.

καὶ τὸν χιτῶνα. Evidently the accusative is dependent only on ἔλαβον, not on ἐποίησαν; the construction could be improved. The χιτών was an under-garment, corresponding both etymologically and in usage with the Hebrew כתנת (*kᵉthoneth*). At Lev. 16.4 both Hebrew and Greek words are used of the high priest's tunic, כתנת בד קדש ילבש, χιτῶνα λινοῦν ἡγιασμένον ἐνδύσεται. See below.

ἦν δὲ ὁ χιτὼν ἄρραφος. ἄρραφος is from ῥάπτειν, 'to sew together'. It can hardly be insignificant that Josephus (*Ant.* iii, 161) describes the high priest's tunic in similar language: ἔστι δ' ὁ χιτὼν οὗτος οὐκ ἐκ δυοῖν περιτμημάτων, ὥστε ῥαπτὸς ἐπὶ τῶν ὤμων εἶναι καὶ τῶν παρὰ πλευράν, φάρσος δ' ἐν ἐπίμηκες ὑφασμένον (note that Josephus does not use ἀρ(ρ)αφος as L.S. *s.v.* assert): and that Philo (*Fug.*, 110–12) treats the tunic as a symbol of the Word which is the δεσμὸς τῶν ἀπάντων, which συνέχει τὰ μέρη πάντα καὶ σφίγγει κωλύων αὐτὰ διαλύεσθαι καὶ διαρτᾶσθαι. It seems probable that the make-up of the tunic was a matter of common knowledge and, in Hellenistic Judaism, of allegory. It goes too far simply to assert, 'Jesus is not only a king but a priest' (Brown). Hahn (*Titel*, 235; E. T. very briefly, 237, n. 26) is much more cautious. John's thought was set in motion not by any description of the high priest's vest-ments but by the fulfilment of Ps. 22 (see v. 24), and he would probably think, not of the Word as the unifying element of the universe, but of the death of Christ as bringing into one flock the scattered children of God (cf. 11.52). It seems very unlikely that there is an allusion to Joseph, with his coat, his brothers (prefiguring the disciples), and his two fellow-prisoners. Schlatter (349) quotes *Betzah* 1.10, but his translation (ἱμάτια εἴτε ῥαφέντα εἴτε ἄραφα) is misleading; the reference is not to garments such as that which Jesus wore, but to garments whether made up (sewn up) or not משלחין (כלים בין תפורין בין שאינם תפורין).

ἐκ τῶν ἄνωθεν. ἄνωθεν, or ἐκ τῶν ἄνω (8.23) would have expressed the fact better, but the meaning is clear.

24. ἵνα ἡ γραφὴ πληρωθῇ. Many MSS. add ἡ λεγοῦσα. The quotation is from Ps. 22(21).19, given exactly according to the LXX. It need not be supposed that this Old Testament passage gave rise to the whole incident as recorded by all the evangelists; it was an incident that might very well happen at any execution. But it does seem likely that the distinction drawn between the ἱμάτια (which were merely divided—διεμερίσαντο, τέσσερα μέρη) and the χιτών (for which the men cast lots—ἔβαλον κλῆρον, λάχωμεν) arose out of a failure to understand that in the parallel form of Hebrew verse ἱμάτια and ἱματισμός (בגדי and לבושי) are to be regarded as synonyms, and not to be distinguished. To say (Lindars) that John did understand the synonymous

parallelism but took advantage of it to fill out the tradition comes near to accusing him 'of saying what he knew to be untrue. In fact, Hebrew parallelism was little if at all understood at this time (see p. 150). Both Ps. 22 and Exod. 39.22f. (about the high priest's tunic) are said to be associated with the feast of Purim (Guilding, 169f.).

οἱ μὲν οὖν στρατιῶται. The soldiers are mentioned again (with the resumptive use of μὲν οὖν) in order to bring out yet another of John' s dramatic contrasts. Over against the soldiers stand the faithful disciples.

25. Just as the division of the clothes of Jesus is in itself a probable event, so the presence near (Sanders points out that the preposition παρά need not signify immediate neighbourhood, but the conversation that follows requires this) the cross of friends of Jesus is improbable. In Mark 15.40f. the women are said with greater plausibility to be ἀπὸ μακρόθεν θεωροῦσαι. It is true that E. Stauffer (Jesus and His Story (E.T. 1960), 179, note 1) adduces passages (T. Gittin 7.1 (330); Y. Gittin 7, 48c, 39; Baba Metzia 83b (S.B. II, 580) could be added) which represent friends of the victim as standing near enough to converse with him, but these do not outweigh the military requirements of the execution of a rebel king (v. 19). Josephus (Vita, 420f.) records that with special permission he was able to release three friends from their crosses; one survived. This shows both that there was a real danger of continued rebellious action, and that permission would be needed to approach the crosses. 'The soldiers ... then had to keep watch by the cross, lest his sympathising friends should come to the help of the tortured man' (O. Holtzmann, The Life of Jesus (E.T., 1904), 487). It is of course not impossible that known associates of Jesus might be able to creep up unobserved, but in addition to the general probabilities Mark 14.50 must be borne in mind. On crucifixion as a military operation see New Schürer, 1, 370ff.

ἡ μήτηρ αὐτοῦ ... ἡ Μαγδαληνή. It is possible that only two women are referred to (Jesus' mother=Mary the daughter (or sister) of Clopas, and her sister, Mary Magdalene) or three (Jesus' mother, her sister=Mary the daughter (or sister, or wife) of Clopas, and Mary Magdalene); but more probable that John intended his readers to think of four. Perhaps he thinks of them as corresponding with the four soldiers. Identifications are easy to conjecture but impossible to ascertain. See a very full note in Brown. John never mentions the name of the mother of Jesus.

ἡ τοῦ Κλωπᾶ. It is possible that this Clopas should be identified with the Κλεοπᾶς of Luke 24.18.

Μαρία ἡ Μαγδαληνή. This Mary has not previously been mentioned in John; she reappears as the first witness of the risen Christ (20.1–18). In Matthew and Mark also she is mentioned only as a witness of the crucifixion and resurrection, and is so mentioned at Luke 24.10; but at Luke 8.2 she is named with other women who ministered to Jesus and it is said that seven demons had gone out of her. It is to be noted that this is all we know of her; there are no serious grounds for identifying her with Mary the sister of Martha and Lazarus, the woman who anoints Jesus at Mark 14.3, or the sinner of Luke 7.37.

26. τὸν μαθητὴν ... ὃν ἠγάπα, the beloved disciple, on whom see Introduction, pp. 116–19, and on 13.23. It is not certain that John the son of Zebedee was intended; if it was it remains beyond proof that he was related to the

mother of Jesus. Here, with Mary, he is the sole representative of the associates of Jesus; even Peter, with whom he appears elsewhere, is absent.

γύναι. Cf. 2.4. She takes her place among the disciples.

ἴδε, as at v. 14, an interjection, not governing an accusative.

ὁ υἱός σου. The form of words recalls formulas of adoption. Brown thinks it better to speak of a revelatory formula; the two are not mutually inconsistent. Adoption means the creation of a new relationship; the formula reveals what the new relationship is to be. It is true (as Brown remarks) that adoption formulas are usually couched in the second person (e.g., 'You are my son'); but here the words are not spoken by the adoptive parent.

27. ἴδε ἡ μήτηρ σου. Henceforward, the mother of Jesus and the beloved disciple are to stand in the relation of mother and son; that is, the beloved disciple moves into the place of Jesus himself. It is not inconceivable that Jesus, as the head of the family (supposing his brothers to have been younger than he, not sons of Joseph by a former wife), should have made provision for care of his mother after his death. It is however surprising that the brothers should be overlooked, for their lack of faith in Jesus (7.5) could not annul their legal claim, and indeed Mark suggests (3.20–35) that their unbelief was shared by the mother also. When we add to this the improbability that friends of Jesus would be allowed near the cross it seems that the historical foundation of the incident is slight; and we note that at Acts 1.14 the mother of Jesus appears in company with his brothers. Cf. Lucian, *Toxaris* 22, where Eudamidas makes provision for his mother and daughter: ἀπολείπω Ἀρεταίῳ μὲν τὴν μητέρα μου τρέφειν καὶ γηροκομεῖν, Χαριξένῳ δὲ τὴν θυγατέρα μου ἐκδοῦναι μετὰ προικός.

ἀπ' ἐκείνης τῆς ὥρας; from that moment; possibly, from the significant hour of the crucifixion.

εἰς τὰ ἴδια, to his own home. Cf. 1.11; 16.32; also Rev. 12. If we are justified in seeing in John's reference to the indivisible χιτών of Jesus a symbol of the unity of the church gathered together by his death, we may here see an illustration of this unity. The Christian receives in the present age houses and brothers and sisters and mothers and children and lands (Mark 10.30). There seems no sufficient ground for the view that the mother of Jesus represents allegorically the faithful remnant of Israel from which the Messiah sprang, now absorbed into the New Israel. Other views may be briefly mentioned. Lightfoot compares 16.21—the cross brings a new sorrow but also a greater joy than physical birth. After this can be said τετέλεσται (vv. 28,30), since the church has now come into being. Brown writes, 'The Johannine picture of Jesus' mother becoming the mother of the Beloved Disciple seems to evoke the Old Testament themes of Lady Zion's giving birth to a new people in the messianic age, and of Eve and her offspring'. It will be wise, however, not to go beyond the recognition of an allusion to the new family, the church, and of the sovereign power of Jesus, '*Christus regens in cruce*' (Haenchen, *Weg*, 507). But see now J. McHugh, *The Mother of Jesus in the New Testament* (1974), 370–8; I. de la Potterie, in *Neues Testament und Kirche* (Festschrift R. Schnackenberg, 1974), 191–219.

28. μετὰ τοῦτο. For this characteristic connecting link see on 2.12.

εἰδὼς ὁ Ἰησοῦς. From first to last in this passion narrative Jesus is in control of all that takes place. The whole train of events is set in motion by him, and at the appropriate moment he will terminate it.

ὅτι ἤδη πάντα τετέλεσται. Cf. v. 30; Acts 13.29, ὡς δὲ ἐτέλεσαν πάντα τὰ περὶ αὐτοῦ γεγραμμένα; also Luke 22.37. Jesus had completed all the work he had been sent into the world to do; the revelation and the deed of love were complete. There is perhaps a special reference to the complete fulfilment of Scripture, with the note that one prophecy remains to be enacted.

The use of the singular, ἵνα τελειωθῇ ἡ γραφή, makes it probable that this final clause is to be connected with what follows. It is not impossible, but less likely, that it should be connected with what precedes: All things had been accomplished in order that the Scripture should be fulfilled. The unusual τελειοῦν is used instead of πληροῦν, probably in view of the repeated τετέλεσται.

διψῶ. See Ps. 69(68).22, εἰς τὴν δίψαν μου ἐπότισάν με ὄξος (quoted in 1QH 4.11). There can be little doubt that this is the γραφή in mind. In no other gospel does Jesus declare his own thirst—in John as usual he takes the initiative. In Mark a sponge of vinegar is offered (Mark 15.36, γεμίσας σπόγγον ὄξους περιθεὶς καλάμῳ ἐπότιζεν αὐτόν; cf. Matt. 27.48; Luke 23.36) As in the mention of the casting of lots for the clothes of Jesus John makes the Old Testament allusion more explicit than do the earlier evangelists. He is probably dependent on Mark or a similar source, and whether the Marcan incident is historical narrative or a construction based simply on the Old Testament passage is a question that need not be discussed here.

29. σπόγγον. In the New Testament the word is used in this context only; it seems very likely that both Matthew and John (Luke does not use it) drew it from Mark 15.36.

ὄξους, apparently the sour wine used by soldiers. It has been said that it would have the effect of aggravating thirst (Lightfoot), and thus of adding to the suffering endured by Jesus; but if this was so one wonders why the soldiers drank it. There is no point in trying to harmonize this passage with Jesus' last supper promise (not recorded by John) to drink no more wine until he should drink it in the kingdom of God.

ὑσσώπῳ. Hyssop is 'a small wall-growing plant, well adapted for sprinkling' (E. Bib., s.v.). It is therefore ill adapted for presenting a wet sponge to the lips of a crucified man; a bunch of hyssop would lack the necessary stiffness (contrast the καλάμῳ of Mark 15.36). In view of this it has been suggested that through a primitive error ὑσσώπῳ has taken the place of ὑσσῷ (ὑσσός, 'a javelin', Latin pilum). This conjectural reading (it occurs, probably by accident, in one late minuscule) would undoubtedly ease the sense of the passage; but it is not therefore necessarily justified. It seems to have been John's purpose to set forth Jesus as the true Paschal lamb, slaughtered for the deliverance of his people (see 1.29,36; 19.14,36), and it will be recalled that hyssop played an important part in Passover observance; see Exod. 12.22, λήμψεσθε δὲ δέσμην ὑσσώπου, καὶ βάψαντες ἀπὸ τοῦ αἵματος τοῦ παρὰ τὴν θύραν καθίξετε τῆς φλιᾶς καὶ ἐπ' ἀμφοτέρων τῶν σταθμῶν. . . . ὕσσωπος was probably an intentional alteration of Mark's κάλαμος; the fact that hyssop could hardly be used in the manner described is not one that would greatly concern the evangelist.

30. τετέλεσται. See on this word in v. 28, and cf. the use of τελειοῦν in Hebrews. Now that the last prophecy had been fulfilled it could be spoken by Jesus himself. His work was done. The cry is to be thought of in this positive sense, not as the mere announcement of the imminence of death, though this too is intended—the word bears a characteristically Johannine double meaning. If it once was the concluding formula of a mystery it has been very thoroughly historicized and Christianized. Cf. 4.34; 17.4, ἐγώ σε ἐδόξασα ἐπὶ τῆς γῆς, τὸ ἔργον τελειώσας ὃ δέδωκάς μοι ἵνα ποιήσω; also 13.1 (εἰς τέλος).

κλίνας τὴν κεφαλήν, in the moment of death; yet even here Jesus remains the subject of an active verb. Cf. 10.17f. This remains true, whether or not bowing the head was a conscious act that prevented breathing and so caused death.

παρέδωκεν τὸ πνεῦμα. This is probably equivalent to Mark's ἐξέπνευσεν (15.37; cf. Luke 23.46), paraphrased in Matthew (27.50) as ἀφῆκεν τὸ πνεῦμα. The words are not, however, the same, and it is possible that in John's mind πνεῦμα was not the human spirit of Jesus, given up when his body died, but the Holy Spirit, which, when he died, he was able to hand over (παραδιδόναι) to the few representative believers who stood by the cross. This suggestion is attractive because it corresponds to the undoubted fact that it was precisely at this moment, according to John, that the gift of the Spirit became possible (7.39). But it must reckon with these objections: (a) The expression may be based upon, and explained by, Luke 23.46, πάτερ, εἰς χεῖράς σου παρατίθεμαι τὸ πνεῦμά μου. (b) John describes circumstantially and impressively the occasion on which Jesus imparted the Holy Spirit to the church: 20.22, λάβετε πνεῦμα ἅγιον. There is no room for an earlier giving of the Spirit.

40. THE BURIAL OF JESUS

19.31–42

Since it was necessary that the bodies should be speedily removed from the cross and disposed of the Jews asked that the necessary steps might be taken to ensure death. The soldiers, however, who had broken the legs of the two crucified with Jesus, found him already dead. Instead of breaking his legs, one pierced his side with a lance, which caused the effusion of blood and water—a fact upon which John lays stress. Afterwards Joseph of Arimathea obtained permission to remove and bury the body of Jesus, and with the assistance of Nicodemus effected the burial in the most sumptuous manner.

There are undoubted contacts here between John and both Mark and Luke (see the notes); but much of the material, especially the breaking of the legs and the lance thrust, is new. The question of its historical value is of the utmost difficulty. On the one hand John emphasizes that the effusion of blood and water caused by the lance thrust was a historical event, vouched for by impeccable testimony (v. 35). On the other, the presence of an eye-witness is not probable, and the alleged fact is clearly related to, and could conceivably have arisen out of, John's theology. It seems, if we may judge from the character of the gospel as a whole, unlikely that John is simply manufacturing an event for the sake of its allegorical significance. For a full discussion of the problems involved see Introduction, pp. 118f., and on the verse. The fact that no bone of Jesus was broken is also of theological significance for John; see the notes. John does not seem fully to have understood the Jewish reason for removing the bodies from the crosses before nightfall, and the narrative of the burial shows a marked development in the tradition from its earlier stages. Contacts with the Marcan narrative will be noted; it is possible that the lance thrust and testimony based upon it are John's substitute for the centurion's confession (Mark 15.39), but the connection is remote.

This section is for the most part simple narrative; but John means to bring out that Jesus truly died, that his death was in accordance with the will of God revealed in Scripture and was the source of life and cleansing for men; and that he was appropriately buried.

31. οἱ οὖν 'Ιουδαῖοι. See on 1.19.

παρασκευή ἦν. Cf. v. 42. At v. 14 the word is used in a different sense (παρασκευή τοῦ πάσχα). Here since there is no genitive, it must mean 'the day before the Sabbath', that is the twenty-four hours between 6 p.m. on Thursday and 6 p.m. on Friday. The death of Jesus therefore took place on Friday afternoon; the Sabbath was near. Cf. Mark 15.42 (ἐπεὶ ἦν παρασκευή, ὅ ἐστιν προσάββατον), on which John is probably dependent.

ἵνα μὴ μείνη ἐπὶ τοῦ σταυροῦ τὰ σώματα (that is, of all three victims) ἐν τῷ σαββάτῳ. The prohibition of Deut. 21.22f. is that bodies should not remain beyond nightfall (οὐ κοιμηθήσεται τὸ σῶμα αὐτοῦ ἐπὶ τοῦ ξύλου); the Sabbath is here mentioned because it happened to be the immediately following day; or perhaps because John misunderstood the prohibition. Of course, it is true that what would have been objectionable on any day was doubly so on so important a day.

ἦν γὰρ μεγάλη ἡ ἡμέρα ἐκείνου τοῦ σαββάτου. 'If this Sabbath, as the Fourth Gospel supposes, was Nisan 15, it could be called "great" since it was at the same time the first Passover festival day. If it fell on Nisan 16, as the synoptics suppose, the title "great" is still suitable, since on it according to Pharisaic tradition the Omer sheaf was presented (Lev. 23.11)' (S.B. II, 581f.). Cf. Mart. Pol. 8.1; 21.1 (ὄντος σαββάτου μεγάλου; σαββάτῳ μεγάλῳ); on these, Lightfoot, Apostolic Fathers II, i, 690–3; Abrahams, Studies II, 67–9.

ἵνα κατεαγῶσιν αὐτῶν τὰ σκέλη. On the verbal form see M. II, 189, 226; B.D., §§66.2; 101. The crurifragium was sometimes an independent form of punishment, sometimes, as here, an accompaniment of crucifixion. It had the merciful effect of hastening death, partly through shock and loss of blood, partly also (according to some) by increasing the difficulty of breathing. Brown (934) notes the discovery in Jerusalem of the bones of a man crucified in the first century A.D. whose legs were broken.

καὶ ἀρθῶσιν. The subject changes and is now τὰ σώματα, which, as a neuter plural, took a singular verb (μείνη) earlier in the verse.

555

32. In the Gospel of Peter 14 one of the malefactors does not have his legs broken but is left to die in torment.

33. εἶδον ἤδη αὐτὸν τεθνηκότα. So speedy a death was unusual. Victims of crucifixion sometimes lingered for days. Cf. Mark 15.44, ἐθαύμασεν εἰ ἤδη τέθνηκεν.

οὐ κατέαξαν αὐτοῦ τὰ σκέλη. John brings out the significance of this fact (which he alone records) in v. 36; see below. He may also be countering the charge that disfigurement of Jesus' body disproved his resurrection; see Daube, *N.T.R.J.*, 308.

34. λόγχη. 'Lance, spear, javelin' (L.S.); the use of this word here makes it the more unlikely that John wrote ὑσσός at v. 29.

τὴν πλευράν. The word is more frequently used in the plural. Cf. 20.20,25,27 where the wounded side is a mark of identification of the risen Christ. This incident is mentioned elsewhere only in the *textus receptus* of Matt. 27.49, where it is undoubtedly due to textual assimilation to this passage in John.

ἐξῆλθεν εὐθὺς αἷμα καὶ ὕδωρ. This obscure statement was evidently regarded by John as a matter of very great importance (see the next verse). (*a*) John certainly intended to describe a real, not merely a symbolic event. This is emphasized by the stress laid on the eye-witness in v. 35. And it must be conceded that the event as described is physiologically possible. Blood might flow from a corpse if only a short time had elapsed since death; and a fluid resembling water might issue from the region described as πλευρά. It may be asked, however, whether John thought he was describing a normal event—one which might have been observed in any corpse, or an abnormal event—one which could have happened only in the body of Jesus, which was not to see corruption. The former alternative is more probable, in view of the anti-docetic interest of the Johannine literature generally; John intended to provide evidence that Jesus was a real man, and that he really died. Cf. Irenaeus, *adv. Haer.* III, xxii, 2, . . . nor [if he had not been truly man], when his side was pierced, would there have come forth blood and water. (*b*) But John's intention is not to be confused with fact. We have already seen (on v. 25) that it is improbable that any disciple should have been in the immediate vicinity of the cross. We may note further that there is no room for the whole incident in the synoptic narrative (the centurion himself observes the death of Jesus and informs Pilate—Mark 15.39,45), and that if Jesus was already dead, as John says he manifestly was, there was no motive for the lance thrust, unless we are to suppose that the soldier struck Jesus out of mere spite or casual cruelty. (*c*) It is not inconsistent with John's intention to narrate a historical event that he should intend also to communicate a theological truth. There can be little doubt that he did so intend, in view of the significance of αἷμα and ὕδωρ elsewhere in the gospel (and in 1 John 5.6,8, a passage which is probably in some way dependent upon or related to this verse, but unfortunately does little to explain it). There is 'living water' which springs up within the believer (4.14), and a water which is identified with the Holy Spirit (7.38f.—this passage is especially important if the words ἐκ τῆς κοιλίας αὐτοῦ refer to Christ—see the note). It is of water and the Spirit that men are begotten from above (3.5), and water is the means by which men are cleansed (13.5). Again, the blood of Christ is the true drink of men (6.53ff.). Through it alone, with the flesh of Christ, which equally is given for the life of the world, may men have life in themselves. It is highly probable then that in the effusion of blood and water from the pierced side of Christ John saw a symbol of the fact that from the Crucified there proceed those living streams by which men are quickened and the church lives. Brown, who gives a great deal of valuable information on the history of the interpretation of this verse, is probable right in seeing here a secondary, but only a secondary, reference to the sacraments, clearer for baptism than for the eucharist. Detailed allusions, e.g. to the mixed chalice (of wine and water), were not intended by John who was not concerned to support this or that detail of sacramental practice or terminology, but to emphasize, perhaps against those who controverted it, that the real death of Jesus was the real life of men. See Introduction, pp. 82–5. There is thus little need to conclude that vv. 34b,35 were added by an ecclesiastical redactor. Again, it does not seem probable that John saw special significance in the sequence, first blood, then water, and intended thereby to indicate that it was when the sacrifice was completed that the Spirit could be given, though this is certainly in accord with 7.39; 16.7. It is doubtful whether Ps. 22(21).14 is in mind; Zech. 13.1 (note that Zech. 12.10 is quoted in v. 37) is a more probable allusion. An important suggestion is made by Dr J. M. Ford (*N.T.S.* 15 (1969), 337f.), who, quoting *Oholoth* 3.5; *Hullin* 2.6; *Pesahim* 5.5,8, sees an allusion to the Passover. 'If these rabbinical ideas do lie behind this passage of St John then we have three allusions to the Passover, (1) the hyssop (v. 29); (2) the unbroken bones (vv. 33 and 36); (3) the mingled blood (v. 34). The testimony, therefore, in v. 35 could be a witness to all three events in which St John sees Jesus as the Passover lamb. The lamb being כשר can cleanse us from all sin (1 John 1.7)' (op. cit., 338).

35. ὁ ἑωρακὼς μεμαρτύρηκεν. For the collocation of these two characteristically Johannine words cf. 1.34; 3.11. On μαρτυρεῖν see on 1.7. ὁ ἑωρακὼς is presumably a person who beheld the event just mentioned, the effusion of blood and water from Jesus' side, and communicated the information either *as* the author of the gospel, or *to* the author of the gospel. It is not stated, nor is it clear, who this person was; it is generally assumed that he was the beloved disciple (mentioned at v. 26), and this assumption may well be true, since v. 27 does not necessarily mean that he took the mother of Jesus to his home immediately. Cf. 21.24, where the identification is much clearer.

ἀληθινή . . . ἀληθῆ. For these words see on 1.9.

καὶ ἐκεῖνος οἶδεν. ἐκεῖνος has been variously held to be (*a*) the witness himself; (*b*) the author of the gospel (supposed to be other than the witness); (*c*) Christ; (*d*) God. The suggestion that ἐκεῖνος οἶδεν is a corruption of ἐκεῖνου οἴδαμεν ('we know that his testimony is true') assimilates to 21.24 but has little beyond its ingenuity to commend it. In favour of (*a*) is the grammatical construction; ἐκεῖνος resumes αὐτοῦ. This suggests that the witness was not the author, but this conclusion is not required by the sentence. ἐκεῖνος may be used by an author about himself (e.g. Josephus, *Bel.* III, 202, οὐ φθόνῳ τῆς ἐκείνου [Josephus'] σωτηρίας, ἔμοιγε [Josephus] δοκεῖν; quoted by Bernard, 649). (*b*) It does not seem easy to render 'his witness is true and *I* know that he is speaking the truth', yet this is in fact done by C. C. Torrey (50, 52f.), who takes ἐκεῖνος as an over-literal rendering of ההוא גברא, literally 'that man', but occasionally 'I'. This view however depends upon the opinion that John

557

as a whole was translated from Aramaic, and is otherwise improbable. (c) ἐκεῖνος is used of Christ in 3.28,30; 7.11; 9.28, and (d) of God in 1.33; 5.19,37; 6.29; 8.42; but it is manifestly ridiculous to suggest that it must refer to God or Christ unless this is required by the context. Of all these four interpretations (a) is the best; but it is not easy to say what it implies about the authorship of the gospel. 'It is inadvisable to build any theories of authorship on the notorious ἐκεῖνος' (M. iii. 46; cf. Turner, Insights, 137f.).

ἵνα καὶ ὑμεῖς πιστεύητε. This clause is only loosely constructed with the sentence, as will appear if an attempt is made to take it closely with ἀληθινή ἐστιν, οἶδεν, or λέγει. It indicates the general aim of the veracious testimony of the witness. 'You' (the readers of the gospel) 'are not merely to believe that blood and water did in fact issue from the side of the Crucified, but to believe in the full Christian sense' (cf. 20.31 for the aim of the gospel as a whole). There is no doubt that this verse claims eye-witness authority for at least one incident, and it is unlikely that John simply invented it (cf. Dodd, Tradition, 133f.); for its bearing on the authorship and authority of the gospel as a whole see Introduction, pp. 118f. The whole verse is omitted by e and by Codex Fuldensis, a very important MS. of the Vulgate. This evidence is certainly slight and perhaps does not justify von Soden who states that the omission is made by the 'African Old Latin'. It is true that neither Tertullian nor Cyprian quotes the verse, but this does not prove that it did not stand in their texts; it is perhaps more significant that it hardly appears in the writings of Augustine. In In Ioan. Euang. Tractatus cxx, 3, where Augustine seems to be following a Vulgate text, it receives but a perfunctory comment. It may or may not be significant that the Valentinians quoted by Clement of Alexandria in his Excerpta ex Theodoto refer to vv. 34, 36, 37, but not to v. 35. If any conclusion at all is to be drawn from these observations it might be that the gospel was at first issued (perhaps in gnostic circles) without 19.35 and that this verse was subsequently added to secure for the book authority (that of the eye-witness = the beloved disciple = an apostle) among the orthodox. But the evidence is so far much too slight to permit any such conclusion.

36. ὀστοῦν οὐ συντριβήσεται αὐτοῦ. It is difficult to give the source of this quotation. Three or four Old Testament passages come under consideration: Exod. 12.10 (cf. v. 46), Num. 9.12; Ps. 34(33).21. The Pentateuchal passages refer to the passover sacrifice, of which no bone may be broken; that in the Psalter refers to God's care of the faithful (κύριος φυλάσσει πάντα τὰ ὀστᾶ αὐτῶν). It is probable that the reference is primarily to the Passover (since Jesus died at the time of the sacrifice; hyssop has already been mentioned at v. 29; and Jesus had not been preserved from death, even though his bones had not been broken); yet we cannot exclude the influence of the Psalm since here only is the verbal form συντριβήσεται used. It may be that John's source referred to the Psalm but that he, with his paschal interests, preferred the Passover reference.

37. It is clear that in this verse (and this is probably true elsewhere) γραφή (singular) means a particular passage of Scripture.

ὄψονται εἰς ὃν ἐξεκέντησαν. John accurately follows Zech. 12.10 in the Hebrew (והביטו אלי את אשר דקרו), in agreement with Aquila and Theodotion (Symmachus has ἐπεξεκέντησαν). The LXX at this point diverges and reads κατωρχήσαντο, a reading which must have arisen from a confusion of consonants in the Hebrew; דקר ('to pierce') was taken to be רקד ('to mock'). Clearly John is not dependent upon the LXX, but whether he himself translated the Hebrew or used some existing version (perhaps a testimony book) it is impossible to say. Cf. a different handling of this *testimonium* in Rev. 1.7, also Mark 13.26; *Didache* 16.7; and Justin, I *Apol.*, 52 (where also ἐξεκέντησαν is used). John does not indicate the subject of ὄψονται, or whether men look in hatred, remorse, or faith (cf. 3.14f.; Num. 21.8f.). It is not the look but the piercing that fulfils prophecy that interests him.

38. Ἰωσὴφ (א Θ ω add ὁ) ἀπὸ Ἀριμαθαίας, not previously mentioned in John but cf. Mark 15.43, whence this section is drawn.

ὢν μαθητὴς τοῦ Ἰησοῦ κεκρυμμένος δέ. According to Mark (loc. cit.) Joseph was εὐσχήμων βουλευτής, ὃς καὶ αὐτὸς ἦν προσδεχόμενος τὴν βασιλείαν τοῦ θεοῦ, but Mark does not say that he was a disciple, though John may have taken him to mean this. For secret disciples of rank cf. 12.42. The participle κεκρυμμένος is used adverbially.

ἵνα (used to introduce the content of the request) ἄρῃ τὸ σῶμα τοῦ Ἰησοῦ. Bodies of criminals condemned and executed by the Romans were commonly left to the vultures; cf. however Philo, *In Flaccum*, 83. Victims of Jewish executions were buried in places provided by the court (*Sanhedrin* 6.5).

ἦλθεν ... ἦρεν. Plural verbs are read by א it sah, probably with reference to Nicodemus.

39. Νικόδημος. John himself supplies the cross-reference to 3.1f. It is perhaps implied here that Nicodemus too was a secret disciple; but (in spite of 7.50f.) this has not been said earlier in the gospel.

μίγμα is the reading of most MSS.; א* B W have ἕλιγμα, φ has σμίγμα. μίγμα is a usual word for a 'mixture' or 'confection' (e.g. of drugs), but neither L.S. nor M.M. quote any other use of ἕλιγμα for a 'packet' of herbs or drugs. ἕλιγμα is therefore to be reckoned the *lectio difficilior* (though it is regularly formed from ἑλίσσειν), and is perhaps to be preferred.

σμύρνης καὶ ἀλόης. σμύρνα is myrrh, used for embalming the dead, e.g. Herodotus II, 86; cf. Matt. 2.11, the only other New Testament use of the word. ἀλόη is *hap. leg.* in the New Testament; in the Old Testament aloes are referred to as providing perfume for the bed (Prov. 7.17) or for the clothes (Ps. 45.9), but not as in use at burial. See the note on the next verse.

ὡς λίτρας ἑκατόν. For the λίτρα see on 12.3. The total weight was about 75 lb. Cf. the immense quantity of wine produced in 2.1–11.

40. ὀθονίοις. Cf. κειρία in 11.44. ὀθόνιον is in the New Testament peculiar to John (also in 20.5,6,7; and in the Western Non-Interpolation in Luke 24.12). It means a linen bandage, such as might be used for wrapping a corpse. See e.g. *P. Giss.* 68.11f. (second century A.D.), ὀθόνια εὔωνα, 'fine linen wrappings for a mummy' (M.M.). The body is wrapped in the bandages, the spices being sprinkled between the folds. For a long note on the meaning of ὀθόνια, and its possible relation to the tradition of the Holy Shroud of Turin, see Brown, 941f. For the interrelation between this account of the burial of Jesus and the anointing see pp. 409, 413f., and Daube, *N.T.R.J.*, 310–24.

καθὼς ἔθος ἐστὶν τοῖς Ἰουδαίοις ἐνταφιάζειν. Cf. 11.44 for the burial of Lazarus. Apparently this means of entombment is contrasted with the Egyptian method of embalming; perhaps also with the Roman method of cremation.

Other sources suggest that among the Jews it was customary to use oil, not spices, for this purpose; but S.B. II, 53, and S. Krauss, *Talmudische Archäologie* (1910–12) II, 55, 474, are satisfied that the New Testament passages alone are sufficient evidence for the use of spices (Daube, op. cit.).

41. κῆπος. Among the canonical evangelists only John remarks that the crucifixion and burial took place in a garden. According to the Gospel of Peter 24 the garden was Joseph's. κῆπος (see on 18.1) means a large garden, orchard, or plantation. If John had intended an allusion to the Garden of Eden it is probable that he would have used the LXX word, παράδεισος. He is preparing for 20.15.

μνημεῖον καινόν. Cf. Matt. 27.60, τῷ καινῷ αὐτοῦ μνημείῳ. If John saw some special meaning in the fact that the tomb was new he does not point it out. That the tomb was unused is in keeping with the luxurious preparations of v. 39.

ἐν ᾧ οὐδέπω οὐδεὶς ἦν τεθειμένος. Cf. Luke 23.53, οὗ οὐκ ἦν οὐδεὶς οὔπω κείμενος. The ugly collocation of sounds in both gospels suggests that John was dependent on Luke.

42. τὴν παρασκευὴν τῶν 'Ιουδαίων. Cf. v. 31 and the note. In view of the near approach of the sabbath rest it was desirable to dispose of the body (whether temporarily or permanently) as quickly as possible. It was laid in the nearby tomb; it would be permissible on the Sabbath, if necessary, to wash and anoint it (*Shabbath* 23.4f.).

41. THE EMPTY TOMB AND THE FIRST RESURRECTION APPEARANCE

20.1–18

The early traditions of the resurrection of Jesus took two forms, traditions of resurrection appearances to various disciples (as in 1 Cor. 15.5–8), and traditions of the discovery that the tomb in which the body of Jesus had been placed was empty (as in Mark 16.1–8). In this paragraph, which John intends as his main statement of the church's Easter faith (v. 8; vv. 19–23 contain the apostolic commission), the two traditions are skilfully combined. A general review of all the New Testament resurrection narratives is given by Brown (966–78); after detailed discussion of other suggestions he comes to the conclusion (998) that in the present section John combines two accounts of visits to the tomb, which is found empty, with one of an appearance to Mary Magdalene. This view is not inconsistent with the possibility that John, in making his combination, was slightly affected by synoptic traditions (see below), and it should probably be accepted. See, in addition to the commentaries, G. Hartmann, 'Die Vorlage der Osterberichte in Joh 20', *Z.N.T.W.* 55 (1964), 197–220; also O. Michel, in *Studien zum Neuen Testament und zur Patristik* (Festschrift E. Klostermann, 1961), 35–42.

Mary, visiting the tomb early on Sunday morning, finds it open. She supposes that either enemies or tomb robbers have been at work, and informs Peter and the beloved disciple, who run to the tomb, find it empty, and see the cloths in which the body of Jesus had been wrapped. The beloved disciple, who was the first to reach the tomb, followed Peter into it, and, when he saw, believed that Jesus had risen from the dead. Mary had followed the two men, and when they left she remained outside the tomb. Looking in she saw two angels. She tells them the reason of her distress; but from that point the angels play no part in the story, for Mary turning round sees Jesus himself, though it is only when he addresses her by name that she recognizes him. He then sends her to the disciples with the message of his coming ascension, which she duly conveys.

This narrative may show some trace of the literary influence of the short Marcan resurrection story (Mark 16.1–8), but in substance it is independent—not necessarily however older (for this view see Jeremias, *Theology* 1, 304f., with his reference to Benoit). In fact its historical value cannot be accurately assessed. The following points however are relevant in this connection. (i) The narrative is permeated with theological themes of a Johannine kind: seeing and believing, and the ascent of Jesus to the Father. (ii) A central place is given to the beloved disciple; this will affect the historical estimate of the story according as it is thought that the beloved disciple represents a serious historical source or not. (iii) The synoptic tradition says nothing of an appearance to Mary Magdalene, and the oldest tradition nothing of the empty tomb. It may be added however that the oldest traditions of the resurrection were probably richer and more varied than those which have come down to us. There is no doubt that the present passage shows dramatic writing of great skill and individuality. On the form of the appearance stories see Dodd, *Tradition*, 143ff.

The beloved disciple appears once more in the company of Peter, and, though Peter is the first to enter the tomb, the former is the first to believe in the resurrection; he holds, in this sense, a primacy of faith. Cf. Peter's confession, Mark 8.29, and especially the Matthean supplement, Matt. 16.17–19.

What was John's intention in writing of the resurrection as he did? See especially v. 17, and the notes. The resurrection is represented as a stage in the process by which Jesus ascends to the Father. Dodd, *Interpretation*, 441ff., makes the interesting suggestion that John is able to introduce so much emotion and 'human interest', and so many physical, or quasi-physical, details into his story precisely because for him the crucifixion, now already in the past, truly is the glory of Jesus. Bultmann thinks that John offers a criticism of the traditional Easter stories. Jesus, encountered in this world, is not yet the exalted Lord who has promised to 'come' to his disciples; the appearances are at best incomplete attestation. In fact John's attitude to the traditional stories is best described in the terms used above (p. 85) to decribe his attitude to the sacraments: it is one of critical acceptance. Had John not held the Easter stories to be true (historically and theologically), still more, had he held them to be misleading (whether historically or theologically), he would not have recorded them. Yet he sees their limitations. Mary is bidden, Stop touching. Jesus says, I have not yet ascended. The resurrection story in itself is not the last word, and men must not regard the risen Jesus as simply the old Jesus all over again. Sight plays its part; but the Christian life is lived by faith.

1. τῇ δὲ μιᾷ τῶν σαββάτων. Cf. Mark 16.2; Matt. 28.1; Luke 24.1. The use of the cardinal numeral for the ordinal is probably to be regarded as a Semitism, in spite of the argument to the contrary in M. I, 95f. M. II, 439 is non-committal, but B.D., §247 allows that Hebrew, which uses cardinals for all days of the month, provided a model. The usage is also Aramaic. It cannot however be said that John was translating a Semitic source; he probably drew the construction from Mark 16.2 (he repeats it at v. 19). The plural σάββατα is used with singular meaning for both 'Sabbath' and 'week'. It probably arose because the Aramaic singular form שבתא (shabbᵉtha, shabbatta—both vocalizations are found) recalled the Greek neuter plural in -τα. The phrase חד בשבתא (literally, 'one in the Sabbath (week)') occurs e.g. in Gen. R. 11.9. The 'first day of the week' extended from 6 p.m. on Saturday to 6 p.m. on Sunday.

Μαρία ἡ Μαγδαληνή. See on 19.25. In Mark three, in Matthew two, and in Luke an indefinite number of women go to the tomb. Both here and in v. 18 ἡ Μαγδαληνή is omitted by sin. The omission may be accidental, or it may be that the Syriac church thought of a different Mary as going to the tomb.

πρωΐ σκοτίας ἔτι οὔσης. John must mean early on Sunday morning, not at the beginning of the day according to Jewish reckoning. According to Mark the first visit to the tomb was at dawn; Luke gives the same sense; Matt. 28.1 is very obscure, and might possibly refer to Saturday evening.

τὸν λίθον ἠρμένον. In 19.38–42 there is no mention of the closing of the sepulchre with a stone. John must be dependent on some such narrative as the Marcan (cf. Mark 15.46, προσεκύλισεν λίθον; 16.4, ἀνακεκύλισται ὁ λίθος). John no doubt implies that the stone had been taken away by supernatural means.

2. τρέχει οὖν καὶ ἔρχεται πρὸς Σίμωνα Πέτρον. For the double name see on 1.42. In Mark 16.7 all the women are bidden to inform 'his disciples and Peter' of the resurrection.

τὸν ἄλλον μαθητὴν ὃν ἐφίλει ὁ Ἰησοῦς. ἄλλον means a disciple other than Peter; there is no reference to a second 'beloved disciple'. For the beloved disciple and his connection with Peter see Introduction, pp. 116–19, and on 13.23. Cf. also the ἄλλος μαθητής in 18.15f. φιλεῖν is not to be distinguished from ἀγαπᾶν; see on 21.15.

ἦραν τὸν κύριον. The third person plural is impersonal and equivalent to a passive; see 15.6 and the note there. Mary not unnaturally suspects activity on the part of the enemies of Jesus, or of tomb-robbers. Cf. the important διάταγμα (rescript or perhaps edict) of Claudius, published at Nazareth (see most conveniently *Documents Illustrating the Reigns of Claudius and Nero* (1939), collected by M. P. Charlesworth; No. 17, p. 15). This document, which may well be in some way connected with Christian origins, threatens special punishments for tomb-breaking. See, for a useful discussion and bibliography, A. Momigliano, *Claudius the Emperor and his Achievement* (E.T. 1934), 36, 100f.

οὐκ οἴδαμεν. Only Mary brings the message, and the plural verb is out of place. It is another trace of the synoptic narrative in which several women visit the tomb, but it is not simply borrowed from the synoptic narrative. Not only does the word οἴδαμεν not occur there, but no such report as this is brought by the women. Bultmann, however, thinks that οἴδαμεν is not a genuine plural, but an Oriental mode of speech with Greek analogies. Cf. 3.2.

3. Cf. Luke 24.24; also Luke 24.12, a Western Non-Interpolation, not for that reason necessarily to be omitted. See K. Aland, *N.T.S.* 12 (1966), 205f. See also Benoit II, 274.

4. προέδραμεν τάχιον. The expression is pleonastic. If the beloved disciple ran more swiftly than Peter, of course he ran before him. Cf. v. 8; in these places the unnamed disciple seems to take precedence of Peter. See Haenchen, *Weg*, 533f. We must however be careful not to suggest that John identified fleetness of foot with apostolic pre-eminence. See v. 8.

5. παρακύψας. The word is often used of one looking down from a height (e.g. Judges 5.28; 1 Enoch 9.1; *P. Oxy.* 475.23; *C.H.* 1, 14), and might therefore be thought to imply a grave dug or hewn in the ground; but it does not necessarily have this meaning. It signifies a glance of any kind for which an inclination of the head is required. εἰσῆλθεν suggests that the grave was not simply vertical.

τὰ ὀθόνια. See on 19.40.

οὐ μέντοι εἰσῆλθεν. This hesitancy, which is perhaps not unnatural, could readily be explained if we supposed that John wished to emphasize that the beloved disciple was both the first to see the empty tomb (he is not in this gospel preceded by Mary) and the first to believe in the resurrection. If the latter point is to be fully made Peter must be brought into the tomb between the arrival of the beloved disciple and his confession of faith.

6, 7. ἀκολουθῶν. This word is usually significant in John (see on 1.37), and it may perhaps be intended here to subordinate Peter to the beloved disciple.
τὰ ὀθόνια κείμενα, καὶ τὸ σουδάριον. For the separate σουδάριον cf. 11.44. It is impossible to say with certainty how John thought the resurrection had taken place. At the raising of Lazarus the body, after being quickened, was drawn out of the tomb still wrapped in, and confined by, the bandages which had been used in preparing it for burial. Here however it seems that the body had in some way disappeared from, or passed through, the cloths and left them lying as they were. Cf. v. 19, where the risen Jesus suddenly appears in a closed room. John's point however may be simply to show that the natural assumption of robbery (v. 2) was mistaken.

εἰς ἕνα τόπον. Either, the σουδάριον was in one place, that is, neatly rolled up (ἐντετυλιγμένον), not simply in a disordered state; or, ἕνα is used for τινά, a Semitic usage.

8. εἶδεν καὶ ἐπίστευσεν. It is implied that Peter had not been convinced of the resurrection by the sight of the empty tomb and the grave-clothes. It does

not seem probable that the subject of these verbs is Peter; see however Benoit, II, 277. For 'seeing and believing' see on v. 29, also Cullmann, *Salvation*, 273, 295.

9. οὐδέπω γὰρ ᾔδεισαν τὴν γραφήν. The disciple's faith was grounded simply upon what he had seen at the tomb. By the time when John wrote the church's faith in the resurrection was supported by the conviction that it had been foretold in the Old Testament. γραφή seems commonly to be used of a single passage of Scripture (see 19.37); but none is quoted here, and it may be that the reference (like that of 1 Cor. 15.4) is to the Old Testament generally. Sanders suggests that Ps. 16.10 is in mind.

10. πρὸς αὐτούς (so ℵ* B; most MSS. have ἑαυτούς). The translation 'went to their own homes' seems impossible; John would have written πρός (or εἰς) τὰ ἴδια (cf. 1.11; 16.32). John's expression corresponds exactly to the Aramaic ethic dative (אזלו להון). But there is no need to suppose that John is translating; cf. Num. 24.25; Josephus, *Ant.* VIII, 124; and perhaps Polybius V, xciii, 1.

11. The men go away; Mary has apparently returned to the grave with them. She has not noticed the abandoned grave-clothes, but remains, overcome with grief. The text printed by Nestle is probably correct, but note that for πρός, ℵ has ἐν, and that ἔξω is omitted by (P⁶⁶) ℵ* it sin pesh. Why did the beloved disciple not speak to Mary? We have here, Brown convincingly suggests, the joining of two originally separate episodes.

παρέκυψεν. See on v. 5.

12. δύο (omit ℵ* e) ἀγγέλους ἐν λευκοῖς καθεζομένους. Cf. Mark 16.5, νεανίσκον καθήμενον . . . περιβεβλημένον στολὴν λευκήν; Matt. 28.2f., ἄγγελος γὰρ κυρίου . . . ἐκάθητο . . . τὸ ἔνδυμα αὐτοῦ λευκόν; Luke 24.4, ἄνδρες δύο . . . ἐν ἐσθῆτι ἀστραπτούσῃ. John is drawing upon either the synoptic or some very similar tradition. The note that the angels sat one where the head and the other where the feet of the body of Jesus had been may be simply an elaboration of a source, not independent tradition.

13. Γύναι. See on 2.4. After τί κλαίεις; D sin add τίνα ζητεῖς; from v. 15.

ὅτι may either introduce direct speech ('Why are you weeping?' 'They have taken away . . .'), or mean 'because' ('Why are you weeping?' 'Because they have taken away . . .').

14. εἰς τὰ ὀπίσω. Cf. 18.6. There is no room for the appearance to Mary in 1 Cor. 15.

15. κηπουρός. *Hap. leg.* in the New Testament, but not uncommon in Hellenistic Greek; the keeper of a κῆπος. To this word κύριε corresponds; not 'Lord' but 'Sir'. Contrast κύριος in vv. 13, 18. See 19.41, and note.

ἐβάστασας. For the meaning 'to take up and take away' see on 12.6. σύ is emphatic: 'If you are the man who has taken him . . .'. In this verse John uses once more his literary formula of enlightenment through initial misunderstanding; indeed this is the supreme example of the device, for it is not a metaphor but Jesus himself who is mistaken.

16. Μαριάμ. The name alone is sufficient to convince Mary of the identity of the speaker. The good shepherd calls his own sheep by name and they recognize his voice (10.3).

στραφεῖσα. Presumably she had turned away from the supposed gardener to the grave; now, when she recognized his voice, she turned back to him. For 'turned' sin has 'she recognized him'; this reading is defended in Black 255f., but it may have arisen as an alleviation of the difficulty caused by the fact that Mary had already (v. 14) turned towards Jesus.

Ἑβραϊστί. See on 19.13. The word is omitted by ω a vg sin.

Ῥαββουνί. Cf. Mark 10.51. Black (23f.; cf. 44, 46) points out that 'the Gospel transcription agrees with the pronunciation in the new [Palestinian Pentateuch] Targum, against that of the Onkelos Targum [*ribboni*]'. See however J. A. Fitzmyer, *C.B.Q.* 30 (1968), 421. Among older books see G. Dalman, *The Words of Jesus* (E.T., 1909), 324ff., 340.

ὃ λέγεται διδάσκαλε. Before διδάσκαλε, κύριε is inserted by D (it); evidently it was thought that a more than human title was called for. For John's translations of Semitic terms see on 1.38, where the same translation is given for Ῥαββί. After this verse ℵ³ Θ sin add καὶ προσέδραμεν ἅψασθαι αὐτοῦ, in preparation for the next verse.

17. μή μου ἅπτου. The present imperative with μή in a prohibition signifies the breaking off of an action already in progress, or sometimes of the attempt to perform an action; see M. 1, 122–6; Bultmann, 687; B.D. §336. Accordingly we may suppose either that Mary had seized Jesus' feet (in which case we may cf. Matt. 28.9) or that she was on the point of doing so when Jesus prevented her. In view of the difficulties raised by these words when taken with the following sentences Bernard (670f.) supposed that textual corruption had taken place. The position of μου varies, and the original MS. reading may therefore have been simply μή ἅπτου, this being itself a corruption of an earlier μή πτόου, 'Fear not'. Such a conjecture, though Sidebottom, 161, is inclined to accept it, should not however be resorted to unless all other attempts to interpret the passage fail. Mary's action is a natural one; Sanders aptly compares Arrian, *Anabasis* VI, xiii, 3. Both by her address to Jesus as teacher, and physical contact, she is trying to recapture the past. But Jesus' reunion with his disciples will be complete only when his reunion with the Father is complete (Lightfoot).

οὔπω γὰρ ἀναβέβηκα πρὸς τὸν πατέρα. This is a statement of some difficulty. It seems to be implied that it will be possible and permissible to touch Jesus after the ascension, though not before; and this is the reverse of what might have been expected. For the ascending of Jesus to the Father cf. 3.13; 6.62 (where ἀναβαίνειν is used), and 7.33; 13.1,3; 14.4,28; 16.5,17,28; 17.13 (where other words are used). It was for John an essential act, completing what was done in the passion, which, though it means the glory of Jesus, is not to be identified with his ascension. It was moreover a condition for the coming of the Spirit (7.39; 16.7). In v. 22 the Spirit is given and in v. 27 (cf. v. 20) Thomas, so far from being forbidden, is invited to touch the hands and side of Jesus. A possible conclusion from these facts is that John believed that between vv. 17 and 22 the ascension or at least the complete glorification, of Jesus had taken place (see Benoit, 1, 373). But it must be admitted that he does not say so, and it is very strange that so vital a fact should be left as a matter of inference. A more profitable line of interpretation is obtained when it is noted (Lagrange, 512) that the δέ which follows πορεύου applies in effect to ἀναβαίνω, the message to the 'brothers' being parenthetical. The verse may then be paraphrased, 'Stop touching me (or attempting to do so); it is true that I have not yet ascended to the Father but I am about to do so [for this use of the present see B.D., §323, and cf. e.g. 1 Cor. 15.32, αὔριον . . . ἀποθνήσκομεν]; this is what you must tell my brothers'. This is perfectly intelligible. The resurrection has made possible a new and more intimate spiritual union between Jesus and his disciples; the old physical contacts are no longer appropriate, though touch may yet (v. 27) be appealed to in proof that the glorified Lord is none other than he who was crucified.

πορεύου δὲ πρὸς τοὺς ἀδελφούς μου. Cf. Matt. 28. 10, ὑπάγετε ἀπαγγείλατε τοῖς ἀδελφοῖς μου. The use of the word ἀδελφός in the earlier tradition may have suggested John's 'My Father and your Father'. It is clear from the context that by 'brothers' the disciples, not the unbelievers of 7.5, are meant.

ἀναβαίνω. See the notes on previous clauses in this verse. The ascension is not referred to again in John, and is not described in the realistic manner of Acts 1.9 (and perhaps Luke, if the words καὶ ἀνεφέρετο εἰς τὸν οὐρανόν are read in 24.51). It is a matter of common belief in the New Testament that after his crucifixion Jesus took his place in glory at the Father's right hand, but only the author of Luke–Acts makes of this belief an observable incident. See further on 3.13f.

τὸν πατέρα μου καὶ πατέρα ὑμῶν καὶ θεόν μου καὶ θεὸν ὑμῶν. There is nothing unusual in the description of God as the God and Father of Jesus Christ, or as the God and Father of Christians. Here John emphasizes that the relation between Jesus and God is different from that between the disciples and God, even though it is described in the same terms and the disciples are said to be his brothers. Jesus eternally is the Son of God; he gives to those who believe in him the power to become the children of God (1.11). Brown, however, referring to Ruth 1.16, sees here identification rather than disjunction. See also W. Grundmann, Z.N.T.W. 52 (1961), 213–30, for the suggestion that John is using an old confession of faith. Torrey (71–3) avoids the difficulties of this verse by noting that the Aramaic from which he believes the present Greek to have been translated could mean equally well 'Touch me not; but before I ascend to my Father, go to my brethren and say to them . . .'.

18. ἡ Μαγδαληνή. For the text see on v. 1.

ἀγγέλλουσα. The future participle expressing purpose would have been more appropriate, but in Hellenistic Greek the future participle was obsolescent, and John probably used the present with a similar meaning.

ὅτι. For the report cf. Luke 24.9. The text runs ὅτι . . . ἑώρακα . . . εἶπεν, that is, ὅτι is loosely used; it introduces first a piece of direct speech (ἑώρακα τὸν κύριον) and then a piece of indirect speech (ταῦτα εἶπεν αὐτῇ). Various attempts were made to mend the grammar; for ἑώρακα there are substituted ἑώρακεν (D Θ ω it) and ἑωράκαμεν, while in the second clause vg sah boh and a few Old Latin MSS. presuppose ταῦτα εἶπέν μοι, and D e sin have ἃ εἶπεν αὐτῇ ἐμήνυσεν (αὐτοῖς).

In these verses the gospel, as at first planned, is brought to an end—a satisfying and indeed triumphant end. It is almost impossible to read vv. 30f. otherwise than as the conclusion of a work, and the preceding paragraphs, in which the followers of Jesus are sent out upon their task in the power of the Holy Spirit, equipped with an adequate confession of faith in their Lord, say all that need be said to effect the transition from the life of Jesus to the history of the church.

In the first incident, which takes place on the first Easter Day, the day on which Peter and the beloved disciple had found the tomb empty and Mary had seen the Lord, the disciples meet behind locked doors. Jesus, evidently able in his resurrection body to pass through solid matter, or, perhaps, to cause his body to materialize where he wills, appears among them, showing them his hands and side to prove that though his body is transformed, he is nevertheless the same. He sends them out upon their mission, and bestows upon them the Holy Spirit and the authority to remit and retain sins.

On this occasion Thomas was absent. Accordingly a week later Jesus returns in similar circumstances to satisfy the doubts of this disciple. The sight of Jesus, whose wounds are still visible, leads Thomas to the culminating confession of the gospel, My Lord and my God. The last words of Jesus are a blessing upon those, who, unlike Thomas, have not seen him, but, like Thomas, have believed.

The evangelist ends his work by recalling that he has given only a small selection of the significant acts of Jesus, and that his selection has been made to the end that his readers may have faith in Christ, and, by faith, life.

It is impossible to identify any of John's sources here, and to estimate their worth. See on v. 30 for the suggestion that this verse marks the end of the hypothetical 'Signs Source'. An appearance to the Twelve (? the Eleven) is attested in 1 Cor. 15.5. John's main concern in the present section, apart from the twofold nature of the resurrection body, which is brought out incidentally, is with what is, from the standpoint of the first Easter, the future: the life, witness, and authority of the church, which are never far from his thoughts at any point in the gospel. It is the mission of Jesus himself which, through the Spirit, is perpetuated in the mission of the church; and the church by its faith is related to Christ as Christ is to God.

19. οὔσης οὖν ὀψίας τῇ ἡμέρᾳ ἐκείνῃ. Only Luke supplies a true parallel to this further appearance on the first resurrection day; cf. Luke 24.31 (the two going to Emmaus), 24.34 (a reported appearance to Simon), 24.36ff. (to the

assembled disciples). The last is in several respects parallel to the present narrative; see below. Cf. also the 'longer ending' of Mark, 16.9-20.

τῇ μιᾷ σαββάτων. See on v. 1. The same day is intended.

τῶν θυρῶν κεκλεισμένων. This fact and the motive given for it (διὰ τὸν φόβον τῶν 'Ιουδαίων) are quite natural and understandable; there is however no parallel, and it is probable that John's motive, whatever his authority may have been, for mentioning that the doors were shut was to suggest the mysterious power of the risen Jesus, who was at once sufficiently corporeal to show his wounds and sufficiently immaterial to pass through closed doors. John offers no explanation of this power, nor is it possible to supply one; though it is legitimate to compare Paul's doctrine of the spiritual body (1 Cor. 15.44).

οἱ μαθηταί (συνηγμένοι is added by Θ ω it). It is important to consider whether 'the disciples' were the Ten only (the Twelve, without Judas and Thomas), or included others also. The Lucan parallel (24.33, τοὺς ἕνδεκα καὶ τοὺς σὺν αὐτοῖς) suggests the larger group; but it might be urged that the description of Thomas as εἷς ἐκ τῶν δώδεκα (v. 24) suggests the smaller. The Twelve are mentioned (at least under that title) very infrequently in John; see on 6.70. It is often impossible to say whether, by μαθηταί, John means the inner or outer circle of the followers of Jesus; consequently it is not surprising (though it remains significant) that it should be impossible to settle the question here with certainty. 'In such a matter the mere fact that doubt is possible is a striking one. It is in truth difficult to separate these cases [after the resurrection] from the frequent omission of the evangelists to distinguish the Twelve from other disciples. . . . Granting that it was probably to the Eleven that our Lord directly and principally spoke on both these occasions [in John and Matthew] . . . yet it still has to be considered in what capacity they were addressed by him. If at the Last Supper, and during the discourses which followed, when the Twelve or Eleven were most completely secluded from all other disciples as well as from the unbelieving Jews, they represented the whole Ecclesia of the future, it is but natural to suppose that it was likewise as representatives of the whole Ecclesia of the future, whether associated with other disciples or not, that they had given to them those two assurances and charges of our Lord, about the receiving of the Holy Spirit and the remitting or retaining of sins . . ., and about his universal authority in heaven and on earth . . .'(Hort, 33). This quotation has been given at length since it seems to express exactly the true sense of the paragraph; the commission of v. 21, the gift of the Spirit of v. 22, the authority of v. 23 are given to the apostolic church.

ἔστη εἰς τὸ μέσον. A pregnant construction (for which cf. Mark 3.3, ἔγειρε εἰς τὸ μέσον), but not unparalleled in classical Greek (e.g. Xenophon, Cyropaedia IV, i, 1, στὰ εἰς τὸ μέσον). Or perhaps εἰς τὸ μέσον is simply an equivalent of ἐν τῷ μέσῳ, εἰς and ἐν being frequently confused in Hellenistic Greek.

εἰρήνη ὑμῖν. שלום, שלמא (shalom, sheˡlama', 'peace') were in very common use as a conventional greeting. The normal meaning is no more than 'May all be well with you', but εἰρήνη had acquired so full a sense in Christian usage (cf. 14.27; 16.33) that much more is intended here. The expression is repeated in vv. 21, 26.

20. Ἔδειξεν καὶ τὰς χεῖρας καὶ τὴν πλευρὰν αὐτοῖς, that is, the parts of his body where wounds or scars were to be seen. Cf. v. 27. The feet are not mentioned. In the earlier tradition there is no reference to the nailing of Jesus to the cross, and it seems not impossible that (as often happened) he was not nailed but tied to it with ropes. Belief that wounds were inflicted by nails might have arisen out of the theological significance ascribed to the blood of Christ (his death being thought of as a sacrifice) and because they provided a valuable piece of evidence that no substitution had taken place—the risen Jesus was the very person who was crucified (cf. the doubts of Thomas, and their resolution, below). Cf. Ignatius, *Smyrnaeans* 3.2.

ἐχάρησαν οὖν. Cf. 16.20,22.

21. καθὼς ἀπέσταλκέν με ὁ πατήρ, κἀγὼ πέμπω ὑμᾶς. The two verbs seem to be used synonymously in this gospel. For Christ's being sent by the Father cf. 3.17,34; 5.36,38; 6.29,57; 7.29; 8.42; 10.36; 11.42; 17.3,8,18,21,23,25 (ἀποστέλλειν); 4.34; 5.23f.,30,37; 6.38f.,44; 7.16,18,28,33; 8.16,18,26,29; 9.4; 12.44f.,49; 13.20; 14.24; 15.21; 16.5 (πέμπειν; note especially the use of this word in the phrase ὁ πέμψας με (πατήρ), and that it is used of the sending of the Paraclete, 14.26; 15.26; 16.7). For Christ's sending his disciples cf. 4.38; 17.18 (ἀποστέλλειν), 13. (16),20 (πέμπειν). The closest parallels to the present passage are 13.20; 17.18. In each the same pattern of sending is noted: the Father sends the Son, and the Son sends the 'apostles' (in John the word ἀπόστολος is used once only (13.16), for convenience, with the simple meaning 'one who has been sent'; it is not used as a technical term). In view of the generally synonymous use of the words ἀποστέλλειν and πέμπειν, and the construction of this sentence (καθὼς ... καὶ ...) it does not seem possible to distinguish between two kinds of sending, one in which the person sent is a delegate with transferred authority (ἀποστέλλειν), and one in which this is not so (πέμπειν). Parallelism, not contrast, between the two missions is emphasized here. It is unnecessary to pursue doubtful parallels in the rabbinic usage of the terms שָׁלוּחַ, שָׁלִיחַ (shaluaḥ, shaliaḥ; the form is that of a passive participle of the verb שָׁלַח (shalaḥ), 'to send') in order to see that the sending of Jesus by God meant that in the words, works, and person of Jesus men were veritably confronted not merely by a Jewish Rabbi but by God himself (1.18; 14.9; and many passages). It follows that in the apostolic mission of the church (see on v. 19) the world is veritably confronted not merely by a human institution but by Jesus the Son of God (13.20; 17.18). It follows further that as Jesus in his ministry was entirely dependent upon and obedient to God the Father, who sealed and sanctified him (4.34; 5.19; 10.37; 17.4, and other passages: 6.27; 10.36), and acted in the power of the Spirit who rested upon him (1.32), so the church is the apostolic church, commissioned by Christ, only in virtue of the fact that Jesus sanctified it (17.19) and breathed the Spirit into it (v. 22), and only so far as it maintains an attitude of perfect obedience to Jesus (it is here, of course, that the parallelism between the relation of Jesus to the Father and the relation of the church to Jesus breaks down). The life and mission of the church are meaningless if they are detached from this historical and theological context. On the words used in this verse, and on the apostles in the ministry and thought of Jesus and in the primitive church, see especially K. H. Rengstorf, *Apostolat und Predigtamt* (1934, reprinted 1954), and the same author's article on ἀποστέλλω, κτλ., in *T.W.N.T.* I, 397–448; R. N. Flew,

Jesus and His Church (1938), 106–20; T. W. Manson, *The Church's Ministry* (1948), 31–52; also the later works of G. Klein (*Die zwölf Apostel*, 1961) and W. Schmithals (*Das kirchliche Apostelamt*, 1961; E.T., 1971), and my own small book, *The Signs of an Apostle* (1970). Here it may be noted that, while the original context of the thought and language of apostleship were Jewish and eschatological, John has characteristically expressed them in terms which are at least as Greek as they are Jewish. The philosophic missionary was *sent* from God; so e.g. Diogenes: πρὸ σοῦ κατάσκοπος ἀποσταλεὶς Διογένης... ἀπήγγελκεν (Epictetus, I, xxiv, 6). The Gnostic Menander claimed that he was ὁ σωτήρ, ἐπὶ τῇ τῶν ἀνθρώπων ἀνωθέν ποθεν ἐξ ἀοράτων ἀπεσταλμένος σωτηρίᾳ (Eusebius, *H.E.* III, xxvi, 1 based on Irenaeus, *adv. Haer.* I, xvii, 1). Cf. also the charge to the Hermetic apostle: λοιπόν, τί μέλλεις; οὐχ ὡς πάντα παραλαβὼν καθοδηγὸς γίνῃ τοῖς ἀξίοις, ὅπως τὸ γένος τῆς ἀνθρωπότητος διὰ σοῦ ὑπὸ θεοῦ σωθῇ (*C.H.* I, 26). E. Percy (*Untersuchungen über den Ursprung der johanneischen Theologie* (1939), 199f.) has brought out the differences between the Johannine concept and that of the Mandaean Envoy. The Hellenistic world was not unfamiliar with the thought of a man who was sent from God, and inspired and empowered for his mission. In John, the inspiration follows at once.

22. ἐνεφύσησεν (D sin pesh, correctly interpreting, add αὐτοῖς) ... λάβετε πνεῦμα ἅγιον. The first word is significant. Cf. Gen. 2.7, ἐνεφύσησεν [*sc.* ὁ θεός] εἰς τὸ πρόσωπον αὐτοῦ πνοὴν ζωῆς, καὶ ἐγένετο ὁ ἄνθρωπος εἰς ψυχὴν ζῶσαν. Ezek. 37.9, ἐκ τῶν τεσσάρων πνευμάτων ἐλθὲ καὶ ἐμφύσησον εἰς τοὺς νεκροὺς τούτους. Wisd. 15.11, ἠγνόησεν τὸν πλάσαντα αὐτόν, καὶ τὸν ἐμπνεύσαντα αὐτῷ ψυχὴν ἐνεργοῦσαν, καὶ ἐμφυσήσαντα πνεῦμα ζωτικόν. See also Philo, *Op.* 135, ὃ γὰρ ἐνεφύσησεν, οὐδὲν ἦν ἕτερον ἢ πνεῦμα θεῖον. 1 QS 4.21 and CD 2.12, sometimes adduced as parallels, are remote from John. That John intended to depict an event of significance parallel to that of the first creation of man cannot be doubted; this was the beginning of the new creation. At the same time, the language of inspiration is not inappropriate to the Hellenistic philosophical apostle; see on v. 21. For the Johannine teaching on the Holy Spirit see Introduction, pp. 88–92, and on 1.32f.; 3.5; 4.24; 7.37ff.; 14.16 among other passages. Dodd (*Interpretation*, 430; *Tradition*, 144) concludes that the conception of the Spirit implied by this passage differs from that of the Last Discourses, in that the latter is personal (as the name Paraclete suggests) whereas the former is quasi-material. But the image of breathing does not necessarily mean that the Spirit is understood in a material sense. It means rather that Jesus is personally communicating and committing himself to his disciples in the person of the Spirit. It had been promised that the Spirit would be given after the glorification of Jesus (7.39; 16.7) and there can be no doubt that this is the gift intended. On its relation to the ascension see on v. 17. It does not seem possible to harmonize this account of a special bestowing of the Spirit with that contained in Acts 2; after this event there could be no more 'waiting' (Luke 24.48f.; Acts 1.4f.); the church could not be more fully equipped for its mission. The existence of divergent traditions of the constitutive gift of the Spirit is not surprising; it is probable that to the first Christians the resurrection of Jesus and his appearances to them, his exaltation (however that was understood), and the gift of the Spirit, appeared as one experience, which only later came to be described in separate elements and incidents.

23. ἂν τινων ἀφῆτε τὰς ἁμαρτίας ἀφέωνται αὐτοῖς· ἂν τινων κρατῆτε κεκράτηνται. For τινων in each place τινος is read by B a (e) sin pesh Cyprian Eusebius. The reading is well attested, but may be ultimately due to Syriac idiom; though it is hard to see how this can have affected B. ἀφέωνται (a Doric-Ionic-Arcadian perfect passive; see B.D., §97; M. 1, 38) is the reading of D and few others, but B (ἀφείονται) should possibly be added, ιο having been written for ω. Most MSS. have the present (ἀφίενται; ℵ* has ἀφεθήσεται), which gives a weaker sense; but see B.D., §323, with a reference to T.W.N.T. III, 753 (J. Jeremias), where it is argued that ἀφίενται (ἀφίονται) is a futuristic present, with eschatological significance (the future reference, however, is denied by Turner, Insights, 8off.). ἂν is used for ἐάν (which appears in some MSS.); cf. 16.23. The best rendering is probably 'If you forgive anyone's sins . . . if you retain . . .'; see Moule, Idiom Book, 152. For the thought of this verse cf. Matt. 16.19; 18.18 (also, for forgiveness only, Luke 24.47). J. A. Emerton (J.T.S. 13 (1962), 325–31) suggests that the Matthean sayings and the Johannine may have a common origin in a saying which recalled Isa. 22.22 and ran as follows: 'And whatsoever thou shalt shut shall be shut: and what-soever thou shalt open shall be opened', the significant Aramaic verbs being אחד (shut) and פתח (open). In John פתח suggested the meaning release, which in turn led to forgive. Dodd, Tradition, 347ff., is probably right in concluding that John is not dependent on Matthew—which indeed few would claim. See also McNamara, T. & T., 130. Cf. also the fact that Matthew (28.19), and the author of the 'longer ending' of Mark (Mark 16.16) both put into the mouth of Jesus before his departure a charge to baptize, which carries with it the offer of forgiveness. There may well be a reference to baptism in the Johannine charge also; the church, by conferring or not con-ferring baptism, opens or closes the door of the redeemed community. But it would be wrong to restrict the meaning of the saying to baptism. The authori-ty conveyed implies an extension of the ministry of Jesus through that of the Holy Spirit. Jesus (in chapter 9) gave sight, and faith, to the blind man who knew he was blind; to those who arrogantly claimed, 'We see', he could say only, 'Your sin remains'. This retaining of sin was both a statement of fact and a punishment. For the work of the Spirit cf. 16.8–11; he perpetuates the ministry of Jesus, and when he convicts of unbelief he convicts of sin, since the relation of men to Christ determines their relation to God. This joint work, of Christ in sending the Holy Spirit and of the Holy Spirit in bearing witness to Christ, is exercised in and through the church as represented by the disciples. ἀφιέναι (literally, 'to release', 'to let go') is used here only in John with the meaning 'to remit'. κρατεῖν signifies the opposite: 'to hold fast', 'to retain'. Brown's long and admirable discussion (1039–45) leads to a con-clusion similar to that adopted here.

24. Θωμᾶς δὲ εἷς ἐκ τῶν δώδεκα. For Thomas cf. 11.16; 14.5; 21.2. The other gospels, and Acts, record only his name. Doubt regarding the resurrection is however a feature of all the gospels: see Matt. 28.17; Mark 16.14; Luke 24.11,25,37,41.

ὁ λεγόμενος Δίδυμος. It is conceivable, though not probable, that Thomas appears as the doubting disciple on account of his name. Δίδυμος, a natural rendering of תומא (Thoma', a 'twin'), means primarily 'double', 'twofold'. On the other hand, the earlier references to Thomas suggest a loyal but

571

obtuse, rather than a doubtful and hesitating, character. His attitude to the resurrection appearances (like that of Mary, v. 17) may be compared with that of the unthinking beholders of signs earlier in the ministry (cf. e.g. 2.9; 3.4; 4.48; 6.26; *et al.*). Dodd (*Tradition*, 145) sees 'here a dramatization (in our author's manner) of the traditional motive of the incredulity of some or all of the disciples'. Betz, 93, aptly quotes Lucian, *Verae Historiae* II, 12 (εἰ γοῦν μὴ ἅψαιτό τις, οὐκ ἂν ἐλέγξειε μὴ εἶναι σῶμα τὸ ὁρώμενον).

25. ἐὰν μὴ ἴδω . . . καὶ βάλω . . . καὶ βάλω . . . οὐ μὴ πιστεύσω. Thomas required the grossest and most palpable evidence that the body he knew to have been killed in a specific manner had indeed been reanimated. He would be satisfied neither with a substituted body which was not the body of the Lord who died on the cross, nor with a spiritual body or apparition. The risen Christ must be both visibly and palpably identical with the old. Such hesitation, so conclusively removed, had of course high apologetic value. Fenton suggests that John may have intended Thomas' stipulation to sound absurd.

For χεῖρα, א* B have χεῖραν. This form is common in uneducated papyri (M. 1, 49) and may well be what John wrote.

26. For the details of this verse see on v. 19. There is no longer any reference to fear as a motive for the closed doors—possibly because the motive was no longer applicable after the bestowal of the Spirit (Fenton). With μεθ' ἡμέρας ὀκτώ contrast John's μετὰ ταῦτα (or τοῦτο) when he is not interested in the precise interval. He means the next Sunday after the first appearances; both Sundays are, according to ancient custom, reckoned in the enumeration. There may be a special intention in John's account of the Lord's special presence on the first day of the week, the day of the church's regular assembly.

27. φέρε τὸν δάκτυλόν σου . . . Jesus accepted the challenge of physical investigation. Contrast v. 17 (see the note) and cf. v. 20. Thomas was offered exactly what he sought. John does not say that he accepted the opportunity; rather he hints (v. 29) that sight was sufficient. But John was evidently of opinion that the resurrection body, though it could pass through closed doors, could also be handled; it was physically 'real'.

ἄπιστος . . . πιστός. Neither word occurs elsewhere in John. ἄπιστος many times in 1 and 2 Cor. and twice in the Pastorals means the 'unbeliever', the person who is not a Christian. It may be that the rather clumsy expression here means that Thomas is (or perhaps represents one who is) neither ἄπιστος nor πιστός; he is urged to become πιστός, a believing Christian. But γίνεσθαι is often used with the meaning 'to show oneself . . .' (John 15.8; Matt. 5.45; 6.16; 10.16; 1 Cor. 14.20; 15.10,58; Col. 3.15; 1 Thess. 1.5; 2.7), and this is probably its meaning here: 'Show that you do believe'. Dodd (*Tradition*, 354f.) finds here a traditional saying; cf. Matt. 24.45–51; Luke 12.42–6.

28. ὁ κύριός μου καὶ ὁ θεός μου. The collocation of κύριος and θεός is common in the LXX where it represents יהוה אלהים and similar expressions. It appears also in pagan religious literature (see e.g. Deissmann 366f.; among other sources, an Egyptian inscription of 24 B.C. (Dittenberger, *O.G.I.S.* 655) speaks of τῷ θεῷ καὶ κυρίῳ Σοκνοπαίῳ; see also Betz, 102) and is well known to

have been an imperial title much affected by Domitian (Suetonius, *Domitian* 13, *dominus et deus noster*). κύριος is a frequent Christian title for Jesus (for κύριος in John see on 13.13f.), and appears in the confession of faith 'Jesus is Lord', probably a primitive credal formula used at baptism and similar occasions (Rom. 10.9; 1 Cor. 12.3). When this confession was interpreted in terms of the Old Testament, where κύριος = θεός, the fuller formula was close at hand. Philonic influence is unlikely, since Philo rarely calls the Word God (J. Lebreton, *History of the Dogma of the Trinity* 1 (E.T. 1939), 449f.); but, as frequently, John's language is carefully chosen so as to be both biblical and Hellenistic. Christ is called θεός only in John (1.1; 1.18 *si v.l.*; cf. 5.18; 10.33) and in the Pastorals (and possibly, but not probably, in Rom. 9.5). The difference between the present verse and 1.1 (where θεός is anarthrous) cannot be pressed; here the articular nominative is used for vocative. The return to the opening proposition of the gospel is intended, and there can be no doubt that John intended this confession of faith to form the climax of the gospel (on ch. 21 see pp. 576ff.); it is his final Christological pronouncement. Dodd, *Interpretation*, 430, distinguishes κύριος and θεός: Thomas recognises the Lord Jesus, and acknowledges that he is divine. It is however better to conjoin the terms than to separate them. The pronouncement may have been taken from a liturgical setting; indeed the whole passage (from v. 19) may be liturgical in origin. The disciples assemble on the Lord's Day. The blessing is given: εἰρήνη ὑμῖν. The Holy Spirit descends upon the worshippers and the word of absolution (cf. v. 23) is pronounced. Christ himself is present (this may suggest the eucharist and the spoken word of God) bearing the marks of his passion; he is confessed as Lord and God (cf. Pliny, *Ep.* x, xcvi, 7, *carmenque Christo quasi deo dicere*). That such a setting as this was in John's mind is supported by the fact that in the next verse the horizon of thought is explicitly extended to include all Christians as they meet under the authority of the word of God.

29. See the last note. At the close of his gospel (see on v. 31) John emphasizes the continuity of the church of his own time with Jesus and his disciples. The wider community was in view from the beginning (cf. 17.20).

ὅτι ἑώρακάς με πεπίστευκας; This clause, punctuated by Nestle as a question, could be taken as a statement, and is perhaps better taken so, though Nestle is supported by many minuscules (the earlier MSS. are seldom punctuated); in this solemn and impressive pronouncement Jesus does not ask questions, but declares the truth. It is possible that John may have intended the meaning, Do you believe simply on seeing me, that is, without the touch you asked for? But this seems over-subtle. The contrast is not between seeing and touching, but between seeing, and believing apart from sight, between Thomas who saw, and the later Christian believers who did not. The words do not convey a reproach to Thomas; the beloved disciple and Mary Magdalene also believed when they saw (see especially v. 8); indeed, but for the fact that Thomas and the other apostles saw the incarnate Christ there would have been no Christian faith at all. Cf. 1.18,50f.; 2.11; 4.45; 6.2; 9.37; 14.7,9; 19.35.

μακάριοι. Cf. Matt. 5.3 and other passages. There are close parallels in Ps. 2.12 (μακάριοι πάντες οἱ πεποιθότες ἐπ' αὐτῷ) and Ecclus. 48.11 (μακάριοι οἱ ἰδόντες σε); but it need not be supposed that John was dependent on either.

οἱ μὴ ἰδόντες καὶ πιστεύσαντες. Cf. 1 Peter 1.8, ὃν οὐκ ἰδόντες ἀγαπᾶτε, εἰς ὃν ἄρτι μὴ ὁρῶντες πιστεύοντες δὲ . . . The aorists in John may be 'timeless' but probably indicate the fact that when John wrote the church was composed of men who had seen no such resurrection appearance as Thomas had seen, and yet had been converted (had come to believe). The blessing is probably intended for all Christians other than eye-witnesses, not for those only who were able to believe without signs and wonders (but cf. Bultmann 696: 'The doubt of Thomas is representative of the common attitude of men. . . . As the miracle is a concession to the weakness of man, so is the appearance of the Risen Jesus a concession to the weakness of the disciples. Fundamentally they ought not to need it! Fundamentally it ought not to be the sight of the Risen Lord that first moves the disciples to believe "the word that Jesus spoke" (2.22), for this word alone should have the power to convince them. Accordingly, as in the story of Mary, vv. 1f., 11–18, there is embedded in the narrative of Thomas also a peculiar critique concerning the value of the Easter stories; they can claim only a relative worth. And if this critical saying of Jesus forms the conclusion of the Easter narratives, the hearer or reader is warned not to take them to be more than they can be: neither as narrations of events that he himself could wish or hope to experience, nor as a substitute for such experiences of his own, as if the experiences of others could, as it were, guarantee for him the reality of the resurrection of Jesus; rather they are to be viewed as proclaimed word, in which the recounted events have become symbolic pictures for the fellowship which the Lord, who has ascended to the Father, holds with his own'). Whatever be the historical value (from the standpoint of modern scientific historical criticism) of the resurrection narratives John himself takes historical testimony with full seriousness. The disciples of the first generation had the unique distinction of standing as a link between Jesus and the church; John indicates in this saying that their successors equally may believe, and that their faith places them on the same level of blessedness with the eye-witnesses, or even above it. The following rabbinic passage is often quoted, and indeed it appears to illustrate John's thought; but it is fairly late (c. A.D. 250), and lays no stress on the thought, vital for John, of a generation which beheld and mediated the faith to the next: R. Simeon b. Laqish said: The proselyte is dearer to God than all the Israelites who stood by Mount Sinai. For if all the Israelites had not seen the thunder and the flames and the lightnings and the quaking mountain and the sound of the trumpet they would not have accepted the law and taken upon themselves the kingdom of God. Yet this man has seen none of all these things yet comes and gives himself to God and takes on himself the yoke of the kingdom of God. Is there any who is dearer than this man? (Tanhuma, לך לך, §6 (32a)). There can be no simple assessment of John's attitude to the resurrection stories, and to the Easter faith. It is easier to express it in negative than in positive statements. It is not true that simple stories of an empty tomb and of encounters with particular people can prove that God raised Jesus from the dead; for disciples should have believed on the testimony of the word, both the word of God in the Old Testament (20.8) and the word spoken by Jesus (2.22). It is not true that these stories are worthless and dispensable; had John believed this he would not have gone to the trouble of recounting them. It is not true that later generations of Christians, who have seen neither the empty tomb nor the Risen Christ, are of a lower order; Jesus himself pronounces them blessed (v. 29). It is not true that the first apostles have no particular and unique importance; for later generations believe through their word (17.20), that is, it is in their word that later generations encounter the Risen Christ and become believers. On p. 562 John's attitude to the Easter tradition was described, with these points in mind, as 'critical acceptance'. The stories were true and essential; but they could be, and perhaps in John's time already had been, turned into a myth, or talisman, a shelter into which Christians ran to escape the necessity of living by faith.

30. πολλὰ μὲν οὖν καὶ ἄλλα σημεῖα. πολύς is regularly joined to another adjective by καί and not simply juxtaposed. For σημεῖον see Introduction, pp. 75–8. Those who believe that John drew on a 'Signs Source' (see Introduction, pp. 18ff.) see here the conclusion of that document, but there is no reason why he should not have been making his own comment on a wider range of material. He was probably familiar with much of the synoptic tradition (Introduction, pp. 42–6), and used other traditions too. Bultmann gives examples to show that John was drawing on a traditional concluding form. Cullmann (Salvation, 156), however, sees in the selection of certain events as making particularly clear the work of God a mark of Heilsgeschichte. The stress on signs done by Jesus and beheld by his disciples is important and illuminates the structure and method of the gospel as a whole; there is no disparagement of the role of eye-witnesses (see above).

ἐνώπιον occurs here only in John, but is a common Hellenistic word (see M.M. s.v.), common in Luke-Acts. It is not to be described as a Semitism, though of course it could represent לִפְנֵי.

31. Both the purpose of the gospel and the author's theology are summed up in this verse. 'Le livre est fini, très bien fini' (Loisy, 514). See also Martyn, 81f. Whoever may have written ch. 21, this verse forms the conclusion and (with the confession of v. 28) the climax of the gospel as originally planned. The words and themes mentioned here run throughout the gospel. For 'believing' see on 1.12; for Jesus as Christ and Son of God, Introduction, pp. 70ff.; for ζωή see on 1.4; 3.15. ἐν τῷ ὀνόματι αὐτοῦ, however, has no real parallel. It cannot be constructed with πιστεύοντες, since John's regular construction (see 1.12) is πιστεύειν εἰς τὸ ὄνομα. Cf. 14.13f.; 15.16; 16.24,26 and especially 16.23, δώσει ὑμῖν ἐν τῷ ὀνόματί μου. The meaning seems to be '. . . that you may have life on account of him, by his agency, in virtue of your believing relationship with him'. Cf. Odes of Solomon, 6; 10.

πιστεύητε; so P66vid א* B Θ, probably rightly; the rest have πιστεύσητε. The present subjunctive (strictly interpreted) means 'that you may continue to believe, be confirmed in your faith', the aorist 'that you may here and now believe, that is, become Christians'. This variant raises acutely the question of the purpose of the gospel; was it written to confirm the faithful, or as a missionary tract, to convert the Hellenistic world? The question is raised but cannot be determined by the tenses, even if we could determine the tenses; see Introduction, pp. 134ff. H. Riesenfeld, St. Th. 19 (1965), 213–20, concludes, probably rightly, that the gospel belongs within the church and is not a missionary tract. Cf. 1 John 5.13. The order of words seems to forbid Léon-Dufour's rendering, '. . . believe that Jesus the Messiah, is the Son of God' (The Gospels and the Jesus of History (ed. J. McHugh, 1968), 81).

πιστεύοντες ζωὴν ἔχητε. Cf. 6.47. 'John directly joins faith and life together, without any interposition of the term righteousness' (contrast Paul) (E. Stauffer, *New Testament Theology* (E.T., 1955), 171).

43. THE APPENDIX

I. THE APPEARANCE OF JESUS BY THE LAKE

21.1–14

It has already been observed that 20.30f. mark the conclusion of the gospel as at first planned. If this is so ch. 21 must be regarded as an addendum. This conclusion has been challenged, notably by S. S. Smalley (*N.T.S.* 20 (1974), 275–88), but not quite convincingly. To narrate the commissioning of apostles to the work of evangelism is a proper part of a gospel, but this is dealt with in 20.21ff.; to demonstrate their success as fishers of men, even under the threat of death (Smalley, p. 284) does not in the same way fit into John's framework, though it is readily understandable as a supplement, especially when it is coupled with a comment on the importance of, and the relation between, Peter and the beloved disciple (see below, p. 583). If ch. 21 is an addendum the question must be raised whether it was composed by the author of chs. 1—20 or by some other. The first criterion available to us, important though not decisive, is a consideration of style and vocabulary. The data may here be briefly set out and examined.

The following words found in ch. 21 are absent from chs. 1—20: αἰγιαλός, ἁλιεύειν, ἀποβαίνειν, ἀριστᾶν, ἀρνίον, βόσκειν, γηράσκειν, γυμνός, δίκτυον, ἐκτείνειν, ἐξετάζειν, ἐπενδύτης, ἐπιστρέφειν, Ζεβεδαῖος, ζωννύναι, ἰσχύειν, ἰχθύς, μακράν, νεώτερος, οἴεσθαι, πῆχυς, ποιμαίνειν, προβάτιον, προσφάγιον, πρωΐα, σύρειν, τολμᾶν, τρίτον (28). Most of these words are of no great significance: δίκτυον and others, for example, occur here only because of the subject matter of the chapter. A few words and constructions however are of interest; the best collection of evidence is Bultmann's (700f.), including, ἀδελφοί as a designation of Christians, v. 23; ἐξετάζειν instead of ἐρωτᾶν v. 12; ἐπιστραφῆναι instead of στραφῆναι (1.38; 20.14,16), ἰσχύειν instead of δύνασθαι v. 6 ("affected" according to Radermacher 37); τολμᾶν v. 12. Further it is surprising to find the disciples addressed as παιδία v. 5 (cf. however I John 2.14,18); causal ἀπό v. 6, and partitive ἀπό v. 10, instead of the usual ἐκ; also ἐπί is used in v. 1 differently from elsewhere in the Gospel; similarly φανεροῦν v. 1. It is strange to read ἕως v. 22 instead of ἕως ὅτου (9.18) or ἕως οὗ (13.38); πλέον v. 15 instead of μᾶλλον (3.19; 12.43), οὐ μακράν v. 8 instead of ἐγγύς (often, e.g. 11.18); ὑπάγειν with infinitive v. 3 (contrast 4.16; 9.7; 15.16). Also τί πρὸς σέ v. 22 is unusual (cp. 2.4).' We may add that whereas in v. 4 πρωΐα is used, the form preferred elsewhere in the gospel is πρωΐ.

These linguistic and stylistic considerations, when weighed against the undoubted resemblances between chs. 1—20 and ch. 21, are not in themselves sufficient to establish the belief that ch. 21 was written by a different author. They do however furnish confirmation for the view that it is extremely unlikely that an author, wishing to add fresh material to his own book, would add it in so clumsy a manner. The supplementary material would have been added by him before 20.30, and the impressive conclusion left undisturbed. Moreover it is difficult to think that an author would wish to spoil the effect of the apostolic mission charge of 20.21-3 by representing the disciples, in a later narrative, as having returned to their former employment and as unable at first to recognize the Lord when he appeared. Ch. 20 is a unit which needs no supplement; and there appear to be some differences in outlook between chs. 1—20 and ch. 21 (see e.g. on v. 23). 21.24 seems to refer to the author of the gospel as a whole, and we must conclude that this verse was not written by the author of chs. 1—20. But this verse belongs (as will be shown below, contrary to the opinion of most scholars) to vv. 1-23, and is not to be thought of as a further addendum. Consequently it seems necessary to detach the whole of ch. 21 from the main body of the gospel.

It remains to ask why the chapter was added. For detailed consideration of this question see below. It is unlikely that the appearance of the risen Jesus in vv. 1-14 would convince of the truth of the resurrection anyone whom ch. 20 had left unpersuaded. The main point seems to lie in the association and contrast of Peter and the beloved disciple. It appears clear that both are, at the time of writing, dead, the latter more recently than the former. They are represented as partners, of whom neither can take precedence of the other. Peter is the head of the evangelistic and pastoral work of the church, but the beloved disciple is the guarantor of its tradition regarding Jesus. Both functions are necessary to the life of the church, and it is probable that the evangelist intended to make this positive point rather than polemical allusion to Mark, the gospel guaranteed, according to tradition, by Peter, from which John differs in certain notable points. See S. Agourides, Πέτρος καὶ Ἰωάννης ἐν τῷ τετάρτῳ Εὐαγγελίῳ (1966), 56–75.

V. 25 is a second conclusion, somewhat feebly imitating the style of 20.30f.

Vv. 1-14. Seven disciples, of whom one is Peter and another the beloved disciple, following the lead of Peter determine to resume their work of fishing in the sea of Tiberias. Their night's work is fruitless, but in the morning an unknown person on the shore instructs them to cast on the right side of the boat, which they do, with instant success. The beloved disciple recognizes Jesus, Peter swims to shore, and the rest follow with the net full of fish. They find preparations for a meal already afoot, and share it with Jesus, who distributes bread and fish to them. Peter meanwhile, under orders from Jesus, draws up the net, which contains 153 fish.

The main point in this narrative, as appears from the text, lies in the representation of the two chief disciples, Peter the quicker to act, the beloved disciple the quicker to see and believe (as in 20.6–8). They, and the other disciples, share with Jesus a meal which has evidently some eucharistic significance, and together, but with the stress laid on Peter's part, they draw in the catch which represents the fullness of the church.

The narrative recalls Luke 5.1–11 (a miraculous catch of fish, but not a resurrection appearance) and 24.13–35 (a resurrection appearance in which a quasi-eucharistic meal takes place), and does not seem to be a unity. There are several hints of unevenness in the story; the miracle is wrought because the disciples have no fish; when they come to land they find fish already cooking yet are bidden to bring fish from their catch, though we do not hear that they do so. No fewer than three words (προσφάγιον, ἰχθύς, and ὀψάριον) are used for fish in different parts of the narrative. It may be that two traditional narratives, similar to those in Luke, have been combined; but whether they were combined by the author of ch. 21, or were found by him in their present state, cannot be determined. It is probable that v. 7 is in any case his work, and was intended to prepare for vv. 15–24. Benoit, II, 274, thinks that Luke 5.1–11 is dependent on John rather than *vice versa*. The two may well be independent. See S. S. Smalley, *N.T.S.* 20 (1974), 275–88.

1. μετὰ ταῦτα. See on 2.12; 3.22; a general transition from the preceding narrative is intended. Contrast 20.26 where a precise indication of time is given.

ἐφανέρωσεν ἑαυτόν. φανεροῦν is a Johannine word (1.31; 2.11; 3.21; 7.4; 9.3; 17.6), but elsewhere in the gospel it is not used of a resurrection appearance (but cf. Mark 16.12,14).

τῆς θαλάσσης τῆς Τιβεριάδος. Cf. 6.1, where however τῆς Τιβεριάδος does not stand independently but is given as an explanation of τῆς Γαλιλαίας. Sanders suggests that the point of an appearance in Galilee is to teach that Jesus is now with his disciples wherever they may be.

2. This verse contains a number of words and constructions characteristic of John's style and matter. For ὁμοῦ cf. 4.36; 20.4. The double name Simon Peter, though used elsewhere, is particularly common in John; see on 1.42. For Θωμᾶς ὁ λεγόμενος Δίδυμος (of whom John has more to say than any other evangelist), see on 11.16; for Nathanael (mentioned by no other evangelist), see on 1.45–9. ὁ ἀπὸ . . . is a Johannine construction; cf. 1.45; (11.1); 12.21; (19.38). Κανά is mentioned only in John; see on 2.1.

οἱ τοῦ Ζεβεδαίου. This is the first and only reference in John to the sons of Zebedee (see among several synoptic passages Mark 1.19). The beloved disciple is mentioned a little later (v. 7), and therefore *may* have been James or John. On this question see Introduction, pp. 116–19.

ἄλλοι ἐκ τῶν μαθητῶν αὐτοῦ δύο. The presence of these unnamed disciples makes it possible that the beloved disciple was not a son of Zebedee. The partitive use of ἐκ is very common in John.

There is a passage very similar to this verse in the Gospel of Peter, 60; ἐγὼ δὲ Σίμων Πέτρος καὶ Ἀνδρέας ὁ ἀδελφός μου λαβόντες ἡμῶν τὰ λίνα ἀπήλθαμεν εἰς τὴν θάλασσαν, καὶ ἦν σὺν ἡμῖν Λευεὶς ὁ τοῦ Ἀλφαίου ὃν κύριος . . . Unfortunately the extant fragment of the gospel breaks off at this point and there is no means of knowing the rest of the story.

3. ὑπάγω ἁλιεύειν. On the infinitive of purpose see M. 1, 205f. This use of the infinitive is in marked contrast with John's frequent use (often where an infinitive would be expected) of ἵνα and the subjunctive; e.g. 11.11, πορεύομαι ἵνα ἐξυπνίσω αὐτόν. That Peter and his brother disciples should contemplate a return to their former occupation after the events of ch. 20 is unthinkable; see the introduction to this section. If ch. 21 is an addition to an originally complete gospel it is of course possible that this event is chronologically earlier than 20.21–3; though it is difficult to see how this can in fact be so. The author of ch. 21 was probably drawing on a different strand of tradition, and it is possible that he intended that Peter's words should be seen to have a double meaning and refer to the apostolic mission of 'catching men'. See below. The commission of 20.21 is being carried out. This is certainly not the face value of Peter's words, but if the author of ch. 21 shared the evangelist's love of double meanings he may have seen this beneath the surface. It supports rather than damages this view that the author wishes to show (Sanders) that the evangelistic task is only made possible by the command and aid of Jesus. When Peter and his colleagues set out on their own they fail completely, and their subsequent (v. 6) success when directed by Jesus stands out the more clearly.

ἐξῆλθον καὶ ἐνέβησαν. The boat seems to be at hand; that is, the disciples are in Galilee, not in Jerusalem, as in 20.1–29.

ἐν ἐκείνῃ τῇ νυκτὶ ἐπίασαν οὐδέν. Cf. Luke 5.5, δι' ὅλης νυκτὸς κοπιάσαντες οὐδὲν ἐλάβομεν. Night is said to have been the best time for fishing, but in the absence of Jesus his disciples can achieve nothing; cf. 15.5. Elsewhere in John (apart from v. 10 in this narrative) πιάζειν is used for the arrest of a person (7.30, 32,44; 8.20; 10.39; 11.57).

4. πρωΐας δὲ ἤδη γινομένης. Elsewhere in John (18.28; 20.1; cf. 1.41) the indeclinable form πρωΐ is used. For γινομένης, γενομένης (ℵ D Θ ω) may be right—morning had come. ἐπί for εἰς is plainly a correction.

οὐ μέντοι ᾔδεισαν. μέντοι is Johannine; it occurs at 4.27; 7.13; 12.42; 20.5; elsewhere in the New Testament only three times. The failure of the disciples to recognize Jesus is difficult to understand if we are to suppose that they had already seen him twice since the resurrection. πρωΐα (especially if taken with the reading γενομένης) need not mean that the light was not good enough to allow recognition; at Matt. 20.1, πρωΐ refers to the beginning of the working day, and in Josephus, Ant. xiv, 65, it refers to the offering of the daily morning sacrifice, when the whole east was alight 'as far as Hebron' (Tamid 3.2).

5. παιδία. This form of address is not used elsewhere in John (the word occurs at 4.49; 16.21). It is used in 1 John (2.14,18; (3.7)). At John 13.33; 1 John 2.1,12,28; 3.(7),18; 4.4; 5.21 τεκνία is used. παιδία as an address (to adults) is used in modern Greek; M. 1, 170.

μή τι προσφάγιον ἔχετε; It would be possible to write μήτι, as at 4.29; 8.22;

18.35. In the last of these passages the answer expected is certainly No; in the others, the question is hesitating and doubtful. The latter appears to be the meaning here (and this is possible also with μή, if the words are separated, as by Nestle; cf. e.g. 6.67); see M. I, 170, but also B.D., §427. προσφάγιον is not found elsewhere in the New Testament, or in the Greek Old Testament; and it is rare elsewhere. According to Moeris and Hesychius it was identical in meaning with ὄψον, which (like its diminutive ὀψάριον, 6.9,11; 21.9f.,13) often meant simply 'fish'. Here προσφάγιον probably means simply 'fish' (used as a relish with bread).

6. βάλετε εἰς τὰ δεξιὰ μέρη τοῦ πλοίου τὸ δίκτυον. For the use of βάλλειν cf. Matt. 4.18; in Luke 5.4f. χαλᾶν is used. The right side is regularly the fortunate side (a secondary meaning of δεξιός is 'fortunate'—see L.S. s.v., quoting among other passages Xenophon, *Cyropaedia* VII, i, 3, βροντὴ δεξιὰ ἐφθέγξατο— many passages are cited in Betz, 38f.), but John means only to suggest that implicit obedience to Jesus brings instant success.

οὐκέτι αὐτὸ ἑλκύσαι ἴσχυον. The magnitude of the catch of fish is described in the Lucan story in other terms: the net broke and the two boats were filled to sinking. ἑλκύειν is a later form of ἕλκειν; in John (6.44; 12.32) it is used of men's being drawn to Christ; this suggests that an allegorical interpretation of the incident may have been intended—the fishing expedition is the apostolic mission, the fish are converts. See on vv. 3, 11, and cf. Mark 1.17 and parallels.

ἀπὸ τοῦ πλήθους, 'by reason of . . .'. This causal use of ἀπό does not occur in John 1—20. It resembles a use of the Hebrew and Aramaic מִן (cf. e.g. Gen. 9.11; Ps. 76.7; Isa. 6.4, with the LXX renderings), but must not be described as a Semitism since it is classical and vernacular (M. II, 461).

7. ὁ μαθητὴς ἐκεῖνος ὃν ἠγάπα ὁ Ἰησοῦς. See Introduction, pp. 116–19, and on 13.23; see on v. 2. As often this disciple is connected with Peter; he is the first to recognize Jesus, as he had been the first to believe in the resurrection (20.8). In John 1—20 ἐκεῖνος is absent from the phrase, but it recurs in v. 23.

ὁ κύριός ἐστιν. D sin pesh have 'Our Lord'; this is a possible instance of Syriac influence on D, since sin and pesh use the common Syriac designation for the Lord (*maran*) and the variant may well have originated in Syriac. But such expansions also occur independently in D. The expression here coincides exactly with the characteristically Johannine ἐγώ εἰμι (for which see on 6.35; 8.24). It can mean only 'It [the hitherto unidentified figure on the shore] is the Lord'.

τὸν ἐπενδύτην διεζώσατο, ἦν γὰρ γυμνός. There is a superficial difficulty in these words: it is customary, when going for a swim, to take clothes off rather than to put them on. The word ἐπενδύτης is not used elsewhere in the New Testament (but cf. 2 Cor. 5.2,4). It is τὸ ἐπάνω ἱμάτιον in contrast with the ὑποδύτης, the ἐσώτερον ἱμάτιον (Suidas s.v. ὑποδύτης; s.v. ἐπενδύτης he says τὸ ἐσώτατον ἱμάτιον—surely a slip, unless Suidas deduced from the present passage that the ἐπενδύτης was the first, that is the inmost, article of clothing that one would put on). Peter had been fishing naked, or nearly so (see L.S. s.v. γυμνός). To offer greeting (שאל שלום) was a religious act and could not be performed without clothing; see *T. Berakoth* 2.20(5): If one goes into the bath, (in a part) where men are clothed, reading (מקרא), prayer, and (it goes without saying) greeting (שאילת שלום) are in order . . .; where there are men naked and clothed, greeting is in order, but not reading and prayer . . .; where men are naked, neither greeting, nor reading, nor prayer is in order. . . . So Peter puts on his ἐπενδύτης, perhaps as the loosest garment and the easiest to put on. Brown, however, who has a particularly good note on this point, observes that the verb used is διαζωννύναι which he renders 'tucked in': Peter, nearly naked, was wearing only his loose ἐπενδύτης, and to make swimming possible he tucked it in. But it is not now clear why John should have added the explanatory ἦν γὰρ γυμνός. The use of the compound δια-ζωννύναι is against Haenchen's suggestion (*Die Bibel und Wir*, 1968, 178) that the author was preparing for v. 18 (where the simple verb, ζωννύναι, is used).

ἔβαλεν ἑαυτόν (ἥλατο, D*). For Peter's haste cf. 20.6. There is no need to cf. Matthew's account (Matt. 14.28–32) of Peter's attempt to walk on the lake.

8. πλοιάριον is used synonymously with πλοῖον (v. 3), as in John 6.24, and perhaps Luke 5.2.

ἀπὸ πηχῶν διακοσίων, about one hundred yards. For the contracted genitive plural (Hellenistic, not Attic) see M. II, 141; B.D., §48. The same construction occurs at 11.18; cf. Rev. 14.20.

9. ἀνθρακιὰν κειμένην. For ἀνθρακιά see on 18.18. For κειμένην the Old Latin has *incensos*, presupposing a Greek text καιομένην.

ὀψάριον. (6.9,11) has the same meaning as προσφάγιον (v. 5). To find fish already cooking on the fire before the fish caught by the disciples had been brought is contrary to what might be expected. It is possible that two stories have been combined, in one of which the disciples caught and brought the fish, while in the other Jesus provided the meal.

ἄρτον. The material of the meal is the same as in 6.9, bread and fish. The combination may have symbolical, or sacramental, significance; see on v. 13.

10. ἀπό. In John 1—20 it is ἐκ, not ἀπό, which is commonly used partitively. The fish which are here called for are never brought, as indeed there is no need for them (v. 9). This may be another indication that the narrative is composite.

ἐπιάσατε, the aorist of 'what has just happened' (M. I, 135), as the addition of νῦν shows.

11. ἀνέβη. Perhaps 'he got into the boat'—to assist his colleagues with the net.

ἑκατὸν πεντήκοντα τριῶν. The number is significant or it would not have been recorded; it is improbable that it represents the fortuitous but precise recollection of an eye-witness. Many suggestions regarding its meaning have been made, but the most probable is that it represents the full total of those who are 'caught' by the Christian fishermen, the apostles (themselves, in this narrative, numbering seven; see below). Explanations which suppose that the 'three' in the number represents the Trinity are probably wrong (since (a) the doctrine of the Trinity was not yet formulated clearly enough, and (b) John would hardly put together divine and human persons in this way), and we are left with the observation that 153 is a triangular number, and $= 1+2+3 \ldots +17$. 17 itself is the sum of 7 and 10, both numbers which even separately are indicative of completeness and perfection. One has only to read Philo to see how seriously first century writers could take such numerical symbolism, though whether the author of chs. 1—20 would have expressed the wholeness of the church in this way is open to question. For further suggestions (based on the numerical value of Gedi and Eglaim, Ezek. 47.10) see J. A. Emerton (*J.T.S.* 9 (1958), 86–9; 11 (1960), 335f.) and P. R. Ackroyd (*J.T.S.* 10 (1959), 94). This observation increases the probability that other features of the story (see vv. 3, 6, 9) should be taken allegorically.

οὐκ ἐσχίσθη τὸ δίκτυον. The church remains one, in spite of the number and variety of its members.

12. δεῦτε ἀριστήσατε. δεῦτε, almost exclamatory rather than an imperative, is often followed immediately by an imperative or cohortative subjunctive (as at 4.29). In this passage ἀριστᾶν must mean 'to take breakfast, the first meal of the day'; cf. v. 4 (πρωΐας). ἀριστᾶν and ἄριστον seem to refer to a later meal at Luke 11.37f.; 14.12, and probably at Matt. 22.4. The Lucan usage seems to be that which was becoming more common in later Greek (see L.S. *s.vv.*), but the position is by no means clear, and M.M. quote a papyrus where they (and editors) give the meaning 'breakfast'.

οὐδεὶς ἐτόλμα. Cf. 4.27. It is possible that there is a reference to 8.25 where the same words (σὺ τίς εἶ;) are used (cf. 1.19, where they are addressed to John the Baptist). Now that Jesus has manifested himself (v. 1) to his own (14.22) such questions are needless. This is not a second recognition (cf. v. 7), and is not therefore an indication that two stories are being combined. ἐξετάζειν is used in the sixth Saying of Jesus in *P. Oxy.* 654 (cf. *Thomas* 6), but there is nothing to link the present passage with the papyrus saying.

13. ἔρχεται seems pleonastic and is possibly Semitic; cf. the use of the Aramaic אזל.

λαμβάνει τὸν ἄρτον καὶ δίδωσιν—the act of the host who pronounces the blessing in a Jewish meal. D (cf. sin) has the more explicit statement εὐχαριστήσας ἔδωκεν.

καὶ τὸ ὀψάριον ὁμοίως. Cf. 6.11, ὁμοίως καὶ ἐκ τῶν ὀψαρίων. The parallel acts recall also the distribution by Jesus of the bread and wine at the last supper. This meal may have been intended to call to the minds of the readers eucharistic associations (cf. the manifestation of Jesus to the two disciples at Emmaus, Luke 24.30f., 35). A fish occurs along with bread in some early representations of the eucharist; and fish-symbolism was very widespread in early Christianity. See Cullmann, *V. & A.*, 510; and Brown. This narrative tells of a meal in which Jesus acted as host; it is not said that he himself ate any of the bread and fish, and equally it is not said that he gave himself to his disciples in the bread and fish. This he neither was able nor needed to do, since they were in his company. The story is thus not parallel to 6.51ff.— the bread that I will give is my flesh—and the eucharistic allusions are more remote than some modern expositors suppose.

14. τρίτον ἐφανερώθη. Apparently the appearance to Mary Magdalene is not counted (perhaps because she was not a μαθητής); that of 20.19–23 is the first, that of 20.26–9 the second. It is impossible to fit the various resurrection narratives of the other gospels (and of 1 Cor. 15) into this scheme. Moreover, the present narrative looks more like a first than a third appearance; see the introduction to this section, and on vv. 1, 3. The impression is given that the present story does not belong to the carefully composed narrative of

ch. 20 but is a distinct incident drawn from another source (perhaps two incidents from two sources; see on vv. 9f.) combined rather clumsily with an already complete whole. The present appearance taken by itself supports the Galilean tradition of the appearances against the Jerusalem. On this issue see *Beginnings*, v. 7–16.

44. THE APPENDIX

II. JESUS, PETER, AND THE BELOVED DISCIPLE

21.15–25

Peter, thrice questioned by Jesus, thrice affirms his love for him, and is entrusted with the pastoral care of Christ's flock. His death by crucifixion is predicted, and he is bidden to 'follow'. Upon this Peter himself notices the beloved disciple doing what he, Peter, has been told to do; he is following. Peter asks concerning his fellow-disciple's lot, and the reply is an evasion, by implication a rebuke. It would be no concern of Peter's should the beloved disciple live till the return of Christ. This, the writer emphasizes, was no prophecy, though it was understood as one. This man, he concludes, was the disciple who wrote 'these things' —probably (see the note) the gospel as a whole, 1.1—21.23.

The connection of this paragraph with 21.1–14 is loose: we hear no more of the meal; disciples other than Peter and the beloved disciple disappear. The writer however used 21.1–14 not only as a narrative introduction but, it seems, to introduce the themes of vv. 15–23. The three affirmations of Peter, and the three charges given him by the Lord, probably (though Bultmann rejects this view) correspond to the three denials. Rehabilitation, however, though it is certainly in mind, is not the primary thought. This is, that a prediction was given of what Peter would become in the church: he would be the great pastor, and he would die a martyr's death. He could thus be bidden to do what previously had been impossible for him (13.36ff.)—to follow. The interest here lies not in the mission of the church (as in 20.21) but in leadership and pastoral care within it (Bultmann). We are now introduced to the beloved disciple, who is already following. It is not predicted that he will be a pre-eminent pastor of the church; but, the writer asserts, though he was not to be a μάρτυς in the same way as Peter, he was a μάρτυς, and was responsible for the μαρτυρία contained in the gospel itself. V. 24 is thus co-ordinate with the prophecy about Peter and is therefore an integral part of the paragraph, not an addition to it. Indeed, its inclusion was one of the principal motives for the addition of ch. 21, since it appears to have been intended to replace an older view, now proved false, of the destiny intended by Christ for his beloved disciple. He was not to survive, a living witness of Christ, till the *parousia*, but he was, through the written gospel, to constitute himself the permanent guarantor of the church's tradition and of the word of Jesus by which alone the church exists.

15. ἠρίστησαν. See on v. 12. Σίμωνι Πέτρῳ. See on v. 2.

Σίμων Ἰωάννου. This reading is to be preferred; cf. 1.42, Σίμων ὁ υἱὸς Ἰωάννου (see the note). Ἰωνᾶ (read by Θ ω) probably came into the text through assimilation to Matt. 16.17.

ἀγαπᾷς . . . φιλῶ. The usage of these verbs throughout the gospel makes it impossible to doubt that they are synonyms; φιλεῖν does not refer to an inferior kind of love. Note particularly (a) the fact that the disciple whom Jesus loved is several times ὃν ἠγάπα, once (20.2) ὃν ἐφίλει (it is highly improbable that there were two 'beloved disciples', one loved in a rather better way than the other); and (b) the parallelism of 14.23, ἐάν τις ἀγαπᾷ με . . . ὁ πατήρ μου ἀγαπήσει αὐτόν, and 16.27, ὁ πατὴρ φιλεῖ ὑμᾶς ὅτι ὑμεῖς ἐμὲ πεφιλήκατε. See a full list of similar passages in Bernard, 703, and cf. the LXX rendering of Prov. 8.17, ἐγὼ τοὺς ἐμὲ φιλοῦντας (אהבי) ἀγαπῶ (אהב). That the author of ch. 21 continued to use the words synonymously is confirmed by the fact that Peter answers Jesus' question affirmatively (Ναί . . .): 'Do you love . . .?' 'Yes, I do love . . .'. The threefold question corresponds to the threefold denial; so does the threefold charge to keep the flock. In spite of the rebuke administered in v. 22 a very high view of the office and importance of Peter is taken. He takes the lead in fishing (v. 3); he is also the chief shepherd. The total effect of the passage is not to question but to affirm his love for Jesus. See the next note.

πλέον τούτων. τούτων may be either masculine or neuter, and several interpretations are possible. The two most important are (a) 'Do you love me more than these other disciples do?' and (b) 'Do you love me more than this fishing gear, which represents your ordinary life and which now once more I am summoning you to leave?' (b) is less probable, because the fishing gear, though no doubt presupposed, has not been mentioned in the immediate context (and in any case represents not so much the instruments of Peter's livelihood as the operations of the apostolic mission—see on vv. 3, 11). Moreover, the comparative form of the question in (a) forms a fitting rebuke for Peter who after the loudest boasts had failed most completely (see 13.8,37f.; 18.10f.,15). There may also be an allusion to Peter's subsequent pre-eminence among the Twelve. Benoit (II, 277–83,301), indeed, sees the ground of Peter's primacy, not only over the church as a whole but over his fellow apostles, in the fact that he loves most. This very fact, however, contradicts Benoit's further argument on succession from Peter (which in any case is not mentioned in the text); it is love, not succession, that constitutes primacy (cf. Mark 10. 41–4, and parallels). Note also the function of the beloved disciple (vv. 21–4), which is neither superior nor inferior to Peter's, but different. It is the two functions, not the persons who exercise them, that are of permanent significance for the church.

σὺ οἶδας. Cf. 2.24f. Peter does not take up the comparison suggested by Jesus, and throws the responsibility for his answer back upon Jesus.

βόσκε τὰ ἀρνία (D it have πρόβατα) μου. It does not appear that any distinction is intended between the words in this and the following verses: βόσκε = ποίμαινε = βόσκε; ἀρνία = προβάτια = προβάτια. None of these words occurs elsewhere in John; πρόβατον, which occurs as a variant in three verses, 15, 16, 17, is probably an assimilation to ch. 10. For Jesus and his sheep see 10.1–16,26. For Christian ministers as shepherds see Acts 20.28f.; 1 Peter 5.2–4. It is because Peter can answer Jesus' question affirmatively that he can be appointed shepherd of the flock. Dodd (*A.S.* 85) sees in βόσκειν an allusion to Jer. 31.10.

16. For προβάτια, ℵ D Θ ω it have πρόβατα.

17. ἐλυπήθη, as at 16.20; cf. 16.6,20ff., λύπη. Peter was grieved because the question was asked three times, not because φιλεῖν was used.

For προβάτια, ℵ D Θ ω it vg have πρόβατα.

18. ἀμὴν ἀμὴν λέγω σοι. See on 1.51. This is a very characteristic, but, it must be admitted, easily imitable, Johannine idiom.

νεώτερος need have no comparative force. Cf. Ps. 36(37).25, νεώτερος ἐγενόμην καὶ γὰρ ἐγήρασα (quoted in Bauer, 238). It may be (Bultmann, 713) that a proverb to the effect that 'In youth man is free to go where he will; in old age a man must let himself be taken where he does not will' underlies this verse; but if this is so, much additional material has been imported into the proverb. Bultmann, it is true, sees no reference here to crucifixion; see however the next two notes.

ἐκτενεῖς τὰς χεῖράς σου. There is abundant evidence for the reference of this expression to crucifixion. Isa. 65.2 (ἐξεπέτασα τὰς χεῖράς μου ...) is taken as foreshadowing the crucifixion by Barnabas (12.4), Justin (1 *Apol.*, 35), Irenaeus (*Demonstration of the Apostolic Preaching*, 79) and Cyprian (*Test.* II, 20); similarly Moses' outstretched hands (Exod. 17.12) by Barnabas (12.2, introducing the verb ἐκτείνειν) and Justin (*Trypho*, 90f.). Non-Christian writers have less occasion to refer to crucifixion, but cf. Epictetus III, xxvi, 22, ἐκτείνας σεαυτὸν ὡς οἱ ἐσταυρωμένοι.

ἄλλος ζώσει σε. According to Bultmann (see above) this cannot be a reference to crucifixion, since ζωννύναι does not mean to bind (criminals were always fastened to the cross in part, and sometimes wholly, by ropes; see on 20.20). The argument is not convincing; in the context a somewhat strained use of the verb is not impossible. The simple verb could (see M. 1, 115) but need not have the same sense as the compound διαζωννύναι (21.7; see the note).

19. σημαίνων ποίῳ θανάτῳ. Cf. 12.33, where the manner of Jesus' death is predicted.

δοξάσει τὸν θεόν. To die in obedience and faith is to glorify God. Cf. 15.8. Jesus' death had been an act by which God had disclosed his glory; the death of the apostle would mean a grateful acknowledgement by man of the glory God had revealed. This passage must be taken as comparatively early and good evidence for the martyrdom of Peter by crucifixion, which it presupposes. Other equally early evidence for this event is extremely slight; see especially 1 Clement 5.4; 6.1, and the writers quoted by Eusebius, *H.E.* II, xxv. 1 Peter (whether authentic or not) is evidence for an early interest in Peter in Asia Minor; cf. Ignatius, *Romans* 4.3. See also Rev. 11.3–13, interpreted by J. Munck, *Petrus und Paulus in der Offenbarung Johannis* (1950). It cannot be said that Peter is here introduced as a representative of the (Roman and Western) Christians who opposed the Quartodeciman views regarding Easter, of which the apostle John was taken to be a supporter; if this controversy had been in mind it would have been much more clearly in evidence.

ἀκολούθει μοι. Cf. 13.36, ἀκολουθήσεις δὲ ὕστερον. It is probable that this command means primarily that Peter must follow Jesus on the path of martyrdom but, as the next verse shows, if this is its primary meaning it is a particularization of a wider conception of discipleship; cf. 12.25f. (cf. Mark 8.34f.). To follow Jesus, whether or not it means martyrdom in blood, is to deny oneself in complete obedience. See on 1.37. Jesus' last word to Peter (cf. v. 22) ranks him with, not above, his fellow disciples.

20. τὸν μαθητὴν ὃν ἠγάπα ὁ 'Ιησοῦς. See on 13.23. The reference is made unmistakable by the allusion to the last supper and the disciple's question.

ἀκολουθοῦντα. This word is omitted by ℵ* W and the Old Latin codex Corbeiensis. The beloved disciple was already doing what Peter had just been bidden to do (once more his superiority to Peter is implied). Cf. 1.38, if one of the disciples there mentioned was John the son of Zebedee, and if the beloved disciple was John the son of Zebedee. It is evident that for him also, as for Peter, following meant following unto death, for (see below) vv. 22f. imply that his death had taken place.

ἀνέπεσεν. See 13.25, and on 6.10.

21. τοῦτον οὖν ἰδών resumes the previous verse, βλέπει.

οὗτος δὲ τί; This elliptic sentence is to be completed by the addition of some such word as πείσεται; or we could write with a *nominativus pendens* in the Johannine manner (see Introduction, p. 10) οὗτος δέ, τί αὐτῷ συμβήσεται; The sense is clear: in colloquial English, 'What about *him?*'

22. ἐὰν αὐτὸν θέλω μένειν (for the addition in D of οὕτως (cf. the text of the vg and other Latin witnesses, *si sic eum uolo manere*, and see the important note in W.W., 647f.), cf. 4.6; 11.48) ἕως ἔρχομαι. ἕως ἔλθω might be expected, for the meaning cannot be other than, 'If I will that he should remain (alive) until I come . . .'. The possibility is contemplated, though (as John hastens to point out) not definitely affirmed, that the beloved disciple might live until the return of Christ; cf. Mark 9.1. Undoubtedly the earliest Christian belief was that the *parousia* would take place before the first generation of Christians had disappeared (cf. especially 1 Thess. 4.15, ἡμεῖς οἱ ζῶντες; 1 Cor. 15.51, πάντες οὐ κοιμηθησόμεθα). See further on v. 23.

τί πρός σέ; 'What has that to do with you?' Cf. 2.4.

σύ μοι ἀκολούθει. σύ is in a very emphatic position: 'Whatever may happen to him, *you* must follow me'. Bultmann rightly observes that it is not the intention of this passage to belittle either Peter or the beloved disciple. 'The really characteristic feature of the passage is that both men are represented as on the same level; the Lord decreed one thing for the one man and another for the other' (716). Bultmann draws the inference that since the position of Peter was assured the intention must therefore have been to claim the same standing for the beloved disciple and thus to 'substantiate the ecclesiastical authority of this Gospel' (717). The inference may be questioned, at least as regards the major intention of the writer. Clearly (v. 24) he was concerned that the testimony of the gospel should be accepted as authoritative, but the equal status of Peter and the beloved disciple attests also the equal importance of pastoral ministry and of the historical-theological testimony of which the gospel provides one crystallization.

23. After ἀδελφούς, D adds καὶ ἔδοξαν, giving a smoother reading.

οὐκ ἀποθνῄσκει. The future would be expected. See on v. 22. The primitive conviction that the *parousia* would happen soon was evidently weakened with the lapse of time to the belief that one of the first generation would survive till it took place. This expectation however was possibly local; there seems to be no evidence for it except in John. Cf. Mark 9.1; 13.30.

οὐκ εἶπεν δέ. D Θ ω have καὶ οὐκ εἶπεν. It seems probable that this disciple, who it was thought would not die, had died. The writer of the present chapter explains carefully that Jesus had made no prediction; he had simply expressed in the strongest terms that the fate of the disciple, whatever it might be, was no concern of Peter's. It seems however probable that the original meaning of the saying (whatever its origin may have been) was that which it was popularly supposed to have. The explanation of this disappointed hope given here is quite different from the bold reinterpretation of Christian eschatology presented in the body of the gospel; see Introduction, pp. 67–70, 139f.

In the latter part of the verse (referring back to v. 22), for ἀποθνῄσκει D e have ἀποθνῄσκεις (turning the sentence into direct speech); τί πρὸς σέ is omitted by ℵ* a e sin.

Lindars (640) has a fine comment on this verse: 'This verse makes an epilogue to the story, which also points its application to the readers. They too must cease to indulge in wild speculations about the Beloved Disciple and attend to their own discipleship. For indeed that is John's object in creating this character in the first place. His reticence about him has a definite purpose. It is his hope that each reader will be so drawn by the Gospel to believe in Jesus and to follow him, that he will discover *himself* in the true discipleship of the Beloved Disciple.' This is well said, but it has the unfortunate effect of separating v. 24 from vv. 21ff., to which it belongs. See below.

24. οὗτός ἐστιν. The beloved disciple. On the interpretation of this verse see also Introduction, pp. 118f.

ὁ μαρτυρῶν περὶ τούτων καὶ ὁ γράψας ταῦτα. The textual evidence is somewhat confused. Before μαρτυρῶν, B adds καί; this is probably a thoughtless slip and should be disregarded. Before γράψας, B D it sin pesh have καὶ ὁ; Θ φ have ὁ καί; ℵ ω have καί. The variable position of ὁ adds weight to the reading of ℵ ω; but the combination of BD it sin is so strong that it seems best to accept καὶ ὁ, though it must be acknowledged to be in John's style to co-ordinate two participles without a second article. For μαρτυρεῖν in John see on 1.7; it is sometimes used absolutely, sometimes with a dative, sometimes, as here, with περί. The most natural meaning of these words, and therefore the meaning to be adopted unless very strong reasons are brought against it, is that the disciple himself not only bore witness to but also wrote down ταῦτα. It is conceivable but perhaps not probable that γράψας should be translated 'caused to be written' (see on 19.19), and means no more than that the disciple was the ultimate and responsible authority for 'these things'. This verse provides an answer to Peter's question in v. 21: the beloved disciple is a trustworthy witness. It thus belongs to, and is part of, the paragraph vv.

15–23, which carries its introduction (21.1–14) with it. The claim made in v. 24 therefore refers to the gospel as a whole, to which 21.1–24 is a supplement by a writer (or writers—οἴδαμεν) other than the author of chs. 1—20. The beloved disciple is (see above, the quotation from Lindars) an ideal of discipleship, but he also is a source of theologically interpreted history (J. Roloff, *N.T.S.* 15 (1968), 129–51, compares the Teacher of Righteousness). The present verse was probably modelled upon 19.35 (unless that verse is to be regarded as a gloss by the author of ch. 21).

οἴδαμεν. The person of the verb separates this verse from the gospel as a whole and calls for different authorship (unless the force of γράψας is to be seriously weakened—see above). According to Clement of Alexandria (*apud* Eusebius, *H.E.* vi, xiv, 7, προτραπέντα ὑπὸ τῶν γνωρίμων) and the Muratorian Canon (ll. 10–15, *cohortantibus condescipulis* [*sic*] *et episcopis suis ... recogniscentibus cuntis* [*sic*] *...*) this gospel was in some sense a joint product; others beside the author took responsibility for it. It is of course possible that these statements are no more than inferences from the present passage. If they are in any degree independent of it they may enshrine a memory of the publication of the book by (it may be) the church of Ephesus. The 'we' is to be taken with full seriousness; there exists an apostolic church whose very existence is a confirmation and affirmation of the apostolic witness. Cf. 1 Cor. 9.2; 2 Cor. 3.2.

ἀληθής. Cf. 19.35, ἀληθινή; on John's use of these adjectives see on 1.9.

After this verse the *Pericope Adulterae* (7.53—8.11) is inserted by λ (probably). See p. 589.

25. The whole of this verse is omitted by א*; but it is added by the first hand and its omission was probably accidental.

ἄλλα πολλά. Cf. 20.30. The repetition is somewhat crude and strongly confirms the view that ch. 21 is an addendum to the gospel. Moreover, ἄλλα πολλά is inferior Greek in comparison with πολλὰ καὶ ἄλλα; this may be a slight indication of different authorship.

καθ' ἕν Cf. Acts 21.19; 'one at a time'.

οὐδ' αὐτὸν οἶμαι τὸν κόσμον χωρήσειν. οὐ is rarely constructed with the infinitive in New Testament Greek; this is perhaps a reason for supposing that it properly belongs to οἶμαι and has not (as is sometimes suggested) been attracted from the subordinate into the principal clause. 'I do not suppose that the world would contain...'. χωρήσειν is the reading of א B; other MSS. have the aorist infinitive χωρῆσαι. But there was in Hellenistic Greek a tendency (M. 1, 204f.; ii, 216, 219; Robertson, 369f.) to write the aorist infinitive with the ending of the present infinitive, so that χωρήσειν may be intended as an aorist, not a future, infinitive. Yet a future is required here and may, in spite of the rarity of the form in the New Testament, have been intended. κόσμος is not used here in the characteristic Johannine sense (for which see on 1.10). For the hyperbole itself many parallels can be quoted; e.g. *Ex. R.* 30.22 (in the age to come 'the whole world [עולם] cannot receive the reward'); Philo, *Post.*, 144 (οὐδὲ γὰρ εἰ τὸν πλοῦτον ἐπιδείκνυσθαι βουληθείη [*sc.* ὁ θεός] τὸν ἑαυτοῦ, χωρῆσαι ἂν ἠπειρωθείσης καὶ θαλάττης ἡ σύμπασα γῆ). Cf. 1 Macc. 9.22. It is neither Greek nor Jewish, but a common human exaggeration.

THE WOMAN TAKEN IN ADULTERY

7.53—8.11

It is certain that this narrative is not an original part of the gospel. Its textual history, of which only an outline can be given here, is decisive on this score. Those authorities which contain it differ markedly among themselves. Those which place it at this point in John include the great mass of late (medieval) Greek minuscule MSS., but in addition, among early Greek MSS., only D (though Jerome knew many Greek as well as Latin MSS. which contained it (*adv. Pelag.* II, 17)). Several Greek MSS. which do contain it mark it with asterisks or obeli. It is found in the Vulgate and in a few Old Latin MSS. (notably b* e); in the Palestine Syriac lectionary, in the Ethiopic, and in a few MSS. of other VSS.; in Ambrose, Augustine, and Jerome, but in no earlier Western Father; and in no Eastern Father before the tenth century at the earliest.

On the other hand, the whole passage is omitted by P⁶⁶ P⁷⁵ ℵ B A Θ and many other early Greek MSS., some of which leave a space after 7.52, indicating that the copyist was aware of the existence of the pericope but thought it right to omit it. It is omitted by the Old and Peshitto Syriac, by the Coptic VSS., by some Old Latin MSS. (including a), and, as has been already indicated, by all early Fathers (including Origen, Cyprian, Chrysostom, and Nonnus, who, in expounding, commenting, or paraphrasing, pass directly from 7.52 to 8.12).

It remains to note that φ places the pericope not in this gospel but after Luke 21.38 (it has been suggested that Luke 21.37f. was composed to fill the gap caused by the removal of this paragraph); that λ (probably) places it at the end of John; that one Greek MS. places it after 7.36, and some Georgian MSS. after 7.44.

The weight of evidence against the originality of the passage cannot be resisted, nor can any good reason be found why the story, supposed original, should have been omitted from so many documents, or should have remained unknown to so many ecclesiastical writers. It cannot have been included in the gospel as at first published. What then was its origin? And what is its historical value? It is probably ancient. Eusebius (*H.E.*, III, xxxix, 16) sets it down that Papias 'records another story also, about a woman, accused in the Lord's presence of many sins, which is contained in the Gospel according to the Hebrews'. In our narrative the woman is accused of only one sin, but the correspondence is none the less fairly close. In the *Apostolic Constitutions* II, 24 (=the Syriac *Didascalia* 7; the documents are to be dated in the third century) a similar story is used to caution bishops against too great severity in dealing with penitents. 'The elders set before him another woman who had sinned, handed over the decision to him (ἐπ᾽ αὐτῷ θέμενοι τὴν κρίσιν), and went out. But the Lord, who knows men's hearts, inquired of her whether the elders had condemned her. When she said, "No", he said to her, "Go then; neither do I condemn you."' This story, which may possibly, like others in the *Constitutions*, have been drawn from the Gospel of Peter, is not identical with the Johannine story but clearly resembles it. It may be that stories on this theme were current in several forms at an early date but did not attain canonical status because they seemed inconsistent with the strict disciplinary treatment of adultery then customary, and that the story as we know it came into the Fourth Gospel because at some time it was combined with it (as originally non-biblical material) in a lectionary.

The historical value of the story cannot be assessed by objective standards, but the opinion may fairly be held that (1) it closely resembles in form and style the synoptic narratives (especially the style of Luke; see the notes); and (2) it represents the character and method of Jesus as they are revealed elsewhere. It may have been inserted at this point in John to illustrate 7.24 (Do not judge by appearance) and 8.15 (You judge according to the flesh, I judge no one), or the Jews' sin contrasted with Jesus' sinlessness (8.21,24,46). Guilding, 110ff., thinks the passage was inserted by one who understood John's lectionary theme, and finds allusions to Gen. 38; 39; 2 Sam. 11; Deut. 9; Jer. 2. See below.

On the textual question see, in addition to the Commentaries, C. Tischendorf, *Novum Testamentum Graece*, (1869), 1, 826–30; WH 11, Appendix, 82–8; H. von Soden, *Die Schriften des Neuen Testaments* (1911–13), 1, 486–524; also Becker and Riesenfeld (below).

That the pericope was used in Christian discussion of the appropriate attitude to sinners, especially in the case of adultery, is clear. See H. Riesenfeld in *Svensk Exegetisk Årsbok* 17 (1952), 106–11, and U. Becker, *Jesus und die Ehebrecherin* (1963). J. Jeremias and T. W. Manson (see below) have laid stress on πειράζοντες in 8.6; Jesus was to be snared into a false position. Derrett (*Law*, 156–88; surprisingly he says that the pericope is ignored in the first edition of this commentary) thinks that Jesus applied Exod. 23.1,7 to remind his hearers of what the law itself required. 'A wicked man, one who "hated his brother in his heart", or one whose motives were devious, could neither accuse, nor testify, nor condemn' (187). The audience would understand what was meant. A similar theme is taken further, and in a particular direction, by D. Daube (who has kindly sent me the typescript of an essay hitherto unpublished). He suggests that, 'in its original context, the slogan "He that is without sin among you, let him be the first to cast a stone at her" is directed specifically against the unfair treatment of women by men and their laws; and that it is representative of a strong movement in Tannaitic Judaism'. The evidence for such a movement (that is, a movement on the part of some but not all rabbis) is convincing, and there is no reason why Jesus should not have played a part in it. There is, however, no hint of it in the framework of the story which, it may be guessed, eventually reached the pages of the Fourth Gospel rather because it depicted Jesus as the merciful judge than because a Christian editor wished to attack discrimination against women.

53. The paragraph opens abruptly, and suggests a piece from the Marcan narrative of the last week in Jerusalem, when Jesus at night went out to Bethany and returned in the morning to the city (Mark 11.11f., 19f.); cf. especially Luke 21.37 (... τὰς δὲ νύκτας ἐξερχόμενος ηὐλίζετο εἰς τὸ ὄρος τὸ καλούμενον Ἐλαιῶν).

ἐπορεύθησαν ἕκαστος εἰς τὸν οἶκον αὐτοῦ. Cf. *C.H.* 1, 29, ἕκαστος ἐτράπη εἰς τὴν ἰδίαν κοίτην.

1. Ἐλαιῶν, neuter plural literally 'the mountain of olive trees'. This is the usual New Testament expression, but ἐλαιών (Olive-orchard) is sometimes found in the Lucan writings.

2. This verse contains several points of contact with the Lucan writings, as follows. (a) ὄρθρος occurs elswhere in the New Testament only at Luke 24.1; Acts 5.21. (b) παραγίνεσθαι is a Lucan word (Luke 8 times, Acts 20; John 2 (including this verse); rest of the New Testament 7). (c) λαός is a Lucan word (Luke 37(36) times, Acts 48; John 3 (including this verse); rest of the New Testament 56(55), of which 22 are in Hebrews and Revelation). (d) καθίσας ἐδίδασκεν. Cf. Luke 4.20; 5.3 (καθίσας... ἐδίδασκεν). In John 7.37; 10.23 Jesus stands.

4. ἐπ' αὐτοφώρῳ should be so written (not as one word). The phrase is *hap. leg.* in the New Testament but by no means uncommon. αὐτόφωρος is an adjective meaning 'self-detected'. If punishment was to be inflicted for adultery eye-witnesses were necessary (Abrahams, *Studies* 1, 73; Deut. 22.22, If a man be *found* ...).

5. ἐν δὲ τῷ νόμῳ. See Lev. 20.10, θανάτῳ θανατούσθωσαν, ὁ μοιχεύων καὶ ἡ μοιχευομένη; Deut. 22.22–4, λιθοβοληθήσονται ἐν λίθοις (spoken of a betrothed virgin, but later in the same verse she is τὴν γυναῖκα τοῦ πλησίον). In the Mishnah the two cases are sharply distinguished (*Sanhedrin* 7.4: These are they that are to be stoned: ... he that has connection with a girl that is betrothed; 11.1: These are they that are to be strangled: ... he that has connection with another man's wife [the woman would doubtless incur the same penalty]). It is natural to infer that the woman in this incident was betrothed, not married; but it seems that the Mishnah requirement that the married woman who commits adultery should be strangled represents a late first-century or second-century change (see Daube, *N.R.T.J.*, 307, and *art. cit.*; also J. Blinzler, *N.T.S.* 4 (1957), 32–47). Abrahams (loc. cit.) thinks that the death penalty 'can never have been frequently enforced'.

σὺ οὖν τί λέγεις; σύ is in a position of emphasis, inviting Jesus to set himself against Moses.

6. πειράζοντες. This sentence recalls several passages in the Synoptic Gospels, e.g. Mark 3.2; 10.2; also Luke 6.7. πειράζειν is used in only one other place in John (6.6.); the wording is very similar, but there Jesus tests his disciples. J. Jeremias (*Z.N.T.W.* 43 (1950/51), 148ff.) thinks that the tempting of Jesus here was on the same lines as Mark 12.13–17. He was asked to pronounce sentence on the woman; it must have been the sentence of death, and to pronounce it would have been to infringe the prerogative of the

Roman governor, since at this time the Jews did not have the right to execute capital sentences (18.31). Thus Jesus would be obliged to incur animosity either by not upholding the Law or by offending the Romans.

κύψας . . . κατέγραφεν. Derrett (op. cit.) thinks that at this point he wrote Exod. 23.1b (Place not thy hand with the wicked (to be a false witness)); at v. 8 he wrote Exod. 23.7a (From a false matter keep far (and the innocent and righteous slay not; for I shall not acquit the guilty)). Guilding (loc. cit.) suggests Deut. 9.10; Jer. 17.13 has also been suggested. T. W. Manson (*Z.N.T.W.* 44 (1952/53), 255f.), taking up Jeremias' interpretation of the incident as a whole, notes that Jesus adopted the Roman custom of first writing and then reading the sentence. The sentence was written, but in such a way that it could not be preserved. In fact it is fruitless to ask what Jesus wrote on the ground. His action was simply a studied refusal to pronounce judgement; cf. 8.15, ἐγὼ οὐ κρίνω οὐδένα.

7. πρῶτος. This recalls Deut. 13.10(9); 17.7, The hand of the witnesses shall be first upon him to put him to death. The aim of this answer was to produce the effect described in v. 9. As v. 8 shows, Jesus maintained silence on the main issue. Cf. the saying (*Sotah* 47b, *et al.*, quoted in Abrahams *Studies* 1, 74) on the trial of a suspected adulteress by the ordeal of the bitter waters: 'Only when the [accusing] husband is himself free from guilt will the waters be an effective test of his wife's guilt or innocence'.

9. After ἀκούσαντες the majority of MSS. add καὶ ὑπὸ τῆς συνειδήσεως ἐλεγχόμε-νοι. συνείδησις occurs nowhere else in the gospels; in the New Testament it is a predominantly Pauline word; elsewhere it was used by the Stoics, though it did not originate with them (see H. Osborne, *J.T.S.* old series 32, (1931), 167–179). On ἐλέγχειν see on 16.8; the function of the conscience was to expose, and it was sometimes called an ἔλεγχος. Evidently none of the accusers could claim to be ἀναμάρτητος.

εἶς καθ' εἶς. Cf. Mark 14.19; Rom. 12.5. For the construction see M. 1, 105; Robertson, 282, 294, 606. Radermacher, 59, thinks that the author may have regarded εἶς as indeclinable (as most other Greek cardinals are).

ἐν μέσῳ. The woman is no longer 'in the midst' in the proper sense (as in v. 3), but she remains standing, as it were, in the centre of the stage.

10. γύναι. For this mode of address cf. 2.4; 19.26. These passages clearly show that it is in no way disrespectful.

After ποῦ εἰσίν some MSS. add ἐκεῖνοι οἱ κατήγοροί σου. If these words are read we should perhaps translate 'Where are they—your accusers?'

11. οὐδὲ ἐγώ σε κατακρίνω. See on v. 6 above. No extenuation of the offence is implied; Jesus has come to save, not to condemn (3.17). Yet his very presence has the effect of judging the self-righteous bystanders; cf. 8.15f., I judge no man; yet if I judge, my judgement is true. This may not have been the original sense of the story (see above, pp. 590f.), but it is probably the sense in which it was understood by those who incorporated it in the gospel.

μηκέτι ἁμάρτανε. Cf. 5.14. If the command is not unrealistic it carries with it the promise that a new obedience is possible.

INDEXES

1. OLD TESTAMENT

2. NEW TESTAMENT

[1] References in this section are to the Introduction (pp. 1–146) only.

3. APOCRYPHA AND PSEUDEPIGRAPHA[1]

1 Esdras		Wisdom (of Solomon)	
3. 7	177	1. 2	465-6
9. 8	362	6	264
		2. 14 f.	312
1 Maccabees		16	256
2. 18	477	18	386, 542
3. 38	477	24	349
4. 36-59	379	5. 4	378
46	173, 330	6. 12	322
50	265	7. 2	164
6. 38	548	22	153
7. 38	456	25	155
9. 22	588	26	157, 336
39	223	27	153, 477
45	548	8. 8	247
47	306	13, 17	157
10. 65	477	9. 4	434
11. 39	522	9-18	161
13. 51	417	11	489
14. 41	173, 330	16	212
		17	206
2 Maccabees		10. 2	498, 502
1. 9	379, 417	10	207, 489
18	379	16	247
27	325	17	489
5. 19	405	15. 11	570
10. 1-8	379	16. 6 f.	213
6	417	19. 3	398
15. 15	173		
		1 Baruch	
3 Maccabees		3. 14 f.	322
6. 18	504		
		Jubilees	
Tobit		8. 19	328
4. 6	218		
6. 3	274	Pseudo-Aristeas	
13. 6	218	112	417
			.
Judith		Martyrdom of Isaiah	
5. 19	325	2. 4	427
Ecclesiasticus		1 Enoch	
1. 10	226	1. 9	302
2. 6	173	9. 1	563
17. 11	157	10. 19	189
24. —	292	39. 4	457
8	166	42. 1 f.	457
21	234, 293	42. 2	166
27	472	48. 1	233
25. 24	349	6	322
37. 15	173	49. 1	233, 427
43. 31	170	58. 3	157
46. 19	393	62. 14	427
48. 1	265	70. 2	213
11	573	71. 1	213
49. 9	173	14	365

[1] The books are given in the order in which they appear in R. H. Charles, *The Apocrypha and Pseudepigrapha of the Old Testament* (1913).

4. JOSEPHUS AND PHILO

5. RABBINIC LITERATURE

7. GREEK AND LATIN AUTHORS

8. INSCRIPTIONS AND PAPYRI

9. EARLY CHRISTIAN LITERATURE

10. MODERN AUTHORS, BOOKS, AND PERIODICALS

Aalen, S., 158, 167

Abrahams, I., xii, 197, 223, 241, 274, 320, 328, 411, 528, 539, 555, 591–2

Ackroyd, P. R., 582

Adcock, F. E., see *C.A.H.*

Agourides, S., 577

Aland, K., 114, 157, 563

Albright, W. F., 231

Allen, E. L., 355

American Journal of Archaeology, 188

Andersen, J. V., 101

Angus, S., 37

Appold, M. L., 67, 97

Bacon, B. W., xi, 3, 24

Bailey, J. A., 46

Baillet, M., 253

Bammel, E., 387, 488, 535, 543

Barnes, T. D., 64

Barr, J., 312

Barrett, C. K., xii, xiv, 3, 20, 22, 25, 27, 29, 31, 51, 63, 67, 69, 71, 73–5, 80–1, 91, 95–8, 114, 126, 132, 134, 139–40, 149, 154, 158–9, 165, 168–9, 173, 176, 178, 196, 238–9, 270, 274, 283–4, 289, 293, 296, 304, 309, 326, 328–9, 382, 384, 403, 425, 427, 439, 455, 462, 482, 498, 500, 570

Barth, K., 96

Bauer, W., ix, x, 127, 140, 207, 231, 242–4, 275, 281, 287, 293, 303, 314, 321, 345, 348, 351, 363, 372–4, 380, 390, 392, 427, 441, 448, 467, 543, 585

Baumbach, G., 92, 162

Baumgartner, W., ix, 342, 429

Becker, J., 74, 149, 455, 501, 590

Bell, H. I., 17, 110

Bengel, J. A., 193

Benoit, P. M., xii, 523–4, 529, 531, 545, 561, 563–5, 578

Bergmeier, R., 62

Bernard, J. H., x, 23, 48, 174, 267, 285, 317, 339, 348, 367, 377, 406, 454, 457, 476, 482, 557, 565, 584

Betz, H. D., 156, 176, 253–4, 356, 358, 373, 504, 572, 580

Betz, O., 462

Biblical Theology Bulletin, 59

Biblische Zeitschrift, 297

Bieler, L., 74

Billerbeck, P., xi, 51, 75, 150, 190–1, 193, 204, 206, 223, 226, 233, 235, 238–9, 241, 244, 256, 260, 288, 310, 322, 328–9, 330, 333, 337, 341, 352, 356, 359, 361–2, 374, 384, 386, 391, 394, 400–3, 407, 443, 463, 472, 532, 555, 560

Birdsall, J. N., 382

Black, J. S., see *E.Bib.*

Black, M., xiii, 9, 10, 51, 168, 222, 224–7, 266, 268, 349, 358, 360, 371, 393, 399, 412, 420, 448, 496, 526, 548, 565

Blass, F., ix, 169–70, 182, 225, 227, 263, 267, 297, 303, 311, 325, 330, 349, 358, 362, 393–4, 398–9, 405, 410–11, 420, 440, 443, 447–8, 474, 481, 484, 493, 505, 539, 555, 562, 565–6, 571, 580–1

Blinzler, J., 259, 591

Boismard, M. E., 67, 220, 437

Bonner, C., 112, 188

Bonnet, M., xiv, 103, 473

Bonsirven, J., xiii, 270, 310, 330, 532

de Boor, C., 103

Borgen, P., 42, 71, 149, 279, 284, 289–90, 292–3, 296–7, 459

Bornkamm, G., 74, 185, 229, 232, 235, 239, 243, 284, 297, 302, 355, 462

Bousset, W., 165, 269, 322, 462, 528

Bowker, J. W., 137

Bowman, J., 138, 239

Brandon, S. G. F., 182

Braun, F. N., 64, 96

Braun, H., 157, 171, 176, 201, 217–18, 231, 233, 328, 357, 371, 442, 447, 489, 493, 503, 528

Briggs, S. A., ix, 101, 177, 248, 429, 489, 505

Brooke, A. E., 59

Brown, F., see Briggs, S. A.

Brown, R. E., 25, 151, 172, 181, 258, 269, 271–2, 274, 279, 284, 293, 302, 322, 325, 329, 342, 355, 371, 373, 388, 391, 404–5, 409–10, 413, 416, 430, 436, 439, 444, 449, 457–8, 461, 471, 475, 477, 480–2, 501, 505, 519, 524, 528, 531, 533, 543, 547–8, 550–2

Brown, S., 9

Brownlee, W. H., 175, 389

Bruns, J. E., 427

Buchanan, G. W., 138

Büchler, A., 75, 532

Bultmann, R., x, xiii, 19, 20, 22–5, 37, 77, 81–3, 97–8, 136, 158, 163, 165, 169, 178, 191–3, 200, 207, 210, 217–18, 220, 226, 233, 236–7, 242–4, 246, 248, 250, 256, 259–61, 268, 271–2, 278, 283, 292, 296, 299, 301, 303–4, 307–8, 313, 317–18, 322, 325–6, 329, 331–2, 335, 338, 342, 345, 349–50, 352, 364, 369, 371, 373, 376–7, 382, 386, 396–7, 403, 409, 425, 427–9, 433, 437–8, 441, 443, 445, 447, 450, 452–8, 464, 470–1, 474–5, 481, 483, 486, 493–4, 497, 499, 504, 512, 514, 516, 531, 541, 549, 563, 565, 574, 576, 583, 585–6

Burkill, T. A., 535

Burkitt, F. C., 145, 155, 417

Burney, C. F., xi, 8–10, 150–1, 176, 288, 297, 349, 359–60, 364, 423, 508

II. SUBJECTS

635

12. GREEK WORDS

637